THE GUIDE TO CELLARS, VINEYARDS

WINEMAKERS, RESTAURANTS

AND ACCOMMODATION

The John Platter SA Wine Guide (Pty) Ltd
www.platterwineguide.com

Publisher
Andrew McDowall

Editor
Philip van Zyl

Tasters
Michael Fridjhon, Angela Lloyd, Jabulani Ntshangase, Neil Pendock, Dave Swingler, Cathy van Zyl; Jörg Pfützner, Mzokhona Mvemve, Jeremy Borg (2005 ed); Cape Wine Masters Tony Mossop (2005 ed), Tim James, Clive Torr, Irina von Holdt & Christine Rudman; honorary member of the Institute of Cape Wine Masters David Hughes; Master of Wine Richard Kelley

Contributors
Lindsaye McGregor, Lynne Kloot, Wendy Toerien, Pippa de Bruyn, Ingrid Motteux-Chappel, Fran Botha, Tseliso Rangaka, Meryl Weaver, Ann Bomford

Advertising
Linda Ransome T 021 438·6161
Young Media T 011 648·3869

Sales
Alison Worrall T 083 530·9761

Co-ordination
Meryl Weaver, Ina de Villiers & Ann Bomford

Maps & typesetting
Gawie du Toit

Photography
Dennis Gordon

PO Box 1466 Hermanus 7200

Tel: 028 313·1281
Fax: 028 312·1395

publisher@platterwineguide.co.za
www.platteronline.com

ISBN 0-9584506-4-1

Typeset by Zebra Publications, Hout Bay

Contents

4 How to use this guide
5 Foreword
6 Editor's note
8 Wines of the year
8 Wine of the year
8 The five stars
9 Highly recommended
10 Buy now, drink later
10 Superquaffer of the year
11 This year's ratings summarised
29 Top performers 2004-5
46 The SA wine industry
46 The industry in brief
47 Wine industry organisations
49 Winegrowing areas
55 Grape varieties
57 Competitions & awards
58 Wine education
59 Selected wine shops
68 Vintages & styles
68 Recent Cape vintages
68 Older vintages
69 SA wine styles
71 Frequently used words & phrases
71 Winetasting terms
74 Winemaking terms
77 Touring wine country
77 Wine routes, trusts & associations
77 Winelands tourism offices
78 Specialist wine tours
80 Eat-outs in the winelands & Cape Town
96 Stay-overs in the winelands & Cape Town
110 Wine & food partners
113 Winelands maps
138 A-Z of Cape wines & wineries
445 Photo gallery: Making a difference
We feature some of the entrepreneurs, investors, researchers, facilitators and transformers whose endeavours are helping to take SA wine to the next level.

How to Use This Guide

Ratings *(Subjective choices in a South African wine context)*

★★★★★	Superlative. A Cape classic	★★★★☆	Outstanding
★★★★	Excellent	★★★☆	Very good/promising
★★★	Characterful, appealing	★★☆	Good everyday drinking
★★	Pleasant drinking	★☆	Casual quaffing
★	Plain and simple	☆	Very ordinary
		No star	Somewhat less than ordinary
✓	Good value	☺	Exceptionally drinkable and well priced

All wines rated 4 stars or more are set in red type.

Symbols & abbreviations

- Bottles own wine on property
- Visiting hours, tasting details (no tasting fee unless noted)
- Restaurant/refreshments
- Accommodation
- BYO picnic
- Wheelchair-friendly (as rated, based on personal inspection, by our consultant Guy Davies)
- Other tourist attractions/amenities on the property
- T Telephone number F Fax number

Visitable wineries in the A-Z are open on public holidays unless noted

All dialling codes (021) unless noted

Abbreviations

% alc	Percentage alcohol by volume	MCC	Méthode cap classique
1stB	First bottled vintage	MIWA	Michelangelo Int. Wine Awards
BYO	Bring your own (wine, picnic)	NE	Non-estate wine
Bdx	Bordeaux	NLH	Noble Late Harvest
Cs	Cases	NV	Non-vintage. Year of harvest not stated on label
CWG	Cape Winemakers Guild	RS	Residual sugar
CWT	Classic Wine Trophy	SAA	South African Airways (selected for First/Business Class)
Est	Date established	SAYWS	SA Young Wine Show
EW	Estate wine	SLH	Special Late Harvest
FCTWS	Fairbairn Capital Trophy Wine Show	Swiss	Swiss Int Airlines Wine Awards
G/ℓ	Grams per litre	Veritas	SA National Bottled Wine Show
IWC	International Wine Challenge	VG	Veritas gold medal
IWSC	International Wine & Spirit Competition	VDG	Veritas double-gold medal
JCWCA	Juliet Cullinan Wine Connoisseur's Award	*Wine*	SA *Wine* magazine
LBV	Late Bottled Vintage	WO	Wine of Origin
Malo	Malolactic fermentation	WOM	Wine of the Month Club
		WS	*Wine Spectator*

See also Editor's Note and start of A-Z section for more about using the guide.

Unless stated otherwise, the following are implied:

- Cabernet/cab = cabernet sauvignon; pinot = pinot noir; chenin = chenin blanc; sauvignon = sauvignon blanc; riesling = Rhine/weisser riesling; touriga = touriga nacional; tinta = tinta barocca (tinta r = tinta roriz; tinta f = tinta francisca)
- Red wines wooded (in 225/300ℓ barrels); Fr = French, Am = American oak; whites unoaked
- Case = 12 × 750ml bottles
- All wines dry unless noted

Foreword

Twenty years. Twenty vintages. My association with the Platter Wine Guide has spanned a hugely significant period in the era of modern wine.

SA's exponential growth, in the number of wineries, improved quality, exports and tourists, are obvious developments but others may prove of greater influence. None springs more readily to mind than the spirited, can-do younger generation. Today's youngsters are knowledgeable, positive and demanding, whether as winemakers, viticulturists, researchers or marketers. I am just so enthusiastic about them all and what they hold for the future.

If these youngsters are fuelled by a sense of assurance and self-belief, and the absence of baggage borne by earlier generations, then tribute is due to Walter and Peter Finlayson, Gyles Webb, Charles Back, Jeff Grier, Neil Ellis and the late Billy Hofmeyr, among others. These are the winemakers I've grown with, most from their early days; they managed to transcend difficulties imposed by a culture bent on a different course to their innovative, quality goals, and set the ball rolling positively for the next generation.

How lucky we are, too, in the worldly, high-calibre individuals who have invested in the beautiful Cape. Californians Phil Freese and Zelma Long, their friendliness as engaging as their Vilafonté wines. Alain Moueix – need one elaborate on such a prestigious Bordeaux name? – whose pedigreed Ingwe blends won't remain a best kept secret for long. Brave Alexander and Ingrid von Essen (the very down-to-earth Baron & Baroness) putting the uncharted wine territory and ward of Philadelphia on the map with Capaia. Giulio Bertrand, Morgenster's simpatico Italian, demonstrating SA can produce very smart wines (and olive oil), the former with the help of Pierre Lurton of steeped-in-quality Chx Cheval Blanc and d'Yquem. These are a few of many foreigners intent on helping to make SA's name with quality, site-specific wines. A challenging and hopefully gratifying task, and one which imparts indispensable depth and persistence to the more evanescent gratification of big-brand success, important as this might be.

Behind the scenes, SA scientists and researchers also command international respect. Our terroir research, which started way back in the 1970s, is the envy of New-World competitors such as Australia and the US. The Institute for Wine Biotechnology, founded only in 1995, is also highly respected internationally and ensures SA remains at the cutting edge of developments at the cellular level.

The pace is hectic; too hectic sometimes. We've become so keen on 'doing', we forget the benefits of standing back and observing, particularly appropriate in relation to anything that grows, as the monks proved in Burgundy all those centuries ago. Here, through long association, our farm workers often know a property equally well or better than the owners or winemakers; we need to value and nurture these true people of the land, for they are a vital link to understanding its many faces.

The guide has enabled me to observe all these developments; it is without doubt my most valued professional involvement with wine over the past 20 years. To John and Erica Platter – founders of this book – thanks for bringing me on board in the first place. I have boundless admiration for you both; your exacting standards were matched by always-generous encouragement.

Platter is more than merely a Guide; for the past 26 years it has chronicled this country's entire wine industry, a unique achievement anywhere. Long may it continue.

Angela Lloyd, Cape Town

Editor's Note

A paradoxical scenario this year: on one hand, a continuing decline in consumer demand for wine, as a consequence of both 'structural' trends (which have seen annual per-capita consumption in SA slide to a new low of just 7.7ℓ) as well as prevailing market conditions, which for now remain somewhat less than ideal. The result is a large quantity of unsold wines, especially (though not exclusively) at the lower end of the market. On the other hand, the past year witnessed unabated – in fact accelerated – growth in the number of new wine producers and merchant houses: in this edition we list a record 72 new players, 15 more than last year. The flood of newcomer brands, combined with new product launches by established producers, pushed the number of new wines on the market since the last edition to a staggering 800, and the total number of wines to be tasted to roughly 5 400. (In the same period, close to 300 wines were discontinued.) Given these big numbers and a tight deadline, it was not possible this year to retaste and re-rate wines which had been submitted previously and are still available for sale. Only wines which last year were reviewed as tank or barrel samples, and thus rated provisionally (or considered too young and unformed to rate), were revisited for the current book.

Though there was a precipitous rise in the number of producers, prices of wines increased much less swiftly, if at all. Accordingly, we maintained last year's value-for-money parameters, and feel that wines flagged with either the good-value symbol (✓, indicating wines of 3½-star quality and better) or the super-quaffing icon (☺, identifying best-buys at 3 stars and below) continue to represent outstanding value in the present market.

Talking value, this edition sees the naming of the guide's first 'Superquaffer of the Year' – the wine which, in the opinion of our tasting team, represents the best value for money and drinkability of all the entry-level wines scrutinised. This, and nine other ultra-easy-drinkers are included under their own heading in the section Wines of the Year (see p 8). Also listed there are the top-ranked wines for 2006 (the Five Stars and Highly Recommended wines), plus a selection of investment wines to lay down for future enjoyment. Given fresh emphasis from this year is the General Index, traditionally 'buried' in the last few pages of the book, and now featured immediately after the Wines of the Year section under a new heading, 'This Year's Ratings Summarised'. The summary, as its name now suggests, affords a quick way to look up the star ratings for the newest vintages included in the A–Z portion of the guide and, equally importantly, to easily compare ratings for different producers within particular style categories. While the Summarised Ratings reflect the form of the most recent vintages, the older vintages which were rated highest in selected local and international competitions and tastings over the past twelve months are reflected in the Top Performers table (p 28). These results are duplicated under the winery headings in the A–Z directory.

Readers who wonder how we arrive at our star ratings should note that each year we mobilise our team of internationally experienced tasters to assess every bottled or boxed wine on sale locally as well as overseas. (Unavoidably examples slip past us, and of course we try to incorporate these and any new releases in the next edition.) The results of our tastings are reflected in the A–Z section, along with news about the wineries and winemakers, general information about products, vinification facilities, vineyards, amenities available to visitors and more. (The ratings are also summarised in the renamed section described above). In line with heightened international interest in SA wine, we continue to highlight names of brands and alternative labels used by local producers for overseas markets (these are also cross-referenced for convenience). Also featured in the A–Z are general style indicators and technical details (note that alcohol, acid, sugar levels, time in wood etc are provided only where they are useful in giving clues to the character of the wine).

For visitors in search of wine-route information, the maps have been fully updated, along with the accompanying tables which provide additional information about the wineries of the particular region, such as whether or not they are open on weekends and public holidays, offer meals or refreshments, specifically cater for children, and are disabled-friendly.

Also of interest to tourists and wine-ramblers is the ever-expanding Eat-out and Stay-over sections, wherein providers of various sorts and styles of hospitality describe their attractions in their own words.

Our ranking system remains largely the same as last year. We cover the full spectrum, from wines we consider 'somewhat less than ordinary' (and award 0 stars) to 'superlative Cape classics', worthy of a full 5. Wines rated ★★★★ and higher are listed first in each entry, with a general rating in the margin, denoting the wine's track record over two or more vintages. Wines ranked 4 stars and higher are set in red type. Vintages deviating from the general rating are individually starred in the text. Very good/promising wines and more modest examples (★★★☆ or fewer) are included in the 'run-on' listings at the end of entries. For easy identification, the quaffing best-buys are both boxed together and individually labelled with the wallet-cordial ☺ sign. See also the section on How to use the guide.

Because of deadlines, many wines in the guide are tasted freshly bottled or as works-in-progress; any considered unrateable as a result are noted as such in the text. It's worth mentioning that we taste from the end of June to early August. Except for the bottlings assessed for five stars (see the preamble to the Wines of the Year), all wines are tasted 'sighted' (with labels exposed), necessarily so, given the high number of unfinished wines submitted for rating. Because of the subjective element associated with wine assessment, we strongly recommend you view our rankings as adjuncts to the tasting notes rather than as oracular pronouncements. For this purpose we include the results of other professional tastings and competitions in both the A-Z and the Top Performers table.

Wines featured in the guide were assessed by our team of internationally experienced tasters whose professionalism and unflagging enthusiasm we again gratefully acknowledge. Our enlarged team this edition include Michael Fridjhon, Dave Hughes, Tim James, Angela Lloyd, Jabulani Ntshangase, Neil Pendock, Dave Swingler, Irina von Holdt, Richard Kelley, Christine Rudman, Cathy van Zyl; newcomers Jörg Pfützner, Mzokhona Mvemve and Clive Torr; and for the 2005 edition only, Tony Mossop CWM and Jeremy Borg. Tasters' initials appear below the wines they tasted.

Warm thanks to the rest of the splendid team: multi-tentacled Tim James, Meryl Weaver and Ann Bomford; Lindsaye McGregor, Lynne Kloot, Wendy Toerien, Pippa de Bruyn, Ingrid Motteux-Chappel, Fran Botha and Tseliso Rangaka; Ina de Villiers; The Elves; Alison Worrall, Linda Ransom, Sally Young; Dennis Gordon; Gawie du Toit; Mark White & XtraSmile; Johan Enslin for the icons; Hanneli Smit & co at VinLAB; Ryk Taljaard for the WO maps; the ever helpful SAWIS. And Angela Lloyd for the foreword and index.

Special thanks to incredibly supportive wife Cathy, still merrily Trekking, and son Luke, who's swapped his lightsabre for a pair of kneepads and bat.

Not least, sincere thanks to SA's wine producers, without whose support the book could not be produced. And the usual invitation to visit our website, www.platteronline.com, now fully revamped, for the latest updates, interactive wine-touring maps and search tools, and other features.

Wines of the Year

In the course of tasting and rating more than 5 000 wines for each edition, the members of our team individually identify a limited number of bottlings showing exceptional quality. These are entered into a second round of tasting, open only to finished/bottled wines, available during the currency of the book. The short-listed wines are retasted 'blind' (without sight of the label) by an assembled panel, and those regarded as superlative in an SA context are awarded the guide's highest grading – five stars. These stand-outs are listed below under the heading 'Five Stars'. The highest scoring five-star wines are subjected to a further tasting to determine the overall top scorer. The wine which emerges from this stringent selection represents the pinnacle of SA winemaking and is the recipient of the guide's highest accolade: Wine of the Year.

The wines which do not make the five-star selection, but which are extremely fine and collectible in their own right, are listed immediately below the Five Stars under the heading 'Highly Recommended'. Implicit in wines of this calibre is the potential to improve with further bottle-maturation – say 8-10 years, perhaps more, in the case of the reds and fortifieds, and around 6-8 years for the whites. (Proper storage is, of course, vital for sound maturation.) During the cycle of tasting, our tasters identify a number of bottlings, over and above the candidate five-stars, which show particular potential for cellaring. These ageworthy wines are listed separately under the heading 'Buy Now, Drink Later'. This year, for the first time, we also list the dozen or so 'superquaffers' which the tasters feel offer the best value for money and drinkability of all the entry-level wines they scrutinised. Further details about all releases listed in this section will be found under the names of the relevant producers in the A–Z directory. The five-star tasting is audited by PKF (Cpt) Inc.

Wine of the Year

Shiraz

- Glen Carlou Syrah 2004

Five stars

Cabernet sauvignon

- Rijk's Private Cellar 2002

Dessert wine unfortified

- Klein Constantia Vin de Constance 2000

Merlot

- Thelema Reserve 2003

Port

- Axe Hill Cape Vintage Port 2003
- De Krans Vintage Reserve 2003

Red blends

- Kaapzicht Steytler Vision 2002

Sauvignon blanc

- Steenberg Vineyards Reserve 2005

Semillon

- Steenberg Vineyards 2005

White blends

- Vergelegen White 2004
- The Sadie Family Palladius 2004

Highly Recommended

Cabernet franc
- Raats Family Wines 2003

Cabernet sauvignon
- Thelema 2003
- Boekenhoutskloof 2003
- Thelema CWG Auction Reserve 2003
- Vergelegen V 2003
- Vergelegen 2003
- Neil Ellis Premium 2003
- Blue Creek 2004
- Rustenberg Peter Barlow 2003
- Waterford 2003
- Stark-Condé 'Condé' 2003

Chardonnay
- Uva Mira 2004
- Springfield Wild Yeast 2003
- Hamilton Russell Vineyards 2004
- Cape Chamonix Reserve 2003

Chenin blanc
- Katbakkies 2004
- Ken Forrester Forrester-Meinert 2003

Dessert wine unfortified
- Kanu Kia Ora Noble Late Harvest 2004
- Nederburg Noble Late Harvest 2004
- Ken Forrester 'T' Noble Late Harvest 2003
- Paul Cluver Weisser Riesling Noble Late Harvest 2004
- Rudera Chenin Blanc Noble Late Harvest 2005

Gewürztraminer
- Paul Cluver 2004

Merlot
- Veenwouden 2003
- KWV Cathedral Cellars 2002

Méthode cap classique
- Graham Beck Blanc de Blancs 2000

Pinot noir
- Hamilton Russell Vineyards 2004

Pinotage
- Camberley 2004
- Simonsig Redhill 2003
- L'Avenir CWG Auction Reserve 2004

Port
- Boplaas CWG Auction Reserve 2003

Red blends
- Vergelegen 'Verglegen' 2003
- Capaia 'Capaia' 2004
- Vilafonté Series M 2003
- Cordoba Crescendo 2003
- Morgenster 'Morgenster' 2003
- Vilafonté Series C 2003
- Buitenverwachting Christine 2001
- Vriesenhof Enthopio 2002
- Mont du Toit Le Sommet 2002
- Neethingshof Laurentius 2001
- Overgaauw Tria Corda 2003

Sauvignon blanc
- Kumkani Lanner Hill 2005
- Tokara White 2004
- Neil Ellis Groenekloof 2005
- Durbanville Hills Biesjes Craal 2005
- Spier Private Collection 2005

Shiraz
- Graham Beck The Ridge Syrah 2003
- The Sadie Family Columella 2003
- KWV Cathedral Cellars 2002
- Robertson Winery No 1 Constitution Road 2003
- Boekenhoutskloof Syrah 2003
- Hartenberg CWG Auction Reserve Gravel Hill 2003
- Cloof Crucible 2003
- The Foundry Syrah 2003
- Scali Syrah 2003
- Delheim Vera Cruz Estate 2003
- Boekenhoutskloof Syrah CWG 2003
- Rijk's Private Cellar 2002

White blends
- Steenberg CWG Auction Reserve Barrel Fermented Sauvignon Blanc-Semillon 2005
- CWG Vergelegen "The White" 2004

Buy Now, Drink Later

Cabernet sauvignon
- Alto Estate 2003
- Graham Beck Coffeestone 2003
- Hartenberg 2003
- L'Avenir CWG Auction Reserve 2003
- Marklew 2004
- Neil Ellis Vineyard Selection 2003

Chardonnay
- Thelema 2004
- Waterford 2004

Chenin blanc
- Beaumont Wines 2005
- Old Vines 2004

Petit verdot
- Zorgvliet Silver Myn 2004

Pinotage
- Camberley 2004

Port
- Allesverloren Vintage 1999
- Muratie Cape Vintage 2002
- JP Bredell CWG Auction Reserve 2003
- JP Bredell Cape Vintage 2000

Red blends
- De Toren Fusion V 2003
- Graham Beck The William 2003
- Hartenberg The McKenzie 2003
- Jordan Cobblers Hill 2003
- Nicolas van der Merwe Wines Mas Nicolas 2003
- Remhoogte Estate Wine 2003
- Simonsig Frans Malan 2003
- Vriesenhof Kallista 2002
- Webersburg 'Webersburg' 2002
- Welgemeend Estate Reserve 2002

Riesling (Rhine or weisser)
- Thelema 2004

Shiraz
- Fairview Beacon Block 2003
- Hartenberg The Stork 2003
- Kaapzicht 2002
- Rudera Syrah 2003
- Waterford Kevin Arnold 2003
- Zondernaam 2003

White blends
- Dornier Donatus White 2004

Superquaffer of the Year

Red blends
- Grande Provence Angels Tears Red NV

Exceptionally Drinkable & Well Priced

Chenin blanc
- Cape Bay 2005

Merlot
- Simonsvlei Lifestyle Merlot 2004

Red blends
- Lorna Hughes Stonehill Bristle 2004
- JP Bredell Vineyard Collection NV
- Muratie Melck's Red 2004
- Boekenhoutskloof The Wolftrap 2004

Shiraz
- De Meye Little River 2003

White blends
- Knorhoek Two Cubs White 2005
- Fairview/Goats du Roam White 2005

This Year's Ratings Summarised

Here we summarise all wines featured in the A-Z section, with their ratings, sorted first by wine style, in alphabetical order, and then by producer or brand. New wines in **bold**. **NS** = no star; **NT** = not tasted; **NR** = tasted but not rated; **D** = discontinued. Where wineries produce more than one version of a particular style, the number of versions is indicated in brackets after the name.

Barbera

★★★☆ Altyd, **Fview**

★★★ **Riverstn** ★★☆ **Hofstraat**

Blanc de noir

★★★ Boschndl, Btnvrwchtng, KWV, Swrtland, Van Lvren ★★☆ Belbon Hills, **De Meye**, Du T'kloof, Grt Cnstntia, Hzndal, Lndskrn, Louiesnhf, Van Lvren, Wlworths ★★ Aan de Drns, Boplaas, Cltzdorp, Jonkhr, **Lynx** ★☆ Ashton, Country C (LowAlc), Goudini, Klawer, **Klein Parys**, Montpllr, Oranje, Oude Kaap ★ Oude Wllngton **NT Clmborg**, Picardi **NR** Montpllr **D** Chamnx, Westcrp Int

Bukettraube

★★★ Cedrbrg ★★☆ Du T'kloof, Smnsvlei ★★ Swrtland ★ Citrus **NT** Klnhof **D** Bovlei

Cabernet franc

★★★★☆ **Plaisir**, Raats Fam

★★★★ Bellnghm, Ekndal, High C, Philip J, Warwick

★★★☆ Avntuur, Cpe Grace, Five Heirs, Le Pommier, Ndrburg, Whlhaven, Zrgvliet

★★★ **Avndale**, Nthlingshof ★★☆ Lndskrn **NR** Rainbow **D** Boschndl, Lvland, Makro

Cabernet sauvignon

★★★★★ Rijk's

★★★★☆ Asara, Bknhtskloof, Blue Creek, Btnvrwchtng, Carisbrke, Cedrbrg, De Traf, Delaire, Havana, Kanu, **Katbakkies**, KWV, L'Avenir, **Le Riche** (2), Mischa, Mrgnhof, Ndrburg, Neil E (2), Ovrgaauw, Rstnberg, Rudera (2), Sprgfield (2), Stark-C, **Thelema** (2), Verglgn (2), Waterfd

★★★★ Alto, Annandale, Anura, Avndale, Bcksbrg, Bellnghm, Bilton, Bloemndal, Boland, Bon Crge, Boschndl, Cedrbrg, Cloof, Coleraine, Cowlin, Crows Nest, Darling C, Daview, Delheim, Dmrsfntn, Drmrshire, Eaglevlei, Ekndal, Fleur dC (2), Flgstone (2), **Fview**, G Beck (2), Goede H, Gracelnd, Grnde Prvnce, Grnghurst (2), Grt Cnstntia, Havana, Hidden V, Hrtnberg, Jordan, JP Bredell, Kaapzicht (2), **Kleine Z**, Kloovnbrg, Knonkp, Knrhoek, **KWV** (2), L'Avenir, La Couronne, Le Riche, Linton P, Lndskrn, L'Ormarins, L'rdge, Lynx, Makro, Marklew, Mischa, Mooipls, Newton J, Nitida, Nthlingshof, Rbtson, Rhbsklf, Rickety, Rmhoogte, Royle Fam, Signal H, Spier, Stark-C, Stkaya, Stony B (2), Sxnburg, The Winery, Vendôme, **Vruchtbaar**, Wbrsburg, Western, Wlworths, **Zrgvliet**

★★★☆ Afrcn Pride, Allesvlrn, **Alluvia**, **Alter Ego**, Assegai, Audacia, **Bernheim**, Bknhtskloof, Black Pearl, Bnnievle, **Bodraai**, Bon Cap (Organic), Bon Crge, Bonfoi, Boplaas, Boschndl, **Bottlry Int**, **BWC**, Cilandia, Citrus, Clmborg, Cloof, Cls Mlvrne, **Conradie**, Dbn Hills, De Wetsh, Du T'kloof, Eikehof, Ekndal, Exclsor, Five Heirs, Fort S, Fredine Fine Wnes, **Gehot Bosch**, **Goedvrwcht**, Havana, High C, Hildenb, **Hofstraat**, Hpnbrg, Jacobsdal, Jonkhr, K Constantia, Kleine Z, KWV, La Bri, La Motte, La Petite F, Laborie, Laibach, Lanzerac, Ldrsburg, Le Bonh, Le Grand Chass, Le Pommier, **Linde**, Linton P, **Lndhorst**, Lndskrn, Lournsfd, L'rdge, Manley, Mdlvlei, Meerend, Mnt Rozier, Mrgnhof, Muratie, **N Ellis Meyer N**, Ndrburg, Ntvbij, Oewerzicht, **Olyvenbosch**, Omnia, Onderklf, Paul C, Perdebrg, **Pick's Pick**, Plaisir, Post Hse, Rbtson (2), **Ridgeback**, Rietvallei, Rtrsvlei, Rust en V, **Savanha** (3), S'bosch Hills, Seidel, Sentinel, Smnsig, Smnsvlei, Stellnzcht, Stnwall, Swrtland, **Sylvnvle**, **Terroir**, Thorn, Tokara,

Tulbagh, Upland, Villiera, Vljsdrift, Vrgnoegd, **Warwick**, Western, **Wlworths** (Organic), Wndmeul, Zevnwacht, Zonneblm, Zrgvliet

★★★ Afrcn Terroir, Altyd, Ashanti, Ashton, Bcksbrg (2), Belbon Hills, Bergsig, Bianco, Boland, Bon Crge, Botha, **Bottlry Int**, **Bscheim**, Bschklf, Cameradi, Chamnx, **Cilliers**, Clairvx, Clovelly, **Coppoolse**, Cpe Coastal, Cru (2), Darling C, Daview, De Compagnie, De Krans, **De Meye** (2), Dieu D, **Dispore Kamma**, Dmrsdal, Dmrsfntn, Domaine B, Doolhof, Douglas G, Drknsig, Drnkraal, **Eaglevlei**, **Ernst Co**, Exclsor, Gecko R, Goedvertw, Groenld, Hildenb, Hldrkruin, Jason's, **Klein Parys** (2), **Kleine Z** (2), **Klmpzcht**, Klnvallei, **KWV** (2), Libertas, Lost H, Lushof, Major's Hill, MAN Vintners, McGreg, **Mellasat** (2), Mrhof, **Napier**, Nelson, New Begin, New Cape, Nthlingshof, Nuy, Obikwa, Omnia (2), Oracle, Ormonde, Oude Kaap, Patrys, Perdebrg, Prospect (2), Pulpit Rock, Rdezandt (2), Rooibrg, **Rstnberg**, Rtrsvlei, Rusticus, Seidel, **Seven Oaks**, **Slaley**, **Smnsvlei**, Spier, Stellar (Organic), Stellndrft, Sthrn Cape Vyds, Sthrn Sky, Stony B, Swrtland, Table Mtn, Thandi, Tulbagh, Uitkyk, Ultra Liq, Van Lvren, **Vinus Via**, Waboom, Wamaker, **Welbedcht**, Welgegund, Wlworths, Yonder, Zndbrg, **Zrgvliet** ★★☆ Afrcn Pride, Afrcn Terroir, **Agterplaas**, Blwklppn, Botha, Bovlei, Citrus, **Cpe Hutton**, Cru, **De Villiers**, Devon H, Drostdy, **FirstCpe**, **Furstnbrg**, Grt Eilnd, Hippo, Jonkhr, **Kango**, Kln Draken (Kosher), Krnskop, **La Providnce**, **Lategnskp**, Linton P, Lngvrwacht, Long Mntn, Ltzvlle, Merwespnt, Mns Ruber (2), **Mntn River**, Montpllr, Opstal, Oranje, **Prtrville** (2), Riebeek, Riverstn, Seidel (2), Shoprite, Smrbsch, Ultra Liq, Vlrsdorp, Wamaker, Welgelee, Westcrp Int, Wldekrans, Wlington ★★ **Afrcn Terroir**(2) (Organic), Bartinney, Boplaas, **Cpe Coastal**, De Zoete, Dieu D, F'hoek Vyds, **Keukenhof**, Klawer, Klnhof, **Leopard's**, Lyngrove, Mostrtsdrift, Oude Wllngton, Pulpit Rock, Ridder's, Riebeek, Rooibrg, Shoprite, Slnghoek, Smnsvlei, **Wandsbeck**, **Wlington**, Wndmeul ★☆ Citrus, Eshkl Kshr, Lost H, Makro, Oranje, **Origin** (Organic), **Tall Horse**, Wlworths ★ Lndzicht **NT** Anthill, Avndvrde, **Belfield**, Bergwater, Bertrams, Blue Crane, Blwklppn, Bnnievle, Bodega, Country C, De Doorns, Drostdy, Fairseat, Gdveld, Hrtswater, Huguenot, IWS (2), Jacaranda, **Jewel Breede**, Koningsrvr, Makro, Môreson (2), Mouton, Niel J, Old Brdge (2), Omnia, Prmium Cpe Wnes, Schoonberg, Stellar, **Stormhoek**, Uitvlucht, **Wine Concepts**, Wine Mnth Club **NR** **Elgin Vntnrs**, **Hemlzcht**, Heron Rdg, Mnt Rochelle, Oudeklf, Rainbow, Romans, Schlkbnbsch, **Stellcpe** **D** Allee B, Ashton, Avntuur, Bowe, DeWaal, Drknsig, Fryer, Fview, Grnde Prvnce, Hpnbrg, Kanu, Lvland, Omnia (3), Savanha, Stellnzcht, Sthrn Cape Vyds, Welgemnd, Whlhaven

Cape 'Bordeaux' – see under Red blends
Cape 'port' – see under Fortifieds

Carignan

★★★★ Fview

★★★☆ Welgegund

Chardonnay, unwooded

★★★★☆ Sprgfield

★★★★ Bchrd-F, Con Uitsig, De Wetsh, Zrgvliet

★★★☆ Bcksbrg (Organic), Cloverfld, De Wetsh (2), Delaire, Jordan, La Couronne, Mnt Rochelle, **Rietvallei**, **Stnberg**, **The Winery**, Von O

★★★ Asara, **Avndale**, Bartinney, Beaumnt, Cpe Bay, De Krans, Dieu D, Doolhof, **G Beck** (2), Goedvertw, Grte Pst, **Hillcrest**, Kleine Z, La Petite F, Long Bch Café, Louisvle, **Main Str**, Millstrm, Môreson, Omnia (2), Rstnberg, Thorn, Tulbagh, Van Z'hof, Vendôme, Vinus Via, Vriesenhof, Wamaker, Wltvrede, Yonder ★★☆ **Agulhas Wines**, Bon Crge, **De Meye**, **FirstCpe**, Hildenb, Janéza, Jonkhr (2), **Juno**, **Leopard's**, Linton P, Lost H, Louiesnhf, Prtrville, Ridder's, Romans, Smrbsch, Swrtland, Tarentaal, Van Lvren, Wlworths, Zndvliet ★★ Afrcn Terroir, Bcksbrg, Botha, Citrus, Cloof, **Cpe Coastal**, Goudini, Lost H, Ltzvlle, McGreg, Mrhof, **New Cape**, Oude Wllngton, Padda, Seidel, **Tall Horse**, **Zidela** ★☆ **Afrcn Terroir**, Boplaas, Mns Ruber (2), **Shoprite**, Vlrsdorp ★ Urbane ☆ Montpllr, **Uitvlucht** **NT** Bloupunt, Bon Crge, **Groot Parys**, Hrtswater, Makro, Montagu, Westcrp Int, Wlworths **D** Afrcn Terroir, Ashton, De Compagnie, Grnde Prvnce, Kango, Riebeek, Sthrn Cape Vyds, Whlhaven

Chardonnay, wooded

★★★★☆ Avntuur, **Btnvrwchtng**, Chamnx, Dbn Hills, Glen C (2), Hrtnberg, HRV, **Jordan** (2), L'rdge, Nthlingshof, R&R, Sprgfield, **Sterhuis**, Sumardg, The Winery, **Uva Mira**, Veenwdn, Verglgn, Wltvrede

★★★★ Amani, Anthill, Asara, Bchrd-F (2), Bcksbrg, Beaumnt, Bellnghm, Bon Crge, Boschndl, Btnvrwchtng, Chamnx, Con Uitsig, De Meye, De Wetsh, Delaire, Dmrsdal, Ekndal, Fleur dC, Fort S, Fview, **G Beck**, Glen C, Grt Cnstntia, Grte Pst, Hrtnberg, Jonkhr (2), Jordan, Kloovnbrg, KWV (2), La Couronne, La Petite F, MC Square, Mnt Rochelle, Môreson, Mrlust, Mulderb (2), Muratie, **Neil E** (3), Nelson, Newton J, Onderklf, Ovrgaauw, Paul C, Quoin, Rstnberg (2), Thelema (2), **Tokara**, Verglgn, **Vins d'Orrance**, Warwick, Waterfd, Wltvrede (2), Wlworths (3), Zndvliet

★★★☆ Afrcn Pride, Afrcn Terroir, Altyd, **Amani**, Anura, Assegai, Avndale, Bergsig, Bnnievle, Boland, Boschndl, Bschklf, Cloverfld, **Conradie**, Cordoba, Cpe Classics, Cpe Point, **Crows Nest**, De Wetsh (3), Delheim (2), Dieu D, Dombeya, Dominion (2), Eikehof, Fat B, F'hoek Vyds, G Beck, Glnwood, Goede H, Grnde Prvnce, Havana, Hegewisch, Hildenb, Hillcrest, **Hpnbrg**, Jack & Knox, Joubert-T, K Constantia, Kanu, Koelfntn, **KWV**, L'Avenir, La Motte, Laibach, Lanzerac, Louisvle (2), Lushof, Lyngrove (2), Marklew, Ndrburg (2), Nitida, Nthlingshof, Omnia, Perdebrg, Plaisir, Pulpit Rock (2), Rhbsklf, Riebeek, Rietvallei (2), Rijk's, **Saronsbrg**, S'bosch Hills, Seidel, Sentinel, Signal H, Slaley, Smnsig, **Smook**, StllnHills (2), Stnwall, Stony B, Sxnburg, Thandi, Tokara, Uva Mira, Van Lvren, Von O, Vriesenhof, Western, Whlhaven, Wldekrans, Wlworths, Wm Everson, Zonneblm

★★★ Afrcn Pride, Arendsig, Bellnghm, Bonfoi, Cpe First, Cpe Grace, Cpe Vyds, Cru, Dalla Cia, Dbn Hills, De Zoete, Ekndal, Exclsor, Five Heirs, Fleur dC, Fview, Gecko R, Goedvrwcht, Grt Cnstntia, Hill & Dale, Hldrkruin, Hpnbrg, Ht Espoir, Hzndal, Kln Draken (Kosher), Klnvallei, Krnskop, KWV (2), **La Chaumiere**, Laborie, Le Grand Chass, Libertas, Linton P, L'Ormarins, **Lorraine**, Makro, MAN Vintners, McGreg, **Mooi Bly**, Mrgnhof, Napier, Ndrburg, New Begin, Nordale, **Oaklnds Exprtrs**, Obikwa, Opstal, Oracle, Ormonde (2), Prospect, Prtrville, Rbtson, Rickety, Riebeek, Romans, Rooibrg, **Savanha**, Smook, Spier, Stellnzcht, Table Mtn, Van Z'hof, Vljsdrift, **Welbedcht**, Western, Winecorp, Wlworths ★★☆ Avntuur, Badsberg, Bcksbrg, Bnnievle, Citrus, Clovelly, Coppoolse, Cpe Vyds, Detendu, Dmrsdal, Douglas G, Du T'kloof, Grt Eilnd, J van Zyl, Klawer, KWV, Le Bonh, Lndskrn, Lngvrwacht, Lyngrove, Major's Hill, Malan, Merwespnt, Mnt Rozier (2), Mntn Oaks, Nelson, Nuy, Origin, Rhbsklf, Slnghoek, Smnsvlei, Two Oceans, Uitkyk, Vrede en Lust, W'drift, Wlington ★★ Ashton, Bcksbrg (Kosher), Boland, Bovlei, Citrus, Clairvx, Clmborg, **Cpe Coastal** (2), Cpe Vyds, **De Villiers**, Deetlefs, Drostdy, Du Preez, Eshkl Kshr, F'hoek Vyds (2), **Furstnbrg**, Goudini, Jason's, **Klein Parys** (2), Lindiwe, Long Mntn, Mdlvlei, **Mntn River**, Origin, Oude Kaap, Rbtson, Rhbsklf, Riebeek, Rooibrg, **SA Premium**, Sthrn Cape Vyds (2), Western, Wlworths ★☆ Afrcn Terroir (Organic), Bovlei, Cltzdorp, **Cpe Vyds**, Ernst Co, **Origin** (2), Tangara, Ultra Liq ★ De Wet, **Kango**, **Lndzicht** ☆ Oranje **NT** Bloupunt, Breelnd, Brndvlei, Daschbsch, De Doorns, Fairseat, **False Bay**, FBW, Hippo, IWS (2), Kln DasBsch, Klnhof, La Bri, Montagu, Niel J, Omnia, Ovrhex, Rdezandt, Umkhulu **NR** Country C, Darling C, Hemlzcht, Lvland, Meerend, New Cape, **Rtrsvlei**, **Ziggurat D** Afrcn Terroir (2), Bowe, Cls Mlvrne, Cpe Point, Daview, Lmrshoek, Maiden, Omnia (2), Origin (2), Oude Wllngton, Rtrsvlei

Chenin blanc, unwooded, dry

★★★★☆ Old Vines

★★★★ Raats Fam, Swrtland

★★★☆ **Altyd**, Avndale, Cedrbrg, **Cloverfld**, Fort S, Mnt Destin, **Mnterosso**, Môreson, Old Vines, **The Winery**, Tierhoek, Vljsdrift, Waterfd, Wndmeul

★★★ Bcksbrg, **Blue Crane**, **Bottlry Int**, **Btnvrwchtng**, Bwland, Cru, Du Preez, Five Heirs, Flgstone, Grte Pst, Hzndal, Jason's, **Kanu**, Laibach, Libertas, Long Mntn, L'rdge, **Mhudi**, Mnt Vernon, Mntn Oaks, Môreson, Napier, Nuy, Obikwa, Onderklf, Ormonde, Perdebrg, Smnsig, Spier, Table Mtn, Tarentaal, **Teddy Hall**, Thorn, Van Z'hof, **Vuurberg** ★★☆ **Alvi's Drift**, Badsberg, Belbon Hills, Boland, **Carolinahve**, Citrus, Coppoolse, Country C, Cpe Bay, Cru, De Krans, Glnview, Jonkhr, Kaapzicht, **Leopard's**, **Main Str**, MAN Vintners, Mooi Bly,

Omnia, Opstal, Oude Kaap, Patrys, Seidel, **Seven Oaks**, Smnsvlei (2), Vrdnheim, Winecorp, Wlington, Wlworths(2) (Organic) ★★ 32 South, Anura, Assegai, Bovlei, Citrus, Drostdy, Fair Valley, **FirstCpe**, Grt Eilnd (2), Jonkhr, Klawer, KWV, Lindiwe, Lndskrn, Lost H, McGreg, Mellasat, Millstrm, Mnt Rozier, New Cape, Niel J, Nieue Drift, Nordale, Oudeklf, Rbtson, Rtrsvlei, Seidel, **Shoprite**, Smrbsch, Swrtland, Tulbagh, Vaughan J, Vinus Via, Wamaker ★☆ Bergsig, Bernheim, Brndvlei, **Citrus**, Clmborg, **De Villiers**, Deetlefs, F'hoek Vyds (2), Hldrkruin, Lngvrwacht, Montpllr, **Prtrville**, Riebeek, Rooibrg, Text, Wamaker ★ **Afrcn Terroir**, Oranje, **Origin**, Prtrville (Organic), **Rhbsklf**, Slnghoek, Ultra Liq, Vlrsdorp, Wandsbeck, **Wlworths** (LowAlc) **NS** Eshkl Kshr, Montpllr Sud, **Stellar** (Organic) **NT** Black Eagle (Organic), Bon Crge, Breelnd, De Doorns, Drostdy (3), IWS, Jacaranda, Mntn River, Montagu, Mostrtsdrift, Old Brdge (2), Rickety, **Wnklshk**, **Zidela** **NR** Groot Parys, Pulpit Rock, Swrtland **D** Bnnievle, Cltzdorp, Cpe Vyds, Kango, Omnia, Sthrn Cape Vyds

Chenin blanc, unwooded, off-dry/semi-sweet

★★★★ L'Avenir

★★★☆ Kanu, Kleine Z

★★★ Ken F, KWV, **Mike's Ktchn**, Perdebrg ★★☆ Boschndl, Botha, Cloof, Du T'kloof, **Klein Parys** (2), **Kleine Z**, Knrhoek, Lndskrn, **Mike's Ktchn**, **Old Vines**, Origin, Rhbsklf ★★ Grt Eilnd, Hzndal, **Klein Parys**, Nordale, Rbtson, S'bosch Hills, Smnsvlei, Uitvlucht, Wlworths ★☆ Bnnievle, Goudini, **Lndzicht**, Ltzvlle (2), Oranje (Nouveau), Smnsvlei ★ **Leopard's** ☆ Oranje (LowAlc) **NS Rietrvr NT** Grndheim, Huguenot, Prmium Cpe Wnes **D** Rietrvr

Chenin blanc, wooded

★★★★☆ Katbakkies, Ken F, Post Hse, Rudera, Spice R, Spier, **Sprngfntn**

★★★★ Beaumnt (2), Bellnghm, Cedrbrg, De Traf, Fleur dC, Fort S, Hildenb, Jean D, Kanu, Ken F, Kleine Z, Lmrshoek, Mrgnhof, Old Vines, Raats Fam, Rijk's, Rudera, **Smnsig**, The Winery, Tukulu, **Tulbagh Mtn Vyds**, Villiera (2)

★★★☆ Assegai, Barton, Glen C, Hzndal, Mulderb, **Perdebrg**, Signal H, Smrbsch, **Stormhoek**, Sylvnvle, Tokara, **Welbedcht**, Wlworths

★★★ **Alvi's Drift**, Anura, Avntuur, Barton, Cpe Classics, Domaine B, Ekndal, Fort S, Fredine Fine Wnes, Jordan, KWV, Mntn Oaks, Nabyglgn, Prtrville, Zevnwacht ★★☆ Cpe Vyds, Klnhof, Riebeek ★★ **Cpe Coastal** ★☆ Bernheim, Eshkl Kshr, Wldekrans, **Wlington NT** IWS **NR Stbosch Cntry Est D** Asara, Avntuur, De Traf, Flgstone, Joostnbrg

Cinsaut

★★★ Perdebrg ★★☆ Lndskrn, Wamaker ★☆ Citrus, Clmborg ★ **Origin**

Clairette blanche

D Montpllr

Colombard

★★★☆ Botha

★★★ Goedvrwcht, McGreg, Nuy ★★☆ Bon Crge, Nuy, Origin, Rbtson (2), Wltvrede ★★ Ashton, Country C, Van Lvren, Wlworths ★☆ Aan de Drns, Oranje, **Origin** (Organic), Rooibrg ★ Lngvrwacht, Oranje **NS** Aan de Drns **NT** Black Eagle (Organic), De Doorns, Gdveld, Montagu, Stellar (Organic) **D** Jonkhr, Montpllr, Sthrn Cape Vyds, Uitvlucht

Fernão pires

★★ Nuy, Swrtland (LowAlc), Van Lvren

Fortified

Hanepoot

★★★★ Deetlefs, Du Preez

★★★☆ Botha, Brndvlei, **Cltzdorp**, Grt Eilnd, Kaapzicht, Sthrn Cape Vyds, Swrtland, Waboom

★★★ Aan de Drns, Badsberg, Boplaas, Citrus, Mns Ruber, Muratie, Opstal, Padda, Rooibrg, **SoetKaroo**, Wamaker ★★☆ Goudini, Lndzicht, Mooitsg, Oranje, Smnsvlei, Vlrsdorp, Wlington ★★ Kango, **Klnhof**, Mooitsg, Rietrvr ★☆ Westcrp Int **NT Bottlry Int**, Daschbsch, De Doorns, **De Wet**, Huguenot **NR** Slnghoek **D** Klawer

Jerepigo, red

★★★★ Rooibrg

★★★☆ Badsberg, Bnnievle, Grndheim, Prtrville, Smnsvlei

★★★ Botha, BWC, Citrus, Lmrshoek, Swrtland ★★☆ Mns Ruber, Oranje, Sdgwick's ★★ Douglas, Kango, Riebeek, Ship Shry ★☆ Lndzicht, Mooitsg **NT** Hrtswater, Huguenot, Slnghoek **NR** Alter Ego

Jerepigo, white

★★★★ Du T'kloof

★★★☆ Cabrière, Dellrust, Grndheim

★★★ De Krans, Prtrville ★★☆ Kango ★★ Mns Ruber, Swrtland ★☆ Cltzdorp, Oranje ★ **Klnhof NT** Drnkraal, Huguenot, Jacaranda **NR** Prtrville **D** Mooitsg

Morio muscat

★★★☆ Lndskrn

Muscadel, red

★★★★☆ Boplaas, Monis, Rietvallei

★★★★ Avndale, De Wet, Du T'kloof, **Grt Cnstntia**, **Jonkhr**, **KWV** (2), Nuy, Rietvallei, Rooibrg

★★★☆ Badsberg, **Bon Crge**, Kango, Riverstn, Sthrn Cape Vyds, Van Lvren, Wltvrede

★★★ Grndheim, McGreg, Mns Ruber, Mooitsg, Ovrhex, Rdezandt, Seidel, Slnghoek ★★☆ Boland, Nordale, Oranje, Rietrvr, Uitvlucht, W'drift ★★ Ashton, Douglas ★☆ Aan de Drns, Klawer, Wandsbeck ★ Lndzicht, **Westcrp Int NT** De Doorns, Montagu

Muscadel, white

★★★★ Avndale, Boland, Bon Crge, De Krans, De Wetsh, G Beck, Jonkhr (2), KWV, Nuy, Sthrn Cape Vyds

★★★☆ Boplaas, Citrus, De Krans, **Saronsbrg**, Thelema

★★★ Boplaas, Clairvx, Cltzdorp, Drnkraal, Grndheim, Ltzvlle, McGreg, Mns Ruber, Rbtson, Rdezandt, Rietrvr, Twee JG, **Westcrp Int**, Wltvrede ★★☆ Kango, Lndzicht, Mns Ruber, Mooitsg, Nordale, Uitvlucht, Yonder ★★ Oranje, Ovrhex **NT** Ashton, Klawer, Montagu **D** Rooibrg

Muscat de Hambourg

★★★★ S'bosch Hills

Non-Muscat, red

★★★★ Drnkraal, Laborie

★★★ Boplaas ★★ Perdebrg ★ Mooitsg

Non-Muscat, white

★★★ **Bcksbrg NT** Daschbsch

'Port', red

★★★★★ Axe Hill, De Krans, JP Bredell

★★★★☆ Allesvlrn, Boplaas (2), **JP Bredell**, Ovrgaauw

★★★★ Bergsig (2), Boplaas, De Krans (3), Drnkraal, JP Bredell, KWV (2), Lndskrn, Makro, Monis

★★★☆ Annandale, **Bcksbrg**, Bergsig, Boplaas (2), Botha (2), **Byrskloof**, De Wet, Dellrust, Du T'kloof, Flgstone, Grt Cnstntia, Jonkhr, Kango, KWV, L'Avenir, Linton P, Louiesnhf, Mrgnhof (2), Muratie, **P Bayly**, Swrtland, Villiera, **Vljsdrift**, Waboom

★★★ Beaumnt, Boland, Bon Crge, Boplaas, **Jean D**, **L'Ormarins**, McGreg, Mns Ruber, Muratie, Riebeek, Rstnberg, Rtrsvlei, Slnghoek, Smrbsch, Sthrn Cape Vyds, Tulbagh, **Van Lvren**, Vrgnoegd, Withoek, Wlington, Wndmeul ★★☆ Ashton, Grndheim, Kango, Padda, Rbtson, Rooibrg, Sentinel, Tulbagh, Wamaker ★★ Badsberg, Bnnievle, Bovlei, De Zoete, **Major's Hill**, Rietrvr, Swrtland, Vlrsdorp ★☆ Aan de Drns, Citrus, Cltzdorp, Klnhof ★ Clairvx, Mooitsg, Oranje ☆ **Montpllr NT** Cltzdorp, Douglas G, Drnkraal, Gdveld (2), Grndheim, Hrtswater, Huguenot (2), Lmrshoek, Uitvlucht **NR** Goudini **D** Bertrams, Cltzdorp, F'hoek Vyds, Rdezandt

Port, white

★★★☆ Asara

★★ Boplaas, De Krans **NT** Drnkraal **D** Mooitsg

Gamay noir

★★★ Kleine Z **D** Wlworths

Gewürztraminer

★★★★☆ Paul C

★★★★ Nthlingshof, Smnsig, Zevnwacht

★★★☆ Btnvrwchtng, Ndrburg, Villiera, Wltvrede

★★★ 32 South, Altyd, Bergsig, Delheim, Oude Wllngton, Wlworths ★★☆ Klnhof, Lndzicht **D** Bon Crge, Rietvallei

Grenache

★★★☆ Signal H

★★★ Citrus ★★ J van Zyl, **Tierhoek D** Signal H

Grenache Blanc

★★★★ Signal H

Hanepoot – see under Fortifieds

Icewine

★★★★ Signal H

Late Harvest

★★★☆ Waboom

★★★ Boplaas, Delheim ★★☆ De Zoete, Drostdy, Du T'kloof, Wlington, Wlworths ★★ Cellr Csk, Citrus, Ovrmeer, Pick 'n P, Rietrvr, Rvnswood ★☆ Bernheim, McGreg, Mooitsg, Rbtson, Riebeek, Westcrp Int ★ Carnival, Country C, K'prinz, Oranje, **Prtrville**, **Vlrsdorp NT** Ashton, De Doorns, Douglas, Grndheim, Hrtswater, Huguenot (2), Montagu, Picardi, Smnsvlei, Swrtland, Ultra Liq, Wndmeul, Wnklshk **D** Bnnievle, Kango, Klawer, Uitvlucht, Wlworths

Malbec

★★★★ Bellevue, Signal H

★★★☆ Ashanti, Bellevue, Hildenb, Ndrburg, **Spier**, Wlworths

★★★ **Anura**, Umkhulu ★★☆ Bcksbrg, **Cpe Vyds D** Fview, Makro

Merlot

★★★★★ Thelema

★★★★☆ Avndale, Cordoba, Havana, KWV, Linton P, Ovrgaauw, Quoin, Slaley, Stnberg, Veenwdn, Verglgn

★★★★ Akkerdal, Amani, **Anura** (2), Asara, Bein, Bellnghm, Bilton, Btnvrwchtng, Cmbrly, Coleraine, Dbn Hills, De Traf, Delaire, Delheim, Du Preez, Ekndal, Fleur dC, Grt Cnstntia, Havana, Hrtnberg, Jordan, Kleine Z, KWV, Laibach, L'Ormarins (2), L'rdge, Main Str, Meinert, Mrgnhof (2), Mrlust, Ndrburg, Plaisir, **Raka**, Ridgeback, Rmhoogte, Rust en V, Savanha, Seidel, Signal H, **Spice R**, Spier, Stkaya, Sumardg, Sxnburg, The Winery, Thelema, **Villiera**, Von O, Yonder

★★★☆ Afrcn Terroir, Altyd, Assegai, Audacia, Avntuur, Bellnghm, Bknhtskloof, Bloemndal, Blubrry Hill, Blwklppn, Boschndl, **Bottlry Int**, Cowlin, Cpe Grace, Darling C, Daview, Dbn Hills (2), DeWaal, Dmrsfntn (2), Dominion, Douglas G, Eaglevlei, Ernie Els, F'hoek Vyds, Five Heirs, Fleur dC, Fort S, **Glnwood**, Gracelnd, Grt Cnstntia, Grte Pst, Havana, **Hillcrest**, **Hofstraat**, Hpnbrg, Hzndal, Iona, JP Bredell, Ken F, Kleine Z, Klmpzcht (2), Koelfntn, Krnskop, KWV, L'Avenir, La Couronne, La Petite F, Laborie, Lanzerac, Lindiwe, **Lndhorst**, L'rdge, Lushof, Manley, Marklew, Meerend, Mischa, Mnt Rozier, **Mooipls**, Muratie, Nthlingshof, Omnia, Ormonde, **Perdebrg**, Rijk's, **Savanha**, Sentinel, Slaley, Stark-C, Stellnzcht, Sthrn Cape Vyds, Stony B, Vrgnoegd, Wlworths (Organic) (2), Zonneblm

★★★ **32 South**, Afrcn Terroir (Organic), Ashanti, Bcksbrg, Blue Crane, Bonfoi, Botha, Bovlei, Bschklf, Coppoolse, Cpe Classics, Daview, **De Grendel**, **De Zoete**, Dellrust, DeWaal,

Dornier, Drostdy, Du T'kloof, Eikehof, Ernst Co, **Flgstone**, Fraai U, **Fview**, G Beck, Goedvrwcht, Grt Eilnd, Hldrkruin, Jason's, Jonkhr, Kaapzicht, Kloovnbrg, Krnskop, KWV, La Bri, **Le Riche**, Libertas, Linton P (2), Lndskrn, Lost H, **Mischa**, Mrgnhof, Nelson, Nico vdM, Obikwa, **Olyvenbosch**, Post Hse, Rbtson, Rickety, Rtrsvlei (2), Rusticus, Savanha, S'bosch Hills, Shoprite, **Smnsvlei**, Spier, **Stellar** (Organic), Sterhuis, Table Mtn, Tulbagh, Upland, Villiera, Wamaker, **Welbedcht**, **Welgegund**, Whlhaven, Wlington, Wlworths (Organic) (3), Wndmeul, Yonder, Zevnwacht ★★☆ Boland, Boplaas, Botha, Clmborg, Cpe Coastal, Devon H, **Ernst Co**, Eshkl Kshr, Exclsor, **FirstCpe**, Fort S, Glnview, Hldrkruin, Klawer, Le Mnoir Brndel, Ltzvlle, **Mdlvlei**, Mnt Rochelle, Niel J, Omnia, Patrys, Rbtson, Riebeek (2), **Rooibrg**, Seidel, Smrbsch, Thorn, Tulbagh, Uitvlucht, Ultra Liq, Wamaker, Western, Wldekrans, Wlworths ★★ **Afrcn Terroir**, **Bovlei**, Citrus, Coppoolse, Dieu D, Hippo, **Kango**, Klnhof, Lost H, Lyngrove, Makro, Mntn River, Pulpit Rock, Rhbsklf, Shoprite, Slnghoek, Swrtland, **Teubes**, Van Lvren, Westcrp Int, **Wlworths** ☆☆ Badsberg, Cltzdorp, Drnkraal, F'hoek Vyds, **Goudini**, **Keukenhof**, Lndzicht, **Origin**(2) (Organic), Seidel, Stellar (Organic), Stellndrft, **Tall Horse** ★ Cru, Montpllr Sud, **Origin**, Wlworths **NT** Avndvrde, Bergwater (2), Bloupunt, Bodega, Country C, Daschbsch, Deetlefs, Doolhof, Drostdy, **Excelsious**, Fairseat, **False Bay**, FBW, IWS (2), Jacaranda, Kln DasBsch, Major's Hill, Makro, Môreson, Norton, Old Brdge (3), Omnia, Oubenhm, Rietrvr, Thabani, **Westcrp Int** (2) **NR Drknsig**, **Flat Roof**, Pulpit Rock, Rainbow, Rooibrg, **Stellcpe**, Vooruitsg, Wstbrdge **D** 32 South, Bcksbrg (Kosher), Bowe, Chamnx, Fryer, Grnde Prvnce, Hpnbrg, Kango, Kanu, Lvland, Main Str, Mnt Rozier, Omnia, Savanha, Schlkbnbsch, Spicc R, Sthrn Cape Vyds

Méthode cap classique – see under Sparkling wines
Morio Muscat – see under Fortifieds

Mourvèdre

★★★★ Beaumnt
★★★☆ **Spicc R**
★★★ **Fview**

Muscat d'Alexandrie

★★★★☆ **Alvi's Drift**
★ **Ovrhex NT** IWS **D** Stellar

Muscat de Frontignan

★★★★ Ndrburg
★★★ Thelema, Uitvlucht ★ Bianco

Muscat de Hambourg – see under Fortifieds

Natural Sweet

★★★★★ K Constantia
★★★★ Nabyglgn, Signal H, **Sprngfntn**, Sylvnvle
★★★☆ Bon Crge, Btnvrwchtng, L'Avenir, Laibach, Meerend, Rstnberg
★★★ Bloemndal, De Krans, **Kaapzicht**, Mrgnhof, Slnghoek, Thnskraal, Twee JG (LowAlc), Wltvrede ★★☆ Ashanti, Goudini, Rooibrg, Sxnburg ★★ Douglas, Grünb, Rbtson, The Saints (LowAlc), Van Lvren (3), Vrdnheim ☆☆ Allee B, Cellr Csk (3), Grünb (LowAlc), Lndzicht (2), Rooibrg ★ **Boplaas**, Darling C (LowAlc), Douglas, Riebeek (LowAlc) (2), Rooibrg, Tulbagh (LowAlc) ☆ Darling C, Douglas **NT** Drnkraal, Hrtswater (LowAlc) (2), Lvland, Prmium Cpe Wnes (4) **NR** Quoin **D** Cltzdorp, Hrtnberg, Merwespnt, Tulbagh, Westcrp Int

Nebbiolo

★★★★ Stnberg
★ Bianco

Noble Late Harvest

★★★★★ Rbtson
★★★★☆ Asara, Bon Crge, Darling C (2), Jordan, Kanu, Ken F, Ndrburg (2), Nthlingshof, Paul C, Rudera (2), Smnsig, Spier, Verglgn
★★★★ Btnvrwchtng, Cpe Point, De Wetsh, Delheim, Fleur dC, Joostnbrg, **Lournsfd**, Ndrburg (2), Rbtson, Rstnberg, Signal H (2), **Villiera** (2), Wlworths

★★★☆ Afrcn Terroir, Badsberg, Beaumnt, Bergsig, **Dieu D**, Du T'kloof, Ekndal, Jason's, Mrgnhof, Nuy, Waterfd

★★★ 32 South, **Dmrsdal**, Stony B, Twee JG ★★☆ Slnghoek ★★ K Constantia **NT** Bknhtskloof, IWS **D** Avntuur, Boland

Non-muscat, red/white, fortified – see under Fortifieds

Nouvelle

★★☆ **Boland**

Perlé wines

★★☆ De Wet (LowAlc) ★★ Autumn Hvst, Grünb (LowAlc), **Jonkhr**, Riebeek (LowAlc) ★☆ Lost H ★ Lost H **NS** Carnival **NT** Ashton, Bergsig (LowAlc), **Zidela**

Petit verdot

★★★★ Du Preez, Ndrburg, Signal H, Zrgvliet

★★★☆ Bellevue

★★★ **F'hoek Vyds**

Pinotage

★★★★☆ Bellevue, Byrskloof, Cmbrly, DeWaal, Dmrsfntn, Fview, Kaapzicht, Knonkp, L'Avenir, Nelson, Omnia, Smnsig, Sthrn Rght (2), Umkhulu

★★★★ Avntuur, Beaumnt, Bellevue, Bellnghm, Boplaas, Cls Mlvrne, Darling C, DeWaal, Dmrsfntn, Domaine B, Flgstone, G Beck, Goede H, Grnghurst, Hidden V, Horse Mtn, Jacobsdal, Kaapzicht, KWV, L'Avenir, Laibach, L'rdge, Lyngrove, Môreson, Mrgnhof, Ndrburg, Neil E, Nthlingshof, Perdebrg, **Rbtson**, S'bonga, Scali, Seidel, Sentinel, Slaley, Spice R, Spier, Stanfrd Hills, Stony B, Vljsdrift, Wstbrdge

★★★☆ Allee B, Altyd, Anura, Assegai, Auberge du P, Bon Crge, Botha, **Bottlry Int**, Byrskloof, Cloof (2), Cls Mlvrne, Cpe Classics, Darling C, Dbn Hills, Delheim, DeWaal, Dmrsdal, Doolhof, Douglas G, Eaglevlei, Five Heirs, Fleur dC, G Beck, Goede H, Grt Cnstntia, Hill & Dale, Hldrkruin, Hrtnberg, **Hzndal** (2), Jonkhr, Kleine Z, **Klmpzcht**, Knrhoek, Ktzenbrg, KWV, Laborie, Lanzerac, L'Auberge, Ldrsburg, Lmrshoek, Lyngrove, Major's Hill, Manley, Meerend, Mntn Oaks, Mooipls, Nitida, Ntvbij, Onderklf, Oracle, Patrys, Perdebrg, Rbtson, Reyneke, Rijk's, Romans, Signal H, Smnsig, **Sprngfntn**, Stellnzcht, Sxnburg, Sylvnvle, **Tempel**, Thelema, Tukulu, Tulbagh, Warwick, Wldekrans (2), Wlworths, Wm Everson, Wstbrdge, Zevnwacht

★★★ Ashanti, Badsberg, Bellnghm, Bergheim, Bergsig, Bianco, Bon Cap (Organic), Botha, **Cilandia**, Citrus, Clmborg, Coppoolse, Cpe Bay, Cpe Vyds (2), Cru, De Krans, **De Villiers**, **De Zoete**, Dellrust, Dieu D, Du T'kloof, FirstCpe, Fort S, Fview, Hldrkruin, Jason's, Ken F, Kleine Z, Klnvallei, KWV, La Petite F, Le Grand Chass, Lndskrn, L'rdge, Lyngrove, Malan, MAN Vintners, McGreg, Mdlvlei, **Mhudi**, Môreson, **Morewag**, Mrgnhof, Mrhof, Ndrburg, New Begin, Nthlingshof, Omnia, Pulpit Rock, Raka, Rusticus, Slnghoek, Smnsvlei, Smook, Smrbsch, Spier, Stettyn, Sthrn Cape Vyds, Sumardg, Tarentaal, Van Lvren, Villiera, Vrdnheim, Vriesenhof, **Wlington**, Wlworths (2), Wndmeul, Zonneblm ★★☆ Afrcn Terroir, **Avndale**, Avntuur, Bernheim, Boland, Bon Cap (Organic), Boplaas, Chamnx, Detendu, **Devon Rocks**, Drostdy, Eshkl Kshr, F'hoek Vyds, G Beck, Hpnbrg, J van Zyl, **Jonkhr**, **Klein Parys**, Kln Draken (Kosher), Libertas, Lndhorst, Louiesnhf, Main Str, Mellasat, Mntn River, Nelson, Niel J, Obikwa, Oranje, Origin, Pulpit Rock, Rhbsklf, Rietrvr, Rtrsvlei, S'bosch Hills, Slaley, Smnsvlei, Sthrn Cape Vyds, Swrtland, Two Oceans, Waboom, Winecorp ★★ **Afrcn Terroir** (Organic) (3), Bcksbrg (Kosher) (2), Bovlei, Citrus, Cloof, Cpe Coastal, Deetlefs, Devon H, Dominion, Drknsig (2), Eshkl Kshr, F'hoek Vyds, Fort S, Grt Eilnd, Klawer, Klein Parys, Le Mnoir Brndel, Long Mntn, Ltzvlle, Oude Kaap, **Prtrville** (2), Riebeek, Rooibrg (2), Seidel (2), Shoprite, Stellar(2) (Organic), Swrtland, Thorn, Tulbagh, Wamaker, Westcrp Int, Wlworths ★☆ Aan de Drns, Fair Valley, Hippo, **Kango**, Klnhof, Lindiwe, Makro, Millstrm, **Origin**, Prtrville, **Stellndrft**, Wlington ★ Goudini, Mntn River, **Origin**, **Shoprite** ☆ **Coppoolse NS** Lndzicht, Wamaker **NT** Anthill, Blue Creek, Bodega, Daschbsch, **De Wet**, Deetlefs, Huguenot, IWS (2), Kln DasBsch, Lemberg, Mdlpos, Nelson, Old Brdge (2), Omnia, Oubenhm, Smrbsch, Westcrp Int, Windfall **NR Stbosch Cntry Est**, Western **D** 32 South, Asara, Beaumnt, Kango, Knonkp,

Marklew, Mellasat, Mnt Destin, Mnt Rozier (2), Omnia (2), Spice R, Sthrn Cape Vyds, Stnwall, Tokara, Vinus Via

Pinot blanc

D Lanzerac

Pinot gris/Pinot grigio

★★★ L'Ormarins, Van Lvren ★★☆ **Stormhoek** ★★ **Flat Roof D** L'Ormarins

Pinot noir

★★★★☆ Bchrd-F (2), HRV, Vriesenhof

★★★★ BWC, Chamnx, De Traf, Kln Optnhrst, Newton J, Topaz, **Weening Barge**, Whlhaven, Wlworths

★★★☆ De Wetsh, Glen C, Grte Pst, Herold, **Makro**, Muratie, Signal H, Sumardg, The Winery

★★★ Bellevue, Btnvrwchtng, Cabrière, Cpe First, Flgstone, Goedvertw, Hpnbrg, K Constantia, Mrlust, Paul C, Rusticus, Sthrn Cape Vyds, Thandi ★★☆ Ashton ★★ **Avntuur** ★ Montpllr **NS** Montpllr Sud **NT** Gdveld, Lemberg, **Minke NR Elgin Vntnrs D** Flgstone

Red blends

Cape 'Bordeaux'

★★★★★ Ernie Els

★★★★☆ Boschndl, Bschklf, Btnvrwchtng, Byrskloof, Capaia, Cordoba, De Toren, Glen C, Grnghurst, Havana, High C, Horse Mtn, Ingwe, Jean D, Jordan (2), Kln Gustrw, Knonkp, Mrgnhof, Mrgnster (2), Mrlust, Muratie, Neil E, Nthlingshof, Ovrgaauw, Sprgfield, **Stkaya**, **Tokara**, Veenwdn, Verglgn (2), **Vilafonte** (2), Vriesenhof, Warwick, Wlworths

★★★★ Adler, Asara, Avntuur, Bcksbrg (2), Beaumnt, Bellevue, Bschklf, Capaia, Cloof, Cls Mlvrne, Cmbrly, Con Uitsig, Conspirare, **Dalla Cia**, **Daview** (2), Delaire (2), Delheim, Ekndal, Flgstone, **G Beck**, Goede H, Grt Cnstntia, **Havana**, Hillcrest, **Hrtnberg**, Kanu, KWV, Laibach (2), Le Bonh, Le Riche, L'Ormarins, Louisvle, Lynx, Makro, Meerend, Meinert, **Mnt Rochelle**, Môreson, **Mrlust**, Mulderb, Nabyglgn, Ndrburg (2), Niel J, Nitida, **Old Vines**, Raka, Ridgeback, **Rijk's**, Rstnberg, S'bonga, Seidel, Smnsig, Stellnzcht, Stony B, Sxnburg, Umkhulu, Veenwdn, Verglgn, Villiera, **Vljsdrift**, Von O, Vrgnoegd, Vriesenhof, Vuurberg, Wbrsburg, **Welbedcht**, Welgemnd (2), Wlworths, Yonder, Zrgvliet

★★★☆ Alter Ego, **Amani**, Bovlei, Btnvrwchtng, Bwland, Cellr-Vie, Chamnx, **Cloof**, Cmbrly, Cowlin, Crows Nest, Cru, Dbn Hills, De Toren, Fryer, Goedvrwcht, Hegewisch, **Iona**, Jean D, Jonkhr, Jordan (2), Joubert-T, **K Constantia** (2), Krnskop, KWV, La Motte, Laborie, Laibach (Organic), Lanzerac, Ldrsburg, Lndskrn, Lyngrove, Makro, Môreson, **Mrgnster**, **N Ellis Meyer N**, Napier, **Nick Forti's**, Nico V, Nthlingshof, Omnia, Ormonde, Paul C, R&R, Rainbow, Saronsbrg, S'bosch Hills, Slaley, Smnsvlei, Smook, Stnwall, Swrtland, **Thandi** (2), **The Winery**, **Tulbagh Mtn Vyds**, Two Oceans, Uva Mira, **Vendôme** (2), Welgemnd, **Wlworths (Organic)** (2)

★★★ **Allee B**, Audacia, Avntuur, Bellnghm, Bnnievle, **Bottlry Int**, Cls Mlvrne, Coleraine, Cordoba, Cpe Bay, Cpe First (2), Cpe Grace, De Compagnie, Detendu, Dominion, Dornier, El Dorado, Grnde Prvnce, Kln Draken (Kosher), La Bri, Lost H, Lyngrove, **Lynx**, Makro, MAN Vintners, McGreg, Merwespnt, Mnterosso, New Cape, Oude Kaap, Perdebrg, Rhbsklf, Rickety, Romond, Rooibrg, Rtrsvlei, Seidel, Stellndrft, Tangara, Ultra Liq, Van Z'hof, Vrede en Lust, W'drift, Wldekrans, Wlworths, Wndmeul ★★☆ Avntuur, Bernheim, Bovlei, Cpe Vyds, Crghall, Dieu D, **Dispore Kamma**, **Dreamview**, **Drnkraal**, **FirstCpe**, Hldrkruin, Jacaranda, Leopard's, Makro, Malan, **Mike's Ktchn**, Mnt Rozier, Mooitsg, **Mostrtsdrift**, Ovrhex, **SA Premium**, Seidel, The Winery, Vriesenhof, Winecorp, Wldekrans, Wlworths ★★ Dominion, Nuy, Slnghoek, Ultra Liq, Vaughan J, **Wlworths**, Zidela, **Ziggurat** ★☆ **Lost H**, Shoprite, **Sthrn Sky**, Westcrp Int ★ **Citrus**, **Hippo**, Horse Mtn, Shoprite **NS** Bon Cap **NT Agterplaas** (2), Bergwater, Bertrams, Blwklppn, Bottlry Hills, Brnthrst, Daschbsch, De Wet, Gusto, Havana, Hrtnberg, Jacaranda, Koningsrvr, La Petite F, Mntn River, Nelson, Old Brdge, Rozendal, Smrbsch, Thabani, **Wedderwill NR**

Hldrkruin, **M Mossop Wines**, Schlkbnbsch (2), **Stellcpe D** Asara, Bon Cap, Cowlin, Ekndal, Grte Pst, Kango, Knonkp, Lmrshoek, Lvland, Omnia (2), Rhbsklf, Swrtland, Wltvrede

Other cabernet-based blends

★★★★☆ Cls Mlvrne, De Traf, Ernie Els, **Flgstone** (2), Ingwe, Waterfd

★★★★ Alto, Barton, Black Pearl, Bonfoi, Carisbrke, Cloof, Cls Mlvrne, **Cmbrly**, De Meye, Dmrsfntn, Ernie Els, Gracelnd, Mulderb, **Nabyglgn**, Ndrburg, **Pick's Pick**, Plaisir, Rmhoogte, Rust en V, Uva Mira, Zonneblm

★★★☆ **Audacia**, Avndale, **Bodraai**, **Boland**, Bon Crge, Cpe Bay, Dmrsdal, **Doolhof** (2), **Douglas G**, Groenld, Hrtnberg, JP Bredell, Kaapzicht, **Knrhoek**, KWV, La Couronne (2), Lournsfd, **Lvland**, Mnt Rochelle, Reyneke, Rstnberg, Slaley, Smnsig, **Smrbsch**, **Stormhoek**, Vrdnheim, Vrgin Erth, Waterfd, Wlworths, Wstbrdge, **Zndvliet**

★★★ **32 South**, Afrcn Terroir, **Allee B** (2), Boschndl, Cloof, Clovelly, Cls Mlvrne, Cordoba, Cowlin, **De Meye**, De Zoete, **Dieu D**, Drostdy, Eshkl Kshr, Flgstone, Glen C, Goede H, Hzndal, Janéza, Klnvallei, Le Grand Chass, Leopard's, **Lmrshoek**, Lushof, Mnt du Toit, Mooitsg, **Mountain Rge**, Mrgnhof, Opstal, Raka, Rbtson, Rietvallei, Rijk's, Uitkyk, Van Lvren, Vrede en Lust, Western, Wine Vllge ★★☆ Agterplaas, Boland, Boschndl, Chamnx, Delheim, Grt Cnstntia, Hill & Dale, Klein Parys, Nordale, **Seven Oaks** ★★ De Zoete, **Fview**, **Kango**, L'Avenir, Slaley, **Stellndrft**, **Umkhulu** ★☆ **Cpe Coastal**, **Origin NT Anwilka**, **Bnnievle**, Drostdy, Maiden **D** Douglas, Omnia (2), Zndvliet

Italian varieties, blends with

★★★★ Bchrd-F, Bcksbrg, Ndrburg

★★★☆ Fview, Wlworths

★★★ **Stormhoek**

Merlot-based blends

★★★★☆ Stnberg

★★★★ Devon H, Joostnbrg, Knonkp, Makro, **Post Hse**, Rmhoogte, **Vuurberg**

★★★☆ Annandale, **Avndale**, Du Preez, Kaapzicht, KWV, R&R, Stony B, Vljsdrift, **Whlhaven**

★★★ Assegai, Bellevue, Bknhtskloof, Ekndal, Fort S (2), Grte Pst, Hill & Dale, Hrtnberg, Jonkhr, Joostnbrg, **JP Bredell**, Mystery, **Onderklf**, Origin, Rmhoogte, Two Oceans, **Vrede en Lust**, Waboom ★★☆ De Krans, Long Mntn, **Tangara**, Western, Whlhaven, Wltvrede, **Wlworths** (2) ★★ Aan de Drns, Boplaas, Dmrsfntn, Drnkraal, **Origin**, **Ovrhex**, Rtrsvlei, Vaughan J ★☆ F'hoek Vyds ★ Westcrp Int **NT Feiteiras**

Pinotage, blends with

Pinotage accounts for a minimum of 30% in these blends; there is no maximum.

★★★★★ Kaapzicht

★★★★☆ Byrskloof, Darling C, DeWaal, G Beck, Grnghurst (2), Meinert, Vriesenhof

★★★★ Asara, Ashanti, **Cloof**, Cls Mlvrne, Dellrust, Flgstone, Kaapzicht, L'Avenir, Nthlingshof, Smnsig, **The Observatory**, Warwick

★★★☆ Byrskloof, Cedrbrg, Cloof, Cls Mlvrne, Devon H, Domaine B, Du Preez, **Fview**, **Klmpzcht**, **Lndskrn**, **Lorraine**, Mdlvlei, Romans, **Sylvnvle**, **Umkhulu** (2), Welgemnd, Wlworths

★★★ 32 South, Afrcn Terroir, Asara, Ashanti, **Babylon's Pk**, Belbon Hills, Bellevue, Blwklppn, Clairvx, Cls Mlvrne, Cpe Grace, **De Krans**, Domaine B, Eden Crst, Goedvertw, **Hidden V**, **Knrhoek**, Makro, New Cape, Opstal, **Spier**, Stellnzcht, Stkaya, Villiera, Waboom, Western, Wldekrans ★★☆ Ashton, **Bianco**, **Carolinahve**, Cloof, DeWaal, Du T'kloof, Goudini, Kleine Z, Malan, Mntn River, **Ndrburg**, Ntvbij, Omnia, Origin, Oudeklf, Padda, Rhbsklf, Slaley, **Stellndrft**, Two Oceans, Western (Organic), Winecorp ★★ Afrcn Terroir, Douglas G, Drnkraal, Hrtswater, **Klein Parys**, Klnhof, Lost H (2), Merwespnt, **Origin**, Prtrville, Rietrvr, S'bosch Hills, Slnghoek, Wamaker, Western (2) ★☆ Cru (2), **La Chataigne**, Lost H, **Origin** (3), Ovrhex **NS Bovlei NT** Bon Crge, Bottlry Hills, Deetlefs,

Dmrsdal, **Drostdy** (2), Huguenot, IWS, Leopard's, Oranje, Rietrvr, S/SW **NR** Tulbagh **D** Boland, F'hoek Vyds, Lmrshoek, Mdlvlei, Origin, Villiera, Welgemnd

Shiraz-based blends

★★★★☆ Bknhtskloof, Cmbrly, Nico vdM, Spice R, The Winery

★★★★ Avndale, Dmrsfntn, Ernie Els, Goats, Hzndal, **Joostnbrg**, **Karusa**, Klmpzcht, **La Motte**, Lmrshoek, Ndrburg, Newton J, Saronsbrg, **Solms-Delta**, Sxnburg, The Observatory, **Tulbagh Mtn Vyds** (2), Wlworths, Yonder

★★★☆ Akkerdal, **Anura** (2), Blyde, **Bscheim**, Doolhof, Flgstone, **G Beck** (2), Goats, Havana, KWV, Long Mntn, Lyngrove, Makro, **Mnt Destin**, Ndrburg, Omnia, Ovrgaauw, Quoin, **Ridgeback**, **Sequillo**, **Spier**, Stettyn, StllnHills, Swrtland, **Tulbagh Mtn Vyds**, Western, Wlworths, Zevnwacht

★★★ Afrcn Terroir (2), Anura, **Cpe Coastal**, Cpe First, Eden Crst, **Exclsor**, FirstCpe, Gallop Hill, Kanu, Klein Parys, **KWV**, **L Hughes**, Lndhorst, Muratie, Oaklnds Exprtrs, Omnia, Prospect, Rickety, **Riebeek** (2), Riverstn, Sxnburg, Tarentaal, The Winery, **Umkhulu**, Van Lvren, Zevnwacht ★★☆ Afrcn Pride, **Bon Cap** (Organic), **Kanu**, Old Vines, Padda, Prtrville, Smrbsch, Sthrn Cape Vyds, Van Lvren ★★ Country C, Douglas, Mrhof, Ovrhex, Smnsvlei (2), **Swrtland**, Tangara, Westcrp Int ★☆ Nordale, **Stellcpe**, **Sthrn Sky**, Ultra Liq, **Zidela** ★ **Origin**, Westcrp Int ☆ Origin **NS Westcrp Int** (LowAlc) **NT** Havana, Makro, Ultra Liq, Wndmeul **NR The Winery D** De Wet, Fview, Omnia, Riverstn, Rtrsvlei, Whlhaven

Other red blends

These may contain pinotage, but always less than 30%.

★★★★☆ Assegai, Ken F, Mnt du Toit

★★★★ **Amani**, **Bartho E**, Boplaas, De Krans, Fview, **Lmrshoek**, Makro, Marklew, Mnt du Toit, Raka, The Winery

★★★☆ Akkerdal, Dellrust, Ken F, **Mnt du Toit**, Signal H, **Spier**, Stkaya, Vrgnoegd

★★★ Botha, **Bottlry Int**, Cpe Bay, Darling C, Du Preez, Goats, Kaapzicht, **Kanu**, KWV, **Latcgnskp**, Lvland, Main Str, Omnia, Raka, Rdezandt, Ridder's, **Ridgeback**, Sxnburg, Thnskraal, Withoek, Wlington ★★☆ Bcksbrg, Bergsig, Blwklppn, Bnnievle (2), Brndvlei, Ch Lib, Citrus (3), Coleraine, Cpe Vyds, Goudini, Kln Optnhrst, KWV, Lndskrn, Millstrm, Mnt Rozier, Nelson, **Oude Kaap**, Patrys, Rbtson, Rooibrg, Schlkbnbsch, Sthrn Cape Vyds (2), The Saints, **Uitvlucht**, Western, Wlworths ★★ **32 South**, Citrus, **Clmborg**, Coppoolse, Drostdy, **Hippo**, KWV, Mdlvlei, Pick 'n P, Rbtson, Rvnswood, **Sthrn Sky**, Swrtland, Tassenbrg, Text, Winecorp, Wlworths (3) ★☆ Carnival, Cellr Csk, Country C (2), Crows Nest, **Eshkl Kshr**, Grt Eilnd, **Mrhof**, **Origin**, Ovrmeer, Riebeek (2) **NT Aufwaerts**, Bottlry Hills, Crows Nest, De Doorns, Douglas, Fairseat, Fredine Fine Wnes, Grndheim, IWS (2), Montagu, Picardi, Prmium Cpe Wnes, Swrtland, Ultra Liq, Windfall, **Wnklshk** (2) **NR Schlkbnbsch D** 32 South, Citrus, F'hoek Vyds, Grt Cnstntia, Klawer, Mnt Destin, Rtrsvlei, The Foundry

Riesling (Cape or SA)

★★★ Ndrburg ★★☆ Bon Crge ★★ Boland, De Wet, Du T'kloof, KWV, Thnskraal, Van Lvren **NT De Villiers D** Sthrn Cape Vyds

Riesling (Rhine or weisser)

★★★★ K Constantia, Ndrburg, Paul C, Thelema, Wltvrede

★★★☆ Btnvrwchtng, De Wetsh, Hrtnberg, Jack & Knox, Villiera, Wlworths (2)

★★★ Bergsig, Deetlefs, Jordan, Lvland ★★☆ **Rietvallei**, Rooibrg ★★ Montpllr ★☆ Rhbsklf **NT** Montpllr Sud **D** Grt Cnstntia

Rosé dry

★★★★ **Solms-Delta**

★★★☆ Goats, **Hpnbrg**, Newton J

★★★ **Allee B**, Asara, Bknhtskloof, Byrskloof, Cabrière, Darling C, Dominion, **Drmrshire**, Drostdy, Flgstone, Goedvrwcht, High C, L'Avenir, Le Pommier, Origin, Raka, Signal H, **Stormhoek**, Sylvnvle, **Villiera**, Vljsdrift, Waboom, **Weening Barge**, **Zrgvliet** ★★☆ Ashanti, Bergsig, **Cpe Grace**, Five Heirs, **Flgstone**, **Fort S**, Hill & Dale, Horse Mtn, Môreson, Mrgnhof, Mrhof, Nelson, **New Cape**, Omnia (2), Slaley, Vrede en Lust, Whlhaven ★★ Afrcn Terroir, Bernheim, Bloemndal, **Crghall**, Deetlefs, Ldrsburg, **Lmrshoek**, **Origin**,

Rooibrg, **Stellar** (Organic), **Welgegund** ★☆ Cloof, **Mnt Vernon**, **Mntn River**, **Rietvallei**, Sumardg ★ **Leopard's**, **Origin**, Seidel **NT** Ht Espoir, IWS, Jason's, Prmium Cpe Wnes, Schlkbnbsch **NR** Môreson, Tangara **D** F'hoek Vyds, Opstal, Origin, Rtrsvlei, Swrtland

Rosé off-dry/semi-sweet

★★★ Bnnievle, **Bon Cap** (Organic), De Krans, Hildenb, **Kanu**, **KWV**, Wlington ★★☆ Badsberg, Bcksbrg, **Chamnx**, Delheim, **Dellrust**, Dieu D, G Beck, Grnde Prvnce, KWV, L'Avenir, Le Grand Chass, Millstrm, Riebeek, **Sylvnvle**, Two Oceans, **Ultra Liq**, Vrdnheim, Winecorp, Wlworths ★★ **Avndale**, Bellnghm, **Bovlei**, Clmborg, Country C, **Exclsor**, Graca, Klnhof, **La Chataigne**, Long Bch Café, Ovrhex, Pick 'n P, Rbtson, Rietrvr, **Rtrsvlei**, Rvnswood, Seidel, Shoprite, Slnghoek, Smnsvlei, Swrtland, The Saints (LowAlc), Van Lvren (LowAlc), Winecorp, Wlworths ★☆ **Eshkl Kshr**, Grt Eilnd, Mooitsg, Ndrburg, Prtrville, Rbtson (LowAlc), Riebeek ★ **Blwklppn**, Clairvx, Cru (2), **Lost H**, Oranje, Sthrn Cape Vyds, **Vlrsdorp**, Westcrp Int ☆ Carnival, Ltzvlle **NS Westcrp Int** (LowAlc) **NT** Hrtswater, Mystery, Riebeek **NR** De Zoete **D** De Wet, Douglas, Drostdy

Roussanne

NR Rstnberg

Ruby cabernet

★★★ Belbon Hills, Goudini, Long Mntn, Ltzvlle, McGreg, Rbtson, Zndvliet ★★☆ Lngvrwacht, Oranje, Rbtson, Waboom ★★ Sthrn Cape Vyds, Wandsbeck ★☆ **Oude Kaap**, Oude Wllngton, Rusticus **NT** Daschbsch, Fairseat, Gdveld, Hrtswater, **Jewel Breede**, Windfall **D** Drostdy, Riverstn

Sacramental wines

★★★ Mooitsg ★★ Citrus ★☆ Eshkl Kshr **NT** Huguenot, Kln Draken (Kosher)

Sangiovese

★★★☆ **Fview**, L'Ormarins

★★★ **Anura**, **Mnterosso** **D** Ashanti, Whlhaven

Sauvignon blanc, unwooded

★★★★★ Stnberg

★★★★☆ Bartho E, **Constnta Glen**, Cpe Point, Dbn Hills, Fleur dC, Fryer, **K Constantia**, Mulderb, Neil E, Nitida, Oak Valley, **Omnia**, Spier, Verglgn, **Zrgvliet**

★★★★ **Alluvia**, Avndale, Bartho E, Bloemndal, Boschndl, **Btnvrwchtng** (2), Cedrbrg, Con Uitsig, **Cpe Point**, Dbn Hills, **De Grendel**, Delaire, Fleur dC, Flgstone, Fort S, Fview, **G Beck**, Grt Cnstntia, Hillcrest, Iona, Jordan, K Constantia, **Kleine Z**, KWV, Landau, Lmrshoek, **Lomond**, L'Ormarins, Lushof, **Meerend**, Ndrburg (3), Newton J, Nitida, **Omnia** (2), Oracle, Ormonde, Quando, Quoin, Raka, Rbtson, Rijk's, **Ross G**, **Saronsbrg**, Sprgfield (2), Sterhuis, Sthrn Rght, Stnberg, Sumardg, **Sxnburg** (2), **Thelema** (2), **Tokara** (2), Uitkyk, Verglgn, Villiera, Wltvrede

★★★☆ **Agulhas Wines**, Altyd, Amavara, **Ataraxia**, Bchrd-F, Beaumnt, Belbon Hills, Bellevue, Bon Crge, Bonfoi, Boschndl, Botha, BWC, Capaia, Chamnx, Clouds, **Crows Nest**, Darling C (2), Dbn Hills, Dellrust, DeWaal, **Doolhof**, Elgin Vntnrs, Ernst Co, **Fat B**, Flgstone, G Beck, Glnwood, Goede H, Grnde Prvnce, Grte Pst, Gusto, Hemlzcht, **Herold**, Hill & Dale, **Hillcrest**, Hpnbrg, Hrtnberg, Hzndal, Kanu, Ken F, Kleine Z, Kln Draken (Kosher), KWV (2), L'Avenir, La Couronne, La Motte (2), Land's E, Lanzerac, Le Pommier, Lournsfd, Main Str, Meerend, Mooipls, Môreson, Ndrburg, Nthlingshof, Omnia, Ovrgaauw, Paul C, **Pick's Pick**, Reyneke, Ridgeback, **Rietvallei**, **Ross G**, **Savanha**, Smnsvlei, Stellnzcht, Sthrn Cape Vyds, **Tierhoek**, Usana, Uva Mira, Villiera, Von O, Warwick, Waterfd, Wlworths, Zevnwacht, **Zoetendal**, **Zrgvliet** (2)

★★★ Afrcn Pride, Afrcn Terroir, Amani, Anura, Asara, Assegai, Avntuur, Badsberg, Bellnghm, Bknhtskloof, Blue Crane, Blwklppn, Boland (2), **Bottlry Int**, Cloverfld, Cls Mlvrne, Cpe Bay (2), Cpe Classics, Cpe First, Crghall, **Cru**, Dalla Cia, De Wetsh, De Zoete, Delheim, Dieu D, Dmrsdal, Dombeya, Dominion (2), Exclsor, **FirstCpe**, Fleur dC, **Gallop Hill**, Goedvertw, Havana, Hldrkruin, Kaapzicht, **Kanu**, Knrhoek, KWV, Laborie, Laibach, Le Bonh, **Lomond**, Long Bch Café, Louiesnhf, L'rdge, Lvland, Lyngrove, Major's Hill, **Mhudi**, Mnt Rozier, Mrgnhof,

New Cape, Ntvbij, Omnia, Onderklf, Ormonde, **Perdebrg**, Plaisir, Rbtson, Rietvallei, Ross G, Rstnberg, Savanha, Sentinel, Smnsig, Smrbsch, **Spice R**, Spier, Stellar, Stettyn, Stony B, Tarentaal, Vljsdrift, **Vrgin Erth**, **Vruchtbaar**, Wlworths (2), **Ziggurat**, Zndvliet ★★☆ Agterplaas, Bcksbrg, **Bon Cap**, **Bottlry Int**, Citrus, Clairvx, Coppoolse, **Cowlin**, **Cru**, Devon H, Drknsig, Du Preez, Du T'kloof, Five Heirs, **Flgstone**, Fort S, Goedvrwcht, Janéza, Jason's, **Kloovnbrg**, KWV, La Petite F, **Langeberg**, Lategnskp, Ldrsburg, Le Grand Chass, Leopard's, Libertas, Lindiwe, Linton P, Long Mntn, **Lorraine**, Lost H (2), Malan, MAN Vintners, **Marais Fam**, McGreg (2), **Mnt Rochelle**, Mnt Rozier, Mnterosso, **Mntn River**, Nabyglgn, Nelson, New Cape, Niel J, Oaklnds Exprtrs, Obikwa, Omnia, Opstal, Origin, Rickety, Riverstn, Romans, S'bosch Hills, Schlkbnbsch, Shoprite, Slaley, Smnsvlei, Swrtland (2), Table Mtn, The Winery, Thorn, Two Oceans, Umkhulu, Van Lvren, Van Z'hof, Wamaker, Western, Winecorp, Wldekrans, Wlington, Wlworths(2) (Organic), Zonneblm ★★ Ashton, Bartinney, Bergsig, Bnnievle, Bovlei, Brndvlei, **Cpe Coastal** (2), **De Villiers**, Deetlefs, Drostdy, Du Preez, F'hoek Vyds (2), Grt Eilnd, Jonkhr, Klawer, **Klein Parys**, Klnhof, Mnt Rochelle, Mnt Rozier, Môreson, Nordale, Nuy, Ovrhex, Patrys, **Prtrville**, Rbtson, Rdezandt, Ridder's, Riebeek, Rietrvr, Rooibrg, Rtrsvlei, Seidel, **Sthrn Sky**, **Stormhoek**, Wltvrede, Wlworths, Wndmeul ★☆ Afrcn Terroir, Boplaas, Bovlei, Citrus, Clmborg, Country C, De Wet, **Dominion**, Fair Valley, Goudini, Ht Espoir, **Kango**, **La Chataigne**, Lndskrn, Ltzvlle, Manley, Merwespnt, Mntn River, Mostrtsdrift, **Origin**, Padda, Rhbsklf, Tulbagh, Ultra Liq, Vlrsdorp, Wandsbeck ★ Afrcn Terroir (Organic), **Cltzdorp**, Hippo, Klnhof, Le Mnoir Brndel, **Origin**, Prtrville, Slnghoek, Urbane, W'drift, **Westcrp Int** ☆ **The Stables** (2) **NT** **ACJ Fine Wines**, Bottlry Hills, Daschbsch, Douglas G, Drostdy, **Excelsious**, **False Bay**, FBW, Havana, IWS (2), Ldrsburg, Lemberg, Mntn River, Old Brdge (2), Omnia, Prmium Cpe Wnes, Sthrn Sky, Thabani, **Wedderwill**, Westcrp Int, **Zidela** (3) **NR** **Adler**, Ekndal **D** 32 South, Afrcn Terroir, **Bcksbrg** (Kosher), Bowe, Cpe Point, Cpe Vyds, Daview, De Zoete, Ingwe, Kango, Ken F, L'Ormarins, Main Str, Montpllr, Omnia (2), Origin, Perdebrg, Rtrsvlei, Savanha, Sthrn Cape Vyds, Wlworths

Sauvignon blanc, wooded

★★★★☆ Chamnx, **Neil E**, **Tokara**, Verglgn

★★★★ Bcksbrg, **Stnberg**

★★★☆ Cpe Point, De Wetsh, Delaire, Flgstone, Jordan, L'Ormarins

★★★ Fort S, **Reyneke**, Smnsig ★★☆ La Petite F **NR** Drmrshire **D** Citrus, Thelema

Semillon, unwooded

★★★ Alter Ego, **Flat Roof** ★★☆ Vljsdrift ★★ Le Pommier, Van Lvren **NT** Breelnd **D** Bon Crge, Glnwood, Montpllr

Semillon, wooded

★★★★★ Cpe Point, Stnberg, Verglgn

★★★★☆ Bknhtskloof, Con Uitsig, Fview

★★★★ **Btnvrwchtng**, Hildenb, Jack & Knox, Landau, Nitida, Rijk's, **Verglgn**

★★★☆ Ekndal, Fleur dC, **K Constantia**, Ndrburg, Rickety, Stellnzcht, Stony B, **Stormhoek**, Wldekrans, Wlworths

★★★ Bloemndal, Eikehof, **F'hoek Vyds**, La Petite F ★★☆ Deetlefs, Wine Vllge ★☆ Ht Espoir **NT** Slnghoek **D** Boschndl, Fview, Glnwood, La Bri

Shiraz

★★★★★ Glen C

★★★★☆ Annandale, Anthony de J, Avndale, **Bknhtskloof** (2), Boschndl, Bschklf, Cloof, Cmbrly, Coleraine, De Traf, Delheim, DeWaal, Fview (2), G Beck, Gilga (2), Horse Mtn, Hrtnberg (2), **Kleine Z**, Kloovnbrg, KWV, Luddite, Neil E, Quoin, Rbtson, Rickety, Ridgeback, Rijk's, Rudi Schultz, Sadie Fam, Scali, Smnsig (2), Stellnzcht, Stony B, Sxnburg, The Foundry, The Observatory, The Winery, Tokara, **Tulbagh Mtn Vyds**, Verglgn, Waterfd

★★★★ Akkerdal, Allesvlrn, Alto, Anatu, Asara, Avndale, Bartho E, Bcksbrg, Beaumnt, Bellevue, Bellnghm (2), Bilton, Bknhtskloof, Black Pearl, Boland, Bon Crge, Bonfoi, BWC, Cedrbrg, **Cloof**, Cowlin, Crows Nest, Darling C, De Meye, **De Traf**, Delheim, DeWaal, Dmrsdal, Dmrsfntn (2), Drknsig, Flgstone, Fview (2), G Beck (2), Grt Cnstntia (2),

Havana, **Hidden V**, Hildenb, **Hrtnberg**, Hzndal, **JP Bredell**, Katbakkies, Klmpzcht, **La Couronne**, La Motte, Laborie, Linton P (2), Lmrshoek, Lndskrn, **Luddite**, Main Str, Manley, **Mason's** (2), Mischa, Mnt Destin, Mnt Rochelle, Mulderb, Muratie, Ndrburg, Neil E, Nitida, Nthlingshof, Omnia (2), Plaisir, Post Hse, Raka, Rbtson, Reyneke, Rudera, Sanctum, Saronsbrg, Sentinel, Slaley, Smook, Spier, **Stark-C** (2), Stnberg, Stony Croft, Sumardg, **Thelema** (2), Veenwdn, Vins d'Orrance, Vrgnoegd, **Weening Barge**, Western, Wlworths, Zevnwacht, Zndvliet (4), Zonneblm

★★★☆ Afrcn Pride, Afrcn Terroir (3), Altyd, Angora, Arendsig, Avntuur, **Babylon's Pk**, Bloemndal, Blwklppn, Bnnievle (2), Bon Crge, Boplaas, Boschndl, Boschrivier, Botha, **Bottlry Int**, Cilandia, Cloverfld, Cls Mlvrne, Coppoolse, Cpe Classics, Darling C, **Daview**, Dbn Hills, **De Grendel**, Dellrust, Dispore Kamma, Dominion, Drmrshire, Du T'kloof, Ekndal, Ernie Els, Ernst Co, Exclsor, Fat B, Five Heirs, Fleur dC, Gilga, Goede H, Gracelnd, Grnde Prvnce, Groenld, Grte Pst, Havana, **Herold**, **Iona**, Jack & Knox, Jordan (2), Joubert-T, JP Bredell, K Constantia (2), Kaapzicht, Kanu, Kleine Z, **Knrhoek**, **KWV** (3), Land's E, Lanzerac, Ldrsburg, Le Grand Chass, Le Mnoir Brndel, Lndhorst, Lndskrn, Lngvrwacht, L'rdge, Lushof, Lvland, Lyngrove, Lynx, Makro, MAN Vintners, Mellasat, **Merwespnt**, Mischa, Mnt Rozier, Mooipls, Ndrburg (2), Nelson (2), **Nick Forti's**, Nico vdM, Niel J, Omnia (2), **Onderklf**, **Perdebrg**, Rbtson, Riebeek, Rietvallei, **Ross G**, Royle Fam, Rstnberg, **Rtrsvlei**, Rust en V, **Savanha**, Seidel, Smnsig, Smook, Stellar (Organic), Stellnzcht, Stony B, Sxnburg, **Sylvnvle**, Tarentaal, Topaz, **Tulbagh Mtn Vyds**, Twee JG, **Uitkyk**, Umkhulu, Villiera, Vljsdrift, Wltvrede, Wm Everson, Wndmeul, **Zoetendal**, **Zrgvliet** (2)

★★★ Allee B, **Andy Mtchell**, Anura, Ashanti, Assegai, Audacia, **Avndale** (2), Badsberg, Belbon Hills, Blue Crane, Blwklppn, **Blyde**, Bnnievle, Boland, Bon Cap (Organic), Boplaas, **Bottlry Int**, Bovlei, Cameradi, Clairvx, Cpe Coastal, Cpe Vyds (2), **De Meye**, De Zoete, Deetlefs, Dennebm, **Detendu**, **Devon H** (2), Dieu D, Domaine B, Douglas G, Drknsig, Eikehof, F'hoek Vyds (2), Glnwood, Goedvrwcht, Hldrkruin, Hpnbrg, Klein Parys, **Kleinrood**, Krnskop, KWV, La Petite F, Laborie, **Linde**, **Lndhorst**, **Lorraine**, MAN Vintners, McGreg, Mdlvlei, Mntn River, New Cape, Nordale, Oaklnds Exprtrs, Obikwa, Omnia (2), Oracle, Origin, Oudeklf, PAX Vrbtm, Perdebrg, Pulpit Rock, Rainbow, Rdezandt, Riebeek, Rtrsvlei, **SA Premium**, Savanha, S'bosch Hills, Schlkbnbsch, Seidel, Slaley, Smnsvlei (2), Smrbsch, Spier, **Sprngfntn**, Stellar (Organic), **Stellcpe**, Sthrn Cape Vyds, Swrtland (2), **Terroir**, The Winery, Thorn, Tulbagh, Van Lvren, Vaughan J, **Vinus Via**, Vrdnheim, Wamaker, Western, **Wlworths**(2) (Organic), Yonder, **Zidela**, **Zrgvliet** ★★☆ **ACJ Fine Wines**, Afrcn Pride, **Agulhas Wines**, Ashton, Bovlei, Buthelezi, Citrus, **Cltzdorp**, Coppoolse, **Cpe Coastal**, **Cru** (2), **De Villiers**, Detendu, **Dispore Kamma**, Drostdy, Eshkl Kshr, F'hoek Vyds, **FirstCpe**, Fort S, Goudini, Grt Eilnd, Hldrkruin, Jason's, **Juno**, **Kango**, **Klein Parys**, Le Pommier, **Leopard's**, **Major's Hill**, Meerend, Migliarina, Mnt Rozier, Mrhof, New Cape, Omnia, Oranje, **Origin** (Organic) (3), **Ovrhex**, Patrys, **Prtrville** (2), **Rbtson**, Rhbsklf, Ridder's, Riebeek, **Rietrvr** (2), Rooibrg, **Rusticus**, Seidel, Shoprite, Slnghoek, Smnsvlei, **Terroir**, Tulbagh, Two Oceans, Vinus Via, **Wederom**, **Westcrp Int**, **Wldekrans**, Wlington, Wlworths, Wstbrdge, Zidela ★★ Afrcn Terroir (Organic), Citrus, Dominion, Du Preez, **Hippo**, **Hofstraat**, Ht Espoir, Lindiwe, Linton P, Ltzvlle, Lyngrove, Matzikama, Mnt Rozier, **Oude Wllngton**, **Rooibrg**, **Stormhoek**, Urbane, Westcrp Int, **Wlington**, Wlworths, Zndvliet ★☆ **Afrcn Terroir**, Lndzicht, **Nieue Drift**, Stellar (Organic), **Tall Horse**, **Vlrsdorp**, Wamaker, **Waterhof** ★ Rusticus, **Teubes**, Wandsbeck **NT** Bergwater (2), **Bernheim**, Bertrams, Bottlry Hills, De Hoopen, Drostdy, **Excelsious**, IWS (2), **Jewel Breede**, Klawer, Klnhof, Koningsrvr, Makro, Old Brdge (3), Oubenhm, Thabani, **Wedderwill**, Welgelee, Westcrp Int, **Wlworths** **NR** Botha, Doolhof, Heron Rdg, **Keisseskrl**, Pulpit Rock, Riverstn, Romans, **Signal H**, **Stbosch Cntry Est D** 32 South, Afrcn Terroir, Bianco, Fview, Ken F, Lvland, Main Str, Marklew, Omnia (2), Origin (2), Raka, Savanha, Sthrn Cape Vyds

Sparkling wines

Méthode cap classique, red

NT G Beck

Méthode cap classique, rosé

★★★★ **Ambeloui**, Cabrière, G Beck, JC le R, Villiera

★★★☆ Wlworths

Méthode cap classique, white

★★★★☆ **Bon Crge**, Cabrière, G Beck, High C, JC le R, Villiera

★★★★ Ambeloui, Avntuur, Bon Crge, Boschndl, Cabrière (2), Chamnx (2), G Beck, JC le R (2), **Jean D**, Laborie, Long Mntn, **L'rdge**, Mrgnhof, Old Vines, Smnsig (3), Stnberg, Twee JG, Villiera, **Wlworths** (2)

★★★☆ Boschndl, Btnvrwchtng, Cabrière, Dieu D, Grt Cnstntia, Hzndal, JC le R, Môreson, Omnia (2), Pongracz (2), Rstnberg, Villiera, Wltvrede, **Wlworths** (2)

★★★ **De Zoete**, Le Grand Chass, Rtrsvlei, Sxnburg ★★ Bloemndal, **Wldekrans** ☆ Montpllr Sud **D** Deetlefs

Non-MCC, red

★★★ JC le R

Non-MCC, rosé, dry

★★★ Laborie, Twee JG ★★ Boplaas

Non-MCC, rosé, off-dry/semi-sweet

★★★ Le Grand Chass, Waboom, Wlworths ★★ Bon Crge, Cold Duck (LowAlc), Drnkraal, Rooibrg, Van Lvren ★☆ Klnhof **D** Swrtland

Non-MCC, white, dry

★★★ Botha, Dominion, Ekndal, Lyngrove ★★☆ Bergsig, Citrus, **Cru**, Du T'kloof, Goudini, JC le R, **Klein Parys**, Ndrburg, **Oranje**, Riebeek, **Westcrp Int** ★★ KWV, Makro, Rhbsklf, Rooibrg, Swrtland, Van Lvren, Wlworths ★☆ **Origin**, Rbtson, Riverstn ★ Bnnievle, Mooitsg **NT** Westcrp Int **D** Brndvlei, Citrus, McGreg, Tulbagh

Non-MCC, white, off-dry/semi-sweet

★★★ Botha, Kango, Rietrvr ★★☆ Aan de Drns, Badsberg, Citrus, JC le R, Klnhof, Nuy, **Ovrhex**, Slnghoek, Vrdnheim, Westcrp Int, Wlworths ★★ Afrcn Terroir, Boplaas, Grand Msx, JC le R, **KWV** (LowAlc) (2), Makro (2), Mooitsg, Oranje, Rooibrg, Van Lvren, Westcrp Int (LowAlc) ★☆ Capnheimr, **Ovrhex**, Rbtson (2), Swrtland, **Vlrsdorp NT** De Doorns, Douglas, Hrtswater, Klawer, Lndzicht, Montagu, Uitvlucht (2) **NR** Wamaker **D** Cinzano, De Krans, Grand Msx, Tulbagh

Special Late Harvest

★★★☆ Bon Crge

★★★ **Bergsig**, Ndrburg, Rbtson, **Rhbsklf**, Van Lvren ★★☆ Badsberg, Du T'kloof, Rdezandt, Slnghoek ★★ Botha (2), De Wet, Drostdy ★☆ Ashton, Oranje **NT** Douglas, Hrtswater, **Klawer D** Merwespnt

Sweet red

★★★★ Sylvnvle

★★★ Fview ★★ Avntuur, **Hrtswater**, Rbtson (LowAlc) (2), The Saints, Wlworths ★☆ Taverna **NT** Prmium Cpe Wnes **D** J van Zyl

Sylvaner

★★★☆ Ovrgaauw

Tempranillo

★★★☆ De Krans

Tinta barocca

★★★☆ Allesvlrn, De Krans, Lmrshoek

★★★ Beaumnt, Louiesnhf ★★☆ Boplaas **NR** Swrtland

Touriga nacional

★★★★ De Krans

★★★☆ Boplaas

★★★ Allesvlrn ★★☆ **Cltzdorp**

Vin de paille

★★★★☆ De Traf, Fview, Stellar

★★★★ Fview, Hzndal, Rstnberg

★★★☆ Lmrshoek, Signal H

★★★ Mellasat, Stettyn **NT** La Petite F

Viognier

★★★★☆ Ridgeback

★★★★ Bellnghm, **Fleur dC**, Fview, **Lournsfd**, **Smnsig**, **Spice R**, Spier, The Foundry

★★★☆ **Adler**, Bon Cap (Organic), **Dmrsfntn**, G Beck, **Mischa**, Ndrburg, **New Cape**, Omnia, **Perdebrg**, Rstnberg

★★★ DeWaal, **Exclsor**, **Katbakkies**, **Swrtland** ★★☆ Bcksbrg, Riverstn, Seidel ★★ **Wamaker NT** Niel J **NR Royle Fam**, **Signal H D** Boschndl, Whlhaven, Wlworths, Zrgvliet

White blends

Chardonnay-based blends, unwooded

★★★☆ KWV

★★★ Cabrière (2), Cpe Grace, FirstCpe, Omnia, Wlworths ★★☆ Ashanti, Bellnghm, Crghall, Mooitsg, Rhbsklf (2), Westcrp Int ★★ Clairvx, Drnkraal, **Mountain Rge**, Ntvbij ★☆ **Eshkl Kshr**, Sthrn Cape Vyds ★ Sthrn Cape Vyds **NT** Cowlin, IWS, **Rhbsklf**, S/SW **D** Avntuur, Omnia

Chardonnay-based blends, wooded

★★★☆ **Boschndl**

★★★ **Avntuur**, **Drostdy**, Wlworths ★★☆ Bartinney, Eden Crst, Westcrp Int ★★ Western **D** Rtrsvlei, Wltvrede

Chenin blanc-based blends, unwooded

★★★ Cpe First (2), Jordan, Kaapzicht, **Knrhoek**, **La Chataigne**, Mrgnhof, Nabyglgn, Omnia, Ridgeback, Swrtland, Sxnburg, Two Oceans ★★☆ Afrcn Pride, Belbon Hills, **Clmborg**, **Dellrust**, Du Preez, Du T'kloof, Kleine Z, **Ndrburg**, Old Vines, **Spier**, **Tulbagh**, Zonneblm ★★ Bnnievle, Boland (2), Darling C, Douglas, **Ernst Co**, KWV, Mntn Oaks, Nelson, Ntvbij, **Origin** (2), **Ovrhex**, **Sthrn Sky**, Swrtland, **Vrede en Lust**, Westcrp Int, **Wlworths**, Zevnwacht ★☆ Brndvlei, Cellr Csk, **Country C**, Douglas, Drostdy (LowAlc), KWV, Makro, **Origin**, Prtrville, **Rooibrg**, Smnsvlei, **Stellar** (LowAlc), **Stellndrft**, Sthrn Cape Vyds ★ **Origin**, **Sthrn Sky**, Westcrp Int **NS Bovlei**, Lndzicht, **Westcrp Int** (LowAlc) **NT** Bottlry Hills, Deetlefs, Hrtswater, Huguenot, Lvland, Mystery, Prmium Cpe Wnes, Ultra Liq **NR** Mnt Rozier **D** Omnia, Schlkbnbsch, Bovlei

Chenin blanc-based blends, wooded

★★★★ Dornier, S'bonga, **The Observatory**

★★★ Jean D, KWV, Winecorp ★★☆ Two Oceans ★★ **Origin**, **Prtrville** (2), Western ★☆ **Origin**

Sauvignon blanc-based blends, unwooded

★★★☆ Fort S, Jordan

★★★ Asara, Boschndl, De Wetsh, **Grte Pst**, La Couronne, **Thandi**, Villiera ★★☆ Bellnghm, Cpe Grace, **Dmrsdal**, Ekndal, Malan, Rietvallei, Schlkbnbsch, **Seidel**, Waboom, Wltvrede, Wlworths ★★ Deetlefs, DeWaal, Ovrhex, S'bosch Hills, **Sthrn Sky**, The Saints, Western (2) ★☆ Horse Mtn ★ Blwklppn **NT** Drostdy, Mooitsg **D** Ekndal

Sauvignon blanc-based blends, wooded

★★★★☆ **Stnberg**

★★★★ **Ingwe**, Ndrburg (2), Newton J

★★★☆ Nico V, Nico vdM

★★★ Raka ★★☆ Ndrburg

Semillon-based blends, unwooded

★★★☆ Grt Cnstntia, Raka, Thnskraal

★★★ Glnwood, Hrtnberg, The Winery ★★☆ Long Mntn ★★ **Wlworths D** Afrcn Terroir, Leopard's, Omnia

Semillon-based blends, wooded

★★★★☆ Con Uitsig

★★★★ Allee B, **K Constantia**

★★★ Stettyn ★★ Origin, Two Oceans

Viognier, blends with

★★★★★ Sadie Fam

★★★★ **Lmrshoek**, **M Mossop Wines**, Omnia, **The Winery**

★★★☆ **Akkerdal**, Fleur dC, **G Beck**, **Hidden V**, **Joostnbrg**, Ndrburg, **Spier**, Whlhaven, Wlworths, Zevnwacht

★★★ **Akkerdal**, **Bon Cap**, **Sxnburg** ★★☆ **Drostdy**, Glen C, **Origin**, Riverstn ★☆ Boplaas **NT** Leopard's **NR Quoin**, **Solms-Delta D** Riverstn

Other white blends, unwooded, dry

★★★☆ Bchrd-F, Btnvrwchtng, Goats

★★★ Bnnievle, Bon Crge, Boschndl, Delheim, Goats, Romans, Twee JG (LowAlc) (2), Vljsdrift, Zonneblm ★★☆ Ashton, Citrus, Coppoolse, Douglas G, Drostdy, Grt Eilnd, Lngvrwacht, McGreg, Ridder's, Van Lvren, Vaughan J, Wldekrans, Wlworths (LowAlc) (4) ★★ Bellnghm, F'hoek Vyds, Leopard's, Merwespnt, Ndrburg, Pick 'n P (LowAlc), Rbtson (LowAlc), Rietrvr, Rvnswood (LowAlc) (2), Swrtland, Tulbagh (LowAlc) (2), Van Lvren (2), Wlworths ★☆ Botha, Goudini, **Hippo**, Ovrhex, Ovrmeer, Pick 'n P, Rbtson (LowAlc) (2), **Smnsvlei** (LowAlc), Swrtland, **Umkhulu**, Van Lvren, Vaughan J ★ Carnival, Country C (2), **Goudini**, Oude Kaap, Uitvlucht ☆ Drnkraal **NS** Westcrp Int (LowAlc) **NT ACJ Fine Wines**, **Aufwaerts**, **De Villiers**, Douglas, Fairseat, Hrtswater, Huguenot, Picardi, Slnghoek, Swrtland (2), Ultra Liq, Wndmeul, Wnklshk **D** 32 South, Citrus, De Wet, Douglas, F'hoek Vyds, Jonkhr, Kango (2), Klawer, Omnia, Origin, Zndvliet

Other white blends, unwooded, off-dry/semi-sweet

★★★☆ Onderklf, Verglgn

★★★ Flgstone, Kln Draken, L'Avenir, Twee JG, Zevnwacht ★★☆ Blwklppn, Boschndl, Graca, Grnde Prvnce, Malan, Montpllr, Mooitsg (2), Nuy, Rbtson, Rdezandt, Seidel, Smnsig (2), **Spier**, Villiera, Wlworths, Zndvliet ★★ Altyd, Bellnghm, Bnnievle, **Bovlei**, Cellr Csk, Cpe Bay, De Wet, Fleur dC (LowAlc), Grünb (LowAlc), Kupfer, Mooitsg, Ndrburg (2), Oranje (LowAlc) (2), Ovrmeer, Rbtson (LowAlc) (2), Riebeek, Rietrvr, **Rtrsvlei** (2), Rvnswood, Seidel, The Saints, Westcrp Int, Wlworths ★☆ Drostdy, F'hoek Vyds, Oude Kaap, Ovrhex, Pick 'n P, Rbtson, Rvnswood, Smnsvlei, Westcrp Int, Wlworths ★ Afrcn Terroir, Carnival, Country C, Mystery, Oom T, Smnsvlei (2), Virginia ☆ Riebeek (LowAlc) **NT** Douglas, Huguenot, La Petite F, Montagu, Mystery, Nelson, Picardi, Smrbsch, Swrtland (LowAlc) (3), Ultra Liq, Westcrp Int, Wnklshk **D** Avntuur, Douglas, Grt Cnstntia, Spier, Sthrn Cape Vyds, Vlrsdorp

Other white blends, wooded, dry

★★★★★ Verglgn

★★★★☆ Verglgn

★★★★ Flgstone, Quoin

★★★☆ Boschndl, Chamnx, **Flgstone**

★★★ Jason's ★★☆ Le Grand Chass, Western ★★ Western (Organic) ★☆ **Origin** (2) ★ Aan de Drns **NT** Stellar (Organic)

Zinfandel/Primitivo

★★★★ **Zevnwacht**

★★★☆ Glen C

★★★ Blwklppn **D** Ashanti, Fview, Hrtnberg

Top Performers 2004–5

The following are SA's top wines as measured by their showing in selected wine competitions and professional tastings in 2004/5, as well as in this guide. The listing covers the following results (latest available – see section on SA wine competitions for more details): Veritas 2004 – we indicate only double-gold medals; Fairbairn Capital Trophy Wine Show (FCTWS) 2005 – trophies & gold medals; Michelangelo International Wine Awards 2004 – trophies & double-golds (Grand d'Or); SA *Wine* magazine (www.winemag.co.za) – 4-5 stars Jun 2004-05; UK *Decanter* magazine (www.decanter.com) – 4-5 stars Jun 2004-05; US *Wine Spectator* magazine (www.winespectator.com) – 90-100 points Jun 2004-05; International Wine Challenge 2004 (IWC, www.wineint.com) – gold medals; and International Wine & Spirit Competition 2004 (IWSC, www.iwsc.net) – gold medals. Our own 4½ and 5 star ratings for the 2005 edition are also shown. The results below, as well as rankings in other local and international competitions are included in the A-Z section under the relevant producers and brands. Be aware that some wineries do not enter competitions and might not be represented here.

	Vintage	Platter	Veritas	Wine	FCTWS	Michelangelo	Decanter	Wine Spectator	IWC	IWSC
Cabernet Franc										
Zorgvliet	03	4½								
Cabernet Sauvignon										
Alto	01	4½								
Asara	98	4½								
Blue Creek	02	4½								
Blue Creek	03			4						
Boekenhoutskloof	01							90		
Boekenhoutskloof	02	4½								
Boland No 1 Reserve	02		DG	4½						
Boschendal	02			4						
Carisbrooke	01	4½								
Cederberg	03			4						
Cederberg V Generations	01	4½								
De Trafford	00							91		
De Trafford	02			4½						
De Trafford	03	4½								
Delaire Botmaskop	02	4½								
Diemersfontein Carpe Diem	03				T					
Eikendal	00			4						
Flagstone Music Room	02		DG	4						
Grangehurst	92							90		
Havana Hills Bisweni	01	4½								
Jordan	99							90		
Jordan	01							90		
Jordan	02			4						
KWV Cathedral Cellar	00									G
KWV Cathedral Cellar	01	4½								
Kaapzicht	01	4½								
Kaapzicht CWG	01	4½								
Kanonkop	91				T					

	Vintage	Platter	Veritas	Wine	FCTWS	Michelangelo	Decanter	Wine Spectator	IWC	IWSC
Kanonkop	95							91		
Kanu Limited Release	01	4½								
Le Riche	01	4½								
Le Riche Reserve	02	4½								
Longridge	02			4						
Morgenhof Reserve	01	4½								
Mount Rozier	02			4						
Neil Ellis Jonkershoek Valley	00							90		
Neil Ellis Jonkershoek Valley	01	4½						90		
Neil Ellis Stellenbosch	99							90		
Neil Ellis Stellenbosch	01							90		
Overgaauw	03	4½								
Post House	02			4						
Rijk's	02				G					
Rudera	01	4½						91		
Rudera CWG	02	4½								
Rust en Vrede	00							90		
Rustenberg Peter Barlow	99							92		
Rustenberg Peter Barlow	01			4				92		
Rustenberg Peter Barlow	03	4½								
Springfield Méthode Ancienne	99	4½								
Springfield Whole Berry	02	4½								
Stark-Condé Condé	00							92		
Stark-Condé Condé	01							92		
Stark-Condé Condé	02	4½								
Stark-Condé Stark	99							90		
Stark-Condé Stark	00							91		
Stellekaya	02	4½				DG				
Stony Brook Ghost Gum	02	4½		4½						
Thelema	94							90		
Thelema	97							90		
Thelema	98							90		
Thelema	99							91		
Thelema	00							91		
Thelema	01							91		
Thelema	02	4½		4				91		
Thelema Reserve	91							91		
Vergelegen	01							90		
Viljoensdrift River Grandeur	02					DG				
Wamakersvallei La Cave	02		DG							
Chardonnay										
Avondale	03			4						
Boschendal Jn le Long Bin 102 Auction Rsrv	91							90		
Bouchard Finlayson Crocodile Lair	01									
Bouchard Finlayson Missionvale	02							90		
Buitenverwachting	03							90		

	Vintage	Platter	Veritas	Wine	FCTWS	Michelangelo	Decanter	Wine Spectator	IWC	IWSC
Chamonix Reserve	02									
Constantia Uitsig Reserve	03	4½								
De Wetshof Danie de Wet Limestone Hill	04		DG							
Durbanville Hills Rhinofields	03	4½								
Eikendal	03			4						
Eikendal	04			4						
Fairview Akkerbos	01							90		
Fleur du Cap Unfiltered	03			4						
Glen Carlou	94							90		
Glen Carlou	96							90		
Glen Carlou	97							90		
Glen Carlou	98							90		
Glen Carlou	02							91		
Glen Carlou Reserve	94							90		
Glen Carlou Reserve	95							90		
Glen Carlou Reserve	02	4½								
Glen Carlou Reserve	03			4						
Glen Carlou Reserve Black Label	03	4½								
GlenWood Vignerons Reserve	03			4						
Groote Post	03			4						
Hamilton Russell Vineyards	95							92		
Hamilton Russell Vineyards	98							90		
Hamilton Russell Vineyards	01							90		
Hamilton Russell Vineyards	02							91		
Hamilton Russell Vineyards	03	5						91		
Jordan	03		DG							
Jordan Nine Yards	03	5	DG	4						
Kanu	01							90		
Longridge	02	4½								
Meerlust	92							93		
Mulderbosch	97							90		
Mulderbosch	00							92		
Mulderbosch	01							92		
Mulderbosch	02							92		
Mulderbosch Barrel Fermented	98							90		
Mulderbosch Barrel Fermented	00			4				91		
Mulderbosch Barrel Fermented	03			5						
Neil Ellis Elgin	01							90		
Neil Ellis Elgin	02							91		
Neil Ellis Elgin	03	4½								
Paul Cluver	02					DG				
Rijk's	03									
Rupert & Rothschild Baroness Nadine	03	4½								
Rustenberg Five Soldiers	99							90		
Rustenberg Five Soldiers	01							91		G
Rustenberg Five Soldiers	02			4½						

	Vintage	Platter	Veritas	Wine	FCTWS	Michelangelo	Decanter	Wine Spectator	IWC	IWSC
Rustenberg Stellenbosch	01							90		
Rustenberg Stellenbosch	02							90		
Seidelberg	01							90		
Springfield Méthode Ancienne	02	4½								
Sterhuis Barrel Selection	04			4½						
Thelema	97							91		
Thelema	01							90		
Thelema	03	4½								
Veenwouden Special Reserve	03	4½								
Vergelegen Reserve	03	4½								
Weltevrede Poet's Prayer	02	4½								
Woolworths Signature	02	4½								
Chenin Blanc										
Anura	04				T					
Bellingham The Maverick	03			4						
De Trafford	03							90		
De Trafford	04							90		
Fleur du Cap	02		DG							
Fleur du Cap	03			4						
Fleur du Cap	04		DG							
Fort Simon	04		DG							
Jean Daneel Signature	03	5		4½						
KWV Steen	04		DG							
Kanu Wooded	02							90		
Kanu Wooded	04			4						
Ken Forrester	00			4						
Ken Forrester	03	4½		4						
Ken Forrester Forrester Meinert	02	4½								
Ken Forrester Forrester Meinert	03			4						
Kleine Zalze Bush Vines	04			4						
Knorhoek	03					DG				
Mulderbosch Steen op Hout	03			4						
Old Vines Blue White	98		DG							
Raats	02							91		
Riebeek Reserve	04			4						
Rijk's Barrel Fermented	03			4						
Rudera	03			4						
Rudera Robusto	02			4½						
Rudera Robusto	03			4						
Spice Route	03	4½								
Spier	03	4½								
Villiera	04			4						
Villiera Cellar Door	03		DG							
Villiera Cellar Door	04			4						
Zondernaam (Tokara)	04			4½						
Fortified Desserts										
Badsberg Red Muscadel	03		DG							

	Vintage	Platter	Veritas	Wine	FCTWS	Michelangelo	Decanter	Wine Spectator	IWC	IWSC
Boplaas Red Muscadel Vintner's Reserve		4½								
Monis Muscadel	92	4½								
Nuy Red Muscadel	03	4½	DG							
Nuy White Muscadel	02		DG							
Rietvallei 1908 Red Muscadel	02	4½								
Gewürztraminer										
Zevenwacht	03	4½								
Merlot										
Alexanderfontein/Ormonde	03		DG							
Avondale Les Pleurs	00	4½								
Bilton	02					DG				
Coleraine Culraithin	03				T					
De Trafford	00							90		
Durbanville Hills Luipaardsberg	00		DG							
Havana Hills Bisweni	01	4½								
KWV Cathedral Cellar	01	4½								
Longridge	01		DG							
Omnia Genesis	01	4½								
Overgaauw	02	4½								
Saxenburg Private Collection	00			4						
Slaley Reserve	99	4½								
Spice Route Flagship	00							90		
Spice Route Flagship	02	4½								
Spier Private Colllection	02		DG			DG				
Spier Private Collection	03									
Steenberg	02			4						
Steenberg	03	4½								
Thelema	99							90		
Thelema	01							90		
Thelema	02							90		
Thelema Reserve	02	4½		4						
Veenwouden	02	4½								
Vergelegen	01	4½								
Méthode Cap Classique										
Ambeloui	01			4						
Bon Courage J Bruére Brt Rsrv Blnc de Blnc	00	4½		4½						
Graham Beck Blanc de Blancs	99	4½								
Graham Beck Brut	94			4						
Graham Beck Brut	99			4						
Graham Beck Brut	03			4						
Graham Beck Brut Blanc de Blancs	99			4						
Graham Beck Brut Rosé	04			4						
High Constantia Clos André	03	4½								
JC le Roux Chardonnay	98		DG							
JC le Roux Desiderius Pongracz	98			4						
JC le Roux Pongrácz	NV			4						

	Vintage	Platter	Veritas	Wine	FCTWS	Michelangelo	Decanter	Wine Spectator	IWC	IWSC
Môreson Soleil du Matin Brut	NV			4						
Simonsig Kaapse Vonkel Brut	01			4						
Villiera Brut Natural Chardonnay	02	4½								
Woolworths Brut Rosé (Villiera)	NV	4		4						
Woolworths Vintage Reserve (Villiera)	97			4						
Petit Verdot										
Simonsig CWG	02	4½								
Zorgvliet Silver Myn	03		DG							
Pinot Noir										
Bouchard Finlayson Galpin Peak	03	4½								
Flagstone Poetry Collection	00	4½								
Groote Post	03			4						
Hamilton Russell Vineyards	03	5		4½	T					
Meerlust	00	4½								
Pinotage										
Allée Bleue	03	4½								
Bay View (Longridge)	03			4						
Bellevue PK Morkel	03	4½								
Bergsig	02	4½								
Beyerskloof Reserve	03	4½								
Boland	02		DG			T				
Camberley	03	4½								
DeWaal/Uiterwyk	02	4½								
DeWaal/Uiterwyk Iop of the Hill	02	4½								
Diemersfontein	03	4½								
Fairview Primo	00							91		
Fairview Primo	01							91		
Fairview Primo	03	4½								
Kanonkop	95							91		
Kanonkop	00							90		
Kanonkop	01							91		
Kanonkop CWG	95			4						
Kanonkop Reserve	93							91		
L'Avenir CWG	03	4½								
Longridge	02	4½								
Neethlingshof Lord Neethling	00									G
Nelson Estate Limited Edition	02	4½								
Nitida	03		DG							
Omnia Kumkani	02	4½								
Reyneke	03	4½								
Rijk's	02			4						
Seidelberg Roland's Reserve	03				T					
Simonsig Redhill	02	4½								
Simonsig Redhill	03			4						
Southern Right	03	4½								
Southern Right Ashbourne	01	4½								

	Vintage	Platter	Veritas	Wine	FCTWS	Michelangelo	Decanter	Wine Spectator	IWC	IWSC
Tukulu	02	4½								
Umkhulu	02	4½								
Wamakersvallei La Cave	03		DG							
Woolworths Reserve	02	4½								
Port										
Allesverloren	98	4½								
Axe Hill Cape Vintage	02	5		4						
Axe Hill Cape Vintage	03			4						
Bergsig Cape Vintage	99	4½								
Boplaas Cape Vintage	03			4½						
Boplaas Cape Vintage Reserve	01							90		
Boplaas Cape Vintage Reserve	02	5	DG	4						
Boplaas Cape Vintage Reserve	03			4						
Boplaas Cape Vintage Reserve CWG	01	4½								
Boplaas Cape Vintners Reserve Selection Cape Vintage Reserve	03			4						
De Krans Cape Tawny	NV			4						
De Krans Vintage Reserve	01							91		
De Krans Vintage Reserve	02	4½	DG	4						
De Krans Vintage Reserve	03			4						
JP Bredell Cape Vintage Reserve	98			5						
JP Bredell Cape Vintage	00			4						
Landskroon	00		DG							
Monis Tawny	95		DG							
Monis Very Old Tawny	96			4						
Overgaauw Cape Vintage	97	4½								
Vergenoegd Old Cape Colony Vintage	01	4½								
Red Blends										
Avondale Avondale	00		DG							
Beyerskloof Beyerskloof	97							91		
Beyerskloof Beyerskloof	02	4½								
Beyerskloof Synergy Reserve	02	4½		4						
Boekenhoutskloof Chocolate Block	03	4½								
Boschendal Grand Reserve	01	4½								
Buitenverwachting Christine	00	4½								
Camberley Cabernet Sauvignon-Merlot	01	4½								
Capaia Capaia	03	4½		5						
Clos Malverne Auret Cape Blend Ltd Release	01	4½								
Cordoba Crescendo	95			4						
Cordoba Crescendo	02	4½								
Darling Cellars Kroon	02	4½								
David Frost Par Excellence	02							90		
De Toren Fusion V	99							90		
De Toren Fusion V	00							91		
De Toren Fusion V	01							91		
De Toren Fusion V	02	4½		4						

	Vintage	Platter	Veritas	Wine	FCTWS	Michelangelo	Decanter	Wine Spectator	IWC	IWSC
De Trafford Elevation 393	00							93		
De Trafford Elevation 393	01			4				90		
De Trafford Reserve	99							91		
Durbanville Hills Caapmans	99	4½								
Eikendal Classique	01		DG							
Ernie Els Ernie Els	00							93		
Ernie Els Ernie Els	01							93		
Ernie Els Ernie Els	02	5		4½				91		
Flagstone Mary le Bow	03			4						
Glen Carlou Grand Classique	02	4½								
Glen Carlou Grand Classique	02			4						
Glen Carlou Grand Classique	02				G					
Goats do Roam (Fairview) Goat-Roti	02							91		
Goats do Roam (Fairview) Goat-Roti	03			4						
Goats do Roam (Fairview) Goats do Roam In Villages Red	03							90		
Grangehurst Cabernet Sauvignon-Merlot	95			4						
Grangehurst Cabernet Sauvignon-Merlot	00	4½								
Grangehurst Nikela	00	4½								
Guardian Peak (Ernie Els) SMG	03			4						
High Constantia Sebastiaan	01	4½								
Ingwe Amehlo	02			4						
Jean Daneel Cabernet Sauvignon-Merlot	01	4½								
Jordan CWG Sophia	02	4½								
Jordan Cobblers Hill	00							90		
Jordan Cobblers Hill	01			4						
Jordan Cobblers Hill	01							91		
Kaapzicht CWG	01	4½								
Kaapzicht Steytler Vision	01	5	DG	4						G
Kaapzicht Steytler Vision	02			4						
Kanonkop CWG	01	4½								
Kanonkop Paul Sauer	91							90		
Kanonkop Paul Sauer	95							90		
Kanonkop Paul Sauer	98							91		
Kanonkop Paul Sauer	00							92		G
Kanonkop Paul Sauer	01	4½								
Klein Constantia Marlbrook	96							90		
L'Ormarins Optima	02			4						
Lammershoek Roulette Rouge	03			4						
Makro Overgaauw Touriga-Cabernet	01	4½								
Marklew Capensis	03	4½		4						
Meerlust Rubicon	00	4½			G					
Meinert Synchronicity	01	4½		4						
Mont Du Toit Le Sommet	98							90		
Morgenhof Première Sélection	01	4½		4						
Morgenster	01	4½								

	Vintage	Platter	Veritas	Wine	FCTWS	Michelangelo	Decanter	Wine Spectator	IWC	IWSC
Morgenster Lourens River	02	4½								
Mulderbosch Faithful Hound	00							90		
Mulderbosch Faithful Hound	01							90		
Napier Red Medallion	01				T					
Neethlingshof Lord Neethling Laurentius	00			4						
Neethlingshof Lord Neethling Laurentius	01				T					
Nico van der Merwe Mas Nicolas	01	4½								
Overgaauw Tria Corda	03	4½								
Raka Quinary	03			4		DG				
Raka Spliced	03			4						
Rust en Vrede Estate Wine	96							92		
Rust en Vrede Estate Wine	98							91		
Rust en Vrede Estate Wine	99							91		
Rust en Vrede Estate Wine	00							92		
Rust en Vrede Estate Wine	01	5		4				91		
Rustenberg John X Merriman	99							90		
Rustenberg John X Merriman	01			4				91		
Simonsig Frans Malan Reserve	00							90		
Simonsig Frans Malan Reserve	02			4						
Simonsig Tiara	02		DG							
Spice Route Malabar	02	4½						91		
Springfield Work of Time	01	4½								
Stellenbosch Hills 1707 Reserve	01	4½		4						
The Winery Radford Dale Gravity	03	4½								
Thelema	92							90		
Uitkyk Cabernet Sauvignon-Shiraz	01		DG							
Umkhulu Tian	01							90		
Veenwouden Classic	02	4½								
Vergelegen Vergelegen	01			4						
Vergelegen Vergelegen	02	4½								
Vergelegen Vergelegen CWG	01	4½								
Vilafonté Series C	03			4						
Warwick Estate Reserve/Trilogy	00							91		
Warwick Estate Reserve/Trilogy	01							90		
Warwick Estate Reserve/Trilogy	02	4½						90		
Warwick Three Cape Ladies	00							92		
Warwick Three Cape Ladies	01							91		
Waterford CWG	03	4½								
Welgemeend Estate Reserve	01	4½								
Welgemeend Pinotage-Shiraz	01	4½								
Woolworths Cabernet Sauvignon-Merlot	02	4½								
Woolworths Signature	01	4½								
Yonder Hill Shiraz-Merlot	03				T					
Sauvignon Blanc										
Bartho Eksteen Premier Choix	03	4½								
Bloemendal Suider Terras	03			4½						

	Vintage	Platter	Veritas	Wine	FCTWS	Michelangelo	Decanter	Wine Spectator	IWC	IWSC
Buitenverwachting	03							90		
Cape Point Vineyards	04	4½								
Delaire	02							90		
Durbanville Hills Biesjes Craal	04	4½								
Fleur du Cap Unfiltered	04	4½		4						
Fleur du Cap Unfiltered Limited Release	04	4½								
Fryer's Cove	04	4½								
Groote Post	04					T				
Iona	04	4½		4						
Jordan	02							90		
Jordan	04							90		
L'Avenir	04			4						
Mulderbosch	01							90		
Mulderbosch	02							92		
Mulderbosch	03							92		
Mulderbosch	04	4½						91		
Mulderbosch Barrel Fermented	00							90		
Mulderbosch Barrel Fermented	01							91		
Neil Ellis Groenekloof	02							90		
Neil Ellis Groenekloof	04	4½								
Nitida	04	4½								
Nitida Club Select	04	4½								
Oak Valley	03	4½								
Ormonde	04	4½								
Rijk's	00			4						
Spier	04	4½								
Springfield Life from Stone	04			4½						
Springfield Special Cuvée	04			4½						
Steenberg	04			4						
Steenberg Reserve	04	5		4½						
Thelema	03							90		
Vergelegen Reserve	04	4½		4						
Vergelegen Schaapenberg Reserve	03	4½								
Warwick Professor Black	03							91		
Semillon										
Boekenhoutskloof	03	4½								
Cape Point Vineyards	03	5		5						
Fairview Oom Pagal	03	4½								
Hildenbrand	04				T					
Jack & Knox Green on Green	03			4						
Landau du Val	03			4						
Nitida	03	4½								
Steenberg	04	4½		4						
Vergelegen CWG	03	5								
Shiraz										
Alto	01			4						

	Vintage	Platter	Veritas	Wine	FCTWS	Michelangelo	Decanter	Wine Spectator	IWC	IWSC
Anatu	03					T				
Annandale	01	4½								
Anthony de Jager	03	4½								
Anura	02			4						
Avondale	02			4		DG				
Avondale Les Pleurs	02	4½								
BWC	01			4						
Babylon's Peak Babylon	03		DG							
Babylon's Peak Syrah	03					DG				
Backsberg Pumphouse	02						4			
Beaumont	03						4			
Bellingham The Maverick	02			4						
Boekenhoutskloof Syrah	01			4				92		
Boekenhoutskloof Syrah	02	5		5						
Boschkloof Syrah	03							91		
Camberley	03	4½								
Cederberg	02			4½						
Cederberg	03			4½						
Cloof Crucible	03		DG							
Coleraine Culraithin	02	4½								
De Trafford	98							90		
De Trafford	00							93		
De Trafford	01							94		
De Trafford	02							92		
De Trafford Blueprint	03							91		
DeWaal/Uiterwyk	02	4½								
Delheim	01							90		
Delheim Vera Cruz Estate	99							90		
Delheim Vera Cruz Estate	00							91		
Delheim Vera Cruz Estate	01	4½								
Devon Hill	02		DG	4½						
Diemersfontein Carpe Diem	03			4						
Eikendal	02			4½						
Excelsior Paddock	03		DG							
Fairview Cyril Back	99							90		
Fairview Cyril Back	00							90		
Fairview Cyril Back	01							90		
Fairview Jakkalsfontein	02			4				92		
Fairview Solitude	01							92		
Fairview Solitude	02	4½								
Fairview The Beacon	01	4½						91		
Fairview The Beacon	02	4½						93		
Flagstone The Foundation	02			4						
Gilga Super	02	4½								
Glen Carlou Syrah	02							90		
Glen Carlou Syrah	03	4½		4						

	Vintage	Platter	Veritas	Wine	FCTWS	Michelangelo	Decanter	Wine Spectator	IWC	IWSC
Graham Beck The Ridge Syrah	01			4						
Graham Beck The Ridge Syrah	02	4½								
Hartenberg	02	4½								
Hartenberg Gravel Hill Syrah	02	4½								
Havana Hills Du Plessis Reserve	01			4½						
Havana Hills Du Plessis Reserve	02		DG							
Hofstraat	03					DG				
KWV Cathedral Cellar	01	4½								
Kanu	02							90		
Katbakkies Syrah	02	4½								
Kleine Zalze	03					DG				
Kleine Zalze Family Reserve	03			4						
Kloovenburg	03	4½								
La Motte	02			4						
Luddite	02	4½		4						
Lynx	03	4½								
Manley	02			4						
Manley	03			4		T				
Mont Destin Destiny	02			4						
Mooiplaas	02		DG							
Mulderbosch	02							90		
Neil Ellis Jonkershoek Valley	00							90		
Neil Ellis Jonkershoek Valley	01	4½						90		
Nelson Estate	02		DG							
Omnia Genesis	02	4½								
Porterville Unfiltered Reserve	02					DG				
Quoin Rock Syrah	03				T					
Rickety Bridge	02	4½								
Ridgeback	03			4						
Rijk's	01			4						
Robertson Winery No 1 Constitution Road	02	4½								
Rudi Schultz Syrah	02							93		
Rust en Vrede	00							90		
Rust en Vrede	01	4½								
Sadie Family Columella	01			4						
Sadie Family Columella	02	5						91		
Sanctum	02							92		
Saxenburg Private Collection	01	4½		4½						
Saxenburg Private Collection	93							90		
Saxenburg Private Collection	96							90		
Saxenburg SSS	01	4½								
Simonsig CWG	02	4½								
Simonsig Merindol Syrah	01			4½						
Simonsig Merindol Syrah	02	4½								G
Spice Route Flagship Syrah	99							90		
Spice Route Flagship Syrah	01			4				91		

	Vintage	Platter	Veritas	Wine	FCTWS	Michelangelo	Decanter	Wine Spectator	IWC	IWSC
Steenberg	03			4						
Stellenzicht Golden Triangle	02			4						
Stellenzicht Golden Triangle	03			4						
Stellenzicht Syrah	94							92		
Stellenzicht Syrah	02	4½								
Stony Brook Reserve	01	4½								
Stony Croft	01	4½								
The Foundry Syrah	02	4½						90		
The Observatory Syrah	02	4½								
Thelema	00							90		
Thelema	01							91		
Thelema	02			4						
Topaz Syrah	03	4½								
Vins d'Orrance Cuvée Ameena Syrah	02			4						
Waterford Kevin Arnold	01			4						
Waterford Kevin Arnold	02	4½	DG							
Unfortified Desserts										
Avontuur	01	4½								
Darling Cellars NLH	02	4½								
Darling Cellars NLH Barrel Selection	02	4½								
De Trafford Straw Wine	98							90		
De Trafford Straw Wine	01							93		
De Trafford Straw Wine	03	4½						92		
Fairview La Beryl	03	4½								
Joostenberg Chenin Blanc NLH	03	5		4						
Kanu Kia-Ora NLH	99							90		
Kanu Kia-Ora NLH	03	4½								
Ken Forrester 'T' Noble Late Harvest	01			4½				91		
Klein Constantia Vin de Constance	97							92		
Klein Constantia Vin de Constance	98							93		
Klein Constantia Vin de Constance	99			4				92		
Klein Constantia Vin de Constance	00	4½								
Nederburg Edelkeur	02									G
Nederburg Edelkeur	03		DG							
Nederburg Eminence	03					DG				
Neethlingshof Weisser Riesling NLH	03			4						
Paul Cluver Weisser Riesling NLH	03									G
Robertson Winery Wide River Reserve NLH	01	5								
Rudera Chenin Blanc NLH	02			4						
Rudera CWG Chenin Blanc NLH	03	4½								
Rudera Chenin Blanc NLH	03	4½						92		
Rustenberg Straw Wine	02	4½								
Signal Hill Mathilde Aszú 6 Puttonyos	02	4½						91		
Signal Hill NLH Crème de Tête	00							90		
Signal Hill Straw Wine	01					DG				
Signal Hill Vin de l'Empereur	03	4½								

	Vintage	Platter	Veritas	Wine	FCTWS	Michelangelo	Decanter	Wine Spectator	IWC	IWSC
Simonsig Vin de Liza NLH	03	4½		4						
Slanghoek Private Selection Natural Sweet	03		DG							
Stellar Organics Heaven on Earth Vin de Paille	03	4½								
Vergelegen Semillon NLH	00	4½								
Villiera Inspiration	01							90		
Viognier										
Fairview	03					DG				
White Blends										
Bon Courage	04		DG							
Omnia Kumkani VVS	04			4						
Sadie Family Palladius	02	4½								
Vergelegen White	03	5		4						
Vergelegen White	04				1					

The South African Wine Industry

The industry in brief

South Africa became the world's 9th largest wine producer in 2002 (latest available year), its ±719m litres representing 2.7% of total global output. (France, with just over 19%, and Italy, with 17%, were number one and two). Newest official SA statistics show that in 2004 there were 4 406 primary producers, about 30 fewer than the previous year, and 561 wine cellars crushing grapes, 56 more than in 2003. There were 477 private cellars, 66 co-operatives and 18 producing wholesalers. Of total cellars, 48% crushed fewer than 100 tons, compared with just 24% only five years ago – further evidence of the increasingly important role played by micro-wineries and *garagistes*.

The vineyards

For the first time since 1998, white-wine varieties are being established at a faster rate than red. Total new white plantings (in 2004, latest available year) were 2 575ha, compared with a relatively modest 1 772ha for reds (at the height of red-vine fever, 5 054ha were established in a single year - 2001). Unlike 2003, when the grape most enthusiastically planted was (again) cab, it is chenin which now takes root fastest (693ha), closely followed by chardonnay (631ha). Shiraz is the third most planted grape (571ha), followed by another white, sauvignon (508ha). 'King' cab now comes a distant 5th, matched by, of all things, colombard (both 496ha). Chenin, historically the lynchpin of the industry in terms of quantity and extent, remains number one in terms of hectares planted (19.1% of the total vineyard). It also has the paradoxical distinction of being the most *uprooted* variety, by a huge margin. Overall, the percentage of young, scarcely productive vines continues to decline, albeit slowly. In 2003, ±14.8% of vines were under 4 years of age while 40.6% were 4-10 years old. Only ±16.4% of SA vineyards were 20 years or older.

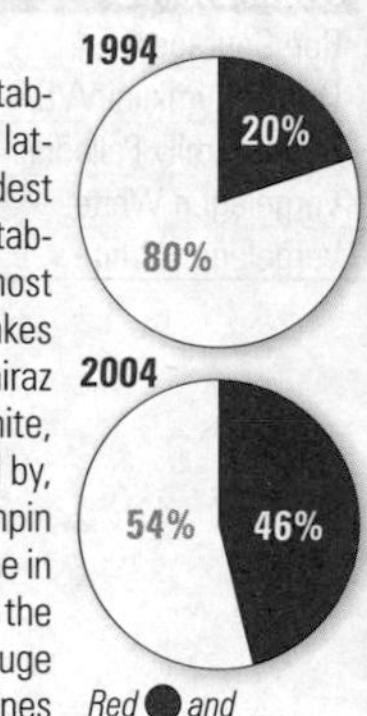

Red ● and white ○ grape varieties as % of total area

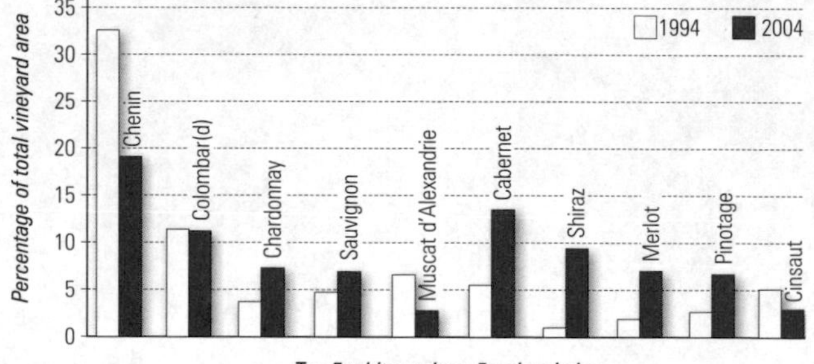

Top 5 white and top 5 red varieties

Exports

Exports of Cape wine remain buoyant despite the global over-supply of wine and relative strength of the rand (see graph). Unsurprisingly, chenin continues as the most exported

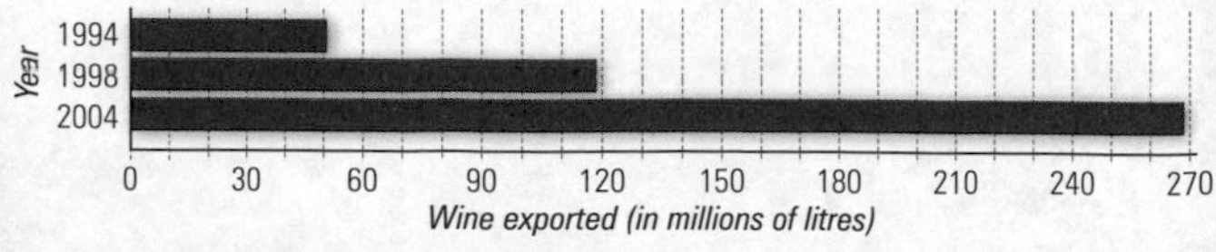

varietal wine, followed by chardonnay and, in roughly equal quantities, sauvignon and cab. The top five markets for SA wine are, in descending order, the UK, Netherlands, Sweden, Germany and the US (where uptake jumped 63% between 2003 and 2004).

Local wine consumption

As SA exports soar, domestic per-capita wine consumption continues to slump, to 7.65ℓ in 2004, lower than the previous year. SA has now slid to No 33 in world wine-imbibing, just one notch ahead of the US. (Luxembourg, at around 60ℓ/liver, still convincingly tops the order.) Of the natural wine sold on the local market, about 39% is in glass containers – and close to 60% of this comes in the standard 750ml bottle.

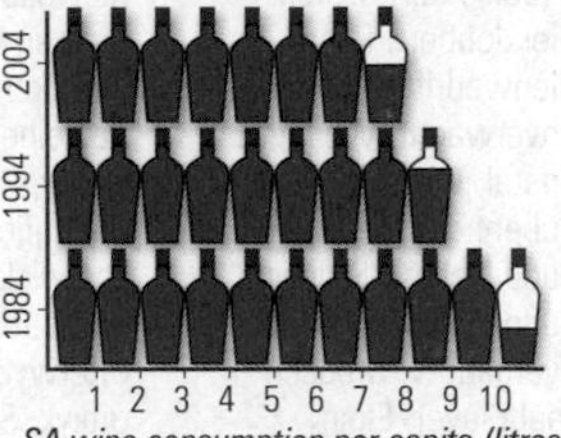

SA wine consumption per capita (litres)

Note

Information above and elsewhere in this guide is based on newly revised SA Wine Industry Information & Systems (SAWIS) reporting procedures, in which sultana (extensively used for table/dried grape production) is now omitted from certain calculations or shown separately for greater clarity. Visit www.sawis.co.za for complete SA wine industry statistics.

Wine industry organisations

ARC Infruitec-Nietvoorbij Research & technology manager: Dr Johan van Zyl ▪ PR: Daleen Bosman **T 809·3018** F 809·3002 ▪ bosmand@arc.agric.za ▪ www.arc.agric.za www.heritagegarden-stellenbosch.com

Internationally-regarded one-stop research institute, generating advanced technology for deciduous fruit- and grape-growers and related processors.

Cape Estate Wine Producers' Association (CEWPA) Chair: Braam van Velden **T 881·3815** F 881·3436 ▪ info@overgaauw.co.za ▪ Manager: Pierre Loubser T 855·1128 ▪ F 855·4351 ▪ pierre.l@mweb.co.za

Units registered for the production of estate wine (total: 109)

Akkerdal, Frhoek
Allesverloren, Swtlnd
Alto, Stbosch
Altydgedacht, Dbnvlle
Ardein, Rbtsn
Asara, Stbosch
Avontuur, Stbosch
Bellevue, Stbosch
Bergsig, Wrcstr
Bloemendal, Dbnvlle
Bon Courage, Rbtsn
Bonfoi, Stbosch
Boschendal, Grt Drknstn
Cabrière, Frhoek
De Compagnie, Paarl
De Heuvel, Tbgh
De Wetshof, Rbtsn
De Zoete Inval, Paarl
Deetlefs, Wrcstr
Devonvale, Stbosch
Diemersdal, Dbnvlle
Du Preez, Wrcstr
Elsenburg, Stbosch
Excelsior, Rbtsn
Fort Simon, Stbosch
Goede Hoop, Stbosch
Goedvertrouw, Bot R
Goedverwacht, Rbtsn
Goudveld
Graham Beck Wines, Frhoek & Rbtsn
Grande Provence (BoweJoubert), Stbosch
Groot Constantia, Constia
Hamilton Russell, W Bay
Hartenberg, Stbosch
Hildenbrand, Wellngtn
Hillcrest, Dbnvlle
Jacaranda, Paarl
Jacobsdal, Stbosch
Jasonsfontein (Jason's Hill), Wrcstr
Johann Graue (Nederburg), Paarl
Joubert, Stbosch
Kaapzicht, Stbosch
Kanonkop, Stbosch
Keerweder, Frhoek
Klawervlei, Stbosch
Klein Constantia, Constia
Klein Gustrouw, Stbosch
Kloofzicht, Tbgh
Kranskop, Rbtsn
L'Avenir, Stbosch
Le Bonheur, Stbosch
Le Grand Chasseur, Rbtsn
Lemberg, Tbgh
Lievland, Stbosch
Loopspruit, Mpumalanga
Lushof, Stbosch
Major's Hill, Rbtsn
Manley, Tbgh
Meerendal, Dbnvlle
Meerlust, Stbosch
Middelvlei, Stbosch
Mischa, Wellngtn
Mon Don, Rbtsn
Mons Ruber, L Karoo
Mont Blois, Rbtsn
Monterosso, Stbosch
Mooiplaas, Stbosch
Morgenhof, Stbosch
Morgenster, Stbosch
Mount Rozier, Stbosch
Muratie, Stbosch

Neethlingshof, Stbosch
Nelson, Paarl
Nicholaas L Jonker (Jonkheer), Rbtsn
Niel Joubert, Paarl
Nieuwedrift, Swtlnd
Onverwacht, Wellngtn
Opstal, Wrcstr
Oubenheim, Olfnts R
Oude Nektar, Stbosch
Oude Wellington, Wellngtn
Overgaauw, Stbosch
Paul Cluver, Elgin
Rainbow's End, Stbosch
Remhoogte, Stbosch
Rhenosterkop, Paarl
Rietvallei, Rbtsn
Rust en Vrede, Stbosch
Schalkenbosch, Tbgh
Seidelberg, Paarl
Slaley, Stbosch
Springfield, Rbtsn
Theuniskraal, Tbgh
Twee Jonge Gezellen, Tbgh
Uiterwyk, Stbosch
Uitkyk, Stbosch
Upland, Wellngtn
Van Zylshof, Rbtsn
Vera Cruz, Stbosch
Vergenoegd, Stbosch
Warwick, Stbosch
Waterford, Stbosch
Welgemeend, Paarl
Weltevrede, Rbtsn
Wildekrans, W Bay
Wonderfontein, Rbtsn
Zandvliet, Rbtsn

Cape Winemakers Guild (CWG) See separate entry in A-Z section

Chenin Blanc Association (CBA) Chair: Zakkie Bester **T (022) 448·1213** ▪ F (022) 448·1281 ▪ zakkie@riebeekcellars.co.za ▪ Manager: Wilmari Borel-Saladin T 872·9779 082·770·8001 ▪ F 871·1619 ▪ wilmaribs@mweb.co.za ▪ www.chenin.co.za

Institute of Cape Wine Masters Chair: Margaret Fry **T 083·628·6511** ▪ F 086·686·3412 capewinemasters@gmail.com

Successful completion of examinations set since 1983 by the Cape Wine & Spirit Education Trust and, latterly, the Cape Wine Academy, have qualified 54 Cape Wine Masters (3 are honorary). The Institute holds seminars, runs tasting workshops, charts trends and names a Wine Personality of the Year. The Institute's current members are (latest inductee in bold): Chris Bargmann (UK) ▪ Berenice Barker ▪ Margie Barker ▪ FC 'Duimpie' Bayly ▪ Paul Benade ▪ Cathy Brewer ▪ Marietjie Brown (Aus) ▪ Robin Brown (US) ▪ Sue Brown (Aus) ▪ Michael Claasens ▪ Marilyn Cooper ▪ Henry Davel ▪ Dick Davidson ▪ Greg de Bruyn ▪ **Ginette de Fleuriot** (Ger) ▪ Heidi Rosenthal Duminy ▪ Stephan du Toit ▪ Pieter Esbach (UK) ▪ Margie Fallon ▪ Margaret Fry ▪ Peter Gebler (Ger) ▪ Penny Gold ▪ Jeff Grier ▪ Bennie Howard ▪ Dave Johnson ▪ Val Kartsounis ▪ Peter Koff (US) ▪ Gerald Ludwinski ▪ Alf Mauff ▪ Tony Mossop ▪ Allan Mullins ▪ Boets Nel ▪ Carel Nel ▪ Elsie Pells ▪ Jenny Ratcliffe ▪ Christine Rudman ▪ Lynne Sheriff (UK) ▪ Caroline Snyman ▪ Cornel Spies ▪ Clive Torr ▪ Charl van Teijlingen ▪ Sue van Wyk (Aus) ▪ Junel Vermeulen ▪ Irina von Holdt ▪ Cathy White ▪ Geoff Willis ▪ Honorary: Colin Frith, Phyllis Hands and Dave Hughes.

Integrated Production of Wine (IPW) Manager: Andries Tromp ▪ trompa@arc.agric.za ▪ T 809·3143 ▪ F 809·3113

Pioneering, widely supported initiative aimed producing wine in an environmentally sustainable, profitable way by means of guidelines for both farm and cellar, embracing all aspects of grape production and winemaking.

Méthode Cap Classique Producers' Association Chair: Jeff Grier **T 865·2002** ▪ F 865·2314 ▪ wine@villiera.com

Muscadel Association Chair: Swepie le Roux **T (044) 251·6715** ▪ F (044) 241·2548 ▪ swepie@odn.co.za ▪ Vice-Chair: Henri Swiegers **T (023) 344·3021** ▪ winemaker@badsberg.co.za

Pinotage Association Chair: Beyers Truter **T 865·1235** ▪ F 865·2683 ▪ beyers@beyerskloof.co.za ▪ Manager: Pierre Loubser **T 855·1128** ▪ F 855·4351 ▪ info@pinotage.co.za ▪ www.pinotage.co.za

Shiraz Association Chair: Jacques Borman **T 881·3268** ▪ **F** 881·3032 ▪ jborman@adept.co.za

SA Port Producers' Association (SAPPA) Chair: Tony Mossop **T/F 780·1178** ▪ tony@axehill.co.za

SA Wine & Brandy Company (SAWB) CEO Johan van Rooyen **T 886·8992** ▪ F 882·9510 ▪ johan@sawb.co.za or lcoetzee@sawb.co.za ▪ www.sawb.co.za

Section 21 company uniting growers, cellars, labour and merchants in a bid to make the wine and brandy industries more globally competitive through implementation of the Wine Industry Strategy Plan (WIP).

SA Wine Industry Information & Systems (SAWIS) Executive manager Yvette van der Merwe **T 807·5703** ▪ F 807·6000 ▪ info@sawis.co.za
Company not for gain, collects, processes and disseminates industry information, and administers the Wine of Origin (WO) system.

SA Wine Industry Trust (SAWIT) Chair: Gavin Pieterse **T (011) 726·7830** ▪ F (011) 726·8790 ▪ gavinp@arim.co.za ▪ Administration: **T 889·8101** ▪ F 889·5900 ▪ sawit@infruit.agric.za ▪ www.sawit.co.za
Aims to transform the wine industry through its Section 21 companies: BUSCO (Wine Industry Business Support Company), concentrating on research, development and technology transfer as well as generic local/export marketing; DEVCO (Wine Industry Development Company), focusing on establishing new wine farmers from previously disadvantaged groups, support/upliftment of farm workers and communities, and black economic empowerment within the wine industry; and WEF (Wine Education Fund).

Wine Industry Ethical Trade Association (WIETA) CEO: Nicky Taylor **T 447·5660** ▪ F 447·5662 ▪ nicky@wieta.org.za anthea@wieta.org.za ▪ www.wieta.org.za
Non-profit, voluntary organisation established in 2002 to promote ethical trade in the wine industry. WIETA has adopted a code of labour standards for the industry, and its main task is to conduct ethical audits to assess members' compliance with the code.

Wine & Spirit Board Chair: Njabulo Nduli ▪ Secretary: Hugo van der Merwe **T 889·6555** ▪ F 889·5823 ▪ vdmerweh@arc.agric.za
Mainly administers the Wine of Origin, estate brandy and Integrated Production of Wine (IPW) schemes.

Wines of South Africa (WOSA) Chair: Paul Cluver Snr **T/F 844·0605** ▪ drcluver@cluver.co.za ▪ CEO: Su Birch **T 883·3860** ▪ F 883·3861 ▪ info@wosa.co.za ▪ www.wosa.co.za
Generic marketing organisation, responsible for raising the profile of SA wine in key export markets.

Winegrowing areas

Note: The area maps in this section are not to the same scale

From a 17th-century experimental vineyard in the Dutch East India Company's gardens below Table Mountain, SA's vineyards have spread over a wide area. Grapes are now grown in over 60 official appellations covering 100 207ha. Since the introduction of the Wine of Origin (WO) scheme in 1972/3, production zones have been designated 'regions', 'districts' and 'wards'. The latter are now the smallest category of the WO system, following amendments to the 'estate' regulations. Below are brief notes on the most important grape cultivation zones. Note: Figures mentioned here are supplied by SA Wine Industry Information & Systems (SAWIS), and reflect the latest available (2004) status for the WO areas. See also note under The industry in brief.

Cape Point Small (±30ha), cool disctrict on mainly west slopes of the Cape Peninsula. Recognised for sauvignon and semillon; the first red-wine vineyards recently came on-stream. Major varieties (ha): sauvignon (11), cab (7), shiraz (4), pinot (4), chardonnay (3).

Constantia Premier viticultural ward on the eastern flank of the Cape Peninsula, summer-cooled by south-easterly sea breezes. Recognised for whites generally, notably sauvignon, semillon and muscat. Sauvignon (131), cab (59), chardonnay (57), merlot (47), shiraz (29).

Darling This district around the eponymous town is best known for the wines from its higher-lying ward, Groenekloof, long the source of top-class sauvignon, also showing promise with reds such as shiraz. Groenekloof: cab (567), shiraz (313), sauvignon (240), chenin (238), pinotage (232).

Durbanville Ward within the Tygerberg district, with enviable reputation for striking sauvignons and merlots. Important quality factors include deep, moisture-retaining soils, cooling summer night-time mists and proximity to the ocean. Cab (307), sauvignon (275), merlot (217), shiraz (216), pinotage (99).

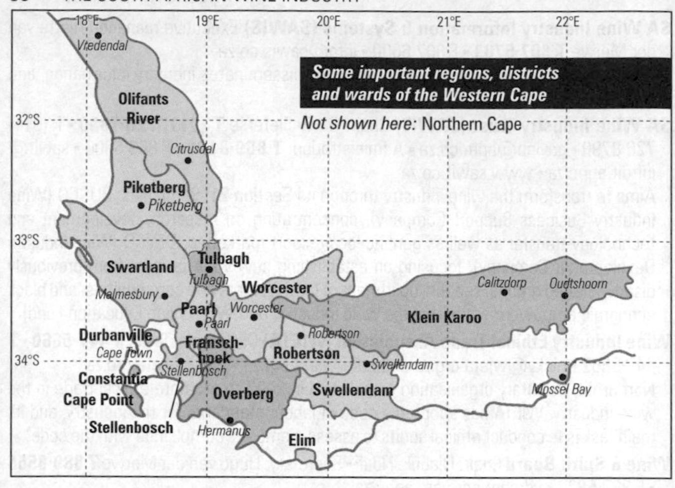

Elgin Upland fruit- and vine-growing area yielding exciting aromatic whites, cool-climate elegant reds. Now a ward within the Overberg district. Sauvignon (108), cab (44), merlot (42), chardonnay (29), pinot (27).

Elim Young maritime ward within the newly proclaimed Cape Agulhas district, its vineyards arrayed around the old mission village of Elim near Africa's most southerly point. Most promising. Sauvignon (53), cab (16), shiraz (15), semillon (10), pinot (10).

Little Karoo Scrubby semi-arid region, ideal for ostrich farming but something of a challenge for viticulture, which is reliant on irrigation. Similarities (in climate, if not soil) with Portugal's Douro Valley have inspired some local growers, chiefly around the hamlet of Calitzdorp, to apply their talents to 'port', with results that impress even the Portuguese. Interesting stirrings in the tiny (47ha) Upper-Langkloof ward. Region also recognised for fortifieds generally. Calitzdorp district: hanepoot (115), colombard (41), cab (26), palomino (19), chardonnay (16). Tradouw ward: colombard (26), chardonnay (23) merlot (14), cab (12), sauvignon (11).

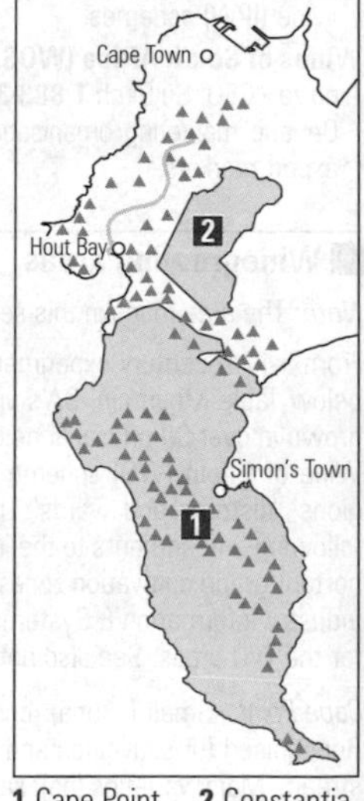

1 Cape Point **2** Constantia

Lower Orange This ward along the Orange River (Gariep) is a production zone within the Northern Cape Geographical Unit. Overwhelmingly a white-grape area but red plantings are increasing. Sultana (9 690), colombard (2 268), chenin (700), hanepoot (251), palomino (47), ruby cab (46).

Northern Cape See Lower Orange.

Olifants River Quality moves are afoot in this north-westerly Cape grape-growing region, particularly in the Bamboes Bay 'micro-ward' (just 6ha) and Lutzville Valley district nearer the coast, as well as the cool upland wards of Cederberg and Piekenierskloof. Further inland, a climate conducive to organic cultivation is now beginning to be exploited to that

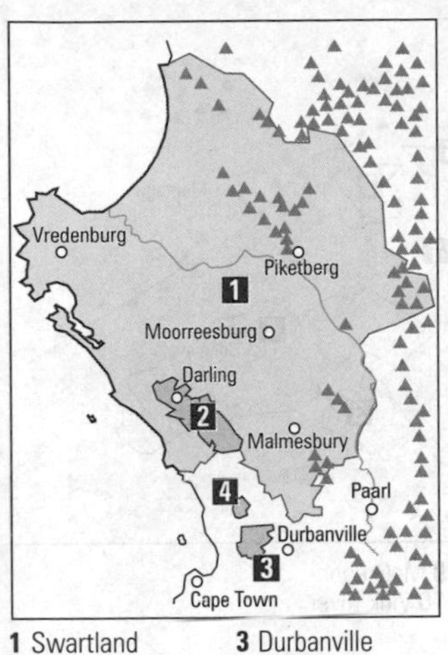

1 Swartland
2 Darling

3 Durbanville
4 Philadelphia

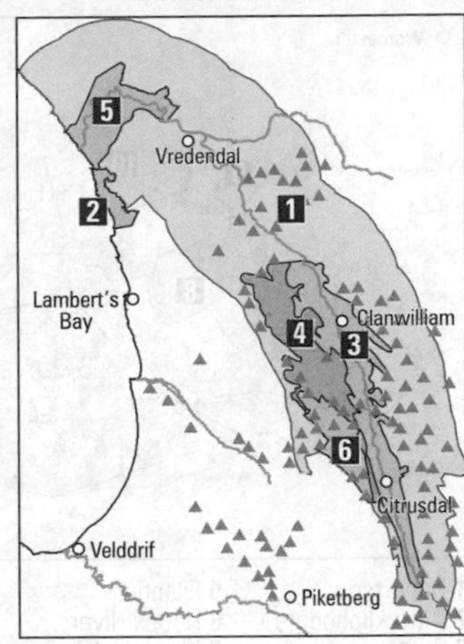

1 Olifants River
2 Bamboes Bay
3 Citrusdal Valley
4 Citrusdal Mntn
5 Lutzville Valley
6 Piekenierskloof

cnd. Koekenaap ward (Lutzville Valley): chenin (184), colombard (150), sauvignon (80), cab (74), hanepoot (45). Cederberg: merlot (14), shiraz (12), chenin, pinotage & sauvignon (all 9). Piekenierskloof: palomino (85), cab (84), pinotage (67), chenin (55), sauvignon (48).

Paarl This district has many mesoclimates, soils and aspects, and thus succeeds with a variety of styles and grapes. Paarl proper is recognised for shiraz and, more recently, viognier and mourvèdre grown on warmer slopes. Chenin (1 744), cab (1 292), shiraz (790), cinsaut (563); pinotage (548). The following are all wards: Wellington is showing promise, especially with shiraz and gutsy red blends generally. Chenin (1 179), cab (862), cinsaut (524), shiraz (478), merlot (35). Franschhoek, founded by 17th-century French Huguenots and now a millionaire's playground, recognised for cab and semillon. Sauvignon (223), cab (206), chardonnay (172), merlot (147), shiraz (142). Simonsberg-Paarl, on the warmer slopes of the Simonsberg, recognised for red blends, shiraz and chardonnay. Cab (387), chardonnay (249), shiraz (169), sauvignon (167), merlot (166). Voor

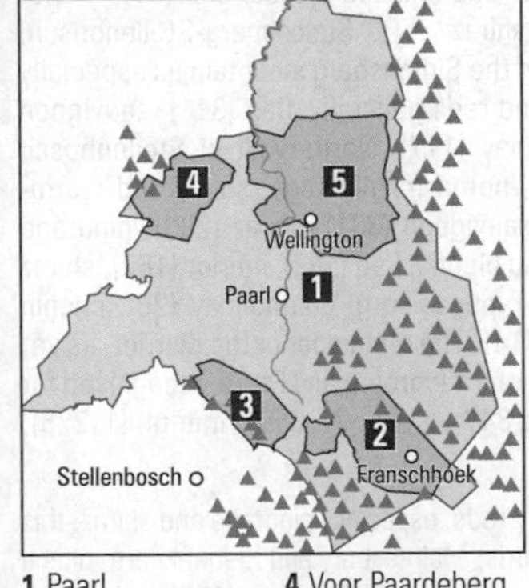

1 Paarl
2 Franschhoek
3 Simonsberg-Paarl
4 Voor Paardeberg
5 Wellington

2
6
3
Stellenbosch
Kuils River
5
4
1
Somerset West
Strand
Gordon's Bay
Elgin/Grabouw

1 Stellenbosch
2 Bottelary
3 Devon Valley
4 Jonkershoek Valley
5 Papegaaiberg
6 Simonsberg-Stellenbosch

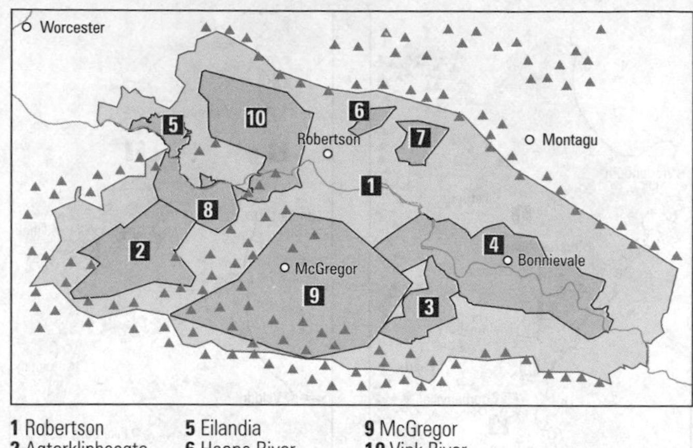

1 Robertson
2 Agterkliphoogte
3 Boesmans River
4 Bonnievale
5 Eilandia
6 Hoops River
7 Klaasvoogds
8 Le Chasseur
9 McGregor
10 Vink River

Paardeberg, long an uncredited source of top grapes for merchants, co-ops and private cellars, now becoming a star in own right. Cab (416), shiraz (270), chenin (236), merlot (220), pinotage (194).

Philadelphia Recently delimited ward of Tygerberg, cooled by the Atlantic and noted for cab, merlot and Bordeaux-style reds. Cab (100), sauvignon (70), merlot (29), shiraz (15), cab franc (9).

Robertson Traditionally white-wine country, increasingly recognised for shiraz and cab. Chardonnay, sauvignon and sparkling remain stand-outs. Colombard (2 081), chardonnay (1 847), chenin (1784), cab (1 336), sauvignon (1 023).

Stellenbosch To many, this intensively farmed district is the wine capital of SA. Key contributors to quality are the cooler mountain slopes, varied soil types and breezes off False Bay which moderate summer temperatures. Jonkershoek Valley, a ward east of Stellenbosch town, is recognised for cab and cab blends. Cab (61), merlot (27), chardonnay (19), sauvignon (17), shiraz (14). Simonsberg-Stellenbosch, encompassing the south-western foothills of the Simonsberg mountain, is especially recognised for cab, cab blends, pinotage and reds generally. Cab (311), sauvignon (167), merlot (156), shiraz (144), chardonnay (117). North-west of Stellenbosch town are three adjoining wards: Bottelary, noted for pinotage, shiraz and warm-blooded blends. Chenin (517), cab (447), sauvignon (331), shiraz (296), pinotage (270); Devon Valley, recognised mainly for red blends. Cab (192), merlot (162), shiraz (114), pinotage (77), sauvignon (74); and Papegaaiberg. Chardonnay (28), chenin (27), merlot (22), sauvignon (21), pinotage (14). The remainder of the district, as yet unappellated, includes Stellenboschberg/kloof, Helderberg and Faure, recognised for red blends, chenin and sauvignon. Cab (2 347), shiraz (1 350), merlot (1 225), sauvignon (1088), chenin (940).

Swartland Traditionally associated with beefy reds, especially pinotage and shiraz, this sunny district north of Cape Town has two wards, Malmesbury and Riebeekberg, plus a large 'Swartland' appellated area. Riebeekberg: chenin (254), shiraz (180), cab (171), pinotage (159), chardonnay (157). Malmesbury: cab (788), chenin (588), shiraz (522), pinotage (470), merlot (301). Swartland: chenin (2 690), cab (917), pinotage (891), shiraz (700), sauvignon (386).

Tulbagh This inland district, traditionally known for sparkling and lightish whites, is rapidly moving towards quality reds. Major varieties: chenin (587), colombard (331), cab (161), shiraz (147), chardonnay (119).

Walker Bay Since the 1980s, some of the Cape's finest wines have come from this maritime area south-east of Cape Town, recently 'upgraded' from a ward to a district. Recognised for pinot, aromatic pinotage, sauvignon and chardonnay. Walker Bay: sauvignon (73), cab (52), merlot (49), shiraz (50), chardonnay (42).

1 Elim **2** Cape Agulhas **3** Walker Bay **4** Kleinrivier

Worcester Still the largest winegrowing district, measured by number of vines (more than 63m, over 20% of the total), producing chiefly for the brandy industry and merchant trade, but small quantities bottled under own labels often represent good quality/value. Recognised for everyday reds/whites and fortifieds. Chenin (4 067), colombard (2 418), chardonnay (1 411), cab (1 179), shiraz (991).

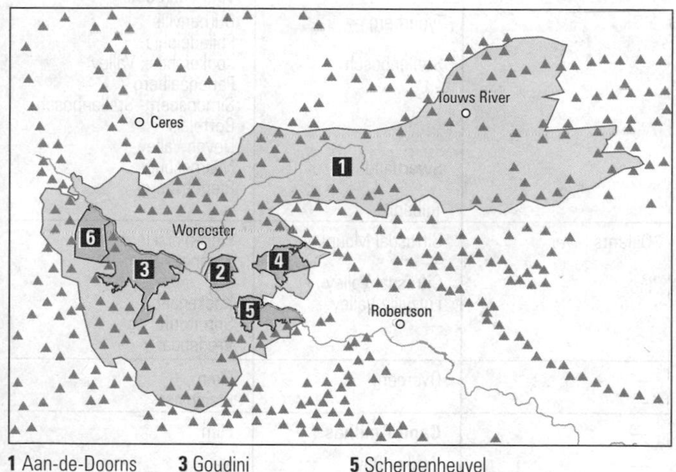

1 Aan-de-Doorns **2** Worcester **3** Goudini **4** Nuy **5** Scherpenheuvel **6** Slanghoek

Wine of Origin-defined production areas
(New appellation in **bold**.)

Region	District	Ward
Breede River Valley	Robertson	Agterkliphoogte Bonnievale Boesmansrivier Eilandia Hoopsrivier Klaasvoogds Le Chasseur

Region	**District**	**Ward**
		McGregor
		Vinkrivier
Breede River Valley	Swellendam	Buffeljags
		Stormsvlei
	Worcester	Aan-de-Doorns
		Goudini
		Nuy
		Scherpenheuvel
		Slanghoek
Little Karoo	—	Montagu
		Tradouw
	Calitzdorp	—
	—	Upper Langkloof
	—	Outeniqua
Coastal	Cape Point	—
		Constantia
	Darling	Groenekloof
	Paarl	Franschhoek Valley
		Wellington
		Simonsberg-Paarl
		Voor Paardeberg
	Tygerberg	Durbanville
		Philadelphia
	Stellenbosch	Jonkershoek Valley
		Papegaaiberg
		Simonsberg–Stellenbosch
		Bottelary
		Devon Valley
	Swartland	Malmesbury
		Riebeekberg
	Tulbagh	—
Olifants River	Citrusdal Mountain	Piekenierskloof
	—	Bamboes Bay
	Citrusdal Valley	—
	Lutzville Valley	Koekenaap
	—	Spruitdrift
	—	Vredendal
—	Overberg	Elgin
—		Kleinrivier
—	**Cape Agulhas**	Elim
—	Walker Bay	—
—	Douglas*	—
—	—	Cederberg
—	—	Ceres
—	—	Hartswater*
—	—	Herbertsdale
—	—	Lower Orange*
—	—	Prince Albert Valley
—	—	Rietrivier (Free State)*
—	—	Ruiterbosch
—	—	Swartberg
Boberg (fortified wines from Paarl & Tulbagh)		

*Production zones within the officially designated Northern Cape Geographical Unit (GU); all other areas are part of the Western Cape GU. A new GU, KwaZulu-Natal, was being gazetted as the guide went to press. Source: SAWIS

Grape varieties

Legislation requires the presence in the wine of 75% of the stated variety (85% if exported). Blends may only name component parts if those components were vinified separately, prior to blending; then they are listed with the larger contributor(s) named first. If one of the blend partners is less than 20%, percentages for all the varieties must be given. Figures given for proportion of the national vineyard are for 2004, and are provided by SA Wine Industry Information & Systems (SAWIS). See note under Winegrowing areas about their newly revised reporting procedures.

Red-wine varieties

Cabernet sauvignon Adaptable and internationally planted black grape making some of the world's finest and longest-lasting wines. And retaining some of its inherent qualities even when overcropped in less suitable soils and climates. Can stand alone triumphantly, but frequently blended with a wide range of other varieties: traditionally, as in Bordeaux, with cab franc, merlot and a few minor others, but also in SA sometimes partnering varieties such as shiraz and pinotage. Number of different clones, with differing characteristics. 13.5% of total vineyard area, steadily increasing (5.7% in 1990).

Cabernet franc Like its descendant cabernet sauvignon, with which it is often partnered, a classic part of the Bordeaux blend, but in SA and elsewhere also used for varietal wines – particularly on the Loire. Tiny vineyard area (0.9%), increasing.

Carignan Hugely planted in the south of France, where it is not much respected. But there, as in SA, older, low-yielding vines can produce pleasant surprises. Insignificant vineyard area.

Cinsaut 'Cinsault' in France. Another of the mass, undistinguished plantings of southern France, which only occasionally comes up trumps. Used to be known locally as hermitage, the name reflected in its offspring (with pinot noir), pinotage. 3% of vineyard area, decreasing (4.6% in 1997).

Gamay noir Although it produces some serious long-lived wines in Beaujolais, its use for (mainly) early- and easy-drinking 'nouveau' wines there, often using carbonic maceration, is the model mostly copied in SA. Insignificant vineyard area.

Grenache (noir) The international (ie French) name for the Spanish grape garnacha. Widespread in Spain and southern France, generally used in blends (as in Rioja and Châteauneuf), but occasionally solo. A favourite for rosés. When vigour restrained, capable of greatness, but this is rare. Tiny plantings here. (White/pink versions also occur.)

Malbec Once a significant part of Bordeaux's blend, now most important in Cahors in western France (where it is known as cot), and as Argentina's signature variety. In SA a few varietal and blended examples; very small plantings.

Merlot Classic blending partner (as in Bordeaux) for cabernet, fashionable around the world, where it tends to be seen as an 'easier' version of cab – although this is perhaps because it is often made in a less ambitious manner. Merlot varietal wines increasingly common in SA too. 7% of vineyard area, increasing (2.5% in 1997).

Mourvèdre Internationally known by its French name, though originally Spanish (monastrell). In Australia and California also called mataro – which was, until recently, its

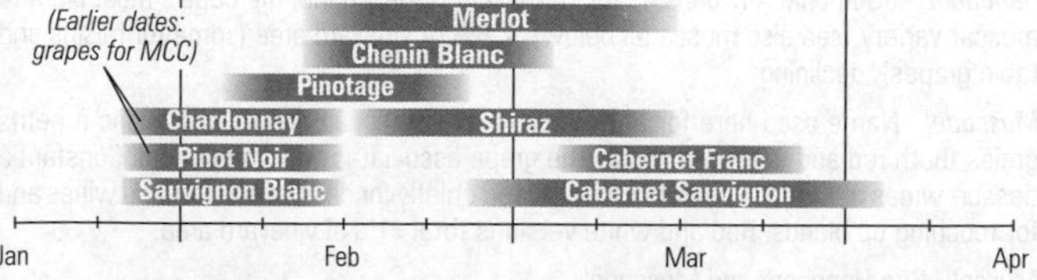

Approximate ripening dates in the Stellenbosch area for some important grape varieties

official name in SA. Particularly successful in some serious southern French blends, and increasingly modish internationally. Minuscule plantings here.

Nebbiolo Perhaps the greatest red grape to have scarcely ventured from its home – Piedmont in this case, where it makes massive, tannic, long-lived wines. Minute plantings here.

Petit verdot Use of this excellent variety in the Médoc limited by its late ripening. Now appearing in some local blends, and a few varietals. Tiny but increasing quantities.

Pinotage A 1920s cross between pinot noir and cinsaut ('hermitage'). Made in a range of styles, from simply fruity to ambitious, well-oaked examples. 6.7% of vineyard area, decreasing (7.3% at zenith in 2001).

Pinot noir Notoriously difficult grape to succeed with outside its native Burgundy, but SA, along with the rest of the New World, now producing some excellent examples, especially as use of BK5 'champagne' clone wanes. Usually matured in wood; seldom at a bargain price. Still very small proportion of the vineyard (0.5%).

Ruby cabernet US cross between cabernet sauvignon and carignan, designed for heat tolerance. Rather rustic, used mostly in cheaper blends. 2.6% of vineyard area, rising.

Shiraz Better known as syrah outside SA and Australia (and on some local labels too). Internationally increasing in popularity, with northern Rhône and now also Australia as its major domiciles. Clearly happy in warmer climates, shiraz is seen by many as the great hope for SA wine. Made here in a variety of styles – generally wooded, often with American oak. 9.4% of vineyard area, sharply up from 1.6% in 1997.

Tinta barocca Elsewhere spelt 'barroca'. One of the important Portuguese port-making grapes, which is now its primary role in SA, usually blended. Also used for some varietal unfortified wines, and namelessly in some 'dry reds'. Insignificant vineyard area.

Touriga nacional Important Portuguese port-making grape, now usefully grown here for similar ends, along with tinta francisca, tinta roriz (tempranillo) and souzão. Tiny plantings.

Zinfandel The quintessential Californian grape (of European origin, and the same as Italy's primitivo), used here in a small way for some big wines. Tiny plantings.

White wine varieties

Chardonnay In the Cape, as elsewhere, many new vineyards of this grape have come on-stream in recent years, with wines showing a wide range of styles, quality and price. Generally used varietally, but also in blends. Often heavily wooded in more ambitious wines. 7.3% of vineyard area, has increased greatly (5.8% in 1997), now stabilising.

Chenin blanc SA has more chenin (locally also called steen) than even France's Loire Valley, the variety's home. Used here for everything from generic 'dry whites' to ambitious sweet wines, to brandy. Some notable table-wine successes in recent years, in a sea of overcropped mediocrity. 19.1% of vineyard area, still declining (30.1% in 1997).

Colombar(d) One of the mainstays of brandy production in the Cape, colombard (usually without the 'd' in SA) also used for numerous varietal and blended wines, ranging from dry to sweet – seldom wooded. 11.2% of vineyard area, declining.

Gewürztraminer Readily identifiable from its rose-petal fragrance, best known in its Alsatian guise. In the Cape usually made in sweeter styles. Insignificant vineyard area.

Hanepoot Traditional Afrikaans name for muscat d'Alexandrie, the Cape's most planted muscat variety (see also muscadel below). 2.8% of vineyard area (some for raisins and table grapes), declining.

Muscadel Name used here for both muscat de Frontignan and muscat blanc à petits grains (both red and white versions). The grape associated with the famous Constantia dessert wines of the 18th century today is used chiefly for dessert and fortified wines and for touching up blends. Red and white versions total ±1% of vineyard area.

Muscat See Hanepoot and Muscadel.

Riesling The name a source of confusion to consumers, and of distress to the producers of what is known in its great homeland, Germany, simply as riesling and here officially as Rhine or weisser riesling. In SA, standing alone, 'riesling' usually, and officially, refers to Cape riesling (sometimes called SA riesling), a much inferior grape properly known as crouchen blanc, mostly used here anonymously in blends, and sometimes varietally. Rhine/weisser riesling frequently in off-dry style here, in blends or varietally, some noteworthy botrytised dessert examples – and developing terpene character much earlier in SA than in cooler climates. Cape riesling: 1.2% of vineyard area, decreasing; Rhine: stable at miniscule 0.3%. Note: in this guide 'riesling' without qualification refers to the latter.

Sauvignon blanc Prestigious vine most associated with eastern Loire regions, Bordeaux and, increasingly, New Zealand – whose wines have helped restore fashionability to the grape. The Cape version no longer a poor relation of these. Usually dry, but some sweet wines; sometimes wooded, more often not (former sometimes called fumé blanc/blanc fumé). 6.9% of vineyard area, increasing.

Semillon Spelt sémillon in French. The present small hectarage devoted to semillon in SA is a far cry from the early 19th century, when the grape, also known as 'groen' (green), a reference to its bright foliage, represented 93% of all Cape vines. Now only 1%. Sometimes heavily wooded.

Viognier Increasingly fashionable variety internationally, spreading out from its home in the northern Rhône, now showing promise here. Usually wooded. Still just 0.5% of total SA vineyard.

SA wine competitions & awards

An increasing number of wine competitions are run by liquor industry bodies, independent companies, publishing houses and individuals. Below are the main national events:

ABSA Top Ten Pinotage Competition Run annually by the Pinotage Association and a major financial institution to help set international quality targets for growers of pinotage. Local judges. See under Industry Organisations for contact details.

Calyon Trophy Bordeaux Blend Challenge New competition lauding the best blends of at least two of the 'Bordeaux reds', cabernets sauvignon and franc, merlot, malbec and petit verdot. Local/overseas judges. ▪ alex@outsorceress.co.za ▪ T (011) 482·5936 ▪ F (011) 482·2272

Classic Wine Trophy Staged under rules of the Office Internationale de la Vigne et du Vin (OIV), recognising ageworthy, Old World-inclined SA wines. Overseas judges. ▪ info@winemaker.co.za ridon@iafrica.com ▪ T 083·675·0280 (Jean-Vincent Ridon)

Diners Club Winemaker of the Year Inaugurated 1981, this prestigious competition features a different category each year. Local panel with some overseas representation. celiag@rsp.co.za ▪ www.winemag.co.za ▪ T 530·3145 ▪ F 531·2212

Fairbairn Capital Trophy Wine Show Launched 2002 to identify the best wines in SA and award trophies to the top wines in each of the major classes, as well as the top producer overall. Local and international evaluators. www.trophywineshow.co.za ▪ Contact details as per Diners Club Winemaker of the Year.

Juliet Cullinan Wine Connoisseur's Award National competition organised by local wine-entrepreneur Juliet Cullinan and judged by a panel of Cape Wine Masters. cullwine@global.co.za ▪ T (011) 447·1885/083·255·9430 ▪ F (011) 442·7669

Landbouweekblad Woman Winemaker of the Year Launched 2004 to acknowledge the role and skills of women winemakers, and highlight the special qualities they bring to their craft. ▪ lorman@yebo.co.za ▪ www.sawinewoman.co.za ▪ T (039) 314·9913/5 ▪ F (039) 314·9914

Michelangelo International Wine Awards Well-established event (1997) featuring international panel and one local judge. Aims to identify SA wines which will appeal to foreign palates. ▪ www.miwa-sa.co.za ▪ See Woman Winemaker of the Year above for contact details.

Muscadel Award for Excellence Annual competition aimed at raising consumer awareness and recognising quality in the creation, packaging and promotion of SA's muscadel wines. Local judges. ▪ swepie@odn.co.za ▪ T (044) 241·2156 ▪ F (044) 241·2548

Peter Schulz Excellence Awards for Port Sponsored by importer-wholesaler NMK Schulz, and organised by the SA Port Producers' association with the assistance of SA *Wine*, to select the best wine in each of the various port categories, and an overall winner. Local judges. ▪ tony@axehill.co.za ▪ www.sappa.co.za ▪ T 780·1051 ▪ F 780·1178

South African Airways (SAA) Wine Awards Annual selection of wines to fly with the national carrier (drinkability in flight conditions an important consideration). The top red, white, bubbly and port each receive a trophy. Local & overseas palates. ▪ DetlevKohler@flysaa.com ▪ www.flysaa.com ▪ T (011) 978·3264 ▪ F (011) 978·3115

SA Young Wine Show Inaugurated 1975 to gauge the quality of embryo wines, prior to finishing and bottling, thereby also recognising wineries which sell their products in bulk. The grand champion receives the General Smuts Trophy. Local judges. ▪ ferreira@vinpro.co.za ▪ www.youngwineshow.co.za ▪ T 807·3104 ▪ F 863·2079

Swiss International Air Lines Wine Awards Run in conjunction with Cape Town's annual Good Food & Wine Show; local/international panel chaired most recently by UK wine merchant Derek Smedley MW. ▪ info@gourmetsa.com ▪ www.gourmetsa.com ▪ T 797·4500 ▪ F 797·4179

Wine Magazine-Amorim Cork Cap Classique Challenge Annual competition to anoint SA's top bottle-fermented sparkling wines. Local judges. Contact details as per Diners Club Winemaker of the Year.

Wine Magazine Best Value Awards SA judges gather annually to select the best value wines based on quality vs price. Results published in *Wine*'s *Best Value Wine Guide*. Contact details as per Diners Club Winemaker of the Year.

Wine Magazine-Tops at Spar Chenin Blanc Challenge Annual event in which wooded and unwooded chenins in the drier spectrum (max 20g/ℓ sugar) are assessed by a mostly SA panel. Contact details as per Diners Club Winemaker of the Year.

Wine Magazine-Tops at Spar Shiraz Challenge Another SA *Wine*/Tops at Spar collaboration, uncovering benchmark SA wines made from shiraz/syrah. Local judges. Contact details as per Diners Club Winemaker of the Year.

Wine Magazine-Tops at Spar Value for Money Pinotage Awards Reconfigured Pinotage Champion of the Year competition, now dedicated to showcase the best-value pinotages of a given vintage. SA judges. Contact details as per Diners Club Winemaker of the Year.

Veritas SA's biggest competition for market-ready wines, awarding double-gold, gold, silver and bronze medals across a wide range of categories. Local palates with some overseas input. See SA Young Wine Show for contact details.

Note: For a list of wines rated highest in selected professional tastings and competitions in the past year, plus our own 4½ and 5-star ratings, see Top Performers.

Wine education

Cape Wine Academy Long-established (1979) general wine education body. Based in Stellenbosch and Johannesburg with satellites in Durban, Pretoria, Windhoek and Harare. Runs wine theory and tasting courses with examinations at several levels, from Introduction to SA Wine to Cape Wine Master, as well as skills workshops for front-of-house sales staff. The MD is Marilyn Cooper.

Stellenbosch **T 889·8844** ▪ F 889·7391 ▪ info@cwa.org.za ▪ Johannesburg T (011) 783·4585 ▪ F (011) 883·2356 ▪ busi.cwa@iafrica.com ▪ Durban T/F (031) 564·5067 ▪ Pretoria T/F (012) 333·1978 ▪ www.capewineacademy.co.za

The Wine Ambassador See Specialised wine tours section.

Selected wine shops

The following retail outlets stock a wide range of fine-wines and/or provide specialised services to the wine-consuming public. 'Bricks-and-mortar' shops are listed first, by area, followed by on-line emporia.

Eastern Cape

Da Vino's Cnr Beach Hotel, Marine Drive, Summerstrand, Port Elizabeth ▪ Mon-Fri 9-6 Sat 8.30-5 ▪ Closed pub hols ▪ **T (041) 583·2166** ▪ F (041) 583·6220

Makro Port Elizabeth Cnr Cape Rd & Samantha Way, Kabega Park ▪ Mon, Tue, Thu & Fri 8.30-5.30 Wed 9-5.30 Sat 8-5 Sun 9-2 Pub hols 9-4 ▪ cbarton@makro.co.za ▪ www.makro.co.za ▪ **T (041) 360·0605** ▪ F (041) 360·9569

Prestons 121 Main Road, Walmer ▪ Mon-Fri 9-6 Sat 8.30-4 (phone ahead on pub hols) ▪ www.eliquor.co.za ▪ **T/F (041) 581·1993**

Spargs Liquor Mart The Bay Shopping Centre, Major Square Rd, Beacon Bay, East London ▪ Mon-Fri 8-7 Sat 8-5 ▪ Closed Good Fri, Dec 25 & Jan 1 ▪ rene@spargs.co.za ▪ www.spargs.co.za ▪ **T (043) 748·1383** ▪ F (043) 748·5059

Ultra Liquors East London 250 Oxford Str, East London ▪ Mon-Fri 9-6 Sat 9-5 Pub hols 9-2 ▪ Closed Easter Fri, Dec 25 & Jan 1 ▪ eastlondon@ultraliquors.co.za ▪ www.ultraclub.co.za ▪ **T (043) 743·5174/722·3476** ▪ F (043) 743·4283

Ultra Liquors Newton Park 140 Hurd Str, Newton Park ▪ Mon-Fri 9-6 Sat 9-5 Pub hols 9-2 ▪ Closed Easter Fri, Dec 25 & Jan 1 ▪ newtonpark@ultraliquors.co.za ▪ www.ultraclub.co.za ▪ **T (041) 364·1103** ▪ F (041) 364·2277

Free State

Liquor City Bloemfontein 6 Showgrounds Shopping Centre, Currie Ave, Bloemfontein Open Mon-Sat, call store for trading hours ▪ **T (051) 448·6222**

Ultra Liquors Bloemfontein Cnr Markgraaf & St Andrew Strs, Bloemfontein ▪ Mon-Fri 9-6 Sat 9-5 Pub hols 9-2 ▪ Closed Easter Fri, Dec 25 & Jan 1 ▪ bloem@ultraliquors.co.za ▪ www.ultraclub.co.za ▪ **T (051) 447·3328** ▪ F (051) 447·3600

Garden Route

Picardi Rebel Fine Wines & Liquors George Garden Route Mall, Shop 51, Intersection N2 & N12, George ▪ Mon-Fri 9-6, Sat 8-5 ▪ Open pub hols ▪ mark.no@picardirebel.co.za

Picardi Rebel Fine Wines & Liquors Knysna Waterfront Drive Lane, Knysna, Fruit & Veg City, Waterfront Drive, Knysna, ▪ Mon-Fri 9-6, Sat 8-5 ▪ Open pub hols ▪ mark.no@picardirebel.co.za ▪ **T (044) 382·3318** ▪ F (044) 382·3319

Picardi Rebel Fine Wines & Liquors Plettenberg Bay Cnr Kloof & Wilder Streets, Plettenberg Bay ▪ Mon-Thu 9-6, Fri 9-6.30, Sat 8-2 ▪ Open pub hols ▪ mark.no@picardirebel.co.za ▪ **T (044) 533·1600**

Picardi Rebel Fine Wines & Liquors Plettenberg Bay Beacon Isle, Beacon Isle Convenience Centre, Beacon Isle Cresent, Plettenberg Bay ▪ Mon-Thu 9-6.30, Fri 0.30-7, Sat 8-5 ▪ Open pub hols ▪ mark.no@picardirebel.co.za ▪ **T (044) 533·1225**

The Lagoon Wine Shop Market Square, Beacon Way, Plettenberg Bay ▪ Mon-Sat 9-8 in season, otherwise 9-6 ▪ lagoonwine@mweb.co.za ▪ www.lagoonwineshop.co.za ▪ **T (044) 533·2440** ▪ F (044) 533·2442

34° South Wine Shop Shop 19, Knysna Quays, Waterfront Drive, Knysna ▪ Mon-Fri 8-8 Sat/Sun 8-5 ▪ wine@34-south.com ▪ www.34-south.com ▪ **T/ F (044) 382·7331**

Ultra Liquors George 7 Courtenay Str, George ▪ Mon-Fri 9-6 Sat 9-5 Pub hols 9-2 ▪ Closed Easter Fri, Dec 25 & Jan 1 ▪ george@ultraliquors.co.za ▪ www.ultraclub.co.za ▪ **T (044) 874·5514** ▪ F (044) 874·5511

Gauteng

Alberts Liquors Braam Pretorius Rd, Magalieskruin, Pretoria ▪ Open Mon-Sat, call store for trading hours ▪ **T (012) 543·0813**

Alpha Liquor Store Cnr Main Reef Rd & Willem van Reekum Str, Roodepoort ▪ Open Mon-Sat, call store for trading hours ▪ **T (011) 763·8740** ▪ F (011) 763·8741

Bamboo-WINE+ Bamboo Centre, 53 Rustenburg Road, Cnr 9th St, Melville ▪ Mon-Fri 10-6 Sat 9-4 ▪ wine@wineplus.co.za ▪ www.bamboo-online.co.za ▪ **T (011) 482·1020** ▪ F (011) 482·5958

Central Liquors @ The Square Cnr Rietfontein & Rigg Rds, Boksburg ▪ Mon-Fri 9-7 Sat & pub hols 9-5 ▪ val@centralliquors.co.za ▪ www.centralliquors.co.za ▪ **T (011) 826·5070** ▪ F (011) 826·7151

Glenfair Wine & Liquor Shop 53/54, Glenfair Centre, Lynnwood Rd, Lynnwood Manor, Pretoria ▪ Mon-Fri 8.30-6 Sat 8-3 Pub hols 9-1 ▪ Closed religious holidays ▪ mickey@glenfairliquor.co.za ▪ www.glenfairliquor.co.za ▪ **T (012) 361·4509/4563** ▪ F (012) 361·4509

John Wilson Sandton City Shop L68, Sandton City, cnr Rivonia Rd & 5th Ave, Sandton ▪ Mon-Thu 9-7 Fri 9-8 Sat 9-5 Pub hols 10-5 ▪ Closed Good Fri & Dec 25 ▪ sandton@wpcellars.co.za ▪ **T (011) 783·7035** ▪ F (011) 783·7036

Liquor City Bassonia Comaro View Shopping Centre, Comaro Rd, Bassonia ▪ Open Mon-Sat, call store for trading hours ▪ **T (011) 432·0457/71**

Liquor City Beyers Naude 181 Beyers Naude Drive, Northcliff ▪ Open Mon-Sat, call store for trading hours ▪ **T (011) 888·9374**

Liquor City Boksburg Cnr Rondebult & McGaghy Strs, Parkdene, Boksburg ▪ Open Mon-Sat, call store for trading hours ▪ **T (011) 917·0866**

Liquor City Boksburg West 53 Rietfontein Rd, Boksburg West ▪ Open Mon-Sat, call store for trading hours ▪ **T (011) 826·2336**

Liquor City Brackengate Cnr Andries Ave & Waal Str, Brackendowns, Alberton ▪ Open Mon-Sat, call store for trading hours ▪ **T (011) 900·4493**

Liquor City Brixton 121 High Str, Brixton, Johannesburg ▪ Open Mon-Sat, call store for trading hours ▪ **T (011) 837·7079**

Liquor City Broadacres Cnr Valley Rd & Cedar Ave, Broadacres, Randburg ▪ Open Mon-Sat, call store for trading hours ▪ **T (011) 465·3795**

Liquor City Cleo's Cnr Kingfisher & Heidelburg Strs, Elspark, Boksburg ▪ Open Mon-Sat, call store for trading hours ▪ **T (011) 916·2358**

Liquor City Cornwall View Cnr Boeing & Piering Strs, Elardus Park, Pretoria ▪ Open Mon-Sat, call store for trading hours ▪ **T (012) 345·5198**

Liquor City Crystal Park Cnr Totius & Strand Strs, Crystal Park, Benoni ▪ Open Mon-Sat, call store for trading hours ▪ **T (011) 969·3700**

Liquor City Dawnpark Cnr Gallahad Way & Hassink Highway, Dawn Park Shopping Centre, Dawn Park, Boksburg ▪ Open Mon-Sat, call store for trading hours ▪ **T (011) 862·2044**

Liquor City Eden Medows Shop 11, Eden Medows Shopping Centre, Cnr Van Riebeeck Ave & Modderfontein Rd, Edenvale ▪ Open Mon-Sat, call store for trading hours ▪ **T (011) 452·1993**

Liquor City Fourways Cnr Uranium & Buchwillow, Fourways ▪ Open Mon-Sat, call store for trading hours ▪ **T (011) 465·6910**

Liquor City Geduld Cnr 4th & 6th Streets, Geduld, Springs ▪ Open Mon-Sat, call store for trading hours ▪ **T (011) 811·5869**

Liquor City Glen Marais Cnr Dann & Veld Strs, Glen Marais Shopping Centre, Kempton Park ▪ Open Mon-Sat, call store for trading hours ▪ **T (011) 391·6005**

Liquor City Glen Marais Hyper Shop 7 Glen Acres Shopping Centre, Cnr Dann & Monument Strs, Kempton Park ▪ Open Mon-Sat, call store for trading hours ▪ **T (011) 391·7819**

Liquor City Glen Nerine Shop 1 Glen Nerine Shopping Centre, Cnr Witkoppen & Nerine Drive, Douglas Dale ▪ Open Mon-Sat, call store for trading hours ▪ **T (011) 658·1706**

Liquor City Heidelberg Shop 29 Victorian Centre, Voortrekker Str, Heidelberg ▪ Open Mon–Sat, call store for trading hours ▪ **T (016) 349·2512**

Liquor City Highlands Shop 1, Phase 2 Highlands Shopping Centre, Cnr Rabie & Glover Strs, Lyttleton Manor, Centurion ▪ Open Mon–Sat, call store for trading hours ▪ **T (012) 664·3424**

Liquor City Jean·Len Shop 8 Jealen Shopping Centre, Cnr Jean & Lenchen Strs, Centurion ▪ Open Mon–Sat, call store for trading hours ▪ **T (012) 663·9389**

Liquor City Lambton 6 Piercy Ave, Parkhills Garden, Lambton, Germiston ▪ Open Mon–Sat, call store for trading hours ▪ **T (011) 827·4566**

Liquor City Leondale Cnr Curry & Blaauwbok Ave, Leondale ▪ Open Mon–Sat, call store for trading hours ▪ **T (011) 865·1690**

Liquor City Lonehill Shop 1 Lonehill Shopping Centre, Lonehill Boulevard, Lonehill, Sandton ▪ Open Mon–Sat, call store for trading hours ▪ **T (011) 467·9887**

Liquor City Montana Shop 3 Montana Corner Shopping Centre, Cnr Zambesi & Dr Swanepoel, Montana, Pretoria ▪ Open Mon–Sat, call store for trading hours ▪ **T (012) 548·7780**

Liquor City Moreleta Cnr Garsfontein & Rubenstein Strs, Moreleta Park, Pretoria ▪ Open Mon–Sat, call store for trading hours ▪ **T (012) 993·0201**

Liquor City Mount Dev Cnr Beyers Naude & Mountain View Rds, Northcliff ▪ Open Mon–Sat, call store for trading hours ▪ **T (011) 782·6485/4**

Liquor City Northpoint Cnr Trichardt & Findel Strs, Impala Park, Boksburg ▪ Open Mon–Sat, call store for trading hours ▪ **T (011) 864·1672**

Liquor City Pretoria North Cnr Gerrit Maritz & Ben Viljoen Strs, Pretoria ▪ Open Mon–Sat, call store for trading hours ▪ **T (012) 546·8839**

Liquor City Princess Crossing Shop 39 Princess Crossing Shopping Centre, Ondekkers Rd, Roodepoort ▪ Open Mon–Sat, call store for trading hours ▪ **T (011) 768·6813**

Liquor City Radiokop Honey Junction Shopping Centre, Cnr John Vorster & Christiaan de Wet Str, Roodepoort ▪ Open Mon–Sat, call store for trading hours ▪ **T (011) 675·0493**

Liquor City Rooihuiskraal Shop 72 The Mall @ Reds Shopping Centre, Cnr Hendrik Verwoerd & Rooihuiskraal Ave, Centurion, Pretoria ▪ Open Mon–Sat, call store for trading hours ▪ **T (012) 656·8835**

Liquor City Ruimsig Cnr Hendrik Potgieter & Peters Str, Ruimsig, Roodepoort ▪ Open Mon–Sat, call store for trading hours ▪ **T (011) 958·2453**

Liquor City Ryngate Cnr Pretorius & Vlei, Rynfield, Benoni ▪ Open Mon–Sat, call store for trading hours ▪ **T (011) 969·1550**

Liquor City Satelite Cnr 11th Ave & Charl Cilliers Str, Boksburg North ▪ Open Mon–Sat, call store for trading hours ▪ **T (011) 917·0791**

Liquor City Selcourt 197 Nigel Rd, Selcourt ▪ Open Mon–Sat, call store for trading hours ▪ **T (011) 818·2961**

Liquor City Silverton Cnr Pretoria & Watermeyer Rd, Silverton ▪ Open Mon–Sat, call store for trading hours ▪ **T (012) 810·0090**

Liquor City Towers Shop 3 Towers Shopping Centre, North Rand Rd, Boksburg North ▪ Open Mon–Sat, call store for trading hours ▪ **T (011) 823·5221**

Liquor City Triomf Cnr Edward & Muller Strs, Triomf, Johannesburg ▪ Open Mon–Sat, call store for trading hours ▪ **T (011) 673·1893**

Liquor City V.C. Shop 3 V.C. Centre, 3 Craigholm Str, Dalview, Brakpan ▪ Open Mon–Sat, call store for trading hours ▪ **T (011) 744·0776**

Liquor City Waverley Cnr Hertzog & Codonia Strs, Waverley, Pretoria ▪ Open Mon–Sat, call store for trading hours ▪ **T (012) 332·0535**

Liquor City Westwood Shop 7 Westwood Shopping Centre, Atlas Road, Westwood, Boksburg ▪ Open Mon–Sat, call store for trading hours ▪ **T (011) 894·6567**

Liquor City Woodhill 948 St. Bernard Str, Woodhill Park, Garsfontein ▪ Open Mon–Sat, call store for trading hours ▪ **T (012) 993·5042**

Liquor Inn Heidelberg 50 Voortrekker Str, Heidelberg ▪ Open Mon–Sat, call store for trading hours ▪ **T (016) 341·2343**

Liquor World Camaro Square, Boundary Lane & Hartjies Rd, Oakdene ▪ Open daily, call store for trading hours ▪ **T (011) 436·1776**

Lynnridge Wine & Liquor Shop 46 Lynnridge Mall, Lynnwood Rd, Lynnwood Ridge, Pretoria ▪ Mon–Fri 8.30–6 Sat 8–3 Pub hols 9–1 ▪ Closed religious holidays ▪ mickey@glenfairliquor.co.za ▪ www.glenfairliquor.co.za ▪ **T/F (012) 348·3456**

Makro Centurion 2 Bloukrans St, Highveld Ext 2, Centurion ▪ Mon–Fri 9–6 Sat 8–4 Sun 9–1 Pub hols 9–4 ▪ cbarton@makro.co.za ▪ www.makro.co.za ▪ **T 0860·305·999** ▪ F 0860·405 ·999

Makro Crown Mines Cnr Main Reef Rd & Hanover St, Selby, Crown Mines ▪ Mon–Fri 8.30–5.30 Sat 8–4 Sun 9–1 Pub hols 9–4 ▪ cbarton@makro.co.za ▪ www.makro.co.za ▪ **T (011) 309·1108** ▪ F (011) 309·1089

Makro Germiston 16 Herman Rd, Meadowdale, Germiston ▪ Mon 9–5.30 Tue–Fri 8.30–5.30 Sat 8–4 Sun 9–1Pub hols 9–4 ▪ cbarton@makro.co.za ▪ www.makro.co.za ▪ **T (011) 372·0314** ▪ F (011) 453·1698

Makro Wonderboom Cnr Lavender Rd & Zambezi Drv, Annlin West ▪ Mon 9–5.30 Tue–Fri 8.30–5.30 Sat 8–4 Sun 9–1 Pub hols 9–4 ▪ cbarton@makro.co.za ▪ www.makro.co.za ▪ **T 0860·306·999** ▪ F (012) 567·9038

Makro Strubens Valley Cnr Christiaan de Wet & Hendrik Potgieter Rds, Roodepoort ▪ Mon 9–5.30 Tue–Fri 8.30–5.30 Sat 8–4 Sun 9–1 Pub hols 9–4 ▪ cbarton@makro.co.za ▪ www.makro.co.za ▪ **T (011) 671·8375** ▪ F (011) 671·8480

Makro Woodmead Waterfall Crescent South, Woodmead Ext 5, Sandton ▪ Mon–Fri 9–6 Sat 8–4 Sun 9–1 Pub hols 9–4 ▪ cbarton@makro.co.za ▪ www.makro.co.za ▪ **T (011) 208·9169** ▪ F (011) 208·9092

Manuka Fine Wines Woodlands Boulevard Shopping Centre, Garsfontein Rd, Woodhill, Pretoria East ▪ Mon–Fri 9–8 Sat 9–5 Sun 10–5 ▪ woodhill@manuka.co.za ▪ **T (012) 997·4669** ▪ F (012) 997·1480

Norman Goodfellow's 192 Oxford Road, Illovo, Johannesburg ▪ Mon–Fri: 8.30–6 Sat 8.30–2 ▪ goodfellow@icon.co.za ▪ **T (011) 788·4814** ▪ F (011) 442·8868

Norman Goodfellow's Hyde Park Lower level, Hyde Park Shopping Centre, Johannesburg ▪ Mon–Fri: 8.30–6 Sat 8.30–2 ▪ goodfellow@icon.co.za ▪ **T (011) 325·6462** ▪ F (011) 325·5450

Picardi Rebel Fine Wines & Liquors Bedfordview Bedfordview Shopping Centre, Smith Street, Bedfordview ▪ Mon–Fri 9–6 Sat 8.30–5 Sun 9–2 ▪ Open pub hols ▪ mark.no@picardirebel.co.za ▪ **T (011) 615·9160** ▪ F (011) 622·2475

Picardi Rebel Fine Wines & Liquors Blackheath Cnr Beyers Naude & Pendoring Road, Blackheath ▪ Mon–Fri 9–6 Sat 8.30–5 Sun–9 1 Open pub hols ▪ mark.no@picardirebel.co.za ▪ **T (011) 678·6817** ▪ F (011) 678·5017

Picardi Rebel Fine Wines & Liquors Fourways ▪ Fourways Mall Shopping Centre, William Nicol Drive, Fourways ▪ Mon–Fri 9–6.30 Sat 8.30–4 Sun 9–1 Open pub hols ▪ mark.no@picardirebel.co.za ▪**T (011) 465·6921** ▪ F (011) 465·6922

Picardi Rebel Fine Wines & Liquors Morning Glen Shop 17, Morning Glen Centre, Cnr Calvin Drive & Bowling Avenue, Gallo Manor ▪ Mon–Fri 9–6, Sat 8.30–4, Sun 9–1, Open pub hols ▪ mark.no@picardirebel.co.za ▪ **T (011) 802·0964** ▪ F (011) 802·0965

Picardi Rebel Fine Wines & Liquors Northmead G32, Northmead Square, Cnr 14 Avenue & O'Reilly Merry, Northmead ▪ Mon–Fri 9–6.00, Sat 8.30–4, Sun 9–1, Open pub hols ▪ mark.no@picardirebel.co.za ▪ **T (011) 849·5392** ▪ F (011) 849·7332

Picardi Rebel Fine Wines & Liquors Sandton Village Walk Centre, 125 Rivonia Rd, Sandton ▪ Mon–Fri 9–6.30 Sat 8.30–4 Sun 9–1 ▪ Open pub hols ▪ mark.no@picardirebel.co.za ▪ **T (011) 884·2151** ▪ F (011) 884·1067

Rivonia Cellars 349 Rivonia Boulevard, Rivonia ▪ Mon–Fri 9–6 Sat 9–2 Closed religious holidays ▪ rcellars@global.co.za ▪ **T (011) 803·6121/2** ▪ F (011) 803·7600

Ultra Liquors Corlett Drive Cnr Louis Botha Ave & Corlett Drive, Bramley ▪ Mon–Fri 9–6 Sat 9–5 Pub hols 9–2 ▪ Closed Easter Fri, Dec 25 & Jan 1 ▪ corlett@ultraliquors.co.za ▪ www.ultraclub.co.za ▪ **T (011) 887·1001/2/3** ▪ F (011) 887·4947

Vintages – The Wine Seller Shop 30 Sandton Square ▪ Daily 9-midnight ▪ Closed Dec 25th/26th, Jan 1st/2nd ▪ thebutchershop@mweb.co.za ▪ www.thebutchershop.co.za ▪ **T (011) 784·8676/7** ▪ F (011) 784·8674

Wine Direct Unit F76, Allandale Park, Le Roux Ave, Midrand ▪ Mon-Fri 8-5 ▪ wine@winedirectonline.co.za ▪ www.winedirectonline.co.za ▪ **T (011) 315·3088** ▪ F (011) 315·3098

KwaZulu-Natal

Blue Bottles Wine Cellar Within Surf Bay Butchery, Shelly Beach ▪ Mon-Fri 7.30-5 Sat & pub hols 8-1 ▪ Closed Good Fri, Dec 25 & Jan 1 ▪ bard@venturenet.co.za ▪ **T (039) 315·1336**

Buxtons La Cave Liquors buxton@3i.co.za ▪ F (031) 561·1252 ▪ Buxtons Village, Umhlanga: Mon-Fri 8-7 Sat 8-5 ▪ Closed Good Fri, Dec 25 ▪ **T (031) 561·6791/2** ▪ La Lucia Mall: Mon-Fri 9-6 ▪ **T (031) 572·6073/4** The Pavilion, Westville: Mon-Thu 9-6 Fri 9-7 Sat 8-5 ▪ **T (031) 265·0571**

Canaan Cellars 23 Springfield Rd, Winterton ▪ Mon-Fri 9-4.30 Sat 9-1 ▪ wine@canaancellars.co.za ▪ www.canaancellars.co.za ▪ **T/F (036) 488·1988**

Makro Pietermaritzburg 5 Barnsley Rd, Campsdrift Industrial Park ▪ Mon-Fri 9-6 Sat 8-5 Pub hols 9-4 ▪ cbarton@makro.co.za ▪ www.makro.co.za ▪ **T (033) 346·0220** ▪ F (033) 386·8120

Makro Rossburgh 101 Archary Rd (off Edwin Swales VC Drive), Rossburgh ▪ Mon-Fri 9-6 Sat 8-5 Pub hols 9-4 ▪ cbarton@makro.co.za ▪ www.makro co.za ▪ **T (031) 480·7000** ▪ F (031) 465·5955

Makro Springfield 90 Electron Rd, Springfield ▪ Mon-Fri 9-6 Sat 8-5 Pub hols 9-4 ▪ cbarton@makro.co.za ▪ www.makro.co.za ▪ **T (031)203·2896** ▪ F (031) 203·5905

Parklane Cellars 237 Greyling Str, Pietermaritzburg ▪ Mon-Fri 9-6 Sat 8.30-1 ▪ Closed pub hols ▪ min@satweb.co.za ▪ **T (033) 394·1691** ▪ F (033) 394·1623

Picardi Rebel Fine Wines & Liquors Glenwood Shop 24, Davenport Centre, Glenwood ▪ Mon-Fri 9-6.00 Sat 8.30-4 ▪ Open pub hols ▪ mark.no@picardirebel.co.za ▪ **T (031) 201·5487** ▪ F (031) 201·5488

Picardi Rebel Fine Wines & Liquors Liberty Mall Pietermaritzburg ▪ Mon-Fri 9-6.00 Sat 8.30-4 ▪ Open pub hols ▪ mark.no@picardirebel.co.za ▪ **T (033) 342·1698** ▪ F (033) 342169

The Village Vineyard Shop 25, Kloof Village Mall, Kloof ▪ Mon-Fri 9-7 Sat 8-5 Pub hols 9-5 ▪ Closed religious holidays ▪ **T (031) 764·6679** ▪ F (031) 764·7196

The Wine Cellar Midlands Meander, Old Main Road (R103), Rosetta ▪ Daily 9-4.30 (Wed/Thu during school term by appointment only) ▪ info@thewinecellar.co.za ▪ www.thewinecellar.co.za ▪ **T/F (033) 267·7044**

The Wine Domain 22 Salisbury Ave, Westville, Durban ▪ Mon-Fri 9-5 Sat 9-12.30 ▪ Closed pub hols ▪ sales@winedomain.co.za ▪ www.winedomain.co.za ▪ **T (031) 266·4394** ▪ F (031) 266·6124

Ultra Liquors New Germany 4 Regent Str, New Germany ▪ Mon-Fri 9-6 Sat 9-5 Pub hols 9-2 ▪ Closed Easter Fri, Dec 25 & Jan 1 ▪ newgermany@ultraliquors.co.za ▪ www.ultraliquors.co.za ▪ **T (031) 705·3777** ▪ F (031) 705·6640

Ultra Liquors Tollgate 39 Jan Smuts Highway, Mayville ▪ Mon-Fri 9-6 Sat 9-5 Pub hols 9-2 ▪ Closed Easter Fri, Dec 25 & Jan 1 ▪ tollgate@ultraliquors.co.za ▪ www.ultraclub.co.za ▪ **T (031) 261·2233/67** ▪ F (031) 261·7980

Ultra Liquors Westville 40A Buckingham Terrace, Westville ▪ Mon-Fri 9-6 Sat 9-5 Pub hols 9-2 ▪ Closed Easter Fri, Dec 25 & Jan 1 ▪ westville@ultraliquors.co.za ▪ www.ultraclub.co.za ▪ **T (031) 266·4364/60** ▪ F (031) 266·4300

Mpumalanga

Big M Liquor Store Cnr 1st & 3rd Strs, Delmas ▪ Open Mon-Sat, call store for trading hours ▪ **T (013) 665·2461**

Hi·Octane Store Secunda Plaza, Cnr Ettienne Rossouw & Frans du Toit Rds, Secunda ▪ Open Mon-Sat, call store for trading hours ▪ **T (017) 634·7033**

Liquor City Nelspruit Shop 14 Nelspruit Crossing Shopping Centre, Cnr N4 & General Dann Pienaar Rd, Nelspruit ▪ Open Mon-Sat, call store for trading hours ▪ **T (013) 752·2034**

Liquor City Witbank Shop 1 Cnr President & Swartkas Str, Witbank ▪ Open Mon-Sat, call store for trading hours ▪ **T (013) 690·2855**

Liquor City White River Shop 2 White River Square, Cnr Kruger Park & Hennie van Till Strs, White River ▪ Open Mon-Sat, call store for trading hours ▪ **T (013) 750·2184**

Windmill Wine Shop R536 between Hazyview & Sabie ▪ Mon-Sat 9-5 ▪ scrumpys@mweb.co.za ▪ www.thewindmill.co.za ▪ **T (013) 737·8175** ▪ F (013) 737·8966

Northern Cape

Zebrani Liquor City Shop No. 10 Pick 'n Pay Kalahari Centre, 29A Le Roux Str, Upington ▪ Open Mon-Sat, call store for trading hours T **(054) 331·2831** ▪ F (054) 331·1546

North West

De Wijnwinkel & Deli 4 Leask Str, Wolmaransstad ▪ Mon-Sat 9-7 Sun & pub hols 10-4 ▪ **T 083·262·0387** ▪ F (018) 596·2890

Liquor City Bushveld Bushveld Pick 'n Pay Centre, Cnr Potgieter & Marx Strs, Warmbaths ▪ Open Mon-Sat, call store for trading hours ▪ **T (014) 736·3215**

Liquor City Euronooi Cnr Lombard Drive & Wilkson, Mooinooi, Brits ▪ Open Mon-Sat, call store for trading hours ▪ **T (014) 574·3060**

Liquor City Geelhout Cnr Manuka & Wisteria Strs, Geelhout, Rustenburg ▪ Open Mon-Sat, call store for trading hours ▪ **T (014) 594·1768**

Liquor City Mafikeng 7 Robinson Str, Mafikeng ▪ Open Mon-Sat, call store for trading hours ▪ **T (018) 381·2326/7**

Liquor City Rustenburg Square Cnr Wolmerans & Von Willigh Strs, Rustenburg ▪ Open Mon-Sat, call store for trading hours ▪ **T (014) 594·2531**

Liquor City Safari Tuine Cnr Arend & Boekenhout Strs, Safari Tuine, Rustenburg ▪ Open Mon-Sat, call store for trading hours ▪ **T (014) 533·3467**

Western Cape

Aroma Fine Wine Centres Info@aroma.co.za ▪ **T 981·4510/0800·224·880** ▪ F 981·5411 ▪ Outlets: Constantia (Aroma Alphen Cellars): Old Village Shopping Centre, Spaanschemat Rd ▪ Mon-Thu 9-6 Fri 9-6.30 Sat 8.30-5 ▪ alphen@aroma.co.za ▪ **T 794·8693** ▪ Canal Walk: Shop 277, Entrance 1 ▪ aromacwa@aroma.co.za ▪ **T 551·7511** ▪ Mon-Fri 10-7 Sat 9-5 Sun 10-5 ▪ Somerset Mall, Somerset West: Mon-Fri 9-8 Sat 8.30-5 ▪ Aromasom@aroma.co.za ▪ **T 852·7551**

Bergkelder Vinoteque Wine Bank Papegaaiberg, Adam Tas Rd, Stellenbosch ▪ Tours/tastings by appt Mon-Fri 8-5 ▪ Closed pub hols but sales 24 hrs via website ▪ info@vinoteque.co.za ▪ www.vinoteque.co.za ▪ **T 809·8283** ▪ F 883·9533

Caroline's Fine Wine Cellar ▪ carowine@mweb.co.za ▪ www.carolineswine.com ▪ City Bowl: 15 Long Street, Cape Town ▪ Open Mon-Fri 9-5.30 Sat 9-1 ▪ Closed Sunday & pub hols ▪ **T 419·8984** ▪ F 419·8985 ▪ V&A Waterfront: Shop KWH8 ▪ Open Mon-Fri 9-8 Sat/Sun 9-5 ▪ carowine3@mweb.co.za ▪ **T 425·5701** ▪ F 425·5702 Also see Eat-out section.

Cellar in the City @ Cape Town Tourism Cnr Burg & Castle Streets, Cape Town ▪ Mon-Fri 9-5 Sat 9-1 Closed Dec 25th, Good Fri ▪ cellarinthecity@cape-town.org ▪ **T 426·2295**

Chapmans Peak Wine & Spirits Main Road, Hout Bay ▪ Mon-Fri 9-6.30 Sat 8.30-4 Closed Sun & religious holidays ▪ lidian@iafrica.com ▪ **T 790·1088** ▪ F 790·1089

Darling Wine Shop on Route 27 Vyge Valley, Darling ▪ Mon-Fri 9-6 Sat 9-5 Sun 10-4 Closed religious holidays ▪ darlingwines@westc.co.za ▪ **T (022) 492·3740** ▪ F (022) 492·3524

De Oude Paarl Wijn Boutique 132 Main Road, Paarl ▪ Mon-Sat 10-8 Sun 10-3 ▪ info@deoudepaarl.com ▪ **T 872·1002** ▪ F 872·1003

De Wijngarten Boetiek Main Road, Bonnievale ▪ Mon-Fri 9-5 Sat 9-1 ▪ timjan@lando.co.za ▪ **T (023) 616·2367** ▪ F (023) 616·3160

DonVino, The Wine Merchant Shop 581A, Tyger Valley Centre, Willie van Schoor Drive, Bellville ▪ Mon-Fri 9-7 Sat 9-5 ▪ Donvino@mweb.co.za ▪ **T 914·6952** ▪ F 914·6951

Gehot Bosch Wine Boutique & Winery See A-Z section for details

Grand World of Wines ArabellaSheraton Grand Hotel, 1 Lower Long Street, Convention Square, CT ▪ 8am-8pm 365 days/year ▪ jabspice@iafrica.com ▪ **T 412·9302** ▪ F 412·9305

Harbour Road Wines Harbour Road, Kleinmond ▪ Mon-Sat 10-5 Sun 10-4 ▪ werner@micron.co.za ▪ **T (028) 271·5151** ▪ F 086·620·5251

I Love Wine 40 Main Str, Paarl ▪ Mon-Sat 9-5 ▪ Closed Dec 25/26 & Jan 1 ▪ info@ilovewine.co.za ▪ www.ilovewine.co.za ▪ **T 863·2375 ▪ F 863·3120**

La Cotte Inn Wine Sales 35 Main Rd, Franschhoek ▪ Mon-Fri 9-6.30 Sat 9-1 ▪ info@lacotte.co.za ▪ www.lacotte.co.za ▪ **T 876·3775** ▪ F 876·3036

Main Ingredient Shop 5, Nedbank Centre, 15 Kloof Rd, Sea Point, Cape Town ▪ Mon-Fri 9.30-6 Sat 9.30-1 ▪ Closed Easter Fri/Sat, Dec 25/26, Jan 1 ▪ **T 439 5169** ▪ F 439·5169

Makro Milnerton Montague Drv, Montague Gardens, Cape Town ▪ Mon-Fri 9-6 Sat 8.30-4 Pub hols 9-4 ▪ cbarton@makro.co.za ▪ www.makro.co.za ▪ **T 550·6348** ▪ F 550·6362

Makro Ottery Cnr Ottery & Old Strandfontein Rds, Ottery ▪ Mon-Fri 9-6 Sat 8.30-5 Pub hols 9-4 ▪ cbarton@makro.co.za ▪ www.makro.co.za ▪ **T 703·6852** ▪ F 703·2508

Manuka Wine Boutique Noordhoek The Cellars, Noordhoek Farm Village, Noordhoek, CT ▪ Mon-Fri 10-6 Sat 9-5 Sun 10-5 ▪ noordhoek@manuka.co.za ▪ **T 789·0898**

Manuka Wine Boutique Somerset West Southeys, Main Rd, Somerset West, CT ▪ Mon-Sat 8-6 Sun 9-3 ▪ southeys@manuka.co.za ▪ **T 851·6060**

Manuka Wine Boutique Tygervalley Willowbridge Centre, Tygervalley, CT ▪ Mon-Fri 9-8 Sat 8-5 ▪ tygervalley@manuka.co.za ▪ **T 083·556·9088**

Manuka Wines & Liquors Tokai Steenberg Village, Reddam Ave, Tokai, CT ▪ Mon-Fri 8-7 Sat 8-5 ▪ info@manuka.co.za ▪ **T 701·2046**

Mooiberge Cnr Annandale Road & R44, Stellenbosch ▪ Daily 8-6 ▪ **T 881·3222** ▪ F 881·3656

Picardi Rebel Fine Wines & Liquors Cape Town Spearhead House, Shop no 6, 42 Hans Strijdom Avenue, Cape Town ▪ Mon-Fri 9-6.30, Sat 9-5, Sun 10-5 ▪ Open on pub hols ▪ mark.no@picardirebel.co.za ▪ **T (021) 425·1639** ▪ F (021) 421·5841

Picardi Rebel Fine Wines & Liquors Claremont 218 Main Road, Claremont ▪ Mon-Fri 9-6, Sat 9–5 ▪ Open pub hols ▪ mark.no@picardirebel.co.za ▪ **T (021) 671·9918** ▪ F (021) 683·9025

Picardi Rebel Fine Wines & Liquors Durbanville Midville Centre, Wellington Street, Durbanville ▪ Mon-Thu 9-7, Fri 9-8, Sat 9-5 ▪ Open pub hols ▪ mark.no@picardirebel.co.za ▪ **T (021) 976·5318** ▪ F (021) 976·5341

Picardi Rebel Fine Wines & Liquors Longbeach Shop G2, Longbeach Mall Centre, Noordhoek ▪ Mon-Fri 9-6, Sat 9-5 ▪ Open pub hols ▪ mark.no@picardirebel.co.za ▪ **T (021) 785·3323** ▪ F (021) 785·3318

Picardi Rebel Fine Wines & Liquors Rosmead 27 Rosmead Avenue, Claremont ▪ Mon-Fri 9-6, Sat 9-5 ▪ Open pub hols ▪ mark.no@picardirebel.co.za ▪ **T (021) 683·1406** ▪ F (021) 674·2094

Picardi Rebel Fine Wines & Liquors Tokai Blue Route Centre, Tokai ▪ Mon- Mon-Fri 9-6, Sat 9-5 ▪ Open pub hols ▪ mark.no@picardirebel.co.za ▪ **T (021) 712·5082** ▪ F (021) 712·2536

Picardi Rebel Fine Wines & Liquors Tygervalley Shop 496, Tygervalley Centre, Willie van Schoor Avenue ▪ Mon-Fri 9-7 Sat 9-5 ▪ Open pub hols ▪ mark.no@picardirebel.co.za ▪ **T (021) 914·1649** ▪ F (021) 914·2420

Riedel@Aroma Old Village Shopping Centre, Spaanschemat Rd, Constantia ▪ Mon-Thu 9-6 Fri 9-6.30 Sat 9-5 ▪ riedel@aroma.co.za ▪ **T 794·8693** ▪ F 794·8694

Rubin's Liquors Westbank House, 21 Riebeek Str, Cape Town ▪ Mon-Fri 8.30-5.30 Sat 8.30-12.30 ▪ Closed pub hols ▪ vinru@new.co.za ▪ **T 425·4692** ▪ F 419·9405

Spier Wine Centre R310 Lynedoch Rd, Stellenbosch ▪ Daily 9-5 ▪ info@spier.co.za ▪ www.spier.co.za ▪ **T 809·1143** ▪ F 809·1144

Stellenbosch Wine Export Centre 86-88 Dorp Street, Stellenbosch ▪ Mon-Fri 9-7 Sat 9-5 Closed Dec 25 ▪ WineCape@global.co.za ▪ **T/F 883·3814**

Steven Rom Wine Merchants & Exporters Checkers Galleria Centre, 76 Regent Rd, Sea Point, Cape Town ▪ wine@stevenrom.co.za ▪ www.stevenrom.co.za ▪ Mon-Fri 9-6 Sat 9-4 ▪ **T 439·6043** ▪ F 434·0401 ▪ Three Anchor Bay: Bay Point, Cnr Beach & Stanley Rds, Cape Town ▪ Mon-Fri 9-7 Sat 9-5 ▪ **T 434·0001** ▪ New wine depot, The Cape Grape & Wine Co: Polkadraai Rd (M12), Stellenbosch (next to Amani) ▪ **T 0860·10·30·34 / 905·0290** ▪ F 905·0293 ▪ info@capegrape.co.za ▪ www.capegrape.co.za

The Cape Grape & Wine Company See Steven Rom Wine Merchants & Exporters

The Vineyard Connection Delvera, cnr R44 & Muldersvlei Rd, Muldersvlei ▪ Mon-Fri 8-5 Sat 9-5 Sun 10-5 ▪ info@vineyardconnection.co.za ▪ www.vineyardconnection.co.za ▪ **T 884·4360** ▪ F 884·4361

The Wine Shop at Constantia Uitsig Constantia Uitsig Farm, Spaanschemat River Rd, Constantia ▪ Mon-Fri 9-5 Sat, Sun & pub hols 10-4 ▪ Closed Good Fri, Dec 25 & 26 ▪ thewineshop@uitsig.co.za ▪ www.uitsig.co.za ▪ **T 794·1810** ▪ F 794·1812

Ultra Liquors Goodwood No 1 Goodwood Mall, McDonald Str, Goodwood ▪ Mon-Fri 9-6 Sat 9-5 Pub hols 9-2 ▪ Closed Easter Fri, Dec 25 & Jan 1 ▪ goodwood@ultraliquors.co.za ▪ www.ultraliquors.co.za T **591·5581** ▪ F 591·8492

Ultra Liquors Greenpoint 122 Main Rd & Varney Str, Greenpoint ▪ Mon-Fri 9-6 Sat 9-5 Pub hols 9-2 ▪ Closed Easter Fri, Dec 25 & Jan 1 ▪ greenpoint@ultraliquors.co.za ▪ www.ultraclub.co.za ▪ **T 434·4847/4302/4838** ▪ F 434·7548

Ultra Liquors Parow 305 Voortrekker Rd, Parow ▪ Mon-Fri 9-6 Sat 9-5 Pub hols 9-2 ▪ Closed Easter Fri, Dec 25 & Jan 1 ▪ parow@ultraliquors.co.za ▪ www.ultraclub.co.za ▪ **T 930·2415/6** ▪ F 930·4007

Ultra Liquors Wynberg Cnr Malton & 300 Main Str, Wynberg ▪ Mon-Fri 9-6 Sat 9-5 Pub hols 9-2 ▪ Closed Easter Fri, Dec 25 & Jan 1 ▪ wynburg@ultraliquors.co.za ▪ www.ultraclub.co.za ▪ **T 762·5885/1473** ▪ F 761·6005

Vaughan Johnson's Wine & Cigar Shop V&A Waterfront Pierhead, Cape Town ▪ Mon-Fri 9-6 Sat 9-5 Sun 10-5 ▪ vjohnson@mweb.co.za ▪ www.vaughanjohnson.com ▪ **T 419·2121** ▪ F 419·0040

Vino Pronto 42 Orange Str, Gardens, Cape Town ▪ Mon-Fri 10-8 Sat 10-5 ▪ Closed Dec 25th, Jan 1st & Good Fri ▪ vinopronto@global.co.za ▪ **T 424·5587** ▪ F 423·5707

Wine Cellar (incl insulated/secure maturation cellars) Unit 4, Prices Park, Nelson Road, Observatory, Cape Town ▪ Mon-Fri 8-5 Sat by appointment ▪ info@winecellar.co.za ▪ www.winecellar.co.za ▪ **T 448·4105 / (028) 312·1663**

Wine & Company 7 High St, Hermanus ▪ Mon-Fri 9-6 Sat 9-2 Closed pub hols ▪ winenco@telkomsa.net ▪ **T (028) 313·2047** ▪ F (028) 312·4029

Wine Concepts Cardiff Castle, Cnr Kildare Rd & Main St, Newlands, Cape Town. Also at Lifestyle on Kloof, 50, Kloof St, Gardens, Cape Town ▪ Mon-Fri 10-8 Sat 9-5 Non-religious pub hols 11-3 (doors close hour earlier in winter) ▪ Newlands: sales@wineconcepts.co.za ▪ www.wineconcepts.co.za ▪ **T 671·9030** ▪ F 671·9031 Gardens: kloofst@wineconcepts.co.za ▪ **T 426·4401** ▪ F 426·4402

Wines@Oude Libertas Oude Libertas Centre, cnr Adam Tas & Oude Libertas Rds, Stellenbosch ▪ Mon-Fri 9.30-5 Sat 9.30-1 ▪ Closed Christian holidays & Jan 1 ▪ wines@oudelibertas.net ▪ www.oudelibertas.net ▪ **T 886·7404** ▪ F 886·7405

Wine Village Hermanus Hemel-en-Aarde Village, Cnr Hemel-en-Aarde and Sandbaai crossing, Hermanus ▪ Mon-Fri 9-6 Sat 9-5 Sun 10-3 ▪ Closed Easter Fri, Dec 25 ▪ wine@hermanus.co.za winenews@hermanus.co.za ▪ www.wine-village.co.za ▪ **T (028) 316·3988** ▪ F (028) 316·3989

Online Wine Shops

Cybercellar.com fiona@cybercellar.com ▪ www.cybercellar.com ▪ **T/F 874·2106**

I Love Wine See listing under Western Cape above

Manuka Wine Exports info@manuka.co.za www.manuka.co.za ▪ **T 701·2046** ▪ F 701·0386

Wine.co.za info@wine.co.za ▪ www.wine.co.za ▪ **T 855·0509** ▪ F 855·0519

Wine Direct See listing under Gauteng above

WINEmag.co.za Online Auctions ▪ webeditor@winemag.co.za ▪ www.winemag.co.za/auction ▪ **T 530·3287** ▪ F 531·2212

Wineseller-Fine Wine On-Line orders@wineseller.co.za ▪ www.wineseller.co.za ▪ **T 905·0290** ▪ F 905·0293

Wine with Personality hello@winewithpersonality.co.za ▪ www.winewithpersonality.co.za ▪ **T 082·371·5017** ▪ F 086·671·8358

Vintages & Styles

Recent Cape vintages

SA wines do not exhibit the major vintage variations seen in cooler northern climes such as Burgundy or Bordeaux. There are, nevertheless, perceptible differences from year to year. These, in terms of reds, relate more to relative ageing potential than the declaration of generally poor vintages; whites, if anything, are more prone to vintage variation, summer heatwaves robbing them of freshness and flavour. Dry, hot summers are the norm but a variety of factors make generalisations difficult and dangerous.

2005 Short, early and particularly challenging. Bone dry winter followed by early-season rains, sparking disease and excessive plant vigour; then prolonged heatwaves. Concentrated if alcoholic reds; whites mostly average, some stellar exceptions.

2004 Long and late, bedevilled by uneven berry-set and an early aroma-stripping heatwave. Yet cooler dry conditions yielded healthy, elegant, possibly ageworthy wines with lower alcs and yielding tannins. Chardonnay, merlot and shiraz especially promising.

2003 Hailed as an outstanding year, with concentrated, structured and generous reds as well as whites. The general euphoria tempered by some difficulties with late-ripening varieties in certain areas.

2002 Challenging and patchy year, marred by disease and high harvest temperatures. Generally, individual producers' track record rather than variety or terroir should guide the purchase/cellaring decision.

2001 Hot, dry, largely disease-free vintage, yielding some excellent reds – fruity and concentrated, possibly long-lived. White-wine producers who picked between heatwaves delivered flavourful if alcoholic wines.

2000 Another hot year with predictably powerful, concentrated reds, sometimes with big tannins. The best should keep very well. Whites, by contrast, generally less stellar and not for long ageing.

1999 Near-perfect ripening conditions meant fat, alcoholic reds with ripe fruit for earlier drinking. Some attractive, fruity whites from chardonnay, semillon and chenin, but generally not too much excitement.

1998 Excellent vintage. Deep, lusty (sometimes tannic) reds with enough fruit for extended cellaring. Whites somewhat less sexy; some good fuller-bodied versions but even these not for keeping.

1997 One of the coolest and latest on record. Serious problems with downy mildew. Slender, supple (rather than light) reds, the best showing pristine fruit, smooth tannins and elegance. Some excellent, stylish whites with beautiful aromas and balance.

Older vintages

1996 Generally awkward reds, not for keeping (but some notable exceptions); whites, except for top NLHs, best drunk up. **1995** For many, vintage of the 90s. Very dry, long and warm; ripe, fruity, concentrated reds, maturing spectacularly. **1994** Hottest, driest vintage in decades; variable quality; new-clone cabs, early ripening reds fared well. **1993** Year without serious mishaps; some excellent sauvignons; above-average reds. **1992** Coolish vintage favouring whites, especially sauvignon; reds (esp pinotage) very good to outstanding; **1991** Dry, warm to hot year, favouring early to mid-season ripeners; some concentrated, long-lasting reds. **1990** Uneven year, alternately cool, warm; average whites; middling reds with some very characterful examples. The **1980s**: even years (82, 84, 86) usually more favourable for reds; uneven years, marginally cooler, favoured whites, but 'white' years 87 and, especially, 89 produced remarkable reds. The **1970s**: again, even years generally favoured reds. The best of the 70s was undoubtedly 74; but top wines from some other vintages are still delicious. The **1960**s and earlier yielded some astonishingly long-lived wines, prompting a new generation to look at the traditional 'dikvoet' winemaking style with fresh eyes.

SA wine styles

Blanc de blancs White wine made from white grapes only; also used for champagne and méthode cap classique.

Blanc fumé or **fumé blanc** Dry white from sauvignon, not necessarily finished in wood (nor smoked, smoky).

Blanc de noir A pink wine (shades range from off-white through peach to pink) made from red grapes.

Brut See sugar or sweetness, sparkling wine.

Cap classique See Méthode cap classique.

Cape Blend Evolving term, increasingly used to denote a (red) blend with pinotage, the 'local' grape making up 30%-70% of the assemblage; sometimes simply a blend showing a distinct 'Cape' character.

Carbonated See Sparkling wine.

Cultivar Grape variety (a contraction of 'cultivated variety').

Cuvée French term for the blend of a wine.

Demi-sec See Sugar or sweetness.

Dessert wine A sweet wine, often to accompany the dessert but sometimes pleasurably prior, as in the famous Sauternes/foie gras combo.

Dry to sweet See sugar or sweetness.

Fortified wines Increased in alcoholic strength by the addition of spirit, by SA law to minimum 15% alcohol by volume.

Grand cru See Premier Grand Cru

Jerepiko or **jerepigo** Red or white wine, produced without fermentation; grape juice is fortified with grape spirit, preventing fermentation; very sweet with considerable unfermented grape flavours.

Late Harvest Sweet wine from late -harvested and therefore sweeter grapes. See Sugar or sweetness.

Méthode cap classique (MCC) See Sparkling wine.

Noble Late Harvest (NLH) Sweet dessert wine exhibiting a noble rot (botrytis) character, from grapes infected by the *botrytis cinerea* fungus. This mould, in warm, misty autumn weather, attacks the skins of ripe grapes, causing much of the juice to evaporate. As the berries wither, their sweetness and flavour become powerfully concentrated. SA law dictates that grapes for NLH must be harvested at a minimum of 28° Balling and residual sugar must exceed 50g/ℓ.

Nouveau Term originated in Beaujolais for fruity young and light red, usually from gamay and made by the carbonic maceration method. Bottled a few weeks after vintage to capture the youthful, fresh flavour of fruit and yeasty fermentation.

Perlant, perlé, pétillant Lightly sparkling, carbonated wine.

Port Fortified dessert with improving quality record in Cape since late 1980s, partly through efforts of SA Port Producers' Association which recommends use of word 'Cape' to identify the local product. Following are SAPPA-defined styles: **Cape White**: non-muscat grapes, wood-aged min 6 mths, any size vessel; **Cape Ruby**: blended, fruity, components aged min 6 mths, up to 3 years depending on size of vessel. Average age min 1 year. **Cape Vintage**: fruit of one harvest; dark, full-bodied, vat-aged (any size); **Cape Vintage Reserve**: fruit of one harvest in year of 'recognised quality'. Preferably aged min 1 year, vats of any size, sold only in glass; **Cape Late Bottled Vintage** (LBV): fruit of single 'year of quality', full-bodied, slightly tawny colour, aged 3-6 years (of which min 2 years in oak); **Cape Tawny**: wood-matured, amber-orange (tawny) colour, smooth, slightly nutty taste (white grapes not permitted); **Cape Dated Tawny**: single-vintage tawny.

Premier Grand Cru Unlike in France, not a quality rating in SA – usually an austerely dry white.

Residual sugar See Sugar or sweetness.

Rosé Pink wine, made from red or a blend of red and white grapes. The red grape skins are removed before the wine takes up too much colouring.

Sparkling wine Bubbly, or 'champagne', usually white but sometimes rosé and even red, given its effervescence by carbon dioxide – allowed to escape in the normal winemaking process. **Champagne** undergoes its second fermentation in the bottle. Under an agreement with France, SA does not use the term which describes the sparkling wines from the Champagne area. Instead, **méthode cap classique** (MCC) is the SA term to describe sparkling wines made by the classic method. **Charmat** undergoes its second, bubble-forming fermentation in a tank and is bottled under pressure. **Carbonated** sparklers are made by the injection of carbon dioxide bubbles (as in fizzy soft drinks). See also Sugar or sweetness.

Special Late Harvest (SLH) SA designation for a lighter dessert style wine. There is no longer a legal stipulation for residual sugar content, but if the RS is below 20g/ℓ, the label must state 'extra dry', 'dry', 'semi-dry' or 'sweet', as the case may be. The minimum alcohol content has been raised from 10% to 11% by volume.

Stein Semi-sweet white wine, usually a blend and often confused with steen, a grape variety (chenin blanc), though most steins are made partly from steen grapes.

Sugar or sweetness In still wines: extra-dry or bone-dry wines have less than 2.5g/ℓ residual sugar, undetectable to the taster. A wine legally is dry up to 5g/ℓ. Taste buds will begin picking up a slight sweetness, or softness, in a wine – depending on its acidity – at about 6g/ℓ, when it is still off-dry. By about 8-9g/ℓ a definite sweetness can usually be noticed. However, an acidity of 8-9g/ℓ can render a sweet wine fairly crisp even with a sugar content of 20g/ℓ plus. Official sweetness levels in SA wine are:

Still wines	Sugar (g/ℓ)	Sparkling wines	Sugar (g/ℓ)
Extra dry	≤ 2,5	Extra dry/brut	≤ 15
Dry	≤ 5	Dry/sec	15-35
Semi-dry	5 ≤ 12	Semi-sweet/demi-sec	35-50
Semi-sweet	< 5 < 30	Sweet/doux	50
Late Harvest	≥ 20		
Special Late Harvest (SLH)	–		
Natural Sweet (or Sweet Natural)	> 20		
Noble Late Harvest	> 50		
Naturally dried grape wine (straw wine)	> 30		

Varietal wine From single variety of grape. In SA must consist of 75% or more of the stated grape – but 85% or more if exported.

Vintage In SA primarily used to denote year of harvest. Not a substantive quality classification (a 'vintage' port in Europe means one from an officially declared great port grape year).

Frequently Used Words & Phrases

Winetasting terms

Short of a ready description? Here are a few frequently-used words, phrases and explanations that may be helpful. See also Winemaking terms; SA wine styles.

Accessible, approachable Flavours and feel of the wine are harmonious, easily recognised; it is ready to drink.

Aftertaste The lingering flavours and impressions of a wine; its persistence – the longer, the better.

Alcoholic 'Hot' or, in excess, burning character caused by imbalanced or excessive alcohol. Also simply spiritous.

Astringent Mouth-puckering sensation in the mouth, associated with high tannin (and sometimes acid); also bitter, sharp.

Aroma Smells in the bouquet, or nose, especially the odours associated with the grape rather than the winemaking process.

Attack First sensations on palate/nose – pungent, aggressive, quiet etc.

Austere Usually meaning unyielding, sometimes harsh. Sometimes, more favourably, to imply a notable restraint/refinement.

Backbone The wine is well formed, firm, not flabby or insipid.

Baked 'Hot', earthy quality. Usually from scorched/shrivelled grapes which have been exposed too long to the sun, or from too warm a barrel fermentation, especially in some whites.

Balance Desirable attribute. The wine's chief constituents – alcohol, acid, tannin, fruit and wood (where used) – are in harmony.

Bead Bubbles in sparkling wine; a fine, long-lasting bead is the most desirable. See also Mousse.

Big Expansive in the mouth, weighty, full-bodied, as a result of high alcohol or fruit concentration.

Bite or **grip** Imparted by tannins and acids (and alcohol in fortified wines); important in young wines designed for ageing. If overdone can impart undesirable bitterness, harshness or spirity 'glow'.

Bitter Sensation perceived mainly on the back of the tongue, and in the finish of the wine. Usually unpleasant, though an accepted if not immediately admired character of certain Italian wines. Sometimes more positively associated with the taste of a specific fruit or nut, such as cherry-kernel or almond.

Body Fullness on the palate.

Botrytis/ed Exhibits a noble rot/botrytis character, from grapes infected by the *botrytis cinerea fungus*.

Bottle age Negative or positive, depending on context. Positively describes development of aromas/flavours (ie complexity) as wine moves from youth to maturity. Much-prized attribute in fine whites and reds. Negatively, bottle age results in a wine with stale, empty or even off odours.

Buttery Flavour and texture associated with barrel-fermented white wines, especially chardonnays; rich, creamy smoothness.

Charming Usually used in the context of lighter, simpler wines. Sometimes synonymous with 'sweet' (both as in 'sugary' and 'dear').

Claret Another name for a dry red Bordeaux or Bordeaux-like red

Classic Showing characteristics of the classics of Bordeaux, Burgundy etc; usually implying balance, elegance, subtlety.

Coarse Rough, unbalanced tannins, acid, alcohol or oak.

Complexity Strong recommendation. A complex wine has several layers of flavour, usually developing with age/maturation. See Bottle age.

Concentration See Intensity.

Confected Over-elaborately constructed, artificial, forced; also overly sweet.

Corked Wine is faulty; its flavours have been tainted by yeast, fungal or bacterial infections, often but not necessarily from the cork. It smells damp and mouldy in its worst stages – but sometimes it's barely detectable. In a restaurant, a corked wine should be rejected and returned immediately; producers are honour-bound to replace corked wine.

Creamy Not literally creamy, of course; more a silky, buttery feel and texture.

Crisp Refers to acidity. Positively, means fresh, clean; negatively, too tart, sharp.

Deep and depth Having many layers; intense; also descriptive of a serious wine.

Dense Well-padded texture, flavour-packed.

Deposits (also sediment or crust) Tasteless and harmless tartrates, acid crystals or tannin in older red wines. Evidence that wine has not been harshly fined, filtered or cold-stabilised.

Dried out Bereft of fruit, harder constituents remaining; tired.

Earthy Usually positive, wine showing its origins from soil, minerally, damp leaves, mushrooms etc.

Easy Undemanding (and hopefully inexpensive).

Elegant Stylish, refined, 'classic'.

Esters Scents and smells usually generated by alcohols and acids in wine. A wine may be 'estery' when these characteristics are prominent.

Extract An indication of the 'substance' of a wine, expressed as sugar-free or total extract (which would include some sugars). 18g/ℓ would be low, light; anything much above 23g/ℓ in whites is significant; the corresponding threshold for reds is around 30g/ℓ.

Fat Big, full, ample in the mouth.

Finesse Graceful, polished. Nothing excessive.

Finish The residual sensations – tastes and textures – after swallowing. Should be pleasant (crisp, lively) and enduring, not short, dull or flat. See also Length.

Firm Compact, has good backbone.

Flabby Usually, lacking backbone, especially acid.

Flat Characterless, unexciting, lacks acid. Or bubbly which has lost its fizz.

Fleshy Very positive, meaning a wine is well fleshed out with texture and grape flavours.

Flowery Floral, flower-like (i.e. the smell of rose, honeysuckle, jasmine etc). Distinct from 'fruity' (ie smell/taste of papaya, cantaloupe, grape! etc)

Forward rather than shy; advancing in age too; mature.

Fresh Lively, youthful, invigorating. Closely related to the amount of acid in the wine and absence of oxidative character: a big, intensely sweet dessert without a backbone of acidity will taste flat and sickly; enough acid and the taste is fresh and uncloying.

Fruity See floral.

Full High in alcohol and extract.

Gamey Overripe, decadent; not universally unattractive.

Gravel/ly With suggestions of minerally, earthy quality; also firm texture.

Green Usually unripe, sour; sometimes simply youthful.

Grip Often almost literally gripping, firm on palate, in finish. Acid, tannin, alcohol are contributors.

Heady Usually refers to the smell of a wine. High in alcohol; intense, high-toned.

Herbaceous Grassy, hay-like, heathery; can also indicate under-ripeness.

Hollow Lacking substance, flavours.

Honey or **honeyed** Sometimes literally a honey/beeswax taste or flavour; a sign of developing maturity in some varieties or more generally a sign of bottle age.

Hot Burning sensation of alcohol in finish.

Intensity No flab, plenty of driving flavour; also deep colour.

Lean Thin, mean, lacking charm of ample fruit; also, more positively, compact, sinewy.

Lees/leesy Taste-imparting dead yeast cells (with grape skins and other solid matter) remaining with wine in tank/barrel (or bottle in the case of *méthode champenoise* sparkling wines) after fermentation. The longer the wine is 'on its lees' (sur lie) the more richness and flavour it should absorb.

Light/lite Officially wines under 10% alcohol by volume, also light in body (and often short on taste); a health-conscious trend in both reds and whites.

Lively Bouncy, fresh flavours.

Long or **length** Enduring; wine's flavours reverberate in the palate long after swallowing.

Maderised Oxidised and flat; colour is often brownish. Over-mature.

Meaty Sometimes suggesting a general savouriness; but also literally the aroma of meat – raw, smoked etc.

Mousse Fizz in sparkling wines; usually refers also to quality, size and effervescence of the bubbles. See also Bead.

Mouthfeel, **mouthfilling** Texture, feel; racy, crispness (fine with appropriate dishes) or generous, supple, smooth.

Neutral What it says, neither here nor there.

New World Generally implies accessible, bold, often extrovert (in terms of fruit and use of oak). **Old World** embraces terms like subtle, complex, less oaky, more varied and generally more vinous (than fruity). See also Classic.

Oaky Having exaggerated oak aromas/flavours (vanilla, spice, char, woodsmoke etc). Oak balanced by fruit in young wines may lessen with age, but over-oaked young wines (where fruit is not in balance) will become over-oaked old wines.

Palate Combination of flavour, taste and texture of a wine.

Pebbly See Gravelly.

Perfumed or **scented** Strong fragrances (fruity, flowery, animal etc)

Plump Well fleshed in a charming, cherubic way.

Porty Heavy, over-ripe, stewed; a negative in unfortified wine.

Rich Flavourful, intense, generous. Not necessarily sweet.

Robust Strapping, full-bodied (but not aggressive).

Rough Bull-in-a-china-shop wine, or throat sand-papering quality.

Round Well balanced, without gawkiness or jagged edges.

Sharp or **tart** All about acid, usually unbalanced. But occasionally sharpish, fresh wine is right for the occasion.

Short or **quick** Insubstantial wine, leaving little impression.

Simple One-dimensional or no flavour excitement.

Stalky Unripe, bitter, stemmy.

Stewed Over-ripe, cooked, soft, soggy fruit.

Structure Vague word, usually refers to the wine's make up (acid, tannin, alcohol) in relation to its ageing ability; if a wine is deemed to have 'the structure to age' it suggests these principal preservatives are in place.

Stylish Classy, distinguished; also voguish.

Supple Very desirable (not necessarily subtle), yielding, refined texture and flavours. See also Mouthfeel.

Tannic Tannins are prominent in the wine, imparting, positively, a mouth-puckering, grippy, tangy quality; negatively, a harsh, unyielding character.

Tension Racy, nervous fruity-acid play on the palate.

Terpene(s)/terpenoid Strong, floral compounds influencing the aromas of especially riesling, gewürztraminer and the muscats; with bottle-age, terpenes often develop a pungent resinous oiliness.

Texture Tactile 'feel' in the mouth: hard, acidic, coarse and alcoholic; or, smooth, velvety, 'warm'.

Toasty Often used for barrel-fermented and aged wines showing a pleasant biscuity, charry character.

Vegetal Grassy, leafy, herby – in contrast to fruity, flowery, oaky. Overdone, a no-no.

Yeasty Warm bakery smells, often evident in barrel-fermented whites and *méthode champenoise* sparkling wines, where yeasts stay in contact with the wine after fermentation.

Winemaking terms

A few brief reference explanations. See also sections Winetasting terms, SA wine styles.

Acid and **acidity** The fresh – or, in excess, sharp or tart – taste of wine. Too little acid and the wine tastes dull and flat. In SA, winemakers are permitted to adjust acidity either by adding acid – at any stage before bottling – or by lowering the acid level with a de-acidifier. See also Volatile acid and Malolactic.

Alcohol Essential component of wine, providing fullness, richness and, at higher levels, sometimes an impression of sweetness. Also a preservative, helping keep wines in good condition. Produced by yeasts fermenting the sugars in the grape. Measured by volume of the total liquid. Most unfortified table wines in SA have between 11% and 14% alc by vol; fortifieds range from about 16% to 21%.

Barrels (**barrel-aged**; **barrel-fermented**) Wines are transferred into barrels to age, pick up oaky flavours etc. When must or fermenting must is put into barrels, the resulting wine is called barrel-fermented. A barrel or cask is generally a 225–500ℓ oak container; *barrique* is a French word for a 225ℓ barrel; a pipe, adapted from the Portuguese *pipa*, usually indicates a vessel of 530–630ℓ; vat is a term generally used for larger (2 000–5 000ℓ) wooden vessels.

Batonnage See Lees.

Biodynamic See Organic.

Blend A wine made from two or more different grape varieties, vintages, vineyards or containers. Some of the world's finest wines are blends.

Bottles While the 750ml (75cl) bottle is now the most widely used size of container for wine, it is by no means the only one. Smaller bottles (375 & 500ml) are popular with restaurants and airlines, and larger sizes are prized by collectors because of their novelty value and/or their tendency to promote slower wine ageing. The following are the larger bottle sizes (note: some no longer in production):

Capacity		Bordeaux	Champagne/Burgundy
litres	*bottles*		
1.5	2	magnum	magnum
3	4	double magnum	Jéroboam
4.5	6	Jéroboam	Rehoboam
6	8	Impériale	Methuselah
9	12	–	Salmanazar
12	16	–	Balthazar
15	20	–	Nebuchadnezzar

Brettanomyces or **'brett'** Currently much focussed-on naturally occurring yeast, usually associated with red wine and regarded as a spoilage factor, because its growth triggers the formation of volatile acids, phenols and other compounds which, in sufficient concentration, impart a range of unpleasant characters, from barnyard to sweat to cheese.

Carbonic maceration or **maceration carbonique** Method of fermenting wine without first crushing the grapes. Whole clusters with stalks etc are put into closed vat; intracellular fermentation occurs within the grape berries, which then burst.

Chaptalisation Originally French term for the addition of sugar to grape must to raise the alcohol of a wine. Selectively legal in northern Europe, where acid adjustments are not allowed as they are in SA. Winemakers in both hemispheres bend the rules.

Charmat Method of making sparkling wine in a sealed tank (*cuvée close)* under pressure. Easier, cheaper than méthode champenoise.

Chips See Oak chips

Cold ferment 'Cold' is a relative term; applied to fermentation of mainly white wines in temperature-controlled tanks, it refers to a temperature around usually 13–16°C. The benefits, especially important in a warm country, include conserving the primary fruit aromas and ensuring fermentation is carried out steadily and thoroughly.

Cold soak or **cold maceration**. Red winemaking method carried out prior to fermentation. Skins and juice are held, usually for a few days, at a sufficiently cool temperature to prevent fermentation. The theory is that this extracts more favourable colour and aromas than after fermentation.

Cold stabilisation Keeping a wine at about -4°C for a week or more to precipitate tartaric acid and 'clean up' the wine, preventing later formation of (harmless) tartrate crystals in bottle. Some winemakers believe this process damages flavour and prefer to avoid it.

Disgorgement (*dégorgement* in French) Important stage in the production of traditionally fermented sparkling where accumulated sediment (or lees), which could cloud the finished wine, is removed from the neck of the bottle.

Dosage The sugar added to sparkling wine after the second fermentation.

Fermentation The conversion of sugar in grapes into alcohol and carbon dioxide, a function of enzymes secreted by yeasts. Wild yeasts occur in vineyards and wineries, but in modern Cape winemaking cultured yeasts are normally added to secure the process. Beyond about 15% of alcohol, yeasts are overwhelmed and fermentation ceases, although it usually is stopped (for instance by cooling, filtration or the addition of alcohol) before this stage. See also Malolactic.

Filtration Removes last impurities including **yeast** cells. Done excessively, can thin a wine. Some traditionalists bottle without cold- or protein-stabilisation or filtration.

Fining and **protein stabilisation** Fining is ridding wine of suspended particles by adding substances that attract and draw the particles from the wine.

Free run After grapes have been de-stalked and crushed, juice runs freely.

Garage wine Generic term for wine made in minuscule quantities, sometimes literally in a garage; grower of such wine sometimes called a *garagiste*.

Glycerol Minor product of alcoholic fermentation; from the Greek for sweet. Has an apparent sweetening effect on even dry wines and also gives a viscous, mouthfilling character.

Icewine Sweet, concentrated wine from grapes picked and pressed while frozen. Not a recognised category for SA wine production.

Leafroll virus Virus (or complex of viruses), widespread throughout the winegrowing world, which causes the vine to perform below its potential and thereby produce wine which is lower in colour, body and flavour than that derived from virus-free or 'cleaned-up' plants.

Lees Spent yeast cells and other matter which collect at the bottom of any container in winemaking. Yeast autolysis, or decomposition, can impart richness and flavour to a wine, sometimes referred to as leesy. Lees stirring or *batonnage* involves mixing the bed of lees in a barrel or tank through the wine, which is said to be sur lie; it is employed primarily on barrel-fermented white wines. The main effects of mixing lees and wine are to prevent off-odours developing from lack of oxygen, to limit the amount of wood tannin and flavour extracted, and to increase flavour.

Malolactic fermentation (malo) Occurs when bacteria convert malic into lactic acids. This reduces the acidity of a wine, a normal and healthy process, especially in reds – provided, of course, it occurs before bottling.

Maturation Ageing properties are closely related to tannin and/or fixed acid content of a wine. A relatively full red wine with tannin has lasting power. With age, it may develop complexity, subtlety and smooth mellowness. Lighter wines with lower tannins are drinkable sooner but probably will not reach the same level of complexity. A number of Cape whites, especially chardonnays and rieslings, now mature well over several years, but most are best drunk in their fruity youth, up to 18 months.

Méthode champenoise Classic method of making champagne by inducing secondary fermentation in the bottle and producing fine bubbles. Due to French restrictions on terminology, Cape sparkling wines made in this way are called méthode cap classique (MCC).

Micro-oxygenation Relatively new (1990) technique enabling introduction of precise, controlled doses of oxygen to must/wine. Advocates claim softer tannins, more stable colours and other advantages.

Oak chips, either in older barrels or stainless steel tanks, are used increasingly in SA, as are oak **staves**. Still frowned on by some purists, the 'additives' approximate the flavour effects of a new barrel, far more cheaply, more easily handled.

Oak-matured See Barrels.

Organic viticulture/winemaking Increasingly popular alternative to 'conventional' or 'industrialised' winegrowing, emphasising natural and sustainable farming methods and cellar techniques. A variant is biodynamic viticulture, influenced by anthroposophy, focused on improving wine quality through harmony with nature and its rhythms.

Oxidation Change (usually for the worse) due to exposure to air, in whites often producing dark yellow or yellowish colour (called maderisation), altering, 'ageing' the taste. Controlled aeration is used to introduce acceptable and desirable development in wine.

pH A chemical notation, used in winemaking and evaluation. The pH of a wine is its effective, active acidity – not in volume but by strength or degree. The reading provides a guide to a wine's keepability. The optimum pH in a wine is somewhere between 3.1 and 3.4 – which significantly improves a wine's protection from bacterial spoilage, so permitting it to mature and develop if properly stored.

Racking Drawing or pumping wine off from one cask or tank to another, to leave behind the deposit or lees.

Reductive Wine in an unevolved, unoxidised state is said to be 'reductive'; usually with a tight, sometimes unyielding character. The absence of air (in a bottled wine) or the presence of substantial sulphur dioxide (anti-oxidant) levels, will inhibit both oxidation and reduction processes, which are linked and complementary.

Skin contact After crushing and de-stemming, white grapes may be left for a period with the juice, remaining in contact with skins (before being moved into the press, from which the grape juice is squeezed). Some winemakers believe the colours and flavours in and under the grape skins should be maximised in this way; others believe extended (or any) contact can lead to coarseness, even bitterness.

Sur lie See Lees.

Tannin Vital preservative in wine, which derives primarily from the grape skins. Necessary for a red wine's longevity. A young wine's raw tannin can give it a harshness, but no red wine matures into a great one without tannin, which itself undergoes change, combines with other substances and mellows. Tannin leaves a mouth-puckering dryness about the gums, gives 'grip' to a wine. A wooded wine will also contain some wood tannin. Various types or qualities of tannin are increasingly commented on.

Tartrates Harmless crystals formed by tartaric acid precipitating in non-cold- stabilised wine. Because of lack of public acceptance, usually avoided through cold stabilisation.

Terroir Important, controversial (and in SA over-used) French term embracing soil, climate, topography and other elements which constitute the natural environment of a vineyard site and give it a unique character.

Unfiltered See Filtration.

Virus or **virused** See Leafroll.

Volatile acid (VA) The part of the acidity which can become volatile. A high reading indicates a wine is prone to spoilage. Recognised at high levels by a sharp, 'hot', vinegary smell. In SA, most wines must by law be below 1.2g/ℓ of VA; in practice, the majority are well below 1g/ℓ.

Whole-bunch pressing or **cluster pressing** Some SA cellars use this age-old process of placing whole bunches directly in the press and gently squeezing. The more usual method is to de-stem and crush the grapes before pressing. Whole-bunch pressing is said to yield fresher, cleaner must, and wine lower in polyphenols which, in excess, tend to age wines faster and render them coarser.

Wood-fermented/matured See Barrels.

Yeasts Micro-organisms that secrete enzymes which convert or ferment sugar into alcohol. See fermentation.

Touring Wine Country

Wine routes, trusts & associations

For localised information about regional official wine routes and wineries, contact these organisations:

Breedekloof Wine and Tourism T (023) 349·1791 ▪ F (023) 349·1720 info@breedekloof.com ▪ www.breedekloof.com

Calitzdorp Wine Route T (044) 213·3775 ▪ F (044) 213·3302 calitzdorpinfo@kannaland.co.za ▪ www.calitzdorp.co.za

Constantia Wine Route T (021) 794·5190 (Lars Maack) ▪ F (021) 794·1351 lars@buitenverwachting.co.za

Darling Wine Experience T (022) 492·3430 (Shaun Mc Laughlin) ▪ F (022) 492·2935 mclaughlin@worldonline.co.za ▪ www.darlingtourism.co.za

Durbanville Wine Valley Association T 083·310·1228 ▪ F (021) 976·1467 info@durbanvillewine.co.za www.durbanvillewine.co.za

Franschhoek See Vignerons de Franschhoek

Helderberg See Stellenbosch

Little Karoo Wine Route T/F (028) 572·1284 (Ellen Marais) info@kleinkaroowines.co.za ▪ www.kleinkaroowines.co.za

Northern Cape Wine Association T (054) 337·8800 (Herman Cruywagen) ▪ F (054) 332·4408
marketing@owk.co.za

Olifants River Vodacom Wine Route T/F (027) 213·3126/082·611·3999 wineroute@matzikamamun.co.za ▪ www.olifantsriverwineroute.com

Orange River Wine Route See Northern Cape Wine Association

Outeniqua Wine Route ▪ T/F (044) 873·4212/072·833·8223 harpie@xsinet.co.za

Paarl Vintners ▪ T (021) 863·4886 ▪ F (021) 863·4883 paarl@wine.co.za ▪ www.paarlwine.co.za

Rawsonville Wine Route See Breedekloof Wine & Tourism

Robertson Wine Valley T (023) 626·3167/083·701·5404 ▪ F (023) 626·1054 manager@robertsonwinevalley.com ▪ www.robertsonwinevalley.com

Stellenbosch American Express Wine Routes T (021) 886·4310 ▪ F (021) 886·4330
info@wineroute.co.za ▪ www.wineroute.co.za ▪ Helderberg office: T (021) 852·6166 ▪ F (021) 852·6168 ▪ hwr@mweb.co.za ▪ www.helderbergwineroute.co.za

Swartland Wine Route T (022) 487·1133 ▪ F (022) 487·2063 swartlandinfo@westc.co.za ▪ www.swartlandwineroute.co.za

Tulbagh Wine Route ▪ T/F (023) 230·1348 info@tulbaghwineroute.com ▪ www.tulbaghwineroute.com

Vignerons de Franschhoek T (021) 876·3062 ▪ F (021) 876·2964 franschhoek@wine.co.za ▪ www.franschhoekwines.co.za

Walker Bay Wine Wander T (028) 316·3988 ▪ F (028) 316·3989 wine@hermanus.co.za

Wellington Wine Route T (021) 873·4604 ▪ F (021) 873·4607 welltour@mweb.co.za ▪ www.visitwellington.com

Worcester Winelands T (023) 342·8710 ▪ F (023) 342·2294 manager@worcesterwinelands.co.za ▪ www.worcesterwinelands.co.za

Winelands tourism offices

For additional accommodation options, brochures and local advice, contact the information offices and/or publicity associations of the wine areas you plan to visit.

Franschhoek Wine Valley Tourist Association T (021) 876·3603 ▪ F (021) 876·2768 info@franschhoek.org.za ▪ www.franschhoek.org.za

Helderberg Tourism T (021) 851·4022 ▪ F (021) 851·1497 info@helderbergtourism.co.za www.helderbergtourism.co.za

Hermanus Tourism Bureau T (028) 312·2629 ▪ F (028) 313·0305 infoburo@hermanus.co.za ▪ www.hermanus.co.za www.tourismhermanus.co.za

McGregor Tourism Bureau T/F (023) 625·1954 mcgregortour@telkomsa.net ▪ www.mcgregor.org.za

Northern Cape Tourism T (053) 832·2657 ▪ F (053) 831·2937 tourism@northerncape.org.za ▪ www.northerncape.org.za

Paarl Tourism Bureau T (021) 872·4842 ▪ F (021) 872·9376 paarl@cis.co.za ▪ www.paarlonline.com

Robertson Tourism Bureau ▪ T (023) 626·4437 ▪ F (023) 626·4290 info@robertson.org.za ▪ www.robertsonr62.com

Stellenbosch Tourism Info Bureau ▪ T (021) 883·3584 ▪ F (021) 883·8017 info@stellenboschtourism.co.za ▪ www.stellenboschtourism.co.za

Wellington Tourism Bureau T (021) 873·4604 ▪ F (021) 873·4607 welltour@mweb.co.za ▪ www.visitwellington.com

West Coast Peninsula Tourism Bureau T (022) 714·2088 ▪ F (022) 714·4240 bureau@kingsley.co.za

Worcester Tourism Bureau T (023) 342·8710/20 ▪ F (023) 342·2294 assistant@worcestertourism.com ▪ www.worcestertourism.com

Specialist wine tours

Adamastor & Bacchus John Ford conducts tailor-made tours for small groups to wine farms not usually accessible to the public. Afrikaans, Dutch, Norwegian, Swedish & German spoken. Photography an additional speciality. ▪ johnford@iafrica.com ▪ **T 439·5169/ 083·229·1172** ▪ F 439·5169

African Wonder Tours Trivial pursuits made unforgettable. Half- or full-day wine and food tours, Stellenbosch, Franschhoek, Cape Town and other wine areas, competitively priced and enthusiastically presented. ▪ **T 082·325·1485** ▪ africanwonder@telkomsa.net ▪ www.africanwonder.co.za

Amber Wine Tours Explore boutique wineries not on the usual tourist route with wine-passionate Lesley Cox, specialist in private, personalised wine tours by luxury vehicle for small groups or individuals. ▪ ambertours@wol.co.za ▪ www.ambertours.co.za ▪ **T 083·448·7016**

Gourmet Wine Tours Exploratory tours for individuals or small groups covering principal Cape wine areas and properties, plus meals in top restaurants. By Stephen Flesch, registered guide and Cape Town Slow Food Convivium secretary. Some French, German spoken. ▪ sflesch@iafrica.com ▪ www.gourmetwinetours.co.za ▪ **T 705·4317/083·229·3581** ▪ F 706·0766

Gudrun Grünewald Conducts tailor-made, personalised wine and gourmet tours to carefully-selected wine farms and restaurants. German, English and Afrikaans spoken. happyholiday@adept.co.za ▪ www.happyholiday.co.za ▪ **T 082·699·3098**

It Just Did! The wine tourism specialists. Memories and fun are all part of their personalised private wine tours. Meet the winemakers. Township tastings, harvest tours, wine and river tastings and much more. ▪ info@itjustdid.com ▪ **T 082·390·6092**

Judy's Tours Judy Krohn, experienced (RSA, Europe & Australia) specialist registered wine guide personally conducts private tours to all Cape wine regions. Day or overnight itineraries to suit individual requests and cellar preferences, emphasis on fine food and wine (German & English). ▪ judyk@zsd.co.za ▪ **T 084·500·1941/851·4205**

Ocean & Vine Tours Wayne Donaldson, registered specialist guide offers private, tailor-made tours to all of the Cape wine regions. Wine, golf and fly-fishing combination options also offered. ▪ wayne@wine.co.za ▪ **T 082·900·6999**

Redwood Tours Daily wine tours by Keith van der Schyff, specialist guide, privileged to live on a wine farm in Stellenbosch. Private, tailor-made tours to suit all tastes and interests. ▪ rwt@adept.co.za ▪ www.redwoodtours.co.za ▪ **T 886·8138/082·443·6480**

Southern Destinations Vanessa Ratcliffe and her team add innovative and creative flair to a Cape winelands experience. Wine- and food-intensive itineraries designed for those travelling solo, with friends, or as a corporate group. French spoken. ▪ vanessa@southerndestinations.com ▪ www.southerndestinations.com ▪ **T 422·3233/083·309·3331**

The Capevine Special-interest tour operator Annette Stals organises the consummate winelands experience for groups of 7 or more, to facilitate your enjoyment of wine, architecture, history, gardens, regional cuisine and beautiful scenery. ▪ capevine@iafrica.com ▪ **T 913·6611** ▪ F 913·4580

The Wine Ambassador Wine educator and specialist registered tourist guide Karen Veysey offers wine knowledge, tasting training and wineland tours for restaurants, tasting room staff, companies, individuals and groups, all tailored to participants' needs. ▪ thewineambassador@telkomsa.net ▪ www.thewineambassador.co.za ▪ **T 975·3906/ 084·499·6014**

Vineyard Ventures First — and, for a long time, only — specialist wine tour company. Gillian Stoltzman (082·893·5387) and Glen Christie (082·920·2825) use their matchless contacts and all-inclusive costing to customise sipping-safaris to visitors' tastes — off the tourist beat. ▪ vinven@iafrica.com ▪ www.vineyardventures.co.za ▪ **T 434·8888** ▪ F 434·9999

Vintage Cape Tours Paarl Private and tailor-made tours for the discerning food and wine lover, conducted by specialist wine guides in English, German, French and Afrikaans. ▪ info@vintagecape.co.za ▪ www.vintagecape.co.za ▪ **T 872·9252/082·553·8928/082·656·3994** ▪ F 862·1484

Vintour Helmut Feil, qualified guide with 37 years' experience in the wine industry, offers small tailor-made tours for the serious wine and food connoisseur or professional, in German or English. ▪ helmut@vintour.co.za ▪ **T/F 976·5709/083·626·0029**

Walker Bay Wine Destination Full and half-day tours to the Walker Bay wine region and surrounds. Twenty-five of SA's highly rated wine producers, at the centre of the fynbos kingdom, on the edge of the best whale watching town in the world. ▪ wine@hermanus.co.za ▪ **T (028) 316·3988**

Wellington Wine Walk Three-day guided hiking trail through the Wellington winelands, including accommodation at upmarket guest houses and luggage portage between overnight stops. Enjoy wine, olive and cheese tastings en route. ▪ judy@winescapetours.co.za ▪ **T 083·313·8383** ▪ F 461·5555

Window on Cape Wine With dozens of new wine producers this year, Meryl Weaver offers up to date, quality and tailor-made 'edutainment'. Full/half-day tours; tutored wine tastings for corporate or tour groups. Registered specialist guide, CWM student and wine lecturer. ▪ mvweaver@iafrica.com ▪ **T/F 866·1002/082·782·5198**

Wine Desk at the Waterfront Exclusive wine tour specialists, offering advice on what to do, where to go and where to stay in the winelands. Complimentary tastings daily. Cape Town Gateway Visitor Centre, Clock Tower, V&A Waterfront. ▪ winedesk@tourcapetown.com; ligia@winedesk.co.za ▪ www.winedeskwaterfront.co.za ▪ **T 405·4550/082·822·6127**

Wine Walks For something completely different, experience the SA wine scene 'in the vineyard, on the farm' with Annelee Steyn. Day tours packed with fresh air and fun, views, interesting people, top wines, snacks and lunch. ▪ **T 083·631·5944**

Eat-outs in the winelands and Cape Town

Below are some dining out options in Cape Town and the winelands. For more eat-outs among the vines, consult the A-Z section of the guide for wineries which offer light lunches, picnics etc. Look for the symbol beside the individual entries. Unless stated to the contrary, all allow you to bring your own (BYO) wine – the corkage fee is indicated at the start of each entry. Any claims to disabled-friendliness are unverified by the publishers of the guide.

***Note:* The eat-outs featured here describe their own culinary styles, menus and attractions.**

Index of eat-outs

Listed alphabetically, with region.

@ M12 Djakarta Indonesian Restaurant	Stellenbosch
@ The Hills Restaurant	Durbanville
33 Stellenbosch	Stellenbosch
96 Winery Road Restaurant	Somerset West
Aubergine Restaurant	Cape Town
Avontuur Restaurant, Cellar & Lounge	Cape Town
Balducci's	Cape Town
Belthazar Restaurant & Wine Bar	Cape Town
Boschendal Restaurant	Franschhoek
Bosman's Restaurant & Bistro Allegro	Paarl
Bread & Wine	Franschhoek
Buitenverwachting Restaurant & Café Petit	Constantia
Café Allée Bleue	Franschhoek
Caroline's Cape Kitchen	Cape Town
Catharina's Restaurant	Constantia
Constantia Uitsig Restaurant	Constantia
De Oewer	Stellenbosch
De Volkskombuis	Stellenbosch
Emily's	Cape Town
Fishmonger	Stellenbosch
Flavours Restaurant	Stellenbosch
Fraai Uitzicht 1798	Robertson
French Connection Bistro	Franschhoek
Grande Provence – The Restaurant	Franschhoek
Groote Post Restaurant	Darling
Haute Cabriere Cellar Restaurant	Franschhoek
Hazendal – Hermitage Restaurant	Stellenbosch
Jonkershuis Restaurant	Stellenbosch
La Colombe Restaurant	Constantia
La Couronne Restaurant	Franschhoek
La Petite Ferme	Franschhoek
L'Auberge du Paysan	Somerset West
Le Café at Boschendal	Franschhoek
Le Manoir de Brendel	Franschhoek
Le Pique-Nique at Boschendal	Franschhoek
Le Quartier Français – Ici	Franschhoek
Le Quartier Français 'The Tasting Room'	Franschhoek
Marc's Mediterranean Cuisine & Garden	Paarl
Meerendal Restaurants	Durbanville
Mimosa Lodge Restaurant	Montagu
Monneaux Restaurant	Franschhoek
Morgenhof Restaurant	Stellenbosch
Moyo at Spier	Stellenbosch
Nuy Valley Restaurant	Worcester
Olivello Restaurant	Stellenbosch
Ons Genot Restaurant	Stellenbosch
Peddlars on the Bend	Constantia
Piccata Restaurant & Bar	Franschhoek
Restaurant Barrique	Stellenbosch
Reuben's Restaurant & Bar	Franschhoek
Rhebokskloof Restaurant	Paarl
Savoy Cabbage Restaurant & Champagne Bar	Cape Town
Schulphoek Seafront Guesthouse & Restaurant	Hermanus
Seasons @ Diemersfontein	Wellington
Sir Herbert's Wine Cottage & Red Pepper Deli	Stellenbosch
Terroir Restaurant	Stellenbosch
The Avontuur Restaurant	Somerset West
The Cape Malay Restaurant	Constantia
The Duck Pond	Stellenbosch
The Greenhouse	Constantia
The Guinea Fowl Restaurant	Kuils River
The Nose Restaurant & Wine Bar	Cape Town
The Restaurant at Pontac	Paarl
The River Café	Constantia
Under the Vines Bistro	Bonnievale
Veranda Restaurant	Cape Town
Vineyard Kitchen at Dombeya Farm	Stellenbosch
Wakame Restaurant	Cape Town
Wasabi Restaurant	Constantia
Wild Apricot Restaurant	Montagu
Zevenwacht Restaurant	Kuils River

Bonnievale

Under the Vines Bistro Weltevrede Wine Estate, Bonnievale ▪ Cape country cuisine ▪ Open Tue-Sat 9:00–15:00 ▪ Closed Good Friday, Christmas, Boxing & New Year's days ▪ Booking advised for groups ▪ Children welcome ▪ Wheelchair-friendly ▪ Major credit cards accepted ▪ No BYO ▪ Owner Lindelize Jonker ▪ info@weltevrede.com ▪ www.weltevrede.com ▪ **T (023) 616·2141** ▪ F (023) 616·2460

Come and experience farm hospitality and real food. Relax under the vine trellis in summer overlooking the vineyards and enjoy the comfort of a roaring log fire in winter. The menu changes daily using fresh regional produce such as grape and goats cheese salad or waterblommetjie bredie. Enjoy the wines of the Weltevrede Estate with your meal. (See also A–Z section.)

Cape Town

Avontuur Restaurant, Cellar & Lounge 67 Dock Road, Entrance to V&A Waterfront, next to City Lodge, Cape Town ▪ Global cuisine with African flair ▪ Open Mon-Sat 9:00–23:00 ▪ Closed Sun; 24, 25 & 26 Dec ▪ Booking advised ▪ Children welcome ▪ Wheelchair-friendly ▪ Major credit cards accepted ▪ Corkage R20 ▪ Owners Tony Taberer & Albert Robertson ▪ cinc@avontuurestate.co.za ▪ www.avontuurestate.co.za ▪ **T (021) 421·0044** ▪ F (021) 421·0046

The fine dining restaurant offers international grillroom fare with a South African flavour and the bistro is perfect for coffees or light meals. The historic cellar is now a tasting room, where all Avontuur Estate's wines are offered for tasting and sale. Private function rooms upstairs. Comfy leather sofas create a cosy lounge area. (See also A–Z section.)

Aubergine Restaurant 39 Barnet Street, Gardens ▪ Innovative, Continental cuisine with Asian influences ▪ Lunch on Thu 12:00–15:00; 'Cinq à Sept' daily 17:00–19:00 & dinner Mon-Sat 19:00–late ▪ Closed Sun ▪ Booking advised ▪ Children welcome ▪ Wheelchair-friendly ▪ Major credit cards accepted ▪ Corkage R40 ▪ Owner Harald Bresselschmidt ▪ aubergin@mweb.co.za ▪ www.aubergine.co.za ▪ **T (021) 465·4909** ▪ F (021) 461·3781

Aubergine Restaurant offers innovative continental cuisine with Asian influences. Our original concept 'Cinq-A-Sept', served between 5–7pm, is a sophisticated solution to rush hour traffic or for early evening relaxation, offering delectable hors d'ouevres, drinks and ambrosial desserts on the elegant garden terrace or in the lounge. Our culturally diverse dinner menu bursts with colours, aromas and flavours to tantalise even the most seasoned palate. Our cellar boasts a vast selection of South African and international wines served by our sommelier.

Balducci's Shop 6162, Victoria Wharf, V&A Waterfront ▪ Cal-Med cuisine ▪ Open daily 9 am till late ▪ Booking advised ▪ Children welcome (but no under 12 at night) ▪ Wheelchair-friendly ▪ Major credit cards accepted ▪ Corkage R30 ▪ Owners Ian Halfon & Doron Duveen ▪ info@slickrestaurants.co.za ▪ www.balduccis.co.za ▪ **T (021) 421·6002/3** ▪ F (021) 421·6010

Balducci's, overlooking the harbour, is an award-winning international café-restaurant situated in the V&A Waterfront. This elegant sit-down eatery has an understated European grace which complements an outstanding menu and attentive service. Balducci's Royal Sushi Bar, situated adjacent to the restaurant, is internationally acclaimed and regarded as one of the best around.

Belthazar Restaurant & Wine Bar Shop 153, Victoria Wharf, V&A Waterfront ▪ Grill & seafood ▪ Open daily 12:00–late ▪ Booking advised ▪ Children 12+ welcome ▪ Wheelchair-friendly ▪ Major credit cards accepted ▪ No BYO ▪ Owners Ian Halfon, Doron Duveen & Jonathan Steyn ▪ info@slickrestaurants.co.za ▪ www.belthazar.co.za ▪ **T (021) 421·3753/6** ▪ F (021) 421·3748

Belthazar, the biggest wine-by-the-glass bar in the world, is a totally new concept in wining and dining. Experienced sommeliers expertly serve up to 100 of the Cape's finest wines by the glass and advise customers on a winelist of up to 600 fine wines and sought-after rare vintages. Indulge your palate, enjoy the best in life – from the slick service to superb Karan beef aged in our butcher's shop, a variety of South African game, export quality Mozambican seafood and the freshest South African seafood.

Caroline's Cape Kitchen Caroline's Fine Wine Cellar, 15 Long Street, Cape Town ▪ Modern Cape cuisine ▪ Lunch Mon-Fri 12:00–14:30, evening functions by prior arrangement ▪ Closed Sat & Sun, public holidays ▪ Booking advised ▪ Wheelchair-friendly ▪ Major credit cards accepted ▪ No BYO ▪ Owner Caroline Rillema ▪ carowine@mweb.co.za ▪ www.carolineswine.com ▪ **T (021) 419·8984** ▪ F (021) 419·8985

Caroline's Fine Wine Cellar is a well-established specialist wine shop in the Cape Town CBD. Proprietor Caroline Rillema has 25 years' experience in the wine trade and manages this store personally. She has converted their large wine cellar adjoining the shop into a restaurant where diners can enjoy lunch at tables surrounded by large stocks of the finest of Cape wines. Delicious homemade lunches are prepared in an open kitchen and six different wines can be tasted by the glass. A special tasting at R50 per person can be arranged before lunch, booking essential.

Emily's Top Floor, Clock Tower Centre, V&A Waterfront ▪ SA cuisine with an African reference ▪ Open Mon-Sat ▪ Closed Sun ▪ Booking advised ▪ Children welcome ▪ Wheelchair-friendly ▪ Major credit cards accepted ▪ Corkage R50 ▪ Owner Peter Veldsman ▪ caia@mweb.co.za ▪ www.emily-s.com ▪ **T (021) 421·1133** ▪ F (021) 421·1131

During the past 14 years, Emily's has earned a multitude of prestigious awards for both food and wine. The innovative cuisine is contemporary South African with reference to the rest of Africa. Emily's goes to great lengths to source the best ingredients and finest, well-matured red meat. Oysters, fresh or baked; gravad of crocodile and harissa-flavoured African red soup with corn-off-the-cob ice cream; grilled crayfish with linefish ragout; newly recreated old traditional dishes like bobotie and denningvleis; game such as ostrich, impala, gemsbok, kudu, wildebeest and kid; creative desserts; an extensive collection of cheese and a choice of more than 2 000 wines and spirits – all of this awaits the visitor to Emily's.

Savoy Cabbage Restaurant & Champagne Bar 101 Hout Street, Cape Town ▪ Contemporary cuisine ▪ Lunch Mon-Fri 12:00–14:30, dinner Mon-Sat 19:00–22:30 ▪ Closed Sun ▪ Booking essential ▪ Major credit cards accepted ▪ Air-conditioned ▪ Smoking section ▪ Secure parking ▪ Corkage R20 ▪ Owner Caroline Bagley ▪ savoycab@iafrica.com ▪ **T (021) 424·2626** ▪ F (021) 424·3366

Winner of a string of accolades, including CNN's only 'Hot Spot' for Cape Town and a place in every annual *Wine* Top 100 Restaurants ranking to date, this city centre establishment offers gracious dining in impressive surroundings featuring historic brick, concrete and glass. Impeccable service and attention to detail are hallmarks. The daily changing menu is inspired by the freshest produce and known to feature game, offal and good vegetarian dishes. Boutique winelist.

The Nose Restaurant & Wine Bar Cape Quarter, Dixon Street, Green Point, Cape Town ▪ Contemporary home-styled cuisine ▪ Open daily 11:00–late ▪ Closed Christmas & New Year's days ▪ Booking advised ▪ Children welcome daytime only ▪ Wheelchair-friendly ▪ Major credit cards accepted ▪ No BYO ▪ Owners Cathy & Kevin Marston ▪ info@thenose.co.za ▪ www.thenose.co.za ▪ **T (021) 425·2200** ▪ F (021) 425·2210

Thirty-five wines by the glass, many more by the bottle, first releases, South African exclusives, unusual grape varieties, wineries you've never even heard of – you don't know Cape wine until you've picked The Nose! And if all that isn't enough, they also offer a full menu of delicious homemade food – including Thai fish cakes, Cape Malay curry, chilli lemon prawns, gourmet bangers 'n' mash, char-grilled steaks – plus their signature platters of tasty finger food to accompany your glass of wine. Full bar including draught beer also available. The Nose is situated on a beautiful open-air piazza in Cape Town's trendiest area – De Waterkant. It's laidback, friendly and relaxed – the perfect place to enjoy the finer things of life. Cheers!

Veranda Restaurant Metropole Hotel, 1st Floor, 38 Long Street, Cape Town ▪ Continental cuisine ▪ Open Mon-Sun for breakfast, lunch & dinner ▪ Booking advised ▪ Children welcome ▪ Wheelchair-friendly ▪ Major credit cards accepted ▪ Corkage R35 ▪ Owners

Steve van der Merwe & Jens Merbt ▪ info@metropolehotel.co.za ▪ www.metropolehotel.co.za ▪ **T (021) 424·7247** ▪ F (021) 424·7248

Situated on the first floor of the new refurbished hip Metropole Hotel, the Veranda offers uninterrupted views of Long Street. Whatever your taste buds crave you are bound to find something you like, well priced, in generous portions, with charming presentation. Great views, an urban edginess and a big dose of romance. (See also Stay-over section.)

Wakame Restaurant 2nd Floor, Surrey Place, cnr Beach Road & Surrey Place, Mouille Point, Cape Town ▪ Pacific Rim & sushi bar ▪ Mon-Sun 12:00-15:00 & 18:30-22:30 ▪ Closed Christmas & New Year's days ▪ Booking advised ▪ Children welcome ▪ Major credit cards accepted ▪ Corkage R25 ▪ Owners Gregory Slotar, Deon Berg & Roy de Gouveia ▪ info@wakame.co.za ▪ www.wakame.co.za ▪ **T (021) 433·2377** ▪ F (021) 434·5148

Wakame's breathtaking views add a unique dimension to the epicurean delights that await you. From whale-watching to yacht-racing or watching the seals and dolphins frolicking just metres away, Wakame's view comes out tops. Pacific Rim blended with Asian fusion and a hint of French and Western influences are what hold true to form in the kitchen. You are sure to be dazzled.

Constantia

Buitenverwachting Restaurant & Café Petit Klein Constantia Road, Constantia ▪ European contemporary cuisine ▪ Open for lunch & dinner Tue-Sat (Apr-Sep) & Mon-Sat (Oct-Mar) ▪ Café Petit – open for lunch only ▪ Closed Sun, some public holidays & Jul-Aug ▪ Booking advised ▪ Children 12+ welcome ▪ Wheelchair-friendly ▪ Major credit cards accepted ▪ Corkage R35 ▪ Owners Lars Maack/Edgar Osojnik (partner) ▪ restaurant@buitenverwachting.com ▪ www.buitenverwachting.co.za ▪ **T (021) 794·3522** ▪ F (021) 794·1351

Overlooking Buitenverwachting's vines and the Constantiaberg, this well-known award-winning restaurant has a menu which is as exotic as it is continental. The relaxed ambience and dedication to quality by executive chef Edgar Osojnik make this restaurant in Constantia an absolute must. (See also A-Z section.)

Catharina's Restaurant Steenberg Estate, Tokai Road, Constantia Valley ▪ Contemporary Cape & cosmopolitan cuisine ▪ Open daily 7:00-23:00 ▪ Booking advised ▪ Children welcome ▪ Wheelchair-friendly ▪ Major credit cards accepted ▪ Corkage R40 ▪ Owner Graham Beck's Kangra Group ▪ info@steenberghotel.com ▪ www.steenberghotel.com ▪ **T (021) 713·2222** ▪ F (021) 713·2251

Catharina's is located in the original winery, built in 1682, now tastefully decorated in Cape colonial mode, with a cosy cigar bar and a terrace overlooking the estate. The restaurant serves innovative Cape colonial cuisine of the very highest standard and is featured among Cape Town's top restaurants. Popular Sunday jazz luncheons. (See also Stay-over & A-Z sections.)

Constantia Uitsig Restaurant Spaanschemat River Road, Constantia ▪ Mediterranean cuisine ▪ Open daily for lunch 12:30-14:30, dinner 19:30-21:30 ▪ Closed for lunch 31 Dec, New Year's day ▪ Booking advised ▪ Children welcome ▪ Wheelchair-friendly ▪ Major credit cards accepted ▪ Corkage R25 (wine), R50 (Champagne) ▪ Owners Marlene & David McCay ▪ frank@uitsig.co.za ▪ www.uitsig.co.za ▪ **T (021) 794·4480** ▪ F (021) 794·3105

Constantia Uitsig Restaurant, housed in the original 19th-century manor house, offers varied and innovative Mediterranean cuisine with a combination of local and international flavours. It has, since its inception 12 years ago, consistently featured among the Top 10 Restaurants in South Africa. (See also Stay-over section for Constantia Uitsig Country Hotel & A-Z section.)

La Colombe Restaurant Spaanschemat River Road, Constantia ▪ Southern-inspired French cuisine ▪ Mon-Sun lunch 12:30-14:30, dinner 19:30-21:30 ▪ Closed Sun eve (winter) & New Year's day lunch ▪ Booking advised ▪ Children welcome ▪ Wheelchair-friendly ▪ Major credit cards accepted ▪ Corkage R30 ▪ Owners Marlene & David McCay ▪ lc@uitsig.co.za ▪ www.lacolombe.co.za ▪ **T (021) 794·2390** ▪ F (021) 794·7914

La Colombe Restaurant has been voted *Top Restaurant in South Africa* three times, and serves traditional French-Provençal cuisine of the very highest standard. French-born chef Franck Dangereux changes the menu daily to incorporate fresh seasonal ingredients with natural sun-ripened flavors. (See also Stay-over section for Constantia Uitsig Country Hotel & A-Z section.)

Peddlars on the Bend 3 Spaanschemat River Road, Constantia ▪ Cosmopolitan cuisine ▪ Open daily 11:00-23:00 (bar), 12:00-23:00 (kitchen) ▪ Closed Christmas & New Year's days ▪ Booking advised ▪ Children welcome ▪ Wheelchair-friendly ▪ Major credit cards accepted ▪ Corkage R15 from 2nd bottle ▪ peddlars@mweb.co.za ▪ **T (021) 794·7747/50** ▪ F (021) 794·2730

Peddlars is popular with locals and visitors alike. Warm country charm, a lovely garden setting, and a reputation for quality food and service, are all part of the attraction. The menu is prepared from fresh ingredients daily, and the kitchen is open all day for those who would like a late lunch or early dinner. Specialities include great steaks, seafood and hearty country-style dishes. The award-winning winelist showcases the local wineries and offers a good selection of cognac, malt whisky, cigars and liqueurs. Peddlars is a non-smoking restaurant with a small smoking area. Pub menu available for bar and garden area. The bar draws an eclectic crowd who mix well and know how to party. Plenty of free parking available.

The Cape Malay Restaurant The Cellars-Hohenort Hotel, 93 Brommersvlei Road, Constantia ▪ Traditional Malay cuisine ▪ Open 7 days a week for breakfast 7:00-10:00, lunch 12:00-14:30, dinner 19:00-21:30 ▪ Booking advised ▪ Wheelchair-friendly ▪ Major credit cards accepted ▪ Corkage R30 ▪ Owner Liz McGrath ▪ cellars@relaischateaux.com ▪ www.collectionmcgrath.com ▪ **T (021) 794·2137** ▪ F (021) 794·2149

Cape Malay cuisine is unique to the Western Cape. It dates back to the 17th century and has evolved to reflect the influences of the times. Martha Williams, Cape Malay head chef, lovingly prepares authentic boboties, smoorsnoek, samoosas and a variety of other dishes. Relax in the 'spice' colours of the decor; the friendly and well-informed staff will put you at ease in this five-star luxury hotel, The Cellars-Hohenort. (See also Stay-over section.)

The Greenhouse The Cellars-Hohenort Hotel, 93 Brommersvlei Road, Constantia ▪ Global/international fine dining ▪ Open 7 days a week for breakfast 7:00-10:00, lunch 12:00-14:30, dinner 19:00-21:30 ▪ Booking advised ▪ Wheelchair-friendly ▪ Major credit cards accepted ▪ Corkage R30 ▪ Owner Liz McGrath ▪ cellars@relaischateaux.com ▪ www.collectionmcgrath.com ▪ **T (021) 794·2137** ▪ F (021) 794·2149

The new and exciting 'Greenhouse' restaurant, with an emphasis on the indigenous, the organic and the fresh, offers a different dining experience in Cape Town. Regarded as one of the top 10 restaurants, it is spacious, with sweeping views through clear plate glass windows of beautiful gardens right up to the 200-year-old camphor trees. The award-winning winelist features some 300 wines selected by a professional sommelier. (See also Stay-over section.)

The River Café Spaanschemat River Road, Constantia ▪ Wholesome country food ▪ Mon-Sun 8:30-17:00 ▪ Closed Good Friday, Christmas, Boxing & New Year's days ▪ Booking advised ▪ Children welcome ▪ Wheelchair-friendly ▪ Major credit cards accepted ▪ Corkage R15 ▪ Owners Marlene & David McCay ▪ www.uitsig.co.za ▪ **T (021) 794·3010** ▪ F (021) 794·2920

The River Café, famous for its hearty breakfasts and delicious lunches, is a premier outdoor venue in an idyllic garden setting. The emphasis is on fresh ingredients which are organic where possible. You are also in easy reach of the Constantia Uitsig Wine Shop, which sells a selection of boutique wines from the Constantia valley as well as the rest of the Cape. (See also Stay-over section for Constantia Uitsig Country Hotel & A-Z section.)

Wasabi Restaurant Shop 17, Old Village Centre, Main Road, Constantia ▪ Asian seafood and sushi bar ▪ Mon-Sun 12:00-15:00 & 18:30-22:30 ▪ Closed Christmas & New Year's days ▪ Booking advised ▪ Children welcome ▪ Wheelchair-friendly ▪ Major credit cards accepted ▪ Corkage R19 ▪ Owners Gregory Slotar, Deon Berg & Roy de Gouveia ▪ info@wasabi.co.za ▪ www.wasabi.co.za ▪ **T (021) 794·6546** ▪ F (021) 434·5148

Breaking through the boundaries of life, the owners of Wasabi decided to take their patrons on a different trip to Asia. Simplicity is the order of the day, and the attention to detail and relentless effort put into preparing and cooking the food to perfection are Wasabi's greatest assets.

Darling

Groote Post Restaurant Groote Post Wine Cellar, Darling Hills Road, Darling ▪ Modern country cuisine ▪ Open Wed-Sat 12:00–14:30 ▪ Closed Sun-Tue & July ▪ Booking advised ▪ Children welcome ▪ Wheelchair-friendly ▪ Major credit cards accepted (excl Amex) ▪ No BYO ▪ Owner Shaun McLaughlin ▪ mclaughlin@worldonline.co.za ▪ www.grootepost.co.za ▪ **T (022) 492·2825** ▪ F (022) 492·3430

The restaurant is located in the historic manor house on this wine farm just outside Darling. Voted best new restaurant on the West Coast, this winelands eatery serves modern country cuisine using the freshest of ingredients prepared daily by chef Debbie McLaughlin. Come and experience Darling at its best! (See also A–Z section.)

Durbanville

@ The Hills Restaurant Durbanville Hills, M13, Durbanville ▪ Contemporary cuisine ▪ Lunch Tue-Sun 12:00–15:00; dinner Wed-Sat 19:00–22:00 (Sep-Apr) ▪ Closed Mon, religious & public holidays ▪ Booking essential ▪ Children welcome ▪ Wheelchair-friendly ▪ Visa & MasterCard accepted ▪ No BYO ▪ Owners Natasha Jewaskiewitz, Marike Roggen & Marlene Brynand ▪ info@durbanvillehills.co.za ▪ www.durbanvillehills.co.za ▪ **T (021) 558·1300** ▪ F (021) 559·8169

From its outlook on the Luipardsberg, this contemporary restaurant offers panoramic views of Table Bay, Table Mountain, the Atlantic Ocean and the Durbanville Hills vineyards. Modern-style regional food with Mediterranean nuances is presented in an innovative way. The menu changes regularly to reflect the seasons and is designed to complement the cellar's award-winning wines. Specialities include smoked kudu salad, biltong and blue cheese soup, lamb neck in red wine sauce, the catch of the day and the popular sago pudding. (See also A–Z section.)

Meerendal Restaurants Meerendal Wine Estate, Vissershok Road, Durbanville ▪ Bistro, deli & fine dining cuisine ▪ **The Barn & Lawn** lunch Tue-Sun 11:00–17:00; dinner Wed-Fri 18:00–close; **Deli** breakfast & lunch daily 08:00–17:00; **Wheatfields** lunch & dinner Tue-Sun ▪ Booking advised ▪ Children welcome ▪ Wheelchair-friendly ▪ Major credit cards accepted ▪ Corkage R15 ▪ Owners David Higgs, Wade van der Merwe & Wynand du Plessis ▪ info@meerendal.co.za ▪ www.meerendal.co.za ▪ **T (021) 975·1655** ▪ F (021) 975·1657

The new and exciting restaurants at Meerendal offer a variety of dining experiences on this historic wine estate. Renowned chefs David Higgs and Wade van der Merwe are cooking up a storm in Durbanville with food for every palate. Menus change daily to reflect the availability of fresh ingredients. **The Deli** offers delicious breakfasts all day, light lunches, scones, cakes, coffees and teas. **The Barn and Lawn** is a must for bistro-style dining, offering great views of the Cape winelands and an appetising 'Cape Table' Sunday lunch buffet. It is also the ideal venue for weddings and corporate functions, with a lawn area where a marquee can accommodate up to 600 people. **Wheatfields**, in the Meerendal Manor House, features the innovative fine dining cuisine which you can expect from award-winning chefs. (See also A–Z section.)

Franschhoek & Environs

Boschendal You'll be spoilt for choice with three culinary options on this historic wine farm: Boschendal Restaurant, Le Café and Le Pique-Nique. (See separate listings.)

Boschendal Restaurant Pniel Road (R310), Groot Drakenstein ▪ Cape-French buffet ▪ Open 7 days a week, 12:15 for 13:30 ▪ Closed Good Friday, 1 May & 16 Jun ▪ Booking advised ▪ Children welcome ▪ Wheelchair-friendly ▪ Major credit cards accepted ▪ No BYO ▪ Owners Boschendal Ltd ▪ reservations@boschendal.com ▪ www.boschendal.com ▪ **T (021) 870·4272/3/4/5** ▪ F (021) 874·2137

Situated in the original cellar of the Boschendal Manor House, the restaurant serves delectable Cape-French buffet luncheons, seven days a week. Your experience of Cape hospitality begins in the reception area with a pre-lunch drink. Yellowwood tables groan under the weight of mouth-watering dishes in the elegant ambience of the dining room. The cheese table is packed with local specialities, complemented by fresh and dried fruit and preserves. Malva pudding on the dessert table crowns this unforgettable experience.

Bread & Wine Môreson Wine Farm, Happy Valley Road, La Motte, Franschhoek ▪ Cuisine du terroir ▪ Open Wed-Sun 12:00-17:00 ▪ Closed Mon & Tue (except during season) ▪ Booking advised ▪ Children welcome ▪ Wheelchair-friendly ▪ Major credit cards accepted ▪ No BYO ▪ Owner Richard Friedman ▪ breadandwine@moreson.co.za ▪ www.lequartier.co.za ▪ **T (021) 876·3692** ▪ F (021) 876-3105

Bread & Wine vineyard restaurant reflects the global return to cuisine du terroir. Imaginative mixes of local ingredients are skillfully presented and complemented. The innovative menu tempts you to explore a range of tastes and textures, while lingering over Môreson's fine wine, served by the glass or bottle. New farm stall opened – take home farm-cured meats, breads and mouthwatering home-cured bacon. (See also Le Quartier Français – Ici, Le Quartier Français 'The Tasting Room', Stay-over section for Le Quartier Français & A-Z section for Môreson.)

Café Allée Bleue T-Junction R45 & R310, Groot Drakenstein ▪ Fresh cuisine ▪ Open daily 08:00-17:00 ▪ Closed 25 Dec ▪ Booking advised ▪ Children welcome ▪ Wheelchair-friendly ▪ Major credit cards accepted ▪ Corkage R25 ▪ Owners Elke & Wilfred Dauphin ▪ madelain@alleebleue.com ▪ www.alleebleue.com ▪ **T (021) 874·1886** ▪ F (021) 874·1850

Set in the beautiful Franschhoek valley on the Allée Bleue Estate, Café Allée Bleue is a metaphor for the majesty of life. It is the spirit of the blue eucalyptus trees, which welcome guests to the estate. Most of the ingredients on the menu are produced on the estate. Concentrating mainly on light alfresco cuisine, the menu offers a variation of some of the world's favourite foods in one place.

French Connection Bistro 48 Huguenot Street, Franschhoek ▪ French influenced ▪ Open daily for lunch 12:00-15:30 & dinner 18:30-21:30 ▪ Closed Christmas eve ▪ Booking advised ▪ Children welcome ▪ Wheelchair-friendly ▪ Major credit cards accepted ▪ BYO discouraged – corkage R25 ▪ Owners Matthew Gordon & Trevor Kirsten ▪ french@worldonline.co.za ▪ **T (021) 876·4056** ▪ F (021) 876·4036

Enjoy the glass-fronted French countryside kitchen and terraced verandah as chef-patron Matthew Gordon tantalises your palate with a variety of carefully selected ingredients and simple but gorgeous fare. Experience the true *'La Provence'* feeling at this delightful eatery. (See also Haute Cabrière Cellar Restaurant, Piccata Restaurant & Bar, & Stay-over section for Auberge Clermont.)

Grande Provence – The Restaurant Grande Provence Estate, Main Road, Franschhoek ▪ Global contemporary cuisine ▪ Open daily 11:00-21:30 ▪ Children welcome ▪ Wheelchair-friendly ▪ Major credit cards accepted ▪ Corkage R15 ▪ Owner Grande Provence Properties Ltd ▪ enquiries@grandeprovence.co.za ▪ www.grandeprovence.co.za ▪ **T (021) 876·8600** ▪ F (021) 876·8601

While the 17th-century Manor House and The Owner's Cottage reflect their Huguenot heritage, The Restaurant at Grande Provence Estate projects a chic industrial presence. Steel joinery, galvanised metals and skylights distinguish this design approach. Vanie Padayachee is our 5-star chef, heading the kitchen. The style that Vanie leans towards is a simple, fresh approach to cooking using traditional methods. The menu exudes culinary excellence, with the signature dishes of the restaurant hitting all the right notes – fresh, palatable and beautiful. Prepared from local fare and flavoured with global influences both modern and classical, the cuisine is characterised by a philosophy of innovation through passion and simplicity. (See also Stay-over & A-Z sections.)

Haute Cabrière Cellar Restaurant Pass Road, Franschhoek ▪ Modern French/international cuisine ▪ Summer: lunch & dinner daily; Winter: lunch daily, dinner Fri & Sat ▪ Booking advised ▪ Children welcome ▪ Wheelchair-friendly ▪ Major credit cards accepted ▪ No

BYO ▪ Owners Matthew, Nicky & Penny Gordon ▪ hautecab@iafrica.com ▪ www.hautecabriere.com ▪ **T (021) 876·3688** ▪ F (021) 876·3691

High up on the Franschhoek pass two unique talents, cellarmaster Achim von Arnim and chef-patron Matthew Gordon, reinvent the eating out experience. It's a gastronomic adventure with a menu created to complement the Haute Cabrière wines and Pierre Jourdan Cap Classiques. No starters or main courses, just a variety of dishes in full and half portions to pair with the wines. (See also French Connection, Piccata Restaurant & Bar, Stay-over section for Auberge Clermont & Cabrière Estate.)

La Couronne Restaurant Dassenberg Road, Franschhoek ▪ Classic European cuisine ▪ Open daily for breakfast, lunch & dinner ▪ Booking advised ▪ Children welcome ▪ Wheelchair-friendly ▪ Major credit cards accepted ▪ Corkage R25 (wine), R50 (Champagne) ▪ Owners Erwin Schnitzler & Miko Rwayitare ▪ reservations@lacouronnehotel.co.za ▪ www.lacouronnehotel.co.za ▪ **T (021) 876·2770** ▪ F (021) 876·3788

High in the Franschhoek foothills, blessed with magnificent views, this small luxury hotel boasts one of the 50 most exciting restaurants in the world, according to *Condé Nast Traveller*. 'Classic international' is the tone. The extensive winelist and imaginative cuisine may be enjoyed on the terrace in summer or beside the fire in winter. This must be one of the most romantic settings on the planet. (See also Stay-over section.)

La Petite Ferme Pass Road, Franschhoek ▪ Rustic contemporary cuisine ▪ Lunch daily from 12:00–16:00 ▪ Closed 25 Dec & 1 Jan ▪ Booking advised ▪ Major credit cards accepted ▪ Corkage R15 ▪ Owners Mark & Josephine Dendy Young ▪ lapetite@iafrica.com ▪ www.lapetiteferme.co.za ▪ **T (021) 876·3016** ▪ F (021) 876·3624

Unsurpassed service, bred from three generations of passion and commitment, is superbly combined with culinary craftsmanship to ensure that every experience relished here is fondly remembered. Perfectly complementing the menu is the renowned La Petite Ferme wine cellar, which boasts award-winning wines cultivated in the heart of one of the world's most beautiful wine regions. A dedicated and dynamic 'femme-force' – head chef Olivia Mitchell and sous chef Carina Bouwer – have brought a tangible *joie-de-vivre* and vigour to this restaurant, adding an exciting flair to a menu flavoured with African, Malay and international influences. Inside, a relaxed ambience extends a warm welcome. A panoramic glass verandah offers magnificent vistas, while underfloor heating, a cosy fireplace and air-conditioning ensures year-round comfort. Sultry summer days are best enjoyed relaxing on the lush, rolling lawns below. (See also Stay-over & A–Z sections.)

Le Café at Boschendal Pniel Road (R310), Groot Drakenstein ▪ Continental, Cape cuisine ▪ Open Mon-Sun 10:00–17:00 ▪ Closed Good Friday, 1 May & 16 June ▪ No bookings taken ▪ Children welcome ▪ Wheelchair-friendly ▪ Major credit cards accepted ▪ No BYO ▪ Owners Boschendal Ltd ▪ reservations@boschendal.com ▪ www. boschendal.com ▪ **T (021) 870·4282/3** ▪ F (021) 874·2137

Tucked away in the original slave quarters of Filander, Karlien and Kandas, Le Café serves tasty light lunches and country-style teas with the best scones in the valley and our famous home-made lemonade. Le Café is the ideal setting for wintry days as you can relax indoors in the cosy atmosphere of a log fire with our traditional bobotie. In fine weather, it is delightful to sit outside under the dappled shade of ancient oaks and enjoy a slice of quiche or mouth-watering baguettes and crisp salads. Watch the ducks and children play on the grass as you savour Boschendal's finest wines.

Le Manoir de Brendel Spa, Wine and Guest Estate, R45, Main Road, Franschhoek ▪ Cosmopolitan cuisine ▪ Open daily for lunch ▪ Booking advised ▪ Children welcome ▪ Wheelchair-friendly ▪ Major credit cards accepted ▪ No BYO ▪ Owner Christian Brendel ▪ lemanoir@brendel.co.za ▪ www.le-manoir-de-brendel.com ▪ **T (021) 876·4525** ▪ F (021) 876·4524

The restaurant at Le Manoir de Brendel, in the most idyllic of settings, offers you exquisite cuisine prepared with French flair. Spoil yourself and your family and enjoy all that we have to offer, from walks through the vineyards to relaxing in our spa and gym. Be extravagant and purchase a gift at our curio shop or an exquisite piece of jewellery from our Uwe Koetter range. Our chapel and conference facilities offer the best venues for weddings and other functions. (See also Stay-over & A–Z sections.)

Le Pique-Nique at Boschendal Pniel Road (R310), Groot Drakenstein ▪ Picnic hampers ▪ Open Mon-Sun, mid-Oct to mid-May. Collect picnic baskets from 12:15–13:30 ▪ Closed mid-May to mid-Oct; Good Friday & 1 May ▪ Booking advised ▪ Special children's hampers ▪ Wheelchair-friendly ▪ Major credit cards accepted ▪ No BYO ▪ Owners Boschendal Ltd ▪ reservations@boschendal.com ▪ www.boschendal.com ▪ **T (021) 870·4272/3/4/5** ▪ F (021) 874·2137

During the summer months, Boschendal's Le Pique-Nique area provides the ideal setting for an alfresco lunch of pre-packed picnics served in wicker baskets. Tables and chairs are set in the shade under the lofty, fragrant pine trees – perfect for a relaxed summer afternoon. Collect your basket filled with pâtés, French bread, cold meats, salads, cheese and biscuits, and relax and enjoy. To complete the meal, dessert and coffee are served from the gazebo. The winelist offers the full range of Boschendal's finest wines to enjoy with your picnic and to enhance your 'Boschendal experience'.

Le Quartier Français – Ici 16 Huguenot Street, Franschhoek ▪ Contemporary cuisine ▪ Open Mon-Sun 12:00–22:00 ▪ Booking advised ▪ Children welcome ▪ Wheelchair-friendly ▪ Major credit cards accepted ▪ Corkage R30 ▪ Chef Margot Janse ▪ restaurant@lqf.co.za ▪ www.lequartier.co.za ▪ **T (021) 876·2151** ▪ F (021) 876·3105

Honest, good food cooked in a wood-burning oven from the finest seasonal produce. (See also Bread & Wine, Le Quartier Français 'The Tasting Room' & Stay-over section.)

Le Quartier Français 'The Tasting Room' 16 Huguenot Street, Franschhoek ▪ Contemporary cuisine ▪ Open Mon-Sun for dinner only ▪ Booking advised ▪ Children 12+ welcome ▪ Wheelchair-friendly ▪ Major credit cards accepted ▪ No BYO ▪ Chef Margot Janse ▪ restaurant@lqf.co.za ▪ www.lequartier.co.za ▪ **T (021) 876·2151** ▪ F (021) 876·3105

A cutting edge experience. Choose four or six courses off an à la carte menu or indulge in an eight-course Gourmand with or without wines. Voted 'Best Restaurant in Africa and the Middle East – 2005' by Restaurant magazine. (See also Bread & Wine, Le Quartier Français – Ici & Stay-over section.)

Monneaux Restaurant Franschhoek Country House, Main Road, Franschhoek ▪ Contemporary cuisine ▪ Open 7 days a week for breakfast, lunch & dinner ▪ Booking advised ▪ Children welcome ▪ Wheelchair-friendly ▪ Major credit cards accepted ▪ Corkage R30 ▪ Owner Jean-Pierre Snyman ▪ info@fch.co.za ▪ www.fch.co.za ▪ **T (021) 876·3386** ▪ F (021) 876·2744

Voted as one of South Africa's Top Restaurants, it has become known for its innovative modern French cuisine, prepared with fresh, well-sourced ingredients and exquisitely presented. A la carte lunches are served on the magnificent new fountain terrace while dinner is served in the understated yet elegant dining room or enclosed verandah. The winelist emphasises local wines which can also be enjoyed by the glass in the cosy wine bar or underground cellar. (See also Stay-over section for Franschhoek Country House.)

Piccata Restaurant & Bar 42 Huguenot Street, Franschhoek ▪ Mediterranean/Italian ▪ Open daily for lunch 12:00–15:30, light meals 15:30–18:00 & dinner 19:00–22:30, bar open till late ▪ Booking advised ▪ Children welcome ▪ Wheelchair-friendly ▪ Major credit cards accepted ▪ BYO discouraged – corkage R15 ▪ Owners Hugo van Niekerk & Matthew Gordon ▪ piccata@mweb.co.za ▪ **T (021) 876·3534** ▪ F (021) 876·3541

This stylish new restaurant on Franschhoek's main road is vibey, exciting and serves Mediterranean-style food. It's the brainchild of leading chef Matthew Gordon and rising culinary star Hugo van Niekerk. Specialising in fresh fish and Italian-inspired dishes with a South African touch, dishes are available in full or half portions. The extensive winelist features a wide variety of Franschhoek's finest, the best of the rest of the Cape winelands and a touch of Italian. (See also French Connection, Haute Cabrière Cellar Restaurant & Stay-over section for Auberge Clermont.)

Reuben's Restaurant & Bar 19 Huguenot Street, Franschhoek ▪ Classical & contemporary fair ▪ Open daily for lunch & dinner ▪ Booking advised ▪ Children welcome ▪ Wheelchair-friendly ▪ Major credit cards accepted ▪ Corkage R30 ▪ Owners Reuben Riffel, Marc Kent & Tim Rands ▪ reubens@mweb.co.za ▪ **T (021) 876·3772** ▪ F (021) 876·4464

This 'modern yet classic' restaurant has an alfresco dining area, as well as a separate bar. The restaurant received a 5-star chef rating from *Wine* Magazine, and was voted Top Restaurant and Top Chef of the Year in the 2004/5 Eat Out guide.

Hermanus

Schulphoek Seafront Guesthouse & Restaurant 44 Marine Drive, Sandbaai, Hermanus (entrance off Piet Retief Crescent) ▪ TGCSA 5-star guesthouse ▪ Global cuisine ▪ Restaurant is limited to stay-over guests ▪ Closed month of June ▪ Booking advised ▪ Children by arrangement ▪ Major credit cards accepted (excl Amex) ▪ No BYO ▪ Interactive hosts Petro & Mannes van Zyl ▪ schulphoek@hermanus.co.za ▪ www.schulphoek.co.za ▪ **T (028) 316·2626** ▪ F (028) 316·2627

Situated at Schulphoek, a beautiful quiet bay with spectacular sea views, five km from Hermanus' centre. The dining room with uninterrupted sea view is staffed by a chef and offers a four-course menu du jour, delectable seafood and venison dishes, fresh herbs and vegetables from the potager, and over 7 000 bottles of regional wine. For stay-over guests, a complimentary four-course dinner on day of arrival is included. (See also Stay-over section.)

Kuils River

The Guinea Fowl Restaurant Polkadraai Road (M12), Kuils River ▪ Continental cuisine ▪ Lunch Wed-Mon, dinner Wed-Sat ▪ Closed Tue ▪ Booking advised ▪ Children welcome ▪ Wheelchair-friendly ▪ Major credit cards accepted ▪ Owners Adrian & Birgit Bührer ▪ restaurant@saxenburg.com ▪ www.saxenburg.co.za ▪ **T (021) 906·5232** ▪ F (021) 906·0489

Well-known restaurateur Leo Romer has the pleasure of welcoming connoisseurs to the Guinea Fowl for the best fish in town. After satisfying patrons for 16 years at Le Chalet, he's now cheffing up a storm on Saxenburg wine farm. New are the light lunches in the garden *lapa*, a convivial venue for private functions and weddings. 'There are lots of restaurants – like sand on the beach,' Romer says. 'But no-one is closer to the fish than we are!' (See also A–Z section for Saxenburg.)

Zevenwacht Restaurant Zevenwacht Wine Farm, Langverwacht Road, Kuils River ▪ Global cuisine ▪ Open year-round for breakfast, lunch & dinner ▪ Booking advised ▪ Children welcome ▪ Wheelchair-friendly ▪ Major credit cards accepted ▪ No BYO ▪ Owner Manie Wolmarans ▪ restaurant@zevenwacht.co.za ▪ www.zevenwacht.co.za ▪ **T (021) 903·5123** ▪ F (021) 903·5257

The restaurant is housed in the elegant Cape Dutch manor house in a tranquil setting overlooking the lake. Global cuisine is served in a friendly, relaxed atmosphere. Quality picnic baskets are available in the gardens. (See also Stay-over & A–Z sections.)

Montagu

Mimosa Lodge Restaurant Church Street, Montagu ▪ French Continental cuisine ▪ Open daily 19:30–21:30 ▪ Booking advised ▪ Children by prior arrangement ▪ Wheelchair-friendly ▪ Major credit cards accepted ▪ Corkage R25 ▪ Owners Bernhard & Fida Hess ▪ mimosa@lando.co.za ▪ www.mimosa.co.za ▪ **T (023) 614·2351** ▪ F (023) 614·2418

Mimosa Lodge is renowned for its creative cuisine. Swiss owner-chef Bernhard Hess uses only the freshest ingredients, often coming from our own garden. Here you will be pleasantly surprised to find world-class cuisine in the small country village of Montagu, situated in the heart of Route 62. (See also Stay-over section.)

Wild Apricot Restaurant @ The Montagu Country Hotel 27 Bath Street, Montagu ▪ Traditional country cuisine ▪ Open daily 07:30–21:30 ▪ Booking advised ▪ Children welcome ▪ Wheelchair-friendly ▪ Major credit cards accepted ▪ Corkage R10 ▪ Owner Gert Lubbe ▪ montinn@iafrica.com ▪ www.montagucountryhotel.co.za ▪ **T (023) 614·3125** ▪ F (023) 614·1905

The Wild Apricot specialises in traditional country cuisine complemented by top quality wines of the region. Dine in the 'Art Deco' dining room, patio or front deck overlooking the mountains. Golden oldies played on a baby grand piano take you on a nostalgic trip down memory lane. (See also Stay-over section.)

Paarl & Environs

Bosman's Restaurant & Bistro Allegro Plantasie Street, Paarl ▪ Global cuisine ▪ Breakfast 7:00-10:30, lunch 12:00-14:00 & dinner 19:00-21:00; Bistro Allegro 11:00-close ▪ Closed 13 May-31 Jul ▪ Booking advised ▪ Children welcome (4+ for dinner) ▪ Wheelchair-friendly ▪ Major credit cards accepted ▪ No BYO ▪ Restaurant Manager Thorsten Fundament ▪ reserve@granderoche.co.za ▪ www.granderoche.com ▪ **T (021) 863·2727** ▪ F (021) 863·2220

Wind your way through the winelands and stop at Bosman's for light, elegant, informal lunches complemented by splendid wines from the superbly stocked cellar (Diner's Club Winelist Diamond awards from 00-04). Bosman's is a world-class restaurant providing contemporary Cape gourmet cuisine in the gracious atmosphere of a magnificent manor house. The Grande Roche, a 5-star estate hotel (see separate Stay-over entry), has become a legend on the hospitality scene, winning a formidable array of awards and culinary accolades. Bosman's is the only restaurant to attain full marks for all categories in Wine magazine's Top 100 Restaurants and five stars six times for its winelist – the latest in the 05 edition. It was also listed one of the 'Editor's Top 10 Restaurants' by leading food writer Lannice Snyman in her Eat Out guide from 99–04. Bosman's is also the first and still the only hotel-restaurant on the African continent to achieve Relais Gourmand status, one of the world's highest Relais & Chateaux culinary appellations. The Bistro Allegro is a new informal dining alternative offering lunches and dinners.

Marc's Mediterranean Cuisine & Garden 129 Main Street, Paarl ▪ Mediterranean cuisine ▪ Open for lunch Tue-Sun; dinner Mon-Sat; light meals served in afternoons ▪ Closed July (yearly holiday), public holidays (please call) ▪ Booking advised ▪ Children welcome ▪ Wheelchair-friendly ▪ Major credit cards accepted ▪ Corkage R25 ▪ Owner Marc Friederich ▪ chezmarc@mweb.co.za ▪ **T (021) 863·3980** ▪ F (021) 863·3990

At this Provençal farmhouse-styled restaurant, situated on Main Street in Paarl, one immediately senses the passion that has gone into creating an excellent dining experience, with fine fare, superb wines and good company, warm elegant lounge and convivial wine and cigar bar. Owner Marc, an award-winning sommelier, and chef extraordinaire Thomas, who is of Austrian origin, share a philosophy of keeping food simple and light.

Rhebokskloof Restaurant Rhebokskloof Private Cellar, Wine Route No 8, Agter-Paarl Road, Paarl ▪ Global cuisine ▪ Open daily for tea & lunch, dinner Thu-Mon (Sep-May), dinner Fri-Sun (Jun-Aug) ▪ Booking advised ▪ Children welcome ▪ Wheelchair-friendly ▪ Major credit cards accepted ▪ No BYO ▪ Owners Rhebokskloof Farming & Trading (Pty) Ltd ▪ restaurant@rhebokskloof.co.za ▪ www.rhebokskloof.co.za ▪ **T (021) 869·8386** ▪ F (021) 869·8906

Rhebokskloof Restaurant offers an unforgettable chance to enjoy top-quality wines from a winelist highlighting Rhebokskloof's own wines, combined with excellent innovative global cuisine created by our executive chef in one of the most beautiful locations in the winelands. Come and enjoy a journey of the senses. (See also A-Z section.)

The Restaurant at Pontac 16 Zion Street, Paarl ▪ International cuisine with local flair ▪ Open daily for lunch & dinner ▪ Booking advised ▪ Children welcome ▪ Wheelchair-friendly ▪ Major credit cards accepted ▪ Corkage R30 ▪ Owners Tim & Deseré Orrill-Legg ▪ reservations@pontac.com ▪ www.pontac.com ▪ **T (021) 872·0445** ▪ F (021) 872·0460

Part of a beautifully restored historic estate, which today also houses a 22-room boutique hotel, The Restaurant at Pontac is renowned for its provocative cuisine and delightful ambience. Patrons dine alfresco on a whitewashed patio, or inside in a restaurant with original wooden floors and fireplaces, and unique African artefacts. With classical French roots, the culinary style is enhanced by local influences and flavours, and various items on the menu are available in full or half portions. Smoking section. Top 100 Restaurants.

Robertson

Fraai Uitzicht 1798 Klaas Voogds East, on Route 62 between Robertson & Montagu ▪ Sophisticated country cuisine ▪ Open Wed-Sun from 11:00 ▪ Closed Mon & Tue; Jun & Jul; 24, 25 & 31 Dec, 1 Jan ▪ Booking advised ▪ Wheelchair-friendly ▪ Major credit cards accepted ▪ No BYO ▪ Owners Axel Spanholtz & Mario Motti ▪ info@fraaiuitzicht.com ▪ www.fraaiuitzicht.com ▪ **T/F (023) 626·6156**

Fraai Uitzicht 1798, the historic wine and guest farm with restaurant, welcomes you to the real vineyard experience. Attentive hosts provide a relaxed ambience for a fine wine and dine experience in the award-winning restaurant. Sophisticated country cuisine, prepared with personal attention using fresh produce from the vegetable and herb garden, is complemented by a selection of the best wines the Robertson valley of wine and roses has to offer. (See also Stay-over & A-Z sections.)

Somerset West & Environs

96 Winery Road Restaurant Zandberg Farm, Winery Road, off the R44 between Somerset West & Stellenbosch ▪ Country, global cuisine ▪ Lunch daily from 12:00–15:00, dinner Mon-Sat from 19:00 ▪ Closed Sun eve ▪ Booking advised ▪ Children welcome ▪ Wheelchair-friendly ▪ Major credit cards accepted ▪ Corkage R25 ▪ Owners Ken Forrester, Martin Meinert, Allan Forrester & Natasha Harris ▪ wineryrd@mweb.co.za ▪ www.96wineryroad.co.za ▪ **T (021) 842·2020** ▪ F (021) 842·2050

From the start in May 1996 it has been our goal to delight each guest with a superb dining experience in our warm, relaxing venue in the heart of the Helderberg winelands. Nominated a Top 10 restaurant in the 04 Eat Out awards, 96 has become a sort of HQ for local and international wine luminaries. Food is fresh, colourful, uncomplicated, and cooked with care and generosity. The menu changes frequently according to the whim and creativity of chef Natasha Harris and Mother Nature. The winelist is extensive with choices from the Helderberg region and the 'rest of the world', and something to suit every pocket and palate.

L'Auberge du Paysan Raithby Road, off the R44 between Somerset West & Stellenbosch ▪ French cuisine ▪ Lunch Tue-Fri 12:00–14:00, dinner Mon-Sat 18:30–22:00 ▪ Closed Sun, July ▪ Booking advised ▪ Children 10+ welcome ▪ Wheelchair-friendly ▪ Major credit cards accepted ▪ Corkage R35 ▪ Owners Frederick Thermann & Michael Kovensky ▪ www.aubergedupaysan.co.za ▪ **T (021) 842·2008** ▪ F (021) 842·3008

Patron Frederick Thermann's style and panache suffuse this French country restaurant, ranked among the finest in the country. The appointments, decor and ambience complement the traditional classic French menu, with specialities from Alsace and Provençe (a rare treat: crêpes Suzette prepared at your table). In summer, sip pre-dinner drinks on the patio; in winter, wine and dine in the romantic warmth of the open log fire. The unusually good winelist now features the own-label L'Auberge du Paysan Pinotage. (See also Stay-over section for La Bonne Auberge & A-Z section.)

The Avontuur Restaurant Avontuur Wine Estate, Stellenbosch Road (R44), Somerset West ▪ Contemporary Cape country cuisine ▪ Open Mon-Fri 9:00–17:00, Sat & Sun 9:00–16:00 ▪ Closed Good Friday & Christmas day ▪ Booking essential ▪ Children welcome ▪ Wheelchair-friendly ▪ Major credit cards accepted ▪ No BYO ▪ Owners/chefs Zunia Boucher-Myers & Melanie Paltoglou (restaurant) ▪ restaurant@polka.co.za ▪ www.avontuurestate.co.za ▪ **T (021) 855·4296** ▪ F (021) 855·4600

Set adjacent to the wine cellar, this intimate restaurant with views of the vineyards, ocean and Table Mountain specialises in fresh, uncomplicated and generous meals with emphasis on using local and, where possible, organic ingredients. The à la carte menu boasts three delectable breakfast choices, a full traditional, Greek meze and a health option. The lunch menu comprises a mouthwatering selection, from soup, quiche, platters and sandwiches to a specials blackboard listing the chefs' choices of the day – succulent beef fillet accompanied by a cream and mushroom brandy sauce, fresh linefish with peppadews and capers, and ending off with our renowned crème brûlée – all to be enjoyed beside the fire or out on the sun-drenched patio. (See also A-Z section.)

Stellenbosch & Environs

33 Stellenbosch Vlottenburg Road (off R310), Stellenbosch ▪ Bookings for functions on any day except 26 Dec, 1 Jan & some public holidays ▪ Wheelchair-friendly ▪ Major credit cards accepted ▪ BYO discouraged ▪ Owners Simon Lavarack & Louise Obertüfer ▪ info@33.co.za ▪ www.33.co.za ▪ **T (021) 881·3793** ▪ F (021) 881·3177

33 Stellenbosch is the perfect setting for weddings, birthdays, functions, product launches and corporate events. The restaurant is no longer open on a daily basis but can be booked for any function. The beautiful Italian piazza-styled courtyard, with 100-year-old pepper trees and a fountain, makes for wonderful alfresco lunches and dinners in summer, while the elegant ambience and charm exuded by comfortable sofas, a stylish bar and a roaring fire are the perfect venue for any function in winter. During the season, light meals will be served to residents and non-residents around the pool. (See also Stay-over section.)

@ M12 Djakarta Indonesian Restaurant La Provence Road, Stellenbosch (behind Polkadraai farm stall on the M12 Stellenbosch-Kuils River) ▪ Asian, authentic Indonesian food ▪ Open daily for breakfast & lunch, dinner Mon-Sat till late ▪ Closed Sun dinner, New Year's day ▪ Booking advised ▪ Children welcome ▪ Wheelchair-friendly ▪ Major credit cards accepted ▪ Corkage R15 ▪ Owner Duncan Fransz (A Dutchman born in Djakarta) ▪ sunhillf@iafrica.com ▪ www.M12Djakarta.co.za ▪ **T (021) 881·3243** ▪ F (021) 881·3299

@ M12 Djakarta – the only restaurant serving the world-famous rijsttafel in South Africa. Seating is outside in a rose garden setting and oak-shaded terrace or on an oriental style sundeck which can be used for functions. Inside, a large log fire, intimate, informal and relaxed service – amid fantastic antiques and valuables. Everything you see is for sale – except the staff. @ M12 Djakarta – the best-kept secret? The secret is out!

De Oewer Aan de Wagenweg (next to De Volkskombuis), Stellenbosch ▪ Global cuisine ▪ Lunch 7 days a week 12:00–15:00, dinner Mon-Sat 18:30–22:00 & Sun (Sep-May) ▪ Closed Good Friday ▪ Booking advised ▪ Wheelchair-friendly ▪ Major credit cards accepted ▪ Corkage R20 ▪ Owners Dawid & Christelle Kriel ▪ mail@volkskombuis.co.za ▪ www.deoewer.co.za ▪ **T (021) 886·5431** ▪ F (021) 883·3413

Settled on the banks of the Eerste River under venerable oaks, this restaurant is well known for its alfresco-style lunches and barbeque menus. Wide selection of Mediterranean dishes and an extensive winelist. Ideal for functions.

De Volkskombuis Aan de Wagenweg, Stellenbosch ▪ SA cuisine ▪ Lunch 7 days a week 12:00–15:00, dinner Mon-Sat 18:30–22:00 & Sun (Sep-May) ▪ Closed Good Friday ▪ Booking advised ▪ Wheelchair-friendly ▪ Major credit cards accepted ▪ Corkage R20 ▪ Owners Dawid & Christelle Kriel ▪ mail@volkskombuis.co.za ▪ www.volkskombuis.co.za ▪ **T (021) 887·2121/887·5239** ▪ F (021) 883·3413

Situated in the heart of Stellenbosch, just off Dorp Street, De Volkskombuis has specialised in traditional fare for more than a quarter-century. Dawid and Christelle Kriel took over the family business in 2001 and, with their personal touch, their passion for food, wine and people, De Volkskombuis is – more than ever – the place to go for a good meal in good company, seven days a week. Diners Club Platinum 02 award-winning winelist.

Fishmonger NPK Building, cnr Ryneveld & Plein streets, Stellenbosch ▪ Mediterranean cuisine ▪ Mon-Sat 12:00–22:00, Sun 12:00–21:00 ▪ Closed Christmas, New Year & Good Friday ▪ Booking advised ▪ Children welcome ▪ Wheelchair-friendly ▪ Major credit cards accepted ▪ Corkage R10 ▪ Owners André Viljoen, Craig Seaman & Nico Strydom ▪ fishmonger@adept.co.za ▪ **T (021) 887·7835** ▪ F (021) 887·7834

Fishmonger is a bustling Mediterranean-style alfresco taverna in the heart of the winelands, where patrons enjoy the best and freshest seafood (sushi an added attraction), with service to match. The winelist showcases local producers and changes seasonally. Good food, good service and good wine are the watchwords here.

Flavours Restaurant Devon Valley Hotel, Devon Valley Road, Stellenbosch ▪ Contemporary Cape cuisine ▪ Open daily for breakfast 07:00–11:00, lunch & dinner 11:00–22:00 ▪ Booking advised ▪ Children welcome ▪ Wheelchair-friendly ▪ Major credit cards accepted ▪

Corkage R20 ▪ Owner LGI Hotels & Vineyards ▪ info@devonvalleyhotel.com ▪ www.devonvalleyhotel.com ▪ **T (021) 865·2012** ▪ F (021) 865·2610

The Devon Valley Hotel's restaurant, Flavours, offers guests and visitors authentic, contemporary Cape cuisine with an award-winning winelist to complement a memorable dining experience. The restaurant has a gentle and homely ambience, affording any special occasion understated elegance in a picturesque setting. Leisurely light lunches on the terrace in summer and cosy fireside dinners in winter are a firm favourite. The focus is on bold flavours, celebrating classic, uncomplicated dishes and fresh clean tastes. (See also Stay-over section & A-Z for SylvanVale.)

Hazendal Hermitage Restaurant Bottelary Road (M23), Stellenbosch ▪ SA & Mediterranean cuisine ▪ Mon-Sun 9:00-14:30, breakfast 9:00-11:00 ▪ Closed Good Friday, Christmas & New Year's days ▪ Booking advised ▪ Children welcome ▪ Wheelchair-friendly ▪ Major credit cards accepted ▪ No BYO ▪ Owner Dr Mark Voloshin ▪ restaurant@hazendal.co.za ▪ www.hazendal.co.za ▪ **T (021) 903·5112** ▪ F (021) 903·5060

This intimate restaurant is situated between the original cellar, which has now been renovated into a tasting centre and restaurant, and the state-of-the-art cellar, built in 1996. A lovely fireplace in the lounge creates a warm welcome and is a great place to relax after mealtimes. There's seating for some 50 people inside the restaurant, with two adjoining courtyards. Outdoor seating on the patios affords beautiful views of the surrounding mountains and hills. Meals vary from light fresh salads, hearty homemade soups and specialities, to pasta and traditional Cape Malay dishes. Hazendal also offers this superb venue for functions. Russian-born owner Dr Mark Voloshin's passion for his homeland's culture saw him establish the Marvol Museum of Russian Art, which is situated inside the wine cellar, along with the conference facility, which hosts up to 40 people. Here you can see a display of Russian icons and paintings by well-known Russian artists – Mark Voloshin's private collection of Fabergé eggs and jewellery are also on permanent display. (See also A-Z section.)

Jonkershuis Restaurant Spier Estate, Lynedoch Road (R310), Stellenbosch ▪ Cape Malay buffet ▪ Open daily for lunch 12:30-15:30, dinner Tue-Sat 18:30-22:00 (summer), Wed-Sat 19:00-22:00 (winter) ▪ Booking advised ▪ Children welcome ▪ Wheelchair-friendly ▪ Major credit cards accepted ▪ No BYO ▪ info@spier.co.za ▪ www.spier.co.za ▪ **T (021) 809·1100** ▪ F (021) 881·3634

Offering a traditional Cape Malay buffet which includes soup, farm breads, cold dishes, stews, curries, Malay specialities, Cape cheeses, and hot and cold desserts. Enjoy your meal inside the 150-year-old Jonkershuis or out on the oak-shaded terrace, the favoured summer venue. A veritable feast awaits you here. (See also Stay-over section for The Village Hotel & A-Z section.)

Morgenhof Restaurant Klapmuts Road, Stellenbosch ▪ Country cuisine ▪ Open Mon-Sun 12:00-14:30 ▪ Closed Good Friday, Christmas & New Year's days ▪ Booking advised ▪ Children welcome ▪ Wheelchair-friendly ▪ Major credit cards accepted ▪ No BYO ▪ Owner Anne Cointreau-Huchon ▪ info@morgenhof.com ▪ www.morgenhof.com ▪ **T (021) 889·5510** ▪ F (021) 889·5266

Enjoy mouthwatering food with a glass of one of Morgenhof's award-winning wines. Summer lunches are served in our garden under the shade of the oak and mulberry trees. In winter, relax alongside a roaring log fire in the warmth of our Gazebo restaurant. We also have a coffee shop which is open daily for breakfasts. (See also A-Z section.)

Moyo at Spier Spier Estate, Lynedoch Road (R310), Stellenbosch ▪ Modern sophisticated African cuisine ▪ Open daily for lunch 12:00-14:00, dinner 18:00-23:00 ▪ Live entertainment daily ▪ Booking advised ▪ Children welcome ▪ Wheelchair-friendly ▪ Major credit cards accepted ▪ No BYO ▪ moyo@spier.co.za ▪ www.spier.co.za ▪ **T (021) 809·1100** ▪ F (021) 809·3634

Lunch or dine in uniquely Cape African surroundings, and relish the diversity and excitement of a truly African experience. Select your meal from the sumptuous buffet menu, and be entertained royally by performers showcasing Cape Town's cultural talent, with a programme of theatre and dance staged from noon to midnight. (See also Stay-over section for The Village Hotel & A–Z section.)

Olivello Restaurant Marianne Wine Farm, Valley Road (R44), Klapmuts, Stellenbosch ▪ Cape Mediterranean ▪ Seasonal opening times, generally closed Mon & Tue ▪ Booking advised (essential weekends) ▪ Children welcome ▪ Wheelchair-friendly ▪ Major credit cards accepted ▪ Corkage R30 ▪ Owners Laurille Krug & Lynne Aberdeen ▪ restaurant@olivello.co.za ▪ www.olivello.co.za www.olivello.co.za ▪ **T (021) 875·5443** ▪ F (021) 875·5483

Ex Café Paradiso partners Laurille and Lynne couldn't resist the opportunity to put their passion to work in these picturesque surroundings. They take great pride in ensuring that friendly service, delicious food and a magnificent setting next to the lake will be a total feast for the senses. Their Sunday speciality is the Mediterranean Table, laid out buffet-style in the kitchen. Sit back, relax, play boules, row the boat or just laze on the lawns. Olivello is the perfect setting for celebrations such as weddings, birthdays or corporate events with every detail enthusiastically co-ordinated by them. English, Afrikaans, German and French spoken. (See also Stay-over section for Marianne Wine Farm Guest Apartments.)

Ons Genot Restaurant Bottelary Road, Stellenbosch ▪ Local cuisine with Belgian flair ▪ Open Wed-Mon for breakfast, lunch & dinner ▪ Closed Tue ▪ Booking advised ▪ Children welcome ▪ Wheelchair-friendly ▪ Major credit cards accepted ▪ Corkage R30 ▪ Owners Jef & Ilse van Nuffelen ▪ restaurant@onsgenot.com ▪ www.onsgenot.com ▪ **T (021) 865·2456** ▪ F (021) 865·2457

Ons Genot Restaurant is on the outskirts of historic Stellenbosch, the heart of the Cape winelands. The combination of local ingredients and Belgian cuisine makes dining at Ons Genot an unforgettable experience. Enjoy your meal inside in the cosy dining room or outside on the wooden deck overlooking the dam. Jef and Ilse will give you a warm welcome. Ons Genot Restaurant, where friends meet for good food and wine! Four-star accommodation available (see also Stay-over section).

Restaurant Barrique Vredenheim Estate, Vlottenburg, Stellenbosch ▪ Italian & local cuisine ▪ Lunch Tue-Sun 12:00–15:00, dinner Tue-Sat 18:00–22:00 ▪ Closed Sun eve, Mon ▪ Booking advised ▪ Children welcome ▪ Wheelchair-friendly ▪ Major credit cards accepted ▪ Corkage R20 ▪ Owner Peter Brittz ▪ barrique@netactive.co.za ▪ **T/F (021) 881·3001**

A fully à la carte restaurant in a beautiful setting on a wine estate. Comfortable atmosphere with personal touch service. Both menu – highlights are oxtail, lamb shank, calamari and great pizzas – and winelist offer good value for money. Suitable for quiet dinners, larger groups or tours, and birthdays and other occasions. Many of our patrons return regularly. (See also A–Z section.)

Sir Herbert's Wine Cottage & Red Pepper Deli Aan de Wagenweg @ Volkskombuis, Stellenbosch ▪ Mon-Fri 9:00–17:00 ▪ Closed Sat, Sun & public holidays ▪ No BYO ▪ Owners Marlé Fourie & Dawid Kriel ▪ mail@volkskombuis.co.za ▪ **T (021) 883·9119** ▪ F (021) 883·3413

As part of De Volkskombuis, brother-and-sister team Dawid Kriel and Marlé Fourie have opened a delicatessen and wine shop next to the restaurant. Famous for their catering services, quiches and stuffed breads, they also do winetastings and private cheffing for house parties. Best of local wines available, gourmet cooking for take-aways.

Spier Two restaurants – Jonkershuis & Figaro's – and The Village Hotel feature at this pleasure resort on a wine estate. (See separate listings.)

Terroir Restaurant Kleine Zalze Wine Farm, Techno Park turn-off, Strand Road (R44), Stellenbosch ▪ Classic French-Provençal bistro ▪ Open for lunch Tue-Sun from 12:30, dinner Tue-Sat from 19:00 ▪ Closed Mon ▪ Booking advised ▪ Children welcome ▪ Wheelchair-friendly ▪ Major credit cards accepted ▪ No BYO ▪ Owners Michael Broughton & Nic van Wyk ▪ terroir@kleinezalze.co.za ▪ www.terroir.co.za ▪ **T (021) 880·8167** ▪ F (021) 880·0719/880·0862

A modern take on Provençal classics is what chefs Michael Broughton and Nic van Wyk are producing at this restaurant under the oaks on the Kleine Zalze estate. Matched with excellent wines from the region and beyond, 'deceptively simple' dishes such as confit of duck, prawn risotto, wood-roasted springbuck and lemon tart form part of an innovative chalkboard menu inspired by the best of what's fresh, seasonal and local. Eat outdoors in summer, indoors at the fire in winter. The same talented team caters for larger private parties and weddings in the function venue (up to 150 guests). Suspended above the wine cellar, this attractive room offers a fascinating view into the heart of the winemaking process through floor-to-ceiling glass walls, and fantastic views of the vineyards and golf course from the large balcony, particularly at sunset. (See also Stay-over & A–Z sections.)

The Duck Pond R310 (Spier Road), Welmoed Farm – Omnia Wines, Lynedoch, Stellenbosch ▪ Country cuisine ▪ Open daily for lunch, breakfast by appointment and evening functions (barbeques, weddings or corporate) for groups of 25+ ▪ Closed Tue (May-Oct) ▪ Booking advised ▪ Children welcome ▪ Wheelchair-friendly ▪ Major credit cards accepted ▪ Corkage R10 ▪ Owner Ronel van der Walt ▪ charlene_ronel@hotmail.com ▪ www.duckpond.co.za ▪ **T/F (021) 881·3310**

The restaurant is situated inside the winetasting building at Welmoed Winery. Ronel van der Walt, who'd managed the restaurant since 1999, became the proud owner in 2001. Her sister, Charlene, is the assistant manageress. Both have many years of experience in the hospitality trade and are putting it to good use at The Duck Pond. Up to 50 people can be accommodated inside the restaurant. The lawn in front can seat a further 60 people on wooden benches and can also be used for marquee functions for bigger groups. A self-contained paved island in the middle of the pond (reached by a footbridge) can accommodate approximately 80 people and may be used for functions and barbeques. The Duck Pond serves country-style food focusing on a lighter, healthier approach while using the freshest ingredients from the area. (See also A–Z section.)

Vineyard Kitchen at Dombeya Farm Dombeya Farm, Annandale Road, Stellenbosch ▪ African cuisine ▪ Open Mon-Sat 9:00-17:00 ▪ Closed Sun, Christmas day & religious holidays ▪ Booking advised ▪ Children welcome ▪ Wheelchair-friendly ▪ Major credit cards accepted (excl Diners Club) ▪ Corkage R20 ▪ Owner Herbert van Schalkwyk ▪ purple_pippa@hotmail.com ▪ www.dombeyayarns.co.za ▪ **T (021) 881·3746** ▪ F (021) 881·3747

We invite you to share in a passion for creativity inspired by beautiful surroundings. The Vineyard Kitchen enhances the well-known Dombeya farm, home of the little wool shop in the mountains, a traditional spinning/weaving workshop selling hand knits and natural yarns. Herbie (the chef) serves delicious lunches, cakes and teas, always an exciting menu. Enjoy good food made with love and served with pleasure! Fully licensed. (See also A-Z section.)

Wellington

Seasons at Diemersfontein Diemersfontein Wine & Country Estate, Jan van Riebeeck Drive (R301), Wellington ▪ Country cuisine ▪ Open daily 8:00–late ▪ Closed Sun & Mon eve (except for in-house guests) ▪ Booking advised ▪ Wheelchair-friendly ▪ Major credit cards accepted ▪ Corkage R20 ▪ Owners David & Susan Sonnenberg ▪ seasons@diemersfontein.co.za ▪ www.diemersfontein.co.za ▪ **T (021) 864·5060** ▪ F (021) 864·2095

Seasons restaurant, set in the wine courtyard and overlooking pastures and the farm dam, offers visitors à la carte country cuisine which specialises in fresh local ingredients, beautifully presented. Open seven days a week for breakfast, lunch and dinner and 'side attractions' for visitors wanting a snack. Gourmet picnics, complete with rug and basket, are also available through Seasons. (See also Stay-over & A–Z sections.)

Worcester

Nuy Valley Restaurant & Guest Farm Werda farm, Nuy, Worcester ▪ Country cuisine ▪ Open daily 8:00–17:00, evenings by prior arrangement ▪ Booking advised ▪ Children welcome ▪ Wheelchair-friendly ▪ Major credit cards accepted ▪ Corkage R10 ▪ Owner Irma Conradie ▪ nuyvallei@xpoint.co.za ▪ www.nuyvallei.co.za ▪ **T (023) 342·1258** ▪ F (023) 347·1356

Our traditional top quality menus offer à la carte options all day until 17:00. Bookings are required for evening dinner. For groups and functions there are specially compiled menus. Sundays are open for à la carte and buffet meals. Nuy Valley has beautiful entertainment areas for large as well as small groups, such as weddings, birthday parties, business functions and touring groups. (See also Stay-over section & A–Z section for Conradie Family Vineyards.)

Stay-overs in the winelands and Cape Town

Featured below are some guest lodges, hotels, country inns, B&Bs and self-catering cottages in the winelands, many of them on wine farms (look for the symbol beside the individual entries in the A-Z section of this guide). Unless stated to the contrary, all speak English and Afrikaans, have parking and gardens/terraces. Rates are for standard double rooms unless otherwise specified – for example per person (pp) or breakfast included (B&B). Tourism Grading Council of South Africa (TGCSA) ratings where provided.

Note: The stay-overs featured here describe their own attractions.

Index of stay-overs

Listed alphabetically, with region.

33 Stellenbosch........ Stellenbosch
Akademie Street Guesthouses......... Franschhoek
Akkerdal Guest House.... Franschhoek
Assegai Lodge......... Somerset West
Auberge Clermont...... Franschhoek
Auberge Rozendal...... Stellenbosch
Batavia Boutique Hotel .. Stellenbosch
Beaumont Guest Cottages........... Bot River
Burgundy Bourgogne Manor House & Cottages........... Franschhoek
Caledon Villa Guest House.............. Stellenbosch
Camberley Guest Cottage Stellenbosch
Constantia Uitsig Hotel Constantia
Dankbaarheid Self-catering Guest House. Stellenbosch
Darling Lodge .... Darling
De Goue Druif .... Stellenbosch
Devon Valley Hotel ..... Stellenbosch
Diemersfontein Guest House............... Wellington
Dunkley House Guest House............... Cape Town
Fraai Uitzicht 1798 ..... Robertson
Franschhoek Country House & Villas .... Franschhoek
Grande Roche Hotel .... Paarl
Grange Cottage........ Stellenbosch
Hampshire House Guest Lodge............... Constantia
Iris and Heidi Cottages .. Franschhoek
Ivory Heights Guesthouse & Conference......... Somerset West
Jan Harmsgat Country House.............. Swellendam
Klein Rhebokskloof Country House .... Wellington
Kleine Zalze Lodges..... Stellenbosch
Klippe Rivier Country House.............. Swellendam
Knorhoek Guest House .. Stellenbosch
La Bonne Auberge....... Somerset West
La Couronne Hotel...... Franschhoek
La Fontaine Guest House. Franschhoek
La Maison Bleue .... Franschhoek
La Petite Baleine ...... De Kelders
La Petite Ferme Guest Suites .... Franschhoek
Landskroon Self-catering Cottage............... Paarl
L'Avenir Wine Estate Guest House.......... Stellenbosch
Le Manoir de Brendel ... Franschhoek
Le Quartier Français..... Franschhoek
Lemberg Wine Estate and Guest House......... Tulbagh
Marianne Wine Farm.... Stellenbosch
Metropole Luxury Boutique Hotel .... Cape Town
Mimosa Lodge.......... Montagu
Montagu Country Hotel . Montagu
Montmartre Luxury Lodges .... Franschhoek
Mooi Bly .... Paarl
Murate Wine Estate ..... Stellenbosch
Natte Valleij Farm ...... Stellenbosch
Nuy Valley Guest House . Worcester
Oak Tree Lodge .... Paarl
Ons Genot Country Lodge Stellenbosch
Pat Busch Private Nature Reserve .... Robertson
Plumwood Inn .... Franschhoek
Schulphoek Seafront Guesthouse & Restaurant .... Hermanus
Sonop Guest House..... Paarl
Spanish Farm Guest Lodge .... Somerset West
Steenberg Hotel .... Constantia
The Cellars-Hohenort Hotel................ Constantia
The Owner's Cottage at Grande Provence...... Franschhoek
The Retreat at Groenfontein.......... Calitzdorp
The Village Hotel at Spier Stellenbosch
Tierhoek Cottages ...... Robertson
Zandberg Farm Country House............... Somerset West
Zevenwacht Country Inn . Kuils River

Bot River

Beaumont Guest Cottages Compagnes Drift Farm, Main Road, Bot River ▪ From R190–R300 pp ▪ Major credit cards accepted ▪ Self-catering ▪ Owners Beaumont family ▪ beauwine@netactive.co.za ▪ www.beaumont.co.za, www.wheretostay.co.za ▪ **T (028) 284·9194 / -9370 a/h** ▪ F (028) 284·9733

The historic farm Compagnes Drift (circa early 1700s) in the heart of the Bot River valley is home to internationally renowned Beaumont wines. Enjoy the tranquil ambience of a bygone era in the country comfort of the Mill House and Peppertree Cottage – an authentic farm experience which offers much to wine tasters, bird-watchers, artists, ramblers, horse riders and those who simply need a guaranteed quiet 'getaway'. (See also A–Z section.)

Calitzdorp

The Retreat at Groenfontein Groenfontein Farm, District Calitzdorp ▪ TGCSA 4-star ▪ R450–R620 pp sharing DB&B, single R530–R720 DB&B (winter rates on request) ▪ Visa & MasterCard accepted ▪ Pool ▪ French, German, Italian & Swedish spoken ▪ Owners Grant & Marie Burton ▪ groenfon@iafrica.com ▪ www.groenfontein.com ▪ **T/F (044) 213·3880**

Victorian farmhouse, 7 comfortable en-suite rooms, lovely lounge and dining room overlooking sweeping lawns and the majestic Swartberg. Three- and 4-star graded accommodation. Winner AA Accommodation Award 03, 04 & 05. Grant and Marie pamper guests with hearty breakfasts and tasty dinners. Enjoy peaceful walks, challenging trails, or simply relax at the pool and let the peace and silence soak into your soul.

Cape Town

Dunkley House Guest House 3B Gordon Street, Gardens, Cape Town ▪ TGCSA 4-star ▪ Double R800 B&B ▪ Visa, MasterCard & Diners Club accepted ▪ Pool ▪ DSTV & DVDs ▪ Fans ▪ French & German spoken ▪ Owner Sharon Scudamore ▪ reservations@dunkleyhouse.com ▪ www.dunkleyhouse.com ▪ **T (021) 462·7650** ▪ F (021) 462·7649

Retreat to an oasis of luxury with friendly service in a welcoming atmosphere. Sip sundowners by the courtyard pool and chill out under the cool shade of banana palms. Set in a turn-of-the-century Dutch-colonial house surrounded by a private, tropical garden, Dunkley House offers spacious en-suite rooms with all the creature comforts, sumptuous breakfasts, homemade breads and muffins, ensuring your stay is a complete pleasure.

Metropole Luxury Boutique Hotel 38 Long Street, Cape Town ▪ TGCSA 4-star ▪ High season: double R1 376 B&B, single R975 B&B ▪ Major credit cards accepted ▪ Veranda Restaurant ▪ TV ▪ Air-conditioning ▪ German spoken ▪ Owners Steve van der Merwe & Jens Merbt ▪ info@metropolehotel.co.za ▪ www.metropolehotel.co.za ▪ **T (021) 424·7247** ▪ F (021) 424·7248

New meets old in Cape Town's hottest luxury boutique hotel. A hip hotel with modern sex appeal, situated in the heart of Cape Town. The renovated 29-room Georgian building is stylish, luxurious and fun! Includes the Veranda Restaurant (see Eat-out section), M-Bar & Lounge, and a small boardroom. Described as the 'coolest kid on the block'.

Constantia

Constantia Uitsig Hotel Spaanschemat River Road, Constantia ▪ TGCSA 4-star ▪ Double R2 400 per room B&B, single R1 600 B&B ▪ Major credit cards accepted ▪ Two award-winning restaurants ▪ World-renowned cricket oval ▪ Conference venue ▪ Pool ▪ TV ▪ Owners David & Marlene McCay ▪ reservations@uitsig.co.za ▪ www.uitsig.co.za ▪ **T (021) 794·6500** ▪ F (021) 794·7605

Set among the vineyards of a private wine estate in the shadow of Table Mountain, the highly acclaimed hotel is just 20 minutes from the city centre and Waterfront. Renowned for its atmosphere of quiet elegance and gracious hospitality, the hotel has 16 individually decorated garden rooms, each with a private patio and sweeping views of the Constantia valley. (See also Eat-out section for Constantia Uitsig, La Colombe & The River Café, & A–Z section.)

Hampshire House Guest Lodge 10 Willow Road, Constantia ▪ TGCSA 4-star ▪ Double from R700 B&B, single from R395 B&B ▪ Visa & MasterCard accepted ▪ Pool ▪ TV ▪ Air-conditioning ▪ Owners Ricky & Carole Chapman ▪ stay@hampshirehouse.co.za ▪ www.hampshirehouse.co.za ▪ **T (021) 794·6288** ▪ F (021) 794·2934

Set in the Constantia wine valley, this 4-star guesthouse was a finalist in the AA Accommodation Awards three years running. It provides the perfect base from which to explore the Cape Peninsula, with easy motorway access to Table Mountain, the Waterfront, winelands, beaches and local restaurants. Five individually decorated en-suite bedrooms have king-sized or twin ¾ beds, satellite TV, CD player, hairdryer and many other amenities. Swimming pool and secure off-street parking. English and continental buffet breakfasts served. The Hampshire Arms is a cosy pub with an interesting winelist.

Steenberg Hotel Steenberg Estate, Tokai Road, Constantia Valley ▪ TGCSA 5-star ▪ Double from R1 750 B&B, single from R1 680 B&B ▪ Major credit cards accepted ▪ Catharina's Restaurant ▪ Pool ▪ TV ▪ Air-conditioning ▪ Relaxation room ▪ 18-hole golf course ▪ German & French spoken ▪ Owner Graham Beck ▪ info@steenberghotel.com ▪ www.steenberghotel.com ▪ **T (021) 713·2222** ▪ F (021) 713·2251

The 5-star Steenberg Hotel is a 30-room boutique hotel, minutes from the centre of Cape Town, amid splendid vineyards and an 18-hole championship golf course. Catharina's Restaurant (see Eat-out section) is open for breakfast, lunch and dinner seven days a week. (See also A–Z section.)

The Cellars-Hohenort Hotel 93 Brommersvlei Road, Constantia ▪ TGCSA 5-star ▪ R2 800 B&B ▪ Major credit cards accepted ▪ The Cape Malay Restaurant & The Greenhouse ▪ Pool ▪ TV ▪ Air-conditioning ▪ French, German, Italian & Xhosa spoken ▪ Owner Liz McGrath ▪ cellars@relaischateaux.com ▪ www.collectionmcgrath.com ▪ **T (021) 794·2137** ▪ F (021) 794·2149

The hotel is next to the world-famous Kirstenbosch Botanical Gardens and minutes away from the Constantia wine route. It has nine acres of splendid landscaped gardens and a small vineyard. In its renaissance as one of the great country house hotels of the Cape, the 5-star Cellars-Hohenort is a member of the International Relais & Châteaux Association. (See also Eat-out section.)

Darling

Darling Lodge 22 Pastorie Street, Darling ▪ TGCSA 4-star ▪ Double from R370 B&B, single from R270 B&B ▪ Visa & MasterCard accepted ▪ Pool ▪ TV ▪ Dutch, French & German spoken ▪ Owners Alfred & Jutta Legner ▪ info@darlinglodge.co.za ▪ www.darlinglodge.co.za ▪ **T (022) 492·3062** ▪ F (022) 492·3665

Set in a gentle valley in the West Coast hills of Darling, this beautifully restored Victorian home is an hour from Cape Town and minutes from the Atlantic Ocean. Stylish and thoughtfully decorated rooms offer a harmonious blend of old and new in an environment of vineyards, dairy pastures, wheat fields and spectacular wild flower displays. Enjoy award-winning wines and olives from the area in a delightful garden with a sparkling pool. Winetastings, private functions by arrangement. Winelands, beaches, golf, whale-watching nearby.

De Kelders

La Petite Baleine Botha Street, De Kelders ▪ TGCSA 5-star ▪ Double R1 500–R2 000 B&B, single from R1 500 B&B ▪ Major credit cards accepted ▪ Pool ▪ TV ▪ Whale-watching ▪ Owners Mark & Josephine Dendy Young ▪ lapetite@iafrica.com ▪ www.lapetiteferme.co.za ▪ **T (021) 876·3016** ▪ F (021) 876·3624

Even when departing the winelands, the splendour never stops. A scenic 90-minute drive from La Petite Ferme leads you to the coastal-based La Petite Baleine and the ideal opportunity to bid a fitting farewell to the area. Soaked generously in sunshine with sweeping, uninterrupted ocean views of Walker Bay near Hermanus, La Petite Baleine villa has two sea-facing bedrooms and an infinity-edged swimming pool set on a private patio. This entire area is worldwide home to whale-watching at its best and the prime-positioned villa constantly boasts seasonal views of both whales and dolphins at play in the bay. The villa is serviced daily and fully equipped for self-catering. (See also Eat-out & A–Z sections for La Petite Ferme).

Franschhoek & Environs

Akademie Street Guesthouses 5 Akademie Street, Franschhoek ▪ R1 200–R2 100 per guesthouse B&B ▪ Winter specials ▪ Visa, MasterCard & American Express accepted ▪ Pool ▪ TV ▪ Air-conditioning ▪ Owners Katherine & Arthur Mc William Smith ▪ info@aka.co.za ▪ www.aka.co.za ▪ **T (021) 876·3027** ▪ F (021) 876·3293

Five-star, 2005 highly commended in AA Accommodation 'South Africa's Best' awards, the guesthouses are within easy, safe walking distance of most of the great village restaurants. Each house has its own private garden and pool. They all join onto pathways leading through lush gardens to the Cape Dutch home, Twyfeling, where breakfasts are served on a vine-covered patio. Oortuiging, the restored 1860s cottage, has two private bedrooms and sleeps three. Vreugde is an intimate garden suite which sleeps two. Gelatenheid, with wide balconies and superb mountain views, is a spacious double-storey villa which sleeps two.

Akkerdal Guest House Akkerdal Estate, R45, Franschhoek ▪ Double R750 per room, single R450 per room ▪ Self-catering ▪ Major credit cards accepted ▪ TV ▪ Owner Pieter Hanekom ▪ wine@akkerdal.co.za ▪ www.akkerdal.co.za ▪ **T (021) 876·3481; 082·442·1746** ▪ F (021) 876·3189

Akkerdal Estate is situated in the picturesque Franschhoek valley. It is surrounded by mountains with oak trees and the constant flowing Berg River. At this artisan winery, we believe that the finest wines emanate from quality grapes. Accept this as an invitation to share and enjoy the perfected bottled art and poetry of Akkerdal Estate. (See also A–Z section.)

Auberge Clermont Robertsvlei Road, Franschhoek ▪ TGCSA 4-star ▪ Double R980 B&B, single R680 B&B ▪ Major credit cards accepted ▪ Pool ▪ TV ▪ Tennis court ▪ Owner Penny Gordon ▪ clermont@mweb.co.za ▪ www.clermont.co.za ▪ **T (021) 876·3700** ▪ F (021) 876·3701

Delightful Provençal-style auberge in stunning setting surrounded by chardonnay vineyards and ancient oaks. Lavender, rosemary and rose bushes perfume the air. Beautiful pool and tennis court, and great vineyard walks. Six stylish rooms, splendid en-suite bathrooms plus a three-bedroom self-catering villa beside a formal French garden. Associate guesthouse of the award-winning Haute Cabrière Cellar Restaurant (see also Eat-out section for French Connection Bistro, Haute Cabrière Cellar Restaurant & Piccata Restaurant & Bar).

Burgundy Bourgogne Manor House & Cottages Burgundy Bourgogne Farm, Excelsior Road, Franschhoek ▪ TGCSA 4-star ▪ R684 pp sharing ▪ Self-catering ▪ Visa & MasterCard accepted ▪ Pool ▪ TV ▪ Fly-fishing ▪ Owner Trevor Kirsten ▪ burgundybourgogne@saol.com ▪ www.burgundybourgogne.co.za ▪ **T (021) 876·4623** ▪ F (021) 876·3817

Set amid olive orchards, vines and centuries-old oaks, Burgundy Bourgogne Farm offers luxury self-catering accommodation in the historic manor house and cottages which charmingly recapture the style and atmosphere of life on a 17th-century Huguenot wine farm.

Franschhoek Country House & Villas Main Road, Franschhoek ▪ TGCSA 5-star ▪ From R695 pp sharing B&B, single from R1 042 B&B ▪ Major credit cards accepted ▪ Monneaux Restaurant ▪ 2 Pools ▪ TV ▪ Air-conditioning ▪ Conference facilities ▪ Owner Jean-Pierre Snyman ▪ info@fch.co.za ▪ www.fch.co.za ▪ **T (021) 876·3386** ▪ F (021) 876·2744

The Country House and Villas comprises14 luxury rooms and 12 new villa suites. All the rooms offer the features and facilities expected of a first-class hotel. The luxurious new villa suites are each a $100m^2$ in size and are arguably the best available in Franschhoek. During summer, guests laze at one of the two pools (one heated) with beautiful mountain vistas, visit the boutique wine farms in Franschhoek, or stroll in the charming town founded by the French Huguenots. Conference facilities for up to 45 delegates are available in the new modern but elegant club room complete with all the required equipment. (See also Eat-out section for Monneaux Restaurant.)

Iris and Heidi Cottages 56 Akademie Street, Franschhoek ▪ From R900–R1 500 per cottage (low-high season) ▪ Self-catering ▪ Visa & MasterCard accepted ▪ Pool ▪ TV ▪ Fans ▪ Dutch & German spoken ▪ Owners Tom & Heidi Clode ▪ iris@plumwoodinn.com ▪ www.capestay.co.za/iriscottage/ ▪ **T (021) 876·3883** ▪ F (021) 876·3803

Charming Cape Dutch-style cottages located in a tranquil corner of Franschhoek village. Each cottage has two bedrooms, two bathrooms, large kitchen and lounge. The verandahs overlook secluded flower-filled gardens, each with a delightful swimming pool. Just a short walk from the art galleries, shops and restaurants, Iris and Heidi Cottages are the perfect bases from which to enjoy everything the valley has to offer.

La Couronne Hotel Dassenberg Road, Franschhoek ▪ TGCSA 5-star ▪ From R1 100 per room B&B ▪ Major credit cards accepted ▪ Restaurant ▪ Colonial wine & cigar bar ▪ Pool ▪ TV ▪ Air-conditioning ▪ Gym ▪ Health & beauty facility ▪ German, Xhosa & Zulu spoken ▪ Owners Erwin Schnitzler & Miko Rwayitare ▪ reservations@lacouronnehotel.co.za ▪ www.lacouronnehotel.co.za ▪ **T (021) 876·2770** ▪ F (021) 876·3788

La Couronne, 'the crown' of Franschhoek, is positioned in what is undoubtedly one of the most beautiful settings in the world. This small luxury hotel, set among the vines, offers a complete winelands experience. Activities in the area include horse riding, fly-fishing, hiking, walking, mountain biking, winetasting and fine dining (see also Eat-out section).

La Fontaine Guest House 21 Dirkie Uys Street, Franschhoek ▪ TGCSA 4-star ▪ R375–R400 pp sharing B&B, single R600 B&B ▪ Major credit cards accepted ▪ Children 12+ welcome, under 12 by arrangement in garden suites only ▪ Pool ▪ TV ▪ Air-conditioning ▪ Owner Linquenda Guest House cc ▪ lafontaine@wam.co.za ▪ www.lafontainefranschhoek.co.za ▪ **T/F (021) 876·2112**

La Fontaine welcomes you into the heart of Franschhoek (one hour from Cape Town). Experience country hospitality in this gracious, centrally situated home with spectacular mountain views. Within walking distance of acclaimed restaurants, galleries and shops. La Fontaine has eight en-suite double rooms; three garden rooms and one family suite set in tranquil garden near swimming pool. Each garden room has a fireplace, TV, fridge, separate entrance and patio. Generous buffet breakfasts served indoors or under vine-covered pergola. Wheelchair-friendly and secure off-street parking.

La Maison Bleue 30 Uitkyk Street, Franschhoek ▪ R300 pp self-catering ▪ No credit card facilities ▪ Children 12+ welcome ▪ No smoking ▪ German & Dutch spoken ▪ Owners Richard & Rebekah Kelley ▪ rosemary_beetge@absamail.co.za ▪ **T/F (021) 876·3849; 083·456·9371** (Contact person: Rosemary)

SA residence of Platter Guide contributor and Master of Wine Richard Kelley. La Maison Bleue is situated in a quiet location on the edge of the village. The house has an extensive living area with three bedrooms (two doubles, one twin), well-equipped kitchen and garden with mountain views, terrace, pool and *petanque piste*. Long- or short-term lets.

La Petite Ferme Guest Suites Pass Road, Franschhoek ▪ TGCSA 5-star ▪ Double R1 200–R2 600 B&B, single R1 050–R2 200 B&B ▪ Major credit cards accepted ▪ Restaurant ▪ Pool ▪ TV ▪ Air-conditioning ▪ Owners Mark & Josephine Dendy Young ▪ lapetite@iafrica.com ▪ www.lapetiteferme.co.za ▪ **T (021) 876·3016** ▪ F (021) 876·3624

Set within an intimate, interlacing labyrinth of garden pathways are five secluded luxury guest suites. Stunning interior decor and full amenities ensure exclusive comfort with romantic charm. The suites, each with their own signature decor and full en-suite bathroom, are elegantly poised on the mountainside, overlooking the sauvignon blanc vineyards and the valley below. This combination of 5-star luxury and home comforts offers a private plunge pool and verandah with panoramic views, a lounge with fireplace, a mini bar, tea- and coffee-making facilities, air-conditioning, underfloor heating and television. Crisp white percale linen covers the extended-length beds, with ceiling fans for cool summer comfort. (See also La Petite Baleine & Eat-out section.)

Le Manoir de Brendel Spa, Wine & Guest Estate, R45, Main Road, Franschhoek ▪ Rates on request ▪ Major credit cards accepted ▪ Restaurant ▪ Pool ▪ TV ▪ Air-conditioning ▪

Conference room ▪ Spa ▪ Gym ▪ Chapel ▪ Owner Christian Brendel ▪ lemanoir@brendel.co.za ▪ www.le-manoir-de-brendel.com ▪ **T (021) 876·4525** ▪ F (021) 876·4524

Le Manoir de Brendel offers you 5-star accommodation. For the energetic, we provide a gym, tennis court and walking trail through the vineyards. For your relaxation, come and indulge yourself at the spa. Our curio shop gives you the opportunity to buy jewellery by Uwe Koetter. Thereafter, visit our restaurant or enjoy a cigar in our bar. The chapel and conference facility provide you with excellent venues for weddings and other functions. (See also Eat-out & A–Z sections.)

Le Quartier Français cnr Berg & Wilhelmina streets, Franschhoek ▪ R1 350 pp sharing B&B, single R2 205 B&B ▪ Major credit cards accepted ▪ Le Quartier Français Restaurant ▪ Pool ▪ TV ▪ Air-conditioning ▪ 30-seat screening room ▪ Dutch & French spoken ▪ Owner Susan Huxter ▪ res@lqf.co.za ▪ www.lequartier.co.za ▪ **T (021) 876·2151** ▪ F (021) 876·3105

Embraced by majestic mountain views, Le Quartier Français lies at the heart of the enchanting village of Franschhoek, Cape winelands. Six luxurious suites, two with private pool, and 15 elegantly decorated en-suite bedrooms overlook a central garden. Here, the old world meets the new in a marriage of sophistication and comfort. In the famous restaurant, experience award-winning cuisine from Margot Janse – 2004 Top Chef South Africa. 'Best small hotel in the world' – Tatler, UK. Satour 5-star. (See also Eat-out section for Bread & Wine, Le Quartier Français – Ici & 'The Tasting Room'.)

Montmartre Luxury Lodges Montmartre Estate, Pass Road, Franschhoek ▪ TGCSA 4-star ▪ Double R798 B&B, single R450 B&B ▪ Major credit cards accepted ▪ Pool ▪ TV ▪ Ceiling fans ▪ Fly-fishing ▪ Horse riding ▪ Owners Franschhoek Water (Pty) Ltd ▪ peter@montmartre.co.za ▪ www.montmartre.co.za ▪ **T (021) 876·3614** ▪ F (021) 876·3620

Montmartre Luxury Lodges are set high on the northern slopes of the magnificent Franschhoek mountains in a beautiful garden which extends upwards into the Cape's unique *fynbos*. Overlooking a trout-filled lake and the charming village of Franschhoek below, it is an ideal setting for a relaxing weekend of leisure. Each lodge has its own unique decor.

Plumwood Inn 11 Cabrière Street, Franschhoek ▪ TGCSA 4-star ▪ Double R750–R1 150 B&B, single R565–R650 B&B ▪ Visa & MasterCard accepted ▪ Pool ▪ TV ▪ Air-conditioning ▪ Dutch & German spoken ▪ Owners Lucienne & Roel Rutten ▪ info@plumwoodinn.com ▪ www.plumwoodinn.com ▪ **T (021) 876·3883** ▪ F (021) 876·3803

This romantic delight is minutes from the heart of Franschhoek's main street. Eight luxurious rooms with private entrances, each uniquely designed and tastefully decorated, with TV, hair-dryer, mini-safe, heater, air-conditioning and bathroom. Delicious alfresco breakfast served in a secluded picturesque garden. Dinner on request. Laze around one of the two pools soaking up the African sun. Personal service and attention to detail.

The Owner's Cottage at Grande Provence Grande Provence Estate, Main Road, Franschhoek ▪ Rates on request ▪ Major credit cards accepted ▪ Restaurant ▪ Pool ▪ TV ▪ Air-conditioning ▪ Art Gallery ▪ Owner Grande Provence Properties ▪ enquiries@grandeprovence.co.za ▪ www.grandeprovence.co.za ▪ **T (021) 876·8600** ▪ F (021) 876·8601

Gracefully governing this idyllic setting is the 18th-century Manor House, which together with The Owner's Cottage welcomes guests to boutique accommodation. Five sumptuous rooms provide a quiet and intimate repose, while the tranquility of the lake provides a restful escape for the soul. It is a beautiful testament to period grandeur and contemporary luxury. Comprising the well-appointed Cottage are four rooms, a deluxe suite, conservatory, lounge and spa pool area. Blanketed in a palette of charcoal slate and white linen, the rooms promise an indulgent experience. Carpeted with lush lawns and vegetation, the spa pool area punctuates the landscape with an elevated view of the surrounds. Curtains of dark green hedges contrast with creamy travertine tiles and inset pebbles, while white walls delineate the deck chairs and lounging areas, juxtaposing the cool and crisp swimming pool. Harmony permeates every angle. (See also Eat-out & A-Z sections.)

Hermanus

Schulphoek Seafront Guesthouse & Restaurant 44 Marine Drive, Sandbaai, Hermanus ▪ TGCSA 5-star guesthouse ▪ Superior, luxury & standard: R503–R1 150 pp sharing B&B (plus complimentary 4-course meal for first night); incentive rates for longer stays and low season specials ▪ Major credit cards accepted (excl Amex) ▪ Restaurant ▪ Wine cellar ▪ Body therapy ▪ Heated pool ▪ Interactive hosts Petro & Mannes van Zyl ▪ schulphoek@hermanus.co.za ▪ www.schulphoek.co.za ▪ www.schulphoek.co.za ▪ **T (028) 316·2626** ▪ F (028) 316·2627

Situated at Schulphoek, a beautiful quiet bay with spectacular sea views, five km from Hermanus' centre. Individually styled suites are luxurious and spacious. The lounge and dining room have a magnificent uninterrupted sea view. The professional kitchen, staffed by a chef, offers a four-course menu du jour, with herbs and vegetables picked daily. Choose from 7 000 bottles of South African wine. Diners Club Platinum cellar award 02. (See also Eat-out section.)

Kuils River

Zevenwacht Country Inn Zevenwacht Wine Farm, Langverwacht Road, Kuils River ▪ R590 pp sharing B&B, single R990 B&B ▪ Major credit cards accepted ▪ Restaurant ▪ Pool ▪ TV ▪ Air-conditioning (excl cottages) ▪ Sauna ▪ Tennis court ▪ Conference facilities ▪ German spoken ▪ Owner Harold Johnson ▪ reservations@zevenwacht.co.za ▪ www.zevenwacht.co.za ▪ **T (021) 903·5123** ▪ F (021) 906·1570

Zevenwacht, on the Stellenbosch wine route, is home not only to reputed wines but also many other attractions, including the Country Inn, offering accommodation in 13 luxury suites or seven vineyard cottages. Dining options include the historic Manor House Restaurant, open daily for breakfast, lunch, dinner and picnics. Our Country Inn has unsurpassed ocean views of Table Bay and False Bay. Other features include a sauna and floodlit tennis court, winetastings, facilities for weddings, product launches and conferences (a 64-seat auditorium is housed in the Country Inn), a cheesery and a chefs' school. (See also Eat-out & A–Z sections.)

Montagu

Mimosa Lodge Church Street, Montagu ▪ TGCSA 4-star ▪ Seasonal rates from R310–R750 pp sharing B&B, single R330–R1 022 B&B ▪ Major credit cards accepted ▪ Restaurant ▪ Pool ▪ TV lounge ▪ German & Swiss German spoken ▪ Owners Bernhard & Fida Hess ▪ mimosa@lando.co.za ▪ www.mimosa.co.za ▪ **T (023) 614·2351** ▪ F (023) 614·2418

Mimosa Lodge is a perfect stop between Cape Town and the Garden Route. A warm welcome awaits you in this historic, carefully renovated house. This is a place to relax in the magnificent garden and enjoy the creative cuisine which is highly acclaimed nationally and internationally. (See also Eat-out section.)

Montagu Country Hotel 27 Bath Street, Montagu ▪ TGCSA 3-star ▪ Classic R400 pp sharing B&B, luxury R640 pp sharing B&B; single classic R480 B&B, luxury R770 B&B ▪ Major credit cards accepted ▪ Wild Apricot Restaurant ▪ Conference venue ▪ Pool ▪ TV ▪ Air-conditioning ▪ Xhosa spoken ▪ Owner Gert Lubbe ▪ res@montagucountryhotel.co.za ▪ www. montagucountryhotel.co.za ▪ **T (023) 614·3125** ▪ F (023) 614·1905

Montagu is situated on the legendary 'Route 62' between Cape Town and the Garden Route. The 3-star Montagu Hotel's colonial 'Art Deco' style is based on 1920s Paris design. The hotel specialises in traditional cuisine, while golden oldies played on a baby grand piano take you back in time. The Wellness Centre specialises in health treatments. Conferencing is in a unique garden venue. (See also Eat-out section.)

Paarl & Environs

Grande Roche Hotel Plantasie Street, Paarl ▪ Standard Room R1 680 B&B ▪ Major credit cards accepted ▪ Bosman's Restaurant ▪ 2 Pools (1 heated) ▪ TV ▪ Air-conditioning ▪ Sauna ▪ Fitness centre ▪ Tennis courts (floodlit) ▪ German, Dutch & French spoken ▪ reserve@granderoche.co.za ▪ www.granderoche.com ▪ **T (021) 863·2727** F (021) 863·2220

Grande Roche has become a legend in South Africa with an array of awards including Satour's first Hotel of the Year Award for 'incredible attention to detail, impeccable grounds, excellent food and superb levels of luxury' as well as the American-based international Andrew Harper Award given to outstanding country estates exuding warmth, charm and excellence. It was also placed 50th in Travel & Leisure's 2004 'The World's Best' awards. This South African gem overlooks vineyards and rugged mountains, and its sprawl of individually decorated suites offer a gentle alternative to big city life. Relax in the pools, go biking or play tennis on site, enjoy excellent golf nearby, visit the fitness centre or the hotel's private masseur. It's the ideal base from which to explore the entire Cape region. Grande Roche is also the first and only hotel restaurant on the African continent to achieve Relais Gourmand status, one of the world's highest Relais & Chateaux culinary appellations. (See also Eat-out section for Bosman's Restaurant.)

Landskroon Self-catering Cottage Landskroon Wines, Suid-Agter-Paarl Road, Suider-Paarl ▪ R500 per cottage – ideal for 2 adults + 2 children ▪ Major credit cards accepted ▪ TV ▪ Owners Paul & Hugo de Villiers Family Trusts ▪ landskroon@mweb.co.za ▪ www.landskroonwines.com ▪ **T (021) 863·1039** ▪ F (021) 863·2810

Fully equipped, self-catering cottage situated in the heart of the Cape winelands along the southern slopes of Paarl Mountain. Serviced daily, carport, TV and security. (See also A–Z section.)

Mooi Bly Mooi Bly Estate, Horseshoe at Bo Dal Road, Dal Josafat, Paarl ▪ From R150–R300 pp ▪ Visa & MasterCard accepted ▪ Pool ▪ TV ▪ Private horseback riding (max 2 riders) ▪ Dutch (basic French & German if required) spoken ▪ Owners Luc Wouters & family ▪ info@mooibly.com ▪ www.mooibly.com ▪ **T/F (021) 868·2808**

In between Paarl and Wellington, tucked away on the mountain slopes, Mooi Bly estate offers five unique thatched cottages in the middle of its vineyards, with a self-catering or B&B option. Each cottage has its own braai, private stoep, garden and view over the Paarl valley or vineyards. Daily serviced cottages from two up to six persons; 45 minutes from Cape Town and airport. They opened their own wine cellar in 2005. (See also A–Z section.)

Oak Tree Lodge 32 Main Street, Paarl ▪ From R275 pp sharing B&B, single from R395 B&B ▪ Major credit cards accepted ▪ Pool ▪ TV ▪ Air-conditioning ▪ Owners Yvette & Gerd Baudewig ▪ info@oaktreelodge.co.za ▪ www.oaktreelodge.co.za ▪ **T (021) 863·2631** ▪ F (021) 863·2607

Oak Tree Lodge is centrally situated in the historic winelands town of Paarl. Spacious en-suite bedrooms offer TV with satellite and German satellite channels, telephone, air-conditioning, underfloor heating, bar fridge, hairdryer and tea trays. Choose between standard rooms or recently built luxury garden rooms next to the pool with lovely vineyard and mountain views. Restaurants and winetasting within walking distance.

Sonop Guest House Sonop Wine Farm, Voorpaardeberg Road, Paarl ▪ TGCSA 3-star ▪ Seasonal rates from R180–R250 pp sharing B&B ▪ Major credit cards accepted ▪ Pool ▪ TV ▪ French spoken ▪ Owner Jacques Germanier ▪ office@african-terroir.co.za ▪ www.african-terroir.co.za ▪ **T/F (021) 869·8534**

Unpretentious, genuine hospitality – a unique place where you can visit the cellar and do a winetasting, learn more about life on a farm, or overnight in our guesthouse. (See also A–Z section for African Terroir.)

Robertson

Fraai Uitzicht 1798 Klaas Voogds East, on Route 62 between Robertson & Montagu ▪ TGCSA 4-star ▪ Double from R800 B&B, single from R600 B&B ▪ Major credit cards accepted ▪ Restaurant ▪ Pool ▪ TV (in cottages) ▪ Game drives in Private Nature Reserve ▪ German, French, Swedish & Xhosa spoken ▪ Owners Axel Spanholtz & Mario Motti ▪ info@fraaiuitzicht.com ▪ www.fraaiuitzicht.com ▪ **T/F (023) 626·6156**

Nestling among the majestic Langeberg hills, in the heart of the Robertson valley, the historic wine and guest farm with an award-winning restaurant welcomes you to the real vineyard experience! Stylishly appointed guest cottages and suites, set amid vineyards and orchards, offer luxurious comfort with spectacular views. Attentive hosts ensure fine dining in the award-winning restaurant. Fraai Uitzicht 1798 offers a tranquil retreat, balm for the soul, the ideal place to spend a relaxing, comfortable and culinary few days. (See also Eat-out & A-Z sections.)

Pat Busch Private Nature Reserve Klaas Voogds West, Robertson ▪ R110–R150 pp sharing, single R130–R150 ▪ Self-catering ▪ Guided game drives ▪ Conference facilities ▪ German spoken ▪ Owners Busch family ▪ patbusch@intekom.co.za ▪ www.patbusch.co.za ▪ **T (023) 626·2033** ▪ F (023) 626·1277

Comfortable self-catering accommodation set in over 3 000 hectares of private nature reserve. Guests are spoilt for choice with beautiful scenery, mountain trails and swimming in mountain dams. Taste Rusticus red wines, join a guided game drive at sunset or book a massage therapy. A perfect retreat any time of the year. Small conference facilities available. (See also A-Z section for Rusticus Wines.)

Tierhoek Cottages Tierhoek Farm, Noree Valley, Robertson ▪ Double from R350, single from R175 ▪ No credit card facilities ▪ Pool ▪ TV (in 2 cottages) ▪ Owners Bruce & Alison Gilson ▪ gilson@intekom.co.za ▪ www.tierhoekcottages.co.za ▪ **T/F (023) 626·1191**

Pepper Tree, Lucky Bean and Tierhoek House are private, self-catering cottages situated on a working organic fruit and vine farm. Elegantly furnished, well equipped and romantic with open fireplaces, private verandahs and braai areas. Use of own private pools. Enjoy spectacular scenery with walks in the mountains and an abundance of bird- and wildlife. Breakfast and dinner 'baskets' on request.

Somerset West & Environs

Assegai Lodge 10 Harewood Avenue, Helderberg Estate, Somerset West ▪ R260–R320 pp sharing B&B, single R290–R350 B&B ▪ No credit card facilities ▪ Pool ▪ TV ▪ German spoken ▪ Owners Sue & Raimund Buchner ▪ rbuchner@worldonline.co.za ▪ **T (021) 855·2249** ▪ F (021) 855·4924 Fax/e-mail 086 616·1743

Come and enjoy a secluded and private atmosphere surrounded by trees and abundant birdlife. Centrally situated in the winelands, only 10 minutes drive to Stellenbosh or the False Bay beaches, with Cape Town and its international airport 30 minutes away. The lodge, because of its size, is a 'home from home' yet spacious and charming. Tiled floors with tastefully furnished reception rooms and bedrooms, all en suite with fridge and TV. Pool and barbeque facilities in tranquil gardens. Winetasting as well as arranged wine cellar and golf tours. (See also A-Z section.)

Ivory Heights Guesthouse & Conference 17 Louis Botha Avenue, Somerset West ▪ TGCSA 5-star ▪ R480 pp sharing B&B, single R580 B&B ▪ Major credit cards accepted ▪ Heated pool ▪ TV ▪ Air-conditioning ▪ Conference facilities ▪ Tennis & squash courts ▪ Gym ▪ Dutch & some German spoken ▪ Owners André & Sonnia du Plessis ▪ info@ivoryheights.co.za ▪ www.ivoryheights.co.za ▪ **T (021) 852·8333** ▪ F (021) 852·8886

Top quality accommodation and service with breathtaking views. The luxurious bedrooms are beautifully appointed with cotton linen, mini bar, air-conditioning, pool gowns and slippers. We offer tennis and squash courts, table tennis, a heated swimming pool, a pool table, dart boards, four lounges, two bars with big-screen TVs. Situated in the heart of the winelands, close to beaches and many golf courses.

La Bonne Auberge 21 Van Zyl Street, cnr Drama Street, Somerset West ▪ R295 pp sharing B&B, Deluxe R350 pp sharing B&B, single R395 B&B ▪ 1 Garden Cottage, 4 Suites B&B; 1 Petite Maisonette (self-catering) ▪ Major credit cards accepted ▪ Pool ▪ TV ▪ Air-conditioning ▪ German & French spoken ▪ Owners Yvonne & Frederick Thermann of well-known L'Auberge du Paysan restaurant ▪ info@labonneauberge.co.za ▪ www.labonneauberge.co.za ▪ **T (021) 852·0078** ▪ F (021) 850·0460

Under the oak trees in a leafy suburb with views of the Helderberg mountains, the restored, sunny Cape Dutch manor house bids you a warm welcome. The new garden cottage and suites are stylishly decorated and have private entrances, patios, fridges, safes, TVs, air-conditioning, off-street secure parking. Enjoy continental breakfast under the trees, swim in the large pool or relax in the leafy garden. Ideally situated for exploring the famous wine estates and fine restaurants of the Stellenbosch area. Professional, friendly service, comfort and value for money are what we are about. Satour 4-star. (See also Eat-out & A-Z sections for L'Auberge du Paysan.)

Spanish Farm Guest Lodge Silverboomkloof Road, Somerset West ▪ R460 pp sharing B&B, single R560 B&B (winter rates on request) ▪ Major credit cards accepted ▪ 2 Pools ▪ TV ▪ Air-conditioning ▪ Sauna ▪ Owner Clara Wiehahn ▪ info@spanishfarm.co.za ▪ www.spanishfarm.co.za ▪ **T (021) 852·7353** ▪ F (021) 851·3534

Spanish farm offers authentic Cape ambience and enjoyment on a private estate set on the slopes of the Helderberg mountain. Enjoy relaxed luxury while overlooking glorious views of mountain, valley and ocean. The staff offers friendly service. Bedrooms have satellite TV, air-conditioning, telephone. En-suite bathroom facilities, sauna, two swimming pools and putting green. Close to excellent golf courses, restaurants and wine farms.

Zandberg Farm Country House Winery Road, off R44 between Stellenbosch & Somerset West ▪ TGCSA 4-star ▪ Double R350–R650 B&B, single R450–R850 B&B ▪ Visa, MasterCard & American Express accepted ▪ Restaurant ▪ Pool ▪ TV ▪ Ceiling fans ▪ Gym ▪ Spa ▪ Putting green ▪ German spoken ▪ info@zandberg.co.za ▪ www.zandberg.co.za ▪ **T/F (021) 842·2945**

'A perfect little paradise', the farm dates back to 1690, with 11 beautifully installed cottages and two large suites in main house. Set in four acres of old park-like gardens, lake, swimming pool, wellness studio, gym, putting green and fine restaurant '96 Winery Road' on site, 10 minutes to beaches and golf course. Children under 12 stay free. Champagne breakfasts. (See also Eat-out & A-Z sections.)

Stellenbosch & Environs

33 Stellenbosch Vlottenburg Road (off R310), Vlottenburg, 5 km from Stellenbosch ▪ TGCSA 4-star ▪ From R350 pp sharing B&B, single from R500 B&B ▪ Major credit cards accepted ▪ Pool ▪ TV ▪ Air-conditioning ▪ Airport transfers ▪ Home cinema & conference centre ▪ French & German spoken ▪ Owners Simon Lavarack & Louise Obertüfer ▪ info@33.co.za ▪ www.33.co.za ▪ **T (021) 881·3792** ▪ F (021) 881·3177

33 Stellenbosch, built in 1903, is now an immaculately restored homestead, situated in the very heart of the historic and picturesque Stellenbosch winelands. Four luxury air-conditioned bedrooms overlook either the majestic Stellenbosch mountains in the distance or the beautiful piazza-styled courtyard and fountain. The two downstairs air-conditioned bedrooms are smaller with separate showers. A new pool was installed for summer where guests will be able to relax and unwind with light meals and an excellent winelist. 33 is renowned for its gracious hospitality and fine country living. Portfolio Collection, AA Quality Assured, 4-star TGCSA. (See also Eat-out section.)

Auberge Rozendal Rozendal Farm, Omega Street, Stellenbosch ▪ Double R945, single R575 ▪ Breakfast R35 continental/R60 full ▪ Major credit cards accepted ▪ Restaurant ▪ Pool ▪ German & Xhosa spoken ▪ Owners Ammann family ▪ rozendal@mweb.co.za ▪ www.rozendal.co.za ▪ **T (021) 809·2600** ▪ F (021) 809·2640

Auberge Rozendal is a charming country inn situated on our biodynamic wine farm on the outskirts of Stellenbosch. Comfortable rooms have a terrace and overlook Stellenbosch and the surrounding mountains. Our restaurant serves freshly prepared menus focusing on organic ingredients from our gardens. Relax around the pool or enjoy the surrounding nature. Thirty minutes from Cape Town International Airport, near many world-class golf courses. Stellenbosch Tourism Grading – Oak Leaf 3. (See also A-Z section.)

Batavia Boutique Hotel 12 Louw Street, Stellenbosch ▪ TGCSA 5-star ▪ R350-R700 pp sharing B&B, single R525-R1 050 B&B ▪ Major credit cards accepted ▪ Pool ▪ TV ▪ Air-conditioning ▪ General Manager Neil Büchner ▪ batavia@mweb.co.za ▪ www.bataviahouse.co.za ▪ **T (021) 887·2914** ▪ F (021) 887·2915

Off Dorp Street, the historic main street and village centre of Stellenbosch, you will find this luxurious, five-bedroom boutique hotel. If attention to detail, first-class service and an intimate experience in sincere hospitality are what you are looking for to make your stay in the Cape winelands memorable, look no further than Batavia Boutique Hotel. AA Accommodation Awards Winner – Best Boutique Hotel 2005.

Caledon Villa Guest House 7 Neethling Street, Stellenbosch ▪ TGCSA 4-star ▪ National monument ▪ R350 pp sharing (in season), R300 pp sharing (out of season) ▪ 15 rooms – suite, luxury, honeymoon, standard or family ▪ Major credit cards accepted ▪ Large pool ▪ Secure off-street parking ▪ Library ▪ Children by appointment ▪ German spoken ▪ Owners Johan & Ode Krige ▪ info@caledonvilla.co.za ▪ www.caledonvilla.co.za ▪ **T/F (021) 883·8912**

Enjoy a holiday rich in cultural exchange and personal care. Owners Johan and Ode share with you their passion for arts and culture but also their love for wine, grown from the Krige family's strong involvement in wine farming for 300 years and their historical link with many of today's well-known vineyards. Discover the winelands from this splendid Edwardian guesthouse with Art Nouveau decor, located in the historical centre of Stellenbosch. Within walking distance from fine restaurants, shops, sports facilities and university. Centrally located to golf and wine estates. Whether you are looking for sheer leisure, are on honeymoon or doing business, Caledon Villa will cater for your individual needs.

Camberley Guest Cottage Camberley Wines, off R310, Banhoek, Stellenbosch ▪ R350 pp sharing, single R450 – breakfast optional ▪ Major credit cards accepted ▪ Pool ▪ TV & DSTV ▪ Xhosa spoken ▪ Owners Gaël & John Nel ▪ john@camberley.co.za ▪ www.camberley.co.za ▪ **T/ F (021) 885·1176**

Tucked away on the Helshoogte Pass, surrounded by beautiful gardens and vineyards with spectacular mountain views, is our elegantly decorated cottage. Often referred to as one of the area's best-kept secrets, the cottage offers guests home-from-home comforts with a fully equipped kitchen, dining area and lounge with DSTV and fireplace. The verandah overlooks the plunge pool in a private garden.

Dankbaarheid Self-catering Guest House Eikendal Road, off R44 between Stellenbosch & Somerset West ▪ TGCSA 3-star ▪ Price per unit from R290 (studio) to R800 (luxury apartment) ▪ No credit card facilities ▪ TV ▪ French & German spoken ▪ Owners Kristo & Tita Truter ▪ dankbaar@adept.co.za ▪ www.dankbaar.co.za ▪ **T/F (021) 855·4907**

Voted one of South Africa's best farm stays and 3-star graded, Dankbaarheid wine farm is set in the 'golden triangle' wine area of Stellenbosch and offers four comfortable self-catering apartments (sleeping 2-5) with quality fixtures, automatic shutters, braai, private patios, secure parking, views and more. Resident owners and hosts Kristo and Tita Truter give their guests personal attention and advice.

De Goue Druif 110 Dorp Street, Stellenbosch ▪ TGCSA 4-star ▪ National monument ▪ R375 pp sharing B&B, single R650 B&B ▪ Visa & MasterCard accepted ▪ Pool ▪ TV ▪ Air-conditioning ▪ Gym ▪ Sauna ▪ French, German & Flemish spoken ▪ Owner Katrien Cools ▪ gouedruif@new.co.za ▪ http://gouedruif.hypermart.net ▪ **T (021) 883·3555** ▪ F (021) 883·3588

A 4-star graded guesthouse in a national monument situated in the centre of Stellenbosch. Restaurants in walking distance. Cape history is gracefully blended with luxury. The suites have all the modern facilities: air-conditioning, heating, superb breakfasts, gym, sauna, steam bath, pool, lush garden, undercover parking. Impressive collection of South African wines.

Devon Valley Hotel Devon Valley Road, Stellenbosch ▪ TGCSA 4-star ▪ R585 pp sharing B&B, single R795 B&B ▪ Major credit cards accepted ▪ Flavours Restaurant ▪ Pool ▪ TV & DSTV ▪ Air-conditioning ▪ German spoken ▪ Owner LGI Hotels & Vineyards ▪ info@devonvalleyhotel.com ▪ www.devonvalleyhotel.com ▪ **T (021) 865·2012** ▪ F(021) 865·2610

This much-loved Stellenbosch landmark has recently been rejuvenated. Over 50 years old, the charming Devon Valley Hotel offers spectacular valley and mountain views, 38 stylishly decorated rooms, innovative contemporary Cape cuisine and an award-winning winelist. Walk through beautiful gardens, swim in one of the two pools, gaze over their own vineyards or just sit on the terrace, admire the view and enjoy their award-winning SylvanVale wines. At night, relax in front of the log fire in the Cedarwood Lounge and savour one of the largest collections of single malt whiskies in the country. (See also Eat-out section & A–Z for SylvanVale.)

Grange Cottage Grangehurst, Eikendal Road (off R44), Stellenbosch ▪ R490 per cottage plus additional R50 for 1-night stay ▪ Self-catering ▪ Major credit cards accepted ▪ Pool ▪ Satellite TV ▪ Owner Jeremy Walker ▪ winery@grangehurst.co.za ▪ www.grangehurst.co.za ▪ **T (021) 855·3625** ▪ F (021) 855·2143

Situated on a working winery in the heart of the winelands, this well-equipped self-catering cottage offers a large airy bedroom, a balcony which leads from the living room where guests can enjoy the wonderful views, a full bathroom and large kitchen/dining area. Underfloor heating is available for winter months and a large swimming pool for the summer months. Stellenbosch Tourism Grading – Oak Leaf 3½. (See also A–Z section.)

Kleine Zalze Lodges Kleine Zalze Wine Farm, Technopark Road, off R44, Stellenbosch ▪ From R345 pp sharing, single from R690 ▪ Breakfast R55 pp ▪ Major credit cards accepted ▪ Terroir Restaurant ▪ Pool ▪ Satellite TV ▪ Air-conditioning ▪ Conference/wedding venue (100 pax) ▪ De Zalze Golf Course ▪ German spoken ▪ Owner Kleine Zalze Lodges (Pty) Ltd ▪ slailvaux@kleinezalze.co.za ▪ www.kleinezalze.com ▪ **T (021) 880·0740** ▪ F (021) 880·2215

Situated three km from Stellenbosch, our stylishly decorated 53-roomed lodges are surrounded by vineyards, the magnificent Stellenbosch mountains and De Zalze golf course. Enjoy tasting our award-winning wines and dining at *Terroir*, our classical Provençal restaurant. Other facilities include an 18-hole golf course, 17-metre long swimming pool, mountain biking and vineyard walks. (See also Eat-out & A–Z sections.)

Knorhoek Guest House Knorhoek Farm, Knorhoek Road, off R44, Koelenhof ▪ TGCSA 3-star ▪ R310 pp sharing B&B, single R410 B&B ▪ Major credit cards accepted ▪ Restaurant – dinners Mon-Thu ▪ Pool ▪ TV ▪ Xhosa spoken ▪ Owners Carol & Ingrid van Niekerk ▪ guesthouse@knorhoek.co.za ▪ www.knorhoek.co.za ▪ **T (021) 865·2114** ▪ F (021) 865·2627

A wine and accommodation experience! Enjoy the seclusion of this beautiful historic farm, ideally situated to explore the Cape. Individually decorated en-suite rooms with all required amenities and a wine cellar at the bottom of the garden. Hearty Cape breakfasts indoors or alfresco, dinners Mon-Thu, winetasting, summer lunches at the unique rock pool. Ten top golf courses within 30 min. (See also A–Z section.)

L'Avenir Wine Estate Guest House Klapmuts Road (R44), Stellenbosch ▪ R500-R950 per room B&B (seasonal) ▪ Major credit cards accepted ▪ Meals on request ▪ Pool ▪ TV ▪ Ceiling fans ▪ French spoken ▪ Owner Marc Wiehe ▪ lavenir@adept.co.za ▪ www.lavenir.co.za ▪ **T (021) 889·5001** ▪ F (021) 889·5258

This is a wine lover's heaven: nine en-suite bedrooms around a large pool on a wine estate with 70 hectares of prime vineyards to wander in, cellar tours and award-winning wines at cellar prices. Relaxed and unhurried luxury, only five minutes from Stellenbosch, 20 minutes from the airport and the beaches of the Strand, 50 minutes from Cape Town. (See also A–Z section.)

Marianne Wine Farm Marianne Wine Farm, Valley Road, off R44, between Stellenbosch & Klapmuts ▪ High season: double R690 B&B, single R525 B&B ▪ Visa & MasterCard accepted ▪ Olivello Restaurant ▪ Pool ▪ TV ▪ German spoken ▪ info@mariannewinefarm.co.za ▪ www.mariannewinefarm.co.za ▪ **T (021) 875·5040** ▪ F (021) 875·5036

Surrounded by citrus orchards and vineyards, our spacious and comfortable apartments are uniquely African in style. Enjoy scenic walks through the vineyards, relax at the swimming pool, winetasting and horse riding nearby. Breakfast is served at the nearby waterside restaurant – Olivello – offering Cape comfort food enhanced by delicious Mediterranean flavours. Children are welcome. Secure parking. (See also Eat-out section.)

Muratie Wine Estate Knorhoek Road, off R44, Koelenhof ▪ R295 pp B&B ▪ Major credit cards accepted ▪ Owners Melck Family Trust ▪ muratie@kingsley.co.za ▪ www.muratie.co.za ▪ **T (021) 865·2330** ▪ F (021) 865·2790

This unusual setting, a converted artist's studio in the winelands, offers peaceful tranquility. Situated on a working wine estate, the ambience is absolutely awesome. With a direct view of Table Mountain in the distance, the evenings are an absolute treat at sundowner time. Being able to walk across to the cellar for a winetasting is just as enjoyable. Stellenbosch Tourism Grading – Oak Leaf 4. (See also A–Z section.)

Natte Valleij Farm Klapmuts Road (R44), 12 km north of Stellenbosch towards Paarl ▪ R240 pp B&B ▪ Self-catering: Vineyard Cottage from R475 & Cellar Cottage from R420 per cottage per day ▪ Owners Charles & Charlene Milner ▪ milner@intekom.co.za ▪ www.nattevalleij.co.za ▪ **T (021) 875·5171** ▪ F (021) 875·5475

Situated below the Simonsberg mountains in the prime winegrowing Muldersvlei bowl where the Stellenbosch wine route meets the Paarl wine route, Charles and Charlene Milner's historic farm, the first land grant of the area, offers a B&B option as well as self-catering. Vineyard Cottage can sleep 6 in 3 double bedrooms, with 2 bathrooms, sitting room and dining room; Cellar Cottage sleeps 2 with the option of 2 extra beds in the sitting room. Both cottages have their own stoep (patio) and braai (bbq). There is a secluded swimming pool in the large garden and horse riding can be done from the farm. Outrides go through vineyards and mountain foothills in the most beautiful surroundings.

Ons Genot Country Lodge Bottelary Road, Stellenbosch ▪ TGCSA 4-star ▪ From R290 pp B&B (low season) to R450 pp B&B (high season) ▪ Major credit cards accepted ▪ Restaurant ▪ Pool ▪ TV ▪ Air-conditioning ▪ Conference Room ▪ Dutch, French & German spoken ▪ Owners Eric & Marleen Bovijn ▪ info@onsgenot.com ▪ www.onsgenot.com ▪ **T (021) 865·2233** ▪ F (021) 865·2250

Ons Genot is an exclusive 4-star country retreat on the outskirts of historic Stellenbosch and a finalist in the AA Accommodation Awards 02, 03 & 04. Features include luxury en-suite air-conditioned rooms with private terrace and attractive garden, television, mini-bar, wall safe, phone, bathroom with bath and shower. In addition, the honeymoon suite has a private jacuzzi. Conference room for 20 people. The restaurant at Ons Genot offers breakfast, lunch and dinner (see also Eat-out section).

The Village Hotel at Spier R310, Lynedoch Road, Stellenbosch ▪ R1 450 per room B&B ▪ Major credit cards accepted ▪ 4 Restaurants ▪ 7 Swimming pools ▪ 3 Tennis courts (1 floodlit) ▪ Air-conditioning ▪ TV ▪ Camelot Spa ▪ Banqueting & conference facilities ▪ Cheetah Outreach Centre ▪ Eagle Encounters ▪ Xhosa spoken ▪ info@spier.co.za ▪ www.spier.co.za ▪ **T (021) 809·1100** ▪ F (021) 881·3634

With 155 rooms nestled in traditional Cape-styled buildings centred around six private courtyards, the Village offers a tranquil escape to those in need of some time out from the world. Figaro's restaurant is situated adjacent to the reception area of the hotel and offers a breathtaking view of the surrounding Helderberg mountains. (See also Eat-out & A-Z sections).

Swellendam & Environs

Jan Harmsgat Country House On the R60, between Swellendam & Ashton ▪ TGCSA 4-star ▪ R750 pp sharing B&B, single R900 B&B ▪ Major credit cards accepted ▪ Restaurant (dinner only) ▪ Pool ▪ Air-conditioning ▪ German spoken ▪ Owners Brin & Judi Rebstein ▪ brinreb@iafrica.com ▪ www.jhghouse.com ▪ **T (023) 616·3407** ▪ F (023) 616·3201

A true country house. Set among pecan nut, almond and fruit orchards, famous for the production of a range of cheeses and preserves. Four-star graded luxury accommodation, delectable cuisine and superb collection of wines. Multiple award winners for outstanding service in the development and inclusion of local communities in tourism. Awarded Fair Trade in Tourism Trademark during 2005. Two hours from Cape Town between Swellendam and Ashton on the Robertson wine route.

Klippe Rivier Country House From N2 take R60, turn left at 4-way stop, cross bridge over River Road (becomes gravel for 1,7 km), Swellendam district ▪ TGCSA 5-star ▪ R895 pp sharing B&B (R850 pp for 2 or more nights), single R1 195 B&B (R1 150 for 2 or more nights) ▪ Major credit cards accepted ▪ Restaurant ▪ Pool ▪ TV in library ▪ Air-conditioning ▪

Children 8+ welcome ▪ German spoken ▪ Owner Liz Westby-Nunn ▪ info@klipperivier.com ▪ www.klipperivier.com ▪ **T (028) 514·3341** ▪ F (028) 514·3337

A magnificent Cape Dutch country house. Converted *'waenhuis'* and stables have six luxury air-conditioned bedrooms. Three downstairs rooms have an open fireplace, dressing room and generous bathroom with separate shower and toilet. Three loft rooms, under thatch, have stunning mountain views and private balconies. A secluded cottage, ideal for honeymooners or the more romantic, has an open fireplace and DSTV.

Tulbagh

Lemberg Wine Estate and Guest House Off the R46 near Nuwekloof Pass, Straatskerk Road, 4 km west of Tulbagh ▪ R300 pp sharing B&B ▪ Major credit cards accepted ▪ German spoken ▪ Owners Uschi & Klaus Schindler ▪ schindler@lando.co.za ▪ www.kapstadt.de/lemberg ▪ **T (023) 230·0659** ▪ F (023) 230·0661

Set fairly privately in the lush garden of this boutique wine estate, a stylish and spacious rondavel offers discerning guests (up to four people) a perfect and peaceful retreat. Overlooking the lake with plenty of birds and panoramic mountain views for an unforgettable delicious breakfast experience in the garden. Gourmet evening dinners are served in the rondavel (self-catering option). Pre-booked lunches for day visitors also available. German owner (professional hunter) offers hunting trips (one or more days) to nearby hunting farms. (See also A–Z section.)

Wellington

Diemersfontein Guest House Jan van Riebeeck Drive (R301), Wellington ▪ R350 pp B&B ▪ Major credit cards accepted ▪ Restaurant ▪ Pool ▪ Air-conditioning (some rooms) ▪ Conference centre ▪ Wedding venue ▪ Owners David & Susan Sonnenberg ▪ ringrose@iafrica.com ▪ www.diemersfontein.co.za ▪ **T (021) 864·5050** ▪ F (021) 864·2095

The Diemersfontein Guest House accommodation is spread out over beautifully appointed garden rooms and vineyard cottages totalling 18 double rooms (16 en suite). Centrally situated Tulani Cottage boasts lounge, TV room, honesty bar and verandah, while the beautiful Diemersfontein gardens provide a fitting backdrop to the swimming pool area. Winter weekend packages offer guests the opportunity to leave the stresses of city life behind and enjoy log fires, great wine and food in breathtaking surrounds. (See also Eat-out section for Seasons at Diemersfontein & A–Z section.)

Klein Rheboksskloof Country House Hildenbrand Wine & Olive Estate, 5km outside Wellington, follow signs ▪ R280 pp sharing B&B, single R380 B&B ▪ Visa & MasterCard accepted ▪ Restaurant ▪ Pool ▪ German spoken ▪ Owner Reni Hildenbrand ▪ info@wine-estate-hildenbrand.co.za ▪ www.wine-estate-hildenbrand.co.za ▪ **T (021) 873·4115** ▪ F 086 670·0147

A separate traditional building offers four spacious bedrooms with all the comforts including verandah, ceiling fan, fridge, radio and tea tray. Two cottages and one bedroom suite have their own fireplaces, a living room and a kitchenette. The swimming pool with sundeck and sitting area under mature trees offers peace and quiet with spectacular views. A full country-style breakfast is served inside or outside. (See also A–Z section.)

Worcester

Nuy Valley Restaurant & Guesthouse Werda farm, Nuy, Worcester ▪ TGCSA 3-star ▪ R200 pp sharing, single R220 ▪ Major credit cards accepted ▪ Restaurant ▪ Pool ▪ TV ▪ Air-conditioning ▪ German spoken ▪ Owners Irma & Pieter Conradie ▪ nuyvallei@xpoint.co.za ▪ www.nuyvallei.co.za ▪ **T (023) 342·1258** ▪ F (023) 347·1356

This family-owned wine farm is situated in one of the most beautiful valleys of the Cape winelands on the popular Route 62. The Nuy Valley turn-off is about 20 km from Worcester. Nuy Valley Guest Farm offers accommodation with a warm and homely atmosphere. We have 18 en-suite rooms and cater for weddings and conferences. A la carte restaurant and boutique wine cellar. (See also Eat-out section & A–Z section for Conradie Family Vineyards.)

Wine & food partners

Here are some recommendations on matching cuisine and wine:

Artichokes Make most wines taste metallic. Drink water or squeeze lemon onto the chokes, which seems to tone down the tinny edges, and team with a high-acid, fresh dry white.

Asparagus A difficult customer. A dry white with lots of flavour like fresh sauvignon.

Avocado Riesling, white port.

Barbecue See Braai below.

Beef Roast: Cape Bdx blend, cab, cab franc, merlot, pinot; just about any serious red. Cold roast beef: room for a bit of light here, reds that can take a spot of chilling, pinot; also rosé, blanc de noir, sparkling dry rosé. See also Stews below.

Biltong (savoury air-dried meat snack, usually sliced) Not usually partnered with wine, but try robust shiraz (or beer).

Bobotie (spicy ground-meat, usually lamb) Many possible wine-partners: try dry sparkling, fresh young chenin, riesling, pinotage or other fruity, easy-drinking reds.

Bouillabaisse Fresh young white, sauvignon, dry rosé.

Braai (the traditional barbecue, a national institution) Depends on what's being braaied, but whether meat, fish or fowl, choose a wine with character and muscle, not a fragile little thing that would be overwhelmed by the smoke for a start.

Carpaccio Meat: Just about any red. Fish: chardonnay, MCC.

Charcuterie Simple fresh reds.

Cheese A good cheddar can be excellent with an elegant red or ruby port. Cream cheese is better with full-bodied whites – try semillon or chardonnay. Goat's cheese: full-bodied white or dry red. Blue cheese: as long as it's not too powerful, good with rich dessert whites such as NLH and port.

Chicken Roast: best red or white. Pie: try light to medium shiraz or young pinotage.

Chinese MCC, dry (or dryish) white with flavour; riesling.

Chocolate Difficult. Demi-sec bubbly, fruity dry red, red muscadel, Cape Pineau des Charentes. Or wait and have a glass of dry bubbly after the choc mousse.

Crudités Simple dry white.

Curry Fish curry: wooded chardonnay is good, especially when coconut milk is an ingredient. A cheerful, slightly off-dry (and slightly pétillant) chenin blend is fine too. Also blanc de noir. Sweetish Cape Malay curries: try matching the spice with gewürz or young riesling, or contrasting with sauvignon.

Desserts See Chocolate above.

Duck Fruity young red, champagne, shiraz, off-dry riesling, pinot.

Eggs Not great for or with any wine, but a simple omelette calls for a simple glass of red.

Foie gras Sweet white, NLH/SLH, MCC, merlot.

Fruit MCC, sweet sparkling wine, Late or Special Late Harvest, hanepoot jerepiko or rosé. Strawberries: with cream: NLH; without cream: light red.

Game birds Rosé, pinot or Cape Bdx blend. Remember, the darker the meat, the darker/stronger the wine. Guinea fowl: pinot, merlot or powerful oaked chenin.

Ham Young pinot; fresh, juicy red.

Hamburgers Dry, simple red.

Ice-cream (If not too sweet) Good bubbly.

Kidneys Full red, riesling, chardonnay.

Lamb and **mutton** Roast: best red (cabernet, merlot etc). Chops: shiraz or young cab. Try to avoid mint sauce – it distorts the taste of even minty, new-clone contenders. Stews: light red.

Liver Fruity, forceful young red such as pinotage.

Mushrooms Pinot or just about any well-aged red.

Mustard sauce Light red, pinotage.

Nuts Port after a meal; sherry before; nutty desserts: MCC.

Oxtail Shiraz, zinfandel.

Pasta Seafood: sauvignon, down-table chardonnay; cream, cheese, egg, meat, tomato sauces: sturdy red.

Pastries and **cakes** SLH.

Pâté Champagne, gewürz, riesling, pinot.

Phutu or mealie meal (SA equivalent of **polenta**) Sturdy red.

Pizza Depends on ingredients, but also see pasta above.

Pork Off-dry white, fruity red, rosé, zinfandel. Pinotage with spare ribs. In Portugal, roast sucking pig is often teamed with bubbly.

Quiche Full fruity white, riesling, gewürz, sylvaner.

Rabbit Depends on how it's cooked, and the ingredients. Anything from great to simple, red or white.

Ratatouille Light, fruity red, rosé, blanc de noir.

Risotto Fish: medium-bodied dry white; mushrooms: pinot.

Salads Go easy on the vinaigrette – vinegar affects wine. A prickly fresh white or rosé with a salade niçoise. Chardonnay with a grand shellfish salad. Or something non-serious like a blanc de noir. Or top up one's water table.

Seafood

- **Fish** Dry sparkling, MCC or dry white (sauvignon or chardonnay, or a chardonnay blend) are safe choices for saltwater; more delicate white or MCC for freshwater. Grilled: sauvignon; cream sauce: chardonnay, chardonnay blend. With red-wine sauce: red used in recipe or pinot. Smoked: crisp aromatic white, sauvignon, full-bodied (wooded) chardonnay, gewürz or riesling, dry or with a touch of sugar. Sushi: a not-too-grand (or too rich) chardonnay, brut sparkling.
- **Shellfish** Grilled, boiled, steamed or cold (with mayonnaise): sauvignon, crisp young chenin or off-dry riesling. Rich sauce: MCC or chardonnay-semillon blend. Piri-piri: this spicy/hot sauce calls for a light pétillant white.
- **Calamari** (squid) Sauvignon, dry white blend or light red.
- **Cape salmon** (geelbek) Racy sauvignon.
- **Caviar** MCC.
- **Crab** Riesling or off-dry chenin.
- **Crayfish** (Cape rock lobster or *kreef)* Sauvignon or chardonnay.
- **Elf** (shad) Chardonnay, dry chenin or Cape riesling.
- **Galjoen** Sauvignon, chardonnay or full-flavoured blanc de noir.
- **Kingklip** Chardonnay or wood-matured white.
- **Langoustine** (deep-sea, from SA's East Coast) MCC, chardonnay.
- **Mussels** Sauvignon or chenin. Smoked: wooded chardonnay
- **Oysters** MCC, sauvignon, lightly wooded or unwooded chardonnay.
- **Perlemoen** (abalone) Chardonnay or sauvignon.
- **Prawns** Chardonnay or sauvignon.
- **Salmon** Chardonnay or fruity non-tannic young red.
- **Sardines** (grilled) Crisp pétillant white, young red.
- **Smoorvis** (braised fish, usually lightly spicy) Frisky (off-dry) chenin, chardonnay or young pinotage.
- **Snoek** Assertive dry white, young red or pinotage.
- **Sole** Grilled: sauvignon or Cape riesling. Sauced: chardonnay.
- **Trout** Young riesling

Snacks Of the canapé sort: aperitif white, fruity, dry to off-dry, kir, sparkling white/rosé, blanc de noir, dry sherry.

Snails Chardonnay, pinot, dry riesling.

Sosaties Local version of the south-east Asian satay; as for curry.

Soufflés Cheese: red; fish: white; dessert: dessert white.

Steak Red wine: cab, merlot, shiraz – take your pick. Pepper steak: somehow smoothes tannins, so doesn't need a mellow old bottle.

Stews and **bredies** Hearty red. Fish casserole: fresh young white, sauvignon or dry rosé. Waterblommetjie bredie: sauvignon, chardonnay, young pinotage or merlot.

Sweetbreads Chardonnay, fine claret, pinot.

Thai Draughts of cool fresh dry white for the chilli-hot dishes. Lemongrass, coconut milk and good (wooded) chardonnay go surprisingly well together. A chilled nouveau style could hold its own. Or riesling.

Tongue Gently dry white, fruity red.

Tripe Hearty red, simple dry white or dry rosé. With tomato: dry red. With onions or white sauce: off-dry chenin or chenin-blend.

Turkey Zinfandel, dry rosé, pinot.

Veal Take your pick, depending on preparation. With vitello tonnato try a chilled, light red.

Vegetables Sauvignon, probably.

Venison Powerful pinot, pinotage, shiraz or mature Cape Bdx blend.

Winelands Maps

The maps in this section show locales where wine is available for tasting/sale either at set times or by appointment. The larger-scale map below shows the areas covered by the maps, and the table starting on the next page lists some details for prospective visitors.

Areas covered by the maps

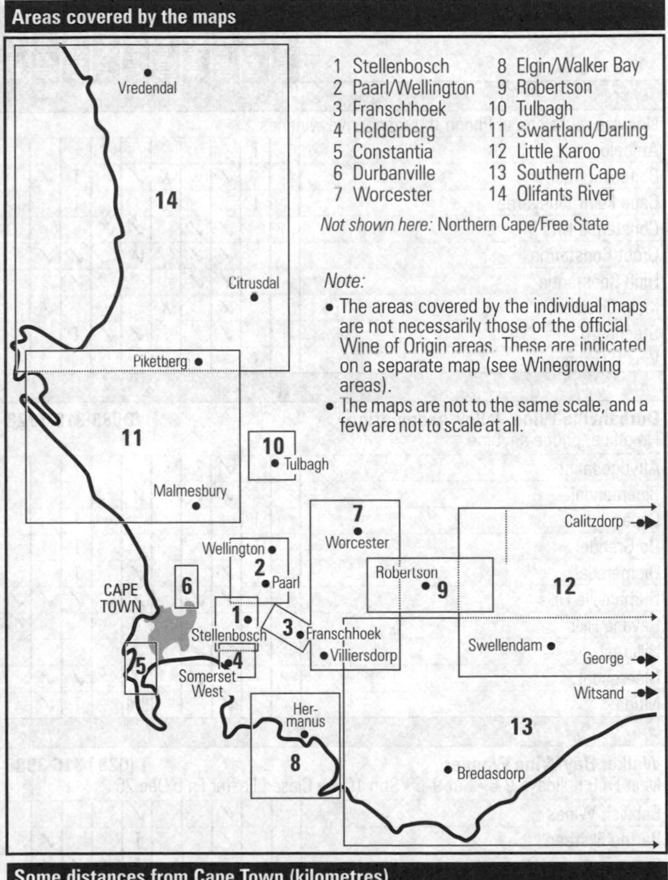

Some distances from Cape Town (kilometres)

Calitzdorp	370	Paarl	60	Tulbagh	120
Franschhoek	75	Robertson	160	Vredendal	300
Hermanus	120	Stellenbosch	45	Worcester	110

Key for maps

- Main access roads
- Roads
- Gravel roads
- R62 R60 Road numbers
- Towns

Details of locales shown on maps

The table below summarises the following details by region: map grid-reference, if applicable; whether open by appointment only (T), open on Saturdays, Sundays (✓ = at set times; T = by appointment), public holidays (✗ = closed all public holidays; otherwise assume open all or some holidays); availability of meals/refreshments (BYO = bring picnic), accommodation, cellar tours, facilities for children; and disabled friendliness, as audited by our disability consultant. For detailed information, see the A–Z and Eat-out/Stay-over sections.

	Grid ref	Open by appt only	Open Saturdays	Open Sundays	Open pub. holidays	Meals/refreshments	Accommodation	Cellar tours	Disabled friendly	Child friendly
Constantia/Cape Point										
No wine route office. Phone the respective wineries.										
Ambeloui		T								
Buitenverwachting			✓		✗	✓		T	✓	
Cape Point Vineyards		T						T		
Constantia Uitsig			✓	✓		✓	✓			
Groot Constantia			✓	✓		✓		✓	✓	
High Constantia			✓	✓				✓		
Klein Constantia			✓		✗				✓	
Steenberg			✓			✓	✓	T	✓	
Vins D'Orrance		T								
Durbanville/Philadelphia										
Durbanville Wine Valley Association — **T 083·310·1228** No office, phone anytime										
Altydgedacht			✓					T		
Bloemendal			✓	✓		✓				
Capaia		T						T		
De Grendel		T						T		
Diemersdal			✓			✓		T		
Durbanville Hills			✓	✓		✓		✓	✓	✓
Havana Hills		T								
Hillcrest			✓	✓		✓				
Meerendal			✓	✓		✓		✓	✓	
Nitida			✓			BYO		T	✓	
Elgin/Walker Bay										
Walker Bay Wine Wander — **T (028) 316·3988** Mon-Fri & holidays 9-6 • Sat 9-5 • Sun 10-3 • Closed Easter Fri & Dec 25										
Babylon Wines			✓			✓				
Bartho Eksteen			✓			T			✓	
Beaumont			T			T	✓	✓	✓	
Bouchard Finlayson			✓		✗				✓	
Dispore Kamma		T								
Feiteiras Vineyards			✓	✓		T		✓		
Gehot Bosch			✓	✓				✓		
Goedvertrouw		T				T	T			✓
Hamilton Russell Vineyards			✓			BYO		T		
Hemelzicht			✓		✗					

	Grid ref	Open by appt only	Open Saturdays	Open Sundays	Open pub. holidays	Meals/refreshments	Accommodation	Cellar tours	Disabled friendly	Child friendly
Iona						BYO	✓	✓		
Keisseskraal Vineyards			T			BYO		✓		
Luddite		T								
Newton Johnson/Cape Bay			✓		✗					
Oak Valley										
Paul Cluver			✓			BYO	✓		✓	
Raka			✓			BYO		T		
Ross Gower/Elgin Vintners					✗	✓	✓	T		
Springfontein		T				T	✓	T		✓
Stanford Hills/Mauroma		T					✓			
Sumaridge			✓	✓		✓	✓			
Thandi			✓	✓		✓		T		
Whalehaven/Idiom			✓			BYO		T		
Wildekrans (Farm/cellar differ - see A-Z entry)			✓	✓		✓	✓	T		✓
Wildekrans (Orchard Farm Stall)			✓	✓						✓

Franschhoek

Vignerons de Franschhoek **T 876·3062**

Mon-Fri 9-6 (Oct-Apr); 9-5 (May-Sep) ▪ Sat 10-5 ▪ Sun & holidays 10-4 ▪ Closed Good Fri and Dec 25

	Grid ref	Open by appt only	Open Saturdays	Open Sundays	Open pub. holidays	Meals/refreshments	Accommodation	Cellar tours	Disabled friendly	Child friendly
Akkerdal		T	✓		✗		✓			
Allée Bleue			✓	✓		✓				
Blueberry Hill		T					✓			
Boekenhoutskloof		T								
Boschendal			✓	✓		✓		T	✓	
Cabrière			✓			✓		✓	✓	
Cape Chamonix			✓	✓		✓	✓	T	✓	✓
Dieu Donné			✓	✓		✓		T		
Eikehof		T						T		
Franschhoek Vineyards			✓	✓		✓				
GlenWood			✓	✓		BYO		✓		
Graham Beck Wines			✓					T		
Grande Provence			✓	✓		✓	✓	T	✓	
Haut Espoir		T						T		
La Bri					✗					
La Chaumiere		T						T		
La Couronne			T		✗	✓	✓	T		✓
La Motte			✓			✓			✓	
La Petite Ferme			✓	✓		✓	✓			
Landau du Val		T								
Le Manoir de Brendel			✓			✓	✓			
L'Ormarins			✓			✓				
Lynx Wines			✓				✓			
Mont Rochelle			✓	✓		✓		✓		
Môreson			✓	✓		✓		T	✓	
Plaisir de Merle			✓				T	T		

	Grid ref	Open by appt only	Open Saturdays	Open Sundays	Open pub. holidays	Meals/refreshments	Accommodation	Cellar tours	Disabled friendly	Child friendly
Rickety Bridge			✓			BYO		T		
Solms-Delta			✓	✓		✓		✓		
Stony Brook			✓							
Von Ortloff		T						T		
Helderberg										
Stellenbosch American Express Wine Routes (Helderberg office) T 852·6166 Phone for information										
Agterplaas		T							✓	
Assegai		T					✓			
Avontuur			✓	✓		✓		T	✓	
Conspirare		T								
Cordoba		T			✗			T		
Dellrust			✓		✗			T	✓	✓
Eikendal			✓	✓		✓	✓	✓	✓	✓
Flagstone			T	T				T		
Grangehurst			✓				✓			
Helderberg/Omnia			✓			✓				
Ingwe		T								
JP Bredell					✗			T		
Ken Forrester/Meinert/Zandberg (96 Wnry Rd)			✓	✓		✓	✓	T	✓	
L'Auberge						✓			✓	
Longridge			✓			BYO			✓	
Lourensford			✓	✓				✓		
Lushof			T		✗			T		
Lyngrove		T					✓			
Morgenster			✓		✗			T		
Mount Rozier		T			✗			T		
Onderkloof						✓		T		
Post House			T							
Romond		T								
Somerbosch			✓	✓		✓		T	✓	✓
Stonewall		T	T							
Vergelegen			✓	✓		✓		✓	✓	
Waterhof		T				✓		T		
Wedderwill		T								
Yonder Hill					✗			✓		
Little Karoo										
Little/Klein Karoo Wine Route T (028) 572·1284 Phone Ellen Marais Mon-Fri 9-5										
Calitzdorp Wine Route T (044) 213·3775 Open daily 9-5										
Outeniqua Wine Route T 072·833·8223/(044) 873·4212 Phone for information										
Axe Hill		T								
Barrydale			✓			BYO		T		

	Grid ref	Open by appt only	Open Saturdays	Open Sundays	Open pub. holidays	Meals/refreshments	Accommodation	Cellar tours	Disabled friendly	Child friendly
Bloupunt		T								
Boplaas			✓			T		T		
Calitzdorp			✓			BYO		T		
De Krans			✓			✓		T	✓	
Domein Doornkraal			✓			✓		T		
Grundheim			✓							
Herold		T						T		
Joubert-Tradauw			✓			✓	✓	T		✓
Kango			✓			BYO		T		
Ladismith					✗	BYO		T		
Schoonberg		T								
Mons Ruber			✓							
Montagu			✓		✗	BYO			✓	
Peter Bayly		T								
Rietrivier					✗	✓		T		
Uitvlucht			✓						✓	
Withoek							✓	T		

Northern Cape/Free State/North West

Northern Cape Wine Association T (054) 337·8800
Mon-Fri 7.30-5

	Grid ref	Open by appt only	Open Saturdays	Open Sundays	Open pub. holidays	Meals/refreshments	Accommodation	Cellar tours	Disabled friendly	Child friendly
Douglas Cellar					✗	BYO		T		
Goudveld			T					✓		
Groblershoop			✓		✗			✓		
Grootdrink			✓		✗			✓		
Hartswater			T			✓		T		
Kakamas			✓		✗			✓		
Keimoes			✓		✗			✓		
Landzicht			✓		✗	T		T		✓
Oranjerivier/Upington			✓		✗			✓	✓	

Olifants River

Olifants River Vodacom Wine Route T (027) 213·3126/082·611·3999
Mon-Fri 8-5 ▪ Sat 8-1 Closed Good Fri & Dec 25

	Grid ref	Open by appt only	Open Saturdays	Open Sundays	Open pub. holidays	Meals/refreshments	Accommodation	Cellar tours	Disabled friendly	Child friendly
Cederberg			✓			✓	✓	✓		
Citrusdal Cellars			✓			BYO	✓	T	✓	
Excelsious			✓							
Johan van Zyl Wines		T								
Keukenhof		T						T		✓
Klawer			✓		✗	BYO			✓	
Lutzville			✓		✗	✓		T	✓	
Stellar Winery			✓					T		
Teubes Family		T			✗					
WestCorp/Vredendal			✓		✗	T		T	✓	

Paarl & Wellington

Paarl Vintners ▪ T 863·4886
Mon-Fri 8-5

Wellington Wine Route ▪ T 873·4604
Mon-Fri 8-5 ▪ Sat 9-2 ▪ Closed Christian holidays

	Grid ref	Open by appt only	Open Saturdays	Open Sundays	Open pub. holidays	Meals/refreshments	Accommodation	Cellar tours	Disabled friendly	Child friendly
African Terroir	C1					✓	✓	T		
Anura/Sequillo	C7		✓	✓		✓		T		
Ashanti	F5		✓	✓		✓		T	✓	
Avondale	F6		✓					T	✓	
Avondvrede	C8	T				T		T		
Backsberg	D8		✓	✓		✓		✓	✓	✓
Bergheim	E5	T						T		
Bernheim	E3		✓					T	✓	
Black Pearl	D5	T						T		✓
Blyde Wines	E5		✓					T		
Boland	E4		✓					T		
Bovlei	G2		✓					T	✓	
Carolinahoeve	E1		✓	✓	✗	✓				
Coleraine	D6	T						T		
Cowlin	D8		✓			BYO		T		✓
Crows Nest/De Reuck	D3	T				BYO		✓		✓
Cru Wines	D7					✓				
Daview Vineyards/Leidersburg	D1	T						T		
De Compagnie	H1	T				T		T		
De Zoete Inval	E6	T						T	✓	
Détendu	C1	T						T		
De Villiers	E6	T								
Diemersfontein	F2		✓	✓		✓	✓	T		
Domaine Brahms	C3		T					T		
Doolhof	H1		✓				✓	✓		
Drakensig	D8		✓							
Eshkol	F1	T				T		T		
Fairview/Spice Route/Goats/Fairvalley	D6		✓	✓		✓			✓	
Freedom Hill	F7		✓		✗	BYO				
Gallop Hill	D4	T				✓	✓			
Glen Carlou	D7		✓					T	✓	
Hildenbrand	G2		✓	✓		✓	✓	T		
Horse Mountain	D1	T	✓			BYO				
I Love Wine	E6		✓			✓				
Jacaranda	F1		✓			BYO	✓	✓		
Joostenberg	A8		✓			✓		T		
Kleine Draken	D6				✗	BYO		T	✓	
Klein Parys	E5		✓			✓				
Kleinvallei	F4	T								
KWV	E6		✓	✓		✓		✓	✓	
Laborie	E6		✓	✓		✓		T	✓	
Landskroon	D6		✓			BYO	✓	T		✓
Lindhorst	D7		✓	✓		T	✓	T		✓
Linton Park	G1	T				T		T		
Main Street	E5	T						T		

	Grid ref	Open by appt only	Open Saturdays	Open Sundays	Open pub. holidays	Meals/refreshments	Accommodation	Cellar tours	Disabled friendly	Child friendly
Mellasat	G5	T						T		
Mijn-Burg	A7	T						T		
Mischa	F1	T			✗	T		T		
Mont Destin	C8	T								
Mont du Toit/Blouvlei	G2	T								
Mooi Bly	F4	T					✓			
Mount Vernon	C7	T				BYO		BYO		
Nabygelegen	H1		✓			BYO		T		
Napier	G2		✓	✓			✓			
Nederburg	F5		✓	✓		T		T	✓	
Nelson/New Beginnings	D3		✓	T		T		✓	✓	✓
Niel Joubert/Klein Simonsvlei	D8	T								
Olsen Wines	G5	T				T		T		
Oude Wellington	G2	T				✓	✓			✓
Perdeberg	B2				✗			T		
Rhebokskloof	D3		✓	✓		✓		T	✓	✓
Ridgeback	D3		✓			✓		T		
Rose Garden Vineyards	C3	T				T		T		
Ruitersvlei	D6		✓	✓		✓		T	✓	✓
Rupert & Rothschild	D8	T								
Scali	C1	T					✓			
Seidelberg	D6		✓	✓		✓		✓		✓
Simonsvlei/Lost Horizons	D7		✓	✓		✓		T	✓	✓
Smook Wines	C1	T								
The Mason's Winery	E5	T						T		
Under Oaks	D3	T						T		
Upland	G2	T					✓			
Veenwouden	E2				✗			T		
Vendôme	E6		✓		✗			T	✓	
Vrede en Lust	D8		✓	✓		✓	✓	T		✓
Wamakersvallei	E2		✓		✗	BYO		T		
Welbedacht Wines	F1		✓	T		BYO		T		✓
Welgegund	G2	T					✓			
Welgeleë	D7	T								
Welgemeend	C7		✓		✗				✓	
Wellington	E2									
Welvanpas	H1		✓							
William Everson Wines	E6	T				BYO		T		
Windmeul	D3		✓		✗			T		
Ziggurat	D3		✓				✓	T		
Robertson										
Robertson Wine Valley Mon-Fri 8-5 ▪ Sat & Sun 9-2	**T (023) 626·3167**									
Angora		T			✗					
Arendsig		T						T		

	Grid ref	Open by appt only	Open Saturdays	Open Sundays	Open pub. holidays	Meals/refreshments	Accommodation	Cellar tours	Disabled friendly	Child friendly
Ashton			✓		✗	BYO		T		
Bon Cap/Karusa			✓	✓		✓	✓	✓		✓
Bon Courage			✓			✓			✓	✓
Bonnievale			✓					T	✓	
Clairvaux			✓			BYO		T	✓	
Cloverfield			✓							
De Wetshof			✓					T		
Fraai Uitzicht			✓			✓	✓	T		
Goedverwacht			✓			BYO		T		
Graham Beck			✓					T		
Janéza		T				T				
Jewel of the Breede River		T				BYO	✓			
Jonkheer		T			✗					
Kranskop			✓			T		✓		✓
Langverwacht					✗			T	✓	
Le Grand Chasseur			✓			✓		T		
Major's Hill			✓					T		✓
McGregor			✓						✓	
Merwespont					✗	BYO		T	✓	
Mooiuitsig							✓	T		
Nordale					✗	✓		T		
Quando		T						T		
Rietvallei			✓			✓				✓
Robertson			✓			BYO		T		
Roodezandt			✓					T	✓	
Rooiberg			✓			✓		T	✓	✓
Rusticus			✓			BYO		T		
Springfield			✓			BYO				
Tanagra			✓	✓		BYO				✓
The Marais Family			✓			BYO				
Van Loveren			✓			✓			✓	
Van Zylshof			✓					T		
Viljoensdrift			✓	T		✓		T		
Vruchtbaar		T				BYO		T		
Wandsbeck/Agterkliphoogte								T	✓	
Wederom			✓			T				✓
Weltevrede			✓			✓	✓	T		
Wolvendrift			✓			BYO		T	✓	
Zandvliet			✓			BYO			✓	
Southern Cape										
Agulhas Wines						BYO	✓	T		
Andy Mitchell		t								
Black Oystercatcher		T								
Jean Daneel		T								

	Grid ref	Open by appt only	Open Saturdays	Open Sundays	Open pub. holidays	Meals/refreshments	Accommodation	Cellar tours	Disabled friendly	Child friendly
Oewerzicht		T				✓	✓			
Zoetendal			✓	T		T		✓		
Stellenbosch										

Stellenbosch American Express Wine Routes **T 886-4310**
Mon-Fri 8.30-5 ▪ Sat, Sun & holidays: enquire at Tourism Office ▪ Closed Good Fri, Dec 25 & Jan 1

	Grid ref	Open by appt only	Open Saturdays	Open Sundays	Open pub. holidays	Meals/refreshments	Accommodation	Cellar tours	Disabled friendly	Child friendly
Alluvia	H5	T					✓	T		✓
Alto	E8		✓							
Amani	B6		✓					T	✓	
Anatu (Stellekaya)	E5	T								
Annandale	E8		✓					T	✓	
Asara	D6		✓			✓		T		
Audacia	E7		✓					T	✓	
Beau Joubert	B6	T					✓			
Bein	B6	T								
Bellevue/Middelpos	C3		✓							
Bergkelder	E5		✓			T		✓	✓	
Beyerskloof	F3		✓						✓	
Bilton	E8		✓		✗	✓			✓	
Blaauwklippen	E6		✓	✓		✓		T	✓	
Blue Creek	E7	T								
Bonfoi	C5		✓		✗	✓			✓	
Boschheim	E5	T								
Boschkloof	C6	T						T		
Bottelary	D3		✓			✓		T		
Camberley	H5		✓	T			✓	T		
Cape First	E7	T								
Cape Hutton	E7	T								
Carisbrooke	C6		✓							
Clos Malverne	D4		✓			BYO		T		
Clouds	G5	T				T	✓			
Clovelly	D3	T						T		
De Meye	E1		✓							
De Toren	B6	T						T		
De Trafford	G8		✓					✓		
Delaire	G5		✓	✓				T	✓	
Delheim	F2		✓	✓		✓		✓	✓	
Devon Hill	D4		T		✗			T	✓	
DeWaal/Uiterwyk	C5		✓							
Dombeya	E8		✓			✓				
Dormershire	A5		✓	✓				✓		
Dornier Wines	F7		✓	✓				T		
Ernie Els	F8		✓							
EagleVlei	E1	t								
Fort Simon	C4		✓			T		T	✓	

	Grid ref	Open by appt only	Open Saturdays	Open Sundays	Open pub. holidays	Meals/refreshments	Accommodation	Cellar tours	Disabled friendly	Child friendly
Goede Hoop	C3					BYO		✓		
Graceland	E7	T			✗		✓			
Groenland	B3		✓			✓		T		
Hartenberg	D3		✓	✓		BYO		T		
Hazendal	B3		✓	✓		✓		✓		
Helderkruin	E8		✓		✗	T		✓	✓	
Hoopenburg	E1		✓			BYO		T		
Jacobsdal	B6	T								
JC le Roux	D4		✓	✓					✓	
Jordan	C5		✓	✓		BYO		T	✓	
Kaapzicht	B4		✓			BYO	✓	T		
Kanonkop	F2		✓			✓			✓	
Kanu	C6		✓		✗					
Klawervlei	D1		✓					T	✓	
Klein Gustrouw	G6	T						T		
Kleine Zalze	E6		✓	✓		✓	✓	T	✓	✓
Kleinood	F7	T						T		
Knorhoek	F3		✓			✓	✓		✓	✓
Koelenhof	D1		✓			BYO			✓	✓
L'Avenir	E3		✓			BYO	✓	T		✓
Laibach	F1		✓					T		
Lanzerac	G5		✓	✓		✓	✓	✓	✓	
Le Bonheur	F1		✓			T				
Le Pommier	H4		✓	✓		✓	✓	T		
Le Riche	G6				✗		✓			
Lievland	F1		✓	✓		T		T	✓	
Louiesenhof	E4		✓	✓		BYO			✓	✓
Louisvale	D4		✓			✓		T	✓	
Marklew	F1	T						T		
Meerlust	B8	T			✗			T		
Middelvlei	E5		✓					T	✓	
Monterosso	E4		✓					T		
Mooiplaas	B4		✓			BYO				
Morgenhof	F3		✓	✓		✓			✓	
Mostertsdrift	E4	T				T		T		
Mulderbosch	E3	T								
Muratie	F3		✓	✓		T	✓	T		
Neethlingshof	D5		✓	✓		✓		T	✓	✓
Niel Ellis/Meyer-Näkel	G6		✓							
Nietvoorbij	F4		T		✗					
Overgaauw	D6		✓					T	✓	
Quoin	F3	T						T		
Raats Family	B6	T								
Rainbow's End	H5	T						T		
Remhoogte	F3	T						T		

	Grid ref	Open by appt only	Open Saturdays	Open Sundays	Open pub. holidays	Meals/refreshments	Accommodation	Cellar tours	Disabled friendly	Child friendly
Reyneke	B6	T					✓			
Rozendal	G5	T				✓	✓	T		
Rust en Vrede	E8		✓							
Rustenberg	G4		✓						✓	
Saxenburg	A6		✓	✓		✓				
Sentinel	E3		✓	✓		✓				✓
Simonsig	E2		✓			✓		✓	✓	✓
Slaley	E2		✓					T		
Spier/Savanha	C7		✓	✓		✓	✓	T	✓	
Stark-Condé	G6	T								
Stellcape/JJ Wines	C3		✓		✗	✓		✓		
Stellekaya/Anatu	E5		✓		✗	T				
Stellenbosch Hills	D6		✓						✓	
Stellenzicht	E7		✓	✓						
Sterhuis	C4	T								✓
SylvanVale (Devon Valley Hotel)	D4		✓	✓		✓	✓	T	✓	✓
The Foundry	B8	T						T		
Thelema	H4		✓		✗	BYO			✓	
Tokara	G4		✓		✗	✓			✓	
Uitkyk	F2		✓	✓		BYO			✓	
Uva Mira	F8		✓							
Vergenoegd	B8		✓		✗			T	✓	
Villiera/M'hudi	D1		✓			BYO		✓	✓	
Vredenheim/Stellendrift	D6		✓			✓			✓	
Vriesenhof	F7		✓			T		T		
Vuurberg Vyds	H4	T								
Warwick	F1		✓	✓		T		T		
Waterford	F7		✓						✓	
Webersburg	E8	T			✗					
Welmoed/Omnia	C7		✓	✓		✓				
Westbridge	E1		✓				✓			
Zevenwacht	A5		✓	✓		✓	✓	T	✓	
Zorgvliet	H4		✓	✓		✓	✓	T		✓

Swartland/Darling

Swartland Wine Route T (022) 487·1133
Mon-Fri 8-5 ▪ Sat & holidays 8.30-12 ▪ Closed Good Fri, Dec 25 & Jan 1

Darling Wine Experience T (022) 492·3430
Mon-Fri 9-4.50 ▪ Sat 9-2.30 ▪ Closed Easter Fri-Mon, Dec 25 & Jan 1

	Grid ref	Open by appt only	Open Saturdays	Open Sundays	Open pub. holidays	Meals/refreshments	Accommodation	Cellar tours	Disabled friendly	Child friendly
Allesverloren			✓			BYO		T		✓
Babylon's Peak		T				BYO	✓	T		
Cloof			T			T			✓	
Darling Cellars			✓			BYO		T	✓	
Groote Post			✓			✓			✓	
Hofstraat		T								
Kloovenburg			✓			BYO		T		

	Grid ref	Open by appt only	Open Saturdays	Open Sundays	Open pub. holidays	Meals/refreshments	Accommodation	Cellar tours	Disabled friendly	Child friendly
Lammershoek			T	T		T		T		
Meerhof			✓			T		T		
Nieuwedrift			✓			T	✓			✓
Org de Rac			✓					✓		
Ormonde			✓			BYO		T		✓
Porterville			✓			T		T		
Pulpit Rock			✓			BYO		T		
Riebeek			✓			✓		T		
Sadie Family		T								
Sequillo		T								
Swartland			✓			BYO		T		✓
The Observatory		T								
Winkelshoek			✓							
Tulbagh										
Tulbagh Wine Route — T (023) 230·1348 Mon-Fri 9-5 ▪ Sat & holidays 10-4 ▪ Sun 11-4 Closed: Good Fri, Dec 25 & Jan 1										
Alter Ego			✓			T				
Blue Crane		T								
Bianco			✓					✓		
Buck's Ridge		T				✓				
Drostdy			✓						✓	
Lemberg			✓	✓		✓	✓	✓		
Manley			✓	✓		✓	✓	✓		
Montpellier			✓	✓		✓	✓	✓		✓
Montpellier du Sud/Constantia de Tulbagh		T								
Paddagang			✓	✓		✓	✓			
Rijk's			✓			BYO	✓	✓	✓	
Saronsberg			✓			BYO		T		
Schalkenbosch			✓	✓		T	T	T		
Theuniskraal			✓			BYO			✓	
Tulbagh			✓		✗				✓	
Tulbagh Mountain Vineyards		T						T		
Twee Jonge Gezellen			✓					✓		
Worcester/Breedekloof/Villiersdorp										
Worcester Winelands — T (023) 342·8710 Mon-Fri 8-5 ▪ Sat 9-4 ▪ Sun & holidays: 10-3 **Breedekloof Wine & Tourism** — T (023) 349·1791 Mon-Fri 8.30-4.30 ▪ Sat 9-4 ▪ Sun 10-4 ▪ Closed Good Fri & Dec 25										
Aan de Doorns					✗			T	✓	
Alvi's Drift		T				BYO		T		
Aufwaerts		T								
Badsberg			✓			BYO		T		✓
Bergsig			✓			✓		T		
Botha			✓			BYO		T		✓
Brandvlei						BYO		T		

	Grid ref	Open by appt only	Open Saturdays	Open Sundays	Open pub. holidays	Meals/refreshments	Accommodation	Cellar tours	Disabled friendly	Child friendly
Conradie Family			✓	✓		✓	✓	✓		
Daschbosch								T		✓
De Doorns			✓							
Deetlefs			✓			BYO		✓		
De Wet			✓		✗	BYO			✓	
Du Preez/Rockfields					✗	BYO		T	✓	✓
Du Toitskloof			✓			BYO		T	✓	
Goudini			✓			✓				
Groot Eiland					✗	T		T	✓	
Jason's Hill			✓	T		T				✓
Lateganskop								T		
Lorraine		T				BYO		T		
Mountain Oaks		T					✓	T		
New Cape Wines			✓					✓		
Nuy			✓			✓			✓	
Opstal			✓			✓		T		
Overhex					✗	BYO		T	✓	
Riverstone/Merwida			✓				✓		✓	
Romansrivier			✓			BYO		T		
Slanghoek					✗	BYO		T	✓	
Stettyn						BYO		T	✓	
Villiersdorp Cellar			✓	✓		✓			✓	
Waboomsrivier			✓		✗	BYO		T	✓	

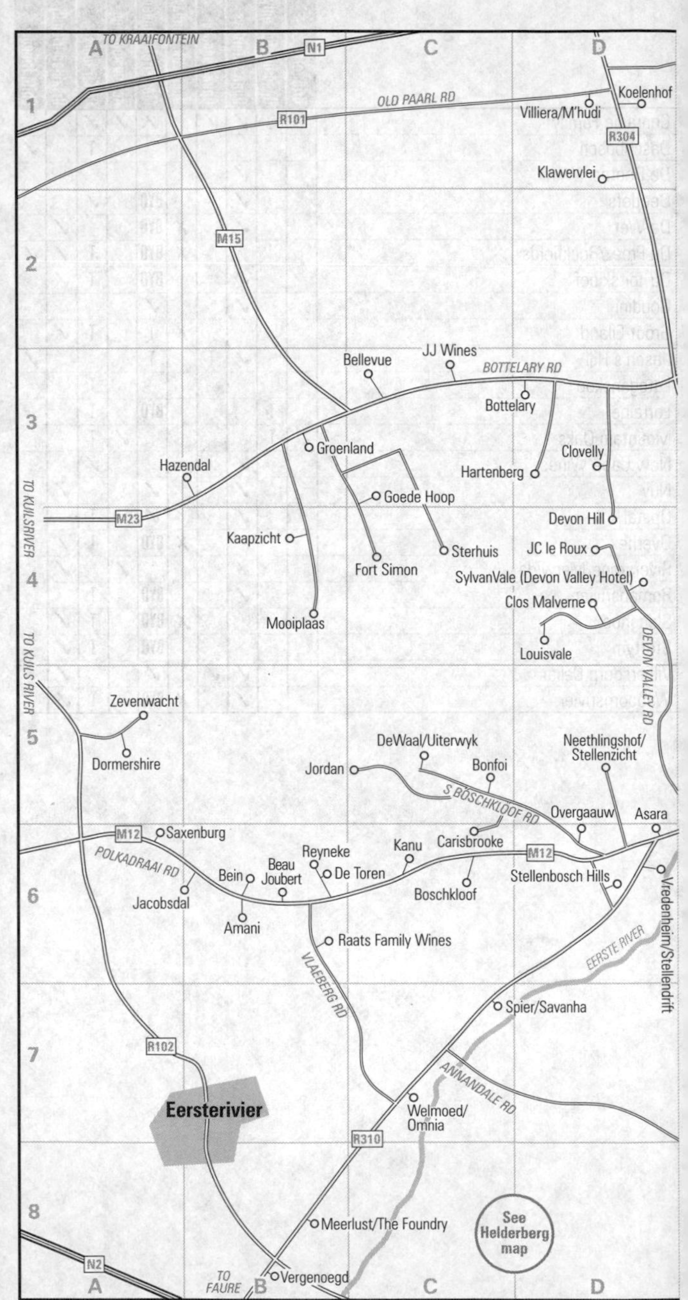
TO KRAAIFONTEIN
N1
OLD PAARL RD
R101
Koelenhof
Villiera/M'hudi
R304
Klawervlei
M15
Bellevue
JJ Wines
BOTTELARY RD
Bottelary
Groenland
Hazendal
Hartenberg
Clovelly
Goede Hoop
M23
TO KUILSRIVER
Devon Hill
Kaapzicht
Sterhuis
JC le Roux
Fort Simon
SylvanVale (Devon Valley Hotel)
Clos Malverne
Mooiplaas
Louisvale
DEVON VALLEY RD
TO KUILS RIVER
Zevenwacht
Dormershire
DeWaal/Uiterwyk
Neethlingshof/
Stellenzicht
Bonfoi
Jordan
S BOSCHKLOOF RD
Overgaauw
Asara
M12
Saxenburg
Carisbrooke
Kanu
Reyneke
Beau
Joubert
De Toren
Bein
POLKADRAAI RD
Jacobsdal
Amani
Boschkloof
Stellenbosch Hills
Vredenheim/Stellendrift
Raats Family Wines
VLAEBERG RD
EERSTE RIVER
Spier/Savanha
R102
ANNANDALE RD
Eersterivier
Welmoed/
Omnia
R310
See
Helderberg
map
Meerlust/The Foundry
N2
TO
FAURE
Vergenoegd

Stellenbosch

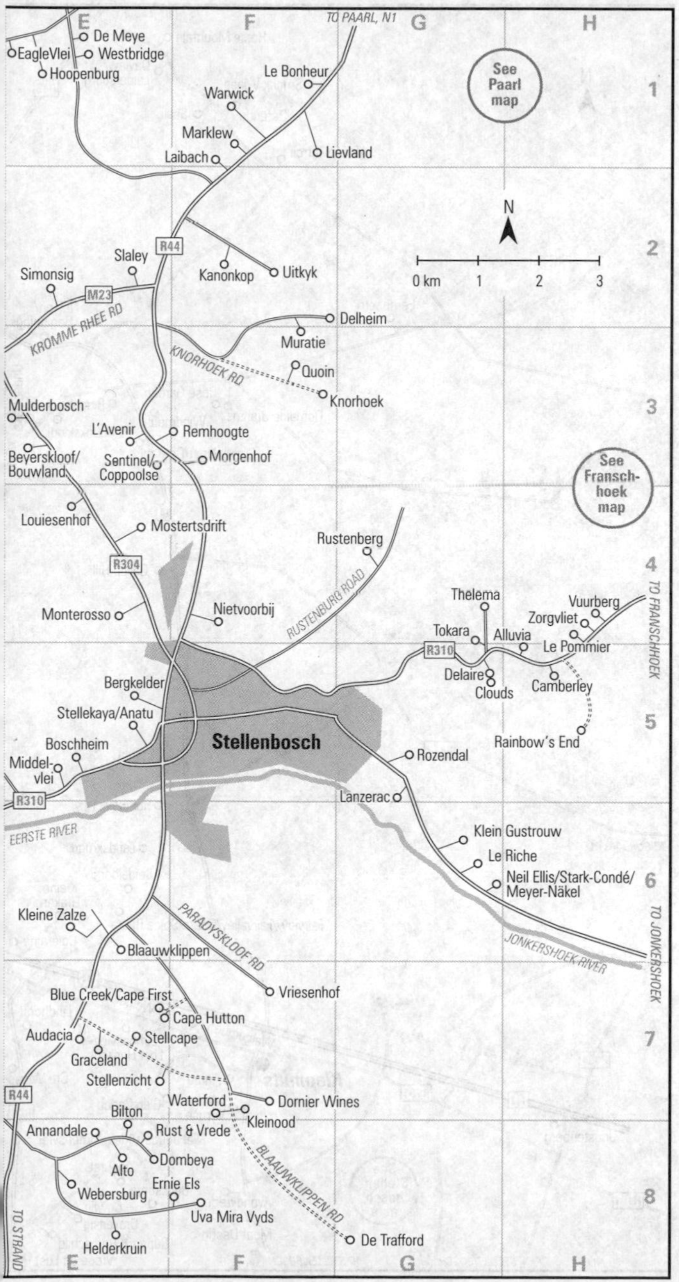

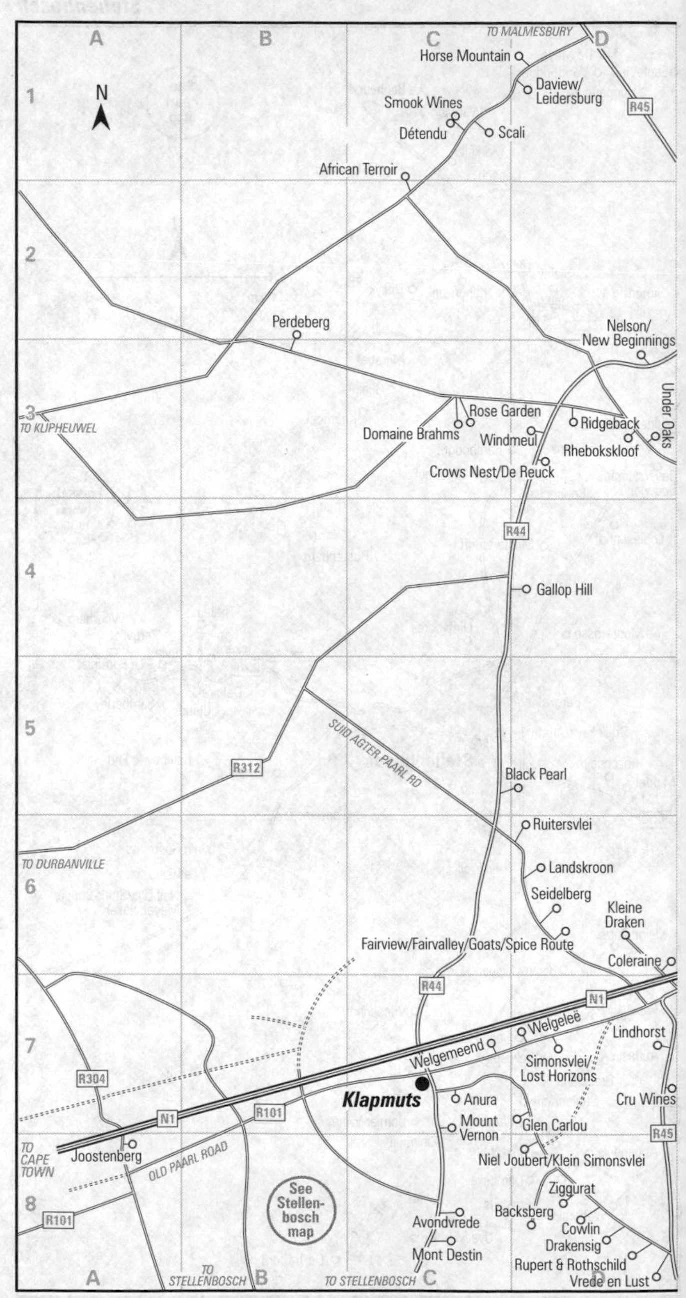
TO MALMESBURY
A
B
C
D
1
2
3
4
5
6
7
8
N
Horse Mountain
Daview/
Leidersburg
R45
Smook Wines
Détendu
Scali
African Terroir
Perdeberg
Nelson/
New Beginnings
Under Oaks
Rose Garden
Ridgeback
TO KLIPHEUWEL
Domaine Brahms
Windmeul
Rhebokskloof
Crows Nest/De Reuck
R44
Gallop Hill
SUID AGTER PAARL RD
R312
Black Pearl
Ruitersvlei
TO DURBANVILLE
Landskroon
Seidelberg
Kleine
Draken
Fairview/Fairvalley/Goats/Spice Route
Coleraine
R44
N1
Welgeleë
Lindhorst
Welgemeend
Simonsvlei/
Lost Horizons
R304
Klapmuts
Anura
Cru Wines
N1
R101
Mount
Vernon
Glen Carlou
R45
TO
CAPE
TOWN
Joostenberg
OLD PAARL ROAD
Niel Joubert/Klein Simonsvlei
See
Stellen-
bosch
map
Ziggurat
Backsberg
Cowlin
R101
Avondvrede
Drakensig
Mont Destin
Rupert & Rothschild
TO
STELLENBOSCH
TO STELLENBOSCH
Vrede en Lust

Paarl & Wellington

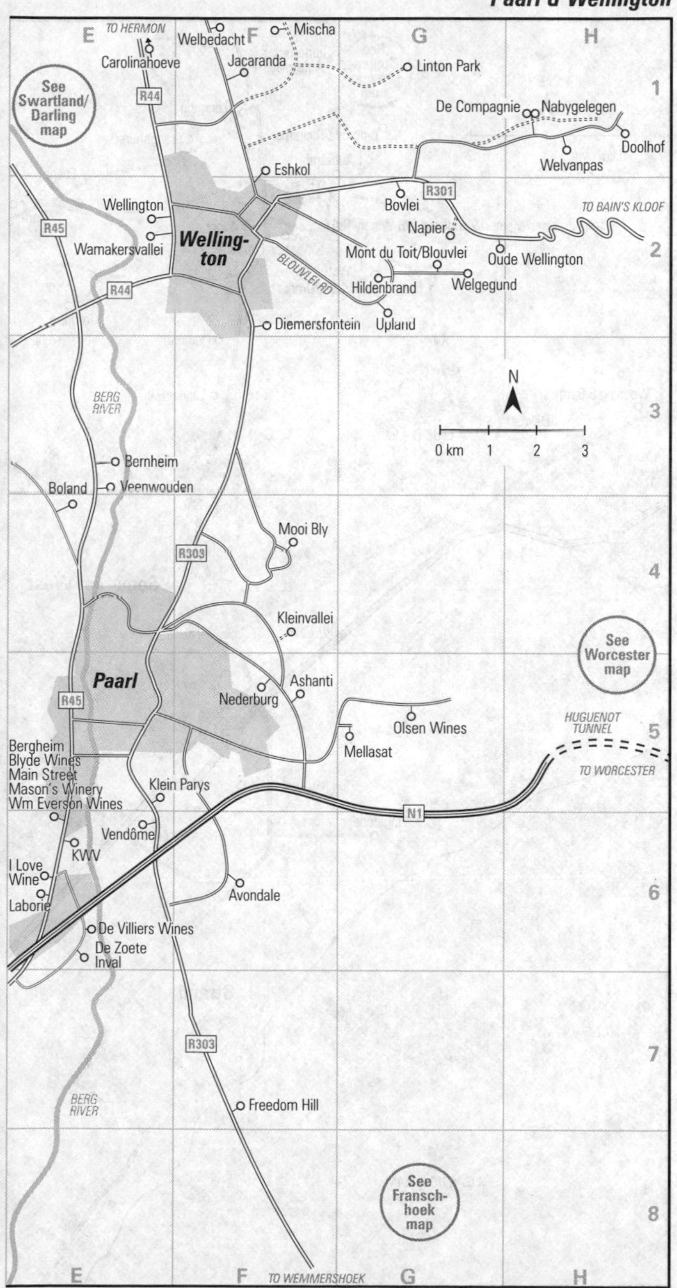

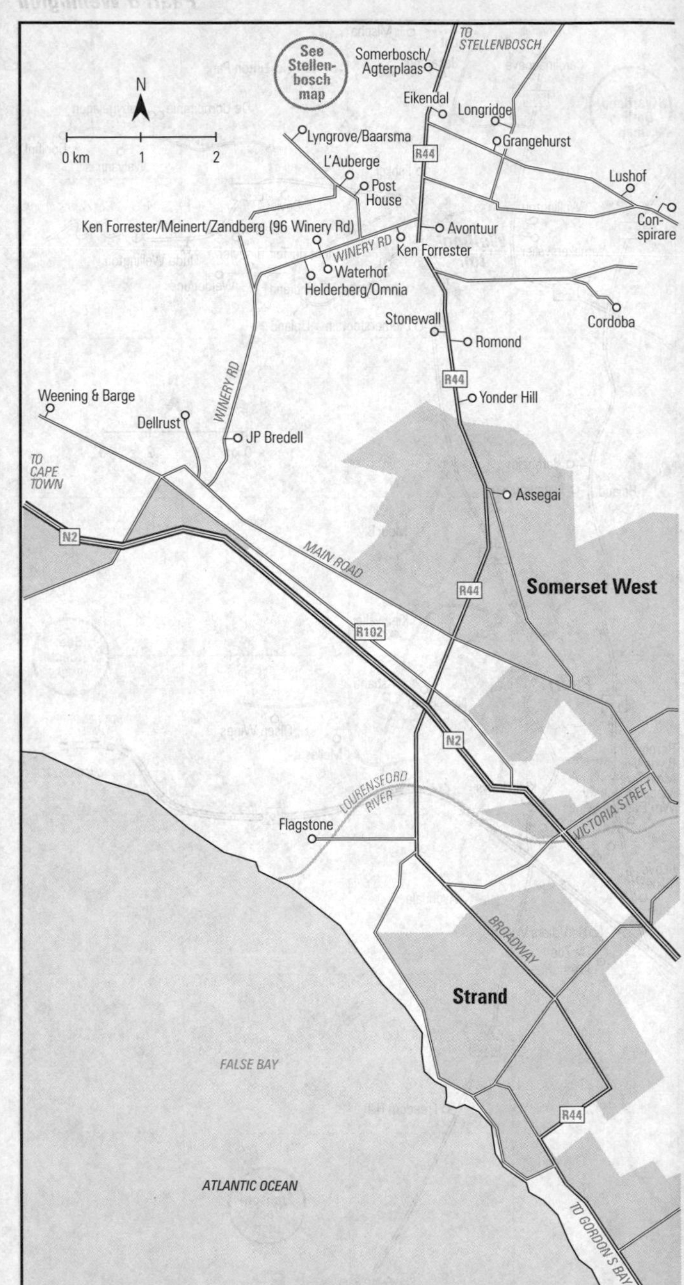

TO STELLENBOSCH
See Stellenbosch map
N
0 km
1
2
Somerbosch/ Agterplaas
Eikendal
Longridge
Grangehurst
Lyngrove/Baarsma
R44
L'Auberge
Post House
Lushof
Con- spirare
Ken Forrester/Meinert/Zandberg (96 Winery Rd)
Avontuur
WINERY RD
Ken Forrester
Waterhof
Helderberg/Omnia
Cordoba
Stonewall
Romond
WINERY RD
R44
Weening & Barge
Yonder Hill
Dellrust
JP Bredell
TO CAPE TOWN
Assegai
N2
MAIN ROAD
R44
Somerset West
R102
N2
LOURENSFORD RIVER
VICTORIA STREET
Flagstone
BROADWAY
Strand
FALSE BAY
R44
ATLANTIC OCEAN
TO GORDON'S BAY

Helderberg

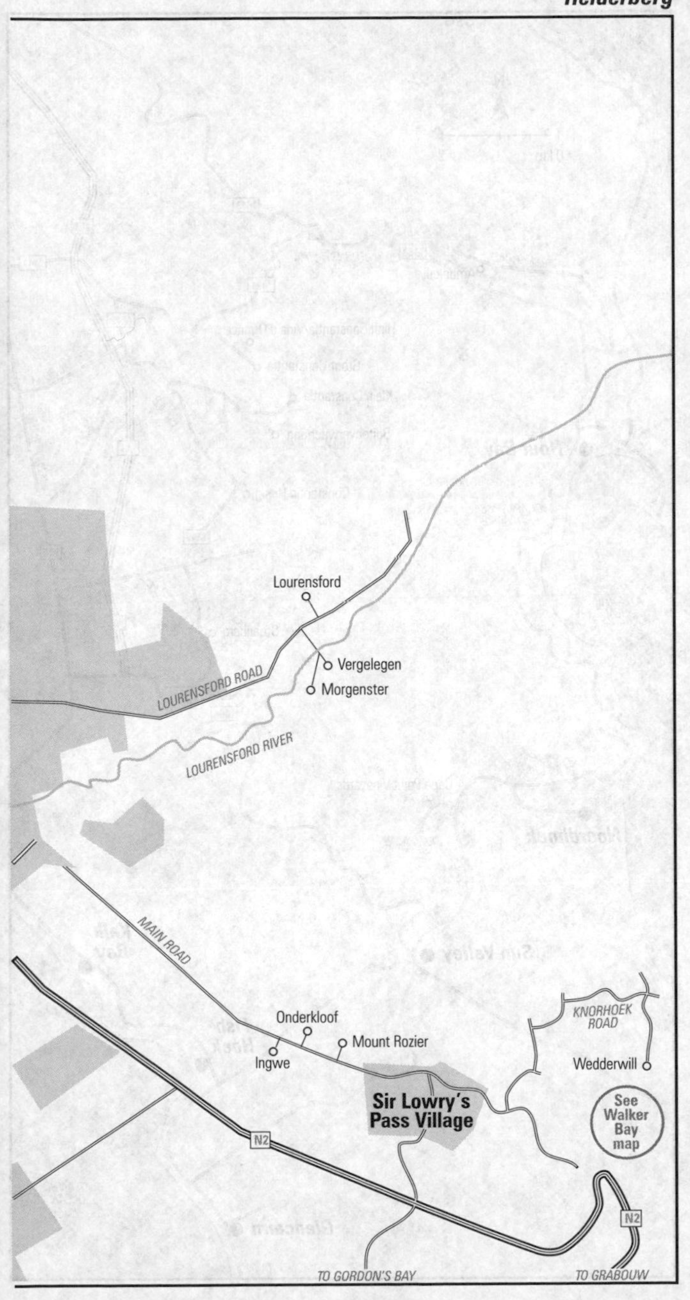

Lourensford
Vergelegen
Morgenster
LOURENSFORD ROAD
LOURENSFORD RIVER
MAIN ROAD
Onderkloof
Mount Rozier
Ingwe
Sir Lowry's Pass Village
KNORHOEK ROAD
Wedderwill
See Walker Bay map
N2
N2
TO GORDON'S BAY
TO GRABOUW

Constantia/Cape Point

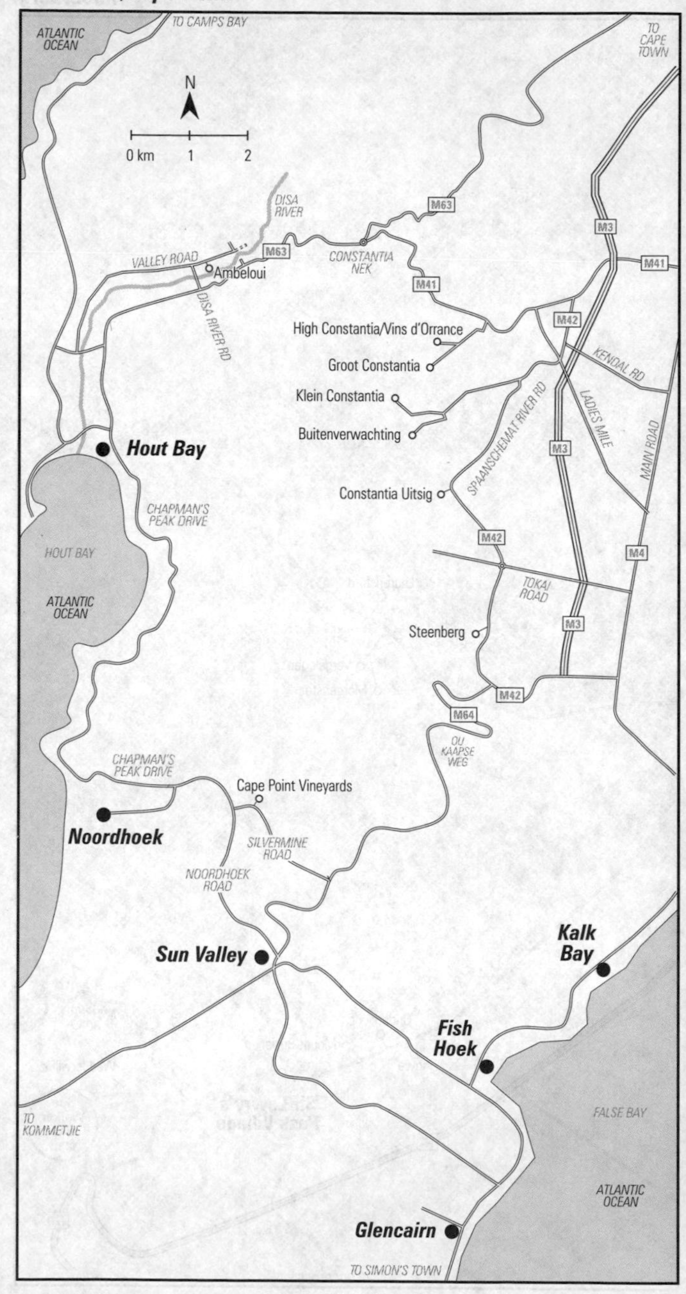

Durbanville/Philadelphia

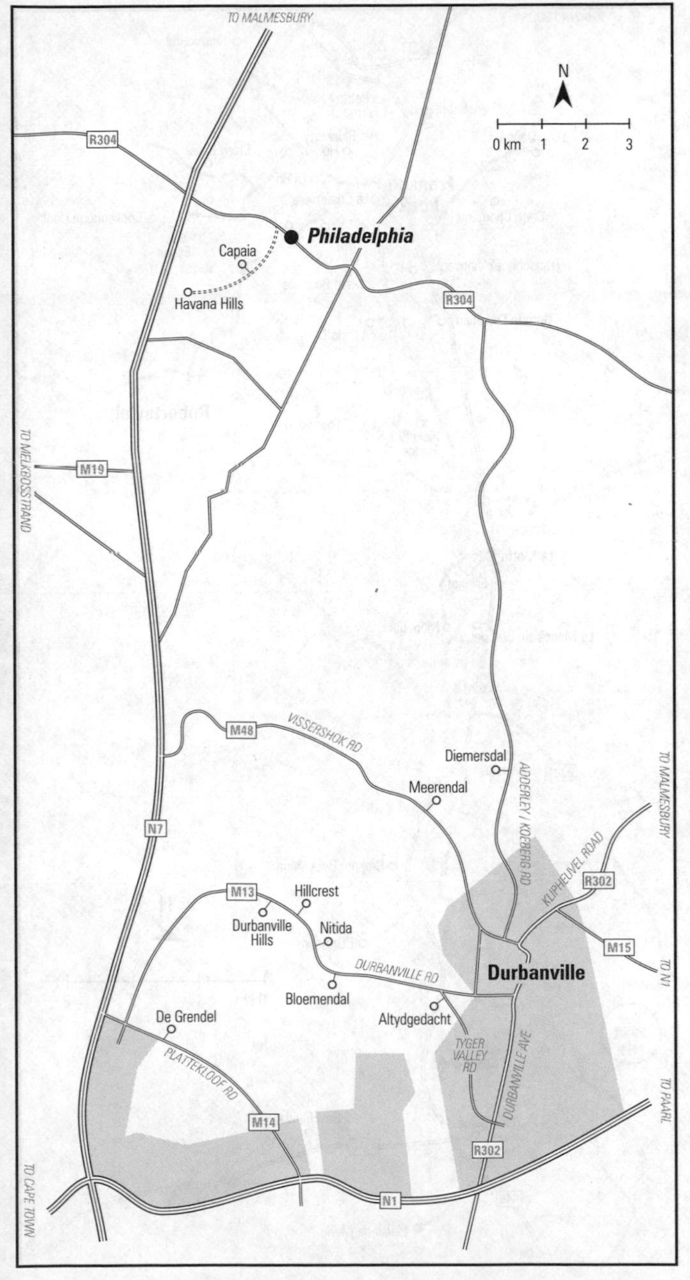

Franschhoek

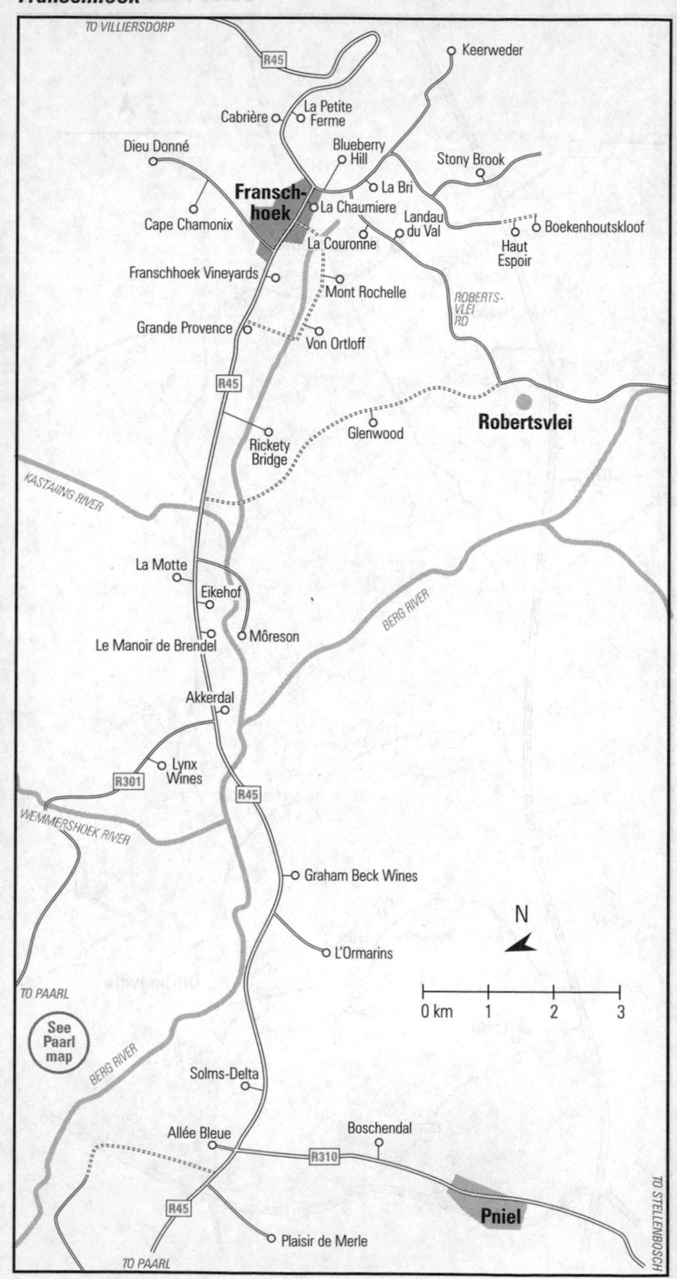

Elgin/Walker Bay

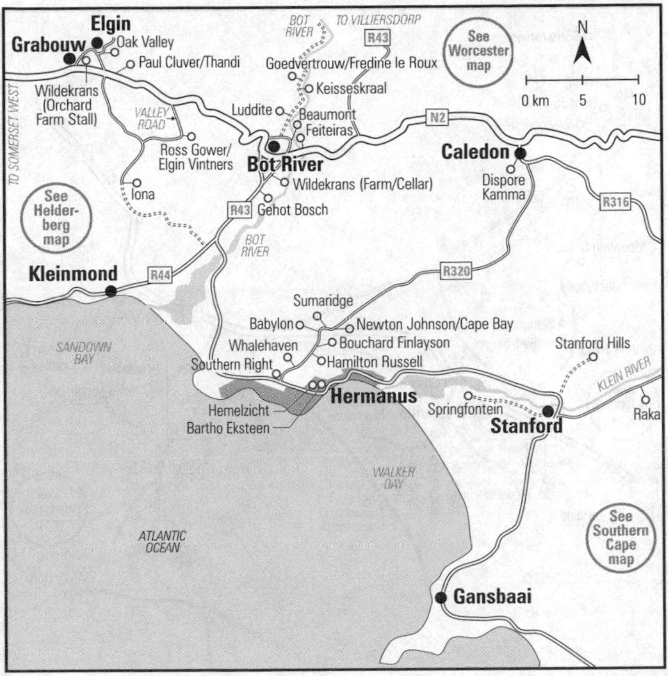

Elgin
Grabouw
Oak Valley
Paul Cluver/Thandi
BOT RIVER
TO VILLIERSDORP
R43
Goedvertrouw/Fredine le Roux
Keisseskraal
See Worcester map
N
0 km 5 10
TO SOMERSET WEST
Wildekrans (Orchard Farm Stall)
VALLEY ROAD
Luddite
Beaumont
Feiteiras
N2
Ross Gower/ Elgin Vintners
Bot River
Caledon
Wildekrans (Farm/Cellar)
Dispore Kamma
Iona
R43
Gehot Bosch
R316
See Helderberg map
BOT RIVER
R320
Kleinmond
R44
Sumaridge
Babylon
Newton Johnson/Cape Bay
SANDOWN BAY
Whalehaven
Bouchard Finlayson
Stanford Hills
Southern Right
Hamilton Russell
KLEIN RIVER
Hermanus
Springfontein
Raka
Hemelzicht
Stanford
Bartho Eksteen
WALKER BAY
See Southern Cape map
ATLANTIC OCEAN
Gansbaai

Southern Cape

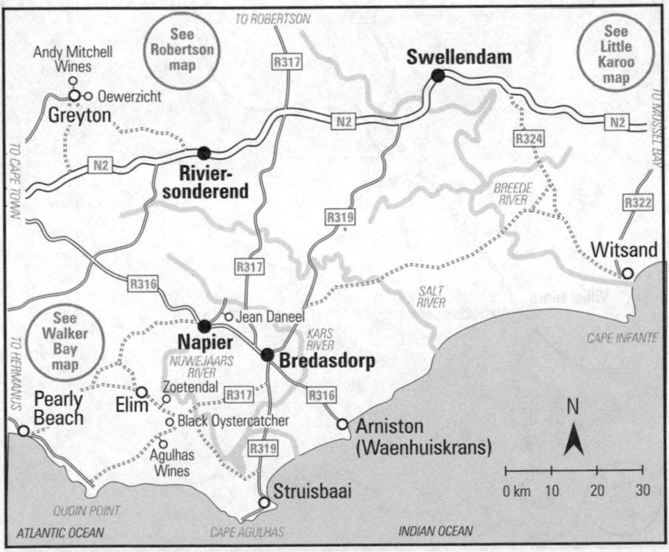

TO ROBERTSON
See Robertson map
See Little Karoo map
Andy Mitchell Wines
R317
Swellendam
Oewerzicht
TO MOSSEL BAY
Greyton
N2
N2
R324
TO CAPE TOWN
N2
Riviersonderend
BREEDE RIVER
R322
R319
Witsand
R317
R316
SALT RIVER
See Walker Bay map
Jean Daneel
Napier
KARS RIVER
CAPE INFANTE
TO HERMANUS
NUWEJAARS RIVER
Bredasdorp
Zoetendal
R317
R316
Pearly Beach
Elim
N
Black Oystercatcher
Arniston (Waenhuiskrans)
Agulhas Wines
R319
0 km 10 20 30
Struisbaai
QUOIN POINT
ATLANTIC OCEAN
CAPE AGULHAS
INDIAN OCEAN

Worcester, Breedekloof & Villiersdorp

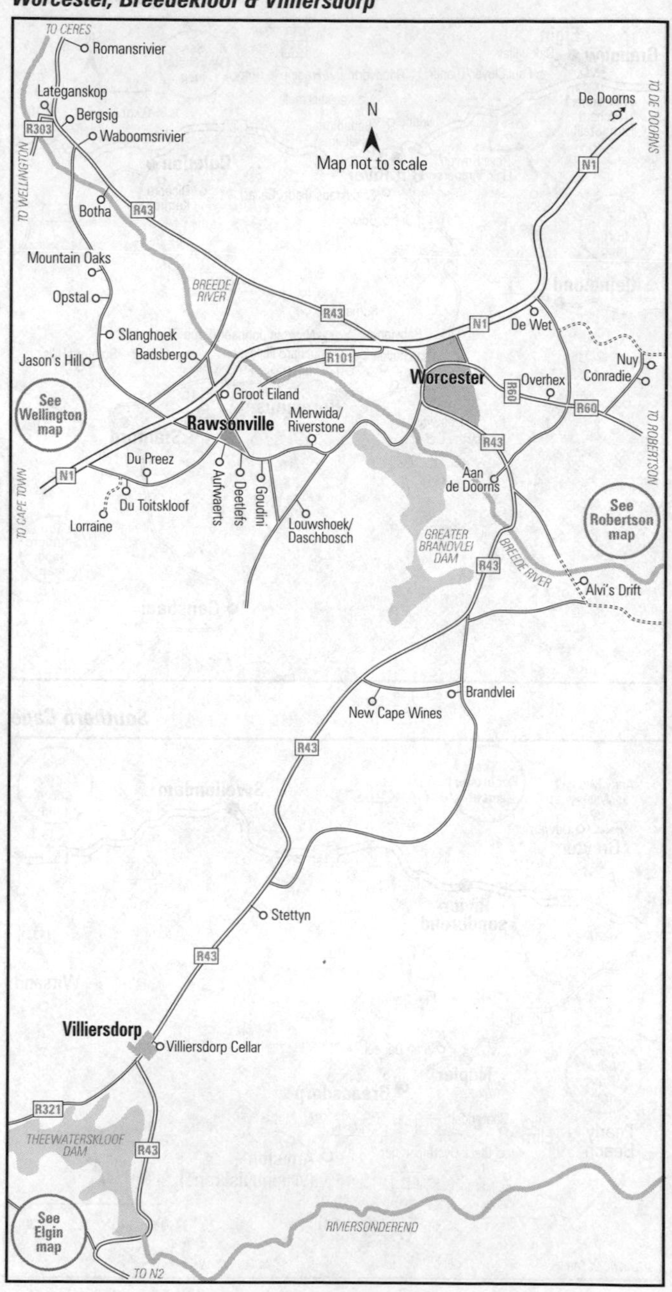

Robertson

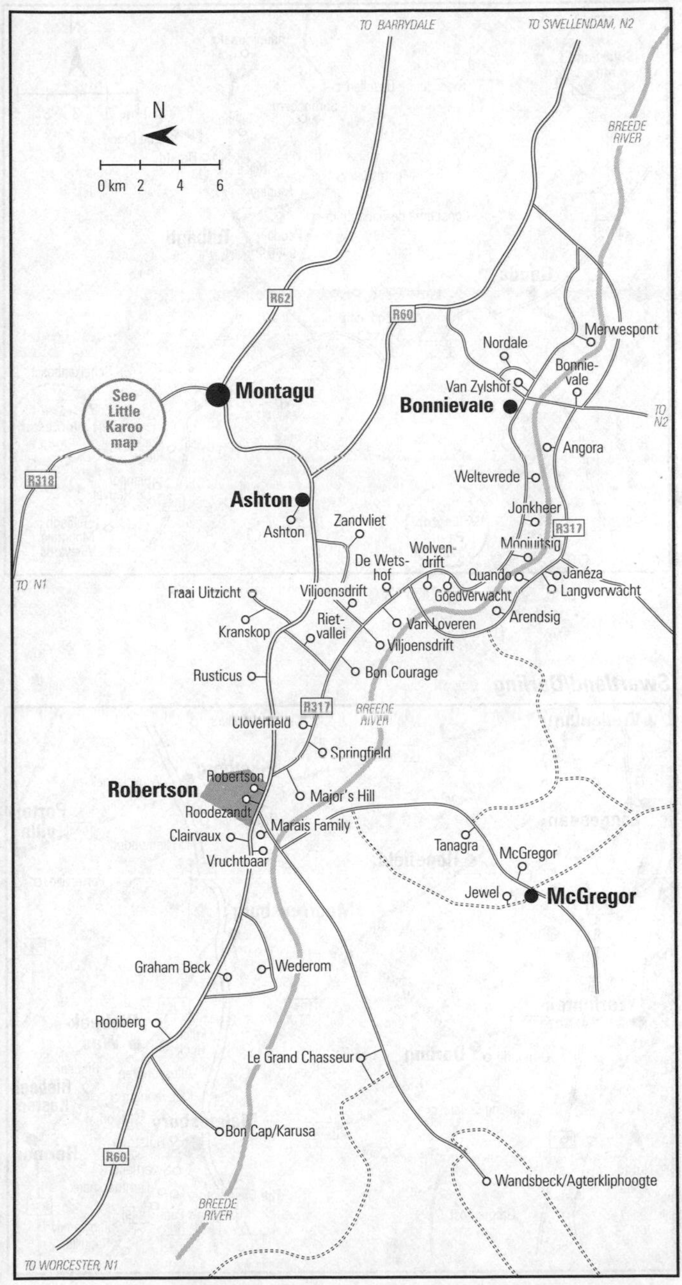
TO BARRYDALE
TO SWELLENDAM, N2
BREEDE RIVER
N
0 km 2 4 6
R62
R60
Merwespont
Nordale
Bonnievale
Van Zylshof
Bonnievale
TO N2
See Little Karoo map
Montagu
Angora
Weltevrede
R318
Ashton
Jonkheer
R317
Zandvliet
Ashton
Wolvendrift
Mooiuitsig
De Wetshof
Quando
Janéza
TO N1
Traai Uitzicht
Viljoensdrift
Goedverwacht
Langverwacht
Arendsig
Kranskop
Rietvallei
Van Loveren
Viljoensdrift
Rusticus
Bon Courage
R317
BREEDE RIVER
Cloverfield
Springfield
Robertson
Robertson
Major's Hill
Roodezandt
Marais Family
Clairvaux
Tanagra
Vruchtbaar
McGregor
Jewel
McGregor
Graham Beck
Wederom
Rooiberg
Le Grand Chasseur
Bon Cap/Karusa
R60
Wandsbeck/Agterkliphoogte
BREEDE RIVER
TO WORCESTER, N1

Tulbagh

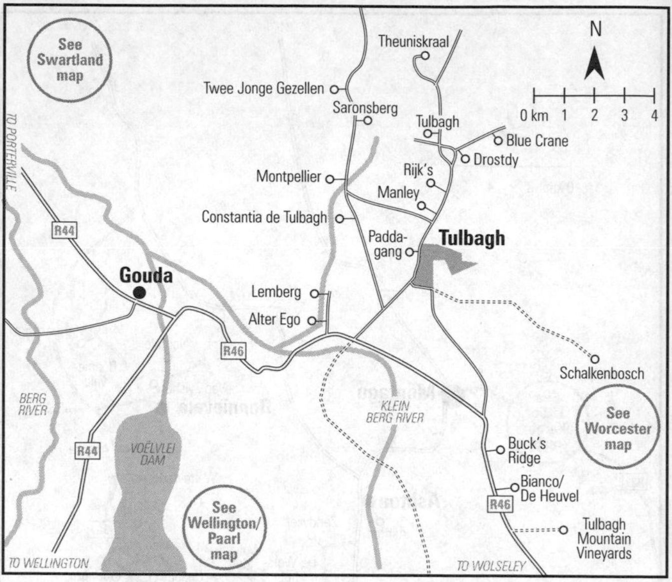

See Swartland map
N
0 km 1 2 3 4
Theuniskraal
Twee Jonge Gezellen
Saronsberg
Tulbagh
Blue Crane
Drostdy
Rijk's
Montpellier
Manley
Constantia de Tulbagh
Padda-gang
Tulbagh
TO PORTERVILLE
R44
Gouda
Lemberg
Alter Ego
R46
Schalkenbosch
BERG RIVER
KLEIN BERG RIVER
See Worcester map
R44
VOËLVLEI DAM
Buck's Ridge
Bianco/ De Heuvel
R46
See Wellington/ Paarl map
Tulbagh Mountain Vineyards
TO WELLINGTON
TO WOLSELEY

Swartland/Darling

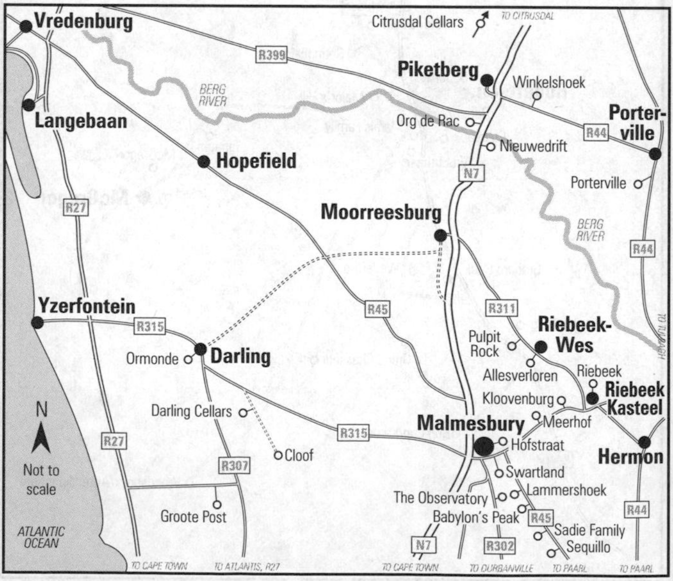

Vredenburg
Citrusdal Cellars
TO CITRUSDAL
R399
Piketberg
Winkelshoek
BERG RIVER
Langebaan
Org de Rac
Porterville
R44
Nieuwedrift
Hopefield
N7
Porterville
R27
Moorreesburg
BERG RIVER
R44
Yzerfontein
R45
R311
R315
Pulpit Rock
Riebeek-Wes
TO TULBAGH
Ormonde
Darling
Allesverloren
Riebeek
Kloovenburg
Riebeek Kasteel
N
Darling Cellars
Malmesbury
Meerhof
R315
Hofstraat
Not to scale
R27
Cloof
Hermon
R307
Swartland
The Observatory
Lammershoek
Groote Post
Babylon's Peak
R45
R44
ATLANTIC OCEAN
Sadie Family
N7
R302
Sequillo
TO CAPE TOWN
TO ATLANTIS, R27
TO CAPE TOWN
TO DURBANVILLE
TO PAARL
TO PAARL

Olifants River

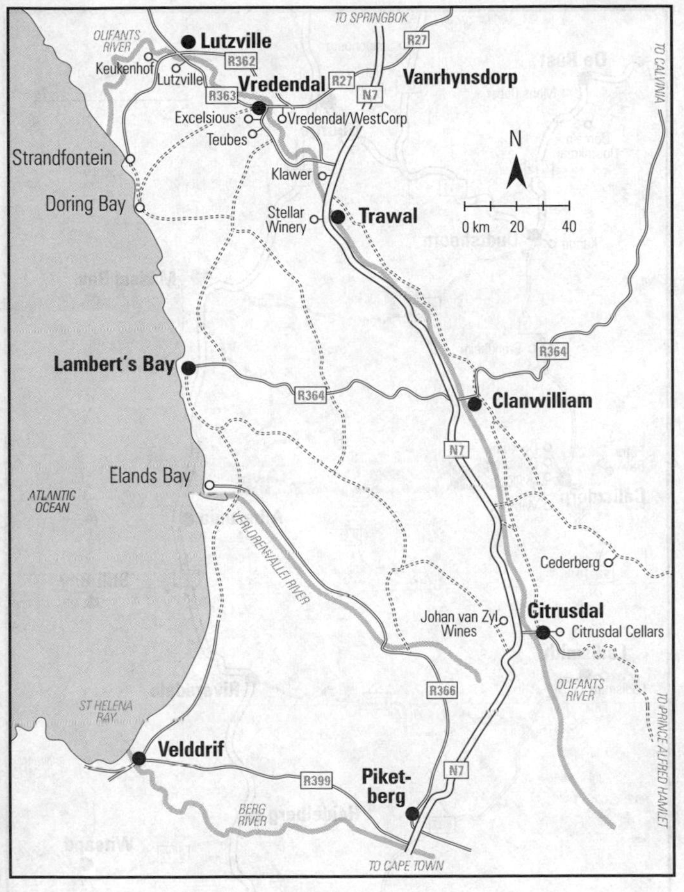

Little Karoo

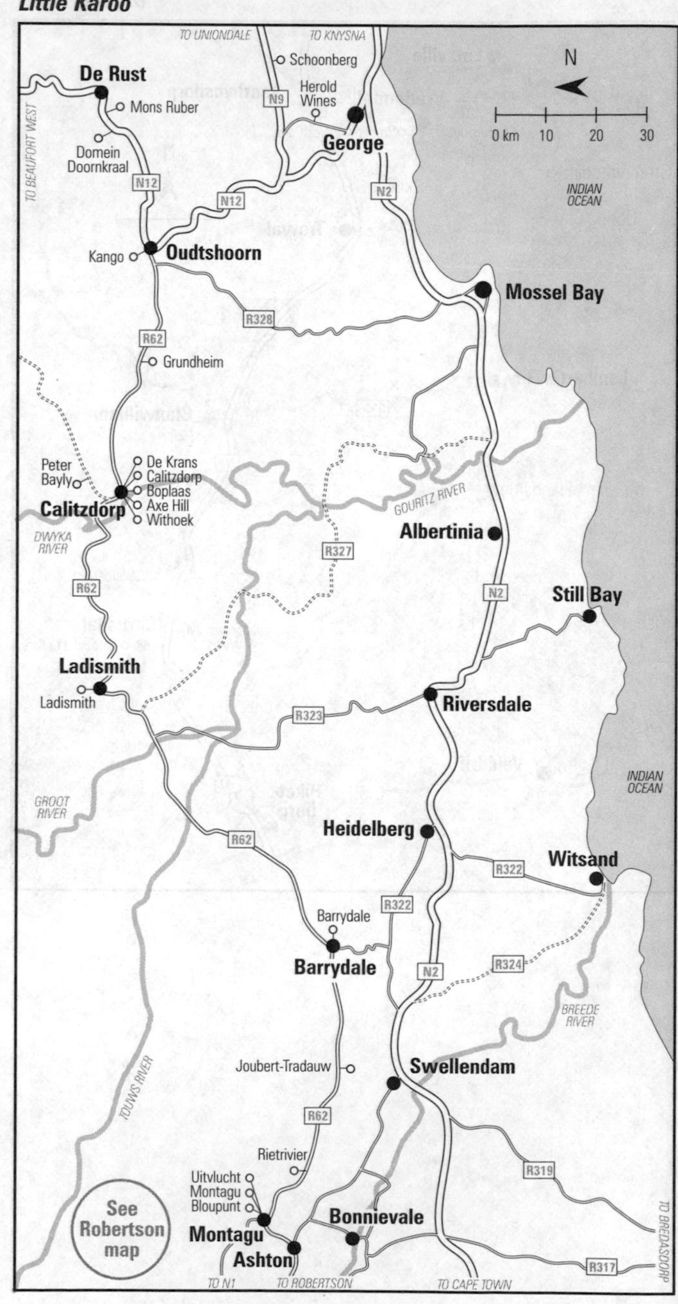

Northern Cape, Free State, North West

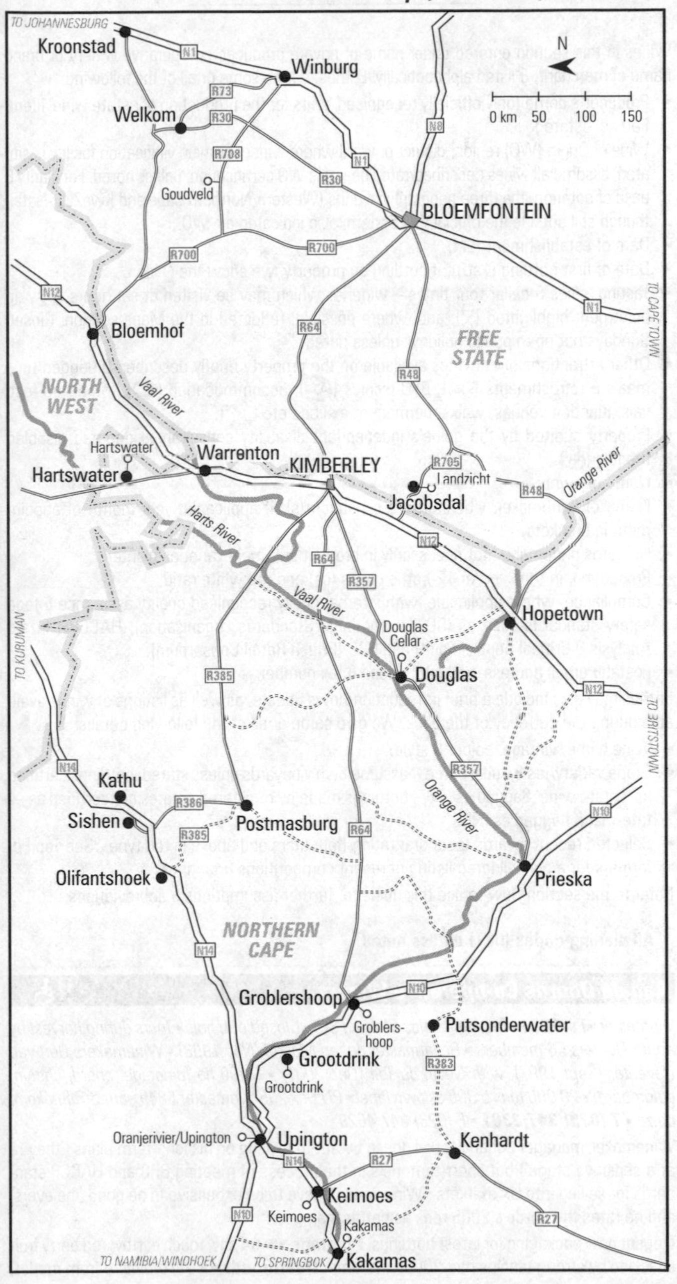

A–Z of Cape Wines

Wines in this section entered under name of private producer, co-operative winery or brand name of merchant, & listed alphabetically. Entries feature some or all of the following:

- Producer's name (only officially recognised 'units for the production of estate wine' identified as 'estate').
- Wine of Origin (WO) region, district or ward where winery or main vinification facility is situated; assume all wines described/rated bear this WO certification, unless noted. For clarity & ease of notation, the three geographical units (Western/Northern Cape and KwaZulu-Natal), though still outside the official WO system, also indicated as 'WO'.
- Date of establishment (Est).
- Date of first bottling (1stB); if bottling on property, we show the icon.
- Tasting, sales & cellar tour times – wineries which may be visited at set hours or by appointment highlighted, and, where possible, reflected in the Maps section. Closed Sundays but open public holidays unless noted.
- Other attractions or activities available on the property briefly described & flagged thus: meals & refreshments, BYO picnics; accommodation; 'other' eg festivals, function venues, walks, permanent exhibits etc.
- Property audited by the guide's independent disability consultant & deemed disabled-friendly.
- Name of owner.
- Name of winemaker, viticulturist & consultant(s), if applicable; year/month of appointment in brackets.
- Hectares under vine (not necessarily in production); main varieties planted.
- Production, in tons and/or 12-bottle cases (cs) and red:white ratio.
- Compliance, where applicable, with internationally recognised quality assurance & food safety standards such as ISO (International Standards Organisation), HACCP (Hazard Analysis & Critical Control Point) and BRC (British Retail Consortium).
- Postal & email address, website, phone & fax number.

Entries may also include a brief introduction/news update, as well as listings of wines available during the currency of the book. We give some or all of the following details:

- Wine name, vintage, colour & style.
- Grape variety/ies & fruit-source – assume own vineyards unless stated; bottlings certified as 'estate wine' flagged as 'EW'; bottlings made by registered estates not certified as estate-made flagged as 'NE'.
- Selected recent awards & our star rating (four stars and above in red type). See Top Performers for a consolidated listing of recent competitions & tastings.

Refer to the section How to use this guide for further assumptions & abbreviations.

All dialling codes (021) unless noted

Aan de Doorns Co-operative Winery

Worcester • Est 1954 • Tasting & sales Mon–Fri 8–5 • Closed pub hols • Tours during harvest by appt • Owners 56 members • Cellarmaster Johan Morkel (Nov 1993) • Winemakers Gert van Deventer (Sept 1997), with Nevin du Toit (Dec 2001) • 1 200 ha (pinotage, chard, chenin, colombard) • 20 000 tons 5 300 cs own label • PO Box 235 Worcester 6849 • aded@intekom.co.za • ***T (023) 347·2301*** *• F (023) 347·4629*

Winemaker/manager Johan Morkel doesn't want to expand on his long-term plans ('they're at a sensitive stage') but short-term he's in the process of meeting BRC and HACCP standards for selling into UK markets. 'Wine doesn't have to be expensive to be good,' he avers, and he rates the co-op's 2005 reds as better than good.

Elegant new packaging for latest bottlings. **Pinotage** ★★ **04** shy, touch earthy; red berry fruit shackled by strong tannins mid-2005; give time. **Doornroodt** ★★ *Vin ordinaire* from merlot, ruby cab; latter's thatch/stalk tone pervades **03**, tight savoury-dry finish. **Blanc de Noir** ★★ **05** pretty Natural Sweet-style blush from muscadel; lovely muscat aromas, lively acidic finish. **Colombar** Sherbety dry white, **05** barely vinous. **Colombar-Chardonnay** ★ **05** equal blend (80/20), unsparingly Fr oak staved. **Colombar Semi-Sweet** ★★ Fresh, off-dry tasting (rather than sweet) **05**, hint tropical fruit, flick of acidity. **Sparkling** ★★★ Demi-sec-style carbonated bubbly from colombard, ruby cab; bright, fresh, tropical fizz for the sweeter toothed. **NV**. **Muscat d'Alexandrie** ★★★ Fortified dessert with penetrating honeysuckle/jasmine scent, **04** well-balanced spirit & acidity for distinctly uncloying pleasure. 16.5% alc. **Red Muscadel** ★★ **03** shadow of former self; very sweet, simple fortified dessert with soapy texture. 16.5% alc. **Cape Ruby** ★★ 'Port' pvs ed. Now 'correct' varieties (tinta b, touriga) but old-style low fortification (17.5% alc); **03** savoury with bracing tannins. — *DH*

ACJ Fine Wines new

Durbanville ▪ Est/1stB 2004 ▪ Closed to public ▪ Owners Allan Hodgson, Billy Martin & Jeff Gradwell ▪ ±9 200 cs own label ▪ Brand for customer: Cattle Baron Group ▪ 33% red 66% white ▪ PO Box 3546 Tyger Valley 7536 ▪ cwacj@telkomsa.net ▪ ***T/F 919·6731***

Bryde wines, named after the whale species, are the product of a fledgling negociant partnership boasting 50 years' wine experience between its members (all ex-Distell). Sourcing from vineyards around the Western Cape, ACJ also supplies The Cattle Baron eateries with house and own-brand wines, and represents selected local cellars here and overseas (currently Canada and the US).

Bryde Shiraz ★★★ **04** shy woodsmoke/choc nose, flavours; smooth, rounded for early drinking. Unoaked. Slnghoek vyds. **Sauvignon Blanc 05** & **Colombard-Chenin Blanc 04** not tasted. — *AL*

Adler

Wellington ▪ Est/1stB 2004 ▪ Closed to public ▪ Owners/winemakers Oliver Meckler & Hans J Mamsell ▪ 1 100 cs 55% red 45% white ▪ adler@olimeck.co.za ▪ www.olimeck.co.za/adler ▪ PO Box 104 Linbro Park 2065 ▪ ***T (011) 579·1980*** *▪ F (011) 579·1981*

It's been a busy year for Geisenheim-trained Oliver Meckler and close friend Hans Mamsell. Having launched their Adler ('Eagle') label with a red, 2005 saw them spread their wings with the still whites below and an MCC sparkling (untasted). Sticking to the philosophy of using as little technology as possible, Meckler is delighted with the results. Next year he plans a white *cuvée* — for him, blending is the ultimate test of the winemaker's craft.

★★★★ **Modus M** Bdx blend cab, merlot, petit v (55/40/5) in **04**; classic mineral tone & fine complexity, structure. Shade smaller, more elegant than **03** with booming blackberry/blackcurrant fruit & 14.5% alc.

Sauvignon Blanc 05 unstabilised sample too unformed to rate. **Viognier** ★★★★ Attractive honeysuckle-scented **05** with viscous palate dominated by peaches & lanolin. A good aperitif style. All new to the guide. All EW except 03 red. — *NP*

Admiralty House see Cape Bay
Adventure see Kango
A Few Good Men see Riebeek Cellars
Affinity see African Terroir, La Bri
African Collection see Rooiberg
African Dawn see Rooiberg
African Gold see Old Bridge, Dominion
African Horizon see Origin Wine

African Pride Wines

Constantia ▪ Est/1stB 2002 ▪ Closed to public ▪ Owner Afrifresh Holdings ▪ Winemaker Mike Graham (May 2002) ▪ 60% red 40% white ▪ PO Box 518 Constantia 7848 ▪ info@africanpridewines.co.za ▪ www.africanpridewines.co.za ▪ ***T 794·0323*** *▪ F 794·0344*

Having established itself in the US and Europe, African Pride is expanding in the local market. Naas Erasmus, now marketing/commercial director, heads this drive while voluble Mike Graham fights the oenological battles. And what a war, with a dry 2004 winter followed by a rain-soaked pre-harvest followed by atypical humidity, threatening rot. 'Too late to spray; let us pray' was the mantra. Whites were hardest hit, with production down 30%. Reds fought back, though, and morale was boosted further by a medal at Vinalies in Paris for the Lady Anne Syrah and a Singapore Airlines Business listing for the Footprint Chardonnay.

Lady Anne Barnard range

Not retasted, notes from pvs ed: **Cabernet Sauvignon** ★★★★ Elegant & understated **02**, hints wet heath & leafy footpath to red-berried ripeness; tannins supple but structured to age few yrs. 18 mths Fr oak. **Syrah** ★★★★ (Noted 2005 ed as 'Shiraz') **02** creamy mulberry aroma, lively, juicy palate features ripe Hldrberg fruit, well expressed. 16 mths oak, new/2nd fill. **Chardonnay** ★★★★ Statement wine with big oak presence; **03** flavours of lemon, lime & buttered toast. Another yr should help integrate oak & fruit, & possibly up the star rating. Fermented/9 mths new Fr oak, portion native yeasts. These WO Stbosch, all below W Cape.

Footprint range

Cabernet Sauvignon ★★★ Appealing early-drinking style; **04** fresh red-fruit profile, toasty dry finish from 20% barrelled portion. **Shiraz** ★★★ Repeats last yr's friendly tone; **04** smoky plum fruit, medium weight, gentle tannins. Following duo not retasted: **Chardonnay** ★★★ **04** aromatic & lively on nose; succulent mid-palate with lime acidity, sweet finish. 10% barrel fermented. **Sauvignon Blanc** ★★★ **04** early harvested for piercing grassiness, forthcoming herbaceous tone repeats on palate through to thirst-quenching finish.

Cape MacLear range

Shiraz-Cabernet Sauvignon ★★★ **04** identical blend to pvs (66/33), unwooded; shiraz nose, cab active on palate, which slightly firmer than last though still accessible. **Chenin Blanc-Chardonnay** ★★★ Last ed **04** offered fruit salad aromas, rounded peach flavours in lively & juicy 60/40 blend. *— CR*

African Sky see Drostdy

African Terroir

*Paarl ▪ Est 1991 ▪ 1stB 1991 ▪ Visits Mon-Fri 9-5 (phone ahead) ▪ Fee R15 refunded on purchase of 2+ btls ▪ Closed Dec 25/26 & Jan 1 ▪ Picnic baskets, platters & beverages by appt; or BYO ▪ Guest house ▪ Tourgroups ▪ Conferencing ▪ Owner Jacques Germanier ▪ Winemakers Helène van der Westhuizen, with Mathieu Labaki (Jan 2003/May 2004) ▪ Viti consultants Thys Greef & Francois Brink (Sep 2000/Dec 2002) ▪ 75 ha (own vyds: cab, shiraz) ▪ 400 tons ▪ BRC & HACCP certified; ISO 9001:2000 in progress ▪ Ranges for customers: Indaba, Mooiberge, Unity & Affinity ▪ PO Box 2029 Windmeul 7630 ▪ office@african-terroir.co.za ▪ www.african-terroir.co.za ▪ **T 869·8103** ▪ F 869·8104*

New winemaker Mathieu Labaki, French-born, isn't new to SA – he's worked here for a couple of seasons and hopes he'll be at African Terroir for at least three years. Word from the winery's international sales arm is that consumers want more fruit and less wood, so that's what they're getting from the winemaker: 'Fruity, juicy wines with varietal character'. AT is an organic pioneer – one of its four wineries, Sonop, celebrates its 10th anniversary as an organic operation this year – and Labaki is firm about using as little sulphur as possible, or any product which is genetically modified. Intent on promoting its range to the local market, AT now offers tours of its Cilmor cellar at Worcester and its new filling line, which handles 20 000 bottles an hour.

Diemersdal range

Cabernet Sauvignon ★★★ **04** variety's cool cedar & berry character on nose, palate lean-fruited, dominated by wood tannins (though only 2nd fill oak). **Merlot 04** ★★★★ Appealing (cab-like) tones of cassis & dried leaf, charming silky dark-fruited palate, well-balanced acid & wood. Allier oak aged. **Pinotage** ★★ **04** nothing like refined pvs; ultra-ripe with 'hot'/baked fruit, touch green stalkiness on prune-tinged palate. 40% oaked. **Shiraz** ★★★★ **04** reprises balanced, harmonious character of pvs (02); velvet-textured dark berry/black cherry fruit, good oaking (only 2nd fill casks), short, slightly sweet finish only detraction. **Harmony** ★★★ Aptly named blend; **04** sees shiraz return to cab, merlot, cab f line-up, all in equal portions; fleshy & soft, big but easy (14.1% alc). Older Allier barrels. **Chardonnay** ★★★☆ Still-available **04** shy, hint resinous oak over peach fruit; light-bodied, minerally, elegant, not overblown. **Sauvignon Blanc** ★★★ **05** oaked, according to winemaker, but no wood detected; evident is Dbnville's dusty capsicum on nose, generous tropical fruit on palate. All above EW, WO Dbnville.

Elixir range

Sauvignon Blanc Noble Late Harvest ★★★☆ Soft, silky **00**, last yr fairly developed aromas, some dried apricot whiffs & good botrytis dusting, clean fruity acidity. Yr barrel aged. 15% alc. Grapes ex-Dbnville.

Milton Grove range

Range (temporarily?) slimmed down to the following wine, not restasted: **Shiraz** ★★★☆ **04** appealing plummy shiraz fruit, leathery whiff; good juice & suppleness.

Out of Africa range

Following reds were samples pvs ed, retasted this yr: **Cabernet Sauvignon** ★★★ **04** warm ripe fruit, eucalyptus touch; lots of austere cab tannins (oak staved) – will they soften? **Pinotage** ★★☆ **04** fat, juicy & stuffed with fruitcake, berry & spice; hugely drinkable & fun. Unwooded. **Shiraz** ★★★☆ Yr on, **04** more 'elegant' than 'exuberant'; notes of truffle & mocha, pleasant if shade more foursquare than pvs. **Pinotage-Shiraz** new ★★ Baked prune nose on old-style **04**, warm-climate character continues on palate with pulpy sweet-ripe fruit. **Chardonnay** ★★ Unwooded **05** warm, friendly, sunny style; dried peach flavours, clean finish. **Merlot** ★★★ **04** last yr showed leafy undergrowth & hint meat, medium body; savoury dark-choc flavours. Combo Vdal/Dbnville fruit. **Sauvignon Blanc** ★☆ **05** usual water-white transparency & pear-drop aroma, otherwise very little character this yr.

Sonop Organic range

All **05**; reds 15% Fr oaked. **Cabernet Sauvignon** ★★ Hot-climate feel, raisined & porty, commensurably soft acid. **Merlot** ★★★ Psvly described as having bright plum-jam-on-toast character; plump & soft. **Pinotage** ★★ Unshowy, almost delicate red-berried appeal, easy to drink if quick finishing. **Shiraz** ★★ Smoky entry to this gentle, softly plummy version; lower alc (13.7%) than pvs, less uptight tannin. **Chardonnay** ★☆ Lacks verve but won't offend; soft ripe stone-fruit tone. Lightly Fr oaked. **Sauvignon Blanc** ★ Trades flinty/dusty austerity of pvs for soft, slightly boneless approachability.

Tribal Winemakers Collection new

Reds all **04**, lightly oak staved. Whites **05** unwooded. **Cabernet Sauvignon** ★★ Cedary whiffs, lively/tangy flavours with savoury notes; lower keyed but pleasant; grows on you. **Merlot** ★★ Unlike so many SA examples, soft & juicy, quaffable; ripe plum & cassis tones, brush of tannin. **Pinotage** ★★ Cheery sort of wine, quaffable, honest varietal expression; lots of squishy fruit. **Shiraz** ★☆ Soft & easy; vague hints of spice, quick finish. **Chardonnay** ★☆ Lighter style, undemanding; delicate whiff white peach & fresh clean acidity. **Chenin Blanc** ★ Plain & simple citrus flavours, hint pithy bitterness.

Tribal range

All NV/uncertified. No newer vintages available; notes from pvs ed: **African Red** ★★★ Understated plum jam aromas, livelier mulberry flavour, low tannins for easy/early drinking. **Rosé** ★★ Light-bodied pink from pinotage. cinsaut, pinot; fairly succulent cherry palate, food-friendly dry finish. **African White Semi Sweet** ★ Shy, lightly fruited, quick finishing. Above available in glass & 1ℓ flexible packs. **Sparkling White Off-Dry** ★★ Light semi-sweet fizz with soft lingering sweetness.

Winds of Change range

Both **04**, Neither retasted; notes from pvs ed: **Pinotage-Cabernet Sauvignon** ★★★ Pinotage's smoky mulberry fruit to fore (70/30 blend); soft, silky & lightly spicy. **Shiraz-Merlot** ★★★ Smoked meat, touch white pepper; soft, ripe & drinkable.

Fruit for above ranges sourced widely; WO W Cape unless noted. — *IvH/TM*

African Treasure see Vin-X-Port
African Wine Adventure see Mooiuitsig

African Wines & Spirits

Cape Town ▪ Est 1999 ▪ Closed to public ▪ Owners Edward Snell & Co ▪ Directors DV Hooper & CC Weeden ▪ 40% red 60% white ▪ PO Box 318 Paarden Eiland ▪ T 506·2600 F 510·4560

This wholesaling and marketing company is now owned by Edward Snell & Co, and has the Craighall range made to spec by Omnia Wines in Stellenbosch. Other brands in the stable include the Cinzano sparkling wine range, which in future will be bottled in Italy and imported into SA.

Africa Vineyards see Winecorp
Agterkliphoogte see Wandsbeck

Agterplaas Wines

Stellenbosch (see Helderberg map) ▪ Est/1stB 2003 ▪ Visits by appt ▪ Owner/winemaker James Basson ▪ PO Box 863 Stellenbosch 7599 ▪ 4.5 tons 250 cs ▪ agterplaas@webmail.co.za ▪ ***T/F 886·9015***

Highlights of 2005 for cellar designer James Basson were sourcing red grapes at very low prices, producing 4 000 bottles of wine, and designing and building his own crusher (output: 10 tons an hour). Next up is a destemmer and, somewhere in between, a sorting table. All this in his Parow *agterplaas* (backyard) and a corner of his friends' Somerbosch cellar. The search for his own production premises continues, on the path towards creating a 'stunning Bordeaux-style wine'.

Cabernet Sauvignon new ★★★ Appealing maiden from Hldrberg vines, with moderate alc (13.5%), dried leaf/macadamia aromas, mulberry & sweet/sour fruit flavours. Firm yet friendly wood tannins from 18 mths 3rd fill Fr oak. **Mike's Red** ★★★ Cab the senior partner in old-Cape formula cab/cinsaut (79/21). Tasted mid-2004, cool cedar notes, softish tannins & fresh acidity. 8 mths used Fr oak. No **04**, **05** unready. **Sauvignon Blanc** ★★★ **04** mid-2004 assertive, lean & bone-dry with rapier-direct acid. Next will be **06**. For 2005/6 release (not tasted): **Cabernet Sauvignon-Merlot 04** & unnamed **'Bordeaux Blend' 05**, melange cab, merlot, petit v, malbec (& cab f if James B can find some!). — *CT/IvH*

Agulhas see Merwespont

Agulhas Wines

new

Elim ▪ Est 2002 ▪ 1stB 2003 ▪ Tasting & sales Mon-Fri 8-5 ▪ BYO picnic ▪ 2 self-catering guest cottages ▪ Tours by appt ▪ Tourgroups by arrangement ▪ Walks ▪ Owners Strandveld Vineyards & Rietfontein Trust ▪ Winemaker/viticulturist Conrad Vlok (Dec 2004) ▪ 65 ha (pinot, shiraz, chardonnay, sauvignon) ▪ 90 tons 6 000 cs 45% red 55% white ▪ Export brands: Strandveld & First Sighting ▪ PO Box 1020 Bredasdorp 7280 ▪ info@agulhaswines.com ▪ ***T/F (028) 482·1902/6***

During the first month of his appointment, winemaker Conrad Vlok (ex-Baarsma) had to battle the worst floods in almost 50 yrs, train vine canes in gale-force winds and draw from a labour pool that knows more about wheat farming than vineyards. But these obstacles were quickly overcome and he is now a passionate supporter of the area. 'I've never come across sauvignon grapes of such high quality. It was nerve-wracking working with them.' The winery claims Africa's southern-most vineyard at Uintjieskuil. Adds Vlok: 'This is the coolest I've ever experienced in SA.' While CV acknowledges climate as his greatest asset, he praises the vineyards planted in gravel and stone for coaxing the most delicate of flavours out of the grapes.

First Sighting Range

Sauvignon Blanc ★★★★ **05** recognisable cool-climate minerals, figgy vivacity. Medium weight, brisk dryness. Well balanced to make most of young Elim vyds. **Shiraz** ★★★ Uncomplicated, ready **03**. Some red fruits/choc character; smooth, full-bodied with rather cloying finish.

Fr oak 16 mths. WO Coastal, as is ... **Chardonnay** ★★★ Medium-bodied, unwooded **04**. Melon/peach bouquet quietened by hint bottle age; simple, rather gravelly, dry. Drink up.—*AL*

Aigle Noir see Remhoogte

Akkerdal Estate

Franschhoek ▪ Est 2000 ▪ 1stB 2001 ▪ Tasting & sales by appt Mon-Fri 8-5 Sat 9-1 ▪ Sales also at Franschhoek Vineyards (see A-Z entry) & La Cotte Inn Wine Sales (see Wine shops section) ▪ Closed pub hols ▪ Self-catering guest house ▪ Owner/winemaker/viticulturist Pieter Hanekom, advised by Eben Archer & Dawid Saayman ▪ 18 ha (malbec, merlot, mourvèdre, petit v, pinotage, shiraz, chard, sauvignon, semillon, viognier) ▪ ±750 cs own label 95% red 5% white ▪ ISO certification in progress ▪ PO Box 36 La Motte 7691 ▪ wine@akkerdal.co.za ▪ www.akkerdal.co.za ▪ ***T 876·3481/082·442·1746*** *▪ F 876·3189*

Franschhoek wine farmer Pieter Hanekom, who lives his passion 'from the vineyard into the bottle', concluded after three warm winters that the key to success last harvest was hands-on 'terroir management', from canopy to sunlight and water. This balanced approach paid off and the more he worked with the wines the more impressed he became with the exceptional aromas, colours and flavours emanating from vintage 2005. His aim now to make a stand-out blend, his vision remains to stay an artisan winery producing 7 000 bottles of wine a year (a percentage of his remaining grapes goes into Fleur du Cap's highly rated Unfiltered Collection.).

★★★★ **Merlot 04** back on track; toasty oak combines with racy yet ripe fruit to deliver rich, rounded mouthful, lingering goodbye; structure for development over 3-5 yrs. 14 mths mainly 1st fill oak. **03** (★★★★) savoury notes, green olive/herbal whiffs, dry herbaceous finish from 18 mths older barrels. No **02** (went into Passion).

Syrah ★★★★ With perfect ripeness, balance, powerful & ripe tannic punch, **03** (★★★★) step up on pvs. Garrigue & liquorice wafts, concentrated berry fruit softened with drop viognier & dollop mourvèdre. Harmonious, a wine to watch. Barrels as above, 18 mths. **Wild Boar** ★★★★ Unconventional blend excites the tastebuds – malbec, mourvèdre, petit v, tempranillo, roobernet, barbera & cab f (we did ask!). Juicy, smooth; accessible but with tannins to carry ± 5 yrs. Oaking as for Syrah. **Passion Red** ★★★★ **04** rings the changes: to blend: (now shiraz led) & to quality level (up). Shiraz pepper dominates wild/mulberry nose; mourvèdre, malbec & pinotage add spice & zest. Robust, muscled tannins great with steak. 14 mths combo Fr/Am/Hungarian oak. **Passion White** new ★★★★ **04** unoaked blend equal (almost) portions chardonnay, sauvignon, semillon & viognier; balanced with waxy roundness, pleasing, dry finish; complex with citrus fruit/floral fragrances/favours. **Kallie's Dream** new ★★★ Oaked dinner table companion; viognier/sauvignon (35/30) lead chardonnay/semillion (23/12). Nuanced bouquet of buttered toast, lime, artichoke, earth; palate rich & smooth.—*CT*

Alexanderfontein see Ormonde

Allée Bleue

Franschhoek ▪ Est 2000 ▪ 1stB 2001 ▪ Tasting & sales daily 9-5 ▪ Café Allée Bleue (Tue-Sun 9-5) & other attractions (see intro) ▪ Tours by appt ▪ Tourgroups ▪ Owners DAUPHIN Entwicklungs-und Beteiligungs GMH (Germany) ▪ Winemaker Gerda Willers (Dec 2001) ▪ Consultant Rob Meihuizen (2001) ▪ 30 ha (cab, merlot, pinotage, shiraz, sauvignon, semillon) ▪ 88% red 9% white 3% rosé ▪ PO Box 100 Groot Drakenstein 7680 ▪ info@alleebleue.com ▪ www.alleebleue.com ▪ ***T 874·1021*** *▪ F 874·1850*

All the signs here of a business that's on the move – a new cellar under construction; the farm's own vines yielding their maiden vintage in 2005; volumes up from 50 000 to 80 000 bottles; the release of a new premium blend, L'amour Toujours; and a newly launched second-label wine, the Starlette Rouge. It's all go on the visitor front too, with varied attractions such as an al fresco restaurant, picnics by arrangement, and conference/event facilities which, the A-B team believes, are among the finest and most attractive in the winelands, combining 300-year-old architecture with modern art and the latest technology.

★★★★☆ **Pinotage** Robust earthy style, fruit off Piekenklf vyds. **04** (★★★☆) shows ample mouth-filling fruit but dominated by alcohol (15%), which lends aggressive texture. Barrel aged, 50% new, 20% Am. Lacks dimension of lighter but more compelling **03** (13% alc).

★★★★ **Isabeau** Fine semillon/chardonnay blend (±60/40). **04** sumptuous but not confected; dense thatchy notes, generously but well oaked, harmonious supple fruit lifted by elegant crisp finish. Worthy successor to similarly structured **03**.

L'amour Toujours new ★★★ Seamless blend mainly cab & merlot (55/24) with shiraz & grenache; from Hermon, Piekenklf vyds. **04** amply oaked (yr, 50% new), alc (15%) masks fruit. **Shiraz** ★★★ Robust texture, munificent oak (as above), rampant alc (15.5%) characterise **04**, less spicy than pvs. **Cabernet Sauvignon-Merlot** new ★★★ Sweet-fruited, muscular red, dominated by cab (66%); **04** ripe despite slight herbal notes. 50% new Fr barrels, Hermon grapes. **Starlette Rouge** new ★★★ Pleasing, accessible red, blend mainly cab & shiraz (44/25) dashes pinotage & grenache adding spice/texture to **04**. 15% alc partly concealed by dense fruit. Hermon/Piekenklf vyds. Wood aged, mainly older. **Rosé** new ★★★ Unusual shiraz/semillon combo (80/20) yields mouth-filling, dusky **04**, with food-friendly tannins; dry (1.8g/ℓ RS), ample grip but alc (14.5%) too evident for lunchtime drinking. **Pinotage Natural Sweet** ★☆ **03**, not retasted, tannic with sugar (22g/ℓ) softening but not lifting fruit, intriguing textures, 15.5% alc, 50% new oak. **Cabernet Sauvignon** discontinued.—*MF*

Allesverloren Estate

Swartland ▪ Est 1704 ▪ Tasting & sales Mon-Fri 8.30–5 Sat 8.30–2 Phone ahead on pub hols ▪ Tours by appt ▪ BYO picnic ▪ Play area for children ▪ Owner/winemaker/viticulturist Danie Malan (Nov 1987) ▪ 187 ha (cab, shiraz & various port varieties) ▪ 50 000 cs 100% red ▪ PO Box 23 Riebeek West 7306 ▪ info@allesverloren.co.za ▪ www.allesverloren.co.za ▪ ***T (022) 461·2320*** *▪ F (022) 461·2444*

A year ago, family Malan hosted a grand celebration: the 300th anniversary of the Allesverloren name. It's a name that's doing marketer Distell proud, particularly in northern Europe, where consumers know and love the Tinta and now, like German and British port-drinkers, they're getting what's labelled Fine Old Vintage. 'We can't make enough for them,' says Orland Firmani, Danie M's father-in-law, who's involved in the marketing effort. Back on the farm, the tasting and sales venue (new, but with the historic look of the buildings around it) has been moved closer to the cellar. New, too, is farm manager Flip Smit, one of whose first projects was removing shiraz from an old block and replanting.

★★★★ **Shiraz** Generous build & chunky ripe fruit are hallmarks; **03** returns to form with complex bouquet & palate of red fruit & wild scrub, lifted by fresh acidity, firm tannin. Needs time to settle, rein in its considerable power (14.4% alc). Difficult red vintage reflected in **02** (★★★☆), firm acidity with drying finish. **01** had more typical Allesverloren flesh, heart. ±18 mths oak, some new, mainly Fr.=

★★★★☆ **Port** A 'quaffing' port, if there is such a thing; ingratiating & effortless LBV style; **99** much like pvs but nuttier – also with dash malvasia rey souping up customary souzão, pontac, touriga & trio of tintas (roriz introduced with **96**). **98** rich prune/savoury nose with madeira-like tang; sweet & delicious. **97** was drier (82g/ℓ sugar) than 104 g/ℓ of **99**, still typical, if more delicate. Old-oak aged.

Cabernet Sauvignon ★★★☆ Recent vintages of this beefy Swtlnd standard more variable; **02** muted on nose; palate packed with prunes, cherries & gruff tannins; not for the faint-hearted; should soften, meld with fruit core over 3-5 yrs. 18 mths Fr oak, 30% new. **Tinta Barocca** ★★★☆ Danie M among handful of producers soldiering on with variety. Attractively rustic **04** has cranberries, lilies & vanilla; easy tannins & zesty acidity, persistent red berry tail. Fr oak 18 mths, 50/50 2nd/3rd fill. **Touriga Nacional** ★★★ Raspberry toned **03** light, sweet & still fairly taut last ed; admirably moderate alc (±13%). Traditionally styled, may develop interestingly.—*CvZ*

Alluvia

new

Stellenbosch ▪ Est 2002 ▪ 1stB 2005 ▪ Tasting by appt ▪ Sales office open daily ▪ Tours for pvt clients only ▪ Luxury guest suites ▪ Facilities for children ▪ Gifts ▪ Conferences ▪ Walks ▪ Moun-

tain bike trails ▪ Owners Delarey & Sandie Brugman ▪ Winemaker Bruwer Raats, with Neil Moorehouse (2002/2003) ▪ Viti adviser Kevin Watt (2002) ▪ 8 ha (cab) ▪ 18 tons 1 100 cs 88% red 12% white ▪ PO Box 6365 Uniedal 7612 ▪ info@alluvia.co.za ▪ www.alluvia.co.za ▪ ***T 0861·80·70·60/885·1661*** *F 885·2064*

Delarey Brugman, a dynamic young businessman, swapped his Johannesburg based corporate 'gold' in 2002 for the 'brown gold' of a rare alluvial soil deposit, on a property high up in the Banhoek Mountains. The move allowed him to provide wife Sandie and family with the tranquil quality of country life, and an opportunity to live out his dream: expressing the unique viticultural site through a small range of top-notch wines, primarily Cab. Their maiden vintages are named Ilka, after twin daughters Ilse and Karla. The farm offers luxury accommodation; facilities, private tuition and equipment for fly fishing; golf and mountain biking, plus helipad.

Ilka range

★★★★ **Sauvignon Blanc** Dusty tropical fruit preface to gentle **05**, floral scents & moderate acidity; 4.5g/ℓ sugar gives richness & some palate weight. 13.5% alc.

Cabernet Sauvignon ★★★★ Restrained fruit but good depth & balance on **04**, incipient complexity from tiny splashes petit v & merlot (3%); needs another yr to start showing its best. 14 mths oak, third new. —*NP*

Alphen Hill see Cru Wines

Alter Ego Wines

Tulbagh ▪ Est 2001 ▪ 1stB 2002 ▪ Visits by appt Mon-Sat 9-5 ▪ Meals by appt or BYO ▪ Mountain biking by appt ▪ Owner Vin de Parr cc ▪ Winemaker/viticulturist John Parr (Sep 2001) ▪ 4 ha (cabs s/f, merlot, pinotage, chard) ▪ 35 tons 2 000 cs 50% red 40% white 10% port ▪ PO Box 364 Tulbagh 6820 ▪ playberg@icon.co.za ▪ www.kloofzichtwines.co.za ▪ ***T (023) 230·0658*** *▪ F (023) 230·0774*

With alcohol levels slightly higher than usual – 'Where was the rain?' the Parrs bemoaned from their Tulbagh property, Kloofzicht – the philosophy behind the wines remained the same: 'Keep it simple, stupid!' Their Semillon 03 – 'so versatile, it's the chameleon of white wines' – was served on BA, creating a firm base of repeat business (although no Semillon was made last year as fruit did not meet expectations). John P spent most of the year in Johannesburg completing a series called 'Sokka Kings', the highest rated local television show after 'Generations'. Having expanded the range to include their first Cabernet and new well-priced red and white blends, they're exploring foreign markets. They're also moving the winery and this filmmaker promises 'a very surprising and rather wonderful' location, to be revealed next edition....

Cabernet Sauvignon new ★★★★ **03** forceful but undemanding; generous cassis fruit encased in carefully managed oak (15 mths Fr, 10% new), structure to improve 3+ yrs. **Ethan Asher** ★★★★ Was 'Cape blend' of pinotage, cab, merlot; now cab/merlot 60/40 blend. Very claret-like with subtle fruit, leafy core & mineral finish. Judicious oak details from 15 mths in Fr wood, 20% new. Should improve 5-7 yrs. **Semillon** ★★★ (Pvsly 'Old Parr's Head). **04** whiffs of honey, lemon, unoaked but 3 mths on lees. Responsible 12.5% alc, refreshing acidity when young. **Alter Ego Elroy's Pawt 00** still available; unrated sweet fortified from cab & merlot, 'made with a few eucalyptus leaves in barrel'. Like the Labrador it's named for, brimming with personality. 375ml. 17% alc. —*DH*

Alto Estate

Stellenbosch ▪ Est 1906 ▪ 1stB 1918 ▪ Tasting & sales Mon-Fri 9-5 Sat & pub hols 10-4 ▪ Fee R10 (R20 incl glass) ▪ Owner Lusan Premium Wines ▪ Winemaker Schalk van der Westhuizen (Jul 2000) ▪ Vineyard manager Danie van Zyl ▪ Viticulturist Eben Archer ▪ 93 ha ▪ 25 000 cs 100% red ▪ PO Box 104 Stellenbosch 7599 ▪ altoestate@telkomsa.net ▪ www.alto.co.za ▪ ***T 881·3884*** *▪ F 881·3894*

This grande dame of Cape red-wine estates continues to quietly produce the goods, keeping abreast of the new without losing sight of what went before. The 2005 vintage saw the first harvest of cab franc (promising, says winemaker Schalk van der Westhuizen in typically laconic fashion); the introduction of a new Bucher press and Diemme destemmer; the enlarging of the maturation cellar, which sees the tasting room moved to another part of the cellar; and visiting hours extended to 4pm Saturdays and public holidays. Danie van Zyl does duty in the vineyards, being replanted under the guidance of Eben Archer, viticultural eminence of the Lusan stable of farms.

★★★★ **Cabernet Sauvignon** Stylistically one of SA's slow-maturing wines, its cellarability conferred by cab's typical austere tannins. Epitomised by outstanding **01** (★★★★☆), **98**, **95** & now **03**, with lovely youthful red/black fruits, dusty spices poised to evolve with distinction over ±10 yrs. No **02**. **00** an anomaly: less obviously tannic, more accessible on release. Oaking regimen 18–24 mths 300ℓ Fr oak, 50% new, rest 2nd/3rd fill.

★★★★ **Shiraz** Off 8 yr old unirrigated vyd, 400–450m up the Hldrberg. Maiden **01** set tone: big but not bold, more elegant than powerful despite ±14% alc. Follow-up **02** has similar vanilla-washed ripe redcurrant tone; very nice. 18 mths new oak, 60% Am. Not retasted; last ed we suggested ageing further 2-3 yrs; should last another 4–6 yrs min. **03** unready.

★★★★ **Alto Rouge** ('Estate' outside SA) ✓ One of Cape's oldest & best-loved labels. Has morphed from cab/cinsaut of yesteryear via traditional Bdx blend to current merlot, cabs s/f, shiraz mix (45/25/15/15). **03** won't disappoint: the scrubby/cherry nose gives way to stern tannins, fresh acidity against ripe background fruit. As usual, a promising future. **02** attractively rustic & organic; **01** soft & faintly 'hot', not as complex. 18 mths oak, mainly Fr, 1st-3rd fill. — *CvZ*

Altydgedacht Estate

Durbanville ▪ Est 1698 ▪ 1stB 1981 ▪ Tasting & sales Mon-Fri 9-5 Sat 9-3 ▪ Closed Easter Fri, Dec 25 & Jan 1 ▪ Tours by appt ▪ Pampoenkraal boma-style function restaurant T 913·4962/3 ▪ Conferencing ▪ Conservation area ▪ Owners Parker family ▪ Winemaker Oliver Parker, with Mark Carmichael-Green ▪ Viticulturists John Parker, with Adanté Roux (2002) ▪ 158 ha (12 varieties, r/w) ▪ 1 250 tons ±5 000 cs own label 60% red 40% white ▪ Export label: Tygerberg ▪ PO Box 213 Durbanville 7551 ▪ altydgedacht@mweb.co.za ▪ www.altydgedacht.co.za ▪ ***T 976·1295*** *▪ F 976·4318 /8521*

It's Oliver Parker's fervent hope that urban sprawl won't encroach on the farms and conservation areas cheek by jowl with Durbanville's vineyards. They give the area its charm, just as the sales venue at Altydgedacht, in spite of a recent upgrade, has the homely, low-key atmosphere of a 5th-generation family farm. Another of winemaker Ollo P's wishes is that the 6th generation – his three sons and his brother John's three daughters – will buck the trend towards the transfer of family properties to companies. The intention is to consolidate Altydgedacht's position as a producer of unusual styles such as barbera and dry gewürz, and as well as varieties which perform well in Durbanville, such as sauvignon and shiraz.

★★★★ **Pinotage 01** was juicy, generous, with ripe tannins. From lesser vintage, **02** (★★★☆) full, well structured, supported by skilful oaking (yr, mostly Fr) & balanced 14% alc, though fruit less rich & touched by animal/plastic character.

★★★★ **Shiraz** ✓ **01** matched aromatic, sweet redcurrant fruit, oak & gently gripping tannins. **02** not tasted. Balanced, savoury **03** (★★★☆) with strawberry jam tone, integrated yr Fr/Am oak, but good red fruit marred by elastoplast undertone.

Cabernet Sauvignon ★★★ Dry-finishing **02** has good tannins, but less fruit presence than pvs. Yr Fr/Am oak. **Barbera** ★★★☆ Engaging SA pioneer of this Italian grape. **02** (not retasted) a little lighter, leaner, less sweet, more tannic than usual – & perhaps more interesting. Mix Fr/Am oak, quarter new. **Merlot** ★★★☆ Barrel sample youthful **04** has herbal, tobacco, red-fruit aromas/flavours; savoury & well-balanced, with ripe tannins. Yr in mix Fr/ Am oak. **Chardonnay** ★★★☆ Mostly oak-fermented/aged 5 mths. Last-tasted **03** round, pleasant, fresh, well balanced. No **04**. **Chenin Blanc** new ★★★☆ Richly textured, warmly rounded & fresh **05** from 32 yr old bushvines, with good green-edged thatchy flavours. **Sauvignon Blanc** ★★★☆ **05** ripely flavourful as ever, freshly & fruitily succulent, with touch sugar (3.7g/ℓ) adding to immediate appeal. **Gewürztraminer** ★★★ Reliably charming example; just-dry **05** includes splash viognier, offers typical rose-petal & spice. **Chatelaine** ★★ Off-dry, aromatically perfumed **05** (tank sample) from gewürz, riesling, viognier; light-bodied (12% alc) & light-hearted. — *TJ*

Alvi's Drift Private Cellar

Worcester ▪ Est 1928 ▪ 1stB 2002 ▪ Tasting, sales & tours by appointment ▪ Canoe trips, game drives, visits to dairy/cheesery, BYO picnics, walks, eco-friendly 4×4 excursions by arrangement ▪ Owners Alvi & Johan van der Merwe ▪ Winemaker Alvi van der Merwe ▪ Viti consultant Pierre Snyman ▪ 350 ha (17 varieties w/r) ▪ 5 000 tons ▪ PO Box 827 Worcester 6850 ▪ alvi@intekom.co.za ▪ ***T (023) 340·4117*** *▪ F (023) 340·4557*

Former Worcester GP Alvi van der Merwe has two passions: winemaking and conservation. He and brother Johan's extensive vineyards produce primarily for bulk but Alvi vdM vinifies some special Alvi's Drift bottlings (with input from ex-Nederburg Newald Marais and AvdM's father, Bertie, a local wine-industry legend). Besides 05 Chenins and Muscadel, he may bottle a Chardonnay (due this year), as well as Shiraz and a shiraz-pinotage-merlot blend (out 2007). See above for extras on this game-stocked, floral-rich property.

★★★★☆ **Muscat de Frontigan** ✓ **04** perfect example of SA muscadel; complex nose, sweet entry, tangy & uncloying finish. Barley sugar, peaches, jasmine waft in/out of bouquet; palate perfectly balanced. Enjoy in winter or summer, even over ice. 14 mths Fr oak.

Chenin Blanc ☺ ★★★ Unoaked, appealing **05**; juicy tropical fruit salad, zingy acid. Happy mouthful, thanks to high extract & 14.3% alc!

Chenin Blanc ★★★ Barrel-fermented, complete, well-structured **05** with bountiful flavour, acid & fruit tannins; oak adding interest/mouthfeel. Charming maiden. All above new. — *CR*

Amalienstein see Southern Cape Vineyards
Amandalia see Rooiberg

Amani Vineyards

Stellenbosch ▪ Est/1stB 1997 ▪ Tasting & sales Mon-Fri 9–4 Sat (Oct-Apr) 10.30–3 ▪ Closed Easter Fri/Sun, Dec 25 & Jan 1 ▪ Tours by appt ▪ Owner Jim Atkinson ▪ Winemaker Carmen Kelley, with Dirk Tredoux (both 2005) ▪ Viticulturist/GM Rusty Myers, advised by Kevin Watt (Oct 2002/May 2003) ▪ 32 ha (cab f, merlot, shiraz, chard, sauvignon) ▪ 7 000 cs 30% red 70% white ▪ PO Box 12422 Die Boord 7613 ▪ wine@amani.co.za ▪ www.amani.co.za ▪ ***T 905·1126*** *▪ F 905·4404*

'We are seeing our production creep up and the vines become more uniform in health and size…' says Rusty Myers, guardian of these vineyards, who with consultant Kevin Watt strictly controls production to six or seven tons per hectare. Last harvest was the 'best ever': the Sauvignon exceeded expectations and their first Shiraz impressed with fruity and full results. The maiden Atkinson Ridge Chardonnay – genuinely 'limited quantity', it represents 1% of their chardonnay production – was released to silver applause at Chardonnay-du-Monde. Winemaker Carmen Kelly exchanged big-volume production at Stellenbosch Vineyards for this 81ton boutique cellar. Vineyard-focused, she's looking forward to the freedom to 'do whatever it takes to make the best wines possible'. They're now open for leisurely Saturday tastings.

★★★★ **Merlot** After dip in **03** (★★★☆), **04** back to heights of pvs; seamless, deep & ripe; creamy texture, concentrated fruit, ripe tannins. **03** somewhat lacking complexity, conviction. These approachable on release, structured for min 3–4 yrs. ±30% new barriques, 11–18 mths; usually with splash cab s or f for complexity/stiffening.

★★★★ **Chardonnay** Excellent track record since maiden **98**; **04** quintessential Amani with white peach tone, rounded/weighty mouthfeel – but not blowsy, satisfying dry finish. Bold oak with fruit to bolster. **03** (★★★☆) was eager & easy drinking. Fermented/aged ±10 mths Fr barrels, some new.

Cabernet Franc-Merlot new ★★★★ 57/43 assemblage in maiden **04**. Bursting with merlot's dark plum fruit & cab f's scrub notes. Integrated oak, balanced; accessible but with structure to improve 3-4 yrs. **I Am 1** new Fine, classy red blend led by cab f (44%) with merlot/cab s/shiraz (35/16/5). Understandably dominated by cab f's green walnut/fynbos notes; juicy berry fruit, judicious oak treatment. Silky, smooth yet powerful. Accessible now with all the attributes to unfold & continue to reward for 5-7 yrs. Potential ★★★★. Yr Fr oak, some new. **Sauvignon Blanc** ★★★ **04**'s leafy/nettle aromas/flavours give austerity to palate, abetted by uncompromising acidity. Splash viognier not overtly apparent, enjoy soonish with food. **Atkinson Ridge** new ★★★★ Oaked chardonnay showing more savoury, steely European character than stablemate. Maiden **04** nutty, some citrus, cool lime palate. Sophisticated, all components in place for development over 2-5 yrs. Wine to watch. All WO Stbosch. — *CR*

Amarava Wines

Stellenbosch ▪ Est 1999 ▪ 1stB 2004 ▪ Closed to public ▪ Owner Bernard Rodenberg ▪ Vini/viti consultants Teddy Hall & Dawie le Roux (2003/2002) ▪ 17 ha (cabs s/f, merlot, shiraz, sauvignon) ▪ 20 tons ▪ PO Box 1083 Somerset West 7129 ▪ info@amaravawines.com ▪ www.amaravawines.com ▪ ***T 084·587·7270***

These carefully tended vineyards on a section of the prime Knorhoek property, long a viticultural secret nestling among the Hottentots Holland mountain slopes near Sir Lowry's Pass, are slowly giving up some of their riches. A full-fruited Sauvignon (now bottled under screwcap and exported to Holland, where owner Bernard Rodenberg resides) will be followed by a young Merlot, made by Teddy Hall (Rudera). Vintage 2006 sees a maiden crop of shiraz. A winery is still in the planning stages.

Sauvignon Blanc ★★★★ Arresting fruity style. No shortage of gooseberry, lime flavours in **05**; its site-specific green edginess makes it a tasty & perfect food companion, as attested to by invigorating 8.7g/ℓ acidity. — *IvH*

Amasimi Cellars see Longridge
Ama Ulibo see Goedverwacht

Ambeloui Wine Cellar

Hout Bay (see Constantia map) ▪ Est 1995 ▪ 1stB 1998 ▪ Visits by appt ▪ Owners Nick & Ann Christodoulou ▪ Winemaker/viticulturist Nick Christodoulou ▪ 0.6 ha (pinot, chard) ▪ 600 cs 100% MCC ▪ PO Box 26800 Hout Bay 7872 ▪ wine@ambeloui.co.za ▪ www.ambeloui.co.za ▪ ***T 082·441·6039*** *▪ F 088 021 790·7386*

A founding tradition on this postage-stamp-size farm in the Hout Bay valley is the naming of its wines (all sparkling) for family members. In 2005, owners Nick and Ann Christodoulou released 'Nicholas' and 'Ann', jesting that 'Nicholas may not be as mature as Nick, but Ann is definitely as elegant as Ann'. Another tradition is that a few select customers help the family bring in the harvest, the last being good enough and big enough to ensure a promising 'Ashley' vintage in 2007. Regrettably, Ann has had to suspend her practice of providing lunches or picnics for visitors — with output now at 600 cases there just isn't time for extras.

★★★★ **MCC** Artful, artisanal brut sparkling from pinot & chardonnay; vintages named for Christodoulou family members. **03** 'Nicholas', degorged early 2005, in mould of **01** 'Alexis' (★★★★★) 60% pinot, 36 mths on lees. Similar apple compôte/honey nose; persistent mousse; fresh lemon-toned palate; pinot-imparted weight. 10% barrel-fermented, as was chardonnay-led (66%) **02** 'Ann', degorged 2004, which had more brioche flavour. RS ±9g/ℓ.

★★★★ **Rosanne Rosé** new Vibrant blush-coloured MCC, varieties as above, with fine bead, bold raspberry/meat aromas & flavours despite preponderance of chardonnay (80%). Sweet impression on finish from ripe fruit (RS ±10g/ℓ). Limited release (only 100 cs); **NV**. Both WO Coastal. — *CvZ*

Amira see Avondale

Anatu Wines

Stellenbosch ▪ Est/1stB 2002 ▪ Visits by appt ▪ Owners André & Freda Hamersma, Wickus & Anina Guelpa, André van Zyl ▪ Winemaker Anina Guelpa ▪ 270 cs 80% red 20% white ▪ PO Box 5792 Cresta 2118 ▪ sales@anatu.co.za ▪ www.anatu.co.za ▪ ***T (021) 889·8398***

Sisters Freda Hamersma and Anina Guelpa (neé van Zyl) and their respective husbands André and Wickus have had an 'awesome' year: their Shiraz 03 took the Michelangelo trophy for the best *garagiste* wine. Cherry on the top was Anina G's nomination as one of six finalists for Woman Winemaker of the Year. For her, the cream on top of the cherry was the arrival mid-2005 of her first baby. Their Shiraz 05 is 'maturing nicely' in barrels – they have use of Stellakaya's cellar – while the 04 (not ready for tasting) was about to be botted as the guide went to bed.

★★★★ **Shiraz** Robust **03**, deep flavoured & husky. Warm, sweet black cherries, spicy oak & whiff smoke; ripe tannins linger in finish. Dbnville grapes, unfiltered/fined. 14 mths oak, 50% new Fr/Am. 15%alc. *— IvH*

Ancient Africa see Baarsma
Andrew Bain see Cape Vineyards

Andy Mitchell Wines

Greyton ▪ Est/1stB 2003 ▪ Visits by appt ▪ Owners/winemakers Andy & Vikki Mitchell, advised by Marais de Villiers (vini) & Terroir Wines (viti) ▪ 150 cs 100% red ▪ PO Box 543 Paarden Eiland 7420 ▪ andy@za.northsails.com ▪ www.andymitchellwines.com ▪ ***T (028) 254·9045/ 083·558·5085*** *F (028) 254·9045*

The best-laid plans … ! Owner/winemaker Andy Mitchell had intended to up his initial production total of 150 cases of shiraz by 50%, but while racking the new wine off the skins lost a tank to the floor of the barrel cellar. 'At a loss for words,' as he tells the story, 'I picked up my phone and called our consultant Marais de Villiers to ask for advice. He told me all I could do was take a photograph of the cellar at high tide for posterity!' Long-term, AM would like to produce a sparkling; in the near future there's a white waiting, as well as his Cape Wine Master's qualification.

Breakfast Rock Syrah ★★★ Compact but amply tannined **04** barrel sample robust (14.5% alc) yet shows finer aromas, more varietal spice & character than **03**, with earthy sweet raspberry notes. Partial malo in barrel, third new. *— MF*

Angels Tears see Grande Provence

Angora

Robertson ▪ Est/1stB 2002 ▪ Tasting & sales by appt ▪ Closed pub hols ▪ Owner Gerrit Joubert ▪ Winemakers Gerrit Joubert & sons, with Danie Slabber ▪ Viticulturist Danie Slabber ▪ 16 ha (cab, port varieties, ruby cab, shiraz, chenin, muscadel) ▪ 300 tons 300 cs own label 100% red ▪ PO Box 343 Bonnievale 6730 ▪ chris.joubert@gilga.com ▪ ***T 881·3475*** *▪ F 881·3248*

The Joubert family, père Gerrit and fils Johan and Chris (latter also Overgaauw winemaker), continue to revitalise their family farm and dream of making white wine to partner their red-only offering. They also want to raise their winegrowing game such that it helps draw 'serious attention' to the Bonnievale area. They will not release an 03 version of their Shiraz but the 04, 'an amazing vintage', is a cracker, they believe.

Shiraz ★★★★ **04** big improvement on pvs. Fleshier palate with distinctive earth/game flavours, individual cream soda-like finish. Bonnievale grapes, 16 mths seasoned Fr barrels. *— DS*

Annandale Wines

Stellenbosch ▪ Est/1stB 1996 ▪ Tasting & sales Mon-Sat 9-5 ▪ Fee R10 refundable on purchase ▪ Closed Christian holidays ▪ Tours by appt ▪ Collection of antique wine objects ▪ Owner/ winemaker/viticulturist Hempies du Toit ▪ 45 ha (cabs s/f, merlot, shiraz) ▪ 5 000 cs own label ▪

100% red ▪ PO Box 12681 Die Boord 7613 ▪ annandale@telkomsa.net ▪ www.annandale.co.za ▪ ***T 881·3560*** *▪* ***F*** *881·3562*

Springbok rugby legend 'Hempies' du Toit laughs about his nickname: 'My shirt tail used to hang out all the time, so on the school bus I was given this nickname. Some foreigners think it's my Christian name. I don't tell them that it's actually Pieter Gerhardus!' This year sees the 10th anniversary of the farm following his Alto days, but also marks Gerhard du Toit Jnr joining the team to handle marketing after a vintage in Bordeaux and wine sales experience at Harrods of London. HdT prefers to hold his wines back until ready: 'I know it's costing me a lot of money, but I don't care.' Any regrets? 'I've achieved everything that anyone could wish for, but I really want to fly a helicopter someday.'

★★★★ **Cabernet Sauvignon** Elegantly structured cabs, carefully oaked (usually 2 yrs new Fr), off own vyds since **01**, currently available, along with following trio: **97** lighter bodied, fragrant; **98** touch organic, savoury; **99** silk-textured, seamless & firm flavoured. No **00**. Burly **01** (15% alc) no-holds-barred 3 yrs new Nevers oak.

★★★★☆ **Shiraz 01** current (& so far only) vintage, beautifully packaged. Quintessential Cape shiraz: warm, spicily intense, properly dry, neither over-rich nor showy, 30 mths 2nd fill barrels, all Fr. Deserves time, as do all HdT's wines, 5–7 yrs min.

Cavalier ★★★☆ Unshowy but substantial blend merlot, cab s & f, shiraz (40/25/25/10) in **01**, 36 mths oak, all Fr; finely judged fruit & clean spicy oak; balanced, classy. **CVP** ★★★☆ Acronym (for Cape Vintage Port) calculated to avoid inflaming EU sensibilities. **01** from shiraz; sweet & delicious; ready, but better to cellar another 4–6 yrs. Only in 375ml. No new vintages tasted this ed. — *IvH*

AntHill Wines

Somerset West ▪ Est/1stB 2000 ▪ Tasting by appt ▪ Owners Mark Howell & Hylton Schwenk ▪ Winemaker Mark Howell ▪ 300 cs 100% red ▪ 14 Somerset Street, Somerset West 7130 ▪ anthill@absamail.co.za ▪ ***T 855·4275/082·895·9008*** *▪ F 855·5086*

It's a barrel here, a barrel there for Mark Howell, irrepressible supplier of cooperage to a lengthy list of SA clients, and Hylton Schwenk, a construction project manager. One (barrel) holds pinot from the remote Koue Bokkeveld, the other shiraz from two Stellenbosch grape growers. That's the total production for 2005. 'We are tiny by any standards,' Howell says, 'and we decided, given the current oversupply of wine, to keep it small.' Unless they feel the wine is good enough, they won't market it: 'This is our hobby — thank heavens for our day jobs!' Worst case, 'we'll drink it all ourselves and share some with our mates!'

★★★★ **Ietermago Chardonnay** new Elegant & classy **03**, with dash sauvignon, has all the right ingredients — incl, of course, oak (new Fr, ±13 mths), handled with flair. Classic citrus & buttered toast character, lively, light (12.5% alc), fresh, long limy flavours. Enough substance to enjoy over good few yrs. Fruit from Koue Bokkeveld. — *CR*

Anthony de Jager Wines

Paarl ▪ Est/1stB 2001 ▪ Closed to public ▪ Owner/winemaker Anthony de Jager ▪ 175 cs 100% red ▪ PO Box 583 Suider-Paarl 7624 ▪ homtini@absamail.co.za ▪ ***T 863·2450*** *▪ F 863·2591*

Anthony de Jager's pace and enthusiasm make many of his younger colleagues look like couch potatoes. Last year, pedalling furiously up and down Paarl Mountain in pitch dark, he won provincial colours in cross-country mountain-biking. 'The first time I really achieved anything in sport — at age 40!' With proprietor Charles Back, he makes the internationally acclaimed Fairview wines, and after-hours makes time to produce the brilliant Shiraz below under his own name. The key, AdJ believes, is to have fun, and that means getting his wife and mates actively involved in the making, not to mention the consuming.

★★★★☆ **Homtini Shiraz** AdJ first to commercially pair shiraz & white grape viognier (±7%, co-fermented), à la northern Rhône's Côte Rôtie. From spectacular debut **00** (★★★★★) always with utmost finesse; ethereal quality to lifted spice, red fruits, lilies; extra-delicate mouthfeel. Sample **04** beguiling as pvs; maintains silkiness, suppleness, fine fruit in warmer, drier vintage. Lovely potential. **03** great depth, personality & balance. Fermented/18 mths matured in older oak. 20–25 yr-old vines on Paarl Mountain. — *AL*

Anthony Smook Wines

Paarl ▪ Est/1stB 2000 ▪ Visits by appt; tasting/sales also at I Love Wine (see Wine shops section) ▪ Owner Anthony Smook ▪ Winemaker Anthony Smook, with Francois Louw (2000) ▪ Viti consultant Johan Wiese (2001) ▪ 30 ha (cab, merlot, pinotage, shiraz, chard, chenin) ▪ 36 tons 2 500 cs 80% red 20% white ▪ PO Box 7038 Noorder-Paarl 7623 ▪ asmook@mweb.co.za ▪ www.smookwines.co.za ▪ ***T 872·1804*** *▪ F 872·2867*

It was a now you have it, now you don't sort of harvest, says assistant winemaker Francois Louw of the 2005 season: the heat just before the harvest drained the crop of its flavours, but back they came after rains at the end of January. Owner/winemaker Anthony Smook had a satisfying fillip with a gold at Veritas for his Chardonnay Reserve. He now conducts personal barrel tastings as well as food and wine matchings – please note, always by appointment.

★★★★ **Shiraz Reserve** More structure, complexity, ripeness than regular version. **03** potential noted as sample last yr now realised; wattage upped with 100% new oak (90% Fr), towering alc (15.5%), retains elegance, balance through clever tannin/acid management, properly ripe fruit.

Pinotage ★★★ **03** continues in burgundian style; soft, silky, elegant despite 14.2% alc. 15 mths oak, 2nd-3rd fill. **Shiraz** ★★★★ **03** cask aged (50% new), even heftier alc than pvs (15.3%) yet not clumsy or over extracted; appealing black cherry hint; savoury tannins add to clean dry conclusion. **Merlot-Cabernet Sauvignon** ★★★★ **03** unready for tasting. **02** (50/40, with dashes malbec, cab f) soft & sweet-fruited, fragrant cigarbox whiff from 50% new Fr oak. **Chardonnay Reserve** new ★★★★ Similar lime/mineral profile as regular, but greater intensity, focus & freshness. **Chardonnay** ★★★ **04** acquiring 'damp cellar' character to lime/mineral fruit; soft, persistent, warming finish (14% alc); not for keeping. All off single-vyds in Voor-Pdberg area. *—IvH*

Anura Vineyards

Paarl ▪ Est 1990 ▪ 1stB 2001 ▪ Tasting & sales daily 9–5 ▪ Closed Easter Fri/Mon, Dec 25/26 & Jan 1 ▪ Fee R15 (cheese & wine) ▪ Lilly Pad Restaurant (see Eat-out section) ▪ Tours by appt ▪ Farm produce sold ▪ Owners Tymen & Jenny Bouma ▪ Winemakers Tymen Bouma & Carla van der Mescht (Jan 2002) ▪ Viticulturist Hannes Kloppers (Oct 1997) ▪ 118 ha (cab, malbec, merlot, mourvèdre, sangiovese, shiraz) ▪ 600 tons total 450 tons/35 000 cs own label 80% red 20% white ▪ PO Box 244 Klapmuts 7625 ▪ info@anura.co.za sales@anura.co.za ▪ www.anura.co.za ▪ ***T 875·5360*** *▪ F 875·5657*

This well-groomed property is poised for major new developments including cellar expansion. In the winery, Carla Pauw (née Van der Mescht) is coming into her own after four harvests, with noticeable results: 'I know how to treat the grapes and which barrels to use for which blocks now,' says this intuitive winemaker who 'asks the wine what it wants!' Viognier, planned for blending with their Shiraz, promises to be so delicious it's been singled out for stand-alone bottling. In the *fromagerie*, master cheesemaker Ian Nicol launched new flavoured marisch cheeses under the Forest Hill label. A visit to the extended tasting room and restaurant reveals just how appealingly these wines and cheeses go together.

★★★★ **Cabernet Sauvignon Reserve** Last tasted was **02** sample, less opulent than pvs, some black cherry among the cassis, more juicy, less tannin. **01** shy cassis, violet bouquet, whiffs cigarbox; sweet fruit tapering to dry finish. 13 mths new Fr oak. VDG. These ±15% alc; worth cellaring 6-7 yrs.

★★★★ **Merlot 04** sample rather sullen – let's hope it opens up when bottled (now ★★★★). Some dark choc & mulberry ripeness, sleek, fine-grained tannins in firm backbone. Quite rich & meaty, with unsettling acidity. 18 mths Fr oak. 14.8% alc. Pvsly tasted was fragrant **02**.

★★★★ **Merlot Reserve** new Sleek new entry to merlot stakes with this luxuriously chocolaty **03.** Swanky oaking (18 mths new Fr), fragrant, densely & creamily textured, excellent balance between plush cassis & fine oak tannins – enough to make a hedonist palpitate.

Pinotage ★★★★ **04** dramatic change of style, no longer mere quaffer. Plummy richness, dense & chewy, good oak support – fragrant, balsamic – needs yr to settle, should last 5-7. **05** sample lighter, still grippy. **Shiraz** ★★★ **02** well-bred dry, dense & compact fruit, firmish tannins; classic style. 20% barrel fermented; matured Fr oak, 50% new. *Wine* ★★★★. Tasted last ed, ditto … **Syrah-Mourvèdre** Maiden **03** sample (provisional ★★★★) showed good depth with loads of dark berried juiciness, enough grip to please the classicists. Part native yeast ferment; 18 mths Fr oak, 40% new. **Syrah-Mourvèdre Reserve** new ★★★★ **03** separate bottling from above, with dark-berried appeal, understated tannins, discreet structure. Very approachable, but more complexity, subtlety than mere quaffer. 14.9% alc. **Malbec** new ★★★ **03** almost ready mid-2005; lead pencil whiffs, neat compact profile, firmly constructed, black-berried charms. 14.8% alc well hidden. **Sangiovese** new ★★★ **03** shows grace & charm, dried plum fruit, nicely rounded build, tannins already approachable; without the dryness of Italian versions of this Tuscan grape – 15.2% alc helps explain sweetish finish. Fermented/18 mths Fr oak. **Chardonnay** ★★★★ **04** drier, more classic than **03**. Dried peach, ripe citrus; firm flesh; 9 mths Fr oak needs time to fully integrate. Should last 2-3yrs. **Chenin Blanc** ★★★ **04** sample in same big, bold style as **03**; harvested ripe: 14.7% alc. Aromas/flavours of sweet yellow peaches, nuts, plus whack of oak (fermented/9 mths, some new). Touch more acidity needed for extra excitement. Has build to last 3-4 yrs. Trophy at FCTWS. **Sauvignon Blanc** ★★★ **05** (sample) impressive figgy/tropical notes, excellent concentration, exciting fruit acid balance. If unscathed into bottle, should rate higher. But watch 14.5% alc.

Frog Hill range

Shiraz-Merlot-Cabernet ☺ ★★★ Varieties given in different order in **03** name. **04** blend has meaty richness with plummy sweetness, still some powerful tannin; attractively oaked. 'Masculine' style, with charm – braais and bonhomie come to mind …

Chenin Blanc ★★ **04** developing honeyed notes, some tropical flavours, spiced melon, but already a little tired mid-2005. – *IvH*

Anwilka new

Stellenbosch ▪ Est 1997 ▪ 1stB 2005 ▪ Closed to public; sales from Klein Constantia ▪ Owners Bruno Prats, Hubert de Boüard & Lowell Jooste ▪ Winemaker Trizanne Pansegrouw (2005), with Hubert de Boüard & Bruno Prats ▪ Piet Neethling, advised by Johan Wiese (May 1998/ Dec 1997) ▪ 40 ha (cab, merlot, shiraz) ▪ 250 tons total ±80 tons own label 100% red ▪ PO Box 5298 Helderberg 7135 ▪ info@anwilka.com ▪ www.anwilka.com ▪ T 842·3225 ▪ F 842·3983

The growing tide of French investment has attracted two formidable figures from Bordeaux: Bruno Prats, former owner of second-growth Château Cos-d'Estournel, and Hubert de Boüard de Laforest, co-proprietor of one of St-Emilion's top estates, Château Angelus. In a 50% joint venture with Lowell Jooste of Klein Constantia, plans are ripe for the release of their first wines around mid-year. The Anwilka property in the Helderberg, bought by Lowell J in late 1997 in near derelict condition, has been extensively replanted and now boasts 40ha under cab, shiraz and merlot. In 2004, a cellar was fast-track-constructed to accommodate the following harvest. The partners will release about 4 000 cs of the maiden red, a 75/20/5 blend still in barrel at press time, with most sold through the Bordeaux wine trade. While Anwilka is not open to the public, the wine will be available from Klein Constantia.

Apiesklip see Baarsma
Aprilskloof see Lammershoek

Arendsig Hand-Crafted Wines

Robertson ▪ Est/1stB 2004 ▪ Visits by appt ▪ Vineyard tour & tasting with winemaker by appt Mon-Fri 9-4 ▪ Open for tasting by appt Sat 9.30-1 ▪ Owner GF van der Westhuizen Trust ▪ Winemaker Lourens van der Westhuizen ▪ 15 ha (cab, shiraz, chard, sauvignon, viognier) ▪ 15 tons ±500 cs ▪ PO Box 170 Robertson 6705 ▪ info@arendsig.co.za ▪ www.arendsig.co.za ▪ ***T (023) 616·2835/084·200·2163*** *▪ F (023) 616·2090*

'If you want to make the best wine in the world, you need as many different components as you can get, to develop unique flavours,' is the philosophy Lourens van der Westhuizen brought back from a stint with Copain, a Californian boutique operation. He plants different slopes on the family farm with different clones; coaxes 20% more free-run juice from a ton of chardonnay with a new tank, its positioning adapted; puts his all into exclusive vineyard tours and barrel tastings; participates enthusiastically in the region's marketing promotions ... The rewards are beginning to come in: his Chardonnay recently bested 20 wooded rivals in a regional tasting.

Shiraz ★★★★ Maiden **04** shows classic shiraz profile: gamey dark fruit, smoky spice, in an elegant, lively package. Drinks well, belies yr Fr barrique treatment (40% new), but underlying structure will support 3+ yrs further development. Only 250 cs made. **Chardonnay** ★★★ **04**, as per last ed, pure & confident with ripe peach & melon aromas, fruity zest. Fermented/6 mths Fr barrels. Unfiltered/fined. — *CR*

Arlington Beverage Group

Est 1996 ▪ 1stB 1997 ▪ Closed to public ▪ Owner Richard Addison ▪ 200 000 cs 45% red 55% white ▪ UK head office: 162-164 Arthur Rd, London SW19 8AQ ▪ PO Box 1376 Stellenbosch 7599 ▪ sarah@arlingtonbeverage.com ▪ www.arlingtonbeverage.com

Arlington markets and sells SA wines to countries such as the UK, Ireland and Argentina. With local partners, it has built a number of successful on-trade brands including Broken Rock, Landsdowne, Millbrook and Rocheburg. Arlington also represents a number of leading Cape properties in the international markets, including Riebeek and Ridgeback.

Arniston Bay see Omnia
Arumdale see Thelema

Asara Estate

*Stellenbosch ▪ Est 1691 ▪ 1stB 1970 ▪ Tasting & sales Mon-Fri 9-5 Sat 10-5 (Nov-Apr), 10-2 (May-Oct) ▪ Fee R15 ▪ Closed Easter Fri, Dec 25/26 & Jan 1 ▪ Tours by appt ▪ BYO picnic ▪ Owner Markus & Christiane Rahmann ▪ Winemaker Jan van Rooyen (Oct 1999) ▪ Viticulturist Pieter Rossouw (1995) ▪ 120 ha (cab, merlot, shiraz, chard, sauvignon) ▪ 500 tons 25 000 cs 75% red 25% white ▪ PO Box 882 Stellenbosch 7599 ▪ info@AsaraWine.com ▪ www.AsaraWine.com ▪ **T 888·8000** ▪ F 888·8001*

2005 brought not only a clutch of new awards to decorate the tasting centre (including a prestigous grand gold at the 2005 Concours Mondial for the 00 Merlot), but also 'a smashing good harvest', enthuses Jan van Rooyen, the shiraz, merlot, cab, chardonnay and sauvignon being the ones to watch. Last year also saw the relaunch of their Cape Blend as Cape Fusion, 'a more exciting wine,' JvR opines, 'expressing SA style with pride. The varieties are now clearly stated on the front label, to familiarise people with the concept.' New in the range is the amarone-style 'meditation wine' from pinotage; another expression of the grape is in the works but the winemaker refuses to divulge details. 'Top secret,' he winks.

★★★★ **Bell Tower Collection Estate Wine** Sets the tone of restrained, classic-mindedness of this estate's reds. Splendid, serious **98** (★★★★★) had fine fruit & balanced structure. 90% cab in **99** (not retasted), with merlot, cab f, petit v, malbec, in same classy tradition, but a trifle lighter in feel despite bigger 14.5% alc. Integrated support from 2 yrs Fr oak, 50% new. Should easily see out their decades.

★★★★ **Amaro** new Provisional rating for unbottled sample – & provisional name reflecting Italian amarone inspiration, for **04** vine-dried pinotage. Beguiling aromas pointed by some not atypical volatility, fairly concentrated flavours on richly firm, fleshy palate, with smooth ripe tannins, 15+% alc, & dry finish despite 7 or so g/ℓ sugar. Good as 'vino di meditazione' with nuts & cheese.

★★★★★ **Cabernet Sauvignon** Last tasted was **98**, offering finesse, ripe, dark fruit with mineral streak; strong, savoury structure. 22 mths oak, third new.

★★★★ **Merlot** Serious & elegant, in house style, **00** has notes of choc-mint & warm ripe black berries, firm but subtle tannins. Like graceful but firmly knit **99** (Concours Mondial gold) well-managed 18 mths Fr oak. Ready, will keep well few more yrs.

★★★★ **Cape Fusion** ('Cape Blend' last ed) Maiden **01**, equal merlot, cab & the vital pinotage, showed whiffs of red fruit wildness. Some customary elegance structuring ripe berry fruits, but richness here a little (deliciously) decadent, though tannins ripely firm, finish dry. Unobtrusive 18 mths oak.

★★★★ **Shiraz 02** continues tradition of engagingly forward & drinkable yet restrained maiden **01** – most attractive already, will keep. Lovely cherry aromas, succulent & firm dry tannin, with rich fruit. 15 mths Fr/Am oak, third new. Like many of these, also in 375ml.

★★★★ **Chardonnay Reserve** Last sampled was silky, well balanced (though big 14.5% alc) **03**, with citrus, spicy wood, oatmeal; long dry finish. Fine food wine. Fermented/yr Fr oak.

★★★★☆ **Noble Late Harvest** Luscious dessert from barrel-fermented chenin. **03** (tasted last ed) lightly intense, with honeyed apricot/pineapple, gorgeous flavours governed by 11.5% alc, fine acidity. 130g/ℓ sugar. **02** (★★★★) particularly rich, raisiny & sweet: unctuous & lingering.

Ebony ★★★ **00** (not retasted) everyday red blend with moderate structure, flavour, lightly wooded. **Rosé** ★★★ Last **NV** version tasted was lightly red-gleaming, made from dark grapes; full-flavoured, savoury & dry; 14% alc. **Chardonnay Unwooded** ★★★ **05** sample promises usual pleasingly steely, chablis-style alternative to wooded version. Well balanced; some citrus, green notes, dry & vinous. **Ivory** ★★★ Latest not ready for tasting mid-2005. Crisp, freshly balanced **04** was from sauvignon, with some chardonnay, semillon. **Sauvignon Blanc** ★★★ Sample of **05** typically refined, bright, with green notes & passion fruit. **Spirit of Chenin** ★★★☆ Last was unctuous, mature **98**: petrol notes, nuts, tinned peaches. 132g/ℓ sugar. 15 mths new Fr oak; 17% alc (fortified). Discontinued: **Carillon**, **Pinotage**, **Chenin Blanc Reserve Selection**. – *TJ*

Ashanti

*Paarl ▪ Est 1997 ▪ 1stB 1998 ▪ Tasting & sales daily 10–4 Sep-May (closed Sat/Sun Jun-Aug) ▪ Fee R10 ▪ Closed Easter Fri-Mon, Dec 25 & Jan 1 ▪ Tours by appt ▪ Restaurant at Ashanti lunches Tue-Fri 11–4 year-round; in season also Sat dinners/sundowners 6.30pm-9pm & Sun à la carte lunches; booking advised ▪ Owner Ashanti Estates ▪ Winemaker Nelson Buthelezi (1999) ▪ Manager/viticulturist Johan Cronjé (Dec 2002) ▪ 96 ha ▪ 70 000 cs ▪ PO Box 934 Huguenot 7645 ▪ info@ashantiwines.com ▪ www.ashantiwines.com ▪ **T 862·0789** ▪ F 862·2864*

It's not a prettification, but the recent installation of photon lights in the production cellar, barrelling area and bottling plant has taken the winery forward in the fight against bacterial contamination. No prettification needed in the Tuscan-inspired gardens and restaurant overlooking the dam – a picture-perfect setting for drinks or a meal. As far as the nitty-gritty of winegrowing is concerned, manager/viticulturist Johan Cronjé is looking afresh at current vineyard practices to pinpoint areas of further improvement, while Nelson Buthelezi, now chief of the cellar after deputising for some years, notched up multiple awards at the 2005 Young Wine Show.

★★★★ **Chiwara** Attractively different blend; pinotage, cab, shiraz in appetising, plump **01**, with ripe red fruit flavours. **02** more elegant, still full of taste, life; noted last ed as approachable with potential over possibly 5-6 yrs. ±15 mths Fr oak.

★★★★ **Pinotage** Fruity & modern, lots of flesh to match the chewy tannins; **04** (★★★) sample still in development stage. Sweet, ripe plummy fruit, tannins busy integrating, need time; could have rewarding 3-4 yrs ahead. Oaked yr Fr/Am. **03** appealing plum pudding & custard tone; quite firm on release, begging yr/2. 10–12 mths Fr oak.

Cabernet Sauvignon ★★★ **04** (sample) likeable red berry profile, but tannins still dominant at this early stage, likely to be more amenable in finished wine. Yr Fr/Am oak. 2-3 yrs ageing potential. **Malbec** ★★★☆ Last tasted was **02**, with veritable berry orchard of fruit. **Merlot** ★★★ **04** has variety's trademark elegance, mixed red fruit tones. Already accessible, no hard edges; sinewy tannins provide support for next 3 yrs. Oak as for Cab. **Shiraz** ★★★ **04** (sample) simpler than pvs. Medium weight, ripe, red-fruited, with juicy, youthful appeal. Oak (as above) adds layer of spice, gives structure for 2-3 yrs cellaring. **Zinfandel**, **Sangiovese** discontinued.

Concept wines

Joseph's Hat ★★★ Fruit is the main focus in **04**, lovely raspberry, mulberry tones, the 8 mnth oaking in support role. A tasty early drinker. 70/30 pinotage, merlot. **Sunset Hat** ★★☆ Charming & perfectly named dry rosé. **05** light-hearted, redcurrant-toned sipper to mark the end of the day. 80/20 pinotage, cab. **Nicole's Hat** ★★☆ Working well together, **05**'s chardonnay/chenin equal partnership contributes pear-drop, melon flavour to this light-textured, refreshingly dry quaffer. **French Kiss** ★★☆ Natural Sweet chenin returns to guide after several vintages. **05** curvaceous, fruit-salad toned, uncomplicated & sweet. 60g/ℓ sugar. Friendly 11% alc. — *CR*

Ashbourne see Southern Right

Ashton Winery

Ashton ▪ Est 1962 ▪ 1stB ca 1970 ▪ Tasting & sales Mon-Thu 8-5.30 Fri 8-5 Sat 8.30-12.30 ▪ Closed pub hols ▪ Tours by appt ▪ BYO picnic ▪ Owners 68 members ▪ Winemakers Philip Louw (Aug 2000) & André Scriven (Jan 2003) ▪ Viticulturist Hennie Visser (Jan 2002) ▪ 1 200 ha (cab, ruby cab, shiraz, chard) ▪ 18 000 tons (6 000 cs own label) 35% red 65% white ▪ PO Box 40 Ashton 6715 ▪ ashkel@mweb.co.za ▪ ***T (023) 615-1135/7*** ▪ *F (023) 615-1284*

The appointment of marketing man Jakes de Wet as CEO is a sure sign that this Robertson-area winery means business when it says it's hitting the overseas market. It's bottling more wine to meet the challenge, and has set up a Stellenbosch-based Ashton Wines Company to co-ordinate things. Winemaker André Scriven rates the chardonnay and shiraz from the variable 2005 vintage, and was rather proud of one of his grower's winning the Robertson regional vineyard block competition with some young cab.

Cabernet Sauvignon ★★★ **03** (sample) back to old Fr barrels (**02** version staved) with splash of petit v. Grainy tannins matched by ripe red/black fruit; juicy acid. Has potential to improve 3-5 yrs. **Pinot Noir** ★★★ **03** tasted as a sample last yr still impressively dark colour, alcoholic (15%); agreeable, with soft red fruit. Not very pinot-like. 7 mths 4th fill casks. **Shiraz** ★★★ **03** sample last yr didn't quite make the ★★★☆ mark when tasted for this ed. Still chunky, savoury & spicy with lively dark fruit; tannins gruff & mouth-coating. Yr Fr oak, none new. **Satyn Rooi** ★★★ As name suggests, smooth equal blend 50/50 ruby cab/pinotage, unoaked; **03** deftly executed; supple & juicy, medium bodied. Drink up soon. Also in 6x500ml packs. **Blanc de Noir** ★★ Unchallenging, off-dry picnic-partner from red muscadel. Dried raisin dominates pale garnet **05**. **Chardonnay Reserve** ★★★ 6 mths 1st/2nd fill Fr oak for **03**, last tasted mid-2004, with soft coconut tone; unsophisticated yet appealing. **Chardonnay Unwooded** ★★★ **04** fruity, very mouthfilling (14.7% alc) but bright; pear & passionfruit tones. **Colombard** ★★☆ **05** grapes treated with ascorbic acid in vineyard/cellar to preserve fruity zing; sample lacks distinct varietal characters but bursts with crisp fruit; drink young. Quaffable 12% alc. **Sauvignon Blanc** ★★ Always early-picked, kept under dry ice for lively crispness. Sample **05** sherbety, lightish, bone-dry. **Colombar-Chardonnay** ★★☆ **05** (sample) charming pool-side sipper with light pear & citrus scents, toned body. **Pétillant Blanc** ★★ Soft, muted, lowish alc (±11.5%) blend colombard, white muscadel under screwcap. Not tasted for this ed. **Late Harvest** Non-spritzy version of above, latest not ready for tasting; pvs **04** ★★☆. Spicy almond hint, fuller than alc would suggest (11.7%); manageably sweet. **Special Late Harvest** ★☆ Ethereal **05** from white muscadel; talcum powder, green apple hints, very sweet & light (11%alc). **Red Muscadel** ★★ **05** strictly for the sweet toothed: rich, viscous, cloying; one-dimensional spicy tea-leaf character. 16.8% alc. **White Muscadel** ✓ ★★★☆ none since **02**, tasted mid-2004 had jasmine & honeysuckle aromas, silky peach & honey flavours. Luxurious. 16.8% alc. **Port** ★★☆ Not a classical style; equal portions pinotage/ruby cab plus 20% shiraz. Raspberry, treacle lifted by spirituous body, finish. Should settle with time. **Cabernet Sauvignon Reserve** discontinued. — *MM/TM*

Assegai Selection

*Stellenbosch (see Helderberg map) ▪ Est 1999 ▪ Tasting & sales by appt ▪ Assegai Guest Lodge ▪ Owner Woodlands Import Export ▪ 15 000 cs 80% red 20% white ▪ 10 Harewood Ave Somerset West 7130 ▪ rbuchner@worldonline.co.za ▪ **T 855·2249** ▪ F 855·4924*

An export label featuring that ancient African weapon, the long throwing spear or assegai. No new versions available; notes from previous edition. Also in owner Raimund Buchner's armoury are the Patrys and Tarentaal brands, described separately.

★★★★☆ **Ineva** ✓ The flagship, a succulent, well-judged merlot/cab blend, with dash pinotage; elegantly showy. Fr oak 6 mths. 53/42/5 ratio in violet-perfumed **03**, more expressive & vivacious than pvs; deserves more time. **02** (★★★★) closed & tight; should be aged further.

Cabernet Sauvignon ★★★☆ ✓ Classically styled, 18 mths Fr/Am oak, barrels only. **01** rich fruitcake aromas, generous rounded cassis flavour; refreshingly unalcoholic, as are most of these. **Pinotage** ★★★☆ ✓ **02** wet heath aromas, succulent wild berry flavour; good quaffing style. 6-18 mths Fr oak, staves/casks. **Merlot** ★★★☆ ✓ Well-fleshed **01**, choc/mocha notes, creamy liquorice in full, soft palate. Tasty. 18 mths Fr/Am oak, none new; same regimen for … **Shiraz** ★★★ Structured, flavourful **02**; fresh-picked berry tones, good dry finish; for earlier drinking. **Merlot-Pinotage** ★★★ **01** smoked meat on nose with sweet spicing; juicy; oak (combo staves/barrels 9 mths) doesn't interfere with enjoyment. **Chardonnay** ★★★☆ Seamlessly wooded **03**, soft, appealing peach/honey palate verging on voluptuous. Big step up on pvs. **Chenin Blanc Barrel Fermented** ★★★☆ ✓ Melon/hay aromas with buttery touch; weighty & ripe, deftly oaked. Delicious **03**. **Chenin Blanc** ★★ **04** fruit salad tones with attractive lime top-note, rather more foursquare palate. **Sauvignon Blanc** ★★★ **03** has green fig & melon tones, crisp herby palate, refreshing. All above EW, WO Stbosch. — *CR*

Astonvale see Zandvliet

Ataraxia

new

*Walker Bay ▪ Est 2004 ▪ 1stB 2005 ▪ Tasting by appt ▪ Owner Kevin Grant Wines (Pty) Ltd ▪ Winemaker/viticulturist Kevin Grant ▪ 29 ha planned ▪ 24 tons 1 700 cs 40% red 60% white ▪ PO Box 603 Hermanus 7200 ▪ ataraxia@kingsley.co.za ▪ **T (028) 313·0143** ▪ F (028) 313·0146*

After ten successful vintages at Hamilton Russell Vineyards, Kevin Grant is going it alone because 'being a good jockey on someone else's horse is okay, but it's not the ultimate'. After scouring the Walker Bay area, he has purchased his own 47ha 'thoroughbred' in the Hemel-en-Aarde Valley and established Ataraxia – an ancient Greek term describing emotional tranquillity. Buying in grapes until his own vineyards are established, he says his handcrafted wines will include 'cool-climate, alchemy-free' Sauvignon Blanc, Chardonnay ('life without Chardonnay is like not being able to breathe'), Pinot Noir ('I believe I can take pinot to heights not yet seen in this country') and a red blend ('transcending the potentially restrictive parameters of a single-variety wine').

Sauvignon Blanc ★★★☆ Attractively lean **05** with fine herbal greenpepper notes; elegance imparted by cool-climate (Hemel-en-Aarde) fruit, promising longevity, finesse. — *MF*

Atkinson Ridge see Amani
At The Limiet see Nabygelegen
Auberge du Paysan see L'Auberge du Paysan

Audacia Wines

*Stellenbosch ▪ Est 1930 ▪ Tasting & sales Mon-Fri 9-5 Sat 10-3 ▪ Fee R10 refundable on purchase ▪ Closed Christian holidays & Jan 1st ▪ Tours by appointment ▪ Owners Strydom & Harris families ▪ Winemaker Elsa Carstens (since Apr 1999), with Louis van Zyl ▪ Viticulturist Elsa Carstens, with Willem Booysen ▪ 20 ha (five Bdx reds, roobernet, shiraz) ▪ 135 tons 11 000 cs 100% red ▪ PO Box 12679 Die Boord 7613 ▪ info@audacia.co.za ▪ www.audacia.co.za ▪ **T 881-3052** ▪ F 881·3137*

With no flash or fanfare, the family owners have turned this once run-down property into an award-winning red-wine boutique winery (their Cab and Shiraz, among a lengthy list of commendations, were applauded by the judges of the inaugural *Wine & Dine* South Asia Wine Awards staged in Singapore last year). 2005 was also the first harvest entirely of own grapes, from vineyards replanted since 2000 under the watchful eye of viticulturist and winemaker Elsa Carstens, holder of an MSc in Wine Microbiology and, in the words of the appreciative owners, 'a perfectionist with a great love for the art of winemaking'.

Cabernet Franc (Rouge Noble) new ★★★★ **04** intriguing blend of cabs f & s plus roobernet (77/14/9); bright leafy spice, curious nutmeg/pimento hints, unshowy claret-like palate, 100% new Fr oak well integrated, succulent finish. **Merlot** ★★★★ ✓ **02** some mulberry aromas & gamey whiffs, succulent soft-textured flavours, fine tannins. Food-friendly successor to well balanced, more leafy **01**. Fr oak, 2nd/3rd fill. No newer releases of the following available for tasting: **Cabernet Sauvignon** ★★★★ **01**, Young Wine Show gold, SAA 1st/Premium Class, brambly/earthy with potential to develop. Yr Fr oak, 20% new. **Shiraz** ★★★ Pleasantly savoury **02**, lighter colour/body, slightly less fruit in line with vintage but still tasty. **Coeur de Rouge** ★★★ Cab/merlot partnership (80/20), seasoned in Fr oak, 2nd-4th fill. **01** good mature touches to bright cassis fruit, prominent tobacco/cigarbox characters. — *MF/TM*

Aufwaerts Co-op

Rawsonville ▪ Visits by appointment ▪ PO Box 15 Rawsonville ▪ aufwaerts@breede.co.za ▪ ***T (023) 349·1202/082·349·4001*** *▪ F (023) 349·1202*

This well-established winery, owned by the De Villiers family, now markets a portion of its bulk production under an own-label, and invites visitors to pop in anytime for a tasting of the Dry Red and Dry White. ('Best to phone ahead though,' says Hennie de V, 'as we bottle very small batches at a time.') Also available is the Twee Eeue 5-year-old potstill brandy.

Autumn Harvest Crackling

Forerunner of SA's mid-priced wines. Latest ★★ perky, gently petillant blend chenin, colombard, crouchen, with fresh fruit salad tones, bright appley acidity. **NV** under screwcap, by Distell. — *CvZ*

Avoca see Douglas Winery

Avondale

Paarl ▪ Est 1997 ▪ 1stB 1999 ▪ Tasting & sales Mon-Sat & pub hols 10–4 ▪ Fee R8, refunded on purchase ▪ Tours by appt ▪ Conferencing ▪ Owner John Grieve/Avondale Trust ▪ Winemaker Bertus Albertyn, with Corné Marais (Jun/Jan 2004) ▪ Viticulturist Johnathan Grieve (2000) ▪ 100 ha (cab, merlot, mourvèdre, shiraz, chard, chenin, muscat d'A, semillon, viognier) ▪ 290 tons 15 000 cs 74% red 20% white 6% fortified ▪ PO Box 602 Suider-Paarl 7624 ▪ wine@avondalewine.co.za ▪ ***T 863·1976*** *▪ F 863·1534*

The 'nature's way' philosophy on which the Grieve family's health products business is based is mirrored in their Klein Drakenstein vineyards and the cellar at their heart. There's a push for biodiversity certification, hence the practice of organic viticulture in all new vineyards. Viticulturist Johnathan Grieve is also reintroducing fynbos between the rocky vineyard rows, interspersing it with organic soil cover, insect-repelling/attracting plants and nitrogen-rich cover crops. Next step will be certified-organic wines, not yet feasible because of low volumes thus far from the organically-farmed shiraz and mourvèdre blocks. With picnics available in season visitors can admire more than the state-of-the-art cellar and attractive tasting room — the gardens are magnificent too.

Les Pleurs range

★★★★★ **Syrah** The flagship from a single vyd, bearing Avondale signatures of rich savouriness, warming alc (±14.5%). **02** supple & svelte, released ahead of **01** (deemed unready), with dense meaty/savoury flavours. VDG. Fr cask-fermented/aged, 80% new, 17 mths. Neither this, Merlot, retasted.

★★★★☆ **Merlot** A wine for romantics. **00** mid-2004 was understated & seamless. Notes of spiced dried fruits & 'rain forest'; sumptuous; extraordinary long, fennel finish. Fermented new Fr oak.

Avondale range

★★★★ **Graham Reserve** (Pvsly 'Avondale', now named for the Grieves' Scottish clan). Selection of vintage's best reds, which in **01** were equal portions shiraz/cab plus melot/cab f (27/27/18/18); now shows multi-layered flavours, great tapered length; also fairly firm tannins & warm finish from ±14.5% alc. 70% new wood. **00** last ed was maturing auspiciously; blend cabs s/f, merlot (45/19/18/) showing mature Bdx-like hints tomato & 'oyster shell'; savoury tannins from 18% shiraz, 6 mths Fr oak. VDG.

★★★★ **Cabernet Sauvignon** Demanding warm-climate cab (±14.5% alc), usually unready on release but promising good development. **00** incl soupçon cab f; should be coming round now. Unblended **01** had herbaceous cassis notes, riper tannins than pvs. **02** lighter, softer, consonant with vintage. Fermented/matured ±14 mths Fr oak, 55-65% new. None retasted.

★★★★ **Syrah** 'Shiraz' pvs ed. Change to Fr nomenclature appropriate for Rhône-like **03**, offering handsome black pepper, lily & mineral fragrances. Abundant red fruit, persistent finish. Should develop well over 5-7 yrs. The usual beefy alc – 15%, cf 14.5% alc for lavender-perfumed, multi-gonged **02** (*Wine* ★★★★, MIWA DG) & 15% for **01**, with roast-spice, black pepper exuberance. VDG. Barrel-fermented/aged new/used oak, 15% Am.

★★★★ **Sauvignon Blanc** ✓ Classy act from S/West, Stbosch, Mbury grapes. Intense passionfruit/blackcurrant aromas, grapefruit flavours; lip-smacking textures of 'wet pebble' & slate on both **05** & **04**. These easily clear bar raised by mouth-watering **03**, despite lower alcs (12.5% vs 13.7%). Good for 2-3 yrs. No **02**.

★★★★ **Muscat Rouge** ✓ Single-vyd fortified dessert from red muscat de F, cropped quite early to retain fruit, manage sweetness. Less alcoholic (±14%) than stablemate below. **02** light-hued (barely coppery) with vivid litchi aroma; pithy finish belies highish RS (186g/ℓ). **03** bit drier (175g/ℓ) yet has characteristic honeyed finish. 9% barrel-fermented. 500ml.

★★★★ **Muscat Blanc** ✓ Hand-crafted nightcap from low-cropped (3-4 t/ha) single block muscat de F. **04** inviting golden hue; scents of almond & marzipan, melon & litchi. Driest of recent vintages (184g/ℓ RS, 17% alc highest, too). Bracing acidity delivers uncloying finish. **02** delicate spanspek bouquet; more ethereal sweetness (192g/ℓ RS) than **03** (205g/ℓ). 500ml.

Julia ★★★☆ Uncomplicated red sipper, blend changes with vintage. Fruity **02** cab, shiraz, merlot (41/34/14) plus dollops cab f & ruby cab. Elegantly rustic. Alc (14.9%) way up on pvs 13.5%. Fr/Am oak, some new. **Pinotage** new ★★☆ Mainly for UK, but some available from cellar door. **05** cheerful quaffer with lively strawberry flavours/aromas, 14% alc grip. **Proprietor's Shiraz** new ★★★ Exclusively for Irish Superquinn group from fruit not selected for Avondale Syrah. **03** soft floral/fruity notes, rustic tannins & warm tail (14.5% alc). Yr mainly old Fr/Am oak. **Chardonnay** Barrel sample **05** hints at buttery richness, hefty 14.8% alc masked by sweet oak & fruit. Potentially ★★★☆. **Chardonnay Sur Lie** new ★★★ **05** shows gentle touch (just 4 mths on lees); quiet lemon notes, zippy acid & short, lemon-pith tail. **Chenin Blanc** ★★★☆ **05** maintains style, standard of pvs; delicate, soft bouquet of flowers & tropical fruit; more vibrant palate & pithy finish, imparted by 4 mths lees-ageing. **Rosé** ★★ From muscat d'F. Pvsly partied only in UK, now SA too. **05** cheery grapey aromas & flavours, rose & peppermint perfumes.

Amira range new

Export wines. **Cabernet Franc** ★★★ **04** for US restaurant/bar market. Deep & dark with scrubby notes, juicy raspberry/cranberry fruit. Honest & straightforward. Moderate oaking. **Syrah** ★★★ **03** laid-back number; supple fruit, soft furry tannins from gentle oaking (mostly older Fr/Am), warming finish (14.5% alc). **Cape Red** ★★★☆ **01** for German retail trade. Lively blend merlot/shiraz/cab (33/32/25), extra oomph from dollops cab f/pinotage. Complex & integrated; drinks well now. Mix new/old, Fr/Am barrels. – *CvZ*

Avondvrede Private Wine Farm

Paarl ▪ Est 1995 ▪ 1stB 1999 ▪ Tasting, sales, cellar tours & light lunches by appt ▪ Tourgroups ▪ Function room ▪ Owners John & Christine Enthoven ▪ Winemaker John Enthoven ▪ 4 ha (cabs s/f, merlot) ▪ 20 tons ±3 600 cs 100% red ▪ PO Box 152 Klapmuts 7625 ▪ ***T 083·658·0595*** *▪ F 875·5609*

No update available on this winery; contact details from previous edition.

Avontuur Estate

Stellenbosch (see Helderberg map) ▪ Est 1850 ▪ 1stB 1990 ▪ Tasting & sales Mon-Fri 8.30-5 Sat & Sun 8.30-4 ▪ Fee R20 for 5 tastings, incl glass ▪ Closed Easter Fri, Dec 25 & Jan 1 ▪ Tours by appt ▪ The Avontuur Restaurant (see Eat-out section) ▪ Owner Tony Taberer ▪ Winemaker Willie Malherbe (Jul 2002) ▪ Viticulturist Pippa Mickleburgh (Sep 1999) ▪ 50 ha (cab s/f, merlot, pinot, pinotage, shiraz, chard, sauvignon) ▪ 20 000 cs own label 70% red 30% white ▪ Export brand: Klein Avontuur ▪ PO Box 1128 Somerset West 7129 ▪ info@avontuurestate.co.za ▪ www.avontuurestate.co.za ▪ ***T 855·3450*** *▪ F 855·4600*

Pinot noir is winemaker Willie Malherbe's favourite variety, so he's cheerleading now that the estate's five-year drought is broken with the release of a Pinot Reserve named 'Minelli'. A good glassful might help him forget the challenges of last harvest, marked by simultaneous ripenings, bigger volumes and high sugars. In the vineyards, there are new plantings of cab, chardonnay and sauvignon, and new in the cellar is the first fruit from a shiraz block which shows promise. The tasting room, open plan to Avontuur restaurant, has been renovated with better lighting and more space for visitors at its characterful tasting counter, made of old wine vats.

★★★★ **Baccarat** Brooding bdx blend of cabs s/f & merlot; 16 mths new Fr oak. **01** when tasted last yr still remarkably deep & dark for its age; some bottle-maturity revealed on nose via forest-floor hint. Drinks well, should improve another few yrs.

★★★★ **Pinotage** Attractive **01** a fine Cape offering. Mid-2004 showed vivid raspberry, strawberry & vanilla-cream flavours backed by judicious wood (±18 mths Fr, some new). Probably best over next ±4 yrs. **00** luscious but burly tannins demanded time.

★★★★☆ **Luna de Miel** Barrel-fermented chardonnay. **04** clearly a wine for lovers (picked on Valentine's Day!). Exotic & pungent bouquet of asparagus, mandarin & lime; grapefruit pith texture/flavour adds interest. Sweet tickle in tail coaxed by touch sugar (5.8g/ℓ) & viscous alc (14.5%). Less overt wood than **03**, which had a caramelised tone, furry finish from lees maturation. 8 mths Fr oak.

★★★★ **Brut Cap Classique** Refined **99** from chardonnay & pinot in equal measure. Hypnotic bubbles, pronounced toffee-apple nose with honey note from long bottle-maturation (4 yrs); zesty lingering lemon-toned flavours. Pvs was another 99, from chardonnay.

Sauvignon Blanc ★★★ Lightish **05** (sample) fairly complex greenpepper, asparagus, cutgrass bouquet; piercing acid backbone well padded by fruit. 3 mths on lees. Following 3 wines are new: **Minelli 04** ★★ Peach, strawberry & raspberry aromas abound on this rustic pinot. Tough tannins dominate ripe-prune palate mid-2005. Probably not for cellaring. **Vintner's Blend** ★★★ **05** (sample) onion-skin-hued blend chardonnay/pinot (70/30) aged briefly in older oak. Biscuity bouquet; chardonnay adds lime/lemon tone to mid-palate, pinot a gentle tannic tug to finish. Tasty sunset sipping. **Chenin Blanc** ★★★ **04** Lightly oaked & food-friendly. Tropical fruit salad nose invites quaffing; refreshing lime-zest flavour lightly teased with oak spice & vanilla. 50% fermented/aged 4 mths 2nd fill Fr oak. Following still-available wines not retasted: **Cabernet Franc** ★★★★ **01** with attractive 'fresh compost' fragrance. Nimble tannins spotlight gentle, perky flavours. Less than yr in older oak. **Merlot** ★★★★ Confident **00** brims with choc/spice, maraschino cherries. Lightly oaked (±yr older Fr barrels) for early drinking with potential for cellaring. **Vintner's Pinotage** ★★★ Gluggable mulberry-hued & raspberry-toned **03**; fruit undominated by yr older wood. **Shiraz** ★★★★ **03** fruit-powered (plums/cherries) with approachably soft sweet tannins; noticeable 14.5% alc. 50% new Am oak. **Cabernet Sauvignon-Merlot** ★★★ Lighter in tone than single-variety bottlings. **01** mélange black/red fruits, ripe tannins suggest ±3 yr longevity. Yr used Fr oak. **Vintner's Red** ★★★ Fruity palate/wallet-pleaser. **03** 50/50 blend two cabs (s/f), with dusty bouquet from the latter & from oak (6 mths older Fr). **Chardonnay** ★★★ **03** early drinking, uncomplicated tropical fruit flavours with hint of wood; light textured/bodied. **Dolce Vita Red** ★★ Sweet & light-bodied red. **NV** blend cab, merlot, ruby cab makes a friendly glassful. Enjoy chilled, soonest after purchasing. **Above Royalty**, **Cabernet Sauvignon**, **Chenin Blanc Barrel Select**, **Vintner's White**, **Dolce Vita White** discontinued.—*CvZ*

Axe Hill

Calitzdorp (see Little Karoo map) ▪ Est 1993 ▪ 1stB 1997 ▪ Open by appt; when closed, sales from Queens Bottle Store, Voortrekker Road (R62), Calitzdorp ▪ Owners Axe Hill Trust ▪ Winemaker Tony Mossop ▪ 1.3 ha (touriga, tinta, souzão) ▪ 6-7 tons 400-450 cs 100% port ▪ PO Box 43942 Scarborough 7975 ▪ tony@axehill.co.za ▪ ***T 780·1051/(044) 213·3585/ 082·490·4248*** *▪ F 780·1178*

Going from strength to strength seems an appropriate way to describe a producer of fortified wine, especially if that producer is port specialist, wine-writer and -judge (including for previous editions of this guide) Tony Mossop. With the latest 03 getting the nod, his Cape Vintage has an unmatched six Platter five-star wines. And the magic is set to continue: 2005 was 'an extremely good vintage, yielding dense wine with plenty of extract and concentration'. This, Tony M reckons, was in part thanks to a tip he and wife Lynn picked up on a recent trip to Portugal – picking a touch earlier and keeping the tanks slightly cooler during fermentation. And, as always, being meticulous about hygiene ('keeping the bugs at bay', as he puts it). Looking ahead, the Mossops are particularly excited about the launch of a solera-aged white port in the course of this year.

★★★★★ **Cape Vintage Port** Multiple accolades celebrate this as SA's top port, stamped with balance rather than opulence. **03** continues stunning run: restrained yet intricate melange of spice, smoke, nuts & elderberry fruits. Flavour, structure, proportion; the 'wow factor' comes as standard. **02** gorgeous, serious yet retiring **01** (★★★★★), less voluptuous than **00** FCTWS trophy winner. Traditionally vinified touriga/tinta blend (70/30) from low-yielding (±5 t/ha) vyds. 14 mths seasoned casks. 20% alc, 91g/ℓ sugar.—*DS*

Baarsma Wine Group

Stellenbosch ▪ Closed to public ▪ Owner Baarsma's Holding B.V. ▪ MD Chris Rabie (since Jul 2001) ▪ Cellarmaster: Hannes Louw (since Jan 2005) ▪ PO Box 7275 Stellenbosch 7599 ▪ phelia@baarsma.co.za ▪ www.baarsma.com ▪ ***T 880·1221*** *▪ F 880·0851*

Baarsma SA, headquartered in Stellenbosch, is a major export marketer of SA wines, shipping more than 1m cases a year to the major international wine markets, notably Europe. Ranges owned or exported include Ancient Africa, Apiesklip, Blydskap, Boschveld, Drie Berge, Goede Moed, Goedgenoegen, Jacobus de Wet, Kaapse Pracht, Lazy Bay, Lyngrove (see entry), Meerland, Podium, Rotsvast, The Mask, Veelplesier, Volmaak, Voorspoed, Vreughvol and Wild Thing. Baarsma also represents a number of top SA brands in Europe.

Babbling Brook see Makro

Babylon's Peak Private Cellar

new

Swartland ▪ Est/1stB 2003 ▪ Visits by appt ▪ BYO picnic ▪ Self-catering guest house ▪ Walks ▪ Conservation area ▪ 4x4 trail ▪ Owner/winemaker/viticulturist Stephan Basson ▪ 200 ha (cab, carignan, merlot, pinotage, ruby cab, shiraz, chard, chenin, sauvignon) ▪ 80 tons 1 200 own label (100% red) + ±40 000ℓ bulk wine ▪ PO Box 161 Malmesbury 7299 ▪ info@babylonspeak.co.za ▪ ***T/F (022) 487·1614***

A towering granite peak known to locals as Babylonstoren, and some of the highest vineyards in the Swartland (including a block of 15 year old pinotage at 750m above sea-level) are found on the farm Nooitgedacht, home to the Basson family for four generations. Stephan B's great-grandfather made wine here until 1948, when the local co-op was established. Restoring the original cellar, with its open cement fermenters, has been a dream come true for Stephan B, whose philosophy is 'passion, perfection and tradition'.

TBWA\HUNT\LASCARIS\DURBAN 005098
think all liquor stores are the same?
you need to get out more...
For info on your nearest TOPS liquor store, phone our Share Call number 0860 313141
we'll change the way you look at liquor stores.
tops! at SPAR
The most exciting liquor store!

Alexander Baron von Essen and his wife **Ingrid**, he a leading independent fine-wine merchant in Germany, she an accomplished architect, so love the winelands that they named their splendid new winery and vineyards in the Philadelphia area Capaia - 'A lot of Cape'. Their pursuit of quality without compromise is reflected in the cellar, which houses the world's largest array of wooden fermenters, installed in-situ by French coopers.

Investec
Private Client Securities

Extra pairs of eyes all round suggest their wearers might be burners of midnight oil - and indeed they are. **Johann Marais** of the Post-Harvest & Wine Technology Division of ARC Infruitec-Nietvoorbij (right), and **Florian Bauer** of Stellenbosch University's Institute for Wine Biotechnology (centre) are researchers of international repute and providers of specialised insights to a great many individuals and organisations throughout the SA wine industry. Their work, and that of colleagues in other arenas, is orchestrated by the Wine Industry Network of Expertise & Technology (WINETECH), headed by **Jan Booysen**, the third person in our photograph.

BANKING | PROPERTY FINANCE |

THE BETTER YOU DO.

related events both locally and overseas to facilitate contact between importers and exporters, and to better understand your business, the way you do. This understanding means that whether you're an investor, estate owner or importer, we can assist you in finding the right solutions. Add value to your business by emailing us at wine@nedbank.co.za. You'll find we're the South African bank most wine industry experts prefer.

The goat, in mythological literature and lore, symbolises vitality and energy. Appropriate, then, that one of SA wine's prime movers and shakers, **Charles Back**, has a strong connection with this characterful animal. His goat herd at Fairview farm not only produces the wet goods for world-class cheeses, but gives its name to the iconoclastic Goats do Roam wines, one of SA's standout export successes. Pioneer, visionary and mentor of winemaking talent, Back is (to borrow the name of one of his newest French-baiting creations) something of a 'Goat d'Or'.

As part of the Biodiversity & Wine Initiative (BWI), the SA wine and conservation sectors' pioneering initiative to minimise the further loss of threatened fynbos and renosterveld, members of the Groenlandberg Conservancy in the Elgin/Bot River area have joined forces to establish the world's first biodiversity wine route. Charting the Green Mountain Wine Route's proposed path, with the eponymous peak in the background, are **José de Andrade** (Feiteiras Vineyards) and **Tony Hansen** (BWI). Behind them, in the usual order, are **Ben Klindt** (Villiersdorp Cellar), **Paul Cluver Jnr** and **Andries Burger** (Paul Cluver Estate), **Anthony Rawbone-Viljoen** (Oak Valley Wines), **Sebastian Beaumont** (Beaumont Wines), **Elreda Pillmann** (Goedvertrouw Estate), **Niels Verburg** (Luddite Wines) and **Leon Lourens** (Cape Nature).

CHAS EVERITT
International Collection

liquor stores in
WINE OF ORIGIN COASTAL

Syrah ★★★★ Sumptuously oaked **03** with coconut/marzipan aromas, soft raspberry fruit, sweet easy finish. MIWA double-gold, from Swtland fruit. **Babylon** ★★★ Intriguing blend of equal parts pinotage, cab, merlot, from low-yielding Pdberg vyds. **03** red berry whiffs, slight minty notes, dense tannins, austere puckering finish. VDG. — *MF*

Babylons Toren see Backsberg

Babylon Wines

new

Walker Bay ▪ Est 1997 ▪ Visits Mon-Fri 9-5 Sat 9-1 ▪ Closed Easter Sun/Mon, Dec 25/26 & Jan 1 ▪ The Champagne Veranda open daily 10-8 in season ▪ Tourgroups ▪ Permanent art exhibition ▪ Owners Babylon Wines (Pty) Ltd & Viking Pony Properties 355 (Pty) Ltd ▪ Winemaker Marc van Halderen (Jun 2005) ▪ Viti adviser Andrew Teubes (Jul 2005) ▪ 27ha (pinot, chard, sauvignon) ▪ PO Box 1580 Hermanus 7200 ▪ marcthesparc@yahoo.com ▪ ***T (028) 312·4631***

A new venture in the Hemel-en-Aarde valley that has all the signs of a great future. The established property, bought by a group of investors from the Johnson family, has tempted Elsenburg's top student, Marc van Halderen to create its portfolio. Promising wines of 'integrity and finesse', MvH says he 'can't wait to get started!' Wines under the Temptation and Redemption labels will pave the way for a premium brand featuring fruit from own vineyards. Summer sees the opening of The Champagne Veranda, offering a selection of champagnes and MCCs, light meals and a selection of cheeses.

Backsberg Cellars

Paarl ▪ Est 1916 ▪ 1stB 1970 ▪ Tasting & sales Mon-Fri 8-5 Sat 8-2 Sun 11-2 (Sep-Apr only) ▪ Fee R10 refunded on purchase ▪ Closed Easter Fri, Dec 25 & Jan 1 ▪ Self-guided tours during tasting hours ▪ New restaurant to open 2006 (phone for opening hours); cheese platters at tasting room ▪ Play area for children ▪ Maze ▪ Gifts ▪ Conferencing by appt ▪ Owner Backsberg Estate Cellars ▪ Winemaker Alicia Rechner ▪ Viticulturist Clive Trent (Jul 1992) ▪ 130 ha (cab, merlot, shiraz, chard) ▪ 1 000 tons ±90 000 cs 65% red 30% white 5% rosé ▪ PO Box 537 Suider-Paarl 7624 ▪ info@backsberg.co.za ▪ www.backsberg.co.za ▪ ***T 875·5141*** *▪ F 875·5144*

'Cool and clean,' was always Alicia Rechner's philosophy when it came to making wine. This often meant working fast. But motherhood changed things slightly (son Enzo turned one last year), slowing down the pace in the cellar, with longer setting times, slower fermentation, more time on the lees and extended skin contact. 'The added complexity to the wines was a great reward,' she says. Another revelation was working with sauvignon from a joint-venture vineyard in Durbanville: 'The quality was unlike anything I've ever worked with!' A high note was Backsberg being listed among *Wine & Spirit* magazine's top 100 wineries in its buying guide for 2005, the only SA winery to be thus honoured.

★★★★ **Elba** Feisty Mediterranean blend of mainly malbec, shiraz, mourvèdre, viognier (04) & sangiovese; **03**, unrated sample last ed; has bloomed into something slightly wild, juicy & rather good; chewy fruit flavours; choc/spice undertone with plentiful chunky tannins. Yr older wood.

Pinneau ★★★ new to the guide (but a long-time tasting room favourite). Pineau des Charentes-style aperitif; unfermented semillon fortified with yr old Backsberg potstill brandy. **04** fruity/toffee flavours with a medicinal Stroh rum-like finish. A curiosity. **Port** new ★★★★ Attractive & different **04** from cab f, fortified with 3 yr old house brandy. Burnt toffee nose/palate sloshed with choc, medium bodied (18% alc) with pungent flavours & grip.

Babylons Toren range

★★★★ **Cabernet Sauvignon-Merlot 03** held back till next yr; last we admired **02**'s serious demeanour, expensive new oak trim & rich flavours still guarded by vibrant tannins. Most ageworthy of range; should peak around 2008-09. 16 mths Fr oak, 50% new.

★★★★ **Cabernet Sauvignon** ✓ **02** features evolved, bright, lifted plum/mulberry bouquet. Supple, substantial but not overly dense mouthful; ripe tannin support. Probably at best over the next ±18 mths. Oak-matured. **01** *Decanter* ★★★★.

★★★★ **Chardonnay** Characterful **03** in pvs ed was said to pick up where modern, sleek **02** left off. Touch more elegant; full, creamily rich flavours, freshened by fine natural acid. Fermented/matured Fr oak, 70% new; malo.

★★★★ **Viognier** Unexpected vegetal notes & medicinal finish (perhaps from 5% sauvignon) mar **05** (★★★), some mitigation via ingratiating sweetness (7g/ℓ RS) & toasty vanilla tone from barrel fermentation. Whopping 15.5% alc a worry here & in **04**

Black Label range

★★★★ **Klein Babylonstoren 03** balance is the watchword, both in make-up (50:50 blend cab, merlot) & character. Fine tannins, rich sour cherry flavours, good length – all well integrated with serious structure. A stayer. 16 mths Fr oak, 25% new vs. 50% new for **02**.

★★★★ **Pumphouse Shiraz 03** (★★★★) crackerjack shiraz with layers of mocha, vanilla & spice. Portion malbec reduced to 5% from 15% in elegant **02**, both with robust 14.5% alc. 16 mths oak, 25% new Am for **03**, copes well given its riper fruit.

John Martin Sauvignon Blanc 05 (sample) shows fresh ruby grapefruit & tropical notes (guava/pawpaw), racy acidity. Grapes from Dbnville/Paarl, 15% oak fermented, 13.5% alc. Could rate ★★★★ when bottled.

Varietal range

Cabernet Sauvignon ★★★ **03**'s adolescent tannins a fur coat for the tongue. Some spice from 4% malbec & 5% petit v, & perfume from 6% cab f. Yr Fr oak, 25% new. More austere than pvs. **Malbec** ★★★ No further releases tasted since **01**, with subdued wet-earth bouquet, minerally red fruits. **Merlot** ★★★ Porty nose, spicy black olives & some dark fruit with good concentration. Yr oak maturation & big 14.5% alc combine to make **04** tougher going than easy, satisfying **03**. **Pinotage** ★★ **04** has sweet aromas & flavours of 'Banana Split', contrastingly unyielding finish. **Dry Red** ★★★ Sweet-fruited unoaked, everyday drinking. Touch of mint adds to fresh appeal, early enjoyment. Latest bottling (**NV**) not tasted. **Rosé** ★★★ **NV** melange of mourvèdre, chardonnay & chenin (54/40/6), ripe berry compôte with 20g/ℓ RS well cloaked. **Organic Chardonnay** ★★★★ Fresh earthy attractions with lively lime/butterscotch on characterful **03**. Medium body, balanced creamy/crisp contrast, roundly dry. Not retasted. **Chardonnay** ★★★ **04** takes 'unshowy' to the extreme, in spite of 50% fermentation in Fr oak. **Chenin Blanc** ★★ **05** cold tea aroma & fennel on palate, some richness from 4g/ℓ sugar. 13% alc. **Sauvignon Blanc** ★★★ **05** big & generously fruity wine spoilt by bitter finish.

Camp range

Chardonnay ★★ Unlike comfortable pvs, hard finish brings abrupt halt to flow of apple, lemon & pear flavours on **05**. **Cabernet Sauvignon** ★★★ **02** pvs ed was scented & soft; 15% merlot for extra-juicy palate. Flourish toasty oak in tail.

Kosher range

Made under supervision of Cape Town Beth Din. **Pinotage** ★★ Highlights variety's sometimes tropical tone; **04** fruit salad melange with banana hint. **Chardonnay** ★★ **04** whiffs of lawn cuttings; fresh compost, fennel & more grass on palate; drier & less creamy than pvs. Oak-influenced. — *NP*

Badsberg Co-op Winery

Worcester ▪ Est 1951 ▪ Tasting & sales Mon-Fri 8-5 Sat 10-1 ▪ Closed Easter Fri/Sun, Aug 9, Dec 25, Jan 1 ▪ Tours by appt during Dec ▪ BYO picnic ▪ Tourgroups ▪ Play area for children ▪ Gifts ▪ Conferencing ▪ Walks ▪ Conservation area ▪ Owners 26 members ▪ Winemakers Willie Burger & Henri Swiegers, with Johann Fourie (Jan 1998/Dec 2002/Dec 2003) ▪ 1 000 ha ▪ 16 000 tons 40% red 40% white 10% rosé 10% fortified ▪ PO Box 72 Rawsonville 6845 ▪ enquiries@badsberg.co.za ▪ www.badsberg.co.za ▪ ***T (023) 344·3021*** *▪ F (023) 344·3023*

No update available on this winery; contact details and wine notes from previous edition.

Merlot ★★ **02** mirrors pvs's austere, super-dry tones. **Pinotage** ★★★ **02** crammed with ripe plums & mulberries; smooth, decidedly quaffable. **Shiraz** ★★★ Debut **02** dark berry fruits with slight peppery hint & touch vanilla from yr Fr oak. **Rosé** ★★★ Sunset-pink **03** switches to off-dry (pvs semi-sweet), with ripe-plum flavours. **Chardonnay Sur Lie** ★★★ **02** barrel matured , with vanilla, lemon & lees hints. **Chenin Blanc** ★★★ **03** understated tropical nose; livelier palate, full, smooth. **Sauvignon Blanc** ★★★ **04** cut grass & nettles, fresh intensity, brightness; delightful in its youth. **Special Late Harvest** ★★★ Hanepoot & chenin blend in **04**, honeysuckle & ripe tropical fruit, deliciously fresh & summery. **Noble Late Harvest** ★★★★ From chenin & hanepoot (50/50), singled out for praise at Rendez-vous du Chenin 2004; **03** muted botrytis character; powerfully sweet (128g/ℓ RS). **Vin Doux Sparkling** ★★★ **03** summer picnic bubbles for the sweeter-inclined. **Red Muscadel** ★★★★ **03** honeysuckle & peach aromas, intense sweetness saved by lively alc (16.5%) & acidity. **Red Jerepigo** ★★★★ **02** lavender whiffs, sweet but focused by alc (15.6%) for agreeably warming fruity finish. **Hanepoot Jerepigo** ★★★ **03** oozes hanepoot; youthful & delightful. 17% alc. **Port** ★★ **01** unclassic mix shiraz, cab f, ruby cab, Fr-oaked; plain but pleasant. 17.8% alc.—*DH*

Bain's Way see Wamakersvallei
Bakenskop see Jonkheer
Balance see Overhex
Baobab see Stettyn
Barefoot Wine Company see BWC
Barrydale Winery see Southern Cape Vineyards

Bartho Eksteen Family Wines

Walker Bay ▪ Est/1stB 1998 ▪ Tasting & sales Mon-Fri 9-5.30 Sat 9-2 at Wine & Company, 7 High Street, Hermanus ▪ Fee for groups R15 ▪ Closed Easter Sun/Mon, Dec 25/26 & Jan 1 ▪ Light meals by appt ▪ Deli produce & wine gifts ▪ Owners Bartho Eksteen & Ailsa Butler (UK) ▪ Winemaker Bartho Eksteen ▪ 30 tons 2 000 cs 20% red 80% white ▪ Suite 47, Private Bag X15, Hermanus 7200 ▪ winenco@telkomsa.net ▪ ***T (028) 313·2047*** *▪ F (028) 312·4029*

Seven years ago the Eksteens had the foresight to specialise in top-end sauvignon and shiraz, both varieties from which local benchmarks have attracted international interest. From humble beginnings (wine was initially made in other people's cellars) the business grew steadily, inhibited only by the fact that they weren't assured a constant supply of grapes. 'It was hard work to establish a style and stick to it,' says Bartho E, who nonetheless achieved remarkably consistent ratings. The old strictures are about to be lifted: they're hooking up with a Walker Bay producer and an own cellar and 'unique' vineyard are in the offing. It's a bit too early to spill the beans though, says Eksteen, obviously delighted at the direction things are taking.

★★★★ **Classified** new No details from Bartho E about this appropriately characterful good-humoured, approachable red: 'All info is classified!' **03** not trivial or over-ambitious: juicy ripe red fruit, moderately wooded, well balanced with softly ingratiating tannins & pleasing length.

★★★★ **Shiraz** Exuberant & flamboyant, from Dbnville, W Bay grapes. **02**'s plentiful fruit lurked in youth beneath roast coffee aromas/flavours. **03**, tasted last yr, similar profile; lingering, well-balanced but evidencing yr oak, small % Am. Few yrs ageing will benefit these.

★★★★★ **Premier Choix Sauvignon Blanc** ✓ Only in exceptional yrs. Last **03** styled like standard version, with semillon touch, but extra authority, intensity. Gorgeous & forceful but elegant, with yrs to go.

★★★★ **Sauvignon Blanc** ✓ Always fine, rich combo grassiness, subtle tropicality. Sample **05** suave, gripping but not aggressive; will benefit from yr/2, 13% alc. From various vyds (WO W Cape); 8% wood-fermented semillon; on lees 5 mths.—*TJ*

Bartinney Cellars

Stellenbosch ▪ Est/1stB 1999 ▪ Sales Mon-Fri 9-5 ▪ Tours by appt ▪ Owner Thabana Li Meli (Pty) Ltd ▪ Winemaker/viticulturist Carl Potgieter (1999) ▪ 13 ha (cab, chard, sauvignon) ▪ 4 000 cs 33.3% red 66.6% white ▪ PO Box 2297 Dennesig 7601 ▪ thabana@mweb.co.za ▪ ***T 885·1013*** *▪ F 885·2852*

No update available on this winery; contact details from previous edition.

Barton Farm

Walker Bay ▪ Est 2001 ▪ 1stB 2003 ▪ Closed to public ▪ Owners Peter Neill & Charles Lousada ▪ Vini consultants Danie Truter & Niels Verburg ▪ Viticulturist Noeil Vorster (Oct 2005) ▪ 24 ha (cab, malbec, merlot, shiraz, chenin, sauvignon, semillon) ▪ 2 430 cs ▪ PO Box 368 Caledon 7230 ▪ Peterjneill@aol.com ▪ ***T (028) 284·9776***

British businessman Peter Neill went home from a holiday in Hermanus with more than just a suntan: he also had the title deeds to this Walker Bay property, which he bought with UK partner Charles Lousada. The area under vine has increased significantly since the purchase, and coming on board to look after the enlarged vineholding is viticulturist Noeil Vorster, ex-Hamilton Russell Vineyards. 'UK customers seem to like our tipple,' says Peter N, who plans to cultivate a bigger SA clientele in the future.

★★★★ **Cabernet Sauvignon-Shiraz** Fruit-driven **04**, delicious raspberry/marzipan aromas, Ribena-rich mid-palate, soft but not insubstantial tannins, long finish. 60% home-farm cab, 40% Mbury shiraz. Yr oak, 25% new, 75/25 Fr/Am. 'A very nice drop,' says Niels V, accurately. Bigger, more concentrated than shiraz-led **03** (★★★), 'Shiraz-Cab' pvs ed.

Chenin Blanc ★★★★ **05** (sample) fine pear-drop aroma, tangy but unaggressive acidity, apricot whiffs on finish; step up on pvs. **Chenin Blanc Reserve** ★★★ Succulent selection of above; **03** tasted for pvs ed showed fine lime & pineapple hints, elegance & length. — *MF*

Bastenburg see Southern Right
Bastiaans Klooff see Lateganskop
Bats Rock see Lutzville
Bay View see Longridge
BC Wines see Brandvlei
Beacon Hill see Jonkheer
Beaufort see Ultra Liquors

Beau Joubert Vineyards & Winery

Stellenbosch ▪ 1stB 2000 ▪ Visits by appt ▪ Self-catering guest houses ▪ Conference facility for max 100 ▪ Functions & weddings for max 150 ▪ Owners Andrew Hilliard & Joubert family ▪ Winemaker Jannie Joubert, advised by Mark Carmichael-Green ▪ Viticulturist Lukas Joubert ▪ 80 ha (cab, merlot, chard, sauvignon) ▪ 600 tons 20 000 cs own label 50/50 red/white ▪ Export brands: Beau Joubert, Oak Lane & Veelverjaaght ▪ PO Box 1114 Stellenbosch 7599 ▪ info@beaujoubert.com ▪ www.beaujoubert.com ▪ ***T 881·3103*** *▪ F 881·3377*

A new name for, and a new leaf at this Polkadraai Hills wine farm previously known as BoweJoubert. The Joubert family and US investor Andrew Hilliard (Bahaman entrepreneur Alphonso Bowe no longer involved) have big plans – not just to develop the vineyards and winery but to build a more visible profile. They will participate in more wine shows and trade events, and enhance and expand the tasting area, overnight accommodation and function facilities ('unforgettable weddings' a prime emphasis). The goal is to make B-J 'a major landmark in the region'.

Beaumont Wines

Walker Bay ▪ Est 1750 ▪ 1stB 1994 ▪ Tasting, sales & tours Mon-Fri 9.30-12.30; 1.30–4.30 Sat by appt ▪ Fee R20 for groups of 10+ ▪ Closed Easter Sat/Sun, Dec 25 & Jan 1 ▪ Meals for small groups by appt ▪ 2 self-catering guest houses ▪ Art/jewellery exhibits ▪ Conservation area ▪ Owners Raoul & Jayne Beaumont ▪ Winemaker Sebastian Beaumont (Aug 2003) ▪ Viticulturist Leon Engelke (May 2003) ▪ 34 ha (13 varieties, r/w) ▪ 200 tons 12 000 cs 55% red 45% white ▪ PO Box 3 Bot River 7185 ▪ beauwine@netactive.co.za ▪ www.beaumont.co.za ▪ ***T (028) 284·9194*** *▪ F (028) 284·9733*

Time moves slowly on this authentically rural farm. 'There's too much flashy "schicky micky" in this industry,' explains winemaker Sebastian Beaumont. 'We want people to have a glimpse of what it is like in a real winery.' Describing his family's 'adventure' here as a 'long-term, many-generations project', he says each year brings a 'deeper love and understanding of the vineyards and wines'. The white wine focus is already on Chenin, with the barrel-matured version named after grandmother Hope Marguerite. Next step will be 'looking at the reds as the vines get older to see which direction we need to move in'. Equally appropriate, then, that the Bordeaux-style blend is named after younger sister Ariane, who recently got married.

★★★★ **Pinotage** Traditional open *kuip* cold soak/ferment. **03** not as bold as pvs, yet solid enough to carry 14.5% alc. More delicate flavours, fine tannins. Whisper of vanilla from 25% Am oak. Excellent mid-2004; should improve over 2-3 yrs. (This, next 3 reds, not re-tasted; notes from last ed.)

★★★★ **Shiraz** Unlike many super-charged versions, this has never sacrificed finesse at the altar of ultra-ripe fruit. Expressive & spicy, **03** emulates **02** with dense black fruit flavours, hint smoked meat & rich, fennel-laced finish. Includes touch mourvèdre. Despite 14.8% alc, focused & balanced. Yr oak, 25% new, 25% Am.

★★★★ **Mourvèdre** SA's first varietal bottling. Foursquare, high alc (15.1%) & substantial tannin. These varietal qualities & more in **03**: scrub & raspberry aromas, pervasive savouriness tempered by 16 mths Fr oak (20% new). Powerful yet balanced, needs time to ease into its frame.

★★★☆ **Ariane 03** (★★★★) step up for this blend merlot, cab, cab f (40/40/20). Generous merlot plum nose/flavours when tasted mid-2004; typical cab backbone, powdery tannins; enticing cab f herbal whiffs. 14 mths Fr oak, 25% new, easily absorbed by punchy fruit.

★★★★ **Hope Marguerite Chenin Blanc Barrel Reserve** 'Let the vineyard talk' is Sebastian B's philosophy; here a distinctive, single-vyd selection from older vines. **04** honeycomb, stewed quince, sprinkling spice follow through into creamily textured mouthful. Enlivened by thrilling acidity. Give 3-5 yrs to show its best. Fermented/10 mths 400ℓ Fr oak, 30% new; half with native yeasts.

★★★★ **Chenin Blanc** ✓ Benchmark example from old vines. **05** subtle spice, bruised apple, cool menthol flavours. Pleasantly rounded, classy fruit still hiding its charms, lively acidity. 15% barrel-fermented portion adds to mouth-filling structure. Try keeping some for pleasant surprise after 5 yrs.

★★★★ **Chardonnay** Arresting bouquet of Seville orange marmalade, caramel, peach compôte on **04**. Big & rounded, wearing its bigness well, thanks to lively acidity – will be elegant table companion. Fermented/10 mths oak, 30% new. Should age well over 2-3 yrs.

Raoul's Old Basket Press Rustic Red ☺ ★★★ As colourful & individual as Raoul B himself; 100% unwooded tinta in **04**, bursting with sweet/sour fruit, nice dusty earthy finish. Terrific tipple, but not for swigging at 14.5% alc.

Sauvignon Blanc ★★★☆ Individual flavours in **05** feature juicy greengage, lime, with more conventional gooseberry, neatly packed around minerally core. Juicy, graceful, curvaceous, a pleasure to drink – but not one for keeping. **Goutte d'Or** ★★★☆ Botrytised semillon/sauvignon blend (80/20), in oak (some new) 10 mths. **04** candied pear, apricot, distinct lanolin notes of semillon, subtle botrytis. Not over-sweet at 122g/ℓ, needs another 5 yrs to reach peak. **Cape Vintage** ★★★ 50/50 tinta/pinotage: a foot in both Cape & Portuguese camps – foot-trodden it was, too, before 2 yrs in old casks. **02** sweet vanilla & spiced plum, lively clean-cut flavours, sweet finish. 20% alc, 88g/ℓ sugar.

Jackal's River range – for UK market

Unwooded Chardonnay ★★★ **05** delicate citrus, lime perfume; juicy lime & grapefruit palate: mouth-watering. **Pinotage** discontinued. – *IvH/CvZ*

Bein Wine

Stellenbosch ▪ Est/1stB 2002 ▪ Open by appt only ▪ Owners/ winemakers/viticulturists Luca & Ingrid Bein ▪ 2.2 ha (merlot) 1 000 cs 100% red ▪ PO Box 3408 Matieland 7602 ▪ lib@beinwine.com ▪ www.beinwine.com ▪ ***T 072·629·3867/881·3025*** *F 881·3025*

Where many farmers churn up the dust with their quad bikes, Luca Bein uses Shanks' pony (he does have just 80 rows of merlot to tend!) and Ingrid B occasionally rides their donkey, Gloria. 'We're different,' she explains, and *vive la difference*! For the Beins, Swiss vets turned Stellenbosch winemakers, 2005 was a special year, not only because of the opulence and density of the vintage, but because they could enjoy their own on-site production facilities. The style of the new cellar is Cape Dutch but its elements are all that today's oenology demands, including a modern basket press and air-conditioning in the barrel cellar and storage room. Final touch to the picture is the splendid view from the new tasting room, across the winelands to False Bay.

★★★★ **Merlot** Growing to be among best Cape merlots as vines mature, since maiden **02** (★★★★). A year on, **03** silky & smartly dry, with rich fruit firmly supported for further development. Concours Mondial gold. **04** similarly well balanced & restrained, lovely fresh & sweet cassis fruit emerging over ripe tannic core; promising harmony. These sensitively oaked — yr, ±40% new. — *TJ*

Belbon Hills

*Worcester ▪ Est/1stB 1999 ▪ Closed to public ▪ Directors Mirella Corsetti Kruger & Pedro Estrada Belli ▪ 30 ha (cab, pinotage, ruby cab, shiraz, chenin, colombard, sauvignon) ▪ 260 tons 10 000 cs own label 60% red 40% white ▪ PO Box 457 Bloubergstrand 7436 ▪ winery@belbonhills.com ▪ **T 557·7143** ▪ F 557·1351*

No update available on this winery; contact details from previous edition.

Belfield

new

*Elgin ▪ Est 2000 ▪ 1stB 2005 ▪ Closed to public ▪ Owners Mike & Mel Kreft ▪ Winemaker Mike Kreft, with Lawrence Lebenya & Kreft family, advised by Mark Carmichael-Green (2004) ▪ Viti adviser Paul Wallace (2002) ▪ 1.64 ha (cab, merlot) ▪ 9 tons total 75 cs own label 100% red ▪ PO Box 191 Elgin 7180 ▪ phkreft@mweb.co.za ▪ **T/F 848·9840***

'All good things start small,' believes Mike Kreft, owner of this minute Elgin property (just 5.5ha, of which 3.5 will ultimately be under vine). Viti-consultant Paul Wallace is positively enthralled by the potential of this cool-climate area, as is vini-adviser Mark Carmichael-Green, who assisted with the maiden 2005 Cab (still in barrel as the guide went to bed). The whole Kreft family – Mike, Mel, Al and Jenna – is involved, aided by Lawrence Lebenya, described as 'a stickler for accuracy and precision'. Winemaking happens at nearby Stranthian farm pending conversion of an old shed into a cellar. Ultimate production will be 2 000 cases, all filled with 'hand-crafted, value-for-money' wines.

Bellevue Estate

*Stellenbosch ▪ Est 1701 ▪ 1stB 1999 ▪ Tasting Mon-Fri 10–4 Sat & non-religious pub hols 10–3 ▪ Owner Dirkie Morkel ▪ Winemaker Wilhelm Kritzinger (Feb 2002) ▪ Viticulturist Dirkie Morkel (1979) ▪ 193 ha (14 varieties, incl 5 bdx varieties, pinotage, shiraz, sauvignon) ▪ 13 000 cs own label 97% red 3% white ▪ PO Box 33 Koelenhof 7605 ▪ info@bellevue.co.za ▪ www.bellevue.co.za **T 865·2055** ▪ F 865·2899*

Despite the smaller yield, Dirkie Morkel and Wilhelm Kritzinger (proud father of Ben, born last May) were delighted with the quality of the 2005 harvest. Dirk is also very proud of Sizanani, their new BEE project, and energised by the presence of new Elsenburg-trained vineyard manager Chris Immelman, and – on the admin side – his eldest daughter, Rozanne, after whom he named the charming red that has proved particularly popular with the SAA wine selectors. With the talents of a 5th-generation Morkel now firmly harnessed, it seems fitting that the estate wines are now marketed exclusively under the Morkel name.

Morkel range

★★★★☆ **PK Morkel Pinotage** Single-vyd selection, worthily representing world's first commercial pinotage partly grown here (released 1961 under Lanzerac label). **04** & **03** make interesting comparison. **04** more accessible with up-front fruit, soft velvety texture; ripe tannins mere ruffling of the surface. **03** reticent, hiding its charms, more classically constructed; same dark opulence, tannins less immediately accessible. Differing oak regimens: former yr Am oak, 50% new; latter all new Fr. Cellar up to 10 yrs.

★★★★ **Pinotage** In bright, modern guise, more immediately accessible than version above. **04** soft plush plummy fruit showcases variety's attractions. Not over-ripe or -extracted, slight sweetness to fruit balanced by dry oak tannins, adding subtle texture, seriousness. Just about perfect balance. Ready to drink. Subtle – will impress even variety's non-believers. Yr Am oak, 50% new.

★★★★ **Tumara 02** full house of main Bdx varieties. **03** also cabs s/f, merlot, malbec, petit verdot (69/6/10/5/10). Sleek, subtle & stylish, more restrained, classically inclined than single variety cellar mates; dry & savoury, not over-rich, with submissive tannins: elegant table companion. Yr Fr oak 50% new. Cellar 5–7 yrs.

★★★☆ **Shiraz** Controlled opulence in **03** (★★★★); black cherry, wood spice & dark choc with mint overlay, waves of rich, dark-berried flavour, soft, velvety tannins for textural contrast – a hedonist's delight. Yr Fr oak, 50% new. Cellar 4–6 yrs. **02** rather more 'red wine' than classically 'shiraz'.

★★★★ **Sauvignon Blanc 05** (★★★☆) less arresting than hugely concentrated **04**. Mix tropical passionfruit, gooseberry with signature fig, grass, but all in lower key. Pleasing fullness to lively palate, nicely rounded with some sweet/sour tension.

★★★★ **Limited Release Malbec** Stylish **03** (sample tried last yr) minted black plum fruit, fine-grained tannins, savoury finish; beautiful concentration in lengthy dry finish. Yr new Fr oak. Cellar 5–7 yrs.

Malbec ★★★☆ **03**'s whiff smoked beef & mint follows through onto palate plus red & black berried fruits; house's typical soft tannins. **Petit Verdot** ★★★☆ Maiden **03** now tasted as finished wine: attractive whiff vanilla oak, deep coloured, with youthful charm. Softly fruity, beguiling red-berried fruit given fine oak treatment (yr new Fr) Still young, bit one-dimensional. **Pinot Noir** ★★★ **02** (tasted last ed) rather more vinous than varietal; soft berry palate, then grippy tannins gather momentum to finish. Fr oak, third new. **Atticus** ★★★ Intended as less serious blend – within estate's serious context. Latest **03** (no **02**) sweet plummy fruit, whiff good oak, soft tannins. Blend cab/pinotage/petit v, 49/34/17. For now, next 2 yrs. **Rozanne** ★★★ Maiden **03** (not retasted) charming & fruity blend merlot, shiraz, pinotage 59/22/19, lightish stave-wooded quaffer with sprig of mint, will find many friends. – *IvH*

Bellingham

Wellington ▪ Est 1693 ▪ 1stB 1947 ▪ Closed to public ▪ Owner DGB ▪ Winemakers Niël Groenewald & Lizelle Gerber, with Mario Damon (Jul/Aug 2004, Jan 2002) ▪ Viti consultants Johan Wiese & Kevin Watt (1994/2002) ▪ 5 000 tons 350 000 cs 50% red 49% white 1% rosé ▪ HACCP & ISO 9002:2000 certified ▪ PO Box 246 Wellington 7654 ▪ bellingham@dgb.co.za ▪ www.bellingham.co.za ▪ ***T 864·5300*** *▪ F 864·1287*

Niël Groenewald's first harvest at Bellingham was one of 'living with your feet in the vineyard. Grapes could take on different characteristics within hours.' Challenging, he agrees, but 'the results look stunning'. His baptism by fire and water coincided with registration of the first Bellingham estate wines, the sauvignon receiving particular attention. In fact, a 'region-specific' sauvignon is to be released, as is a new wine in the Maverick range which has benefited from experimentation with Rhône-style blends (neither tasted by us). There's been more trying and testing, with Italian and French merlot clones, which have yielded promising results. Groenewald and colleagues Lizelle Gerber and Mario Damon intend to extend the Spitz and Maverick ranges, leading in turn to extensions of the cellar where more options for fermentation are being investigated.

Spitz range

No new vintages released; not retasted for this ed.

★★★★ **Merlot 02** weighty offering of distinction; sultry dark fruit wrapped up in chewy tannins, bolstered by 15% alc. Fruit intensity promised development over 2–4 yrs. 14 mths new Fr oak.

★★★★ **Cabernet Franc** None since **99**, pvsly noted as sensuous, elegant.

★★★★ **Pinotage** When last **99** tasted, had savoury tones, mulberry fruit, spicy vanilla sweetness.

★★★★ **Chardonnay 03** extended lineage of seriously elegant wine; stony ring to creamy – not broad – texture. Stbosch fruit, labelled WO Coastal, as was debut **02** from W Bay & Darling grapes. Natural ferment; yr new Fr oak.

Maverick range

★★★★ **Syrah** The red iconoclast pushes into deep, dark territory. **03** intensely spiced, potent pears-in-red-wine, clove interest to structured palate; ripe but manageable balance. **02** handsome fruit & floral tints spiced up with tensioned berry fruits, sweet tannins. Latest 18 mths new wood, 90% Fr, rest Am.

★★★★ **Chenin Blanc 04** brims with ripeness: golden patina heralds billowing cling peach aromas, huge apricot tart palate – oodles of fruit, 15% alc & sweet finish (5g/ℓ sugar). Quite a mouthful. 6 mths all new Fr oak.

★★★★ **Viognier** Always bold, now verging on huge. Ultra-ripe **04** bursts with tropical fruits, ample girth to off-dry 14.5% alc finish. 6 mths new Fr casks. **03** demure by comparison: peach characters mingled with pistachio/roast cashew flavours, fleshy farewell carried 6g/ℓ sugar & 14.5% alc.

Our Founders (varietal) range

★★★★ **Shiraz** Yr Fr oak contribution (75%, rest Am; 30% new), introduced with punchy, peppery **02**, palpable in **03**; plumply juiced blackcurrant & loganberry fruits in smoky frame.

★★★★ **Cabernet Sauvignon 03** cements promise of improvement since **01**; shows cab fruit nestled among firm tannins; still needs 2–4 yrs to soften. **02** sweetly-fruited. Extended maceration, malo in wood, yr Fr oak, 30% new.

Merlot ★★★☆ **03** sampled in pvs ed as supple & plummy, with velvety mouthfeel, gently-oaked finish (Fr, 30% new, 14 mths), now drying out, needs drinking. **Pinotage** ★★★ **04** fruit-driven, strawberry-toned; overt oak (yr, 1/3 new) adds purchase to palate; touch hard but eschews bitterness. **Chardonnay** ★★★ **04** less obvious oak (25%, 6 mths), more yellow peach flesh to limey fruit than forerunners. **Sauvignon Blanc** ★★★ Now in more refreshing style. **05** tropical fig spiked with cut grass. All above WO Coastal, below W Cape.

The Blends range

Cabernet Sauvignon-Merlot (Classic) ★★★ **03** equal blend spotlights latter's choc coating for reticent cassis. Firmer grip than pvs. **Rosé** ★★ The first Cape rosé. **05** coral-ruby hue; candyfloss nose, sweet cherry send-off. From pinotage. **Sauvignon Blanc-Chardonnay (Sauvenay)** ★★☆ Dependable easy-going style. **04** polished; bright pear flavour, med-bodied, dry-enough tail. **05** not ready at press time. **Chardonnay-Semillon** ★★☆ Export only. Unwooded 50/50 mix in **04**, full & firm, waxy sheen to figgy flesh with citrus tension in sweetish finish. **Premier Grand Cru** ★★ Crisp & dry **NV** blend (including chenin, sauvignon, colombard), delivering the goods – & refreshingly light 12% alc – consistently since 1951. **Johannisberger** ★★ Launched 1957, soon to be rebranded with added 'Legacy', still SA's biggest semi-sweet. Light-bodied **NV** (8% alc); aromatic, grapey sweetness in tangy tail. – *DS*

Bell Tower see Asara
Ben du Toit see Helderkruin

Bergheim

Paarl ▪ Est/1stB 2000 ▪ Visits by appt; tasting/sales also at I Love Wine (see Wine shops section) ▪ Owners E&H Jordaan ▪ Winemaker Edwin Jordaan ▪ 200 cs 100% red ▪ PO Box 6020 Main Street Paarl 7622 ▪ ***T 082·770·8001*** *▪ F 862·7852*

There is no cure for the vinous bug, even for a practicing doctor. Having started with a Pinotage four years ago, Edwin 'Jorries' Jordaan, Paarl-based GP and *garagiste* winemaker, is gearing up to launch a Shiraz (with a possible quirky name to express his displeasure at the proliferation of this variety). And, to celebrate his 50th, a Semillon. Clearly terminally afflicted! He continues to operate from the Schoongezicht cellar; wine sales are from the shared tasting facility in Paarl's main street, 'I Love Wine'.

Pinotage ★★★ Rustic, salt-of-the-earth **03** showing the same character it did as sample last ed. Extracted & dense, chewy; pungent stewed mulberry & toast aromas, volatile touch. Structure to improve 2-3 yrs. 20% Am oak, 20% new; WO Voor Pdberg. — *DH*

Bergkelder

Stellenbosch ▪ Tasting & sales Mon-Fri 8-5 Sat 9-3 ▪ Fee R20 ▪ Open pub hols ▪ Tours Mon-Fri 10 (Eng or Afr), 10.30 (Eng, Ger or Fr), 3 (Eng or Afr); Sat 10 (Eng or Afr), 10.30 (Eng, Ger or Fr), 12 (Eng or Afr); incl AV presentation available in 7 languages (5 tours a day in Dec/Jan) Bookings: tours@bergkelder.co.za ▪ Special group tours, private functions by appt ▪ Owner Distell ▪ Cellarmaster Andrea Freeborough ▪ Winemakers Kobus Gerber (white wines) & Justin Corrans (red wines), with Tariro Masayiti & Jaco van der Walt ▪ Viticulturist Bennie Liebenberg ▪ PO Box 184 Stellenbosch 7599 ▪ www.bergkelder.co.za ▪ ***T 809·8492*** *▪ F 883·813*

Literally 'Mountain Cellar', after the maturation halls cut into Stellenbosch's Papegaaiberg, Bergkelder is responsible for the Fleur du Cap range, listed separately. Also the home of the Vinoteque Wine Bank, now in its 22nd year, marketing fine wines with the option of having purchases stored in perfect cellar conditions at surprisingly low cost. See Selected wine shops section for details or visit www.vinoteque.co.za.

Bergsig Estate

Worcester ▪ Est 1843 ▪ 1stB 1977 ▪ Tasting & sales Mon-Fri 8-5 Sat 9-5 ▪ Tasting fee for groups ▪ Closed Easter Fri & Dec 25 ▪ Tours by appt ▪ Tea garden for light meals/refreshments, or BYO picnic ▪ Owners Lategan family ▪ Winemaker De Wet Lategan, with Chris du Toit (Jan 1989/Jul 2003) ▪ 253 ha (cab, pinotage, shiraz, chard, chenin, sauvignon) ▪ 3 200 tons 50 000 cs own label ▪ 35% red 60% white 4% rosé 1% port ▪ Exported as Lategan & White River ▪ PO Box 15 Breede River 6858 ▪ wine@bergsig.co.za ▪ www.bergsig.co.za ▪ ***T (023) 355·1603*** *▪ F (023) 355·1658*

A pace-setter in the region, this family-run winery at the junction of the Worcester-Wolseley-Wellington roads is worth a stop. You'll now find a tea garden and conference venue, and a varied range of wines catering to most tastes (you'll also find their produce under some Woolworths labels). Vintage 2005 was 'possibly one of the best red-wine years in ages', says cellarmaster De Wet Lategan. 'Cab and merlot stand out.' The downside: drought caused a 26% crop-drop (a punishing 50% for hardest-hit sauvignon). Growing wine as nature intended, the Lategans are avid conservationists. Their estate is a habitat for the endangered geometric tortoise, and last October the first of an annual birdwatching day treated twitchers to 88 species in six hours.

★★★★ **Pinotage** Elegant, minerally wine, from selected ±30-yr-old shy-bearing vyds. **03** (★★★) an unheralded blip: all good qualities present (incl ripe berry fruit) but texture marred by astringency, slight bitterness on finish; tannins integrate with time in bottle, though certainly not for long keeping. Contrast with stellar **02** (★★★★☆) & **01**, both noted as having potential to develop beautifully. 10-15 mths oak, 50% new; moderate 12.8-13.8% alc.

★★★★ **Chardonnay** Numerous local/overseas awards for this new-oak-fermented version. **04** (★★★☆) barrel character very obvious mid-2005, jousts with delicate tropical/stone fruits; finish is a tad unyielding — needs more time. **03** good combination of ripe peach, vanilla & butterscotch, lively acidic bite. Aged 6-9 mths Fr barrels.

★★★★ **Cape Ruby** ✓ Latest version of this multi-vintage **NV** blend their finest to date; from tinta b, as usual, fermented in open cement tanks, with no oak maturation 'to allow fruit to be main focus'. Which it is: lovely fresh berry/cherry, rich & ripe, cinnamon dusting adds to the exceptional appeal. 19.3% alc.

★★★★ **Cape Late Bottled Vintage** Traditionally made, from tinta, 36-48 mths cask-aged; around 95g/ℓ sugar, ±18% alc. **98** full & round, slightly firmer tannin, higher alc (±20%) than pvs; **99** (★★★☆) somewhat gawky mid-2005, very firm yet also sweet, charry oak evident, components still unmeshed; perhaps just need more time.

★★★★ **Cape Vintage** As above, from tinta, traditionally vinified, fortified with brandy spirit, 36 months older oak; **00** rich & smooth, generously fruited, delicious peppery choc hints; already harmonious, should mature fruitfully – similar promise noted for **99**, very youthful, elegant, could mature into ★★★★★ (or better) quality.

Cabernet Sauvignon ★★★★ **04** attractive red berry fruit intro, stern & gripping tannins take over on finish; might attain greater harmony with time. 9 mths 2nd fill barrels. **Ruby Cabernet-Merlot** ★★★ **04** offers the usual ripe plum & cherry fruit, but this vintage tannins chewier, touch gruff; give more time or decant well ahead of serving. **Shiraz Rosé** ★★★ Quaffable bone-dry blush with strawberry flavours in **05**; good refreshing summertime drink. **Chenin Blanc** ★★ **05** (sample) slight tropical tone, slender fruit, very firm in the mouth. **Sauvignon Blanc** ★★ Always a more genteel expression of the variety; **05** zesty & light, better with the meal than before. **Gewürztraminer** ★★★ Charming sweetish summer aperitif; **05** signature rose-petals & litchis, rounded but crisp; fresh, fragrant farewell. **Weisser Riesling** ★★★ Last tasted was **03**; with potential for cellaring few yrs. **Bouquet Light** None made in **05**. **Special Late Harvest** ★★★ Made intermittently; **05** from riesling & chenin, botrytis-touched; gorgeous peach/passionfruit aromas, ripe but lively fruity flavours, active ±7g/ℓ acidity imparts jewel-bright palate tone. **Noble Late Harvest** ★★★★ Last tasted was **99**, mostly sauvignon (40%) with buket, chenin, gewürz. 375ml. **Sauvignon Blanc Brut** ★★★ Energetic carbonated dry sparkler; **05** with lighter than usual tropical flavours, lightly less generous & well-padded finish. All WO Brde Rvr Vlly. – *DH*

Bergwater Vineyards

*Prince Albert ▪ Est 1999 ▪ 1stB 2002 ▪ Closed to public ▪ Owners Heimie & Stephan Schoeman & DKPG (Dutch Investors Group) ▪ Winemaker Mariska Schreuder (Jan 2003) ▪ Viti advisers VinPro (1999) ▪ 68 ha (cab, merlot, shiraz, sauvignon) ▪ 90% red 10% white ▪ PO Box 40 Prince Albert 6930 ▪ wine@bergwater.co.za ▪ www.princealbertvalley.com ▪ **T (023) 541·1703** ▪ F (023) 541·1081*

No update available on this winery; contact details from previous edition.

Bernheim Wines

*Paarl ▪ Est/1stB 2004 ▪ Tasting & sales Mon-Fri 8.30-5 Sat 9-12 ▪ Fee R5 refunded with purchase ▪ Closed Christian holidays ▪ Tours by appt ▪ Owners Pieter & Anneke Taljaard, Hermann Helmbold, Jacques Kruger/Pacas Winery (Pty) Ltd ▪ Winemaker Jacques Kruger (Feb 2004) ▪ Viti consultant Gawie Kriel (Mar 2004) ▪ 11 ha (cabs s/f, merlot, pinotage, shiraz, chenin) ▪ 6 000 cs 70% red 25% white 5% rosé ▪ PO Box 7274 Noorder-Paarl 7623 ▪ bernheim@iafrica.com ▪ www.bernheimwines.com ▪ **T 872·8358** ▪ F 872·5618*

Their second harvest on this Paarl farm was all about family and friends – wives, shareholders, brothers-in-law and nephews – all pitched in. Remarkably, with all the untrained cellar hands around, the only casualty was the chenin, which had to be very carefully selected after falling victim to 'heat-stroke' in the abnormally hot, dry conditions. Winemaker Jacques Kruger says extensive vineyard replanting, re-trellising and maintenance are paying dividends. In the winery, the barrelling programme for the 04 versions of the premium range, JH Pacas & Co (initials of family and shareholders), is well underway. The preceding vintage of the Pacas Cab was launched last year, and very favourably received, reports wife and marketer Adna K.

JH Pacas & Co range new

Cabernet Sauvignon ★★★★ Harmonious, soft & supple **03**, with well-handled oak (17 mths Fr, 85% new); restrainedly flavourful. Stbosch fruit. **04** and the **Shiraz 04** still maturing at press time.

Bernheim range

Following **04**s reviewed as samples last ed; retasted this yr: **Pinotage** ★★★ Uncomplicated, light & drinkable, with mildly gripping tannins. Try with traditional smoorsnoek (braised fish) or at a braai, Kruger says. **Merlot-Cabernet Sauvignon** ★★★ Eucalyptus-fragrant 60/40 blend's tautness has relented somewhat, yet still better with food, or allow to mature further.

Fermented/aged with Fr staves, 4 mths. **Rosé** ★★ Lightish equal mix colombard/chenin, dollop cab for colour; starting to tire, drink up. New releases of following not available: notes from pvs ed (all **04**) **Chenin Blanc** ★☆ Light, shy pear-drop aroma with leesy note, bone dry. **Chenin Blanc Oak Fermented** ★☆ Slightly floral nose, marginally fuller than unwooded version, very dry finish. **Late Vintage** ★☆ Medium-bodied semi-sweet with hint of clove.—*CT*

Berrio see Flagstone

Beyerskloof

*Stellenbosch ▪ Est 1988 ▪ 1stB 1989 ▪ Tasting & sales Mon-Fri 8.30-4.30 Sat 10-2 ▪ Closed Easter Fri/Sun/Mon, Dec 25/26 & Jan 1 ▪ Farm produce ▪ Owners Beyers Truter & Simon Halliday ▪ Winemaker Beyers Truter, with Anri Truter (Jan 2004) ▪ Viti consultant Johan Pienaar (2000) ▪ 70 ha (cab, merlot, pinotage) ▪ 490 tons 100 000 cs + 225 000ℓ for customers ▪ 98% red 2% white ▪ PO Box 107 Koelenhof 7605 ▪ wine@beyerskloof.co.za ▪ **T 865·2135** ▪ F 865·2683*

The much anticipated return to making wine 'at home' after more than a decade has pleased Beyers Truter no end. Beyerskloof's top-end wines will be produced here, with the rest still being vinified elsewhere. They'll share home-site production with the launch of Lagare, their first port-style venture, which is made in the traditional shallow foot-pressing vats which give it its name. Brand manager Francois Naudé, who has six vintages' experience of rolling up his trousers and dyeing his feet red, makes this wine. Son Anri T now works full-time alongside proud dad after completing his studies at Elsenburg, and construction is underway to double the maturation cellar capacity and renovate the tasting room to welcome the growing number of visitors.

★★★★☆ **Beyerskloof** Fine, modern blend cab, merlot, from 5ha planted 80/20, harvested en-bloc, vinified traditionally, 2+ yrs new Fr oak. Cedary wood & big smooth tannins obvious on youthful **01**, as was plenteous red fruit & mineral streak. Gold on 2004 CWT. **02**'s 15% alc higher than pvs, adding to forceful, macho presence; darkly savoury, yet sweet-fruited. These need vigorous decanting in youth – but 8-10 yrs in bottle even better. This & blends below not retasted.

★★★★ **Synergy** 'Cape blend', with cab & merlot in varying, but fairly equal, proportions with pinotage. Maiden **01** was succulent, refined. ± Yr Fr oak, some new. **02** (★★★☆) spicy, ripely soft attractions; decently structured, well balanced, but not very serious or conclusive.

★★★★ **Synergy Reserve** Cab in majority here, pinotage 37%, merlot 8%. So maiden **01** firmer, more focused than version above; yr Fr oak, half new. VDG. Fresh, dynamic **02** (★★★★☆) with meaty, smoky nose is forceful but focused, with delicious rich-fruited savouriness, firmly & gently underpinned by tannin. *Wine* ★★★★. Enjoyable on release, should develop well over 5+ yrs.

★★★★☆ **Pinotage Reserve** Serious & suavely refined. IWC 2004 & IWSC 2003 golds for **02**, also top-ranked in *Wine*. Some sombre, forest-floor/earthy notes apparent now, with dense fruit over strong dry tannins. **03** (not retasted) lighter-hearted, with lovely scented nose (incl spicy wood), deep dark cherry fruit. Sophisticated yet likeable, intense & well-formed.

Pinotage ✓ ★★★☆ Reliably outgoing, delicious, as with tasty, fresh, strawberry/cherry-charactered **04**. Ripely firm tannins, big but balanced 14.4% alc, lightly oaked. **Rosé** ★★★ Another guise for Truter's much-loved pinotage. **05** attractive & tastily dry, well balanced with subtle tannin; notes of sweet red berries, nice earthy undertone. **Lagare Cape Vintage** new ★★★☆ Traditional port style, with touriga, shiraz supplementing pinotage. Ripe, simple sweet fruitiness; winningly balanced for early approachability with some lightly, drily gripping tannins, acid. 19% alc; 77g/ℓ sugar. In handy 500ml.—*TJ*

Bianco Fine Wines

Tulbagh ▪ Est/1stB 1997 ▪ Tasting & sales Mon-Fri 8.30-5 Sat 9-2 ▪ Fee R10 p/p for groups ▪ Closed Easter Fri/Sun, Dec 25 & Jan 1 ▪ Tours Mon-Fri 9-4.30 ▪ Olive oil/olive products for sale

▪ *Owner Toni Bianco ▪ Winemaker/viticulturist Marinus Potgieter (2005) ▪ 16 ha (cab, nebbiolo, pinotage, shiraz) ▪ 70 tons 2 000 cs 70% red 30% white ▪ PO Box 103 Tulbagh 6820 ▪ bianco@lando.co.za ▪ www.bianco.co.za ▪* ***T (023) 231·0350*** *▪ F (023) 231·0938*

Deciding the time has come 'to do more supervision than physical work', owner Tony Bianco has given Marinus Potgieter, newly graduated from Stellenbosch, his first job as winemaker/viticulturist and appointed a marketing manager in Julie Walton. Potgieter is satisfied that his maiden vintage produced full-bodied wines with very fruity bouquets, particularly the reds. Taking the Bianco name from Tulbagh to Toronto and Tokyo is Singapore Airlines, which last year reordered the Cab 02.

Cabernet Sauvignon ★★★ **03** returns to house's low-fruit, high-tannin styling; needs time or mama's cooking. Yr Fr/Am oak. **Shiraz** ★★☆ **03** dark berry/plum fruit, charry oak woven with the abundant dry tannins; needs yr/2. Yr Fr/Am oak. **Nebbiolo** ★ **04**, like pvs, very pale, almost rosé; faint strawberry flavours masked by harsh astringency. **Pinotage** ★★★ Last bottled was **02**. **Boulder Red** new ★★☆ Everyday **NV** blend cab, shiraz, pinotage (48/20/32), savoury notes of salty dried fruit, big but manageable dusty tannins. **Dry Muscat** ★ Wolseley fruit, vinified traditional Italian way (fermented on skins 1st 2 days). **05** soft muscatty scents, a little honeyed sweetness. for early enjoyment. Only bottled wine tasted; all others samples, ratings provisional. **Joya** discontinued. — *DH*

Big Six see Old Bridge Wines

Bilton Wines

Stellenbosch ▪ 1stB 1998 ▪ Tasting & sales Mon-Fri 8.30–4.30 Sat 9–1 ▪ Fee R10 ▪ Closed pub hols ▪ Teas, coffees & soft drinks; summer picnics by appt; wine & choc tastings by appt ▪ Walks ▪ Owner Mark Bilton ▪ Winemaker Rianie Strydom, advised by Giorgio Dalla Cia (Jan 2005/Oct 2004) ▪ Viticulturist Ruan du Plessis (Dec 2004) ▪ 80 ha (cab, merlot, mourvèdre, petit v, pinotage, shiraz, chenin, sauvignon, semillon) ▪ 100 tons own label 80% red 20% white ▪ PO Box 60 Lynedoch 7603 ▪ sales@biltonwines.com ▪ www.biltonwines.co.za ▪ ***T 881·3714*** *▪ F 881·3721*

Taking it to the next level. That's Mark Bilton on what is the largest farm (140ha) in the Helderberg mountainside area. Celebrating his 10th anniversary here in 2006, he has an exciting new team in place, including vini-consultant Giorgio Dalla Cia (ex-Meerlust), and winemaker Rianie Strydom (ex-Morgenhof). Joining some ripping reds (2002 Cab and Merlot rated 90 points by US guru Robert Parker) is a new Sauvignon — though a Bordeaux-style blend is the ultimate aim for this red-wine specialist. Upping own-label production to 100 tons (total crop = 500 tons), the new cellar has extended barrel maturation and steel tank facilities. Vine rejuvenation on 80ha includes regrafting mourvèdre, new viognier.

★★★★ **Cabernet Sauvignon** Vintage & vinification make for more structured wine than pvs in **03**, with longer life (±4-6 yrs). Impressive fruit intensity gets extra dimension from 10% petit v & 17 mths Fr oak: violets, white pepper, a tarry note. Has verve, style. **02** opulent & impressive without real complexity/structure. This, below, from single-vyd.

★★★★ **Merlot** Succulent, sophisticated & classy. **03**, with 10% cab, shows the layering of well made merlot: fresh-picked raspberries perked up by wet moor nuances, smoky oak. Tannins firm but harmonious, accessible — give framework for 4-5 yr ageing. 20 mths Fr oak, half new. **02**, rich, creamy mulberry fruit with touch spice from 30% new Fr oak. 14% alc. Drink soon — like other 02s here.

★★★★ **Shiraz** Modern style, voluptuous, lashings creamy vanilla-oak: all that in **03**, with plenty of spice, mocha choc tones to deep plummy fruit. Generously proportioned (15%), lush fruit easily handling 17 mths Fr/Am oak. For those who can resist, a 5+ yr future. **02** enlivened by crackle of acidity & hint of spice/savouriness. Generally showy, so golds at IWSC, IWC for **01** not surprising. — *CR*

Birdfield see Klawer
Bisweni see Havana Hills

Blaauwklippen Agricultural Estate

*Stellenbosch ▪ Est 1690 ▪ 1stB 1974 ▪ Tasting & sales Mon-Sat 9-5 Sun 9-4 ▪ Fee R20 (informal tasting); R25 (tutored; incl tour) ▪ Closed Dec 25 & Jan 1 ▪ Tours by appt 10-3 ▪ Two restaurants & many other amenities (see intro) ▪ Owners Mr & Mrs Stephan Schörghuber ▪ Winemaker Rolf Zeitvogel, with Piet Geldenhuys (Oct/Dec 2003) ▪ Viticulturist Kowie Kotzé (1987) ▪ 80 ha (cabs s/f, malbec, merlot, mourvèdre, petit v, pinot, shiraz, zin, viognier) ▪ 340 tons 20 000 cs own label ▪ 90% red 10% white ▪ HACCP certification in progress ▪ PO Box 54 Stellenbosch 7599 ▪ mail@blaauwklippen.com ▪ www.blaauwklippen.com ▪ **T 880·0133** ▪ F 880·0136*

This historic and characterful wine property is part of the Arabella portfolio, which includes luxury hotels, conference venues and golf resorts (to name a few), and is owned by the international Schörghuber group. Rolf Zeitvogel, promoted to farm manager, continues to make the wine, assisted by Piet Geldenhuys, with part-of-the-terroir Kowie Kotzé (appointed 1987!) still on vineyard patrol. The pressure was on last harvest when all varieties ripened within a month. Visitors, blissfully unaware of the logistical challenges thus created, continued to enjoy the many and varied facilities, which now include a more attractive tasting room, enlarged wine shop and upgraded restaurant.

Vineyard Selection range

★★★★ **Cabernet Sauvignon** Handsome, muscular cab from home vyds. **01** (★★★★) reported last yr as edgier though maintained cellar's trademark elegance. 2 yrs new Fr oak. ±13% alc. **00**, which developed nicely, showed cigarbox whiff & attractive earthiness to fruit-filled palate.

Cabriolet ★★★★ Elegant blend cab f, cab, merlot, 18 mths oak, portion new. **01** not retasted; pvslyrecorded as needing food, due to firmer, grainier tannins, fair thread of acid. **Zinfandel** ★★★ Brash & ostentatiously fruity **03**, fat, sappy cranberry flavours, booming tannins, big 14.2% alc, yet light-textured thanks to racy 7.2g/ℓ acid. 15 mths oak. **Sauvignon Blanc** ★★★ **04**, winner of 2004 B'klippen Blending Competition, squeaky clean, crisp, gastronomy-friendly; delicious now & within 1-2 yrs.

Blaauwklippen range

Barouche Cape Blend ★★★ Has origins in 2000 B'klippen Blending Competition; continues as pinotage blend, with tweaks & tucks. **03** with cab, shiraz, cinsaut; 14 mths Fr oak. Very ripe fruit, juicy tannins, clean dry conclusion. **Cabernet Sauvignon** ★★★ **04** not ready. **03** neatly combined New World fruit on nose, Old World dry mineral palate. 66% in Fr oak. **Merlot** Moves here from above range. **04** (sample) spicy, herbaceous character with lead pencil whiff from 55% 1st fill Fr oak (rest 2nd fill); fine dry tannins, big 14.6 alc. Likely ★★★★ on release. **Shiraz** ★★★★ **03** a food wine: well-fused but still tight tannins, lively red-plum fruit with farmyard whiffs & gently astringent 'tea leaf' finish. 14 mths Fr/Am oak. Preview of **04** most promising; shows ★★★★ potential. **Red Landau** ★★★ Still-selling **02** contains an A-Y of varieties (no zin), all eager to please; lightly savoury with grainy, pasta-friendly tannins. Low 12.5% alc. **Landau Rosé** new ★ From (unusually) shiraz & cab f, **04** Turkish Delight & floral perfumes, technically semi-sweet though finishes almost dry. **White Landau** ★ **04** fruity-dry melange of mainly sauvignon plus semillon & chenin. Less satisfying than pvs. **Landau Semi-Sweet** new ★★★ Delicate & balanced muscat ottonel, gewürz concoction, **04** rose-petal & muscat wafts, lovely soft, gently sweet grapey flavours, perfect for spicy/Oriental food. Mix Coastal, W Cape & Stbosch WOs. *— CvZ/CT/TM*

Black Eagle

*Piketberg ▪ Est 2000 ▪ 1stB 2001 ▪ No tasting/tours, but stay-overs available at Libre Guesthouse B&B ▪ Owner Breda van Niekerk ▪ Winemaker André Oberholzer (Oct 2000) ▪ Viticulturist Johan Viljoen (Oct 2000) ▪ 40 ha (shiraz, chenin, colombard) ▪ 45 000ℓ 5% red 95% white ▪ PO Box 61 Saron 6812 ▪ lushof@iafrica.com ▪ **T (023) 240·0925** ▪ F (023) 240·0238*

No update available on this winery; contact details from previous edition.

Black Oystercatcher

new

Elim (see Southern Cape map) ▪ Est 1998 ▪ 1stB 2003 ▪ Tasting by appt ▪ Owner/winemaker/viticulturist Dirk Human ▪ 14.5 ha (cab, merlot, shiraz, sauvignon, semillon) ▪ ±90 tons 48% red 52% white ▪ PO Box 199 Bredasdorp 7280 ▪ dhuman@brd.dorea.co.za ▪ ***T 082·779·5439***

A fitting name for Dirk Human's wines from Moddervlei farm near Elim. This promising maritime wine ward between Hermanus and Cape Agulhas is part of the protected red-billed black oystercatcher's range. One of the first to cultivate vines in this area – the Humans have farmed here for generations – Dirk H has both reds and whites planted on a cool ridge of laterite (koffieklip), sandstone and broken shale soils. He says the wines from this site are 'full and fat, crisp and minerally'. Too late for inclusion in this guide were the 05 Sauvignon and Semillon and 03 Shiraz. Other wines 'under consideration' are a red blend and limited-release wooded Sauvignon. Plans for a cellar are also being incubated.

Black Pearl Wines

Paarl ▪ Est 1998 ▪ 1stB 2001 ▪ Tasting, sales & tours just about anytime but please phone ahead (no credit cards) ▪ Closed Dec 25 ▪ Facilities for children ▪ Walks ▪ Conservation area ▪ Owner Lance Nash ▪ Winemaker/viticulturist Mary-Lou Nash Sullivan ▪ 8 ha (cab, shiraz) ▪ ±1 800 cs 100% red ▪ PO Box 609 Suider-Paarl 7624 ▪ info@blackpearlwines.com ▪ www.blackpearlwines.com ▪ ***T 863·2900 / 083·395·6999 / 083·297·9796***

'If there was a prize for the smallest cab berries in SA, we'd win,' chuckles Lance Nash. Though crop size here, as elsewhere, was down (thanks to a combo of drought and dryland farming), quality was 'unbeatable'. On these western slopes of Paarl Mountain, the shale-derived, clay-rich soil also nurtures swathes of fragile renosterveld, which is why the Nash family have joined the Biodiversity & Wine Initiative to help conserve this pristine floral heritage.

★★★★ **Cabernet Sauvignon-Shiraz** Aussie-styled **03** intensely ripe berry flavours, big 14.5% alc, ingratiatingly smooth. Shiraz (55%) dominates with spice/leather tones. 13 mths oak. Probably best enjoyed over next 2-3 yrs.

★★★☆ **Shiraz 03** (★★★★) showy, forward, big aromas/flavours on offer. Mid-2004 needed yr/2 to develop potential of spicy red fruit. **02** with mocha, raspberry, coconut nuances, sold out. ±13 mths Fr oak, 60% new.

Cabernet Sauvignon ★★★☆ **03** step-up on pvs; cassis perfume, good fruit concentration. 13 mths oak, 60% new. None of above revisited this ed. – *NP*

Black Rock see The Winery

Bloemendal Estate

Durbanville ▪ Est 1902 ▪ 1stB 1987 ▪ Tasting & sales Mon-Fri 9-5 Sat 9-4 Sun 11-3 ▪ Fee R15 pp for groups ▪ Closed Dec 25 ▪ Deli/oyster bar & full conference facilities etc (see also intro) ▪ Owner Bloemendal Trust ▪ Winemaker Jackie Coetzee ▪ Viti consultant Johan Pienaar ▪ 140 ha (cab, merlot, shiraz, sauvignon) ▪ 5 000 cs own label 73% red 25% white 2% rosé ▪ PO Box 466 Durbanville 7551 ▪ bloemendal@isoft.co.za ▪ ***T/F 976·2682***

This estate's enviable assets, including its pastoral setting in the midst of suburbia and its proximity to Cape Town, are augmented by extensively upgraded visitor facilities. It's now possible to book the tasting area for evening functions for up to 60 guests; by day, the same area (revamped) now opens on to landscaped gardens, a farm dam with a wooden deck for sun-loving winetasters and, in East-meets-West style, a Zen garden and a *boules* court. The menu ranges from the full à la carte (platters à la Française) with cheese boards as a simpler option.

★★★☆ **Cabernet Sauvignon** Touches tobacco, cedar on latest **01** (★★★☆); stylish dark cassis, velvet texture & soft supple tannins. Showcases house's signature drinkablilty with stylish aplomb. Ready, should last ±3 yrs. Yr Fr oak. Traditional open *kuip* fermentation, as are all reds.

★★★★ **Shiraz** Smoked beef, veld fire aromas/flavours on **03** (★★★☆), savoury & very dry, verging on austere – less rich than burly **02**. Tannins already approachable, dry tang on finish. Yr Am oak.

★★★★ **Sauvignon Blanc Suider Terras** Named for mature s-facing vyd, 30 yr old bushvines benefiting from bracing sea breezes. Latest **05** right on the money. Distinctive dusty capsicum, green fig, nettles, translate easily onto assertive but elegantly built palate; rapier acidity, some softer ripeness on finish.

★★★★ **Semillon** Latest **05** (sample, potentially ★★★) very quiet, lacking flamboyance of Sauvignon above; some spiced lemon, hint apricot. Silky texture, modestly rounded profile, helped by brush oak – third Fr oak fermented. Friendly (but big 14.6 alc) **04** also tasted as sample.

Merlot ★★★★ Properly dry & savoury **02** has charming cassis flavours, good oak (yr Fr) helping gentle firmness on dry finish. Ready to drink. **Blosend Rooi** ★★ (Translates as 'Blushing Red'). Barrel-fermented dry rosé, **04** blending shiraz (70%), merlot; more a light red than rosé, barrel ferment giving more weight, less fresh fruitiness. **Brut** ★★ Distinctly blanc de blanc style cap classique, light textured & focused, attractive citrus tones, busy bubbles, by mid-2006 should have settled, gained weight. **NV** from chardonnay, 9 mths lees before disgorging. **Natural Sweet** ★★★ Semillon/sauvignon melange. **03** last yr offered whiffs dried apricot, warm hay & caramel; luscious sweetness with some fresher sappy notes. – *IvH*

Blouberg see Graça

Bloupunt Wines

Montagu ▪ Est/1stB 1997 ▪ 12 Long Street Montagu 6720 ▪ bloupunt@lando.co.za ▪ www.bloupuntwines.co.za ▪ ***T/F (023) 614·2385***

Range in abeyance till the next vintage.

Blueberry Hill

Franschhoek ▪ Est/1stB 1998 ▪ Visits by appt ▪ 2 self-catering cottages ▪ Owners Blueberry Hill Trust (Brian & Lindy Heyman) ▪ Vini/viti advisers Nigel McNaught & Paul Wallace (1998/2000) ▪ 0.6 ha ▪ 350–400 cs 100% red ▪ PO Box 580 Franschhoek 7690 ▪ bhwine@iafrica.com ▪ ***T 876·3362*** *▪ F 876·2114*

You don't get much more focused than this: a winery with just one tiny block of merlot. Which meant the heat was on last harvest when it came to deciding exactly when to pick in a very hot, dry year. 'We managed to hang on, which I believe was the right thing to do,' says Brian Heyman, who also reports they're now keeping their Merlot longer in barriques – up to 2 years. With the goal still to 'keep it small, big on quality', Heyman suggests the maiden vintage below needs further maturation to truly reward.

Merlot ★★★★ Auspicious **03** mouth-watering plum/choc/mint flavour, clean oak backing (yr new barrels, 20% Am), long firm finish. Really attractive unforced tone – no striving for effect. – *DH*

Blouvlei Wines

new

Wellington ▪ Est/1stB 2003 ▪ Visits Mon-Fri 8-5 Sat by appt ▪ Fee R7/tasting ▪ Closed pub hols ▪ Meals by appt ▪ Guesthouse ▪ Owner Stephan du Toit ▪ Winemaker Pieter-Niel Rossouw, with Jerome van Wyk ▪ 8 000 cs 100% red ▪ PO Box 817 Wellington 7654 ▪ blouvlei@cknet.co.za ▪ ***T 873·7745*** *▪ F 864·2737*

This new producer of largely export wines is an initiative by Mont du Toit's Stephan du Toit, involving his farm's vineyard and cellar employees in the making and sale of their own wine through a worker's trust. Using Mont du Toit's cellar, technological and managerial facilities (as well as neighbouring farms' white winemaking capabilities), three easy-drinking, affordable wines are produced for the UK, German, Danish and US markets. Traditional (often labour-intensive) handling and vinification methods are used, overseen by Mont du Toit's Pieter-Niel Rossouw assisted by Jerome van Wyk. Most of the trust members, represented by director Abdelia Lawrence, are locals, born and bred in the Wellington Valley, after which this community-based venture is named.

Red ☺ ★★★ Ripe, warmly inviting aromas on **03** bargain blend cabs s & f, merlot; firm palate with fresh acidity, dry tannic grip. Unobtrusive yr in oak. **White** ☺ ★★☆ Crisp **04** from sauvignon, typical light tropical, grassy aromas/flavours. Nicely textured, helped by light wooding; prominent savoury acidity, dry finish.

Klassique ★★★☆ The senior bdx-style **03** blend (60/40 cab/merlot) has good ripe red fruit character, with serious-minded structural support in satisfying balance; savoury dry finish. ±17 mths barrelled. Mainly Wllngtn fruit. — *TJ*

Blue Crane Vineyards

Tulbagh ▪ Est 2001 ▪ 1stB 2004 ▪ Visitors welcome but phone ahead ▪ Owners Henk & Anita Jordaan ▪ Winemaker/viticulturist Henk Jordaan, advised by viticulturist Andrew Teubes & suppliers ▪ 6 ha (cab, merlot, shiraz, sauvignon) ▪ 2 000 cs 75% red 25% white ▪ PO Box 306 Tulbagh 6820 ▪ info@bluecrane.co.za ▪ www.bluecrane.co.za ▪ ***T (023) 230·0823/ 083·266·0156 ▪ F*** *(023) 230·0825*

Working out of their tiny cellar in the shadow of Jagger's Peak, Henk and Anita Jordan are relentless in their pursuit of 'quality at every level'. From reduced yields for concentrated flavours, to chilling the grapes before sorting, attention to detail and lots of patience is what allows them to 'do things impossible or unaffordable in large cellars'. The Jordaans are even going as far as delaying the release of their first (flagship) Blue Crane wines until they're satisfied with the quality. Meanwhile they offer the Jagger's Peak wines — 'Jagger' also being their border collie who struts about like a rock star.

Jagger's Peak range new

Cabernet Sauvignon 04 untasted, will join range before end 2006. **Merlot** ★★★ Accessible & refreshing **04** well stocked with cassis, red berry flavours; judicious oaking gives structure for 2-3 yrs cellaring. Lighter-fruited but not light on alc – 14.5%. Yr Fr oak, 10% new. **Shiraz** ★★★ Crowd-pleasing **04** early drinker; effusive fruit & flesh, lots of upfront charm (& alc: 14%). Yr combo Fr/Am oak, some new. **Chenin Blanc** ★★★ **05** complex, distinctive nose: baked apple, hint resin, fynbos; palate similar, savoury, not fleshy, should come into its own with food. **Sauvignon Blanc** ★★★ **04** still lively but needs drinking. Elegant, lemongrass & gooseberry whiffs, tangy finish. — *CR*

Blue Creek Wines

Stellenbosch ▪ Est 1995 ▪ 1stB 1996 ▪ Visits by appt ▪ Owner/winemaker Piet Smal ▪ Viti consultant Johan Smith (1996) ▪ 7.5 ha (cab, merlot, pinotage) ▪ 1 000 cs own label 100% red ▪ 26 Piet Retief Str Stellenbosch 7600 ▪ blue_creek@email.com ▪ ***T 887·6938*** *▪ F 886·5462*

If the winemaker's notes from this cellar include more numerous references to 'great extraction' or 'mouth-filling', that's because a dentist, Piet Smal, is the after-hours winemaker. In the Blaauwklippen Valley, 2005 was a particularly good red wine year, Smal says, and given his track record over the past decade, this signals another class act in the making. 'I always try to give back what nature provided, and keep it as simple as possible,' is his down-to-earth philosophy.

★★★★ **Cabernet Sauvignon** ✓ Hedonistic **04** (★★★★☆) sumptuously fruited; cassis, curry leaf, lead pencil & tomato bouquet, all mirrored on palate. Opulent proportions given focus by strong cab acid backbone & powdery tannins. Fruit concentration easily matches 14 mths Fr oak & 13.5% alc. Depth & structure for cellaring 7+ yrs. **02** equally classy; heady bouquet & chewy yet pliable fruit. *Wine* ★★★★. From vyds in Stbosch's reputed 'Golden Triangle'. — *CvZ*

Blue Grove Hill see Capaia
Blue White see Old Vines

Blyde Wines

Paarl ▪ Est/1stB 2000 ▪ Tasting & sales at I Love Wine (see Wine shops section) ▪ Tours by appt ▪ Owner/ winemaker Lieb Loots ▪ 60 cs 90% red 10% white ▪ ISO 9000 certified ▪ PO Box 3231 Paarl 7620 ▪ lajanc@iafrica.com ▪ www.blyde.com ▪ ***T 083·270·5706*** *▪ F 872·8799*

Northern Cape crop farmer Lieb Loots last year opted to make a limited quantity of shiraz and try his hand at chenin. Reason? 'I just felt like it.' Sourcing the grapes was the easy part, Lieb L discovered. Finding a place to turn them into wine was less straightforward. He found temporary abode for his barrels but the challenge next year is a more permanent home. Any offers?

Bona Dea ★★★★ Classy blend rings the changes in **03**: shiraz takes the lead (46%), relegates cab to support role with merlot; Fr oak (18 mths) now all-new, which effortlessly absorbed by layered spicy fruit. Structure for the long haul, complete with generous 14.6% alc. **Jacobus Petrus Shiraz** new ★★★ **03** heavy on the toast, smoke, thatch character, somewhat lighter on fruit. Refreshing acidic zip, dry & spicy tannins bring up the rear. — *CT*

Blydskap see Baarsma

Bodega

Paarl ▪ Closed to public ▪ PO Box 590 Kraaifontein 7569 ▪ ***T 988·2929*** *▪ F 988·3527*

No update available on this winery; contact details from previous edition.

Bodraai Private Cellar new

Stellenbosch ▪ Est 1999 ▪ 1stB 2001 ▪ Closed to public ▪ Gabriël Kriel & Theo Beukes ▪ Vini consultant PG Slabbert (2001) ▪ Viticulturist Gabriël Kriel ▪ 4 ha (cab, shiraz) ▪ 1 000 cs 100% red ▪ PO Box 321 Stellenbosch 7599 ▪ minpro@adept.co.za ▪ ***T 083·601·9030*** *▪ F 881·2095*

They say good fences make good neighbours. Gabriël Kriel & Theo Beukes, who share a fence in the Stellenbosch Hills area, are also good friends and make good wine. Their mutual passion for the stuff, Gabriël K says, encouraged them 'to team up to make a wine as well-balanced as our friendship'. Their output is limited, but there's enough to share with like-minded folk in the UK, Canada and Benelux countries. It's a dream come true: 'To have your own grapes in liquid form is the best feeling in the world!'

Cabernet Sauvignon ★★★★ Forthcoming varietal flavours, cedary hints on mature, ready **01**. Decent, appealing wine: fresh, light-bodied (12.4% alc), well balanced with gentle but firm tannins. Yr Fr oak in unobtrusive support. **Cabernet Sauvignon-Shiraz** ★★★★ **02** blend (85/15) has inviting herby/spicy character. A little longer oaking, more power, than above, but as unpretentious & rewarding – these should be good food partners: eminent drinkability clearly a house speciality. — *TJ*

Boekenhoutskloof

Franschhoek ▪ Tasting by appt ▪ Sales Mon-Fri 9-5 ▪ Owner Boekenhoutskloof Investments (Pty) Ltd ▪ Winemakers Marc Kent & Rudiger Gretschel, with Heinrich Tait & Heinrich Hugo ▪ Viticulturist Pieter Siebrits ▪ PO Box 433 Franschhoek 7690 ▪ boeken@mweb.co.za ▪ ***T 876·3320*** *▪ F 876·3793*

One word encapsulates this winery – stellar. Significantly, it's not only the top-of-range Boekenhoutskoof wines which win exceptional ratings and critical praise (note the *Wine Spectator* points). The well-priced *sous-marque* Porcupine Ridge, too, earns high grades and, in updated packaging (including screwcaps), is flying high locally and in the US and UK. Which will please winemaker Rudiger Gretschel, who's playing a more prominent role (Marc Kent devoting more time to management and marketing), assisted by two Heinrichs – Tait, here, and Hugo, at the Porcupine facility in nearby Franschhoek town. Working for the first time last season with carignan and mourvèdre, both mainly from Malmesbury, was 'good fun'. And that's what it's all about here – stellar wines and a friendly, down-to-earth attitude.

★★★★★ **Cabernet Sauvignon** A thoroughbred with looks, tone & track record to match. **03** one of Kent's finest performance to date (which says something); epitomises top-class vintage. Customary dark-berry/cedar complexity with extra spicy lift from infusion cab f, usual expensive oak. Beautiful fresh/ripe contrast; chiselled cab tannin matched by broad, sustained ripe fruit. Embryonic still; set to reward decade-plus maturation. **02** well balanced if probably earlier-peaking. **01** 90 pts *WS*. From single hillside vyd in Frhoek; 27 mths new Fr oak (mostly extra-thin-stave barrels), unfiltered.

★★★★★ **Syrah** Breed, consistency as above, expressed with variety's more sensuous abandon. **03** clearly revelled in wonderful summer: full of measured oomph, finishes with ripe flourish; on nose, veritable vortex warm woodsmoke, cured meat, dark berries animated by vibrant dark spice; also more nuance than in full-blooded **02** (★★★★★). Greater savoury satisfaction likely over next 8-10 yrs; (worth the wait: outstanding maiden **97** still magnificent, though different fruit source). Since **98** from single old Wllngtn vyd with low production (±600 cs, all allocated). Individuality heightened by traditional vinification: native yeasts, only used Fr oak, 27 mths. WO Coastal. **02** *Wine* ★★★★★, **01** 92 pts *WS*.

★★★★★ **CWG Auction Reserve Syrah** NEW to the guide. Same vinification, 27 mths oaking as above; **03** selection best 2 barrels, one new (unusually for Kent's syrah – Chocolate Block usual destination). Makes its point subtly, without oaky imposition; gives greater lift, more sumptuous texture to warm-area game/spice attractions. Plush, polished & as friendly & delicious as above wine. $64 000 question: will MK be tempted to incorporate some new oak in his regular Syrah? WO Coastal

★★★★★ **Semillon** ✓ Charm, personality of this individual manifests properly only after few yrs; which why Kent is holding back **04** for Oct 2006 release. **03** less sumptuous than pvs yet delivers great crescendo of flavour/texture, length. Frhoek vyds, some century-plus old; fermented/aged new Burgundian barrels; malo.

★★★★★ **Noble Late Harvest** Last tasted was intensely vinous botrytis-brushed **02** dessert from semillon, with creamy viscosity contrasted by breathtakingly fresh conclusion. Uncloying despite massive 240g/ℓ sugar, low 9% alc. Fermented/14 mths new Fr oak. 375ml. **03** not ready for tasting.

★★★★★ **The Chocolate Block** Swiss or Belgian? Whichever choc benchmark, **04** has dark, (positive) bitter qualities of both, backed by heady pepper spice. Blend exudes warm southern France (& Kent's own take on that region's voluptuous wines): 45% syrah, 25% grenache, 11% cinsault, 2% viognier; 17% cab adds individuality. Kaleidoscope of savoury sensuality melded into firm yet friendly build. Intriguing development possibilities over 6-8 yrs. **03** had a creamy concentration with bright peppery contrast. 15 mths Fr oak, some new. 14.8% alc. WO W Cape.

The Wolftrap ☺ ★★★ Delicious 'country-style' red named after trap set by early settlers for non-existent Frhoek predator. **04** melodious combo of reds; choc, red fruit, spice ensemble richly refrained on palate; chunky tannins emphasise down-to-earth nature. Screwcapped for quick access. Fr oak. WO W Cape. **Wolftrap Rosé** ☺ ★★★ **04** from syrah, cinsaut, grenache (70/21/9) still available; not re-tasted. Loads wild strawberry, spicy appeal; rounded, fresh, dry.

Porcupine Ridge range

★★★★ **Syrah** ✓ Among SA's top good-value reds; holds its own in best/most expensive company. Marvellous **04** drier, fresher, more-structured than pvs, no less immediately irresistible. Exhilarating white spice features. Who cares about potential; of course it'll keep 3-4 yrs, but why wait? **03** rounder, readier than Syrah above. *Decanter* ★★★★. Mainly Mbury, with Stbosch, Wllngtn/home vyds (as for Merlot). Small portion oaked. WO Coastal.

Cabernet Sauvignon ★★★★ ✓ For immediate enjoyment without compromising on essential cab attributes (incl yr/2 ageability). **04** expressive soft black berry freshness; ripe, compact tannins; lovely sweet-fruited length. 11% malbec. Fr oak influenced. Stbosch, Paarl, Wllngtn fruit. WO Coastal, as are following pair. **Merlot** ★★★★ ✓ Generously-proportioned **04**; ripe plum/choc intensity; mouth-filling, fleshy; freshened by balanced dry tannin, 10% cab. 14.8% alc. Fr oaked 9 mths. **Sauvignon Blanc** ★★★ Gentle, persuasive tropical sauvignon tones on **05**. Bit fuller bodied than usual but harmonious, fruitily dry. — *AL*

Boland Cellar see Boland Kelder

Boland Kelder

Paarl • Est 1947 • 1stB 1948 • Tasting & sales Mon-Fri 8-5 Sat 9-2 • Closed Easter Fri/Sun, Dec 25/26 & Jan 1 • Tours by appt • Underground cellar for functions & gatherings (max 45 people) • Events programme during Dec/Jan; phone for details • Tourgroups • Owners 96 producing shareholders • Cellarmaster Altus le Roux (Sep 1984) • Winemakers Naudé Bruwer & Bernard Smuts (Dec 1996/Nov 1999), with JG Auret & Chris Crawford (Dec 2002/July 2005) • Viticulturist Jurie Germishuys (Jul 1998) • 2 400 ha (cab, merlot, pinotage, shiraz, chard, chenin, sauvignon) • ±17 600 tons 50% red 50% white • Export brands: Boland Cellar, Lindenhof & Montestell • PO Box 7007 Northern Paarl 7623 • info@bolandkelder.co.za • www.bolandkelder.co.za • T 862·6190 • F 862·5379

Big news from Boland was the release of the first bottled nouvelle, a Cape cross (of crouchen and semillon) a half-century in the cultivation by local researcher and academic Chris Orffer. Also added to this Paarl-based cellar's range of wines was a Cabernet-Shiraz blend – yet another indication of the move away from supplying wholesalers to establishing a strong Boland own brand. Success in Europe and Japan has encouraged export initiatives to the US and Canada. Sourced from seven separate areas within the Paarl district, fruit is handled on an 'estate' basis, vinified individually in its own designated cellar space.

Reserve range

★★★★ **Cabernet Sauvignon** Showstopper **02** a study in classy oak; powerful but undomineering coconut, spice, vanilla notes enhance opulent dark fruit. Modern, already harmonious, should gain further complexity from ±5 yrs cellaring. **01** sleek & well groomed; great concentration; also deserves keeping. Oak, 60/40 Am/Fr all new. 24 mths. *Wine* ★★★★★, VDG.

★★★★ **Shiraz** Powerful, showy **02** chockablock with beef, coconut & vanilla aromas, savoury & sweet/sour red fruit flavours; long powerful tannin finish. Concours Mondial gold. **01** individual & beautifully put together. Natural ferment, new Am oak, 20 mths. At 15.8% alc, not for the faint-hearted.

Chardonnay ★★★★ Delicacy on nose belies gravitas of **04**. Hints of lemon zest, mandarin & cream, concentrated citrus palate gains weight & complexity from partial barrel ferment, ±16 mths lees suffusion, all new Fr oak. **Sauvignon Blanc** ★★★ **05** shows heavy hand with wood; resin hint on nose; char on palate, though zingy acidity does provides freshness to floral/tropical flesh. Barrique fermented/aged, all new Fr, no malo.

Boland range

★★★★ **White Muscadel** Elegant version always flies out of the cellar. **04** myriad nut, citrus aromas/flavours incl macadamia & lime. Modest alc for style (15%), sweet but not sugary (even at 179g/ℓ!) thanks to freshening acidity.

Pinotage ☺ ★★★ Characteristic juicy strawberry, rubber/acetone & lip-smacking acidity on **04**. Dry tannins, touch earthiness on finish add interest. 10 mths old oak.

Cabernet Sauvignon ★★★ Ready **04** ripe cassis, sweet vanilla/coconut & accessible tannins. Balance marred by astringent edge. Yr Am/Fr staves. **Merlot** ★★★ Dusty/leafy black fruit, plums & mulberries on **04**. Lighter textured, fresh acidity, charry tannins, touch bitter lift at end. 10 mths Fr staves. **Shiraz** ★★★ Leathery/organic **04** brimful with dark-berried fruit; properly dry, savoury beef with attractive dry, friendly tannins. Drink young. Am/Fr staves 7 mths. **Cabernet Sauvignon-Shiraz** new ★★★★ Complex bouquet showing leather/earth of shiraz, black fruits/spice of cab. **04** sweet/sour/zingy pomegranate palate, gripping tannins need ±yr to settle. **Chardonnay** ★★ **05** light-textured peachy style with smooth accessibility, pithy finish. Stave-fermentation/ageing add some spicy complexity. Undaunting 13.5% alc. **Chenin Blanc** ★★★ **05** shy but firm-fleshed & lively, tart Granny Smith apple flavours, eminently gulpable at 12.5%

alc. Dash sugar adds to palate roundness. **Nouvelle** new ★★★ **05** first varietal bottling of this semillon-crouchen (Cape riesling) cross. Exotic fruits & khaki bush tones, semillon lends weight to palate, warm finish despite moderate 13.5% alc. **Riesling** ★★ Made from crouchen – an enduring favourite; **05** light-textured but no longer bone-dry; this yr with 3.5gℓ sugar. Whiff of pear-drop, soft acidity. **Sauvignon Blanc** ★★★ **05** more mineral in style than pvs full-blown tropical fruit. Vibrant lime/grapefruit flavours & long tangy finish. Comfortable 13% alc. **Red Muscadel** ★★★ **04** dessert wine for sweeter toothed (179g/ℓ sugar). Crystallised fruit tone, dusty/earthy nuance & stalky finish. Modest 15% alc. **Port** ★★★ **03** from shiraz; mid-2004 not overly sweet or alcoholic at 98g/ℓ sugar, 16.5% alc. Prune fruit with dry tannic grip. Matured 14 mths 2nd fill casks. **Pinotage Cinsaut**, **Noble Late Harvest** discontinued.

Bon Vino range

In 500ml 'Bordeaux lite' bottles; 2ℓ & 5ℓ packs. All **NV**, bargain priced.

Dry Red ☺ ★★★ Despite recipe change – cinsaut, merlot out; shiraz in; cab only constant – still perfect for glugging round the braai. Unwooded fruit full of fun, cab tannins lend structure. 14% alc all but guarantees jollity. **Dry White** ☺ ★★ Designed for carefree drinking (incl moderate alc), enticing floral nose & crisp finish. Mainly chenin, with colombard.

Semi-Sweet ★★ Will appeal widely. Mainly chenin; charming floral, grapey character & soft sweetness abets easy drinking. Low 11.5% alc. – *CvZ*

Bon Cap Organic Winery

*Robertson ▪ Est 2001 ▪ 1stB 2002 ▪ Tasting & sales Mon-Fri 8-5 Sat/Sun 9-5 ▪ Fee R10 for groups of 8+ ▪ Closed Dec 25/26 ▪ Tours 10.30 & 3 (groups by appt) ▪ Function/conference centre serving meals Mon, Tue, Thu & Sun 8-5; evenings by appt; or BYO picnic ▪ Guest house (self-catering & B&B by appt) ▪ Farm produce ▪ Facilities for children ▪ Tourgroups ▪ Conferencing ▪ Walks ▪ Owners Roelf & Michelle du Preez/SHZ Winecellar (Pty) Ltd ▪ Winemakers Roelf du Preez & Jacques Conradie (2002/2004) ▪ Viticulturists Roelf du Preez & Henning Retief ▪ 45 ha (cab, pinotage, shiraz) ▪ 300 tons 15 000 cs + 135 000ℓ bulk + 500 cs for clients, incl Woolworths & De Mooie Opstal (Belgium) ▪ 80% red 10% white 10% grapejuice ▪ PO Box 356 Robertson 6705 ▪ boncap@intekom.co.za ▪ www.boncaporganic.co.za ▪ **T (023) 626·1628** ▪ F (023) 626·1895*

In common with others from Robertson, Jacques Conradie found the 2005 vintage a challenge – compounded by falling headlong into a tank of fermenting pinotage just before a tasting with German clients. He's nevertheless excited to be leading the winery in a slew of new projects, all of which play on Robertson's strengths, with a premium organic Chardonnay and a bottle fermented Cap Classique (amongst others) in progress. Extending the estate's organic ethos into the winery, he reckons the injudicious use of sulphur prevents the development of site-specific character in wines, and prefers to invest in more natural avenues of preservation – clean fruit, sterilised equipment, cold temperatures and full tanks. Materially, the main development on the estate has been the opening of a bistro and a conference venue.

Organic range

Cabernet Sauvignon ★★★★ **03** continues neatly-tailored style; ripe brambleberry, cassis bound by mouth-coating tannin; honestly dry. Barrel matured. Fruit quality of these organically grown wines impresses. **Pinotage** ★★★★ After deeply fruity yet unshowy **03**, sample **04** (provisional ★★★) firm & serious, nicely concentrated, some sweet prune, biltong with good oak (70/30 Fr/Am, 10mths). Pristine fruit. **Syrah** ★★★★ **03** was restrained, fine darkberried fruit, dry savoury grip. Latest **04** (sample; possible ★★★) in similar style; in its shell mid-2005. Good dark fruit, sprinkling white pepper; dry tannins not overwhelming but acid on the high side – a signature for the producer. 10 mths oak, 80/20, Fr/Am. **Viognier** ★★★★ Maiden **04** SA's first organic version of this Rhône variety. **05** firm peach & greengage; drier profile than pvs — more classic. Still oaky mid-2005 (fermented/6 mths new Fr), needs ±yr. 14.5% alc.

The Ruins range

Sauvignon Blanc new ☺ ★★★ **05** zippy dry white with tropical overtones, delicious quaffer. From leased (non-organic) vyds in Tradouw. **Rosé** new ☺ ★★★ SA's first organic rosé — pretty stylish too. Gorgeous pink coral hue in **05** from pinotage, almost dry strawberry, raspberry flavours; juicy & tangy, begs to be sipped again & again.

Pinotage ★★★ **04** savoury meaty version, still quite tough mid-2005, firm tannins on finish. Less accessible than pvs. Organic, as all of these, unless noted. **Syrah-Cabernet Sauvignon** new ★★★ **04** ripe baked plum, firm tannins & acid show cab in control here. Not yet ready mid-2005. **Chardonnay-Viognier** new ★★★ Non-organic, attractive **05**, concentrated, firm-fleshed peach/apricot fruit, lively acidity, clean finish. Complementary varieties work well together — watch this one. **Cabernet Sauvignon-Merlot** discontinued. — *IvH*

Bon Courage Estate

Robertson ▪ Est 1927 ▪ 1stB 1983 ▪ Tasting & sales Mon-Fri 8-5 Sat 9-3 ▪ Restaurant Mon-Fri 9-4.30 Sat 9-3 ▪ Closed Easter Fri & Dec 25 ▪ Play area for children ▪ Owner/viticulturist André Bruwer ▪ Winemaker Jacques Bruwer ▪ 150 ha ▪ PO Box 589 Robertson 6705 ▪ boncourage@mindsmail.co.za ▪ www.boncourage.co.za ▪ ***T (023) 626·4178*** *▪ F (023) 626·3581*

Having recently celebrated ten years at the helm, Jacques Bruwer, son of this estate's founder André, has many reasons to pop a cork or two. Judges at the Chardonnay-du-Monde awarded his Chardonnay Prestige Cuvée a gold medal, and, on the sparkling wine front, the all-French panel of the Classic Wine Trophy Show couldn't choose between the Brut Reserve Blanc de Blanc and the Brut Reserve — so, for the first time ever, they awarded a trophy to each! Hardly surprising that production of the estate's cap classiques is set to rise. But the original winegrowing philosophy still stands: to correctly match varieties and terroir, and as much as possible, make single-vineyard wines.

★★★★ **Shiraz Inkará** ('Syrah Inkará' pvs ed) The flagship; shows muscle, polish & attention to detail — cold soaked, whole berry fermented, partly barrel fermented Am oak, finished yr in new Fr. For the long haul. **03** so seductively accessible, doubt there'll be any left to age. Generous mocha, creamy spice & dark plum styling, seamlessly integrated with oak. Class apparent in the elegance, silky texture, long finish. General Smuts trophy at SAYWS.

★★★★ **Chardonnay Prestige Cuvée** Classy barrel-matured version, 6-8 mths on lees in 2nd/3rd fill Fr oak. Back on form with bold & showy **04**: citrus peel & English toffee styling; generous oaking balanced by fruit concentration. Drinks beautifully. Good enough to age 2-3 yrs. Chardonnay-du-Monde gold. **03** (★★★☆) lacked bit of zing.

★★★★☆ **Cap Classique Jacques Bruére Brut Reserve Blanc de Blanc** Hugely impressive debut with **00**, clearly a standout vintage for the estate; interesting contrast between this chard-only bottle-fermented sparkling & version below (neither retasted this ed); here a restrained steelikness, heightened by vein of green fruit, spicy lemongrass coolness; palate leavened by delicate lees/biscuit/lemon cream type flavours. Base-wine whole bunch pressed in stainless steel.

★★★★ **Cap Classique Jacques Bruére Brut Reserve** This MCC has developed own unique fruity style. Current **NV** (00) again more supple than sparse 7.6g/ℓ sugar would suggest; hallmark doughy notes, bright lime & grapefruit aromas & crisp, citrus finish. Plenty of frothy mousse. Whole-bunch-pressed pinot, chardonnay (60/40), 18 mths on 2nd lees. Next is 01.

★★★★ **Noble Late Harvest** From botrytised riesling, sumptuously sweet (±147g/ℓ sugar), with rapier-like fruit acid to balance. **01**, **02** shared similar dried apricot & peach profile. Standout **04** (★★★★★) last yr noted as delightfully different; ethereal quality on both palate & nose. Peaches & cream texture, some terpene oiliness, followed by waves of cleansing acidity for a racy/steely finish. 9.5% alc.

★★★★ **White Muscadel** Long lineage of concentration, richness; **05** (sample) is very aromatic, waves of raisin & honey, caramel & floral bouquet; voluptuous mouth-coating sweetness. 18% alc. Last tasted **03** won Muscadel Association gold.

Cabernet Sauvignon Inkará ★★★★ Premium, limited release. **03** is well made, harmonious: creamy cappuccino & sweet spice nuances; juicy red fruit core; supple tannins & elegant structure. Already accessible, potential for 4-6 yrs more. Yr Fr oak. **Cabernet Sauvignon** ★★★ **03** last ed's notes read: straightforward but juicy early drinking style; lighter-weight than pvs, not as much structure. **Pinotage** ★★★★ Back after two vintage break, **04** a step up. Modern style: fresh-toned rhubarb, white pepper, red fruit; silky texture & fully integrated oak; all designed to please, & do. 18 mths Fr/Am mix new/used. Drink till ±2010. Sample tasted; ditto for .... **Shiraz** ★★★★ **04** fruit-dominant style, big in structure & flavour. Ripe black plums, some peppery tones; plenty of oak extraction, chewy but not harsh; sample should be more harmonious on release. Yr oaked, mix new/used. **Cabernet Sauvignon-Shiraz** ★★★★ Last yr **02** had a warm, spicy Xmas pud nose, sweet ripe profile without jamminess or confection; good dry finish. 60/40 blend, 8 mths Fr oaked before blending. **Sauvignon Blanc** ★★★★ **05** shows big quality jump, reductively made for maximum flavour extraction: gooseberries & zesty lime, long intense finish. Edginess & nervy intensity are pure sauvignon. Alc 12%. **Chardonnay** ★★★ Unwooded, slenderly built **05** plenty of lemony freshness, best enjoyed in its youthful prime. **Colombard** ★★★ **05** simpler than pvs: lemon-drop styling & bracing acidity, better accompanying food than solo. **Riesling** ★★★ From Cape riesling/crouchen. **05** lacks complexity of pvs, but has good typicity, fresh-mown hay aromas, crisp palate structure. Can be enjoyed on its own or with food. **Colombard-Chardonnay** ★★★ **05** step up on pvs. Unwooded 60/40 blend, fragrantly floral, appealing lemon freshness & 'drink me' written all over it. **Gewürztraminer Special Late Harvest** ★★★★ **05** classic aromatic, rose-petal aromas & sweet-sour acid/sugar effect that is so appealing & tasty. In spite of the 54g/ℓsugar, has elegance, refinement. Moderate 12% alc. **Weisser Riesling Natural Sweet** ★★★★ **03** has lots happening: lush fruit, pineapple & lime; smoothly rounded body, lovely to drink; racy acidity (12.2g/ℓ) which freshens the 117g/ℓ sugar richness, finishes crisply clean. Only 11% alc. **Blush Vin Doux** ★★ Frothy pink **NV** sweet bubbly with fruit-gum, musk-sweet flavours. Light-hearted, uncomplicated. From pinot & muscadel. **Red Muscadel** ★★★★ new **03** (sample) intensely sweet, like drinking a pudding of stewed plums, raisins, dried apricots. Spirity bite on finish provides nice contrast. **Vintage Port** ★★★ **03** has both tasty drinkability & distinctive character: coffee grounds, black plums & molasses aromas, flavours, richly savoury. Tinta b, some cab f. **Chenin Blanc Semillon**, **Gewürztraminer** discontinued. **Three Rivers Ruby Cabernet-Pinotage**, **Chardonnay** untasted. — *CR/TM*

Bonfoi Estate

Stellenbosch ▪ Est 1699 ▪ 1stB 1974 ▪ Tasting & sales Mon-Fri 9-5 Sat 10-2.30 ▪ Fee R10, refunded with purchase ▪ Closed pub hols ▪ BYO picnic ▪ Walks ▪ Conservation area ▪ Owner/winemaker/viticulturist Johannes van der Westhuizen ▪ 98 ha (cabs s/f, merlot, pinotage, shiraz, chard, chenin, sauvignon) ▪ 700 tons 3 000 cs own label 60% red 40% white ▪ PO Box 9 Vlottenburg 7604 ▪ albec@mweb.co.za ▪ www.bonfoiwines.co.za ▪ ***T 881·3774*** *▪ F 881·3807*

Moving away from the hi-tech and back to more traditional winemaking, Johannes van der Westhuizen is destemming after crushing the reds, adding no enzymes or tannins, allowing only gentle pumping, and experimenting with natural fermentation of his Chardonnay. 'The closer we get to the natural, the better for long-term stability,' he believes. He has high hopes of vintage 2005, noting flavours more flinty than tropical in the sauvignon and predicting that the reds will age really well.

★★★★ **Ouverture** Beautifully crafted & elegant blend, selection of best barrels. **02** seamless blend cab/merlot/shiraz (45/30/25); latter adds warmth, generosity — but still bdx-like, with mulberry, blackberry & cedar of cab now in control. Yr wood for components, 6 mths for blend. Unfolding stylishly, keep till ±2008.

★★★★ **Cabernet Sauvignon** Style established: dark mulberry, cool cedar, fine oak to black velvety fruit. Latest **02** (★★★★) slightly green, stalky flavours reflect vintage problems, but lively, clean-cut; fresh acid; good depth. Yr Fr oak.

★★★★ **Shiraz 03** terrific – gorgeous warm spice, smoked beef & fynbos bouquet, ripe dried plum, dry tannic grip on finish. Real substance here, meaty richness tempered by fine oak, manages true elegance. Cellar 3-5 yrs. Yr Fr/Am oak (75/25).

Merlot ★★★ Attractive dark cassis, some mulberry leaf tones adding freshness on **03**; ripe mulberry flavours; acidity perhaps unbalanced, diminishing generous feel. Yr oak. **Chardonnay** ★★★ Somewhat diffident **04** less convincing than pvs, but gentle citrus, subtle oak, smooth acidity, longish finish. Fermented/5 mths in barrel. **Sauvignon Blanc** ★★★☆ **05** (sample) subtle gooseberry & fig; curves in all the right places, bouncy & juicy passionfruit, tangy grapefruit flavours, beautifully balanced. – *IvH*

Bonne Esperance see KWV International
Bonne Nouvelle see Remhoogte

Bonnievale Cellar

Robertson • Est 1964 • Tasting & sales Mon-Fri 8-5 Sat & pub hols 10-1 • Closed Easter Fri-Mon, Dec 25/26 & Jan 1 • Tours by appt • Conferencing • Owners 60 members • Manager/winemaker Henk Wentzel, with Gerhard Swart & Wilson Madlathu (Aug 1999, Dec 2002/2003) • Viti consultant Willem Botha • 800 ha (cab, merlot, pinotage, ruby cab, shiraz, chard, chenin, colombard, sauvignon, semillon) • 10 000 tons 20 000 cs own label + 5m litres bulk 40% red 60% white • PO Box 206 Bonnievale 6730 • info@bonnievalecellar.co.za • www.bonnievalecellar.co.za • ***T (023) 616·2795*** *• F (023) 616·2332*

A happening cellar – in every sense of the word: new vines (nouvelle, viognier and petit verdot); new label designs; a pruning of the Bonnievale range (now only varietal bottlings); a new release in the flagship Vertex Reserve range; the launch of the new blended Bonnievale CCC wines, and an upgrade of the tasting room and cellar facade. All part of shifting the focus from bulk to bottled wine, and building the brand – the latter one of the key objectives of new marketing manager Mignon du Plessis.

Vertex Reserve range

Cabernet Sauvignon 04 not ready for tasting. The following retasted this ed (pvsly barrel samples): **Shiraz** ★★★☆ Aussie-style fruity density on **03**, protracted savoury fruit flavours tinged with spice & whiffs eucalyptus; fragrant vanilla-oak (100% new barrels, 67% Am, 15 mths) well-synched with wine's 'amicable monster' personality (15% alc). **Chardonnay** ★★★☆ Lives up to early expectations; **03** cleverly crafted: neither too fat nor too full (despite 14.5% alc), oak supportive of delicate citrus-tinged mineral fruit, finishes elegantly. Oak-fermented, 50% new.

Bonnievale range

No follow-ups yet to following pair of reds, both **02**: **Cabernet Sauvignon Reserve** ★★★☆ Seriously made, new Fr oak 9 mths; New-World-style; padded with spicy berry fruit, big whack oak & chunky tannins. **Shiraz Reserve** ★★★☆ Attention-grabber, new oak matured (Fr/Am casks); dark berries with Karoo bush & pepper hints, firm but ripe tannins. **Shiraz** ★★★ **03** last year had ripe plum & prune intro, whiffs sweet spice & pepper, full, round & fruity. Combo Fr/Am barrels & staves; similar regimen for ... **Cabernet Sauvignon-Merlot** ★★★ 60/40 blend; **03** minty touch, floral background to sweet fruit, smooth & drinkable with potential to develop. **Cinsaut-Cabernet Sauvignon** ★★☆ **04** satisfying everyday drink. 55/45 blend last yr had red plum & strawberry attractions. **Kelkierooi** ★★☆ Lightish quaffable mulberry-toned melange of cinsaut, cab & ruby cab, unwooded. Can take light chilling in summer. 500ml. **NV**. **Cabernet Sauvignon Rosé** ★★★ Not retasted. Ripe red berry lead-in to **04**, redcurrant touch, smooth-tasting rather than sweet. **Chardonnay** ★★☆ Aperitif-style crispness, zing on **04**; hints lemon-rind & fruit pastille. 50% Fr staved. **Chenin Blanc** ★★☆ To be discontinued after lightly refreshing **04**, last yr with lemonade flavours & twist citrus-zest. **Sauvignon Blanc** ★★ **05** seemingly earlier picked than pvs – distinct green tone, garden peas & salad leaves, tart appley finish. **Kelkiewit** ★★ Keep-em-guessing blend in 500ml. New version is **NV**; equal chenin/colombard with light vinous tones. **Pik 'n Wyntjie** ★☆ Late Harvest-style **NV** from chenin. Light & simple; straw/dry grass whiffs; manageable sweetness. **Late Harvest** ★★★ **04** will be last; from chenin; balanced acidity for light & lively drinking. **Sauvignon Blanc Brut** ★ Our samples of this carbonated sparkling uncharacteristically tired; usually full of verve & fizzy sauvignon flavour. Pvs *Wine* best value selection. **NV**. **Cape Vintage Port** ★★ **03** early sample fine, rich raisin/Xmas cake aromas, undone by excessive sweetness; perhaps just needs time for fruit to assert itself.

CCC range

Cabernet Sauvignon-Cinsaut-Cabernet Franc new Not ready. Replaces Cinsaut-Cab from **05**. **Colombard-Chenin Blanc-Chardonnay** ★★★ 40/40/20 mix; **05** zinging freshness again the hallmark, plus attractive mix bright tropical pineapple & guava flavours; best young. — *CT*

Boplaas Family Vineyards

Calitzdorp (see Little Karoo map) ▪ Est 1880 ▪ 1stB 1982 ▪ Tasting & sales Mon-Fri 8-5 Sat 9-3 ▪ Fee R15 p/p for tourgroups ▪ Closed Easter Fri/Sun & Dec 25 ▪ Tours by appt ▪ Meals by appt during school holidays ▪ Gifts ▪ Owner Carel Nel ▪ Winemakers Carel Nel & Alwyn Liebenberg (Jan 2004) ▪ Viti consultant Willem Botha ▪ 70 ha (cab, merlot, pinotage, shiraz, touriga, chard, sauvignon) ▪ 35 000 cs 50% red 45% white 5% blanc de noir ▪ PO Box 156 Calitzdorp 6660 ▪ boplaas@mweb.co.za ▪ www.boplaas.co.za ▪ ***T (044) 213·3326*** *▪ F (044) 213·3750*

This family farm's winegrowing tradition dates back to the 1880s, so it's most appropriate that the words 'Family Vineyards' should now appear beside the familiar 'Boplaas' name. Paterfamilias and chief winemaker Carel Nel is well satisfied with continuing kudos for their innovative reds and portwines, most notably the stellar 93/100 rating from Robert Parker for the 02 Cape Vintage Reserve (the US critic's highest for an SA port and one of the highest for any SA wine). Quietly combative against Portuguese pressure to reserve the 'port' moniker for their wines, Carel N privately pitted Portugal's 2003 Vintages against SA's Vintage Reserves at the 2005 London International Wine & Spirits Fair and reiterates that local quality accounts for Portuguese defensive action!

Reserve range

★★★★ **Pinotage** Complexity, balance, suppleness are hallmarks; **02** (★★★★) well & ripely fruited with plums & black cherries, though alc (14.9%) tad fiery. **01** had appealing banana-custard tones, creamy texture, ripe tannins for 3-4 yrs.

★★★★ **Kuip & Clay** Sample tasted last yr was named 'Kuip & Klei'. **03** fascinating & different blend touriga, cab & merlot (30/35/35). Lavish black/red fruit & herby top-note; elegant, commanding but not overpowering, moderate 13.5% alc. Wood (50% new Fr). ± 5 yrs aging potential.

Cabernet Sauvignon ★★★★ **02**, first since **99**, balanced, flavourful & juicy; packed with cassis intensity. **Shiraz** ★★★★ **02** spicy & rich, some choc blended in with the red berries. All above tasted mid-2004; **03** vintages not ready for review this ed.

Boplaas range

★★★★★ **Red Muscadel Vintner's Reserve** Olive-rimmed beauty; **75** not a misprint. Decadently smooth & soft; complex, lifted dried-fruit finish. Delicious when tasted mid-2004.

★★★★★ **Cape Vintage Reserve Port** Distinctive & ageworthy fortified dessert, made only in exceptional yrs by style-guru Carel N, from mature touriga vines (15 yrs) & ungrafted ±30-yr-old tinta (blend also includes dash souzão). **03** (★★★★) a hedonist's delight: acacia blossom, fynbos glosses for heady plum pudding fragrance; smooth with unobtrusive 18.6% alc core. *Wine* ★★★★. Lacks refinement & structure of **02**, which also *Wine*'s 2004 Port of Yr. Oak/fortification as below. These show long-term potential.

★★★★★ **Cape Vintage CWG Auction Reserve Port** Selection of best barrels, tiny quantities, even more sumptuous than above. **03** restrained nose with nutty/coffee whiffs, sweetness (92g/ℓ) corralled by masterly tannins & knife-edge acidity/fortification. Boasts concentration & structure lacking in above std version. **02** despite macerated plums/brandied fruitcake richness, has surprising elegance & verve, which was Nel's intention. Both made to Duoro specs, incl 500ℓ port 'pipes' (18-24 mths) to finish wine. Touriga, tinta b, souzão; fortified with brandy spirit.

★★★★ **Cape Tawny Port** ✓ Often awarded, SA benchmark for style. Latest **02** 100% tinta, wood-matured 12 yrs. Nutty, flor-like bouquet with marzipan hint; velvety smooth, with 18.6% alc wake-up in the tail. Entrancing copper hue; well worth trying.

Dry Red ☺ ★★ Unoaked **NV** a merry blend of merlot, cab, shiraz pinotage & tinta b. Perky acidity, soft tannins & bright fruit.

Cabernet Sauvignon ★★ Effusive jammy bouquet at odds with austere palate & slightly bitter finish on **04**. Some vanilla leavening from 9 mths Fr oak. **Merlot** ★★★ Fruit-driven **04** pleases with plummy aromas, flavours plumped out by 8 mths Fr oak. Slips down easily. **Pinotage** ★★★ Flirtatious **04** from newer vines than pvs. Typical banana/cherry-stone bouquet; juicy & balanced. Low 13% alc. **Shiraz** ★★★ **03** smoke, leather, farmyard run riot on **03**'s bouquet. For early drinking (active 13.8% alc not for quaffing). **Touriga Nacional** ★★★★ Still one of very few varietal bottlings; **03** tasted last yr reprised fynbos/herb character of pvs; nice & chewy, has personality, body & balance. **Tinta Barocca** ★★★ **03** comfortable in its oak cloak (6 mth Fr), raspberry nose & palate, seamless & unchallenging. **Blanc de Noir** ★★ Semi-sweet **04** closer to rosé in appearance/tone; pleasant, but lacks fruity zing of pvs. Low 12% alc. Not tasted this yr. **Rosé** new ★ Natural Sweet **NV** from muscadel, colombard & shiraz. Rose-petal & blue-vein cheese nose, strawberry flavours, sweet goodbye (42g/ℓ sugar). **Chardonnay Unwooded** ★★ **04** shy & restrained; shortish orange-pith finish. **Sauvignon Blanc** ★★ **05** unsubstantial; barely discernible pear-drop tone, racy acid. **Classic Dry White** ★★ **05** quaffable melange sauvignon, chardonnay, colombard, viognier; fruit-salad nose, viognier adds weight to palate. **Late Harvest** ★★★ Hanepoot/colombard equal blend; **05** not tasted. Aromatic **04** with fruit-pastille tone, clean finish. **Pinot Noir Sparkling** ★★ Friendly blush-coloured brut; **05** lively mousse, rasp/strawberry aromas, flavours. **Sweet Sparkling** ★★ Uncomplicated, light (10% alc) all-day quaffer, fleeting finish. From hanepoot & colombard (60/40), **NV**. **Red Dessert** ★★★ 50/50 mix tinta/muscadel fortified to 16% alc (vs pvs 17.2%). Bread pudding in a glass, delicious, uncloying. **NV**. **Hanepoot** ★★★ **05** silky fortified dessert; luscious raisins & dried fig aroma; persistent barley sugar finish. Lightish but balanced. ±16% alc. **Muscadel** ★★★ Velvety fortified white dessert. **05** shy grapey nose; cloying raisin finish. Enjoy over ice with slice of lime to cut its richness. **Cape Vintage Port** ★★★★ ✓ Produced annually from tinta, touriga, souzão (50/35/15), ageing/fortification as per Rsv above; 'correct' lower sugar. Latest **03** red velvety hue introduces tea-leaf nose & palate softened with marzipan, black fruit. Plush but finishes tad short. 18.6% alc. *Wine* ★★★★★, Peter Schulz 'Best Port in SA'. **Cape Ruby Port** ★★★ SA's best-selling **NV** ruby, always in drier Douro style. Souzão joins tinta (60%), touriga (25%) in latest bottling. Plum pud nose & palate, delightfully dry & sippable. ±18.5% alc. **Late Bottled Vintage Option Port** ★★★★ ✓ Still available, garnet-hued **93** tasted mid-2004 spicily opulent, deliciously harmonious & balanced. Tinta, touriga, 4½ yrs Portuguese oak. 18.5% alc. **Cape White Port** ★★ Latest (**NV**) brassy 'Banana Boat' styling, creamy, pithy with distinct spirituous tail. Delightful over crushed ice in summer. 17.2% alc. **Muscadel Reserve** discontinued. — *CvZ/CR*

Boschendal Wines

*Franschhoek ▪ Est 1685 ▪ 1stB 1976 ▪ Tasting & sales daily 8.30–4.30 ▪ Fee R15 for 5 wines ▪ Closed Easter Fri, May 1, Jun 16 & Dec 25 ▪ Tours (vyd & cellar in minibus) 10.30 & 11.30 by appt ▪ Restaurants & picnics (see Eat-out section) ▪ Tourgroups ▪ Gifts ▪ Conservation area ▪ Museum visits 9.30–5 ▪ Owner DGB ▪ Cellarmaster JC Bekker (Oct 1996) ▪ Winemaker James Farquharson (Jan 2004), with Lionel Leibbrandt & Francois Conradie (Dec 1999/Nov 2001) ▪ Viticulturist Spekkies van Breda (1995) ▪ 200 ha (cab, merlot, shiraz, chard, sauvignon) ▪ 3 600 tons 250 000 cs 50% red 33% white 14% rosé 3% sparkling ▪ ISO 9001 & 14001 certified ▪ Pvt Bag X1 Groot Drakenstein 7680 ▪ taphuis@boschendalwines.co.za ▪ www.boschendal.com ▪ **T 870·4200** ▪ F 874·1531*

Having acquired the Boschendal wine business, DGB's strategy is to build on research feedback indicating high levels of awareness enjoyed by the historic property locally and abroad, says CEO Tim Hutchinson. Recent investments in the vineyards are bearing fruit (as evidenced by, among others, Boschendal taking the SA Producer of the Year trophy at the 2004 IWSC). Coupled with a successful winemaking team led by JC Bekker and James Farquharson, Hutchinson says the plan is to 'dramatically' increase Boschendal's share of the premium wine category. Potentially suitable wines are maturing in the cellar, and wines singled out for release will be linked to key aspects of the Boschendal heritage (read: Rhodes Cottage, Cecil John Rhodes, Lanoy). The Jean le Long range will be available only from the cellar door and. at the lower end, well-known Le Pavillon will become a stand-alone easy-drinking range. Ultimately, Hutchinson reveals, the team hopes to release a wine of a quality to challenge Penfold's Grange.

★★★★☆ **Grand Reserve** Classically crafted & ageworthy flagship from cask selections, increased cab f component to 45% in deep-coloured **00** (with 40/15 cab, merlot). Made for long haul, with velvet fruit-sweetness supported by sensitive oaking – mix new, 2nd fill Fr. **01** (not retasted) broadly similar stats, also grandly serious, but perhaps a little easier-going. Lovely bright, savoury fruit, firm tannic backbone; also needs time to show its best. Like all these, now WO Coastal.

★★★★ **Cabernet Sauvignon Reserve** Elegantly styled maiden **00** had spicy leafiness with cassis fragrance, well-balanced palate, delicate but with firm grip & persistence. Darkly rich **01** burlier, was still youthfully tight mid-2004, with tobacco notes, hints of lurking fruit – few yrs required to show more attractions, longer maturation best. Mix new/older barrels for these.

★★★★ **Merlot 01** was powerful, offering leafy edge to attractive plum, choc. Ripe-scented **02** (★★★☆, not retasted) called 'Reserve', sweet fruitcake, mocha flavours, big tannins with touch bitterness. Obvious 15% alc. Yr oak, 30% new.

★★★★☆ **Shiraz Reserve** 'Syrah' last ed. **01** had ripe, smoky bouquet & plenty of savoury red berries, 15% alc giving powerful glow to finish. Yr mix new, older Fr oak. Deeply coloured **02** offers dried herb, red-fruited aromas; big structure, needing time to harmonise with sappy plum fruit.

★★★★ **Chardonnay Reserve** Attractive nutty, toasty notes on creamily rich, full-flavoured **04**, from single, low-yielding home vyd. Technically almost off-dry, but well balanced & not obviously sweet. Partly native yeast-fermented; 11 mths Fr oak, half new. **03** was big, modern but not over-brash, with fruit power, rich texture, balancing fresh acidity.

★★★★ **Jean le Long Sauvignon Blanc** Named after property's Huguenot founder. Fine example, frequently gilded. Barrel sample **05** promises usual restrained, deeply flavoured & well-balanced impressiveness, with quiet pungency & grass/gooseberry character. Combines freshness & focused power, as did **04**.

★★★★ **Brut** Supple, yeasty, vintaged MCC from pinot (60% in **99**), chardonnay. Biscuit/brioche bouquet presages almost decadently rich but well-balanced palate offering strawberry, ripe apple notes, sweet touch from 13g/ℓ sugar. Our bottle tasted mid-2004 was disgorged Jan 2003 (date on label). 2002 MCC Challenge runner up.

Cabernet Sauvignon ★★★☆ Good drinking while waiting on Reserve. **02** more sombre, tannic than pvs, but packed with solid fruit & good varietal flavours. *Wine* ★★★★. These will keep good few yrs. Mix new/older oak. 14.5% alc. **Shiraz** ★★★☆ Good varietal character on **03**, warm red fruit, but essentially vinous, with pleasantly austere tannins. Yr Fr oak. **Lanoy** ★★★ Big-volume blend named after 17th century part-owner Nicolas de Lanoy. Like beguiling pvs, **02** cab-based with merlot (28%), shiraz (12%); appealing nose, then straightforward, shorter & more drily tannic than usual. Yr Fr oak, 25% new. **Blanc de Noir** ★★★ Pale salmon-coloured **05**, from red grape all-sorts, offers boiled sweets, berries in pleasant, just-off-dry package. **Pinot Noir-Chardonnay** ★★★☆ SA pioneer. Pink-gold tinge to flavoursome, just off-dry **05**, following rich, fresh & dry **04**, similar notes of peach, strawberry, earth. 20% barrel fermented. **Chardonnay** ★★★☆ **05** has tropical fruit & pear-drop notes, firm acid balancing 4g/ℓ sugar; pleasantly rounded, but 'hot' finish from big 15% alc. 60% barrel fermented. **Chenin Blanc** ★★☆ **05** attractively flavoursome, softly rich & nearly dry, but big 14% alc gives rather warm & hard finish. **Sauvignon Blanc Reserve** ★★★☆ Formerly 'Sauvignon Blanc'. Tropical-fruited, crisply appealing **05** as fresh, tasty & pleasantly balanced as was **04**. **Jean le Long White** ★★★☆ new to guide. Blend will vary with vintage. Maiden **04** sauvignon 50%, chenin 30%, viognier 20%. Pleasantly interesting flavours, lovely off-dry creaminess shot through with fresh acid, rather brisk finish. **05** replaces sauvignon with chard, but same 10g/ℓ sugar more obvious on concentrated rich palate – charming but too sweet, bland for a wine with serious ambitions. Both barrel fermented/matured older oak. **Grand Vin Blanc** ★★★ Delightful as ever, light & freshly off-dry **05** from sauvignon, dollop semillon, with lingering passion fruit flavour. **Blanc de Blanc** ★★★ Last tasted was cheerful, just-dry **04** blend full of fresh, bright fruit. **Le Bouquet** ★★☆ Softly grapey off-dry blend of aromatic whites, **05** packed with pretty flavour as usual.

Le Pavillon range

Rouge ★★☆ **04** customary blend cab, merlot, shiraz; unassuming & friendly, with ripe baked aromas/flavours padding a firmly tannic core. **Blanc** ★★☆ **05** happily fruity blend of many convivial varieties; full-bodied, fresh, with sweet edge. **Le Grand Pavillon** ★★★☆ Reliable **NV** Cap Classique brut; attractively yeasty, mature bouquet & spicy baked apple notes on light, fresh dryness. Discontinued: **Jean le Long Cabernet Franc**, **Jean le Long Semillon**, **Viognier**. – *TJ*

Boschetto see Stellekaya

Boschheim

new

Stellenbosch ▪ 1stB 2003 ▪ Visits by appt ▪ Owner/winemaker Andy Roediger ▪ 220 cs 100% red ▪ PO Box 3202 Matieland 7602 ▪ ahar@sun.ac.za ▪ ***T 808·3175*** *F 886·4731*

Andy Roediger, in the final throes of his Cape Wine Master studies, doesn't believe the qualification means much without experience of the practical aspects of winemaking – exactly what he's been doing since 2003. He doesn't tend his own vineyards yet but, determined to find the exact moment of ripeness (his CWM thesis topic), he personally selects both the grapes and the harvest date. A portion of his small output is exported to Germany.

Elemental ★★★☆ Shiraz/viognier combo indubitably fashion trend of yr. **04** with obvious 5% white grape influence, plus tarry, sweet oak. Both may settle over yr/2 to reveal underlying, much more attractive shiraz delicacy. Yr oak, third used Fr. **Cabernet Sauvignon** ★★★ No -frills **03**. Freshly crushed, soft black berry aromas, sweet-fruited juiciness trimmed by enthusiastic oaking. Roughish, slightly bitter tail. Yr oak, portion Fr, 33% new. – *AL*

Boschkloof

Stellenbosch ▪ Est/1stB 1996 ▪ Tasting & sales by appt only Mon-Fri 8-6 (sales 8-5) Sat 8-1 ▪ Tours by appt ▪ Owners Reenen Furter & Jacques Borman ▪ Winemaker Jacques Borman ▪ Viticulturist Reenen Furter ▪ 19 ha (cab, merlot, shiraz) ▪ 120 tons ▪ 8 000 cs 89% red 11% white ▪ PO Box 1340 Stellenbosch 7599 ▪ boschkloof@adept.co.za ▪ www.boschkloof.co.za ▪ ***T 881·3293*** *▪ F 881·3032*

After two seasons partnering father-in-law Reenen Furter, winemaker Jacques Borman realises the importance of knowing your vineyards, 'when optimum ripeness has been reached and when to harvest'. He's been experimenting: dividing a block of merlot into three, he cropped three times, at weekly intervals. The difference made to the final product, he says, was 'unbelievable' and supported his belief that SA wine farmers harvest 'far too early'. He notes the trend of late to huge investments in high-tech cellars: 'They're good for the industry and its image but no guarantee of quality; terroir, micro-climate and viticulture count the most.'

★★★★ **Syrah** Considerable power within svelte frame of **03** (★★★★☆) wowed *Wine Spectator* palates: 91 pts, 'Smart Buy' status – & sold out … Follow-up **04** (from own grapes) proffers arresting perfumes, white pepper spice. Big up front, but without resonating length of **03**, a beauty; gentian tones add thrill, subtlety, to balance & power of finish. Dbnville, Swtland grapes support home vyds. Fr & Am oak 14 mths, 30% new.

★★★★ **Boschkloof Reserve** Usually a special selection, a vehicle for cellar's entire cab & merlot crush in excellent **01** (★★★★☆): enticing truffle nose heralds rich mouthful of gleaming fruit on supple frame, super length of finish. Fine tannins will protect until 2010. 70/30 blend. **00** (78/22) also a sleeper at first. **99** (87/13) deeply concentrated. 2 yrs Fr oak, 80% new.

★★★★ **Cabernet Sauvignon-Merlot** ✓ Stylish, accessible blend, easier – not lesser – than Reserve. **03** appealing dark choc flourish to plum/red berry fruits, all drawn together with tingling austerity, gliding elegance. More merlot (40%) than firm **02** (30%) with tarry notes in satisfying finish. 16 mths Fr oak, 20% new.

Cabernet Sauvignon ★★★ Measured house elegance woven into lighter **02**; palate texture leads covert fruit, 14.5% alc. **Merlot** ★★★ **02** sappy vinosity lends austerity to quiet berry fruit, no loud choc-nut flavours of pvs. **Chardonnay** ★★★★ **04** retains bold styling – butterscotch fruit & 14% alc in dry finish – in spite of reduced (20%) new Fr oak. *– DS*

Boschrivier Cellar

Stanford ▪ Est 1997 ▪ 1stB 2002 ▪ Closed to public ▪ Owner NJT de Villiers ▪ Viti consultant Mike Dobrovic, with Clinton le Sueur (both Jan 2002) ▪ Viticulturist Johan van der Merwe ▪ 14 ha (cab, shiraz) ▪ 367 cs 100% red ▪ PO Box 809 Caledon 7230 ▪ drmjtdevilliers@mweb.co.za ▪ www.boschrivier.co.za ▪ ***T (023) 347·3313*** *F (023) 342·2215*

Vinified for paediatrician Theo de Villiers by Mulderbosch's Mike Dobrovic, Boschrivier Shiraz attempts to emulate the inky-coloured, spicy northern Rhône wines. A cellar on the farm Boskloof, inherited by De Villiers in 1997 as a wheat-and-onion concern dating back to the 18th century and renowned in the early 1900s for its must-wine, remains a dream … for now.

Shiraz ★★★★ No follow up yet to **02**, with retiring wool-oil nose, expansive huckleberry fruit tinged with cassia, roast spice. Soft, easy, approachable. 18 mths Fr oak, 50% new. *– DS*

Boschveld *see* Baarsma
Bosman's Hill *see* Saxenburg

Botha Wine Cellar

Rawsonville (see Worcester map) ▪ Est 1949 ▪ 1stB 1974 ▪ Tasting & sales Mon-Fri 7.30-5.30 Sat 9-1 ▪ Closed Easter Fri/Sun, Dec 25 & Jan 1 ▪ Tours by appt ▪ BYO picnic ▪ Facilities for children ▪ Tourgroups ▪ Conservation area ▪ Owners 71 members ▪ Manager/cellarmaster JC 'Dassie' Smith (Nov 1996) ▪ Winemakers Johan Linde & Michiel Visser (Nov 1996/Nov 1999), with Pierre Hugo & Jacobus Brink ▪ Viticulturist Francois Nel (Nov 2000) ▪ 1 775 ha ▪ 31 000 tons 30% red 70% white ▪ PO Box 30 Botha 6857 ▪ bothawyn@mweb.co.za ▪ ***T (023) 355·1740/498*** *▪ F (023) 355·1615*

No update available on this winery; contact details and wine notes from previous edition.

Dassie's Reserve range

Cabernet Sauvignon ★★★ **02** whiffs currant jam & tobacco; dry powdery tannins, obvious wood, lacks polish. Fr barriques, as are all these reds. **Merlot** ★★★ Some complexity on nose of **02**, but vanilla oak dominates palate, ends with firm acidity. **Pinotage** ★★★★ Oak/acid better handled here; **02** plum jam/spice tones complemented by wood, spicy dry finish. **Shiraz** ★★★★ **02** attractive peppery red-berry nose, mocha from oak, classy. **Chardonnay** ★★ **04** starts auspiciously with fresh apple & pear whiffs, turns slightly coarse & phenolic on palate. **Chenin Blanc** ★★★ **04** aromatically subdued but well fruited, lively & light. **Colombard** ★★★★ **04** one of their best; appealing & forthcoming, bolstered by well-hidden 10g/ℓ sugar. **Sauvignon Blanc** ★★★★ Crushed nettles & mown lawn on **04**, attractively taut & austere. **Special Late Harvest** ★★ Last tasted was lightish **02**, tropical fruit flavours & light bottle-age.

Standard range

Following reds unwooded. **Cabernet Sauvignon** ★★★ **04** punchy, but tannins well managed, in harmony with fruit. **Merlot** ★★★ **04** vibrant mulberry jam nose, palate tight & grainy, slightly under-ripe. **Pinotage** ★★★ **04** Aussie-style fruit-bomb made of mulberries. **Shiraz** **04** sample too unformed to rate. **Dassie's Rood** ★★★ **03** swiggable braai companion from mainly cinsaut, dollops cab & ruby cab. **Blanc de Blanc** ★★ **03** bone-dry equal mix colombard, chenin, crouchen. **Special Late Harvest** ★★ **04** honeyed & very sweet chenin & hanepoot, with light barley sugar softness. **Chardonnay Brut** ★★★ Refreshing dry carbonated sparkling with busy, creamy bubbles. **Chardonnay Demi-sec** ★★★ Appealing, not over-sweet sparkling with masses of prickly bubbles. Both sparklers **NV**. **Hanepoot**

Jerepigo ★★★★ Gorgeous **02** fortified dessert, billows jasmine & honeysuckle, hugely sweet & raisiny. **Red Jerepigo** ★★★ **02** full-sweet, redolent of treacle & fruit cordial. 16% alc. **Ruby Port** ★★★★ **99** spirity & warming, with dryish finish. **Late Bottled Vintage** ★★★★ **98** equal blend pinotage, shiraz, ruby cab; characterful & appealing. Matured 300ℓ Fr oak. All WO Wrcstr/Brde Rvr Vlly.—*TM*

Bottelary Hills Wines

*Est/1stB 2003 • Tasting, sales & tours see Bellevue, Goede Hoop, Groenland, Kaapzicht & Mooiplaas • Owners Bottelary Hills Wines (Pty) Ltd • 70% red 30% white • PO Box 42 Koelenhof 7605 • kaapzicht@mweb.co.za • www.bottelaryhills.co.za • **T 906·1620** • F 903·6286*

Six wineries (Kaapzicht, Bellevue, Goede Hoop, Mooiplaas, Groenland and Sterhuis) in Stellenbosch's Bottelary Hills are the drivers behind the premium Bottelary Hills range and the second label M23 (the road runs through it). Individual 'estate' labels remain, but the B-H offerings, blended from contributions by participating wineries, are intended to help establish the Bottelary Wine Route as a distinctive area where 'the terroir is reflected in the wines'. To date the Bottelary Hills Cab-Pinotage and Shiraz; and the M23 Cab-Merlot, Rhapsody (cinsaut, cab, merlot), Sauvignon and Limerick (chenin, sauvignon).

Bottelary Winery International

*Stellenbosch • Tasting & sales Mon-Fri 8-5.30 Sat 9-1 • Closed Easter Fri & Sat, Dec 25 & Jan 1 • Tours by appt • Light meals during office hours • Private functions after-hours/weekends by appt • Owner Perdeberg Winefarmers' Co-op • Winemakers Kobus de Kock, Ewald Kellerman & Pieter Carstens, with Jehan de Jongh (all Aug 2004) • Viticulturist Stephan Joubert (2004) • ±3 000 tons own vyds 100 000 cs 48% red 48% white 4% rosé • Also exported as Rocco Bay • PO Box 214 Paarl 7620 • bottelary@mweb.co.za • **T 865·2781** • F 865·2780*

Under the stewardship of Perdeberg Co-op, Bottelary Winery is once again open for tastings of its own brands, Rocco Bay and Bottelary Winery. 'Established in 1948, the winery went into hibernation several years ago,' explains cellarmaster Kobus de Kock. 'But the roots of history run deep, and it was only a matter of time before Bottelary re-emerged. Energy and enthusiasm are blended with experience and patience. The old is merged with the new.' He believes in keeping things as natural as possible to produce 'quality wines at affordable prices'.

Reserve range

Cabernet Sauvignon ★★★★ Modern yet elegant **03**, combines fruit richness with restraint & seriousness; deserves yr/2 to show its best. 14 mths Fr/Am small-oak (ditto all Rsv reds). **Merlot** ★★★★ Supple tannins underpin **02**, impart backbone to ripe red/black fruit & platform for growth; pity to open too soon. **Pinotage** ★★★★ **02** a polished performance; delicious black cherry fruit, elegant dry tannins, tangy sweet-sour touch. **Shiraz** ★★★★ **02** ripe red fruit firmly supported by savoury tannins, twist liquorice in tail. Good potential. **Sauvignon Blanc** new ★★★ Still vibrant, fruitily persistent **04**, passionfruit & gooseberry combo, well-balanced acidity.

Bottelary range

Cinsaut-Shiraz ☺ ★★★ **03** lively, jovial 70/30 blend; smooth & seamless without being simple. **Chenin Blanc Dry** ☺ ★★★ Ideal summer picnic wine; **04** ripe pear & apple flavours; refreshing & zesty.

Reds in this range unoaked. **Cabernet Sauvignon** ★★★ Spicy, juicy **03** well-made, unpretentious, light-textured (despite 14% alc). **Shiraz** ★★★ **03** forthright & attractive expression of the variety; smooth, friendly tannins. easy-drinking. **Cabernet Sauvignon-Merlot** ★★★ **04** modern fruity styling, satisfying; juicy black fruit, easy tannins for standalone or food partnering. **Sauvignon Blanc** ★★★ **04** flagging a bit; drink soon. **Hanepoot Jerepiko 05** untasted. Both ranges WO Coastal.—*JN*

Bouchard Finlayson

Walker Bay ▪ Est 1989 ▪ 1stB 1991 ▪ Tasting & sales Mon-Fri 9-5 Sat 9.30-12.30 ▪ Fee R20 for groups of 8+ ▪ Closed pub hols ▪ Owner Bouchard Finlayson (Pty) Ltd ▪ Winemaker/viticulturist Peter Finlayson ▪ 17 ha (pinot, nebbiolo, sangiovese, chard, sauvignon) ▪ 180 tons 12 000 cs 20% red 80% white ▪ PO Box 303 Hermanus 7200 ▪ info@bouchardfinlayson.co.za ▪ www.bouchardfinlayson.co.za ▪ ***T (028) 312·3515*** *▪ F (028) 312·2317*

After 25 years in the Hemel-en-Aarde Valley, Peter Finlayson can look back on 'a journey fulfilled', as well as 'a multitude of personal escapades'. Last harvest's adventure was a burst tyre, resulting in a load of grapes for their acclaimed Kaaimansgat Chardonnay landing on the tar outside Hermanus. 'We saved about two thirds of the grapes, perhaps this year to be called Crash Chardonnay!' As a new architect-designed homestead neared completion at press time, Finlayson was excited about having 'a beautiful venue to complement the superlative wines'. Ever practical, however, he's more excited that he'll have access to a hot shower when 'inconveniences' occur, such as receiving the odd blast of grape juice from the press. 'Must just remember to keep a fresh change of clothing at hand....'

★★★★☆ **Galpin Peak Pinot Noir** A leading Cape example with grip & substance; more recently softer in style with riper – yet exemplary – red berry fruit moderating classic pinot tension. Burgundy remains the spiritual home here, & it shows. **03** luxurious creamy texture cradles pithy black cherry fruit, plushness carries through to taut finish. **02** less oaky, more elegant than muscular **01**. Own vyds, concentrated yield 1kg grapes/vine. Steadily diminishing new oak (now only 30%), 10 mths.

★★★★★ **Tête de Cuvée Galpin Peak Pinot Noir** Cellarmaster's barrel selection in best yrs, strenuously oaked (75% new Burgundian barrels, 14 mths). Last was terrific **01**, redolent of truffles; velvet texture of super-fine tannins. Garlands aplenty. Not revisited for this ed.

★★★★ **Hannibal** Substantial power of Cape's first sangiovese-led blend threaded with finesse. Pinot & 'Mediterranean partners' – nebbiolo, mourvèdre, barbera – add interest. Exotic toasted sesame aromas lead to juicy fruit in **03**; succulence aplenty within muscular structure. **02** gentler, well-ordered forest-floor fruits ready earlier. Tank-fermented, matured 14-16 mths Fr oak, quarter new.

★★★★ **Missionvale Chardonnay** A fitting white flagship – complete, substantial, yet carries house's understated, elegant stamp. **04** burnished golden hue; nutty nose, mineral refinement in undulating finish; enough freshness, verve to joust with the opulence. Equally unflashy **03** replete with finesse. Home grapes, barrel-fermented/matured 6 mths, 25% new.

★★★★ **Kaaimansgat Chardonnay** ('Crocodile's Lair') High, cool Villiersdorp mountain grapes massaged into most overt style of the trio: vanilla butter nose, ripe fruit tempered by lime twist in **04**. Like gravelly **03**, not gauche – carries 14% alc well. Barrel-fermented, 8 mths oak, 25% new. WO Overberg, as is following.

★★★★ **Sans Barrique Chardonnay** Less complicated & unoaked: clean, fresh fruit to the fore. **04** initially quiet, citrus flavours without flab. Refreshing: dash sauvignon, shorter lees contact (now 5 mths), no malo. **03** filled out into a beauty.

Sauvignon Blanc ★★★☆ Pvs were 'always crisp, never outspoken', but in louder style since **04**. **05** herbaceous whiffs, litchi flesh, tingling dry finish. **Blanc de Mer** ★★★☆ **05** intriguing blend of steely riesling, flinty sauvignon with unoaked pinot blanc & chardonnay adding flesh; consummate aperitif. Tangy, invigorating. WO Overberg. *– DS*

Bouwland

Stellenbosch ▪ Est 1996 ▪ 1stB 1997 ▪ Tasting & sales at Beyerskloof ▪ Owners Bouwland Deelnemings Trust & Beyerskloof ▪ Winemaker Beyers Truter, with Anri Truter (1997/2004) ▪ Viti consultant Johan Pienaar (2003) ▪ 40 ha (cab, merlot, pinotage) ▪ 350 tons 30 000 cs 90% red 10% white ▪ PO Box 62 Koelenhof 7605 ▪ bouwland@adept.co.za ▪ ***T 865·2135*** *▪ F 865·2683*

Still making use of Beyerskloof's facilities, this early and successful empowerment winery would dearly love to have its own offices and tasting area. 'We're enormously grateful to

Beyers Truter and company for their help,' says marketing manager Veronica Campher, 'but at some time or another we must learn to stand on our own feet.' With that in mind, they're working hard at local marketing – participating in all the big shows including the first Soweto Wine Festival as well as WineX in Johannesburg and Cape Town – and going abroad to expos like the WOSA Mega Tasting in London. Production-wise, they have a varietal pinotage and a Cape blend in the pipeline.

Cabernet Sauvignon-Merlot ★★★☆ Versatile dinner companion or solo sipper. **03** intrigues with green olive aromas, leather & pleases with supple tannin, smooth/dry finish. Light oaking (6- 8 mths) gently backs up opulent red/black berries. 13.6% alc is considerably lower than pvs. **Chenin Blanc** ★★★ No follow up to easy-drinking **03**. Tasted mid-2004 had honey, dried grass, pear-drop aromas. Freshly flavoursome, but not overly fruity, & balanced. *— MM*

Bovlei Winery

Wellington ▪ Est 1907 ▪ Tasting & sales Mon-Fri 8.30-5 Sat 8.30-12.30 Non-religious pub hols 9-4.30 ▪ Tours by appt ▪ Olive & grape seed products ▪ Owners 39 members ▪ Winemaker Hendrik de Villiers (Dec 1996) ▪ Viti consultant Dawie le Roux ▪ 560 ha (cab, merlot, shiraz, chard) ▪ 120 000 cs own labels + 920k ℓ bulk ▪ 40% red 60% white ▪ PO Box 82 Wellington 7654 ▪ wines@bovlei.co.za ▪ www.bovlei.co.za ▪ ***T 873·1567/864·1283*** *▪ F 864·1483*

With distribution partner Vinimark, historically export-orientated Bovlei has launched a concerted drive to market its wines locally. The results to date, reports production manager Frank Meaker, are encapsulated in the winery's slogan: 'Above Expectations'. An on-going focus is to add value to what Meaker describes as the 'exceptional quality fruit' produced by the winery's growers, whose vineyards are scattered about the greater Wellington area. Shiraz, he believes, is the undiscovered jewel, but with correct vine management merlot, cab, chenin, chardonnay and sauvignon all have potential to yield 'classic, complex wines'. In line with its value-added campaign, Bovlei is involved with a number of high-flying projects, including Stormhoek, African Pride and Cape Coastal Vintners.

Reserve range

Merlot ★★★ **03** more elegant than pvs, sympathetically wooded, alc a much more manageable 13%. Currently reclusive fruit should emerge over next yr/2. Small barrel matured, portion new. **Shiraz** ★★★ **03** scaled down, less effusive version of pvs; still shows ripe fruit, sweet tannins for early enjoyment. Oak as for Merlot. **Cabernet Sauvignon-Merlot** ★★★☆ **02** last yr showed classic claret tone, clean oak backing, ripe fruity tannins; few more yrs cellaring will help realise its potential. **Chardonnay** ★★ **04** demure compared with pvs; slight peaches & cream hint, attractive oaking (40% barrel fermented/aged 6 mths, 3rd fill), must be enjoyed soon. **Sauvignon Blanc** ★★ **04** lively nose of ripe tropical fruit unmatched by restrained, somewhat downbeat palate.

Bovlei range

Reds in this range lightly wooded. **Cabernet Sauvignon** ★★☆ **04** honest, well-made cab. Soft & rounded, good everyday drink. **Merlot** new ★★ Early-drinking **04**, shy red fruit aromas, relatively firm tannin, sweet-sour finish. **Grand Rouge** ★★☆ Bdx-style blend merlot/cab f showing red berry/choc fruit; **03** soft & effortless. **Pinotage** ★★ Classic mulberries & plums on **04**, noticeably firm dry tannins, better in yr/2 or with food. **Shiraz** ★★☆ Most approachable of these reds; **04** sweet fruited, slightly smoky, toasty backing from well-executed oak staving. **Pinotage Rosé** new ★★ Pale cerise **05**, youthfully fresh & appealing, light, its sweetness well balanced by keen acidity. **Chardonnay** ★☆ **04** light tropical tones with honeyed notes; pleasing, but not for further keeping. **Chenin Blanc** ★★ **05** light in body/flavour this yr; fleeting lemon hints, clean & dry. **Sauvignon Blanc** ★☆ Light-bodied/flavoured **03** some tropical tones, crisp dry finish. 12.5% alc. **Beaukett** new ★★ Medium-sweet muscat/chenin blend with delicate honeysuckle perfume, pleasantly rounded soft flavours. **Port** ★★ Ruby-style **NV** offers fresh ripe-plum flavour, as expected from ruby cab (50%, with cab f, roobernet & grenache); traditional low fortification (15.3%). **Bukettraube** discontinued. *— DH*

BoweJoubert see Beau Joubert
Bradgate see Jordan

Brahms see Domaine Brahms
Brampton see Rustenberg

Brandvlei Cellar

Worcester ▪ Est 1955 ▪ 1stB 1956 ▪ Tasting & sales Mon-Thu 7.30–12.30; 1.30–5.30 (doors close 4.30 on Fri) ▪ Closed pub hols ▪ Tours & group tastings by appt ▪ BYO picnic ▪ Owners 32 members ▪ Manager/winemaker Jean le Roux, with Jandré Human & Tertius Jonck ▪ Viticulturist Danie Conradie (2005) ▪ 1 400 ha (13 varieties r/w) ▪ 10 000 cs own label 20% red 75% white 10% jerepiko ▪ PO Box 595 Worcester 6849 ▪ brandvlei@cybertrade.co.za ▪ www.brandvlei.co.za www.bcwines.co.za ▪ ***T/F (023) 340·4215/4108*** *▪ F (023) 340·4332*

There were 'ripe grapes galore' clamouring at this Worcester winery's doors last harvest, despite a 24% drop in crop volume. The vines delivering this bounty are now the responsibility of viticulturist Danie Conradie, who joined from Villiersdorp Cellar in time to savour the news of the creditable 3-star rating at the Chenin Challenge for their bargain priced 04. The wine-making mantra here continues to be 'honest, fresh and fruity wines' (only 2% of production gets bottled under the BC label, the rest is sold in bulk).

BC range

Ruby Cabernet-Merlot ★★★ Always a happy marriage; **04** 60/40 blend, lightly wooded; ripe plum flavour, floral scents, subtle toasty touch. **Chardonnay** ★★★ **05** not ready. **04** sweet fruit tastily melded with butterscotch & vanilla. **Chenin Blanc** ★★ **05** smooth, fresh & frisky, with light 12.8% alc. **Sauvignon Blanc** ★★ A top seller here; **05**, like pvs, picked early for racy freshness & low alc. **Bacchanté** ★★ Zesty **05** semi-sweet white from chenin, drop colombard; fresh & easy to drink. **Hanepoot Jerepiko** ★★★★ ✓ **05** tangy citrus/honeysuckle aroma; well-managed sweetness & alc. For delicious aperitif, pour over crushed ice. **Sec Sparkling** discontinued. *DH*

Bredell's see JP Bredell

Breeland Winery

Rawsonville ▪ Closed to public ▪ PO Box 109 Rawsonville 6845 ▪ mlalee@xpoint.co.za ▪ ***T/F (023) 344·3137***

No update available on this winery; contact details from previous edition.

Brenthurst Winery

Paarl ▪ Est 1993 ▪ 1stB 1994 ▪ Open to public only by special appt ▪ Owner/winemaker José Jordaan, with viti consultant Johan Wiese (1991) & other advisers ▪ 5 ha (cabs s/f, merlot, petit v) ▪ 50–70 tons ▪ PO Box 6091 Paarl 7622 ▪ ***T 863·1154/1375*** *▪ F 424·5666*

No update available on this winery; contact details from previous edition.

Britz Vineyards see Under Oaks
Broken Rock see Arlington, Riebeek Cellars
Broken Stone see Slaley
Bryde see ACJ Fine Wines

Buck's Ridge Wines & Olives

Tulbagh ▪ Est 2005 ▪ Visits by appt ▪ Self-catering cottages & camping site ▪ Olives & olive products ▪ Walks, mountain biking & other attractions (see intro) ▪ Owners Brendon & Sue McHugh ▪ Winemaker/viticulturist Brendon McHugh, with Craig Bianco ▪ 10 ha (cab, mourvèdre, petit v, shiraz, zin, viognier) ▪ 2555 cs (est) 80% red 20% white ▪ PO Box 222 Tulbagh 6820 ▪ info@bucksridge.co.za ▪ www.bucksridge.co.za ▪ ***T (023) 230·1160*** *▪ F (023) 230·0444*

Not content with the tranquillity that pervades their Tulbagh property, Wild Olive Farm owners Brendon and Sue McHugh decided to up the stress levels a notch and established their first shiraz and cab sauvignon vineyards in 2003. Three years and several plantings including viognier, mourvèdre and relatively rare zinfandel later, their Buck's Ridge label is nearly ready for its maiden showing. '2005 was my very first vintage and there were many stressful moments, as you can well imagine,' says Brendon M. 'Well worth it,' you may say as you sample the 70/30 tank and barrel fermented 2005 Chenin Blanc while strolling past a flock of wild geese or unwind with a relaxing Shiraz in one of the beautiful Cape Dutch guest cottages on the farm.

Bugatti's see De Compagnie

Buitenverwachting

Constantia ▪ Est 1796 ▪ 1stB 1985 ▪ Tasting & sales Mon-Fri 9-5 Sat 9-1 ▪ Closed pub hols ▪ Tours by appt ▪ Buitenverwachting Restaurant Mon-Sat ▪ T 794·3522. Summer only: Café Petite for light lunches (tel as above) & picnic baskets by appt ▪ T 083·257·6083 ▪ Teddy Bear Fair May 1; Valentine's Day Picnic ▪ Conferences ▪ Owners Richard & Sieglinde (Christine) Mueller, Lars Maack ▪ Winemaker Hermann Kirschbaum (Dec 1992) ▪ Vineyards Peter Reynolds (Jun 1997), advised by Johan Pienaar ▪ 120 ha (cabs s/f, merlot, pinot, chard, sauvignon, riesling) ▪ 1 300 tons 90 000 cs 18% red 80% white 1% rosé 1% sparkling ▪ PO Box 281 Constantia 7848 ▪ info@buitenverwachting.com ▪ www.buitenverwachting.com ▪ ***T 794·5190*** *▪ F 794·1351*

Constantia's strength, sauvignon, seems to be Buitenverwachting's patron grape, and it is the capacity of their examples to evolve over time that fascinates Lars Maack. (A 96 took Museum Class trophy at the Trophy Show.) 'Our approach,' he says, 'is diametrically opposed to the "show young, die early" school of winemaking, with attractive but short-term fruit and no site-specific character.' Unsurprisingly, they're planting more sauvignon where red varieties once grew. The potential of these new blocks got a public thumbs-up when the Hussey's Vlei took Veritas gold. The installation of smaller tanks will allow for more experimentation and the chance to develop site-specific strengths by vinifying smaller batches. Brad Paton has joined as stalwart winemaker Hermann Kirschbaum's assistant, bringing with him seven years' experience in Germany, including studies at Geisenheim.

★★★★★ **Christine** A Cape fixture as one of its best classically minded bdx-style blends. **00** bigger, deeper, riper & sweeter fruited than **99**, took good few yrs to even start revealing its authoritative, richly firm best. **01** organises merlot, cabs s/f (40/36/20) & dollop malbec into a particularly fine, impressive whole, whose appealing, developing bouquet presages a deep, ripe-fruited but subtle palate; majestically balanced, coping well with big 14.5% alc & ±22 mths new Fr oak. Should have a long, happy future.

★★★★ **Merlot** Typically unshowy, elegant **00** revealed plenty of spicy, plummy charm; powerful 14.5% alc, yet harmonious & very drinkable. **01** in same tradition, perhaps a little less potent (beneficially so), with sweetly ripe flavours packed round firm but far from austere core. Will develop for few yrs, keep longer. Wood as for Cab.

★★★★ **Cabernet Sauvignon** Dark, deep, ripe **00** had cedar & blackcurrant dominating savoury balance in youth. *Wine* ★★★★★. Slightly lower alc (14%), & well-judged oak (18+ mths mix 1st/2nd fill) contribute to harmony of splendid **01** (★★★★★). Restrained but lovely, forceful fruit, excellent structure. Ready to drink, thanks to farm's comparatively late release policy, but should easily last out its decade.

★★★★ **Sauvignon Blanc 04** now shows understated but lingering scents/flavours dried grass, passionfruit; bright well-balanced acidity. Sample **05** promises more of the same – perhaps a little fruitier in its youth, with intense savour. Good food wines: satisfyingly dry, moderate 13% alc. **03** got *WS* 90 pts.

★★★★ **Husseys Vlei Sauvignon Blanc** new **04** selection from particular vyd's contribution to above. Rather bigger & bolder, more pungent green-tinged flavours.

★★★★ **Chardonnay** Forward, lightly toasty aromas/flavours on **04**, with lime marmalade notes; rich creaminess veined with enlivening acid, good dry finish. As with well balanced juicy & silky **03** (*WS* 90), two thirds fermented/11 mths oak (80% new); all through malo.

★★★★★ **Husseys Vlei Chardonnay** new **04** vyd-based selection of above. More elegant, less toasty (though 100% new oak), oatmeal & floral nose. Lovely balance, silky-smooth, long subtle flavours.

★★★★ **Semillon** new Flavourful, crisp, very approachable **03**, with cool-climate character. ±15% wooded, ultra-ripe sauvignon inventively added to augment richness, complexity. Like most of this cellar's wines, will partner & not overwhelm fine food.

★★★★ **Rhine Riesling Noble Late Harvest** Beautiful pale gold **02** with aromas of honey, pineapple, peach when last tried. Lightly, seductively delicious, with filigree acidity. Fermented/6 mths oak.

Meifort ✓ ★★★★ Second-best but serious, blend of cab (68%) some cab f, a little merlot; **01** particularly approachable, with ripe fruit but firmly structured as ever. **Pinot Noir** ★★★ No follow-up yet to earthy, chunkily acidic **01**. **Blanc de Noir** ★★★ The blanc being a pretty strawberry pink, the noirs in particularly good **05** being from juice run off fine quality cabs s/f, merlot. Bright fragrant fruitiness, tannic allusions: dry & delicious. **Coastal Chenin Blanc** new ★★★ As name implies, partly from non-home vyds. Good flavours, nicely rounded, but a touch clumsy with bright, hard finish. **Coastal Sauvignon Blanc** ★★★ new to guide, but not to some overseas markets. **05** has lightly tropical aromas, gently fruity & pleasantly fresh. **Buiten Blanc** ★★★★ Big-volume, reliably delicious sauvignon-based blend, with some chenin & drop of riesling. **05** overflows with fresh flavours, easy charm. WO W Cape. **Gewürztraminer** ★★★★ Characteristic rose-petal fragrance, flavours noted last yr on maiden **03**, but more elegant than many, with serious but gently balanced palate. Lightly oaked, almost dry. **Rhine Riesling** ★★★★ **05** attractively aromatic, redolent of peach & crisp apple, freshly balanced and lip-smacking. Effectively only just off-dry, balanced with light 10.8% alc – 'enough high alcohol wines around these days', says Hermann K. **Brut MCC** ★★★★ **NV** bubbly from 66/44 pinot/chard, latest with lovely spiced apple & brioche character, drily elegant but ending with sweet-sour hint. **Natural Sweet** ★★★★ Last-tasted **02** from riesling offered pineapple, honey, nuts & terpene notes in a fine balance that's lightly sweet, lovely to sip. 90g/ℓ sugar; 12% alc; unobtrusively wooded. – *TJ*

BunduStar see Vin-X-Port
Bushman's Creek see Cru Wines
Bush Vines see Cloof

Buthelezi Wines

*Cape Town ▪ Est/1stB 2002 ▪ Closed to public ▪ Owner/winemaker Khulekani Laurence Buthelezi ▪ 800 cs 100% red ▪ PO Box 12481 Mill Street Cape Town 8010 ▪ buthelezi@winery.co.za ▪ **T 461·9590** ▪ F 465·0342*

Laurence Buthelezi is proud of his Tutuka shiraz, now exported to the US and France. The wine sells on its inherent quality, not as the object of 'ethnic curiosity' or political correctness, as he feels is the case with some black empowerment labels. He lauds the joint SAWIT and French government program to train previously disadvantaged SA winemakers, having successfully completed another theoretical and practical stint in the heart of Burgundy. This, with mentoring from Jean-Vincent Ridon (of Signal Hill), has reinforced his winemaking approach of minimum intervention and judicious oaking. His increased knowledge and experience enabled him to meet the challenges of the difficult 2005 harvest, with production now doubled to 800 cases.

Tutuka Syrah ★★★ Where pvs vintages more muscular, **04** is fragrant, even perfumed: cassis, liquorice, violets & incense all leap out of the glass; soft flavours, textures, though active tannins appear on finish, will need ±yr to soften. 16 mths older Fr oak, 14% alc. WO W Cape. – *JP*

BWC Wines

*Paarl ▪ Est/1stB 1997 ▪ Tasting by appt ▪ Owners Jeff Jolly, Cathy Marshall, Greg Mitchell & Peter Oxenham ▪ Winemaker Cathy Marshall (1997) ▪ 40 tons ▪ 2 500 cs + 300 cs for Woolworths ▪ 75% red 25% white ▪ 2 Blaauwklippen Meent, Paradyskloof, Stellenbosch 7600 ▪ info@bwcwines.co.za ▪ www.bwcwines.co.za ▪ **T/F 880·2579***

Great delight here. Winemaker and genial force behind the peripatetic BWC, Cathy Marshall, reports the group is joining with eight like-minded producers (read: independent, explorative, passionate) to establish a permanent home. It will feature a 'studio' winery, restaurant, rose nursery and wine sales venue open to the public, all on a beautiful site. Over a decade of foot-stomping harvests, BWC has grown from one to 40 tons. Newly contracted vineyards (in Elgin and Somerset West) are taking quality up another notch; Pinot sales have jumped (courtesy of Hollywood's wine-themed *Sideways*?); Sauvignon production has doubled; and the Syrah continues to charm its way into export markets. Last heard, the travel-hungry Marshall was hot-footing it to Burgundy, northern Rhône and Argentina.

★★★★ **Pinot Noir** Cathy M constantly seeks different vyds to 'push complexity envelope'. Incipient in **04** ex-Darling/Stbosch (so WO Coastal), elegant yet with great presence. Fresh raspberry/cherry fragrance, complementary bright, savoury acid, mere suggestion toasty oak (yr Fr). Touch more ethereal than **03**, from Stbosch, Elgin, Darling, which supple & smoothly approachable. Both with potential to ±2007/09.

★★★★ **Syrah** No **04**, but **03** still on the menu. Offers elegant concentration of smoky meat, spice, red fruits aromas; compact, long & savoury flavours. Potential to 2009/11. Fr oak 11 mths. **01** *Wine* ★★★★. Same Paarl vyd as Ridgeback.

Wholeberry Cabernet Sauvignon new ★★★★ Supple-textured **03** with splash merlot (15%); rich plum/walnut flavours; subtle wooding in tune with overall harmony. 24 mths Fr oak. **Sauvignon Blanc** ★★★★ Bright passion fruit/fig exotica on vibrant, steely **05**. Whistle-clean; purity/freshness maintained under attractive screwcap packaging. WO Stbosch. **Myriad** ★★★ Part-fermented, brandy-fortified pinot/merlot, handmade (& 60 pairs feet!). **02** plum pudding character, gentle glow in tail. —*AL*

Cabrière Estate

Franschhoek • Est 1982 • 1stB 1984 • Tasting Mon-Fri 8.30-4.30 Sat & pub hols 10.30-4 Fee R15 for 3 wines • Formal tasting/tour Mon-Fri 11 & 3 Fee R25 p/p • Private tasting/tour (pre-booked) Fee R30 p/p • Achim vA's tasting/tour Sat 11 Fee R25 p/p • Closed Good Fri, Dec 25 & Jan 1 • Haute Cabrière Cellar Restaurant (see Eat-out section) • Tourgroups • Conferencing for groups of fewer than 60 • Owner Clos Cabrière Ltd • Cellarmaster Achim von Arnim (1984), with Takuan von Arnim • Viticulturist Sakkie Lourens (May 2002) • 24 ha (pinot, chardonnay) • 500 000ℓ 40% red 60% white • PO Box 245 Franschhoek 7690 • cabriere@iafrica.com • www.cabriere.co.za • ***T 876·8500*** • *F 876·8501*

Cabrière, the first estate to specialise in traditional-method sparkling wine, celebrated its 21st anniversary in 2005. 'And the show must go on,' says the irrepressible Achim von Arnim, who this year celebrates a personal milestone – his 60th birthday – by launching a book of own poetry and art. Called 'Naked', it promises to contain 'lots of flavours and surprises' – just like his now-legendary tour and tasting on Saturday mornings. He and wife Hildegard still share their enthusiasm for 'Sun, Soil, Vine, Man' personally with visitors, and, with son Takuan as assistant cellarmaster, it promises to become even more of a family affair.

Arnim Sauvignon Rouge ★★★ Asparagus (!) whiffs on latest version of this easy/early drinking 'rosé', **NV** blend unoaked cab & sauvignon (60/40) ex-Bonnievale (so WO W Cape). Bouncy sauvignon palate brought to earth by firm cab tannins. Serve chilled. NE, as is P-J range below.

Haute Cabrière range

★★★★ **Pinot Noir** Burgundian clones, densely planted (10 000 vines/ha), gently handled in cellar, ±10 mths Fr oak, 35% new. **03** (★★★) textbook cherry/tea leaf aromas, elegant acidity; characterful but less fruit/substance than pvs (13.5% vs 14% alc). Lightly chill & serve with oysters, suggests AvA. **02** more generous, with juicy cherry palate.

Chardonnay-Pinot Noir ★★★ Interesting, food-cordial alternative to ubiquitous 100% chardonnay. **05** elegant tropical fruit & citrus aromas, palate fleshed out with touch sugar & fruity substance of pinot (51% of blend).

Pierre Jourdan range

Mostly traditionally made cap classiques from chardonnay and/or pinot, named for estate's French Huguenot founder. **NV** unless noted; bunch-pressed; unoaked; alc ±12%.

★★★★ **Cuvée Reserve** Rich, satisfying, chardonnay/pinot blend (60/40) from first fraction (500ℓ) of press juice. Officially NV, but mostly from single vintage, currently 98. Enchanting cream & honey nose; languid introduction glides to long, rousing lime finish. Whisper of fruit-sweetness (actual sugar only 4.5g/ℓ). Admirable complexity from 5+ yrs on lees (disgorged on demand). No rush to uncork.

★★★★ **Cuvée Belle Rose** SA's first rosé MCC; a charmer from 100% pinot, fruit ex-estate & Frhoek Valley. Latest from 03 vintage (as last two digits on base of bottle indicate). Distinct strawberry & mushroom tones; slightly more assertive than pvs. Best enjoyed soonish – this wine needs its freshness to really shine.

★★★★☆ **Blanc de Blancs** Made exclusively from top chardonnay vyds, base-wine partly wooded in Fr Argonne barrels, 5-6 mths. Latest incarnation extraordinarily fine: pale, delicate, poised – yet no push-over. Marvellous subtle wet-pebble bouquet, kiss of vanilla; touch drier than pvs at 3.4g/ℓ sugar. Will reward those with patience. 'From a village in the Côtes des Blancs?' wondered participants in a recent blind-tasting in Champagne. 'The village was in Africa!' chortles AvA.

★★★★ **Brut Sauvage** 'Savage' by virtue of its absolute & uncompromising dryness, most unusual in SA. Latest release a gorgeous antique satin hue, rousing mineral tone. Highly seductive (perfect for those who prefer their oysters naked). Same blend/origin as Brut below, but longer on lees (36 mths).

Brut ★★★☆ ✓ Estate's best selling MCC; 60/40 chardonnay/pinot. Vibrant mousse; aromas of pear & 'ocean spray'; good palate weight; emphatic brut finish via minimal 4.5g/ℓ RS. Needn't be broached soon. Available in 375ml, 750ml & 1.5ℓ. **Tranquille** ★★★ This, wine below, the non-sparklers in range. Appealing pale red-gold hue, icing-sugar bouquet & palate. Grip & depth imparted by *première taille* juice (from near end of pressing time). Pinot, chardonnay 55/45; lunchtime light 11.5% alc. **Ratafia** ★★★☆ Jerepigo-style aperitif from chardonnay, fortified with estate's (chardonnay) potstill brandy. Latest has Golden Delicious apple aroma, mead-like touches, decidedly sweet tail (115g/ℓ RS). 'To be served with foie gras,' instructs AvA. 20% alc. – *CvZ*

Calitzdorp Cellar

Calitzdorp (see Little Karoo map) ▪ Est 1928 ▪ 1stB 1977 ▪ Tasting & sales Mon-Fri 8-1; 2-5 Sat 8-12 ▪ Closed Easter Fri & Dec 25 ▪ Tours by appt ▪ Tourgroups ▪ BYO picnic ▪ Farm produce ▪ Owners 60 members ▪ Winemaker Alwyn Burger (Nov 1990) ▪ Viti consultant Willem Botha ▪ 160 ha (13 varieties, r/w) ▪ 3 000 cs 60% red 30% white ▪ PO Box 193 Calitzdorp 6660 ▪ ***T/F (044) 213·3301***

Like elsewhere, a lower yield for 2005, but its seems that quality in the Little Karoo varied dramatically: some varieties show real promise, but others suffered from rot. Nonetheless, the shifted from quantity to quality, with the purchase of a range of variously sized tanks and, no doubt, plenty of barrels in order to carry out the vital decision to again mature red wines in oak. The team has also realised the importance of marketing, with new labels for the range, a new marketing person on board (welcome to Christell Nel) and a new-found interest in awards (watch the White Muscadel go!).

Blanc de Noir ☺ ★★ Despite 26g/ℓ sugar, **04** ends more off-dry than semi-sweet; lovely apricot whiffs, refreshing acidity for summer tippling.

Merlot ★★ Nose of ripe plums belies lean palate, sweet/sour finish of **04**. **Shiraz** ★★★ **04** everyday quaffer with *garrigue* aromas, plenty fresh fruit flavours; balance. **Touriga Naçional** ★★☆ Food-friendly **04** has earthy/spice in bouquet, pleasing dry tannins on finish. Above all chipped 3 mths, not for keeping. **Chardonnay** ★☆ **04**'s tropical aromas/flavours tiring, mature honey wafts, drink soon. **Sauvignon Blanc** new ★ Faint capsicum/tropical aromas on **05** barely follow onto palate, slightly dilute. Following 3 sweeties 16% alc, all over 220g/ℓ sugar **Golden Jerepigo** ★☆ Syrupy raisin nose & palate, **NV**; technically the driest of the three, this 80/20 blend hannepoot/muscadel is the most cloying. **White Muscadel** ★★★ No raisins on **03**, just honeysuckle & pink roses; alc & zippy acidity add lift to tail. **Hanepoot** ✓ ★★★☆ **04** classiest of the trio of dessert wines. Fresh raisins & honeysuckle in bouquet, lemony acidity ensures freshness; uncloying. **Cape Vintage** ★★ Dark & brooding **03** with savoury/meaty notes, some caramel on nose & palate, fading berry fruit. Appears tired, oxidised. 2 yrs old oak. **Cape Ruby** not tasted. **Chenin Blanc** & **Natural Sweet** discontinued. *— DH*

Camberley Wines

Stellenbosch ▪ Est 1990 ▪ 1stB 1996 ▪ Tasting & sales Mon-Sat & pub hols 9-5 Sun preferably by appt ▪ Fee R5 ▪ Closed Dec 25 & Jan 1 ▪ Tours by appt ▪ B&B guest cottage ▪ Owners John & Gaël Nel ▪ Winemaker John Nel, with Grant Baxter ▪ 7 ha (cabs s/f, merlot, petit v, touriga, shiraz) ▪ ±35 tons 2 500 cs 100% red ▪ PO Box 6120 Uniedal 7612 ▪ john@camberley.co.za ▪ www.camberley.co.za ▪ ***T/F 885·1176***

Sitting in a restaurant and seeing two tables of people drinking their wines was 'kinda cool' for Johnny and Gaël Nel. Now, they're finally able to release their wines the second year after they're made: expensive to achieve, they say, but well worth it. The sorting table was used for the first time last harvest and they're eager to see if there's a detectable improvement in the wines. That's the kind of attention to detail that goes into these wines, made in the elegant style they themselves like to drink. With sales dramatically increased, improvements include 'bigger and better' stemware in the tasting room and two new war-plane pictures added to Johnny Nel's collection.

★★★★ **Cabernet Sauvignon-Merlot 03** shows all nuances vibrant red fruit & superb oaking can bring: roasted nuts, violets, underbrush, without losing fruit intensity. Svelte, with misleadingly accessible fine-grained tannins – 5+ yr future here. 14 mths Fr, half new. 72/28 blend. **02** impressive complexity, silky & accessible. Also 500ml.

★★★★☆ **Shiraz 03** (as per last ed's notes) classically styled, with elegance & verve. Herbaceous, minty tones, merest savoury hint in juicy wild-berry fruit. Framework for long, gentle development. 14 mths Fr/Am oak, 80/20, 40% new. 14.3% alc. Big, complex **02** also for 5-8 yrs development.

★★★★☆ **Philosopher's Stone** Changing base metals – shiraz (75%) & merlot – into gold. Or at least powerful, impressive wine! Maiden **02** (not retasted) had shiraz at centre: white pepper, underbrush, dark fruit; succulence, creamy richness from merlot. 22 mths 2nd fill Fr oak. 14.4% alc. **03** sold out before we could taste.

★★★★ **Merlot** No **03**. **02** well built, soft & mellow, with supple grip from seasoned oak (14 mths).

★★★★ **Charisma** new Innovative blend cab f, shiraz, merlot 65/20/15, with cellar's trademark fruit intensity, ripe tannins. Individual, terrific **03**'s smoke-infused creamy cassis/cherry flavouring has intriguing sweet/sour/savoury effect, setting it apart. 14 mth Fr oak, 50% new helps build 5+ yr cellar-worthy structure.

★★★★☆ **Pinotage 04** barrel sample already seductive; ink-dark, riveting wild berry intensity, voluptuous build to match. Equal Fr/Am/Hungarian oaking (half new, 13 mths) supplies structure, white pepper/dried herb spicing. Massive 16% alc absorbed by flavour richness, bold styling. Ready young, will age well 6-7 yrs. Also 500ml. **03** impressed too – infanticide to be avoided.

Cabernet Franc-Merlot ★★★★ Maiden **02** (tasted last yr) 80/20 blend with raspberry, green walnut, touch mint, dusted with cedar; minerality; lithe, supple tannins. For 4+ yrs. 14 mths mainly Fr oak, 25% new. 14.9% alc. *— CR*

Cameradi Wines

Wellington ▪ Est 1998 ▪ 1stB 2000 ▪ Closed to public ▪ Owners Stelvest cc (Pieter Laubscher, Niel Smith, Nic Swingler, Hendrik du Preez & Casper Lategan) ▪ Winemaker Casper Lategan (Jan 1999) ▪ 8 tons 600 cs 100% red ▪ 48 Bain Str Wellington 7655 ▪ sonellel@telkomsa.net ▪ ***T 873·1225/082 323·4244*** *▪ F 873·4910*

This comradely wine venture, started by five former university pals, hand-crafts very small quantities of reds.

04s bottled too late for inclusion in guide. Neither **03** retasted; following notes & provisional ratings for samples tasted pvs ed: **Cabernet Sauvignon** ★★★ Strapping, daunting tannins & oak flavours which dominate pungent greenpepper/mulberry fruit. **Shiraz** ★★★ **03** impenetrably dark & deep; redolent of black pepper & lily, vanilla flavours, tarry oak finish. — *CvZ*

Capaia Wines

Philadelphia ▪ Est 1997 ▪ 1stB 2003 ▪ Visits by appt ▪ Owners Alexander & Ingrid von Essen ▪ Winemakers Stephan von Neipperg & Mark van Buuren ▪ Viticulturist Mattie Bothma (Jan 2004) ▪ 58 ha (cabs s/f, merlot, petit v, sauvignon) ▪ 90 tons ±6 000 cs 83% red 17% white ▪ PO Box 25 Philadelphia 7304 ▪ info@capaia.co.za ▪ www.capaia.co.za ▪ ***T 972·1081*** *▪ F 972·1894*

Mark van Buuren faced the daunting task of bringing in the 2005 harvest single-handed after the death of celebrated fellow winemaker and co-owner Tibor Gál. St-Emilion château owner Count Stephan von Neipperg, a close friend of Baron Alexander von Essen's, stepped in to assist and will continue to consult at this no-expense-spared venture. Von Neipperg shares Gál's approach in allowing 'the most natural expression of the grape possible', paying particular attention to the grape skins, which he believes play a major role in quality and texture of the finished wine. Van Buuren is delighted with the concentration and elegance of the latest vintage, and considers the cab franc and petit verdot particularly exciting. Convinced they have hit the site specificity jackpot, he is impatient to have the vineyards in full production.

★★★★☆ **Capaia** Dark-fruited, sombrely handsome & suave **03** launched a line that promises to be illustrious. **04** also supple & beautifully structured, fine acidity, meltingly smooth tannins — but deeper, more authoritative. 54% merlot with cab, and dollops petit v, cab f. Seductive, but criminally youthful (will be so for 5+ yrs), showing 14 mths new Fr oak, after fermentation in big wooden casks: concentrated flavours will emerge fully, more complexly. Big alc well balanced. Convincing, quite refined blockbuster (in corresponding, ultra-heavy bottle).

Blue Grove Hill range

★★★☆ **Blue Grove Hill** (formerly 'Cabernet-Merlot'). After ripely cheerful **03**, finer, more interesting **04** (★★★☆), half merlot, with cabs s & f, gorgeous savoury-sweet fruit along with fine texture, signature silky tannins, deep flavour. Well integrated 9 mths 2nd fill Fr oak. 14.4% alc not obvious.

Sauvignon Blanc ★★★☆ Step-up **04** all first-crop home grapes. Quiet figgy aromas, mineral notes, lightly textured. — *TJ*

Cape 1652 see Origin Wine

Cape Bay

Well-established, nautical-themed range of easy drinkers by Newton Johnson. Ready and well priced.

Admiralty House range

Export only. **Cabernet Sauvignon-Shiraz** ★★★☆ Spicy & elegant **04** has red fruit, lavender & pepper in bouquet, choc-mocha on palate; integrated, with moderate alc, complexity from ±yr mix Fr oak. **Sauvignon Blanc** ★★★ Restrained 'European' feel to mineral **05**, mainly Wrcstr fruit given extra zing from 35% cooler Hemel & Aarde Vlly & Firgrove. Pithy grapefruit farewell.

Cape Bay range

Mellow Red ☺ ★★★ Quaffably smooth unwooded blend led by ruby cab. **05** spearmint top-note to berry aromas & flavours. Less savoury than pvs. **Chenin Blanc** ☺ ★★★ Slips down cheerfully. **05** gently dry with chenin's brisk acidity. Dusty flowers & wet wool to contemplate while sipping.

Cabernet Sauvignon-Merlot ★★★ 'Miniature' bdx blend, complete with splash petit v, unwooded & rather nice. **05** blackcurrant & plum gulpability focused by cab acidity & firm fruit tannins. **Pinotage** ★★★ Plump & sleek **05** similar to pvs with mulberry/strawberry & hint tar; softly fruity with pleasant bitter nuance on finish. **Chardonnay** ★★★ **05** unwooded for fruity pleasure; creamy sweet melon aromas, lively acidity & ripe tangerine tail. **Sauvignon Blanc** ★★★ Refreshing anytime dry white with moderate alc; **05** tropical bouquet; racy acidity & Granny Smith apple flavours. **Bouquet Blanc** ★★ Lightish, juicy off-dry white from colombard (65%), dollop muscadel & splash gewürz. Honeysuckle/rosewater wafts in gentle **05**. Both ranges WO W Cape. — *CvZ*

Cape Boar see Doolhof Estate
Cape Cab see Coppoolse Finlayson

Cape Chamonix Wine Farm

Franschhoek ▪ Est 1991 ▪ 1stB 1992 ▪ Tasting & sales daily 9.30–4 ▪ Fee R10 ▪ La Maison de Chamonix Restaurant ▪ Fully equipped self-catering cottages ▪ Facilities for children ▪ Tours by appt ▪ Gifts ▪ Tourgroups by appt ▪ Farm-distilled schnapps & spring water ▪ Owners Chris & Sonja Hellinger ▪ Winemaker Gottfried Mocke (Sep 2001), with Inus van der Westhuizen (Jan 2002) ▪ Viticulturist Rodney Kitching, with Gottfried Mocke ▪ 50 ha (cabs s/f, merlot, pinot, pinotage, chard, chenin, sauvignon) ▪ 200 tons 17 000 cs 60% red 36% white 4% MCC ▪ PO Box 28 Franschhoek 7690 ▪ marketing@chamonix.co.za office@chamonix.co.za ▪ www.chamonix.co.za ▪ ***T 876·2494*** *▪ F 876·3237*

Traditional winemaking, embracing natural fermentations, long lees suffusion and extended bottle-maturation to bring out secondary flavours, has stood winemaker Gottfried Mocke in good stead. The kite-surfing winemaker excelled himself by scooping a gold medal at the 2005 Chardonnay-du-Monde competition – having also won gold the previous year. 'Individual, interesting and more site-specific wines' are Mocke's goal, and he believes the change-over to fully organic production, although slow, will contribute substantially towards that objective. 'But it is a process that just cannot be rushed,' he notes. Varied facilities, including a restaurant, guest cottages and amenities for children, make this property a delight to visit.

★★★★ **Troika** Substantial **03** (★★★☆) serious-minded blend cabs s/f, merlot, essentially vinous, with good red fruit flavours supported by firm structure; a little awkward, with fairly abrupt, dry tannic finish. Part natural ferment in open wood. 20 mths Fr oak. **02**, previewed last ed, had serious, cool-climate feel, auguring well for development. **01** needed time to integrate.

★★★☆ **Pinot Noir** Traditional open-topped barrel fermentation. **03** attractive forest floor, red fruit aromas/flavours, with earthy note, gentle tannic bite. 16 mths Fr oak, 10% new. **04** (★★★★) a big step up: fuller, richer, more intense, with spicily perfumed nose, deep strawberry flavours, long savoury finish. This 80% native yeasts; 14 mths 95% new oak well integrated.

★★★★☆ **Chardonnay Reserve** Elegantly forceful flagship, internationally applauded. Following suit on beautifully polished **02** (Chard-du-Monde, CWT golds), still-developing & quietly elegant **03** offers oatmeal, subtly citrus complexity, with mineral streak, undominated by subtle oaking: fermented/14 mths new Allier. Lovely silky texture, long flavours; perfectly balanced 13.5% alc.

★★★★ **Chardonnay** An enviably fine 2nd label, should mature well too for few yrs. **02** impressive mineral nose; focused, chalky, chablis-style palate. Oatmeal, light toast & hazelnut, glimmerings of lime on well-balanced, refined but lip-smacking **03** (Chard-du-Monde gold). Fermented/±13 mths new Fr oak.

★★★★ **Méthode Cap Classique Brut** From chardonnay, 11 mths big older oak, 3 yrs on fine lees. **02** undemonstrative & refined, with subtle yeast, green apple character; silky texture beneath the tiny bubbles. Like elegant **01**, lovely yeasty persistence. Very dry – just 6g/ℓ sugar.

★★★★ **Méthode Cap Classique Reserve** Occasional special release, degorged only after 5 yrs lees-ageing. Mid-gold **00** more forward, expressive than younger wine, with brioche, baked apple notes, creamy refined richness & dry elegance.

★★★★ **Sauvignon Blanc Reserve** ✓ For those who like their sauvignons more subtle, steely & complex than most, the finely wooded **04** (★★★★☆) has earthy, passionfruit, melon notes, excellent balance & a satisfying citrus bite. Fermented/11 mths mostly older oak. 13.3% alc. Like intense, persistent **03**, racy mineral texture makes terrific food partner.

Rouge ☺ ★★★ Juicy but unfrivolous blend cab, merlot, pinotage; lightly wooded, decently structured. **NV** (mostly 02, 30% 03).

Cabernet Sauvignon ★★★ Solid, chewy **03** first since **99**; earthily savoury & pleasant; substantial dry tannins from 20 mths wood, 60% new. **Pinotage** ★★★ **03** good varietal character, but nice bright fruit rather ungracefully served by big, chunky dry tannin. 20 mths Fr oak, 30% new. **Rosé** new ★★★ **05** blends pinot, merlot, chenin, for fresh, almost-dry quaffer with red-berried earthiness; lightly tannic, small oak influence; sweet-sour finish. **Sauvignon Blanc** ★★★★ ✓ Vibrant & generously flavourful **05** sample promises forthcoming ripe tropicality, good crisp lemony finish. 3 mths on fine lees before bottling. **Chamonix Blanc** ★★★★ Unfrivolous but very drinkable, fresh & gently fruity & successful **05** blend semillon, chard, chenin, with splash sauvignon; partly barrel fermented. Discontinued: **Merlot**, **Blanc de Noir Natural Sweet**. — *TJ*

Cape Circle see Vin-X-Port & Rooiberg

Cape Classics

*Somerset West ▪ Est 1991 ▪ 1stB 1995 ▪ Closed to public ▪ Owners Gary & André Shearer ▪ Winemaker Mzokhona Mvemve (Jan 2002) ▪ 83 000 cs own label 45% red 55% white ▪ PO Box 5421 Cape Town 8000 ▪ info@capeclassics.com ▪ www.capeclassics.com ▪ **T 847·2400** ▪ F 847·2414*

Cape Classics was the first SA export company to focus on, and successfully reconnoitre, the US market in the 1990s. Their Indaba range and portfolio of other high profile export clients – veritable vinous weapons of mass seduction, continue to captivate wine drinkers – with distribution in 50 of the 51 states. Sporting upgraded packaging and screwtop closure, the brand will now also be available in SA. And, amid much excitement, CC has moved to new offices and cellar facilities at Lourensford winery, Somerset West. Winemaker Mzokhona Mvemve also celebrates some memorable personal milestones this year: being appointed to the Platter tasting team for this edition and the imminent launch of his own wine range, under the 'Sagila' label.

Indaba range

★★★★ **Shiraz 04** (★★★★) tasted pvs ed – out of vintage sequence – dusty/brambly fruit with peppery hint; well-formed red berry/plum palate. Our first looks at **03** & **05**: former has appealing & generous flavours of the vintage, smooth tannins. **05** (★★★) smoky nose promises excitement but lack of fruit, excess wood & bitter finish disappoint.

Merlot ★★★ Crowd-pleasing **05**, dollops ripe mulberries with smoky overtones & subtle vanilla, silky tannins. **Pinotage** ★★★★ Ebullient **04** last yr had typical estery mulberries on nose; supple & juicy fruit, slightly sweet tail. Fruit ex-Tlbgh. **Chardonnay 05** (sample) obvious chardonnay fruit & white melon/vanilla hint, well balanced. Compact 13% alc. Likely ★★★★. **Chenin Blanc** ★★★ Good journeyman white. **05** boiled sweets on nose/palate; unindimidating 13% alc. **Sauvignon Blanc** ★★★ **05** dusty, restrained nose with vegetal character well suited to sauerkraut, civilized 12% alc. All WO W Cape. — *NP*

Cape Coastal Vintners

*Paarl ▪ Est/1stB 2004 ▪ Closed to public ▪ Owners: see intro ▪ Winemaker Koos Jordaan, with Johan Pietersen (Feb/Jun 2005) ▪ 65 000 tons 300 000 cs 45% red 55% white ▪ Export brands: Matuba & Kleinbosch ▪ ISO, HACCP, BRC certified ▪ PO Box 6141 Paarl 7620 ▪ office@ccvintners.com ▪ www.matuba.co.za ▪ **T 860·8840** ▪ F 872·9262*

Boland, Bovlei, Riebeek, Wamakersvallei and Wellington cellars (plus other shareholders, including an empowerment organisation), have joined forces with business group Strategy Partners to establish an export marketing platform, Cape Coastal Vintners. While each member winery continues to market its own brands locally and overseas, they jointly supply CCV, under a unique 'first-option' agreement, with top-notch fruit for their new collective brand, Matuba. The Matuba wines are selected and blended by Koos Jordaan, and with a combined harvest of just under 70 000 tons a year, the seasoned cellarmaster (Nederburg, the Rupert portfolio) has plenty to choose from. There are three tiers within the range, separated by style and price: Premium Select, Vineyard Specific and Barrel Selection. Far from fading away, the Kleinbosch range marketed by the precursor to CCV, Cape Wine Cellars, has been expanded.

Vineyard Specific range new

Shiraz-Viognier ★★★ Well-made **04** (sample), expressive varietal character (white pepper, savoury spice), peachy uplift from 8% very ripe-picked viognier. Combo staves/barrels (40%). **Chardonnay** ★★ Agter-Paarl fruit, 5% oaked for **04**; balanced sugar (3.5g/ℓ) helps vanilla-brushed fresh lemon fruit to shine; appealing, friendly wine.

Matuba Premium Select range new

Cabernet Sauvignon ★★ **03** savoury old-Cape styling, whispers dried leaf & damp earth, dry leathery tannins. Briefly oaked. **Shiraz** ★★☆ **04** restrained fruit (despite big 14% alc), roast-beef whiffs, enough tannin to go 2+ yrs if needed. 25% unwooded. **Chardonnay** ★★ Soft, slightly sweet, accommodating **04**, with moderate melon flavours. **Chenin Blanc** ★★ Lightly fruity everyday sip. **04** shy floral introduction, easy white-peach flavours. Incl dash barrelled chardonnay. **Sauvignon Blanc** ★★ **05** (sample) low-key wet hay aroma, food-styled crispness, brisk dry finish.

Kleinbosch range

Cabernet Sauvignon ★★★ **03** still in stock; attractive warm-country jammy/meaty nose; dry savoury finish. Fr oak staves. **Merlot** ★★☆ New vintage not ready. Unwooded **03** was tight, grainy, with sour-plum palate. **Pinotage** ★★ **04** green banana/wild berry hints, quite lean & short, very dry. **Shiraz** ★★★ Last tasted was **02**, fairly rich dark plum colour/aroma; well-oaked to highlight chunky choc/blackberry flavours. **Cabernet Sauvignon-Shiraz** new ★☆ **04** youthfully astringent, stalky/green leaf character, needs the proverbial fatty chop. Following both tasted as samples: **Chardonnay** ★★ Fruit-sweet entry to oak-staved **04**, whiff orange zest, briskly dry lemon-zest flavours. **Sauvignon Blanc** new ★★ Light, peppery **05**, touches green fig & cat's pee, clean & quaffable. All ranges WO W Cape. — *CT*

Cape Fest see Oranjerivier Wine Cellars

Cape First Wines

*Stellenbosch ▪ Est 2003 ▪ 1stB 2004 ▪ Visits by appt at Blue Creek (see entry) ▪ Owners Cape Five Export, Barry Kok, Johan le Hanie & Christo Versfeld ▪ Winemakers Johan le Hanie & Christo Versfeld (both 2004) ▪ 30 000 cs own label ▪ 40% red 60% white ▪ PO Box 3294 Somerset West 7129 ▪ barrykok@capefirstwines.co.za ▪ www.capefirstwines.co.za ▪ **T 880·2549 / 083·290·7695** ▪ F 880·2547*

This likely looking partnership — experienced winemakers Christo Versfeld and Johan le Hanie, marketer Barry Kok and big fruit exporter Cape Five — got off to a fine start when their Bordeaux-style red was placed in the top ten of the inaugural Calyon competition. After what Versfeld calls 'a tricky 2005 vintage' the outlook remains sanguine. The grapes are handled with particular care, according to the Versfeld maxim of keeping interference with the natural process to the minimum, doing no more than manipulate negative factors that might influence quality. Local sales have increased nicely while the UK, Japan and Sweden are now international markets. Late news is the receipt of a big order from the UK for two new blends under the private label, Livingstone.

Makana range

Pinot Noir ★★★ **04** a step up. Cherry, sherbet & subtle spice; strawberry, earthy notes & mineral finish. Fruit concentration easily soaks up 14.5% alc. 11 mths Fr oak (25% new). WO W Cape, rest Coastal. **Cabernet Sauvignon-Merlot-Cabernet Franc** ★★★ **04** (sample) ripe berry compôte & spice on 50/30/20 blend; mouth-puckering tannins & acidity need some time to settle; big finish (15% alc). Calyon plaudit for **03**. **Chardonnay** ★★★ Pvsly tasted as sample, rerated. Complex butter, citrus, mineral interplay on **04**; big oak, fruit concentration & 14% alc (plus dollop actual RS) all add up to sweet, drink-soon tone. 8 mths Fr wood, 40% new. **Sauvignon Blanc** ★★★ Fresh & friendly **05**, white pepper & tropical notes; plenty of extract to balance 13.3% alc. Pithy finish from 7 wks on lees.

Three Anchor Bay range

Cabernet Sauvignon-Merlot ★★★ **04** attractive & fresh, with savoury berry notes & soft tannins. 14% alc hidden by abundant fruit. Light oaking. **Chenin Blanc-Chardonnay** ★★★ **05** (sample) 60/40 mix; youthful citrus/floral nose; shortish lemon/lime palate with sweet/sour tussle. This, range below, WO W Cape.

Hill Station range

Shiraz-Pinotage ★★★ **03** tasted last yr; spicy/brambly whiffs, fairly rich texture, tannins softened by slight sweetness (6g/ℓ RS). Oaked with staves in tank. **Chenin Blanc-Chardonnay** ★★★ **05** inviting bouquet on 60/40 blend; lime, flowers & wisp smoke. Crisp acidity, citrus flavours, could do with bit more persistence. — *CvZ*

Cape Grace Wines

Stellenbosch ▪ Est/1stB 2004 ▪ Closed to public ▪ Owners Thierry's Wine Services & Afrifresh ▪ Winemaker Carno du Toit ▪ 200 000 cs for export only, incl Waitrose, Asda, Sainsbury's, Tesco & Somerfield ▪ 50% red 45% white 5% rosé ▪ PO Box 1376 Stellenbosch 7599 ▪ info@capegracewine.co.za ▪ www.capegracewine.co.za ▪ ***T/F 855·5639***

This UK/SA joint-venture range is to be found in an enviable position: on the shelves of all five major UK supermarket chains, and expanding into the US and Far East. Absence of a physical home has led manager Lucy Warner to pioneer the moveable tasting venue – a yacht in False Bay, the banks of the Breede River and a Guguletu township home – chosen to reflect SA's diversity. She and recently appointed winemaker Carno du Toit stepped into the unknown late last year when the pair abseiled off Table Mountain to raise funds for the Pebbles Project, a charity established by Warner's sister to meet the needs of children affected by foetal alcohol syndrome.

Pinotage Rosé ★★★ new **05** sensuous little number: coral pink glint, musky scent, suavely dry flavour. Ideal sundowner; screwcap. **Sauvignon Blanc-Chenin Blanc** ★★★ **05** similar to pvs: 50/50 light-bodied blend, forthcoming, firmly dry & refreshing lime. **Pinotage-Shiraz** ★★★ Preview **05** consistent with style of pvs: ripe rasp/blackberry notes, sweet-fruited palate, comfortable furry tannins. Oak influenced. Following tasted as samples pvs ed (so ratings provisional), not revisited; unwooded, alcs 12-13.5% unless noted: **Cabernet Franc** ★★★★ **02** notes of black plum & dried leaves; firmish, concentrated; lead pencil whiffs from 16 mths in 2nd/3rd fill barrels. Stbosch grapes. **Merlot** ★★★★ ✓ Effortlessly drinkable **03**, ripe plum jam whiffs; big, soft jammy choc flavours, more sweetness in the slippery finish (3.5g/ℓ sugar). **Cabernet Sauvignon-Merlot** ★★★ Modern styling with complexity; **03** plump, juicy, supple & full-bodied; hints of stewed plum, earth & forest floor. **Chardonnay** ★★★ An easy drinker, should appeal widely. 10% new-oak-fermented shows subtly as hazelnut/butterscotch tint to **04**'s pear flavours. **Chardonnay-Semillon** ★★★ Varieties in equal measure impart vibrant & zesty mouthfeel in **04**, with delicate hints pear & quince. All WO W Cape unless noted. — *MM/TM*

Cape Haven see Pulpit Rock
Cape Heights see False Bay Vineyards

Cape Hutton

Stellenbosch ▪ Est 2003 ▪ 1stB 2004 ▪ Visits by appt ▪ Owners/viticulturists Gerrit & Lesley Wyma ▪ Winemaker Piet Smal (Blue Creek), with owners ▪ 4ha (cab, merlot) ▪ 19 tons 1 000 cs 100% red ▪ PO Box 2200 Somerset West 7130 ▪ info@capehutton.com; lesley@capehutton.com ▪ www.capehutton.com ▪ ***T 880·0527/082·322·8489*** *▪ F 880·0666*

'Our wine should be approachable to all palates,' says Gerrit Wyma, who has an unusually nuanced understanding of such things, being an oral and maxillofacial surgeon. He does his after-hours wine thing with wife Lesley and their children under the expert guidance of neighbour Piet Smal (who happens to be a dentist). Smal's enthusiasm for cab was their inspiration, and the elegantly packaged varietal bottling below is their maiden vintage. It's from their own 4ha vineyard, planted with cab and merlot, just coming on stream.

Cabernet Sauvignon ★★★ **04** elegant blackcurrant, lead pencil aromas suggest classically styled if slightly austere red. More spice, tea-leaf & cedar character than fruit, restrained finish. 14 mths Fr oak. —*MF*

Capell's Court see Linton Park

Cape Legends

Stellenbosch ▪ Closed to public ▪ Owner Distell ▪ PO Box 184 Stellenbosch 7599 ▪ ekrige@capelegends.co.za ▪ ***T 809·7000*** *F 882·9575*

Stand-alone marketing and sales organisation within the Distell group, representing a portfolio of well-regarded brands including Alto, Allesverloren, Flat Roof Manor, Hill & Dale, Jacobsdal, Le Bonheur, Lomond, Neethlingshof, Plaisir de Merle, Stellenzicht, Theuniskraal, Tukulu and Uitkyk, all listed separately.

Cape Maclear see African Pride
Cape Mist see Thorntree & Overhex
Cape Nature Organic see Origin Wine

Capenheimer

SA's original perlé wine (launched 1962), based on the Italian Lambrusco style. Latest (**NV**) ★★ 50/50 chenin/colombard; fresh-cut pear & pink musk sweet aromas; gently petillant, light & soft. By Distell. —*CvZ*

Cape Original see Origin Wine

Cape Point Vineyards

Cape Point ▪ Est 1996 ▪ 1stB 2000 ▪ Visits by appt ▪ Owner Sybrand van der Spuy ▪ Winemaker Duncan Savage (Dec 2002), with viticultural adviser Kevin Watt ▪ 31 ha (cab, pinot, shiraz, chard, sauvignon, semillon) ▪ 140 tons 7 000 cs own label 1 500 cs for Woolworths ▪ 20% red 80% white ▪ PO Box 100 Noordhoek 7985 ▪ info@cape-point.com ▪ www.capepointvineyards.co.za ▪ ***T 785·7660*** *▪ F 785·7662*

Summer visitors to Cape Point will appreciate the cooling effects of the south-easter blowing off the cold southern ocean. So too do the vines, and for Duncan Savage the wines really are made in these maritime vineyards, where the cool mesoclimates of his three different vineyard sites translate into great flavour concentration. Intent on optimising these unique assets, Savage insists on matching the style of wine to the character of the grapes each vintage – not the other way round. He is planting more sauvignon on a high Noordhoek site, which he believes to be particularly well suited to this variety. Recent branding changes include the introduction of the CPV Stonehaven label for earlier-drinking sauvignon, and dropping the second-tier Scarborough whites, to be revived in the future as a separate red-only label.

★★★★★ **Sauvignon Blanc** ✓ Styled for long-term evolution, with Loire-inspired restraint & complexity. Release always yr after vintage, allowing for extended lees enrichment. **04** deep, rich, sonorous; mouth-filling flavours overlaid with pebble-like minerality. Needs time to show full impressive colours. **03** expressive yet unevolved; energised by fine, tense acid; remarkable length. These need 3–4 yrs to show at best. All with dash barrel-fermented sauvignon, 7–10% semillon for richness, structure.

★★★★ **Stonehaven Sauvignon Blanc** new ✓ Vinified for easy/early but not simple drinking. **05** deliciously juicy; tropical fruit/fig bounce enlivened by area's cool mineral tang, zippily clean length. Maiden **04** still frisky, though fruit mellowing.

★★★★ **Semillon** After **03**'s dazzling performance (★★★★★), **04** regrettably channelled elsewhere, incl sauvignon above. Next **05** untasted. **03** with 15% sauvignon, complex mix wild herb, citrus, honey & mineral. Silkiness enhanced by judicious 30% barrelled portion. Potential to at least 2007. Balanced 13.5% alc.

★★★★ **Semillon Noble Late Harvest** Made only when sufficient botrytis. None since **01**. 123g/ℓ sugar; fermented/aged yr new Fr oak.

Chardonnay ★★★☆ **04** (sample) modern, well-oaked style. Forthcoming vanilla-cream richness balanced by energetic freshness, medium-bodied refinement. ±2 yrs potential. **Isliedh** ★★★☆ (Pronounced 'Islay', after Sybrand vdS's granddaughter) Maiden **04** from sauvignon, fermented/matured Fr oak, 30% new, 8 mths. Powerful though mid-2005 rather sombre; oak curbs characteristic bright mineral/fig attractions. May open up over next yr/2.—*AL*

Cape Promise see WaverleyTBS
Cape Roan see Doolhof Estate
Cape Table see Riebeek Cellars
Cape View see Kaapzicht

Cape Vineyards

Rawsonville ▪ Est 1994 ▪ 1stB 1996 ▪ Closed to public ▪ Owners 7 shareholders ▪ 15 000 cs + 8.5m litres bulk ▪ 70% red 30% white ▪ Ranges for customers: Pearl Springs (UK/Japan); Andrew Bain Reserve, Jantara, Wildfire (all UK) ▪ ISO 9001/2000 certified ▪ PO Box 106 Rawsonville 6845 ▪ admin@cape-vineyards.com; vicgentis@cape-vineyards.com ▪ www.cape-vineyards.com ▪ ***T (023) 349·1585/1466*** *▪ F (023) 349·1592*

Seven Breedekloof wineries fall under this wholesaler's umbrella, so Cape Vineyards involves itself enthusiastically in the area's tourism initiative. On the wine marketing front, its local Andrew Bain and Rawson ranges have been trimmed to allow for more dedicated focus rather than a general spread. The new Wildfire brand, introduced into British Asda supermarkets in 2004, has lived up to its name; unavailability of large volumes of malbec led to its being replaced in 2005 with a Shiraz, Pinotage or red blend. The other UK range, Jantara, falls under the aegis of Aussie vini adviser Mark Nairn, one of a team producing 'trend-setting, affordable wines that can be enjoyed in the spirit of goodwill and humour with which they were created'.

Andrew Bain Reserve range

For UK market. **Pinotage** ★★★ Sappy & suave **04** includes 15% ruby cab for extra juice, sweetness; more than stands up to 14% alc. Fermented with Fr/Am oak chips. Slnghoek fruit. **Chardonnay** ★★★ Tasted last ed, **04** vibrant & quaffable, youthful citrus/melon tones enhanced by dexterous oaking; enjoy young.

Andrew Bain range

Cabernet Sauvignon-Merlot ★★☆ **05** 60% cab with equal dollops merlot/malbec; flavourful coffee, choc, red fruits spread. Generous, with warm tail (14.5% alc). Merlot matured with Fr/Am 'beans' — similar to chips. **Chardonnay** ★★☆ Briefly 'beaned' (see above) **05** attractive, tropical fruit salad melange; weighty, with zesty lift.

Jantara range

For UK market; mostly **05**. **Pinotage** NEW ★★★ With splash malbec, muscular, dense, rich in colour & fruit; dry tannins & bitter lift make it a food wine. Responsible 13.5% alc. Fr/Am oak 2 mths. **Shiraz** ★★★ Juicy & chunky; gets density, flavour boost from 15% malbec & semblance of sweetness from 14% alc. Smoky nuances, dry raspy tannins need 2–3 yrs or rustic food. Oak as above. **Chardonnay** NEW ★★ Subdued varietal character, gentle creaminess with hint lemon; not for keeping. Wood as below. **Chenin Blanc** NEW ★★★ Attractive nectarine & lime tones, light oak vanilla whiffs (6 wks combo Fr/Am oak). Mouth-filling & balanced, very drinkable with sensible 13% alc. **Sauvignon Blanc** ★★☆ No **05**. Pvsly tasted **03** had unusual peach whiff; bright, zesty finish.

Rawson's range

Ruby Cabernet-Merlot ★★★ Unoaked; ruby cab leads blend, provides sweet fruit & accessibility; merlot/malbec (20/10) add structure. **05** to enjoy soon.

Wildfire range new

Malbec ★★★ Boisterous braai buddy **04** features dollop ruby cab for interest, fruit; full bodied (14.5% alc), juicy centre & dry finish. Drink soon. **Chardonnay** ★★ **05** light & tropical summer sipper, oak influenced. Incl soupçon chenin. All above WO W Cape/Brde Rvr Vlly. — *DH*

Cape Wine Cellars see Cape Coastal Vintners

Cape Winemakers Guild (CWG)

Chair: Gary Jordan ▪ General Manager: Kate Jonker ▪ ***T 883·8625*** *▪ F 883·8626 ▪ info@capewinemakersguild.com ▪ www.capewinemakersguild.com*

Independent, invitation-only association, founded in 1982 to promote winemaking excellence among its members. Since 1985, the CWG has held a highly-regarded annual public auction. A Development Trust, formed in 1999 with auction sponsor Nedbank, benefits disadvantaged communities living and working in the winegrowing regions. The current guild members are: Beyers Truter, Beyerskloof; *Marc Kent*, Boekenhoutskloof; *Carel Nel*, Boplaas; Peter Finlayson, Bouchard Finlayson; *Christopher Keet*, Cordoba; *David Trafford*, De Trafford; *Etienne le Riche*, Etienne le Riche Wines; *Bruce Jack*, Flagstone Winery; *David Finlayson*, Glen Carlou; *Jeremy Walker*, Grangehurst; Charles Hopkins, Graham Beck Coastal; *Pieter Ferreira*, Graham Beck Robertson; Kevin Grant, Kevin Grant Wines; *Carl Schultz*, Hartenberg; *Anton Bredell*, JP Bredell Wines; *Gary Jordan*, Jordan Winery; Jean Daneel, Jean Daneel Wines; *Danie Steytler*, Kaapzicht; *Francois Naudé*, L'Avenir; *Philip Costandius*, Lourensford; ***Niels Verburg***, Luddite Wines; Neil Ellis, Neil Ellis Wines; **Bernhard Veller**, Nitida; Braam van Velden, Overgaauw; Ross Gower, Ross Gower Wines; *Teddy Hall*, Rudera; Louis Strydom, Rust en Vrede; *Johan Malan*, Simonsig; Abrie Bruwer, Springfield; ***John Loubser***, Steenberg; *Gyles Webb*, Thelema; *André van Rensburg*, Vergelegen; *Jeff Grier*, Villiera; *Nicky Versfeld*, Omnia; *Jan Coetzee*, Vriesenhof; *Norma Ratcliffe*, Warwick; *Kevin Arnold*, Waterford. New members in bold; those with wines on current (2005) Auction italicised.

Cap Vino see Winkelshoek
Cardouw see Citrusdal Cellars
Caresse Marine see Wildekrans

Carisbrooke Wines

Stellenbosch ▪ Est 1989 ▪ 1stB 1996 ▪ Tasting & sales Mon-Fri 9.30–2 (all day & Sat 9–12 during Dec/Jan) ▪ Closed Easter Fri-Mon, Dec 24/25 & Jan 1 ▪ Owner/winemaker Willem Pretorius ▪ Viti/vini consultant Kowie du Toit (Jan 1997) ▪ 6 ha (cab, shiraz) ▪ 40 tons 1 500 cs own label 100% red ▪ PO Box 25 Vlottenburg 7604 ▪ wjpret@mweb.co.za ▪ ***T/F 881·3798***

The little train station of Carisbrooke, made famous by Alan Paton's masterpiece *Cry, the Beloved Country*, gives its name to this small range, owned by Stellenbosch senior counsel Willem Pretorius and vinified by Kowie du Toit. Predating present-day empowerment initiatives, a farmworker profit-sharing scheme has been in place here for several years.

★★★★★ **Cabernet Sauvignon** Modern but classically inclined. **00** well-padded with sweet, soft fruit, elegantly oaked. We also previewed **01** & noted it as promising. Own single-vyd.

Neither wine retasted for current ed; notes from pvs ed: **'Red Blend'** Unnamed seamless union of cab (80%) shiraz, dollop merlot; barrelled 2 yrs. Preview **01** impresses: very ripe fruit, New-World ambience with restraint (moderate 13.5% alc). Probable ★★★★. — *TM*

Carl Everson see Opstal

Carnival

The Spar chain of convenience stores' boxed wines, available in 1, 3 & 5ℓ packs. See also Country Cellars and Spar.

All **NV**; alc around 12% unless noted. **Classic Red** ★★ Usually a crowd pleaser, but latest version less juicy-fruity, more tannic; needs taming with a hearty stew. **Rosé** ★★

Blush-coloured semi-sweet from colombard, tinted by pinotage. **Grand Cru** ★ No-frills easy drinker from chenin; colombard; lively, dry, with tropical nuance. **Perlé** Spritzy colombard, chenin in 750ml bottle under screwcap. Our samples very tired & characterless. **Stein** ★ Unpretentious semi-sweet with peachy tone, from colombard & chenin. **Late Harvest** ★ Latest version unusually sugary, lacks verve of pvs. —*JP*

Carolinahoeve Boutique Cellar

new

Wellington ▪ Est 2004 ▪ 1stB 2005 ▪ Tasting & sales Tue-Sun 11am-midnight ▪ Closed public holidays ▪ Light meals ▪ Exhibition of railway artefacts & water colour paintings ▪ Owners Lee-Ann Millin & Carolina Dagevos ▪ Winemaker Johnnie Loubser, advised by Pierre Marais (Jan/Jul 2005) ▪ 4 ha (cinsaut, chenin) ▪ 6 tons ±1 000 cs 75% red 25% white PO Box 974 Wellington 7655 ▪ info@carolinahoeve.com ▪ www.carolinahoeve.com ▪ ***T 873·0741*** *▪ F 873·0742*

Partners Carolina Dagevos, a Dutch émigré, and Lee-Ann Millin, an SA Brit, bought a 37-year-old Wellington property in October 2004. Unable to continue supplying the local co-op and seeing 'the beautiful grapes growing', the pair decided in December to cock a snook at the establishment and convert the garage into a small winery. 'With tremendous hard work by Lee-Ann', they were ready for the first grapes at the end of January! The crop was vinified in association with Pierre Marais of Distell (full-time winemaker Johnnie Loubser joined mid-year). With typical gusto, the owners attacked the export market with their brand Carolinahoeve (hoeve = estate in Dutch), and in short order secured deals with restaurants and specialised wine shops in three European countries.

Pinotage-Cinsaut ★★★ Vivid ruby hue announces cheerful character of **05** pleasantly dry *vin ordinaire.* Bright spicy red fruits, well-contained 14% alc. Unwooded; also available aged on staves & barrelled. **Chenin Blanc** ★★★ **05** with understated delicacy; some pretty though fleeting floral features, medium-weight, roundly dry. Wllnton; Pville bushvine vyds. Both WO Coastal; 750/187ml. —*AL*

Casa Portuguesa see Paarl Wine
Casa do Mar see Ruitersvlei
Cathedral Cellar see KWV International
Cattle Baron see ACJ Fine Wines
CCC see Bonnievale

Cederberg Private Cellar

Cederberg (see Olifants River map) ▪ Est/1stB 1977 ▪ Tasting, sales & tours Mon-Sat 8-12.30; 2-5 Pub hols 9-12;4-6 ▪ Fee R10 ▪ Closed Easter Fri/Sun/Mon & Dec 16/25 ▪ BYO picnic ▪ Fully equipped self-catering cottages ▪ Walks/hikes ▪ Mountain biking ▪ Owners Nieuwoudt family ▪ Winemaker David Nieuwoudt, with Jan Taylor (1997/1998) ▪ Viticulturist Ernst Nieuwoudt ▪ 52 ha (cab, shiraz, chenin, sauvignon) ▪ 12 000 cs 60% red 40% white ▪ PO Box 84 Clanwilliam 8135 ▪ info@cederbergwine.com ▪ www.cederbergwine.com ▪ ***T (027) 482·2827*** *▪ F (027) 482·1188*

Oops, almost caught with his pants down, laughs David Nieuwoudt, champion of the rugged Cederberg-ward vineyards, which last year mimicked their lower-altitude counterparts across the Cape by ripening early. A (pleasant) surprise for David N was the promise shown by the first crop from a new, higher, south-east-facing sauvignon block on shale soils. Displaying great typicity, it lends a mineral nuance to the 05 Sauvignon below. Another memorable moment was the bottling of David N's first Shiraz Reserve ('or should we name it "Syrah"? he wonders, a touch impishly). But last year's biggest day probably was August 6th. With assistant/entertainer Jan Taylor on guitar, and fortified by plenty of aforementioned white, David and *vrinne* [friends] spent the day merrily bottling Cederburg's first MCC. Worth waiting three years for, reckons its creator.

★★★★★ **V Generations** David N's homage to his family's guardianship of this snowline wilderness area. Cab, from 28 yr old vyd, worthy vintages only, such as **03**, where fruit quality able to take 100% new oak. More obvious mocha effects than regular version; some liquorice too; layered, juicy cassis-mulberry mélange to balance; trademark clean lines, firm tannins. Big but elegant, should grow over 7-9 yrs. No **02**.

★★★★ **Cabernet Sauvignon** Now into well-established quality level & style; cool, pure, focused fruit, ample & sweet, ripe dry tannins. **04** warmer vintage evinces slightly riper mulberry/blackberry profile, oaked to complement; maintains usual freshness, elegance. Possibly ready slightly earlier than sleek, tight **03**. Yr Fr oak, 60% new; malo in barrel. *Wine* ★★★★. MIWA gold.

★★★★ **Shiraz** Stamped early authority on SA shiraz scene when **02** won two 2004 FCTWS trophies (Shiraz, Best Red), scored ★★★★☆ at Shiraz Challenge, garnered *Wine* ★★★★ for both **02**, **03**. Latest **04** released younger than DN would like; Am oak, 14.5% alc still evident. Further yr should bring harmony, reveal more of the dainty yet persuasive & supple spicy red fruit. Probably not for extended ageing, though. 15 mths, 70/30 Fr/Am oak, 70% new.

★★★★ **V Generations Chenin Blanc** Richer, ageworthy version from older low-yielding vyd. **04** complex peachy/floral concentration boosted by complementary oak vanilla. Flavour-packed but not heavy, partly thanks to long fermentation (44 day), striking mineral acid (7g/ℓ), medium body. Will benefit from yr/18 mths settling; lovely potential to 2008/09. **03** contrasting fruit richness with clean, savoury acid. Fermented in 60% new Fr oak, 11 mths matured.

★★★★ **Sauvignon Blanc** Downside of drought-ravaged **05** is 25% crop reduction; upside sauvignon of vigour, finesse. Touch more passionfruit/ripe fig intensity than usual, offset by cool, steely freshness typifying these vyds in the sky; moderate 13% alc.

Bukettraube ☺ ★★★ **05** from vastly reduced crop, fuller, more obviously semi-sweet. Maintains pleasant peppery spice, sufficient balancing acid for uncomplicated sipping. 13.5% alc.

Chenin Blanc Unwooded ★★★☆ One of most interesting in fresh & fruity style. **05** enticing floral, honey, winter melon complexity; vivid, zesty; daintily flavoursome, long. Regular VDG/G. **Cederberger** ★★★☆ **04** step up from pvs; merlot, pinotage, with newcomer shiraz (50/30/20); Tasty, plump rasp-/blackberry flavours; rounded, dry. Enough aplomb to mix in best company. Used oak matured14 mths.—*AL*

Cellar Cask

Well-established budget range; first in SA, in 1979, with a bag-in-box. Soft, light (±11.5% alc) fruitiness are keynotes. By Distell.

All **NV**. **Select Johannisberger Red** ★★ Fresh-tasting & juicily sweet (48g/ℓ RS) with ripe red berry flavours, gentle tea leaf grip. **Select Johannisberger Rosé** ★★ Hint smoke, fruit pastille bouquet, slightly cloying palate. **Select Johannisberger White** ★★ Wallet-pleasing easy-drinker with soft, melon finish. All above Natural Sweets, 750ml bottles & 5/2ℓ packs. Following in 5/2ℓ packs; none available for tasting: **Premier Claret** ★★ Pvsly rustic four-way blend; plum/prune aromas & earthy, dry, slightly minerally palate. **Premier Grand Cru** ★★ No-frills glugger from chenin, colombard (50/50); last tasted had lemon-drop freshness & austerity in line with style. **Premier Semi-Sweet** ★★ Pvs with fresh-smelling nose of hay & apple; soft, accessible; tastes off-dry rather than semi-sweet. Varieties as for PGC. **Premier Late Harvest** ★★ Sweeter version of Semi-Sweet; last tasted boxing had pineapple & pear on nose/palate, appealing fruity freshness.—*CvZ*

Cellar Door see Villiera
Cellar Hand see Flagstone
Cellar Selection see Kleine Zalze

Cellar-Vie Wines

*Est/1stB 2004 ▪ Closed to public ▪ Owners Hendri Nagel, Adam Simcock & Karl Watkin ▪ Vini consultant Bartho Eksteen ▪ 245 cs 100% red ▪ PO Box 10136 Edleen 1625 ▪ hermitage@absamail.co.za ▪ **T 083·713·9256** ▪ F (011) 975·4482*

No update available on this winery; contact details from previous edition.

Chacma's Bark see African Pride
Chamonix see Cape Chamonix
Chapman's Peak see Cape Classics

Chateau Libertas

Consistent & affordable red blend made every year since 1932. Latest **03** ★★★ cab-dominated (60%); sloshes merlot, cinsaut, shiraz (20/15/5), partly oak-staved; moderate alc 13.6%. Plum & mineral bouquet, sour cherry & vanilla flavours. Firm & food-friendly, with impression of sweetness on finish. WO Coastal. By Distell. — *CvZ*

Chiwara see Daschbosch

Christo Wiese Portfolio

*Owner Christo Wiese • Winemakers Philip Costandius (Lourensford) & Wynand Lategan (Lanzerac) • Contact Anton du Toit • PO Box 16 Somerset West 7129 • cwp@lourensford.co.za • **T 847·2200** • F 847·0910*

This is the umbrella for big-businessman Christo Wiese's extensive wine interests, which include Stellenbosch farms Lanzerac and Lourensford, and branded ranges Five Heirs and Eden Crest, listed separately.

Churchaven see The Winery

Cilandia

*Robertson • Est 2002 • 1stB 2003 • Visits by appt • Owners AA Cilliers Jnr & AA Cilliers • Winemaker Albie Cilliers • Viticulturist Abraham Cilliers • 60 ha (cab, cinsaut, pinotage, ruobernet, shiraz, chard, chenin) • 700 tons 1 200 cs own label 100% red • PO Box 504 Robertson 6705 • Cilandia@telkomsa.net • **T/F (023) 626·5209***

Fruit for the Cilandia brand (concatenation of family name, Cilliers, and Robertson winegrowing ward Eilandia) is from selected fruit off 60 hectares on the home farm, vinified by third-generation AA 'Albie' Cilliers, who is intent on restoring winemaking pride to the family spread.

Cabernet Sauvignon ★★★★ Tasted for pvs ed, **02** subtly structured, tannins carefully managed to ensure early-ish drinkability, say 2 yrs. Should easily hold for 4-5. Yr Fr/Am oak, 50% new. **Pinotage** new ★★★ Will appeal to fans of the old style; smoke, tar, fynbos notes on big & gutsy **03** (14.5% alc), needs 2-4 yrs; meanwhile will easily stand up to BBQ steak or oxtail stew. Fermented/aged Fr/Am oak, all new. **Shiraz** ★★★★ Maiden **02**, tasted mid-2004, promising debut given dim vintage; richly endowed with dark choc, prune & leather fruit. Should improve with 3-5 yrs cellaring. Yr oak, all Fr, 40% new. All above WO Eilandia. — *CR*

Cilliers Cellars see Stellendrift
Cilmor see African Terroir
Cinzano see African Wines & Spirits

Citrusdal Cellars

*Citrusdal (see Swartland map) • Est 1957 • 1stB 1958 • Tasting & sales Mon-Fri 8-5 Sat 9-12.30 (sales also at retail outlet in Citrusdal village Mon-Fri 9-7 Sat 8-1) • Closed all pub hols except Easter Sat • Tours by appt • Picnic baskets by appt during Dec holiday, or BYO anytime • Citrusdal Cellars Guest House • Tourgroups • Conferencing • 4×4 trail • Owners 80 members • Winemakers Ian Nieuwoudt & Pieter Carstens (2005/2003) • Viticulturist Bartho van der Westhuizen (Dec 2003) • 1 200 ha (grenache, pinotage, chenin) • 7 000 tons 20 000 cs own label + 5m litres bulk + 20 000 cs for clients • 50% red 40% white 5% rosé 5% dessert • Export brand: Danckaert • HACCP certified • PO Box 41 Citrusdal 7340 • citrusdalcellars@yebo.co.za • www.citrusdalcellars.co.za • **T (022) 921·2233** • F (022) 921·3937*

A concerted effort has been made, says GM De Witt la Grange, to develop the particular characteristics of this winery's main production areas — Bo-Rivier, Piekenierskloof, Cederberg and Citrusdal Mountain — and to use the best fruit from each zone to produce the wines of the Goue Vallei range. The renewed focus has resulted in 'unparalleled growth', La Grange reports, the newer addition to the range, Classique Blanc, 'exceeding all expectations'. A well-established and ongoing initiative involves community development in the Citrusdal area. Four of the winery's growers are recognised by the Fair Trade Labelling Organisation (FLO), and their combined output of 1m litres of wine generates substantial funds for community projects.

Cardouw range

Range named after the local Cardouw Pass ('Narrow Road' in Khoisan language). **Cabernet Sauvignon Reserve** ★★★☆ 1st from their Piekenklf vyds (certified as such). Interesting & substantial **00**, mid-2004 still showed structure, generosity, chewy ripe tannins. **Cabernet Sauvignon** ★☆ None since **99**, to be enjoyed with food. **Grenache** ★★★ Among 1st varietal bottlings in SA (WO Piekenklf). Well structured **03** last ed showed bright red-fruit tones, touch of spice. Could take light chilling in summer. Yr Fr/Am (80/20) oak. **Pinotage** ★★ **02** touch of ester, slight green edge, fairly strong tannic finish. Not retasted. **Chardonnay** ★★ No follow-up to **03**, barrel-fermented/matured (Fr oak, 8 mths). WO Cdrberg. **Chardonnay Reserve** ★★☆ Ex Cdrberg/Piekenklf vyds, blended after yr in new Fr oak; **03** last ed more rounded than above version, good dry finish. **Chenin Blanc** ★★ Still-listed **03**'s fruit very ripe but lifted by racy acidity; dainty pear flavours. **President's Red**, **Blanc Fumé** discontinued. All ranges WO W Cape unless noted.

Ivory Creek range

Following reds not retasted: **Cabernet Sauvignon** ★★☆ **02** porty whiffs, dried plum tones on palate; suggest drink soon. **Pinotage** ★★★ Wide-girthed **02** holding up; plump red berry palate, pleasantly dry tannic finish. 7 mths Fr oak. **Merlot** ★★ **03** light-hued but full-bodied dry red; slight green tinge & strongish tannin grip. 6 mths Fr oak. WO Piekenklf. **Shiraz** ★★ **02** shows a dry leaf character, fair amount of tannin though big alc (15.8%) not as evident. **Royal Rouge** ★★☆ For export. Quaffable unwooded **03** mix cinsaut, merlot, tinta, ruby cab, with latter's spicy aroma jumping from glass. **Chardonnay** ★★ **04** again unwooded; dry, softly fruity with hint lemon zest. **Chenin Blanc** ★★☆ **04** racy bone-dry white; last ed showed crisp apple & pear aromas/flavours; WO Ctrsdal Mntn (first ever wine with this appellation). **Sauvignon Blanc** ★★☆ **04** (sample last ed, retasted) night harvested for freshness; zingy nettles & green figs, bright acidic backbone ensures a perky mouthful. 13% alc. Piekenklf fruit. **Royal Blanc** ★★☆ 4-way blend for Dutch market. Last yr **04** was lightish, pleasant; gentle liveliness on deciduous fruit palate.

Goue Vallei range

Cabernet Sauvignon ★☆ Big, tight tannins on **04**, dry, food-imploring character accentuated by 8 mths oak (2nd/3rd fill barrels). **Pinotage** ★★★☆ **02** was last vintage tasted; weighty & firm, with fairly rich, minerally red-berry aromas/flavours. 8 mths oak, mainly Fr. **Shiraz** ★★☆ Last ed reported as discontinued; reappears revived & refreshed with **04**, trailing leathery woodsmoke whiffs, well stocked with savoury fruit. **Cabernet Sauvignon-Merlot** new ★ Compact, light-bodied **04**, 60/40 blend marked by light fruiting & unrestrained tannins. 6 mths 2nd/3rd fill oak. **Classique Rouge** ★★☆ House's best-seller; latest is **NV**, blend undisclosed. Crowd-pleaser with wild/mulberry fruit, drier & leaner than last. Quaffably light 13% alc. Also in 3ℓ bag-in-box. **Chianti** ★★ Appealing, effortless everyday red; brambly/savoury flavours, well-managed tannins add BBQ-friendly grunt. Cinsaut joined by merlot in latest **NV**, unwooded. **Classique Rosé** ★★ Lightish, semi-dry **04** again from pinotage, with cherry fragrance; ends fairly crisply. For export; not retasted. **Chardonnay** ★★ **04** last ed pleasingly light textured; apple/peach flavours & smoky aftertaste from 50% fermentation with Fr oak chips (rest unwooded). **Chenin Blanc** ★☆ Undemonstrative **05** vague tropical hints, smooth, dry. **Sauvignon Blanc** ★☆ Ethereal **05** 'crisply dry' rather than pvs 'perky', with suggestion of grassiness. 11.5% alc. **Classique Blanc** ★☆ Latest is **NV**, untasted; pvs (04) lightish-textured, muted guava & apple whiffs (sampled freshly bottled), dry finish. **Bukettraube** ★ **05** off-dry white, feather-light in every respect. **Late Vintage** ★★ Semi-sweet last ed returned to line-up as 3ℓ bag-in-box; candied fruit flavours, hints spice/mint – good with glazed chicken or Thai curry. **NV**/uncertified. **Brut** ★★☆ Chardonnay & clairette; stylish dry fizz with appetising fresh baked bread tone. **NV**/uncertified; not retasted; ditto ... **Vin Doux** ★★★ Lovely bouncy bubbles with honeysuckle fragrance, uncloyingly sweet. **Blanc de Blanc**, **Brut Pinot Gris** discontinued.

Following fortifieds all **NV**/uncertified; none revisited for current ed: **Sacramental Wine** ★★ For the Roman Catholic Church; aromatic blend pale dry sherry, muscadel & colombard. 14.8% alc. **Red Jerepiko** ★★★ Exotic & interesting dessert from pinotage, with distinctly warming malt & treacle flavours. 19.5% alc. **Hanepoot Jerepiko** ★★★ Wickedly smooth & sweet; mid-2004 wonderful grapey nose; herbal palate with hints mint & buchu. 17.8% alc. **White Muscadel** ★★★★ Almost a dessert in itself, complete with ripe mango, pineapple & apricot flavours; silky smooth (partly due to low 15% fortification). **Ruby** ★★ From shiraz, straightforwardly sweet, dry for style (86g/ℓ sugar).

Zaximus range

Export brand for UK & Italy now discontinued. – *CT/JN*

Clairvaux Private Cellar

Robertson • Est 2000 • 1stB 2001 • Tasting & sales Mon-Fri 8-5 Sat & pub hols 9-12.30 • Closed Easter Fri-Mon, Dec 25/26 & Jan 1 • Tours by appt • BYO picnic • Owners Wouter de Wet Snr & Jnr • Winemaker Pieter van Aarde (Jan 2004) • Viti consultant Briaan Stipp • 100 ha (cab, malbec, merlot, pinotage, petit v, shiraz, chard, colombard, muscadel, sauvignon) • 3 100 tons • PO Box 179 Robertson 6705 • clairvaux@lando.co.za • www.wine.co.za • ***T (023) 626 3042*** *• F (023) 626·1925*

Good wine is made in the vineyard, believes Pieter van Aarde, but there's something of the winemaker's personality and taste in every bottle. And it's bottles he and owners Wouters de Wet Snr and Jnr are focusing on: they want to up their production of cork closed wines, and develop markets for these products locally and overseas. At the winery, they added a function/conference area, and paused to pop a cork in celebration of the arrival of 4th generation de Wet yes, Wouter.

Sandberg Purple ☺ ★★★ **04** delightful easy-drinker; spicy red fruit flavour, slippery tannins; usual more-or-less equal pinotage, ruby cab, merlot concoction, briefly staved. 13.5% alc.

Cabernet Sauvignon ★★★ **04** opposite of nervy, lean pvs: ripe & succulent berry fruit, silky tannins, good persistence. Oak staved. **Shiraz** ★★★ Wooding formula (combo staves/barrels, all Am) imparts pleasant sweet vanilla tone, well-tuned with very ripe dark fruit on **04** (sample). **Rosé** ★ Returns to overtly sweet, somewhat simple mode; **05** with talcum powder whiff from white muscadel. **Chardonnay** ★★ **05** its former amiable self; bit podgy but nice to have around; Fr oak staving better than last yr. **Sauvignon Blanc** ★★★ Uncomplicated picnic wine. **05** light-bodied, lemon-toned; briskly dry with good long finish. **Chardonnay-Colombar** ★★ Friendly dry white (amenable 13% alc too); **05** orange zest aroma, gentle dryness; suggest drink soon. **Soleil** ★★ Returns to guide with sweet but refreshing **05**, mainly white muscadel & colombard; straightforwardly pleasant. **Madonna's Kisses** ★★★ Full-sweet muscadel jerepigo; **03** billows Turkish Delight, luscious muscat character through to well-balanced, silky finish. 16% alc. **Port** ★ **03** old-style fireside fortifier from ruby cab, with treacle-like sweetness. 16% alc. – *MM*

Clemence Creek see Mooiuitsig

Cloof

Darling • Est 1997 • 1stB 1998 • Tasting & sales Mon-Thu 10-4 Fri 10-3 Sat by appt • Closed Easter Fri/Sun, Dec 25/26, Jan 1 • Occasional gourmet BBQ events – pre-bookings only • Owner Cloof Wine Estate (Pty) Ltd • Winemaker Christopher van Dieren (Jan 2002) • Viticulturist Peter Duckitt (2005) • 166 ha (cabs s/f, cinsaut, merlot, pinotage, shiraz, chard, chenin) • 600 tons 90 000 cs 88% red 5% white 7% rosé • PO Box 269 Darling 7345 • info@cloof.co.za • www.cloof.co.za • ***T (022) 492·2839*** *• F (022) 492·3261*

Most 'New World' wines are perceived to be for everyday enjoyment, reflects Cloof marketer Oscar Foulkes. 'But above entry-level wines – and especially at the level of special-occasion – consumers seem to prefer Old World. This is a big challenge.' And one this West Coast winery is tackling head-on. Cloof is now the best-selling New World brand in Hong Kong, Oscar F reports; their Dusty Road Pinotage the fastest-moving SA red above 90 kroner in Norway; and their wines have been chosen by both BA and SAA to meliorate in-flight rigours. High-flyers, these, and with another 18 hectares planted, a new viticulturist on board and promising 05 reds in the pipeline, they've no reason to look down.

★★★★☆ **Crucible Shiraz** Shades of the deepest, darkest Rhône; **03** remarkably concentrated; sniffs of roast meat to the big, booming fruit & spicy fynbos flavours. Powerful but balanced oak (15 mths new Fr), sweetness & richness from 5.6g/ℓ sugar, brawny 15.5% alc. Widely gonged: VDG, MIWA, SAA 1st Class.

★★★★ **Burghers Post Shiraz** new **04** eponymous wine from neighbouring farm. Abundance of big grippy tannins & expressive plummy fruit, hints pepper & allspice. Yr Fr oak, 75% new.

★★★★ **Pinotage** From single bushvine vyd established 1976. **03** (★★★☆) old-style, with serious tannins only partly ameliorated by sweet red fruit; funky flavours, as in **02** with candyfloss aftertaste.

★★★★ **Cellar Blend** new Appealingly rustic **04** mix pinotage, tinta, cab & shiraz (45/23/20/12). Sweet & wild red fruit, exotic nose, richness from 5.1g/ℓ sugar. Yr Fr oak, 29% new.

★★★★ **Cabernet Sauvignon-Cabernet Franc-Merlot 03**, sample last ed, hoists this label to new level. Herbal tones with dark choc depths; good & grippy balance despite 15% alc. 14 mths Fr oak, 90% new. Concours Mondial gold. **02** (★★★) considerably less arresting.

Bush Vines range

★★★★ **Cabernet Sauvignon 03**, previewed last ed, still boarded shut but promising; lurking blackcurrants & intriguing leather nuance. Beefy 15% alc. 13 mths Fr oak, 10% new. A keeper.

★★★★ **Cabernet Sauvignon-Shiraz** 80/20 blend **02** red/black berry array, nice balance & length. 15 mths Fr oak. This, following pair, not retasted.

Pinotage ★★★☆ Good concentration of varietal flavour, some acetone hints on **03**. 13 mths older Fr oak. **Bushvine** ★★★☆ Fruity & friendly **02** blend pinotage, cab, cinsaut (44/33/23); ripe, generous tannins, toasty finish; some promise for development. **Merlot-Cabernet Sauvignon** ★★★☆ new **04** rustic blend (71/29) proffering generous fruit & good persistence. Yr Fr oak, 44% new.

Dusty Road range

★★★★ **Chardonnay Unwooded 05** (★★) zesty pineapples with disturbing chemical notes, sweetish tone (4g/ℓ RS). Not a patch on fresh, flavoursome **04**, which over-delivered on price.

Cabernet Sauvignon ★★★☆ **03** attractive dusty quality with a pleasant fruit sweetness & mineral austerity. Fine balance. **Pinotage** ★★ **04** old-style, with rubbery undertone; not the easy-drinker of pvs vintage. **Cabernet Sauvignon-Shiraz** ★★★ Smoky & austere **03**, some stone fruit flavours from 80% cab, pepper from shiraz. Massive 14.9% alc; just-dry 4.1g/ℓ sugar. Preceding pair still available, not revisited. **Pinotage-Shiraz-Cabernet** ★★☆ Pinotage now in control **03** 40/20/40 blend (pvs was cab-led); juicy red fruit up, alc down to 13.5%, but tougher tannins. **Rosé** ★☆ **05** cinsaut, shiraz, pinotage melange with juicy-dry fruit flavours; touch confected. Lowish 13% alc. **Chenin** ★★☆ **05** oily texture with contrasting sour/tart flavours, bigger than pvs but still low 12.5% alc. – *NP*

Clos Cabrière see Cabrière Estate

Clos Malverne

Stellenbosch ▪ Est/1stB 1988 ▪ Tasting & sales Mon-Fri 10-4.30 Sat 10-1 ▪ Fee R13 ▪ Closed Christian hols & Jan 1 ▪ Tours by appt ▪ BYO picnic ▪ Owners Seymour & Sophia Pritchard ▪

Winemaker/viticulturist Isak 'Ippie' Smit (Nov 1997) ▪ 25 ha (cab, merlot, pinotage, shiraz, sauvignon) ▪ 350 tons 24 000 cs 90% red 10% white ▪ Export brands: Shepherd's Creek & Kleinrivier ▪ PO Box 187 Stellenbosch 7599 ▪ closma@mweb.co.za ▪ www.closmalverne.co.za www.capeblend.co.za ▪ ***T 865·2022*** *▪ F 865·2518*

At Clos Malverne they're going all out with sauvignon blanc. Finding that it does particularly well in their vineyards, and with a market for twice their current production, they're hurrying along with new graftings and plantings – the aim being to boost overall production from the current 10% to 25% over the next few years. Encouraged by the positive reception of their style generally, they are experimenting with earlier picking as they continue to hone their idea of what constitutes optimal ripeness. Despite their ambivalence towards its bottling as a varietal wine, they haven't given up on their long-standing affair with pinotage, nor their determination to advance the market for pinotage-based blends.

★★★★ **Auret Cape Blend** Standard-bearer of this cellar – cab, pinotage, merlot blend, usually 60/25/15. Magisterial **01** was firm & unyielding in youth. Latest **02** (★★★★) still stylish, but less presence; more approachable than pvs. Rounded cassis, plum flavours, tannins not overdone, slight sweetness on finish. As other reds here, basket-pressed, fermented in traditional open-topped *kuipe*. Yr Fr/Am oak.

★★★★★ **Auret Cape Blend Limited Release 01**, tasted mid-2004, features SAYWS-winning cab (60%) & merlot, plus cellar's best pinotage (25%). dense, compact flavours; yr Fr oak adds opulence. Impressive, understated power; lots of life ahead.

★★★★ **Pinotage Reserve** Showy, deep-flavoured barrel selection bristles with awards. After impressive, seamlessly elegant **01**, dark, brooding & unyielding **02** rather more understated, more bdx-like. Lead pencils, prune; ripe & savoury, dried fruit character rather than juicy, firm tannins. Cellar 3-5 yrs. Yr Fr/Am oak.

★★★★ **Cabernet Sauvignon-Merlot Limited Release 01** once off showcase for 60/40 blend which won Jan Smuts Trophy at SAYWS 2001; held back for further bottle maturation. Retasted mid-2005: deep-pile velvety richness, intense black mulberry, beautifully proportioned, oak still exercising subtle discipline, set to be a stunner in 2-3 yrs.

★★★★ **Cabernet Sauvignon-Shiraz 03** continues style of seamless integration, shiraz softening cab's more austere notes in 75/25 blend. Cigar-tinged oak offsets ripe mulberry, dusted with white pepper. Classy dark fruit, subtly supported by fine oak. Well balanced, just right. Cellar 2-3 yrs. 6 mths Fr/Am oak.

★★★★ **Cabernet Sauvignon-Pinotage Cape Blend 01**, tasted mid-2004 when sleek & suave, almost ready. 65/35 blend: cab's cassis complementing pinotage's mulberry notes, gentle Fr oak (yr) adding classic savoury finish.

Devonet Merlot-Pinotage ☺ ★★★ Intended as entry-level Cape blend; **04** bright Satsuma plum, whiff vanilla; plump & juicy; good oak sleeks young fruit. 4 mths Fr/Am oak. **Shepherds Creek Classic Red** ☺ ★★★ Robust **NV** all-sorts blend led by cab, pinotage. High-quality fruit, braaied chop-impervious tannins. WO W Cape. Only to restaurants.

Pinotage ★★★★ **01** ripe mulberries & hints vanilla oak, when tasted mid-2004 tannins bit gruff. 4-6 mths Fr/Am oak adding body & spice. **Cabernet Sauvignon** ★★★★ Correct, unshowy **01** (not retasted) endowed with classic cassis padding around firm tannic & mineral core. Properly dry. **Shiraz** ★★★★ **03** fragrant dark cherry, soft ripe tannins sculpt fruit to pleasing roundness, controlled generosity. Very easy to drink. Yr Fr/Am oak. **Cabernet Sauvignon-Merlot** ★★★ Tasted last ed, **03**, much more cab (80%) than minerally **02** – firmer but also quieter; cassis abounds, rather more classic & perhaps less interesting than pinotage blends. **Sauvignon Blanc** ★★★ From home-grown & neighbouring grapes, **05** continues zesty, lively style; gooseberry & grapefruit notes, fresh & zingy, hint sugar for soft landing. Moderate 12.5% alc. **Shepherds Creek Chardonnay** discontinued. *— IvH*

Clouds Vineyards

Stellenbosch ▪ Est 2002 ▪ 1stB 2003 ▪ Visits by appt ▪ Lunches/dinners for small groups by appt ▪ Luxury self-catering & B&B suites ▪ Weddings & functions ▪ Owners Bernard & Petro

Immelman ▪ Vini consultants Gyles Webb & Rudi Schultz ▪ Viticulturist Matthew Castle ▪ 2.5 ha (sauvignon) ▪ 750 cs 100% white ▪ PO Box 540 Stellenbosch 7599 ▪ info@cloudsvineyards.co.za ▪ www.cloudsguesthouse.com ▪ ***T 885·1819*** *▪ F 885·2829*

Blessed with a great location high on Helshoogte Pass, Bernard & Petro Immelman are making the most of their assets. They've registered their sauvignon block as a single vineyard, and continue to harness the considerable talents of Rudi Schultz and Gyles Webb of neighbouring Thelema to vinify the crop. They've also added a new 5-suite guesthouse (catering for weddings and functions too), and built a tasting area, so the welcome has never been warmer.

Sauvignon Blanc ★★★★ One for fans of the *sauvage* style (& one to watch); **05** nettle/green pepper pungency, funky whiff of caper; racy fruit & zesty acidity. Raises the bar with more concentration, complexity. — *CT*

Clovelly Wines

Stellenbosch ▪ Est/1stB 2000 ▪ Visits by appt ▪ Owners Mineke Toerien-Fourie & Deon Toerien ▪ 3 ha (cab) ▪ 6 tons 2 600 cs 70% red 30% white ▪ Postnet Suite 215 Private Bag X5061 Stellenbosch 7599 ▪ info@clovellywines.com ▪ www.clovellywines.com

Bureaucratic issues all but resolved, this small Devon Valley winery is looking forward to the year ahead and nurturing the dream of an own cellar to join the Tuscan-style homestead featured on their label. Last harvest holds happy memories of their first harvest of shiraz — '1.2 tons and looking good', they say. There was further cause to celebrate: Clovelly Wines' fifth anniversary, and as if to mark it, sales to the UK, Canada and Gauteng doubled.

Cabernet Sauvignon ★★★ **03** crafted from very ripe fruit to be opulent but not blowsy. Dark choc/cherry aromas & flavours countered by tangy acids & savory tannins. Well balanced, should hit its stride ± 3 yrs. At 13.5%, alc lower than pvs. WO Stbosch; 14 mths oak, some new. **Triangle** ★★★ Name refers to trio of partners in this venture; could be either single variety or three-way blend; no new bottling to taste for this ed; pvs **NV** from cab/merlot/cinsaut. **Chardonnay** ★★★ **04** not up to quality of **02**. Hot alcoholic finish (14%), sharp acidity, obtrusive oaking detract from lovely peachy fruit. Portion barrel fermented/aged. WO W Cape unless noted. — *IvH*

Cloverfield Private Cellar

Robertson ▪ Est ca 1920 ▪ 1stB 2002 ▪ Tasting & sales Mon-Fri 9-5 Sat 10-2 ▪ Closed Easter Fri-Sun, Dec 25 & Jan 1 ▪ Owner Pieter Marais ▪ Winemaker Cobus Marais (Jan 2002) ▪ Viticulturist Pieter Marais ▪ 120 ha (cinsaut, merlot, petit v, shiraz, chard, chenin, sauvignon, semillon) ▪ ±1 700 tons ±2 000 cs own label 40% red 60% white ▪ PO Box 429 Robertson 6705 ▪ info@cloverfield.co.za ▪ ***T (023) 626·4118/3*** *▪ F (023) 626·3203*

Hanging out their board on the wine route has helped Pieter and Liz Marais to pull visitors into their year-old tasting room — their recent awards should further increase traffic flow. For the second year running their wooded Chardonnay took a Michelangelo gold and their Chenin came up for a Tastevins du Cap trophy. Expansion of their red wine cellar is the first in a series of upgrades.

Winemaker's Selection

★★★★ **Chardonnay** ✓ From a single vyd, fermented/aged on Fr oak, sold only ex-cellar & in Joh'burg. **04** worth the trip, though no rush: time needed for overt (& delicious) barrel characters to settle; similar voluptuous profile to **02**, striking brioche & burnt match aromas; buttery peach flavours.

Shiraz ★★★★ Maiden **02** still in stock; last yr showed lovely mix of red fruits, some pepper & game — fine complexity, zesty sour-plum farewell. Fr vats/staves, 9 mths.

Four Clover range

★★★★ **Sauvignon Blanc 04** powerful nose of grapefruit zest, carries into zingy citrus-zest palate with twist of nettles. **05** (★★★) more tropical, some mineral hints; broad entry tapers quite quickly to firm acidic conclusion.

Chardonnay Unwooded ★★★★ **04** (pvs ed a sample) crisply dry & composed; fresh melon flavour with citrusy acid, hauling in the usual bulging alc (14.5%). **Chenin Blanc** new ★★★★ ✓ **04** a little gem: richly fruited & characterful, some bottle age complexity, bright tingle of acidity. Delightful (& imperative) to drink now.—*MM*

Cogmans Kloof see Zandvliet
Cogmans River see Zandvliet

Cold Duck (5th Avenue)

Exuberant, gently sweet, low alc (8%) carbonated sparkler from Distell. Its signature: heady pineapple scents from Ferdinand de Lesseps grapes (50%, with pinotage, chenin); latest (**NV**) ★★ lots of frothy flavour, red berry sweetness in character with easy charm.—*CvZ*

Coleraine Wines

Paarl ▪ Est 1998 ▪ 1stB 1999 ▪ Visits by appt; tasting/sales also at I Love Wine (see Wine shops section) ▪ Walks ▪ Owners C & HK Kerr ▪ Winemaker/viticulturist Clive Kerr ▪ 30 ha (cab, cinsaut, merlot, mourvèdre, petit v, ruby cab, shiraz, chard, sauvignon, viognier) ▪ 4-5 000 cs own label 100% red ▪ PO Box 579 Suider-Paarl 7624 ▪ info@coleraine.co.za ▪ www.coleraine.co.za ▪ ***T/F 863·3443***

Approbation for winemaker/viticulturist Clive Kerr last year arrived in the form of the trophy (and only gold medal) at the Trophy Wine Show for the Culraithin Merlot 03, and a call-up for the same wine from local convenor Michael Fridjhon to strengthen SA's hand at the Tri-Nations Challenge in Australia. 'For our small cellar this is an amazing achievement,' notes Kerr's wife Lyn.

★★★★ **Syrah (Culraithin)** Deeply scented, amply fruited & opulent. Last was exceptional **02** (★★★★★) which mid-2004 offered cornucopia of features, shored up by clean oak, sturdy tannins – & 16% alc. Latest for the long haul – 2008 onwards. More complex than **01** VDG. 8-15 mths Fr oak, 20-25% new.

★★★★ **Merlot (Culraithin)** 2005 FCTWS Trophy for **03**; inky-black viscosity ushers in plump magenta-toned fruits, butcher-shop richness & finely tuned tannins; manages balance in spite of decadence & 15% alc. Promise of expanded allure with time in bottle. No **02**. 2 yrs in cask, 10% new Fr.

★★★★ **Cabernet Sauvignon (Culraithin) 03** not ready. Ripe-fruited **02** (★★★★) flaunted spicy cassis, damson depth & savoury hints pvs ed, lacy tannins in fine finish restraining 15% alc. Yr Fr barriques, 20% new.

Still available from tasting room, not retasted: **Cabernet Sauvignon-Merlot (Culraithin)** ★★★ Once-off, now tiring **99** 60/40 blend, 40% new Fr oak. **Fire Engine Red** ★★★ **00** easy-drinking merlot, ruby cab, cinsaut blend, lightly oaked.—*DS*

Compagnies Wijn see Oude Compagnies Post
Condé see Stark-Condé
Confluence see Douglas Winery, Landzicht

Conradie Family Vineyards

new

Worcester ▪ Est/1stB 2004 ▪ Tasting, sales & tours daily 9-5; sales also after-hours by appt ▪ Closed Good Fri, Ascension Day, Dec 25 & Jan 1 ▪ Fully licensed restaurant, guest house & other amenities (see intro) ▪ Owners Conradie family ▪ Winemaker CP Conradie, with Colin Ciliers (both Jan 2004) ▪ Viticulturist CP Conradie ▪ 91 ha (cabs s/f, merlot, pinotage, red muscadel, chard, chenin, colombard, crouchen, sauvignon) ▪ 1 500 tons 2500 cs own label ▪ Export brands: Conradie Family Vineyards & Saw Edge Peak ▪ 45% red 45% white 10% rosé ▪ PO Box 5298 Worcester 6851 ▪ wine@conradievineyards.co.za ▪ www.conradie-vineyards.co.za ▪ ***T (023) 342·1258/342·7025*** *▪ F (023) 3471356*

CP Conradie, 5th generation tender of the family vineyards on the Langeberg's lower reaches, returned in 2004 from winemaking spells in Germany and the US to reopen the small cellar on the farm – exactly 40 years after the doors had closed due to the establishment of the Nuy Co-op. The first Chenin Unwooded of the new era promptly won gold at the Michelangelo Awards, spurring CPC to expand the range. Quantities remain limited, however, and distribution mostly local. A fair portion is consumed on the spot by guests of the farm's restaurant and guest house, offering a wide variety of amenities.

Cabernet Sauvignon ★★★★ **04** attractively & carefully assembled; restrained berry fruit, soft herbal whiffs, dense without being confected. Grapes hand-selected in vyd, cold soaked pre-fermentation, aged in new oak, 25% Am. **Chardonnay** ★★★★ Finely made & classically styled **05**, shows bright citrus notes, subtle oak (only third barrel fermented), food-friendly mien. Both from home-farm fruit. — *MF*

Conspirare

Stellenbosch ▪ Est/1stB 2002 ▪ Tasting by appt ▪ Owners HB Dowling/LRD Trust ▪ Winemaker Henry Dowling ▪ Viticulturist Francois de Villiers ▪ 24 ha (cab s/f, merlot, shiraz, chenin) ▪ 250 tons 425 cs own label 100% red ▪ PO Box 1210 Stellenbosch 7599 ▪ dowls@mweb.co.za ▪ ***T 855·0722*** *▪ F 855·0706*

Taking stock, Helderberg farmer Henry Dowling's to-do list reads: further improve on quality, sharpen marketing skills and then gradually up production. He didn't make any wines in 2005 but, pressed for an opinion on the vintage, believes that it was 'fairly good' (grapes not used for his and singer wife Lesley-Rae's Conspirare label are sold off). Their improbably beautiful eyrie on the Helderberg now opens to visitors by appointment.

★★★★ **Conspirare** Elegant **02** sweet-fruited blend cabs s/f, merlot, discreetly confident, satisfying. Still-youthful deep-coloured **03** adds 14% shiraz & some intensity & power to equation, no reduction of appeal. Subtle red fruit, cedar notes; savoury ripe tannins, judicious supportive oaking: 27 mths, 30% new. Will benefit from good few yrs maturation yet. — *TJ*

Constantia de Tulbagh see Montpellier du Sud

Constantia Glen

new

Constantia ▪ Est 2000 ▪ 1stB 2005 ▪ Closed to public ▪ Owners Tumado Investments ▪ Winemaker John Loubser (Steenberg), 2005 harvest ▪ Viticulturist Andrew Teubes (1999) ▪ 29 ha (cabs s/f, malbec, merlot, petit v, sauvignon) ▪ 102 tons 250 cs 100% white ▪ PO Box 780 Constantia 7848 ▪ wine@constantiaglen.com ▪ www.constantiaglen.com ▪ ***T 794·7865*** *▪ F 794·9705*

Constantia's physical beauty and special place in the history of SA winemaking were the inspiration for the founding of Constantia Glen. Planned in the mid-90s, this boutique venture aims to combine the steep (often misty) mountain aspects and coastal exposure of its location with modern vinification techniques and vineyard practices. The intention is to produce just two wines — a Sauvignon and a Bordeaux-styled red — both reflecting this unique location. Fruit for the maiden wine below, vinified by John Loubser at Steenberg, came off the property — and most went straight to the UK. This year sees a winery built in time for the 2007 harvest, which will be the first to be bottled on-site.

★★★★★ **Sauvignon Blanc** Classic cool-climate style, **05** with racy food-friendly acidity softened by succulent mid-palate richness; greenpepper & gooseberry notes in persistent fine finish. Bunch pressed, cold fermented 21 days, further aged *sur lie*. — *MF*

Constantia Uitsig

Constantia ▪ Est 1988 ▪ 1stB 1993 ▪ Tasting & sales Mon-Fri 9-5 Sat & Sun 10-4 ▪ Closed Easter Fri, Dec 25/26, Jan 1 ▪ Constantia Uitsig & La Colombe restaurants (see Eat-Out section); Spaanschemat River Café for light meals 8-5 ▪ Constantia Uitsig Country Hotel (see Stay-over section) ▪ Gift/wine shop ▪ Conference facilities ▪ Owners David & Marlene McCay ▪ Vini/viti consultants André Rousseau & John Loubser (Mar 1998/2001) ▪ 32 ha (cab, merlot, chard, sauvignon, semillon) ▪ ±200 tons ±12 000 cs 30% red 70% white ▪ PO Box 402 Constantia 7848 ▪ wine@icon.co.za ▪ www.uitsig.co.za ▪ ***T 794·1810*** *▪ F 794·1812*

The ripe 2005 harvest brought out the improviser in viticulturist and winemaker André Rousseau, compelling him to pick his sauvignon in three phases of ripeness. This allowed him to capture some of the greener flavours, resulting, he feels, in a more balanced wine. While professing to be happy with the overall success of his wines, new projects seem to be much on his mind, with some chardonnay going to make Uitsig's first MCC. 'Producing cap classique has always been my passion, and I look forward to realising this dream at Uitsig,' he says. The relaunch of their Semillon-Sauvignon as 'Constantia White' – 'a wine that keeps surprising me' – is another milestone for André R, who also hints that Semillon is to get his renewed attention.

★★★★ **Constantia Red** (Formerly 'Cabernet Sauvignon-Merlot') After gap year (no **02**), name change for **03** plus new embossed Constantia bottle. Change in emphasis too: more showy, lushly ripe, oaky than pvs. Half merlot, with cab s & 9% cab f ex Steenberg; rich fruit, fresh acidity, soft reclusive tannins. 19 mths oak, mostly Fr 70% new, a little Am. Characterful & complete **01** more elegantly understated. 2 yrs Fr oak, 50% new. Should develop few yrs or more.

★★★★☆ **Chardonnay Reserve** Lovely aromas of oatmeal, citrus on **04** (★★★★), full flavours & silky texture on palate, complemented by admirable oaking (11 mths, 70% new) – but a rather hard, hot alcoholic glow tends to dominate finish (alc 14.5%). **03** coped well with same alc, full, rich & deep, subtly alluding to citrus, honey, butterscotch, with mineral thread.

★★★★☆ **Semillon Reserve** Always serious & rather grand, needing yr/2 to open up. Youthful **04** promises good development, from incipiently complex nose (nuts, lanolin, citrus) to lingering finish, via rich, deep fruited palate – where wood flavours blissfully lacking: fermented/11 mths in 2nd/3rd fill Fr oak. Dry – as with fine, powerful **03**, a little sugar not apparent, subsumed in richness. **02** was Diners Club winner.

★★★★ **Constantia White** (Was 'Semillon-Sauvignon Blanc') Maiden **03** flagship blend showed semillon as dominant partner (72%), with nutty, biscuitty notes; 5g/ℓ sugar not quite disguised. More equal partnership in **04** (★★★★☆), some tweaking of cellar practices (as before only semillon component fermented/4 mths oak, but now blend spends 5 mths in 2nd/3rd fill oak), touch less sugar & alc (now 13.8%), bit more acid – all making for finer balance, better focus, more serious effect. 6 000 bottles, screwcapped – as are all these whites.

★★★★ **Sauvignon Blanc** Elegantly intense **05**, aromas fig, gooseberry, passionfruit. Gratifying acidic grip on full flavours, focused green citrus conclusion. Same moderate 13% alc as **04** with finely balanced richness & thrilling acidity. These, like all the Uitsig whites, benefit greatly from yr+ in bottle.

★★★★ **Chardonnay Unwooded** Convincing & charming example in increasingly popular genre; **05**, from unirrigated vyds, typically nervy, dry & fine, though generous in mouthfeel, lingering flavour, freshness. Powerful, well balanced **04** gracefully full & round. 2-3 mths on lees. – *TJ*

Co-operative Group see International Wine Services

Coppoolse Finlayson Winery

Stellenbosch ▪ Est 1991 ▪ 1stB 1994 ▪ Tasting etc at Sentinel Vineyards (see entry) ▪ Owners Rob Coppoolse, Walter Finlayson & Viv Grater ▪ Cellarmasters Walter Finlayson & Jean-Claude Martin (1998/2004) ▪ Winemakers Adele Dunbar & Danielle du Toit (Aug 1998, Apr 2002) ▪ Viti consultant Johan Pienaar (2001) ▪ 850 000 cs + 150 000 own label 70% red 30% white ▪ Ranges for customers: Kaaps Geskenk, Kaapse Pracht, Songloed & Nuwe Wynplaas ▪ ISO 9001:2000, HACCP & BRC certified ▪ PO Box 4028 Old Oak 7537 ▪ wine@sentinel.co.za ▪ www.cfwines.co.za ▪ ***T 982·6175*** *▪ F 982·6296*

A substantial joint venture with an international company was imminent at press time, promising even bigger things for this, the biggest exporter of SA wine to the Netherlands and one of the largest SA wine exporters overall. Their focus is on Kaya, a range linked to the celebrated Cheetah Outreach Programme at Spier (€1 per bottle goes to fund the adoption of cheetah cubs). Sales of Kaya wines in Holland are so strong, a new cub may soon join their original adoptee, Kaya. Plans are afoot to grow the brand in the local market – currently only

2% of their business. They're also moving more strongly into the US, with an agent in place and sales of their Cape Cab brand growing. Canada and Mexico are next. Public tastings of their wines are at sister winery, Sentinel Vineyards (see entry.)

Cape Cab ★★★ new Indisputably cab(ernet sauvignon), with all edges well smoothed for soft & pleasant drinkability. **04** even has some elegance. Export only.

Kaya Traditional range

Wine for this, ranges above & below, bought from selected W Cape cellars & blended. **Shaka** ★★ Three-way mix, mainly cinsaut & pinotage, dash cab f; **04** juicy, rounded & perhaps just a shade too easy for higher rating – needs bit more oomph. **Nandi** ★★☆ **05** pleasant, light dry white with crisp melon/peach finish.

Kaya Cape Vineyards Level range

No new releases of following tasted; notes from pvs ed: **Merlot** ★★★ Textbook varietal characters; smooth, juicy; big ripe tannins augur well for development. **Pinotage** ★★★ Ripe plum & banana whiffs, deft touch oak, rounded ripe tannins; youthfully exuberant & drinkable. **Shiraz** ★★★☆ Bright purple hues; nose of blackberries & pepper; toasty, well rounded; shows some structure & heft. **Chardonnay** ★★☆ Toasty touch to tropical fruit, nicely put together. **Sauvignon Blanc** ★★☆ **04** amenable tropical fruit, lightish, easy drinking. All **04**s, tasted as samples, ratings provisional.

Songloed range

Merlot ★★ Undemanding, quaffable **04** with herbaceous edge to plummy fruit, dry, slightly stalky finish. **Pinotage** new ☆ Old-style **04**, insubstantial with hot finish from 14.7% alc. **Shiraz** ★★☆ **04** sound everyday red, no histrionics; subtle mulberry whiffs, soft touch tannin, clean dry finish. **Dry Steen** ★★☆ Last tasted was Fresh & fruity **04**, attractive tropical nose, quaffably light bodied (12.6% alc). – *CT*

Cordoba Winery

Stellenbosch (see Helderberg map) ▪ Est 1982 ▪ 1stB 1994 ▪ Tasting only by appt Mon-Fri 8.30-5 ▪ Sales Mon-Fri 8.30-5 ▪ Closed pub hols ▪ Tours by appt ▪ Owner Jannie Jooste ▪ Winemaker/viticulturist Christopher Keet (Oct 1993) ▪ 31 ha (cabs s/f, merlot, shiraz, chard) ▪ 100 tons 7 000 cs 90% red 10% white ▪ PO Box 5609 Helderberg 7135 ▪ mail@cordobawines.co.za ▪ www.cordobawines.co.za ▪ ***T 855·3744*** *▪ F 855·1690*

'Our vineyard redevelopment programme is complete,' announces Chris Keet with undisguised satisfaction. It's taken years of back-breaking work – painstaking planting of cab, cab franc and merlot on these prime sea-facing Helderberg mountainside sites, then nursing 30 000 individual vines weekly for four months during one season – and Chris K does it all himself, with just a handful of helpers. Attention to detail is a way of life here, with the smallest reward welcomed with deep delight. Like the first crop off young cab franc vines, subjected to a whopping 70% cut-back at the onset of ripening, and delivering wines with great fruit concentration and high natural acid. Chris K is now all set to nearly double production to 12 000 cases. Happy news.

★★★★☆ **Crescendo** Classically oriented fine blend based on cab f (proportions may vary). Quietly assertive **03** has 15% each cab s & merlot. Unusually early emergence of charm for this long developer: lovely berry fruits, cherries, minerality supported in harmonious whole by fine tannins, savoury acid, good oak (18 mths new Fr), 13.9% alc. Delicate, fresh, exciting now, but a fine future too. Contrasting, bigger (14.5% alc) & less elegant **02** was muscularly gaunt & sulky at same stage, needing more time to reveal its best.

★★★★ **Merlot** This always one of Cape's more serious. After refined, refreshing & persistent **01** (★★★★☆) with characteristic roast coffee/dark choc notes over cherries & minty-leafy element, **02**, not retasted, was more severe, though fragrant, savoury & well structured, deserving attention, time, decanting, & food. 17 mths Fr oak, 20% new.

Mount Claire Mountain Red ☺ ★★★ **03** cab-merlot-shiraz blend charming & unpretentious, but a 'proper' wine: pure, fresh fruit, well-balanced, dry. Lightly oaked; 13.3% alc.

Merlot-Cabernet Sauvignon ★★★ Typically dry, firm **02** has plummy & slightly dour flavours; lightish fruit flesh over strong bones. 17 mths Fr oak, 20% new. **Chardonnay** ★★★★ Oak-fermented/matured (9 mths, 33% new) **04** as usual rounded but elegant, with lime-marmalade & toast-vanilla notes of oak; drinkability helped by easy 13% alc. — *TJ*

Country Cellars

These are the Spar chain of convenience stores' cork-closed wines. See under Carnival for the boxed range, and under Spar for news and contact details.

Country Cellars range

Claret ★★ **04** easy, satisfying blend shiraz, ruby cab; red fruit & choc on entry, mocha after-taste, not too dry. **Shiraz-Cabernet Sauvignon 05** not ready for tasting. **Chardonnay 05** sample too unformed to rate. **Sauvignon Blanc** ★★ **05** (sample) less fruity & more straight-forward this yr; light & dry. **Chenin Blanc-Chardonnay** new ★★ Incl dollop colombard; **05** pleasant summer refresher with whiff of cucumber (!), vibrant lemon acidity.

Non-vintage range

All **NV**, featuring more serious-looking packaging; alc around 12% unless noted. **Classic Red** ★★ Best-seller in this stable. Outdoorish wine from ruby cab (80%), pinotage; latest bottling atypically subdued & tannic, needs robust/fatty food. **Rosé** ★★ Colombard replaces chenin in latest incarnation, tinting still by pinotage. Ripe banana/cassis aromas, dry & savoury flavours. **Caresse** ★★ Low-alc (9%) blanc de noir-style semi-sweet, in 1 000 ml bottle. Shy strawberry scent, drier taste than pvs. **Dry White** ★ Light-bodied glugger from chenin, colombard, with tropical hint, dry, lively. **Blanc de Blanc** ★★ From colombard; round & lightly fruity, slightly sweet. **Light** ★ Light, bright, dry & crisp, with easy-to-tipple low alc (8%). **Stein** ★ Colombard, chenin & 28g/ℓ sugar do the business here; soft peachy aromas, distinctly sweet finish. **Late Harvest** ★ Plain & simple sweet white from chenin, colombard; lacks pvs version's sprightliness, refreshment. — *JP*

Cowlin Wines

Paarl ▪ Est 2001 ▪ Tasting & sales Summer: Mon-Fri 10–4 Sat 10–1 Winter: Sat 10–1 or by appt ▪ Picnics: please phone for details ▪ Closed Easter Fri, Dec 25 & Jan 1 ▪ Tours by appt ▪ Facilities for children ▪ Farm produce ▪ Small tourgroups ▪ Walks ▪ Owners Cowlin & Malherbe families ▪ Vini consultant Hardy Laubser, with Rodney Zimba (2002/2003) ▪ Viti consultant Gideon Malherbe ▪ 17 ha (cab, merlot, shiraz, mourvèdre, chard, viognier) ▪ 130 tons 3 500 cs 90% red 10% white ▪ PO Box 174 Simondium 7670 ▪ cowlinwines@iafrica.com ▪ www.cowlinwines.co.za ▪ ***T 874·3844*** *▪ F 874·2948*

Joining 'Jack's Jug' in this family winery's portfolio is 'Poodle's Passion', a Sauvignon named after wine-passionate Cowlin daughter Lisa, whose nickname is almost as characterful as the wine. (Her grandfather Jack is the man behind the Jug.) 'Wonderful wines at good prices' are the goal, along with 'excellent service', which includes providing a wide range of family-friendly facilities on their home farm in the northern Simonsberg foothills.

★★★★ **Shiraz** The new kingpin here; **02** last yr exhibited good varietal character, generous but accommodating tannins; all in elegant, not overblown package (13.5% alc). 6 mths oak, casks/staves. Next will be **05**.

Cabernet Sauvignon ★★★★ Cedar notes (from yr Fr oak, 30% new) on **02**; wood tannins still in charge, firmly trussed black fruit needs time to develop undoubted potential. **Merlot** ★★★★ Pleasingly vinous **03** opens with classic pencil shavings & dark berried fruit, concludes with serious-minded dryness. Oak as per Cab. **Noble Hill** Stylish (wine & packaging) cab-driven blend with merlot; **03** repeats 50/50 mix, at once beefy (14% alc) & silky, rounded & sustained dry finish. 14 mths oak, otherwise as for Cab. **Jack's Jug** ★★★ Juicy, lip-smacking dry red; latest (**NV**) brings shiraz (25%, with cab, merlot) to the steakhouse table. 6 mths staved. **Poodle's Passion Sauvignon Blanc** new ★★★ **04** growls at you with array of assertive sauvignon aromas (incl tomato leaf & dusty nettle), then backs down & covers you with soft, slightly sweet licks. **Semillon-Chardonnay** ★★★ Pvs (& only) was 70/30 blend, **NV**, with brioche & lees whiffs & creamy palate. 15 mths 2nd/3rd fill Fr oak. Next will be **05** 'Chardonnay-Semillon'. **Cabernet Sauvignon-Petit Verdot** a once off, sold out.—*IvH/TM*

Craighall

Popular range of early/easy drinkers, budget priced, from African Wines & Spirits.

Cabernet Sauvignon-Merlot ★★★ Comfortable standalone drink or food partner; medium-bodied **03** showed bottle-age dried-fruit, gamey tones last ed; pleasantly astringent dark cherry flavours. 66/33 mix. **Rosé** new ★★ Ripe, slightly jammy **NV** from shiraz, soft, gentle, uncomplicated dry flavours. **Chardonnay-Sauvignon Blanc** ★★★ Formula change for **04** (pvs teamed chard & chenin); lightish harmoniouis blend; fleshy citrus fruit, sherbety texture. **Sauvignon Blanc 04** (sample, provisional ★★★★) shows no sign of flagging; appealing lively, zesty gooseberry/asparagus fruit, well calculated acidity for worry-free quaffing. Usual low alc (12.6%). All WO W Cape.—*MM*

Credo see Omnia Wines

Crows Nest

*Paarl · Est/1stB 2003 · Tasting & sales by appt · Tours Mon-Sat 9-5 · BYO picnic · Farm produce · Facilities for children · Tourgroups · Owners Marcel & Deidre de Reuck · Winemaker Marcel de Reuck · Viti consultant Paul Wallace (Aug 2003) · 11 ha (cab, mourvèdre, shiraz, chard, viognier) · 48 tons 4 000 cs 85% red 15% white · PO Box 2571 Paarl 7620 · dereuck@mweb.co.za · **T 869·8712** · F 869·8714*

Consistency remains the main drive in what Marcel and Deidre de Reuck still refer to as 'this silly, loving and passionate industry'. The 2005 harvest, as elsewhere, was small but shows great promise, and Marcel dR assures that what lies in store is more complex and bold than anything the Nest has nurtured thus far. The tasting room is now complete; visits still by appointment, so plan ahead.

Marcel de Reuck range

★★★★ **Marcel de Reuck** 'Cabernet Sauvignon' in pvs ed, where **03** noted as showing succulent blackcurrant fruit, dense tannins, elegance despite opulent texture. Yr Fr oak, 20% new. Dbnville fruit, ditto for following reds.

★★★★ **Syrah** ('Shiraz' pvs ed) **03** (★★★★) more savoury/peppery profile than pvs & to us more appealing; also better fruit extraction, guts, persistence; **02** fruity, with overt barrel characters. Fr oak, 20% new.

Cabernet Sauvignon-Merlot ★★★★ **02** last ed noted as mouth-puckering & somewhat austere. 60/40 blend, Yr Fr oak. **Chardonnay** new ★★★★ Well-crafted & harmonious **04**, restrained, minerally styling, lime marmalade finish. Frhoek grapes; yr new oak. **Sauvignon Blanc** ★★★ new to guide but **04** shows some bottle-age (so drink soon); nice gooseberry flesh, clean acid grip. Rbtson-SWest fruit.

Crows Nest range

Two **03** red blends. **La Karnel** Sold out. **Torres Claude** ★★ Last ed was unsupple with chunky dry tannins. Paarl/Dbnville grapes, varieties 'secret'.—*CT/MF*

Croydon Vineyard Residential Estate new

*Stellenbosch (see Helderberg map) · Est 2005 · Visits by appt · Owners Croydon Vineyard Estate Homeowners Association · Winemaker Corius Visser (2005), advised by Beyers Truter · Viti consultant Johan Pienaar (2005) · 7 ha (cabs s/f, merlot, pinotage, shiraz) · 72 tons ±5 000 cs · 100% red · PO Box 30201 Tokai 7966 · general@jbb.co.za · www.croydon-estate.co.za · **T 701·3227** · F 701·3236*

The latest in residential vineyard estates (à la Steenberg, Zevenwacht) is going up near Vergenoegd in the Faure area. With the redoubtable Beyers Truter as partner and consultant, the Croydon development is also being dubbed a 'Beyers Truter Signature Estate' (in the vein of an Ernie Els-designed golf course!). It includes a 7 ha vineyard precisely planted with a mix of cab, merlot, pinotage, shiraz and cab franc. A winery is on the cards, designed to produce some 5 000 cases, of which a fifth will be allocated to residents; the rest will be available commercially. A Fine Living Red blend, vinified off-site in 2004 (untasted by us), will become available this year.

Crucible see Cloof

Cru Wines

Paarl ▪ Est 2004 ▪ Tasting & sales Mon-Fri 11-5 ▪ Bistro & other attractions (see intro) ▪ Owner DS Sarnia (Pty) Ltd ▪ Cellarmaster Wrensch Roux ▪ Viticulturist Wilhelm van Rooyen ▪ Export brands: Due South, Rising River, Withof, Something Else/Ietsie Anders, Klippendal & ranges below ▪ PO Box 1317 Paarl 7620 ▪ jtaljaard@cruwines.co.za ▪ ***T 863·1471*** *▪ F 863·1473*

With offices on the historic Zonnebloem Vineyards property between Franschhoek and Paarl, this production and marketing company aims to build on the farm's 185-year old heritage, giving it a make-over which includes an expanded tasting and sales area, and the opportunity to purchase picnic hampers to enjoy on a deck overlooking the Berg River. Wrensch Roux has joined the team to head the production of the various brands. Franschhoek's Rickety Bridge Winery is an autonomous member of the group and its wines form part of the brand portfolio.

Alphen Hill range

Cabernet Sauvignon ★★★ **03** last ed showed fresh red berries & pencil shavings on nose, accessibly smooth ripe tannins, undemanding & ready. **Merlot** ★ **03** dusty herbaceous tone, unripe flavours/tannins despite high alc (14% alc). 6 mths Fr/Am oak. **Pinotage** ★★★ **01**, not retasted, warmly ripe; spiced berry pudding aroma; lightly fruity palate, very dry finish. Only 3 mths oak. **Shiraz** ★★★ **03** savoury undertone to warm baked fruit, fairly generously flavoured, undaunting dry tannins. 6 mths Fr/Am oak. **Chenin Blanc** ★★★ **05** pre-bottling sample quiet, neutral; off-dry taste (despite low 2.9g/ℓ RS); may perk up once bottled. **Sauvignon Blanc** new ★★★ **05** plump & jolly, tropical fruit delivered with charm & some flair.

Bushman's Creek range

Shiraz new ★★★ Lightish, compact profile despite fattening 5.8g/ℓ sugar; **03** dried currant hint, harmonious 18 mths Fr/Am oak. **Cabernet Sauvignon-Merlot** ★★★★ **03** continues modern styling, though firmer tannins this vintage need food or yr/2 to soften; seamless 60/40 blend, elegant mulberry flavour, whiff pencil shavings from yr Fr oak. **Chardonnay** ★★★ **04** more heavily wood influenced than pvs, but well integrated; butterscotch/caramel patina to peach fruit; plump, fleshy yet finishes dry. **Sauvignon Blanc** new ★★★ Appealing & flavourful **05**, light but lingering zesty passionfruit tones, lots of vitality & youth – pity not to enjoy soon.

Dolphin Bay range:

Pinotage-Ruby Cabernet ★★★ Juicy 70/30 blend with wild berry, green banana on nose; smooth **04** not retasted; ditto ... **Pinotage Rosé** ★★ Bouquet of fruit pastilles; **04** some gentle red berry tastes; lightish casual quaffing. **Chenin Blanc** ★★★ Delicious, generously proportioned **05**, combo Golden Delicious apple & herb; fleshy, almost fat flavours, semi-dry finish. **Sparkling Brut** new From chenin, with variety's giveaway honeyed fruit; lively refreshing bubbles. All ranges WO W Cape. – *IvH/CR*

Culemborg

This big-volume range of easy-drinkers (822 000 cases) is for export only; made by DGB. Some reds lightly seasoned with Fr oak. Following pair of **03**s not retasted: **Cabernet Sauvignon** ★★★★ Classic cab aromas/flavours, dry but soft dusty tannins, easy drinking. **Pinotage** ★★★ Muted but quintessential mulberry aromas/flavours; soft, sweet jammy finish. **Merlot** ★★★ Balanced, well-made everyday red; **03** smooth choc/plum flavours, mere suggestion of tannin. **Cinsault** ★★ Undemanding **05**, plum & fruitcake flavours, soft dry tannins. **Cape Red** new ★★ Mainly cinsaut & ruby cab, **04** with those varieties' ripe-berried friendliness & generosity. Massive 500 000 cs. **Rosé** ★★ Off-dry & gluggable **05**, hints strawberry & dried fruit, tangy fruit-cordial flavours from pinotage. **Blanc de Noir** ★★ **05** similar to Rosé. **Chardonnay** ★★ Quaffable commercial style. **04** subtle but fresh melon/peach tone. Fermented with Fr oak. **Chenin Blanc** ★☆ Not overtly chenin, but **05** a pleasant, fresh, juicy dry white. **Sauvignon Blanc** ★☆ **05**, light (12.4% alc) zesty dry white, for casual quaffing within yr of harvest. **Cape White** ★★☆ new to the guide but already pleasantly rounded from bottle-age; **04** equal chenin/colombard mix; light, with sweet grape/floral aroma. All WO W Cape. — *DH*

Culraithin see Coleraine

Dalla Cia Wine & Spirit Company

Stellenbosch ▪ Est 2004 ▪ Closed to public ▪ Owner Giorgio dalla Cia ▪ 7 000 cs 11 Papegaai St Stellenbosch 7600 ▪ gdallacia@iafrica.com ▪ www.dallacia.com ▪ ***T/F 843·3462***

Retiring as Meerlust cellarmaster, where 25 years ago he oversaw saw the creation of the famous Rubicon, hasn't cured Giorgio Dalla Cia of his passion for Bordeaux-style blends. He's back on the shelves this year with a cab-merlot combination bearing his own name — made at Meerlust from Helderberg fruit. Providing the quality's right, cab franc and petit verdot will be adding something to the blend in future, though GDC's already pleased — his wine is deliberately made to age, in line with his disdain for the fashion of releasing ready-to-drink fruit bombs. Traditionalism doesn't preclude him from being innovative: he's first in SA to use the new hi-tech Guala Seal closure for his Sauvignon. It's also business as usual in the family grappa business, with son George.

★★★★ **Giorgio** new Harmonious, deliciously drinkable **02** cab, merlot blend (70/30) that exudes charm, generosity. Lovely spicy oak, smoky notes, a cherry-pip piquancy. Doesn't put a foot wrong: fruit purity, amenable tannins, well-structured for ageing. 18 mths Fr barrels, 80% new. Also in magnums.

Chardonnay ★★★ **03** (tasted last ed) fruitier style; lemons, limes with hint toasty oak. Juicy, flavoursome mouthful; tail-end sweetness only detraction. 5% fermented/9 mths oak. **Sauvignon Blanc** ★★★ **05** rooted in Old World rather than New, with its elegant gunflint, nettly minerality. Classic sauvignon styling — ideal food companion (not surprising given this family's gastronomic bent). — *CR*

Danckaert see Citrusdal Cellars
Danford's see Klein Constantia
Danie de Wet see De Wetshof

Darling Cellars

Groenekloof/Darling (see Swartland map) ▪ Est/1stB 1996 ▪ Tasting & sales Mon-Thu 8-5 Fri 8-4 Sat 10-2 ▪ Closed Easter Fri/Sun, Dec 25 & Jan 1 ▪ BYO picnic ▪ Tours by appt ▪ Owners ±20 shareholders ▪ Cellarmaster Abé Beukes (Dec 1997) ▪ Winemakers Johan Nesenberend (reds, Dec 1996) & Albé Truter (whites, Dec 2003) ▪ Viti consultant Gawie Kriel (Sep 2001) ▪ 1 300 ha (cab, merlot, pinotage, shiraz, cinsaut, chard, chenin, sauvignon) ▪ 6-7 000 tons 300 000 cs ▪ 65% red 33% white 2% rosé ▪ BRC & IFS certified ▪ PO Box 114 Darling 7345 ▪ info@darlingcellars.co.za jsheppard@darlingcellars.co.za mnel@darlingcellars.co.za ▪ www.darlingcellars.co.za ▪ ***T (022) 492·2276*** *▪ F (022) 492·2647*

Given the harvest season heatwave of 2005 ('the longest in my memory — 8 days!,' exclaims cellarmaster Abé Beukes) he's surprised at the quality of the vintage and feels positive about the wines but believes they're probably for earlier consumption. The season saw new plantings of barbera, while grenache and mourvèdre came into production. Tweaks to the cellar lay-out now allow free-run juice to be moved via gravity-flow instead of pumps, promising heightened wine quality. Danie de Kock joined as sales and marketing manager, and Johan Nesenberend took a walk to the award-winner's platform when he was named Young Winemaker of the Year for the Beukes/Nesenberend private-label For My Friends Shiraz. In a coda to a season of extremes, the team harvested their NLH in the opening days of June — later than ever before.

For My Friends Shiraz ★★★★ Maiden **02** modern, bright, generous, with very ripe dark, spicy fruit; good support from piquant acid, tannin & good oak; big 14.5% alc comes in warmly on finish. Savoury-sweet **03** ('work in progress') could rate ★★★★: more elegant, lingering, harmonious – though also on large scale. These 18 mths Fr oak, 60% new.

Onyx range

★★★★☆ **Kroon** Cellar's flagship, an unusual blend shiraz, pinotage, grenache & cinsaut, fermented *en famille* & matured in small oak. **03** not ready for tasting. **02** tweaked formula slightly: no Am oak, slightly less pinotage, fractionally more shiraz for final 50/40/5/5 ratio; yr barrelled, 80% new. Wood well meshed mid-2004; huge alc (15.2%) no detraction.

★★★★ **Cabernet Sauvignon** In a lesser vintage, **02** fares well. Plump, bouncy ripe blackberry fruit, cedar whiff from 70% new Fr oak (up from 60% for **00**); finishes noticeably dry, so cellar with care to catch at peak. 14.4% alc. From ±10-yr-old dryland bushvines. **03** not ready for tasting.

★★★★ **Pinotage** Good advert for extrovert, fruitier style. Mulberry fruit threads through **03** from colour to finish; whiffs cardamom, vanilla, violets & strawberry add impressive complexity; makes an elegant statement even at 14.8% alc. New oak regime – 100% new Fr vs pvs 80/20 Fr/Am mix. **02**, though enormous (15.4% alc), balanced, not overripe.

★★★★ **Shiraz** Raises the bar on version below; **03** bold & impressive, showing pedigree in fresh acidity, finely focused tannins. Gamey, less alcoholic but with the same peppery black fruit as **02**. This quiet on nose; palate livelier; sweetish finish (partly from big alc: 14.9%). Only Fr oak for this premium label; 60% new, ±yr.

★★★★☆ **Noble Late Harvest** From chenin; **03** not ready. **02**'s daunting sweetness (240g/ℓ RS) brought alive with tangy fruit-acid (9.5g/ℓ) so it races across palate. Smooth, viscous concentrated tropical fruit, slight terpene hint; richer than pvs. 11.5% alc. Aged 5–9 mths Fr barrels, none new. **Barrel Selection** The 2 best **02** casks, 14 mths older wood; drier (120g/ℓ), firmer, less voluptuous; botrytis' darker tones more evident among candied fruit flavours.

Sauvignon Blanc ★★★☆ **05** sample suggests style departure; latest green & racy, hints herb, nettle & 'wet slate', vibrant acidity vs more tropical, weighty **04**, robust **03**. All above WO Groenekloof.

DC range

★★★★ **Black Granite Shiraz 04** (★★★☆) attractive Old Boys' Club aromas of coffee, spice, smoke & bacon, left wanting by fruit-shy palate & short, 'green-stick' tannins, alcoholic farewell (14.6%). **03** richly coloured, opulent & complex. Combo staves, casks. ±14% alc.

Terra Hutton Cabernet Sauvignon ★★★ Vinified for approachability, with few yrs in reserve. **03** malty, port-like fruit character; cab tannin/acid stand out on palate. Drier than pvs (2.6 vs 4g/ℓ sugar). Combo steel/staves & older Fr oak. **Six Tonner Merlot** ★★★☆ Appealing version of this variety; **04** with fruit concentration & structure to handle substantial 14.8% alc. ±10 mths older Fr oak. Plummy fruit profile broadened by mineral, meaty notes. **Old Block Pinotage** ★★★☆ 35 yr old vyd delivers smoke & raspberry fruit in **04** sample. Alc down (from 15.7% for some pvs) to more respectable 14.6% Yr older Fr oak, well structured with firm tannins, bright acidity. **Quercus Gold Chardonnay** ★★★ Unwooded, early picked & fairly straightforward; unfinished preview **05** whiffs acacia, lemon/lime; promising palate, citrus grip & chalky finish. More alc (13.3%) than lightish, oak chipped pvs. **Bush Vine Sauvignon Blanc** ✓ ★★★☆ **05** continues pace set by racy **04**. Grassy, hint of lemongrass; lime/flint flavours & textures, crunchy acidity. Early picked (±12.5% alc) dryland bushvines. This, ranges below, WO Coastal.

Flamingo Bay range

Cinsaut-Cabernet Sauvignon ★★★ Sappy, easy 80/20 blend. **04** with spicy stewed plum notes, hint cinnamon, slightly savoury tail. **Lagoon Rosé** ★★★ Appropriately flamingo-pink easy-drinker; **04** changes from blend to straight pinotage, & from sweetish to dry; shy redberry aromas, appealing strawberry-toned palate. Both above tasted mid-2004, no **05**s ready this ed. **Chenin Blanc-Sauvignon Blanc** ★★ Uncomplicated 80/20 blend. Retiring **05** dry & limey, coarse finish.

Zantsi Natural Sweet range

Rosé ☆ Coral hued sweetie from buket & pinotage; suggestions of sherbet. Less flavour/structure than … **White** ★ 100% buket; sweet-sour nose & palate, short. Finds favour in France as aperitif. Both **NV** (03), ±9% alc. — *CvZ/TJ*

Daschbosch Wine Cellar

Goudini (see Worcester map) • Est 1956 • 1stB 1965 • Tasting & sales Mon-Fri 8-5 Sat 10-2 • Tours by appt • Closed pub hols • BYO picnic • Facilities for children • Tourgroups • Walks • Conference facilities • Owners 32 shareholders • Winemakers Gerrit van Zyl & Johan Lötz (Jun 2000/Jun 2004), with Wilhelm le Roux (Sep 2002) • Viticulturist Gerrit van Zyl (Jun 2000) • 890 ha (15 varieties, r/w) • 14 700 tons 3 500 cs own label 50% red 40% white 10% fortified • Ranges for customers: Welgevonde (Nthrlnds/Belgium); Louwshoek (Nthrlnds); Elephant Trail, Chiwara, Safeway & Kumala (UK) • BRC certified • PO Box 174 Rawsonville 6845 • cellar@daschbosch.co.za • www.daschbosch.co.za • ***T (023) 349·1110*** *• F (023) 349·1980*

The home of not-to-be-missed Nectar de Provision (SA's very own Cognac look-alike Pineau des Charentes, offered with blue cheese in the tasting room, now open on Saturdays too) and contributor to one of SA's biggest UK export brands (Western Wine's Kumala) met its major targets for 2005. A new, hi-tech fully computerised white wine production cellar swung into operation; and applications for BRC and HACCP food safety accreditation were approved. Celebrating the winery's 50th anniversary in 2006, the team promises an 'interesting' year.

No new wines tasted; notes from pvs ed: **Ruby Cabernet** ★★★☆ Well-made & -presented; ripely padded **01**, variety's grassy whiffs quite forward, juicy tannins, pleasurably drinkable now & for few yrs. **Pinotage** & **Merlot** not tasted. **Cabernet Sauvignon-Cabernet Franc** ★★☆ 60/40 mix; muted aromas of mint & ripe plum; well rounded, drinkable. **Chardonnay** ★★★ Light-toned everyday white; **03** fairly prominent vanilla-butterscotch tone, subtler bottle-age character. **Sauvignon Blanc** ★★★☆ **03** rounder & more interesting with yr in bottle; fresh, clean acidity. **Louwshoek-Voorsorg Hanepoot** ★★★ Traditional fortified dessert; last tasted was **99**, very sweet yet clean finishing. 17% alc. **Nectar de Provision** ★★★☆ Cellar's long-time signature. First local version of Cognac's classic aperitif, Pineau des Charentes; from colombard, fortified with 5/3 yr old brandy, yr barrelled post-fortification. Ages well & interestingly. Recent releases finer, more sophisticated than pvs; last tasted **NV** opened with orange & choc-mint flavours, hint vanilla; long, elegant, soothing finish. 16.5% alc. — *DH*

David Frost Wines see Daview Vineyards

Daview Vineyards

Paarl • Est 1994 • 1stB 1997 • Visits by appt • Owner David Frost • Winemaker Jan du Preez, with Jacques du Preez (both 2005) • Viticulturist Jacques du Preez (2005) • ±24 ha (five Bdx reds, shiraz) • ±100 tons ±7 500 cs own label 100% red • PO Box 7358 Noorder-Paarl 7623 • davidfrost@global.co.za • www.frostwine.com • ***T 869·8339*** *• F 869·8732*

Golf pro and long-time wine lover David Frost has made some changes to his support team, bringing in Jan du Preez (winemaker) and son Jacques (viticulturist). Like Frost (through golf), Du Preez (through marketing) has extensive experience of overseas markets and impressive contacts in the US, a field Frost would like to compete in. A name change to Daview (with estate registration under way) heralds a consolidation of his range to reflect his passion for reds: a cab-merlot blend, a Shiraz and the classic Bordeaux-style blend aptly named David Frost Par Excellence (which recently scored a 90/100 in *Wine Spectator*). The tasting room has been given a total makeover, and now sports a treasure trove of golfing memorabilia.

★★★★ **Cabernet Sauvignon Reserve** With dash merlot, **00** intensely plummy, fine-grained tannins but mid-2004 needing 2-3 yrs more to harmonise. 22 mths Fr oak.

★★★★ **Cabernet Sauvignon 02** (★★★) tasted last yr; powdery tannins & big alc (15%) fight for dominance over ripe blackcurrant flavours. Cellaring should give fruit the upper hand. 18 mths 42% new Fr oak. **01**'s velvet tannins & slightly lower alc (14.5%) tapered slowly to persistent finish.

★★★★ **Par Excellence 02** cab-dominated bdx-style blend, aptly named, given co-owner David F's golfing links. Last ed showed excellence in flavour department too. Deep, slightly decadent choc-truffle tones; so keenly balanced, nearly 15.5% alc goes unnoticed; structure & intensity to improve 6-7ys. 18 mths new Fr oak.

Merlot Reserve ★★★★ Massive **00** ripe plum, prune flavours & hot 15.5% alc. Generous tannins from 20 mths Fr oak (30% new) & sweet jammy finish. No new vintage in sight; ditto for … **Merlot** ★★★ **02** savoury & high-toned, packing tremendous fruit & alc (15.4%) on the finish. Expect mellowing with time in bottle – but not overnight. **Shiraz** new **04** barrel sample shows ★★★★ potential. Powerful with very ripe, concentrated fruit; bold tannins. Needs 2-3 yrs to integrate, grow into its frame. **Cabernet Sauvignon-Merlot** new Elegant structure & opulent fruit bode well for fine integration; already creamy, velvety, nodding at ★★★★. **Chardonnay** & **Sauvignon Blanc** discontinued.*—CR/CvZ*

DC Wines see Darling Cellars
Decent Red see Southern Cape Vineyards

De Compagnie

Wellington ▪ Est/1stB 2002 ▪ Tasting & tours by appt ▪ Fee R10 ▪ Sales Mon-Fri 8-4.30 or by appt ▪ Meals for groups of 2-30 by appt ▪ Owners 2 shareholders ▪ Vini consultant Anna-Mareè Mostert-Uys (Aug 2002), with Matewis Thabo (Jun 2003) ▪ Viti consultant Theo Brink (Jan 2005) ▪ 16 ha (cabs/f, merlot, pinotage, shiraz, chard, chenin) ▪ 85 tons 1 000 cs own label 70% red 30% albece brandy ▪ Range for customers: Bugatti's ▪ PO Box 395 Wellington 7654 ▪ mail@decompagnie.co.za ▪ www.decompagnie.co.za ▪ ***T 864·1241*** *▪ F 864·3620*

It was a case of mistaken identity when Johann Loubser, co-owner with wife Riana Scheepers of this 300-year-old Wellington property, was 'swapped' with Johann Laubser of Dominion Wine Company in last year's entry – apologies to all concerned. Now on to the good stuff: they're thrilled with their maiden Shiraz, due for release at the end of this year. Scheepers, a well-known Afrikaans-language author, and Nicci Thabo, farm worker and winner of a Bloemfontein Writer's Circle award, collaborated on a collection of vineyard and farm vignettes to which all writers in SA were invited to contribute. Said Riana S: 'There are wonderful stories I hear every day in our vineyards – and they're being lost.'

Cabernet Sauvignon ★★★★ Powerful **03** needs 6-8 yrs to knit; warm plum fruit dusted with earth/fynbos, juicy fruit wrestles mouth-puckering tannins on palate. 18 mths old/new Fr oak, 14% alc unobtrusive. Same regime, alc for… **Privaatkeur** ★★★ Bdx-styled **03** cab led with dollop merlot & splash cab f. More tannic, less succulent than pvs; needs 5-7 yrs to hit its stride. Both WO Wllngtn. **Chardonnay** discontinued. *– CT*

De Doorns Winery

Worcester ▪ Est 1968 ▪ Tasting & sales Mon-Fri 8-5 Sat 8-12 ▪ Winemaker/manager Danie Koen, with Ferdie Coetzee ▪ PO Box 129 De Doorns 6875 ▪ ddwk@mweb.co.za ▪ ***T/F (023) 356·2835*** *▪ F (023) 356·2101*

This co-op in the scenic Hex River Valley has a friendly, welcoming face in the form of a Cape Dutch 'wine house' near the N1 highway, open on weekdays and Saturday mornings. Regulars on the wine list are a Cab, Roodehof Dry Red, Chardonnay, Chenin, Colombar, Late Harvest, Red Muscadel, Hanepoot and Demi-sec Sparkling, none tasted.

Deetlefs Estate

Rawsonville (see Worcester map) ▪ Est 1822 ▪ Tasting, sales & tours Mon-Fri 8-5 Sat 10-4 ▪ Closed Easter Fri, Dec 25 & Jan 1 ▪ Picnic baskets by appt or BYO ▪ Owner Kobus Deetlefs ▪ Cellarmaster Willie Stofberg (Aug 2004) ▪ Viticulturist Coenie van Dyk (Sep 2003) ▪ 100 ha (cab, malbec, merlot, pinotage, shiraz, chard, chenin, sauvignon, semillon) ▪ ±1 000 tons 40% red 50% white 5% rosé 5% fortified ▪ BRC certified ▪ PO Box 36 Rawsonville 6845 ▪ sales@deetlefs.com ▪ www.deetlefs.com ▪ ***T (023) 349·1260*** *▪ F (023) 349·1951*

It may not be the norm for the region, but 2005 was an excellent year for red wine at Deetlefs, says Kobus Deetlefs, citing careful vineyard management as a prime reason. Sauvignon and riesling were well up to par, too, while the semillon was judged outstanding — perhaps why he and cellarmaster Willie Stofberg decided to break new ground by making the estate's first Semillon Noble Late Harvest. Only 400 litres were vinified, so fans might want to start working on their arm-wrestling techniques….

★★★★ **Muscat d'Alexandrie 74** a superb old muscat, a rarity; individual & exotic, to drink by the thimbleful at end of a fine dinner. Next release: 2025!

Merlot ★★★★ **02** last ed was a satisfying light-textured mouthful; gentle tannins for easy accessibility. **Pinotage** ★★ Earth & leather whiffs on **04**, modestly fruited with some dry tannins — better with a food accompaniment. **Shiraz** ★★★ Winemakers' goal of elegance achieved with 50% barrel-fermented **02**, last yr showed red fruit & pepper tones, pronounced but accommodating tannins. **Chardonnay** ★★ As pvsly, portion barrel fermented/matured, yet wood hardly discernible in **05**'s restrained styling: just gentle tropical tones, hints pear-drop & boiled sweet. **Chenin Blanc** ★★ **04** muted hints apple & melon, crisp dry finish with only a suggestion of palate-broadening 90-day *sur lie* maturation. **Sauvignon Blanc** ★★ Fresh, uncomplicated summer sipper with pleasantly low alc (12%); **05** briefly lees-aged. **Semillon** ★★★ Well-balanced fruit/acid gives lively feel to **05**, with lemon/herb nuance. Appealing everyday drink. **Weisser Riesling** ★★★ Slightly higher residual sugar (±20g/ℓ) buoys **04**'s zesty lemon/lime fruit, makes the whole wine's profile friendlier & more appealing. WO Brde Rvr Vlly. **Brut Cap Classique** discontinued.

Stonecross range

New releases of only the **Rosé** & **Sauvignon-Semillon** tasted; other notes from last ed: **Pinotage** ★★★ Cherry-toned **04** undoubtedly pinotage, grape's firm tannins impart a certain tautness; needing yr/2 to soften, settle. **Merlot-Pinotage** ★★★ **04** (sample) attractively chewy mix cherries & juicy tannins, braai-friendly but could also be cellared. **Rosé** ★★ Pinotage does the trick in this dry version, **05** deftly combining variety's forthright acid & tannin to sculpt the ripe berry fruit. **Chenin Blanc-Chardonnay** ★★★ **04** delicious, soft peachy curves, plump profile, easy but good underlying fruit, attractive touch fruit-sweetness. **Sauvignon Blanc-Semillon** ★★ **05** satisfying dry aperitif; 60/40 blend with lightish lemon-lime flavours. All WO W Cape.—*DH*

De Grendel Wines

Durbanville ▪ Est 1720 ▪ 1stB 2004 ▪ Visits daily by appt 9-5 ▪ Closed Good Fri, Dec 25 & Jan 1 ▪ Farm produce ▪ Walks ▪ Conservation area ▪ Owner Sir David Graaff ▪ Winemaker Charles Hopkins (Oct 2005) ▪ Viticulturists Johnnie de Flamingh & Granville Klerk ▪ 104 ha (cabs s/f, grenache, malbec, merlot, petit v, pinot, shiraz, mourvèdre, chard, semillon, viognier) ▪ 570 tons 24 000 cs 90% red 10% white ▪ PO Box 15282, Panorama, Cape Town 7506 ▪ info@degrendel.co.za ▪ www.degrendel.co.za ▪ ***T 558·6280*** *▪ F 558·7083*

One could be forgiven for thinking that things at De Grendel (Dutch for 'lock' or 'latch') move quite slowly. The farm was bought in 1875, the first wines bottled in 2004, and bottling does not yet take place on the property. Actually, Sir David Graaff, son of the late Sir De Villiers Graaff, and the fourth generation on the property, began the transformation of the huge 800 ha former wheat and stud farm only in 2000. Now more than 100ha are under vine, planted with classic varieties, and new cellar facilities are expected to be completed for this harvest. Only 25% of production is sold under the premium De Grendel label (the rest is snaffled by Graham Beck, whose former winemaker, Charles Hopkins, is now cellarmaster here). New worker-owner empowerment initiative Nuutbegin will see workers owning 60% of a 30 ha section.

★★★★ **Sauvignon Blanc Sauvignon Blanc** Maiden **04** impresses with aromatic khaki bush, asparagus, litchi pungency, classic whiffs of 'Dbnville dust'. Complex palate lifted by 4 mths *sur lie* ageing; acid refreshes, doesn't jar; long grassy finish. Alc a moderate 12.5%. **05** maintains standard; higher acidity (6.4g/ℓ vs 5.6) yields juicier, racier finish. High fruit quality easily carries slightly weightier alc (13%).

Merlot ★★★ Creamy plums & dusty spices on nose of attractive **04**; summer fruit compôte on palate; powdery tannins from 50% new Fr oak; long warm finish (14.5% alc). **Shiraz** ★★★★ **04** handsome in cardinal-red cloak; upfront shiraz red fruit & tang of black pepper, broad fruity tannins. Careful oaking (50% new Am, 50% 2nd fill Fr) tops off bouquet/finish with vanilla; sweet impression unobtrusively bolstered by alc (14.5%). – *CvZ*

De Groene Heuwel see Linton Park
De Heuvel Estate see Bianco
Dekker's Valley see Mellasat

De Krans

Calitzdorp (see Little Karoo map) ▪ Est 1964 ▪ 1stB 1977 ▪ Tasting & sales Mon-Fri 8–5 Sat 9–3 ▪ Tasting fee for groups R10 pp ▪ Closed Easter Fri/Sun, Dec 25 ▪ Tours by appt ▪ Vintners platters 12–2 Wed & Sat during Feb (also pick your own hanepoot grapes) ▪ BYO picnic ▪ Olive oil for sale ▪ Tourgroups ▪ Self-guided vineyard walks year round ▪ Owners/winemakers Boets & Stroebel Nel (1982, 1988) ▪ Viti consultant Willem Botha (2001) ▪ 42 ha (cab, pinotage, tempranillo & port varieties, chard, chenin & muscats) ▪ 500 tons ▪ 20–25 000 cs 50% red 10% white 3% rosé 37% fortifieds ▪ PO Box 28 Calitzdorp 6660 ▪ diekrans@mweb.co.za ▪ www.dekrans.co.za ▪ ***T (044) 213·3314/64*** *▪ F (044) 213·3562*

'Jack of all trades' Boets Nel, co-owner/winemaker with brother Stroebel, calls himself. 'Master of most', one is tempted to add. Certainly they're masters of port, as a lengthening array of awards attests (2005 FCTWS 'museum class' trophy for the 97 a particular highlight – 'shows it's maturing well, as a Vintage Reserve should'). But the brothers Nel are turning out increasingly interesting reds, too, including a touriga/cab blend and single-varietal tempranillo and touriga. Key here are greater attention to vines, improved irrigation management, and new plantings of tinta, tempranillo and chardonnay. Equally important, 'we're known as the friendliest cellar in Calitzdorp – we like to be that.' New wheelchair facilities bear testimony. A *Wine* best-value red rating for the 2003 Cab illuminates another stated aim: 'Providing genuine value.'

★★★★ **Red Stone Reserve** Flagship red blend touriga (70%), cab; after the dramatic rubicund cliffs visible from the cellar. **04** (★★★★) raises the bar on maiden **03**, a gentle giant, with eucalyptus & mixed berry aromas, cassis flavour. **04** similar but better focused; maintains balance, restraint despite fruit opulence, substantial tannins (10 mths Fr oak, 50% new). Should soften, improve over next 5–7 yrs. 'Benchmark red from the Little Karoo,' say the Nels; we concur.

★★★★ **Touriga Nacional** ✓ From stalwart port variety, maiden **00** among SA's first unfortified varietal bottlings. **04** (★★★★) similar to **03**; Xmas cake & plum nose, savoury palate & solid tannins. The latest vintage more complex, however, better groomed & meshed, with choc/prune/spice bonuses. Recommend cellaring 3–4 yrs. 5 mths wood; alc 14%.

★★★★ **White Muscadel Jerepigo** ✓ Picked before too many grapes raisin, to preserve pure varietal character. **05** intense muscat aromas with curry leaf, nut, khaki bush whiffs. Great length. Refreshing smack of tea-leaf on finish. Drink now & over 10 yrs. Touch sweeter than **03** (205 vs 195g/ℓ RS). **02** & pvs sweeter still. **04** untasted. Unwooded.

★★★★ **White Muscadel Reserve** ✓ From 19 yr old muscat de F vines, fortified to 15.5% alc; popular unwooded export to northern Europe. **04** (★★★★) delicate apricot/almond/lychee nose, touch sweeter than pvs (165g/ℓ RS), shortish finish. **03** Exquisite rose-petal, nut & litchi melange with warming alc.

★★★★★ **Vintage Reserve Port** A Cape benchmark, declared only in outstanding vintages. Classic varieties tinta, touriga, souzão (50/37/10) & drop tinta r, fortified with unmatured spirit; 16 mths 4 000ℓ vats. Excellent structure & brooding fruit suggest **03** (★★★★★) will blossom over 10+ yrs. Now still shy; hints mulberry, coriander, prunes;

engulfing tannins. Same sugar, alc (90g/ℓ, 20%) as **02**, but less showy in youth. **02** already open, flaunting opulent fruit, yet has structure/substance for decade-plus aging, as multiple accolades suggest: Peter Schulz 2004, *Wine* ★★★★, VDG.

★★★★ **Cape Vintage Port** ✓ Made every year, hardly fails to delight. **03**, like pvs, from tinta b, touriga, souzão, tinta r (55/35/10) but longer seasoned in old 500ℓ oak (18 vs 12-15 mths). Fruit- & choc-cake aromas/flavours; wonderfully smooth alc (19%). **02**, with spicy boiled sweet/citrus nose, pepped up flyers on Air Namibia. These drinkable early though better after min 2-3 yrs.

★★★★ **Cape Tawny Port** ✓ Predominantly tinta b with touriga, tinta r; avg age of wines 8 yrs, freshened with dash younger touriga port. Rich, with authentic tangy dark toffee & caramel bouquet; weighty & sweet (104g/ℓ sugar). **NV**. Also in 375ml. Wine ★★★★, Peter Shultz Trophy.

★★★★ **Cape Ruby Port** ✓ Lively, reliable **NV** blend tinta, touriga, souzão (50/45/5); favourite of Peter Schulz judges. Latest fruitcake/marzipan aromas with tea leaf hint; layered citrus & Indian spice finish. ±18.5% alc, 95g/ℓ sugar. Half the blend spends yr in 500ℓ casks, the rest in 4 500ℓ. Also in 250ml under screwcap.

Relishing Red new ☺ ★★★ Soft, juicy easy drinker from pinotage, ruby cab & merlot. **04**'s punchy 14.5% alc more wisely sipped than gulped. **Rosé** ☺ ★★★ Cab, merlot, pinotage mix with strawberry/earth tones in **04**, sweet lift to finish. **Golden Harvest** ☺ ★★★ Engaging **NV** natural sweet from 50/50 hanepoot & gewürz. Not cloying, despite 40g/ℓ sugar. Best young.

Cabernet Sauvignon ★★★ **03** sweet vanilla/clove bouquet, comfortable tannins (only 4 mths oak) & ripe cassis palate. **Pinotage** ★★★ Unpretentious easy drinker. **04** with restrained plum & licorice character, hint bitter tail, forgiving tannins (4 mths, older oak). **Tempranillo** ★★★★ ✓ Only stand-alone bottling in SA. **04** medium bodied with properly dry tannins, sour cherry palate. 5 mths oak, 25% Am. **Tinta Barocca** ★★★★ ✓ Jovial unadorned raspberry fruit make this a favourite with the Nels' European customers. Peppery **04** a step up on brambly pvs. **Merlot-Pinotage** ★★★ **04** same blend as pvs (60/40, unwooded) but drier. Plums & strawberries with respectably dry tannins; slight bitter grip from pinotage. **Chenin Blanc** ★★★ Refreshing & charming **05**; flowers & bubble gum on nose; lightish; texture supplied by 2 mths on lees; bone-dry. **Chardonnay** ★★★ Unwooded version; three mths on lees for roundness. **05** with ethereal lemon peel bouquet, cinnamon palate, pebbly finish. **Heritage Collection White Jerepigo** ★★★ From lightly botrytised gewürz. Label features Honey Badger; profits go to nature conservation education. Will be discontinued after current **01** now with mature notes of dried apples/pears; glacé fruit on palate. **White Port** ★★ **NV** from chenin; drier (65g/ℓ) than red stablemates. Latest with macadamia nut, cream & tea aromas; not as oxidative as pvs. Over ice, an alternative to sherry. 19.5% alc. **Spumanté** discontinued. — *CvZ*

Delaire Winery

*Stellenbosch ▪ Est 1982 ▪ 1stB 1986 ▪ Tasting & sales Mon-Fri 9-5 Sat/ Sun 10-5 ▪ Fee R10 + R10 glass deposit ▪ Closed Easter Fri, Dec 25/26 & Jan 1 ▪ Tours by appt ▪ Gifts ▪ Owner Laurence Graff ▪ Winemaker Gunter Schultz (Jan 2004) ▪ Viticulturist Bennie Booysen (Oct 2002) ▪ ±19 ha (cabs s/f, merlot, petit v, shiraz, chard, sauvignon) ▪ 95 tons 7 500 cs 60% red 40% white ▪ PO Box 3058 Stellenbosch 7602 ▪ info@delaire.co.za ▪ www.delairewinery.co.za ▪ **T 885·1756** ▪ F 885·1270*

Against the general trend, the 'Vineyards in the Sky' reported a good white-wine vintage in 2005 (perhaps not surprising for these cool Helshoogte heights). The general spruce-up/overhaul/clean sweep started in 2004 by new owner, London diamond man Laurence Graff, continues. A semi-gravitational, user-friendly cellar. A focus shift towards an iconic red blend (cab franc joins the cab-merlot blend, and a small petit verdot crop is harvested). The raising of trellises on older vines to increase leaf:bunch ratio. Some more sauvignon, chardonnay, shiraz planted. Jaco van Rensburg (ex-Quoin Rock) joins as GM. And they still have time for sport: winemaker Gunter Schultz goes to SA surfing champs; viticulturist Bennie Booysen makes WP Rugby Sevens side.

★★★★☆ **Botmaskop** Cab made only in best yrs: 'one third Old World-style & two thirds New', named after peak above farm, with view of False & Table Bays. Small quantities. Last tasted was gorgeous **02**; soft, silky, elegant, with moderate 13% alc; balanced fruit & oak (70% new, mostly Fr, some Am, 18 mths).

★★★★ **Delaire** Was awaiting naming last ed, when sample **03** tasted. Like the maiden, **04** blends cab, merlot, cab f (43/41/16). Seductive flavour complexity makes one regret the tannins still too tight, need another yr to soften. Delights in store include mulberry/cherry fruit, violets, smoky spice, whiff of tar. 14 mths barriques Fr/Am/Hungarian (50/38/12), 45% new.

★★★★ **Merlot** Massive, premium-priced, showcase wine, bottled only in top yrs. Nothing since **00**.

★★★★ **Cabernet Sauvignon-Merlot** Pvsly an all-purpose ready-on-release red, but **03** shows a stylistic change, increased complexity, more serious albeit elegant structure, built for the longer haul. 50/33 blend, +17% cab f adding herbaceous lift to deeply rich cassis, smoked beef aromas, flavours. 15 mths Fr barriques, third new. No **02**. 85% cab in **01**: good strong cassis nose, pleasing dry firmness.

★★★★ **Chardonnay Barrel Fermented** (Pvsly 'Barrique'). **05** still in development stage, oak busy integrating, but already showing toasty peach & lemon cream tones that promise a good result. 85% in oak 8 mths, 40% new. Sample rating ★★★★ mid-2005; perhaps higher for finished wine. **04** all fermented/9 mths Fr barrels; soft, sweet, easy 6g/ℓ sugar.

★★★★ **Sauvignon Blanc** ✓ From mountain vyds picked at varying degrees of ripeness. **05** sauvignon at its powerful best: gooseberries, kiwi, pear, a vein of lime, all compacted into a mouth-tingling, ultra-fresh (7.1g/ℓ acidity) body. Bone dry, gorgeous long finish.

Chardonnay Unwooded ★★★★ Strives for unadorned fruit impact; from separate vyds yielding spectrum of flavours. **05** has attractive fresh-picked melon, dessert peaches character supported by well balanced structure, lively finish. **Sauvignon Blanc Barrel-Matured** ★★★★ Last tasted was food-friendly **02**. – *CR/TM*

De Leuwen Jagt see Seidelberg

Delheim

*Stellenbosch ▪ 1stB 1961 ▪ Tasting & sales Mon-Fri 9-5 Sat 10-4 Sun (Sep-Apr) 10-4 ▪ Fee R15 (tasting) R20 (tour & tasting) ▪ Tours Mon-Fri 10.30 & 2.30 Sat 10.30 ▪ Closed Easter Fri/Sun, Dec 25 & Jan 1 ▪ Delheim Garden Restaurant for country/traditional meals Mon-Sat 12-3 Sun (Sep-Apr) 12-3 ▪ Tourgroups ▪ Gifts ▪ Farm produce ▪ Winemaker Brenda van Niekerk, with Karen Swanepoel (Oct 2002/Sep 2004) ▪ Viticulturist/cellarmaster Victor Sperling (Aug 1993) ▪ 148 ha (15 varieties, r/w) ▪ 810 tons 60 000 cs 70% red 28% white 2% rosé ▪ Wines for client: Woolworths ▪ PO Box 10 Koelenhof 7605 ▪ delheim@delheim.com ▪ www.delheim.com ▪ **T 888·4600** ▪ F 888·4601*

Much to celebrate last year: the irrepressible 'Spatz' Sperling's 75th birthday and the 100th birthday (in memory) of Delheim's founder Hans Hoheisen. 'With recent renovations in the cellar, we also discovered the date 1.3.1944 plastered on the wall, signifying the completion date of our first concrete fermentation cellar – another good reason for a celebration.' Looking ahead, this year will see viticulturist son Victor planting cab franc and petit verdot, possibly for winemaker Brenda van Niekerk's Grand Reserve. 'The person who buys my wine must want and be able to drink more than one glass,' is her philosophy. Meanwhile, the Sperling daughters are probably on tour right now – Nora looking after wine exports and Maria, a musician, demonstrating the perfect combination of wine, women and song....

Vera Cruz Estate range

★★★★☆ **Shiraz** Plush velvet fruit draped over unobtrusive but firm structure – impressive since maiden **98** (★★★★★). Current **03** deeply fruity, meaty & rich with hints of spice/smoke; big (14.5% alc) & darkly handsome, still manages elegance. Will be hard to defer drinking until 2007, when at peak; will easily last for 8-10 yrs. 17 mths oak, Fr/Am 90/10, all new. WS plaudits: **01** 91 pts, 00 90 pts.

Delheim range

★★★★ **Grand Reserve** Enduring success for this trail-blazing flagship; **03** repeats recent formula of 98% cab with 2% merlot (some pvs only cab). Whiffs mulberry with gentle mint overtones, makes interesting comparison with Cab below: similarly dark berried but GR still hiding much while cab is more about accessibility. Tannins firm, will allow for cellaring up to 10 yrs, drink Cab while waiting. 18 mths Fr oak, 40% new. No **02**.

★★★☆ **Cabernet Sauvignon** Latest **03** (★★★★) right on form after difficult **02**; impresses with intense blackcurrant fruit, attractive sweetness from ripe grapes, ripe tannins to match. Well judged oaking (house's current 16 mths regimen well suited to variety). Already approachable, should peak around 2007. All Fr oak, 20% new.

★★★★ **Merlot** Some attractive dark cassis fruit, whiffs mulberry, leaves & cedar. Neat build, ripeness adds pleasing sweet notes. Fresh acidity & firmer tannins in **03** (★★★☆) after longer stay in cask, 16 mths vs yr for **02**, perhaps not best option despite auspicious red-wine vintage.

★★★★ **Shiraz** Less show, more gravitas in **03**. Poised & stylish, sleek dark-berried fruits in profusion, neatly disciplined by good oak, lingering spicy finish & proper dryness. 16 mths oak, mainly Fr, 20% new. Extrovert **02** had all the aromas of the spice souk.

★★★★ **Edelspatz Noble Late Harvest** Gorgeous bounty of deliciously scented fruit on **05**, pineapple & honey with fresh orange zest. Luscious & sweet (though somewhat lower RS than pvs at 117g/ℓ) but fresh acidity imparts lift, excitement; added bonus of firm, clean finish. 11.5% alc. Unoaked, from riesling. Pvs tasted was **03**, **04** sold out.

Pinotage Rosé ☺ ★★☆ Almost-dry **05**, charming picnic wine with raspberry pastille flavours, tangy, juicy. 9% muscat adds some perfume. **Sauvignon Blanc-Chenin Blanc Heerenwijn** ☺ ★★★ Comes up smiling yet again; **05** really grown up & filled out in all the right places; ripe, juicy; seamless blend 55% sauvignon, 25% chenin, 20% colombard, properly dry, too.

Pinotage ★★★☆ Back to the Real Deal in **03** after vintage-impacted pvs, irrepressible pinotage with sweet-sour nuances, crushed red/black-berry flavours, not showy or overdone. Good fruit showcased, slight sweetness on finish. **Cabernet Sauvignon-Pinotage Dry Red** ★★☆ Pvsly simply 'Dry Red'. Trusty all sorts red; **03** properly dry, meaty/savoury flavours. Staves/Fr oak, 8 mths. Quaffable 12.5% alc. **04** not tasted. **Chardonnay sur Lie** ★★★☆ More weighty than version below, flavours resonate in lower key. **04** rich panoply of ripe citrus flavours, concentrated fruit from 20 yr old vines, generous oaking (10 mths, 40% new Fr), not yet fully integrated but well balanced. These need yr in bottle before opening. **Chardonnay** ★★★☆ **04** ripe & creamy, layers of peach/tangy citrus flavour in nicely rounded profile. For those who prefer light oak. **Sauvignon Blanc** ★★★ Style well established: firm & dry, for food partnering. **05** ripe gooseberry/grapefruit flavours, smooth acidity, some creaminess. **Gewürztraminer** ★★★ Less arresting in **05**, marred by slight off-odour; Turkish Delight spiciness with added zing of grapefruit, slightly less sweet at 21g/ℓ. **Spatzendreck Late Harvest** ★★★ **05** sees pinot blanc (29%) blended with chenin. Wafting pineapple/honey, attractive fresh sweetness; slightly less charm this time around. — *IvH*

Dellrust Wines

*Stellenbosch (see Helderberg map) ▪ Est/1stB 1998 ▪ Tasting & sales Mon-Fri 8-5 Sat 10-2 ▪ Closed pub hols ▪ Tours on request ▪ Play area for children ▪ Owner Albert Bredell ▪ Winemaker Albert Bredell ▪ Viticulturist Francois Hanekom (Jul 2003) ▪ 97 ha (11 varieties, r/w) ▪ 800 tons 6 000 cs own label 75% red 25% white ▪ PO Box 5666 Helderberg 7135 ▪ dellrust@mweb.co.za ▪ www.dellrust.co.za ▪ **T 842·2752/842·2457** ▪ F 842·2456*

Owner Albert Bredell returned to vinification duties last harvest and promptly shook things up with two Dellrust firsts: a Rosé and a white blend named 'Steen & Groen', after the old-Cape monikers for chenin and semillon. In the vineyard, 40-year-old cinsaut vines were grubbed up (to be replaced with merlot this year). Albert B bottles only ±10% of his production under the Dellrust label (the rest is sold in bulk to KWV), and long-term goal is to push this to 50%. Equally important, he believes, is to address empowerment issues within the next two years via 'a good, defined strategy'. And what would a harvest be without one of the team falling into a fermenter? 'Luckily he survived,' observes the boss dryly, 'and the wine still has good body.'

★★★★ **Three Vines** Cellar's flagship, harmonious blend merlot, pinotage, shiraz; selected blocks vinified & blended pre-maturation in small Fr oak, ±14 mths. Last tasted was **03**, 40/30/30 ratio; darker, chunkier than pvs; plummy with hint toast/lead-pencil (from 5% Am barrels?). **02** skipped. **01** (★★★★) with hint cigarbox, was well-fruited & elegant.

Merlot ★★★ **02** revisited (pvsly a sample) reveals rich plummy introduction, softish if not juicy tannins; will be enhanced by food. 13 mths Fr oak, further yr bottle age. **Pinotage** ★★★ **03** pleasingly rustic & earthy, barnyard sniff, well behaved tannins & acidity, dry finish. Pvs were 14 mths Fr oak. **Shiraz** No follow-up to **03** barrel sample, last ed provisionally rated ★★★★. **Tinta Barocca-Cinsaut** ★★★★ Last ed we featured **02**, 50/50 blend with appealing spicy nose & supple juicy flavours; & sample **03**, seemingly lighter textured/structured. **Rosé** new ★★★ Fun & friendly red-berried number from merlot & shiraz; fresh, off-dry; stodgy 14% alc needs proper chilling. **Sauvignon Blanc** ✓ ★★★★ Gutsy **05** positive mineral attack; generous tropical fruit aromas switching to flint in full-flavoured finish. **Steen & Groen** new ★★★ **05** 67/33 blend tasted very young, still needed to get into stride. Baked apple note, dumpy body needing verve. **Jerepigo** ★★★★ ✓ Different & interesting **NV** (02) still on offer, from botrytised chenin, 16% alc. Dried peach/apricot aromas; lovely richness, silkiness to palate. **Cape Vintage** ★★★★ Last ed we previewed **02**, livelier fruit, bigger structure than pvs; total 24 mths Fr casks. 88/12 tinta, touriga. 500ml. Next port release will be LBV-style **02**. *—MM/TM*

De Meye Wines

Stellenbosch ▪ Est/1stB 1998 ▪ Tasting & sales Mon-Fri 9.30–5 Sat 9.30–2 ▪ Closed Easter Fri, Dec 25/26 & Jan 1 ▪ Home-grown lavender & lavender essential oil ▪ Owner Jan Myburgh Family Trust ▪ Winemaker Marcus Milner, with Aby Bodlani (Sep 1999/Sep 2000) ▪ Viticulturist Philip Myburgh ▪ 60 ha (cab, shiraz, pinotage, chard) ▪ 13 000 cs 90% red 10% white ▪ PO Box 20 Muldersvlei 7607 ▪ info@demeye.co.za ▪ www.demeye.co.za ▪ ***T 884·4131*** *▪ F 884·4154*

A 700% increase in sales from 2003 to 2004, followed by the launch of the successful Little River label – things are looking rather rosy here. Last year saw a few changes and upgrades: a new cooling system for the winery, new cab franc and merlot vineyards, and the advent of the charming Thildée Visser as marketing manager. As animated in promoting De Meye (including their excellent lavender oil) as she is in clinching a deal with crafters in Khayelitsha township to produce promotional items for their foreign distributors, Thildée V says 2005 was a year with great potential, the smaller crop showing concentrated character and beautiful fruit.

★★★★ **Trutina 02** coming into its own, somewhat lesser than pvs (reflecting vintage; drink before **01**), but usual generous warm fruit & firm structure. Cab with touch shiraz, more refined than 14.5% alc suggests, & hint of the herbal minerality shared by all these characterful reds. Effective but smooth tannins, savoury acidity, well-judged oak (20 mths Fr, 35% new): the Latin name appropriately means 'balance'.

★★★★ **Shiraz** ✓ Suave, fresh & charming, **03** convincingly shows variety in its more delicate, fragrant guise, with sweet fruit & decent structure. As **02**, deliciously approachable but understated. 18 mths Fr oak (25% new) well integrated.

★★★★ **Chardonnay** ✓ **05** barrel sample suggests honeyed element added with customary spice, nuts, orange-peel of this reliably attractive, well wooded (50% new) example. Pvs have had powerful, balanced structure, confident finish.

Cabernet Sauvignon ★★★ **02** less powerful (13.5% alc), lighter texture than classic firm, savoury pvs, but good varietal character. 16 mths Fr oak, 20% new. **Blanc de Noir** new ★★★ Pale, coppery-red **05** all from shiraz; easy-going with its touch of sugar, but no pushover. 8 mths older wood. **Chardonnay Unwooded** new ★★★ Light, bright & pleasant **05** a little bubblegummy in youth along with typical citrus; well-textured; 13% alc.

Little River range new

Shiraz ☺ ★★★ **03** pure- and sweet-fruited, straightforward, most attractive. Like all these, ± yr in older wood; 14% alc. Like them, happily & immediately drinkable but not careless or dumbed-down: intelligent, with gentle but informing structure. **Blend** ☺ ★★★ Of cab, shiraz & pinotage in **03**, flavourful, ripe fruit held in place by modest tannin, fresh acidity. **Cabernet** ☺ ★★★ **02** Unshowy, nice varietal character, brightly red-fruited. A thoroughly welcome range. — *TJ*

De Mooie Opstal see Bon Cap

De Morgenzon

Stellenbosch ▪ Closed to public ▪ Owners Wendy & Hylton Appelbaum ▪ Manager Anton Ferreira ▪ Vini consultant Teddy Hall (2005) ▪ Viti consultant Kevin Watt (Sep 2003) ▪ PO Box 1388 Stellenbosch 7599 ▪ demorgenzon@absamail.co.za ▪ ***T 881·3030*** *▪ F 881·3773*

The only survivors of the new-broom replanting programme here in Stellenboschkloof (Jordan a neighbour) were some 30-year-old chenin vines, in 2005 fashioned by Rudera's Teddy Hall into De Morgenzon's maiden wine. Choice of site, variety, rootstock, row spacing and direction have been aided by the extensive use of hi-tech tools and analyses — all with the holistic aim of establishing the new vines in harmony with the fundamental elements of topography, soil and climate. A nursery, established to provide seedlings for restoration of surrounding fynbos and renosterveld, supports this endeavour. The intensiveness of the five-year renovation and rebuilding programme affords co-owner Hylton Appelbaum the confidence to anticipate that De Morgenzon will ultimately 'emerge as an industry showpiece'.

Denneboom see Oude Denneboom
De Sonnenberg see Premium Cape Wines, Rooiberg
Destiny see Mont Destin

Détendu Wines

Paarl ▪ Est 1995 ▪ 1stB 2001 ▪ Visits by appt ▪ Owner Western Investments Company ▪ Winemaker Anthony Smook, with Francois Louw (Jan 2001/2003) ▪ Viti consultant Johan Wiese (2002) ▪ 33 ha (cab, merlot, pinotage, shiraz, chard, chenin, colombard) ▪ 300 tons 1 500 cs own label 90% red 10% white ▪ PO Box 2917 Paarl 7620 ▪ detendu@sybaweb.co.za ▪ ***T 863·3282*** *▪ F 863·2480*

A fast, intense harvest here last year due to the heat, with plenty of berry sorting necessary. Good quality shiraz — which won't surprise owner-company director Garry Roberts, as he's convinced the Voor Paardeberg ward is destined to become known for the fine wines it produces from this fashionable variety. He has in the past also extolled the area's potential for top-notch chardonnay, but ruefully admits that 2005 was 'not a great year for whites'. Just as well, then, that the focus here is predominantly on producing top quality reds in limited quantities — at least until a loyal following is firmly in place.

Cabernet Sauvignon-Merlot ★★★ Like a cat on a hot tin roof, this blend once again cab-led (60%) in **03**. Interesting green olive (Aussie wine stalwart James Halliday refers to 'oliveaceous' character), coffee & dusty oak; pliable tannins, black concentration in mouth. Should develop over 2-3 yrs. **Pinotage** ★★★ **03** bursting with jammy red fruit/toasty vanilla. Abrasive tannins bring up the rear; would show better alongside oxtail or game. The winemaking team has produced two WO W-C shiraz; one bottled as 'reserve'. **Shiraz** ★★★ **03** has caramelised fruit, oak aromas, prominent fruit acid, touch sweetness from 14.5% alc. **Shiraz Reserve** ★★★ **03** hints at freshly brewed coffee, spice. Approachable sweet berry flavours, smooth tannins, persistent finish; oak (18 new mths Fr) more in tune with fruit stable mate. Could improve 2-3 yrs. **Chardonnay** ★★★ **04** is rich/nutty thanks to well balanced wooding (50% matured in new Fr oak, 6 mths). Nose/palate livened by grapefruit aromas & flavours. Restrained; finishes tad short. WO W Cape. — *MM*

De Toren Private Cellar

Stellenbosch ▪ Est 1996 ▪ 1stB 1999 ▪ Visits by appt ▪ Fee R180, waived on purchase ▪ Owner Edenhall Trust ▪ Winemaker Albie Koch (Aug 1998) ▪ Viticulturist Ernest Manuel (Mar 2003), advised by Johan Pienaar ▪ 20 ha (cabs s/f, malbec, merlot, petit v) ▪ 7 000 cs 100% red ▪ PO Box 48 Vlottenburg 7604 ▪ info@de-toren.com ▪ www.de-toren.com ▪ ***T 881·3119*** *▪ F 881·3335*

'Not the easiest, but definitely a very good one,' is how winemaker Albie Koch sums up the long 2005 harvest. Apart from relying on supplementary irrigation and aerial imaging at this high-tech, high-flying rated winery, he says it boiled down to 'gut feel'! Meanwhile, director Emil den Dulk points out: 'Disease and pest control were quite easy. For the first time ducks were used with great success – and noise – to control the snails.' As always, there's much to be proud of, but this year's highlight was son Dale dD's completion of a B.Comm Enterprise Management honours degree (cum laude). 'With a passion for the industry, combined with his business aptitude he has slotted into the position of marketing manager at De Toren. You will be hearing a lot from him in the future,' says dad.

★★★★☆ **Fusion V** Listing on global A-list by US *Food & Wine*; international Wine of Year in Dutch *Proefschrift*; collector's item locally, this glossy, modern blend remains a top-ranker. Features full house of bdx red grapes (cab, merlot, malbec, cab f, petit v), composed according to vintage but invariably cab-led; **03** 55/18/14.5/9.5/3 make-up; great concentration of pure sweet red fruits; powerful; dense yet fine tannins. Needs more time to settle than herb-scented **02**, which chewy but ripe, quite approachable. Mainly Fr oak, 50% new. Regular *WS* 90-plus pts. These worth cellaring decade min. **01** gold at 2005 IWSC.

★★★★ **Diversity** Second label, sequentially labelled according to Greek alphabet; fruit selected with help of satellite imaging; varieties as per Fusion. Current **03** 'Delta' (★★★☆) so seamless, open-fruited it lacks depth mid-2005; may gain dimension, lose detracting sweetish edge of Am-oaked malbec (13%). **02** 'Gamma' light, stalky but ripe, with potential to evolve. Yr Fr/Am oak, 2nd/3rd fill. Own, Elim fruit. —*AL*

De Trafford Wines

Stellenbosch ▪ Est/1stB 1992 ▪ Tasting, sales & tours Fri & Sat 10-1 ▪ Owners David & Rita Trafford ▪ Winemaker David Trafford ▪ 5 ha (cabs s/f, merlot, pinot, shiraz) ▪ 80 tons 3 500 cs 75% red 25% white ▪ PO Box 495 Stellenbosch 7599 ▪ info@detrafford.co.za ▪ www.detrafford.co.za ▪ ***T/F 880·1611***

Quiet-spoken architect David Trafford, probably the Cape's most respected and influential 'untrained' winemaker, is confident that there are enough aficionados out there who are above 'shallow stylistic preconceptions', and that though some of his wines end up with high alcohols, they are still balanced and integrated – 'to be enjoyed for what they are'. Important for him is that his wines express a sense of place. 'Which,' he adds provocatively, 'includes our abundant sunshine and deep, clay-rich soils – we are not the shagged-out alluvial plains of the Médoc, with their miserable climate.' This sense of place is about to get scope for expansion with the planting – to hardy, high-quality Mediterranean varieties – on the stony plateau between Malgas and Cape Infanta. With this and more fruit coming on line from his own and contracted vineyards, already working at double its design capacity, the winery is ripe for expansion.

★★★★☆ **Cabernet Sauvignon** Aristocratic Cape cab with lineage of superior quality. Barrel sample **04** concentrated & complex; finely etched blackcurrant aromas a harbinger of ripe-fruit elegance & beauty likely to unfurl 6–8 yrs from harvest. Pity to open too soon. **03** showed intense cassis fruit in grassy cab structure. **02** leafy, to us more austere (but recent *Wine* ★★★★☆). Low-yield Stbosch cab supported by 12% merlot, splash petit v. ±20 mths oak, mainly Fr, 40% new.

★★★★ **Merlot** These elegant wines noted for their crafted plum & mulberry fruits, shaped by careful wooding (35% new Fr, 18 mths) & splashes cab f & petit v. **04** (sample) densely coloured, deep violet scents mingle with black fruits in lithe tannin frame.

★★★★☆ **Shiraz** A singular exposition of cellar's handmade craft lauded with regular *WS* 90+ ratings. Lately Am oak fraction reduced for more elegance, sleekness. Preview **04** magical; lilting plumes of roast spice & succulent mulberry fruits tucked into embroidered framework; sensational lingering depth of finish. **03** evinced thrilling white pepper intensity within tailored structure. ±19 mths wood, 60% new, lightly toasted to add structure, not flavour. 200 cs.

★★★★ **Blueprint Shiraz** new Fruit of younger Keermont vyds accorded cellar's standards: gentle hand-picking/crush, native yeast ferment, full malo in barrel, very limited racking/handling. Maiden **03** (*WS* 91 pts) launched & sold out between eds. Sample **04** fragrant herbal tones to spiced liquorice tints; focused elegance in finish. Barrelled 18 mths 50/50 Fr/Am casks, 20% new.

★★★★ **Pinot Noir** Mere 5 barrels given individual attention; natural processes guided with minimal intervention. Sample **04** black cherry gloss to earthy/tar aromas, breath-taking concentration of supple tannins give upholstered feel mid-2005, promise super maturation beyond 2010. 18 mths Fr wood, none new. 15% alc. **03** shiny red/black fruits sewn into firm yet delicate texture, lingering finish. 20% new oak. Mix Burgundian (±80%) & older BK5 clones.

★★★★ **Elevation 393** Allusion to height above sea level of Mont Fleur home vyd. Selection best cab, merlot, shiraz, cab f lavished with 100% new Fr oak for first yr, then mix seasoned casks (total 22 mths). **03** (★★★★★) more subtle than stablemates, needs time but worth it; creamy texture, elegant fruits lined in the gentle fabric of its casing. No **02**. Elevated alc (15.5%) part of persona. *Wine* ★★★★★, *WS* 90. 120 cs.

★★★★ **Chenin Blanc** A new-wave chenin, now exclusively from venerable Hldrberg vyds, full & complex but laced with elegance: sample **05** proffers rich truffly custard aromas, luscious peach fruits supported by clean oak lines; excellent acid seam freshens finish. Equally delicious **04** & **03** 90 pts *WS*. Fermented/8 mths half each Fr/Am oak, 20% new; native yeasts; unfiltered.

★★★★★ **Straw Wine** Passion & commitment taken to the edge with this elixir coaxed from 'air-dried' chenin grapes; recent stylistic shift to stronger (±17% alc), drier (±85g/ℓ sugar vs 200+ pvsly) rendition. **04** in cask mid-2005 billows apricot/white pear aromas, luxe mouthful beautifully balanced; stunning length to dry feel in finish. **03** incredibly rich, full & complex yet elegant; only 13% alc, 202g/ℓ sugar. *WS* 92 pts. 280 cs × 375ml. Mostly new oak, 50% Fr/Am, 17 mths.

Keermont range, **Chenin Blanc (Walker Bay)** discontinued. — *DS*

De Villiers Wines

Paarl ▪ Tasting & sales by appt ▪ Owner De Villiers Family Trust ▪ 50 000 cs 60% red 40% white ▪ PO Box 659 Southern Paarl 7624 ▪ devwines@mweb.co.za vadev@mweb.co.za ▪ www.devwines.co.za ▪ ***T 863·4441*** *▪ F 086·6538·988*

With a new GM, Morne Kotze, and merchandising manager, Wayne Fredericks, at the helm, this Paarl winery has set a course for growth. Packaging has been revamped, and the SA retail sector identified as the main target market. The goal is to a take their De Villiers Heritage brand national, and secure listings with all the major supermarket chains.

Cabernet Sauvignon ☺ ★★★ Drink-soon **04** quaffably smooth red berry & spice concoction, hint sweetness on tail from 4.2g/ℓ sugar. Fat, firm but ripe tannins. **Pinotage** ☺ ★★★ Classic pinotage strawberry, smoke & ripe banana whiffs, **04** food & wallet-friendly. Modest 11.9% alc; enjoy now or allow tannins to soften over next yr/2.

Shiraz ★★★ **04** promising nose of dark choc, red fruit, dust & coffee; slightly less convincing palate, touch warming on finish (14.7% alc). **Chardonnay** ★★ **04** citrus & buttery oak aromas & flavours, perky acidity, woody finish. **Chenin Blanc** ★★ Understated **04** merest hint of sweet-sour fruit on nose/palate. **Sauvignon Blanc** ★★ Lightish **04** has asparagus & passionfruit in bouquet; crunchy & uncomplicated palate. **Blanc de Blanc 05** and **Riesling 05** unready for tasting. — *MM*

Devon Air see Terroir Wines

Devon Hill Winery

Stellenbosch ▪ Est 1996 ▪ 1stB 1997 ▪ Tasting & sales Mon-Fri 10-4 Sat by appt ▪ Fee R10 ▪ Closed pub hols ▪ Tours by appt ▪ Walks ▪ Winemaker Erhard Roux (May 2004) ▪ 46 ha (cabs s/f, merlot, pinotage, shiraz, sauvignon) ▪ ±300 tons 80% red 20% white ▪ PO Box 541 Stellenbosch 7599 ▪ info@devonhill.co.za ▪ www.devonhill.co.za ▪ ***T 865·2453*** *▪ F 865·2444*

'I've watched nature filter a good red wine by settling, and all it took was patience,' observes Erhard Roux, who subscribes to an old-school style of winemaking: 'I really try and let nature do its thing.' He'd be first to admit that's not always easy. Last January, 'all was quiet and calm and the next day all hell broke loose as we realised the grapes were ready! Two weeks earlier than usual.' Still in the planning stages is a new restaurant overlooking Devon Valley – it's set to be 'a stunning addition' to the cellar.

★★★★ **Blue Bird 01** blend merlot, pinotage, cab (73/17/10), delivering fresh blueberry aromas/flavours on cleanly elegant palate. Yr Am/Fr oak. **00** was pinotage-led, with cab f, merlot.

Four Stars ★★★★ Flavoursome, fruity, easy-drinking pleasure; **02** light-textured blend pinotage, merlot, shiraz, cab (40/30/15/15). Yr oak, none new. Above pair not retasted. **Cabernet Sauvignon** ★★★ Morphs from popular, commercial style of pvs to more elegant & restrained **03**, dusty cassis notes & noticeably dry wood tannins from yr new Fr oak. Bigger alc (14.2%) than **02** VDG. **Shiraz Reserve** new ★★★ Cellar's flagship. Spartan rather than sensuous **03**; emphatic varietal pepper/leather/spice introduction; leanish dusty dry palate. Would benefit from further maturation, as would … **Shiraz** ★★★ No doubt about the variety – **03** forthcoming pepper & spice aromas, followed by red fruit with some fairly strong tannins. Yr oak, third new. **Sauvignon Blanc** ★★★ **05** (sample) green-tinged aromas, hint crunchy apple to sherbet-textured dry palate; pleasant, in more compact package than pvs. **Pinotage** ★★ Last ed 'nail varnish' tone dominated palate of **02**, with bitter element. Yr Fr oak. **Merlot 03** sample shrouded in dusty dry oak mid-2005, impossible to rate conclusively. On current form ★★★. – *MM*

Devon Rocks

Stellenbosch ▪ Est 1998 ▪ 1stB 2003 ▪ Visits by appt ▪ B&B ▪ Owners Jürgen & Brita Heinrich ▪ Vini consultant John Robert Frater (De Zoete Inval) ▪ Viti advisers Gawie du Bois & Paul Wallace ▪ 3.5 ha (pinotage, shiraz) ▪ 600 cs 100% red ▪ PO Box 12483 Die Boord 7613 ▪ info@devonrocks.co.za ▪ www.devonrocks.co.za ▪ ***T 865·2536*** *▪ F 865·2621*

Early retirement from the corporate world brought Jürgen Heinrich and his Swedish wife to the Devon Valley, and a new career in wine. The vineyard's small enough to oversee (under consultants' guidance); the wine's made elsewhere for the moment, leaving Jürgen H with the biggest challenge – distribution. He sees finding niche markets the solution to keeping marketing expenditure in proportion to his small volumes. He still swears by the 'striving for excellence' slogans of his corporate past. 'As a small producer,' he says, 'I cannot afford to make a mediocre product,' and is eyeing his native Germany as a possible export destination.

Pinotage ★★★ Maiden **03** a more knit, settled version of pretty **04**, with its hints crushed red berries, toasty oak, jammy black/red berry; 15% alc sneaks in at the finish to give warm goodbye. From Stbosch dryland bushvines; yr new Fr oak. – *IvH*

Devon View see Devon Hill

DeWaal Wines

Stellenbosch ▪ Est 1682 ▪ 1stB 1972 ▪ Tasting & sales Mon-Fri 9-4.30 (Oct-Apr) Mon-Fri 10-12.30; 2-4.30 (May-Sep) Sat 9-4.30 (Aug-May only) ▪ Fee R10 ▪ Closed Easter Fri/Sun, Dec 25/26 & Jan 1 ▪ Owners De Waal brothers ▪ Winemakers/viticulturists Chris de Waal & Daniël de Waal (whites/reds, Jan 1976/1989) ▪ Marketing Pieter de Waal ▪ 120 ha (pinotage, shiraz, sauvignon) ▪ 800 tons 20 000 cs 50% red 50% white ▪ PO Box 15 Vlottenburg 7604 ▪ dewaal@uiterwyk.co.za ▪ www.dewaal.co.za ▪ ***T 881·3711*** *▪ F 881·3776*

Just a glance at the tasting notes below is enough to show the high regard many judges hold for the De Waal brothers of Uiterwyk estate. Then again, the family for many years has had a reputation for quality and innovation: to celebrate the fact that a clansman made SA's first pinotage back in 1941 while lecturing at Elsenburg College, they've rechristened one of their flagship Pinotages 'CT de Waal'. Using specialist pickers to ensure that only the best bunches make it to the cellar, red-wine maker Daniël expects the 05 pinotage and shiraz to be exceptional (though he notes that it was not the greatest year for merlot), while brother Chris, who makes the whites, was delighted with the calibre of the viognier.

★★★★★ **Top of the Hill Pinotage** One of the more elegant & serious (yet gorgeous) expressions of this grape, from small bushvine vyd over 50 yrs old. **01** made Daniël de W Diners Club Winemaker of the Year (2003). **02** with spicy/toasty wood notes, followed by deep savouriness, ripe tannin underpinning solid fruit. Pinotage Top Ten. Spicy oak, bright fruit also prominent on youthful **03**, the variety's rustic element & power combining with graceful charm; finishes with sweet fruit over big dry tannins. 27 mths Fr oak, 80% new. These need good few yrs in bottle.

★★★★★ **CT de Waal Pinotage** Formerly 'Pinotage'. This, from small-cropping ±40 yr old vines, a label to rival illustrious partner – some will prefer its somewhat lesser oakiness (50% new Fr, 15 mths). **03** (★★★★) has perfumed/spicy nose, rich fruit, all freshly & pleasingly balanced with support of ripe tannin, savoury acidity, 14.2% alc. Allow few yrs of maturation. First was intense **01**; follow-up **02** characterised by happily refined rusticity.

★★★★★ **Cape Blend** Maiden **93** was first of the 90s wave of blends with pinotage – this one a serious-minded, soberly elegant version. **02** with 30% each shiraz & merlot graceful, well & firmly balanced. Youthful **03** has merlot at 50% (pinotage/shiraz 30/20), dominant on dark-fruited, softly dense structure, adding choc notes; though pinotage also assertive. Plenty of oak character (50% new Fr). Should develop well at least 5 yrs, keep longer.

★★★★★ **Shiraz** Sample **02** last yr promised powerful but restrained characterfulness, sweet fruit, rich ripe tannins. No **03** made.

★★★★ **Merlot** Brightly fruited but restrained **02** (★★★★), with modest plummy, leaf-edged nose, elegantly structured. More choc-mint on **03**, bags of plummy flavour to match big structure. Integrated 40% new oak.

Pinotage ★★★★ Elevated from Uiterwyk range with tasty **03**, the lightest of home-variety trio, but not inconsiderable: lighter, fruitier, less tannic power. 45% new Fr oak. **Sauvignon Blanc** ★★★★ Always a serious-minded example: grass, capsicum on fresh & severely elegant **05** tank sample; dry lingering finish & balanced 13% alc. **Viognier** First Stbosch version of this white Rhône variety, now with 15% new Fr oak. After forceful **04** (★★★★) sample **05** quiet, dry, steely, with only hints of typical aromatics – likely ★★★. Discontinued: **Cabernet Sauvignon**.

Standard Uiterwyk range

★★★★ **Shiraz** Last tasted was well-structured, velvety **00**, viognier perfume adding to spice, plum & toasty-oakiness. Firm tannin, savoury acidity; 40% new Fr oak.

Merlot ★★★ Fr-oaked **00** had spicy, dusty plum notes, pleasing balance.

Uiterwyk Young Vines range

Red ★★★ Low-key & friendly, but in house's refined style: lightly wooded **02** blends pinotage, shiraz, merlot in plummy, fresh & pleasant package. **White** ★★ **05** easy-going, dry & crisp blend sauvignon plus pals; modest 12.5% alc. – *TJ*

De Wet Co-op Winery

Worcester ▪ Est 1946 ▪ Tasting & sales Mon-Fri 8-5 Sat 9-12 ▪ Fee 50c/wine ▪ Closed pub hols ▪ BYO picnics ▪ Conferencing ▪ Owners 60 members ▪ Winemaker/manager Piet le Roux (1995) & Hugo Conradie (2003) ▪ Viti consultant Newald Marais (Jan 2003) ▪ ±1 000 ha (chard, chenin) ▪ 19 000 tons 20% red 80% white ▪ PO Box 16 De Wet 6853 ▪ dewetwynkelder@mweb.co.za ▪ www.worcesterwinelands.co.za ▪ ***T (023) 341·2710*** *▪ F (023) 341·2762*

After 2004's record crop, a period of drought resulted in a 20% lower production last harvest – but the wines were up on quality. As a 50% shareholder in FirstCape, fastest-growing SA brand in the UK, this Worcester winery now applies focused management practices in the vineyards, thereby exercising better quality control. Vinifying wines in different styles and at varying price points has posed logistical problems in the cellar, reports Piet le Roux, but they've risen to the challenges. New are blocks of fashionable viognier and nouvelle, a crossing of semillon and crouchen blanc developed locally.

★★★★ **Red Muscadel** ✓ **01** fortified dessert was very clean & light tripping. **02** (★★★★), retasted last ed, luscious & tropical, full & round, delicious; could be cellared further. **03** untasted.

Pinotage Returns to line-up with **03**, untasted. 'Fruity wine, lightly wooded,' advises Piet le R. **Dry Red** ★★★ Formula varies from yr to yr, **04** not ready; **03** was bdx-style blend, cab f & petit v; with delicate brush oak. **Cape Riesling** ★★ Usually swiggable & light; **03** needed drinking soon last ed; **05** now selling. **Petillant Fronté Light** ★★★ Slightly spritzy, extra-low alc white (±8%) endorsed by the Heart Foundation. 100% muscat de F, pvs **NV** was fragrantly smooth & sweet. **Chardonnay** ★ Wooded **02** still available; last ed already v oaky; better in youth. **Sauvignon Blanc** ★★ **05** untasted; **04** lighter than pvs, not much varietal zing. **Bouquet Blanc** ★★ Scented, lightish off-dry white from fernão p, colombard & gewürz; **03** was last featured; **05** untasted. **Special Late Harvest** ★★ 100% gewürz; **04** still selling; spicy floral nose, balanced off-dry taste. Pleasantly light 11% alc. **Hanepoot** Fortified dessert stages return with **04**, untasted by us. **Port** ★★★★ Traditional-style fortified with extra character/interest imparted by rare-in-Cape variety pontac; newest **03** not reviewed. **02** had lots of complexity (including tomato-sauce like nuance!), 17.4% alc. **Shiraz-Pinotage**, **Rosé**, **Colombard-Chardonnay** discontinued. – *DH*

De WetsBerg see Excelsior

De Wetshof Estate

Robertson ▪ Est 1949 ▪ 1stB 1972 ▪ Tasting & sales Mon-Fri 8.30-4.30 Sat 9.30-12.30 ▪ Closed Dec 25/26, Jan 1 & Easter Fri/Mon ▪ Tours by appt ▪ Owner Danie de Wet ▪ Winemaker Danie de Wet (1973), with Mervyn Williams (2001) ▪ Viticulturist George Thom (1996), advised by Phil Freese & Francois Viljoen (both 1997) ▪ 180 ha (cab, merlot, pinot, chard, sauvignon, semillon, riesling) ▪ 10% red 90% white ▪ ISO 9001, BRC & HACCP certification ▪ PO Box 31 Robertson 6705 ▪ info@dewetshof.com ▪ www.dewetshof.com ▪ ***T (023) 615·1853*** *▪ F (023) 615·1915*

'We do not strive to win competitions,' insists Danie de Wet – for all the trophies on his mantelpiece. 'We endeavour to create the best possible wines for people to enjoy.' As part of efforts to this end, De Wetshof has now received three certificates for quality management systems, safety and hazard standards. 'It is no longer possible to tell consumers you are doing everything in your power to provide a wine which is not going to harm them – if enjoyed in moderation, naturally! They insist on checks and balances.' A founding member of Proudly South African, De Wetshof has been named Company of the Year. Proud, too, 'of what we do and of where we come from'. And they're immensely proud of Employee of the Year runner-up Mervyn Williams, who arrived seeking work as a gardener and is now an integral member of the winemaking team.

★★★★ **Bateleur Chardonnay** Estate's flagship, always a personal Danie dW barrel selection – finesse, complexity the aims. **03**, tasted last ed, didn't falter. Immediate orange zest/yellow cling peach appeal, deft oaking (fermented/11 mths), sinewy structure; racy acidity lifting palate. One to age 4+ yrs. CWT gold. **02** was taut but packed with citrus.

★★★★ **Rhine Riesling** ✓ Well-regarded example; in good yrs allows ageing over 5-7 yrs. Usually delicate & refined but **04** (★★★★) more austere than pvs. Floral, summer garden aromatics, bone dry & light (12.7% alc), could unfold over time. No **03**. **02**'s acidity balanced by 8g/ℓ sugar, finishing dry.

★★★★ **Edeloes** Gorgeous, full-blown botrytis dessert from riesling. Triumphant **00** (★★★★★) honeyed, with lovely balance between opulent sweetness & firm, clean acid; ageing magnificently when last tasted.

Chardonnay D'Honneur ★★★★ Oaky style, but also generous ripe fruit. Last-tasted **03** peach-laden, with roasted nuts, lemon peel. Ripe, tasty, finishing crisply. Fermented/10 mths oak. **Finesse Chardonnay** ★★★★ Lighest-oaked version of the trio of barrel-fermented chardonnays; named **Lesca** for export. **04** tropical character, biscuity oak-spice flavours harmonising nicely with fruit. Rounded, full-flavoured & satisfying. **Bon Vallon Chardonnay** ★★★★ SA's first unwooded version, **05** in fresher style than before, no less appealing; combines floral & citric tones; lively, aromatic & great with food. **Blanc Fumé** ★★★★ Lightly wooded, bone-dry sauvignon. **04** lemon, lime with leafy/green edginess, smoothed by gentle biscuit overlay. Friendly 11.6% alc. This, next 2, tasted last yr. **Sauvignon Blanc** ★★★ **04** still available, with green fig intro, herbaceous, nettly; lovely racy, tangy-lime flavours, finish. Good food partner. 12% alc. **Blanc De Wet** ★★★ **04** was good value; equal partners sauvignon/semillon working well together: juicy gooseberry/guava flavours, zinging citrus freshness. 12.2% alc.

Danie de Wet range

★★★★ **Danie de Wet Cape Muscadel** Excellent, refined new-wave Cape fortified. Last was **00**, aromas, flavours marmalade & jasmine; lovely sweet/sour tussle, uncloying. 15.3% alc. 500ml.

★★★★ **Limestone Hill Chardonnay** Scented unwooded version; always very ripe, terrific, bold. **05** (★★★★) a peaches & cream delight, abounds with flavour, curvaceous silky texture; just-dry 5g/ℓ sugar & enough balancing acidity for delicious solo drinking or food.

Cabernet Sauvignon Naissance ★★★★ **03** nicely put together: opulent cassis/black cherries, deep, sweet spicing, all held by an elegant framework of firm but ripe tannins. Plenty of concentration & interest. Malo/maturation in seasoned oak, 3-4 yr ageing potential. One to watch. **Nature in Concert Pinot Noir** ★★★★ **03** (tasted as sample last ed), had toasty vanilla-spiced aromas vying for attention with raspberry/strawberry fruit, whiffs forest floor; supple, amenable tannins. Oak as above. **Call of the African Eagle** ★★★★ Briefly oak-aged chard. Last tasted was **02**. **Chardonnay Sur Lie** ★★★★ Unwooded, 3 mths on lees ('longer than on shop shelves!' says Lesca dW). **05** more grip & structure than pvs, more serious: heady floral perfume, juicy structure, racy, bone-dry: excellent food fare. — *CR*

Deza see Oaklands Wine Exporters

De Zoete Inval Estate

Paarl ▪ Est 1878 ▪ 1stB 1976 ▪ Tasting & sales at I Love Wine, Paarl (see Wine shops section for opening hours); farm tastings & tours by appt ▪ Owner AR Frater Trust ▪ Winemaker/viticulturist John Robert Frater (1999/2004) ▪ 20 ha (cab, petit v, port varieties, shiraz, chard, sauvignon) ▪ 100 tons 5 000 cs own label 50% red 50% white ▪ PO Box 591 Suider-Paarl 7624 ▪ dezoeteinval@wine.co.za ▪ www.dezoeteinval.co.za ▪ ***T 863·1535*** *▪ F 863·2158*

'Minimal intervention and keeping it all as natural as possible' summarises John Robert Frater's approach to winemaking. The long-term plan to trim the range of wines, with improved focus on fewer products still guides the team, with a flagship white and a red blend firmly in their sights. Modernising and simplifying the cellar forms part of this plan, and a new tasting room is imminent. The range-trimming hasn't prevented the release this year of their maiden cap classique, a wine to JFR's mind satisfying enough to consider making plenty more of.

Only three wines tasted for this edition: **Vintage Brut**, **Rosé** & **Yvette**. **Vintage Brut** new ★★★ Maiden MCC **03** from chardonnay, WO Paarl. Fine bubble & raspy, rather than creamy, mousse. Arresting acidity, bone-dry with just 3g/ℓ sugar, balanced finish. **Rosé** ★★★ Historically a quirky blend sauvignon/port varieties, but **05** from shiraz. 13.3% alc, unrated. **Yvette** ★★★ **05** a step up on pvs; distinctive sauvignon tinned pea/asparagus notes, zesty acidity & faint lemon palate. Wonderful fruit concentration, fresh finish despite 13g/ℓ sugar. 12.9% alc. No new vintages of following: **Cabernet Sauvignon** ★★ **01** potpourri nose with tobacco & cherry; dry, light bodied, somewhat lacking ripeness & fruit; drink up. Yr 1st fill Fr oak. **Cabernet Sauvignon-Shiraz** ★★★ Almost porty nose of prunes & plums, savoury touch; chunky/chewy wine (15.2% alc), quite rustic yet not unappealing. **NV. Grand Rouge** ★★ Individual blend cab & port grapes, yr wooded, 3rd fill Fr; light (11% alc) with hints coconut & tea-leaves, sour plum palate. **Chardonnay** ★★★ **03** reveals some complexity; 'burnt match' character, dry, attractively austere on finish. **Late Harvest** ★★★ From sauvignon. Last was **03**, with supple, light fruit salad tastes. **Cape Vintage** ★★ **01** acquiring mature tawny tint; dusty dried fruit on nose, soft, silky, attractively dry. Fortified to low 16.8% alc; 26 mths 500ℓ casks. **Sauvignon Blanc** discontinued.

Eskdale range

All **03**, aged ±10 mths in Fr oak. No new vintages: **Merlot** ★★★ With house's slight savoury edge, obvious acidity, grainy tannins; clearly a food style. **Pinotage** ★★★ Bluegum aromas, bouncy mulberry flavours, lighter-bodied (13.5% alc); creamy oak (10% Am) on finish. **Shiraz** ★★★ Roast meat & smoky edge to the dry, firm, full-bodied palate; dry tannins, sweet-sour note on finish. —*DH*

DGB

*Wellington ▪ Est 1942 ▪ Closed to public ▪ Owners DGB management, Brait Capital Partners & Kangra ▪ Winemakers/viticulturists: see Bellingham ▪ PO Box 246 Wellington 7654 ▪ exports@dgb.co.za ▪ www.dgb.co.za ▪ **T 864·5300** ▪ F 864·1287*

Well-established merchant house with a wide portfolio of own-brand table wines, ports and sherries. See separate listings for Bellingham, Culemborg, Douglas Green, Millstream, Oude Kaap, Tall Horse, Text and The Saints.

Die Breedekloof see Viljoensdrift
Die Krans see De Krans

Diemersdal Estate

*Durbanville ▪ Est 1698 ▪ 1stB 1990 ▪ Tasting & sales Mon-Fri 9-5 Sat 9-3 ▪ Closed Easter Fri/Sun, Dec 25 & Jan 1 ▪ Tours by appt ▪ Meals/refreshments: see intro ▪ Walks ▪ Owner Tienie Louw ▪ Winemaker Johan Kruger (Sep 2004) ▪ Viticulturist Div van Niekerk (1980) ▪ 172 ha (cab, merlot, pinotage, shiraz, chard, sauvignon) ▪ 1 730 tons 15 000 cs own label 85% red 15% white ▪ PO Box 27 Durbanville 7551 ▪ wines@diemersdal.co.za ▪ **T 976·3361** ▪ F 976·1810*

A harvest which was warm by cool-climate Durbanville standards gave wines riper in character and with good ageing potential, from the Sauvignon Blanc through to the Pinotage. With winemaker Johan Kruger at the cellar controls (in tandem with family label Sterhuis), the new grape-sorting facility was worth every cent: 'No more bad berries!' More small tanks allowed separate fermentation of fruit from various blocks (two single vineyards have been officially registered). And ('very exciting!') there were five barrels of chardonnay, the base-wine for a Cap Classique. In the vineyards, a new block of sauvignon is 'coming on nicely', and soils were prepared for a few hectares each of petit verdot, malbec, and Burgundian-clone chardonnay. Not to mention a new restaurant opening its doors (but BYO picnics still allowed).

★★★★ **Shiraz** ✓ Modern accessible style with a nod to the classics. Like pvs, **03** with fynbos & scrub intro, also savoury mineral wafts; deceptively soft entry, earthy middle & peppery, dry finish. **02** harmonious mouthful, fruit carries through to spicy conclusion. 14% alc, yr 50% new oak, mainly Fr.

★★★★ **Private Collection** ✓ Red blend, usually led by cab; make-up varies with vintage. In **03** (★★★★), cab 53% with shiraz/cab f/pinotage/merlot (19/11/10/7). Sweet red fruit & tobacco aromas, juicy, sweet/sour palate pulled up respectable acid/tannins. Structure to improve 3–5 yrs, respectable 13.4% alc. **02** cab-dominated, with 29% shiraz; attractively plump, ripe, fruit. Yr oaked.

★★★★ **Chardonnay Reserve** new Wonderfully rich & indulgent **04** maiden; melange buttered toast, lime, butterscotch on nose & palate; satiny mouthfeel, poised & elegant.

Barrel fermented/aged 100% new Fr oak for 10 mths. Certainly a step up on other whites in the range.

Cabernet Sauvignon ★★★★ Attractive cassis fruit, hints of spice/tobacco/meaty aromas on **03**. Sweet & sour fruit character & austere tannins; touch eucalyptus; slightly jammy finish, 13.5% alc well integrated. 16 mths Fr oak, 50% new. **Pinotage** ★★★★ Hallmark charm & grace (rather than the variety's more usual power) on **03**, this with ripe, dried fruit aromas & distinctive oak toastness (yr 50% new Fr oak). Brusque tannins need ± yr to soften. 14.5 % alc. MIWA gold. **Matys** ★★★ Pronounced Mah-*tace*, lightly wooded blend pinotage, shiraz, merlot (51/39/10). Tasted mid-2004, **03** leafy whiffs, notes cigarbox & dark plums; big plum flavours; slightly rustic but appealing. 14% alc. MIWA gold. **Chardonnay** Charming, subtly oaked example. **05** (unrated preview) almond nuttiness & citrus notes, sherbety palate; 14% alc showing on finish. Portion (40%) barrel fermented/aged 4 mths. **Sauvignon Blanc** ★★★ **05** passionfruit & other tropical notes spill out of the glass; zesty acidity, medium bodied & dry, sensible 12.5% alc. **Blanc de Blanc** new ★★★ Sauvignon/chardonnay/semillon/gewürz (49/27/12/12) mingle to serve up a weighty (13.5% alc) food wine; attractive fruit salad nose, well pitched acidity. **Elixir** new ★★★ partially barrel-fermented NLH. **03**'s ripe peaches of botrytis overlaid with freshly baked bread yeastiness; racy acidity & nutty palate with long, elegant goodbye. 14% unobtrusive. —*MM*

Diemersdal wines see Diemersdal Estate, African Terroir

Diemersfontein Wines

Wellington ▪ Est/1stB 2001 ▪ Tasting & sales daily 10–5 ▪ Fee R15 ▪ Closed Dec 25 ▪ Tours by appt ▪ Restaurant & guest house (see Eat-out & Stay-over sections) ▪ Conferencing ▪ Walks ▪ Mountain biking ▪ Owners David & Susan Sonnenberg ▪ Winemaker Bertus Fourie, with Francois Roode (Nov 2000/Sep 2003) ▪ Viticulturist Bertus Fourie (Mar 2001) ▪ 55 ha (cab, merlot, mourvèdre, petit v, pinotage, shiraz, viognier) ▪ 380 tons 15 000 cs + 3 000 cs for Woolworths ▪ 95% red 4% white 1% rosé ▪ HACCP & ISO 9001 accredited ▪ PO Box 41 Wellington 7654 ▪ wine@diemersfontein.co.za ▪ www.diemersfontein.co.za ▪ ***T 864·5050*** *▪ F 864·2095*

Bertus Fourie continues to put Wellington on the map, and not only with his Pinotage (which continues to wow judges around the world, most recently at the International Wine Challenge in London where the Carpe Diem won the South African trophy). Closer to home, it was his Carpe Diem Cab which top-scored at the Trophy Wine Show, where Diemersfontein was also named most successful winery overall. So what's Fourie's secret? 'Making good and consistent quality wines is actually simple,' he says modestly. 'Take good care of the soils and the vines, harvest when optimally ripe, and keep it straight and simple in the winery. Oh yes — and enjoy every bit of it because it is not a job, it's a way of living.'

Carpe Diem range

★★★★ **Cabernet Sauvignon 04** (sample) pencil shavings/minerals plus minty choc & taut austerity; weightier (14.5% alc) than **03**, with pleasant sweetness, red berry rather than usual cassis flavour profile. FCTWS trophy. 70/30 Fr/Am oak, 60% new.

★★★★★ **Pinotage** Sample **04** destined for greatness. Toasty nose leads on to fruity sweetness, well structured tannins with lingering aftertaste. Serious oaking: all new, 15 mths, 70/30 Fr/Am. Touch hotter (14.5% alc) & drier than pvs, but poised to continue assertive wine-show presence (incl FCTWS, Pinotage Top Ten, Classic Trophy). **03** luscious, with measured ripe tannins, balanced 14% alc keeping teeming flesh & touch sugar (3.1g/ℓ) in check.

★★★★ **Shiraz** Sample **04** returns to form after vegetal & milky **03** (★★★); smoky aromas & big mocha addition from 15 mths Fr oak, huge extract, tight tannins.

Merlot ★★★★ **03** in house style of delivering smouldering herbal warmth to tightly arrayed palate. ±18 mths oak. **Viognier** ★★★★ new **04** mirabelle & violets rather than more usual peach/apricot perfumes; good concentration & integration.

Diemersfontein range

★★★★ **Pinotage 04**, previewed last ed, packed with notes of mocha, burnt match & banana; pleasing sweetness from super-ripe fruit. Likely ★★★. Not as arresting as **03** MIWA gold.

★★★★ **Heaven's Eye** Cabs s/f, petit v & shiraz alliance, tannins as tight & sleek as James Bond's tuxedo mid-2004. **03** monster dark ripe fruit, cloves, choc – & midi-monster 14.5% alc. Components matured mainly Fr oak, 10 mths. Keep up to 10 yrs.

★★★★ **Summer's Lease 03** shiraz-dominated blend (77%), with pinotage, dollop mourvèdre. Meaty, tight, explosive fruit, pleasant sweetness from 14.5% alc. Mix Fr/Am oak, 10 mths. Last ed we felt it should develop, keep ±6 yrs yet.

Cabernet Sauvignon ★★★ **02** slightly green, but classic cab cassis emerged from austerity & tea leaves last yr. **Merlot** ★★★★ Ripe red plums & freshness hid **03**'s 14.7% alc. Riper than **02**, with choc richness emerging through tannins. Half tank, half new Fr oak. Not retasted. **Shiraz 03** sample promised ★★★★ quality mid-2004. Attractive sweetness with floral & herbal note. New Fr/Am oak. **Maiden's Prayer** ★★ Unoaked merlot, cab, shiraz, pinotage blend, fruit-driven & designed for early drinking – though **04** is neither: unripe vegetal tone & bitter finish. – *NP*

Die Tweede Droom see Groot Parys

Dieu Donné Vineyards

Franschhoek ▪ Est 1984 ▪ 1stB 1986 ▪ Tasting & sales Mon-Fri 9-4 Sat/Sun 10.30 4 ▪ Fee R10 ▪ Closed Dec 25/26 & Jan 1 ▪ Cheese platters & picnics in summer by appt ▪ Tours by appt ▪ Tourgroups ▪ Owner Robert Maingard ▪ Winemaker Stephan du Toit (May 1996) ▪ Viticulturist Hennie du Toit (Apr 1988) ▪ 40 ha (cab, merlot, pinotage, shiraz, chard, sauvignon) ▪ ±280 tons 16 500 cs 60% red 35% white 3% rosé 2% MCC ▪ PO Box 94 Franschhoek 7690 ▪ info@dieudonnevineyards.com ▪ www.dieudonnevineyards.com ▪ ***T 876·2493*** *▪ F 876·2102*

Harvest blessings in 2004 for winemaker Stephan du Toit included the first conditions conducive to 'very nice botrytis' since 1997, enabling him to make a small quantity of NLH, which has now been released. A restaurant, being built literally in the hill next to the tasting room, with glass-panelled frontage and a deck, promises to take full advantage of some of the finest views in the Cape. These can also be admired over a pre-booked picnic or cheese platter – with some wine, of course.

Cabernet Sauvignon-Shiraz new ☺ ★★★ **03** smooth & accessible maiden should please the crowds with balance, New World fruitiness, light oak touch.

Cabernet Sauvignon ★★★ House style lean, tight tannins, but **01** steps up in quality with lovely perfumed nose, good balance of fruit & structure. 18 mths Fr oak. **Merlot** ★★ Generous plum fruit on nose/palate of **02**, bitter almond goodbye. Styling has its admirers: Concours Mondial gold. 18 mths Fr oak. **Pinotage** ★★★ **03** charms with delicate raspberry aroma, lightish frame (13.6% alc) & dry, elegant finish. Hint Am oak; more 'pinot' than 'cinsaut'. **Shiraz** ★★★ **03** all earthiness & spice, lighter this vintage (14% alc vs pvs 15.5%), very dry but not stalky. Yr mainly Fr oak. **Rosé** ★★★ Usually from two sauvignons, one red (cab-), other white (-blanc); **05** cherry whiffs, raspberry-toned sweet/sour flavours; for immediate enjoyment. **Chardonnay Unwooded** ★★★ **05** gains weight/texture from 4 mths *sur lie* ageing; balanced with refreshing Granny Smith apple acidity. **Sauvignon Blanc** ★★★ Zingy cat's pee, green fig, nettle combo in bouquet of **05**, dry but not austere, for early drinking. **Maingard Brut MCC** ★★★★ **02** our first ever look at their bottle-fermented sparkling (pvs consistently missed deadline) – we are not disappointed! Light & delicate with fine toasty mousse, brioche whiff. Some honey, cream on finish. 30 mths matured. **Noble Late Harvest** new ★★★★ Varieties unnamed. **04** possibly incl riesling given this delicate unfortified dessert's light, oily palate & lively acidity. Hint botrytis apricot mingles with pineapple, citrus, almond aromas & flavours. Sweet (113g/ℓ sugar) but not cloying; long farewell. No new vintages of following; notes from pvs ed: **Cabernet Sauvignon Reserve** ★★★ **99**

similar qualities/oaking to std version, mid-2004 still powerfully tannic. Other palates find considerable merit in its qualities: gold at Concours Mondial 2003, UK *Decanter* ★★★★. **Cabernet Sauvignon-Merlot** ★★★ Current release is **98**, 85/15 blend with cab's trenchant tones; mid-2004 showed tertiary aromas, still youthful raspberry fruit on palate. 18 mths Fr oak. **Chardonnay Wooded** ★★★★ **03** light, delicate, attractive citrus freshness; fine oak treatment results in appealing oatmeal whiffs. —*JN/RK*

Die Vlakte see Cloverfield
Disa see Porterville Cellars

Dispore Kamma Boutique Winery

Caledon ▪ Est/1stB 2002 ▪ Visits by appt ▪ Owners Philip Mostert & Hannes Coetzee ▪ Winemaker Philip Mostert, with Hannes Coetzee (Jan/Jun 2002) ▪ Viti consultant Willie de Waal ▪ ±100 cs 100% red ▪ PO Box 272 Caledon 7230 ▪ philmos@mweb.co.za ▪ ***T (028) 214·1057 (a/h) / 083·448·1670*** *▪ F (028 214·1077*

Vinifying's a part-time business for Philip Mostert — he's a doctor in Caledon, owner of a newly-acquired parcel of land there. But as a winemaker he has four vintages under his belt, using grapes bought in from Paarl, Robertson and the Overberg. His passion for shiraz was rewarded with a 2004 Michelangelo gold for his Syrah 03, and a good placing for the 02 in the Caledon Wine Club's shiraz tasting. All fertilising his ambitions to 'make the best shiraz that's possible, and use fruit from five regions to produce different wines'.

Cabernet Sauvignon new ★★★ Well-balanced **04** is eminently approachable; acids are fresh, black fruit is generous & tannins firm yet ripe. Nose packed with jam & spice, latter thanks to 14 mths old Fr oak. Should improve 2-3 yrs. Do be alert when seeking out the **Syrah**, as Philip M now has two — one from vines on Schooneoord (the home of Scali, near Paarl), the other from Hldrberg fruit. The maiden **02** from this source was much applauded & awarded. Follow-up **03** (★★★★) also succulent & fragrant but barrel sample **04** too unkit to rate: brawny 14.7% alc, ultra-ripe bordering on jammy, aggressive tannins. 12-14 mths new Fr/new & 2nd-fill Am oak, unfiltered. By contrast, **04** from WO Paarl grapes rates ★★★★. Restrained & elegant at only 13. 7% alc, it has mineral/spice/red fruit/ripe tannins/savoury, persistent goodbye. Aged in a combo Am/Fr new/old; structure to improve 3-5yrs. **Merlot-Cabernet Sauvignon** new ★★★ Lean, dinner table partner, merlot (70%) champions the blend. **04** with more-ish black fruit & green mealies aromas, surprisingly austere palate; astringent tannin/low fruit concentration. We question if it has the structure to soften. All old Fr oak. —*MM*

Distell

Stellenbosch ▪ PO Box 184 Stellenbosch 7599 ▪ www.distell.co.za ▪ ***T 809·7000***

It's hard to keep up with the ever-increasing scope of this monolith (made up of former producing wholesaler giants Distillers and SFW). So here's a breakdown. Operating from two corporate-owned wineries (Bergkelder and Adam Tas), Distell vinifies some of SA's most successful and enduring wine brands. They are: 5th Avenue Cold Duck, Autumn Harvest Crackling, Capenheimer, Cellar Cask, Chateau Libertas, Drostdy-Hof, Flat Roof Manor, Fleur du Cap, Graça, Grand Mousseux, Grünberger, Hill & Dale, Kellerprinz, Kupferberger Auslese, Libertas, Monis, Oom Tas, Obikwa, Oracle, Overmeer, Sedgwick's, Ship Sherry, Table Mountain, Tassenberg, Taverna, Two Oceans, Virginia and Zonnebloem. Heading things up at The Bergkelder cellar is Linley Schultz, who manages a phalanx of winemakers, each dedicated to a specific brand/s. At the Adam Tas cellar, red-winemaker Michael Bucholz remains a constant for Zonnebloem. Recent in-house reshuffles include assistant Deon Boshoff replacing Zonnebloem white-winemaker Louw Engelbrecht (who's moved to Durbanville Hills), Andrea Freeborough (ex-Nederburg) joining Bergkelder, Justin Corrans (ex-Zonnebloem) focusing on Fleur du Cap. Distell also owns the House of JC le Roux, a dedicated MCC cellar in Devon Valley. Then there are the stand-alone 'estate' labels: Nederburg, Plaisir de Merle (both former SFW properties), and now Lomond, in the exciting new cool-climate Elim ward. Distell is also the co-owner, together with Hans Schreiber's Lusan Holdings, of a handful of top Stellenbosch properties (Alto, Le Bonheur, Neethlingshof, Stellenzicht, Uitkyk), and has agreements with a few independently-owned cellars (Allesverloren, Jacobsdal and Theuniskraal) for which it provides a range of services. Finally, there's the black empowerment West Coast venture on Papkuilsfontein farm near Darling, jointly owned with a local community trust and a consortium of taverners, which produces the Tukulu range of wines. See Bergkelder for details about the Vinoteque Wine Bank (previously listed here), and separate entries for the above brands/properties.

Dolphin Bay see Cru Wines

Domaine Brahms Wineries

Paarl ▪ Est 1998 ▪ 1stB 1999 ▪ Tasting & sales Mon-Fri 9.30-5 Sat & pub hols by appt (closed Easter Fri-Mon, Jun 16, Sep 24, Dec 25/26 & Jan 1) ▪ Fee R5/wine ▪ Tours anytime by appt ▪ Owners Braam & Gesie Lategan ▪ Winemaker/viticulturist Gesie Lategan (1998) ▪ 15 ha (cab, merlot, pinotage, shiraz) ▪ 100% red ▪ PO Box 2136 Windmeul 7630 ▪ brahms@iafrica.com ▪ ***T 869·8555*** *▪ F 869·8590*

'I don't make show wines to impress judges. I make wine because it's a passion.' Indomitable Gesie Lategan may not try, but she does impress: named Cape Farmer of the Year in 2003, she was selected last year to participate in the nationwide 'Salute To Success' programme – the only winemaker to be invited. A busy year it was: she also released her first blend; if her track record is anything to go by, Quartet will be well received. Not that Gesie will take the credit. 'It's arrogant to think we make wine – nature does. We simply help nurture it into being.' Some mothers are just better at it than others.

★★★★ **Shiraz 02** (★★★) now bottled, retasted. Bayleaf, white pepper in lean profile; difficult vintage has high acidity & greenish tannins robbing varietal generosity. Developing similarly to **01**, whose herbal notes, greener tannins marred succession from standout **00**. From low-yielding vyds (±6 t/ha); Fr oak, 15-20% new.

★★★★ **Pinotage** Sample **04** discreet plum, red cherry fruit; rich, concentrated; almost chocolaty texture & feel aided by clever tannin manipulation (whole berry fermentation, 2 punch-downs daily, 26 days on skins); fine-grained. Suave, well behaved but still varietally true pinotage. Seems drier, more classic than warm, plummy debut **03**. 9 mths Fr oak.

Cabernet Sauvignon ★★★ Shyish **02** needs coaxing from glass; palate more amenable with dark berried charms, tannins nearing approachability. 9 mths oak, used Fr. **Quartet** new ★★★★ **03** stylish blend merlot, pinotage, cab, shiraz (50/30/10/10). Some attractive cassis, spice, wisp of smoke, hint biltong migrate easily onto palate, nicely proportioned, unobtrusive oak (only 40% wooded). **Judex Provisional Judgement** ★★★ Earthy blend pinotage, merlot, ruby cab, shiraz (39/30/28/3); for last ed, **02** attractive berry, herb & oaky tones. **Chenin Blanc** ★★★ **04**'s shy peach whiffs with lively peachy fruit to match; good concentration, firm acidity allow for good 4 yrs of life. 50% fermented/9 mths Fr oak – this well tucked away. – *IvH*

Domaines Paradyskloof see Vriesenhof

Dombeya Vineyards

Stellenbosch ▪ Est 2002 ▪ 1stB 2003 ▪ Tasting & sales Mon-Sat 10-4 ▪ Closed Easter Fri/Sun, Dec 25/26 & Jan 1 ▪ Vineyard Kitchen tea-garden & fully licensed restaurant ▪ Gifts ▪ Owner EOPM Ltd ▪ Vini consultant Rianie Strydom (2005) ▪ 15 ha (cab, merlot, shiraz, chard, sauvignon) ▪ 70% red 30% white ▪ PO Box 12766 Die Boord 7613 ▪ www.dombeya.co.za ▪ Cellar: cellar@dombeya.co.za ▪ T 881·3895 ▪ F 881·3986 ▪ Office: info@dombeya.co.za ▪ ***T 881·3490*** *▪ F 881·3491*

A production cellar, maturation area and tasting locale were completed just in time to handle the 2005 harvest at this prime Stellenbosch location (Dombeya Yarns, known internationally for its on-site-made wool, cotton and mohair products, also on the premises). The winery has been designed with quality in mind: gravity flow, sorting tables and small tanks enabling fermentation of individual vineyard blocks – in keeping with John Sainsbury's mission to produce top wines through rigorous attention to winemaking techniques. Overseeing the operation is winemaking consultant Rianie Strydom (ex-Morgenhof).

03 Cabernet Sauvignon-Merlot & **Shiraz** not ready for tasting. **Chardonnay** ★★★★ New oak (65%, 9 mths) comes into play in **04**, & it's well applied to make most of zesty grapefruit flavours. Firmer fleshed than pvs, lingering, pleasantly low 13% alc. **Sauvignon Blanc** ★★★ **05** well-rounded flesh, lush passionfruit/pineapple tones, softish acidity make for easy, delicious summer drinking. — *IvH*

Domein Doornkraal

Little Karoo ▪ Est 1890 ▪ 1stB 1973 ▪ Tasting & sales Mon-Fri 9-5 Sat 8-1 ▪ Fee R15 p/p for groups of 8+ ▪ Closed Easter Fri/Sun, Dec 25/26 & Jan 1 ▪ Tours by appt ▪ Jemima's Restaurant, Baron van Rheede Str, Oudtshoorn T (044) 272·0808 ▪ Farm produce ▪ Indigenous plant nursery ▪ Tour groups ▪ Gifts ▪ Owners Swepie & Piet le Roux ▪ Winemakers Swepie & Piet le Roux, with Schantelle Swiegelaar (2005) ▪ Viticulturist Piet le Roux ▪ 22 ha ▪ 1 500 cs own label 50% white 50% red ▪ PO Box 14 De Rust 6650 ▪ doornkraal@xsinet.co.za ▪ www.doornkraal.co.za ***T (044) 241·2156*** *(farm)* ***(044) 251·6715*** *(tasting room) ▪ F (044) 241·2548*

The passion for life that goes into the making of these wines by father-and-son team Swepie and Piet le Roux (assisted by Schantelle Swiegelaar) evokes a similar response in those who imbibe their idiosyncratic elixirs. A judge for the Swiss Airline Awards was in tears after tasting the eventual gold-medal-winning Ten Year Old Tawny, while a cute young thing with a baby on each hip, upon sipping the Majoor (a fortified dessert), was heard to exclaim: 'My sainted aunt, this is nice!' That's what it's really all about for these characterful Little Karoo vintners/ostrich farmers/local flora conservators.

★★★★ **Pinta** ✓ Luscious jerepiko-style dessert from pinotage, tinta; lately dash touriga too (necessitating name change?); damson jam aromas, prune flavours, hint of violets; harmonious; fresh dry finish. 30/50/20 mix; alc now set at 17%. **NV**.

★★★★ **Ten Year Old Tawny Port** Among handful of SA vintaged tawnies; old-fashioned but delicious. **92** vibrant amber hues; coffee/crème caramel melange with twists cedarwood, tobacco; beautifully balanced sweetness. Pinotage, tinta; ±18% alc. VDG. Premium priced: R150 ex-tasting room.

Following pair still available, not retasted: **Cabernet Sauvignon** ★★★ **02** ripe cassis aromas; focused & quite rich; quick finish but pleasant enough. **Merlot** ★★ Awards? 'Not likely,' quip Le Rs good-naturedly of quirky, sweet & simple **03**, fermented with native yeasts. **Kannaland (Red)** ★★★ **05** switches to cab, merlot (60/40), unwooded; undemanding, lightish; red berry flavours finish slightly sweet. **Kannaland (White)** new ★★ **05** chardonnay/semillon liaison under screwcap; semi-dry boiled-sweet flavours, lively, for early enjoyment. **Tickled Pink** ★★ Light (12% alc), friskily foamy blanc de noir sparkler, intense grapey aromas, sweet but very fresh finish; sold with shocking pink home-grown ostrich feather. **Muscadel Jerepigo** ★★★ Comfortable & warming fortified dessert; subdued, almost minerally nose, rich raisiny flavours with hint of pipe-tobacco. 18% alc. **NV**. Also available but not tasted: **Kuierwyn** (dry & Natural Sweet), **Ruby/White Port**.

'Military' range

NV fortified desserts. **Majoor** ★★★ Idiosyncratic white jerepiko from chenin, with cold-tea flavours & (in latest bottling) twist of lemon. 16% alc. 'Great Martini mixer,' avers Piet le R, 'or pour over crushed ice.' **Kaptein** & **Luitenant** not assessed (both still AWOL). — *DH*

Dominion Wine Company

Stellenbosch ▪ Est/1stB 2002 ▪ Closed to public ▪ Winemaker Lelanie Germishuys (2004) ▪ 12 000 cs own label 50% red 49% white 1% rosé ▪ Export brands: African Gold, Imvelo, Harvest Moon, Keteka, Kleinbok, Welgedacht etc ▪ Postnet Suite 280 Private Bag X29 Somerset West 7135 ▪ info@dominionwineco.co.za ▪ www.dominionwineco.co.za ***▪ T 883·8879*** *▪ F 883·8782*

This export-focused wine company met with such a positive response abroad to the initial small volumes of their Harvest Moon range that the brand was launched locally in time for summer (at prices as attractive as the packaging). Another new product, also available locally, Big Red, is just that — a generous 1,5ℓ of cab-merlot. With several Wine of the Month

Club wins as affirmation, winemaker Lelanie Germishuys' philosophy remains maximum flavour extraction with finesse and balance.

Sauvignon Blanc Brut ☺ ★★★ Really refreshing & quaffable; crisp, lively pin-point bubbles, lightish litchi flavour, semi-dry finish. **NV** (04).

Merlot ★★★★ **03** last ed showed notes of plum, game & leaves, dark-choc flavours & tight tannins needing 2-3 yrs to soften. Ex-single vyd in Paarl. 14.8% alc. **Kingsview Pinotage** new ★★ **03** lusty version with high-toned red-berry pungency, big tannins, warming 14.3% alc. Fr barrels, 9 mths. **Milestone Syrah** ★★★★ Still enjoying **02**'s red berry aromas, hint fairly restrained palate with sour-plum twist, subtle oak (yr Fr). **Shiraz** ★★★★ **03** not revisited; elegant, slightly grainy wine, good now with richer food or better cellared few yrs. Lightly oaked. **Cabernet Sauvignon-Merlot** ★★★ **03** 51/49 blend, last yr noted as pleasant middle-of-the-road red; medium bodied, mocha & choc flavours, slightly sweet finish. Yr Fr oak. **Big Red** new ★★ Cab/merlot mix sold in magnum only; **02** (sample) 'big' in volume rather than extract/substance; sweet stewed fruit to swig while watching sport on TV. **Rosé de Syrah** ★★★ **03** last yr was pungently aromatic, bone-dry & mouth-filling, versatile with food or solo. **Rolling Hills Chardonnay** ★★★★ **03** big flavoursome wine, will be liked by lovers of woodier styles. 7 mths Fr oak. Not retasted; ditto ... **Milestone Chardonnay Limited Release** ★★★★ **03** less oak-powered than above; fruit salad & peach tones; lightly toasty caramel finish. Yr 1st/2nd fill barrels.

Sugar Bush Ridge range

Cabernet Sauvignon-Merlot ★★★ Easily-approachable **04** (sample), soft & balanced, delicious black-fruit flavours. Fr oak, 9 mths. **Sauvignon Blanc** ★★★ Appealing ripe-tropical style; passionfruit tinged with lemongrass in firmly dry, mouth-watering **05** (sample). 12% alc.

Harvest Moon range new

Charming labels for these quick-quaffs. **Shiraz** ★★ **05** (incl dash malbec) shows typical Swtlnd 'grunt', touch sweetness (7g/ℓ RS), gulpably soft tannins. Fr oak staves 8 mths. **Sauvignon Blanc** ★★ **04** light & dry, some fleeting yellow stone-fruit flavours. All above wines sourced widely, so various WOs. *– IvH/CR/TM*

Doolhof Estate

Wellington ▪ Est 1996 ▪ 1stB 2001 ▪ Visits Mon-Fri 9.30–5 Sat 9.30–1.30 ▪ Fee R25 ▪ Guest cottages ▪ Conferences ▪ Walks ▪ Mountain biking ▪ Owners Kerrison family ▪ Winemaker Therese Swart (Aug 2004) ▪ Vineyard manager Hendrik Laubscher (Aug 1996) ▪ ±35 ha (cabs s/f, malbec, merlot, petit v, pinotage, shiraz, chard, sauvignon) ▪ 220 tons 10 800 cs ▪ PO Box 975 Wellington 7654 ▪ wine@doolhof.com ▪ www.doolhof.com ▪ ***T 873·6911*** *▪ F 864·2321*

Last year was a landmark at this Wellington property. Under direction of winemaker Therese Swart, a new cellar was commissioned – a little nerve-wracking, with the electricity switched on just two days before picking started. But harvest was smooth, with reds impressing and the sauvignon harvested before the rains. Viticulturist Hendrik Laubscher, 10 years at the estate, adapted smoothly to the changeover from supplying grapes to third parties to growing them for in-house vinification. 'Yields are now lower to enable far better quality.' The freshly renovated guest house, revamped tasting facilities and new opening hours (tastings by appointment) are set to attract visitors.

Renaissance Cabernet Sauvignon new ★★★ Unusual but attractive sweetcorn aromas/flavours mingle with toasty oak; lacks cab fruit characters, still a refreshing, interesting mouthful. Full 14.5% alc; combo old/new Fr/Am oak. **Renaissance Pinotage** new ★★★★ Early-drinking **03** charms with intense dark fruit/mocha bouquet, noticeable but integrated oak & satisfying rich, creamy finish. 6 mths Fr staves. Both above WO Wllngtn. **Cape Boar** ★★★★ Partly oaked blend led by cab (60%) in **04**, equal portions shiraz/merlot. Explosive plum pudding fruit, gutsy tannins make for robust quaffing wine. 15% alc not unbalanced. **Cape Roan** ★★★★ Not enough shiraz to make a **04** vintage. Shiraz led the charge in **03** (70%) with cab/merlot (20/10); similar character to above, slightly more pepper; massive alc (15%) but more control, less overt sweetness. Both 'Capes' WO Coastal. **Maiden's Prayer** new ★★★★ **03** joint venture with Diemersfontein; intended as light-textured blend merlot, cab, shiraz, pinotage (40/30/25/5) – 'for the ladies', says David K; dark fruit, mocha & choc with lively acidity & juicy tannins. Enticing, with structure to improve 2-3 yrs. **Signatures Chardonnay** ★★★ **05** step up in quality from crowd-pleasing pvs. Latest more sophisticated passionfruit & citrus notes, tasty & satisfying, zestier, drier. Lees contact minimised to preserve freshness. Blend Wllngtn/Stbosch fruit. **Signatures Sauvignon Blanc** new ★★★★ Food-friendly version midway between leafy 'cool' & tropical 'warm' styles. **05** nervy acidity plumped out with 5.6g/ℓ sugar. Balanced & long. – *CR*

Dormershire

Stellenbosch ▪ Est 1996 ▪ 1stB 2001 ▪ Visits Mon-Fri 10-5 Sat 10-4 Sun 11-4 ▪ Owner SPF Family Trust ▪ Winemaker Sunette Frost, advised by Hilko Hegewisch) ▪ Viti consultant Johan Pienaar ▪ 7 ha (cab, shiraz, sauvignon) ▪ 60 tons 4 000 cs 75% red 20% white 5% rosé ▪ PO Box 491 Bellville 7535 ▪ frostyr@iafrica.com wine@dormershire.co.za ▪ ***T/F 903·1784*** *▪ F 945·1174*

After putting the finishing touches to their 100-ton cellar, Paul & Sunette Frost barely had time to breathe before tackling their next project – an upmarket sales and tasting facility. Situated between Saxenburg and Zevenwacht, this small property has a picture-perfect view of Table Mountain, depicted on the front-label. While reds play the lead role here, Sunette F, guided by Hilko Hegewisch, made the Sauvignon on the property for the first time last harvest, along with a new wooded Rosé.

Cabernet Sauvignon 04 classically constructed, class immediately apparent despite youth (barrel sample tasted). Brooding black fruit, pencil shavings; sour-cherry acidity & abundant fruit to flesh out austere tannins; promises ★★★★ quality when bottled. 13 mths, all Fr oak, 15% new. **Shiraz** ★★★★ **03** uninhibited bouquet with biltong, warmed plums & spice notes; fresh palate with persistent smoked-bacon tail. Friendly, well-managed tannins. 15 mths Fr oak, 20% new. **Rosé** new Work-in-progress **05** from shiraz/cab (80/20); unusual cherry biscuit aroma; properly dry finish, integrated tannins. 4 mths Fr oak, third new. Likely ★★★. **Sauvignon Blanc** Vinous rather than fruity **05**, still in barrel & too unknit to rate; deep straw pigment from oak, flinty whiff. Weighty palate – but only 13% alc – with 'iron filing'/mineral finish. – *CvZ*

Dornier Wines

Stellenbosch ▪ 1stB 2002 ▪ Tasting & sales Mon-Fri 9-4.30 Sat 11-4 Sun 11-4 (Nov-Apr only) ▪ Fee R20 ▪ Closed Easter Fri-Mon, Dec 25/26, Jan 1 ▪ Tours by appt ▪ Tourgroups ▪ Owner Christoph Dornier ▪ Winemaker JC Steyn (2005) ▪ Viticulturist Bob Hobson (Sep 2005), advised by Kevin Watt (2005) ▪ 67 ha (cabs s/f, malbec, merlot, petit v, shiraz, chenin, sauvignon, semillon) ▪ 10 000 cs 85% red 15% white ▪ PO Box 7518 Stellenbosch 7599 ▪ info@dornierwines.co.za ▪ www.dornierwines.co.za ▪ ***T 880·0557*** *▪ F 880·1499*

After an 'interesting' consultancy stint at Ch Kalechick in Turkey, Stellenbosch University-trained JC Steyn took up residency here as winemaker last year. 'My philosophy is to guide the wine along its own natural path; to allow it to express itself over time; and to make food wines that age well.' But if his general style is 'a fusion between New and Old World', the winery itself is all new – a sinuous assemblage of brick, steel and glass – and last year beat stiff international competition to win a Great Wine Capitals of the World architecture award. As the guide went to press Bob Hobson (ex-Lievland) became their viticulturist, advised by Kevin Watt, and Raphael Dornier, son of owner Christoph, took over as MD.

★★★★ **Donatus** Bdx-inspired red as imposing as its name. Selection of best blocks, vinified & matured separately before blending. Classic claret aromas of pencil shavings, black berries, liquorice preface **03**, melding of cab f, merlot & cab (43/37/20 – dollop Am-oaked shiraz featured in **02** notably absent); attractive herbal palate with fresh acidity. Mainly new Fr oak, 18 mths. Modern, serious; deserves 5+ yrs cellaring. Creditable maiden **02**, shiraz-dominated nose deferred to a Bdx-like palate, structure.

★★★★ **Donatus White** Maiden **03** showered with compliments locally/overseas (considered one of world's best wines by UK's Matthew Jukes). Blend chenin, semillon, sauvignon 56/28/16 (chenin portion cleverly oaked, 5 mths). **04** lovely lifted almond, wax

& apricot bouquet; taut mineral palate, weighty core from the barrelled fraction. Well-structured for bottle maturation. **03** similarly poised, focused.

Merlot ★★★ **03** vivid & opulent mulberry/plum compôte aromas, repeat on palate; richness cut by slightly astringent tannin. 'Second red' varies with vintage, so pvs was 'Cabernet Sauvignon-Merlot'. — *CvZ*

Douglas Green

Wellington ▪ Est/1stB 1938 ▪ Closed to public ▪ Owner DGB ▪ Cellarmaster (blending cellar) Gerhard Carstens, with Liesl Carstens-Herbst (2003) ▪ Oenologist Jaco Potgieter (2000) ▪ Vini advisor John Worontschak ▪ Viti advisers VinPro (May 2000) ▪ 6 000 tons 580 000 cs 50% red 50% white ▪ ISO 9002 & HACCP certified ▪ PO Box 246 Wellington 7654 ▪ douglasgreen@dgb.co.za ▪ www.douglasgreen.co.za ▪ ***T 864·5300*** *▪ F 864·1287*

Custodian of this piece of vinous Africana (68 vintages this year) is producing wholesaler DGB (now also owner of the Boschendal wine business). In charge of DGB's newly dedicated wine marketing arm (formerly integrated with the spirit brands) is Jacques Roux, previously sales and marketing director at Graham Beck. Also core to Douglas Green's longevity and success are its relationships with contracted growers, control of vinification at six appointed cellars, and its extensively production facilities in Wellington. 'Viticulturally diverse SA allows for an infinite number of styles, so winemaking here is always an interesting challenge,' says oenologist Jaco Potgieter, the liaison between the growers and the cellar team, which includes flying Australian winemaker John Worantschak

Cabernet Sauvignon ★★★ Latest repeats somewhat restrained style of pvs; **04** savoury/meaty fruit spectrum, enough cab backbone to go few yrs. Contrast with ... **Merlot** ★★★★ ✓ **03** again well-fruited, aromatic red berry nose, well constructed & balanced, with integrated oak (Fr staves, 3 mths). Not retasted. **Pinotage** ★★★★ ✓ **03** banana custard aroma imparts impression of richness, belied by leaner, fairly firm palate; accessible but best in 3–4 yrs. 3 mths Fr staves. **Shiraz** ★★★ Still-current **03** tasty commercial style with typical smoky/meaty whiffs, soft, accessible flavours, lots of vanilla from 3 mths on Am/Fr staves. **St Augustine** ✓ Favourite SA red since the 1940s; now equal cab & merlot, with 20% shiraz in unwooded **03**, warm & generous red (14% alc), approachable, with few yrs in hand. Ripe black plum & mulberry on taste. **Chardonnay** ★★★ **04** last ed offered melon & lightly buttered-toast whiffs; soft & easy but quite quick. Stave fermented. **Sauvignon Blanc** ★★★ No follow-up to **04**, with crunchy acidity, appley fruit salad tones, low 12.4% alc. **Cape Ruby Port** ★★★★ No new version of **NV** winter snuggler; last we noted an LBV (rather than Ruby) style, fragrant & warming. Both ranges WO W Cape.

Faces of Africa range

Cinsault-Pinotage ★★ 50/50 blend in **04**, wood (Fr/Am staves) a more commanding presence than pvs, firmish fruit-pastille palate ends furrily. **Colombar-Chardonnay** ★★★ Light-textured **04**, up-tempo lemon-drop flavours, refreshing crisp acidity. — *CR*

Douglas Wine Cellar

Northern Cape ▪ Est 1968 ▪ 1stB 1977 ▪ Tasting & sales Mon-Fri 8-5 ▪ Fee R5 ▪ Closed pub hols ▪ Tours by appt ▪ BYO picnic ▪ Gifts ▪ Owners 45 shareholders ▪ Winemaker Chrisna Botha ▪ Viticulturist Stefan Gerber (Mei 2005) ▪ 360 ha (cab, merlot, ruby cab, shiraz, chard, chenin, colombard, gewürz) ▪ 6 000 cs own label 19% red 43% white 8% rosé 30% dessert ▪ PO Box 47 Douglas 8730 ▪ wynkelder@gwk.co.za ▪ www.confluencewines.co.za ▪ ***T (053) 298·8314*** *▪ F (053) 298·1845*

Talking the talk is marketing man Pieter Louw: this Orange River Valley winery near Kimberley is intent on proving that the Northen Cape can produce the goods. Walking the walk are viticulturist Wrensch Roux, focussing on individual block management, and winemakers Pou le Roux and Danie Kershoff, planning a few single-vineyard bottlings in 2006. To this end: more small steel tanks; expanded barrel maturation facilities; possible investment in new specialised winemaking equipment. Says Louw: 'You're going to hear a lot more from us...'

Confluence range

Shiraz-Cabernet Sauvignon ★★ 60/40 mix with briary red fruit aromas; soft, juicy, medium bodied; lightly oaked. **Chenin Blanc-Colombard** ★★ Clean but quiet & foursquare 65/35 blend; light bodied. Both **03**s tasted mid-2004. **Classic Red** ★★ **03** braai-side quaffer with wild berries, spicy, dry finish. **Classic White** ★★**05** attractive summer sipper from chenin/colombar/chardonnay (50/30/20). Tropical bouquet, guava & melon palate. Three Natural Sweets in the range vary in sweetness, alcohol levels: **Johannisberger Red** ★ **05** Tutti-frutti medium bodied (12.5% alc; 45g/ℓ sugar), soft tannins. Cloying, strawberry **Classic Rose** ☆ **05**, barely vinous; 80g/ℓ sugar, 8% alc. **Johannisberger White** ★★ **05** Crowd pleasing sun-kissed peachs & melons with good sugar/acid balance; 30g/ℓ sugar, 11% alc. **Red Muscadel** ★★ Well-crafted winter warmer. **04** full of raisins & treacle, well integrated alc, not cloying despite 200g/ℓ sugar. **Red Jerepigo** ★★ Fortified dessert sipper. **04** Xmas cake aromas, full-sweet molasses palate. 230g/ℓ sugar. **Avoca Classic** range discontinued.

Provin range

Available but not tasted: in 2/5ℓ bag-in-boxes: **Dry Red**, **Grand Cru**, **Stein**, **Special Harvest** & **Late Harvest**. Also **Vin Doux Sparkling**. —*CT/DH*

Drakensig Wines

Paarl • Est 1999 • 1stB 2000 • Tasting & sales Mon-Fri 9-5 Sat 9-1; low season by appt • Closed Easter Sun, Dec 25/26 & Jan 1 • Farm-grown olive oil for sale • Conference facilities for groups of 5-10 • Owner/winemaker/viticulturist Marais Viljoen • 13 ha (cab, pinotage, shiraz) • 4 000 cs 80% red 20% white • HACCP implementation in progress • PO Box 22 Simondium 7670 • drakensig@mweb.co.za • ***T 874·3881*** *• F 874·3882*

No news is good news, according to Marais Viljoen, holder of the opinion that there's nothing wrong with constancy and the general preoccupation with newness and change in the industry is perhaps not an entirely good thing. He continues to tend the vines, make the wines in low-key fashion on his Paarl property, producing some highly-rated examples in the process.

Marais Viljoen Reserve range

★★★★ **Shiraz** Sophisticated & stylish **02**, fruitcake aromas/flavours, drier, more structured than version below. 14 mths Am/Fr barrels, 50% new. Fruit ex-Mbury.

Pinotage ★★ **01** statement wine, big & unsubtle; porty character, gamey palate-coating flavours.

Drakensig range

Shiraz ★★★ Still-current **02** smoky mocha whiffs & bramble fruit; easy drinking despite high 14.5% alc. None of the above tasted anew, notes from pvs ed; following quartet reviewed pre-bottling: **Cabernet Sauvignon** ★★★ Vaguely floral aromas on **03**, juicy latent fruit core suppressed by powerful wood tannins; could take yr/2 post-bottling to come round. Yr Fr oak, 1st/2nd fill. **Merlot** new **03** difficult to call: mid-2005 big chunky tannins tussle with plummy choc fruit. Which will prevail? Oak as for Cab, ditto ... **Pinotage** ★★ **03**, like pvs, big (14.5% alc), rustic & sweet; notes of savoury mulberry jam. **Sauvignon Blanc** ★★★ Muted varietal character but pleasant enough 'dry white'; **05** subtle tropical tone & lively acid crunch. All WO Coastal. —*DH/TM*

Dreamview Hill

Somerset West • Est 2004 • Winery closed to public; sales from Capelands restaurant • Owners Capelands Estate (Johann Innerhofer & Laura Mauri) • 4 ha (cab, malbec) • 18 tons 200 cs 100% red • PO Box 3835 Somerset West 7129 • office@capelands.com • www.capelands.com • ***T 858·1477***

Newcomers to the local wine scene, Italians Johann Innerhofer and wife Laura Mauri indulge their passions in this small-scale wine and food venture, established in July 2004. Grapes from their property on Schapenberg Hill (the views *are* dreamy) are vinified by across-the-road winery Ingwe. Johann I, whose background includes wine-imports and -auctions in Italy, also has a gourmet flair, which sees their Capelands restaurant on the property play a significant role in sales.

Redstone ★★★ Ready-to-drink **03** succulent if straightforward bdx-style blend lifted by 10% shiraz, with ripe red berry & plum flavours. Barrel sample tasted (unfined/filtered). — *MF*

Drie Berge see Baarsma

Drostdy Wine Cellar

Tulbagh ▪ Est 1804 ▪ Tasting & wine sales at De Oude Drostdy Mon-Fri 10-5 Sat 10-2 ▪ Owner Distell ▪ PO Box 9 Tulbagh 6820 ▪ www.drostdywines.co.za ▪ ***T (023) 230-0203*** *▪ F (023) 230-0510*

De Oude Drostdy, Tulbagh's old magistracy, built in 1804 and now a national monument, is the spiritual home of Drostdy-Hof wines. The range, intended to be fruity and accessible early, is now distributed globally.

Drostdy-Hof range

Cape Red ☺ ★★★ Harmonious blend cab, merlot, pinotage, shiraz. **04** not just a quick gulp: packed with juicy red fruit/rhubarb & fynbos flavours, refreshing goodbye. Small portion oaked. **Chardonnay-Semillon** new ☺ ★★★ Lively seafood lunch companion. **04** attractive white peach/pear bouquet; bold citrus palate. Touch weight/vanilla notes & flavours from 6 mths chips/lees contact.

Cabernet Sauvignon ★★★ **03** shows hint of cab's austerity; minty tinge to cassis, but lightish palate, tannic finish; best with food. Fr barrels/staves, 9 mths. **Merlot** ★★★ Standout red in range; yr mix old/new Fr oak. **04** seductive plum & mulberry whiffs; integrated, elegant & satisfying. **Pinotage** ★★★ Deep **04** youthful & shy, delicate fruit, for early drinking, soft caramel tone from Fr oak staves, 9 mths. **Shiraz** ★★★ **04** burly with chunky tannins; smoked meat & game notes should go well with savoury foods. Fr/Am staves 9 mths. **Claret Select** ★★ Lightish vat-matured blend, latest (**NV**) rich stewed fruit pudding, touch leathery oxidation but finishes pleasantly dry, with tangy lemon lift. **Rosé** ★★★ **05** notch up on pvs. Engaging melange carignan, cinsaut, pinotage & pinot delivers savoury 'carpaccio' nuances; finishes dry. **Chardonnay** ★★ **04** abundant aromas of vanilla, lemon, pear; oak (chips) not an overwhelming presence; acid stands apart, though. **Sauvignon Blanc** ★★ **05** intense granadilla notes; zesty & refreshing yet lighter textured than pvs. **Chardonnay-Viognier** new ★★★ Serious oak regime adds weight & texture. **04**'s bouquet entices, hints apricot, tangerine. Sharp acidity; touch gruff, austere finish for such fleshy varieties. **Extra Light** ★★ Big-selling, low-alc (9.5%), bone-dry **NV** for the figure conscious; latest from barely ripe chenin, colombard. Traditionally picked early. **Steen/Chenin Blanc** ★★ Always crisp & lightish; hay/grass bouquet. **05** quiet with dried pear aromas. Arresting acidity, almost too austere. **Premier Grand Cru** ★★★ Latest **NV** blend more mineral, 'wet slate' character herbaceous pvs. Bone-dry dieter's friend with slightly salty farewell. **Stein Select** ★★ Generous semi-sweet from quintet of varieties incl palomino & ugni blanc, tropical fruit salad with honeyed aromas. **Late Harvest** ★★★ Flirtatious **NV** from chenin; fruity on nose with lively, sweet (but not cloying) finish. **Adelpracht** ★★★ Unctuous SLH from chenin; shy lemon-drop scents on **04**; light-bodied & cloying when pvs have been tangy. Above mainly WO Coastal. Some also available in 340ml, 2ℓ and 5ℓ packs.

African Sky range

Untasted export wines: **Cabernet Sauvignon**, **Merlot**, **Shiraz**, **Cirrus** (mainly pinotage, with cab, merlot, cab & shiraz), **Crux** (chiefly cab, splash ruby cab), **Cape Red**, **Cumulus** (chenin), **Chenin Blanc**, **Cape White** (chenin), **Sauvignon**, **Celeste** (sauvignon, semillon). — *CvZ*

Dry Creek see Du Preez Estate
Due South see Cru Wines
Dumisani see Winecorp
Duncan's Creek see Rickety Bridge
Du Plessis see Havana Hills

Du Preez Estate

Goudini (see Worcester map) ▪ Est 1995 ▪ 1stB 1998 ▪ Tasting & sales Mon-Fri 8-12.30; 1.30-5 Sat 10-1 ▪ Closed public holidays ▪ Tours by appt ▪ BYO picnic ▪ Facilities for children ▪ Tourgroups ▪ Owners Du Preez family ▪ Winemaker Hennie du Preez Jnr (1995) ▪ Viticulturist Jean du Preez (Dec 1996) ▪ 300 ha (cab, merlot, petit v, chard, chenin, sauvignon) 56% red 40% white 2% rosé 2% sparkling ▪ Export brands: Du Preez Estate, Rockfield Wines, Dry Creek, Route 101 ▪ PO Box 12 Rawsonville 6845 ▪ dupreezestate@intekom.co.za ▪ ***T (023) 349·1995*** *▪ F (023) 349·1923*

The Du Preez family celebrated the 10th anniversary of their own wines in 2005 with a fresh new livery, introduced on the Sauvignon. They like to be creative with packaging: their varietal Petit Verdot, the familialy named Hendrik Lodewyk, is bottled in classy French glass. The Du Preezs (winemaker Hennie Jnr and viticulturist Jean), experienced growers though they are, were still delighted to win the 2005 regional Vineyard Block competition.

★★★★ **Merlot Reserve** Easily recognisable by its spicy, high-toned pungency; edgy style, zingy but ripe; **01** FCTWS trophy clincher; fermented with oak chips, then barrelled 18 mths, some Am. Skip to current **03** (★★★) less woody (14 mths 2nd fill barrels); eucalyptus whiff & spicy olive; deeply extracted fruit.

★★★★ **Hendrik Lodewyk Petit Verdot** One of still handful of solo bottlings of grape in SA. Promising when tasted last ed, deserved time. **01** Seriously wooded (30 mths small oak), giving clean & attractive spiciness. NE.

★★★★ **Hanepoot** Invariably smooth jerepigo-style dessert. Last we tasted the **03**.

Shiraz ★★ **04** lacks excitement of pvs; smoking matchstick nose, mocha & vanilla – & not much fruit. 6 mths 2nd fill barrels. **Polla's Red** ★★★★ Individual & fragrant blend pinotage, shiraz, ruby cab, petit v. Loads of satisfying spicy flavour. **01** coffee-choc palate with charry/ smoky touch, good ripe tannins. Oak/alc as for 01 Merlot. Not retasted. **Chardonnay** ★★ **05** simple & straightforward, with acids quite apparent. Less impressive than pvs. **Sauvignon Blanc** ★★★ **05** smoky aromas with rotund palate & sweaty notes, low 12.5% alc.

Rockfield range

Red Stone ★★★★ **02** spicy red-berried blend merlot, shiraz, ruby cab, petit v; last ed was characterful & stylish yet easy. Combo barrels & staves. **Chenin Blanc** ★★★ **05** creamy & quite rich, with flavours of peach & pear, quaffably low 12.5% alc. A step up. **Sauvignon Blanc** ★★ **05** sample shows vegetal tone, 13% alc. Lacks pleasing light tropicality of pvs.

Dry Creek range

Red ★★★ **04** last yr offered abundant ripe red berry fruit with floral touch, all tweaked for unproblematic quaffing. **White** ★★ Pineapple whiffs dominant on **05**, from chenin, colombard & sauvignon, still unknit mid-2005. Last two ranges NE. – *NP*

Durbanville Hills

Durbanville ▪ Est 1998 ▪ 1stB 1999 ▪ Tasting & sales Mon-Fri 9-4.30 Sat & pub hols 9.30-2.30 Sun 11-3; fee R10 ▪ Tours Mon-Fri 11 & 3; Sat/Sun by appt; fee R20 ▪ Closed Easter Fri/Sun, Dec 25/ 26 & Jan 1 ▪ @ The Hills Restaurant (see Eat-out section) ▪ Facilities for children ▪ Tourgroups ▪ Owners Distell, 8 farmers & workers' trust ▪ Winemakers Martin Moore & Louw Engelbrecht, with Günther Kellerman (Nov 1998/Jun 2005/Nov 2003) ▪ Viti consultant Johan Pienaar ▪ 770 ha (cab, merlot, pinotage, shiraz, chard, sauvignon) ▪ 5 600 tons 140 000 cs own label 50% red 50% white ▪ ISO 9000 & 14000 certified ▪ PO Box 3276 Durbanville 7551 ▪ info@durbanvillehills.co.za ▪ www.durbanvillehills.co.za ▪ ***T 558·1300*** *▪ F 559·816*

When Shakespeare's Coriolanus said that 'with wine and feeding, we have suppler souls', he could have had in mind Martin Moore, who is as supple in the cellar as he is in a kitchen. Talking cellar, a new soul has taken up residency there: red winemaker Louw Engelbrecht (ex-Zonnebloem). 'I like his winemaking philosophy', says Martin M, 'which is that he is neither alchemist nor non-interventionist, but believes in guiding the wine to bring all its best qualities to the fore. I equally like his dry sense of humour, a prerequisite if you want to survive in this game.' Other developments include a move to screwcap for Sauvignon. 'Relax,' MM hastens to assure, 'the wine is intended for the UK and US markets!'

'Single Vineyard' range

★★★★☆ **Caapmans Cabernet Sauvignon-Merlot 00** (★★★★) a step down: the expected fruit intensity beautifully delivered (cherries, redcurrants, cool touch of mint), but structurally in an awkward phase – slenderly built, dominated by tannins. Needs 2+ yrs to unfold. 64/36 blend. 90% new Fr oak, 2 yrs. Follows impressive debut **99**. MIWA gold.

★★★★ **Luipaardsberg Merlot** Extraordinary, showy **99** with big savoury palate, almost treacly intensity. **00** (★★★★) in same mould, but better executed, showing remarkable flavour intensity, attention to cellar detail. Complex layers of mint-choc, lush black cherries, smoke tendrils; slenderly built & accessible, but musculature for 5–7 yr development. 2 yrs new Fr oak. VDG.

★★★★☆ **Biesjes Craal Sauvignon Blanc** In cool vintages only, & steep south-facing vyd. **05** (sample) has minerality at core, but top-notes capture attention: artichoke, wet heath, nettles. Less vivid than pvs, but impressive (& made for food): invigorating acidity, long finish. **04** had quivering intensity, piercing green character, racy acidity, low 11.5% alc.

Rhinofields range

★★★★☆ **Chardonnay** Delicious **03** (not retasted) with lemongrass, citrus, & peach-tropical aromatics. Flavours more toasty, with citrus undertones, but smoothly ripe, good length. Combo tank/barrel fermented/matured, new oak. 3+ yrs ageing potential. No **02**.

★★★★ **Sauvignon Blanc** Fruit from 2 producers, selected vyds. **05** (sample) recalls leafy summer salad with chopped asparagus & herb dressing – many layers of interest, all appealing. Bone dry, with refreshing acidity & only 12.3% alc – to enjoy solo or with ... salad? **04** with Dbnville 'wet heath' pungency, intense, zinging freshness.

Merlot ★★★★ Last **00** had appealing elegance, accessibility. Yr Fr oak, 75% new.

Premium range

Cabernet Sauvignon ★★★★ Like rest of range, intended for earlier drinking. **02** delivers that stylishly: smooth with no hard edges, plummy fruit & wafts white pepper, mint choc contributing to the pleasure. Yr oak, 40% new. **Merlot** ★★★★ More than merely charming. **03** exuberantly fruity: mulberries/cherries, hint of mint, with oak only showing on finish & not detracting from juicy drinkability. **Pinotage** ★★★★ Lively & delicious **03** (sample) reaches goal of 'very friendly, accessible wine' with its smoothly rounded body, while over-delivering on aromas, flavours: vibrant rhubarb, wild berries & fynbos. **Shiraz** ★★★★ **02** drinking nicely; spice-perfumed, sweet ripe fruit & lots of smoky, meat-extract flavour. Friendly tannins, well-judged oak (yr mix Fr/Am, some new). **Sauvignon Blanc** ★★★★ Entry-level, high-volume (±26 000 cs) version. **05** (sample) shows attractive typicity, nettles, green figs & grapefruit, with food-friendly lively acidity. **Chardonnay** ★★★ **04** true to friendly house-style of showcasing fruit: peach-tropical flavours, nice rounded mouthfeel. 25% oaked, new Fr – this remains supportive. – *CR*

Dusty Road see Cloof

Du Toitskloof Winery

Rawsonville (see Worcester map) ▪ Est 1962 ▪ 1stB 1970 ▪ Tasting & sales – Winery: Mon-Fri 8–5 Sat 9–12.30 Wine Shop: Mon-Fri 9–5.30 Sat 10–5 Sun 11–4 ▪ Closed Easter Fri/Mon, Apr 27, Sep 24, Dec 16/25/26, Jan 1 ▪ BYO picnic ▪ Tours by appt ▪ Formal tasting for groups max 40 ▪ Owners 17 members ▪ Winemakers Philip Jordaan & Shawn Thomson (May 1983/Oct 1999), with Derrick Cupido & Christo Basson (1993/Jan 2002) ▪ Viti consultant Leon Dippenaar (2005) ▪ 750 ha ▪ 13 500 tons 30% red 70% white ▪ PO Box 55 Rawsonville 6845 ▪ dutoitcellar@intekom.co.za; info@dutoitskloof.co.za ▪ www.dutoitskloof.com ▪ ***T (023) 349·1601*** *▪ F (023) 349·1581*

Wine lovers with an appreciation for both quality and fair price remain loyal fans of these wines, which offer remarkable consistency across the board. A smart selection, for example, is the Sauvignon – still a steal at R22 ex newly refurbished tasting room. Accolades are regularly raked in from competitions, and several of the wines fly with SAA. New in the team is Leon Dippenaar, replacing Schalk du Toit as viticulturist.

★★★★ **Red Muscadel** ✓ Among the Cape's top fortified muscats: opulent but rather refined, wonderful in effusive youth (esp lightly chilled), graceful in maturity. After complex **02**, **03** came & went without us. Raisiny, grape- & jasmine-scented **04** happily up to standard. Like white version below ±240g/ℓ sugar, 15.5% alc. Off single bushvine block 10 yrs old.

★★★★★ **Hanepoot Jerepigo** ✓ Gorgeous fortified; **99**, **00** were absolute crackers; **01** (★★★★) less riveting, with palate too silky, easy-drinking. **02** sold out untasted by us. Penetratingly powerful **03** (★★★★) interesting & ingratiating, with muscat & Cointreau-like citrus notes, lingering fruitiness. Massive sweetness but not too cloying or heavy.

Merlot ☺ ★★★ Gains extra juiciness from partial carbonic maceration. **03** interesting & charming aromas; succulently tasty, in pleasingly, decently balanced whole. This & next, 8 mths Fr oak; 14% alc. **Pinotage** ☺ ★★★ Banana, raspberry aromas/flavours, firm & fresh, for light-hearted pleasure. **Chenin Blanc** ☺ ★★★ **05** pear-drop, tropical fruit package of softly off-dry, easy-going pleasure; low 12% alc. **Sparkling Brut** ☺ ★★★ Muscat gives nice grapey aromas to this dryish carbonated **05** bubbly; sauvignon & chard add green-apple crispness.

Cabernet Sauvignon ★★★★ ✓ **03** Pleasing dusty-blackcurrant aromas; savoury & succulent with firm, ripely dry tannin in support. Avoids all vulgarity as do most of these. Like shiraz below, ±8 mths Fr oak. **Shiraz** ★★★★ ✓ **03**'s shy smoky nose leads to well-balanced, savoury flavours: lightish, even elegant, though 14% alc. **Pinotage-Merlot-Ruby Cabernet** ★★★ Straightforward **04** blend, with forthcoming baked aromas, some tannin & 2 mths oaking giving focus to soft, sweetish palate. **Blanc de Noir** ★★★ Refreshing **04** from cinsaut: bone-dry tastes, elegant sappy red-fruit character, refreshing. **Chardonnay** ★★★ **05** has integrated oak element (50% barrel-fermented; 2 mths on lees); citrus & dried fruit flavours, creamy texture abetted by sweet touch, sharp finish. **Sauvignon Blanc** ★★★ **05** green beans & passion fruit aromas, fresh & gently crisp despite some sugar, with not unpleasant green-sour finish. **Riesling** ★★ Not retasted, like all the following 04 or NV whites. Unusually characterful for crouchen; **04** herby whiffs; dry & pleasantly austere, hint of almonds. **Blanc de Blanc** ★★★ Last was attractive, softly dry, effortless chenin, semillon blend; 500ml screwcap, **NV**. **Bukettraube** ★★★ **04** was surprisingly full-flavoured for variety, fruit salad tone, well-balanced sweetness. **Late Vintage** ★★★ Fruitily sweet & light **NV** from chenin & muscat d'A. 500ml screwcap. Last had perfumes of jasmine & spice, supple fruit salad & melon flavours. **Special Late Harvest** ★★★ Light-bodied semi-sweet muscat d'A. **04** hints of apple & pear, jasmine: poised sweetness. **Noble Late Harvest** ★★★★ Botrytised dessert from muscat & chenin; to date the debut **99**, SAYWS champ. **Cape Ruby** ★★★★ ✓ **03** (not retasted) moved to more modern style, with tinta, souzão, touriga; inviting stewed plum, raisin hints; rich, supple, dryish & smooth, molasses note on finish. 18% alc; yr small oak. All WO Worcester. – *TJ*

D'Vine see Swartland Wine Cellar
Dwyka Hills see New Cape Wines
Eagle's Cliff see New Cape Wines

EagleVlei

Stellenbosch ▪ Est/1stB 1997 ▪ Visits by appt ▪ Owners Steve & Jean Weir, André & Tessa van Helsdingen ▪ Winemaker André van Helsdingen ▪ Viticulturist Henry Fisk, advised by Paul Wallace ▪ 11 ha (cab, merlot, pinotage) ▪ 40 tons 3 000 cs 100% red ▪ PO Box 969 Stellenbosch 7599 ▪ avanhels@adept.co.za ▪ www.eaglevlei.co.za ▪ ***T/F 880·1846***

Wines made on the property in the Muldersvlei area by André van Helsdingen, a partner with wife Tessa; marketing handled by UK-based Steve and Jean Weir. Now open for tasting by appointment.

★★★★ **Cabernet Sauvignon** Cassis-perfumed **02** (with splash merlot) with gushing sweet fruit, but good ripe tannin support. Pure cab **03** more subtly savoury, also delicious;

plentiful berry flavours, balanced smooth strong tannins, lingering finish. Open-vat ferment (as all these), yr Fr oak. Like all below except Reserve, this last tasted for pvs ed.

★★★★ **Cabernet Sauvignon Reserve** new ★★★ **02**'s wood-influenced aromas tobacco, spice are attractive, but mid-2005 oak overwhelms sweetly ripe fruit on palate, gives drying hard tannic finish. **Pinotage** ★★★★ Friendly but firm. **02** has sweet-sour element, ripe tannin core, supportive wooding (yr, 20% Am); 14.5% alc. More exuberant **03** drier, less powerful 13.5%; boiled sweet & disconcerting rubber notes, then lushly ripe flavours. **Merlot** ★★★★ Fruity, choc-coated aromas on flavoursome **03**, soft ultra-ripeness clinging to firm tannic core, yet a slightly green note too. Well integrated yr oak. — *TJ*

Eden Crest

Part of the Christo Wiese Portfolio (see entry), this blended range takes its name from its 'fertile garden origins' in the Stellenbosch area.

Merlot new ☺ ★★★ **04** has 'Drink me' written all over it: easy accessibility, minted red berries, with herbaceous/peppery tones adding lift & freshness. Unwooded.

Cape Blend ★★★ Last available, maiden **03**. Tasty early-drinking blend merlot, pinotage, cab (55/33/12), lightly oaked. **Shiraz-Merlot** ★★★ **03** not retasted this ed. Pvsly showed sweet ripe fruit, light oaking, youthful freshness, in 58/42 blend. **Chardonnay-Chenin Blanc** ★★★ Maiden **03** still available; summer fruits character in 55/24 blend enhanced with 21% sauvignon, touch oak. Good food partner. — *CR*

Edenhof see Schalkenbosch

Eikehof Wines

Franschhoek ▪ Visits by appt ▪ Owner/winemaker/viticulturist Francois Malherbe ▪ 43 ha (cab, merlot, shiraz, sauvignon) ▪ 70 tons 4 000 cs 60% red 40% white ▪ PO Box 222 Franschhoek 7690 ▪ eikehof@mweb.co.za ▪ www.eikehof.com ▪ ***T/F 876·2469***

Outdoorsman Francois Malherbe was one winemaker guaranteed his Easter breakaway during what was for many a long and drawn out 2005 harvest. Picking started sooner — some blocks ripened a whole month earlier — and the harvest was not nearly as protracted as the previous year's.

★★★★ **Cabernet Sauvignon** Pvs were dense, showy, chunky, but **03** (★★★★) none of these: soft, muted briary nose, savoury plum fruit, dry but ripe balanced tannins, slight sweetness on exit. **02** well layered with ripe berry flavours, fairly evident oak. ±5 mths wooded (same for all the reds).

Merlot ★★★ **03** unready for tasting. Med-bodied **02** returned to earlier-approachable mode; choc/plum flavours, forward soft tannins. **Shiraz** ★★★ Yr in bottle softened **02**; smoky touches, long finish concluded with sweet-fruity touch. **03** is next. **Chardonnay** ★★★ Attractively steely **04**, whiffs Seville orange marmalade, clean & juicy citrus flavours. Bunch-pressed, fermented on staves, 10 mths *sur lie*. **Bush Vine Semillon** ★★★ Features ancient low-cropped bushvines, bunch-pressed, fermented/aged 5 mths Fr/Am casks. **03** light-toned; bouquet of lime & lemon with lees nuance. Next will be **05**. — *IvH*

Eikendal Vineyards

Stellenbosch (see Helderberg map) ▪ Est 1981 ▪ 1stB 1984 ▪ Tasting & sales — Sep-Apr: Mon-Fri 9.30-4.30 Sat/Sun 10.30-3; May-Jun Mon-Fri 10.30 — 3.30 Sun 11-2.30 Jul-Aug Mon-Fri 10.30-3.30 ▪ Fee R10 (5 wines) ▪ Tours 10 & 3 ▪ Closed Easter Fri -Mon, Jun 16, Aug 9, Dec 25/26 & Jan 1 ▪ Restaurant (Oct-May); Cheese fondue Fri evenings (Jun-Aug)▪ Eikendal Lodge Guest House/B&B ▪ T 855·3617 ▪ Facilities for children ▪ Tourgroups ▪ Small conferences ▪ Walks ▪ Winemaker Henry Kotze (Sep 2004) ▪ Viti consultant Johan Pienaar (Sep 2001) ▪ ±65 ha (cabs s/f, merlot, shiraz, chard, chenin, sauvignon, semillon) ▪ ±500 tons ±35

000 cs 65% red 35% white ▪ PO Box 2261 Stellenbosch 7601 ▪ info@eikendal.co.za ▪ www.eikendal.com ▪ ***T 855·1422*** *▪ F 855·1027*

This year is the winery's silver anniversary, so expect an even bigger bash than that thrown in 2005 for farm manager Le Roux Wentzel, celebrating his 50th. The season was a first run here for experienced winemaker Henry Kotze, and 'I must say I had a few punctures', soon mended (last out of the puncture kit, a new in-house bottling capability: 'having full control over the process lets one rest easier at night'). The chenin botrytised nicely; the ensuing 'Noble Late Harvest' is what was previously called 'Puccini', from the Italian Composer range which has sung its swansong. Mid-year, Eikendal relaunched its Rouge and Blanc, a dry red and a dry white, the aim being to regain in-store visibility at the lower end of the market.

★★★★ **Cabernet Sauvignon Reserve** In best yrs only. Last was **00**, with big dense tannins, sweet fruit, good acidity.

★★★★ **Merlot** After less concentrated **02**, darkly handsome **03** developing well: lightly rich freshness, with choc-mint notes, supportive ripe & savoury tannic structure, good length. 14 mths Fr oak.

★★★☆ **Cabernet Franc** Maiden **02** was fragrantly spicy, **03** (★★★★) similar but even more delicious – slightly decadently gentle fruit, but elegantly built round a firm core. 14 mths older oak.

★★★☆ **Classique** Deep-hued **01** (★★★★, not retasted) blends cab, merlot, cab f (60/30/10 – much same as **00**). Tobacco/cedar/spice from 20 mths new Fr oak, with sweet fruit wrapping firm, dry tannic core. Savoury, generous – very non-classique but balanced 15% alc! Deserves few yrs in bottle.

★★★★ **Chardonnay** Vanilla-toasty **04** rich & round, with lingering lime/lemon flavours & bright vein of acid – good food wine. 9 mths partly new Fr oak. Track record for good development over 3-5 yrs.

Rouge ☺ ★★★ Warm & friendly merlot-based blend, with cab, shiraz (last featured in 2003 ed). Lots of herb-tinged ripe fruit, but savoury & firm. Lightly oaked.

Cabernet Sauvignon ★★★☆ Last tasted was **01**, whose savoury freshness, deep fruit dominated by tannin. Solid 14.5% alc; 16 mths oak. **Shiraz** ★★★☆ Soft, smooth, very ripe **03** showing better after yr in bottle: mocha, spice evidencing 14 mths mostly Fr oak, 30% new. **Janina Chardonnay** ★★★ Scarcely oaked **04** packed with butterscotch, melon lime flavours; richness cut by vivid acidity. **Chenin Blanc** ★★★ Lightly oaked, smooth **04** last yr had peach & melon notes, green-fruit undertones. **Sauvignon Blanc** Unrated **05** tank sample promises usual racy amalgam of gooseberry & grass flavours, greenly fruity finish. **Semillon** ★★★☆ **04** showing oak (though only 7 mths older, mix Fr/Am), citrusy honeyed nuttiness; round texture, but big acid. **Blanc** ★★☆ Returns to guide (pvs were 'Blanc de Blanc') with full sauvignon/chardonnay flavours tussling pleasantly in rounded, just-dry **NV** blend. **Noble Late Harvest** 'Puccini' by another name. Pleasingly balanced, rich but fresh not-too-unctuous dessert wine from lightly oaked chenin, with sweet-sour marmalade flavours; tank sample **05** likely ★★★☆. **Sparkling Brut** ★★★ Latest bottling of **NV** bubbly not sampled; last was most attractive & great value, from sauvignon, chardonnay. Discontinued: **Verdi**, **Rossini**. – *TJ*

Eikestad see Omnia
Elandsberg see Viljoensdrift

Eldorado Wines

Paarl ▪ Est 1999 ▪ 1stB 2001 ▪ Closed to public ▪ Owner Proteus Trust ▪ Winemaker/viticulturist Shannon Booth (1999) ▪ 1 ha ▪ 4 tons 300 cs 100% red ▪ PO Box 2042 Windmeul 7630 ▪ tmurray@iafrica.com ▪ www.eldorado.co.za ▪ ***T/F 869·8830***

Shannon Booth last year decided to take her winegrowing more seriously, and invested in a quantity of new wood. She also showed her wines to numerous friends in the industry (including neighbour Gesie Lategan of Domain Brahms), actively seeking opinions and suggestions before releasing her 03 vintage. This year she'll make a Syrah, focus on improving canopy management and work on raising her brand's profile with an export plan.

Aquila ★★★ Attractive cab/merlot (80/20) blend with whiff of mocha, mulberry & intriguing balsamic notes of damp fynbos on **02**, last ed noted as praiseworthy first effort. **03**, not retasted, hinted at better acid balance. All ±yr Fr oak, third new. — *IvH*

Elements see Hartswater
Elephant Trail see Daschbosch

Elgin Vintners

Elgin ▪ Est 2003 ▪ 1stB 2004 ▪ Tasting & sales Mon-Fri 9-5 by appt ▪ Closed pub hols ▪ Owners Derek Corder, Max Hahn, Alastair Moodie, James Rawbone-Viljoen, Rob Semple & Paul Wallace ▪ Winemaker TBA ▪ Viticulturist Paul Wallace ▪ 42 ha (cab, merlot, shiraz, pinot, sauvignon) ▪ 3 650 cs ▪ PO Box 121 Elgin 7190 ▪ wallovale@mweb.co.za ▪ ***T/F 848·9744***

This group of 'otherwise apple farmers going gr … ape', as business manager Nicky Wallace puts it, had a true grape man join as shareholder in 2004 in the person of viticulturist Paul Wallace. The plus was balanced by a minus — winemaker Ross Gower detached himself to concentrate on his own brand after producing the 2005 (that vintage's Sauvignon is E-V's launch wine; the 04 was not released). Besides a new winemaker, the group needs a brand name and a marketing campaign. What they have found is an abandoned apple shed where their barrels are stored under optimum conditions. Also decided is that the Sauvignon will be screw-capped.

Sauvignon Blanc ★★★★ **05** first to market after maiden **04** not released. Latest: expressive interplay flinty fruit with tropical tones, focused by cool-climate acidity. Following unfinished barrel samples not rated, both new: **Cabernet Sauvignon 05** black fruits elegantly swaddled in gentle tannins, lined with promising mineral seam. **Pinot Noir 05** attractive clean cherry fruit stitched into creamy texture, unobtrusive oak. Demure 12% alc. — *DS*

Elixir see African Terroir
Engelbrecht-Els see Ernie Els
Enon see Zandvliet
Equus see Zandvliet
Erica Vineyards see Raka

Ernie Els Wines

Stellenbosch ▪ Est 1999 ▪ 1stB 2000 ▪ Tasting & sales Mon-Fri 9-5 Sat: May-Sep 9-3 Oct-Apr 9-4 ▪ Closed Easter Fri, Dec 16/25 & Jan 1 ▪ Gifts ▪ Owners Ernie Els & Jean Engelbrecht ▪ Winemakers Louis Strydom & Coenie Snyman (2000/2005) ▪ Viti consultant Paul Wallace (2004) ▪ 72 ha (cab, merlot) ▪ 45 000 cs 100% red ▪ PO Box 7595 Stellenbosch 7599 ▪ info@ernieelswines.com ▪ www.ernieelswines.com ▪ ***T 881·3588*** *▪ F 881·3688*

This past season saw the partnership between pro golfer Ernie Els and Jean Engelbrecht, son of Rust-en-Vrede's Jannie, get all its birdies in a row. While the duo's Bordeaux-style blend immediately impressed upon debut in 2000, it's taken time to consolidate vineyards, cellars, brand ownerships and winemakers. Having purchased prime Helderberg land from Webersburg (now based in restored historic Groenrivier nearby), the E-E wines were vinified in their own brand-new cellar in 2005 by former Rust-en-Vrede winemaker Louis Strydom, now caddying full-time for the Els-Engelbrecht pairing. Ex-Bergkelder Coenie Snyman joined the team, in charge of the Guardian Peak range, transferred here from the Rust-en-Vrede stable. They're finally ready for the world stage, says marketer Duncan Woods, with a range of specialist red blends competing at various price points. Clearly inspired by the vision of this exciting young set-up, Strydom has already started experimenting, co-fermenting shiraz and viognier.

★★★★★ **Ernie Els** Bdx blend which mirrors its namesake's lofty reputation. **03** (★★★★★) heralded by radiant ruby hue, initial distinctive plush cab scents, with their hint of truffles, more expressive than brooding **02**; claret tension returns on palate with vibrant mineral grip reins in the elegantly textured red fruit. Excellent light-toned yet full-flavoured concentration. Cab-led with 25% merlot, equal parts cab f, petit v, malbec, latter duo unoaked. Bal 20 mths new Fr 300ℓ casks. Possible 7-9 yr maturation. **02** *Wine* ★★★★☆, 91 pts *WS*; **01**, **00** 93 pts *WS*. Smnsberg, Hldrberg fruit (WO Stbosch).

★★★★☆ **Engelbrecht-Els Proprietor's blend** Cab/shiraz (60/20) with merlot/petit v, malbec, cab f equal cohorts. Sophisticated **03** more than lives up to promise of last ed's sample; evinces both subtlety & distinction. Fine roast nut, dark berry scents; concentrated, persistent yet not heavy; velvet tannins. Delicious now, could be tucked away ±3-4 yrs. Riper **04** ex-cask, fine classic structure; flavour crescendo presages plenty pleasure around 2010. 20 mths used Fr barrels. Dbnville, Elgin, Stbosch vyds. WO W Cape.

Guardian Peak range

★★★★ **Syrah-Mourvèdre-Grenache** One of earliest local takes on southern Rhône-style blend; made mark with first, distinctive **01**, VDG; FCTWS 2003 gold. **03**, ex-barrel last ed, delivering on promise: full spread porcini mushroom, rare game, black pepper & other aromatic extras. More peppery punch, grip, delivered with grace; delicious savoury tail. Homogenous, no negative effects of 14.8% alc. Malo in barrel. 18 mths new oak. **02** *Wine* ★★★★.

★★★★ **Frontier** ✓ Glossy, modern cab, shiraz, merlot blend with loads of personality. Preview **04** hedonistic Black Forest cake; opulence cut by clean black cherry flavours, bright creamy tannins. Very moreish, long; well contained 14% alc. 50/40/10 blend, 15 mths Fr/Am oak. Dbnville, Stbosch vyds, same as for classy **03**, ex-barrel last ed, now with finely nuanced mocha, soft dark berry tone; savoury harmony.

Merlot ★★★★ ✓ So friendly, & so smart! Dark choc allure on creamy, supple **04**; lively build/finish should provide delicious drinking for further yr/2. Stave-matured. Ex-Stbosch/Klawer. **Shiraz** ★★★★ ✓ Nothing overly showy in **04**s spice, red fruits, woodsmoke geniality; caresses palate with freshness, gentle tannins. Aged on staves. Klawer; Dbnville vyds. These all WO W Cape. —*AL*

Ernst & Co Wines

Stellenbosch ▪ Est/1stB 2004 ▪ Tasting by appt ▪ Owners Ernst & Gwenda Gouws ▪ Winemaker Ernst Gouws ▪ 12 ha (chenin, sauvignon) ▪ 10 000 cs 50% red 50% white + 10 000 cs export brand Imbizo ▪ Other export range: Timbili ▪ PO Box 7450 Stellenbosch 7599 ▪ info@ggwines.co.za ▪ www.ernstco.co.za ▪ ***T 865·2895*** *▪ F 865·2894*

It's been only two vintages since Ernst Gouws sold his stake in Hoopenburg to strike out solo with wife Gwenda, but already their flagship label Ernst & Co is firmly established, and cases of Imbizo and Timbili, their 'mass market' wines, wend their way overseas. Just as well. Ernst G, who recently celebrated his silver anniversary as winemaker (and completed a 6th Comrades Marathon at the tender age of 53), has given himself a decade to build an inheritance worthy of his children. They, in turn, are helping to build their future: daughter Ezanne recently joined him as assistant winemaker. The wines may now by tasted at Koelenhof Winery.

Cabernet Sauvignon new ★★★ Appealing maiden **03** has all the right aromas/flavours; just lacks concentration of older vines. Fruity, layered with cedar/herbaceous notes; dry & fresh balanced palate. Potential for ±4 yrs cellaring. Yr new Fr oak. **Merlot** ★★★ **03** savoury, with meat/liquorice hints. Persistent blackberry finish; warm goodbye from 14.5% alc, tannins more sinewy less supple than pvs. Should improve over 3-5 yrs. Yr Fr oak. **Shiraz** ★★★★ New World style given floral/fruit lift from touch viognier. **04**'s raspberry & coriander nuances tipped with apricot, dry tannins softened by hint sugar. Accessible but should hold ±3 yrs. Yr new Fr oak. **Chardonnay** ★★★★ **05** leap up in quality; richer than pvs, also more alcoholic (14.5% alc vs 12%). Fuller aromas & flavours too; deft oaking (5 mths new Fr barrels) complements this fleshier/flashier style. Fruit ex-Mbury. **Sauvignon Blanc** ★★★★ **05**, like above, raises the bar; tropical but with dense, flinty notes; texture from 6 mths lees maturation. Fresh lemony farewell, brisk as a sea breeze. Easy 12.5% alc. Both ranges WO Stbosch unless noted.

Imbizo range

Merlot ★★★ **03** charming everyday tipple; generously fruited with cassis & blueberries, soft tannins & smooth finish. Yr Fr oak. **Chenin Blanc-Sauvignon Blanc** ★★★ **03** delightful summer quaffer with straightforward tropical fruit salad aromas/flavours; zesty & refreshing. **Timbili** range export only, not tasted.—*JP*

Eshkol Kosher Winery

Wellington ▪ Est/1stB 2003 ▪ Tasting & sales only by appt Mon-Fri 10-7 Fri 10-12 Sun by appt ▪ Fee R15 ▪ Closed Jewish holidays ▪ Tours by appt ▪ Cheese platters by appt; also (non-kosher) meals at Onverwacht Restaurant ▪ Small tourgroups ▪ Owner ERIE Trading ▪ Winemakers Shalom Epstein & Hein Hesebeck (2003/2004) ▪ Viticulturist Hein Hesebeck (2004) ▪ 15 ha (merlot, pinotage, ruby cab, shiraz, chenin) ▪ 10·000 cs 90% red 10% white ▪ PO Box 151 Wellington 7654 ▪ eshkol@ezinet.co.za ▪ www.eshkol.co.za ▪ ***T 864·3356*** *▪ F 873·0871*

The young observing Jewish wine drinker in SA now has another kosher option with the release of the maiden Shiraz Rosé, says Eshkol director Shalom Epstein, whose sights are set on producing kosher brandy and what could possibly be SA's first kosher bubbly. According to the world's oldest winemaking laws, for wine to retain its kosherness, it should be made *mevushal* by undergoing flash pasteurisation, here carried out using the hi-tech Thermoflash system. It's a technique, Epstein points out, not uncommonly used in non-kosher commercially-styled wines.

King Solomon range

Cellar Masters Choice Red new ★★ **04** roughly equal four-way blend with dusty dried-currant fruit, sweet-stalky finish. **Shiraz Rosé** ★★ new Crushed raspberry whiffs on semi-sweet **05**, juicy, balanced by touch dry tannin on finish. **Chardonnay** ★★ **05** tasty dry white from Rbtsn grapes, 100% Am oak a surprisingly subtle backdrop; grapefruit hints, citrus-salad flavours. **Premier Chenin Blanc** Grapes from Rose Garden Vyds, Paarl, **05** boiled sweet/caramel hints, dry finish. **Cellar Masters Choice White** new ★★ Chardonnay, chenin blend (53/47), **04** high-toned, with pleasing fresh acidity. **Kiddush** new ★★ Sacramental wine from cinsaut, shiraz, ruby cab; very soft & sweet.

Eshkol range

Cabernet Sauvignon ★★ Hot-country 'baked' quality on **04**, flavours of plum jam with slight stalky edge, sweet concluding nuance. **Merlot** new ★★★ Restrained but appealing **03**, leafy cassis hint; light (12%), harmonious, accessible dry flavours. Am oaked. **Pinotage** ★★ **04** lightish country-style red with choc-prune fruit, tangy dry savoury flavour. Paarl fruit, unwooded, whereas ... **Walker Bay Pinotage** new ★★★ Gets 100% Am oak treatment – yet amazingly unwoody; pinot-like delicacy on **04**; red berry flavour, juicy & dry; pretty redcurrant fragrances. **Shiraz** ★★★ Touch sweetness enlivens **03**'s dark berry/plum taste, dusty/earthy tannins impart vinosity. **Classic Dry Red** ★★★ Light but succulent cab, merlot, shiraz convivium; **03** classy cedar whiff & berry ripeness from cab, balanced by leafy tannins.—*IvH/CR*

Eventide see Mischa
Evolution see Origin Wine

Excelsior Estate

Robertson ▪ Est 1859 ▪ 1stB 1997 ▪ Closed to public ▪ Owner Freddie de Wet ▪ Winemaker Johan Stemmet (Nov 2003) ▪ 170 ha ▪ 60 000 cs own label 67% red 33% white ▪ Exported as Stonehurst & De WetsBerg ▪ HACCP certified ▪ PO Box 17 Ashton 6715 ▪ info@excelsior.co.za ▪ www.excelsior.co.za ▪ ***T (023) 615·1980*** *▪ F (023) 615·2019*

This sizeable Robertson estate has been divided between the De Wet brothers. Freddie de W and his son Peter retain 170ha of vineyard and the Excelsior name. Their first Viognier bottled, their priority now is to market the brand (De Wet Jnr's business science degree from UCT and seasonings in Napa and southern Australia should come in useful). Brother Stephen de Wet and his son Jamie will be setting up a cellar and launching their own new wine brand from their portion of the property, complete with *its* 170ha of vineyards.

Sauvignon Blanc ☺ ★★★ Affordable, satisfying everyday tipple. **05** repeats successful formula of tropical breadth, cool crispness & moderate 13% alc. **Paddock Viognier** ☺ new ★★★ Fresh, zesty **05**, super varietal expression (white peach, apricot), lots of characterful fun. Screwcap for easy access.

Cabernet Sauvignon Reserve ★★★★ None since modern style, well formed **02**, with rounded approachability & potential for short-term maturation. **Cabernet Sauvignon** ★★★ Always eager to please; **04** pulpy fruit, ultra-supple tannins, touch sugar smoothes away any remaining edges. 8-10 mths oak (as are most reds). **Merlot** ★★★ **04** starts well with smoky merlot aromas, ends rather flat & overly ripe. **Paddock Shiraz** ★★★★ ✓ Unsubtle but attractive **04**, bouquet a repeat of pvs gamut of berries, coffee, choc, herbs & scrub; fresh fruity tastes. **Merlot Rosé** new ★★ Light coral pink **05**, lightweight summer refresher with clean semi-dry finish. **Purebred Red** new ★★★ Shiraz, merlot, cab harnessed for early drinkability, **02** gentle tannin gives structure, focus. Best within yr/2. **Chardonnay** ★★★ Reliable & delicious; lightly wooded **04** ingratiates with peachy vanilla aromas, sweet tropical flavour, clean citrus finish. Best young. *— DH*

Excelsious Wines

Vredendal (see Olifants River map) ▪ Est 1997 ▪ 1stB 1998 ▪ Tasting & sales Mon-Fri 8-12; 2-5 Sat 9-11 ▪ Fee R10 ▪ Closed Easter Fri-Mon, Dec 25 & Jan 1 ▪ Owners Stoumann & Sons ▪ Winemaker Napoleon Stoumann ▪ Viticulturist Gideon Stoumann ▪ 112 ha (cab, merlot, shiraz, chard) ▪ ±1 900 tons ±300 cs own label 96% red 2% white 2% rosé ▪ PO Box 307 Vredendal 8160 ▪ stoutmans@kingsley.co.za ▪ ***T/F (027) 213·2323***

No update available on this winery; contact details from previous edition.

Faces of Africa see Douglas Green
Fair Hills see Origin Wine
Fairbridge see Paarl Wine

Fairseat Cellars

Cape Town ▪ Closed to public ▪ Owner Dick Davidson ▪ PO Box 53058 Kenilworth 7745 ▪ fairseat@mweb.co.za ▪ ***T 797·1951***

Negociant and Cape Wine Master Dick Davidson sources wines locally for export to Europe, chiefly buyers' own brands (BOBs) for the German market. Current production (untasted) includes the Fairseat Cellars Ruby Cab; Mountainside Cab, Merlot and Chardonnay; and Ruiters Red and White, all 03. Some previous releases have flown with Lufthansa.

Fairvalley Farmworkers Association

Paarl ▪ Est 1997 ▪ 1stB 1998 ▪ Tasting & sales at Fairview (see entry) ▪ Owners Fairvalley Community ▪ Winemaker Awie Adolph (Feb 1997) ▪ 18 ha ▪ ±50 000ℓ for own label 50/50 red/white ▪ PO Box 6219 Paarl 7620 ▪ marlene@fairview.co.za ▪ ***T 863·2450*** *▪ F 863·2591*

Now here's an industrious crew: if they're not busy upgrading the tasting facilities or tending to the vines and the wines, they're hard at work in the popular new Goatshed Restaurant at next-door Fairview, which initiated this farmworkers empowerment project, among the first in the winelands. With wine sales soaring in the USA, they're rapidly reaching their financial target to start phase two of their housing development.

Pinotage ★★ **04** tannic & astringent, lean fruit; less friendly than pvs. Combo tank/oak aging (older Am/Fr). **Chenin Blanc** ★★ **05** pleasant tipple with lemon/herbaceous fragrance & mineral core; palate more satisfying. **Sauvignon Blanc** ★★ **05** fairly neutral, whiffs tropical fruit & grass. All WO Coastal. *— JP*

Fairview

Paarl ▪ Est 1693 ▪ 1stB 1974 ▪ Tasting & sales Mon-Fri 8.30-5 Sat 9-4 Sun 9.30-4 ▪ Fee R15 ▪ Closed Easter Fri, Dec 25, Jan 1 ▪ Goatshed Eatery for meals/refreshments daily 9-5 (T

863·3609) ▪ Groups by appt ▪ Also tasting & sales of Fairview cheese ▪ Owner Charles Back ▪ Winemakers Charles Back & Anthony de Jager (Dec 1996), with Erlank Erasmus (Jan 2001) ▪ Viticulturist Johan Botha, advised by Andrew Teubes ▪ 300 ha (cab, barbera, malbec, merlot, mourvèdre, nebbiolo, pinotage, shiraz, sauvignon, viognier) ▪ 1 500 tons 80% red 15% white 5% rosé ▪ ISO 9001:2001 & HACCP certified ▪ PO Box 583 Suider-Paarl 7624 ▪ info@fairview.co.za ▪ www.fairview.co.za ▪ ***T 863·2450*** *▪ F 863·2591*

'Sorry, it's been pretty much line and length,' apologises winemaker (and cricket enthusiast) Anthony de Jager when asked 'what's new at Fairview?' The man's low-key approach belies a talent (see also his own Homtini Shiraz) and level of contribution to the constant excitement generated by Fairview's wines that surpasses any 'assistant/side-kick' job description. His constancy of presence, proved over nearly a decade, gives free(-er) rein to restless, creative boss Charles Back to 'go where the terroir is': Paarl, Stellenbosch, Malmesbury, Darling, Piekenierskloof, Upper Langkloof ... While at home there's the large, airy new tasting room, and the dual indoor-al fresco Goatshed eatery in the renovated old cellar. Not forgetting 600ℓ open-top fermenters; more depth of character from maturing cab/merlot vines on their Lynedoch farm; good growth in the US market, growing interest in Canada ... that's line and length.

Red Seal range

★★★★ **Caldera** Maiden **03**, from selected Swtlnd vyds of grenache, mourvèdre, shiraz. Lightish, earthy – some would say rustic; pepper & spice extras; fresh acidity & taut tannins cry out for bottle-ageing. **04** shows label settling into its stride. Sweet, ripe nose with integrity, elegance; choc & orange notes; recalls Châteauneuf-du-Pape. Potential to evolve.

★★★★ **Pegleg Carignan** Features some of the oldest carignan in SA. **03** low key, with firm acidity. **04** shows high toned, sweet nose of ripe fruit & oak. Typical firm acid of the variety.

★★★★☆ **Primo Pinotage** Massively flavourful & aromatic; off bushvines on eponymous Agter-Paarl farm. **03** with solid stewed aromas, rich dense fruit. **04** deep & concentrated, with good varietal definition. Serious wine with positive savoury elements. Firm tannins suggest it needs time to settle.

★★★★☆ **Solitude Shiraz** From dryland Perdeberg vyd. **02** bright shiraz fruit; complex, forward yet elegant with good texture; well-handled oak (14 mths Fr/Am; 50% new). **03** appears the most facile of the trio of single vineyard Shiraz's. Firm, but forward with juicy, firm acidity. Needs time to show itself.

★★★★☆ **Beacon Block Shiraz** From low-vigour Koelenhof vyd. Luxuriously oaked **02** impressed us (& *WS*: 93 pts). **03** obviously riper, sweeter, but elegantly styled with pure, solid fruit expression – whose generosity masks tannins. Will grow over ± 4 yrs.

★★★★ **Jakkalsfontein Shiraz** Mature bushvine vyd on western Perdeberg slopes. **02**, youthful, firm & restrained on release, but with great potential for complexity. 92 pts *WS*. **03** serious, sturdy but shows integrity of its Swtlnd origin. Reserved, juicy fruit, great structure and linear acidity. Holds its 15% alc well. Will benefit with keeping.

★★★★ **Akkerbos Chardonnay** Allusion to the numerous oaks shading Fairview. Own grapes given full Burgundian oak treatment – fermented/*sur lie* 10-14 mths, full malo in barriques. **02** showed delicate wooding, creamy texture with mineral persistence. **03** slightly more overtly oaky, silk textured, fresh & limy with similar attractive minerality. No **04**.

★★★★☆ **Oom Pagal Semillon** One of the serious Cape examples. Attractive, subtle **04**, with hint of wood not pervading varietal expression of lanolin, honey. Just-dry opulence. Fermented/7 mths Fr oak, some new. Already evolved, ready now. **03** wonderfully clean, healthy fruit, focused, with firm mineral acidity. WO Coastal.

Discontinued: **Cyril Back Shiraz**

Fairview range

★★★★ **Shiraz** ✓ This winery's signature & Cape benchmark since **74**. **02** open and approachable, polished in older oak for a more Old World quality. ±14 mths mostly Fr oak. **03** not tasted. **04 h**igh toned, light & elegant, with lily note. Obvious shiraz fruit with juicy acid, soft tannins.

★★★★ **Stellenbosch Cabernet Sauvignon** new From recently acquired Firgrove vyds. Solid, authentic maritime-influenced fruit. Attractive, well wooded complexity; mineral quality over good structure, texture. Promises devt, but already approachable.

★★★★ **Sauvignon Blanc** From unirrigated Swtlnd bushvines, some Dbnvlle fruit. Youthful, screwcapped **05** floral, delicate & elegant, with modest 12% alc. **04**, **03** occupied the more vegetal end of spectrum.

★★★★ **Viognier** Long welcomed as good example of the fashionable Rhône variety. **04**, from Paarl & Mlmsbry fruit, underplays oak, relying more on fresher, less 'oily' character with good varietal definition. Two thirds fermented/4 mths Fr barrels, 15% new; rest in tank. 14.8% alc. Screwcapped to preserve aromatics.

★★★★ **La Beryl Rouge** Returns after some yrs hiatus with **04** – a single barrel of straw-dried syrah. Concentrated, smoky nose, well focused & juicy. A worthy curiosity.

★★★★☆ **La Beryl Blanc** Chenin grapes (50% semillon in **04**), air-dried on straw mats. Sweet (206g/ℓ RS), but with fantastic balancing acid & concentrated fruit. 12% alc. Gorgeous, pure & delicate **03** with complex flavour array of apples, pears, toffee apple and crème caramel.

Rosé ★★ An occasional presence in the range. Dry, **05** with brisk acidity, mainly from gamay (for fruit, freshness) & shiraz (gives backbone, body). **Formosa Peak Cabernet-Shiraz** new ★★ **03** from high, Garden Route vyds – 600 kms away (WO Upper Langkloof). Smoky, cool climate nose with charry, high toned wood (14 mths Fr oak). Minty & leafy character; soft tannins. **Mourvèdre** new ★★★ Sturdy & tarry **04** expresses variety's typical monolithic girth; flattered in youth by oak (9 mths older Am). From dryland Swrtlnd grapes. **Stellenbosch Merlot** new ★★★ **04** from Firgrove, as with Cab above. Good, bright merlot fruit; taut palate that would benefit with some ageing. **Pinotage** ★★★ **03** last yr seemed a touch old fashioned, with hints of acetone, grainy tannin & chunky oak. **Pinotage-Viognier** new ★★★☆ After 3 yrs experimenting **03** is first commercial release. 25 year old bush vine pinotage co-fermented with (4%) aromatic white grape in open fermenters. Aged in Fr oak for 19 mths. Floral, open nose with sweet/ripe palate; powerful (15% alc), needing time to open up. Concours Mondial gold. **Chardonnay** ★★★ **03**, as per last ed, showed clean citrus & slightly mineral tone on palate. Bunch-pressed, fermented/aged 6 mths Fr/Am oak, some new. No **04**. **Sweet Red** ★★★ Fairview's fortified winter warmers tend to change variety every year; latest from merlot. A touch rustic & very sweet with firm acid. Just about holds its 17% alc. **Agostinelli** ★★★☆ Italianate blend of barbera, sangiovese, nebbiolo, primitivo (aka zinfandel) 43/25/18/14 in **04**. From young vyds, grapes fermented in 'neutral' oak for fruitier profile. High toned, juicy & fresh, with sweet & sour notes, grainy tannins. Demands food. **03** Gold at Concours Mondial 2004. WO Coastal. **Agostinelli Barbera** new ★★★☆ Deep, youthful **04** with black fruits. Dense of entry with wood evident. Firm but supple tannins. Chunky finish. Concours Mondial gold. WO Swtlnd, as is … **Agostinelli Sangiovese** new ★★★☆ **04** less expressive than above, but more linear, supple & harmonious. This range WO Coastal unless noted. Discontinued: **Zinfandel**, **Semillon**, **Cabernet Sauvignon**, **Malbec**, **SMV**. *– RK*

False Bay Vineyards

Est/1stB 2000 ▪ Closed to public ▪ Owner Boutinot UK ▪ Winemakers Werner Engelbrecht & Paul Boutinot (2004/2000) ▪ Viti consultant Johan Pienaar, with Werner Engelbrecht ▪ 40 ha (cabs s/f, grenache, merlot, mourvèdre, petit v, shiraz, chard, sauvignon) ▪ 350 000 cs 50% red 42% white 8% rosé ▪ Export brands: Cape Heights, Hoop Huis, Paarl Heights, Peacock Ridge, Post Stones, Vals Baai/False Bay & Waterkloof ▪ PO Box 1286 Wellington 7654 ▪ ceo@boutinotsa.co.za admin@boutinotsa.co.za ▪ ***T 873·2418*** *▪ F 873·7580*

This sizeable but low-key winery's well-laid plans are coming together apace. Currently Wellington-based, it bought farm Waterkloof on Schapenberg Hill in the Somerset West area, and devoted much of last year to almost doubling the area under vine there. This year construction begins on the cellar. Roll-out of their Peacock Ridge range has begun (the Sauvignon released last year, to be followed by Chardonnay and Merlot); the first wines under the flagship Waterkloof label are expected this year. Both ranges are from Schapenberg grapes; fruit for the top range is from specific sites.

Family Reserve see Jonkheer, Kleine Zalze, Riverstone, Waterford
Fantail see Morgenhof

Fat Bastard

Tongue-in-jowl international label created by European wine-partners Thierry Boudinaud and Guy Anderson. Now made in serious quantities (500 000+ cartons) and distributed in Europe, America and the Far East. The SA versions, featuring a cartoon hippo on the front-label, are from Robertson Winery.

Shiraz ★★★★ Lumbering wine lives up to its name. **03** last ed noted as ripe, brambly, aromatic; touches meat, clove & anise, supple tannins, big alc (14%). **Chardonnay** ★★★★ Much nicer than name suggests, & not so podgy either. Still-available **04** ripe & tropical; waddles on to rich, vanilla-toned finish. Partially oak-fermented. **Sauvignon Blanc** new ★★★★ Well textured & flavoured **05**, passionfruit/pineapple ripeness, upbeat lemon-zest exit. Enjoy in fruity youth.—*DH*

Fat Ladies see Winecorp

Feiteiras Vineyards

*Walker Bay ▪ Est 2003 ▪ 1stB 2004 ▪ Visits Mon-Fri 9-5 Sat/Sun 9-12 ▪ Closed Easter Fri/Sun, Dec 25 & Jan 1 ▪ Private functions (Portuguese meals) for min 14 people by appt; also BYO picnic ▪ Owners De Andrade family ▪ Winemaker Jose de Andrade (Mar 2003) ▪ Viticulturist Manuel de Andrade (Mar 2003) ▪ 4.5 ha (cab, merlot, mourvèdre, petit v, shiraz, verdelho) ▪ 600 cs ▪ 75% red 25% fortified ▪ PO Box 234 Bot River 7185 ▪ feiteiraswine@icon.co.za ▪ www.feiteiraswine.co.za ▪ **T 082·453·1597** ▪ F (028) 284·9525*

Far away, in the borough of Feiteiras in Madeira, Portugal, the septuagenarian parents of José and Manuel de Andrade still make wine. 'They do it out of sheer love for people, the land, the food and of course the wine. And in their later years, this is what brings them the most pleasure.' This was the inspiration behind the brothers' decision to start making wine in the Cape after 23 years in the restaurant and retail liquor trade. 'We share that same love for life, wine, food and people, and a winery marries all of the above,' says winemaker José. Manuel, meanwhile, looks after the vines – which includes some Portuguese verdelho for a future white port. Their maiden wine, an 04 named Troca Tintas, from merlot and tinta barocca, is available from the farm, and selected restaurants and wine shops.

Fernkloof see Cape Wine Exports
Ferry see Merwespont
Fired Earth see Villiera
Firefly see Stellar Winery

FirstCape Vineyards

*Paarl ▪ Closed to public ▪ Est 2002 ▪ Owners De Wet Co-op Winery, Goudini Wines, Newton Johnson family & BrandPhoenix ▪ Winemakers Piet le Roux & Gordon Newton Johnson, advised by Newald Marais ▪ 60% red 40% white ▪ PO Box 6213 Paarl 7622 ▪ info@firstcape.com ▪ www.firstcape.com ▪ **T 872·0837** ▪ F 872·2534*

This extraordinarily successful joint venture has become the fastest-growing SA brand in the UK (deservedly named *Wine & Spirit* magazine's Brand Champion of the Year 2004). If you're in the Worcester area you'll see the new FirstCape 'On the Move ...' branded tankers (the local De Wet and Goudini cellars, the Newton Johnson family and UK-based BrandPhoenix are the key players). The HQ has moved to Paarl, and Bevan Johnson, brother of winemaker Gordon N-J, now sits in the PR director's chair. Export manager Charmaine Alger reports they've launched their first 3-litre boxed wines, and just been listed by retail colossi Somerfield, Kwiksave, Asda and Thresher.

FirstCape Limited Release range new

Sauvignon Blanc ☺ ★★★ Intense cat's pee/greenpepper aroma & bracing acidity given interest/weight by pithy grapefruit & lime fruit in **05**. Perfect for oysters.

Cabernet Sauvignon ★★☆ Luscious blackcurrant teams with cab's typical astringency to deliver a fruity, uncomplicated **04** sipper. **Merlot** ★★☆ Friendly early drinker with ripe plum/blackberry fruit, approachable tannins & gentle acidity. **04** slips down easily. **Shiraz** ★★☆ Not-for-ageing **04** quaffer with bright red fruit, furry tannins; short, warm finish (from 14.2% alc). **Chenin Blanc** ★★ **05** shy & retiring dieter's friend (only 1.5g/ℓ sugar). Dusty fynbos bouquet, hint apple on palate

FirstCape range

Pinotage ★★★ Juicy, elegant **04**, strawberry/raspberry tone with firm fruit tannins for structure & grip. Persistent earthy finish. **Shiraz-Pinotage** ★★★ **04** last ed was a supple red-fruited mouthful, soft & youthfully delicious, chillable in summer. **Cabernet Sauvignon-Merlot** new ★★☆ **04** early drinking summer red; pleasant savoury nose with dab plum/prune & gentle rounded fruit tannins. **Chardonnay-Semillon** ★★★ Easy-going 53/47 blend, **04** last yr showed vintage's shy aromas but bouncy/zesty apple flavours, good dry flinty finish. **Colombard-Chardonnay** new ★★☆ **04** sidewalk café wine; bright citrus fruit, breezy acidity & lots of attitude. Drink young, serve well-chilled. Both ranges WO W Cape. — *CvZ*

Fish Eagle see Le Grand Chasseur
Fish Hoek see Flagstone

Five Heirs

This brand, part of the Christo Wiese Portfolio (see entry), takes its name from the Wiese family, 'heirs to the cultural riches of Lanzerac and Lourensford', their wine farms in the Jonkershoek and Lourens River valleys. The grapes are grown and the wines vinified on the two properties before selection and blending.

Cabernet Sauvignon ★★★☆ **04** fruit is main focus here, ripely attractive plums, cassis, while firm vein of oak tannin ensures food compatibility, ±2 yrs ageing potential. **Cabernet Franc** ★★★☆ Serious yet friendly & unintimidating. **01** last available, had trademark green walnuts, supported by red fruit profile. Ageing potential from 15 mths Fr oak. **Merlot** ★★★☆ **04** back on track after lighter **03**. Layered white pepper, herbaceous tones, red berries. Vibrant palate, but enough tannin backbone from 40% oaking for few yrs ageing. Soupçon cab. **Pinotage** ★★★☆ **04** retains signature fruit purity of pvs, red currants, rhubarb, with eminently drinkable juiciness. Partly oaked. **Shiraz** ★★★☆ **04** classic shiraz profile: peppery wild berry fruit, campfire smoke, complemented by gutsy but smoothly accessible structure. Lightly oaked. Robust 15.3% alc. **Rosé** ★★☆ Uncomplicated al fresco lunch companion. Last tasted **03**, tasty, appealing, fruit pastille tones. **Chardonnay** ★★★ **04** step up on pvs. Lemongrass & fresh peach character, softly rounded & approachable. Portion barrel fermented & matured; dash viognier. **Chenin Blanc** ★★★ **04** still available not retasted. Softly rounded, had pear-drop & melon typicity, refreshing finish. **Sauvignon Blanc** ★★☆Last tasted **04**, light-textured quaffing wine. Showed nettly/herbaceous character, crisp finish. All WO Stbosch. — *CR*

Five Senses see Overhex

Flagstone Winery

Somerset West ▪ Est 1998 ▪ 1stB 1999 ▪ Tasting & sales Mon-Fri 10-5 Sat/Sun by appt ('phone to avoid disappointment') ▪ Fee R50 redeemable with any purchase ▪ Tours by appt ▪ Owners Jack family ▪ Winemakers Bruce Jack & Wilhelm Coetzee ▪ Viticulturist Bruce Jack ▪ 130 ha under management ▪ 400-600 tons 40-70 000 cs (varying % reds/whites) ▪ PO Box 3636 Somerset West 7129 ▪ admin@flagstonewinery.co.za sales@flagstonewinery.co.za ▪ www.flagstonewines.com ▪ ***T 852·5052*** *▪ F 852·5085*

Long an outsider, plying his craft in quirky spaces (below the V&A Waterfront!), Flagstone winemaker Bruce Jack must feel he's arrived. He has his own young vines on the family farm near Napier (though continuing to source grapes from across the Cape and, now, beyond), and a commodious own cellar at Somerset West. And he's one of the newest members of the by-invitation-only Cape Winemakers Guild, debuting with two wines on their annual auction. One auction offering, named with typical Jackian flair, A Month of Sundays, embodies the creativity and scope of the man's vini/viti ventures: it combines Swartberg riesling and muscat, Elim sauvignon and Helderberg chardonnay. Now Bruce J's casting his net even wider: 2006 sees pinotage planted in California and Germany, for future single-vineyard wines and multi-national blends. The move dovetails with his fledgling 'Flagstone Friends' import business, managing new foreign-wine sections for SA supermarket chains Makro and Pick 'n Pay.

★★★★☆ **CWG Black South Easter** new Equal portions cab & shiraz pampered – whole-berry crush, 2 wk cold soak, 100% new Am casks – into combustible auction offering. **03** opaque wet-coal hues, ruminative dark fruits guarded by plush tannins mid-2005; finely etched texture dominates echoing length now, likely to bloom from 2010. WO W Cape.

★★★★☆ **Mary Le Bow** Inimitable cooperation with the Fraters of Rbtsn 'to reflect the compelling beauty of the place'. Elegantly restrained **03** 'trembles with power'; blackcurrant fruit neatly ordered in refined structure, honeyed rather than simply sweet tones folded into unremitting viscosity of finish. Cab, shiraz, merlot (62/25/13) cold soaked for 2 wks, then mix Fr/Am barrels, third new, 14 mths. Moderate 13.4% alc. Swiss 2005 gold.

★★★★ **Bowwood Cabernet Sauvignon & Merlot** Promise of something special delivered by **03**, sample pvs ed, as was above wine, now in finished form. 63/37 blend. merlot cold-soaked until later-ripening cab picked, then fermented together before yr wood, mostly Am, rest Fr, 15% new. Bold juicy mulberry fruits burst through oak spice; quality key is the ripe, soft, sweet tannins. **02** also full & warm-hearted. Partnership with the Johnsens in Pdberg.

The Berrio range

★★★★ **Cabernet Sauvignon** This, below, joint venture with Francis Pratt, grower of 'magical grapes' near Elim. Sample **04** in individual groove: succulent huckleberry fruit contained in elegant focused form, bags of flavour rifled into svelte frame. 14 mths Am oak, 60% new. 14% alc. **03** not reviewed, no **02**.

★★★★ **Sauvignon Blanc** Deliciously measured stone character, neither opulent nor austere. **05** textbook cool-vyd bottling; intense capsicum character with ham-and-pea-soup stamp, mellifluous elegance to tapered tail. **04** smooth & velvety, super fruit concentration in fine finish.

Foundation range

★★★★ **Dragon Tree** Not for classicists perhaps, but Cape individuality in complex blend cab, pinotage, shiraz & merlot (35/31/18/16). **03** mellow, earthy aromas lifted by currant concentration; muscular ripple to medium-firm tannins. **02** sold out, not reviewed. Yr wood, 70% Am, 40% new.

★★★★ **Longitude** ✓ Consistent value, deftly orchestrated fruit ensemble with sound vinosity. **04** (★★★★) sees shiraz to the fore, supported by cab s, pinotage & 4 others; wild berry/dark cherry features, tannins more open than pvs. Sold out **03** not tasted. 9 mths oak, 70% Am, 20% new.

★★★★ **Dark Horse Shiraz** (Prosaic 'Shiraz' pvs ed.) As wild as the cellar mantra: 'a moving target, our dreams reflected'. **03** full, deep & brooding, lovely spirals of ethereal spice intertwined with choc-sheen fruit, lithe tannic support; excellent duration to aftertaste. **02** a sultry monster of hotland fruit trussed up in oak, ripe tannin. 50% whole-berry crush, all oaked (60% new Am) for 14 mths.

★★★★ **The Music Room Cabernet Sauvignon** Jack's 'best attempt yet' (**02** pvs ed) topped, in our view, by vintage-finessed **03**: packed with explosive cassis, succulent red berries tucked up in decadently smooth structure; unobtrusive Am oak paves lingering finish. **02** VDG. Barrelled 14 mths, half new Am.

★★★★ **Writer's Block Pinotage** Emphatic in fidelity to its grape origin, ever popular with pundits. **03** flew the coop before it could be tasted. **04** confirms upward quality trajectory: spicy plum richness mingles with sweet ripe pinotage fruit in medium-tannined tail. As opulent as **02**; with pears-in-wine glazed fruit. Third whole-berry crush, 14 mths barrelled, 30% new Am in the mix.

★★★☆ **Two Roads** Cellar's 'icon white blend' gears up with **04** (★★★★): fascinating bootwax nose, layers of undulating flavour build to crescendo, simmer into lingering finish. Subtle, not overt: the sum being more than the (pinot blanc-led) 7 parts. No **03**. **02** pvsly noted as elegant. 50% oak-fermented 4 mths.

BK5 Pinot Noir ★★★ No follow up yet for **03**, where BK5 clone's propensity for organic notes held sway. **Semaphore** ★★★ A refreshingly dry rosé to bring a smile to any face. **05** bounced off shelves before we could taste. **04** set the tone: copper-pink, cherry/berry aromas, enough grip in mouth for food – from picnics to silver-service salmon. **Free Run Sauvignon Blanc** ★★★☆ Natural oak-free handling of small parcels of Rbtsn, Elim free-run juice. **05** less aromatic than pvs, tropical appley palate drawn together by flinty edge in tart tail. **Heywood House Barrel Fermented Sauvignon Blanc** ★★★☆ Sophisticated handling of often fractious sauvignon/wood marriage. Current **04** golden sheen; warm custard breadth of spiced oak softens sauvignon spikes. Barrelled 8 mths, 70% Am, 10% new. **Noon Gun** ★★★ Riesling-based miscellany of 7 white grapes, winner at The Houston Livestock & Rodeo Show! **05** aromatic floral tints to peachy palate, oak whispers in crisp tail. One-size-fits-all versatility. **The Last Word Port** ★★★☆ Exotica such as tannat jostle with mourvèdre, sangiovese & friends in eclectic take on higher alc/lower sugar genre. None since **02**. **The Poetry Collection Pinot Noir** discontinued.

Cellar Hand range

Joint venture with employees committed 'beyond the monotonous security of a monthly salary', not retasted; no new vintages available at press time. **The Backchat Blend** ★★★ Mix 8 varieties, mostly cab, shiraz, merlot. **02** developed toned berry fruits mingled with silky-soft tannins in composed grip. **Chenin Blanc** ★★★ **04** tropical, pulpy guava flavours, gently firmed by reductive palate, refreshingly moderate 12% alc.

Strata Series

'Experimental, once-off & seriously adventurous' wines. **Cape Blend** See under Makro. **The Wallflower** new ★★★☆ Not to be found in the winemaker's primer; 65/35 morio muscat & sauvignon blend of Oudtshoorn, Elim fruit – muscat Am oaked 8 mths to boot – but the latest envelope-edge being pushed here. Sample **05** eclectic pastiche grapey fruit & charry wood whipped into upright form by sauvignon tartness in dry tail. **The Glass Carriage Chenin Blanc** discontinued.

Fish Hoek range new

Entry level wines – in fun fishmonger packaging – mainly for export; all W Cape.

Merlot ☺ ★★★ **04** chunky everyday red with fruity flesh beyond its price point; cab s & f add some authority, Am oak (65% new, 10 mths) gives vanilla warmth. 14.5% alc.

Rosé ★★☆ **05** sun, fruit & fun; grippy tail (partial used Am cask fermentation) encases just-dry finish. **Sauvignon Blanc** ★★☆ **05** tropical girth seamed with racy tones, 12% semillon confers gravitas to unpretentious quaffer. – *DS*

Flamingo Bay see Darling Cellars

Flat Roof Manor new

'Laid-back, unpretentious and quirky' screwcapped range made by Estelle Swart of Uitkyk (where the wines may be tasted). The name an allusion to the flat-roofed, neoclassical manor house on the property.

Merlot 04 unrated sample still in vice-like grip of tannins. Assertive plum/vanilla nose & palate with spicy finish. **Semillon** ★★★ Waxy lemon blossom whiffs in delicious **04**. Medium-bodied, hint spice & pithy texture, 5 mths lees contact; zesty acidity thanks to suppressed malo. Drink over next ±12 mths. **Pinot Grigio** ★★ **04** 'skinny' version, despite 6 mths fattening on lees, more typical of Italian examples. Retiring pear & litchi bouquet; austere slatey/citrus palate. Moderate 12% alc. All Stbosch vyds. — *CvZ*

Fleur du Cap

Stellenbosch ▪ 1stB 1968 ▪ Tasting & sales at Bergkelder ▪ Owner Distell ▪ Winemakers Kobus Gerber (white wines) & Justin Corrans (red wines), with Tariro Masayiti & Jaco van der Walt ▪ Viticulturist Bennie Liebenberg ▪ 18 000 tons 200 000 cs 60% red 40% white ▪ fleurducap@distell.co.za ▪ www.fleurducap.co.za ▪ ***T 809·7000*** *▪ F 883·9651*

Flagship label for mighty wine producer/wholesaler Distell, familiar Fleur du Cap retains a consistently fine level of quality, possibly underrated by local wine aficionados coping with the plethora of new names out there. A glance at the Unfiltered Collection line-up should rectify that misperception. The cellar team, with Kobus Gerber dedicated to whites and new-blood Justin Corrans (ex-Zonnebloem) on reds, draws on some of the finest fruit from across the winelands. Besides helping launch the Lomond label (see separate entry), Kobus G has been delving into the influence of site on varying styles possible from a single variety. The results, starting with sauvignon, will be individually bottled and offered in a 'terroir pack', headed for shop shelves via the annual Nederburg Auction.

Unfiltered Collection

★★★★ **Cabernet Sauvignon** Unmistakably cab from first sniff — **03** distinctive mulberry, touches cedar, tobacco. Mulberry returns on palate with cassis, very concentrated. Tannins still fairly abrasive, should unravel over next 2-3yrs — cellar up to 8. At 13.2%, lower alc than some pvs. **02** (★★★☆) less ripe; tannic grip, too-high acid. These ex-single Bottlry vyd, as Merlot below. 16 mths Fr oak, all new.

★★★★ **Merlot** After poor vintage **02** (★★★☆) **03** on form: immense concentration of dark choc, lead-pencils. Dense, thick & beefy rather than berried; very dry; firm tannic backbone. 18 mths new Fr oak. For keeping, say 3-6 yrs.

★★★★ **Chardonnay 03** was more New Worldish than usual. **04** more classic again — rich lime, lemon with charry oak. Firm-fleshed & classy, citrus joined by mineral notes, chalkiness; supportive oak (fermented/9 mths new, 80/20). Needs another yr to hit its stride, should last 2-4 yrs.

★★★★☆ **Sauvignon Blanc** Tropical nuances to core flavours green fig, grass in **05** (★★★★), racy acidity helping to hide big 14.2% alc. Hint sweetness on finish ensures soft landing. From vyds in Gansbaai & Koekenaap — highlights widening search for fine fruit. Gorgeous **04** with mouth-watering flavours, *Wine* ★★★★.

★★★★☆ **Sauvignon Blanc Limited Release** Arresting aromas in **05** — capsicum, gooseberry & cat-pee. Full-blast herbal, capsicum green (but not unripe) flavours undiminished by tropical tones, and bone-dry. Contrast to wine above less obvious than in **04**. Similarly well built, also 14.2% alc.

★★★★ **Semillon** After graceful, fleshy but firm **03**, **04** (★★★☆) has slimmed down a bit. Lime marmalade, subtle oak, no trace of variety's usual lanolin. Firm citrus flavours & brisk acidity for mouth-watering freshness, balancing ripe fruit. Fermented/6 mths 50% new Fr/Am oak.

★★★★ **Viognier** new **04** worthy addition to range. Whiffs white peach, evening flowers; firm flesh, packed with ripe peach flavours, creamy texture undisturbed by smooth acidity. Oak supportive, only appears at end of long finish. Fermented/9 mths used Fr oak. Big 14.9% alc.

★★★★ **Viognier-Chardonnay-Sauvignon Blanc-Semillon** Equal blend again in **04** (★★★☆). Quieter, less stuffing than **03**; some citrus, delicate peach aromas; elegant rather than bold, tangy citrus flavours, firm acid on finish. Fermented/matured separately, 9 mths Fr oak, some new.

Standard range

★★★★ **Cabernet Sauvignon** Reliable but stylish, good bargain — as is this whole range. Dark mulberry, cool cedar on **03**, graceful blackcurrant fruit; classically constructed, with fine-grained dry tannins, lingering dry finish with brush of oak (18 mths, mostly Fr, third new). Almost ready, but these go 7 yrs. No **02**.

★★★★ **Noble Late Harvest** From unwooded riesling. **05** stunning glacé apricot, pineapple, tangerine, wafting botrytis already discernable. Lengthy finish tinged with orange zest. In modern, less sweet style with thrilling acidity (107g/ℓ sugar, 10g/ℓ acid), the balance poised on a knife edge.

★★★☆ **Chenin Blanc** ✓ These have found their style: intense fruit from older vines, subtle oak support allowing fruit to shine. **05** (★★★★) greengage, chamomile, mineral, with touches of spice in youth; firm flesh, mouth-watering acidity. Has years ahead. Watch whopping 14.7% alc. Quieter **04** tasted as sample, soft spicy flavours. VDG

Merlot ★★★☆ **03** continues fine tradition. Attractive cool-grown fruit, cassis with touches mint; smooth & serene with dark-berried appeal, attractive dry tannins, fair finish. Approachable early, will keep 3-5 years. **Pinotage** ★★★☆ **03** richly robed in plummy fruit, ripe almost porty aromas/flavours, whiff of good oak. Dry & meaty, firm tannic grip, some earthiness on finish. **Shiraz** ★★★☆ **03** pleasurable as ever – black cherries with hints liquorice, leather; nicely proportioned with smooth approachable tannins. Ready, should keep 2-3 yrs. From selected Stbosch vineyards. Fr/Am oak 18 mths, 30% new. **Chardonnay** ★★★ All the necessary aromas/flavours lime & toast in **04**; oak unobtrusive (6 mths, mainly Fr); soft finish, will please many palates. **Sauvignon Blanc** ★★★ **05** less arresting than usual; grass & scrub notes; firm flesh, very dry, brisk acidity. Ideal for luncheon fish & salads.

Natural Light ★★ 'Light' referring to low ±9% alc, not 9.8g/ℓ sugar; ideal therefore for lunchtime tippling, not dieting! **05** crunchy acidity, appley tail, sugar almost not noticeable. — *IvH/CvZ*

Foot of Africa see Kleine Zalze
Footprint see African Pride
Forellen see Lanzerac
Forge Mill see Franschhoek Vineyards
For My Friends see Darling Cellars
Forrester see Ken Forrester
Fortress Hill see Fort Simon

Fort Simon Estate

*Stellenbosch ▪ Est/1stB 1998 ▪ Tasting & sales Mon-Fri 9.30-5 Sat 10-2 Pub hols 10-4 ▪ Fee R1/wine ▪ Closed Easter Fri/Sun, Dec 25/26 & Jan 1 ▪ Tours by appt ▪ Meals & venue for after-hours receptions/conferences (max 40 guests) by appt ▪ Walks ▪ Owners Renier & Petrus Uys ▪ Winemaker Marinus Bredell, with Wilhelm Hörstmann (Jun 1997/Feb 2005) ▪ Viticulturist Renier Uys ▪ ±78 ha (cabs s/f, malbec, merlot, pinotage, shiraz, chard, chenin, sauvignon, viognier) ▪ 280 tons 20 000 cs own label 50% red 50% white ▪ PO Box 43 Sanlamhof 7532 ▪ fortsimon@telkomsa.net ▪ www.fortsimon.co.za ▪ **T 906·0304** ▪ F 903·8034/906·2549*

It was 'stress, stress and more stress' last year when simultaneous ripening filled this recently extended cellar to capacity. But 'a winemaker always has a plan' avers Marinus Bredell (now assisted by Wilhelm Hörstmann), and as a result they made what they believe are some of the most promising wines to date. First crops of viognier, petit verdot and malbec were sold off, but the hope is to make wines from the varieties in the future, says Bredell, a keen angler who admits he's 'still waiting for that big one which gets away every time'. Upside is, he's not about to get roped in when time comes to stock the swimming pool beside the tasting room, being converted into a pond....

★★★★ **Chardonnay** House style is elegant, understated, so **04** a delightful exception: pungent citrus zest & pineapple tones, great fruit concentration & richness; biscuity oak, savoury nuance to finish. **03** leaner, attenuated build yet ultra-long finish. Fermented/aged 9 mths new Fr barriques.

★★★★ **Chenin Blanc Barrel Fermented** Not made in **04**. Last ed **03** quietish dried pear aroma; poised, vigorous fruit with lively acidity, resonating finish. Standout **02** (★★★★★) had a silky palate, very long finish. These should easily last 5–7 yrs. Fermented/aged 4 mths, new Am oak.

★★★★ **Sauvignon Blanc** Showy & intense **04**, vibrant, tangy, mouth-watering green fig/capsicum flavours, long limy finish.

Cabernet Sauvignon ★★★★ Maiden **01** understated, compact; ripe cassis, touches capsicum & cedar, medium-weight with silky tannins. 18 mths Fr/Am oak, none new. **Merlot** ★★★★ **01** cassis & choc beckon, palate with savoury dryness & fresh acidity; neat, compact, lighter textured (13.2% alc). 18 mths oak vs 9 for pvs; 25% Am, 2nd/3rd fill. **Pinotage** ★★★ **02** 'cooler' fruit in lighter yr: rhubarb & green fynbos; slender, sappy palate, approachable but probably better in yr/2. Oaking scaled back to 6–8 mths (vs 15), third Am. **Shiraz 02** ★★★ Last yr cool herbaceous character, slender build, quite austere. Alc 12.9%. Yr small-oak, 30% Am. **Rosé** new Pretty cerise-tinged **05**, mainly merlot with pinotage; soft berry flavours, easy dry finish. **Anna Simon Merlot-Pinotage** ★★★ **01** interesting savoury, ground coffee aromas/flavours, tell-tale touch pinotage sweetness in finish. Staves/barrels 8–10 mths. Not retasted. **Chenin Blanc** ★★★★ Portion barrel fermented, **04** light textured appley fruit salad flavours, subtle oak overlay, exuberant acidity. VDG. **Restelle** ★★★★ **04** sauvignon, chard, chenin (65/25/10), 50% fermented together 'due to lack of space'; sauvignon dominates, adds limey edge throughout; chard/chenin contribute palate weight & tropical flavours. **Sauvignon Blanc Barrel Fermented** ★★★ **03** fermented & aged 4 mths Eur oak. Wood prominent last ed, had tamed wilder edges of sauvignon, plumped up profile of otherwise slender style. This, Chenin Barrel Fermented, are alternating releases.

Fortress Hill Reserve range

Second label; only Merlot tasted for current ed. **Merlot** ★★★ **01** notch up approachability scale; liquorice & cream nose, rounded (4.7g/ℓ RS) & tasty dark fruit palate. 18 mths 3rd/4th fill barrels, third Am. **Pinotage** ★★ Lightly oaked **02**, ripe & plummy; approachable tannins, savoury twist to tail. 30 yr old vines, since uprooted. **Merlot-Pinotage** ★★★ **01** amiable easy red, smooth tannins for early accessibility. Lightly oaked. **Chenin Blanc** ★★★ Gorgeous ripe melon, spice on rich but lively **03**. Vibrantly fruity. Terrific tipple (note 14% alc). **Sauvignon Blanc** ★★★ Whiff passionfruit, greengage in **03**; easy-drinking version plumped with touch sugar. – *CR/IvH*

Foundation Series see Flagstone
Four Clover see Cloverfield
Four Cousins see Van Loveren

Fraai Uitzicht 1798

Robertson • Sales at reception/restaurant during opening hours (see Eat-out section) • Closed Easter Fri/Sun, Dec 25 & Jan 1 • Tours strictly by appt • For amenities & activities, see Stay-over section & intro below • Owners Axel Spanholtz & Mario Motti • Winemakers/viticulturists Axel Spanholtz & Mario Motti, advised by local experts • 10 ha (cab, merlot, shiraz) • 500 cs 100% red • PO Box 97 Robertson 6705 • info@fraaiuitzicht.com • www.fraaiuitzicht.com • ***T/F (023) 626·6156***

The romance of a ramshackle wine cellar circa 1798 had Axel Spanholtz and Mario Motti hooked a full two hundred years later. In 1998, in search of the 'enjoyable way of life which wine brings', the partners swapped Europe for the hills surrounding the Klaas Voogds valley. Despite this being the oldest cellar in the Robertson district, recent renovations have brought the property into the 21st century. Catering mostly to international guests, this has become a popular destination for its excellent cuisine, warm hospitality and hand-crafted wines.

Merlot ★★★ Smooth drinking **03** with dark berry sauce warmed for ice-cream, gentle oak whiffs & inky notes in bouquet; supple, approachable tannins & broad fruit centre. Drink soon. – *IvH*

Franschhoek Vineyards

Franschhoek ▪ Est 1945 ▪ 1stB ca 1975 ▪ Tasting & sales Mon-Fri 9.30-5 Sat 10-4 Sun 10.30-3 ▪ Fee R10 ▪ Closed Easter Fri & Dec 25 ▪ La Cotte Restaurant (booking advised) ▪ Owners 95 shareholders ▪ Winemaker Jolene Calitz (Nov 2002) ▪ Viticulturist Annette van der Merwe (Aug 2003) ▪ 2 300 tons 44 000 cs own label 45% red 55% white ▪ Ranges for customers: Keates Drift & Millberg ▪ ISO 14000 certification in progress ▪ PO Box 52 Franschhoek 7690 ▪ info@franschhoek-vineyards.com ▪ www.franschhoek-vineyards.co.za ▪ ***T 876·2086*** *▪ F 876·3440*

The transformation from co-op to serious cellar targeting mid- to upper-price points has culminated in satisfied 'engineer' Daan Coetzee feeling it's all been worth it. Sales are booming – up 30%. Housewines for Woolworths now number five, and exports to the UK and Belgium flourish. Germany is a new market. Branding has been consolidated under a re-designed Franschhoek Cellars (FHC) label with a distinctive heraldic shield shape (replacing old brands like La Cotte). The black-label Cellars Reserve range contains selected bottlings (including a Petit Verdot and new barrel-fermented Semillon). The FHC Gold range contains single varieties. The FHC Silver covers entry-level wines. Credit to the vini/viticultural teams inspired by consultant Jacques Borman, insists Coetzee.

Franschhoek Cellar Reserve range

Merlot ★★★★ **03** again big-boned (16% alc) but well-behaved; prune & bitter cherry whiffs, copious ripe fruit manages to rein in the oak (17 mths Fr), tame the lively tannins. Should develop, hold, good few yrs. **Petit Verdot** new ★★★ Velvety hues on **03**, inviting red fruit with liquorice hint, firm smoky tannins & pleasing 'tea-leaf' astringency. **Chardonnay** new ★★★★ **04** tinged with lime, lemon & vanilla oak; lively palate; pithy finish with well-meshed oak & exotic tangerine aftertaste. 6 mths Fr oak, 50% new. **Semillon** new ★★★ Incl 7.8% (!) sauvignon – surprisingly active on **04** palate, imparting welcome verve to semillon's weight. Delicate lemon blossom character somewhat dominated by oak mid-2005 – give bit of time to harmonise. 100% new oak, 33% Am.

Franschhoek Cellar Gold range

Cabernet Sauvignon ★★ **04** similar to pvs; bright cherry & currant intro, charry oak, healthy fruit waiting for puckering tannins to relax, unwind. Incl dash petit v, as do following pair of reds: **Merlot** ★★ Robust **04** gamey/savoury aromas, juicy plump fruit, big astringent tannins from 8 mths on oak, same as for … **Shiraz** ★★★ Most generous, open, of these reds; **04** fleshy berry fruits with hints farmyard, smoke; unobtrusive 15% alc. Bitter nuance only detraction. **Pinotage** ★★ **04** forthcoming on nose yet fairly withdrawn on palate, chewy tannins & hint of pinotage bitterness. Third unoaked. **Chardonnay** ★★ Wood-fermentation character still fairly obvious on **05**, time needed for delicate pear/citrus fruit to come to fore. **Sauvignon Blanc** ★★ Green-tinted **05** delicate & light, some grassy hints, zingy tropical finish. Most also sold under Forge Mill label.

Franschhoek Cellar Silver range (pvsly La Cotte)

Grande Rouge ★★ Varietal quintet led by merlot, 8-9 mths oaked. Friendly red fruit given some backbone by light wood tannins. **NV**. **Chenin Blanc** ★★ **05** lightish dry white with retiring pear & quince aromas. Incl dash sauvignon. **Blanc de Blanc** ★★ Light-bodied **05** mainly semillon, with trio of white partners; waxy semillon whiffs, pleasing mineral-tinged fruity finish. **Semi-Soet** ★★ Chiefly hanepoot, with chenin & crouchen; **05**, grapey muscat perfumes, spring blossom whiff, short but polite farewell. **Chenin Blanc** also available under Forge Mill label. **Anvil** range discontinued. – *CvZ*

Fredericksburg see Rupert & Rothschild Vignerons

Fredine le Roux Wines

Walker Bay/Caledon ▪ Est/1stB 2004 ▪ Tastings/sales at Goedvertrouw ▪ Owners Josias & Fredine le Roux ▪ Winemaker Fredine le Roux ▪ 240 cs 60% red 40% white ▪ PO Box 338 Caledon 7230 ▪ Josiasfredin@mweb.co.za ▪ ***T (028) 284·9026/083·274·9606*** *▪ F (028) 284·9029*

'If your vision doesn't scare you, it's not big enough!' says Fredine le Roux, who bottled her 04 Cab shortly before giving birth to a daughter – a week after being named a finalist in the Woman Winemaker of the Year competition. There's no secret recipe for success here, though: 'Things must be done at the right time, you must never be in a hurry, and make 100% sure you have the right grapes for the style of wine that you have in mind…'

Cabernet Sauvignon ★★★★ Big-boned **04** oozes ultra-ripe but gorgeous cassis/plum fruit on nose & palate; toasty oak & pipesmoke whiffs add complexity. Tannins a touch aggressive, need ± 2 yrs to soften; finishes warmer than 13.1% alc suggests. 18 mths Fr oak. **Grenache-Cabernet Sauvignon** Too young last yr to rate, now sold out! **Chenin Blanc** ★★★ Tasted mid-2004, **04** marked by sinewy elegance; kiwi & passionfruit on nose, fairly prominent oak but enough vivacious lemon fruit to carry it. Slender 13% alc. Grapes from Barton Farm, W Bay. *— MM*

Freedom Hill Wines

Paarl ▪ Est 1997 ▪ 1stB 2000 ▪ Tasting & sales Mon-Thu 9-5 Fri 9-4 Sat by appt ▪ Closed pub hols ▪ BYO picnic ▪ Owner Francois Klomp ▪ Winemaker/viticulturist Ryan Wyness (Aug 2005) ▪ ±19 ha (cab, merlot, pinotage, shiraz) ▪ 140 tons 6 000 cs 100% red ▪ PO Box 6353 Uniedal 7612 ▪ info@freedomhill.co.za ▪ www.freedomhill.co.za ▪ ***T/F 867·0085/882·8207***

The welcome mat is out at Francois Klomp's estate on the Paarl/Franschhoek road (stone's throw from the site where Nelson Mandela walked to freedom in 1990). There's now a 'rustic and cosy' tasting area, open weekdays and, by appointment, Saturdays. Visitors can picnic on the lawns (with wonderful valley views) and take a dip in the 'reservoir' pool. Winemaker Ryan Wyness, now permanently ensconced as oenologist/viticulturist after serving an apprenticeship under consultant Hempies du Toit, is on hand for personal attention. The past year has seen production upped to 6 000 cases. Shiraz still stars, though the Merlot garnered high praise at the Swiss Air tastings, winning gold and a 'best value red' award.

Freedom Hill range

★★★★ **Shiraz-Cabernet Sauvignon** No new vintage since **01**; 50/40 blend (& splash merlot), generous New World ripeness, fairly extracted but harmonious, well contained.

★★★★ **Shiraz 03**'s Ribena fruit has evolved into creamy plum pudding notes; now more savoury & gamey than when tasted last yr. Brisk acidity, ripe tannins auger well for 5-6 yrs cellaring. 2 yrs Fr/Am oak. **04**, not retasted, seemed lighter, different character.

Cabernet Sauvignon new ★★★ **05** early drinking style; comfortable tannins, fruitcake & cream nose, slender mouthfeel despite 14.5% alc. No follow up to … **Merlot** ★★★☆ **02** soft plum & currant aromas; very ripe, plump style, wood (2 yrs Fr, 2nd/3rd fill) a pleasing background scent. **Pinotage** new ★★★☆ Introverted; muted cappuccino/earth tones, well structured with fleshy fruit, lively acidity, generous tannins. Drinking well but should hold 2–3 yrs. **Liberty** new ★★★☆ 'Cape blend' of pinotage/shiraz/cab (52/27/21). Attractive rhubarb & wild berry fruit aromas/flavours; toasty tannin adding structure. Not a keeper; enjoy with food. These staved ± 10 mths unless noted.

Shibula range

Merlot ★★★☆ Last ed ripe plums, as above, but with meaty hint in **01**; big, juicy, supple wine; fair amount of complexity which should increase with time. 2 yrs 3rd fill Fr barrels. *— CR*

Frog Hill see Anura
Frost Vineyards see Daview Vineyards

Fryer's Cove Vineyards

Bamboes Bay/Stellenbosch ▪ Est 1999 ▪ 1stB 2002 ▪ Tastings at Knorhoek (see entry) ▪ Owners Jan Ponk Trust, JH Laubscher Family Trust & Wynand Hamman ▪ Winemaker Wynand Hamman (Apr 1999) ▪ Viticulturist Jan van Zyl (Apr 1999) ▪ 6 ha (cab, merlot, pinot, sauvignon) ▪ 25 tons 1 500 cs 66% red 34% white ▪ PO Box 213 Doringbaai 8151 ▪ janponk@kingsley.co.za ▪ ***T 082·550·8749/(027) 213·2312*** *F (027) 213·2212*

The romantic dream of a Bamboes Bay beach cellar has been abandoned … for now. The practicalities of a ready-built winery won out. Wynand Hamman (ex-Lanzerac winemaker) and brother-in-law Jan 'Ponk' van Zyl (a Vredendal farmer) have formed a company with Knorhoek in Stellenbosch and together they're restoring the old farm cellar which they shared in 2005. Fryer's Cove wines can now be tasted and purchased here. Hamman is happy to be settled: the focus is now on quality. Their cool-climate, practically wave-washed West Coast vineyards near the Hamman/Van Zyl family's Strandfontein beach cottage have delivered stunning sauvignon, attractive cab and merlot, and now the first pinot noir (planted in 2002) – experimental, but promising, says Hamman, equally cool.

★★★★★ **Sauvignon Blanc 05** shows stylistic change: riveting nettly, wet heath character, 'green' yet ripe, sauvignon at its showiest. Finishes with minerality owing more to Old World than New. Impressive. **04** (sample) had layered depth, subtlety; flavours were pure sauvignon, arresting just-picked freshness.

Richard Fryer ★★★★ **04** near-equal blend cab, merlot (barrel sample, as was **03** tasted last ed) difficult to rate, still in development mid-2005. Dense plummy fruit, whiffs tar, smoked beef. Tannins dominant, not yet integrated but building blocks in place. Yr Fr barriques. **Merlot**, **Cabernet Sauvignon** discontinued. – *CR*

Furstenburg Wines new

Stellenbosch ▪ Est 2004 ▪ 1stB 2005 ▪ Closed to public ▪ Owners Victor van Aswegen & Anton van Aswegen family trusts ▪ Vini consultant Jeff Wedgwood (Oct 2004) ▪ 1 600 cs 67% red 33% white ▪ PO Box 212 Stellenbosch 7599 ▪ victor@furstenburg.com ▪ www.furstenburg.com ▪ ***T 082·552·7063*** *F 465·2428*

There's a self-styled 'MoE' in charge of winemaking here. He's Jeff Wedgwood and, given his more than 45 years in the wine business, he certainly is a Man of Experience. As consultant to the Van Aswegen brothers of Furstenburg, who have legal and financial backgrounds, the avuncular Jeff W oversees the sourcing of top-notch wines in bulk from leading Stellenbosch estates for bottling under the Furstenburg label, for local and overseas markets

Cabernet Sauvignon ★★★ From old Stbosch vines, **03** herbaceous tea leaf/tobacco aromas & whiffs black cherry, dense tannined finish. 18 mths new Fr barrels. **Chardonnay** ★★ Aromas of stone fruit on **05**, golden straw colour with matching developed notes, some intensity. 15 year old Stbosch vines, barrel aged. – *MF*

Gallop Hill

Paarl ▪ Est 2001 ▪ 1stB 2002 ▪ Visits by appt ▪ Attractions/amenities: see intro ▪ Owners Dijonne du Preez & Jim Deane ▪ Winemaker Loftie Ellis ▪ Viti consultant Neil Malan ▪ 20 ha (cab, shiraz) ▪ ±50 tons 2 500 cs 100% red ▪ PO Box 7539 Stellenbosch 7599 ▪ info@gallophill.co.za ▪ www.gallophill.co.za ▪ ***T 869·8956*** *▪ F 869·8133*

'Gallop Hill maintains its aspiration to embody the perfect synergy between boutique-style wines and polo,' says GM Cronje van Heerden. Sceptical? Experience the smell of the soil on an exhilarating outride – as co-owner Dijonne du Preez did one fateful sunset from the adjoining stud farm, where he was honorary patron – and you'll understand. A variety of polo and horse-riding activities are offered (5-star accommodation available). Winetasting – by appointment – is in the new tasting area, and visitors are welcome to tour the new barrel cellar and view the owners' personal art collection. To follow: an indoor polo arena.

The First Chukka ★★★ **03** seamless blend shiraz, pinotage, cab (70/15/15). Warm baked plum note, hints leather, mint; ripe & fleshy, tannins suitably ripe to match; oak supportive rather than obvious – components matured separately 14 mths in used Fr/Am barrels. Ready, will keep 2-3 yrs. **Sauvignon Blanc** new ★★★ **04** a delicate example, with gentle tropical nuances to smooth rounded profile; silky mouthfeel despite firm acidity. Very polite, but lacks varietal punch. – *IvH*

Garob see Kango

Gecko Ridge

Owner Pernod-Ricard SA ▪ Winemaker Eben Rademeyer (Jun 2004) ▪ 50% red 50% white ▪ PO Box 1324 Stellenbosch 7599 ▪ vanda.davies@pernod-ricard-southafrica.com jaco.boonzaaier@pernod-ricard-southafrica.com ▪ ***T 880·8800*** *▪* ***F*** *880·8860*

This range, specifically aimed at the on-trade, is a big hit in Ireland and Canada. Though at present limited to two varietal bottlings, both labelled 'Reserve', the intention is to add other varieties to the line-up in the future.

Cabernet Sauvignon ★★★ **03** shows vintage's ripeness, generosity; lovely balanced red-berried drinkability. **Chardonnay** ★★★ **04** appealingly soft & rounded white peach flavour with spicy oak, some creamy lees, gently & supportively wooded. Both WO Brde Rvr Vlly. — *DH*

Gehot Bosch Winery

new

Bot River (see Elgin/Walker Bay map) ▪ Est 2005 ▪ Visits Tue-Sat 9.30–5 Sun 10–3 ▪ Closed Easter Fri & Dec 25 ▪ Owners Pierre & Paulette van den Bosch ▪ Winemaker Pierre van den Bosch ▪ 185 cs 100% red ▪ PO Box 1895 Hermanus 7200 ▪ vdbosch@lando.co.za ▪ ***T/F (028) 284·9409***

After emigrating from Zaire 14 years ago, Pierre and Paulette van den Bosch farmed fruit in Robertson, where Pierre also made tiny quantities of Cab. But their ultimate dream was to live near Hermanus – a vision they have now realised. Paulette, née Gehot, works as a property agent at this new Bot River landmark, while Pierre focuses on his handmade wines. They also stock 'selected wines at competitive prices' from local cellars and the Robertson Valley.

Cabernet Sauvignon ★★★★ Cheerful but not frivolous **03**, open tank-fermented, deftly packs lots of ripe red fruit around a firm armature. Spice/tobacco hints from 18 mths Fr oak. Lightish in feel: surprisingly low 12.5% alc, given ripeness & Rbtson fruit-origin. — *TJ*

Genesis see Omnia
GG Wines see Ernst & Co

Gilga Wines

Stellenbosch ▪ Est/1stB 1998 ▪ Closed to public ▪ Owner/winemaker/viticulturist Chris Joubert ▪ 700 cs 100% red ▪ PO Box 3 Vlottenburg 7604 ▪ chris.joubert@gilga.com ▪ www.gilga.com ▪ ***T 881·3475*** *▪ F 881·3248*

As 'a South African syrah (shiraz) specialist', Chris Joubert identifies single vineyards remarkable for their quality and individuality, buys in the grapes and then, in leased space and using the least possible intervention, makes 'terroir-specific world-class' wines. He also dons the viticulturist's hat on a couple of hectares of his own.

★★★★ **Syrah** Hand-crafted, deep-fruited wine forged by fine, tight-grained Fr oak into statement of note. Sultry, brooding **03** (★★★★★) growing in bottle; gentian hue & mulberry fruits entice but marbled tannins, stylish structure suggest true pleasure still yrs off. 13.8% alc. Burly **02** showed similar huge trellis of minerally, well-sprung tannin – & much higher alc (15.2% alc). 18 mths new/used wood. — *DS*

Glen Carlou

Paarl ▪ Est 1984 ▪ 1stB 1988 ▪ Tasting & sales Mon-Fri 8.45–4.45 Sat 9–12.30 ▪ Fee R10 ▪ Closed Easter Fri/Sun, Dec 25/26 & Jan 1; phone ahead on other pub hols ▪ Tours by appt ▪ Tasting/sale of home-made cheese (other attractions see intro) ▪ Owners The Hess Group (Switzerland) ▪ Winemaker David Finlayson, with Arco Laarman (1994/2000) ▪ Viticulturist Marius Cloete (2000), with Richard Camera ▪ 70 ha ▪ 900 tons 45 000 cs 60% red 40% white ▪ PO Box 23 Klapmuts 7625 ▪ welcome@glencarlou.co.za ▪ www.glencarlou.co.za ▪ ***T 875·5528*** *▪ F 875·5314*

There's a sure sense of achievement at this glossy winery, now wholly owned by former Finlayson family partner, Swiss-based The Hess Group. David Finlayson, MD, second-generation vintner and new dad to third-generation Callum, is enormously proud of having helped build GC up to its maximum production capabilities (65 000 cases). Volumes are evenly distributed across six to seven wines, with the scales tipped in favour of reds. The wines are neatly divided into three categories: Prestige (selected, single-vineyard/variety wines), Classic (for chardonnays, pinot, syrah, the Grand Classique red blend) and Contemporary (two all-purpose blends). While GC is renowned for its chardonnay and pinot, shiraz is particularly suited to the farm's warm sites and the Syrah is turning heads – and wowing the tasters for this Guide ahead of all the five star candidates. Visitors will see a rebuilt tasting room, incorporating an art museum housing top SA and African contemporary works.

★★★★ **Pinot Noir 04** (★★★☆) not as fine as pvs. Textbook pinot entry: perky raspberries, redcurrants, underbrush notes, with attractive oak spicing, but the palate more awkward, with tannins, ripe fruit not yet fully reconciled – could do so with time. 11 mths oak, 25% new. Elegant & charming **03** with ripe, seductive raspberry/cherry fruit profile, silky texture.

★★★★☆ **Syrah** Deep, complex, intriguing, individual wine with soupçons mourvèdre, viognier. Picks up accolades around the globe – & stunning **04** (★★★★★) our Wine of the Year. Same savoury styling as **03**, taken to a new level. Seductive layers of dark fruit, mocha-choc, *garrigue*, wood-char, in misleadingly accessible structure – resist for 6-8 yrs, there are still rewards in store. The balance is perfect: disciplined tannins, flavour opulence, yet sophisticated nuancing. Yr Fr/Am oak, 75% new. **03** also approachable in youth, with foundation for longer haul. SAA trophy, *Wine* ★★★★.

★★★★ **Grand Classique** Historically, flagship red of range. **02** (★★★★☆) step up; classic 5 Bdx varieties, but merlot dominating, as in **01**. Intense cedar-spiced cassis, cherries, with herbal, minty hints. Juicy, ripe, lots of vitality & interest; lithe deep-veined tannins, with expert oaking (2 yrs Fr, half new). Already delicious, but has 10+ yr ageing potential. 14.8% alc. *Wine* ★★★★, FCTWS gold. **01** reticent in youth, with taut tannins & firm acid, somewhat unknit.

★★★★ **Chardonnay** No restraint in **04** – a sumptuous melange of peach & citrus, roasted nuts, barley-sugar. With such fruit concentration, the dry finish surprises. Gorgeous now, can age 3-4 yrs. 10 mths oak, mainly Fr. **03** Also a keeper, with lemon-sharpened taut minerality on palate. **02** CWT gold; *WS* 91.

★★★★☆ **Chardonnay Reserve** Intense, rich & serious, under CWG Auction label for most of past 10 yrs. Last tasted was **02**.

★★★★☆ **Chardonnay Reserve 'Black Label'** Mainly for export to UK/US. Impressive **04** manages both lip-smacking palate freshness & intense fruit concentration, richness with ease. Yellow cling peaches, tangy grapefruit zest, nutty overlay. Seamlessly integrated oak (yr new Fr), ultra-long tail. Native yeast ferment. **03** with concentration, length, classic biscuit richness & sinewy structure. *Wine* ★★★★.

Tortoise Hill White ☺ ★★★ Unpretentious varying blend. Step-up **05** blend sauvignon, chard, viognier (65/30/5 mix) tastily meets quaffing wine brief; lemony freshness coupled with tangy guava/pear tones, brisk finish. Touch oak.

Tortoise Hill Red ★★★ **04** charms with fleshy youth, sweet ripe mulberries, plums, creamy spice ex-oak, textured finish. For easy-drinker, gets surprising care: 14 mths Fr/Am oak, some new. Blend cab, zin, shiraz, touriga, 50/20/15/15. **Zinfandel** Last tasted was **01** for CWG auction. **Devereux** Occasional chenin label; last was **00** ★★★☆. – *CR*

Glenhurst see Quoin Rock

Glenview Wines

*Cape Town ▪ Est/1stB 1998 ▪ Closed to public ▪ Owner Robin Marks ▪ Vini consultant Hein Hesebeck ▪ 7 000 cs 50% red 50% white ▪ PO Box 32234 Camps Bay 8040 ▪ bayexport@kingsley.co.za ▪ www.glenview.co.za ▪ **T 438·1080** ▪ F 438·3167*

Owner Robin Marks hasn't shifted focus: his aim is to please with soft, fruity easy-drinkers that amaze because they're so low-priced (think R26 for a merlot!). He laments the reluctance of supermarket retailers to list new and lesser-known brands: 'We're a wine-producing country but our wine departments are very poorly stocked by comparison with those in

European or British supers. I pity the housewife who wants to buy a bottle of wine with her weekly groceries!

Merlot ★★★ **04** food-friendly; mocha, bitter-choc hints, slender palate; for early consumption. Staved 6 mths. **Chenin Blanc** ★★★ Uncomplicated **05** tangy with fruit pastille aromas, bright melon fruit & crisp acidity, cheeky 14% alc. Both WO Paarl. — *CR*

GlenWood

Franschhoek ▪ Est/1stB 2000 ▪ Tasting & sales Mon-Fri 11-4.30 Sat/Sun (Sep-Apr only) 11-3 Pub hols (except Christian holy days) 11-3 ▪ Fee R10 ▪ Tours daily 11 ▪ BYO picnic ▪ Walks ▪ Owner Alastair G Wood ▪ Winemaker/viticulturist DP Burger (May 1992) ▪ 21.5 ha (chard, sauvignon, semillon) ▪ ±150 tons 4 500 cs own label 30% red 70% white ▪ PO Box 204 Franschhoek 7690 ▪ info@glenwoodvineyards.co.za ▪ www.glenwoodvineyards. co.za ▪ ***T 876·2044*** *▪* ***F*** *876·3338*

Viticulturist DP Burger grew into the winemaking job at this Robertsvlei Valley winery with the help of adviser Cathy Marshall, on a property which is unusual in 'enjoying' 2 000mm of rain per annum! Planting with vines necessitated the time-consuming and costly elimination of 45 ha of alien vegetation – a project overseen by Kirstenbosch consultant Fiona Powrie. The results of this hard work can be appreciated in the course of the extensive vineyard and cellar tour conducted daily during the season. Having committed to increasing production, the team are heartened by a 50% increase over only 4 harvests – in what seems to be an ever-smaller cellar! – with loyal consumers locally and new friends abroad both doing their bit to help.

★★★★ **Chardonnay Vignerons Reserve 04** (★★★★) quirky spirituous nose; hints orange liqueur & almond. Buttery palate sweetened by 4.4g/ℓ RS, finishes warm, lacks vibrancy of **03**, also seriously & well oaked (new Fr, 11 mths), balancing citrus freshness with structure. Swiss gold, *Wine* ★★★★.

Merlot new ★★★★ Star in the making. **04** medium-bodied with red fruit & refreshing acidity to match the bright aromas of plum & mineral. Soft, round tannins, attractive creamy mouthfeel. **Shiraz** ★★★ **04** from 9 yr old vines; similar to pvs in reticent nose & foursquare meaty palate, short tail; standout tannins need time to knit. 10 mths 2nd fill Fr oak. **Sauvignon Blanc** ★★★★ Grapes picked at 5am, kept under cover of dry ice to conserve freshness. These efforts reflected in **05**'s attractively cool blackcurrant/nettle bouquet, zippy but harmonious acidity, long mineral/grapefruit finish. **Semillon-Sauvignon Blanc** ★★★ Self-effacing **05** the ideal wine for delicate fish dishes, low 12% alc also pitched to not overpower food. Subtle lanolin whiffs, lively acidity, gravel-textured goodbye. Unoaked, semillon bunch-pressed. **Semillon Barrel Fermented** & **Semillon Unwooded** discontinued. — *CvZ*

Goat Roti see Goats do Roam
Goats do Roam see The Goats do Roam Wine Company

Goede Hoop Estate

Stellenbosch ▪ Est 1928 ▪ 1stB 1974 ▪ Tasting, sales & tours Mon-Thu 10-4 Fri 10-3 ▪ Open pub hols ▪ Tours, meals & refreshments by appt ▪ BYO picnic ▪ Conferencing for 20 people max ▪ Owner Pieter Bestbier ▪ Winemaker Carel Hugo (Dec 2002) ▪ Viticulturist Johan de Beer (Apr 2000) ▪ 80 ha (cab, carignan, malbec, merlot, pinotage, shiraz, chard, chenin, sauvignon) ▪ 11 000 cs + 90-100 000ℓ bulk 91% red 9% white ▪ PO Box 25 Kuils River 7579 ▪ goede@adept.co.za ▪ www.goedehoop.co.za ▪ ***T 903·6286*** *▪ F 906·1553*

Renewal is the name of the game here. Beginning, appropriately enough, in the vineyard, where several blocks have been uprooted and replanted – sauvignon on 'fantastic terroir' a particular source of excitement for Elsenburg-trained winemaker Carel Hugo. His sights are on gold and double-gold medals, hence the investment in more new wood and experimentation with combinations of yeasts. 'If you're not experimenting, you've already lost the fight,' he declares The cellar and packaging will both see an upgrade shortly. A sprucing-up and expansion of the conference facilities have already taken place, and the estate is now open on public holidays.

★★★★ **Cabernet Sauvignon 00** nose more open than pvs; balanced tannin, fine structure for ageing. **99** Xmas cake aromas over leafy, cassis notes, classic cigarbox notes, dry finish. 2nd/3rd fill Fr, 18 mths.

★★★★ **Merlot-Cabernet Sauvignon** ✓ Charming & delicious **01** juicy, ripe, accessible with plenty to give. **00**'s 60/40 blend shows spice & complexity; restrained wooding makes for plush style. 19 mths 2nd/3rd fill barrels.

★★★★ **Pinotage Private Collection** ✓ Limited release; last tasted was **01**, which exhibited a classical, almost burgundian tone.

Shiraz ★★★★ **02** interesting combo black fruit & white pepper, some savoury spicing; quite chewy/youthful, needs time; classy, has good credentials. **Pinotage** ★★★★ Current release **02** somewhat leaner than pvs, slight vegetal hint with savoury undertone. 8 mths oak, 2nd/3rd fill. **Domaine** ★★★ Lightish unwooded cab/carignan blend (53/47). **02** redcurrants & cherries, accessible weave, savoury & peppery fruit, firm dry finish. **Chardonnay** ★★★★ Quite a powerful wood presence in **03**, 10 mths new Fr barriques, 30% malo; lots of butterscotch & toast but good limy fruit backing too, rounded mouthfeel, richness. **Sauvignon Blanc** ★★★★ ✓ Expressive **05** with nettle, 'sea spray' whiffs, zesty acidity & pithy mid-palate. Granny Smith apple goodbye. All except Sauvignon tasted mid-2004.—*CR/CvZ*

Goede Moed see Baarsma
Goedgenoegen see Baarsma

Goedvertrouw Estate

Walker Bay ▪ Est 1990 ▪ 1stB 1991 ▪ Visits by appt ▪ Home-cooked meals & accommodation by appt ▪ Play area for children ▪ Farm produce ▪ Small conferences ▪ Conservation area ▪ Small art gallery ▪ Owner/winemaker/viticulturist Elreda Pillmann ▪ 8 ha (cab, pinot, chard, sauvignon) ▪ 70% red 30% white ▪ PO Box 37 Bot River 7185 ▪ Josiasfredin@mweb.co.za ▪ ***T/F (028) 284·9769***

'I'm still surviving,' twinkles Elreda Pillmann, whose rosy cheeks and warm heart would surely make her the best candidate for the role of fairy godmother in Cape wine. In fact, her hands-on winemaking career began just three years ago after the death of her beloved husband Arthur. Now well into her 60s, she laughs when asked about her winemaking philosophy: 'I wish I knew!' But she pays tribute where she believes it's due: 'My winged as well as two-legged angels work very, very hard. Thanks to them.' In particular, they're (all?) working hard to turn Goedvertrouw into a biodiverse estate.

★★★★ **Cabernet Sauvignon** Native yeast-fermented (as are stablemates), matured ±yr seasoned Fr oak. **03** (sample) dense, ripe cassis fruit swathed in grainy tannins. **04** (★★★) leaner & more restrained; firm acid & dusty finish; unknit, needs yr/2 to marry.

Pinot Noir ★★★ Barrel sample **04** more 'correct' than pvs; fragrant mineral bouquet, hints game & damp earth; elegant, firm finish redolent of freshly baked bread. Much lighter (12.7% alc) than pvs. Yr in old vats. **Chardonnay** Last sampled was **01** (★★★); next probably the **06**. **Sauvignon Blanc** Individual style, more 'white wine' than 'sauvignon'; **03** (★★★) was last tasted. **05** not ready. **Pardoemps** ★★★ Limited stock remains of once-off individual **03** blend pinot, pinotage, cab (50/25/25); with eucalyptus-spiced plum & strawberry notes. Onomatopoeic name a favourite of the late Arthur Pillmann's.—*MM*

Goedverwacht Estate

Robertson ▪ 1stB 1994 ▪ Tasting & sales Mon-Fri 8.30–4.30 Sat 10–2 ▪ Closed Easter Fri/Sun, Dec 25 & Jan 1 ▪ Tours by appt ▪ Snacks served with wine tasting; also BYO picnic ▪ Owner Jan du Toit & Sons (Pty) Ltd ▪ Winemaker Jan du Toit ▪ Viticulturist Pieter Venter (Dec 2002), advised by Francois Viljoen ▪ 110 ha (cab, merlot, shiraz, chard, colombard, sauvignon) ▪ 1 500 tons 40 000 cs own label 43% red 50% white 7% rosé ▪ Exported as Soek die Geluk, Pier 42, Thys Drift & Ama Ulibo ▪ PO Box 128 Bonnievale 6730 ▪ goedverwachtestate@lando.co.za ▪ www.goedverwacht.co.za ▪ ***T (023) 616·3430*** *▪ F (023) 616·2073*

Determined not to be overtaken by corporate players with money to burn – that's owner/winemaker Jan du Toit. He's also driven to excel. 'I know very well that Goedverwacht's philosophy of producing value for money wine is the right one, but we need to win good awards.' And they are: the maiden (03) Acre of Stone Shiraz, for instance, was selected as one of 20 Great SA Wines by *Decanter*. After a 2005 harvest plagued by nature's vagaries, Jan dT remains stoic. 'The older you get, the more you realise that you have to accept the things you cannot change.'

★★★★ **Triangle** ✓ Cab f (04) joins merlot/cab from **03** (★★★★) in 49/41/10 blend to authenticate new name (pvsly 'Cab-Merlot'). Sturdy, ripe, plentiful wood-laced berry fruits. Gentle tannins, fresh acid spine, spurt sweetness on finish. **02** 60/40 blend with floral touch & hint coffee; 14.9% alc; yr Fr/Am oak.

Shiraz Rosé ☺ ★★★ Delicious rose-tinged pink. **05** brims with fresh raspberries & cherries. Good presence, sufficiently dry to make versatile food partner. **Great Expectations Chardonnay** ☺ ★★★ Wood-influenced just enough to highlight expressive mineral/lime freshness. Sample **05** big, ripe, but balanced; best during first yr. **Crane White Colombard** ☺ ★★★ As zesty, fruity & enjoyably quaffable as any self-respecting colombard should be. **05** stimulatingly fresh, moreishly dry.

Maxim Cabernet Sauvignon new ★★★★ From south-facing single vyd; classy intro to **03** via ripe mulberry scents, quality cedary Fr oak. Pliant tannins, balanced freshness; good fruit ultimately diminished by finishing sweet impression, slight glow from 14.8% alc. May mellow over yr/2. **Crane Red Merlot** ★★★ Plump, juicy, with soft tannins. Preview **05** bright plum/choc flavour & hint oak. Friendly fruit lifted by soupçon sugar. **Acre of Stone Shiraz** ★★★ **04**'s well-judged toasty, sweet vanilla Am oak flavours, fruit-flattering trace sugar, will undoubtedly prove consumer hit. Attractive red fruits/lilies nose suggests more serious possibilities as vines mature. 14%+ alc. **The Good Earth Sauvignon Blanc** ★★★ **05** forward guava, tropical tones. Varietal briskness trimmed by touch sugar. Single riverside vyd, 12 yrs old. —*AL*

Goeie Tye see Rooiberg
Golden Kaan see KWV International
Golden Triangle see Stellenzicht
Gordon's Bay see Zidela

Goudini Wines

Rawsonville (see Worcester map) ▪ Est 1948 ▪ Tasting & sales Mon-Fri 8-5 Sat 9.30-12.30 ▪ Closed Easter Fri-Mon, Dec 25/26, Jan 1 ▪ Coffee shop ▪ Conferencing ▪ Gifts ▪ Owners 40 members ▪ Winemakers Hennie Hugo & Dominique Waso (Dec 1984/Oct 2001), with Ruaan Terblanche (Nov 2001) ▪ Viti advisor Hendrik Myburgh (Nov 2001) ▪ 1 040 ha (merlot, ruby cab, shiraz, chard, chenin, semillon) ▪ 20 000 tons 33 000 cs own label 45% red 45% white 10% rosé ▪ Ranges for customers: Safiki (UK), Hummelhof (Germany) ▪ PO Box 132 Rawsonville 6845 ▪ winesales@goudiniwine.co.za ▪ www.goudiniwine.co.za ▪ ***T (023) 349·1090*** *▪ F (023) 349·1988*

This co-op was one of the first in SA to experiment with Pera thermoflash technology, which briefly heats the red wine must to extract more of the colour and 'friendly' tannins available, as well as rendering the wine more biologically stable. They're sufficiently enamoured to have upgraded the system in their bid to bring value-for-money wines to market. Winemaker Dominique Waso says much hard work in both cellar and vineyard has gone into improving quality, and feels that his personal benchmark – double-gold recognition – is now more within reach than ever.

Reserve range new

Ruby Cabernet ★★★ **04** (sample) has winemakers excited – 'potentially our best ruby ever'. Does indeed look promising: clear & generous varietal expression (sweet ripe plum, touch stalk/thatch), well massaged tannins/oak (1st-3rd fill, 20% Am). **Chardonnay Barrel Fermented** ★★ **03** last yr appeared to be ageing rapidly, though still a pleasant drink. 100% new oak, 15% Am, 4 mths.

Goudini range

Pinotage ★★☆ Mellow & tasty casual quaff. **04** plummy, soft, with gentle fruity tannins. **Shiraz** ★★☆ **04** (sample) shows potential; good peppery varietal fruit, healthy tannins. Mix Am/Fr (60/40) barrels, none new. **Ruby Cabernet-Merlot** ★★☆ Oak-brushed **04**, again 60/40 blend, ripe plum fruit, hint ruby cab stalkiness; dry, mildly grippy tannins. **Blanc de Noir** ★☆ Partridge-eye-pink **04**; light, honeyed, some mouthfeel from 10g/ℓ sugar. **Unwooded Chardonnay** ★★ **04** last ed showed ripe peach & pineapple flavours; bit plodding: could do with more acidity to enliven big alc (14.3%), sugar (±5g/ℓ). **Chenin Blanc** ★☆ Customer-driven change from off- to semi-dry from **05**, easy, lightly tropical, for drinking soon. **Sauvignon Blanc** ★☆ **05** fresh, pleasant & drinkable dry white. **Natural Sweet** ★★☆ Pvs labelled 'Special Late Harvest'; **05** still from chenin; gorgeous pineapple aroma/flavour, crisp acidity for balanced, fresh profile. **Brut Sparkling** ★★☆ Reliable carbonated sparkling from sauvignon; **05** racy 'brut' palate; good appetiser. Features 'shrink-sleeve' labelling – 'an SA first'. **Hanepoot** ★★★☆ **02** last ed was delicious & velvety, with intense muscat & raisin aromas. 17% alc. **00**, in 250ml, not tasted this yr. **Port** ★★★ **02** unbottled at press time. **01** with traditional low fortification (18%), last ed showed good bottle-maturity.

Umfiki range

All **NV**, some also in 3ℓ bag-in-box. **Merlot** new ★☆ Unwooded, with big dry tannins & hint of plum. Needs a food foil. **Pinotage-Cinsaut** ★★☆ Last yr noted as delightful quaffer, full of strawberries & plums, glides down effortlessly. **Clairette Blanche-Colombar** ★☆ Slight tropical tone, touch of acidity adds liveliness. **Dry White** new ★ Simple but clean all-sorts blend, with muted tropical fruit. *— DH*

Goudveld Winery

Free State ▪ Tasting & sales Mon-Fri 8-6 Sat by appt ▪ Tours on request ▪ Conferences & receptions for 100-120 guests ▪ Owner Jan Alers ▪ Winemaker/viticulturist Merkil Alers (1985) ▪ 15 ha ▪ 120 tons 1 000 cs own label ▪ PO Box 1091 Welkom 9460 ▪ ***T/F (057) 352·8650***

No update available on this winery; contact details from previous edition.

Goue Vallei see Citrusdal Cellars

Graça

Vinho Verde-inspired lightly spritzy swiggers, the original white version still among SA's top-selling cork-closed wines. By Distell; exported as Blouberg.

Graça ★★☆ Semi-dry crowd-pleaser, anytime-light (12% alc); hay & grassy freshness from sauvignon (60%, with semillon, crouchen), ends with sweet-sour tang. **Rosé** ★★ Slightly sweeter, less zippy version; dollop pinotage providing the blush & dusty cherry goodbye. Low alc (±11%). Also in 375 ml. Both NV; WO W Cape. *— CvZ*

Graceland Vineyards

Stellenbosch ▪ Est 1997 ▪ 1stB 1998 ▪ Visits by appt only ▪ Fee R30 ▪ Closed pub hols ▪ Two-bedroom B&B + self-catering vyd cottage ▪ Owners Paul & Susan McNaughton ▪ Winemaker/viticulturist Susan McNaughton (2001) ▪ 10 ha (cab, merlot, shiraz) ▪ 60 tons 4 300 cs 100% red ▪ PO Box 7066 Stellenbosch 7599 ▪ graceland@iafrica.com ▪ www.gracelandvineyards.com ▪ ***T 881·3121*** *(admin)* ***881·3394*** *(cellar) ▪ F 881·3341*

When it comes to wine, we should analyse less and drink more. That's owner Paul McNaughton's philosophy, and one which wife Susan puts into practice in the vineyard and cellar: 'We strive to produce a wine that when you open a bottle, you finish the bottle, as opposed to over-extracted wine that you can only drink one glass of at a time.' With this outlook, they sailed through the tricky 2005 harvest that 'led to a shortened life expectancy for some winemakers'. They're also confident this is now a nice self-sustaining family business. 'At least until the next shock like a wine lake, a strong rand or global warming,' they laugh. 'This is farming after all – it's riskier than going to the casino!'

★★★★ **Three Graces** Cellar's designated flagship a stylefully named & packaged melange of the varietal trio below. **03**, dramatic improvement on maiden **02** (★★★), shows restrained though ample blackcurrant/mulberry fruit; oak is evident but successfully integrates components (cab 59%, shiraz 22%, merlot 19%) into food-friendly whole; persistent spiciness, succulence, unlike overly restrained **02**.

★★★★ **Cabernet Sauvignon** Open vat fermented, traditional punch-down vinification; **03** big step up on pvs: ripe black fruit aromas, silken tannins sweetened by 3.5% shiraz; sumptuous though not flamboyant; 16 mths in oak, mainly Fr, unfiltered/fined. More seductive than light, hard-fruited **02** (★★★).

Merlot ★★★☆ More opulent **03** has smidgens cab, shiraz (each 4%); ripe plum aromas, soft tannins, sweet mid-palate with lingering fruitiness; distinctly better than leaner, more obviously oaked pvs. **Shiraz** ★★★☆ **03** soft peppery notes, marzipan whiffs, Am oak adding richness/spice; riper, fuller than more austere **02**. *—MF*

Graham Beck Wines

Franschhoek/Robertson ▪ Est 1983 ▪ 1stB 1991 ▪ Owner Graham Beck ▪ Viticulturist Marco Ventrella (Sep 2004) ▪ ISO 14001 certified ▪ market@grahambeckwines.co.za ▪ www.grahambeckwines.com ▪ Robertson Estate: Tasting & sales Mon-Fri 9–5 Sat & 1st Sun of mnth 10–3 ▪ Closed Easter Fri/Sun, Dec 25/26 & Jan 1 ▪ Tours by appt ▪ Cellarmaster Pieter Ferreira (Aug 1990) ▪ Winemaker Irene Waller (Dec 2004) ▪ 156 ha (cab, merlot, pinot, sangiovese, shiraz, chard, viognier) ▪ 1 300 tons ▪ 72% red 11% white 17% MCC ▪ PO Box 724 Robertson 6705 ▪ ***T (023) 626·1214*** *▪ F (023) 626·5164 ▪ Franschhoek Estate: Tasting & sales Mon-Fri 9–5 Sat 10–4 ▪ Closed Easter Fri/Sun, Dec 25/26 & Jan 1 ▪ Tours by appt ▪ Winemaker Erika Obermeyer (Jan 2005) ▪ 192 ha (cabs s/f, merlot, petit v, pinotage, shiraz, sauvignon, viognier) ▪ 1 200 tons ▪ PO Box 134 Franschhoek 7690 ▪* ***T 874·1258*** *▪ F 874·1712*

A season of changes this year in a team well known for its stability: Erika Obermeyer was appointed winemaker at the Franschhoek cellar; Robertson cellarmaster Pieter Ferreira hired top Stellenbosch graduate Irene Waller as his assistant – this former teacher and accountant's first winemaking job at age 35, though she's had plenty of hands-on experience in Stellenbosch and Australia. Very sadly, young marketing dynamo Peter Hafner died after only two months here, already having won huge admiration for his enthusiasm and fresh approach. Promotion to viticulturist has pleased Italian ex night-club boss Marco Ventrella no end, with his consummate commitment to the vineyards. And, as if to celebrate another successful year in the valley of (sparkling) wine and roses, Ferreira lived up to his nickname 'Bubbles' by winning the Diners Club winemaker of the Year award for his Blanc de Blanc.

Single Vineyard range

★★★★☆ **The Ridge Syrah** Icon wine named after its Rbtsn vyd. With finesse & style, **03** doesn't put a foot wrong; prosciutto, black plums, mocha choc held in place by an elegant, wonderfully harmonious structure. 14 mths oaking, 60/40 new Am/Fr, lays groundwork for 6–8 yr ageing potential. **02**, ex-cask, an iron fist in velvet glove. **01** *Wine* ★★★★.

★★★★ **Coffeestone Cabernet Sauvignon** (Renamed from 'Cornerstone'.) From Firgrove, Stbosch 'coffee stone' (decomposed granite). **03** shows admirable concentration, cassis/blackberries, liquorice spice, smoky depths. Serious oaking evident as steely backbone, cloaked by lush fruit. An infant, 10 yr development ahead. **02** svelte structure, well judged oaking (these 15 mths, mainly new Fr).

★★★★ **The Old Road Pinotage** From 1963-planted, low-yielding Frhoek vines. **02** shows its class in sinuous structure, complex interweaving of sweet & savoury spices with concentrated red berry fruit, easily assimilated yr Fr/Am barriques. VG, Pinotage Top Ten. **01**, with 5% cab, remarkable fruit intensity, richness, depth. Built for longer haul: 8+ yrs.

★★★★ **Lonehill Chardonnay** new Bold & showy **03**, roasted nuts, peach profile; silky texture, long & full-flavoured finish. Bunch-pressed, fermented/10 mths Fr barrels, 80% new. WO Rbtsn.

★★★★ **Peasant's Run Sauvignon Blanc** new **05** (sample, so potential rating) awakens the senses with piercing capsicum, nettly character, mouth-tingling limy tang. Intense, uncompromising, impressive. WO Dbnville.

★★★★ **Rhona Muscadel** Not made every year, only released when fruit & spirit integrated, so glorious, perfumed **99** only followed now by **01**. The care shows: sumptuous apricot, honeysuckle & sultana aromas, flavours; grippy alcohol lift to the 145g/ℓ sweetness – remarkably easy to drink. 16.7% alc. 500ml.

Barrel Select Range

★★★★☆ **The William** Named for a Beck grandson. Barrel-selected 60/40 blend cab, pinotage, vinified separately at the Rbtsn & Frhoek cellars prior to blending. **03** rich dark fruit, meat extract, lashings oak spice. Sleekly muscular, plenty more to give; drink now if you must, but should develop beautifully 8+ yrs. WO Coastal. **02** (★★★★) was less impressive, ripe, sinewy tannins needed time to meld, soften. These yr oak: Fr (cab)/Am (pinotage).

★★★★ **The Joshua** Adopts Beck's second name. Cellar flagship, with price to match. 7% viognier in maiden **02** – varieties crushed, fermented together. CWT gold. 9% infusion in finer **03**, not to soften but to bring perfume, more complexity, à la Côte Rôtie. Tasted last ed, very ripe (enormous 15.5% alc) sour cherry, roasted spice flavours. Yr Fr/Am barrels, 60/40. Good in youth, will develop 6+ yrs. WO Frhoek.

★★★★ **The Andrew** new Cellar's first bdx-style blend, another Beck grandson behind name. Serious, classy rather than flashy. **03** has cassis, savoury spice & meat extract complexity, polished, sleekly appealing texture from supple tannins & very good length. Yr Fr oak, 60% new. Cab, merlot, cab f in 41/35/24 blend. WO Coastal.

Graham Beck range

★★★★ **Cabernet Sauvignon** Serious & classic **01** tasted few yrs back: pulpy blackcurrant intro, cedary, herbaceous nuances; elegant, firm ripe tannins. 14 mths oak, half new. WO Coastal (as Shiraz below).

★★★★ **Shiraz 03** (not retasted) with wild berries, smoky spice; seamlessly integrated fruit & tannin. Tiny portions tannat, mourvèdre, viognier for added complexity. 13 mths mostly Am oak. 15% alc. Can age 3-4 yrs, but tempting in youth.

★★★★ **Blanc de Blancs** Brut MCC from chardonnay, amongst Cape's best reputed. Lots of depth & interest on **00** (★★★★★): creamy mousse, invigorating vein of freshness, & honey-biscuit, citrus peel, apple pie flavours that stay till the last drop. 50% of bunch-pressed grapes fermented in oak; ±4 yrs on lees. Delicious **99** also had impressive concentration, vibrant freshness, creamy mousse & long full-flavoured finish. *Wine* ★★★★. Diners Club Winemaker of Year. WO Rbtsn, as is Brut below.

★★★★ **Brut** Stylish **NV** MCC, for many the winery's hallmark. Lively, with chardonnay's lemony freshness, gentle yeasty overlay from 2 yrs on lees. Pinot (46%) plumps up body, lends flavour. 20-25% 'reserve' wine added for consistency. *Wine* ★★★★.

★★★★ **Brut Rosé** Tasty, characterful **03** combines brioche richness with fruity charm of fresh-picked red berries. 20 mths on lees. Light-textured 12% alc. Pvs (was **NV**) also had delicacy & finesse. *Wine* ★★★★. These 70/30 pinot/chard, crushed together, 30 mths on lees.

Merlot ★★★ Blend of wines vinified at both cellars. **04** in restrained, cool fruit style: violets, fresh red berries, herbaceous thread & juicy palate in light tannin framework. **Pinotage** ★★★☆ Sunshiny, unambiguous pinotage. **04** perfectly ripe red berry fruit & good appetite appeal. 13 mths Am oak, third new, provides sinewy structure, cedar spicing. Pepped up by 5% each cab, tannat. WO Coastal. **Shiraz-Cabernet Sauvignon** new ★★★ UK only. White pepper tones over soft plummy fruit in **04**; supportive tannins help the accessibility, add spice, interest. 9 mths seasoned Fr/Am oak. **Railroad Red** ★★★☆ **04** harmoniously blends 60/40 shiraz, cab: layers of fynbos, cherries, smoky spice combine in medium-weight, attractively accessible structure. Lightly oaked. **Pinno** ★★☆ **04** unwooded & fruit-focused pinotage: vibrant wild berry, rhubarb tones, offering undemanding, juicy quaffability. A chillable red. **Pinno Rosé** ★★☆ Light (12.5% alc) & very pretty **05**; dayglo cerise, young pinotage red berry/herbaceous tones & easy off-dry drinkability. WO Rbtsn. **Chardonnay**

★★★★ Curvaceous **04** has buttered toast, citrus peel & underlying tropical tones, with well integrated oak. Rates high on the drinkability scale. 6 mths Fr, 40% new. WO Rbtsn. **Chardonnay-Viognier** new ★★★★ UK only. **05** something different (& nice): unwooded 80/20 combo where viognier's aromas, jasmine/peach pip, play bigger role than expected & chardonnay supplies structure, texture. **Sauvignon Blanc** ★★★★ Zesty, satisfying **05** reductively made (with 12% semillon) to capture variety's cut-grass lime peel freshness on nose & palate in bone dry, light-textured (12.5% alc). WO Coastal, as is ... **Viognier** ★★★★ **04** sample (not retasted) showed early promise. Silky texture, long mouth-filling finish, 50% deftly oaked allowing fruit character to shine through. **Waterside Chardonnay** ★★★ Pvsly just 'Waterside'. Unwooded **05** with gentle tropical fruit, including peaches, well supported by smooth texture, food-friendly acidity. **Pinno Chardonnay** new ★★★ USA only. Unoaked chard meant for earlier enjoyment. **05** peachy flavours, round & ripe, given lift by crisp acidity. All wines WO W Cape except where noted. — *CR*

Grande Provence

Franschhoek ▪ Est 2004 ▪ Tasting & sales daily: summer 10–6; winter 9–5 ▪ Fee R12 ▪ Closed Easter Fri & Dec 25 ▪ Tours by appt ▪ Grande Provence Restaurant ▪ 'Owners Cottage' accommodation ▪ Art gallery ▪ Winemaker/viticulturist Jaco Marais (Oct 2003), advised by Kevin Watt (2001) ▪ 22 ha (cab, merlot, shiraz, chenin, sauvignon) ▪ 250 tons 22 000 cs own labels 35% red 55% white 10% rosé ▪ ISO 14001 certified ▪ PO Box 102 Franschhoek 7690 ▪ winesales@grandeprovence.co.za ▪ www.grandeprovence.co.za ▪ ***T 876·8600*** *▪ F 876·8601*

A change of name from Agusta back to the original Grande Provence (single-varietal wines and a future flagship Bordeaux-style blend to be marketed under the namesake label) is just one of the sweeping changes at this Franschhoek property. An international team, including New Zealand-based interior designer Virginia Fisher, was called in to revamp all key facilities, from the tasting room to the Owner's Cottage. The result is a confident and stylish blend of 'modern industrial', ethnic and historic Cape Dutch. The cellar remains an integral part of Grande Provence, and winemaker Jaco Marais holds his own here: 'I do the basics correctly, pay attention to detail — and never stop experimenting. I'm a real mad scientist during harvest!'

Following all tasted as samples: **Cabernet Sauvignon 04** very well put together: layers of intense dark fruit, brambleberries, mulberries & some minty nuances, lots of oak as befits wine of this class. Tannins ripe, accessible, but give it time, up to 6 yrs, to show true worth. 16 mths Fr barrels. Own grapes/EW. Possible ★★★★. **Shiraz** ★★★★ **04** explores the savoury spectrum: smoky, gamey, underbrush, roasted spice, resting on a bed of firm but ripe tannins. Already drinking beautifully, has further 4–5 rewarding yrs ahead. 15 mths 80/20 Fr, Am oak. Own grapes/EW. **Chardonnay 04** (sample) still in development, difficult to rate. Some building blocks already in place: lemon/lime character, zinging freshness for food compatibility, but oak is dominant, could show better in finished wine. Frhoek grapes. **Sauvignon Blanc** ★★★★ **05** (sample) classic sauvignon character: grapefruit, nettly aromas, already pointing you towards food, but the minerality & elegant freshness is delicious enough for solo enjoyment too. W Cape vyds.

Angels Tears range

Red ☺ ★★★ This guide's first 'Superquaffer of the Year'. Entente cordiale between merlot & cab; amazing quality at the price. Fleshy fruit given 6 mths oak treatment (80/20 Fr, Am) to add complexity, nutty/savoury nuances, backbone. Silky, delicious.

All in this range **NV**, WO W Cape. **Pink** ★★★ From chenin with dollop pinotage, off-dry. Friendly, likeable, with no pretensions; jelly baby aromas/flavours & enough juiciness & zest to drink easily, well. **White** ★★★ Something of a benchmark in off-dry, fruity white genre. Latest works its chenin/hanepoot charms with grapey, musk-sweet aromatics, softly rounded drinkability. Uncomplicated summer quaffer. **Count Agusta** & **Agusta** ranges discontinued. — *CR*

Grand Mousseux

With culling of the Vin Sec, this dependable, all-occasions sparkling brand now features only **Vin Doux** ★★ Carbonated NV summer sipper. Subdued tropical fruit & teasing honeyed sweetness refreshed by busy bubbles. By Distell. — *CvZ*

Grangehurst Winery

Stellenbosch (see Helderberg map) ▪ 1stB 1992 ▪ Tasting & sales Mon-Fri 9-4 Sat & pub hols 'take a chance' 9-4 ▪ Self-catering guest cottage ▪ Owner Grangehurst Winery (Pty) Ltd ▪ Winemaker Jeremy Walker, with Gladys Brown (1992/2002) ▪ Viti consultant Thys Greeff ▪ ±14 ha (cab, merlot, mourvèdre, petit v, pinotage, shiraz) ▪ 50-60 tons 3 200-3 700 cs 100% red ▪ PO Box 206 Stellenbosch 7599 ▪ winery@grangehurst.co.za ▪ www.grangehurst.co.za ▪ ***T 855·3625*** *▪ F 855·2143*

Jeremy Walker's success as a cab and pinotage exponent, perhaps most visibly at the CWG Auction, attracted a joint-venture partner in the form of Cape Town ophthalmologist, John Hill. In 2000 they bought a 13ha vineyard just outside Stellenbosch ('top-quality soil on west and south-west facing slopes'), and set about establishing mainly Bordeaux reds plus smatterings of pinotage, shiraz and mourvèdre. Amid great anticipation, last season the first 14 tons of cab were harvested from the Sunset Vineyard. Although still on the small side of the projected 70 ton target set for 2008, JW is well satisfied with the quality of the young wines. The venture will supply half of Grangehurst's target production; the balance will continue to come from the selected Stellenbosch vineyards currently supplying the winery.

★★★★★ **Nikela** 'Tribute', in Xhosa, to Jeremy Walker's late parents. Blend cab (50+%), pinotage, merlot, from 4 Stbosch areas. Deep-coloured, engaging **00** (38% pinotage) with red berries over ripely firm tannins. Should keep happily 5+ yrs yet — bonus to consumers in comparatively late release. **99** (★★★★), with 32% pinotage, also bright sweet red fruit, solid tannins, but a little less substantial. These ±2 yrs oak, including some Am. Notes from last ed for all of these except CWG Blend.

★★★★☆ **Cabernet Sauvignon-Merlot 00** authoritative & satisfying, sombrely rich fruit well balanced with grippy tannins, savoury acid, big 14.2% alc. No hurry to drink. 27 mths oak (mostly Fr) finely integrated. 80% cab, as was **99**, with sweet blackcurrant fruit. Grapes for these mostly ex Hldrberg, Firgrove.

★★★★ **Pinotage** Serious-minded, restrained version, with splash cab; grapes from own, Hldrberg, Firgrove vyds. As with all these, fermented in open *kuipe*. Pleasing soft sweet fruit of **00** layered on big dry tannins; greater harmony to hopefully come. 14 mths oak, quarter Am. No **99**. As with all above wines, also available in magnums.

★★★★ **CWG Auction Reserve Cabernet Sauvignon** Since **95**, the main outlet for Walker's Cab. In youth, oak dominated firm, supple **01**, masking the fruit which undoubtedly there. Like **00**, ripe & balanced with well-focused acidity, wanting few yrs to reveal its best. ±22 mths Fr oak, 80% new.

★★★★ **CWG Auction Cape Reserve Blend** (Pvsly simply 'Blend') Flavourful, exciting, well & elegantly structured **01** was a happy ménage à trois of cab, pinotage, shiraz (49/37/14). Next-up **03** (★★★★☆) more equally built, pinotage just ahead. Plenty of spicy cedar, tobacco on offer, but also delicious sweet red berry/plum fruit, making up a characterful, serious whole supported by ripe tannins, untroubling 14.8% alc. Components matured apart 20 mths, together 6 more in mostly Fr, 13% Am, oak. Just 900 bottles. Like all Walker's wines, genuinely dry. Will grow easily 5+ yrs.

★★★★ **Chairman's Reserve Cabernet Sauvignon 00** was fine, handsome bottling mostly for a private organisation. Attractively fresh bouquet blackcurrant, with spicy cedar. Well structured, balanced. 27 mths Fr/Am (75/25) wood. — *TJ*

Green Wine see Southern Cape Vineyards
Griekwaland West Co-op see Douglas
Groblershoop see Oranjerivier Wine Cellars
Groenekloof see Darling Cellars, Neil Ellis, Omnia, Woolworths

Groenland

Stellenbosch ▪ Est 1932 ▪ 1stB 1997 ▪ Tasting & sales Mon-Fri 10-4 Sat & pub hols 10-1 ▪ Fee for large groups ▪ Closed Easter Fri/Sun, Dec 25, Jan 1 ▪ Meals for 20-60 by appt; also BYO picnics ▪ Tours by appt ▪ Conference & reception facilities ▪ Owner Kosie Steenkamp ▪ Winemaker Kosie Steenkamp, with Piet Steenkamp (1975/2001) ▪ Viticulturists Kosie & Piet Steenkamp ▪ 152 ha (cab, merlot, pinotage, shiraz, chard, chenin, sauvignon) ▪ 1 100 tons 6 250 cs own label + 75 000 blts ▪ 100% red ▪ PO Box 4 Kuils River 7579 ▪ steenkamp@groenland.co.za ▪ www.groenland.co.za ▪ ***T 903·8203*** *▪ F 903·0250*

Marié Steenkamp, qualified winemaker involved with marketing and sales of this family winery's produce, has been lured away to lecture at Elsenburg College, prompting her father, owner/winemaker Kosie Steenkamp, to appoint a new PRO in the person of Maritsa Brand. He and his son Piet, viticulturist and winemaking assistant, have a strict policy of not bottling or releasing wines which are not up to their high standard, so the fact that they're considering Reserve versions of their 04 Shiraz, Cab and Antoinette Marié blend suggests their appraisal of the vintage is very high indeed, much more so than hot, dry 2005, which they rate as 'average'.

Antoinette Marié ★★★★ Usually a 60/40 blend of varieties below, **03** has less cab, dollop merlot giving 51/40/9 configuration. Crafted to be taken seriously; all three varieties contributing vibrant fruit on nose & palate, & to palate weight, structure. For cellaring 3-5 yrs. Yr Fr/Am oak. **Cabernet Sauvignon** ★★★ Herbaceous **03** with firm yet ripe tannins, seems to lack the fruity flesh of its stablemates, needs yr/2 to soften. 12 mths Fr oak. **Shiraz** ★★★★ **03** continues overt New World styling. In-your-face red fruit & sweet vanilla wafts, juicy/lively palate. Yr 80% Am/20% Fr. Very amenable now but has structure to improve 3-5 yrs. Untasted **Cape Port 01** also available from the cellar door. — *CR*

Groot Constantia Estate

Constantia ▪ Est 1685 ▪ 1stB 1688 ▪ Tasting & sales daily 9-6 (Dec-Apr) 9-5 (May-Nov) ▪ Fee R25, R30 (tasting & tour) ▪ Closed Easter Fri, Dec 25 & Jan 1 ▪ Tours on hour (large groups plse book ahead), every hour 10-4 (summer); 10, 11 & 3 (winter); or by appt. Also 'theme' tours/tastings ▪ Simon's at Groot Constantia Restaurant ▪ T 794·1143; or BYO picnic ▪ Tourgroups ▪ Gift shop ▪ Conferencing ▪ Walks ▪ Museum ▪ Managed by Groot Constantia ('Section 21' company) ▪ Winemaker Boela Gerber (Jan 2001), with Nadia Cilliers (Aug 2004) ▪ Viticulturists Callie Bröcker & Boela Gerber, advised by Johan Pienaar (1996) ▪ ±90 ha (12 varieties, r/w) ▪ 525 tons 40 000 cs 60% red 40% white ▪ Private Bag X1 Constantia 7848 ▪ enquiries@grootconstantia.co.za ▪ www.grootconstantia.co.za ▪ ***T 794·5128*** *▪ F 794·1999*

'I absolutely love the European approach to winemaking,' says Boela Gerber, who recently spent a harvest in Rioja, Spain. 'I was amazed how jacked up the Spanish are – incredible technology and innovation, mixed with centuries of history and culture. It is a lifestyle.' The same could probably be said of Groot Constantia, which celebrated its 320th anniversary by … building a new laboratory. 'Very excited about that. A lab is more of a necessity than a luxury these days,' Gerber says. Environment friendliness, an emphasis here, is getting a fillip from the Constantia area's pioneering coordinated strategy to control the spread of mealy bug, by setting pheromone traps and introducing large numbers of critter-chomping ladybirds. 'Seems very effective,' says Gerber, 'we had good results after the first season.'

Gouverneurs range

★★★★ **Reserve** Modern bdx-style blend, **03** sees addition of malbec for 60/30/10 cab, merlot, malbec configuration. Cedar, mint, mocha overlay to blackcurrant/red berry, fine tannic grip. More classic & elegant than pvs, promises fine development over 5-7 yrs. 18 mths new Fr barrels impart obvious oak tone in youth. No **02**. Unfiltered, as are most of the premium reds.

★★★★ **Merlot** Opaque **01**, last ed showed cassis & spicy oak on nose. Lithe & graceful, rich warm fruit; savoury, ripely soft tannins; big 14.5% alc. 18 mths Fr oak absorbed with ease. Diners Club Winemaker of the Year award 2002; CWT gold.

★★★★ **Reserve Chardonnay** Huge whack of oak on **04** (★★★★), needs further time to integrate but should be well worth the wait. Dense, tightly woven fruit, ripe citrus &

lime marmalade flavours, firm acid & bone-dry finish, even some oak tannins – all poised to harmonise & bloom. 10 mths Fr oak, 70% new. **03** was quiet on nose but giving on palate.

Groot Constantia range

★★★☆ **Cabernet Sauvignon** Gorgeous **03** (★★★★) richly robed; velvet blackberry fruit draped over elegant dry backbone. Luxurious but understated, classy; almost ready – clever tannins allow early drinking, should last good 6-8 yrs. 15 mths Fr oak, 40% new. **02**, not a great cab vintage, firmer but accessible.

★★★☆ **Shiraz** Classically constructed **03** (★★★★) unshowy, not overripe, exudes style. Black cherry, dark choc, clean wood spice – all harmonious; lingering complexity. Tannins well manipulated for dryness on finish. Yr Fr oak, 40% new. **02** also well executed but less open.

★★★★ **Sauvignon Blanc** After languishing a while, catching up with rest of appellation. Distinctive Constia feel & proportions to **05**, confidently made with nothing out of place. Tropical nuances to classic core of green fig, nettle; tangy & savoury; pleasing fullness & generosity, long, long finish. **04** decently ripe but taut, bracingly dry, lip-smacking.

★★★★ **Grand Constance** new Exciting addition to range, flies flag for famous Grt Constia sweet muscat desserts of yesteryear. Painstakingly researched; revives long-disused moniker. Pretty, sweet & seductive **03** satin textured with beguiling wafts fresh grape, litchi, tangerine peel & spice; ultra-long finish. Purists would demand slightly higher acid, but doubtless future versions will achieve this & more. Red & white muscat de F, oak fermented (none new), aged 18 mths.

Blanc de Noir ☺ ★★☆ Latest **05** much more focused, revved up than pvs; crisp & almost dry, strawberry aromas/flavours, very food friendly, ideal for summer picnics. 60/40 merlot/cab; alc a welcome 12.5%. **Chardonnay** ☺ ★★★ Distinctive & unusual **04**, ripe & fragrant mandarin & orange zest, modest oak (20%), fleshy yet lively.

Merlot ★★★☆ **03** continues in ripe choc-mint style, richness enlivened by fresh acidity. Unobtrusive tannins do not detract from variety's deep, black-berried fleshiness. Oaking now more serious 15 mths Fr, 40% new. **Pinotage** ★★★☆ **03** attractively rustic with ripe baked prune; variety's telltale sweetness downplayed; dense & chewy, good dry tannins but already approachable. Yr Fr oak, 60% new. **Constantia Rood** ★★☆ Cab/merlot with pinotage, earlier-drinking style but still some tannic grip, showcases classy fruit in latest **03**; yr older wood; probably not a quaffer at 14% alc. **Semillon-Sauvignon Blanc** ★★★☆ ✓ Each vintage notch up on previous. Tailored **05** unoaked; showcases fine fruit, richness & creamy texture of semillon (ideal partner for steely backbone of sauvignon). Touches dusty fig, passionfruit; needs to settle, but well poised. 60/40 blend. **Cap Classique** ★★★☆ Last tasted was an **NV** (00); rich & not quite bone-dry. Next to be released 06. **Cape Ruby Port** ★★★☆ **03** unclassically a vintaged ruby, more in LBV mode. Sweetish & definitely moreish; caramel & toffee nuance to rich fruitcake, balanced, ready to drink. Shiraz/touriga. 18.6% alc. **Merlot-Shiraz, Weisser Riesling, Bouquet Blanc** discontinued. *– IvH*

Grootdrink see Oranjerivier Wine Cellars

Groot Eiland Winery

Goudini (see Worcester map) ▪ Est 1962 ▪ 1stB 1980 ▪ Tasting & sales Mon-Fri 8-5 ▪ Tours by appt ▪ Gifts ▪ Owners 30 members ▪ Winemakers Erik Schlünz & Albertus Louw (2000/2003), with Lyndi Kotzé & Jacques Theron (both 2003) ▪ Viti consultant Johan Möller (2003) ▪ 1 000 ha (cab, merlot, pinotage, shiraz, chard, chenin, colombard, sauvignon) ▪ 50 000 cs own label 30% red 50% white 20% rosé ▪ PO Box 93 Rawsonville 6845 ▪ grooteiland@lando.co.za ▪ www.grooteiland.co.za ▪ ***T (023) 349·1140*** *▪ F (023) 349·1801*

A stated aim here is to increase brand awareness and international exposure, so last year's gold medal and Prix de Jury for best value wine at the Classic Wine Trophy could not have come at a better time. The wine which so impressed the all-French judges, whose brief was to reward wines imbued with classic qualities of balance, finesse and longevity, was the 04 Pinotage. Building on their success, the GE team subjected their production equipment to a major overhaul and, Erik Schlünz reports, the effects are already reflected in the quality of the new wines.

Cabernet Sauvignon ★★★ Blueberry, lavender & spice abound in brawny **04**, with earthy hints, powerful tannic finish. 14.5% alc. **Merlot** ★★★ Plum/smoke whiffs & dried fruit reoccur on palate of approachable & supple **04**; shows potential to improve with 2-3 yrs cellaring. **Pinotage** ★★ Fruit-rich **04**, plentiful strawberry fruit with banana hint; strong dry tannins & high-kicking alc (14.9%). **Shiraz** ★★★ Sweet fruit, spicy oak & fynbos combo on nose, attractive savoury end, should slip down more easily once tannin has settled ±1 yr. **Rosé** ★★ Not-too-sweet **05**, earthy strawberry aromas, hint of tannin. More vinous, not as pretty as pvs. **Chardonnay** ★★★ Tasted last yr, **04**'s delicate ripe peach/orange character marred by too much wood, alc (14.2%). **Chenin Blanc** ★★ Back in guide with appealing & honest **05**, quaffable tropical tones & refreshing acidity. **Sauvignon Blanc** ★★ Soft & friendly **05**, lemongrass tones to enjoy within yr of harvest. **Honigtraube** ★★ Supple **04** mainly colombard with 15% chenin; more forthcoming than usual; effusive floral/honey aromas, easy uncloying sweetness. **Hanepoot Jerepigo** ★★★★ **02** sold out; no new vintage in sight.

Meander range

Fruity Red ★★ Quaffable three-way blend fronted by cinsaut, **04** positive earthy notes topped by sweet/sour redcurrant flavours. **Crisp Dry** ★★★ Suitably crisp & dry **04**, with tropical fruit tones, apple zest finish. Tasted mid-2004, as was ... **Fruity White** ★★ **04** sweeter but nicely balanced version of above. Both from chenin. — *DH*

Groote Post Vineyards

Darling (see Darling/Swartland map) ▪ 1stB 1999 ▪ Tasting & sales Mon-Fri 9-5 Sat 9-2.30 ▪ Closed Easter Fri-Mon, Dec 25 & Jan 1 ▪ Fee R10 for groups of 10+ ▪ Groote Post Restaurant (see Eat-out section) or BYO picnic ▪ Tourgroups (40 people) ▪ Conferencing ▪ Walks ▪ Conservation area ▪ Bird hide ▪ Owners Peter & Nicholas Pentz ▪ Winemaker Lukas Wentzel (Nov 2000) ▪ Viticulturist Jannie de Clerk, advised by Johan Pienaar (1999) ▪ 117 ha (cabs s/f, merlot, pinot, shiraz, chard, chenin, sauvignon) ▪ 430 tons 26 000 cs 40% red 60% white ▪ PO Box 103 Darling 7345 ▪ wine@grootepost.co.za ▪ www.grootepost.com ▪ ***T (022) 492·2825*** *▪ F (022) 492·2693*

Father-and-son team Peter and Nick Pentz have committed the 2 000ha of indigenous Swartland (granite/shale) renosterveld and Atlantis (sand) fynbos on their 4 000ha Darling Hills spread to preservation as part of the UNESCO-proclaimed Cape West Coast Biosphere Reserve. All part of the Biodiversity & Wine Initiative to promote sustainable wine production. And it's not just marketing speak. Soil moisture retention supports a healthy mealybug-combatting ladybird population — a practical spin-off for the vineyards, now maturing to give the wines even more of an individual cool-climate quality. Newcomers semillon and malbec, and more sauvignon and chardonnay, will eventually see 140ha under vine. It's prime stuff, intelligently farmed. Game drives through the buck-rich hills, a bird hide, the 18th-century manor house restaurant run by internationally-inspired Sean and Debbie McLaughlin are added attractions.

★★★★ **Chardonnay** Showy **04**, sumptuous flavouring, kumquat/dried peach, buttered whole-wheat toast; silky body & lingering finish. What more could you want? Mainly native yeasts, 8 mth oak. **03** was delicious; palate richness tempered by food-friendly acidity. FCTWS gold.

The Old Man's Blend Red ★★★ Anytime wine to 'drink on the stoep with your old man'. **03** mainly merlot, cab, some shiraz, pinot, creating tasty mulberry/café au lait-toned blend, juicy enough to please most tastes. Partial oaking, seasoned Fr. Also in 1.5ℓ. **Merlot** ★★★★ From young vines, **03** has lots to like: cassis, black cherries, shot through with cedar spicing; accessible, creamy palate; well-judged oak (14 mths mainly Fr, 20% new) for ±4 yr cellaring. **Shiraz** ★★★★ **03** immediately appealing smoke/liquorice/dark fruit perfumes, flavours. Accessible, but tight, will unfold further over next 6 yrs. 14 mths Fr oak, half new. Also in 375ml. **Pinot Noir** ★★★★ **04** attractive typicity: zinging red berry fruit, balanced, elegant structure & organic/mocha thread throughout. Harmoniously oaked, 8 mths older Fr; to age ±3 yrs. **Chardonnay Unwooded** ★★★ **05** a tropical fruit salad with lashings of citrus; zesty

& flavourful enough for solo drinking or food partnership. **Sauvignon Blanc** ★★★★ **05** tauter, more intense than pvs. Green scrub, capsicum, tangy grapefruit styling; sleekly powerful, bursting with freshness. **Chenin Blanc** ★★★ Easy-drinking style. Pear-rich fruit salad & summer freshness are main ingredients in appetising **04** quaffer. WO Coastal, as is ... **Old Man's Blend White** new ★★★ **05** Sauvignon (60%) plays dominant role in aromas with vibrant fynbos, grassy tones, but concedes to chenin for a smoothly accessible, fruity palate. **Cabernet Sauvignon-Merlot** discontinued. — *CR*

Groot Parys

Paarl ▪ Est 1699 ▪ 1stB 2003 ▪ Closed to public ▪ Owners Eric Verhaak & Peter & Mariëtte Ras ▪ Vini consultant Naudé Bruwer ▪ Viti consultant Gawie Kriel ▪ 64 ha (ruby cab, chard, chenin, colombard, hanepoot, sauvignon, semillon) ▪ 900 tons ±1 500 cs ▪ PO Box 82 Huguenot 7645 ▪ grootparys@wam.co.za ▪ www.grootparys.co.za ▪ ***T/F 872·7140***

Mariëtte Ras says her approach since purchasing the farm in 2002, of restoring the balance to both vines and soil, is paying dividends. As a further step in this direction, a block has been allocated for biodynamic cultivation, and if successful this approach will be extended to more of the farm. In keeping with the idea of the winemaker as 'nature's assistant', small batches of wooded chenin and chardonnay have been made to further explore the site-specific expression of these varieties. More obvious developments are also afoot, with villas being built and restoration of the 1699 manor house undertaken. 'Small steps on a long road to realise our Tweede Droom.'

Die Tweede Droom range

Chardonnay Unwooded ★★★★ **05** unready. **04** last yr showed more intensity, character than most. Intense, clean tropical flavours, ripe & enjoyable. **Chenin Blanc** ★★★★ **04** archetypical Paarl chenin, lifted ripe-tropical character with concentration, balance. **05** sample appears somewhat leaner; uncommunicative, too unformed to rate. — *CR/JB*

Grünberger

Originally developed for the Bergkelder, now part of Distell, by German oenologist Alfred Baumgartner, hence the Frankish 'bocksbeutel' bottles for the non-spritzy wines. All are off-dry or semi-sweet, and quaffably light.

Rosenlese ★★ Natural Sweet from sauvignon, splash ruby cab supplies the coral hue; **05** candyfloss aromas, fruit-shy palate. Finishes sweeter than stablemates. **Freudenlese** ★★ **05** also Natural Sweet, also mainly sauvignon for zest, gewürz, muscadel for perfume. Varieties mentioned on the label. **Stein** ★★ **05** cheery semi-dry sipper from chenin & sauvignon with grassy nose, fresh finish. **Spritziger** ★★ Frothy & refreshing poolside drink; **05** with vivacious acidity. Screwcap. All WO W Cape. — *CvZ*

Grundheim Wines

Little Karoo ▪ Est/1stB 1995 ▪ Tasting & sales Mon-Fri 8-5 Sat 9-1 ▪ Fee R10 for groups of 10+ ▪ Closed Easter Sun, Dec 25 & Jan 1 ▪ Owner Danie Grundling ▪ Winemaker Dys Grundling (1997) ▪ 25 ha (cinsaut, tinta, touriga, ruby cab, r/w muscadel, colombard, hanepoot, palomino) ▪ 360 tons 10 000ℓ for own labels 100% fortified ▪ PO Box 400 Oudtshoorn 6620 ▪ grundheim@absamail.co.za ▪ ***T/F (044) 272·6927***

Famous for his fiery 'witblits' and liqueurs, master distiller Danie Grundling has done it again, winning trophies at the 2005 Agricultural Distillers Guild championships for best aged product and best liqueur. 'We now boast an underground maturation cellar,' reveals son Dys, the winemaker, whose focus is more on the Muscadel, Jerepigo and port-style wines. This year, he's particularly excited about the Muscadel from 30-year-old bushvines. 'The quality of my wine is determined by the quality in my vineyard,' he notes, adding that a port made from 100% touriga is also maturing 'beautifully'.

No new releases of their fortifieds tasted; notes from pvs ed: **Red Muscat** ★★★ Subtitled 'Muscat de Frontignan'. **95** lovely tawny hues; aromas of Karoo bush & raisins, soft caramel texture. ±17% alc. **Red Jerepigo** ★★★★ Silky & characterful fireside warmer, damson & dark choc, whiffs mint. **NV**. 17% alc. Ruby cab & tinta. **White Muscadel** ★★★ Attractive **98** redolent of spice, herbs & grapefruit; palate more straightforwardly sweet, with barley-sugar flavours. **Golden Jerepigo** ★★★★ White muscadel in full sunshine mode; wafts of spice & raisins; packed with flavour. NV. **Cape Ruby** ★★★ Minty, rich & sweet, distinctly warming. Also available: **Classic Red**, **Chenin Blanc**, **Late Harvest** & **Cape Vintage**. — *DH*

Guardian see Lost Horizons
Guardian Peak see Ernie Els Wines

Gusto Wines

Stellenbosch ▪ Est 2001 ▪ 1stB 2002 ▪ Tasting by appt ▪ Owners PG Slabbert & Nicolette de Kock ▪ Winemaker Nicolette de Kock ▪ Viticulturist PG Slabbert ▪ 500 cs 30% red 70% white ▪ PO Box 6045 Uniedal 7612 ▪ gusto@base4.co.za ▪ ***T 082·807·4447*** *▪ F 883·8965*

You can take a girl out of the Boland – but Nicolette Waterford (née De Kock, CEO of the Stellenbosch Wine Routes), newly wed to Darryl W (MD of Base 4 Helicopters), intends planting rows at their new Llandudno home so that she can still wake up to vineyard views. Last harvest was a lot easier than she anticipated: 'Must be my new Hilton Weiner pink polka dot gumboots'. The 05 Sauvignon is positively my best effort to date.' While Gusto will always be a labour of love – 'the job must still pay for the habit' – it looks set to expand a little in the near future.

Destino ★★★★ **02** not ready for tasting for this ed; **01** unshowy maiden merlot/cab blend ex-Stbosch. Vegetal & earthy tints warmed red berries; savoury fresh acidity, unassertively firm tannins. 16 mths Fr oak, 70% new, not too obvious. **Sauvignon Blanc** ★★ Dip in quality in **05**; greener, nettle-ly, tarter, more slender (13% vs 14% alc), seems to be lacking fruit core of pvs vintages. — *CR*

Hagelsberg see Middelvlei
Hakuna Matata see Remhoogte

Hamilton Russell Vineyards

Hemel-en-Aarde Valley (see Walker Bay map) ▪ Est 1975 ▪ 1stB 1981 ▪ Tasting & sales Mon-Fri 9–5 Sat 9–1 ▪ Also tasting/sales of estate olive oil ▪ Closed Easter Fri/Sun, Dec 25/26 & Jan 1 ▪ Tours by appt ▪ BYO picnic by appt ▪ Conservation area ▪ Owner Anthony Hamilton Russell ▪ Winemaker Hannes Storm (2004) ▪ Viticulturist Johan Montgomery (2005) ▪ 52 ha (pinot, chard) ▪ 150 tons 13 500 cs 40% red 60% white ▪ PO Box 158 Hermanus 7200 ▪ hrv@hermanus.co.za ▪ ***T (028) 312·3595*** *▪ F (028) 312·1797*

In the wake of the departure of Kevin Grant, his onetime assistant Hannes Storm's debut as winemaker could not have come at a better time for a man to prove his mettle. 2005, Storm's fourth HRV vintage, proved logistically challenging as well as demanding of great vigour. But the sleep-starved HS seems pleased with the classic styling that has emerged to mark the 25th anniversary of HRV Pinot Noir. Future vintages should also be supported by vigorous clonal selection, which saw the planting of cuttings from virus-resistant older blocks. Anthony HR, 14 years at the helm, also has much to cheer about. After achieving five 90+ scores in *Wine Spectator* in recent years, HRV was invited on this commercially important magazine's Grand Tour of the US, with the Chardonnay 04. Top Pinot ratings in *Wine* and a Trophy Wine Show trophy for Best Pinot Noir last year add lustre to the jubilee.

★★★★★ **Pinot Noir** Well textured **04**, pure, fresh, perfumed & elegant; needs time to settle. One of the longest hang-times recorded. 24% new oak. **03** (★★★★★) classy mineral tone; obvious wood, but integrated; excellent structure & balance. FCTWS Trophy. **02** light, but sound pinot fruit, elegant. Reflects weakness of vintage.

★★★★★ **Chardonnay 04** (★★★★★) tight mineral nose. Very restrained, but well focused & powerful, with distinct cool-climate feel. No malo here, which shows in linear acidity. Persistent, elegant finish. 8 mths oak, third new. **03** very smart. Noticeable oak, but with integrated, toasty, silky qualities. Delicately complex; lovely structure & a stony minerality. — *RK*

Hartenberg Estate

*Stellenbosch ▪ 1stB 1978 ▪ Tasting & sales Mon-Fri 9–5 (Nov 1 till Easter 9–5.30) Sat 9–3 Sun Dec 1 till Jan 31 (tasting & lunches) 10–4 Closed all other Sundays & Easter Fri, Dec 25 & Jan 1 ▪ Nominal tasting fee for groups, refunded with purchase ▪ Vintners lunches (al fresco, weather permitting) Mon-Sat 12–2 (picnic platters in summer; soup & vetkoek in winter); booking advisable ▪ Seasonal cellar tours by appt ▪ Excellent birding (obtain permission via tasting room) ▪ Owner Hartenberg Holdings ▪ Winemaker Carl Schultz, with Jaco van der Merwe (Jun 1993/Jan 2001) ▪ Viticulturist Frans Snyman (1996) ▪ 95 ha (cab, merlot, pinotage, shiraz, chard, riesling, sauvignon) ▪ 500 tons 42 000 cs 72% red 26% white 2% rosé ▪ PO Box 69 Koelenhof 7605 ▪ info@hartenbergestate.com ▪ www.hartenbergestate.com ▪ **T 865·2541** ▪ F 865·2153*

Something old, something new … The old rhyme comes to mind at Hartenberg, which has released its last wine from the uniquely South African pontac grape. 'At least until some virus-free planting material is available,' qualifies viticulturist Frans Snyman. Meanwhile, they've bucked the trend with a new riesling vineyard, with advice from German riesling specialist Stefan Radeck. Something borrowed? Well, winemaker Carl Schultz is 'always open to new theories so as to capture maximum intensity through minimum intervention'. And perhaps 'something blue' refers to the sea, where Hartenberg's German intern had just finished a shark dive when a Great White demolished the cage … On land, the priority is 'to make the vineyards sing. We cannot claim to be organic, but judging by the amount of healthy wildlife on the estate we are clearly doing something right!'

★★★★ **Cabernet Sauvignon 03** tighter knit, more focused than **02**, with much longer potential – 10 yrs. Flavour in abundance, dark fruit, cigar-box, white pepper. Accessible beyond the firmness, still an infant. 17 mths Fr oak, half new, half 2nd fill (± this for all the top reds). **02** also misleadingly friendly; elegant, juicy, lively. **01** won SAA red wine trophy.

★★★★ **Merlot 03** continues in sleek style that has become estate's trademark: cool-grown berry fruit, mint-choc, mixed spice, harmoniously oaked to give ready accessibility, but should develop beautifully over 4–6 yrs. 70% new oak. **02** muscular, with ripe tannins.

★★★★ **The McKenzie** new **03** classically styled blend cab (70%) & merlot, named for family responsible for estate's regeneration. Cassis, crystallised violets, mint-choc characters. Tightly structured with plenty of oak, well handled, harmonious. Will grow over 7–10 yrs. As with next, only 450 cs & for release June 06.

★★★★ **The Stork** new Shiraz from vyds with clay soils, to give a contrasting style to Gravel Hill. Memorialises late Ken McKenzie (nicknamed 'Stork' for his height & thin legs!), who loved the estate's shiraz. Generous **03** with deeply rich dark fruit, plums, black cherries, creamy texture; easily accommodates hefty 15.5% alc. Savoury aspects (cigar-box, roasted spice) from 20 mths new Fr oak. A keeper, 8–10 yrs.

★★★★☆ **Shiraz** Always serious & unshowy. Gorgeous **03** expresses variety with wood char notes, trademark roast veg, fennel & enough fleshy dark fruit for immediate enjoyment. Masterly oaking (60% new) gives core of finest polished tannins, already amenable, in unobtrusive support for devt. **02** svelte structure, but iron fist in velvet glove, with good 6+ yr potential. Swiss gold.

★★★★☆ **CWG Auction Reserve Gravel Hill Shiraz** From single vyd with gravelly red soil – 'poorest on the property, producing our best wine', says Schultz. Awesome **03** (for 06 CWG submission) has colour you could write with, indicating concentration. Wild scrub, peppery, mocha-choc tones vie with intense berry fruit; velvety tannins seduce, mislead about the sheathed power, longevity. 17 mths new Fr barrels. wine. Only 47 cs made. Intensely perfumed, savoury **02** with refinement & class. 14.5% alc.

★★★★ **Cabernet Sauvignon-Merlot 03** not ready for tasting. Last was **95**, 60/40 blend.

★★★★ **Chardonnay Reserve** From premium vyd blocks, only in best vintages (last was **98**). **03** (★★★★☆) has elegance & refinement; the oak shows only as gentle nutty flavour thread; the fruit includes peach, citrus peel, but is silk-textured. All in perfect balance & top-drawer. A wine to savour. 8 mths new Fr, dash Am. VG.

★★★★ **Chardonnay** Selection from 5 vyds, 5 clones – all Burgundian or California Davis. Bold, concentrated style. **04**'s aromas & flavours showy, seductive: peach & citrus peel, shortbread biscuit, roasted nuts, with underlying balance & verve reflecting its quality. Oak (10 mths, 70% new), is fully integrated. Richly flavoured **03** with silky, voluptuous body.

Chatillon ☺ ★★★ Easy-drinking characterful white. **04** appealing lemongrass & pear fragrance, flavours; a nicely rounded, friendly semillon-chenin blend. **Bin 9** ☺ ★★★ **NV** dry red; only ex-estate & Gauteng restaurant, Luca's. Varying blend, in this case merlot, cab, shiraz, with loads of peppery wild berry fruit, savoury notes, a touch of mint. Juicy, flavourful quaffer. NE.

Pinotage ★★★★ Fleshy & youthful **03** has lovely drinkability. Flavourful, with cedar-toned red berries, a hint of liquorice; well constructed, fruit masking 15% alc. 19 mths oak, mostly Fr, some Am, 60% new. **Cabernet Sauvignon-Shiraz** ★★★★ 'Ecurie' in USA. **03** a 59/41 blend with plums, red berries & smoky nuances which deepen on the palate. Fully integrated oak – 14 mths seasoned Fr/Am. Lively appetite appeal. **Sauvignon Blanc** ★★★★ **05** in delicious riper-style mould of pvs. Plenty of fruit (gooseberry, litchi), tangy freshness; long finish. **Weisser Riesling** ★★★★ Semi-sweet, usually friendly rather than racy version; **05** still has sugar (18g/l), but now offset by grippy finish, tasting drier than expected. Lovely aromatics, floral/jasmine & a muscat tone; it's a charmer. NE. **Bin 3**, **L'Estreux** made occasionally. Discontinued: **Zinfandel**, **Zinfandel Natural Sweet**. – *CR*

Hartswater Wine Cellar

*Northern Cape ▪ Tasting & sales Mon-Fri 8.30–5 Sat tasting by appt ▪ Sales also from outlet in Hartswater town; orders delivered to liquor stores in Northern Cape (350km radius), Free State & Pretoria ▪ Tours by appt ▪ Fully licensed restaurant with braai ▪ Conference facilities ▪ Owner Senwes ▪ Winemaker Roelof Maree (1978) ▪ 5 000 tons ▪ PO Box 2335 Hartswater 8570 ▪ wynkelder@senwes.co.za ▪ **T (053) 474·0700** ▪ F (053) 474·0975*

Northern Cape news: 2005 a normal year (thus some hail damage, being a summer rainfall region); crop down 600 tons (off a 5 000-ton total). But, exhorts Roelof Maree, they're not to be compared with the Western Cape. *Kuierwyne* (light, low-alc easy-drinkers) are their forte; their aim: to be the biggest seller within a 350km radius of the winery, encompassing an area with an emerging market that might not own corkscrews, hence the new easy-opening screwcap closures. 'Makes sense, doesn't it?' asks Roelof M who, with wife Dalena, regularly does educational tastings. Their wines, including newcomer Thunder, carry a 'Proudly South African' label … proudly.

Elements range

Only wine tasted this ed is … **Thunder** new ★★ Rich & earthy glassful of bold, juicy fruit; weightier than 11% alc would suggest, sweetish finish. **Earth** ★★★ Dry red with herby hint to its red fruits, soft bite of tannin. Pinotage, shiraz, cab. **Fire** ★★★ Natural Sweet rosé from chenin, pinotage; strawberries & cream aromas, crisp finish. **Wind** ★★ Off-dry chenin-based white with peach blossom aroma; light, juicy, refreshing lemon acidity. **Rain** ★ Natural Sweet white from chenin, colombard, with soft, somewhat diluted fruit-salad flavours. All above light-bodied, low-alc wines (9.5–12.5%). All **NV**, for early drinking. Serve whites well chilled.

Hinterland range

Available but not tasted: **Ruby Cabernet**, **Cabernet Sauvignon**, **Chardonnay**, **Chenin Blanc**, **Overvaal Grand Cru**, **Late Harvest**, **Special Late Harvest** (in 3ℓ bag-in-boxes), **Doux Sparkling**, **Red Jeropigo** & **Port**. – *DH/TM*

Harvest Moon see Dominion Wine Company

Haut Espoir

Franschhoek ▪ Est 1999 ▪ 1stB 2004 ▪ Tastings & tours by appt; sales Mon-Fri 9–4 (phone ahead) ▪ Owners Ian & Anne Armstrong ▪ Winemaker/viticulturist Nikey van Zyl (Oct 2003), *advised by Paul Wallace ▪ 12 ha (cab, merlot, petit v, shiraz) ▪ 40 tons 2 000 cs 70% red 30% white ▪ PO Box 681 Franschhoek 7690 ▪ wine@hautespoir.co.za ▪ www.hautespoir.com ▪ **T 876·4000** ▪ F 876·4038*

They've had fun and held their media launch. 'Now award shows have been entered, so we will see what develops,' say owners Ian and Anne Armstrong, fully settled into their Franschhoek eyrie (when not at their second home in New Zealand). 'The new winery is working well and I am now comfortable increasing the tonnage,' says winemaker Nikey van Zyl, who expects to 'coax' about 65 tons of grapes into wine this year. 'But making wine is the easy part,' teases Armstrong son, Rob, in charge of management and marketing. 'Selling it is the difficult part!' (Impressive, then, that he has managed the ice-to-Eskimos scenario of selling Sauvignon to the Kiwis!)

Syrah ★★ From Frhoek vines, 8 mths combo Fr/Hungarian/Am oak (90/5/5). **04** red fruit compôte & lifted notes, some cream & vanilla from oak; squishy mulberry fruit & friendly tannins. **Shiraz Rosé 04** sold out before we could taste. **Chardonnay Reserve** ★★★ Oak the driving force on **04**, butter, cream, touch wood-char; palate similar but refreshed by lemon acidity. New Fr barrels, 9 mths, 50% malo. **Sauvignon Blanc** ★★ Lightish **05** is water-white with cat's pee nose, slightly medicinal finish. **Semillon** ★★ Fruit-shy **04** has nuances of peach & wax; palate propped up by 13.5% alc. Small portion oaked. *— CvZ*

Havana Hills

*Philadelphia ▪ Est 1999 ▪ 1stB 2000 ▪ Visits by appt ▪ Owner Kobus du Plessis ▪ Winemaker Nico Vermeulen (Jun 1999) with Joseph Gertse (Jan 2000) ▪ Viticulturist Rudi Benn (2001) ▪ 58 ha (cabs s/f, merlot, mourvèdre, shiraz, pinot, chard, sauvignon) ▪ 120 tons 20 000 cs 85% red 15% white ▪ Export brands: Lime Road 1481 & Virgin Earth ▪ Postnet Suite 57, Pvt Bag X18, Milnerton 7435 ▪ sales@havanahills.co.za ▪ **T 972·1110** ▪ F 972·1105*

With all building projects completed at long last and space made for more tanks, focus here is on the vineyards, where you'll find rarities like sangiovese and mourvèdre, viognier and nouvelle. The plan behind the additional cellar hardware and fledgling vines is flexibility, both when it come to blending wines and what the market is looking for, explains winemaker Nico Vermeulen. Reds still rule here but sauvignon has also been planted in the best-suited sites on the Atlantic-facing property. Owner Kobus du Plessis, delighted to have taken up residence on the farm with his family, reports that permanent water for irrigation, via the Durbanville joint pipeline venture which feeds from Potsdam, will make a massive difference. 'The vines will do even better in stress situations with supplementation.'

★★★★ **'Flagship'** NEW As yet unnamed – 'Kobus One' (doffing the cap, wryly, to Mondavi-Rothschild's icon) was a contender … **02** a complex ±50/50 cab/merlot ensemble: minuscule 2 t/ha yield; 2 yrs Fr oak (30% new, rest 2nd fill for 1 yr, then all new!). Brambly, bdx-like tomato cocktail character, good substance for young vines in a lesser vintage.

Du Plessis Reserve range

★★★★☆ **Du Plessis** Carrying own West Coast fingerprint & making waves since maiden **00** (★★★★★), FCTWS trophy winning **01**. Current **03** restores form after lighter **02** (★★★★). Latest features red-earth characters, full cassis fruit & succulent spice; considerable oomph in finish (yet not alcoholic: just 13%). 55/36 cab/merlot blend, with 9% cab f. All Fr oak-matured, 30% new, 15 mths.

★★★★ **Cabernet Sauvignon 03** not ready at press time. **02** in sappy mode when last reviewed (mid-2004): aromatic walnut nose, juicy blackcurrant fruit hung on integrated palate. **01** classic cab profile; refined power. Fr oak, 15 mths, 30% new.

★★★★ **Merlot 03** similarly work-in-progress on our deadline. **02** showed power with elegance: structured core encircled by ripe choc-berry/plum flesh, vigorous grip in bone-dry tail. **01** rich & luscious. 15 mths Fr casks, 30% new.

★★★★ **Shiraz** Serial VDG laureate, nuanced & refined. **03** likely to perpetuate medalled lineage: warm vanilla oak nose leads savoury pepper/mulberry fruit interplay, firm tannins need 2–4 yrs. **02** more hefty; plum, milled-pepper & meaty richness provide satisfying finish. Oaking regimen settled into Fr/Am 85/15, 30% Fr new, 15 mths.

Making his debut in this guide (as both wine entrepreneur and contributor) is **Tseliso Rangaka** (left), formerly a Johannesburg advertising copywriter, now Stellenbosch vinegrower and winemaker with his very own brand, M'hudi. With him at Villiera for the first bottling of M'hudi wine was 'old hand' **Khulekani Laurence Buthelezi**, whose own label Tutuka was first featured in the 2004 edition. Buthelezi is also assistant winemaker at Signal Hill.

Looking forward to flying to Burgundy for her first overseas harvest as part of the Beaune Exchange Programme was **Gladys Brown**, winemaking assistant to Grangehurst owner **Jeremy Walker**. Gladys B's mother, Jane, has worked at the Helderberg property nearly 30 years. Gladys's gravitation towards winemaking has been so successful that she's in line for additional responsibilities and opportunities.

Soon-to-be-landowners **Chrisjan Williams** and **Maritsa Jansen** are among the partners in a new Robertson venture, De Goree Farming, between the Retief family of Van Loveren Private Cellar and members of their labour force. A farm currently owned by the Retiefs is being transferred to a trust, to be co-administered and co-managed with the workers. Several months in the gestation, the business is already running, says Van Loveren's **Phillip Retief** (right), and needed only Department of Land Affairs approval to shift into high gear.

The Vineyard Connection

Stellenbosch (at Delvera cnr R44 & Muldersvlei Road Muldersvlei) • Wine tasting & sales Mon-Fri 8-5 Sat & Sun 9-4 Hosts Lara Philp & Johan Rademan • PO Box 1484 Stellenbosch 7599 • Tel (021) 884-4360 • Fax (021) 884-4361 E-mail: wine@vineyardconnection.co.za • Website: www.vineyardconnection.co.za

With an impressive track record as the exporters of wines from the Cape, The Vineyard Connection is recommended as THE one-stop destination for winelovers and travellers alike. Meticulous personal service and a beautiful balanced selection of South African wines, sweeping views of the vineyards and the warmest of welcomes will leave you with a lasting impression of quality. Promises ★★★ service.

Havana Hills range

★★★★ **Sauvignon Blanc 05** (★★★) straightforward tropical style; contrast with more aromatic **04**, well fleshed gooseberry richness edged with racy cut-grass. WO Coastal. Tempered 13% alc.

Lime Road 1481 ★★★☆ Reliable member of this 'fruity & elegant' range. **03** shiraz-driven, with near-equal contributions cab & merlot; raspberry fullness to spicy aromatics, supple tension in savoury finish. Yr Fr/Am oak, 30% new. Noted as discontinued last ed, the next three reds return with **03**: **Cabernet Sauvignon** ★★★☆ Slow to start, opens into wild berry basket wrapped in big tannins, has bite yet accessible on release. Yr Fr casks, 30% new. **Merlot** ★★★☆ Olive & pimento savoury tones to black cherry fruit in similarly styled but easier, gliding texture: versatile at table. Yr Fr oak, 30% new. **Shiraz** ★★★☆ Sweet vanilla feature to well-spiced, fruit-driven mouthful; trademark sleek glaze to smooth finish. Yr 60/40 Fr/Am barrels, 30% new. 13% alc, as for ... **Chardonnay** ★★★☆ **04** individual peachy character to full body, well bolstered by tangy lime spine; nice farewell grip. 60% oaked. **Bisweni** range discontinued. **Khanya** range, for specific European clients, not reviewed this ed. — *DS*

Hazendal

Stellenbosch ▪ Est 1699 ▪ 1stB ca 1950 ▪ Tasting & sales Mon-Fri 8.30–4.30 Sat/Sun 9–3 ▪ Fee R5; R10 incl tour ▪ Tours Mon-Fri 11 & 3 ▪ Closed Easter Fri, Dec 25 & Jan 1 ▪ Hermitage Restaurant (see Eat-out section) ▪ Museum of Russian art & culture ▪ Gifts ▪ Conferencing ▪ 4×4 trail by appt ▪ Owner Mark Voloshin ▪ Vini/viti consultants Ronell Wiid & Schalk du Toit (Jan 1998/2000) ▪ 68 ha (cab, merlot, shiraz, chenin, sauvignon) ▪ 400 tons 25 000 cs own label 40% red 60% white ▪ PO Box 336 Stellenbosch 7599 ▪ info@hazendal.co.za ▪ www.hazendal.co.za ▪ ***T 903·5112*** *▪ F 903·0057*

'If Hazendal was a château in Bordeaux, the 2005 Bushvine Chenin Blanc would cost 140 bucks a bottle,' laughs winemaker Ronell Wiid. Fortunately for us, this Russian-owned property has not translocated. But the 2005 harvest was tiny – 'a mini harvest, especially the buggerol chenin grapes, but maxi labour-intensive, to keep us out of mischief, I suppose!' The 2005 harvest was also RW's 17th – a personal milestone ('around the neck,' she adds wryly) because with it comes the realisation 'that I have experienced more harvests than I still have ahead of me, so I am past halfway to retirement. This is frightening because I'm still learning about stuff – weather, soil, clones, wood, etc. When the hell am I going to become an expert, I wonder?' She's doing fine.

★★★★ **Shiraz-Cabernet Sauvignon** ✓ Back after a 2 vintage break, with 54/46 blend. **03** has everything in place for a good drinking experience: creamy, fully-ripened berries, some savoury oak notes, woodsmoke; balanced structure firm enough for ageing 4–5 yrs but already accessible & finishing on a lively, juicy, high note. Yr Fr barrels, 40% new.

★★★★ **Shiraz** Discreet & classically toned. **03** lovely Rhône-like characteristics: pepper, savoury spice/cloves, dark berry fruit, a touch of tar. Already accessible, has lithe tannins for 4–6+ yrs ageing. Fr oak, half new. **02** sold out before we could taste, following bold but elegantly constructed maiden **01**.

★★★☆ **The Last Straw** Aptly & amusingly named meal-ending straw wine. Notch up **04** (★★★★) neither simple nor mere fun. Luscious, with mouth-coating, resonating apricot, pineapple & honeycomb flavours, almost resinous oak injection; richness (180g/ℓ sugar) tempered by brisk acidity; long finish. Fermented/9 mths Fr oak. Follows rich & unctuous **03**.

Bushvine Chenin Blanc ☺ ★★★ Bargain-priced **05** (sample) from old vines has all the attributes of well-made chenin: apple & lemon-drop tones, plenty of juicy liveliness for with food or solo, plus 2–3 yr ageability.

Merlot ★★★☆ **03** has a firmer structure than **02**, promising longer life, 4–5 yrs. The flavours are seductive, creamy red berries, cigar-box, sweet spice. Yr Fr oak, half new. **Marvol Pinotage** new ★★★☆ Made for Mark V's 60th birthday celebration in Russia. Serious **02**

elegant, with perfectly ripe plummy fruit, attractive smoky spice. 2 yrs 2nd fill oak. Good for 6+ yrs. Includes W Bay grapes. **Chenin Blanc Wood Matured** ★★★★ From low-yielding 30 yr-old bushvines. **04**'s generous oaking (yr Fr), easily assimilated by the fruit, gives a structure for enjoying now or over 3–4 yrs. Tasty array lemon zest, pineapple flavours, biscuit overlay. **Sauvignon Blanc** ★★★★ From 30 yr-old bushvines. **05** (sample) has lovely appetite appeal; vibrant fruit tones, gooseberries, crunchy apples, pears; balancing friendly, rounded texture & crisp freshness. **White Nights Cap Classique** ★★★★ Recalls 'Beliye Nochi' – bright midsummer nights of St Petersburg. Last tasted was fresh, very dry, lively, light-textured & toned **00** chardonnay/pinot (60/40) blend, nearly 4 yrs on lees. **Pinotage** ★★★★ Just 500 cs for UK market. **04** from Paarl/Stbosch fruit. Captures the variety perfectly: rhubarb pie richness, with a touch of green fynbos to lift, enliven. Harmoniously oaked (10 mths), drinks smoothly. **Blanc de Noir** ★★★ **05** (sample) from pinot show redcurrants, herbaceous notes; palate is simpler, friendly (12.5% alc), designed for early drinking. Plumping 7g/ℓ sugar. **Chardonnay** ★★★ **04** oak supplies unobtrusive structural support – peachy/tropical fruit character at centre; lively, tasty, nicely put together. Fermented/aged Fr barrels, 20% new.

Kleine Hazen range

Reserve Red ★★★ Unoaked early-drinking cab, shiraz, merlot ensemble. **02** (not retasted) with nice tannic grip. WO W Cape. **Konynwijn** ★★ **05** (sample) uncomplicated semi-sweet chenin quaffer, with appealing flavours. Mostly for own restaurant. – *CR/IvH*

Hegewisch Wines

*Est 2000 ▪ 1stB 2002 ▪ Closed to public ▪ Owner/winemaker Hilko Hegewisch ▪ Viticulturist Francois van Schoor ▪ 60 ha (merlot, pinotage, shiraz, chard) ▪ 800 tons 300 cs own label 40% red 60% white ▪ 22 Van Coppenhagen Str Rozendal Stellenbosch 7600 ▪ hegewisch@xsinet.co.za ▪ **T 887·9544** ▪ F 883·2310*

No update available on this winery; contact details and wine notes from previous edition.

Cabernet Sauvignon-Merlot ★★★★ **03** medium-full bodied, well-made & balanced, firmly ripe tannin, food-friendly acidity. 55/45 blend, Allier oak matured. **Chardonnay** ★★★★ **03** bigger than pvs (14.3% alc) yet harmonious; creamy cling-peach aromas & hint of citrus; well flavoured. Both WO Rbtsn. – *JB*

Helderberg Winery see Omnia

Helderkruin Wine Cellar

*Stellenbosch ▪ Est 1997 ▪ 1stB 1998 ▪ Tasting & sales Mon-Thu 9- 5 Fri 9-4 Sat 9-1 ▪ Closed pub hols ▪ Tours during tasting hours ▪ Catered functions for groups of 30–120; also BYO picnic ▪ Owner Niel du Toit ▪ Winemaker Koos Bosman, with Bosman Bonthuis (Nov 1997/Jan 2003) ▪ Viticulturist Pietie Goosen (1980) ▪ 100 ha (cab, merlot, pinotage, shiraz) ▪ 1 000 tons 70% red 30% white ▪ PO Box 91 Stellenbosch 7599 ▪ helkruin@iafrica.com ▪ **T 881·3899** ▪ F 881·3898*

No update available on this winery; contact details and notes from previous edition.

Ben du Toit range

Ben du Toit Unrated preview of the flagship promises well; cab-led blend (52%) with petit v (25), merlot; **02** sweet-violet fragrance; spice from 16 mths new oak; whiff eucalyptus in finish. **Merlot** ★★★ Well-constructed **02** shows some bottle-age, also attractive ripe-fruit tone, still something in reserve. 14 mths new oak. **Pinotage** ★★★★ Savoury **02**, good mature qualities & enough ripe plum fruit-stuffing to go another few yrs. **Shiraz** ★★★ **02** dense, chewy, needing more time. 12% alc. Oak as for Merlot.

Helderkruin range

Cabernet Sauvignon ★★★ **00** easy soft tannins, mellow red fruit, touch bottle-maturity all pleasantly harmonised. 16 mths Fr oak. **Merlot** ★★★ **01** usual 18 mths Fr/Am oaking, good plummy fruit waiting to unfold. **Pinotage** ★★★ **01** still redolent of barrel character (20% new wood), time required to settle, meld. **Shiraz** ★★★ **01** strident tannins conceal sweet jammy fruit; further bottle-maturation needed. **Chardonnay** ★★★ Oak-fermented but not -aged; **04**

ripe peach & citrus touches, distinct vanilla on palate but also well-weighted sweet fruit. **Sauvignon Blanc** ★★★ **04** continues quicker pace of pvs; clean & fresh; for early enjoyment.

Yellow Cellar range

Dry Red ★★★ Straightforward, light-textured cab/merlot blend, unwooded; **99** fresh berry nose, better flavour than pvs, low 12.4% alc. **Dry White** ★★ Chenin, **03** with tropical fruit aromas, slight honeyed patina, firm dry finish. — *DH*

Helgerson see La Bri
Helshoogte Vineyards see Vuurberg

Hemelzicht

Walker Bay ▪ Est 1998 ▪ 1stB 2003 ▪ Tasting & sales Mon-Fri 8.30-5 Sat 8.30-1 at 19 Long Street Hermanus ▪ Closed pub hols ▪ Owner Louis Saaiman ▪ Winemaker Hannes Storm (2003) ▪ 16 ha (cab, malbec, shiraz, chard, sauvignon) ▪ 800 cs 100% white ▪ PO Box 469 Onrusrivier 7201 ▪ ***T/F (028) 313·2215*** *(cellar) ▪ T (028) 312·3512 (a/h)*

Louis Saaiman, a relative newcomer to winegrowing yet seemingly supremely practical and unflappable, describes the past year as 'ordinary'. Not that he doesn't recognise that his vineyards are hardly in an 'ordinary' environment: the Hemel-en-Aarde Valley, home of some of SA's top wines, with a climate Saaiman ventures is 'very specific'. He's pleased with his 05 Sauvignon (the valley was cooler than most areas in a hot season). And positively bursting about the giant potential of his 05 Cab. Future plans include 10ha more vines, a maturation cellar/tasting venue and a restaurant.

Chardonnay ★★★★ Steely, minerally **03** showed refined cool-climate tone & fine line of citrus fruit. **05** mid-2005 undergoing barrelling in Fr oak, 40% new. No **04**. **Sauvignon Blanc** ★★★★ **05** far drier than pvs (1.75g/ℓ RS vs 5g/ℓ); 'cool', racy fruit profile crushed nettle, gooseberry, capsicum — mineral texture with fine persistence. — *CR/TM*

Hemisphere see Lost Horizons

Hendrik Boom

Feel-good range (portion of profit goes to Help Aids Kids of Africa, a privately run support group) recognising the vinous contribution of Hendrik Boom, founder of the Cape's first vineyard. See Jonkheer for contact names and numbers.

Red ★★★ Easy **01** glassful with gamey fruitcake whiffs, fullish body, soft dry savoury finish. Equal portions 5 red grapes; *Wine* best value selection in 2004. 1 000ml .

White ★★★ To date a smooth & relaxed **01**, not retasted. — *TM*

Hendri Nagel see Cellar-Vie
Hercules Paragon see Simonsvlei

Herold Wines

Outeniqua (see Little Karoo map) ▪ Est 1999 ▪ 1stB 2003 ▪ Visits every Tue & last weekend of mnth 10-4 (Sep-Apr) or by appt ▪ BYO picnic ▪ Walks ▪ Conservation area ▪ Owner Mark Chandler ▪ Winemakers Mark Chandler & Vivien Harpur ▪ Viticulturist Vivien Harpur (1999) ▪ 6 ha (pinot, sauvignon) ▪ 15 tons 600 cs 80% red 20% white ▪ PO Box 10 Herold 6615 ▪ heroldwines@mweb.co.za ▪ ***T 072·833·8223*** *▪ F 086·620·4248*

It was cliffhanging time at these vineyards high up on the Montagu Pass, where signage is now up to entice passersby to stop for a tasting. With previously contracted winemaker Hannes Storm now at Hamilton Russell Vineyards and his brother Ernst S in the US, brother-and-sister team Mark Chandler and Vivien Harpur set to it alone, making the odd urgent phone call, like when they inadvertently left the cooling on and thought they'd killed the fermentation of their maiden Sauvignon: 'It luckily recovered and is tasting fantastic ... we may have to do that every year!

Pinot Noir ★★★★ **04** forest floor, organic aromas, with more ripeness, & obvious oak on finish than **03** – perhaps less finesse. Rich plum fruit & smooth silky palate with sensual appeal. 11 mths Fr oak. **Shiraz** new Intense choc, mocha on **04** (sample; provisional ★★★★); gorgeous ripeness gives thick rich fruit, ripe tannins; slight abrasiveness on finish. **Sauvignon Blanc** new ★★★ Extraordinary pungency on **05** – capsicum with passionfruit, lime and catpee; dry, mouth-watering acidity to tropical flavours, juicy with long finish. – *IvH*

Heron Ridge

*Stellenbosch (see Helderberg map) ▪ Est 1997 ▪ 1stB 2001 ▪ Visits by appt ▪ Fee R10 p/p for groups ▪ Closed pub hols ▪ Owners Pete & Jane Orpen ▪ Winemaker Pete Orpen ▪ Viti consultant Paul Wallace (Mar 1999) ▪ 4 ha (cab, shiraz) ▪ 30 tons 1 800-2 000 cs 100% red ▪ PO Box 5181 Helderberg 7135 ▪ orps@xsinet.co.za ▪ **T/F 842·2501***

Pete and Jane Orpen say they'd like to make 'a fancy straight Shiraz, hold it back for 3 or 4 years, and then release it at its best time so as to make the most of the wine'. Harvest 2005, frenetic elsewhere, here was calm and controlled, and fermentation took place 'with quiet success'. Quietly incubating in barrel is their maiden Cab.

★★★★ **Shiraz 04** sample last yr offered sumptuous raspberry/marzipan notes; very ripe though big alcohol not dominating; rich, finely textured, with lovely concentration. **05** preview reveals similar broad-shouldered, essency style. ±Yr oak, 30% new; 70% Fr. Unfiltered. – *IvH*

Hidden Valley Wines

*Stellenbosch ▪ Est/1stB 1995 ▪ Sales hours see intro ▪ Owners Dave & Marguerite Hidden ▪ Winemaker/GM Chris Kelly (2005) ▪ Viticulturist Johan 'Grobbie' Grobbelaar (Feb 1999) ▪ 30 ha (barbera, cabs s/f, malbec, merlot, mourvèdre, petit v, pinotage, shiraz, tannat, sauvignon) ▪ 180 tons 8 500 cs 90% red 10% white ▪ PO Box 12577 Die Boord 7613 ▪ info@hiddenvalleywines.com ▪ www.hiddenvalleywines.com ▪ **T 880·2646** ▪ F 880·2645*

This year sees a rebirth for this small Helderberg-based producer, with its prime, organically cultivated Devon Valley and Helderberg sites. Consultative relationships with Grangehurst's Jeremy Walker (since 1994) and Luddite's Niels Verburg (since 2004) have ended with the permanent appointment as manager/winemaker of Chris Kelly (ex-Stellenbosch Vineyards) – Kiwi-born, but now firmly rooted down in SA soil after marriage to former cellar colleague Carmen Stevens. An early task was to oversee the construction of a 200-ton, modern gravity-flow cellar on the mountain slopes to handle the 2006 harvest, wine sales and tastings. And he's delighted to be working with top-quality Helderberg red wine vineyards. International standards remain a focus, with the appointment of an Australian viticultural consultant to assist in doing justice to their 'gift of nature'.

★★★★ **Pinotage** From a 30+ yr old Devon Valley vyd & Elgin grapes. Ripe & concentrated **01** followed by **04** (sample) Multi-faceted & alluring; cool-fruit herb garden/fennel, rhubarb nuances to wild berry personality. Tannins now melding – already add savoury, roasted spice & assist a good 5-7 yr future. 13 mths oak, 80/20 Fr/Am, 25% new.

★★★★ **CWG Auction Reserve Pinotage** Last was serious, succulent **01**, with 13% cab.

★★★★ **Cabernet Sauvignon** Fruit from Firgrove/Hldrberg sites. Traditional vinification, including small open fermenters, basket press. **01** impressively both serious & approachable: reveals savoury/sweet layers, smoked beef, tapenade, rich berry fruit. Built on svelte lines; beautifully judged tannins give silky drinkability, with deep-veined strength for ageing. 18 mths mainly Fr, touch Am, mix new/used oak. With 10% shiraz. Also in magnums.

★★★★ **Shiraz** new **04** (sample) stylish debut; attractive Rhône-like character: garrigue/dried herb shadings, touch of tar, even ripe brie – all anchored by creamy black fruit. Amenable tannins give smooth drinking pleasure, structural longevity. 13 mths new/2nd fill barrels. Made in Elgin by Niels Verberg.

Hidden Agenda range new

★★★★ **Red**★★★ **03** made for food: dry, savoury tannins to soak up oily Mediterranean dishes; zinging fresh-picked berry to awaken senses, give tangy flavour. Mainly pinotage, some shiraz, merlot, dash cab. 6 mths Fr/Am oak, some new. **White** ★★★★ **05** (sample) chenin with 10% viognier, dollop sauvignon. Pear/apple-rich style, with round-textured appeal, freshness & verve. But also tantalising floral whiffs, gentle savoury tone. The thinking person's quaffer, offering something extra. Partial oaking, just off-dry (6.9 g/ℓ). Both screwcapped. — *CR*

High Constantia

Constantia ▪ Est 1683 ▪ 1stB 2000 ▪ Tasting, sales, tours 8-5 ▪ Fee R25 ▪ Closed Dec 25 & Jan 1 ▪ Owner David van Niekerk ▪ Winemakers David van Niekerk & Roger Arendse ▪ 9.5 ha (cabs s/f, merlot, pinot, chard, sauvignon) ▪ 40 tons 3 400 cs own label ▪ 91% red 3.5% rosé 5% MCC ▪ Range for customer: Sherwood-Berriman (UK) ▪ Puck's Glen Groot Constantia Rd Constantia 7800 ▪ david@highconstantia.co.za ▪ ***T 794·7171*** *▪ F 794·7999*

No update available on this winery; contact details and notes from previous edition.

★★★★ **Sebastiaan** Blend of cabs s & f as elegant & understated as its packaging. Last yr **01** showed ★★★★★ class. Leaf, berries, spice & blackcurrant notes all to be found. Fine tannins, sweet savouriness, 13.6% alc, yr Fr oak in excellent balance with fruit. Less earthy than maiden **00** where creamy, denser, more mineral notes abound.

★★★★ **Cabernet Franc** Classically styled **01** (★★★★) showed prominent herbal notes & fragrant leafiness over cedar & sweet red berries, tasted 2003. Sombrely elegant & harmonious; Fr oak; 13.7% alc. Finer, more intense than gamey **00**.

★★★★ **Clos André MCC** Beautifully, elegantly packaged, like all these. Fine maiden effort was NV, but follow-up vintaged **03** (★★★★★) even better (our sample disgorged Jan 2004, says back label). Full, rich style but bone-dry, delicate, long flavours. From 70/30 chardonnay/pinot grown on s-facing Constia slopes. 11.7% alc.

Cabernet Sauvignon ★★★★ Leafy earthiness on **01** (last tasted 2003), blackcurrant on austere palate. Good tannin support, dry finish. 13% alc. Yr new/2nd-fill Fr oak. **Rosé** ★★★ **03** mostly bled-off cab f, 8% from MCC press-wine; earthy, raspberry fragrance; just about dry. — *TJ*

High Gables see Klein Constantia

Hildenbrand Wine & Olive Estate

Wellington ▪ Est 1998 ▪ 1stB 1999 ▪ Tasting & sales daily 10–4 ▪ Closed Easter Fri-Sun, Dec 25, Dec 31, Jan 1 ▪ Tasting fee R15 ▪ Tours by appt ▪ Hildenbrand Restaurant (closed Tue) ▪ Klein Rhebokskloof Country & Guest House ▪ Farm-grown olives & olive oil ▪ Owner/viticulturist Reni Hildenbrand ▪ Winemaker Reni Hildenbrand ▪ 18 ha (cab, malbec, shiraz, chard, chenin, semillon) ▪ 4 800 cs own label 50/50 red/white ▪ PO Box 270 Wellington 7655 ▪ info@wine-estate-hildenbrand.co.za ▪ www.wine-estate-hildenbrand.co.za ▪ ***T 873·4115*** *▪ F 0866·700·147*

Owner/winemaker Reni Hildenbrand is helping lead the charge to rescue undervalued-in-SA variety semillon, and at the 2005 Trophy Wine Show her faith in the 04 Hildenbrand version (and the estate she bought in 1991) was vindicated with an exalted 'Most Successful Cellar' citation. She lets nature have her head – a philosophy which rewarded her last harvest with 'wonderful flavours'. The carbonic maceration method was applied to the shiraz bushvine grapes to impart a beaujolais character (20% of this vinification went into the 05 Shiraz Rosé below). The indefatigable Reni H keeps her eye on a slew of interests: restaurant, guesthouse, vineyards, olive groves, cellar, Cape Wine Academy olive-appreciation course (now extended to Johannesburg), and marketing and competing abroad.

★★★★ **Shiraz** Slow-maturing, graceful **02** still available. Well-flavoured & -structured with broad spectrum pepper/scrub/red fruit aromas. Generously built, with elegant tannins. 14.7% alc.

★★★★ **Chenin Blanc** ✓ Gentle **04** beguiling & understated; feather-soft acid (uncharacteristic for this grape) contrasted by freshening tannin, delicate honeysuckle/earth persistence. Used Fr oak fermented. Might not go distance but why worry? **03** sold out before we could taste. **02** was big & fat, again with soft acidity.

★★★★ **Semillon 04**, previewed in pvs ed, has blossomed into something special. Lovely layered bouquet of lemon/honey/earth; cool impression heightened by lemon grass/spice flavours. Softish but with good length. Golden hue mirrored in medal/Best Semillon Trophy at 2005 FCTWS. Native yeast ferment.

Rosé ★★★ ☺ Bright-hued, lively **05**; delicious spicy raspberry flavours vitalised by hint sugar. From shiraz.

Cabernet Sauvignon Barrique ★★★★ **01** with cassis/classy oak fragrance, dry tannins, some elegance. Fr oak, third new, 13 mths. **Cabernet Sauvignon Unwooded** ★★★★ Pleasingly medium-bodied **01** still with us. Good berry fruit, soft & approachable tannins, dry earthy finish. **Malbec 04** still in barrel, not re-tasted. Pvsly we enjoyed its cordial-like blackberry intensity, earthy dryness. Sold ex-estate only. Provisional ★★★★. **Chardonnay Barrique** ★★★★ Limited qnty of **02** still available; described last ed as delicious; mineral, citrus austerity cut by butterscotch, toast nuances. **03** sold out. **Chardonnay Unwooded** ★★★ **04** pleasant tropical tones freshened with citrus snatches. Medium-bodied, rounded, shortish finish.—*AL*

Hilko Hegewisch see Hegewisch Wines

Hill & Dale

'Classic but accessible' wines are the goal for this range, vinified from fruit off selected Stellenbosch vineyards by Guy Webber at Stellenzicht (see entry for tasting/sales information). All WO Stbosch.

Cabernet Sauvignon-Shiraz ★★★ 80/20 blend, big but not bothersome alc (15%). Burly **03** with intense red/black fruit, smoke & pepper overtones & lots of vanilla oak (Fr/Am). Chunky tannic finish. Not for keeping. **Pinotage** ★★★★ **03** has homey charm of pvs; lots of vanilla & rich fruitcake flavour, dry finish without any hard edges. No **04** tasted. **Stellenbosch Red** ★★★ Appealing forest floor bottle-age on early-drinking **00** merlot-led blend. Soft dried fruit flavours, touch of leather. Dry mineral palate invites plate of good food. Mix Fr, Am, Russian oak, ±17 mths. **Merlot Rosé** ★★★ **05** raspberry nose has savoury, bacon edge; restrained herby palate, very dry sherbet finish. Substantial 14.8% alc. **Chardonnay** ★★★ **04** retiring lemon cream bouquet, whiffs buttery oak. Slippery texture, dry tail; probably at peak now. Fr/Am oak fermented. 13.8% alc. **Sauvignon Blanc** ★★★★ ✓ Textbook **05**; pungent blast of asparagus & figs, vivid 'green' flavour; moderate alc (12.3%) but big on character.—*CvZ*

Hillcrest Estate

Durbanville ▪ Est/1stB 2002 ▪ Tasting & sales daily 9–5 ▪ Closed Easter Fri, Dec 25 & Jan 1 ▪ Restaurant for breakfast & lunches during tasting hours ▪ Tours by appt ▪ Owners PD Inglis, R Haw & G du Toit ▪ Winemaker Graeme Read (Jan 2003) ▪ Viticulturist G du Toit ▪ 25 ha (cab, merlot, shiraz, chard, sauvignon) ▪ 60 tons ▪ ±3 000 cs 45% red 55% white ▪ Private Bag X3 Durbanville 7551 ▪ restaurant@hillcrestfarm.co.za ▪ ***T 976·1110/975·2346*** *▪ F 975·2195*

Talk to Graeme Read (marine biology PhD in another life) about vines and winemaking, and witness the art and science of wine in motion: eyes gleaming like some new stainless steel tank, and all the bubbling energy of a wine mid-ferment, he expounds on the latest fine-tuning of the vineyards and cellar, including (to name just a few) different picking regimes, pre-ferment chilling, yeast experimentation. Read is upbeat about the latest harvest delivering well balanced, fruity wines (see below for some of the results). The plan is for the winery to remain boutique in terms of output, but generous in visitor hospitality: its restaurant is now open for breakfast and lunch, and affords magnificent views of Table Mountain and Robben Island.

★★★★ **Merlot-Cabernet Sauvignon** Barrel sample **04** has potential to attain heights of **03**, **02**; latter only one led by cab. Latest 60/40, elegant, restrained yet with smoky plums

& dark berries in abundance. Oak (50% new Fr) well integrated; shows class in ripe tannic finish. **03** comfortably plump fruit though firmly structured.

★★★★ **Sauvignon Blanc 04** sample continues along trail blazed by maiden **03**. Current exhibits variety's classic cool-climate characteristics of lime & gooseberry, persistent minerality; impressive fruit concentration & mouthfeel. Accessible, but with structure to improve.

Merlot ★★★★ new Early drinking example from young Dbnville vines, **04** delights with exceptionally pure fruit, delicate oaking (60% new Fr). Poised, balanced, ripe. Fine potential to gain in stature as vines mature. **Chardonnay Wooded** ★★★★ **05** work-in-progress abounds with citrus, hot buttered toast character. Full, round, warm finish from 14.7% alc. Portion oaked, mix new/older Fr. **Chardonnay Unwooded** new ★★★ **05** sample shows tropical rather than above's citrus tone. Rounded fresh flavours, pleasantly uncomplicated. **Sauvignon Blanc Reserve** new Coolly austere whiffs nettle & grapefruit on **05** sample; seems tad lean, lacks above version's intensity & fleshiness – but may settle once bottled; ★★★★ potential. – *CR*

Hill Station see Cape First
Hinterland see Hartswater

Hippo Creek

By Vintage International Brands. Originally exclusive to the PicardiRebel chain, now more widely available following its success in the export arena. VIB's Colin Frith, viti consultant Paul Wallace and Hazendal winemaker Ronell Wiid join forces to provide 'good-value wines without cutting corners'. For drinking rather than just tasting, is their credo.

Simply Red new ☺ ★★ Chunky & friendly (14% alc) blend pinotage/merlot/ruby cab, spilling over with plums & prunes; zippy finish. **Simply White** new ☺ ★★ Pleasant tropical quaffer from colombar & chardonnay. Flirtatious, but respectably dry. Both **NV**.

Cabernet Sauvignon ★★★ **02** vanilla & red berries lead aromas/flavours, riper, rounded tannins (only 2nd fill oak) make for easy, early drinking. **Merlot** ★★ **03** less stellar than pvs, still juicy but uncomplex; smoky/savory nuances. ±Yr Fr oak Fr oak, 20% new. Drink soon. **Pinotage** ★★ Unwooded, swiggable **04** earthy & plummy with brusque tannins – good wit hearty braai food. **Shiraz** new ★★ Medium bodied **03**, fruity, dusty, from combo new/old Fr oak. Showing signs of maturity, time to pull the cork. **Coast** new ★ **02** bargain basement dry red from 60% merlot, plus cab. **Chardonnay** ★★★ No new vintage since **03** (untasted). **02** pvsly noted as low-keyed but attractive. **Sauvignon Blanc** ★ Light **05** (sample) lacks varietal character, somewhat dilute. All WO W Cape. – *DH*

Hofstraat Winery new

Malmesbury (see Swartland map) ▪ Est/1stB 2002 ▪ Visits by appt ▪ Owners/winemakers Wim Smit, Loch Nel & Jack de Clercq ▪ 3.5 tons 310 cs 100% red ▪ 30 Rainier Str, Malmesbury 7300 ▪ wimsmit@wcaccess.co.za ▪ T (022) 487·3202 F (022) 487·3015

This tiny winery was born when three Malmesbury friends decided to fulfil a lifelong ambition: to sit around a table and enjoy a wine made with their own hands. The oeno-pals – who have no formal wine training – keep it simple, buying in grapes and enlisting the help of family and friends for everything from pressing the grapes to labelling the bottles. It's clearly a recipe that works: their maiden Shiraz and Merlot each won a medal at the Michelangelo Awards.

Renosterbos range

All wines fermented in 3rd fill Fr oak. **Merlot** ★★★★ **04** well-focused red plum, choc freshness; light-textured but with some fruity succulence; technically dry; finishing twist oaky sweetness detraction from some elegance. WO Voor Pdberg. **Shiraz** ★★ For those who like their spicy vanilla oak laced with a little shiraz. Fresh, bone-dry. Best drink **04** now, before dries out. Yr new Am oak. WO Swtland, as are following tank samples: **Cabernet Sauvignon 04** promises juicy, supple style; flavoursome fresh cassis teamed up with noticeable but good oak. Possible ★★★★. **Barbera** First for area. **04** unusual nose of black cherries macerated in ruby port. Full-bodied, smooth; liberal Am oak spice. Potential ★★★. — *AL*

Homtini see Anthony de Jager Wines

Hoopenburg Wines

Stellenbosch ▪ Est 1992 ▪ 1stB 1994 ▪ Tasting & sales Mon-Fri 9–4.30 Sat (Oct-Apr only) & pub hols 9.30–1 ▪ Fee R10 refunded with purchase of 6+ btls ▪ Closed Easter Fri-Mon & Dec 25/26 ▪ BYO picnic ▪ Tours by appt ▪ Art gallery ▪ Owner Gregor Schmitz ▪ Winemaker/viticulturist Neil Hawkins (Jan 2005) ▪ Farm manager Gert Snijders ▪ 34 ha (cab, merlot, pinot, shiraz, chard) ▪ 150 tons 10 000 cs 75% red 25% white ▪ PO Box 1233 Stellenbosch 7599 ▪ info@hoopenburg.com ▪ www.hoopenburg.com ▪ ***T 884·4221/2/3*** *▪ F 884·4904*

Owner Gregor Schmitz and new vini/viti man Neil Hawkins believe the only way to survive the global wine glut is to trade up. Accordingly, they're paying special attention to vineyard quality-enhancing techniques such as shoot thinning, 'green' harvesting (thinning out bunches pre-ripening) and rigorous fruit selection. For harvest 2005, they cut yields by a massive 50%. In the cellar, they moved from 300ℓ barrels to 'the best 225ℓ cooperage'. A new bag press allowed bunch-pressing (expect a particularly fine 05 Chardonnay, advises Neil H) while two new open fermenters meant the best fruit could be kept separate – all the way to the bottle. 'It's a total rejuvenation for Hoopenburg wines,' promises Neil H.

★★★★ **Cabernet Sauvignon 02** (★★★★) revisited (a sample pvs ed) still for those who enjoy strapping wines with tannins to match; black/sour cherry tones with warm conclusion from 14.5% alc. **01** more restrained yet full-flavoured, less challenging. Yr 2nd & 3rd fill Fr oak.

Merlot ★★★★ **02** deeply pigmented; earthy & savoury with textbook plums, coffee & choc; sweet fruit & balanced tannins. Youthful, should improve with ±2–5 yrs cellaring. **Pinot Noir** ★★★ **Preview 03** similar to pvs; hints cherry, raspberry & charry oak. Taut, persistent tannins need time to knit; more than sufficient fruit to go the distance. **Pinotage** ★★★ Last reviewed was **01**, clean fresh-fruit tone, firm tannins should have relaxed by now. **Shiraz** ★★★ Rustic **03** needs food to cushion noticeably drying tannins. Leather & scrub whiffs, touch bottle-age. finishes with dried prune tinge & noticeable alc. **Chardonnay** ★★★ **03** attractive peaches & cream character, rounded, supportively oaked. **04** sold out before we could taste. **'South Barrel Chamber Chardonnay'** new Tentatively named work-in-progress. **05** acacia flower & lemon blossom on nose, lively lime acidity; all daubed with buttery, creamy oak. Potential ★★★★. **Sauvignon Blanc** ★★★★ **04**, tasted as sample pvs ed, now shows green grass & nettle bouquet; ebullient fruit balances piercing acidity; dry, slate-like finish. WO Coastal, all others Stbosch. **Pinot Noir-Chardonnay** new Attractive sweet-sour raspberry & boiled sweets in **05** bouquet, slightly meaty citrus flavour. 'Slight pink tinge should be a lady-killer' winks winemaker. Unfinished 60/40 blend could rate ★★★★. **Winemaker's Selection** range discontinued. — *CvZ*

Hoop Huis see False Bay Vineyards

Horse Mountain Wines

Paarl ▪ Est 1997 ▪ 1stB 2001 ▪ Visits by appt Mon-Fri 9–5 Sat 9–1 ▪ BYO picnic ▪ Owner Far Horizons Wine Estate (Pty) Ltd ▪ Winemaker Charles Stassen (Jan 2002) ▪ Viti consultant Paul Wallace (Jan 2000) ▪ 45 ha (cabs s/f, merlot, pinotage, shiraz) ▪ 400 tons 20 000 cs own labels + 80 000ℓ for clients ▪ 70% red 20% white 10% rosé ▪ PO Box 2143 Windmeul 7630 ▪ wine@horsemountainwines.com ▪ www.horsemountainwines.com ▪ ***T 869·8328*** *▪ F 869·8329*

Craig Lardner feels like he's picked the winning trifecta. His premium range is up and running, with the Bordeaux-style blend Michele (named for his daughter) and Shiraz having joined his front-runner Pinotage. All were commended at the 2005 IWSC. Meanwhile, his 'lifestyle' Quagga Ridge trio are performing at The Shaftesbury Theatre in London's West End (doing a solo for Prince Charles at the gala opening of the musical production *The Far Pavilions*). Wonderful reassurance for this former property developer who transformed a dairy farm into a vineyard, helped establish the Voor Paardeberg as an official wine ward, and has not been shy to introduce screwcaps on all his wines.

★★★★ **Pinotage ✓ 04** worthy successor to perfumed **03**. Fresh, ripe red flavours, hint of acetone more heritage than hindrance; excellent balance. 20% Am oak for coconut lift.

★★★★☆ **Michele ✓ 04** classic bdx recipe of cab, merlot, cab f provides a wealth of interesting flavours, richness & palate weight. New Fr oak applied with class & restraint.

★★★★☆ **Shiraz ✓ 04** Italian coffee shop in liquid form: all mocha & spice, booming 14.5% alc. Fr and 20% Am oak.

Quagga Ridge range

Rosé ☺ ★★☆ Easy drinking **05**, boiled sweets nose & light, fragrant body (12.5% alc.); 80% pinotage, dash merlot.

Red ★ **04** rustic, earthy melange of cab & merlot; quality-wise, not from same stable as pvs. **White** ★☆ 60:40 blend of sauvignon/semillon in **05**, vegetal flavours & big acidity. Less convincing than unpretentious **04** quaffer. — *NP*

Houmoed see Teubes Family

Huguenot Wine Farmers

Wellington ▪ Closed to public ▪ Owner Kosie Botha ▪ Cellarmaster Bill Matthee (1984) ▪ Trade enquiries Gert Brynard ▪ PO Box 275 Wellington 7654 ▪ jcb@mynet.co.za ▪ ***T 864·1293*** *▪ F 873·2075*

Privately owned wholesaling company which blends, markets and distributes a wide range of wines, liqueurs and spirits. The range, not assessed, includes: Cabernet, Pinotage, Smooth Red (cinsaut/pinotage), Premier Grand Cru (chenin/crouchen), Stein (chenin), Late Harvest (chenin), Hanepoot, Red/White Jeripico (red/white muscadel), Invalid Port, Tawny Port, Nagmaalwyn and Old Brown Sherry. And the Zellerhof 5ℓ vats: Stein, Late Harvest and Premier Grand Cru.

Hummelhof see Goudini
Husseys Vlei see Buitenverwachting
Ibis see Schalkenbosch

Idiom

Sir Lowry's Pass ▪ Est/1stB 2003 ▪ Tasting & sales: see Whalehaven ▪ Tours by appt ▪ Owners Alberto & Valerie Bottega ▪ Winemaker Paul Engelbrecht (Sep 2003) ▪ Viticulturist Tim Clark ▪ 32 ha (cabs s/f, merlot, shiraz, mourvèdre, nebbiolo, pinotage, sangiovese, zinfandel, viognier) ▪ 90% red 10% white ▪ Private Bag X14 Hermanus 7200 ▪ wine@idiom.co.za ▪ www.idiom.co.za ▪ ***T (028) 316·1633*** *▪ F (028) 316·1640*

Retired Italian *émigré* Alberto Bottega of Whalehaven (see separate entry) finds inspiration in tasting blockbuster wines from around the word. So expect something special from Da Capo Vineyards, his vineyards on the Hottentots Holland Mountains near Sir Lowry's Pass. Soil scientist Dawid Saayman, oenological guru Eben Archer and vini-consultant Giorgio Dalla Cia (mentoring Whalehaven winemaker Paul Engelbrecht) are involved. As are deep granitic soils, 350m altitude, sea breezes (really!) and a selection of Bordeaux, Rhône and Italian varieties, plus pinotage (tipping a hat at Bottega's adopted country). The label 'Idiom' is no fancy: personal expression and individual character of clone, variety and vineyard are being strived for here.

★★★★ **Bordeaux Blend** new **04** more elegant & charming than characterful stable mates. Cab dominated (58%) with merlot/cab franc (24/18). Dark maraschino cherries backed by classy tannins, these firm but supple. Poised, even at 14.8% alc, with touch sweetness on finish (3g/ℓ sugar). Yr Fr oak, 60% new. Structure to develop complexity 3-6 yrs cellaring.

Sangiovese ★★★☆ **04** realises the potential suggested by the maiden **03** tasted as sample mid-2004. Well-crafted so that 15% alc barely noticeable; juicy berry fruit, springy tannin, tangy tail. Great solo or with food. Yr Fr/Am, some new. Muscled (15% alc) & toned **Zinfandel** new ★★★☆ **04** bursts with dark berries & sharp red currants, rich, spicy oak. Vibrant acidity & firm tannins suggest will improve 2-3 yrs. 60% new Am oak. **Shiraz-Mourvèdre** ★★★☆ **04** classy Rhône-style blend led by shiraz (71%), dollop mourvèdre (25%) & tickle viognier. Pepper/spice/liquorice in bouquet, mouth full rounded. Powerful; we can sense a latent authority that should show itself with ± 3 yrs cellaring. Combo new/old; Fr/Am barrels. **Wooded Viognier** ★★★☆ **04** celebrates stone fruit on its nose & palate; sweet butter scotch & barley sugar finish. Oak overwhelming at present but there is sufficient fruit to mesh over 2-3 yrs. All above WO Stebosch. – *DH*

Ietsie Anders see Cru Wines
Ilka see Alluvia
Imagine see Southern Sky
Imbizo see Ernst & Co
Imvelo see Premium Cape Wines
Indaba see African Terroir, Cape Classics, Excelsior
Indalo see Swartland Wine Cellar
Infiniti see Omnia Wines
Inglewood see Omnia Wines

Ingwe

Stellenbosch (see Helderberg map) ▪ Est 1998 ▪ 1stB 1999 ▪ Visitors welcome but plse phone ahead ▪ Owner Alain Mouiex ▪ Winemaker PJ Geyer (Sep 2001) ▪ Viticulturist Francois Baard (Sep 1999) ▪ 28 ha (own/leased; cabs s/f, malbec, merlot, shiraz, tempranillo, chard, sauvignon) ▪ 110 tons 18 000 cs 95% red 5% white ▪ PO Box 583 Somerset West 7129 ▪ ingwewine@eject.co.za; ingwewinepg@eject.co.za ▪ ***T 083·280·0137(FB) / 083·327·3887 (PJG)*** *F 858·1063/852·7346*

A White has joined the range from this 'micro-château' near Sir Lowry's Pass – a sauvignon/semillon. 'Expect only blends now,' viticulturist Francois Baard explains, 'no more varietals. Blending gets so much more out of a wine.' Proprietor Alain Moueix, co-owner/director of two Bordeaux estates, would say 'amen' to that. Given a relaxing six-week harvest (unlike the frantic three of the previous year), winemaker PJ Geyer had plenty of time to work with the reds, which had benefited from rain just before harvest (to the level of 'exceptional', he declares, in the case of the merlot and shiraz). Perhaps a start can now be made on building that elusive cellar....

★★★★ **Ingwe** 'Leopard' in Xhosa. Refined melot-led red, with 48% cab in promising **03** (★★★★☆) sample, showing complex array of mineral, savoury & black cherry tones; fine oak integration helped along by micro-oxygenation (piped music & the reassuring presence of their mascot, a fluffy pink & white cow, other possible quality factors!). Classy maiden **02** also displayed refined minerality, mid-palate fruit density; 60% new Fr oak compared to **03**'s 40%. 13.8% alc.

★★★☆ **Amehlo** Meaning 'Leopard's Eye' – a different & varietally more intricate look at the Bdx-style blend. Cab's in front (46%) in elegantly structured **03** (★★★★☆), with merlot, malbec, shiraz (25/15/10) & touch petit v. Entices with spicy perfumes & lilies; focused velvet texture (micro-oxygenation enhanced); improves in glass. Leap up from **02**, which more austere & leafy, in line with vintage. 14–18 mths Fr oak. *Wine* ★★★★.

★★★★ **Amehlo White** new Sophisticated & harmonious blend fronted by sauvignon (60%), semillion portion barrel fermented, blend lees-aged ±5 mths. Maiden **04** (★★★☆) has multifarious bouquet of curry leaf, mango & melon, grapefruit pith on palate. Bright & engaging **05** raises the bar; similar aromas but more impressively taut, minerally and substantial.

Sauvignon Blanc discontinued. – *CvZ*

Initial Series *see* Jean Daneel
Inkawu *see* Laibach
International Wine Services *see* WaverleyTBS

Iona Vineyards

Elgin ▪ Est 1997 ▪ 1stB 2001 ▪ Tasting, sales & tours Mon-Fri 8-5.30 ▪ Closed Easter Fri/Sat/Sun, Dec 25 & Jan 1 ▪ BYO picnic ▪ Self-catering guest house ▪ Walks ▪ Mountain biking ▪ Owner Andrew & Rozanne Gunn, Workers Trust ▪ Vini consultant Niels Verburg, with Thapelo Hlasa (both Feb 2004) ▪ Joseph Sebulawa, advised by Kevin Watt (Nov 2001) ▪ 35 ha (cab, merlot, petit v, shiraz, mourvèdre, chard, sauvignon, semillon, viognier) ▪ 7 000 cs 25% red 75% white ▪ PO Box 527 Grabouw 7160 ▪ gunn@iona.co.za ▪ www.iona.co.za ▪ ***T (028) 284·9678/284·9953*** *▪ F (028) 284·9078*

With plantings up to 35ha, Iona owner Andrew Gunn's broad objective to offer four site-specific wines is excitingly close to being met. The Sauvignon (now mostly under screwcap to promote optimum condition and minimise bottle variation – though, for the purists, some is still closed with cork) and the Bordeaux-style red are up and running. A Chardonnay and Shiraz-Mourvèdre-Viognier are in the starting stalls. Where other areas experienced difficulties with drought and unseasonable rain, cool-climate Elgin recorded an excellent harvest, says Gunn. Tight canopy controls and curtailed crop levels produced reds with increased concentration.

★★★★★ **Sauvignon Blanc** Elegant & poised example from cool upland site; typical Iona vibrant mineral core, gooseberry/nettle notes on **05** (★★★★), lingering flavours; slightly less mid-palate flesh this vintage, might fill out with time (better after yr+ anyway); First yr under screwcap means SO_2 levels lower than pvs. Picked earlier than sumptuous & deep-flavoured **04**.

Merlot-Cabernet Sauvignon new ★★★★ Restrained & elegant (12.5% alc), begs time to show its best. **03** 51/49 blend; deft hand with oak complements dark cherry fruit. Wine to watch as vyds mature. Yr Fr barrels, 25% new. **Shiraz** new ★★★★ Intriguing lily, pistachio, camphor bouquet, **04** dry & smooth, refreshing mineral aftertaste. Accessible now with 3-4 yr potential. **Merlot** discontinued. *—JP*

Isabelo *see* 32 Degrees South
Ivory Creek *see* Citrusdal Cellars
Ivy du Toit *see* Jason's Hill
Jabulani *see* South African Premium Wines

Jacaranda Estate

Wellington ▪ Est 1993 ▪ 1stB 1994 ▪ Tasting, sales & tours Mon-Sat 10-5 ▪ Closed Easter Fri & Dec 25 ▪ Self-catering/B&B cottage ▪ BYO picnic ▪ Farm-grown/made cheeses, jams & olives ▪ Owners Jan & Trish Tromp ▪ Winemaker/viticulturist Jan Tromp ▪ 2.8 ha (cab, merlot, chenin) ▪ 25 tons 300 cs own label ▪ 75% red 25% white ▪ PO Box 121 Wellington 7654 ▪ jacranda@iafrica.com ▪ ***T 864·1235***

'Does a new granddaughter qualify as a milestone?' asks Jan Tromp, in answer to our stock question this year. Why not? After all, this is an estate where an impressive 164 bird species have now been spotted within one kilometre of the cellar, and where Daisy the dairy cow is setting her own record: a lactation lasting 1 003 days. 'Like the vines, quality was good but quantity was reduced,' says retired accountant Jan T of vintage 2005. 'Our vines (like their owners) continue to age well.'

Cabernet Sauvignon ★★ Individual & rustically charming **01** was the last tasted. **04** 'in the pipeline'. **Merlot** ★★★ Soft & light textured, **03** showed good tannin structure & deft wooding (Fr staves) last yr. **Debutante** ★★★ Lightly Fr oaked cab/merlot blend, 67/33 ratio in **03** (sample pvs ed). Farmyard/wild scrub whiffs enliven black cherry/raspberry compôte nose, stewed fruit on palate, tannins firm & dry. Individual & idiosyncratic. Still-available **02** marketed as 'Dry Red' (correct labels not available at bottling time). **Chenin Blanc** ★★ Unwooded **03** tasted mid-2004 was soft, fruity-dry with pear tones. **Jerepigo** ★★★ Winter-warming **96**, 100% chenin; honeyed lanolin tone with slight savoury edge; individual & attractive. 18% alc. — *JN*

Jack & Knox Winecraft

Est/1stB 2001 ▪ Closed to public ▪ Owners Graham Knox & Bruce Jack ▪ See under Flagstone

Vinous chameleon Graham Knox (Siyabonga, Stormhoek, At The Limiet) here collaborates with creative fruit-sourcer(er) Bruce Jack (Flagstone Winery), uncovering exciting and unusual vineyards, capturing the essence of variety, nurturing the young and nursing the old back to life. And bottling under the most descriptive names: Frostline – from high, not-quite-snowline Swartberg mountain vineyard; Outsider – single shiraz block just outside Riebeek-Kasteel, one of the oldest in SA; Green on Green – vineyard situated on lower foothills of Wellington's Groenberg ('Green Mountain'). Huge critical acclaim, great fun.

★★★★ **Green on Green Semillon** Textured rather than bright varietal tones garnered from Wllngtn vyd. Latest **04** beautifully elegant from candlewax notes through ripe quince flesh, tethered by limey seam. **03** subtle, silky, with thread lemony freshness leading to elegant conclusion. Native yeasts; Am/Fr oak, 30% new; now lighter 13% alc.

The Outsider Shiraz ★★★★ Brooding blockbuster **02** noted last ed had ultra-ripe waves liquorice & crushed dark spice; Am oak, tannins bolster chewy viscosity. **04** is next. **Frostline Chardonnay** ★★★★ **04** proffers crème brûlée aromas, roast hazelnut girth cut by litchi & white pear; smooth, less robust (13% alc) than pvs. Barrel-fermented 4 mths Am/Fr oak, 60% new. **Frostline Riesling** ★★★★ Variety's aromatic pepper-lime delicacy given steely glint in **05**: broad fruit richness to tingling bone-dry finish. Reductive; zesty aperitif or for cream sauces. 13% alc. This WO Swartberg, above, Coastal. — *DS*

Jackass see Vinus Via
Jackson's of Stanford see Stanford Hills Winery

Jacobsdal Estate

Stellenbosch ▪ Est 1916 ▪ 1stB 1974 ▪ Tasting & sales at Bergkelder (see entry) or by appt ▪ Owner Dumas Ondernemings (Pty) Ltd ▪ Winemaker/viticulturist Cornelis Dumas, with Hannes Dumas ▪ 100 ha (cab, pinotage, chenin, sauvignon) ▪ 600 tons 7–10 000 cs own label 100% red ▪ PO Box 11 Kuils River 7579 ▪ dumas@iafrica.com ▪ www.jacobsdal.co.za ▪ ***T/F 905·1360***

Continuing to ferment grapes from old dryland bushvines in cement tanks, originally cast by grandfather Dumas in 1921, this father-and-son team resolutely adhere to simple time-honoured methods. A little sulphur aside, nothing is added or subtracted, and the grapes ferment with their own yeasts. And things look set to continue in this vein: with no innovations to report, their only 'plans' are to continue making top quality Pinotage (maiden vintage 1966) and Cab from the estate vineyards.

★★★★ **Pinotage** One of the originals (first was **66**) & still resolutely artisanal. **02** rustic, with pinotage smoke, strawberry & acetone whiffs; savoury, faintly rubbery flavours. 14% alc unobtrusive, pleasantly austere tannins. **01** marked an improvement on pvs two vintages; should evolve into something classic. 25–35 yr old dryland bushvines, free-run juice only, 12–18 mths small Fr oak.

Cabernet Sauvignon ★★★★ Made exactly as above, off dryland bushvines 8–20 yrs old. No pandering to fleshy fruit pundits: **02** lean & grippy, with taut cab backbone; curry spice & cassis/cedar nuances make interesting accompaniment to rich mutton *bredies*. — *CvZ*

Jacobus de Wet see Baarsma
Jacoline Haasbroek Wines see My Wyn
Jagger's Peak see Blue Crane

Janéza Private Cellar

Robertson ▪ Est 2000 ▪ 1stB 2001 ▪ Visits by appt ▪ Fee for tourgroups R5 ▪ Open pub hols by appt ▪ Platters by appt Mon-Fri during opening hours ▪ Owners Jan & Eza Wentzel ▪ Winemaker Jan Wentzel ▪ Viti consultant Briaan Stipp ▪ 18 ha (cab, merlot, shiraz, chard, sau-

vignon) ▪ 3 000 cs own label 80% red 20% white ▪ PO Box 306 Bonnievale 6730 ▪ jan.eza@lando.co.za ▪ www.janeza.co.za ▪ ***T 082·978·7020*** *▪ F (023) 616·2848*

A rich sense of history and tradition pervades Jan and Eza Wentzel's farm near Bonnievale, especially when it comes to winemaking, where minimal influence and natural methods are the way. Their personal goal is 'to get the balance right from the ground to the bottle', and they're striving for full-bodied fruity wines.

Tresuva ★★★ The 3 grapes in winery's Spanish name are cab (50%), shiraz & merlot from selected blocks, made traditionally, 13-16 mths Fr/Am oak. **02** shows vintage's light plummy tone (despite ripe-seeming 14.5% alc), slightly grainy tannins. **Chardonnay** ★★★ **04** shy baked-apple & lees aromas, bright fruit-salad flavours; hint sweetness on finish; unwooded. **Sauvignon Blanc** ★★★ **04** entrée of green herbs & nettles, crisp, steely, piercing freshness perhaps a little overdone given the fruit-weight. 12% alc.—*TM*

Jantara see Cape Vineyards
Jardin see Jordan

Jason's Hill Private Cellar

Slanghoek (see Worcester map) ▪ Est/1stB 2001 ▪ Tasting & sales Mon-Fri 9-5 Sat 10-1 Sun by appt ▪ Fee R10 ▪ Closed Easter Fri, Dec 25 & Jan 1 ▪ Cheese platters by appt ▪ Facilities for children ▪ Farm produce ▪ Conferencing for max 50 ▪ Owner/viticulturist Sakkie du Toit ▪ Winemaker Ivy du Toit Oates (Jan 2001) ▪ 100 ha (13 varieties r/w) ▪ 600 tons 50% red 45% white 5% rosé ▪ Brand for customer: Wolvenbosch (UK) ▪ PO Box 14 Rawsonville 6845 ▪ jasonshill@lando.co.za ▪ www.jasonshill.com ▪ ***T (023) 344·3256 ▪ F*** *(023) 344·3146*

Effervescent Ivy du Toit-Oates, wine-maker and -ambassador for the Cape Winelands District Municipality's marketing campaign, 'Homegrown', is determined to be heard when it comes to her region: 'It's unpretentious, the people are friendly and it's still really undiscovered.' Her own young winery is the smallest in the area but has an enviable reputation (IdT a past Diners Club Young Winemaker and Woman Winemaker of Year). Though 'still experiencing growing pains', she looks forward to someday exporting her wines. Viognier was vinified for the first time in 2005, and wide-ranging trials carried out with chardonnay.

No new vintages reviewed; notes from pvs ed. **Cabernet Sauvignon** ★★★ **01** mocha/mushroom features to dark-berried bouquet; solid mouthful; well-integrated for current drinking. 15% alc. **Merlot** ★★★ **01** ripe, soft, fleshy fruit, balanced tannins. Hint alc glow (14.7%) suggests best open soon. Fr casks, 14 mths. **Pinotage** ★★★ Vanilla-toned **01** smooth, light-textured & less weighty than 14.5% alc would suggest. 10 mths used Fr oak. **Shiraz** ★★★ **01** sweet oak flavours dominate; 15% alc warmth in tail. Drink up. 20% new Am oak, rest old Fr. **Rosé 04** dry blend shiraz, pinotage, merlot not tasted. **Chardonnay** ★★ **03** butterscotch/sweet vanilla tones, uncomplicated, lightweight creaminess. Fermented/5 mths Fr oak. **Sauvignon Blanc** ★★★ **03** won Diners Club Young Winemaker of Year for Ivy dT; also VDG, MIWA gold. Current **04** not tasted. **Chenin** ★★★ **04** invitingly fresh, lively medium-bodied sipping; fruitly dry. 12% alc. **Ivy du Toit White Blend** ★★★ **03** equal parts semillon, sauvignon, chardonnay; prominent sweet oak vanilla, good thread balancing acid. Fermented/8 mths new Fr oak. SA Woman Winemaker of Yr award. **Noble Late Harvest** ★★★★ Golden **03** dessert; 50/50 chenin/muscat d'A. luscious but not over-heavy. 12.8% alc. 109g/ℓ sugar.—*AL*

Jay Gatsby see Third World Wines

JC le Roux

Stellenbosch ▪ 1stB 1983 ▪ Tasting & sales Mon-Fri 8.30-4.30 Sat 9-4 Sun (Sep-Apr only) 10-3 ▪ Fee R20 ▪ Tour & AV show Mon-Fri 10, 11.30, 3 Sat 10, 12 Sun (Sep-Apr only) 11, 12 Mid Dec-Jan 10, 11, 12, 2, 3 ▪ Closed Easter Fri/Sun, Dec 25 & Jan 1 ▪ Tourgroups ▪ Gifts ▪ Owner Distell ▪ Winemaker Melanie van der Merwe (1995), with Hentie Germishuys & Wilhelm Pienaar (Oct 2002/April 2004) ▪ Farm manager Willem Laubscher; viticulturist Bennie Liebenberg (both Jan 2000) ▪ 27 ha own vyds ▪ 766 000 cs 20% red 80% white ▪ ISO 9200 certified ▪ PO Box 184 Stellenbosch 7599 ▪ jclr@distell.co.za ▪ www.jcleroux.co.za ▪ ***T 865·2590*** *▪ F 865·2586*

With more South Africans sipping it than ever before (over 7.5m litres a year), bubbly has shifted from 'wedding wine' to 'anytime enlivener'. Part of the credit has to go to Melanie van der Merwe, long-time cellar chief at this, the largest sparkling-wine house in the country. Her aim is to make 'the perfect cap classique', and she's continually tweaking the vinification to reach her goal. Last year MvdM introduced new pressing techniques which upped the quality of juice from bunch-pressed grapes. Fermentation temperatures were adjusted to yield fuller base-wines. Tasting at their venue in Devon Valley remains a fine winelands experience. The restaurant, temporarily closed last winter, is due to open in time for this summer season. Another option is the independently owned Manor Restaurant on the edge of the property. Note: Pongrácz range now listed separately.

Méthode Cap Classique range

★★★★ **Scintilla** Brut-style MCC dominated by chardonnay (75%, with pinot), bottle-matured 4½ yrs; class alluded to by weighty embossed bottle. **99** invigorates with explosive mousse, cool blackcurrant/savoury scents, lemon acidity & herbal nuance. Fruit weight/concentration bodes well for cellaring. 7g/ℓ RS. Maiden **98** poised & elegant, with rich, firm palate.

★★★★ **Pinot Noir ✓ 97** (★★★★★) step up on pvs with intense honeycomb/choc croissant aromas; languid bead belies lively savoury palate; weight/complexity from 7 yrs *sur lie* ageing. Dry mineral farewell. 7.1g/ℓ RS. Stylish **96**'s black-fruit heft, minerality softened by strawberries-&-cream flavours.

★★★★ **Pinot Noir Rosé** Further evidence that pink sparklers can be serious. Brut-styled **00** was first; next (and current) release is partridge-eye-hued **96**, tasted last yr, enticing pinot earthiness, strawberry/cherry tones; weighty & pleasantly dry (9g/ℓ RS).

★★★★ **La Vallée ✓** Idiosyncratic & popular semi-dry bubbly (33g/ℓ RS) from pinot gris. **99** last ed offered apple-pie & cream aromas mingled with grilled nuts, chamomile; honey notes from 5 yrs bottle-age.

Chardonnay ★★★★ Brut sparkler, classically long-matured (5-9 yrs on lees). Latest **98** VDG, similar to **97** with apple compôte richness; round toffee-apple flavour; persistent chalk/mineral finish. Structure to develop further complexity in bottle. 7g/ℓ RS.

Sparkling range

All carbonated; **NV** unless noted. **Le Domaine** ★★★ Sweet party fizz from mainly muscat with sauvignon, chenin; floral & spicy muscat tones, lively bubbles, low 7.8% alc. **La Chanson** ★★★ Big-volume ruby-hued sweet sparkler. Low 7.7% alc, with abundant berry fruit from mix red varieties. Tannins provide contrast, absorb some of the sweetness. **Sauvignon Blanc** ★★★ Summer holiday bubbly. No mistaking the variety on latest **05** with grass & Granny Smith apple aromas; tastes sweeter than 11g/ℓ sugar suggests. **JC Blue** ★★ Aimed at younger market, packaged in 187ml sapphire bottle with screwcap & easy-sipping straw. Soft, semi-sweet flavour; spicy/floral perfume with touch muscat. Both ranges Coastal or W Cape origin. *— CvZ*

Jean Daneel Wines

Napier ▪ Est/1stB 1997 ▪ Visits by appt ▪ Owners/winemakers Jean & René Daneel ▪ 3.25 ha ▪ 42 tons 3 000 cs 30% red 70% white ▪ PO Box 200 Napier 7270 ▪ jdwines@worldonline.co.za ▪ ***T (028) 423·3724*** *▪ F (028) 423·3789*

As ever, Jean Daneel prefers to let his wines do the talking, while he merely utters (in answer to our question: what's the highlight of the past year) the two words some winemakers only dream of: 'Sold out'. His future plans? 'Make more wine.' Which should be good news coming from this chenin specialist, except that the very wet weather in Napier, where he now has his own small vineyard, resulted in low yields of chenin and sauvignon in 2005. But merlot is looking good, says the former Buitenverwachting and Morgenhof winemaker, who plans to plant more vines this year while continuing to buy in fruit from selected vineyards for his two-tiered portfolio.

Signature series

★★★★ **Cabernet Sauvignon-Merlot 00** was robust & dense, but step-up **01** (★★★★☆) last ed showed great elegance & restraint. Blackcurrant/almond notes, leafy yet still ripe, great length. 75/25 blend, Stbosch fruit (WO Coastal), 22 mths new Fr oak. *Decanter* ★★★★. Future vintages released only when deemed market ready.

★★★★ **Chenin Blanc Signature** This guide's first Wine of the Year accolade for magnificent **03** (★★★★★) ✓, from low yielding Stbosch vyds, 7 mths Fr oak, 20% new. **04** slightly less striking but still excellent, in restrained & classic style. Honeysuckle aromas, measured palate with good, even dense flavour (apricot/pear-drop), bone-dry finish. The now std 20% new oak fully integrated in lime-citrus finish.

★★★★ **Chardonnay Brut** new Elegant cap classique, 100% chardonnay, Frhoek vyds, basewine Fr oak matured (3rd/4th fill). **01** creamy mousse with biscuit notes, delicious suppleness on palate, great lift & focus.

Initial series

★★★★ **Cabernet Sauvignon-Merlot** Still youthful **02** (★★★☆), pungent black fruit aromas, herbal whiffs; ripe tannins promise future softness though 14.5% alc evident mid-2005. Equal blend ex-Frhoek vyds. Less sumptuous than maiden **01** 54/46 blend from Frhoek/Stbosch fruit, more savoury, complex. MIWA gold. 22 mths Fr oak.

Chenin Blanc-Sauvignon Blanc ★★★ Sauvignon's greenpepper whiffs dominate latest **04**, showing JD's hallmark elegance. Now lower alc (13.5%), less of the honeyed tone of more chenin-influenced **03**. WO Frhoek. **Port** new ★★★ From cab ex-Barrydale, 3 yrs wooded & showing rich barrel character; plus some autumnal leaf notes, good length. Raisiny oxidative berry aromas; dense, soft textures. **00** but uncertified at press time. — *MF*

Jewel of the Breede River

Robertson ▪ Est 2004 ▪ 1stB 2005 ▪ Visits by appt ▪ BYO picnic ▪ Guest accommodation ▪ Walks ▪ Owners De Clercq family ▪ Winemaker Ruud de Clercq (2005), advised by Kobus van der Merwe ▪ Viti adviser Anton Laas (2004) ▪ 26 ha (ruby cab, shiraz, chard, chenin, colombard) ▪ 250 tons total 900 cs own label 100% red ▪ PO Box 203 McGregor 6708 ▪ jewelbr@lando.co.za ▪ www-kingsriver-estate.com ▪ ***T (023) 625·1108***

Part of the original Koningsrivier property, Kingsriver Estate has a colourful 150-year history. In the 1950s it was owned by the Gunstons (the famous 'cigarette' family), who enlarged the manor house to accommodate their glamorous parties. Current owner Ruud de Clercq, a trained engineer, traded theme parks in Europe for this tract on the Breede River, where he's growing herbs and grapes to make 'elegantly ecological wines'. A discovery in a ramshackle shed of four large underground storage tanks, an intact part of the original winery, was his vinous 'hit button' (previously all the grapes were delivered to McGregor Winery). He's decided to launch his label, Jewel of the Breede River (the phrase used by the real estate agent to market the property), with a Cab, Ruby Cab and Shiraz, none ready for tasting.

Kiss & Tell see Leopard Frog Vineyards
JH Pacas & Co see Bernheim
JJ Wines see Stellcape

Johan van Zyl Wines

Swartland ▪ Est/1stB 2002 ▪ Visits by appt 10–5 ▪ Owner Johan van Zyl ▪ Vini consultant Gerda Willers ▪ Viticulturist Johan Viljoen ▪ 50 ha (cab, cinsaut, grenache (r/w), pinotage, tempranillo, chard, viognier) ▪ 250 tons 500 cs own label ▪ PO Box 251 Citrusdal 7340 ▪ hannalise@heidedal.co.za ▪ ***T (022) 921·3328/2740*** *▪ F (022) 921·2740*

A name change (from Van Zylskloof to avoid confusion with Bonnievale's Van Zylshof) caused hardly a hiccup in the ongoing progress on this rediscovered vineyard land high up the Piekenierskloof (Fairview's Charles Back has inspired growers, farming here since the 1920s). Labour-intensive night-harvesting (midnight-10am), new cooling/packaging facilities required some 100 new workers. The Van Zyl family responded by transforming maturation space into a crèche and pre-primary (fruit goes to Franschhoek for vinification by consultant Gerda Willers). The 2004/2005 drought conditions cut the crop on these dryland vineyards, but constant temperatures facilitated even ripening and the 35-year-old unirrigated bush-vine pinotage is expected to be 'beeeeg'!

Grenache ★★ **04** Mulberry bouquet introduces sweet/sour palate, aggressive acidity. Appears less generous, leaner than this variety usually is. Drink with food, perhaps rich venison. 14.5% alc. Mainly old oak. **Pinotage** ★★★ **03** tasted last yr, high-toned, slightly spirity raspberry aromas 'sweetened' with oak (yr, 50% new, 20% Am); raspberry/vanilla cuts gutsier elements of 15.5% alc. Will need careful monitoring. Above all from Piekenklf vineyards. **Chardonnay** ★★★ **04** lively, full ripe & tropical, integrated & unobtrusive oak; more user-friendly than pvs hot, unyielding finish. 8 mths Fr oak, 50% new. **Pinotage Natural Sweet** discontinued. —*CT*

John B see Rietvallei
John Faure see Ruitersvlei

Jonkerskloof

These budget-priced quaffers by Robertson Winery for Vinimark now discontinued.

Jonkheer

Robertson ▪ Est 1912 ▪ 1stB 1956 ▪ Visits by appt ▪ Closed pub hols ▪ Proclaimed conservation area ▪ 4×4 trail ▪ Owners Nicholas Jonker & sons ▪ Winemakers Erhard Roothman & Dirk Jonker (1970/1992) ▪ Viticulturists Andries Jonker & Gideon van Niekerk (1985/1981) ▪ 185 ha (cab, chard, muscat de F) ▪ 2 500 tons 15 000 cs own label + 130 000 cs for customers, incl Semaya (US & Scandinavia) ▪ 30% red 70% white ▪ PO Box 13 Bonnievale 6730 ▪ info@jonkheer.co.za ▪ www.jonkheer.co.za ▪ ***T (023) 616·2137/8****/9 ▪ F (023) 616·3146*

'Don't interfere with nature's expression of beauty,' says Dirk Jonker, asked for his winemaking philosophy. Though he then hastily adds (no doubt reflecting on the major recent and ongoing revamp of the cellar, and the positive effect of their new and no doubt very expensive technology): 'however, if you get equipment that enables you to intervene less, use it!' Yes, well. Seems they needed all the help they could get in finding the beauty of vintage 2005 – the toughest crush since 1992, reckons Dirk, though chenin and sauvignon surprised pleasantly, and the touriga was 'brilliant'. Renovation and innovation continue, with exciting news for aspirant *garagiste* winemakers: the plan is not only to provide some training, but also to offer wine lovers facilities for making their own wines.

Jonkheer range

★★★★ **Chardonnay Family Reserve** Serious & classically styled, new oak fermented, *sur lie* 18 mths, native yeasts. Delicious **04** (sample) holds nothing back: sourdough, nutty, crème brûlée intensity; riveting nose & palate. Citrus peel edginess lifts, freshens. Palate-lengthening 6g/ℓ RS, robust 14.8% alc. No **03**. **02** concentrated aromas, complex, creamy palate, exceptional length.

★★★★ **Dead Frogge Chardonnay** Vastly less frivolous than name – selection of best barriques, full-bodied & overtly oaky (15 mths new Fr). Bold & vibrant **04** (sample) already seductive: intense peachy fruit easily handles powerful nutty oak emphasis, surprises with rounded, silky structure, crisp finish. 5.5g/ℓ sugar. Billowing **03** (★★★★) big, heavily wooded.

★★★★ **Muscatheer Family Reserve Muscat de Frontignan 04**, as finished wine, reveals more layers: billowing fragrance/flavours of caramelised peel, dried fruit, toasted nuts. Massively sweet (288g/ℓ) palate supports winemaker's claim of 'Once in a lifetime wine'. IWSC Gold, Muscadel Assoc Platinum. Pvsly tasted **00** lightweight, elegant, evolved. 500ml.

Pinotage ★★★★ **02** sampled last yr ex-barrel, like following reds; has evolved into liquorice-toned, dark fruit style, with an intriguing coffee-grounds savouriness. Ripe, rounded, with enough serious oaking (yr new Fr) for 3+ yr future. **Cabernet Sauvignon Family Reserve** ★★★★ **03** meat-extract savouriness; well constructed palate has juicy accessibility yet enough tannin foundation (18 mths in barrel) for 4 yrs in cellar. 'Best since 1912!' says Dirk J. **Cabernet Sauvignon-Merlot** ★★★★ Yr oaked **03** has evolved beautifully, with wild berries, fennel, loads of cigarbox spicing. Curves in the right places to please most palates.. **Chardonnay** ★★★ Unoaked **04** sample (tasted last ed) showed delicate floral/honeysuckle nose; full-flavoured with refreshing limy acidity. **Buccanheer Touriga Nacional** ★★★★ Ruby style port, 18 mths in 2nd fill oak; **02** complex & layered flavouring: Xmas cake, tea leaves & marzipan. Lighter than expected body doesn't detract from enjoyment. 500ml.

Bakenskop range

★★★★ **Red Muscadel** ✓ Traditional-style fortified muscatty dessert with intriguing complexity. **04** finished wine impressive: tea leaf notes & gluhwein spice add more layers to dried fruit, crème brûlée flavours. Marvellous silky texture, delicious. And bargain-priced, as is White version.

★★★★ **White Muscadel** ✓ Raisiny fortified dessert, beloved of competition judges. Gorgeous **04** delivers on sample's promise: clementine marmalade aromas, flavours; powerful, luscious & full-sweet, with enough alc zip to break the richness. WO Rbtson, as is above.

Merlot ☺ ★★★ **04** a real charmer: sappy red berry fruit, silky mouthfeel helped by 4.7g/ℓ sugar, beautifully balanced & light-textured.

Cabernet Sauvignon ★★★ **04**'s plum & vanilla biscuit aromas, flavours punctuated by firm edginess, making it food-compatible. 7 mths barrel maturation, as are rest of reds. **Roothman Cape Red** ★★★ Fruit the hero of this **NV** blend merlot, cab, pinotage, shiraz: bright, fresh-picked mulberries, blackcurrants, backed up by creamy, smoothly tasty palate. (Pvs sep listing as Roothman Klassieke Rooiwyn; white version of that suspended.) **Pinotage** NEW ★★★ Textbook ripe-style pinotage aromas, dried banana, macerated fruit on **04**. Forceful tannins, could do with another yr in bottle. **Blanc de Noir** ★★ Simple & honest **05** will make many friends. Redcurrant/cherry character from its red muscadel source, light 11.7% alc & off-dry. **Chardonnay** ★★★ Unwooded **04** (sample, not retasted) with pear/marzipan aromas; nice melon mouthful. **Chenin Blanc** ★★ **05** refreshing easy-drinker with pear/guava fruit salad character, approachable 12.3% alc. **Sauvignon Blanc** ★★ **05** shyer than pvs; nettly minerality, light-textured, bone-dry. **Muscat Perlé** NEW ★★ Gentle bubbles emphasise the floral tones, grapey flavours of **04**. Semi-sweet, friendly quaffer, with low 8.9% alc. All WO W-Cape unless noted. **Colombard, Blanc de Blanc** discontinued. *— CR*

Joostenberg Wines

*Paarl ▪ Est 1999 ▪ Tasting & sales at Klein Joostenberg Deli & Bistro Mon-Fri 9-5 Sat 11-3 ▪ Tours by appt ▪ Bistro hours Tue-Sun 8-5 (T 884·4208) ▪ Owner Myburgh Winery (Pty) Ltd ▪ Winemaker Tyrrel Myburgh (Dec 1999) ▪ Viticulturists Tyrrel Myburgh & Stephen Pons (Jun 2002) ▪ 33 ha (cab, shiraz, merlot, chenin, viognier) ▪ 200 tons 8 000 cs own label 35% red 50% white 15% dessert ▪ PO Box 82 Elsenburg 7607 ▪ joostenberg@mweb.co.za ▪ www.joostenberg.co.za ▪ **T 884·4932** ▪ F 884·4052*

Six years of Joostenberg Wines inspired Tyrrel Myburgh to release two new wines, both featuring viognier: the Fairhead pays tribute to his mother (her maiden name) and the Shiraz-Viognier is intended to 'show the two varieties at their best in this Rhône-like terroir'. Last harvest, they avoided the drawbacks of dry conditions by severely limiting the crop. 'We are very strict on this farm,' notes Tyrrel M. The tasting room has moved to the nearby Klein Joostenberg Deli & Bistro, where, *après dégustation*, you can enjoy a meal made by ebullient French brother-in-law and chef Christophe Dehosse. This year the renovated manor house is 250 years old, and this extended family intends celebrating in style.

★★★★ **Bakermat** (formerly 'Joostenberg') Continues as serious, restrained blend merlot/cab/shiraz, proportions varying with vintage. 42/35/23 in savoury, dark-fruited, youthful **03**, promising good, elegant future when big dry tannins harmonise with lurking flavours; already satisfying, as was **02**, well balanced 18 mths oak, 25% new.

★★★★ **Shiraz-Viognier** new Aromatic white variety (co-fermented) just 8%, adding tiny perfume hint to spicy, smoky aromas. Vibrant, ripe, fresh, flavourful, with gently gripping dry tannin, 14.5% alc adding hot note to finish. Native yeast ferment; 10 mths 500ℓ barrels; screwcapped 'to maintain freshness'.

★★★★ **Chenin Blanc Noble Late Harvest** ✓ Standout **03** (★★★★★) delicately powerful, complex, with racy tension on fine honeyed richness. FCTWS trophy; IWC gold. Yellow-gold **04** packed with honey, sultana, marmalade characters, acid freshness adequate now for richly sweet 145g/ℓsugar, but a trifle heavier, less thrilling than pvs. Native yeast-fermented/aged 7 mths older wood.

Merlot-Shiraz After spicy **03** with splashes of cab, touriga & viognier, barrel sample **04** (with 10% cab) pushes limits of ripeness with soft texture, prune flavours; freshness just maintained by high acid. Likely ★★★. Yr older wood. **Fairhead** new ★★★★ Well-matched 60/40 blend viognier/chenin, separately on lees in old wood 10 mths, giving lightly rich texture. Aromatic; light-feeling though 14% alc; strong vein acid holding it together very pleasantly, freshly. One to watch as vyds mature. **Chenin Blanc-Viognier** ★★★★ (Replaces 'Chenin Blanc') **05** has 5% aromatic viognier subtly enriching fresh appley, lightly earthy chenin base. Ripe, rounded, quietly elegant. Discontinued: **Chenin Blanc Natural Sweet**. – *TJ*

Jordan

*Stellenbosch ▪ Est 1982 ▪ 1stB 1993 ▪ Tasting & sales Mon-Fri 10–4.30 Sat 9.30–2.30 Sun 10–2.30 ▪ Fee R15 refundable with purchase ▪ Group tastings for up to 15 by appt ▪ Closed Easter Fri-Mon, Dec 25 & Jan 1 ▪ Tours by appt only (no pub hols) ▪ BYO picnic ▪ Function room for special occasions ▪ Owners Jordan family ▪ Winemakers Gary & Kathy Jordan ▪ Production Sjaak Nelson (2002) ▪ Viticulturists Ted & Gary Jordan (1982) ▪ 105 ha (cabs s/f, merlot, shiraz, chard, chenin, sauvignon, riesling) ▪ 900 tons 65 000 cs 55/45 red/white ▪ PO Box 12592 Die Boord 7613 ▪ info@jordanwines.com sales@jordanwines.com ▪ www.jordanwines.com ▪ **T 881·3441** ▪ F 881·3426*

Jordan's 13th vintage turned out to be anything but unlucky, with everything running tickety-boo throughout – Gary J ruefully admitting that the staff are finally reconciled to working for a pair of control freaks (speaking for wife Kathy?). He singles out the best ever sauvignon, and says he could happily have invested a further million on oak 'to give the reds the treatment they deserve'. Future plans consist mainly of fine-tuning. 'We're now at full capacity – we'll just have to do what we do better.' Tweaks include a revamped label, new labelling machine ('at four times the original cost of the entire property!'), and a screwcap head for the bottling line. Surrounding hillsides have been restored to fynbos, attracting a porcupine with a peculiar fondness for plastic water pipes. To the delight of their game-spotting children, many other animals have returned.

★★★★ **Cobblers Hill** Flagship red blend commemorating the Jordan cobbler heritage. Superb **03** (★★★★★) big, very dry, dominated by majestic cab austerity, though inherently more dimension than pvs. Needs min 2 yrs before broaching; should be long-lived (±2011-13). Blend cab, merlot, cab f (55/30/15) vs 85/15 for **02**. 23 mths new oak. Gold IWSC.

★★★★★ **Sophia CWG Auction Reserve** Selection of best barrels of Cobblers Hill plus extra barrel of structure-imparting cab result in sophisticated, brilliantly executed **03** blend cab/merlot/cab f (61/26/13). Big but graceful; properly tight, dry; ripely vinous with concentration to absorb smart but still conspicuous cedary oak. Potential through 2011-13. 26 mths new Fr barriques, mix coopers. **02** was youthfully austere with underlying sweet-fruited richness.

★★★★ **Cabernet Sauvignon** Premier-league Cape cab, early approachable – in modern mode – yet deserving of 4-7 yrs to show best. Oustanding vintage's extra sophistication, complexity notable in impressive **03**, subtle vinosity allied with lively, dry tannin. Fuller features lightened, freshened by dash minerally, spicy cab f (7%). **02** sensitively vinified to promote medium-term drinking. *Wine* ★★★★. ±20 mths new/used Fr oak.

★★★★ **Merlot** One of few achieving impact via quiet presence, not over-extraction/oaking. **04** not available for tasting. **03** stylish, beautifully balanced; fresh, persuasive plum/damson elegance. Yr Fr oak, new/used. Concours Mondial gold.

★★★★★ **Nine Yards Chardonnay Reserve** Billed as 'the ultimate expression of our terroir' — the Jordans going 'the whole nine yards' to select best barrels from their top vyd site. **04** (★★★★★) announced via pale gold brilliance; harmonious though restrained lime/spice bouquet; more expansive flavours, length; perhaps not quite same gravitas as deep, probing **03**, ready sooner. Well-fused new Fr oak. *Wine* ★★★★; VDG; JCWCA gold for **03**.

★★★★★ **CWG Auction Reserve Chardonnay** new **04** special cuvée from Nine Yards vyd. Of same distinctive & refined family as above wine, but more assertive. Gorgeous spice/lime attractions, balanced buttered toast density, spry acid; medium rather than full-bodied; delicious now, perhaps too forward, though should offer classy mouthful until ±2008. Extra subtleties from native yeast ferment (new Fr oak), 14 mths maturation.

★★★★ **Chardonnay** Possibly most consistently awarded of SA chards. **04** perceptible lees/citrus thumbprint; spice nuances freshen/lengthen usual creamy richness. Beautifully balanced but perhaps earlier peaking than some (±2007). Understated & poised **03** won VDG, Concours Mondial gold for its penetrating lime/lees complexity. Barrel-fermented (Burgundian oak, 50% new), *sur lie* 9 months. Incl ±12% tank-fermented portion.

★★★★ **Sauvignon Blanc** ✓ **05** reflects consistency of house style: stimulating without being too *sauvage*. Freshly bottled, emits vigorous gooseberry/grassy scents; steely, brisk, medium-bodied; excellent flavour growth on palate; long, dry finish. **04** 90 pts *WS*.

★★★★ **Blanc Fumé** ✓ Wooded sauvignon, richer, more sophisticated than above. **04** (★★★★) agreeable though less rich 'fumé' appeal than usual. **03** sleek, elegant, tropical fruit persistence. Incl 40% tank-fermented component.

★★★★ **Mellifera Noble Late Harvest 05** (★★★★★) shimmering green/gold dessert from botrytised riesling best to date. Variety glitters in this role: seductive, subtle; shot with keen botrytis-brushed lime/pepper scents. Sumptuous fruit cleansed, intensified by racy acidity, medium body. **04** was a promising racy mouthful, neither heavy nor over-sweet.

Syrah ★★★★ Maiden **03** (not retasted) generous & rounded with roast meat, dark spice attractions; concentration to balance ±14%. 14 mths Fr/Am oak. **Chameleon Cabernet Sauvignon-Merlot** ★★★★ In house's trio bdx-style blends, this more aligned to Bradgate, though sterner-framed, more obvious oak, ageworthy. **03** medium-bodied, dry; should improve with ±4 yrs. Incl dash cab f. 14 mths Fr oak. **04** not ready for tasting. **Chardonnay Unoaked** ★★★★ Without oak but not sans character. Distinctive **04** touches honey/melon decadence. Balanced textural richness, persistence nourished by 4.3g/ℓ sugar & lees ageing (8 mths). **Chenin Blanc** ★★★ **04** unusually developed, less supple than pvs; best opened whilst honey-fruited palate endures. 71% barrel-fermented, 8 mths on lees. **Chameleon Sauvignon Blanc-Chardonnay** ★★★★ Weighty, food-friendly dry white; **05** full of creamy white flower aromas; mouth-filling, intense flavours with leesy breadth; vigorous, dry. 55/36 partnership with 9% chenin. **Rhine Riesling** ★★★ **04** with maturing kerosene/pepper bouquet/flavour. Livelier palate, racy acid balances 9g/ℓ sugar, lengthens limy tail.

Bradgate range

'Easy-drinkers' developed for world-wide markets but also available locally.

Syrah ★★★★ ✓ **03** convincing fragrance, flavours; supple, dry, yet palate-friendly; delicious. Fr/Am oak finish. **04** not ready for tasting. **Cabernet Sauvignon-Merlot** ★★★★ ✓ Modern, bright-fruited blend with dash shiraz for round/fullness, immediate drinkability. **04** fresh, sassy red/spicy fruit. Intense flavours, ripe tannins, agreeably dry. **Chenin Blanc-Sauvignon Blanc** ★★★ **04** characterful, fruitily dry blend (59/41); stands out in crowded category. **05** unfinished; not tasted. —*AL*

Joubert-Tradauw Private Cellar

Tradouw (see Little Karoo map) ▪ Est/1stB 1999 ▪ Tasting & sales Mon-Fri 9-5 Sat 10-2 ▪ Breakfasts, teas & deli lunches Mon-Sat ▪ Tours by appt ▪ Lentelus B&B, facilities for children & many other attractions ▪ Owner Joubert Family Trust ▪ Winemaker/viticulturist Meyer Joubert (1995) ▪ 30 ha (cab, merlot, shiraz, chard) ▪ 2 500 cs own label 70% red 30% white ▪ Range for customer: Unplugged 62 ▪ PO Box 15 Barrydale 6750 ▪ joubert.r62@lando.co.za ▪ www.joubert-tradauw.co.za ▪ ***T (028) 572·1619*** *▪* ***F*** *(028) 572·1315*

After a decade of farming, Meyer Joubert says he'll be releasing his first Pinot in 2010, if all goes according to plan. Stretching conventional thinking about the suitability of the Little Karoo, perhaps, but Meyer J argues that chardonnay and shiraz produce classic wines in these conditions – dry air, sunny days, cold nights and rich clay soils – so why not pernickety pinot? A warm welcome, accompanied by a glass of wine with ciabatta (freshly baked by wife Beate) and delicious deli fare, backed by views stretching to the hazy blue of the Langeberge, make this an enjoyable stop on Route 62.

R62 Cabernet Sauvignon-Merlot ★★★★ Classically oriented (as all these) blend, 60% cab in lightly firm, happily mouthfilling **01**, with savoury spice, tobacco, attractive ripe berry fruit. Unobtrusive Fr oak support. Same blend, similar character promised in **03**. No **02**, for quality reasons. **Syrah** ★★★★ **04** as delicious as maiden **03**, has plenty of spice, smoky red berries – perhaps not perfectly enough for big 14.5% alc, acid balance. Well-judged Fr oak (a little Am pvsly); unfiltered. One to watch as vines mature. **Chardonnay** ★★★★ Restrained, silky (as usual) **03** shows delicate citrus fruit with mineral touch; big, slightly exposed acidity & judicious oaking – barrel fermented/matured 13 mths, now 65% new. Sample **04** promises similar elegant pleasures. – *TJ*

Journey's End see Western Wines

JP Bredell Wines

Stellenbosch (see Helderberg map) ▪ 1stB 1991 ▪ Tasting & sales Mon-Fri 9-5 Sat 10-2 ▪ Tours by appt ▪ Owner Helderzicht Trust ▪ Winemaker Anton Bredell ▪ 95 ha (cab, merlot, pinotage, shiraz, souzão, tinta, tourigas f/n) ▪ 20 000 cs own label 80% red 20% port ▪ PO Box 5266 Helderberg 7135 ▪ info@bredellwines.co.za ▪ www.bredellwines.co.za ▪ ***T 842·2478*** *▪ F 842·3124*

Bredell (man and wine) radiates a quiet power held in check. Vintner Anton B is a giant. Ditto his wines, primarily ports, among the Cape's finest, but also unfortified reds of monumental proportions. For gentler tastes (and the impatient) he's introduced Bredell's Vineyard Collection – the red blend already released; a Shiraz and Port due this year – offering earlier accessibility and good value. East Asia (China, Korea, India) is a new market focus. MD/marketer Donald Keys says: 'We have to settle in before the Chinese figure out how to make good wine from all the vines they're planting!' Meanwhile Anton B retreats to his beloved Karoo farm, Aasvoëlsvallei, offering wine/nature lovers camping, hikes, buck- and bird-watching.

★★★★ **Bredell's CWG Auction Shiraz** new Emphatic exposition of the variety – & this cellar's individuality. **01** bursting blackberry pastille fruit overlaid with tempered spice & extra-fine tannins; finish tantalisingly 'different' to rafts of competitors in the modern mould. Yr mix Fr/Am wood, 25% new. 20x6 cs to be gavelled off this yr under 'Previous Auction & Vinotique Wines' category.

★★★★ **Cabernet Sauvignon** Current vintage **00** (★★★★) was 'held back to lose a bit of power' & released after **02**, which last we noted as ripe & soft, in easy tannin frame. **00** very different: pulpy purple berry fruit whipped into form by spicy zest: ripe & warm now but more appealing ±5 yrs hence. Yr Fr casks, 50% new.

★★★★ **Merlot** None since fine-boned, delicately scented **00** & big, plummy **01** (★★★★).

★★★★★ **Cape Vintage** Benchmark Cape port for 15 yrs. **00** an inch off fabulous still-in-stock **98** & **97** (both labelled 'Reserve', as in pvs ed). Bold, but the beauty's in the refinement: nuts & raisins, fruit pud & cigar smoke all swirl into a powerful finish of tremendous length. **98** added *Wine* ★★★★★ to other numerous (VDG, FCTWS, JCWCA) awards: recognition for stunning complexity, enduring length. **97** also 'lots of everything': opulent fruit, minty spice, power & grip, only marginally the lesser. 5% touriga f joins tinta, touriga, souzão (50/35/10). 20% alc, ±90g/ℓ sugar.

★★★★☆ **CWG Auction Reserve Port** new Mid-2005 **03** just out of 2 yrs large old Fr oak & barely into bottle – where it needs to slumber for decade/2 in vintage style: quiet aromas simmer around tightly stitched fruit, tannins & 20% alc; hatches battened for now. Tinta, touriga n & f with souzão. 87g/ℓ sugar.

★★★★ **Late Bottled Vintage** Not-so-serious but still weighty, rich & silky 'fireplace port'. **02**, from barrel, seduces: spirited edge to plush, ripe cake-mix fruit features, promising velvety finish. Revisited **00** tense & brooding mid-2005, likely to open into dried fruit flesh, herby tail as did pvs. Tinta/souzão/tourigas; 3 yrs in older wood; 19% alc; ±90g/ℓ sugar.

Vineyard Collection new ☺ ★★★ **NV** 'Quality does not have to cost a fortune' & this merlot-led cheer won't break the bank. Honest fruit, lightly wooded, easy without being a cordial.

★★★☆ Following reds not revisited this ed: **Shiraz** ★★★☆ Old-World style, yet full of juicy blackberry fruit & sweet vanilla Am oak, 14.5% alc to boot in **01**. **De Rigueur** ★★★☆ **00** unfined & unfiltered, leaving all the brambly/woodsmoke flavour shoehorned into sturdy tannin frame, sweet plum-jam finish. – *DS*

Judex see Domaine Brahms
Juno see The Juno Wine Company
Kaapdal see Robertson Wide River
Kaap Hollands see Origin Wine
Kaapse Hoop see Omnia Wines
Kaapse Pracht see Baarsma, Coppoolse Finlayson
Kaaps Geskenk see Coppoolse Finlayson

Kaapzicht Estate

*Stellenbosch ▪ Est 1946 ▪ 1stB 1984 ▪ Tasting & sales Mon-Fri 9-4.30 Sat & pub hols 9-12 ▪ Fee R10 ▪ Closed Easter Fri-Sun, Dec 25 & Jan 1 ▪ Tours by appt ▪ BYO picnic ▪ Self-catering chalet & separate 'Wingerd Kraal' braai area for ±70 people; conference/entertainment venue (T 082·737·8329 – Mandy Steytler) ▪ Farm produce ▪ Conservation area ▪ Owner Steytdal Farm (Pty) Ltd ▪ Winemaker Danie Steytler, with Charl Coetzee (Jan 1979/2003) ▪ Viticulturists George Steytler, Charl Coetzee & Schalk du Toit (Jan 1984; Mar/Jun 2003) ▪ 146 ha (cab, merlot, pinotage, shiraz, chenin, sauvignon) ▪ 1 100 tons 40 000 cs own label 65% red 35% white ▪ PO Box 35 Koelenhof 7605 ▪ kaapzicht@mweb.co.za sales@kaapzicht-wines.com exports@kaapzicht-wines.com ▪ www.kaapzicht-wines.com ▪ **T 906·1620** ▪ F 906·1622*

Bought 60 years ago by the Steytler family, this farm was one of the first in the Bottelary Hills to provide evidence of the potential quality here. Danie Steytler replanted vineyards, tweaked vinification, culled the range and fast-tracked this estate in the 1990s, with strong showings in competitions. Fast forward, and the celebrated Kaapzicht Steytler Vision 01 claimed the coveted trophy for the best red blend at the IWSC 2004, followed by our five-star rating and almost too many medals to fit on the bottle. Not that this consistent Cape *cuvée* should overshadow any of the other wines in this pedigree stable: 'Any blend is only as good as your building blocks,' is Danie S's stance, after all. The Steytler range launched with the Pinotage 98 – the grape that's a vital part of the famous blend; this cultivar wine is maintaining the stellar rating we awarded that maiden effort, and was recently named best red wine at the Swiss International Air Lines' awards. All music to marketer wife Yngvild's ears.

Steytler range

★★★★★ **Vision** Danie S's standout version of the Cape blend features 50% cab, 10% merlot with, of course, pinotage. **02** triumphs in difficult vintage, structure & flavours fully intact – just a slight shyness. Big & sweet-fruited, richly concentrated, massive underlying structure cloaked in dense dark-berried fruit; winds up to long, dry finish still with brush of youthful but ultra-ripe & generally unobtrusive tannin. 5–8 yrs+ maturation potential. Already gold IWSC, Cullinan. Extraordinarily bemedalled **01** another blockbuster, but manages elegance too. Components vinified separately, blended after 18 mths; matured Fr oak.

★★★★☆ **Pinotage** Latest **02** continues long success story of this multiple show-winner. Huge concentration of ripe, cordial-like, chunky, black cherry fruit. Tannins worked for early accessibility, but allow for long cellaring, say 10 years. 14.9% alc. Swiss, Concours Mondial golds. **01** (★★★★★) a great pinotage; excellent structure with round, ripe tannins; massive build (15.3% alc). These 12–18 mths new Fr oak.

Kaapzicht range

★★★★☆ **CWG Auction Reserve Blend** Barrel selection of Vision above, but generally less yielding than that. **03** (★★★★) similarly burly build to massive, magisterial, dark-berried **01** (no **02**). Now with slight reticence on nose, but rich & complex unfolding of flavours – plums, cassis. Touch of sweetness a clue to presence of pinotage, allowed to ripen & soften to velvety richness. Sumptuous, for self-congratulatory occasions. 15% alc. 5–8 yrs good life ahead.

★★★★ **Cabernet Sauvignon 02** has Steytler signature of ripe cassis, dark choc fruit, authoritative oaking allowing for earlier accessibility. Less opulent than outstanding **01** (★★★★☆); even shows some classicism though still New World breadth, generosity. Alc a more manageable 14% vs 01's 15%. 18 mths Fr oak, 50% new. Worth ageing 5–8 yrs.

★★★★☆ **CWG Cabernet Sauvignon 02** (★★★★) mixes intense cedar, tobacco, cassis & pencil shavings. Very dry, despite ripeness of mulberry fruit (14.9% alc), tannins still slightly rough. Not as good as **01**, which promised to open out & be splendid. 19 mths new Fr oak. One for the deep part of the cellar.

★★★★ **Pinotage** Another stylish Steytler exercise in this variety. **02** rich & ripe, with fruit cordial-like intensity. Sleek, suave & tamed, shows how attractive the oft-unruly pinotage can be. Sweet rich fruit, bursting with black cherry, choc – a hedonist's delight. 18 mths Fr oak, 30% new. Massive 14.9% alc. Cellar 2–4 yrs.

★★★★ **Shiraz** Vintage took toll of **02** (★★★☆), showing in shyness & slight awkwardness in fruit/tannin balance. Back on form in **03**, still firm but richly fruity. Loads of black cherry fruit, touches smoked beef & warm spice, good oaking for beautifully dry finish. 18 mths Fr oak, 30% new, enlivened by dash unwooded. Watch 14.7% alc.

★★★★ **Bin-3** ✓ After sleek, fat **03**, **04** (★★★☆) less concentrated, looser textured. Approachable, almost-ready merlot/cab blend with near-inevitable pinotage there too at 7%, adding some sweetness. Plump & good-tempered, waiting to please. Fr oak 9 mths. Keep 1–3 yrs for extra pleasure.

Sauvignon Blanc ☺ ★★★ Big & juicy **05** shows ripe tropical fruit – passionfruit & melon, with tangy grapefruit acidity. Sweet/sour finish – generally mouthwatering.

Merlot ★★★ **03** warm spiced plum & mulberry aromas, flavours, plus atypical smokiness. Firm oaking, tangy acidity, daunting 14.8% alc. Less successful than last-tasted **01** (★★★☆). **Kaapzicht Estate Red** ★★★☆ Cab/shiraz blend (65/35), with (as per last ed) **03**'s components successfully submerging identities; rich, muscular, deep black mulberry fruit flavours; tannins ready only for resilient palates. 9 mths Fr staves. 14.6%. **Cape View Classic Red** ★★★ All-sorts red with cinsaut, **03** a classy quaffing bargain. Shows sweetness of perfectly ripe fruit; rich, meaty. Not retasted – as with ... **Combination** Maiden **04** bright, lively chenin-led blend with sauvignon. **Chenin Blanc** ★★☆ **05** a younger, more plain sister, has had a nip and tuck, now just 12.8% alc. Shyish, some baked apple flavours, soft acidity, pleasant. **Natural Sweet** NEW ★★★ Pineapple, mint intro to **05**, delightful sweetie with tropical flavours & smooth acidity for freshness & lift. Perfect ending to a summer dinner instead of sticky liqueur. Try with creamy cheese. **Hanepoot Jerepigo** ✓ Wafting incense & barleysugar invitation on **05**. Like liquid raisins, sweet & intense, with thread of refreshing mint, but could do with higher acidity. High 19% alc. – *IvH*

Kakamas see Oranjerivier Wine Cellars
Kalkveld see Zandvliet

Kango Winery

Little Karoo • Est 1976 • 1stB 1977 • Tasting & sales Mon-Fri 8-5 Sat 8-4.30 • Tours by appt • Picnic baskets by appt, or BYO • Farm produce • Owners 58 members • Winemaker Flip Smith • Viti consultant Willem Botha (2001) • 295 ha (cab, merlot, pinotage, shiraz, chard, chenin, colombard, hanepoot, muscadel r/w, sauvignon) • 3 000 tons 18% red 82% white • Export label: Adventure • PO Box 46 Oudtshoorn 6620 • flip@kangowines.com • www.kangowines.com • ***T (044) 272·6065*** *• F (044) 279·1038/1339*

Nobody ever said winemaking was easy, even in temperate climes. So spare a thought for Flip Smith, winemaker at Kango Winery in the Little Karoo, where the temperature is below zero in winter and above 45°C in summer. His dogged determination to transform this co-op from a bulk-wine producer into one which 'puts a high-quality product into bottle at an affordable price' is paying off. The Rijckshof White Muscadel was named one of the country's top 10 Muscadels in 2005, the Cab, Merlot and Pinotage having already achieved regional champion or reserve champion status. And, poised to launch the winery into the premium market, a new top range named Swartberg, initially represented by a Pinotage, Shiraz and Chardonnay.

Pvs 'Mont Noir' branding makes way for 'Kango Winery'. **Cabernet Sauvignon** new ★★★ Rounded, plummy **04**, whiff meat extract, firm grape tannin gives definition. **Merlot** ★★ **04** lightish, easy-drinking dry red with ripe plummy fruit, nicely smoothed edges. **Pinotage Reserve** ★★ Hints mulberry & rhubarb on **04**, firm but juicy, shade modestly fruited for lofty 'Reserve' labelling. **Shiraz** new ★★★ Fleshy, sweet & ripe **04**, just enough grape tannin for lifted mouthfeel. **Cabernet Sauvignon-Merlot-Shiraz** new ★★ Generalised red fruit character, no variety dominating; soft, pleasantly rounded for sound short-term pleasure. **Chardonnay Reserve** ★★ Lightly wooded **04**, with baked character underlying subtle peachy fruit. **Sauvignon Blanc** ★★ **05** uncomplicated dry white with pear-drop & tropical fruit tone. **Morio Muscat Sparkling** new ★★★ Characterful bubbly with hints aniseed & muscat, lots of minty freshness, energetic bubbles. **04** made from Swartberg fruit. **Chenin Blanc** & **Grand Cru** discontinued. These, below, all WO W Cape unless noted.

Rijkshof range

All fortified desserts in range **NV**. **Red Muscadel** ★★★★ Coppery fortified dessert with powerful raisined sweetness cut by well-judged fortification (slightly lower for latest bottling – 16.5%). Lacks complexity of some pvs. **Red Jerepigo** ★★ Mahogany-hued warming drop with prune & stewed plum flavours. **White Muscadel** ★★★ Muscadel Association 2005 gold for this wine, which mid-2005 characterised by little more than honey richness, syrupy sweetness, solid 16.5% fortification. **Gold Jerepigo** ★★ Appropriately golden hues; fairly rich barley sugar & prune aromas, approachable, easy. **Hanepoot** ★★ Subdued grapey character, not too sweet, appealing caramel overlay. **Ruby Port** ★★★ Pleasant fireside fortified ('port' something of a misnomer) with moderately sweet Xmas pud tones. 17% alc. **Vintage Port** ★★★★ From tinta, with traditional-style low alc (17.4%); last yr was rich red/black berry bouquet, vanilla throughout (from 18 mths oak); smooth & sweet. **Garob** range discontinued. – *CR*

Kanonkop Estate

Stellenbosch • Est 1910 • 1stB 1973 • Tasting & sales Mon-Fri 8.30-5 Sat 9-12.30 (9-2 Sep-Mar) • Fee R10 • Closed Easter Fri , Dec 25 & Jan 1 • Traditional snoek barbecue only by appt (min 15 people) or BYO picnic • Owners Johann & Paul Krige • Winemaker Abrie Beeslaar (2002), advised by Beyers Truter • Viticulturist Koos du Toit • 100 ha (cabs s/f, merlot, pinotage) • 500 tons ±40 000 cs 100% red • PO Box 19 Elsenburg 7607 • wine@kanonkop.co.za • www.kanonkop.co.za • ***T 884·4656*** *• F 884·4719*

The seamless handing over of executive/leadership responsibilities is the hallmark of a successful business. In winemaking terms, it's perhaps most famously expressed by the Bordeaux first growths where winemaker succession seldom affects the house style/quality. Kanonkop is a Cape equivalent. Abrie Beeslaar, only the third winemaker in nearly four decades, completed his second solo vintage here in 2005, and is sticking to the recipe. So when fourth-generation co-owner Johann Krige, asked about personal milestones, replies: 'Having reached 50, it's better to say "nothing", he may as well have been commenting on the incredible consistency of style/quality of Kanonkop's internationally reputable range of reds. So, no, there's nothing much new to report. It's all issues of finesse now. As Johann K describes it: minimising variables between terroir and variety, becoming even more focussed, and trying to capture the elegance, balance and structure of Sophia Loren in one bottle/bottling....

★★★★☆ **Paul Sauer** Fine bdx-style blend, one of few undoubted Cape classics, dating back to 1981. Vinified traditionally, like all these, in open fermenters. **01**'s 64% cab less than pvsly usual 80%; with equal amounts cab f & merlot. Violets, tea-leaf, black berries, presented subtly & superbly, leading to finely structured & balanced palate, strongly elegant, with succulent acidity & silky tannins, plentiful understated fruit, all heralding rewarding, lengthy maturity. Similar blend in lesser-vintage **02**, which also good & serious, long-flavoured but less sumptuously fruited, more severe, with big dry tannins. These 2 yrs new Fr oak. WO Simonsberg-Stbosch (as all are, bar Kadette which WO Stbosch).

★★★★☆ **CWG Auction 'Kanonkop'** The two auction wines fall away with departure of Beyers Truter. Final **01** — a barrel selection of above, so essentially similar — last yr offered great structural finesse, lovely fruit, masked by oak.

★★★★ **Cabernet Sauvignon** More conservatively styled than siblings perhaps now are, from 30+ yr old vines. Spicy, tobacco, berry bouquet/palate cooperate on **01** (not retasted) with firm ripe tannins to offer youthfully fine, sternly elegant profile. 2 yrs Fr oak, half new. Needs & deserves good few years to give of its best.

★★★★☆ **Pinotage** Long respected, serious-minded example, from old bushvines, typically rich, full-bodied, full-flavoured. **02** (★★★★) had all this last yr, but fruit too overlaid then by oak, & a forest floor note; vintage (+oak?) giving acceptable tiny twist of bitterness. Chunky 14.5% alc. **03** back on song, though oaky in youth (16 mths mostly new Fr, as before); loads of berries, spice, earthy hints, with big plush tannins & succulent acidity making grand, characterful package. Deserves few yrs wait.

★★★★ **CWG Auction Pinotage** The last (not retasted) **02** barrel selection, emphatically structured, with big dry tannins & obvious oak over dense sweet ripe fruit which will hopefully emerge one day.

★★★★ **Kadette ✓ 02** was pinotage-based (with 25% cab, 20% merlot), with bright, wild & spicy aromas & flavours, ripe soft tannins & a bitter hint adding to focus. Pinotage shows strongly on **03**, though only 26%, with merlot, cab s & touches of ruby cab & cab f. The most rustic of range, but sophisticatedly so. Well-structured, with sweet fruit, toasty wood (14 mths Fr), sour-cherry notes. — *TJ*

Kanu Wines

Stellenbosch ▪ Est/1stB 1998 ▪ Tasting & sales Oct-Mar: Mon-Fri 10-5 Sat 9-1; Apr-Sep Mon-Fri 10-4.30 Sat closed ▪ Fee R3/wine ▪ Closed pub hols ▪ Gifts ▪ Cheese Bar for farm-style products ▪ Functions venue (T 881·3464; functions@kanu.co.za) ▪ Permanent art exhibition ▪ Owner Hydro Holdings ▪ Winemaker Richard Kershaw, with Johan Grimbeek & Adéle Swart (Jan 2002/Jun 2003) ▪ Viticulturists Werner de Villiers (Nov 2004) ▪ 54 ha (cab, ruby cab, shiraz, sauvignon, viognier) ▪ 1 000 tons 50 000 cs own label 50/50 red/white ▪ PO Box 548 Stellenbosch 7599 ▪ info@kanu.co.za ▪ www.kanu.co.za ▪ ***T 881·3808*** *▪ F 881·3514*

Everything new at Kanu this year. With Richard Kershaw at the winemaking helm, changes continue apace, beyond some refinements of the range. They've been on an equipment spending spree in the quest for more efficient vinification, without heavy handling and loss of quality. New in the vineyards is viticulturalist Werner de Villiers, engaged in time to deal with a 'strange' 2005 vintage. In a bid to focus the range, current vintages of varietal Cabernet and Merlot 'are sadly the last we will see of these two loyal companions'; they will augment the Keystone Bordeaux-style blend. The mid-range red blend is to be renamed Rockwood, because simply Red, it was felt, no longer did justice to the winery's ambitions for this wine. And, due to hit the receiving blanket just as Platter 2006 hits the bookstores, is the Kershaw's firstborn.

Limited Release range

★★★★☆ **Cabernet Sauvignon** Last tasted was sensational **01** (★★★★☆) – rich fruit supported by fine tannins, unobtrusive 14.5% alc. As with Merlot below, to be discontinued.

★★★★ **Merlot** ✓ Beguilingly perfumed **02** barrel sample was last we tried: elegantly structured, with harmonious oak (20 mths Fr, 20% new); accessible but much to offer over time.

★★★★ **Chenin Blanc Wooded** Much lauded, including Chenin Challenge triumphs for both **01**, **02**. Latest **04** more elegant than pvs, less showy, but a lot of class. Aromatically perfumed, a basket of tropical fruit, some buttered toast, a squeeze of lemon, supported by a balanced structure, lovely tangy finish. Serious oaking: 9 mths Fr, half new, adds structure yet allows fruit to shine through. *Wine* ★★★★ No **03**. **02** toasty oak nose, palate bursting with fruit, wood, sweetness (13g/ℓ sugar). *Wine* ★★★★★; *WS* 90 pts. Grapes from Khof bushvines.

★★★★☆ **Kia-Ora Noble Late Harvest** Botrytised dessert, when vintage permits. Lusciously textured **04**, from chenin, enchants with array of flavours, complex interweavings, riveting sweet/sour balance. Pineapple, apricot & marmalade tones with a botrytis overlay & invigorating 8.7g/ℓ acid. The luscious texture completes the experience. 14 mths Fr oak, 60% new; 120g/ℓ sugar; 12.5% alc. Beautifully balanced **03** includes 15% hárslevelü: a powerhouse of richness, concentration, with racy acidity. 375ml.

Shiraz ★★★☆ Modern **03** with rich plummy fruit, plenty of vanilla spicing & full, rounded palate showcasing amenable tannins. Designed for enjoyment & delivers winningly. 18 mths older Fr oak. From **04** will join **Chardonnay**, **Keystone, Sauvignon Blanc** whch have moved to range below.

Kanu range

★★★★ **Keystone** ✓ Bdx blend cab, merlot. **03**'s 91% cab dictates styling, firm tannin structure, ageabilityl. Blackberry/brambleberry fruit, toasty oak, vanilla spicing. Youthful freshness, but wine needs time, has good 6+ yr future. 18 mths Fr oak, half new. No **02**. **01** was sensual, ripe, densely structured.

★★★★ **Chardonnay 04** (★★★☆) less impressive than deep, sophisticated, just off-dry **03**. Perhaps just at awkward stage mid-2005, oak not yet fully integrated. But zesty acidity & tropical fruit, citrus flavouring in place, given extra dimension by smoky oak (10 mths, mainly Fr, dab Am, equal new/2nd fill). Khof fruit.

Red ☺ ★★★ Not simple, just friendly **03** blend shiraz, merlot, cab 56/28/16. Mainly about fruit: crushed red berries/cherries. Smoky nuance from 18 mths older wood. To be replaced by new label, namely … **Rockwood** new ★★☆ Rejigging of Red's varieties – shiraz/cab/merlot in 49/37/14 blend in **04**, giving a cooler-style fruit expression, juicy red berries, herbaceous/grassy tones. Lightly oaked, drinks smoothly. Both these to be enjoyed in youth.

Sauvignon Blanc ★★★ **05** (sample) lighter (12.6% alc) and less concentrated than pvs. Varietal typicity, grapefruit, green figs, in restrained mode; friendly, rounded texture & crisp finish. 5% chenin infusion. **Chenin Blanc** ★★★☆ ✓From low-yielding 26 yr-old bush-vines. Perennial charmer, with many awards over the yrs. **05** (sample) gets the juices going with crunchy Granny Smith apply freshness – 6g/ℓ sugar not obvious. Perked up by 13% sauvignon addition. Lovely food wine.

Reserve range new

★★★☆ **Sauvignon Blanc** ★★★☆ **05** well put together, has depth & fullness: green fig & summer meadow character, a lively, food-friendly structure (aided by 7g/ℓ acid), long minerally finish.

Escape range

Notes from last ed; none retasted. **Chenin Blanc** ★★★ Ripe, intense sample **04** from 24 yr old bushvines: peardrops, guava & apple-rich summer fruit salad. Invigoratingly fresh, vibrant. Good value, as was … **Sauvignon Blanc** ★★★ **04** with appealing cool-grown character, without being aggressive, unfriendly. Refreshing, finishes with citrus tang. 12.5% alc. **Red** ★★★ For early drinking, **02** is juicy, ripe & fruit-driven. Led by ruby cab, with cinsaut, shiraz, pinotage, with fleshy red berry focus. Touch of oak contributes definition. **Rosé** ★★★ Softly amenable **03** with light-toned redcurrant/cranberry fragrance & flavours, plumped up by soupçon sugar. Blend cab/merlot/shiraz. *— CR*

Karmosyn see Terroir Wines

Karusa Vineyards new

Robertson ▪ Est/1stB 2004 ▪ Tasting by appt ▪ Owner/winemaker Jacques Conradie ▪ 100 cs (projected) ▪ jacques@boncap.co.za ▪ ***T (023) 626·1628***

Jacques Conradie is especially grateful to his employers at organic winery Bon Cap for allowing him to produce his own-label wine in their cellar. The maiden 04 Karusa (Khoisan for 'Arid Land') has been named 'The Fifth Element' — a combination of air, water, fire, earth and a fifth constituent — human passion. Conradie aims to make a maximum 100 cases (up from half of that in 2004) of this 'unique ultra-premium wine' which he hopes will show, above all, individuality and a sense of place: 'I am very emotional about my wine, it reflects who I am'. An ambition is to eventually build a small cellar in his beloved Little Karoo.

★★★★ **The Fifth Element** Impressive debut with refined **04** shiraz/viognier (88/12) blend. Intense black choc, fragrant leather, fine oak intro. Balanced & poised, tannins cleverly worked to manageable levels, lengthy dry finish. Power for several yrs ageing. Yr new Hngrian oak. Unfiltered/fined. *— IvH*

Katbakkies Wine

Est/1stB 1999 ▪ Tasting & sales by appt ▪ Owner Andries van der Walt ▪ Vini consultant Teddy Hall (2002) ▪ 450 cs 33% red 66% white ▪ PO Box 21675 Kloof Street 8008 ▪ Avdwalt@inds-ct.co.za ▪ ***T 424·6883*** *▪ F 426·1967*

While Andries van der Walt bottled his first Viognier and Cab (the latter's 600 bottles 'only for myself and special friends' at this stage), baboon raiders harvested the first crop of petit verdot on the remote Cederberg home-farm. 'This vintage we are ready for them,' he growls … The curious name of the property is thought to derive from the crystal-clear rock pools ('cat bowls') the mountain felines drink from.

★★★★★ **Cabernet Sauvignon** new Impressive debut **03**, convincingly balances sweet-fruit opulence with classic herbal whiffs; amplitude without show. Great persistence, fine dense tannins. Worthy of 5 yrs bottle maturation. Relatively modest 13.5% alc a bonus. 22 mths new Fr oak, Stbosch grapes.

★★★★★ **Syrah** ✓ Big though classically styled red, from trio low-yield Stbosch vyds. Maiden **02** a standout, effusive white pepper/clove notes, dense fruit. Lighter, less complex **03** (★★★★) offers soft, spicy whiffs, sweet red-fruits palate, slightly evanescent finish. 11 mths oak matured, 20% new.

★★★★ **Chenin Blanc** Sumptuous **04** (★★★★★), peach/honeysuckle aromas & intense lime flavours perfectly poised & focused. Marvellously fresh, clean & complex wine, excellent with food. Considerable step up on unshowy **03**, citrus/apricot notes, elegant, dry-ish, low 12.9% alc. Off miserly Stbosch vyds.

Viognier new ★★★ **04** sweet peachy notes layered with almond; rich, viscous flavours softened by (4.8g/ℓ) sugar, seemingly dry finish (via 8.8g/ℓ acid) adds cuisine-cordial tang. *— MF*

Kautzenburg

Stellenbosch ▪ Est 2000 ▪ 1stB 2002 ▪ Closed to public ▪ Owners Peter & Nina Ruch ▪ Winemaker Jeremy Walker (2002) ▪ Viticulturists Peter Ruch, advised by De Waal Koch &

Hannes Bredell ▪ 5 ha (pinotage) ▪ ±25 tons ±300 cs 100% red ▪ PO Box 91 Somerset West 7129 ▪ ***T/F 842·3903***

Grangehurst's Jeremy Walker vinifies the Kautzenburg wine for Swiss summer swallows Peter and Nina Ruch, owners of a small pinotage vineyard in the Somerset West area. Grapes not used for own bottlings are diverted to Grangehurst and other cellars.

Pinotage 04 tight knit sample from low-yielding Hldrberg bushvines. *Garrigue* nose enlivened by dark fruit & tar, layered fruit complexity & fine tannins from deft oak touch; 16 mths Fr oak. Persistent, dry finish; 14.7% alc unobtrusive. For the long haul: 6 yrs at least; potential ★★★★. *– CR*

Kaya see Coppoolse Finlayson
Keates Drift see Franschhoek Vineyards
Keermont see De Trafford
Keimoes see Oranjerivier Wine Cellars

Keisseskraal Vineyards

new

Bot River (see Walker Bay map) ▪ Est 2004 ▪ 1stB 2005 ▪ Tasting, sales & tours Mon-Fri 10–4 Sat/Sun by appt ▪ Fee R15pp ▪ Closed Christian holidays ▪ BYO picnic (if tasting) ▪ Farm produce ▪ Walks ▪ Owners Johann & Ulrike Mendelsöhn ▪ Winemaker Johann Mendelsöhn, advised by Bartho Eksteen (Jan 2005) ▪ Viticulturist Johann Mendelsöhn ▪ 2 ha (cab, malbec, merlot, petit v, shiraz, viognier) ▪ 1.3 tons 100 cs 100% red ▪ PO Box 85 Bot River 7185 ▪ mendelsohn@telkomsa.net ▪ ***T/F (028) 284·9219***

Relocating the renowned Onduno horse stud from Namibia to the Boland in 1997 put Keisseskraal's owners Johann and Ulrike Mendelsöhn in the happy position of discovering a hidden yearning to make wine – previously eclipsed by Johann's career in architecture. A keen eye for the integrity of nature's own building blocks has given rise to a winemaking philosophy built around biodynamic principles and the first-do-no-harm approach. Until other plantings come on stream in 2009, they plan to continue with their limited 100-case production from 5 yr old shiraz vines. First out of the starting stalls is a Galantskloof Shiraz, too unformed to rate mid-2005.

Keizer's Creek see Roodezandt

Kellerprinz

High-volume **NV** glugger from Distell. **Late Harvest** ★ Lightish semi-sweet chenin/colombard in 2ℓ jug; honey/biscuit nose, muted tropical palate. *– CvZ*

Ken Forrester Wines

Stellenbosch (see Helderberg map) ▪ Est 1993 ▪ 1stB 1994 ▪ Tasting & sales daily 10–5 (farm & 96 Winery Road Restaurant – see Eat-out section) ▪ Closed Easter Fri-Mon, Dec 25/26 & Jan 1 ▪ Cellar tours by appt ▪ Tourgroups ▪ Conferencing ▪ Owners Ken & Teresa Forrester ▪ Vini consultant Martin Meinert, with Henk Marconi (1997/1995) ▪ Viticulturist Jannie Fourie (Jan 2001) ▪ 33 ha (grenache, merlot, mourvèdre, shiraz, chenin, sauvignon) ▪ 200 tons 50 000 cs own label + 300 000ℓ for clients ▪ 30% red 70% white ▪ HACCP certified ▪ PO Box 1253 Stellenbosch 7599 ▪ ken@kenforresterwines.com ▪ www.kenforresterwines.com ▪ ***T 855·2374*** *▪ F 855·2373*

Tenth anniversary celebrations in 2005 at the farm off Winery Road showcased a new barrel cellar, bottling hall and cellar door tasting room (under the hand of brand manager/marketer Beverley Berkowitz, Ken Forrester's sometime classmate from Hotel School) for Forrester-hosted functions. His popular restaurant, 96 Winery Road, remains a general tasting venue – and for the tasting that follows the cellar tour (in fact, an in-depth vineyard experience). Also new in 2005 were team members Helet van der Merwe, OC electronic marketing, and viticulturist Jannie Fourie, bringing to the vineyards close on 10 years' experience of growing table grapes. Destined for the bottle – specifically flagship red, The Gypsy – is grenache from Pieknierskloof and Tierhoek. The legions of lovers of Ken F's wines will applaud his philosophy: 'I need to ensure that I would be happy to buy my own wines from a value and quality perspective.'

Icon range

★★★★ **Gypsy** Impressive, individual New World fusion of mostly grenache with shiraz, smattering pinotage; **02** tasted as sample last ed showed spiced prunes, sour cherry confit, with underbrush nuances. Sleekly muscular & generously oaked (18 mths); possible ★★★★☆. Vyd/barrel selection. **01**'s instant appeal belied complexity.

★★★★ **The FMC Chenin Blanc** (formerly 'Forrester/Meinert Chenin Blanc') Designed to 'put Cape chenin indelibly on the map'. **03** (★★★★☆) continues impressive track record: deeply rich, but sheathed power, not OTT; layered citrus, pears, nutty biscuit, a seductive drinkability (helped by 8.8g/ℓ sugar) & long finish. Native yeast ferment/10 mths new oak. *WS* 90 pts, *Wine* ★★★★. **02** had an admirable sweeping canvas of flavours. IWC gold.

★★★★☆ **'T' Noble Late Harvest Chenin Blanc** Mesmerising botrytised dessert, both solo-perfect & food-cordial. **03** assails the senses with waves of flavour: marmalade, barley sugar, pineapple, botrytis, tantalising sweet/sour effect of the acid-sugar balance (8. 5g/ℓ / 130g/ℓ) plus assimilating 18 mths new Fr oak. No effort was spared: native yeast-fermented, up to 5 pickings off old bushvines. IWC gold. No **02** produced. **01** (★★★★★) lush silkiness & flavour intensity, long finish. FCTWS gold, *WS* 91 pts, *Wine* ★★★★☆.

Sauvignon Blanc discontinued.

Ken Forrester range

★★★★ **Chenin Blanc** ✓ From 30+ yr old Hldrberg bushvines, pruned for low yields. Irresistible **04** shows house-style flavour richness: basket of tropical fruits, toffee-apple, well-integrated oak that allows fruit to be the hero, & velvety, elegant structure. Half fermented/9 mths Fr oak. Powerful, impressive **03** (★★★★☆) lush, intense, well judged integrated oak (as above). Will age beautifully 4+ yrs. *Wine* ★★★★.

Merlot ★★★☆ Good varietal character. **03** cassis, mocha & cherry fruitcake flavours, with lovely structural elegance & vitality. Backbone for 5+ yrs cellaring. Yr Fr oak. Tasted last ed. **Grenache-Syrah** ★★★☆ **02** unusual & piquant 55/45 blend. 52% old-vine grenache in **03** (sample); layers of perfume & flavour, coriander, cocoa, *garrigue* wildness; smooth, fleshy, with firm tannin backbone. Now or keep 3-4 yrs. 9 mths Fr oak, some new. **Sauvignon Blanc** ★★★☆ **05** intense & flavourful, capsicum, nettles & tangy lime, green but ripe; nicely rounded , with enough freshness for food. **Shiraz** discontinued.

Petit range

Petit Pinotage ☺ ★★★ Juicy unwooded style. Finished wine **04** has house-style fleshy mulberry/brambleberry fruit, with plenty fresh-picked vibrancy.

Petit Chenin 'Keep in the fridge for anytime', suggests Ken F. **05** (sample; should gain ★★★ and a ☺) shows crunchy apple flavouring, racy acidity, lip-smacking appetite appeal. — *CR*

Keteka see Dominion

Keukenhof Wines new

Olifants River ▪ 1stB 2003 ▪ Visits by appt Mon-Sat 8-5 ▪ Fee R10 p/p ▪ Closed Good Fri-Mon, Ascension Day & Dec 25 ▪ Play area for children ▪ Owners Smuts family ▪ Winemaker Riaan Smuts, with Nadine Smuts (both Jan 2003) ▪ Viticulturist Riaan Smuts (Jan 2003) ▪ 65 ha (cab, merlot, chard, chenin, colombard, sauvignon) ▪ 1 200 tons 250 cs own label ▪ Range for customer: Ulusaba ▪ PO Box 49 Lutzville 8165 ▪ tazu@kingsley.co.za ▪ ***T/F (027) 217·2623***

Garagistes? John and Lulaine Smuts are the real thing. Their maiden Cab (the 03, first ever Wine of Origin Koekenaap) was made in an actual garage and, in the spirit of artisanal wine-making, they, son Riaan and wife Nadine do everything by hand. Rooted in a love of agriculture and vineyards, they've taken up the challenge of carving a niche alongside the big names in the industry. A fine start, via a listing at Sir Richard Branson's private game reserve, Ulusaba, has made them more determined to prove the winemaking potential of the sites nearer the cold Atlantic – up the N7, left turn at the Olifants River....

Both **04**s Fr oak matured, unfiltered. **Cabernet Sauvignon** ★★ Sweet blackcurrant & fine herbal hints, some greenish tannin/alc evident. **Merlot** ★★ Chalky mulberry whiffs, succulent & soft tannins though fruit somewhat overpowered by nearly 15% alc. – *MF*

Keurfontein see Viljoensdrift
Kevin Arnold see Waterford
Khanya see Havana Hills
King Solomon see Eshkol
Kingsriver see Jewel of the Breede River
Kiss & Tell see Leopard Frog Vineyards

Klawervlei Estate

Stellenbosch ▪ Est 1994 ▪ 1stB 1995 ▪ Tasting & sales Tue-Fri 10–5 Sat 10–2 ▪ Closed Dec 25 & Jan 1 ▪ Tours by appt ▪ Klawervlei Pantry ▪ Owner Quickstep 584 (Pty) Ltd ▪ Winemaker Christoph Hammel ▪ 20 ha (cab, merlot, chenin) ▪ 100 tons 3 000 cs own label ▪ 70% red 30% white ▪ PO Box 144 Koelenhof 7605 ▪ chrisdejager@mweb.co.za ▪ www.klawervlei.com ▪ ***T 865·2746*** *▪ F 865·2415*

No update available on this winery; contact details from previous edition.

Klawer Co-operative Cellars

Olifants River ▪ Est 1956 ▪ Tasting & sales Mon-Fri 8–5 Sat 9–1 ▪ Fee R5 ▪ Closed pub hols except during wildflower season ▪ BYO picnic ▪ Conferences ▪ Owners 120 members ▪ Winemakers Bob de Villiers, Hermias Hugo & De Wet Hugo (Dec 2000/Dec 2003/Aug 2003)2003), with Roelof van Schalkwyk & Dewald Huisamen (Jan 1999/Nov 2002) ▪ Viticulturist Klaas Coetzee (Jun 2001) ▪ 2 095 ha ±40 000 tons 14% red 85% white 1% rosé ▪ PO Box 8 Klawer 8145 ▪ klawerwyn@kingsley.co.za ▪ www.wine.co.za ▪ ***T (027) 216·1530*** *▪ F (027) 216·1561*

It's been half a century since the Klawer cellar took in its first harvest, but the recipe remains the same: 'time, late nights, experience, hard work and patience', says winemaker Hermias Hugo. To coincide with the anniversary, the flagship Birdfield range has been extended and now also boasts lively new plumage. Partners in the Western Wines/Kumala export success story, Hugo & co were proud recipients of the Kumala Fruit Growers Challenge trophy for their 04 Pinotage – a welcome accolade but for them the real proof comes when 'good wines sell themselves'. Their pink sparkling, Michelle, is again available from the tasting room. 'A real hit', Hugo says, 'with the fairer sex.'

Birdfield range

Merlot ★★★ **04** undemanding early drinker with dusty nuance from 6 mths Fr oak, big 14% alc. **Pinotage** ★★ **04** fruity, juicy, unpretentious & satisfying country wine. Not oaked. **Shiraz** ★★★ **04** not tasted. **03** had touches pepper & anise, evident but supple tannin, brawny 15% alc, potential for some improvement. **Blanc de Noir** ★★ Coral pink summer sip from pinotage; **05** strawberry fruited with slightly savoury off-dry flavours. **Chardonnay** ★★★ **05** gentle tropical fruit lead-in, citrus-zest flavours, freshening acidity which still slightly apart mid-2005. **Chenin Blanc** ★★ **05** light-textured/bodied (12% alc), lemon-drop flavours, balanced acidity. **Sauvignon Blanc** ★★ Back on song with early-picked **05**, better balanced fruit/acid, lime freshness goes well with lighter foods. **Special Late Harvest 05** from chardonnay not tasted. **Michelle Sparkling** ★★ Jelly baby-flavoured pink froth from red muscadel; **05** light (9% alc) frivolous fun for sweeter palates. **White Muscadel** ★★ **05** not ready. Straightforward **04** was still quite fiery last ed, needed time to settle, develop. 16.6% alc. – *CR*

Klein Avontuur see Avontuur
Klein Begin see New Beginnings, Omnia Wines
Kleinbok see Dominion

Kleinbosch see Cape Coastal Vintners

Klein Constantia Estate

Constantia ▪ Est 1823 ▪ 1stB 1986 ▪ Tasting & sales Mon-Fri 9-5 Sat 9-1 ▪ Fee R20 for groups ▪ Closed pub hols ▪ Owners Duggie & Lowell Jooste ▪ Winemaker Adam Mason, with Floricius Beukes & Corina du Toit (Jul 2003/Jul 2004/Dec 2003) ▪ Viticulturist Kobus Jordaan (Feb 1981) ▪ 82 ha (cabs s/f, merlot, pinot, shiraz, chard, muscat de F, riesling, sauvignon) ▪ 500 tons 40 000 cs 25% red 75% white ▪ Export brands: High Gables & Danford's ▪ PO Box 375 Constantia 7848 ▪ info@kleinconstantia.com ▪ www.kleinconstantia.com ▪ ***T 794·5188*** *▪ F 794·2464*

With the 25th anniversary of ownership of Klein Constantia by the Jooste family comes a burst of enthusiasm and change in both vineyard and cellar. The aim, says Adam Mason, is to preserve KC's hallmark restrained classicism while employing modern technology 'to show-case more of the vivid fruit and racy minerality that are seen as Constantia's hallmarks'. Floricius Beukes, described by Adam M as a fervent oenophile with a soft spot for sauvignon, now assists in the cellar, whilst the vineyard team progress with the replanting programme, which will see white varieties rise to 80% of the total by 2010. New plantings include petit verdot, malbec – and tracts of indigenous fynbos for greater biodiversity. Changes to the line-up include a new earlier-drinking 'KC' range; above this, the premium 'Klein Constantia' varietal bottlings; and top-tier 'Marlbrook' – a white blend now released, with the upgraded red version due in a few years.

★★★★ **Mme Marlbrook** new Madame a charming consort for flagship red (which now undergoing rebirth), formula not settled, but **04** half semillon with sauvignon, chard, & a little florally fragrant muscat de F controlling the hints dried grass, citrus. Rich, full, with touch of sweetness & a green-tinged, lingering finish.

★★★★☆ **Perdeblokke Sauvignon Blanc** new Selection from exposed, higher-altitude vyd with poorer soil – name recalling ploughing Percherons of older times on the estate. Expressive, exuberant aromas passionfruit, hints asparagus on **05**, vibrant green grass-edged richness, lingering flavours. Maiden **04** (★★★★) less showy, similar fine cool-climate balance.

★★★★ **Sauvignon Blanc** Enduring favourite, noted for rewarding ageability in some vintages, with 15% semillon adding complexity. Pvsly sampled **04** now steely cool-climate character showing dried grass, gooseberry, traces of passionfruit. **05** similar well-balanced acidity, flavour spectrum – plus hints asparagus; but more succulent, incipiently complex. Usual fresh, lingering finish.

★★★★ **Rhine Riesling** Under screwcap to safeguard aromatic purity. Adam M's inaugural **04** hinted at change: drier (still perceptibly off-dry), lower alc, ±12%. Aromatic, with tinned pineapple & pepper, delicately fresh & lively. Latest **05** (not ready for tasting) will be totally dry, though still modest alc.

★★★★ **Sauvignon Blanc Noble Late Harvest** Intermittently produced. Follow-up to spicy-sweet **98** is disappointingly heavy **02** (★★★), with woody, burnt toffee character; softly unctuous (though only 87g/ℓ RS), not much verve. 18 mths new Russian oak.

★★★★☆ **Vin de Constance** Continually reclaiming the international renown its ancestor enjoyed 2 centuries back; from usually unbotrytised but superbly ripe muscat de F giving a long-lived, silkily textured wine with fine mineral acidity. Raisiny luxuriance of **99** also evoked dried apricot, marmalade, shot through with thrilling acid; fine lingering farewell. 14.5%; 183g/ℓ sugar. Riveting old-gold-coloured **00** (★★★★★) somewhat drier (141g/ℓ), full, gorgeously complex panoply of aromas/flavours (from muscatty grape to citrus, dried peach to marmalade), refined silky richness, balanced acidity. These some 2 yrs in used 500ℓ Fr oak barrels, after ferment/time in tank. In specially made 500ml old hand-blown-style bottles.

Marlbrook ★★★☆ Seriously styled blend of half cab with merlot & dash cab f. **01**'s cab severity rounded by softer merlot fruit; dry finish. Cedar notes from new Fr oak 2 yrs; 14.3% alc. As with Cab, not retasted; next of both likely to be **05**, after sorting out of ranges, development of vyds. **Cabernet Sauvignon** ★★★☆ Quietly austere **01**, with notes earthiness, cassis; sweet fruit lurking amongst the dry tannins. 20+ mths new Fr oak. Should keep few more yrs, & hopefully soften somewhat. **Pinot Noir** ★★★ Typically light-coloured **04** round & fresh, decent varietal character, well integrated oak (10 mths 30% new Fr); modestly pleasant drinking over short term. **Shiraz** ★★★★ Roast coffee, smoky notes on tasty, outgoing & toastily pleasant **03**; light-feeling, well-balanced. 12 mths Am oak, half new. **Shiraz Reserve** ★★★★ Last was **01** selection from new barrels of above – more grip, intensity, sweet red fruit. **KC Cabernet Sauvignon-Merlot** new ★★★★ First of a 2nd tier of reds with some fruit from their Hldrberg property (so WO Coastal). **03** blend (53/39 balance cab f) pleasing, generous & ripe, though more vinous than fruity, with underlying firm savoury tannins; moderately wooded. **Chardonnay** ★★★★ Attractive **04**'s forward aromas of oatmeal, butterscotch, citrus lead to fresh, creamy mouthful; well integrated oak (50% fermented/yr in barrel). **Semillon** new ★★★★ Notes of lemon, honey, lanolin on **04**; fresh, nicely textured mouthfeel but perhaps a little wood harshness (10 mths oak, half new). Unlikely to develop many yrs. – *TJ*

Kleindal see Robertson Wide River Export Company

Klein DasBosch

Stellenbosch ▪ Closed to public ▪ Owner James Wellwood Basson ▪ Viti/vini consultant Jan Coetzee (1997) ▪ Marketing director Nikki Herbst ▪ 5.5 ha ▪ 35 tons 2 000 cs own label 89% red 11% white ▪ PO Box 826 Brackenfell 7561 ▪ wine@kleindasbosch.com ▪ www.kleindasbosch.com ▪ ***T 880·0128*** *▪ F 880·0999*

Range made at Vriesenhof by rugby and wine legend Jan Coetzee for his neighbour James 'Whitey' Basson, CEO of retailing empire Shoprite. Current releases include an 02 Merlot and Pinotage, and an 04 Chardonnay. Mostly exported, though some do appear on selected local restaurant lists.

Kleine Draken

Paarl ▪ Est 1983 ▪ 1stB 1988 ▪ Tasting & sales Mon-Fri 8-12.30; 1.30-5 ▪ Closed pub hols & Jewish holy days ▪ Tours strictly by appt ▪ BYO picnic ▪ Owner Cape Gate (Pty) Ltd ▪ Winemaker Neil Schnoor, with Mabusa Nyaniso (Sep/Jul 1999) ▪ Viticulturist Frank Pietersen (1984) ▪ 9 ha (cabs s/f, malbec, merlot, chard, riesling, sauvignon) ▪ 90 tons 10 000 cs own label 50% red 50% white ▪ Brand for customer: Tempel Wines ▪ ISO 9000 certification in progress ▪ PO Box 2674 Paarl 7620 ▪ zandwijk@capegate.co.za ▪ www.kosherwines.co.za ▪ ***T 863·2368*** *▪ F 863·1884*

While a hot, dry ripening season may have been detrimental to more delicate varieties like sauvignon, it benefited this Paarl property's cabernet and shiraz. It was the maiden vintage of the latter – due for release mid-year; more progress at a winery where they are 'still striving to produce top quality wines which also happen to be kosher,' according to GM/winemaker Neil Schnoor. Recently secured export markets for these kosher wines, flash pasteurised to meet the exacting standards of the Cape Beth Din, are Australia and New Zealand.

Cabernet Sauvignon ★★★ **02** the only wine ready for tasting for this edition. Full-fruited with cassis & black berries; carefully oaked 6 mths old/new Fr barrels giving good dry tannins. **Pinotage** ★★★ **03** red cherries & red berries, strong tannins & dry finish; like Cab, best cellared further or enjoyed with food. 6 mths Fr oak, some new. **Dry Red** ★★★ **03** lightish-bodied bdx-style blend of equal portions cab f, merlot, malbec, with generous dark-fruit flavours; unlike other reds, immediately approachable, user-friendly. Fr oak 4-6 mths, 2nd-3rd fill. **Kiddush** ★★ Natural Sweet sacramental wine from cinsaut **01**. **Chardonnay** ★★★ New-oak-fermented **04** soft & easy to drink, good dry finish; melon flavour upfront, touch vanilla oak behind. **Sauvignon Blanc** ✓ ★★★★ **04** grassy first sniff; full flavoured – good mouthful of ripe gooseberry – refreshing, well-balanced acidity. Amazing achievement given the vinification process. **Bouquet Blanc** ★★★ **04** sauvignon; upfront 'fruity' rather than 'aromatic', also very pleasant, semi-dry, light bodied. – *DH*

Kleine Hazen see Hazendal
Kleine Parys see Klein Parys

Kleine Zalze Wines

*Stellenbosch ▪ Est 1695 ▪ 1stB 1997 ▪ Tasting & sales Mon-Sat 9-5 Sun 11-4 ▪ Closed Easter Fri, Dec 25 & Jan 1 ▪ Fee R15 ▪ Tours by appt ▪ 'Terroir' Restaurant (see Eat-out section) ▪ Guest cottages & golf lodges ▪ Play area for children ▪ Tourgroups ▪ Conferencing ▪ Functions ▪ Owners Kobus Basson & Jan Malan ▪ Winemaker Johan Joubert, with Bertho van der Westhuizen (Nov 2002/Dec 2004) ▪ Viticulturist John Fullard, advised by Schalk du Toit (both 2000) ▪ 60 ha (cab, merlot, shiraz) ▪ ±1 500 tons 80 000 cs 50% red 50% white ▪ PO Box 12837 Die Boord Stellenbosch 7613 ▪ quality@kleinezalze.co.za ▪ www.kleinezalze.com ▪ **T 880·0717** ▪ F 880·0716*

A year of noteworthy local and international ratings, including winning *Wine* magazine's Shiraz Challenge, and scooping a trophy in the *Decanter* World Wine Awards for the Cellar Selection Chenin Bush Vine. These and other compliments are Kobus Basson & co's rewards for concerted efforts the past few years, including major investments in the cellar, rejuvenating the vineyards, gaining sole ownership of neighbour Groote Zalze (thus reducing the need for fruit from outside Stellenbosch), and playing the right team (ex-Citrusdal Bertho van der Westhuizen joining Johan Joubert in the winery). Vintage 2005 was all about harvesting fully ripe grapes (without over-extracted results), and vinifiying individual blocks according to their soil composition and character. For visitors, KZ now offers a variety of attractions, not least the new luxury lodges with amenities and views of the golf course, vineyards and mountains.

Family Reserve range — new

★★★★☆ **Shiraz** Much gilded **04** (incl MIWA, Wine Shiraz Challenge winner), sleek & confident but not brash, with deep colour, forthcoming fragrant & smoked meat aromas, ripe smooth tannins supporting rich fruit which copes well with 18 mths new oak (85/15 Fr/Am) & 14.2% alc. Should develop well over few yrs, last longer.

★★★★ **Cabernet Sauvignon** Serious, impressive wine, **04** perhaps still subdued in youth, to emerge in yr/2 – potential seems to lurk in tightly packed, satisfyingly savoury balance. 18 mths all-new Fr oak well absorbed, hinted at by vanilla/cedar notes, with smoky plums & berries. 14.5% alc a little too assertive on finish.

★★★★ **Sauvignon Blanc** Reserved, rather stately **05** in riper grassy/green pea style. Big fresh acid lifts fruit on well balanced, textured palate (adding passionfruit to the equation), with a little sugar smoothing any edges. Should only benefit from bottle ageing through 2006. WO W Cape.

Vineyard Selection

★★★★ **Cabernet Sauvignon Barrel Matured** As with Merlot below, **03** tasted as sample last ed; no **02** made. **03** smoky plum aromas, a fruity first impression; palate chewy, extracted, cedarwood & fruit; provisional ★★★★ with potential to add ☆ with bottle-ageing. **01** more elegant, classical & minerally. 12-15 mths oak, Fr/Am, some new.

★★★★ **Merlot Barrel Matured 03** (sample) mint-choc aroma, slight leafy note & lead pencil; dark plummy palate, cedarwood tinge; dry tannins. **01** lighter colour, bricking; plum with dried-fruit character & leafy touch. Yr-18 mths Fr/Am oak, some new.

★★★★ **Barrel Fermented Chardonnay** ✓ ±8 mths Fr oak, 30% new, 50% malo. Last ed, fat & soft **02** (MIWA gold) seemed to need drinking soon. **03** (sample; not retasted) looked promising: generous creamy melon & baked apple notes, big, firm, juicy wine.

★★★☆ **Chenin Blanc Barrel Fermented 04** (★★★★) now showing as rich, serious – dominated by spicy-butterscotch aromas from 100% Fr oaking, 50% new, with plenty of chenin fruit depth; juicy, fresh, substantial. Technically off-dry, but sugar well balanced & not too obvious. **03** luscious, fragrant & appealing.

Pinotage Barrel Matured ★★★☆ More power than charm on **03**, marked by severe tannins, dusty cedar notes from 18 mths new Fr oak – but dark fruit lurks. **Shiraz Barrel Matured** ★★★☆ **03** still in tank, looking promising with scrubby, spicy, ripe red fruit; savoury, firmly structured; good fruit copes well with 14.5% alc. 16 mths oak, some new, 10% Am.

Cellar Selection

★★★★ **Chenin Blanc Bush Vines** ✓ Unwooded version, noticeably off-dry (8.4g/ℓ RS) in most appealingly fragrant-floral, melony, full, rich **05** (★★★★); good compensating acidity gives it verve. **04** luscious melon, lanolin & honeysuckle whiffs.

Merlot ★★★★ Fresh, lively & well-balanced **03**, with light, ripe tannins, integrated wood influence; notes of plumcake & earth. **Cabernet Sauvignon** ★★★ **03** has tobacco, red/blackcurrant aromas leading through firmly tannic but balanced mouthful to slightly sweet-sour conclusion. WO Coastal. Only lightly wooded, as is ... **Pinotage** ★★★ Cheerful, fresh, spicy **04**; ripely sweet fruitiness matched with big dry tannins. **Gamay Noir** ★★★ **05** tank sample with spicy tart plumminess, soft red berries; light & bright & clean, with full – if brief – flavours; ex-Wllnton vyds. **Chardonnay** ★★★ Unwooded, dry & pleasingly zippy version. **05** with typical pear notes, creamily weighty palate. WO Coastal. **Sauvignon Blanc** ★★★★ Billows forth good-natured, charming tropicality in **05**. Ripe pleasure continues on full, well balanced, just-about-dry palate.

Foot of Africa range

Cabernet Sauvignon new ★★★ Good varietal character on **03**, with black fruit & cigar-box wood (18 mths Fr oak); robust but not excessive tannins; nice fruit disappears as alcoholic glow takes over (14.5%). **Pinotage-Shiraz** ★★★ Lightly wooded **04** from 60% home pinotage, 40% Coastal shiraz. Ripe jammy aromas, soft fruit, mild tannins, short sweet adieu. Big 14.5% alc.

Chenin Blanc new ☺ ★★★ Yet another pleasant off-dry KZ chenin – this crisp **05** one with forward, tropical aromas. WO W Cape. **Chenin Blanc-Chardonnay** ☺ ★★★ **05** home chenin + 30% Coastal chard: lots of heavy, vinous power for your buck here (glowing 14.5% alc) & citrus/tropical flavours. – *TJ*

Klein Gustrouw Estate

Stellenbosch ▪ Est 1817 ▪ 1stB 1993 ▪ Tasting, sales & tours by appt '24x7' but phone ahead (closed Dec 25/26) ▪ Conservation area ▪ Owners Chris & Athalie McDonald ▪ Winemaker/viticulturist Chris McDonald ▪ 16 ha (cab, merlot) ▪ 21 tons 1 600 cs 100% red ▪ PO Box 6064 Stellenbosch 7612 ▪ ***T/F (021) 887·4556***

Known for his ruthlessly honest vintage appraisals, Chris McDonald reports 2005 as a winner. The diminished quantity of grapes survived the heat in rude health, rendering almost superfluous his sorting table. Punting it as one of the '10 Coolest Cellars', a local magazine referred to the operation as *garagiste*, but McD insists that this is quite the wrong impression, 'even if part of the cellar *was* a garage'. The keen can motor off to the Jonkershoek cellar to buy his Bordeaux-styled red (at prices unchanged since 2001), from the stock McDonald squirrels away from eager Zurich and London importers. McD and Ghillie, the Scottish Deerhound who yearns for a mate, enjoy receiving visitors '24/7' – but he stresses, please ring first. And bring a dog?

★★★★★ **Cabernet Sauvignon-Merlot** Faceted, finely tailored bdx-style red usually released an indulgent three yrs after harvest. Current **03** brooding mid-2005: smouldering coffee-bean, dark choc aromas herald currant fruit tempered by tense frame; should soften into seamless elegance by 2008. **02** (★★★★) in lighter style, a yard off super **01**. 65/35 cab/merlot blend. 12-17 mths oak, third new (mostly for cab). – *DS*

Kleinood

new

Stellenbosch ▪ Est 2000 ▪ 1stB 2002 ▪ Visits by appt ▪ Owner Gerard de Villiers ▪ Winemaker Willem Grobbelaar (Sep 2004) ▪ Viti consultant Aidan Morton (Dec 2000) ▪ 9.6 ha (mourvèdre, shiraz, viognier) ▪ 62 tons 1 200 cs own label 100% red ▪ PO Box 12584 Die Boord 7613 ▪ winemaker@kleinood.co.za ▪ T 880·2527 ▪ F 880·2884

After 20 years of designing and constructing cellars (for Graham Beck, the Ruperts and Distell, among others), engineer Gerard de Villiers has completed his own small winery and bottled his first wine. Having in 2000 acquired the last section of formerly Stuttaford-owned Stellenrust farm (earlier subdivisions spawned Stellenzicht, Waterford and Dornier), GdV and former actress wife Libby commissioned consultant Aidan Morton to plant ±10ha with shiraz, viognier and mourvèdre. The challenge: 'To create something distinctive from a small viticultural entity.' Aiding are excellent clay-based soils, small blocks and different clones. Abetting is winemaker Willem Grobbelaar, combining De V-designed technology with traditional vinification methods in a simple, whitewashed, barn-like building, lovingly conceived and executed.

Tamboerskloof Shiraz new ★★★ Stylishly packaged **03**, earthy aromas with vegetal/game touches, ample fruit well conceals yr Fr/Am oak. Mix Stbosch, Wllngton, Kmuts fruit. —*MF*

Klein Optenhorst

Wellington ▪ Est/1stB 2001 ▪ Closed to public ▪ ±150 cs 100% red ▪ See Siyabonga for details.

Vino-preneur Graham Knox (Jack & Knox, Siyabonga etc) here links up with Wellington neighbour Naas Ferreira, owner of a tiny but pampered pinot vineyard on the slopes of Groenberg Mountain.

★★★★ **Pinot Noir** Individual SA take on classic grape. Last tasted was truffly **03**, which recaptured the unpretentious allure of **01** in a more delicate body (13% alc). 11 mths Fr oak. Probably for earlier enjoyment (1-3 yrs). **02** diverted to 'Knife's Edge Pinot Noir-Merlot'. **04** unready. —*AL*

Klein Parys Vineyards new

Paarl ▪ Est 1692 ▪ 1stB 2003 ▪ Mon-Fri 10-6 Sat 10-4 ▪ Closed Easter Fri/Sun, Dec 16/25/26 & Jan 1 ▪ Cheese platters, olives, olive oil & other farm-style produce ▪ Tourgroups ▪ Gifts ▪ Art, clothing & other exhibitions ▪ Owner Kosie Möller ▪ Winemaker/viticulturist Kosie Möller, with Herman Roux ▪ 48 ha (cab, chard, chenin, nouvelle, semillon, viognier) ▪ 700 tons 80 000 cs 50% red 50% white ▪ Export brands: Kleine Parys & Miller's Mile ▪ PO Box 1362 Suider-Paarl 7624 ▪ parys@kparys.co.za ▪ ***T 872·9848*** *▪ F 872·8527*

Former KWV chief winemaker Kosie Möller has put down roots on one of the oldest wine farms in Paarl, determined to turn Klein Parys (circa 1692) into the region's icon. Wine tourism is the name of the game. But it's not just about the frills (gardens, restaurant, tastings till sunset, future guesthouse and self-catering cottages). The emphasis is on value-for-money wines, unusual varieties and balancing a winemaker's distinctive style with the consumer's tastes. With established vineyards (including home-grown roobernet and nouvelle) and a recommissioned cellar (last used in 1969), Möller happily handled a difficult 2005 harvest, foreseeing a vintage for 'blockbuster wines'. Cherry on the top was the first birthday of his twin boys.

Kleine Parys range

Cabernet Sauvignon new ★★★ Different & characterful; **04** touches tar & eucalyptus; extracted 'hot' character well balanced by freshening acidity; protracted finish. Yr oak, 20% Am. **Shiraz** ★★★ 80% Am oak for **04**, similar stylish feel to pvs; welcoming, warm; obvious spicy oak; succulent fruit subtly tensioned by well-extracted tannins. **Pinotage** ★★ **04** different kettle of fruit to pvs: old-style with whiffs leather & acetone, savoury-dry, big (14.5% alc) & boisterous. 40% Am oak, yr. **Beatrix Selection** ★★★★ Meaty/spicy blend shiraz (60%), cab, pinotage; **02** last yr delicious fruitcake flavour, rich & ripe. Contrived & obvious in the nicest way. New oak 18 mths, 40% Am. **Classic Red** new ★★★ Pruney baked fruit character with soft, easy, sweet-sour twist; **04** varieties as per Beatrix. WO W Cape. **Pinotage Blanc de Noir** new ★★ Palest shell-pink **05**, off-dry, restrainedly fruity. **Chardonnay** ★★ **05** (sample) barrel fermentation not obvious; sniffs warm hay & peach; soft, fruit-sweet, eager to please. **Chenin Blanc** ★★★ **05** spring flowers & confected peach ice-cream on nose; light-bodied, lingering flavours, good peachy acidity. Following pair new; WO W Cape: **Sauvignon Blanc** ★★ Herbal, slightly rustic **05**, firmly dry, lingering fynbos flavours. **Cuvée Brut** ★★★ Bracing no-frills summer bubbles, bone dry; **NV** from chenin, colombard. **Golden Vintage** new ★★★ Semi-sweet chenin with simple but pleasing melon fruitiness, balanced acidity.

Miller's Mile range

Cabernet Sauvignon ★★★ Honest & typical; **04** lingering cedar/mulberry aromas, medium bodied, dry; youthful slightly savoury tannins. 8 mths oak, 20% Am. **Pinotage** ★★★ Dusty-dry **04**, typical pinotage red fruit; still subdued, gawky, should perk up with few mths in bottle. Oak as for Cab. **Shiraz** ★★★ Lightly wooded **04** unshowy but satisfying, accessible; plump fruit, subtle oak backdrop (Am/Fr staves). **Pinotage-Shiraz** ★★ Light-textured 60/40 blend, oak as for Cab, shy & dry, some red fruit lying in wait – **04** possibly needs time. **Chardonnay** ★★ **05** barrel fermented though not obviously so – whiffs talcum powder & perfume; modestly fruited, soft, inoffensive. 4 mths oak, 40% Am. **Chenin Blanc** ★★ Soft, clean pulpy melon fruit; **05** gentle, light-bodied off-dry pre-dinner quaff. WO W Cape for all. *– IvH/CR*

Kleinrivier see Clos Malverne
Klein Simonsvlei see Niel Joubert
Klein Tulbagh see Tulbagh Winery

Kleinvallei Winery

Paarl ▪ Est/1stB 2000 ▪ Tasting by appt ▪ Owners Piet & Sandra van Schaik ▪ Vini consultant Jean-Vincent Ridon (2000) ▪ 10 ha (cab, malbec, merlot, petit v, pinotage, shiraz, chard) ▪ 17 tons 940 cs 90% red 10% white ▪ PO Box 9060 Klein Drakenstein 7628 ▪ kleinvallei@mweb.co.za ▪ www.kleinvallei.co.za ▪ ***T 868·3662/082·399·5075*** *▪ F 868·3130*

With new vineyards coming into production last year, the Kleinvallei crop more than doubled. More importantly, overall quality was good and there was a fair bit of lucky timing: the team picked the chardonnay just two days before heavy January rain. With so many more grapes pouring in, the cellar needed some serious reorganising to find room for them all. More vines, more wines – it all means more work, especially when, as owner Piet van Schaik puts it: 'We have become even more aware of how important attention to detail really is, and how the learning curve never plateaus.'

Cabernet Sauvignon ★★★ **01** tasted for pvs ed, blackcurrant, cream & toast aromas; slightly leafy & austere; best enjoyed soon. 20 mths Fr, some new. ±14% alc. No new vintage; all used in **Bel Canto** ★★★ **03** raises the bar on pvs; now a wine to lay down 4–5 yrs. Led by cab (60%) with shiraz (27%) & merlot, it's concentrated with fine, dense tannins. 18 mths combo new/old Fr oak. Not yet certified as we went to print. **Pinotage** ★★★ Not at all quirky like pvs, with its 16% alc, 9g/ℓ sugar! **04** dark & extracted style; fleshy fruit/rhubarb, big tannins; not quite ready, try in ± yr's time. Yr older Fr oak. **Chardonnay** ★★★ **04** inviting citrus, warm buttered toast aromas, poised yet lively palate given body/flavour from yr in 5th fill Fr casks. *– CR*

Klippendal see Cru Wines
Klompzicht see Freedom Hill
Kloofzicht Estate see Alter Ego Wines

Kloovenburg Vineyards

Swartland ▪ Est 1704 ▪ 1stB 1998 ▪ Tasting & sales Mon-Fri 9-4.30 Sat 9-2 ▪ Fee for groups R10 ▪ Closed Christian holidays ▪ Tours during tasting hours by appt ▪ BYO picnic ▪ Farm-grown olive products for tasting/sale ▪ Walks ▪ Conservation area ▪ Owner/winemaker Pieter du Toit ▪ Viti consultant Kobus van Graan (Jun 2000) ▪ 130 ha (cab, merlot, shiraz, chard, sauvignon) ▪ 6 000 cs own label 70% red 30% white ▪ PO Box 2 Riebeek-Kasteel 7307 ▪ info@kloovenburg.com ▪ www.kloovenburg.com ▪ ***T (022) 448·1635*** *▪ F (022) 448·1035*

Tucked away beneath the Kasteelberg peak at the entrance to the newly sexy little country retreat of Riebeek-Kasteel, Kloovenburg, with the bright white of its lime-washed *ringmuur* and Iceberg roses offset against a wall of green shade trees, has been turning out some star-studded shirazes. (The 2002 was given the ultimate high five by UK *Decanter* last year.) The Shiraz need barely stand back for the Chardonnay. And now, in addition to the Cab and Merlot, there's a maiden Sauvignon joining this elegant line-up. Owner/winemaker Pieter du Toit and wife Annalene are also into olives, offering all sorts of tasty treats for tasting and sale to locals and visitors.

★★★★★ **Shiraz** Unshowy but consistently superb northern-Rhône style red, with subtle white pepper undertone. **04**, ex-barrel, impressively black-hued & -fruited; spice & nutmeg aromas, elegant tannins seamlessly integrated; alc less evident than similarly styled **03**, marked by well-defined fruit flavours.

★★★★ **Chardonnay** ✓ Sumptuously oaked though amply fruited, **05** mid-2005 shows toasty/smoky edges to grapefruit whiffs, good amplitude & succulence. New Fr barrel fermented/matured. Bigger & brasher than **04**, showing suppleness, persistence, elegance.

Cabernet Sauvignon After sinewy, vinous, restrained **03**, sample **04** (likely ★★★★) is riper, softer, more intense: deep coloured, rich textured with fine soft tannins. Fr oak matured. **Merlot** ★★★ **04** fine if unenduring plum/mulberry notes, herbal finish, less sumptuous than sweeter & riper **03**. **Sauvignon Blanc** new ★★★ Cat's pee aromas on **05**; pungent & racy, edgy acidity (8.1g/ℓ) & austere finish. From cellar door only. — *MF*

Knorhoek Wines

*Stellenbosch ▪ Est 1827 ▪ 1stB 1997 ▪ Tasting & sales daily 9–5 ▪ Fee R10 ▪ Closed Dec 25 ▪ Restaurant/lapa Sep-May 12–4 ▪ Guest house (B&B) with conference, function, entertainment area ▪ Facilities for children ▪ Tourgroups ▪ Walks ▪ Conservation area ▪ Owners Hansie & James van Niekerk ▪ Winemaker/viticulturist Arno Albertyn (2005), advised by Wynand Hamman ▪ 105 ha (cabs s/f, merlot, pinotage, shiraz, chenin, sauvignon) ▪ 900 tons 10 000 cs own label 70% red 30% white ▪ Export label: Two Cubs ▪ PO Box 2 Koelenhof 7605 ▪ office@knorhoek.co.za ▪ www.knorhoek.co.za ▪ **T/F 865·2627***

The 2005 vintage was produced in the newly completed cellar by recent arrival Arno Albertyn, under the sage eye of Wynand Hamman (ex-Lanzerac, who now makes his Fryer's Cove wines here too). Knorhoek's always enjoyed popularity with tourists and trippers — now visitors can taste the fruits of the vine in a new, improved venue, appropriately situated in the cellar and open over weekends. A wide deck makes the link between rustic and hi-tech: 'A bit of Muratie and a bit of something new,' as HvN describes it.

★★★★ **Cabernet Sauvignon** Sleek & stylish **03** showing its class in concentrated cassis/roast tomato fruit, finely handled/cedar tannins. Accessible, but deserves 6–7yrs cellaring to evolve to its full potential. 14.4% alc higher than pvs; 2 yrs Fr oak maturation, 48% new. Sweet-fruited **02** has black berry & spice at its centre, deliciously embroidered with choc-mint.

Two Cubs Cape Blend new ☺ ★★★ **03** deliciously savoury shiraz, pinotage, merlot blend for braai-side quaffing. Biltong, coriander & smoky whiffs, dry tail. Stbosch WO, Coastal for ... **Two Cubs White Blend** new ☺ ★★★ Limy, tangy & friendly. **05** chenin (50%), equal parts sauvignon & semillon.

Pinotage ★★★★ No new vintage. Uncorked last yr, **01** had a bottle-age note adding interest & complexity to earthy mulberry/plum fruit. Yr oak, 40% new. **Syrah** new ★★★★ **03** in fruity New World mould. Generous prune & spice nose, creamy palate designed to please. Drink now or over ± 2yrs. **Reserve** new ★★★★ Tightly wound four-way blend mainly cab (65%), shiraz, merlot, pinotage. **03** not revealing its true charm, should so with 2–5 yrs cellaring. Elegant tannins wrap around mulberry fruit, oak aromas with fynbos hints. 2 yrs 100% new Fr oak. **Chenin Blanc** ★★★ **05** easy drinker with salad of summer fruits character, plumpish, ripe, semi-dry finish. **Sauvignon Blanc** ★★★ **05** leaner than pvs, herbaceous/nettle profile, lip-smacking dry finish. Unless noted, all WO Smnsberg-Stbosch. — *CR/DH*

Knysna Cellars

Knysna ▪ Est 2001 ▪ 1stB 2002 ▪ Tasting & sales Mon-Fri 8.30–1; 2–5 Sat 8.30–1 (summer only) ▪ Fee R100 for 'vintage tutored tasting' (min 6 wines) ▪ Closed Dec 25/26 & Jan 1 ▪ Tourgroups of up to 12 people ▪ Farm-style cheeses ▪ Owner/winemaker Geoff Boomer ▪ Viticulturist Mark van Haldren (Apr 2003) ▪ 590 cs ▪ 12a Watsonia Street Knysna 6570 ▪ gbalstar@pixie.co.za ▪ ***T (044) 382·6164*** *▪ F (044) 382·6193*

'Vines don't grow quick enough in Knysna!' exclaims the area's only grower, Irishman Geoff Boomer, whose vineyards had to be replanted last year. 'Like everything else in life, patience is required.' Meanwhile he conducts tutored tastings of other selected producers' wines, including older vintages, for small groups at his premises.

Koelenbosch see Koelenhof Winery

Koelenhof Winery

Stellenbosch ▪ Est 1941 ▪ 1stB 1974 ▪ Tasting & sales Mon-Thu 9-5 Fri 9-4.30 Sat & pub hols 9-1 ▪ Closed Easter Fri, Ascension Day, Dec 25/26 & Jan 1) ▪ BYO picnic (excellent deli nearby) ▪ Play area for children ▪ Conferencing ▪ Owners 75 shareholders ▪ Winemakers Wilhelm de Vries & Martin Stevens (Jan 2001/Oct 2003) ▪ Viticulturist Herman du Preez (Jan 2002) ▪ 11 000 tons 6 000 cs own label ±9m litres bulk 60% red 38% white 1% rosé 1% sparkling/grape juice ▪ HACCP certification in progress ▪ PO Box 1 Koelenhof 7605 ▪ koelwyn@mweb.co.za ▪ ***T 865·2020/1*** *▪ F 865·2796*

With last year's personnel changes now bedded in, this Stellenbosch outfit is going great guns as a 'service cellar', making more than competent wines-to-order for various wineries with well established names. For their own account they release everyday and mid-range wines with broad public appeal under the Koelenhof brand, but the team feel it's time to go further, bottling a top tier under the newly created 'Koelenbosch' label. They'll oversee all this, and a more focused marketing drive, from their new offices at the winery, which has also been expanded to include a tasting room, large enough to be used for functions.

Koelenbosch range new

Merlot ★★ Appears to have undergone a style change from exuberantly New World of initial releases to leafy/herbal of **02** & now Old Cape on **03**, dried-fruit character with powerful tannins. Will have its followers. New oak, 20 mths. **Pinotage** ★★ 24 mths new oak for **03**, displaying similar 'retro/nostalgic' quality in old-style acetone whiff, dry, fruit-shy profile. **Cabernet Sauvignon** ★★ Oaked as for Merlot, with similar effect: **03** very dry & lean, hints damp earth & dry leaves, begs a hearty country casserole. **Cape Blend** ★★ Merlot/pinotage equal partnership with 20% cab; oak as for Merlot (10% Am). **03** somewhat fruitier than range-mates, juicier tannins, wood not as strident. **Chenin Blanc Wooded** new ★★★ New oak fermented/*sur lie* 9 mths, partial native year fermentation; **04** still redolent of wood, whiff of almond, restrained fruit, needs to be enjoyed soon. **Sauvignon Blanc** ★★ **05** downplayed fruit this vintage (early harvested); faint grass/asparagus suggestions, light-bodied casual quaffing.

Koelenhof range

Koelenkeur In abeyance. **Shiraz** ★★★★ **02** last ed showed dark fruits with touches fynbos & dried herbs, seamlessly oaked. Next is **04**. **Pinotage Rosé** ★★ **05** unready. **04** appealing crushed-fruit sappiness, perhaps touch too sweet, even for fructose fans. **Chardonnay Wooded 04** unready for tasting. **Koelenhoffer** ★ Unpretentious semi-dry white a perennial brisk seller; **05** again from sauvignon, early picked, lightish & bracingly fresh. **Koelnektar** ★★★ Scented semi-sweet gewürz, **05** billows rose-petal & Turkish Delight, very soft this vintage, will be prized by the sweeter toothed. **Sauvignon Blanc Vin-sec** ★★★ ('Sparkling Sec' pvs ed) Lightish semi-dry carbonated sparkling with lots of friendly bubbles, slightly sweet tone & whiffs of pine & melon. **NV**, as is ... **Pinotage Rosé Vin-sec** ★★ ('Sparkling Rosé' last ed) Potpourri & dried fruit in bouquet, sweetish flavours without any grip, very undemanding. **White Jeripigo** ★ Big alc (17%) on **04** certainly glow-inducing; sweet grapey flavours from chenin. **Pino Porto** ★★ LBV-style (**NV**) from pinotage, 2 yrs seasoned small oak. Traditional-style low fortification (16.4%), but what alc there is, is cheek-rougeingly active.*—CR/CT/TM*

Koelfontein

Ceres ▪ Est 1832 ▪ 1stB 2002 ▪ Visits by appt ▪ BYO picnic ▪ Farm produce, walks & other amenities (see intro) ▪ Owners Handri & Zulch Conradie ▪ Vini consultant Dewaldt Heyns ▪ Viticulturist Zulch Conradie ▪ 19 ha (cab, merlot, shiraz, chard, colombard) ▪ 200 tons 2 000 cs own label + 110 000ℓ for customers ▪ 60% red 40% white ▪ PO Box 702 Ceres 6835 ▪ wine@koelfontein.com ▪ ***T (023) 313·3130*** *▪ F (023) 313·4898*

Growing quality fruit is the main business of this high altitude (750m!) property, but vines under the care of the Conradie brothers also produce the only wine bearing the Wine of Origin Ceres seal. The 1840 homestead, which in 2005 saw the arrival of the seventh generation of Conradies, sports a fully operational watermill powered by the spring from which the farm derives its name, and is also home to one of the few remaining (licensed!) working witblits stills in the country. The original wine cellar – a blacksmith's workshop for a time – has been revamped into a tasting facility. With snow-spotting in winter, fresh fruits in summer, and wine year round, the only wine destination in Ceres must be worth a visit.

No follow-up releases; notes from pvs ed: **Merlot** ★★★★ Showy **02** can hardly fail to impress with its oak-boosted pungency; juicy plum flavours perhaps a tad jammy; wood (11 mths Fr oak, 40% new) too forceful for fruit mid-2004, time needed to settle down. **Chardonnay** ★★★★ **03** rich & heavily wooded – overpowering now, but good core of lime fruit waiting to assert itself. Oak stave fermented/aged ±10 mths. *—TM*

Kogmans Kloof see Zandvliet
Koningshof see Avondvrede

Koningsrivier Wines

Robertson ▪ Est/1stB 2002 ▪ Visits by appt ▪ Owner SW Colyn ▪ Winemaker Niël Colyn ▪ Viti consultants Anton Laas & Briaan Stipp ▪ 9 ha (cab) ▪ 435 cs 100% red ▪ PO Box 144 Robertson 6705 ▪ nscolyn@yahoo.com ▪ ***T (023) 625·1748/082·588·1262*** *▪ F (023) 625·1748*

No update available on this winery; contact details from previous edition.

Kosher see Backsberg, Eshkol, Kleine Draken, Tempel
Kosie Möller see Klein Parys

Kranskop Estate

Robertson ▪ Est/1stB 2001 ▪ Tasting & sales Mon-Fri 10-5 Sat 10-2 1st Sun of mth 10-1 ▪ Closed Easter Sun, Dec 25 & Jan 1 ▪ Tours during tasting hours ▪ Light meals by appt ▪ Tourgroups ▪ Facilities for children ▪ Walks ▪ Owner/winemaker/viticulturist Nakkie Smit ▪ 40 ha (cab, merlot, shiraz, chard) ▪ 500 tons 2 500 cs own label 90% red 10% white ▪ PO Box 18 Klaasvoogds 6707 ▪ kranskop@myisp.co.za ▪ www.kranskopwines.co.za ▪ ***T/F (023) 626·3200***

Last year was Nakkie Smit's fifth under the Kranskop banner, and Nature's gift was ... the most difficult harvest yet. His belief that vineyard practices are the major determinant of wine quality remains unchanged, and he's matching attention to detail there with tweaks in the vinification. The portion of new wood rises from 20% to 30%, and total maturation time almost doubles to just under two years. An adherent to the small-is-beautiful aesthetic, Smit assures visitors of his personal attention (and so is pleased that his English 'improves a little every day').

Cabernet Sauvignon ★★★ Returns to guide after 2 vintages. Extended new Fr oak regime (30%, 22 mths) still obvious on **03**, billows smoke, tar, black fruit barely peeping through; needs time to settle, meld. **Merlot Reserve** ★★★★ None since elegant **02**, with dark minerally fruit, well-judged spicy Fr oak (100% new, yr). **Merlot** ★★★ **03** again big wine (14.5% alc); dark choc/prune richness hauled in by house's hallmark lively acid; friendly tannins for earlier approachability. 22 mths Fr oak, 20% new. **Shiraz** ★★★ **03** in mould of pvs; savoury red fruit, whiffs eucalyptus & vanilla; fairly tart tannins & ultra-dry finish. 30% new barriques, 30% Am. **Cabernet Sauvignon-Merlot** ★★★★ Last was light-textured **02**, 50/50 blend with gentle dusting Fr oak. Barrelled yr, 15% new. **Chardonnay** ★★★ Full-bodied &

firm-fleshed. **04** lifted by rush of acidity, good mineral finish . ±Yr Fr oak. All these WO Klaasvoogds.—*CvZ*

Krone see Twee Jonge Gezellen
Kuikenvlei see Terroir Wines
Kumala see Daschbosch, Porterville, Western Wines
Kumkani see Omnia Wines

Kupferberger Auslese

Consistent semi-sweet by Distell. Current (**NV**) ★★ pleasant blend sauvignon, riesling, chenin; the blancs giving tropical aromas & flavours, all contributing to zinging acidity. —*CvZ*

KWV Limited

Paarl ▪ Est 1918 ▪ KWV Wine Emporium daily tastings 9-4; fee R15 ▪ Sales 9-5 ▪ Tours Eng: 10, 10.30 & 14.15; Ger: 10.15 ▪ Tourgroups ▪ Gifts ▪ KWV SA: winemaker Thys Loubser (reds), with Nomonde Kubheka (reds) & Tania Joubert (whites) ▪ Viticulturist Chris Albertyn, advised by Cobus van Graan ▪ ±13 000 tons ▪ KWV International: PO Box 528 Suider-Paarl 7624 ▪ customer@kwv.co.za ▪ www.kwv-international.com ▪ ***T 807·3911*** *▪ F 807·3349*

Following the high-profile departure last year of two of its winemakers, this industry giant (2m cases a year) has adopted what it believes is a 'significant and new approach to wine-making'. Its oeno-team is now mentored by three industry heavyweights – locals Neil Ellis (Neil Ellis Wines) and Charles Back (Fairview), and Australian Ian McKenzie (ex-Southcorp) – part of their brief being to create 'a culture of continuous improvement in KWV's cellars'. A market-oriented approach to brands continues to be encouraged (though the premium Cathedral Cellar and KWV Reserve ranges still reflect vintage vagaries and individual winemaking skills). Company stalwart Sterik de Wet, who oversees cellar and vineyard operations, says they're implementing a partnership programme with growers, highlighting vineyard block management and fruit selection as required by specific ranges and brands. In support are some 2 000 small oak barrels in the newly revamped showpiece Cathedral Cellar at the Paarl headquarters, now featuring spectacular stained glass windows depicting Cape wine's past, present and future.

Cathedral Cellar range

★★★★☆ **Cabernet Sauvignon** Expensively, carefully made cab. **02** more accessible than usual, with no loss of class. Interwoven with polished tannins are cassis, violets, herbaceous note, oak-spiked smoky tones. Juicy palate, with freshening acidity nice contrast to rich fruit & firm structure. New oak 26 mths. Age 5-7 yrs, or drink while waiting for **01's** elegantly layered structure to unfurl. **00** *Wine* ★★★★☆. IWSC gold.

★★★★☆ **Merlot** Refined, elegant **02** doesn't put a foot wrong: lush, ripe red fruit, berries, plums; an oak injection of cigar-box spicing. Palate impresses: superbly judged oak (as for Cab), serious yet ripe tannins, harmoniously integrated. **01** classically styled, lithe structure, with oaking laying foundation for 4/5 yrs ageing. 13.5% alc.

★★★★ **Pinotage** Fruit leaps out of the glass in **02** – redcurrants, cherries, given cinnamon/sweet spicing by the wood. Generous, flavourful, with lovely balance; plenty of oak, but fine-grained, ripe, finishing dry enough for solo drinking or as food accompaniment. Will age well 5-7 yrs. WO Stbosch. 18 mths new. Follows well on modern, impressive, opulent **01**.

★★★★☆ **Shiraz** Always complex, silkily elegant. **02** combines Old World & New, with lots of savoury aromas: complex tones of proscuitto, garrique, white pepper resting on a brambleberry base, reflecting the good marriage of fruit and 2 yrs equal new Fr/Am oak – latter giving attractive vanilla sweetness. **01**'s supple tannins cloaked by lush fruit, deft oaking.

★★★★ **Triptych** Blend cab, merlot, shiraz – near equal partnership in **01** (★★★★☆); sampled last yr, now unfolding beautifully: shimmering cassis, crushed berries; savoury balsamic, meat extract notes deepening, becoming richer, the impressive oaking (26 mths new Fr) not dominating. Iron fist in a velvet glove, with framework for 6+ yrs ageing. 15% alc. Impressive **00**'s lithe, muscular structure suggested serious intent. VDG.

★★★★ **Chardonnay** To date, all showy, powerful. **04** has wealth of flavours, from intense ripe fruit, generous oaking: toffee, dried peach, bread & butter pudding; with house-style silky texture, making for irresistable drinkability. 8 mths new Fr. **03** also moreish. Fermented/8 mths new Fr oak.

Sauvignon Blanc ★★★★ **04** has underlying minerality, svelte sophistication even more impressive than the nettly, grapefruit greeting. Dry; friendly 12.5 % alc. This range WO Coastal/W-Cape unless noted.

KWV range

Roodeberg ★★★★ A Cape institution: admirable quality given large quantities. Usually cab, shiraz, merlot blend. Designed for maximum appeal – as with **03**: lively red fruit, gently oak-spiced; sweetly ripe palate, no hard edges, & juicy drinkability. Yr seasoned oak. Also in 1.5ℓ, 3ℓ, 5ℓ. **Cabernet Sauvignon** ★★★★ **03** built to please, has layers of interest: cassis, plum core, smoky/savoury nuances, approachable yet a firm backbone. As with next 2 reds, could age 2-3 yrs. Yr Fr oak. **Merlot** ★★★ **03** lighter weight than pvs, but still red berry flavour appeal, toasty injection from oak. **Pinotage** ★★★★ **03** attracts with vibrant raspberry/brambleberry fruit, toasty spice layers, juicy palate, yet shows a serious side in fine-grained tannins. **Shiraz** ★★★ Classic profile on **03**, carpaccio, wild berries, white pepper; lighter structure than pvs, best enjoyed within 2 yrs. **Cape Blush** ★★★ Blanc de noir **04** from cinsaut, merlot now has appealing glacé cherry/fruit pastille flavours; rounded from 7.4g/ℓ sugar; juicy, appetising, with good length. **Chardonnay** ★★★ For those who prefer a lightly oaked style, **04** has peach & biscuit fragrance, flavours; roundly accessible, with enough spark for food. **Steen** ★★ Chenin's 'old-Cape' name for this bone dry version, slightly sterner than sibling below. Early-drinking **04** gentle fruit salad fragrance/flavours, refreshingly dry. VDG. **Chenin Blanc** ★★★ **05** good quaffing chenin: summer fruits, frisky acidity, round texture from 6g/ℓ sugar, friendly 12.5% alc. **Val du Chené** ★★★ Name change from 'Chené' for lightly wooded chenin. **04** 's fruit shines through well: crunchy fruit-salad, vibrant food-friendly palate, finishing with lemon-biscuit tang. **Sauvignon Blanc** ★★★ Enough green fig, herbaceous character on **05** to please purists, but approachable, light-textured – & best in the flush of youth. 12.5% alc. **Cape Riesling** ★★ Typical restrained, mown hay of crouchen, with touch leafy freshness in uncomplicated, softly accessible **04** (sample). We'd pvsly noted next 2 **NV** bubblies from chenin discontinued, but ... **Mousseux Blanc Cuvee Brut** Simple but honest crowd-please★★ r. Fruit salad tones, touch of sugar but finishes dry. **Mousseux Blanc Demi-Sec** ★★ Friendly quaffer with tropical fruit, star-sweets flavours, frothy medium-sweet finish.

Reserve range

★★★★ **Cabernet Sauvignon** Impressive fruit purity, depth; cedar-infusing 16 mths new Fr oak. **02** still tightly held, in classic cab mode, with ingredients for good 5-6 yr future: red berry concentration, some herbaceous tones, juicy palate accessibility.

★★★★ **Merlot** Seductive dark tones, black plums, bitter choc, mocha spicing, resting on a bed of firm but ripe tannins in **02**. As was tightly knit **01**, this a keeper, worth cellaring 5-6 yrs. Oak as above.

★★★★ **Sauvignon Blanc** From single vyd. **04** powerful, complex, with notes fresh fennel, grapefruit, zesty lime. Palate pumps with juiciness, awakens the senses. Bone-dry; amenable 12.5% alc.

★★★★ **Chardonnay 04** notch up on **03** (★★★★), but same style. Prominent peach & citrus-peel, with extra fruit/wood dimensions of nutty crème brulee, honey biscuit. Overall impression of richness, concentration, but delightful twist of lime lifts the finish. 6 mths new Fr oak; single vyd. Gold at Chard du Monde.

Shiraz ★★★★ A stylistic change in **02**, moving into fynbos territory, with more herbaceous, white pepper tones than riper **01**. Cherry fruit & harmonious, integrated tannins, but not for long keeping. 16 mths new Am oak. This range WO Stbosch.

Robert's Rock range

★★★★ **Chardonnay-Semillon** Lively, flavoursome. **04** (★★★☆) sample tasted last yr, easier than pvs. Ebullient flavours, smoothly supple unwooded 51/49 blend. **03** affirmed partnership's compatibility.

Cinsaut-Ruby Cabernet ☺ ★★★ **04** continues drinkability track record: exuberantly fruity, red currants, cherries; light, juicy, goes down easily. Lightly oaked.

Cabernet Sauvignon-Merlot ★★★ **04**, near-equal blend, less showy than pvs; cassis base toned down by dried herbs, suggestion of stalkiness. Lightly oaked, could unfold over 2-3 yrs. **Merlot-Cinsaut** ★★★☆ **02** was last tasted. **Pinotage-Pinot Noir** ★★★☆ ✓ Unusual & successful ± 60/40 blend. **04** nice early-drinker, with flavours cherry, red berry, dab of cedar from yr oak; harmoniously put together. **Shiraz-Malbec** ★★★☆ ✓ Compatible **03** partnership noted last yr ex-barrel as delivering good flavours, balance. **Shiraz-Cabernet Sauvignon** new ★★★ **04** holds nothing back in flavouring: upfront Fortris & smoky spice; soft, ripe structure, no hard edges, effortless. Not for long keeping, delicious now. Yr oaked. **Cinsaut-Chenin Blanc** ★★☆ Vibrant cerise colour the first attraction on **04** – but also red berry fruit/fruit gum tastes, smooth off-dry appeal. Unoaked 60/40 blend; friendly 12% alc. **Chardonnay** ★★☆ **04**'s peach & tropical fruit flavours aiding easy uncomplicated quaffability. Lightly oaked sample tasted last ed. **Chenin Blanc-Chardonnay** ★★★ **04** now showing ripe peach, tropical tones, good length & balance in 52/48 blend. Graceful, approachable. All WO W-Cape.

Golden Kaan range

All ★★★, all **04** except Rosé. **Cabernet Sauvignon** Generous & ripe; cassis-infused, deliciously approachable, lively. Oaking (9 mths seasoned Fr) only apparent in dry finish. **Merlot** Plenty to like: cassis/raspberries, light oak dusting, medium weight accessibility, with just enough tannin for food matching. Oak as above. **Shiraz** Biggest selling member of range – easy to see why. Fruit-focused style: luscious strawberries, red berries, sweetly spiced, with 9 mths used Am oak to provide required support.. **Pinotage** Fruit-dominant, basket of berries & plums, with rhubarb tone, touch of oak (Fr/Am 9 mths) adding interest. Simple but tasty palate. **Pinotage Rosé** new **05** pretty in every way: bright cerise colour, fruit pastille nose, juicy off-dry friendliness. **Chardonnay** Amenable & satisfying, with elegantly styled peach & citrus flavours, perked up by brisk acidity; light, harmonious oaking. **Sauvignon Blanc** Attractive pear-drop/lime character, crisply refreshing, herbaceous-toned finish. Easy-going 11.8% alc. All WO W-Cape.

Golden Kaan Reserve range new

★★★★ **Winemaker's Reserve Cabernet Sauvignon** Cassis/raspberry fruit depth & concentration of **03** allow serious oaking (new Fr, 26 mths), contributing lovely cigar-box flavours, & providing for 6+ yrs cellaring – but tannins need yr to become supple, integrate.

All below ★★★☆. **Reserve Selection Cabernet Sauvignon** Well balanced **03** has oak well integrated with creamy red fruit: cedar tones, smoky spicing. Elegantly structured, for solo or food. Yr Fr barrels, half new, as for ... **Reserve Selection Shiraz** Harmonious, accessible **03** where fruit is main focus (plum jam, cherry); deep & rich, yet also some savoury hints, herbs. Oak supports, not hinders. Ready, can age ± 3 yrs. **Winemaker's Reserve Chardonnay** Bold New World style **03**: crystallised lemon rind, roasted nuts, dried peaches, showing on both nose & palate, with a big dollop of oak (8 mths new Fr) & well-rounded body. Will make many friends. **Reserve Selection Sauvignon Blanc 05** has interesting aromas lemonade, fennel, toned-down grassiness, followed by mouthfilling vibrant freshness, nice long finish. Alc a friendly 12%.

Bonne Esperance range

Dry Red ★★ This, below, **NV**, in 1ℓ screwcap, sold internationally; in SA only for KWV staff. A changing blend, usually cinsaut, ruby cab, smattering pinotage. Latest softly friendly; juicy ripe berry flavours. Unwooded; amenable 12.5% alc. **Dry White** ★★ Latest chenin-based easygoing quaffer has summer fragrances, tasty grapy flavours. Refreshing, light 12.1% alc.

Pearly Bay range

Cape Red ☺ ★★★ Vivid hued, flavoursome early-drinking blend similar to Dry Red above; fruit-gum whiffs, juicy cherries, light-hearted. Unwooded. 12.5% alc. **NV** like 2 next.

Cape White ★★ Chenin shines through in crunchy apple freshness, light-toned sociability. 11.8% alc. **Celebration** new ★★**NEW** Cheerful bubbly from muscat d' A, grapey & semi-sweet. Amiable 8% alc.

KWV Fortified range

★★★★ **Millennium Port 99** still available – per last ed, ageing gracefully; cinsaut/tinta; 19.5% alc, 110g/ℓ RS; huge grape-tannin structure for keeping. Unwooded.

★★★★ **Tawny Port** Appeal starts with colour, perfectly reflecting name; continues throughout ... Long ageing (5-8 yrs old oak), expert cellar handling give consistent character yr after yr, at high level. Latest (**NV**) again shows tealeaf, English toffee, honeycomb, nutty oak; long aromatic, brandied finish. Almost syrupy texture; gorgeous. Equal tinta/souzão. 19.3% alc. 120 g/ℓ sugar.

★★★★ **Vintage Red Muscadel** From selected Rbtson vyds; **75** (not retasted) deep amber hue, like tawny port in character. Admirable complexity: tea leaf, nutty oiliness, brandy-soaked raisins. Long savoury/sweet finish, plenty life, sophistication. Large oak 8 yrs. 17.3% alc, 150g/ℓ sugar.

★★★★ **White Muscadel** As pvsly, latest **NV**'s amber colour alerts you to delights to come. Unwooded, to allow full expression to the glorious richness of the fully ripened muscadel grapes. Layered complexity: sultana-essence concentration, toffee, freshening leafy edginess. Ambrosially rich palate, yet savoury, almost tawny-like. Good ageing potential. 17.5% alc. WO Brde Rvr Vlly.

★★★★ **Red Muscadel** Latest **NV** in same footprints as pvs (★★★★) but better: raisins soaked in honey, glace fruit, esp citrus peel. Luscious & full-bodied, but eminently drinkable because of the freshening acidity, livening spirit. 8 yrs large oak. 17.6% alc. NV.

Ruby Port ★★★★ Current delicious **NV** notch up from before. Like drinking Xmas cake rich in brandy-drenched raisins & prunes. 2 yrs large oak. From tinta/souzão. 19.3% alc. All these WO W-Cape unless noted. — *CR*

La Beryl see Fairview

La Bon Vigne see The Marais Family

Laborie Cellar

Paarl • Est 1691 • Tasting & sales daily 9-5 (Nov-Apr) Mon-Sat 9-5 (May-Oct) • Fee R9 (tasting only) R19 (tasting & tour) • Closed all Christian pub hols • Tours for groups 10+ by appt • Laborie Restaurant open daily 10-5 (T 807·3095) • Owner KWV International • Winemaker/viticulturist Dave Boyes • 39 ha (cab, merlot, pinot, pinotage, shiraz, chard, sauvignon, viognier) • 550 tons 40 000 cs • PO Box 528 Suider-Paarl 7624 • samaai@kwv.co.za • www.kwv-international.com • ***T 807·3390/3196*** *• F 863·1955*

Dave Boyes is armed with a wicked sense of humour and an interesting CV – at school, science projects involved all things vinous and, on completion of a BSc Agriculture at Stellenbosch University and stints at Jordan, Tokara and Bellingham, he ventured further afield to Michel-Schlumberger in Sonoma, California, Ch Angélus and Ch de Francs in France, and Wither Hills in Marlborough, New Zealand, where his focus was, of course, on sauvignon (we simply can't tell you what he said about the sheep). Now he's settled enthusiastically into his new role as winemaker and viticulturist at KWV's prestige Paarl property. (Vineyard manager Henri van Reenen took a well-deserved retirement recently; previous winemaker Gideon Theron left after 2004's additive scandal.) With winelands weddings increasingly popular, Laborie hosted the first Bridex, which showcased the best of wedding fare.

★★★★ **Jean Taillefert** A bold New World shiraz flagship. As befits the vintage, **02** more accessible than normal, but no less impressive: deep, rich vanilla-spiced fruitcake nose, voluptuous black plum flavours, smoothly polished. 13 mths new Am oak. Should develop 4+ yrs. Unfiltered, as are other reds. Opulent **01** had cherry/dark-fruited mocha richness, oodles of vanilla-spice. 90 pts US *Wine & Spirits* mag.

★★★★ **Cabernet Sauvignon 02** (★★★★) lighter textured than pvs, restrained; fine layers cassis, violets, cedar, firm but ripe tannin. Accessible early, drink over 3–4 yrs. Yr Fr oak, 20% new. This, all reds below not retasted this ed. **00** VDG; **01** VG.

★★★★ **Blanc de Blanc Brut** All-chard MCC, with plenty of character from ±3 yrs bottle-ageing on lees. Current **00** bone-dry, crisply refreshing palate, without sacrificing any flavour: irresistible, tantalising, marmalade-spread brioche. A delight. **99** was showy, impressive.

★★★★ **Pineau de Laborie** Luxurious, unique dessert from pinotage, mostly unfermented, matured 18 mths in used barriques, fortified with Laborie pinotage potstill brandy to ±17.5% alc. Sugar (±90g/ℓ) tweaked for comfortable solo sipping or with dessert/cheese. **02** deeply spiced plum pudding character with enough spirity bite amidst rich fruitiness to refresh, offset the sweetness. WO Paarl. 375ml.

Merlot ★★★★ **02** had creamy red berries, whiffs spice, elegant accessibility. Oak of this & next as for Cab above. **Merlot-Cabernet Sauvignon** ★★★★ **02** 60/40 blend, succulent berry profile with just enough oak framework to hang it on, some character & charm. **Pinotage** ★★★★ **02** vivid berry fruit, lip-smacking verve & texture. Enjoy in youth, but serious enough for 3–4 yrs cellaring. Yr oak, portion Am; same for … **Shiraz** ★★★ Maiden **02** was delicately fruit-driven with added smoky, spice nuances. Lively, juicy, for early drinking. **Blanc de Noir** ★★★ Dry sparkler now from mainly pinot, dash other reds. Last tasted **00** had tangy fruit flavours, rounded by honeyed bottle maturity. 12.7% alc. **Chardonnay** ★★★ **04** showy but simpler than pvs. Attracts with toffee apple, citrus peel fragrance, flavours; good natured, accessible. 60% given 3 mths oak. **Sauvignon Blanc** ★★★ **05** characterised by cool fruit, nettles, grapefruit; followed by austere, fynbos-flavoured palate. Bone-dry, friendly 12.4% alc: good for food. All WO Coastal unless noted. —*CR*

La Bri

*Franschhoek ▪ Tasting & sales Mon-Fri 10-12.30 Oct-Apr or by appt ▪ Fee R12 ▪ Closed pub hols ▪ Owner Robin Hamilton ▪ 18 ha (cabs s/f, merlot, petit v, shiraz, chard) ▪ 3 500 cs own label 85% red 15% white ▪ Ranges for customers: Helgerson Wines (US), Makro ▪ PO Box 180 Franschhoek 7690 ▪ info@labri.co.za ▪ www.la-bri.co.za ▪ **T 876·2593** ▪ F 876·3197*

Lots of sods being turned here, with two-thirds of the vineyards replanted (including, sadly, some semillon vines that had hung in for over a century). But at least the cab franc and petit verdot are starting to produce quality wine – good enough for the 04 Bordeaux-style blend, now under the 'Affinity' label (the 01 scored gold at the US Star Wine show). The recently refurbished barrel cellar at Franschhoek Vineyards allows for increased capacity and quality control, and manager Johan Haasbroek says he'd like to achieve 8 000 cases a year, as long as there's still time for plenty of discussions with farm manager (and wife) Jacoline – who has her own wine label, My Wyn.

Affinity new ★★★ Leaner than stable mates; 86/14 cab/merlot blend aged 22 mths Fr oak, third new. **03** subtle cassis nose/dry, cinnamon palate; needs time for oak/fruit to knit.

Reserve range

★★★★ **Cabernet-Merlot Reserve** ✓ 82/18 blend in **01**, showed good bottle-development mid-2004, carefully wielded oak, supple tannins firming up ripe plum flavours. *Wine* ★★★★. 94% cab in **02**, yet more approachable (factor of the vintage?), more 'New World', stacked with succulent cassis. 14.5% alc, 20 mths Fr oak, third new. Both, below, not retasted for this edition.

Merlot ★★★★ Ripe plum flavours, fine almost silky tannins, **02** sweet, floral end. Ready, may not be for keeping. 20 mths Fr oak, some new.

Limited Release range

Cabernet Sauvignon ★★★★ Pvs releases attained slightly higher ratings. **03** characteristic tobacco leaf/spice nose; fruity core on palate, supple, drinking well now. **Merlot** ★★★ **03**

tightly wound with zippy acidity, firm tannin, toasty/plum fruit flavours. Structure to improve with cellaring 3-5 yrs. **Chardonnay 05** not ready for tasting. **Semillon**, from 105 yr old heavily virused vines, discontinued. *—MM*

La Cave see Wamakersvallei

La Chataigne new

*Franschhoek ▪ Est 1972 ▪ 1stB 2003 ▪ Visits by appt ▪ 3 guest cottages ▪ Owners Parkfelt family ▪ Vini consultant Gerda Willers (2002) ▪ Viti adviser Pietie Le Roux (1996) ▪ 15 ha (merlot, pinotage, shiraz, chenin, sauvignon, semillon) ▪ 150 tons 1 000 cs own label 25% red 45% white 30% rosé ▪ PO Box 7 La Motte 7691 ▪ richard@solvit.co.za ▪ www.lachat.co.za ▪ **T/F 876·3220***

'Fun, spontaneous and informal ... not too complicated,' reflects the attitude of Richard and Julie Parkfelt, owners of La Chataigne ('Chestnut') since 1972, to their wine, food and life in general. The low sulphur wines (no headaches!), which all bear the chestnut name in different languages, are made by Gerda Willers and styled for early drinking. Production will always be small, with sales directly from the farm and exported to Belgium, Holland and Sweden. The 12ha in production, including some venerable semillon bushvines, are tended by the multi-tasking Richard P. He designates himself a farmer whose duties include 'personnel, admin, production, first aid, plumbing, driver, father, husband and wine consumer'. Whoever said winefarming was easy?

Kasanje ☺ ★★★ **04** blend le by chenin, that variety providing distinctive wet wool hints, piercing acidity & lingering fruit finish; partners lend palate weight (semillon 13%) & greengage/grapefruit aromas/flavours (sauvignon 7%).

Marron ★★ **03** equal portions merlot/pinotage with 20% cab. Warm plum fruit & ripe tannin; 14.5% alc creates sweet impression on finish. 9 mths older oak. **Rosé** ★★ **04** friendly picnic companion; berry/cassis hints from merlot (50%); refreshing entry courtesy two blancs (chenin, sauvignon, 25% each); slightly sweet conclusion from 5.4g/ℓ sugar. **Sauvignon Blanc** ★★ **04** lean & refreshing; very little varietal bouquet, 12.7% alc good for lunchtime quaffing. *—IvH*

La Chaumiere Estate 

Franschhoek ▪ Est 2001 ▪ 1stB 2003 ▪ Tasting & tours by appt (sales only from local outlets) ▪ Owners Ian & Margaret Slack ▪ Winemaker Justin Hoy (Dec 2004) ▪ 3.6 ha (shiraz, chard) ▪ 16 tons 600 cs 100% white ▪ Exported as La Chimere ▪ PO Box 601 Franschhoek 7690 ▪ slacki@telkomsa.net ▪ T 876·2135

In the heart of town, with their vineyard dipping down to the river, owners Ian and Margaret Slack initially sold off their grapes. 'But it soon became clear we should take up the challenge to make our own,' they say. 'The aim is to make wine of a high enough standard to satisfy the hardest critics – ourselves. Some 35 years spent sampling the world's wines must have some influence on the tastes you are trying to achieve from the resources you have.' This is no mom-and-pop operation: 'Our philosophy is not to compromise,' they say. 'We select grapes from our own vineyard, use extended maturation in French oak barrels, and blend and package to the highest standards.'

Chardonnay ★★★ **03** intense, oak-driven style; marzipan notes, viscous & rich mid-palate, buttery finish. Commendably low 12.5% alc. *—MF*

La Chimere see La Chaumiere
La Cotte see Franschhoek Vineyards

La Couronne Estate

Franschhoek ▪ Est/1stB 1999 ▪ Tasting & sales Mon-Fri 10-4 Sat Nov-Apr only by appt ▪ Fee R15 ▪ Tours by appt (R10 p/p) ▪ Closed pub hols ▪ Picnics ▪ La Couronne Hotel ▪ Facilities for children ▪ Tourgroups ▪ Owners The Austrian Trust ▪ Winemaker Dominic Burke (Jul 2001) ▪ Viti consultants Andrew Teubes & Johan Wiese (Jan 1999) ▪ 21 ha (cabs s/f, malbec, merlot, petit v, shiraz, chard, sauvignon) ▪ 60-90 tons ±13 000 cs 60% red 40% white ▪ PO Box 459 Franschhoek 7690 ▪ rikki@lacouronne.co.za ▪ www.lacouronne.co.za ▪ ***T 876·3939/2110*** *▪ F 876·4168*

'Going forward' is enthusiastic Dominic Burke's most-used phrase. Not surprising, as the whole Austrian-owned wine farm and hotel are undergoing major redevelopments. Recently old virused vines were grubbed up and will be replaced (after a fallow period) with new certified clonal planting material. New viognier vines were also established. Vintage 2005 saw several farm firsts: the maiden crop off young shiraz vines on estate; the first bottled Shiraz (fruit bought-in from Malmesbury); and a Pinotage (from stablemate farm Normandy in Groot Drakenstein). Tastings of the restructured range are now upstairs: bigger, better with beautiful views.

★★★★ **Cabernet Sauvignon** Excellent red-wine vintage starts a new ball-game: **03** serious & classically styled; signalled by deep ruby tone, confirmed by ripe cassis palate, finessed tannin management (new oak scaled back to 30%, shorter barrelling – 18 mths). Accessible now, bright future. Mbury grapes/NE. Different league to russet-edged **01** (★★★). No **02**.

★★★★ **Shiraz** ✓ new Showy & bold **03** features rampant warm-climate fruit (14% alc), lots of varietal pyrotechnics (smoke, wild scrub, pepper etc) kept in shape by ripely firm tannins & well-judged oak (20 mths oak, 20% new, 20% Am). Mbury fruit/NE.

★★★★ **Chardonnay Wooded** Replaces 'Chardonnay Reserve'; **04** light (13% alc) & light-textured yet full of ripe mango/pineapple flavours; elegant oaking (30% new, all Fr, 9 mths) adds delicate vanilla note to the lively, balanced proceedings.

Merlot ★★★★ **03** most amenable to date: succulent red fruit (partly via dashes cab, shiraz), well structured & balanced; clean dry tannins. For now & few yrs. Mbury grapes, 18–22 mths Fr oak, 1st-3rd fill. **Ménage à Trois** ★★★★ Blend changes to cab, malbec, shiraz (75/15/10) for **03**. Noticeably ripe (Mbury) fruit; shiraz richness leavens cab/merlot austerity for friendlier New World profile. 19 mths oak, 1st-4th fill; NE. **Chardonnay Unwooded** ★★★★ **05** pure, unadulterated chard; extrovert & zesty, oozes ripe peach & citrus; lovely balanced fruit-acid.

'277' range

Mereaux Red ✓ ★★★★ Replaces 'Rogues Rouge'. **03** elegant, medium-bodied blend cab, merlot, malbec, shiraz; juicy melange red/black fruit, ripe & ready (with some maturation potential). 16 mths Fr oak, 1st-3rd fill. **Sauvignon Blanc** ★★★★ **05** again lively, crisp, zesty & clean; same passionfruit tone as pvs with improved mid-palate concentration. Again laudably light alc (12.5%). **Cevennes Blanc** ★★★ Replaces 'Sauvignon Blanc-Chardonnay' & adds chenin from Wllngtn to the pot; **05** vibrant interplay of ripe/green tones through to firm grapefruit finish, which is decidedly food friendly. *— JN*

Ladismith Winery see Southern Cape Vineyards
Lady Anne Barnard see African Pride

Laibach Vineyards

Stellenbosch ▪ Est 1994 ▪ 1stB 1997 ▪ Tasting & sales Mon-Fri 9-5 Sat 9-1 (Nov-Apr only) Pub hols 9-1 (closed Easter Fri/Sun, Dec 25 & Jan 1) ▪ Fee R10 refunded on purchase ▪ Tours by appt ▪ Owners Laibach family ▪ Winemakers Stefan Dorst & Francois van Zyl (Jan 1997/Jan 2000) ▪ Viticulturist Michael Malherbe (Jun 1994) ▪ 42 ha (cabs s/f, malbec, merlot, petit v, pinotage, chard) ▪ 300 tons 24 000 cs own label ▪ 600 cs for Woolworths ▪ 70% red 30% white ▪ Export brands Inkawu & Special Selection ▪ PO Box 7109 Stellenbosch 7599 ▪ info@laibach.co.za ▪ www.laibach.co.za ▪ ***T 884·4511*** *▪ F 884·4848*

'We want to fight with the big dogs – and we believe we can beat them,' declares Michael Malherbe. Now into the second of a series of 5-year plans, the Laibach MD/viticulturist says the future looks 'great'. 'With good, clean, older vineyards and the benefit of experience, we can only improve.' Motivated by the sell-out-success of their organic Bordeaux-style blend, The Ladybird, they intend to convert the petit verdot and malbec vineyards to organically-farmed. Other plans include a more focused range, emphasising pinotage and blended reds.

'Don't expect any funny varieties or blends, however. Bordeaux won't start planting shiraz because it is fashionable. Use your terroir to the best of its ability.'

★★★★ **Friedrich Laibach** 'Our flagship & joy', declares Francois vZ of bdx-style red; rigorous selection at both vyd, barrel stages produces cab, merlot, cab f, petit v quartet (64/16/13/7) in **03**. More sumptuous, imposing than their other reds; still beautifully tailored, shows off intricate mocha, mulberry features to best advantage. Should continue to improve till ±2009-11, as should following 3 reds. No **02**: 'not good enough'. **01** cab/merlot 82/18; sophisticated & sweet-fruited. 100% new Fr oak, 16 mths, half as blend.

★★★★ **The Dogleg** Named for golf hole presenting greater challenge than this bdx-style blend, refined though built to age. **03** (★★★★) very fine, fresh; layered vinosity currently held in cab's savoury grip, should fill out over next ±5 yrs. Equal cab/merlot partners with cab f/p verdot (7/5); yr Fr oak, 20% new, 4 mths as blend. **02** was also nuanced & structured.

★★★★ **Cabernet Sauvignon** ✓ Red house style reflects area's muscular, broad-shouldered character with admirable restraint, finesse. **03** (★★★★) cedar-dusted claret-like aromas; focused, compact; embryonic dark-berried flesh well-melded with fine grainy tannins, partly from 14 mths new Fr barriques. SAYWS champ. **02** immensely satisfying without huge complexity.

★★★★ **Merlot** FvZ's favourite grape; receives 'all tricks of trade' he absorbed working in Pomerol, incl lengthy post-ferment maceration. **03** (★★★★) illustrates best of lovely vintage. Confident yet understated; fresh mineral profile; sinewy, firm, full fruit richness still to emerge. 14 mths Fr oak buffing, 80% new. **02** good presence in difficult vintage.

★★★★ **Pinotage** Affably modern; tight, minerally rather than ripely flamboyant. **03** neat red damson/raspberry fruit; leanish, light texture balanced by substantial persistence. Belies hearty 14.7% alc. Skilfully handled tannins, Fr oak adds to overall class, personality. ABSA Top Ten, as was **01**. **02** (★★★★) straightforward tangy damsons, redcurrants; nip bitterness would be negated by suitable hearty dish. Wooded 16 mths.

The Ladybird ★★★★ Fulsome merlot-led bdx blend with cabs s/f (47/31/22) in approachable **04**. Warm, sweet plummy notes lifted by spicy, leafy intrusions. Plenty ripe tannins, substance, vibrant youth balanced by sweet-fruited persistence. SGS-certified as organic. Named for mealy bug predator, & suitably (attractively) packaged. Yr Fr oak, 35% new. **Chardonnay** ★★★★ Quietly satisfying youthful **04**. balances oatmeal/citrus freshness, broadening dash oak. Juicy, well-weighted; roundly dry. Good aperitif or with variety of foods. Half barrel-fermented/aged yr new Fr oak. **Chenin Blanc** ★★★ **05** delicate & floral-tinged; crisp minerality, medium body, fruity dryness all enhance charm, ready drinkability. Bottlry hills vyds, so WO Stbosch, as are following two wines (all others Smnsberg-Stbosch). **Sauvignon Blanc** ★★★ Broad tropical, figgy **05** at riper end fruit spectrum; more medium-bodied, gentle freshness; good flavour follow-through, pleasantly lingering. **Natural Sweet** ★★★★ Unusual though not entirely compatible mix of styles: chenin partly new oak fermented, & Mosel-type low alc (7%). **05** suppressed aromas; lemon delicacy released with quavering ethereal lightness on palate. Balanced 9g/ℓ acid, 165g/ℓ sugar. 375ml. **Pinotage Unfiltered** discontinued. —*AL*

Lammershoek Winery

Swartland ▪ Est/1stB 1999 ▪ Tasting, sales & tours Mon-Fri 9-5; Sat/Sun & pub hols by appt ▪ Tours Mon-Fri 9-5 by appt ▪ Special house platter (R50 p/p) Mon-Fri 9-5 by appt; or BYO picnic ▪ Walks ▪ Conservation area ▪ Mountain biking ▪ Owners Paul & Anna Kretzel, Stephan family ▪ Winemaker Albert Ahrens (Jun 2002) ▪ Viticulturists Paul Kretzel & Albert Ahrens ▪ 130 ha (12 varieties, r/w) ▪ 100 tons 10 000 cs own label 75% red 25% white ▪ PO Box 597 Malmesbury 7299 ▪ info@lammershoek.co.za ▪ www.lammershoek.co.za ▪ ***T/F (022) 482·2835***

Still in search of 'that one great wine', Albert Ahrens seems to be finding other things equally great. First, a life partner and colleague in newlywed wife Heidi, who has joined the team ex-Cordoba. Next something to sing about: the new reggae-inspired blend, Red-Red Wine, which made this Malmesbury group feel so fine they decided to embark on a countrywide Local is Lekker wine-and-dine marketing campaign. Now, with a new block of viognier planted, young syrah and mourvèdre vines in production as well as a re-born Zinfandel (with dash of syrah 'to calm the wildness'), it seems the team are set to find many more hits than misses.

★★★★ **Roulette** ✓ Their flagship red, a spicy Rhône melding of syrah, carignan, grenache, viognier, blended 66/14/11/6 in **03**, richly redolent of the Swtland; touch savoury; firm yet unintimidating tannin; revitalising minerally acid; needs to settle but interesting potential till ±2008/9. Fr barriques, mix new/used. *Wine* ★★★★. **02** similar profile; excellent prospects to 2006/7; some Am oak. Both unfined, not cold-stabilised (as are all in range), so may throw harmless sediment.

★★★★ **Syrah 03** reprises above wine's warm-hearted typicity; enticing smoked meat/spice/earth aromas; full, concentred yet surprisingly delicate, thanks to minerally frisson, fresh red-fruit top notes. Fr/Am oak 16 mths, portion new. **02** big but balanced; fruit concentration to match 15.5% alc.

★★★★ **Zinfandel-Syrah** new ✓ Is there a blending possibility left untried by this innovative team? Delicious, savoury tailed **03** augmented by splashes cab, carignan; striking, individual & unusually refined given zin's boisterousness. No need to wait (nor hurry to open: possibilities till 2009). Fr oak, portion new, 14 mths.

★★★★ **Roulette Blanc** ✓ **04** excellent follow up to intriguing maiden **03**, also a chenin-led quartet of hárslevelü, viognier, chardonnay performing in unison, oak a background player. Gorgeous lime/pineapple/apricot tones; distinctive & warm yet unblowsy; cleansing lime-zest finish. Should develop with interest till ±2008. **03** similar make-up, generosity & body, with balanced elegance.

★★★★ **Chenin Blanc Barrique** ✓ Unusual **04** will delight those who enjoyed buxom **03**, though latest is bigger, more powerful. Attractive oxidative complexity to ripe honeysuckle/tropical fruit. Sweeter (7.8 vs 2.8g/ℓ) but spectacular acid nullifies any sense of sweetness. Good till ±2008. **03** sophisticated; beautifully balanced; staying power till 2010. Fr oak fermented/matured, portion new.

★★★★ **Viognier Barrique** Advice last yr of this label's demise premature. Continues with **04** (**03** featured in 2004 ed). Big & rich; varietal aromas quietened by 14% hárslevelü; more typical ripe apricot/floral concentration on silky palate. Skilfully oaked (fermented/matured 300ℓ Fr barrels, some new, 10 mths).

Pinotage Barrique ★★★☆ **04** not ready for tasting. **03** modern, elegant, dry, with fine vibrant tannins. Partially fermented large casks, matured yr Fr barriques, 33% new. **Tinta Barocca Barrique** ★★★☆ Finely balanced, supple **02** sold out. Next is **05**. **Straw Wine** ★★★☆ **04** from sun-dried hárslevelü; quietish nose; blossoms on palate with textured white peach flavour. Lowish (for this area!) 12.5% alc. Native yeast fermented, matured 10 mths used Fr oak; 123g/ℓ sugar. Elegant 375ml bottle. **Cape Ruby Zinfandel** ★★★ Ruby-style port, subtitled 'Sweet Zin'; last reviewed was **01**, next **02** still slumbering in barrel. **Pinodoux** ★★★ Pinotage fermented dry, sweetened with grape juice to 102g/ℓ, fortified with brandy; yr used Fr oak. **03** smooth, rich; red fruits, some toffee. Unheavy 16% alc. **04** not ready for tasting.

Aprilskloof range

★★★★ **Sauvignon Blanc** ✓ Vivacious, charming **05** well-weighted with pure mineral/fig fruit, incisively clean, dry; very moreish, which moderate 12.5% alc permits. Coastal WO. **04** (★★★☆) bright & tropical, with delicious savoury acidity. Again modest alc (12%).

Red-Red Wine new ☺ ★★★ **04** mainly cab with pinotage, zinfandel, merlot, grenache, designed for wide appeal. Full of vitality, juicy ripe red fruits, bouncy tannins. Rounded yr in used Fr oak.

Rosé ★★ Unusual grenache/syrah/chenin blend, used Fr oak fermented, matured 10 mths. Full-bodied, quietish, dry but slight sweet effect/finishing kick from 14.5% alc. **NV**/

uncertified. **Cabernet Sauvignon-Merlot Barrique**, **Zinfandel**, **Chardonnay Barrique**, **Aprilskloof Cabernet Sauvignon-Pinotage** discontinued. —*AL*

La Motte

Franschhoek ▪ Est 1984 ▪ Tasting & sales Mon-Fri 9–4.30 Sat 10–3 ▪ Fee R10 ▪ Closed Easter Fri/Sun, Dec 25 ▪ For attractions & amenities, see below ▪ Owner Hanneli Koegelenberg ▪ Winemaker Edmund Terblanche (Dec 2001), with Werner Geldenhuys (Jun 2003) ▪ Viticulturist Pietie le Roux (May 1986) ▪ 108 ha (cabs s/f, merlot, shiraz, chard, sauvignon) ▪ 900 tons 30 000 cs own label 53% red 47% white ▪ Exported as Schoone Gevel ▪ ISO 14001 certified ▪ PO Box 685 Franschhoek 7690 ▪ cellar@la-motte.co.za ▪ www.la-motte.com ▪ ***T 876·3119*** *▪ F 876·3446*

Award-winning winemaker Edmund Terblanche believes that wine is a perfect blend between nature, science and hard work. Which is why he was excited by the terroir variations he found in the 2005 harvest, put in place a mobile bottling line to enhance quality control, and is managing to simultaneously expand the La Motte range (last year saw the launch of the premium Pierneef Collection) while focusing more on shiraz and sauvignon – the varieties Edmund wants wine lovers to associate with La Motte. Incidentally, owner and mezzo-soprano Hanneli Koegelenberg (née Rupert) recommends a little Brahms as the best accompaniment to their Shiraz – the fine singer is also the inspiration behind the classical concerts hosted in the historic cellar each month.

Pierneef Collection new

Small, special lots, with a Pierneef engraving or painting on each label.

★★★★ **Shiraz-Viognier** Impressive debut for **03** (barrel sample). Made separately from Shiraz below, with 10% of the aromatic white variety. More dark choc than smoked beef; black cherry & shy violet an attractive invitation. Crammed with blackberry, cherry fruit, luscious flesh around dry, minerally core, fine tannins. Warm spicy oak on lengthy dry finish. Matured in used Fr oak.

Sauvignon Blanc ★★★★ Carefully groomed, slender **05**, more classic than version below: dusty capsicum, green fig coolness, assertive & bone-dry, with rapier acidity. Organically grown.

La Motte range

★★★★ **Shiraz 02** had subtly, sensuously caressing fruit, slight savouriness, lingering finish. Tasted ex-barrel, subtly structured but quietly insistent **03** has understated black cherry, smoked beef notes; dry & savoury, dark-berried richness underplayed; tannic backbone & lingering dry finish. Less ripeness, more savoury elegance at 14% alc. 19 mths oak, 30% new, mainly Fr.

★★★★ **Millennium** After classy **01** with sensual & cerebral appeal, **02** (★★★★) less arresting – sullen & sulky even. Some dark-berried appeal, tannins cleverly manipulated to approachability, fine oak – all the components, but refuses to fly, a common 02 vintage problem. May improve. Blend cab, merlot, cab f, malbec (53/33/9/5). 22 mths Fr oak, third new.

Cabernet Sauvignon ★★★★ House-style cedar coolness, dark choc richness, touch roast beef, but more charm, accessibility in **03**. Pleasantly plump; dry savoury finish. 19 mths Fr oak, 30% new. **Chardonnay** ★★★★ **04** reticent in youth; cool citrus, tropical lime, grilled nuts with mineral touches; understated style, still needs time to integrate fully (keep 2–3 yrs). Partly fermented/±yr Fr oak, 50% new. **Sauvignon Blanc** ★★★★ Stylish **05** tank sample shows ripe gooseberry, passionfruit – very tropical, with touches fig, grass for correctness; lifted by tangy sweet-sour interplay & limy acidity. —*IvH*

Landau du Val

Franschhoek ▪ Tasting by appt ▪ Sales at La Cotte Inn Wine Sales, Franschhoek ▪ Owners Basil & Jane Landau ▪ Winemaker to be appointed ▪ Viticulturist Jaco Schwenke ▪ ***T 082·410·1130*** *▪ F 876·3369*

Basil and Jane Landau's semillon bushvines celebrated their centenary last year, but they're far from retiring. In fact, they outshone their younger competitors in a recent *Wine* tasting of 22 semillons from four vintages. Yield for 2005 was the usual miserly 4 tons/ha, and as usual the Landaus are more than satisfied with the quality. Jean Daneel having moved to Napier to nurture his own venture, all that's missing is a winemaker – any takers?

★★★★ **Semillon** Handsome, warm-butter/brioche character flirts with opulence (as does 14% alc) but flash of lemon-toned acidity adds vigour to **04**. Replete with concentrated fruit & waxy lanolin textures, a choice silver-service table accompaniment. Fr oak-fermented/aged 5-6 mths, seasoned barrels. **03** pink grapefruit twist lifts vanilla honeyed fullness. Venerable bushvines, minuscule yields.

★★★☆ **Sauvignon Blanc Private Selection 04** (★★★★) proffers velvety nuance, extra depth to trademark tropical core. More concentrated, unfurling length than fleshy **03**. 14% alc.—*DS*

Landsdowne see Arlington

Landskroon Wines

Paarl ▪ Est 1874 ▪ 1stB 1974 ▪ Tasting & sales Mon-Fri 8.30-5 Sat 9-1 ▪ Fee R3 for groups ▪ Closed Easter Fri, Dec 25 & Jan 1 ▪ Tours by appt ▪ Picnics in summer by appt or BYO ▪ Self-catering cottage ▪ Play area for children ▪ Tourgroups ▪ Gifts ▪ Walks by appt ▪ Permanent display of Stone Age artefacts ▪ Owners Paul & Hugo de Villiers & families ▪ Winemaker Paul de Villiers, with Fanie Geyser (Jan 1980/Dec 2002) ▪ Viticulturist Hugo de Villiers Jnr (1995) ▪ 270 ha (14 varieties r/w) ▪ 1 100 tons 86% red 11% white 3% port ▪ PO Box 519 Suider-Paarl 7624 ▪ landskroon@mweb.co.za ▪ www.landskroonwines.com ▪ ***T 863·1039*** *▪ F 863·2810*

Major developments on the De Villiers family farm include the conversion of the existing bottle-maturation facility into a barrel cellar with improved temperature and humidity control (and inauguration of a completely new bottle cellar), as well as an upgrade of the bottling line – all the better to 'keep improving quality while still keeping prices within the budget of local wine lovers'.

★★★★ **Paul de Villiers Cabernet Sauvignon** The flagship, from selected parcels on the home-farm, comprehensively oaked (all new Fr, ±14 mths), limited quantities (± 600 cs). **03** tannins still tight-knit, will come around with time, showing wine's full potential. No shortage of fruit to help it on its journey; smoky spice, herbaceous notes. Cellaring potential 6+ yrs. No **02**. **01** forthcoming youthful fruit, dry savoury edge with grainy tannins.

★★★★ **Cabernet Sauvignon** Much attention given in vyds & cellar shows in excellent fruit concentration, expensive oak. **03** (★★★★) lighter this vintage, for earlier drinking. Tannins integrated, drinking smoothly; a wine with ripe plummy/red berry fruit & no hard edges. **02** greater concentration of fruit, full, almost robustly flavoured; excellent ageing potential. Fr oak ±10 mths, some new.

★★★★ **Paul de Villiers Shiraz** More concentrated, tougher version of std version below; partially barrel-fermented, barrique aged ±18 mths. **03** big & gutsy, billowing sweet ripe fruit, accompanied by meat, woodsmoke, underbrush aromas, flavours. Easily handles the serious oaking (Am/Hungarian). Already delicious, should age well over next 6 yrs. **02** has lots of oomph, deserves cellaring.

★★★★ **Port** ✓ Usually made from one-third each tintas b/r, souzão; *still* in squat 'quick-quaff' bottle, belying elegant contents. Attractive, idiosyncratic **01** blend includes touriga, proportions roughly quarter each; add meat extract, tapenade textures in the creamy ripe fruit. For early drinking rather than long keeping. Aged 300/500ℓ barrels. **00** red berries & choc tones; rounded, noticeable oak. Both ±100g/ℓ sugar, ±18% alc.

Blanc de Noir ☺ ★★★ **05** successful house style: just off-dry 7.2g/ℓsugar to add body curves, pinotage for its bright, red berry fruitiness & enough acidity for juicy, lively drinkability.

Paul de Villiers Reserve new ★★★★ **03** eclectic mix of shiraz, pinotage, merlot 40/30/25, with dash touriga. Showcases each: lots of juicy red fruit, smoky, savoury overlay, supple tannins for immediate enjoyment, yet with 4-6 yr cellaring potential. Nicely made, harmonious. Oaked in new Fr barriques. **Cabernet Franc** ★★★ Last tasted was **02**, unexpectedly subdued, not a lot of varietal character. **Cinsaut** ★★★ **04** charming lightness, approachability. Redcurrant/fruit pastille flavouring, vibrantly juicy & oh-so-easy to drink. Chillable. Gentle oaking doesn't intrude. Incl13% shiraz. **Merlot** ★★★ **03** light-textured, with attractive varietal-true cassis & violet aromas, flavours. Supple tannins provide structure for 1-2 yrs ageing, but wine is ready. Oaked in seasoned barriques, as are other reds below. **Pinotage** ★★★ **03** pleasantly fruity, plums & rhubarb flavours, with well-integrated oak. Structured for easy accessibility: smooth, ripe & tasty. With 10% shiraz. **Shiraz** ★★★★ **03** step down on pvs, simpler. Full-ripe style, rich red fruit, vanilla-spiced, broad-textured. What it lacks in complexity, it more than makes up in warmth, generosity. Oak as above. **Cabernet Franc-Merlot** ★★★★ **04** (sample) shows good partnership: cab f supplies green walnut/herbaceous aromas, merlot the red fruit base & dash cab an anchor of firmness, giving a sum greater than the individual parts. 45/41/14 blend. Seasoned Fr oak. Ready, but could age 3-4 yrs. **Cinsaut-Shiraz** ★★★ Popular formula: production now tops 16 000 cs. **04** despite being only 42% of blend (rest cinsaut 48%, cab f 10%), shiraz dominates with its smoky/leathery, dark-fruit flavours. Harmonious, good everyday wine. **Chardonnay** ★★★ Unwooded. **05** peachy, tropical tones shine through, ripe & rounded; given lift by the refreshing acidity. **Sauvignon Blanc** ★★ **05** pear-drop flavours, quite low-key, but brisk acidity (7.2g/ℓ) gives a zesty liveliness. WO W Cape. **Chenin Blanc Dry** ★★ **05** bone-dry, with gentle fruit styling. Uncomplicated quaffer. **Chenin Blanc Off-Dry** ★★★ **05** light (12.2% alc) & friendly; just off-dry, with nice fruit salad flavours. **Morio Muscat Jerepico** ★★★★ ✓ Very fresh, intensely sweet fortified dessert with soft acidity, beguiling perfume. **04** retasted as finished wine: attractive, forthcoming honeysuckle, grapey aromas; sugar richness (196g/ℓ) nicely lifted by spirit. Would be delicious chilled. 18.5% alc.—*CR/DH/TM*

Landzicht GWK Wines

*Jacobsdal (see Northern Cape & Free State map) ▪ Est 1976 ▪ 1stB ca 1980 ▪ Tasting & sales Mon-Fri 8-1; 2-5 Sat 8-11 ▪ Tasting fee on application ▪ Closed pub hols ▪ Tours by appt ▪ Meals/refreshments by appt, or BYO picnic ▪ Farm produce sold ▪ Play area for children ▪ Tourgroups ▪ Conferences ▪ Owner GWK Ltd ▪ Winemaker Ian Sieg (1984) ▪ Viti consultant Stefan Gerber ▪ 300 ha (cab, merlot, pinotage, shiraz, chard, chenin, colombard, muscadels r/w) ▪ ±4 300 tons 40 000 cs own label 20% red 40% white 20% rosé 20% fortified ▪ PO Box 94 Jacobsdal 8710 ▪ landzicht@gwk.co.za ▪ **T (053) 591·0164** ▪ F (053) 591·0145*

Ian Sieg, celebrating his half-century as winemaker, feels he's finally getting to grips with conditions in this drought-, flood-, hail- and locust-battered neck of the woods. Having started a steady vineyard renewal (the right variety in the right place) and planning cellar technology upgrades, Landzicht is targeting the quality bottled wine market. First up: 'twenty-one barrels of fantastic-looking cab in the cosy new room for nurturing our babies'.

Features handsome new labels. **Cabernet Sauvignon** ★ Brawny **04** rather enthusiastically Fr-oak-chipped (as elsewhere in range), leaving sweetish red berry fruit somewhat overwhelmed. **Merlot** ★★ **04** touch of sour plum, dry astringent finish. **Pinotage** Huge **04**, wood-driven & touch porty. 15% alc. **Shiraz** ★★ Rustically characterful **04**, sweet-sour plum flavours, some fruit cushioning from the dry tannins. **Chardonnay** ★ Dry, oaky & very firm **04**, distinct warming glow from 14% alc. **Chenin Blanc** ★★ **05** summer quaffer; soft, rounded off-dry style with light tropical tone. **Blanc de Blanc 04** chenin (85%), chardonnay blend with firm acidity, which 4g/ℓ sugar does little to mollify. **Gewürztraminer** ★★★ Tsunami of rose petals & Turkish Delight. Wow! **04** well-rounded, off-dry on taste (though 30g/ℓ sugar), soft. **Blümchen** ★★ Natural Sweet white from colombard & hanepoot; soft, guava-toned easy-drinker with low 8% alc. **NV**, as is ... **Rosenblümchen** ★★ Natural Sweet rosé, cab gives the coral pink glints, otherwise identical to white version. **Vin Doux** Latest version of low-alc semi-sweet carbonated sparkling not tasted. **Sweet Hanepoot** ★★★ One of their better bottlings, **04** enlivened by spirituous bite, lemony tang. **Red Jerepigo** ★★ Good winter warmer; **04** youngberry jam & molasses; glow-inducing finish (16% alc). **Red Muscadel** ★ Coral-tinted **04**, curiously acidic & distinctly warming. **White Muscadel** ★★★ **04** ultra-sweet & honeyed, 16.5% alc overpowered by soft muscat grapiness. All WO N Cape. — *DH*

Langkloof Vineyards see Schoonberg

Langverwacht Cellar

Robertson ▪ Est 1956 ▪ Tasting & sales Mon-Fri 8-12.30; 1.30-5 ▪ Closed pub hols ▪ Tours by appt ▪ Owners 30 members ▪ Manager/winemaker Johan Gerber, with Henry Conradie (Dec 1986, Dec 2003) ▪ Viti consultant Briaan Stipp (2000) ▪ ±600 ha (ruby cab, shiraz, colombard, sauvignon) ▪ ±9 800 tons ±9 000 cs own label 60% red 31% white 9% rosé ▪ PO Box 87 Bonnievale 6730 ▪ langverwacht@lando.co.za ▪ ***T (023) 616·2815*** *▪ F (023) 616·3059*

Farm manager Johan Gerber, incumbent here for 20 years, reports that the wines from last harvest, both red and white, were above average quality despite a reduced crop. Now his fervent wish is for red wine prices to rise so that they can pull out all the stops when it comes to focusing on red wine varietals.

Cabernet Sauvignon ★★★ **03** stewed currants, hints of lead pencil & bluegum, slightly jammy & green. 5 mths Fr oak. Not retasted, ditto: **Shiraz** ★★★★ tasted for pvs ed. This briefly Am-staved; **03** hits all right chords, red fruit & peppery spice; balanced acidity; spicy finish.

Ruby Cabernet ☺ ★★★ **04** like pvs with black plum & thatch nose; succulent plum/choc flavours; softly dry, with savoury twist. 14% alc.

Chardonnay ★★★ Reticent **05** sample, some tropical hints, oakiness on palate & sawdust finish. Drink soon. **Chenin Blanc** ★★ Very muted **05**, light bodied 12.4% alc with high acid zing. **Colombard** ★ Neutral **05**, zesty but lacking fruit. **Colombar-Chardonnay** ★★★ **05** fruity & fun, brisk, herbaceous, sappy & light, despite 12.8% alc. All WO Rbtson. — *DH*

Lanzerac Wines

Stellenbosch ▪ Est 1991 ▪ 1stB 1995 ▪ Tasting & sales Mon-Thu 8.30-5; Fri & pub hols 9-4; Sat 10-2; Sun 11-3 ▪ Fee R15 (incl tasting glass) ▪ Tours Mon-Fri & pub hols 11 & 3 ▪ Closed Easter Fri, Dec 25 & Jan 1 ▪ Five-star Lanzerac Hotel for stay-overs; also Governor's Hall Restaurant & Craven Lounge (T 887·1132) ▪ Tourgroups ▪ Gifts ▪ Conferences (T 887·1132) ▪ Walks ▪ Winemaker Wynand Lategan (Nov 2004) ▪ Viticulturist Tommie Corbett (Aug 2002) ▪ 50 ha (cabs s/f, malbec, merlot, petit v, pinotage, shiraz, chard, sauvignon) ▪ 500 tons 30 000 cs 80% red 20% white ▪ ISO 14000 & HACCP certification in progress ▪ PO Box 6233 Uniedal 7612 ▪ winesales@lanzerac.co.za ▪ www.lanzeracwines.co.za ▪ ***T 886·5641*** *▪ F 887·6998*

Switching from sister property Lourensford just ahead of the 'intense and short' 2005 harvest was a real challenge for Wynand Lategan, and he had to think on his feet and rely on gut-feel much of the time. A very considerable plus was that the maturing vines showed their best, prompting much excitement and enthusiasm about the future. Single-vineyard wines were a focus, and these received Lategan's 'unlimited personal attention'. Vinified separately, they evince significantly more complexity and elegance, the winemaker reports. His goal is to make this historic property more famous for its wines than its elegant hotel, so his advice right now is 'watch this space'.

★★★★ **Merlot** Classically & elegantly styled. **03** (★★★★) lighter, earlier drinking than pvs. Charms with dark choc/red berry core, herbaceous hints. Structural support from yr Fr oak (30% new), doesn't hinder juicy, tasty drinkability. **02**, in generally taxing vintage, stylish, lithe & supple. Dash cab f adds interest, complexity. As with elegant **01** & pvs, no hurry to open.

★★★★ **Chardonnay** Bold & generously oaked style. **04**, good yr for variety, richer, more impressive than pvs. Citrus peel, dried peach intensity complemented by nutty oak-spice, enlivening acidity. Showy, yes, but a flavourful, rewarding experience. 11 mths 300ℓ Fr barrels, 60% new. Whole-bunch pressed, mix 4 clones. **03** (★★★★) lime-peach aromas & flavours vie with oak's buttered-toast richness to create satisfyingly mouth-filling experience.

Cabernet Sauvignon ★★★★ **00** still current, built to last; layers berry & spice, 21 mths oaking, third new, promises 10+ yr potential. MIWA gold. **Pinotage** ★★★★ Modern styling now for this pioneer pinotage label (**59** vintage was first), with lithe structure, firm dry tannins. Last tasted **02** displayed lively mulberry/cherry tones, good oak spicing from 14 mths Fr/Am barrels. Could be cellared 5+ yrs. **Shiraz** ★★★★ Stylish, delicious **03** still available; deep black fruit, whiffs smoke, savoury spice, underbrush. Judicious oaking (yr Fr, touch Am, third new) allows tasty accessibility yet 5+ yrs ageing potential. **Classic** ★★★★ Approachable bdx-style blend, merlot dominant at 47%. Latest **02** has stylish berry compôte, cigarbox character from 18 mths Fr oak, 80% new. Structure for 6+ yrs profitable maturation. **Sauvignon Blanc** ★★★★ **04** last ed was tangy, flavourful, with lemongrass/gooseberry perfume; mouth-watering zestiness. **Forellen Pinot Blanc** discontinued. — *CR*

La Petite Ferme

*Franschhoek ▪ Est/1stB 1996 ▪ Wines below available in the restaurant or from the cellar 12-4 daily ▪ French country-style lunches daily; luxury guest suites (see Eat-out/Stay-over sections) ▪ Gifts ▪ Owners Dendy Young family ▪ Winemaker Mark Dendy Young (Jan 1996) ▪ Viticulturist John Dendy Young ▪ 8 ha (merlot, shiraz, chard, sauvignon) ▪ 5 000 cs 40% red 60% white ▪ PO Box 55 Franschhoek 7690 ▪ lapetite@iafrica.com ▪ **T 876·3016** ▪ F 876·3624*

In food-friendly Franschhoek, what could be more appropriate than wine that's made in a restaurant? Actually Mark Dendy Young's dinky little cellar is next door to, but shares a roof with, his family's French country-style eatery. Unsurprisingly, MDY's wines go well with food, and many of the matchings suggested to restaurant customers are made in gastronomic heaven. The single-vineyard Semillon, for instance, has been offered with gorgonzola tart, lemongrass chicken or grilled cape salmon. Though food-cordial, the wines aren't merely table accessories. They're serious, created with care and skill. Dendy Young claims no credit, however: 'The wine makes itself, the winemaker merely guides it in the right direction.'

★★★★ **Barrel Fermented Chardonnay** Single high Frhoek vyd accorded VIP treatment; incl 100% wood vinification (60% new Fr), full malo, partial native-yeast ferment; **04** (★★★★) delicious, drinks perfectly now (& possibly for up to 5 yrs). Full-ripe but restrained, classy. **03** appetising lemon custard tone seamlessly melded with the fruit.

Cabernet Sauvignon ★★★★ **03** tasted for pvs ed; vanilla-accented blackcurrant & mint aromas, well-defined Ribena flavours, firm but fine tannin, well-balanced wood (Fr/Am). **Merlot** ★★★★ **04**, from single 'Gravel Slope' vyd, in same vein as **03**; unexpectedly dry, firm; spicy wood protruding into the damson plum & choc tones. Keep 3-5 yrs or (following MDY's advice) try with casseroles & spicy sausage. Combo new/older Fr oak. **Bush Vine Pinotage** ★★★ **04** first since **01**, from organic fruit (though uncertified), well padded, lifted strawberry/mulberry nose, creamy vanilla wood still apart. Has structure to improve over 5-8 yrs. 14 mths Fr oak. At 15% alc, biggest red here. **Shiraz** ★★★ **04** upfront spicy black pepper & smoked bacon aromas; leaner-fruited than pvs; elegant, food-friendly style, dry. 13 mths Fr oak, some new. **Chardonnay Unwooded** ★★★ **05** lemon/lime zestiness, lively albeit slightly short flavours. **Sauvignon Blanc** ★★★ **05** crisp & austere, lacks vinosity/concentration of pvs. Brisk acid & brief goodbye. Usual lowish alc, 12.5%. **Blanc Fumé** ★★★ Small Fr oak-matured portion, usually from pvs vintage. **05** faint vanilla & melon notes, buttery mid-palate yet steely finish. Lightish bodied, wood more apparent than pvs. **Semillon** ★★★ **04**, now a bottled product, shows typical floral waxiness under layer of biscuity oak; mouth-filling lees character, well fleshed mid-palate. Potential to develop into something really attractive; part barrelled. No follow-up vintages for **Cabernet Sauvignon-Merlot**, **Nectar du Val**, **La Petite Sieste**. — *CT/JB*

La Providence

Franschhoek ▪ Est 2001 ▪ 1stB 2002 ▪ No tasting/tours at present ▪ Luxury self-catering guest cottage ▪ Owners Andy & Ana Higgins ▪ Vini consultants Justin Hoy & Anton Beukes (Nov 2004/Jan 2002) ▪ Viti consultant Pietie le Roux (May 2005) ▪ 2.2 ha (cab) ▪ 9.5 tons 5 510ℓ 100% red ▪ PO Box 363 Franschhoek 7690 ▪ info@laprovidence.co.za ▪ www.laprovidence.co.za ▪ T 876·4790 ▪ F 876·4898

Call it providence: Andy and Ana Higgins had already taken ownership of their Franschhoek farm when they got the first taste of their own grapes, in the form of the 2000 Cab, vinified under the auspices of the previous owner. They loved 'their' wine so, they resolved to develop a cellar to continue making it themselves. The 02 below is the first under the La Providence label; the next two vintages were made at down-the-road Môreson, but the 05 and future harvests will travel only far as next-door Bo-La Motte's new cellar, where a trio of tanks has been installed for the Higgins' exclusive use. With advisers Pietie le Roux and Justin Hoy, their goal is 'to produce the best cab in the Franschhoek Valley'.

Cabernet Sauvignon ★★★ Comprehensively oaked **02** shows caramel/molasses overtones to grape's signature blackcurrant, ultra-ripe flavours well conceal 14.4% alc. —*MF*

La Siesta see Signal Hill
Lategan see Bergsig

Lateganskop Winery

Worcester ▪ Est 1969 ▪ 1stB 2004 ▪ Tastings & sales Mon-Fri 8-12.30; 1.30-5 ▪ Tours by appt ▪ Owners 5 members ▪ Winemaker Vlam Fourie, with J Manewick (Aug/Dec 1990) ▪ 238 ha (cab, cinsaut, merlot, pinotage, ruby cab, chenin, colombard, hancpoot, riesling, sauvignon, semillon, viognier) ▪ 650 cs + 2.2m litres bulk ▪ 50% red 50% white ▪ PO Box 44 Breërivier 6858 ▪ lateganskop@mweb.co.za ▪ ***T/F (023) 355·1719***

From bottling a few hundred cases of just two wines (Sauvignon and Cab) in 2004, this small familial co-operative (all five members are Lategans) has introduced a new range of reds called Lions Drift. Hence delight with the 2005 vintage: though 15% down on volume, the quality improvement was pegged at a precise 30%! Small berries, excellent colour and aromas, reports winemaker Vlam Fourie.

Lion's Drift Cabernet Sauvignon ☺ ★★★ Med bodied (13.4% alc) quaffer; muted plumy fruit, tannins to hold for a yr/2. 16 mths Fr oak.

Lion's Drift Ruby Cabernet ★★★ Ripe & round fruit bomb focussed by lively acidity & savoury finish. 6 mths Fr oak, 13.9% alc. Enjoy young. **Twin's Peak Sauvignon Blanc** ★★★ Sample **05** similar to pvs summer thirst quencher; shy greengage bouquet, chalky centre, crisp finish. All WO Breede River. —*CR*

L'Auberge du Paysan

Stellenbosch (see Helderberg map) ▪ Est 1995 ▪ 1stB 1998 ▪ Tasting & sales during restaurant hours (see Eat-out section) ▪ Closed Easter Fri-Mon, Dec 25/26, Jan 1 ▪ Art gallery ▪ Owners Frederick Thermann & Michael Kovensky ▪ Winemaker/viticulturist Tjuks Roos, with Ricardo Adams ▪ 3.8 ha (merlot, pinotage) ▪ 14 tons ±1 250 cs 100% red ▪ PO Box 315 Somerset West 7129 ▪ ***T/F 842·2008***

The pinotage grapes for the 2005 vintage were harvested earlier due to dry conditions. The reduced crop resulted in quality grapes and a mouth-filling wine with 'lots of fruit, good tannin and great ageing potential', according to Frederick Thermann, vintner and co-owner of L'Auberge du Paysan country restaurant, with its delightfully French patina.

Pinotage ★★★★ Elegant & amenable **04**, sweet red berry fruit, baked bread whiff, hint Am oak vanilla. Silky, firm tannins are more 'pinot' than 'cinsaut', as is earthy finish. 13% alc, yr 2nd fill oak, 15% Am. —*MM*

L'Avenir Estate

Stellenbosch ▪ Est/1stB 1992 ▪ Tasting & sales Mon-Fri 10-5 Sat 10-4 ▪ Fee R15 ▪ Closed Easter Sun, Dec 25 & Jan 1 ▪ Tours by appt ▪ BYO picnic ▪ Luxury 9-bedroom B&B guest lodge ▪ Play area for children ▪ Tourgroups ▪ Farm-grown olives & olive products ▪ Owner Marc Wiehe ▪ Winemaker Francois Naudé (Jan 1992), with Stephan du Toit ▪ Viticulturist Francois Naudé ▪ 53 ha (10 varieties r/w) ▪ 350-370 tons ▪ ±24 000 cs 50% red 43% white 7% rosé ▪ PO Box 1135 Stellenbosch 7599 ▪ lavenir@adept.co.za ▪ www.lavenir.co.za ▪ ***T 889·5001*** *▪ F 889·5258*

Asked about the past year, assistant winemaker Stephan du Toit claims he's 'another year older, but not necessarily any wiser', while mentor Francois Naudé feels that with another year's hair loss, he's heading, 'like a good wine', towards a smooth finish. 2005 was a 'thinking' harvest, and no pat recipes applied. A record crop was rescued from the weather by their dryland situation and the late-ripening nature of the varieties planted. A new flagship, the Black Label Reserve, has just been released. Assembled according to the principle of including the best fruit across the varietal spectrum, its first incarnation is as a pinotage blend, and it's likely to remain so, given their enviable reputation for the variety.

★★★★ **Cabernet Sauvignon** Top-class **02** followed by perfectly proportioned **03**. Opulent cassis/cedar aromas & flavours matched by firm cab fruit tannins & refreshing acidity. Well-meshed, persistent, elegant finish. Both vintages good now; possible peak around 2008. Now up to 14.5% alc; 18 mths Fr oak, 33% new, rest 2nd fill.

★★★★ **Cabernet Sauvignon CWG Auction Reserve 03** (★★★★☆) step up on pvs; strongly influenced by 20 mths new Fr oak, yet concentrated, fruit able to fully absorb the wood. Black fruit pastille entry reined in by grippy tannin; lingering liquorice/savoury goodbye. Like polished, seamless **01**, has possible 10 yrs potential. **02** (★★★☆) not as convincing.

★★★★ **Pinotage** Few understand, love this sometimes wild local grape like Naudé. **04** textbook pinotage: acetone-touched strawberry bouquet followed by friendly tannins & green olive lift to tail. From bushvines; alc down to more respectable 14.5%. Structure to improve ±5 yrs for those who can resist. Smartly oaked **03** offered generous flesh in tight-knit, though ripe tannin frame. 13 mths Fr oak, 50% new.

★★★★☆ **Pinotage CWG Auction Reserve** On track record, leader of the L'Avenir reds. Perfumed **04** unbelievably rich & concentrated – pushes showy envelope to the extreme, yet not at expense of class, varietal precision. Huge complexity waiting to unfold over next 7-10 yrs. Imposing **03** viscous, concentrated without overt varietal tones; like **04**, laps up 100% new Fr oak.

★★★★ **Black Label Reserve** Previewed last ed, **03** big but light-footed; voluptuous dark fruits lifted by fine ripe tannins. Pinotage important constituent (30%), with cabs s/f, merlot (30/15/25). Amazingly drinkable already. ±2 yrs new Fr oak. Minuscule 160 cs.

★★★★ **Chardonnay** Eight consecutive Chardonnay-du-Monde medals for this consistent white, 10 mths in burgundian oak, lees regularly stirred for creamier feel. **04** (★★★☆) has a more flamboyant feel due to ultra-ripe fruit; charming if slightly warming nut/cream finish. **03** more harmonious, buxom but not flabby.

★★★★ **Chenin Blanc** One of first success stories in chenin's renaissance in Cape. Classy, unoaked **05**, tropical fruit salad & creaminess (from 2 mths lees contact). Broad, rounded. Technically dry, yet delightful sweet nuance on finish. Should age gracefully. **04** fragrant & fresh mouthful; juiciness intensified by 5.5g/ℓ sugar.

★★★★ **Cape Vintage 03** (★★★☆) successor to delicious **99**. From cab, irresistible if not classic: luscious menthol, choc, prune aromas; vanilla tones, approachable tannins. Follows Portuguese lead with low 85g/ℓ sugar; beefy 19% alc.

L'Ami Simon ★★ Cab f joins usual merlot, pinotage, cab partners (50/22/19/9) in unpretentious **03**. Herbaceous lifted nose; lots of chunky sweet fruit, honest country red. **Merlot** ★★★☆ So far only elegant maiden **01**. 10-14 mths oak, 40% new. 14% alc. **Rosé Maison Dry** ★★★ Tasted last yr, old-time Cape favourites clairette, cinsaut with cab, pinotage in appealing pearly pink **04**. Gentle summer fruits/flowers in fresh body for al fresco sipping. **Rosé Maison** ★★☆ Their original, off-dry house pink, from pinotage. **05** attractive coppery-pink hue, juicy red berry fruits, drier this yr (6.2g/ℓ sugar). **Vin d'Erstelle** ★★★ Off-dry white from colombard, riesling (53/39) & splash crouchen. **05** similar to persuasive **04** spicy fruit salad with juicy kick, finishes drier than 6.4g/ℓ sugar would suggest. Low 12.5% alc. **Sauvignon Blanc** ★★★★ **05** recovering from bottle shock when tasted. Subtle mineral, nettle bouquet/grapefruit palate & grassy tail suggests earlier picked than tropical **04**. Both probably better with ± yr bottle maturation. **Vin de Meurveur** ★★★★ Intermittently produced golden dessert, dependent on 'good botrytis'. **04** 100% colombard Sweet Natural [*sic*] from vines yielding just 2t/ha. 'Not enough botrytis to make a Noble,' says Naudé. Intense apricot/melon/papaya aromas & flavours; zesty acidity. 77g/ℓ sugar. — *CvZ*

Lavida see Overhex
La Vinette see Olsen Wines
Lazy Bay see Baarsma
Leatherwood see Prospect 1870

Le Bonheur Estate

Stellenbosch ▪ Tasting & sales Mon-Fri 9-5 Sat 10-4 ▪ Fee R10 ▪ Special tastings on request ▪ Functions & conferences by appt ▪ Owner Lusan Holdings ▪ Winemaker Sakkie Kotzé (1993) ▪ Viticulturist Eben Archer ▪ Vineyard manager Louis Tshamba ▪ 435 tons ±31 000 cs ▪ PO Box 104 Stellenbosch 7599 ▪ info@lebonheur.co.za ▪ www.lebonheur.co.za ▪ ***T 875·5478*** *▪ F 875·5624*

Sakkie Kotze, a traditionalist who's happiest hands-on in the cellar and holds short shrift with 'long and fancy' presentations, believes his wines should speak for themselves. They do so even more elegantly after a recent packaging upgrade, featuring labels which silhouette the cellar's signature 'twin peak' gable. The handsome old manor house with its gleaming dark wood interiors is an atmospheric setting for exclusive dinners (by appointment).

★★★★ **Prima** Well-established merlot-led (±75%) blend with cab; recently softer, more approachable; **01** last yr offered typical Le B lifted fruit with pure redcurrant aroma/flavour; back on track after less focused, lighter & probably earlier-maturing **00** (★★★★); ±18 mths Fr/Am oak, 50% new.

Cabernet Sauvignon ★★★★ Delivers good flavour at pleasingly modest alc (13–13.5%); current **01** aromatic & forthcoming; red-fruit tones with capsicum edge; mid-2004 finished dry with firm acidity. **Chardonnay** ★★★ Fruit from low-yielding vineyards, gently wooded. **04** friendly orange/lime & butter greeting turns rather sullen on palate, with slightly bitter-pith bite. **Sauvignon Blanc** ★★★ **05** step up. Pale & diamond-bright; intense cat's pee & greenpepper give way to arresting acidity, almost bone-dry palate (1.7g/ℓ sugar). Persistent Granny Smith apple finish. — *CvZ*

Lee & Jones see Breeland
Leef op Hoop see Le Riche
Leeurivier see Terroir Wines
Leeuwenberg see Swartland Wine Cellar

Le Grand Chasseur Estate

Robertson ▪ Est 1881 ▪ 1stB 1999 ▪ Tasting & sales Mon-Thu 8.30-5 Fri 8.30-5.30 Sat 9-2.30 ▪ Closed Easter Fri/Sun/Mon, Dec 25/26 & Jan 1 ▪ Tours by appt ▪ Deli & gifts ▪ Owner Albertus de Wet ▪ Winemaker Albertus de Wet, with Wickus Erasmus (Jan 2001) ▪ Viti consultant Francois Viljoen (Jan 1998) ▪ 250 ha (cab, pinotage, ruby cab, shiraz, chard, colombard, sauvignon) ▪ 3 500 tons 8 000 cs own label 43% red 54% white 3% rosé ▪ PO Box 439 Robertson 6705 ▪ lgc@intekom.co.za ▪ www.lgc.co.za ▪ ***T/F (023) 626·1048*** *(cellar) ▪* ***T/F (023) 626·5781*** *(tasting room)*

Wickus Erasmus believes winegrowing is a continuum from the vine to the bottle. So it's no coincidence that a wide spectrum of processes on the estate are under scrutiny, with an eye on all-round improvement. In the vineyard, small top-performing blocks are being identified for the bottled range, the crops from these are now vinified in smaller tanks specially installed for the purpose. Marketing, too, is under review, and the hope is to grow their export business, and to bring one or two fortified wines to market. As for branding, after a brief period as just 'Le Grand', the 'Chasseur' (the regal fish eagle found on this river-fronting estate) is now back in the estate's unusual and rather grand name.

Sauvignon Blanc ☺ ★★★ Cheery, sunny **05** (sample), zesty tropical flavours, light (12.5% alc) & lively; for early enjoyment.

Above, most below, now carry prefix '1881'. **Sauvignon Blanc-Chardonnay** ★★★ Replaces 'LGC White'; 60/40 blend, lightly oaked; **05** complementary & attractive union – green top notes from sauv bl, rounded mouthfeel from chard; equally good solo or with food. **Cap Classique** ★★★ 'Brut MCC' pvs ed. **NV** from chardonnay, highly unusual (not unappealing) styling: touches smoke & toast, buchu-like whiffs, firm mouth-filling mousse with mushroom hint on bone-dry finish. None of following retasted; notes from pvs ed: **Cabernet Sauvignon** ★★★★ **02** sweet berries on nose/palate; big but comfortable tannins should go few yrs yet. Fr oak, 5 mths. **Pinotage** ★★★ Briefly Fr oak matured **03** very drinkable, ripe plum aromas, some charry wood, pliable fruity tannins. **Shiraz 02** red berried, quite chunky tannins need yr/2 to relax. Fr oak, 9 mths; balanced 14% alc. **LGC Red** ★★★ **02** succulent red berry, plum & greenpepper mix; juicy rounded tannin. Equal ruby cab, cab, 8 mths Fr/Am oak. **Rosé** ★★★ Pinotage's candied aromas on **NV** (03), with just enough honeyed development to be attractive; drink up. **Chardonnay** ★★★ Fermented/*sur lie* 8 mths new Fr oak; **03** bright & lively ripe peach tones with subtle butterscotch hint. **Sparkling** ★★★ **NV** from pinotage; bursts with sweet red-berry flavour & excited bubbles. – *DH*

Leidersburg Vineyards

Paarl ▪ Est 1996 ▪ 1stB 1997 ▪ Visits by appt ▪ Owners Jan du Preez & Brian Craddock ▪ Winemaker Jan du Preez, with Jacques du Preez ▪ Viticulturist Jacques du Preez ▪ 6 ha ▪ 2 000 cs 100% red ▪ PO Box 7210 Stellenbosch 7599 ▪ leidersburgwines@intekom.co.za ▪ ***T 869·8339*** *▪ F 869·8732*

It's taken three years of hard slog, but Jan du Preez has now broken into the US market. Equally momentous is his new partnership with pro golfer David Frost, owner of the recently renamed Dayview Vineyards. With pooled resources there's an obvious cost benefit, and JdP will also now be able to work in a state-of-the-art winery. 'Perfect,' he says, 'for what we want to achieve.' Son Jacques, who recently completed his studies at Elsenburg, is being groomed as future viticulturist and winemaker for both labels. Says proud dad: 'He has the touch.'

Cabernet Sauvignon ★★★★ **03** luscious & integrated, no rough edges. good fruit concentration, hints liquorice, smoke & mocha; refreshing acidity, ends with a peppery twist. **Sauvignon Blanc** ★★★★ Elegant, mineral **05** is fresh, tangy with passionfruit hint. Not overtly powerful, but poised & serene with some dimension thanks to *sur lie* ageing.

Migration-Serengeti range

Pinotage ★★★★ Latest is **04**. Last we tasted **02**, less flamboyant than pvs, well pitched/presented. **Shiraz** ★★★★ **01**, featured pvs ed, agreeably old-fashioned, rounded & accessible. Next is **03**. **Cabernet Sauvignon-Merlot** ★★★★ **03** the current release; mellow & easy drinking, juicy tannins & mild alc (±13%) slipped down comfortably last yr. **Pinotage Rosé** ★★ **03** was mature & needed drinking mid-2004. **05** not ready for tasting. **Sauvignon Blanc** ★★★ **05** unready; food-inclined **03** was light bodied with tart, racy finish. – *CR/DH*

Le Manoir de Brendel

Franschhoek ▪ Est/1stB 2003 ▪ Tasting & sales Tue-Sat 11–4 Sun 11–3 ▪ Fee R10 ▪ Lunches daily 12–3 ▪ Luxury accommodation & other amenities/facilities (See Eat-out/Stay-over section) ▪ Owner Christian Brendel ▪ 26 ha (cab, merlot, shiraz, chardonnay, chenin, sauvignon, semillon) ▪ Export brand: Wine 4U ▪ PO Box 117 La Motte 7691 ▪ lemanoir@brendel.co.za ▪ www.le-manoir-de-brendel.com ▪ ***T 876·4525*** *▪ F 876·4524*

At Christian & Maren Brendel's 5-star establishment in Franschhoek, wine is just one of many attractions. See the Eat-out and Stay-over sections for more details.

Merlot ★★★ **03** Appealing red fruit on nose & palate, accessible tannins & dry finish; lighter than 14% alc would suggest. **Pinotage** ★★ Typical pinotage banana/strawberry aromas & flavours, brisk acidity on **03**; needs food to counter rasping tannins – possibly lamb bredie? **Shiraz** ★★★★ Bold & beautiful **03** as friendly/accessible as it is powerful (14.5% alc). Opulent black fruits scented with dabs spices, mint; silky texture, persistent dry aftertaste. **Sauvignon Blanc** ★ **04** light, muted varietal characters. All WO Frhoek, all reds aged 12 mths. — *JN*

Lemberg Estate

*Tulbagh ▪ Tasting, sales & tours Mon-Sat 8-5 Sun 10-5 ▪ Fee R5 ▪ Gourmet lunches (book 2 days ahead) ▪ Luxury guest cottage (see Stay-over section) ▪ Walks/hikes ▪ Owner/winemaker/viticulturist Klaus Schindler ▪ 4 ha (pinot, pinotage, sauvignon) ▪ 50/50 red/white ▪ PO Box 317 Tulbagh 6820 ▪ schindler@lando.co.za ▪ www.kapstadt.de/lemberg ▪ **T (023) 230·0659/083·270·3449** ▪ F (023) 230·0661*

This mini-estate on the Little Berg River – just 4ha of vines – supports all sorts of activities. Owner Klaus Schindler has turned his forester's skills to winemaking (a Pinotage, Pinot and Sauvignon, hand-picked at night) and conducting hunting trips, while wife Uschi runs a pretty-as-a-picture guesthouse, cooks gourmet meals and hand-crafts wine labels. 'Hands-on' and 'by hand' are Lemberg watchwords, extending to the production process where mechanisation is kept to the minimum.

L'Emigré see De Morgenzon

Leopard Frog Vineyards

new

*Stellenbosch ▪ 1stB 2003 ▪ Closed to public ▪ Owner Brookwood Capital Corporation ▪ Winemakers David John Bate & Hempies du Toit ▪ Viticulturist Hempies du Toit ▪ 250 cs 100% red ▪ 8 Royal Ascot Lane, Sandown, Sandton 2196 ▪ firstfrog@leopard-frog.com ▪ www.leopard-frog.com ▪ **T (011) 884·3304** ▪ F (011) 883·0426*

The historic (1688) Annandale farm is now home to a cross-cultural winemaking collaboration between the Old World elegance of Hempies du Toit and New World dash of Canadian David John Bates. Their contrasting styles merge in a hand-crafted red blend destined mainly for fine-dining establishments in North America and Europe. The symbolism depicted on the label continues the collaborative theme, combining the playfulness of the American frog (symbol of wealth, among others) and the elusiveness of the African leopard. With the name 'Kiss & Tell Reserve', the wine is seductive rather than reductive, quips Hempies dT.

Kiss & Tell Reserve ★★★ Blend of near-equal portions merlot & shiraz plus 10% mourvèdre, yet it's the latter two varieties which give **03** its pleasing spicy character, mineral notes, nutmeg/marzipan whiffs & touch cedar. 24 mths Fr oak. — *MF*

Leopard's Leap Wines

*Franschhoek ▪ Est 2000 ▪ 1stB ▪ Closed to public ▪ Owner Historic Wines of the Cape ▪ Winemakers Eugene van Zyl (Nov 2002) ▪ Viti adviser Francois Viljoen ▪ 167 860 cs 70% red 30% white ▪ ISO 1400 certified ▪ PO Box 685 Franschhoek 7690 ▪ info@leopardsleap.co.za ▪ www.leopardsleap.co.za ▪ **T 876·8000** ▪ F 876·4156*

This everyday-drinking-with-style range is part of the Rupert Family Vineyards portfolio. Launched in 2000, the wines are intended to 'over-deliver on quality and packaging'. Vinified by the very experienced Eugene van Zyl, they are available locally and exported to North America, Europe and other markets.

Cabernet Sauvignon new ★★ **04** light, approachable with savoury fruit, mocha finish. **Shiraz** ★★★ new to the guide; easy-drinking **04**, spicy red fruit melange, balanced, modestly low 13.5% alc. **Cabernet Sauvignon-Merlot** ★★★ 50/50 blend in **04**, undemanding, brimming with berry fruit, for early enjoyment. Combo staves/micro-oxygenation (same for most of the reds). **The Lookout Rosé** new ★ Candyfloss nose & palate, 14% alc gives warm lift to tail. From pinotage. **Chardonnay** new ★★★ Crisp & refreshing **05**, pear/citrus notes, zesty acidity. Appealing poolside quaffer. **Chenin Blanc** new ★★★ **05** friendly & fruity, Granny

Smith apple flavours/crunch. Well balanced. **Sauvignon Blanc** ★★★ **05** leaner than pvs; still lively, light & well fruited but with hollow middle. **The Lookout Cape Mountain White** ★★★ Sprightly, light (12% alc) everyday drink. **05** chenin, sauvignon, chardonnay. Tasty if somewhat muted lemon-lime tones. **Chenin Blanc Semi Sweet** new ★ Demure aromas & flavours on light-bodied **04**, only a hint of sweetness (though 15g/ℓ sugar). No new vintages of the following; notes from pvs ed: **Sangiovese-Pinotage-Cabernet Sauvignon** ★★★★ Spicy & wild shiraz-like aromas in attractive & different **03**; sweet-fruited suppleness aided by touch sugar. Equal blend. **Pinotage-Shiraz** ★★★ **03**, as pvs, 50/50 blend neatly balancing approachability & structure. **The Lookout Cape Mountain Red** ★★★ Jumble of 5 varieties (incl nebbiolo) in **03**; plums, berries & spice; firmish tannins cushioned by smidgen sugar (3.3g/ℓ). **Chenin Blanc-Viognier** ★★★ Quaffable **04** loaded with tropical fruit & citrus flavour, plumply round from touch sugar (±4g/ℓ). **Semillon-Chardonnay** ★★★ Regime-change to unoaked in **04**, equal blend; attractively light & supple with the usual gentle acidity. All WO W Cape. — *JN/DH*

Le Pavillon see Boschendal

Le Pommier Fine Wines

*Stellenbosch ▪ Est 2002 ▪ Tasting & sales daily 9-6 (summer) 9-5 (winter) ▪ Fee R10 ▪ Le Pommier Restaurant & Country Lodge (see intro for other amenities/attractions) ▪ Tours by appt ▪ Owner Zorgvliet Wines ▪ Winemaker Bruwer Raats ▪ Viti adviser Roedolph Jansen van Vuuren ▪ PO Box 916 Stellenbosch 7599 ▪ wine@lepommier.co.za ▪ www.zorgvliet.com ▪ **T 885·2070** ▪ F 885·1583*

Banhoek Valley neighbour Zorgvliet has once more taken ownership of this brand and associated restaurant, country lodge and wine shop. New sauvignon, cabernet franc and malbec vines will increase the supply of quality grapes vinified by Bruwer Raats, who believes that the wines should show 'a lot of clean fruit with soft structures which will always be pleasant for everyday wine drinkers'.

Cabernet Sauvignon ★★★★ Fruit-driven **04**, raspberries & some spice. 14 mths older oak. Touch less elegant than pvs. **Cabernet Franc** ★★★★ ✓ **03** has grape's slightly stalky fragrance to fresh strawberry & 'milky' finish; pleasant but not for long keeping. Oak as above. **Shiraz** ★★★ **04** resinous hint to restrained fruit, wood dominant thanks to third new oak, 14 mths. **Dry Rosé** ★★★ Attractively light (±13% alc), licorice-wafting melange mainly cab with shiraz, cab f & merlot (45/25/23/7); fresh & fruity; **04** touch more complexity than pvs. **Sauvignon Blanc** ★★★★ **05** uncomplicated passionfruit & lime pleasure, light (13% alc), for early drinking. Stbosch fruit; screwcap. **Semillon** ★★ **04** last ed showed rubbery aromas/flavours with just an edge of honey & a little shy fruit. WO Coastal. — *NP*

Le Riche Wines

*Stellenbosch ▪ Est 1996 ▪ 1stB 1997 ▪ Tasting & sales Mon-Fri 10-12.30 2-4.30 ▪ Closed pub hols ▪ Self-contained B&B (T 887·8958) ▪ Owner Etienne le Riche ▪ Winemaker Etienne le Riche, with Mark Daniels (1998) ▪ 5 000 cs 100% red ▪ PO Box 6295 Stellenbosch 7612 ▪ wine@leriche.co.za ▪ www.leriche.co.za ▪ **T/F 887·0789***

Bordeaux-red specialist Etienne le Riche has the pleasure and privilege of making two identical Cab-Merlot blends in two hemispheres each year. He uses the same equipment, techniques and blend proportions; the sole difference is the source of the grapes: Stellenbosch and Bergerac (not far from Bordeaux). A continuing source of fascination for this experienced winemaker is how the wines can be so similar yet so dramatically different in character. Visitors to the Jonkershoek farm (where a stay-over is conveniently available) can experience this paradox first hand – and meet the new team member, daughter Yvonne, now involved in all facets of the family business. (The Le Riche Bergerac Grand Vin de Terroir 02 is also available from selected trade outlets).

★★★★★ **Cabernet Sauvignon Reserve** A 2004 review of the first five vintages of this bastion of classical elegance yielded **97** & **01** as favourites, worthy of cellar space. Current **02** (★★★★), reflecting the vagaries of a lighter harvest, is easier, for drinking while **01** –

still a concentrated sleeper – evolves & grows. Rich fruit, underpinned by supple tannin & honed with finesse, marked **00** (★★★★★). Jonkershoek & Firgrove grapes, 24 mths 70% new Fr oak.

★★★★★ **CWG Auction Reserve Cabernet Sauvignon** new 100% cab, 100% new Fr oak, 100% attention lavished on **03** sure to get bidder's paddles twitching. Density of colour reflected in tightly wound blackcurrant fruit, plushly textured structure. Tastes great in youth mid-2005 – a harbinger of rare pleasure to come 2010 onwards. 18 mths Fr oak.

★★★★★ **Cabernet Sauvignon** Fine-grained, unflashy, delicious in sculpted style. **01** still current; when tasted for last ed, we noted cool bramble fruit behind a soft tannic curtain. Approachable, but will reward cellaring 3-5 yrs. **00** had splash merlot. Stbosch fruit, 18 mths in barrel, mostly older. 13.5% alc.

★★★★ **Cabernet Sauvignon-Merlot** Medium-bodied need not be lesser: the easier offering with which to await the above stablemate's maturity. **03** entices with forest-floor whiffs, delivers bright cassis sheen through to juicy tail. Classic, yet accessible. 65/35 blend. Yr seasoned wood. 14% alc. **02** not tasted.

Leef op Hoop Merlot new ★★★ Plummy **04**, rich meaty mouthful, soft & accessible without sacrificing grace. Yr in older oak adds to frame. – *DS*

Le Roux see Vendôme
Les Pleurs see Avondale

Libertas

For selected export markets, this brand fills a value-priced slot in the Distell portfolio.

Cabernet Sauvignon ★★★ Fruit-grenade **04** bursts with cassis, palate lifted by sugar (4. 5g/ℓ), firm fruit-tannins give grip to palate. No wood; following reds mainly Fr oak, staves/barrels. **Merlot** ★★★ Harmonious **04**. Cherry fruitcake nose, hint bacon; lively, smooth, slides down easily. **Pinotage** ★★★ **04** unpretentious, with banana/strawberry jam whiffs; youthfully abrasive tannins, zippy acidity; perfect for cutting fatty foods. **Chardonnay** ★★★ Ripe tangerine aromas, lime & peach on **04**; unoaked portion boosts freshness while imparting ripeness. **Chenin Blanc** ★★★ Lively, refreshing; **05** with Granny Smith apple zing & mineral finish; lovely mouth-juicing crispness; food enhancing. Moderate alc. **Sauvignon Blanc** ★★★ **05** what the variety should be: crunchy, fresh, aromatic & fruity. Light bodied 11.8% alc. All WO W-Cape. – *CvZ*

Lievland Estate

*Stellenbosch ▪ Est 1982 ▪ Tasting & sales Mon-Fri 9-5 Sat & Sun 10-4 ▪ Fee R10 ▪ Closed Dec 25 ▪ Tours by appt ▪ Light meals/picnics by appt ▪ Owner Susan Colley ▪ Winemaker Kowie du Toit (Jan 2004) ▪ Viticulturist to be appointed ▪ 50 ha (cabs s/f, merlot, mourvèdre, roobernet, petit v, riesling, shiraz, viognier) ▪ 250 tons 15 000 cs 50/50 red/white ▪ PO Box 66 Klapmuts 7625 ▪ lievland@icon.co.za ▪ **T 875·5226** ▪ F 875·5213*

Susan Colley, owner of this historic (1715) Simonsberg property, has an upbeat progress report: last year they harvested the first mourvèdre, which is 'looking really good' (as are shiraz, the estate's signature grape, and petit verdot), and bottled a small quantity of a new Cab-Shiraz blend. Much effort and focus is going into further upgrading the vineyards and matching the quality of the various blocks to the envisaged style. Mindful of the potential slumbering here, Colley aims to 'consolidate and get great wines under the Lievland brand again'.

Shiraz ★★★★ Shows renewed vigour & form in **03**. Classic savoury/wild berry aromas, supportive fruit, structure to improve over 3-5 yrs. Oak, 14 mths Fr/30% new, well integrated. **Cabernet Sauvignon-Shiraz** new ★★★★ Complex & taut **03**, shiraz showing in red berry/smoke, cab in minty hints, firm backbone. Tannins ripe, fruit intense; potential to improve 5-6 yrs. 15 mths Fr oak, all new. **Lievlander** ★★★ Food-friendly **02** blend a veritable fruit salad of varieties – cinsaut, ruby cab, roobernet, merlot, cab sauv, cab f & petit v! Creamy plum & nutmeg fruit; accessible tannins. Yr old Fr oak for structure. **Chardonnay 05** (sample) too unknit to rate. Muted lemon drop/lime character; hint of oak gives structure & flavour. Staved 3 mths. Very different from pvs oak-dominated monster. **Sauvignon Blanc** ★★★ **05** raises bar on pvs with better balance, fresher finish. Granny Smith apple/nuts, powerful fruit intensity. **Weisser Riesling** ★★★ **04** ethereal pineapple & tropical fruit fragrances/flavours; quaffably light, refreshing, off-dry. **05** untasted. **Chéandrie** ★★★ Lightish summer drink, **05** untasted; **04** from chenin, semillon (66/34) herbaceous & sherbet nuances, refreshing acidity, dry finish. **Natural Sweet** No **05** Last ed **04** was unrated; from riesling; very light; modest floral aromas; peachy flavours with hint quince on unexpectedly dry finish; partly barrel fermented; 12% alc. — *CR*

Lifestyle see Simonsvlei
Lime Road see Havana Hills
Lindenhof see Boland Kelder

Linde Vineyards

*Tulbagh ▪ Est 1998 ▪ 1stB 2001 ▪ Visits by appt ▪ Walks ▪ Owners Olof Gregor & Sylvia Linde ▪ Winemaker Sylvia Linde ▪ Viticulturist Jean Kotzè ▪ 14 ha (cab, merlot, shiraz, chard) ▪ 80 tons 100% red ▪ PO Box 146 Tulbagh 6820 ▪ diggershome@mweb.co.za ▪ **T(023) 230·0742** ▪ F (023) 230·2838*

Hemisphere-hopping couple Olof Gregor and Sylvia Linde spend part of the year in California, with 6 ha in Geyserville, where the local Italian community put their own handmade *vino* on the *tavola*; the rest in Tulbagh, where the all-red line-up of cab, merlot and shiraz vines has been joined by a small block of chardonnay, all manged by Jean Kotzè.

Cabernet Sauvignon new ✓ ★★★★ **04** Modern style, focused on vibrant intense cassis/black plum fruit; silky, friendly tannins. Concentrated, voluptuous but with dry finish. **Shiraz** new ★★★ Characterful & accessible **04**; cornbread & fennel in bouquet, rounded mouthfeel, smooth tannins, savoury finish. — *CR*

Lindhorst Wines

*Paarl ▪ Est 1996 ▪ 1stB 2002 ▪ Tasting daily 10–5 ▪ Fee R20 (incl tasting & snacks, redeemable against purchase of 6 btls) ▪ Closed Easter Sun, Dec 25 & Jan 1 ▪ Phone for availability of meals/refreshments; or BYO ▪ Accommodation: see intro ▪ Facilities for children ▪ Gifts ▪ Farm produce ▪ Owners Mark & Belinda Lindhorst ▪ Vini consultant Cathy Marshall (Nov 2002), with Ernie Wilken ▪ Viti consultant Kevin Watt (Jan 2001) ▪ 18 ha (cab, merlot, pinotage, shiraz) ▪ 60 tons 4 000 cs 100% red ▪ PO Box 1398 Suider-Paarl 7624 ▪ belinda@lindhorstwines.com ▪ www.lindhorstwines.com ▪ **T 863·0199** ▪ F 863·3694*

Former accountant Mark Lindhorst may be living the wine dream full-time, but others don't have to hang up their suits now that he and wife Belinda have launched their Wine Partners concept. He explains: 'For a small investment, up to 100 people or companies will receive an annual allocation of Partner's Choice, a shiraz blend not available to others; have use of the Vineyard Cottage; enjoy Belinda's superb cuisine when they visit; and have the freedom of Lindhorst Wines — in other words, act like they own the place!' There's an alternative way to get a taste of the place: by opening the Statement blend — 'a wine that states what we are all about'.

Cabernet Sauvignon new ★★★★ Deep-coloured **03** has powerful cassis & herbal aromas, ample tannin; ripe, soft, lingering, chocolate finish. Low 12.6% alc. WO Coastal (27% Hldrberg, balance Paarl). **Merlot** new ★★★★ **03** savoury plum/currant & sumptuous fruit notes layered with spicy olivaceous whiffs; rich, soft tannins abetted by thimble sugar (3.7g/ℓ), good persistence. 20 mths Fr oak, third new. **Shiraz** ★★★★ A food wine, **03** dishes up cassia, allspice & pepper aromas; ripe sweet tannins, good dry finish; more elegant (13% alc) than massively rich **02**. **Max's Shiraz** new ★★★ Mainly Stbsch fruit, 20 mths older oak. **03** mint/eucalyptus nuance; elegant if slightly attenuated palate showing some spice, grippy tannins. **Statement** ★★★ Ripe shiraz (52%) & succulent merlot create supple easy drinking **03**, spiced by 76% new oak; raspberry & marzipan notes; more polished than pvs. **Pinotage** ★★★ **04** rounder & more sumptuous (14.4% alc) than pvs; gamey/herbal nose, acetone whiffs, variety's famously edgy tannins well smoothed. — *MF*

Lindiwe Wines

Paarl ▪ 1stB 2003 ▪ Tasting & sales at KWV ▪ Fee R15 ▪ Winemaker Chris Jansen (Oct 2003) ▪ Viticulturists Chris Albertyn & Cobus van Graan ▪ 20 000 cs 50% red 50% white ▪ ISO 9001 certified ▪ Suite 170 PostNet, Pvt Bag X3036, Paarl 7620 ▪ info@lindiwewine.co.za ▪ ***T 949·6013/4*** *▪ F 949·6036*

Lindiwe ('The One We Have Been Waiting For') is owned by Reinvest, a BEE company with a 25% shareholding for disadvantaged folk. The wines are made by Chris Jansen at KWV's Vinnova contract cellar, the latter company providing important initial guidance. The grapes are sourced from the Breede River Valley, with the ultimate aim of buying from other empowerment projects.

No new wines; notes below from pvs ed. **Cabernet Sauvignon** ★★★ Modestly oaked **02**, with leafy blackcurrant aromas, with some green notes on end, despite 14.2% alc. **Merlot** ★★★☆ **02** pleasing, plummy & ready; soft savoury notes, lightish feel (despite substantial 14.5% alc). Yr Fr oak. **Shiraz** ★★ Light peppery notes & soft raspberry-recalling textures on **02**, but an oaky finish. **Pinotage** ★☆ **02** recalls the old days, with its estery, tannic rusticity. 14% alc; lightly wooded. **Chenin Blanc** ★★ Smoky apricot notes on **03**; food-friendliness abetted by briskly crisp, dry finish & lightish 12% alc. **Chardonnay** ★★ Marzipan aromas on oak-fermented (& 3 mth matured) **03**; wood helps with creamy texture, as just-dry 4g/ℓ sugar helps the soft finish. **Sauvignon Blanc** ★★☆ **03** tropical gooseberry whiffs, pineapple finish, attractively accessible. Easy-going 12.5% alc. All WO W Cape. *—MF*

Linton Park Wines

Wellington ▪ Est 1995 ▪ 1stB 1998 ▪ Tasting & sales Mon-Fri 8-5 by appt ▪ Tours by appt Mon-Fri 9-4; also guided cellar/vineyard tours by appt (incl barrel tasting) ▪ Light lunches/picnics for small groups by appt Mon-Fri 9-4 ▪ Owner Linton Park plc ▪ Winemaker Hennie Huskisson, with Danie Stevens (Jan 2001/Oct 1999) ▪ Viticulturist Arnold Hugo ▪ 89 ha (cab, merlot, shiraz, chard, sauvignon) ▪ ±750 tons 20 000 cs 75% red 25% white ▪ Export brand: De Groene Heuwel ▪ PO Box 1234 Wellington 7654 ▪ lpexport@lantic.net ▪ www.lintonparkwines.co.za ▪ ***T 873·1625*** *▪ F 873·0851*

Grand-gold medal at the Concours Mondial competition in Brussels for the Reserve Merlot was the towering highlight of the past year for Hennie Huskisson & his colleagues. 'Over the moon,' they unison, adding as many exclamation marks are there are words in Hennie H's potted philosophy of winemaking: Quality, quality, quality. The pursuit of which is getting a big fillip with the construction of an on-site bottling and storage facility. This harvest, they're hoping to use a sorting table to maximise the condition of the fruit going into their Reserve range. With his strenuous pursuit of zero defect, Hennie H may even finally bottle a Sauvignon he's happy with.

Reserve range

★★★★ **Shiraz** From same 'Summer Hill' vyd as std version, different wooding (yr Am, finished off with extra yr Fr) adds to **01** brazen New-World styling with potential longevity.

★★★★ **Cabernet Sauvignon** Same block ('Bush Vine') as below, more extensively barrelled (1 yr new Fr oak, further yr 4th fill). **01** similar New World character, spicy oak perhaps more evident; ripe mint-choc character à la Australia, yet fairly easy to drink.

★★★★☆ **Merlot** Maturation regime similar to Cab gives added flavour concentration & savoury olive-like tones. **01** noted last yr as gaining complexity, still showing healthy tannins.

Linton Park range

★★★★ **Shiraz** Yr Am oaked; **02** sweet brambly fruit, hints of flowers & fynbos; softer & lighter than Rsv. On release, **01** had choc, black cherry & spiced-meat tones, smoky youngberry tastes.

★★★★ **Chardonnay** Dense, creamy, elegant & persistent wine from farm's Claire Division vyd; **02** (★★★) billows toasty passionfruit, crème brûlée & 'burnt match'; big, opulent & slightly exotic; very low acidity (4.7g/ℓ) otherwise would have rated higher.

Cabernet Sauvignon ★★★★ **02** bright bramble aromas; plump & juicy fruit with hint cigarbox, attractive New World styling with restraint. Yr new Fr oak. **Merlot** ★★★ From 'River Garden' vyd; yr Fr oak, none new. **02** light-hued; red plum-jam nose, light, simple jammy fruit. **Port** ★★★★ Limited release made in a sweet LBV style, 3 yrs aged in 4th fill Fr oak; **NV** from ruby cab. Nothing like the Portuguese style but appealing. Neither range above retasted for this ed.

Capell's Court range

This range not wooded. **Cabernet Sauvignon** ★★★ Explosion of rich choc/cinnamon fruit on **05** (rather shocking after retiring Old-World nose), waddling fatness thanks to low acid. **Merlot** ★★★ **05** luscious peppermint-crisp character coupled with fruit succulence could seduce even hard-core classicists. **Shiraz** ★★ Hennie H pushing envelope here: usual dollop sugar almost doubled to 11.3g/ℓ, yet **05** retains semblance of balance, some varietal fireworks keeping a lively tone. **Chardonnay** ★★★ Amenable, flavourful **05**, honeysuckle & pear whiffs, honest fresh drinkability; low 13% alc. **Sauvignon Blanc** ★★★ **05** everything you want – zing, flavour (ripe & greener), freshness, modest 13.5% alc – in scaled-down form. All ranges WO Wllngton. – *CT/TM*

Lions Drift see Lateganskop
Lion's Gate see Origin Wine
Liquor Boys see Oranjerivier Wine Cellars
Little River see De Meye
Live-A-Little see Stellar Winery
Livingstone see Cape First

Lomond new

Cape Agulhas ▪ Est 1999 ▪ 1stB 2005 ▪ Closed to public ▪ Winemaker Kobus Gerber, with Tariro Masyiti ▪ Viticulturists Johan Wiid & Bennie Liebenberg ▪ 100 ha (merlot, shiraz, sauvignon, semillon) ▪ 487 tons 832 cs (sauvignon) 100% white ▪ ISO 9002 certified ▪ PO Box 778 Stellenbosch 7599 ▪ ***T 809·7000*** *▪ F 886·5253*

This exciting new property, just 9km from the sea at Cape Agulhas, the southern tip of Africa, launched in 2005 with a limited-released (832 cases) Sauvignon formerly channelled into the Fleur du Cap Unfiltered Collection. A fynbos-rich farm, Lomond's 100 hectares (85 in production) have been nurtured since 1999 by soil guru Dawid Saayman and viticulturists Bennie Liebenberg and Johan Wiid. They reckon it outclasses even Constantia and Elgin as a prime cool-climate site, with narrower day/night and seasonal temperature variations. Bergkelder winemakers Kobus Gerber and Zimbabwean-born Tariro Masyiti kept their maiden Lomond vintage (including shiraz and merlot) simple: 'Natural wines to reflect a unique site.'

Sauvignon Blanc 'Block 3' 05 potential ★★★★ from this maiden; assertive 'green' aromas & flavours – asparagus, capsicum, fig & cat's pee – with taut, racy acidity & mouth-watering fruit intensity unhindered by high 14.8% alc. Harmonious & long, tight & cool, unlike … **Sauvignon Blanc 'Block 5' 05** which shows far warmer fruit characteristics. Tropical fruit, especially granadilla, abounds revved up by whiff lemon grass. Plump & round, 14.9% alc palate, friendly/less daunting than nervy stable mate. Potential ★★★. – *IvH*

Long Beach

Mediterranean-inspired range by Robertson Winery for Vinimark, pitched at SA's 'ever-burgeoning café society'. Attractively presented with latest Stelvin twist-off caps.

Rosé ☺ ★★ From shiraz; **05** dry but well-rounded, generous pepper-laced berry flavour; good with al fresco foods.

Chardonnay ★★★ Latest **05** offers more of everything; loads of toasty citrus flavour to enjoy now & over next yr. **Sauvignon Blanc** ★★★ **05** yards better than pvs; zingy but comfortable tropical flavours, quaffably light 12.5% alc. – *DH*

Long Mountain Wine Company

*Stellenbosch ▪ Est/1stB 1994 ▪ Closed to public ▪ Owner Pernod-Ricard SA ▪ Winemaker/viticulturist Eben Rademeyer (Jun 2004) ▪ 50% red 49% white 1% MCC ▪ PO Box 1324 Stellenbosch 7599 ▪ vanda.davies@pernod-ricard-southafrica.com ▪ jaco.boonzaaier@pernod-ricard-southafrica.com ▪ www.longmountain.co.za ▪ **T 880·8800** ▪ F 880·8860*

The philosophy at this Pernod-Ricard-owned operation is to produce wines which reflect the various meso-climatic conditions of the Cape and in particular the Breede River Valley. A viticultural programme has given Eben Rademeyer and his team tighter control over the quality of the grapes and style of wine they're aiming for. This formula has proved 'extremely successful', and currently wines wing their way to 35 countries. Most exciting are the growing US market and the huge potential of China. Next is the addition of 'premium' and 'super premium' wines to the range.

★★★★ **Chardonnay-Pinot Noir MCC Brut** Affordable, carefully made sparkling with fine creamy mousse, lively citrus/bakery flavours. Latest **NV** bottling especially good. Base-wine Fr-oaked 6 mths, yr *sur lie*.

Ruby Cabernet ☺ ★★★ Appealingly ripe & juicy **04**, vibrant thatchy varietal nose, rounded red berry fruit & tannins for effortless quaffing. **Chenin Blanc** ☺ ★★★ Vinified for fruit-juiciness; **05** delightful; touches pineapple & green apple, super-frisky tropical fruit salad flavour. Enjoy young.

All in LM range light to medium alc (13-14%); WO W Cape. **Cabernet Sauvignon** ★★★ Scaled down but not dumbed down cab; last tasted was **03**, lifted black fruit, fresh acidity & variety's noticeable tannin. Structure to drink/keep ±2 yrs. **Pinotage** ★★ Last reviewed was undemanding **03**, combo peppery & creamy red berry aromas, generous red fruit flavours. **Merlot-Shiraz** ★★★ **04** not available for tasting; last ed **03** was lightweight, slightly more assertive & dry than its range-mates. **Shiraz-Cabernet Sauvignon** ★★★★ Step above pvs yet **04** retains hallmark seamless accessibility, light oaking during fermentation imparts vanilla suggestion to packed red berry fruit. **Chardonnay** ★★ Invariably a tasty mouthful; **04** last ed had tropical melon & mango in medium-full bodied, rewarding package. **Sauvignon Blanc** ★★★ **05** notes of citrus & tropical fruit, clean, fresh & well made, as usual. **Semillon-Chardonnay** ★★★ These have some staying power, but best young; **04** pleasant lime/lees tones, flourish of flavour in finish. — *DH*

Long Neck see Simonsvlei

Longridge Winery

*Stellenbosch (see Helderberg map) ▪ Est 1994 ▪ Tasting & sales: Mon-Fri 9-5 Sat 9-2 ▪ Fee R10 ▪ Closed Easter Sun, Dec 25 & Jan 1 ▪ Cheese platters & picnic baskets (book day ahead) ▪ Sundowner evenings with live music in summer ▪ Owner Winecorp ▪ Winemakers/viticulturists: see Winecorp ▪ 60 ha ▪ 23 000 cs 60% red 40% white ▪ ISO 9001 certified ▪ PO Box 99 Lynedoch 7600 ▪ info@longridge.co.za ▪ www.longridge.co.za ▪ **T 855·2004** ▪ F 855·4083*

Part of the Westcorp stable (with Savanha, Spier), Longridge is a consistently fine wine brand, perhaps deserving of more attention from local wine lovers. Its premium 'boutique' Longridge range and equally pleasing mainly-exported Bay View wines are vinified from grapes grown on selected Helderberg slopes. The 2005 harvest saw the first fruits from new plantings, which will swell volumes, while cellar upgrades (cooling equipment, additional sorting tables) aim at ensure continued quality. A clutch of golds this past year (Veritas, Concours Mondial de Bruxelles, Chardonnay du Monde) was topped by a 'best merlot' trophy (for the 2003) at the IWSC in London.

★★★★ **Cabernet Sauvignon** Serious & delicious. **03** Less overt, showy than pvs but quality there: admirable fruit purity, cassis, red berries; firm, finely orchestrated tannins. Sleek, athletic, already accessible, but as with all these reds, will unfold to true potential over next ±7 yrs. Fr/Am barrels, some new, 12-16 mths. IWSC gold. Dark fruited **02** muscular, velvety fruit-texture, deep-veined tannins. 14.7% alc. VG; Concours Mondial gold; *Wine* ★★★★.

★★★★ **Merlot 03** (★★★★☆) a class above pvs, with thoroughbred lines. Far from peak, but even now shows potential of SA merlot. Cedar-toned, coolly grown fruit, intense & vibrant blackcurrants, mulberries; perfect foil for firm, peppery tannins. Drinking beautifully for those who can't wait. Oak as for Cab. IWSC merlot trophy. Extrovert **02** impressed with vibrancy, intensity, chewy tannins within sleekly muscular framework. Concours Mondial gold, VG.

★★★★ **Pinotage** A modern, stylish (& much awarded) rendition of the variety. **03** impresses not least with complexity, concentration of flavours: piquant red berries, cherries, savoury oak tones, a refreshing touch of mint. Appealingly juicy palate, but built for the longer haul. Oak as for Cab. Concours Mondial gold for impressive, beautifully crafted **02** (★★★★☆) – harmonious despite hefty 14.9% alc.

★★★★ **Brut** new MCC from chardonnay/pinot (65/35), initial 9 mths lees maturation before 2 yr bottle ferment. **01** full-flavoured, well structured. Bouquet of fresh brioche with lemon butter; toasty palate with lively mousse, long finish. blend. 12.1% alc; 15.2g/ℓ RS, but tastes dry.

★★★★☆ **Chardonnay** Frequently gilded label. **04** tighter, more focused than pvs, bridges Old World & New. Grapefruit, buttered toast & citrus peel, with underlying tension, enlivening lemon edginess. Drinking well, but don't rush it, there's plenty of complexity, sophistication. Fermented/11 mths Fr oak, 60% new. **03** went without us tasting. VG.

Bay View range

Cabernet Sauvignon 02 aromas mocha & cassis/dark cherries; sleeker, smoothly ripe; tannins supportive of fruit at centre. These reds all 11 mths oak. Tasted last ed, as was … **Shiraz** ★★★☆ Bold, flavourful **03**: black cherry, scrub, roasted spice; firm but ripe tannins, savoury finish. Drink, or keep 3+ yrs. 14.7% alc. **Merlot 04** offers good typicity, cassis, plums, mint choc, supported by firm but amenable tannins. Essentially light-structured, yet has everything it needs. **Pinotage** ★★☆ Ripe, opulent **04**, dark plums, bananas & cream masking the hefty 15.2% alc. Ready, drink within ±3 yrs. **Chenin Blanc** ★★☆ This & next tasted last yr as samples. **04** exuberant, fresh: juicy fresh-cut pears, guavas, long zesty finish. **Sauvignon Blanc** ★★☆ For export. **04**'s crisp acidity gives focus to fruit salad flavours, helps food compatibility. This range WO W-Cape/Coastal. – *CR*

L'Ormarins Private Cellar

Franschhoek • Est 1965 • 1stB 1982 • Visits only by appt Mon-Fri 9-4.30 Sat 10-3 • Fee R20 • Light lunches Mon-Sat Dec-Mar • Closed Easter Fri/Sun, Dec 25 & Jan 1 • Small tourgroups • Owner Johann Rupert • Winemaker Neil Patterson (Oct 2005) with Christo Hamerse (June 1995) • Viticulturist Rosa Kruger (Oct 2004) • 90 ha (cab, merlot, pinot g, chard, sauvignon) • 1 000 tons 25 000 cs own label 50/50 red/white • ISO 14001 certified • PO Box 435 Franschhoek Valley 7690 • tasting@lormarins.co.za • www.lormarins.com • ***T 874·1026*** *• F 874·1361*

Another milestone is reached at this historic farm, established by French Huguenot Jean Roi in 1694. This year the gates are being opened again to the public (by appointment), after being temporarily shut while owner Johann Rupert breathed fresh life into the property originally brought to prominence by his late brother Anthonij. In a sweeping redevelopment, Johann R has ordered less auspicious vineyards replaced and new, smaller blocks planted on higher ground (much emphasis placed on matching site with suitable grape variety). Charged with actualising all this carefully cultivated potential is viticulturist Rosa Kruger (ex-Cape Point Vineyards, Iona). What winemakers Neil Patterson and Christo Hamerse hail as 'a new revolutionary red-wine cellar' is complete, and at the time of writing all available hands were busy refurbishing the existing cellar. 'Innovative winemaking practices', meanwhile, we being adopted at both facilities.

★★★★ **Optima** Quality claret-style red. **02** still available; 70/30 cab s/merlot (pvs included cab f); refined ripe bouquet; supple palate more flagrantly New World (14% alc). Great prospects. Yr Fr oak, 40% new. *Wine* ★★★★. No **01**.

★★★★ **Cabernet Sauvignon** Last we looked, **02** had a classic cassis/cigarbox bouquet; light texture but ripe & elegant fruit; deserved time. 15 mths Fr oak; 60% new. **01** 91 pts *WS*.

★★★★ **Merlot** Improved track record over past 3 vintages: still-selling **03** fruity, chunky high-toast-oak nose; concentrated grainy texture; give more time. ±15 mths oak, 70% new Fr. **02**, in difficult vintage, achieved richness, complexity.

★★★★ **Barrique Select Merlot** Special selection which so impressed Concours Mondial judges on first (**02**) outing, they conferred Category trophy. Still available; generous & juicy; supple tannins & persistence. 15 mths 70% new Fr oak.

★★★★ **Sauvignon Blanc** (Pvsly 'Cold Soaked') Intriguing dusty dried grass, green fig subtleties on latest **05**; initial austerity from some tannin grip, bone dry finish alleviated by weighty fruit but only moderate alc (12.5%). Unusual & food-friendly. No **04**. **03** had loads of vim & personality. Soaked on skins (at 8°C) for 20 hrs to unleash flavour.

Chardonnay ★★★ **04** medium-weight but satisfying, versatile at table. 30% new-barrel-fermented/11 mths (rest equal 2nd fill & unoaked). Neither this, following wine retasted. **Blanc Fumé** ★★★★ **04** sample was suavely food-cordial — third unwooded, rest fermented/4 mths oak. **Late Bottled Vintage** ★★★ new to guide; pvs sold only ex-cellar. **92** a bit lightweight, otherwise as ready as this port style should be. Clean shoe polish/fresh currant nose, dryish 75g/ℓ sugar. 5 yrs in cask. 17% alc. WO Frhoek. **Pinot Grigio** & **Sauvignon Blanc** discontinued.

Terra del Capo range

Sangiovese ★★★★ Proves the Cape isn't French grape country only. **03** convincingly different; ultra-clear ruby brilliance, lightish, quite lean, soundly dry balanced by sour cherry/damson concentration. Supportive oaking; yr 75% Fr. Food wine par excellence. **Pinot Grigio** ★★★ **05** with trompe l'oeil flicker of smoky pink on pale gold hue. Refreshing easy drinking; mouth-watering Golden Delicious apple zest, lifted by 5g/ℓ sugar. Enjoy as young as possible. Both ranges WO Coastal unless noted. — *AL*

Lorna Hughes new

*Stellenbosch ▪ Est 1990 ▪ 1stB 2003 ▪ Closed to public ▪ Vini consultant Mark Carmichael-Green (2003) ▪ Viticulturist Lorna Hughes ▪ 3.2 ha (cab, shiraz) ▪ 100% red ▪ PO Box 612 Stellenbosch 7599 ▪ llhughes@telkomsa.net ▪ **T 073·420·3300** ▪ F 865·2740*

Devon Valley viticulturist Lorna Hughes, (wife of Dave H, SA wine ambassador and taster for this guide) lends her name to this boutique brand. ('Bristle' a veiled tribute to the distinctively hirsute DH?) Inspiration came in 2003 when a neighbour whose vineyard she manages, 'donated' the fruit from a hectare of shiraz the day before harvest. Mark Carmichael-Green is the vinifier, using the Monterosso facility.

Stonehill Bristle ☺ ★★★ Unpretentious, ready-now **04** blend of gnarled-vine shiraz & younger cab, older Fr oaked 10 mths. Offers clean red fruits & well integrated wood. Pvs **03** slightly denser, more complex & structured. — *NP*

Lorraine Private Cellar

*Goudini (see Worcester map) ▪ Est 1875 ▪ 1stB 2002 ▪ Visits by appt ▪ Tasting fee R15 (incl glass) ▪ BYO picnic ▪ Conservation area ▪ Owners Lorraine Trust (Johan & Lori Ann de Wet) ▪ Winemaker Johan de Wet ▪ Viti adviser Leon Dippenaar (2003) ▪ 150 ha (cab f, merlot, petit v, pinotage, ruby cab, shiraz, chard, chenin, sauvignon, viognier) ▪ 2 000 tons total 50t/±4 200 cs own label ▪ 75% red 25% white ▪ PO Box 2 Rawsonville 6845 ▪ info@lorraine.co.za ▪ www.lorraine.co.za www.lorraine-wines.com ▪ **T/F (023) 349·1224***

Johan de Wet is now the 5th generation owner (& trustee) of the historic 2 400ha Lorraine farm in the foothills of the Du Toitskloof Mountains, at the fertile western edge of Goudini. 2 200ha are devoted to conservation and 150ha to vineyards, cultivated on the farm since the mid-19th century, with cellar and distillery built in 1875. Ever since JdW started farming, he longed to return to his roots and make his own wine. His wife, whom he met while travelling in the USA, inspired and encouraged him to fulfil that dream. With some capital and courage, the old cellar was refurbished and in 2002, he made his first 3 barrels. He now presses 50 tons, and exports, quite fittingly, to the USA.

Chardonnay ☺ ★★★ Bright lemon-butter colour, aromas, smooth mouth-filling flavours in still fresh **03** crowd pleaser. Breakfast concludes on toasty note.

Cape Harmony ★★★☆ Suitably named pinotage, cab, merlot concordance; **03** well-melded; simple agreeable red-wine smells contemporised by generous oak. Light-textured, pleasantly firm. Versatile food partner. **Shiraz** ★★★ Modern, international style. **03** ripe but fragrant floral/red fruit aromas generously decorated with wood; dense, heavy mouthfeel with roughish aftertaste. **Sauvignon Blanc** ★★☆ Clean, undemanding **05**. Forward, easy fig/tropical fruit; initial juiciness diminished by gravelly short finish. *—AL*

Lost Horizons Premium Wines

Paarl ▪ Est/1stB 1995 ▪ Tasting & sales at Simonsvlei International (see entry) Mon-Fri 8-5 Sat 8.30-4.30 Sun 11-3 ▪ Fee R15 for 5 wines (incl glass) ▪ Closed Easter Fri & Dec 25 ▪ Tours by appt ▪ Owner Norton Sky Cooper ▪ Viti consultant Schalk du Toit (Jun 1999) ▪ ±250 000 cs 50% red 30% white 20% rosé ▪ Export brands: Lost Horizons, Quantum, Guardian, Panorama, St Dalfour ▪ ISO 9001:2000, HACCP & BRC certified ▪ PO Box 568 Suider-Paarl 7624 ▪ horizons@global.co.za ▪ www.losthorizons.co.za ▪ ***T 863·3848*** *▪ F 863·3850*

Last year was a memorable one for GM Jacques Jordaan – it marked his 10th year with Lost Horizons and the export company's 10th birthday. A milestone indeed in what he calls 'this complicated and internationally competitive market'. The signpost for the 2005 vintage points to better quality from smaller yields, with Jordaan predicting 'excellent' shiraz, pinotage, sauvignon and chardonnay. His personal wish is to increase production and sales twofold. Looking at the bigger picture, he hopes to contribute to making the SA wine industry more representative.

Classic Red ☺ ★★ Unpretentious unwooded **04** repeats pvs mix pinotage, ruby cab, merlot; friendly red fruit flavours, very smooth & undemanding.

Cabernet Sauvignon ★☆ **03** good everyday red, smooth & easy (slipperiness boosted by ±6g/ℓ sugar – ditto for Cab-Merlot); not oaked, as are all these. **Merlot** Temporarily out of stock. **Cabernet Sauvignon-Merlot** ★☆ 60/40 blend in **03**, trattoria-friendly as always; very soft, juicy, sweetish fruity flavours. **Chardonnay** ★★ **05** uncomplicated but nice; sweet-ripe fruit, peach/mango flavours, crisp, well-juiced finish. **Sauvignon Blanc** ★★★ Bottled **04** (pvs ed a sample) ebullient on palate: zingy green flavours, tart sherbety acidity to counter anything rich &/or fishy. **Classic White** ★★ Latest bottling switches to 100% chenin; guava/pear/apple melange, dry, fresh & fruity. **NV**. **Guardian** range discontinued.

Quantum range

Classic Ruby Red ☺ ★★ **04** unwooded mix pinotage, ruby cab, merlot; gulpable juicy red fruit, delightfully smooth & unpretentious.

Petillant Rosé ★ Of its style, still one of SA's top sellers; delicately spritzy off-dry **04**, flavourful but barely vinous. **Chenin Blanc** new ★★ Workmanlike **05** dry white with clean pear & guava hints, fresh & crisp acidity. **Petillant Blanc** ★☆ **04** from chenin; usual slight prickle on palate, but not quite the aromatic freshness of pvs.

Hemisphere range

Cabernet Sauvignon ★★★ Ripe, Ribena-toned **02**, last ed was similar to LH version but appeared rounder, plusher, better balanced. **Merlot** ★★★ **02** last yr slightly fleshier than the LH version; similar meaty/gamey sniffs; full, ripe, soft fruit. **Cabernet Sauvignon-Merlot** ★★★ Not retasted. **02** perfectly pleasant medium-bodied quaffer, fairly laid-back; some soft leafy strawberry fruit. **Classic Ruby Red** ★☆ Good anytime red, unwooded (as are all these reds); mix pinotage, ruby cab, merlot in **04** (sample), ultra-ripe style, lively red berry flavours. **Select Rosé** ★ (Pvsly Petillant Rosé) Light & delicately spritzy **04**, with stewed fruit flavours, dryish aftertaste. **Chardonnay** ★★★ **05** (sample) soft & buttery (though winemaker says unoaked), attractive lime marmalade flavours, fairly abrupt finish. **Sauvignon Blanc** ★★★ Shy on nose last yr, **04** came alive on palate: bright, green, sherbety flavours; good lightish quaffing. All ranges WO W Cape.—*JN/TM*

Louiesenhof Wines

*Stellenbosch ▪ Est/1stB 1992 ▪ Tasting & sales daily 9–5 (summer) Mon-Sat 10–3 (winter) ▪ Fee R10 ▪ Closed Christian holidays ▪ Light picnic meals in summer ▪ Play area for children ▪ Function facilities ▪ Farm produce ▪ Walks ▪ Conservation area ▪ Owner WS Smit Watergang Trust ▪ Winemaker Stefan Smit, advised by Jos le Roux in 2004 ▪ Viti consultant Gawie Kriel (2000) ▪ 120 ha (cab, merlot, pinotage, tinta, chard, chenin, sauvignon) ▪ 800 tons 3 000 cs own label 70% red 28% white 2% rosé ▪ PO Box 2013 Stellenbosch 7601 ▪ lhofwine@iafrica.com ▪ www.louiesenhof.co.za ▪ **T 865·2632** ▪ F 865·2613*

A maiden harvest last year of sauvignon, from vineyards established on virgin soils in the Bottelary Hills, pleased Stefan Smit no end. He's equally delighted with the quality of the reds, and notes that he's taken to fermenting these at lower temperatures and 'turning'—rather than punching down—the musts to extract flavour and tannins more gently. A novelty in the cellar is a Natural Sweet from late-harvested cab. The tasting area has been extended and can now accommodate functions for up to 60 guests (pizza parties a possibility, thanks to a new domed oven).

Pinotage ★★★ Envisaged as a 'lifestyle' wine with extra-generous flavours; unwooded **04** rich plum & black berry notes, soft ripe tannins, finishes fairly dry, touch dusty. **Sauvignon Blanc** ★★★ Water-white **05** liberal tropical aromas; brisk dusty finish. No newer vintages of the following tasted: **Tinta Barocca** ★★★ **02** Mediterranean-style food-cordial red, pleasing mix red berry & dried fruit on nose; hint choc on finish. Briefly oaked. **Pinotage Blanc de Noir** ★★★ **03** coral glints, sappy strawberry tones with creamy touch, bone-dry conclusion. **Chardonnay Unwooded** ★★★ **04** shy pear/green melon on nose; minerally & restrained, good foil for seafood. **Perroquet Cape Tawny** ★★★★ Rustic glow-inducer from tinta, off very old vyd; fortified with brandy, aged 5 yrs in barrels; **NV**; 19% alc. Fairly developed character with savoury touches.—*MM/TM*

Louisvale Wines

*Stellenbosch ▪ Est/1stB 1989 ▪ Tasting & sales by appt only Mon-Fri 9.30–4.30 Sat 10–1 ▪ Fee R10 ▪ Closed Easter Fri-Mon, Dec 25/26 & Jan 1 ▪ Tours by appt ▪ BYO picnic ▪ Owners Michael A Johnston, Hendrik Kotzé & Martin Delaney ▪ Winemaker/viticulturist Simon Smith (Jul 1997) ▪ 23 ha (cab, merlot, shiraz, chard) ▪ 200 tons 15 000 cs 20% red 80% white ▪ ISO 9000:2001 certification in progress ▪ PO Box 542 Stellenbosch 7599 ▪ winery@louisvale.com ▪ www.louisvale.com ▪ **T 865·2422** ▪ F 865·2633*

'We are winemakers and not carpenters,' says the eminently quotable Simon Smith, no cabinet-maker but a viticulturist and producer of a chardonnay that reflects site and has as much or as little wood as is called for by skill and taste. Three chardonnays, in fact—an unwooded (a successful newcomer to the US market), a lightly-oaked (Chavant) and the most serious one, which was first made in 1989. Simon and assistant winemaker Mogamat Dickson (product of the farm's in-house training scheme) spent the 2005 French season in Burgundy, with Philippe Bouchard, as part of a strategy to return the farm to its chardonnay roots. In line with that resolve is the decision to produce a premium range from the first vines planted on Louisvale.

★★★★ **Dominique** ✓ **00** (not retasted) introduced dash cab f to flagship blend of cab, merlot (55/30); luxurious velvet texture to opulent dark-berried fruit, pleasant dryness. Should still hold 2-3+ yrs. Yr Fr barriques.

★★★★ **Chardonnay** Well established & consistent, with track record for good ageing. Tasted last ed, **03** (★★★★) shade less arresting—more obvious oak (though less time in barrel

– 6 mths vs 8), austere; standout bouquet still features toast, grilled hazelnuts, ripe citrus. **04** unready for tasting.

Chavant Chardonnay ★★★☆ **04** back on form, big bouquet ripe citrus & melon, intriguing hint of damp cellar; lovely juicy ripe fruit, generously fleshy but enlivened by mouth-watering acidity. 85% fermented/4 mths in oak. **Chardonnay Unwooded** (previously GlenDevon) ★★★ **05** gorgeous floral & white peach aromas translate easily onto palate – creamily textured, threaded with lively acidity. Dash sugar adds to easy drinkability. – *IvH*

Lourensford

Stellenbosch (see Helderberg map) • Est 1999 • 1stB 2003 • Tasting & sales Mon-Fri 8.30-5 Sat 10-2 Sun 11-3 Pub hols 9-4 • Fee R15 • Closed Easter Fri, Dec 25 & Jan 1 • Tours Mon-Fri 11 & 3 • Conferencing • Fly-fishing • Annual SAA Cape Town Flower Show • Polo • Cheesery • Cellarmaster Philip Costandius • Oenologist Hannes Nel (Dec 2002) • Viticulturists Barry Humby, Ben de Villiers & Annelie Viljoen • 285 ha (cab, merlot, pinotage, shiraz, sauvignon, viognier) • 1 300 tons 80 000 cs 80% red 20% white • ISO 14000 certification in progress • PO Box 16 Somerset West 7129 • winetastings@lourensford.co.za • www.lourensford.com • ***T 847·0891*** *• F 847·0896*

This Christo Wiese-owned property in the Helderberg foothills is buzzing. Much of the activity and success centres on pinotage, one of cellarmaster Philip Costandius's great passions – as founder-member (1995) of the Pinotage Assocation, he mooted the idea for the influential Pinotage Top Ten benchmarking exercise. His as-yet-unreleased 05 Pinotage, coincidentially, was selected to represent the Helderberg area at the Assocation's 2005 New Vintage tasting. And, in a viticulural coup, a parcel of 6-year-old pinotage won the Stellenboch Vineyard Block competition. Joining the team from Nietvoorbij as assistant winemaker is Adele Louw, while Anton du Toit, ex-Vinfruco, signs on as chief executive of Wine Business at Lourensford (and sister winery Lanzerac).

★★★★ **Viognier** new **04**, with 14% sauvignon has lovely jasmine & honeysuckle fragrance, anchored by peach pip & gentle savoury biscuit notes. They unfold on the palate, never losing delicacy, hallmark refinement. 6 mths Hngrn oak. addition. Very creditable result from 1st crop.

★★★★ **Semillon Noble Late Harvest** new Distinctive, original, hedonistic **04**: lavender scent; shortbread, apricot tart flavours & a lifting, citric freshness on long, silky-textured finish. Partially oaked. 136 g/ℓ RS, 10.6 g/ℓ acid. Power in a 500ml package.

Cabernet Sauvignon ★★★☆ **03** now attractively juxtaposes dark fruit, smoked beef & fynbos nuances. Finely honed tannins integrating well, provide framework for 4+ yr cellaring, fruit masking 14.8% alc. Yr Fr oak. One to watch. **Seventeen Hundred** ★★★☆ Named for date of property's establishment: blend cab (75%), merlot, soupçon shiraz. Faure fruit as yet. **03** shows bold oaking (yr Fr, half new); first impression of toasty, sweet spice aromas, forceful tannins, all in dark-fruited, savoury construct. 14.6% alc. Closed mid-2004, needing time; keep up to 10 yrs. **Sauvignon Blanc** ★★★☆ Classic-styled asparagus, nettles on **04**, & fleeting glimpses herb garden, summer fruits. Reductively made to capture zinging, youthful freshness. Dry – fine for food, as is moderate 12.8% alc. – *CR*

Lourens River Valley see Morgenster
Louwshoek see Daschbosch
Luca & Ingrid Bein see Bein Wine

Luddite Wines

Bot River (see Walker Bay map) • Est 2000 • Tastings by appt • Owners Niels Verburg & Hillie Meyer • Winemaker Niels Verburg • Viticulturist Penny Verburg • 5.5 ha (cab, mourvèdre, shiraz) • 1 800 cs 100% red • Export brand: Niels Verburg • Ranges for customers: Iona, Barton & Hidden Valley • PO Box 656 Bot River 7185 • luddite@telkomsa.net • ***T (028) 284·9308*** *• F (028) 284·9045*

'The reds are sleepers, well-balanced, but will take time to reveal their true potential,' opines Niels Verburg, who sources grapes widely for the Luddite range. His and wife Penny's own young blocks at Bot River are coming into production (and showing 'fantastic potential'), and will make their presence felt for the first time in the upcoming 04 release. Verburg describes his approach as 'very traditional, but always pushing the envelope'. For instance, he's now macerating healthy grapes on their skins far longer than previously – 72 days in the case of one especially promising tank – to extract the maximum flavour and structure. The highlight of 2005 undoubtedly was the invitation to join the exclusive Cape Winemakers Guild. A welcome counterpoint to the harrowing aftermath of a late-2004 shooting incident, in which son Kim was critically injured but miraculously recovered.

★★★★☆ **Shiraz** Classically styled, subtle & seamlessly assembled from variety of sites – Mbury, Hldrberg, Bottlry vyds for **03**, sweet-fruited but still peppery entrée; elegant unshowy raspberry mid-palate (lower alc than pvs – 14%) with nutmeg, allspice hints; polished, lingering. Worthy successor to unflamboyant **02** where sumptuous fruit yields pepper, clove & cassia whiffs, tannin weight conceals 15.5% alc; bigger, more obvious than reined-in **01**.

★★★★ **CWG Auction Reserve Shiraz** new Fine Auction debut for newly Guilded Verburg; **04** tiny production (59 cs) from single Hldrberg site, 100% new Fr oaked, 13 mths; sumptuous fruit (raspberries, blackcurrants), sweet almond notes; ample ripe tannins delivering texture & length; unshowy yet mouth-filling. — *MF*

Lusan Premium Wines

Stellenbosch ▪ Closed to public ▪ info@neethlingshof.co.za ▪ ***T 883·8988*** *▪ F 883·8941*

Umbrella organisation for Alto, Flat Roof Manor, Hill & Dale, Le Bonheur, Neethlingshof, Stellenzicht and Uitkyk. Wines from these farms, totalling some 800 ha of prime Stellenbosch vineyards, marketed by Cape Legends. See individual entries.

Lushof Estate

Stellenbosch (see Helderberg map) ▪ Est 1997 ▪ 1stB 2000 ▪ Tasting & sales Mon-Fri 10-4 Sat by appt ▪ Closed pub hols ▪ Tours by appt ▪ Owners Hennie & Linda Steyn ▪ Winemakers/viticulturists Erika van Zyl & Hennie Steyn, advised by Bruwer Raats ▪ 12.5 ha (cab, merlot, shiraz, chard, sauvignon) ▪ 70 tons 3 500 cs 75% red 25% white ▪ PO Box 899 Stellenbosch 7599 ▪ lushof@icon.co.za ▪ www.lushof.co.za ▪ ***T 855·3134*** *▪ F 855·3623*

Owners Hennie & Linda Steyn were saddened by the sudden death of previous winemaker Daniel Hudson while on a visit to New Zealand. He'd left assistant Erika van Zyl and Hennie S at the helm, and for the time being the duo continues under the eagle eye of consultant Bruwer Raats (Raats Family). Last season's variable weather further complicated matters, but the quality of the fruit turned out to be 'amazing' and the cellar team looks forward to 'some stunning wines'. 'Drinkable wines of excellence' are what vinophiles should expect to find under Lushof labels, both on retail shelves and at the newly updated tasting area on the higher reaches of Helderberg Mountain.

★★★★ **Sauvignon Blanc 05** showcases perfectly ripe grapes worked into expressive, balanced & well-textured drinkability. Hints artichoke & asparagus add herbaceous touches to broad tropical palate. **04** among yr's more subtly expressive. Juicily clean; very moreish.

Cabernet Sauvignon ★★★ **03** continues restrained demeanour of pvs; leafy, minty choc whiffs, usual fine tannin, suave oak (14 mths, 30% new), understated sweet-sour finish. **Merlot** ★★★☆ Well-tailored example, shows good cohesive decorum; mulberry-toned **03** again light-textured, lifted by tasty savoury acid, well-managed tannin support. Oak as for Cab. **Shiraz** ★★★☆ **04** not ready. **03** deftly executed to show off best of young vines. Last yr showed deepish carpet pile texture, balanced natural freshness complementing elegantly expressive dark spice. 11 mths Fr/Am oak, 50 % new. **Signet Red** ★★★ 'Flagship Blend' last ed; cab, merlot, shiraz, yr Fr oak, 80% new. Bottled version shows Hldrberg refinement, classic mulberry tones with mint-choc edge, balanced acid/tannin grip. Attractive, but perhaps lacks gravitas for top status/rating. **Chardonnay** ★★★☆ Elegant & refined **04**, barrel-fermented (60% Fr oak, 8 mths), similar profile to pvs; smoothly rounded; oak characters well supported by limy, tropical succulence; geared for current drinking. — *CT/AL*

Lutzville Cape Diamond Vineyards

Olifants River ▪ Est 1961 ▪ 1stB 1980 ▪ Tasting & sales Mon-Fri 8-5 Sat 9-12 ▪ Tours by appt ▪ 'Café Wijne' coffee shop, picnic baskets by appt ▪ Function/conference venue ▪ Tourgroups ▪ Gifts ▪ Farm-style produce ▪ Owners 109 shareholders ▪ Senior winemaker Emile Schoch (Dec 2003) ▪ Winemakers Albie Rust & Christiaan Visser (Jan 1999/Dec 2003) ▪ Viticulturists Jaco Lategan (Dec 2002) ▪ 2 100 ha (cab, merlot, pinotage, ruby cab, shiraz, chard, chenin, colombard, sauvignon) ▪ 47 500 tons (20 000 cs own label) 10% red 87% white 1% rosé 2% fortified/sparkling ▪ PO Box 50 Lutzville 8165 ▪ info@lutzvillevineyards.com ▪ www.lutzvillevineyards.com ▪ ***T (027) 217·1516*** *▪ F (027) 217·1435*

The team at SA's second biggest cellar feel they've established a broad base of good-quality, value-for-money wines (and won multiple *Wine* magazine value citations for their efforts), and they're ready to start selecting wines for a premium range. The revamped tasting locale is a hub for visitors to the Olifants River Valley, serving as an information centre — and serving fresh coffee, accompanied by something sweet (wine the main ingredient) or a cheese platter with home-baked bread. They're handily open for wine sales on public holidays, too. New function/conference facilities for groups of up to 20 and lovely gardens for pre-booked picnics complete the experience.

Cabernet Sauvignon ★★★ Light-bodied unoaked **04** recalls pvs's amenable herbal black-fruit tones, dry savoury finish, firm ripe tannins. **Merlot** ★★★ Unwooded this time, & friendlier; dark spicy berries on **04**, pleasant dusty whiff, firm but balanced tannins. **Pinotage** ★★ Fast-forward to attractively rustic **04**; not wooded; vibrant aromas of banana & red berry, soft but dry food-preferring tannins. **Shiraz** ★★ 2nd look at briefly Am-oaked **04** (pvs ed a sample): enticing, rich, spicy red-berry nose; big but subtly fruited palate with meaty hint. **Chardonnay** ★★ Lowish acidity & touch sugar impart roundness to **05**; pretty unwooded aromas of orange zest & ripe pear. **Sauvignon Blanc** ★★ Water-white **05** lightish & bone-dry, as usual; slightly dusty tropical fruit flavours. **Chenin Blanc** ★★ **05** more subtly flavoured this yr; some minerally guava hints, nice acidity gives semi-dry impression (8.8g/ℓ RS). **Muscadel** ★★★ Attractive **04** from white muscadel; lovely ripe muscat bouquet; rich nutty barley-sugar flavour, sweet but clean finish.

Bat's Rock range

Ruby Cabernet ★★★ Unwooded **04**'s dollop sugar plumps out rather than sweetens palate, enriches sweet squishy red-fruit character. Real crowd-pleasing stuff. **Rosé** ★ **04** pinotage & colombard in petally, very simple semi-sweet quick-quaff. **Chenin Blanc** ★★ **05** understated green apple tones, just off-dry, crisp. All above WO Olifants River/Lutzville. — *MM*

Lyngrove

Stellenbosch (see Helderberg map) ▪ 1stB 2000 ▪ Tasting & sales by appt (T 842·2116) ▪ Five-star Lyngrove Country House ▪ Owner Baarsma's Holding B.V. ▪ Winemaker Hannes Louw, with Stefan Hartman (Jan 2005/Jan 2004) ▪ Vineyard manager Pikkie Grobler ▪ 76 ha (cab, merlot, shiraz, petit v, pinot, pinotage, chardonnay, chenin, sauvignon) ▪ 50 000 cs 80% red 20% white ▪ PO Box 7275 Stellenbosch 7599 ▪ info@lyngrove.co.za ▪ www.lyngrove.co.za ▪ ***T 880·1221*** *▪ F 880·0851*

Hannes Louw, ex-KWV, is the new winemaker for this Helderberg operation which forms part of the low-profile but highly successful (1m cases a year) Baarsma Wine Group. A feature here is the Lyngrove Country House, offering stylish accommodation in a quiet vineyard setting.

Platinum range

★★★★ **Pinotage** Barrique-matured **03** very obviously pinotage but well behaved; generous fruity flavour in spicy vanilla-toned package. Good lifted finish. Yr Am oak; unfiltered.

Range listed as 'Premium' last ed; all WO Stbosch. **Shiraz** ★★★★ Aussie-style **03** quite a mouthful; zero finesse but loads of interest, extract, alc (14.3%). Yr oak, 80% Am, none new.

Cabernet Sauvignon-Merlot ★★★★ European profile; **03** herbal hint to clean cassis; medium body, fine minerally structure. Yr Fr oak. **Chardonnay** ★★★★ Classically styled **04**, attractive lemon-butter-citrus character throughout, some leesy girth, very well handled new Fr oak (40%, 11 mths).

Reserve range

Coastal & Stbosch WOs. **Cabernet Sauvignon-Merlot** ★★★ Same 60/40 ratio, but more concentration/extract on **03** than pvs; fruity warmth & ripeness lifted by sweet-sour fillip on finish; yr Fr oak. None of following retasted: **Pinotage** ★★★★ Ripe-picked **02**, sweet & flavoursome, obvious yet not a blockbuster; yr combo Fr/Am oak. **Shiraz-Pinotage** ★★★★ 80/20 partnership; **02** peppery mulberry flavours; dry & quite reserved, hint green oak (yr Fr/Am). **Chardonnay** ★★★★ Showy **02** full & rich layers creamy fruit with hint of botrytis. Barrel-fermented/aged Fr oak.

Lyngrove Collection

Unless stated, reds Fr oak staved, yr. Following trio were samples pvs ed, retasted for current book. **Cabernet Sauvignon** ★★ **03** touch lean, fruit still lurking, unyielding – give more time. **Merlot** ★★ Light-hued **03**, eucalyptus whiffs precede greenish, fairly tart sour-plum flavours. Needs hearty stew or pepper steak. **Shiraz** ★★ **03** stalky/spicy mulberry fruit & pronounced acidity. Fr/Am oak. **Pinotage** ★★★ **03** incorrectly reported as 04 pvs ed; jammy, sweet, rescued by acid tweak. Am oak. The real **04** (sample) too unformed to rate. **Chardonnay** ★★★ *Sur lie* 6 mths for **04**, marzipan/marmalade flavours, touches oak, lees & bottle age – enjoy while fruitiness persists. **Sauvignon Blanc** ★★★ **04** was well-balanced, supple & forthcoming; **05** unready. **Brut** ★★★ Characterful carbonated sparkling; **04** from chenin (80%), chardonnay. Not ready for tasting. These mainly Stbosch WO. – *CT/TM*

Lynx Wines

Franschhoek ▪ Est/1stB 2002 ▪ Tasting & sales Mon-Fri 11-5 Sat 10-1, otherwise by appt ▪ Self-catering cottages ▪ Owner Vista Hermosa (Pty) Ltd ▪ Winemaker Dieter Sellmeyer (2002) ▪ Viti adviser Kevin Watt (Apr 2002) ▪ 11 ha (cabs s/f, merlot, shiraz, viognier) ▪ 1 000 cs 100% red ▪ PO Box 566 Franschhoek 7690 ▪ winemaker@lynxwines.co.za ▪ www.lynxwines.co.za ▪ ***T 867·0406*** *▪ F 867·0397*

'Quite literally the cream of the crop' is how owner/winemaker Dieter Sellmeyer describes the grapes he picks for his own wines. Having now planted viognier, he says 'time will tell' whether it becomes a single varietal wine or is blended with the Shiraz. He's impatient to produce a white, and the new Blanc de Noir ('kept as pale, fresh and fruity as possible') is an interim step. Apart from converting a guest cottage into a tasting room, goals for the winery remain deliberately low-key: 'I plan to remain small so I can continue to be 100% hands-on. And I will continue to do all the cellar tours myself.'

★★★★★ **Shiraz** After standout launch with **03**, a more restrained **04** (★★★★); slight gamey notes, earthy whiffs, generally more raspberry-fruit than pepper tone; super-ripeness (15.4% alc) yields softness but not elegance or precision. Superb **03** was both sumptuous & deliciously spicy; barrel aged (incl malo), third new.

★★★★ **Cabernet Sauvignon** More reined-in **04** (13.9% alc) has herbal whiffs, mulberry blackcurrant notes, sweet tannins; textured yet not showy palate; notch up on extra-ripe **03** (15.1% alc), which altogether more opulent. 11 mths Fr oak (25% new).

★★★★ **Xanache** Classic Bdx blend 50% cab, 40% merlot, 10% cab f in **04**, supple sweet fruit with cassis & plum flavours, elegant dense tannins. Polished; builds upon **03** which had more cab (64%), less merlot (22%) though equally ripe, succulent finish.

Following both new: **Tinto** ★★★ Fine fruited **04**, cassis/mulberry notes, marzipan extras; soft (partly due to 100% malo); alc (14.5%) still youthfully apparent but should harmonise with time; cab, merlot, cab f (57/36/7). **Blanc de Noir** ★★ Delicate pale salmon pink **05**, from merlot, screwcap-closed for undemanding, easy drinking. – *MF*

M23 see Bottelary Hills Wines
Maankloof see Mountain River Wines

Maiden Wine Cellars

*Gordon's Bay ▪ Est 1995 ▪ 1stB 1999 ▪ Tasting/tours by appt; also tailor-made wine tours (max 6 people) ▪ Owner Danie Hattingh ▪ 750 cs 100% red ▪ PO Box 185 Gordon's Bay 7151 ▪ mwines@mweb.co.za ▪ www.maidenwines.com ▪ **T 856·3052** ▪ F 856·5085*

Maiden Wine Cellars's 8th birthday coincided with the successful completion of the first export shipment to Malaysia, after which MD Danie Hattingh was lucky enough to be able hang a 'sold out' sign above the door. Most orders to date have been for his Private Reserve, a cab, shiraz, pinotage blend sourced from vineyards in the Olifants and Breede River areas, and he's now decided to focus on this one wine exclusively.

Main Street Winery

*Paarl ▪ Est/1stB 1999 ▪ Tasting & tours by appt ▪ Owner/winemaker Marais de Villiers ▪ 700 cs 50% red 50% white ▪ PO Box 2709 Paarl 7620 ▪ mainstreet@mweb.co.za ▪ **T/F 872·3006***

Small-scale winemaker and oeno-mentor Marais de Villiers has reorganised his portfolio into a mainly varietal Stoep range, which brings in the cash, and a flagship Main Street Bordeaux-style blend-in-the-making, hopefully destined to bring home laurels (and cash). Affable De Villiers says he's the fittest he's ever been, after paddling up and down the swollen Berg River with his 12-year-old son in preparation for last year's Canoe Marathon. His self-designed mobile vinification system has found favour with the current crop of youngsters who've returned to their family farms after seasons in far-flung winelands, MdV reports.

Stoep range

Old-Cape labels a charming feature. Following all tasted as samples; ratings provisional. **Shiraz 03** raises the bar with well-extracted savoury fruit, excellent varietal spice, properly dry finish; shows real elegance & grace. Possible ★★★★. 26 mths 2nd fill Fr oak. **Merlot** Similar dramatic improvement: deep, densely layered mulberry-choc fruit; ripe dry tannins; already well-knit oak (as above). **03** more serious effort could rate ★★★★. **Pinotage** ★★☆ Last was tannin-rich **02**, with Bovril aroma & hint of prune. **Dry Red** ★★★ No new version of amiable **NV** 4-way blend with hint of ruby cab's thatch. **Chardonnay** new ★★★ Plenty of character & flavour coaxed from **05** Tradouw Valley grapes. Lively & pure unwooded fruit, refreshing lemony tang. **Chenin Blanc** new ★★☆ Lighter styled easy-drinker from Swtlnd fruit; **05** apple & pear flavours, zippy acidity. **Sauvignon Blanc** ★★★☆ **05** much improved this yr; Dbnville grapes vinified to show their dusty fig character, cool-area freshness. —*JN*

Major's Hill Estate

*Robertson ▪ 1stB 2002 ▪ Tasting & sales Mon-Fri 9.30-1; 2-5 Sat 10-4 ▪ Closed Good Fri, Dec 25/26 ▪ Tours by appt ▪ Facilities for children ▪ Owners Dewald, Johan & Anton Louw ▪ Winemaker Alkie van der Merwe, with Nico Renoster (both Jan 2003) ▪ Viticulturist Dewald Louw ▪ 52 ha (cab, merlot, pinotage, shiraz, chard, sauvignon) ▪ 7 500 cs + 120 000ℓ bulk ▪ 60% red 40% white ▪ PO Box 561 Robertson 6705 ▪ info@majorshill.co.za ▪ www.majorshill.co.za ▪ **T (023) 626·6093** ▪ F (023) 626·6096*

Another successful year, with the team struggling to keep up with demand despite soaring production — the 03 Merlot alone selling 8 000 bottles in 8 months. With a track record like this, watch the recently released Cab and Shiraz go. We felt lucky to have a sneak preview of the 03 all-pinotage Port; it's due for release in 2008, but there's talk of releasing a few bottles at the end of 2005. Moving more slowly, the permanent tasting room (in the old cellar that birthed Klipdrif brandy) is still not complete, but now you can play boules, or get lost in the maze.

Merlot ★★★☆ **03** still available, not retasted for this ed. Mocha plum notes dominated by oak mid-2004 (Yr 70/30 Fr/Am), though fine savoury fruit starting to emerge, offering coconut/raspberry succulence; lengthy finish bodes well for development. 14% alc well hidden by vinous character. **Cabernet Sauvignon** ★★★ Currently available **03** has spent 22 mths in Am/Fr oak compared to the wine tasted last yr. Latest has roasted chestnuts, fresh corn-on-cob & abundant berry fruit; soft, approachable tannins. Alc too, at 13.5%, is lower than pvs 14.3%. Drink within 2 yrs. **Pinotage** ★★★☆ Tasted mid-2004, varietally typical banana/

varnish aromas on **03**, graced with some cherry; smoky bouillon flavours, textured oaky finish. Very accessible already. **Shiraz** new ★★★ **03** a fruit-shy maiden, more mineral & savoury with fine, dry tannins from 22 mths Am/Fr oak. Should prove delicious with steak. **Chardonnay** ★★★ Easy drinking **05** from youthful vines; clean & crisp lemon aromas & flavours; sweetish entry & finish from 5.5 g/ℓ sugar & solid 14.5% alc. **Sauvignon Blanc** ★★★ **05** Grassy, green hints revved up by racy acidity on the palate; refreshing aperitif style. Drink up. **Pinotage Port** new ★★ Great care taken with maiden **03**, only 225 ℓ will be released at a time after being bottled & labelled by hand! Burnt rubber & raisin aromas, sweet finish (175 g/ℓ sugar), very little support provided by soft tannins & relatively low alc (16.5%). All above whole-berry ferment. – *CT*

Makana see Cape First

Makro

See Specialist wine shops section for opening hours ▪ Enquiries Carolyn Barton ▪ cbarton@makro.co.za ▪ www.makro.co.za ▪ ***T (011) 797·0503*** *▪ F (011) 797·0366*

Retain chain Makro is one of SA's most accessible one-stop wine destinations, offering some 2 000 labels that cover the entire gamut – from unsung workhorses to tiny boutique gems. Wine selection is under the aegis of buyer Carolyn Barton, who heads a panel which meets fortnightly to taste newcomers, report back on shows, and review styles and price categories. To make it onto the shelf the main criterion must be met: does the wine offer value for the price? The wines below are special parcels exclusive to Makro.

Private Reserve range

★★★★ **La Bri Cabernet Sauvignon Reserve** ✓ Last yr noted as well stocked with sweet ripe plums, milk choc hints, sappy oak (30% new Fr, 18 mths). **02** not for long keeping. WO Frhoek.

★★★★★ **Overgaauw Touriga Nacional-Cabernet Sauvignon** ✓ **03** similar blend to pvs (60/40), same elegance & underplayed class; gorgeous perfumes of violets & berries; chunky tannins need 2/3 yrs, plenty of life thereafter. **01** heady bouquet of dried herbs, lots of complexity & flavour. ±18 mths oak. Stbosch fruit.

★★★★ **Yellowwood Ridge Merlot-Cabernet Sauvignon** Made by Vergelegen's André v Rensburg. Formula tweaked to merlot-cab (60/30) for **03**, dollops cab f, shiraz added; still delicious, claret-like & elegant (despite 14.5% alc). 21 mths Fr barriques, 30% new. **01** 58/42 cab/merlot, finely tuned, elegantly fruited. WO Stbosch.

★★★★ **Landskroon Merlot-Cabernet Franc 02** sophisticated wine which improved in bottle; not retasted **03** (★★★★), 65/35 mix, obvious but delicious; Xmas pud sprinkled with cinnamon. WO Paarl.

★★★★ **Boplaas Private Bin Port** ✓ Classic Boplaas: rich & ripe fruitcake flavours, loads of lurking complexity on firm tannic platform – but welcoming, not stern. **99** touriga & tinta (70/30), 18% alc, 18 mths 500ℓ Portuguese barrels. Bargain priced magnum (1.5ℓ). WO Cdorp.

Vriesenhof Vineyards Pinot Noir new ★★★★ Elegant, earthy red from pinotphile Jan Coetzee; **02** farmyard backdrop to ripe cherry, full-bodied/flavoured, long smoky finish. 14 mths 2nd fill barrels. WO Stbosch. **Villiera Cabernet Sauvignon-Merlot** ★★★★ Elegant, med-bodied **01** last ed had brambly red fruit aromas/flavours, all in elegant harmony. Fr oak, 40% new. WO Paarl. **Villiera Merlot-Pinotage** new ★★★ Villiera team letting their hair down with **02**, distinctly un-genteel; firm, punchy (14.6% alc), lots of firm tannins. A collectible quirk. WO Stbosch, as is … **Truter's Reserve** ★★★ From Beyerskloof's Beyers T. **03** again blend cab & merlot, same oaking (6-8 mths oak, none new); similar lean fruit profile, grainy dry tannins. **Flagstone Strata Series Cape Blend** ★★★★ **02** improbably soft & silky fusion shiraz, pinotage & merlot; sweet-fruited, lavender & pepper pervade the assembly. 70% Am oak, 10% new, 8-10 mths. WO W Cape. **Shiraz-Mourvèdre 04** from Diemersfontein not ready for tasting. **Morgenhof Estate Private Bin 44 Chardonnay** ★★★ Crowd-pleaser with lots of everything (incl toast & vanilla), though **04** tad lighter, sterner on finish. Barrel fermented/8 mths oak, 1st-2nd fill. WO Stbosch. **Misty Mountain**

★★ Light off-dry chenin, colombard blend; wet straw/tropical fruit nuance, to sip while opening any of above. 1ℓ, ex-Bon Courage (so WO Rbtson).

Babbling Brook range

Cabernet Sauvignon ★★ **01** slightly stern, touch green, better with food. 14 mths new Fr oak. Ex-Kanu; WO Stbosch. **01 Merlot** ★★ Brambly, lightly oaked **04** (incl dollop petit v) soft & easy, nice picnic red. By Franschhoek Vineyards. **Pinotage** ★★ **04** more 'sip' than 'quaff' (as was pvs); some wild berry fruit in rustic package. By Horse Mountain; WO Paarl. **Shiraz** ★★★★ Currently unavailable; last **02** piquant red fruit flavours; elegant, soft fruity finish. From Bon Courage. WO Rbtsn.

Mont d'Or range

NV carbonated sparklings by Van Loveren. All ★★, ±11.5% alc. **Brut** Festive party fizz with touch pineapple; easy, gently dry. **Vin Sec** Slightly sweeter version from riesling, muscadel, with latter's enticing floral tone. **Vin Doux** Fully sweet & very soft crowd pleaser, wafting muscat & raisin.

Thomas Kipling range

Currently 'under construction'; not available for tasting. — *CT/DH/DS/TM/IvH*

Malan Family Vintners

Colourfully and simply attired export range by the Malan brothers of Simonsig.

Pinotage ☺ ★★★ **03** offers typicity & juicy quaffability. Spicy rhubarb/brambleberry character, lively, tasty. Unwooded. **Sauvignon Blanc** ☺ ★★★ Lighter-bodied **03** still with leafy/grassy vibrancy, tangy freshness on palate. Enjoy solo, or as food partner.

Cabernet Sauvignon-Merlot ★★★ Early drinking 53/47 blend; **03** dark fruited & toasty. **Cape Rouge** ★★★ **NV** with more definition than pvs. Pinotage, merlot, cab 49/31/20. Exuberantly fruity, raspberries/mulberries; grippy tannins to match food, promise few yrs ageing. **Chardonnay** ★★★ **03** still offers uncomplicated enjoyment; lightly oaked, trademark lemon-butter on toast, crisp finish. **Sauvignon Blanc-Semillon** ★★★ **04** light-textured, accessible. Majority sauvignon (66%) gives green fig/gooseberry pungency. **Cape Blanc** ★★★ Lightish, appealingly aromatic blend colombard/semillon/riesling/morio muscat; softly rounded. **NV**. All WO Stbosch. — *CR*

Mankazana see Ross Gower Wines

Manley Private Cellar

Tulbagh ▪ Est/1stB 2002 ▪ Tasting & sales daily 10–4 Sat/Sun 10–12 ▪ Fee R5/wine ▪ Cellar tours by appt ▪ Closed Good Fri & Dec 25 ▪ Light picnic lunches ▪ Luxury B&B ▪ Gifts ▪ Walks ▪ Owner/winemaker/viticulturist David Manley Jordan ▪ 8 ha (cabs s/f, merlot, mourvèdre, pinotage, shiraz) ▪ Target: 5 000 cs ▪ PO Box 318 Tulbagh 6820 ▪ info@manleywines.co.za ▪ www.manleywines.co.za ▪ ***T (023) 230·0582*** *▪ F (023) 230·0057*

Another year, another vintage, and former yachtsman David Manley Jordan sailed solo through his fourth on this Tulbagh property, which its skipper has set firmly on a course to producing 'only the highest quality red wines'. His 2003 Shiraz raked in the hardware at the Michelangelo Awards (double-gold) and the Classic Wine Trophy (Grand Prix). With his 2005 crop equalling previous harvests in quality, David MJ was pleased to be able to up his limited output by another 1 000 cases. Best place to sink a few glasses is undoubtedly on-board at his and wife Esther's exclusive Hunter's Retreat Guest House.

★★★★ **Shiraz** Gutsy, showy **04** preview continues established big-fruit, big-oak aesthetic; massively ripe (16.1% alc), powerful coconut element from Am oak (50%, ±18 mths) — but well-extracted fruit handles the regimen better than **03** (★★★★), where wood overwhelmed sweet mid-palate fruit at same stage of development.

Cabernet Sauvignon ★★★★ **04**'s huge ripeness (15+% alc) well restrained by elegant, dry, well-fused tannins. Delicious cream-topped plum pudding flavours, finish lifted by whiff fennel.

18 mths oak, 10% Am new. **Merlot** ★★★★ **04**, like pvs, prefaced by savoury prosciutto aromas, attractively layered with pepper & spicy red fruit. Sensitively oaked this vintage (13 mths Fr) – merits higher rating. **Pinotage** ★★★★ **04** same mould as pvs: softly opulent plummy fruit with vanilla hint, refined tannins, persistent flavours. Satisfyingly mouthfilling – helped by 15% alc. 18 mths barrel matured, 40% Am. **Sauvignon Blanc** ★★ Last tasted was **03**, herbal & slightly austere; dry, with moderate 13.1% alc. WO Coastal. – *CR*

MAN Vintners

Paarl ▪ Est/1stB 2001 ▪ Tasting & sales by appt ▪ Owners: see below ▪ Winemaker Tyrrel Myburgh ▪ 60 000 cs own ranges + 15 000 cs for Pangolin ▪ 70% red 30% white ▪ PO Box 389 Stellenbosch 7599 ▪ info@manvintners.co.za ▪ www.manvintners.co.za ▪ ***T 886·7532*** *▪ F 887·4340*

Kingpins José Condé of Stark-Condé, Tyrrel Myburgh of Joostenberg and Fairview's Charles Back have a new partner in Perdeberg Winefarmers' Co-op, where production now takes place, mainly from grapes grown in the Agter-Paarl area. The Vintners see PWC's extensive low-cropping dryland chenin and shiraz vineyards as particularly strong assets. From what began as a modest shipment to Japan in 2001, MAN-V now exports to 9 countries, the most recent being the US. The goal is 'simply to make the best value varietal wines in SA', and with the appointment of a domestic distributor imminent at press time, locals should finally get a taste of these good-value easy-drinkers.

Sénga range

Shiraz ★★★★ **04** will please now & for few yrs, with aromatic smoked meat nose, forceful but restrained flavours supported by succulent acidity, gentle tannic grip. **Merlot & Cabernet Sauvignon** ★★★ Friendly & forthcoming **04** notes of choc, plummy fruit; fresh, but alc power (these both 14.5%) asserts itself on palate, as do rather astringent tannins. These from Muldersvlei grapes; yr mostly Fr oak.

Standard range

Cabernet Sauvignon ☺ ★★★ Attractive blackcurrant aromas on **04** a prelude to ripe-fruited flavours settled a touch uneasily with youthful big dry tannins. Incl a little merlot, shiraz. As all this range, straightforward, honest value. **Pinotage** ☺ ★★★ Beguiling **04** offers lashings of red fruit & spice; gently structured & mouth-filling flavours. As these reds all are, very modestly wooded. **Shiraz** ☺ ★★★ Ripe & round, soft tannins & deep plummy flavour on freshly ingratiating **04**, some extra structure from 10% cab. **Chardonnay** ☺ ★★★ **05** generous with warm nutty citrus, dried peach flavours; full-bodied, but fresh & eminently drinkable. Dash sauvignon.

Chenin Blanc ★★★ Easy-going **05** from Pdberg grapes (but W Cape origin given, as whole range). Bags of tropical fruit flavour; full & rich, with bright acid. **Sauvignon Blanc** ★★★ Grassy, lightly pungent & refreshing **05** has dollop of semillon; quaffably moderate 12.4% alc. – *TJ*

Marcel de Reuck see Crows Nest
Marimba see Southern Sky & Overhex

Marklew Family Wines

Stellenbosch ▪ 1stB 2003 ▪ Visits by appt ▪ Tourgroups (max 20) ▪ Pvt/business functions for small groups ▪ Walks ▪ Mountain biking ▪ Conservation area ▪ Owners Marklew family (Edward Dudley, Edward William, Lyn & Haidee) ▪ Winemaker Duan Brits, with Haidee Marklew (both Jan 2003) ▪ Viticulturists Billy Marklew & Duan Brits (Jun 2001/Jan 2003), advised by Cobus van Graan ▪ 45 ha (cabs/f, merlot, pinotage, shiraz, chard, sauvignon) ▪ ±300 tons 2 700 cs own label 70% red 30% white ▪ PO Box 17 Elsenburg 7607 ▪ wine@marklew.co.za ▪ www.marklew.co.za ▪ ***T/F 884·4412***

This bubbling pot of youthful energy stands on three legs: the Marklew brother-and-sister partnership of Billy (farm management, finances, cycling) and Haidee (winemaking assistant, marketing, showjumping); the first-generation Marklews, Dudley and Lyn, now retired (mature vineyards established by them are being freshened with new plantings of shiraz and cab franc). The third leg is youthful Duan Brits, who seeks equilibrium – between wine structure and oaking – and strives to 'keep it simple' in the restored 180 year old cellar, which now also includes a by-appointment function venue.

★★★★ **Capensis Reserve** Marklews' take on Cape blend characterised by underplayed pinotage presence. In maiden **03**, pinotage just 7% (with cab/merlot – 62/31) & hardly discernible; bit more obvious (though only 10%) in previewed **04**, & still to fully homogenise with cab, merlot, shiraz (45/32.5/12.5). Otherwise continues **03**'s fresh elegance, plush velvety feel, classic dryness. Interesting development potential till at least 2010. Components in separate new oak yr, further 6 mths as blend.

★★★☆ **Cabernet Sauvignon** Benefits of mature vyds & team's increased confidence realised in impressive **04** (★★★★); exudes all (refined) oomph missing in **03**, also identifiable Simonsberg well-toned muscularity, classic cassis/mulberry concentration; dry, insistent tannins yield to memorable finish. Should improve over 6-8 yrs. Yr Fr/Am oak, 40% new.

Merlot ★★★☆ **04** better structure, fruit intensity than pvs. Fresh ripe plum/dark choc tones; powerful yet with elegant & seamless, savoury tannins. Sensitively oaked, third new, Fr/Am barrels. **Chardonnay** ★★★☆ Marklew snrs' predilection for this variety indulged here in confident unblowsy style. **05** (sample) judiciously Fr oaked, none new. Good vinosity infused with roast nut/savoury length. **Pinotage** & **Shiraz 04**s sampled ex-barrel last yr blended into Capensis. All WO Smnsberg-Stbosch. *—AL*

Mason's Hill see The Mason's Winery
Matuba see Cape Coastal Vintners

Matzikama Organic Cellar

Olifants River ▪ Est 1999 ▪ 1stB 2001 ▪ Closed to public ▪ Owner/winemaker/viticulturist Klaas Coetzee ▪ 4 ha (shiraz) ▪ 180 cs 100% red ▪ PO Box 440 Vredendal 8160 ▪ info@matzikamawyn.co.za ▪ www.matzikamawyn.co.za ▪ ***T 082·801·3737***

These vineyards at the foot of Mt Maskam, in a region known for its colourful display of wild flowers in springtime, are certified organic annually by a Dutch company, SKAL International, confirms Klaas Coetzee, who intends furthering his studies in viticulture and oenology this year. With significantly less water available for irrigation last year, the wines were far more concentrated.

Shiraz Two batches of **03** made: 60/40 Fr/Am oak, 8 mths (★★★); tasted last yr showed lightish red berry tone, moderate flavour; 70/30 Am/Fr, yr (★★); spicy toffee tone, firm acidity & overt wood tannin, will need time. Light 13% alc. Next is **04**. *—MM*

Mauroma see Stanford Hils Winery

McGregor Wines

Robertson ▪ Est 1948 ▪ 1stB 1978 ▪ Tasting & sales Mon-Fri 8-5 Sat 9-2 ▪ Closed Easter Fri-Mon, May 2, Dec 16/25/26 ▪ Owners 42 members ▪ Manager/winemaker Jacques du Toit, with Chris Smit (Aug 2002/Jan 2003) ▪ Viticulturist Anton Laas (Dec 2000) ▪ 700 ha ▪ 11 000 tons 25% red 75% white ▪ PO Box 519 McGregor 6708 ▪ mcg@intekom.co.za ▪ www.mcgregorwinery.co.za ▪ ***T (023) 625·1741/1109*** *▪ F (023) 625·1829*

Last year (too late for detailed inclusion in the guide) saw the release of this enterprising co-op's new After Five box-wine range (a packaging choice which is making a comeback in price-sensitive US markets) and LBV Port, each of its 1 000 bottles filled, labelled and numbered by hand. The overarching aim, says new PRO Emma Human, is to keep pushing for quality and to build the McGregor brand. Bottled-wine sales doubled last year (to about 10% of total sales) – partly realising a key objective. 'For the next 5-10 years, we want to become a well-known SA brand,' Emma H declares.

Winemaker's Reserve range

Cabernet Sauvignon ★★★ Handsomely packaged & seriously structured; full-bodied **03** spicy tobacco whiffs, ripe black fruit flavours, supple dry finish. ±14 mths Fr barrelling still obvious; should settle, improve over 2/3 yrs. All above tasted as samples.

Chardonnay ☺ ★★★ **05** billows ripe citrus zest; crisp & juicy; brief Fr oak staving imparts attractive nutty hint. **Sauvignon Blanc** ☺ ★★★ Lightish **05** Fr wood fermented, subtly so – ripe tropical fruit the overriding tone; well-balanced acidity for easy enjoyment.

McGregor range

Ruby Cabernet ☺ ★★★ Appealing & versatile quaffer (13.5% alc). **03** pristine fruit, some grassy notes, quite firm, tangy, dry. **Colombard** ☺ ★★★ They do this so well! Lime/citrus tone throughout **05**, usual light body, upbeat off-dry finish. Perfect picnic wine. **Colombard-Chardonnay** ☺ ★★★ **05** (sample) 60/40 blend bit less wow! than pvs 50/50, still lively, tasty & smoothly dry.

Pinotage ★★★ **04**, from barrel (small Fr, 6 mths): honest & well-crafted, everything in position, looking/tasting good; poised 13.5% alc. **Shiraz** ★★★ Engaging & decidedly drinkable **04**, sweet-spicy brioche tones, well-judged oak (6 mths Fr/Am), properly dry. **Cabernet Sauvignon-Merlot** ★★★ Outdoorsy **03** (sample) again lightly oaked; smooth, slightly nutty tannins; good now but may benefit from ageing yr/2. **Chardonnay** ★★ Unwooded, water-white **05**, lightish & pleasantly lean, good summer refresher. **Chenin Blanc** ★★ **05** winter-melon whiffs, crisp, light & very easy to drink. **Sauvignon Blanc** ★★★ Light bodied, for early enjoyment. Preview **05** lime & tropical nuance, vibrant fruit/acid balance, juicily dry. **Late Harvest Bouquet** ★ **03** still on the list; baked apple aromas, very soft sweetness. **White Muscadel** ★★★ Muscat-scented **05**, racy lemon-tinged acidity lifts, refreshes, leaves palate salivating for more. 16.5% alc. **Red Muscadel** ★★★ Brilliant vermillion-hued **05**, usual spicy basket of potpourri & Turkish Delight, slightly sugary this vintage – for the sweeter toothed. 17% alc. **Cape Ruby** ★★★ Still-available **02**, from ruby cab; last ed showed maturing dried fruit/raisin aromas, varnish notes. ±18% alc. Also available, not tasted: **After Five Ruby Cabernet** & **Chenin Blanc**, in 3ℓ packs, not available for tasting; both NEW. **Brut** discontinued. All WO McGregor. – *MM/TM*

MC Square

Est/1stB 1996 ▪ Closed to public ▪ Winemaker/viticulturist Jean-Luc Sweerts ▪ 300 cs 100% white ▪ PO Box 436 Somerset West 7129 ▪ mcsquare@iafrica.com ▪ ***T 083·303·5467*** *▪ F 852·7740*

No update available on this winery; contact details and wine notes from previous edition.

★★★★ **Cuvée Chardonnay** Subtitle – 'Méthode Classique' – sets tone for both vintages tasted to date: **00** fine honeyed patina to elegant marmalade/apricot tones. **01** fuller, richer, more youthfully citrus-fruited with attractive hints toast on nose/palate. Yr Fr barriques, ±20% new; bottle-aged extra yr. – *IvH*

Meander see Groot Eiland

Meerendal Estate

Durbanville ▪ Est 1702 ▪ 1stB 1969 ▪ Tasting & sales daily 8–5 ▪ Fee R10 per person, refunded on purchase of 6 btls ▪ Closed Easter Fri & Dec 25 ▪ Restaurant, bistro & deli (see Eat-out section) ▪ Owners HN Coertze, AF Swanepoel, JG Adriaanse, R Truter & CG Stride ▪ Cellarmaster Karl Lambour (Jul 2005) ▪ Winemaker Liza Goodwin (Nov 1998) ▪ Viti advisers Paul Wallace & Dawie le Roux (Aug 2004) ▪ 142 ha (cab, merlot, pinotage, shiraz, chard, chenin, gewürz, sauvignon) ▪ ±1 000 tons 25 000 cs 80% red 20% white ▪ Private Bag X1702 Durbanville 7551 ▪ info@meerendal.co.za ▪ www.meerendal.co.za ▪ ***T 975·1655*** *▪ F 975·1657*

Rejuvenation of this historic gem continues with a massive cellar-equipment investment by the syndicate which bought out the Starke family trust in 2004 (the long-late Kosie Starke was a 1970s Cape wine pioneer). Vineyard upgrades remain a priority: new sauvignon occupies a prime position, and 2005 heralded maiden single-vineyard wines. Winemaker Riaan van der Spuy (departed for his father-in-law's wine business in Uruguay) has been replaced by Karl Lambour (ex-Zevenwacht). Resident chef David Higgs has set up his school here (now also offering a food-and-beverage course). A wooden deck off the Meerendal Deli and winetasting area (open seven days a week) overlooks the Durbanville winelands. Add the casual Barn & Lawn Bistro and formal Wheatfields and you have one exciting new food-and-wine experience.

★★★★ **Cabernet Sauvignon-Merlot** ✓ The renamed 'Cabochon'. Current release is **03**, described in last ed as bright, modern, silky, with lots of ripe mulberry fruit, cigarbox whiffs; will have many fans. Yr Fr oak, 2nd/3rd fill.

★★★★ **Sauvignon Blanc Reserve** new **05** flaunts Dbnville's classic cool lemongrass/fig ripeness. Big but beautifully balanced, with sleek concentration, vigorous fruity acids; headily long. Single vyd.

Cabernet Sauvignon ★★★★ Preview **04** shows pleasing freshness, structure, incl vigorous dry tannins to accompany lavish blackberry, cedar tones. Sensitively Fr oaked, third new. Promises greater complexity with time. **Merlot** ★★★★ Blockbuster **04** with tightrope balance, harmony. Polished oak lends support to concentrated yet supple bitter choc/red plum fruit; very fresh core. Deserves time to settle. 15% alc. Fr oaked, third new. **Pinotage** ★★★★ **04** appealingly modern. Generous raspberry/cherry freshness; grippy but balanced tannins. Medium body, careful oaking (Fr barrels, third new) add refinement. **Shiraz** ★★★ **03** old style compared with other reds. Sweetish, porty, with some funky notes. Drink up. Older Fr oak. **Chardonnay 04** mouth-filling baked apple/tropical fruit tastes, with taut acid support. Unrated in 2005 ed; **05** unavailable for tasting. **Sauvignon Blanc** ★★★★ Powerfully built **05**; intense tropical/fig aromas, dominated by prominent 14.5% alc on palate; slight alc glow on dry finish. **Natural Sweet** ★★★★ **02** from gewürz not re-assessed; showed Turkish Delight, lemon notes with well-toned sweetness. 14.9% alc. —*AL*

Meerhof Winery

*Swartland ▪ Est/1stB 2000 ▪ Tasting & sales Mon-Fri 8.30–4.30 Sat 10–2 Pub hols 10–2 ▪ Closed Easter Fri-Sun, Dec 25 & Jan 1 ▪ Sun lunch (T 022·482·2088); also BYO picnic ▪ Functions for up to 100 by appt ▪ Tours by appt ▪ Owners Gert & Cobus Kotzé ▪ Vini consultant Wrensch Roux (Jan 2003) ▪ ±65 ha (cab, merlot, pinotage, shiraz, chard) ▪ ±320 tons 90% red 10% white ▪ PO Box 1229 Malmesbury 7299 ▪ meerhof@wcaccess.co.za ▪ www.meerhof.co.za ▪ **T (022) 487·2524** ▪ F (022) 487·2521*

Wrensch Roux is determined to keep producing wines that smack of the Swartland: 'Serious, concentrated, with the ability to age.' So he's thrilled with the 2005 vintage, whose dry conditions resulted in 'powerful wines'. These can now be tasted in the upgraded tasting area, perched on the crest of the Bothmaskloof Pass leading to the Riebeek Valley, or over Sunday lunch (by appointment) at the new Pieternella's Restaurant.

Shiraz Unmistakably 'Swrtlnd', **03** offers bulging berry basket of flavour, matching 14.8% alc & teeth-coating tannins. On current form, unfinished sample merits ★★★. Fr oak, 50% new, 22 mths. **Dry Red** new ★★ **05** (sample) cinsaut-based casual quaff with summer-ripe fruit & generous tannin courtesy pinotage, cab & merlot (each 20%). **Chardonnay** ★★ Unwooded **05** sample well-composed & flavourful; peach notes, bright acidity, clean dry finish. No new vintages of following available; notes from pvs ed: **Cabernet Sauvignon** ★★★ Focused & pure **02** sweet red-fruit aromas, firm slightly dry tannins. **Shiraz-Cabernet Sauvignon** ★★ **02** interesting layered bouquet of fresh-crushed berries, game & forest floor; lacks juice on palate; shortish dry finish. **Pinotage** ★★★ **01** well-shaped; full, fine flavours need time to soften, develop. **Rosé** ★★★ Pale fuchsia-hued **04** (sample), petally, refreshing & dry. Perfect for a hot summer's day. —*DH/JB*

Meerland see Baarsma

Meerlust Estate

Stellenbosch ▪ Est 1693 ▪ 1stB 1975 ▪ Tasting & sales Mon-Fri 9-4 Sat 10-2 ▪ Fee R20 ▪ Closed pub hols ▪ Owner Hannes Myburgh ▪ Cellarmaster Chris Williams (Jan 2004) ▪ Viticulturist Roelie Joubert, advised by Paul Wallace (both 2001) ▪ 110 ha (cabs s/f, merlot, pinot, chard) ▪ 600 tons ±50 000 cs 90% red 10% white ▪ PO Box 7121 Stellenbosch 7599 ▪ info@meerlust.co.za ▪ www.meerlust.co.za ▪ ***T 843·3587*** *▪ F 843·3274*

If there is an estate which can show the newcomers what the game is all about, it has to be this one, owned and farmed by eight generations of Myburghs. Their 'estate blend', Rubicon, is to many *the* iconic SA wine, a vinous national treasure whose future is now in the hands of thoughtful and intuitive Chris Williams. Asked to describe 'the Meerlust philosophy', the young winemaker's exposition is refreshingly empty of buzzwords and jargon. 'We strive,' he explains, 'to discover, accentuate and capture the true character of our vineyards in our wines. We believe this can be done by matching variety to site, by careful viticulture, correct crop yield, age and maturity of vines, fruit selection and harvesting at proper ripeness. In the cellar, minimum handling, traditional methods, the importance of time and the value of blending.' A judicious, time-honoured formula which, one senses, would have carried the approval of Simon van der Stel, the father of SA winemaking, under whose aegis Meerlust was born.

★★★★☆ **Rubicon** After 26 yrs, this ground-breaking bdx-style red still commands cachet & respect: voted 'SA's Most Prestigious Wine Internationally' & 'An SA Icon' by *Wine* readers in 2005; and, in emphatic local show-circuit debut, **00** awarded gold by both FCTWS & Swiss panels. Invariably cab dominated – 70% in current **01**, with 20% merlot, 10% cab f; shows strength of classic cab year: deep, dark fruits nose/flavour; powerful, rich (though retains hallmark moderate alc); still constrained by vibrant grainy tannins; mocha tones from new Fr oak (80%, 2 yrs) add class. Released end 2005, after Red below, needs much longer (min 5 yrs). **00** sleek & agreeably fresh; sufficient tannic grip to lay down until at least 2010.

★★★★ **Red** Occasional label, dusted off when vintage doesn't permit flagship quality. Essentially Rubicon in lighter, more approachable mode; good value at less than half the price. To date only three: **85**, **90**, current **02**. Still classy, impressively cab led (70% with merlot/cab f 20/10); oak sensitively handled to complement less intense though not insubstantial fruit. Should hold, if not improve, till 2008. Yr Fr oak.

★★★★ **Merlot** Always authoritative, never ostentatious. **01** epitome of refinement; 'modern classic' style. Deep, soft, dark berries/choc flavours; vibrancy, freshness promise a good evolution over remainder of decade. Arresting but ripe tannins better balanced than **00**, whose genteel, ripe tones were gripped by big dry tannins, demanding time. 18 mths Fr oak.

★★★★ **Pinot Noir** Since fuller-style **95**, some charming & convincing versions, including aromatic, accessible **99**. Latest **01** (★★★) less so: atypically sombre, sturdy & dense, with formidable dry tannins. May win over those who favour beefier style, but probably lacks usual potential to delight further with age. 50/50 Burgundian clones/BK5. **00** (★★★★☆) delicate, fleshy; structured tannins need yr/2 to unleash greater delights. 15 mths Fr oak (heavy-toast, tight-grain Allier). 14% alc.

★★★★ **Chardonnay** Quite a leap from **00**, featured in last ed, to current **03** (**01** sold out; no **02**); the interval marked by regime change (oaking reduced from 19 mths in Fr wood to only 12), earlier release date. Result is fresher feel, better-balanced fruit/oak, greater elegance; none at expense of signature roast hazelnut richness, sumptuous mouthfeel; in **03** also particularly notable savoury length. Graceful ageing possible till ±2008. Intended to be enjoyed with fine food.—*AL*

Meinert Wines

Stellenbosch (see Helderberg map) ▪ Est 1987 ▪ 1stB 1997 ▪ Tasting & sales at 96 Winery Road Restaurant (see Eat-out section) ▪ Owner Martin Meinert ▪ Winemaker Martin Meinert, with Allison Adams ▪ Vineyard/farm manager Henk Marconi ▪ 13.5 ha (cabs s/f, merlot, petit v, *pinotage) ▪ 70 tons 5 000 cs 100% red ▪ PO Box 7221 Stellenbosch 7599 ▪ info@meinertwines.com ▪ www.meinert.co.za ▪ **T/F 865·2363***

With veteran aide Henk Marconi and new assistant Allison Adams to rely on, Martin Meinert intends delegating much of the day-to-day running of his operation, and directing his energy towards marketing and non-wine activities. Reflecting on the bigger picture, in particular his 21 years in the industry, he says: 'I wish I could claim greater wisdom. Instead I am continually reminded how much remains to be learned.' His quest is for individual wines whose character expresses the Devon Valley sites, refining style to show more elegance, and striving for balance of fruit ripeness at lower alcohol levels. He also thinks his range could find room for a white, and winter will see the planting of sufficient semillon vines for about 300 cases.

★★★★☆ **Synchronicity** The standard-bearer, but nothing 'standard' about this ripe, rich & modern blend since maiden **00**. Sample **03** promises to match standout quality of **01** when finished; as with pvs, barrel-selected cab & merlot, with 15% pinotage in **03** – still smouldering mid-2005, the lip-smacking fruit & gum-numbing tannins suggest extraordinary pleasure around 2011. **01**, seamless ensemble of enduring length, boasted cab f (& only a dash of pinotage). No **02** (vintage not up to standard). 2 yrs new Fr oak. 15% alc.

★★★★ **Devon Crest** Gains its moniker from the home-farm; **03** restores form after lighter **02**. Brambly/leafy tones tantalise; the tense, gently austere structure should unfurl with beauty by 2010. **01** boasted 15% alc, latest now %. Cool s-facing vyds 10–14 yrs old; 69/31 cab/merlot blend. 18 mths new Fr oak.

★★★★ **Merlot** Urbane table companion, loaded with panache. Super black/red berry fruits of **03** woven with wood-smoke, ordered by tannins in final flourish. Yard up on **02**, which slighter than sumptuous **01**. Soupçon pinotage, cab. 18 mths older Fr oak.—*DS*

Mellasat

*Paarl ▪ Est 1996 ▪ 1stB 1999 ▪ Visits by appt, but encouraged ▪ Owner Stephen Richardson ▪ Winemaker/viticulturist Stephen Richardson, with Poena Malherbe ▪ 8 ha (cab, pinotage, shiraz, tempranillo, chenin) ▪ 50 tons 2 500 cs 85% red 15% white ▪ PO Box 7169 Paarl 7623 ▪ mellasat@mweb.co.za ▪ www.mellasat.com ▪ **T/F (021) 862·4525***

Having recently been served to Prince Charles, at Wimbledon and the Houses of Parliament in London, it should come as no surprise that Stephen Richardson's wines made their debut at the Nederburg Auction as well. A quest to produce lower-alcohol wines, and the conversion of a store into a bottle-maturation cellar (freeing up precious space for a temperature-controlled malo-room) has kept Norfolk-born Stephen B busy. However, his recent passion for golf, shared with viticulturist Poena Malherbe, is set to rob whatever free time may be left. Plans include an 'estate blend' under the Mellasat label and an expansion of the Dekker's Valley range for the value end of the market.

Cabernet Sauvignon ★★★ Chunky **03**, savoury & coffee/choc notes, lots of tannins needing time but enough fruit to go the distance. 15 mths Fr oak, none new. **Revelation** ★★★ Cab by another name; **02** individually styled – won't disappoint fans of this characterful winery. Unfiltered. 15 mths oak, 50/50 Fr/Am. **Pinotage** ★★★ **03** (sample) reprises house's wholesome earthiness, adds complexity to ripe plummy fruit, supple tannins. 22 mths Fr oak, 21% new. **Shiraz** Last tasted was work-in-progress **02**, showing improved tannin management, provisionally rated ★★★☆. 18 mths Am small-oak, 2nd fill. **03** sample too unformed to assess. **Tuin Wyn** ★★★ Straw wine from air-dried chenin grapes. None since **00**, which mellowed into velvety mouthful.

Dekker's Valley range

Their easy-drinking wines. **Dekker's Valley Chenin Blanc** ★★ **04** last ed was quietly tropical, soft, gentle & lightish bodied. **05** sample too young to rate. **Pinotage** discontinued.—*DH*

Merwespont Winery

Robertson (see map) ▪ Est 1956 ▪ Tasting & sales Mon-Thu 8-12.30; 1.30-5 Fri 8-12.30; 1.30-4.30 ▪ Closed pub hols ▪ Tours during harvest by appt ▪ BYO picnic ▪ Farm produce ▪ Owners 35 members ▪ Winemaker Esmarie Smuts (Jan 2002) ▪ Viti consultant Willem Botha (May 2005) ▪ 568 ha (cab, pinotage, ruby cab, shiraz, chard, sauvignon) ▪ 8 850 cs own labels 56% red 44% white ▪ PO Box 68 Bonnievale 6730 ▪ merwespont@lando.co.za ▪ ***T (023) 616·2800*** *▪ F (023) 616·2734*

A cellar's 50th birthday is a good reason to celebrate (and revamp its labels across the board). Also to reflect on future plans and priorities. 'Our goal is to introduce more modern technology every year,' says winemaker Esmarie Smuts, who is particularly proud of her two shiny-new cold-stabilisation tanks. 'Wine is made from a natural product, grapes, so to make the best possible wine, you have to retain as much fruit flavour as possible,' she explains.

Cabernet Sauvignon ★★★ Fast-forward to attractive **04** (sample), cool capsicum/cedar whiffs; soft, fleshy plum fruit, tannin brush on finish. Fr oak influenced. **Limited Release Cabernet Sauvignon-Merlot** ★★★ Two **03** SAYWS champs blended 80/20 & matured in 2nd fill Fr barrels, 8 mths; lovely rounded dark berry fruit, complementary oak, fine elegant tannins. **Limited Release Shiraz** new **04** regional Young Wine Show class winner; delicious soft chocolaty fruit, good wooding (11 mths Am/Fr), velvet texture. Promising sample should rate ★★★★ on release. **Chardonnay** ★★★ **04** last ed offered lovely melange of fresh fruit, hint kumquat, crisp & very fresh finish. **Sauvignon Blanc** ★★ **04**, now a finished product, flinty with hint capsicum; bone-dry & austere. **Agulhas White** ★★ Pvs ed noted as light, refreshing just-dry equal blend chenin, colombard, sauvignon. **NV**. Brde Rvr Vlly WO. This & Red in Agulhas range to be replaced with new bottlings below.

Ferry range new

Both sample **05**s. **Red** ★★ Earthy drink-young blend pinotage, ruby cab (60/40); boiled sweets on nose, dry savoury flavour. **White** ★★ Colombard/chenin 80/20; light, very brisk & dry; bracing style for mid-summer refreshment.
— IvH/JB

Merwida see Riverstone Vineyards

M'hudi Wines new

Stellenbosch ▪ Est/1stB 2003 ▪ Visits as for Villiera (see entry) ▪ Owners Rangaka family ▪ Winemakers Jeff Grier & Anton Smal, with Tseliso Rangaka (all 2004) ▪ Viticulturist Simon Grier (2004) ▪ 3 000 cs 33% red 67% white ▪ PO Box 66 Koelenhof 7605 ▪ wine@villiera.com ▪ www.villiera.com ▪ ***T 865·2002/3*** *▪ F 865·2314*

His parents' 2003 purchase of Klapmuts vegetable, fruit and wine farm Vredelust transformed Johannesburger Tseliso Rangaka overnight from a beer-drinking advertising copywriter into a tiller of soil and nurturer of vines. After 'hard lessons and rude awakenings' caused by scant farming experience and limited wine knowledge, Rangaka's partnership with neighbour Villiera has resulted in a trio of maiden wines. 'And if that's not something to smile about ...' Immediate plans include marriage to his lady of four years ('my life and all other aspirations probably depend on this!'); building M'hudi (Setswana for 'harvester') into a brand truly SA in character; and graduating from assistant to proper winemaker 'in the next 50 years or so.'

These all tank/barrel samples, all likely ★★★. **Pinotage** Big, cheerful **04** bruiser with nicely dry finish, but sweet ripe fruitiness jolted by powerful acidity. Yr in mix Am/Fr oak. 14.3% alc. This, following wine, WO Stbosch. **Chenin Blanc** Forward tropical fruit notes, hints honey & interesting earthiness. Rounded & fresh, but with rather hard acidity, big 14.8% alc. **Sauvignon Blanc 05** characterful, pleasant aromas/flavours of passion fruit, melon; bone dry & zippily balanced, 13.5% alc. WO Elim. — *TJ*

Middelpos

Swartland ▪ Est 1978 ▪ 1stB 2001 ▪ Tasting/sales at Bellevue & The Olive Boutique, Riebeek-Kasteel ▪ Owner Stephanus du Toit ▪ Vini/viti consultant Dirkie Morkel, with Wilhelm Kritzinger

▪ *57 ha* ▪ *100% red* ▪ *PO Box 59 Riebeek West 7306* ▪ *mariedut@mweb.co.za* ▪ ***T (022) 461·2375*** ▪ *F (022) 461·2042*

Stephanus du Toit and wife Marie, a crafter specialising in quilts, grow mainly reds on their farm in the Riebeek West area. A small quantity of their pinotage finds its way into bottle under the farm name via brother-in-law Dirkie Morkel of Bellevue. To date an 01.

Middelvlei Estate

Stellenbosch ▪ *Est 1919* ▪ *1stB 1973* ▪ *Tasting & sales Mon-Sat 10-4.30* ▪ *Fee R15* ▪ *Closed Easter Fri & Dec 25* ▪ *Combo cellar tour/barrel tasting Mon-Fri 11 & 3* ▪ *Small conference facility* ▪ *Walks* ▪ *Owners Momberg family* ▪ *Winemaker Tinnie Momberg (Jan 1992)* ▪ *Viticulturist Ben Momberg (Jan 1992)* ▪ *130 ha (cab, merlot, pinotage, shiraz, tinta, chard, sauvignon)* ▪ *1 000 tons 35 000 cs own labels 95% red 5% white* ▪ *PO Box 66 Stellenbosch 7599* ▪ *info@middelvlei.co.za* ▪ *www.middelvlei.co.za* ▪ ***T 883·2565*** ▪ *F 883·9546*

The goal some years down the road is to produce a wider variety of styles of wine. Concomitant with that is a wider appeal in a bigger market. The Mombergs of Middelvlei took the first steps down that road in 2005, with the acquisition of a new destemmer (result: softer wines with lower tannins), a new must-cooler (giving fruitier flavours) and a new refrigeration unit so that fermentation is better controlled. And that, they say, is just the beginning. Whew! was winemaker Tinnie M's take on 2005: 'It was difficult to keep up with personal milestones in a year so busy, that flew by so fast!'

★★★★ **Cabernet Sauvignon** Satisfying wine, shows a sense of place; still-listed **01** (★★★★) last ed noted as richer, better balanced than pvs, with characteristic austere note for food-partnering. 26 mths new wood. FCTWS gold. **00** was firmer & drier.

★★★★ **Shiraz** No follow-up yet to appealingly rustic **02**, which last yr had one's nose follow fascinating trail from gunsmoke through to hints of earth to forest floor, then to dense black plum on palate; 21 mths oak, 42% Am.

Pinotage ★★★ **03** seems determined to hide its pinotageness, but an appealing 'dry red' nonetheless; flavourful, balanced, even better in 2/3 yrs. 14 mths oak, mostly Fr. **Pinotage-Merlot** ★★★★ Understandably popular blend; again roughly equal proportions in **03**, oaky invitation (16 mths, 2nd fill), showy dark choc whiffs; firm, lingering savoury flavours. **Chardonnay** ★★★ **05** plump & jolly, rotund peachy fruit, extra softness from 30% stave-fermented portion, warming finish (14.5%).

Hagelsberg range

Literally 'Hail Mountain', allusion to Stbosch's Papegaaiberg. **Merlot** ★★★ new Bouncy dark-berried fruit on **04**, soft & well padded with supple tannins, quickish finish. Also in 3ℓ bag-in-box; all to Norway. **Robyn** ★★★ **03** fruitily unpretentious & warmly engaging blend tinta, cab, shiraz, pinotage – latter to fore last ed, with touch earthiness. For Germany & Holland. **Merlot-Pinotage** discontinued. – *IvH/TM*

Migliarina Wines

Stellenbosch ▪ *Est/1stB 2002* ▪ *Closed to public* ▪ *Owner/winemaker Carsten Migliarina* ▪ *500 cs 100% red* ▪ *PO Box 673 Stellenbosch 7599* ▪ *carsten@migliarina.co.za* ▪ *www.migliarina.co.za* ▪ ***T 072·233·4138***

After a few crushes at Mulderbosch and Ernie Els Wines, Carsten Migliarina chose a challenging year to go it alone and double his production. The 2005 harvest was tricky, with high alcohols, stressed vineyards and ferments which struggled due to nitrogen deficiencies. But he took it all in his stride and has pinpointed the vineyards which best express the style he's aiming for: more fruit and less oak.

Shiraz ★★★ **04** gentle ripe tannins & opulent berry fruit plumping out the mid-palate do little to soften a searing acidity. Fruit is obviously high quality, oaking has been empathetically managed, 13.8% alc is integrated; pity the acid balance seems out of kilter. – *IvH*

Migration-Serengeti see Leidersburg

Mike's Kitchen

*Head office: 298 Main Rd, Bryanston Ext 1, Sandton ▪ www.mikeskitchen.co.za ▪ **T (011) 463·9269** ▪ F (011) 463·9300*

Exclusive, easy-drinking range for the Gauteng-based restaurant chain returns to the guide after an extended break. Now made by Old Vines Cellars.

Reserve Red ★★★ Blend cab/merlot (70/30) from old vines, lightly wooded in Fr oak. **02** understandably with bottle-age aromas of forest floor, mushroom; palate vinous, food-friendly, as is 12.5% alc. **Classic White** ★★★ 100% chenin in **04**; fresh hay, wet wool & lemon aromas give way to restrained mineral palate, lifted by touch of sweetness. Modest 13.5% alc. **Stein Select** ★★★ From chenin, sweetish (16g/ℓ sugar) with honey, some wax, nuts & floral notes. All WO Coastal. —*CvZ*

Miles Mossop Wines new

*Stellenbosch ▪ Est/1stB 2004 ▪ Closed to public ▪ Owner/winemaker Miles Mossop ▪ 10 tons 700 cs 72% red 28% white ▪ PO Box 7339 Stellenbosch 7599 ▪ sam.jam@mweb.co.za **T 082·413·4335** ▪ F 875·5292*

It's all in the family for Tokara winemaker Miles Mossop, son of Axe Hill wine-man Tony, who has grabbed the opportunity to crush 10 tons of grapes for his own label each year. His first-born, daughter Saskia-Jo, has provided the obvious name for his first release, a white blend, while the arrival of son Max in June last year provided an equally convenient (though at press time unconfirmed) name for a Bordeaux-style blend, due for release this year.

★★★★ **Saskia** Impressive new-generation white blend from impressive new-generation winemaker. **04** chenin leads on paper (67%), though in glass viognier's deluxe apricot tones set pace. Marriage sumptuous hedonism, sleek, dry sophistication; liaison perfected with subtle oaking. Ideal Thai food partner. Native yeast fermented in Burgundy barrels, 20% new; 10 mths matured. Stbosch/Paarl vyds.

'Bordeaux Blend' (To be named) **04** ex-barrel (unrated) effective 21% petit v component lends freshening violet resonance to more familiar cab/merlot scents (58/21). Tight, elegant, full flavoured, with Mossop trademark polished oaking. Same class as above wine. Merlot ex-Paarl; balance Stbosch. —*AL*

Millberg see Franschhoek Vineyards
Millbrook see Arlington
Millers Thumb see Ruitersvlei

Millstream

Range by DGB for export chiefly to the UK, Ireland and the Netherlands. Available locally at News Café branches.

Pinotage ★★★ Balanced easy-drinker; **03** last ed had attractive earthy touch; plump, dry savoury flavours. **Cinsault-Ruby Cabernet** ★★★ Ripely appealing 50/50 melange in **04**, brambly/smoky whiffs, seamless carry-through to red-fruit palate. **Rosé** ★★ **05** strawberry & toffee apple whiffs, lively, uncomplex, lower alc (13.2%) than last. **Chardonnay** ★★★ **05** not tasted. **03** appealed widely with peaches & cream aromas, perky lemon-peach fruit. **Chenin Blanc** ★★★ Lightish **05**, casual-quaffing dry white, some melon fruit, not-too-dry finish. All WO W Cape. —*DH*

Milton Grove see African Terroir

Minke Wines new

*Stellenbosch ▪ Closed to public ▪ Owner Henry Davel ▪ **T 083·273·4561***

'My first wine, but definitely not the last,' promises medical doctor and Cape Wine Master Henry Davel on the debut of his own-label Pinot Noir, from the 2004 vintage (unavailable to us at press time). Made at Muratie to phenomenally precise specs – insistence on the fruity 777 clone probably the least onerous. There are just 80 cases of hand-filled/labelled bottles named after the minke whale, 'smallest and most delicate of the species' (Davel's granddaughter shares the moniker). The man's persuasive powers are clearly substantial, given his source: Vriesenhof's Jan Coetzee, who prefers 777 over other clones even for coq au vin.

Mischa Estate

Wellington ▪ Est/1stB 1999 ▪ Tasting, sales & tours (incl vine nurseries in summer) by appt ▪ Fee R200, waived if 6+ btls purchased ▪ Closed pub hols ▪ Snacks & meals by appt ▪ Walks ▪ Mountain biking ▪ Owners JH & JA Barns ▪ Winemaker Andrew Barns (Jan 1999) ▪ Viticulturist Ruiter Smit (Jun 1960) ▪ 40 ha (cab, merlot, shiraz) ▪ 60 tons 3 000 cs own label 100% red ▪ PO Box 163 Wellington 7654 ▪ mischaestate@telkomsa.net ▪ www.mischa.co.za ▪ ***T 864·1016/19/20*** *▪ F 864·2312*

'Andrew hasn't gone completely mad yet,' chortle this team as they contemplate the past year's highlights for winemaker Andrew Barns. But he's laughing too, after the excitement of producing this Wellington winery-and-vine-nursery's first own-label white, the Eventide Viognier. And that, they're relieved to report, is as exciting as it got in 2005: 'The only thing worth mentioning is that this was our first harvest without incident. We remain committed to minimal intervention and environmentally sensitive vineyard practice, but due to lower yields one can expect fuller more concentrated wines, hopefully displaying good character.'

★★★☆ **Cabernet Sauvignon 03** (★★★★☆) shows characteristic blueberry signature of poised Wllngton cab; extreme elegance; full (14% alc), concentrated yet finely balanced. Idiosyncratic, too. In same vein as extraordinarily scented **02** – currants, satsuma plum jam – pointing to ripeness here.

★★★★ **Shiraz** Quintessential hot-climate shiraz; **03** spice & pungent sweetness, big, bodice-ripping flavours & 15% alc. Worthy successor to **02**, well built & muscular, with ripe tannins. Yr tight grain Fr oak.

Merlot ★★★☆ **03** exotic minerals & earth, spicy red fruit & olivaceous character. More exciting than pvs. Yr Fr barriques. Alc a restrained 13.5%.

Eventide range

★★★☆ **Cabernet Sauvignon 03** (★★★★) a lunchtime cab: accessible 13.5% alc & attractive floral nose with sweet luscious fruit. **02** warm porty fruit, soft irresistible palate, slight sweetness from alc.

Merlot new ★★★ **03** sour cherries with dominant acids, lightish palate, lunchtime-suitable 12.6% alc. **Shiraz** ★★★☆ Vanilla-dominated **03**, simple red fruit flavours, some spice & leather. Fat 14.3% alc. **Viognier** new ★★★☆ **05** spicy with curry leaf hint, rich opulent fruit, 13.7% alc & good length. – *NP*

Misty Point see Southern Cape Vineyards

Monis Wines

Paarl ▪ Est 1906 ▪ Closed to public ▪ Owner Distell ▪ Winemaker Dirkie Christowitz (Aug 1979) ▪ 22 000 cs 100% fortifieds ▪ PO Box 266 Paarl 7620 ▪ dchristowitz@distell.co.za ▪ www.distell.co.za ▪ ***T 860·1601*** *▪ F 872·2790*

To 'enhance its standing and better reflect conditions of spectacular vintages', the VO Tawny Port from this, the Cape's oldest fortified-wine house, has been renamed to simply 'Tawny Port'. It remains vintage-dated, which is unusual for this style

★★★★☆ **Muscadel** ✓ Venerable **92** has garnered as many admirers as show gongs (2000 VDG; gold 2001 Muscats of the World, France, Best Muscat trophy 2002 FCTWS, ★★★★☆ *Wine*) during unpretentious tenure. Mid-2004 was scintillating amber gaining tawny tints, expansive raisin fruit fully integrated, sensual silkiness holding.

★★★★ **Tawny Port** Hero of many competitions (including Veritas, Peter Schultz, FCTWS). Recent versions slightly drier (_g/ℓ sugar), less spirituous (18% alc), shorter time in wood (now 8.5 yrs), so current **96** unexpectedly sweet (109g/ℓ RS). Complex bouquet of spice, burnt caramel, nuts & dried fruit; slippery tail. Paarlberg tinta/cinsaut grapes. **95** (★★★☆) marzipan nose adds icing to Xmas cake tone, venison-pie/pipe tobacco nuances for interest. – *CvZ*

Mons Ruber Estate

*Little Karoo ▪ Est ca 1850 ▪ Tasting & sales Mon-Fri 9-5 Sat 9-1 ▪ Closed Easter Sun & Dec 25 ▪ Self-catering overnight accommodation ▪ Estate produce for sale ▪ Hiking trail in proclaimed conservation area ▪ Owners Radé & Erhard Meyer ▪ Winemaker Radé Meyer ▪ Viti consultant Willem Botha ▪ 38 ha (cab, muscadels r/w, chard, chenin, hanepoot, palomino) ▪ ±500 tons 10 000 cs own label 50% red 50% white ▪ PO Box 1585 Oudtshoorn 6620 ▪ monsruber@lantic.net ▪ www.geocities.com/monsr_za ▪ **T/F (044) 251·6550***

It's the muscadel which excels on this ostrich and wine farm in the Little Karoo. The quest being for quality, the plans for the winery are too long to list: replacement of wine tanks, more cooling capacity, bottling equipment ... An urgent task is to replant old vineyards, to which end new cabernet and chardonnay rows are being established. 'Is having a little more free time an acceptable goal?' muses winemaker Radé Meyer. His Majesty's Quarters, a whimsical reference to the British royal family's visit in 1947, is their self-catering accommodation, 'fit for a king'.

Cabernet Sauvignon ★★★ Last tasted was unoaked **00**, lightish, soft, plummy mouthful. **Conari** ★★★ Uncertified/unvintaged cab, usually light casual quaffing, could be chilled. Not retasted. **Chardonnay** ★★ Maiden **02** still selling ex-cellar; hints ginger & honey; full smoky herbal flavours. **Vino** ★★ **NV**, but 03 (chardonnay), last ed showed bottle-age honey & hints of peach; light, soft, toasted nut flavours. **White Muscadel Jerepigo** ★★★★ ✓ **02** fortified turning striking bronze shade last yr; fragrant honeysuckle, grape & Turkish Delight aromas. Lightish 15.3% alc nicely balanced, gives creamy effect. **Regalis** ★★★ Current bottling (**NV**, 03) of fortified white muscadel sweeter, more unctuous than version above, less muscat character, caramel & tea-leaf on finish. 16.7% alc. **Hanepoot Jerepigo** ★★★ **04** rich, ripe & grapey, lovely balanced acid & spirituous lift. 16.5% alc. Alternative label: Bonitas. **Sultana Jerepigo** ★★ **04** first in guide since **99**, retains slight nutty character with hints honey & liquorice, silky smooth & distinctly sweet. 16.5% alc. **Cabernet Sauvignon Jerepigo** ★★★ Unusual dessert. Caramelised sugar, herbs & rhubarb hints on **04** (under alternative name, Elegantia), unusually sweet & rustic this yr. 16% alc. **Red Muscadel Jerepigo** ★★★ Velvet-smooth fortified dessert with unmistakable muscat tones; **02** sweet waxy/floral bouquet, muscat character growing somewhat less overt last ed. 17.7% alc. **Muscadel Liqueur** new ★★★ One of the individual, long-matured fortifieds gleaned from the depths of Radé Meyer's cellar (last was Elusivo 89 (!); sample **97** glistening tawny depths, treacle-like texture, powerfully sweet with sherry-like feel. 9 yrs oak, only 400 × 375ml btls. **Port** ★★★ Mellow tawny style, less sweet than many traditional Cape ports; from cab; same blend as last yr (98, 99, 00) not retasted. ±17% alc. Mature-looking russet-ruby, stewed fruit & mocha hints. — *MM/TM*

Montagu Winery

*Little Karoo ▪ Est 1941 ▪ 1stB 1975 ▪ Tasting & sales Mon-Fri 8-12.30; 1.30-5 Sat 9-12 ▪ Closed pub hols ▪ Tours by appt during harvest ▪ BYO picnic ▪ Owners 68 members ▪ Winemaker Sonnie Malan , with Collin Wright (Jan 1972/1990) ▪ Viti consultant Willem Botha ▪ 660 ha (cab, merlot, muscadel, shiraz, chard, chenin, colombard) ▪ ±12 000 tons 5 000 cs own label ▪ 10% red 40% white 50% muscadel ▪ PO Box 29 Montagu 6720 ▪ mkwkelder@lando.co.za ▪ **T (023) 614·1125** ▪ F (023) 614·1793*

No update available on this winery; contact details from previous edition.

Mont Destin

*Paarl ▪ Est/1stB 1998 ▪ Visits by appt ▪ Owners Ernest & Samantha Bürgin ▪ Winemaker Samantha Bürgin, advised by Bruwer Raats (Jan 2002/Jan 2003) ▪ Viticulturist André van den Berg (Jan 2000), advised by Johan Wiese ▪ 7 ha (cab, cinsaut, grenache, mourvèdre, shiraz, viognier) ▪ 15 tons 1 000 cs 80% red 20% white ▪ PO Box 1237 Stellenbosch 7599 ▪ info@montdestin.co.za ▪ www.montdestin.co.za ▪ **T 083·288·4985** ▪ F 875·5870*

Richer a son, sonorously named Destin Saint-James, Ernest and Samantha Bürgin are building a micro-cellar (it will crush only 15 tons) on their Simonsberg property. A dream home is going up alongside, also inspired by Mexican architect Luis Barragan. By keeping quantities low, they say, they're better able to devote attention to detail, like bunch-sorting before destemming and berry-sorting afterwards. Their goal is to continue repeating the success of their first Destiny Shiraz, demand for which far outstripped limited supply.

★★★★ **1482** Variable blend shiraz, merlot & cab, proportions guided by vintage. Shiraz (55%) heads **03** (★★★☆), its lily/black pepper tones dominate on nose; palate as yet unknit, so tannins appear rather firm & savoury. Fr oak, 20 mths, 30% new. **02** saw merlot upfront (81%), imparting dark-berried richness, though not quite the density & opulence of **01** (★★★★☆) equal cab, merlot, with 20% shiraz.

★★★☆ **Destiny Shiraz** Strikingly packaged, handmade limited release – only 300 btls of **02**, which earned *Wine* ★★★★. Gutsy **03** (★★★★) in same artisanal, personality-packed mould: leather/resin aromas cavort with black fruit; tannins (from 20 mths new Fr/Am oak) still furry but plenty of fleshy cushioning available. Relatively plentiful 800 btls. 15.5% alc.

Chenin Blanc ★★★☆ ✓ Unwooded chenin from 3 different blocks; 3 mths *sur lie*. **05** delicate citrus & nut aromas; similar palate with lees-enriched core. At 14.5% alc more powerful, weightier than pvs, but also with 2-3 yrs staying power. WO Coastal. **Bushvine Pinotage** & **CMS** discontinued. – *CvZ*

Mont d'Or see Makro

Mont du Toit Kelder

Wellington ▪ Est 1996 ▪ 1stB 1998 ▪ Tasting & sales by appt ▪ Owner Stephan du Toit ▪ Winemaker/viticulturist Pieter-Niel Rossouw (Jan 2000), advised by Bernd Philippi (1997) ▪ 26 ha (alicante bouschet, cabs s/f, merlot, petit v, tinta r, shiraz & mourvèdre) ▪ ±130 tons ±10 000 cs 100% red ▪ PO Box 704 Wellington 7654 ▪ kelder@montdutoit.co.za ▪ www.montdutoit.co.za ▪ ***T 873·7745*** *▪ F 864·2737*

Stephan du Toit says he got a bit of a fright when an unexpected pre-harvest rainstorm threatened his crop. But luckily no damage was done and late-ripeners like cab are looking good. Good news, especially as this Johannesburg-based lawyer has just launched another take on the Cape red blend: the handsomely named Les Coteaux Mont du Toit. He's sticking to traditional methods, applying more punch-downs for greater extraction. And Pieter-Niel Rossouw has taken charge of both vineyards and cellar for a more integrated approach to the business of winemaking. Asked what he regards as success, Du Toit pronounces: 'Survival in a tough market!'

★★★★☆ **Le Sommet** Ambitiously priced, deep dark & inscrutable **02** still holding a lot back: dignified unfolding like watching an eagle prepare to fly. Concentrated black cherry, touches roast beef, oak char. Sweetness of ripe fruit & alc (15%), ripe tannins to balance, easily absorbed by massive fruit, still musters elegance. Blend unspecified, certainly features shiraz. 2 yrs oak, 70% new, 75% Fr, balance east Eur, Am. Cellar 5-7 yrs.

★★★★ **Mont du Toit** Blend varies – usually cab, merlot, shiraz, cab f, but winemaker coy! Plush black velvet texture on **03**, cab evident, but in big boned, warm-climate generous mode; spicy tannic grip balanced, should unfold with ease. Ripe, plummy **02** with soft, ultra-ripe tannins. 2 yrs oak (±30% new) imparting loads of spice. These deserve 4-6 yr wait.

Les Coteaux new ★★★☆ **03** positioned between Hawequas & the summit, adds a rung to scale of affordability. Also adds shiraz, more approachable than wine below; well rounded, generous feel, tannins unintimidating – but no pushover, should last 3-5 yrs. **Hawequas** ★★★ **03** back to more traditional formula cab/merlot (often shiraz sneaks in), & takes on new seriousness. Good whiff classy oak (16 mths), ripe cassis with ripe tannins to match, lengthy finish with faint bitterness? All these Wllngton/Kmuts fruit; WO Coastal. – *IvH*

Monterosso Estate

Stellenbosch ▪ Est/1stB 2000 ▪ Tasting & sales Mon-Sat 8.30-12.30; 1.30-5 ▪ Closed Easter Fri/Mon, Apr 27, May 1, Jun 16, Dec 25 & Jan 1 ▪ Tours by appt ▪ Owners Socrate, Orneglio & Francesco De Franchi ▪ Winemaker Orneglio De Franchi (Jan 2000) ▪ Viticulturist Francesco

*De Franchi ▪ 68 ha (cab, merlot, pinotage, sangiovese, chard, sauvignon, semillon) ▪ 1 800 cs own label 80% red 20% white ▪ PO Box 5 Stellenbosch 7599 ▪ monterosso@mweb.co.za ▪ **T/F 889·5021***

At this family *fattoria*, Francesco and Orgnelio ('Meaty') De Franchi have been making steady progress. 'Baby steps,' the brothers hasten to add, 'we haven't started marketing yet.' Nonetheless, their first two vintages sold out quickly, mainly through word of mouth. Phase three of the cellar completed, they purchased a 10 000-litre white-wine fermenter and additional barriques. Their maiden Sangiovese (03), from immature vines, was lighter in colour than they'd hoped, so in subsequent vintages they dropped 50% of the crop and successfully upped the intensity. Another excitement was the bottling of their first Chenin, made from bushvines which turned 45 last year.

Cabernet Sauvignon-Merlot ★★★ Sinewy rather than 'meaty', shows an attractive handcrafted rusticity. **02** shy black fruit aroma & flavours, austere tannins; lengthy, balanced goodbye. Fermented/matured 16 mths Fr oak (mix old/new). **Sangiovese 'Socrate'** new ★★★ Welcome alternative to the Cape's French-dominated varietal palette; honours the De F paterfamilias. **03** oak-soaked nose & bitter-cherry flavours; authentic Italian dry, tannic finish. Italian yeasts; 14-16 mths 2nd fill wood. **Old Bush Vine Chenin Blanc** new ★★★★ Enticing almond, pear, white peach whiffs off **05**, zesty acidity; persistent & elegant mineral finish. **Sauvignon Blanc** ★★★ **05** characterful quaffer with shy lemon blossom/bubble gum nose & refreshing palate. 13.5% alc, though not high, a touch obtrusive. — *CvZ*

Montestell see Boland Kelder

Montpellier

*Tulbagh ▪ Est ca 1950 ▪ 1stB ca 1968 ▪ Tasting, sales & tours daily 9-12; 2-5 Sat 9-12 ▪ Farm-style guest house ▪ Facilities for children ▪ Tourgroups ▪ BYO picnic ▪ Conferencing ▪ Farm-style guest house ▪ Owner Lucas J van Tonder ▪ Winemaker Anton Krynauw (Jan 2003) ▪ Viti consultant Gawie Kriel (Apr 2003) ▪ 50 ha (11 varieties, mainly white) ▪ 300 tons 10 000 cs 30% red 70% white ▪ PO Box 79 Tulbagh 6820 ▪ montpellierwine@tiscali.co.za ▪ www.montpellier.co.za ▪ **T (023) 230·0723/0656** ▪ **F** (023) 230·0656*

Trademark disputes between two neighbouring Tulbagh wine farms and the Montpellier name were resolved in 2005, with Johannesburg advocate Lucas van Tonder now owning both properties (see also newly named Montpellier du Sud/Constantia de Tulbagh). Renovation of the original Montpellier farm, granted to a French Huguenot in 1714 and featuring a Cape Dutch manor house (now a gracious guest house) continues. Also major replanting to mostly noble reds (in the planning are grenache, malbec, nebbiolo, chardonnay and viognier). The aim is to scale down quantity while upping quality (which includes upgrading the cellar). Early results include promising shiraz and mourvèdre from the prime hilltop 'Chapel Vineyard', and increased MCC production.

Cabernet Sauvignon ★★★ Unpretentious braai buddy; **04** generous cassis/choc mouthful; gently firm dry tannins. 8 mths 2nd fill Fr oak. **Pinot Noir** ★ **02**'s ethereal colour last ed belied immense body (15.5% alc); savoury/forest floor aromas, soft texture. **Blanc de Noir** ★★ Soft, pale strawberry looks/tastes; **05** bled from pinot juice & vinified as white. **Chardonnay** ★ Unwooded **05** sweet & unsubtle, some over-ripe apricot character. **Chenin Blanc** ★★ Simple guava-fragrant quaffer, **05** short on concentration despite high alc (14.5%). **Pinot Noir Blanc** Last was unrated **02**; **05** not ready for tasting. **Weisser Riesling** ★★ Minerally & dry **02**, last ed was gaining more pronounced terpene tone; lightish & soft palate. **Private Reserve** ★★★ Perfumed **02** last ed wafted rose-petals, light body, good balance, soft finish; from gewürz, colombard, clairette. **Port** ★ new More correctly named 'sweet fortified red'; ethereal in all respects (16.5% alc). **NV**. — *JP*

Montpellier du Sud/Constantia de Tulbagh

Tulbagh ▪ Est 1965 ▪ 1stB 2000 ▪ Visits by appt ▪ Owner Lucas J van Tonder ▪ 35 ha (cab, merlot, pinot, chenin, riesling, sauvignon) ▪ 3-5 000 cs own label 15% red 80% white 5% blanc de noir • PO Box 79 Tulbagh 6820 • montpellierwine@tiscali.co.za • www.montpellier.co.za • ***T (023) 230·0723/230·0656/083 353 8688*** *•* ***F*** *(023) 230·0656*

This 330ha property, originally known as Constantia, is now owned by Johannesburg advocate Lucas van Tonder (he also owns neighbouring Montpellier). Extensive renovations are under way; visitors are welcomed by imposing gates and an avenue of 300 plane trees. The cellar has been upgraded to handle 600 tons from well-drained, rocky hillside sites – à la Châteauneuf-du-Pape, says Lucas vT – due for extensive planting. The intention is to create a range of hand-crafted wines under the Constantia de Tulbagh label. Building blocks include sauvignon, chardonnay, chenin, riesling, cab, merlot, shiraz and pinot.

Merlot ★ **02** dark fruit & stalky/herbaceous notes, demandingly dry tannins. Yr 2nd fill Fr oak. **Pinot Noir** Old oak aged **04** oxidised, with meaty whiffs. **Chenin Blanc** Our samples of **04** unrateable. **Weisser Riesling 04** untasted. **Méthode Cap Classique** ☆ **NV** from riesling; oxidised style, lacking freshness, coarse bubbles add some life. – *JP*

Mont Rochelle Mountain Vineyards

Franschhoek • 1stB 1996 • Tasting & sales Mon-Sun 10-6 • Fee R15 • Closed Easter Sun/Mon, Dec 25/26 • Tours 11, 12.30 & 3 • Cheese platters; picnics & gourmet tastings by appt • Functions & events • Farm produce • Art gallery • Owner Miko Rwayitare • Winemaker Anneke du Plessis • Viticulturist Pieter Botha • 19 ha (cab, merlot, chard, sauvignon) • 10 000 cs own label 50% red 50% white • ISO 14001 certified • PO Box 334 Franschhoek 7690 • info@montrochelle.co.za • www.montrochelle.co.za • ***T 876·3000*** *• F 876·2362*

With one of the finest Franschhoek Valley views, Mont Rochelle hopes to re-establish its 'country estate' charm to attract wine lovers and visitors alike. With business commitments keeping owner, Congolese-born telecoms entrepreneur Miko Rwayitare, in Gauteng, the farm's management has been handed over to La Couronne. Tapping into its neighbour's infrastructure, Mont Rochelle now combines cellar tours with food-and-wine tastings and al fresco terrace meals, and caters for special functions. A fresh focus on quality (and probable drop in wine volumes) inspired a cellar refurbishment (with Anneke du Plessis now resident) and closer attention to vineyards (under new man Pieter Botha).

★★★☆ **Syrah** Elegantly hedonistic **03** (★★★★) sourced from Paarl area (as was pvs), marvellously rich black cherry fruit layered with cinnamon & woodsmoke. As deliciously smooth & fine-grained as **02**, with more savoury/meaty character. 20 mths Fr oak.

★★★★ **Oak-Matured Chardonnay 03** unready. **02** at best was full, richly textured, nutty & complex; retasted mid-2004, tiring, needed drinking soon. 10 mths oak, 30% new.

★★★★ **Natural Chardonnay** ✓ Unwooded version with more interest than many. Medium-bodied **05** (★★★☆) shorter lees lie-in (2 mths) for zestier/fruitier (if less complex) profile; lovely apricot/lime flavours, concentrated & rounded, enduring. **03** showed smoky, buttery notes, as if wooded, gutsy 14.5% alc.

Cabernet Sauvignon ★★★☆ **03** too unformed to rate. **02** in now familiar style – minty fragrance, hints sage, fennel; ripe mulberry & dark choc intensity. Should hold another 4-6 yrs. **Merlot** ★★☆ **03** very stern & unyielding, nothing like plump & velvety pvs; oak as for Syrah. **Alchemy** ★★★☆ To date maiden **02**, blend cabs s/f, merlot, shiraz, pinotage. Mid-2004 nascent savoury/meaty, dried biltong notes, smooth & supple. 15 mths oak. Should keep few more yrs. **Merlot-Cabernet Sauvignon** new Promising debut. Sample **03** fragrant & rich choc, cassis & balsamic notes; components (60/40) seamlessly melded. Ripe, glossy tannins show 7-8 yr potential. **Sauvignon Blanc Reserve** new ★★☆ Marginally more concentrated, zingy than below; clean, light bodied, easy to drink. **Sauvignon Blanc** ★★ **05** from Wllngtn fruit, lighter all-round; whiff gooseberry, soft texture, modest 12.5% alc. Mainly W Cape origin. – *IvH*

Mooiberge see African Terroir

Mooi Bly Winery

Paarl • Est/1stB 2003 • 'Vine to wine tour' appt (see intro) • Self-catering cottages (see Stay-over section) • Owner Luc Wouters • Winemakers Erik Schouteden & Theunis van Zyl, with consultants • Viticulturists Erik Schouteden & Theunis van Zyl • 19 ha (cabs s/f, malbec, petit v, tannat, chard, chenin) ▪ 95 tons 1 400 cs own label + 40 000ℓ bulk ▪ 35% red 65% white ▪ PO Box 801 Huguenot 7645 ▪ info@mooibly.com ▪ www.mooibly.com ▪ ***T 868·2808/ 082·371·2299*** *▪ F 868·2808*

Now that they're making all their wine in their own cellar, you can expect more than a traditional tasting at Mooi Bly Winery. 'We offer a vine to wine tour,' beams farm manager Erik Schouteden. 'In this the winemaker takes you from the vineyards to the cellar and eventually a wine tasting with some nibbles and bites. The whole tour takes two hours and is by appointment only.' With tannat, malbec, petit verdot and cabernet franc having recently been planted for blending purposes, there'll be much more red wine to complement the Chenin and Chardonnay in future.

Chardonnay new ★★★ **05** makes a pleasing debut. Lime & dessert island fruits enriched by toast & butter aromas & flavours. Round, full palate from 14% alc & 4 mths on lees, judicious oaking. Lingering, dry finish. **Chenin Blanc** ★★☆ **05** brimful of sunny fruit: melons, guavas, pineapples & other tropical delights. Plump palate, thanks in part to 13% alc, given focus by tangy acidity & crunchy, persistent finish. *— IvH*

Mooiplaas Estate

Stellenbosch ▪ Est 1963 ▪ 1stB 1995 ▪ Tasting & sales Mon-Fri 9-4 Sat & pub hols 10-2 ▪ Closed Easter Fri-Mon, Dec 25/26 & Jan 1 ▪ Fee R10 refundable with purchase ▪ BYO picnic ▪ Conservation area ▪ Owner Mooiplaas Trust ▪ Winemaker Louis Roos (1983) ▪ Viticulturist Tielman Roos (1980) ▪ ±120 ha ▪ 750 tons 8 000 cs own label 57% red 43% white ▪ PO Box 104 Koelenhof 7605 ▪ info@mooiplaas.co.za ▪ www.mooiplaas.co.za ▪ ***T 903·6273*** *▪ F 903·3474*

Celebrations last year at the Roos family estate in Stellenbosch's Bottelary Hills area, on the occasion of the 10th anniversary of their brand (launched with the 95 Cab) and the Veritas double-gold medal awarded their 02 Shiraz. Further gratifying news from winemaker Louis Roos, who is 'pleasantly surprised' by the quality of the 05 wines, specially the Cab, Shiraz and Sauvignon. The introduction of two new varietal bottlings, a Merlot and Chenin (latter untasted for this ed), adds to the upbeat mood. A Johannesburg-based Roos, Louis and viticulturist Tielman's sister Illse, has been roped in to help with upcountry marketing.

★★★★ **Cabernet Sauvignon** Always released with a few yrs on them – a welcome bonus these days. Often take in other varieties for balance's sake: **01** has 10% merlot, 4% shiraz. With lovely aromas of blackcurrant, cedar, profile recalls muscular, rich **00**: ripe, fresh fruit, big & dry but juicy tannins, savoury lingering finish. 2 yrs oak, mostly Fr, 40% new. Fine, honest wine that should see out its decade.

★★★★ **Pinotage 01** was fresh, fruity, sleek; pinotage lushness touched with elegance. Difficult year showing in slightly less charming **02** (★★★☆), whose pleasant darkly bright fruit tinged with sombre green notes. 6% 00 oaked cab added in – remainder unoaked. Serious but approachable tannins.

Merlot new ★★★☆ **02** has 10% cab. Made in serious style, even touch severe in youth, showing lots of tobacco notes, big dry tannins. **Shiraz** ★★★☆ **02** (not retasted) broad, ripe, savoury, with subtle blackcurrant & leather notes; good acid, ripe tannin. 18 mths oak, mostly Fr, 60% new. 15.1% alc. Should keep happily 5+ yrs. 20 mths Fr oak, 9% new. **Sauvignon Blanc** ★★★☆ Tank sample **05** promises usual fresh suppleness, satisfyingly mixing sharp green element (peppers, greengage) with tropical fruit roundness. *— TJ*

Mooiuitsig Wine Cellars

Robertson ▪ Est 1947 ▪ Sales Mon-Thu 8-5 Fri 8-3 ▪ Tours by appt ▪ Stay-overs at De Rust Lodge: info@outdoorarena.co.za ▪ T (023) 616·2444 ▪ Owners Jonker & Claassen families ▪ Winemaker Christiaan van Tonder, with Nico van der Westhuizen (Dec 2002/Feb 2003) ▪ Viticulturist Casper Matthee ▪ 2 500 tons ▪ PO Box 15 Bonnievale 6730 ▪ info@mooiuitsig.co.za ▪ www.mooiuitsig.co.za ▪ ***T (023) 616·2143*** *▪ F (023) 616·2675*

A youthful 79, Boet Jonker (respectfully known as 'Oom') is still master blender at Mooiuitsig, the farm he established with his father in 1947. No longer part of the furniture is Kobus Oosthuizen, who has moved on after a mere 24 years, handing the manager's baton to Marius Burger. Marius B's extensive experience in exports (for Lanzerac and Lourensford) will be employed to expand the marketing focus, which has previously been predominantly domestic. They've adopted a new strategy of producing smaller volumes of premium noble-variety wines from individual vineyard blocks, which they hope will bring them into line with other quality producers in the region.

African Wine Adventure range

No mistaking the Afro-theme here: zebra stripes blazoned on cork as well as label. **Red** ★★☆ **04** light, dusty-dry equal blend cab/merlot with treacle-like hints. **White** ★★☆ Latest (05) not ready; pvs **NV** honest to goodness light dry white from sauvignon, chardonnay (70/30).

Mooiuitzicht range

Overberger ★★ Charmingly subtitled 'Opwindende Witwyn' ('Exciting White Wine') – with some accuracy in **05**, thanks to lively acidity to offset the 9g/ℓ sugar. **Vin Brut** ★ Light-bodied, bone-dry carbonated sparkling from sauvignon. Same variety for ... **Vin Doux** ★★ Spritz rather than full-blown fizz, tropical flavours & gentle sweetness. Following fortified desserts all **NV**; fortified to ±17.5% alc. Not retasted; notes from pvs ed: **Marsala** ★ Spirity red from 'various sweet-wine varieties'. **Nagmaalwyn** (Sacramental Wine) ★★★ Light mahogany colour; pleasant porty character & sweet prune flavours. **Hanepoot** ★★ Sunshine-yellow dessert with low-key sweetness; 'great winter companion' winemakers say. **Old Tawny Port** ★ Wood-matured, with traditional-style low alc. **Bonwin Ruby Dessert Wine** ★☆ Hues nearer mahogany than ruby; rounded & sweet.

Oude Rust range

Certified desserts, fortified to ±17.5% alc. Not retasted; notes from pvs ed: **Red Muscadel** ★★★ **03** pale bronze-pink; gentle liqueur-like palate; more refreshing, sprightly than pvs. **Sweet Hanepoot** ★★☆ Light golden glints to unctuous, warming **01**. **White Muscadel** ★★☆ Early-drinking style. **02** attractive, with honeysuckle scents, lemon freshness to its smooth length.

Rusthof range

Oulap Se Rooi ☺ ★★★ Fun label for this lightly-oaked blend cab, merlot, pinotage, sweet-fruited & juicy. Styled to enjoy with a traditional potjie. Also in more conventional attire as Dry Red.

These cork-closed wines all **NV**. **Rosé** ★☆ Slight berry-like tone on palate but otherwise straightforward semi-sweet. **Premier Grand Cru** ★★☆ Light, flinty thirst-quencher from chardonnay, sauvignon, chenin; brisk racy finish. **Blanc de Blanc** ★★ Slightly sweeter version of PGC. **Potjie Effe Droog** ★★ Similar to BdB; marketed in 500ml screwtop. **Late Harvest** ★☆ Light semi-sweet with subtle caramel tone, varieties as for BdB. All ranges mainly own, Brde Rvr Vlly vyds. **Clemence Creek** range discontinued. *—DH/MM*

Moonlight Organics see Stellar Winery

Môreson

Franschhoek ▪ Est 1986 ▪ 1stB 1994 ▪ Tasting & sales daily 11-5 ▪ Fee R10 ▪ Closed Dec 25 ▪ Tours by appt ▪ Bread & Wine Restaurant & other amenities (see Eat-out section) ▪ Owner Richard Friedman ▪ Winemaker Jacques Wentzel (2003) ▪ General manager/viticulturist Anton Beukes (1994) ▪ 18 ha (chard, chenin, sauvignon) ▪ 300 tons 18 000 cs 40% red 55% white 1% rosé 4% MCC ▪ Export brands: Pinecrest & MorningSide ▪ ISO 14000 & Eurogap certified ▪ PO Box 114 Franschhoek 7690 ▪ sales@moreson.co.za ▪ www.moreson.co.za ▪ ***T 876·3055*** *▪ F 876·2348*

'South Africa's winelands don't deliver bad vintages; it's just that every harvest has its own challenges,' says Vivienne Scholtz, who markets Môreson with breathless enthusiasm. Having made a major investment in their irrigation systems just before the onset of the drought, last year's challenge was easily met. It's still early days, but winemaker Jacques Wentzel believes 2005 may even produce their best wine yet. Last year also saw the team earning more accolades (and a 'hefty' R2 200 for a case of 97 Cab at the Nederburg Auction), and releasing a new bubbly. No big plans for the future, simply doing the same and doing it better, or as Vivienne S would have it, 'nurturing the Môreson magic'.

★★★★ **Magia** Bdx-style red named by unidentified Bulgarian at international wine show, who declared the as yet unlabeled **98** 'magia!' (magical). **02** from Stbosch grapes, cabs s/f, merlot (42/35/23), 2 yrs oak, new oak for cab. Restrained fruiting (in line with vintage), emphatic tannins; will require few yrs to show best; **01** Paarl, Stbosch vyds subjugated into successful blend, finely structured, holds 15% alc well.

★★★★ **Cabernet Sauvignon** These need yr/2 from release to settle, unwind. **01** (★★★☆) still tight, unknit mid-2004, but showing ripely generous cab fruit & oak (18 mths, Fr, 1st/2nd fill). **00** still inky, oaky, embryonic when tasted for 2004 ed. **03** not ready for inclusion in current guide.

★★★★ **Pinotage** Latest vintages much improved; **03** ABSA Top Ten, SAA listing; suave (which not many pinotages are) despite 15% alc; exhibits fine minerality & suppleness; supportively oaked (9–12 mths Fr/Am oak, 33% new). Combo Stbosch/Frhoek vyds; only Stbosch fruit for **02**, juicy & well-defined; supple tannins & poised acidity.

★★★★ **Premium Chardonnay 04** maintains quicker pace set by pvs vintage. Bold (14.2% alc) but elegant, deep-veined lime/apricot fruit, toasted hazelnut complexity, very well-judged oak (75% new Fr, yr, remainder unwooded). **03** also deftly wooded, polished, balanced & focused. WO Frhoek.

★★★★ **Sauvignon Blanc** ✓ Own fruit, night-harvested & made reductively for freshness, zing. **05** (★★★☆) picked early yet shows well-fleshed mid-palate, smooth & zesty; **04** also noted for its well weighted palate, evinced concentration, focus.

Merlot ★★★☆ Enthusiastically oaked, mostly with good results; as in **01**, juicy with well-expressed varietal fruit; last yr just needed time for chunky wood to harmonise. 15–20 mths Fr barrels. **Chenin Blanc** ★★★☆ **05** fresh & harmonious lemon-lime flavour profile with leesy hint (3 mths *sur lie*), from mature Frhoek bushvines. Following MCCs **NV**: **Blanc de Blancs** ★★★ Brut sparkling from chardonnay (90%), chenin. Last tasted has the usual busy bready bubbles, but also some lemony austerity missing from pvs riper releases. *Wine* ★★★★. **Cuvée Cape** new ★★★☆ Versatile standalone celebrator & food friend. Brut from pinotage & chenin (80/20); pale golden hue, assertive bready aromas, soft red berry flavours from pinotage, emphatically dry (7g/ℓ RS).

Pinehurst range

Cabernet Sauvignon ★★★ **03** unready for tasting; no **02**; **01** fairly big departure from pvs' clever bdx-like styling. 14% alc prominent; simple, sweet, porty. 14 mths oak. WO W Cape. **Merlot-Cabernet Sauvignon** ★★★☆ Inaugural Calyon show top ten slot for **02**, merlot-led this yr – just! (51/49); rounded, fruity, with genteel tannins & sustained finish. 3rd/4th fill oak fully absorbed. Stbosch fruit. **Pinotage** ★★★ **03** big, bold & forthright; loaded with banana fruit, juicy tannins; Fr oak staving well judged. **Rosé Sec** ★★☆ **04** from pinotage; coral pink, light, dry, fresh, for easy summer quaffing. Stbosch fruit. **Chardonnay** ★★★ Unwooded **05**, lively pear/peach tone, rounded & fruity, perhaps too soft – could do with some moxie. **Chenin Blanc** ★★★ **05** youthful tropical/stone fruit tone; creamy, leesy textures, bouncy finish; more characterful than pvs. WO Frhoek. **Sauvignon Blanc** ★★ **05**, like pvs, doesn't shout the variety but shows some vinosity. All above WO Coastal unless noted. – *DH*

Morewag new

Stellenbosch ▪ Est 1995 ▪ 1stB 2002 ▪ Closed to public ▪ Owners Michael & Ulrike Merkel ▪ Farm manager Charl Buys ▪ PO Box 290 Klapmuts 7625 ▪ morewag@mweb.co.za ▪ ***T/F 875·5626***

Not exactly newbies – their first pinotage was produced in 2002 by Elsenburg vini/viticulture students – Michael and Ulrike Merkel feature in the guide for the first time. Their farm on the R44 has been repeating the pinotage/student exercise ever since that maiden vintage and the Merkels are now ready to produce from other varieties planted since their arrival in the

Klapmuts area in 1995. Their other crop is lavender, grown on their adjacent farm, where they plan to build a lavender distillery.

Pinotage ★★★ Sinewy, spicy & savoury **03** souped up by fresh acidity & sweet/sour fruit; unwooded. Drinks well now (& for 2-3 yrs) particularly with meaty dishes, where dried herbs/carpaccio notes should add interest. — *CR*

Morgenhof Estate

*Stellenbosch ▪ Est 1692 ▪ 1stB 1984 ▪ Tasting & sales Nov-Apr: Mon-Fri 9-5.30 Sat/Sun 10-5; May-Oct: Mon-Fri 9-4.30 Sat/Sun 10-3 ▪ Fee R10 ▪ Closed Dec 25 ▪ Light lunches/coffees & other amenities (see Eat-out section & intro) ▪ Tourgroups ▪ Owner Anne Cointreau ▪ Winemaker Jacques Cilliers (Jan 2005) ▪ Viticulturist Pieter Haasbroek (1998) ▪ ±70 ha (cabs s/f, merlot, pinotage, touriga, chard, chenin, sauvignon) ▪ 320 tons 25 000 cs 60% red 40% white ▪ PO Box 365 Stellenbosch 7599 ▪ info@morgenhof.com ▪ www.morgenhof.com ▪ **T 889·5510** ▪ F 889·5266*

Accorded winemaker status at the beginning of 2005 (he'd been working at the estate for 18 months), young Jacques Cilliers made the most of what nature gave the Morgenhof vineyards last season. Highs of the harvest — three weeks earlier than usual — were the saving of the sauvignon from a heatwave ('We were rewarded with wonderful flavours') and noble rot in the chenin after January rains, hence 'a lovely NLH'. The cellar, an attractive feature of a picture-perfect estate with chapel, Tastevin reception area and al fresco restaurant under aged oaks, is now 10 years old. Another cause for celebration was vineyard manager Pieter Haasbroek's second prize for a parcel of merlot in the local Vineyard Block competition.

★★★★☆ **Première Sélection** Classically styled, blend varying with vintage. **01** (not retasted) cab, merlot, cab f, malbec (60/25/9/6) configuration less austere, more accessible & graceful than pvs. Concentrated, refined dark fruit with ripe sweetness, firm tannins but balanced, lengthy dry finish. 18 mths oak, 60% new. Cellar 6-8 yrs. *Wine* ★★★★.

★★★★☆ **Cabernet Sauvignon Reserve** Fine, deep **01**, a barrel selection. Lovely berry fruit, cool herbal touches in refined setting. Magisterial, with an almost austere power when retasted mid-2005. 18 mths new Fr oak. 6-8 yrs life ahead.

★★★★☆ **Merlot Reserve** With flagship styling & massive structure. **00** (★★★★) had big tannin structure, suggesting hopeful wait of 5+ yrs. **01**, tasted last ed, re-establishes claim in seductiveness stakes (but classy & serious), helped by less dominating oak (60% new Fr). Ripe, supple tannin integrating with warm, bright fruit, savoury acid. 4-7 yrs ahead.

★★★★ **Merlot** Serious version. **01** tasted mid-2004 delightful: refined, graceful, integrated; beautifully poised & accessible. 18 mths Fr oak, 20% new.

★★★★ **Pinotage** Fragrant, generously but elegantly styled, benefits from few yrs' keeping, as **01** showed mid-2004. Plump, well-balanced, with sweet redcurrant charms, though dry on finish. Yr oak 90/10 Fr/Am, 40% new.

★★★★ **Chardonnay** Following understated but over-sweet **03** (★★★), **04** significant step up: intense ripe citrus with hint yellow peach; firm acid, serious oaking (9 mths Fr), butterscotch malo character, giving lively yet rich & creamy texture. Ultra-long finish, & decently dry.

★★★★ **Chenin Blanc** ✓ From 30+ yr old vines, always impressive, unobtrusively wooded (5-8 mths, 10% new), usually just about dry. Latest **04** ripe quince with hint oak; full-bodied, never cloying thanks to the variety's distinctive clean acidity. Should have long life, with some excitement.

★★★★ **Brut Reserve 02** from chard/pinot (60/40); crisp & dry with brisk bubble, good yeasty attack. Tasted before disgorging & dosage. Base wine oaked 7-9 mths for added complexity, weight. Shows the firm, linear style of chard-dominated blend, burgeoning biscuity complexity; pleasing creaminess after 2 yrs on lees.

Cabernet Sauvignon ★★★☆ **02** now bottled, shows ripe black cherry & mulberry with cool cedar whiffs; ripe & concentrated but retains freshness, savoury appeal. Tannins tightened up, leading to fine dry finish. Fine oak component. **Sauvignon Blanc** ★★★ Good workmanlike version; bone-dry **05** a melange of tropical fruit, wild scrub & grass notes, firm acid.

Noble Late Harvest ★★★★ **02** attractive orange marmalade bouquet, barley sugar twist, not over-sweet at 105g/ℓ with good balancing acidity, slight caramel notes, dry finish. Fermented/6 mths in oak. Tasted last ed, as was ... **Natural Sweet** ★★★ Maiden barrel-fermented **NV**. Less sweet than many at 90g/ℓ sugar, soft acidity, subtle oak on nose/palate. Lightish 12.6% alc. NE. **Cape LBV** ★★★★ (Pvsly 'Late Bottled Vintage') Latest **01** from tinta, touriga, less sweet & rich than many; mocha, dried fruit, Demerara sugar notes; good acidity for lift; dry savoury finish – far too easy to drink! Touch more alc (this 17.6%) needed to complete modernisation of style. **Cape Vintage** ★★★★ Last was **00** tinta/touriga in drier Portuguese style.

Fantail range

Pinotage ★★★ **03** (not retasted; notes from last ed – as for all below except White) more welcoming, more succulence & juice, than rather austere **02**. **Merlot** ★★★ **02** some attractive cassis & berry sleekness, smooth & supple. 18 mths oak, 30% new. Moderate 12.7% alc. **Vineyards Red** ★★★ **03** all-sorts red, but cab dominant; pleasing & fruity, soft approachable tannins, made with accessibility foremost. Sweet tasting, but dry. NE. **Rosé** ★★★ **04** pinotage shows in sweet candyfloss nose; palate a lovely surprise – bone-dry & zingy, lightish 12.7% alc. **Vineyards White 05** ★★★ Blend chenin, sauvignon (75/25), whiff of tropical fruit; attractive lime & melon flavours; juicy but dry; good lingering fruity finish. – *IvH*

Morgenster Estate

Stellenbosch (see Helderberg map) ▪ Est 1993 ▪ 1stB 1998 ▪ Tasting & sales Mon-Fri 10-5 Sat 11-3 ▪ Fee R10 ▪ Closed pub hols ▪ Tours by appt ▪ Estate-grown olive oil & olives products ▪ Owner Giulio Bertrand ▪ Winemaker Marius Lategan, with Cornea Cilliers (Aug 1999, Jan 2004), advised by Pierre Lurton ▪ Vineyard/orchard manager Gerhard Bruwer, advised by Francois Viljoen ▪ 40 ha (cabs s/f, merlot, petit v) ▪ 200 tons 100% red ▪ PO Box 1616 Somerset West 7129 ▪ wine@morgenster.co.za ▪ www.morgenster.co.za ▪ ***T 852·1738*** *▪ F 852·1141*

The Morgenster family is growing and evolving, under the watchful eye of Italian 'paterfamilias', Giulio Bertrand. Responsibility for the vineyards and orchards now belongs to Gerhard Bruwer, supported by VinPro's widely experienced Francois Viljoen. A more aggressive marketing stance, adopted since MD Gerrie Wagener's appointment, aims to cement the two Bordeaux-style reds – Morgenster and Lourens River Valley – in their positions at the top end of the market. A favourable outflow for visitors is what's being punted as 'a total brand experience', which includes their awarded estate-grown extra virgin olive oil, now more readily accessible thanks to extended farm opening hours. Much excitement was caused last season by the birth of their new Italian 'children' – the first very small crops of sangiovese and nebbiolo. Both winemaker Marius Lategan and Bordeaux-based consulting oenologist, Pierre Lurton, of Chx Cheval Blanc and d'Yquem, are 'extremely positive' about the potential for the varieties on Morgenster.

★★★★★ **Morgenster** Classy & delicious bdx-style red bearing the restrained mark of the Old World. **03** returns to cab dominance (s/f 70%, remainder merlot). Subtle, beguiling bouquet of herbs, cassis & eucalyptus overlain with spice; tannins, fruit, alc (14.3%) perfectly aligned; persistent green-tea finish. Reduced time in barrel (to 13 mths), higher new oak portion (90%); needs 5-7 yrs to integrate fully & grow. No **02** (see below). Merlot-rich (51%) **01** was delicate with already tertiary nose.

★★★★★ **Lourens River Valley** This 'second' red blend seems set to keep pace with the flagship. **02** similar make-up to pvs, complex whiffs herb & lavender, structure & balance (14.5% alc unobtrusive) to improve with cellaring – tea-leaf-toned tannins need time to unleash vibrant raspberry fruit. **01** (★★★★), 55% merlot, with cab, dash cab f, had firm tannin grip from 16 mths new Fr oak.

'Third Wine' new ★★★★ To be named. 'Declassified' grapes diverted here for cosseting as above, though no new oak; **02** predominantly merlot (54%) with cab s/f & tiny splash petit v (32/13.3/0.7). Fruit melange given extra dimension, grip by savoury oak. Persistent liquorice finish, alc (14.3%) more apparent than on cellarmates. – *CvZ*

Morkel see Bellevue
MorningSide see Môreson

Mostertsdrift Noble Wines

Stellenbosch ▪ Est/1stB 2001 ▪ Visits by appt ▪ Fee R5 ▪ Meals by appt ▪ Owners Anna-Mareè Mostert-Uys & André Mostert ▪ Winemaker Anna-Mareè Mostert-Uys (Jan 2001) ▪ Viticulturist Nico Mostert (Jan 2001) ▪ 7.5 ha (merlot, pinot, cab, chard, hanepoot) ▪ 29 tons 600-800 cs 70% red 30% white ▪ PO Box 2061 Dennesig Stellenbosch 7601 ▪ mostertsdrift@telkomsa.net ▪ ***T 889·5344*** *▪* ***F*** *887·1780*

A long, tough harvest last year, but Anna-Mareè Mostert ventures that the quality of the grapes, particularly the red, more than made up for it. Serendipitous, especially as she has shifted her focus to red wine (now 70% of production) and is experimenting with new red varieties. She planted new lots of pinot and merlot last year, and is also tinkering with her AnéRouge blend, replacing the cinsaut with merlot and playing with proportions. But the future is not only rosy: Anna-Mareè wants to try her hand at a bottle-fermented sparkling wine.

Cabernet Sauvignon ★★ Bountiful red/black berry fruit, sensible 13% alc don't keep pace with strident tannins in **04**; 14 mths old oak/10 mths with new staves. **AnéRouge** ★★★ Usually a lightly oaked cinsaut/cab, cab dominates **04** with 18% splash of merlot. Friendly strawberry/plums brushed with smoke; supple & savory. Easy drinking thanks to deft oak treatment: 14 mths only old barrels, merlot unoaked. Both reds WO S'bosch. **Sauvignon Blanc** ★★ **05** Somewhat neutral in the aroma/flavour department but zesty & refreshing. Untasted for this edition is the unwooded **Chenin Blanc** ★; honeyed **03** already tired mid-2004. Also untried by us … **Blanc de Blanc** ★★ 100% sauvignon from Frhoek; lightish **04** tropical tones with hints gooseberry, green grass; lively apple zest finish. **Chenin Blanc Wooded** discontinued. — *DH*

Mountain Oaks Winery

Worcester ▪ Est/1stB 2003 ▪ Tasting, sales & tours by appt ▪ Guest cottage ▪ Organic farm produce ▪ Owners Stevens family ▪ Winemaker Christine Stevens (Jun 2003), advised by Ross Gower ▪ Viticulturists Christine & Mark Stevens ▪ 20 ha (cabs s/f, mourvèdre, pinotage, shiraz, chard, chenin, viognier) ▪ 40-50 tons 2 000 cs 30% red 70% white ▪ PO Box 68 Rawsonville 6845 ▪ eikenbosch@iafrica.com ▪ ***T (023) 344·3107*** *▪ F (023) 344·3688*

'Every year with organic farming gets easier,' says winemaker Christine Stevens, 'the weeds are becoming less — or it is my imagination?' Nothing uncertain about the completeness of the new tasting room ('rustic, romantic and charming') and guest cottage. When it comes to winemaking, C-S continues to believe in keeping things simple: 'As we farm organically and do not irrigate, we cannot mess around with the brilliant-tasting fruit we get. Instead, we treat it with love and respect, and that way the wine tells its own story.'

Pinotage ★★★★ **04** dense black fruit & smoky, gamey notes; mouth-filling fruit. Well-handled tannins contribute to dry, fine finish. 11 mths 80/20 Fr/Am oak. **Chenin Blanc** ★★★ Restrained pear bouquet and persistent mineral, 'wet slate' flavour make **04** an elegant glassful. 14% alc unobtrusive. **Chenin Blanc Barrel Reserve** ★★★ **04** from old vines; brilliant straw hue but nose rather closed; creamy lime palate with butterscotch hints; good length & texture. 6 mths Fr oak, 30% new, well integrated. **Chardonnay** ★★★ **04** dominant buttery oak wrestles tangerine, mandarin, dried pear on nose & palate (yr Fr, 30% new). Ripe citrus palate, pithy finish; oak more obvious than on Chenin above. **Le Jardin** ★★ **04** not tasted; **03** was crisp chenin-dominated quaffer (30% chard), food-friendly & undemanding. Name a tribute to the farm gardens. All WO Slanghoek. — *CvZ*

Mountain Range

new

Closed to public ▪ Owners Belinda Traverso, Paul Finlayson & Paul de Waal ▪ 1 000 cs ▪ 67 Belmont Ave Oranjezicht 8001 ▪ shelley@mountainrange.co.za ▪ www.mountainrange.co.za ▪ ***T 461·3531/073·225·6891*** *▪ F 461·3531*

Many wineries claim to market 'icon wines'; this merchant house sells its wines *in* an icon. Its Table Mountain-shaped bottles, filled with wines from a reputable Stellenbosch estate, fly off the shelves – and often fly home with tourists too. The distinctive bottles, available in miniature 50ml size as well, also hold fine local sherry, brandy and extra-virgin olive oil.

Table Red ★★★ This novelty quaffer fruity & fun but not so frivolous. Drink-soon **03** delicious berry aromas/flavours from cab, merlot, shiraz (45/35/20); focused by spicy tannins & vanilla/cedar notes from older oak, mix Am/Fr. Warm goodbye thanks to 13.5% alc. **Table White** ★★ Zippy blend chardonnay, sauvignon, chenin. **04** herb garden bouquet & lime/ orange palate. – *CvZ*

Mountain Ridge see Romansrivier

Mountain River Wines

Paarl ▪ Est 1993 ▪ 1stB 1998 ▪ Closed to public ▪ Owner De Villiers Brits ▪ Winemaker De Villiers Brits with consultants ▪ 38 700 cs 60% red 40% white ▪ 146 Main Road Paarl 7646 ▪ dev@mountainriverwines.co.za mattie@mountainriverwines.co.za ▪ www.mountain-riverwines.co.za ▪ ***T 872·3256/7*** *▪ F 872·3255*

New in De Villiers Brits's portfolio is a proudly SA answer to the 'critter' brands which are springing up all over – and flying off supermarket shelves, especially in the US. Using the motif of a giraffe for the branding and label design, Brits added South Africa's international country code, ZA, to the mix and came up with the name Zaràfa, and the slogan 'Reach for it'.

Cabernet Sauvignon-Merlot ★★★★ **01** not retasted; mellow cherry/strawberry joined by sweet spice & slight savoury touch, light tannins. Stbosch grapes; 16 mths new/older Fr oak. **Merlot** ★★ Classic flavour profile of plums & mocha, **02** round & fruity entry yet fairly strong tannic comeback; give time. 14% alc. **Pinotage-Shiraz** ★★★ Ripe, flavoursome **03**, friendlier & less tannic than pvs, well rounded for everyday drinking. 70% new oak, Fr/Am. **Chardonnay** ★★★ Bonnievale fruit for **03**, 6 mths 2nd fill oak. Holding, but should be opened soon. **Estuary Sauvignon Blanc** new ★★★ Pale lemon hue introduces **04**, whiff of baked apple, soft & gentle styling for pleasant standalone imbibing. WO Olfnts Rvr.

Maankloof range

Cabernet Sauvignon new ★★★ Quietly delicious **04**, dollop ripe berry fruit on nose, firm but approachable tannins. **Shiraz** ★★★ Bouncy, fragrant **02**, last yr showed Karoo scrub & woodsmoke hints; ample rounded flavours, structure for cellaring 2/3 yrs. **Pinotage** ★★★ **04** ripe plummy aromas, spicy cherries on palate, fairly firm ripe tannins; better with a food accompaniment. **Rosé** ★★ new Pale rose petal pink **05**, fresh berry flavours, savoury dry finish. Soft, rounded early enjoyment. **Chenin Blanc** ★★★ Drink-soon **04** last yr was light & pretty with ripe tropical tones, balanced acidity. **Sauvignon Blanc 04** untasted.

Zaràfa range new

Pinotage ★ Soft, uncomplex **04**, baked prune hint, sweeter than analysis (1.7g/ℓ sugar) would suggest. **Sauvignon Blanc** ★★ **05** pleasant, clean dry white, with subtle tropical fruit tone. All ranges WO W Cape unless noted. – *DH*

Mountain Shadows see Omnia
Mountainside see Fairseat Cellars, Ruitersvlei
Mount Claire see Cordoba

Mount Rozier Estate

Stellenbosch (see Helderberg map) ▪ Est/1stB 1997 ▪ Tasting, sales & tours by appt ▪ Closed pub hols ▪ Conservancy area ▪ Owner Atlantic Wine Agencies, Inc ▪ Winemaker Jacques Fourie (Sep 2001) ▪ 45 ha (cab, merlot, shiraz, chard, sauvignon, semillon) ▪ ±1 500 cs own label 40% red 60% white ▪ PO Box 784 Somerset West 7129 ▪ wine@mountrozier.co.za ▪ www.mountrozier.co.za ▪ ***T 858·1130 ▪ F*** *858·1131*

Atlantic Wine Agencies have upped the ante since taking ownership of this Sir Lowry's Pass property in 2004, investing heavily in vineyards, winery and personnel. Phase-one redevelopment is complete – barrel hall renovated, new equipment purchased, new programmes implemented and a first-class tasting facility built. An enlarged management team is in place, and phase two, will see capacity increased to 300 tonnes, is well underway. Last year was a tricky vintage, but the four designated single vineyards were given ultra-VIP treatment, and the results have the team talking about the possibility of releasing the first super-premium wine sometime next year. As the guide went to press, the vines were introduced to their new full-time caregiver, ex-Simonsig/Slaley viticulturist Jaco Mouton.

★★★★ **Shiraz 03**, previewed last ed, sumptuous, a feast, but loss of elegance – massive alc (15.6%), oak evident (new, 15 mths Fr /Am). More New World profile continues with **04** (★★★★) showstopper; very ripe youngberry fruit, athletic tannins, sweet impression to finish (from 15.8% alc). Sample drinks well now, should hold ± 3-4 yrs.

Cabernet Sauvignon ★★★★ Bold & beautiful **04**, balanced, with ripe black fruit, spicy/sweet tobacco hint. Crowd-pleasing supple tannins, tad showy, should gain complexity/gravitas with 2-4 yrs. 15.3% alc, usually Fr oak, small portion new. **Merlot** ★★★★ **04** raises the bar; attractive inky, blueberry nose following on to palate; elegant & structured for long haul with powdery tannins, latent fruit. Oak as above. **Sauvignon Blanc** ★★★ Fresh & lively **05**, intense tropical notes; poised, well-composed fruity finish.

Rozier Bay range

No follow-up to following pair of reds; notes from pvs ed: **Cabernet Sauvignon** ★★★★ Inky black, whiff cedar to **03**; mulberry ripeness, with firm tannic structure, youthful astringency, judicious oak. **Merlot** ★★★ **03** sweet choc-coated prunes, ripe tannins for easy accessibility. 15.5% a brake to easy quaffing. Following previewed as samples; ratings provisional. **Shiraz** new ★★★ Early-drinking **04** tad restrained; muted spice, red fruit; fresh acidity & dry tannins. By contrast ... **Cabernet Sauvignon-Merlot** new ★★★ **04** needs time for wild berry fruit to marry harsh tannins & brawny 14.9% alc. **Chardonnay** ★★★ Engaging **05** vibrant citrus fruit, less billowy, more restrained than pvs 'oak-aholic' style. **Sauvignon Blanc** ★★ **05** softly flavoured tropical version, dry & light (12.3% alc); short. **Pinotage** discontinued.

Rozier Reef range

Pinotage ★★★ Last tasted **04** has ripe prune fruit, very dry, youthful tannic grip on finish. To be discontinued as might be ... **Merlot** ★★★ Ripe blackcurrant fruit in **04**, fat & juicy tannins to match, subtle oak. **Ruby Cabernet** ★★★ No new vintage; **04** robust, crammed with plummy cab-like fruit. Following tasted as samples; ratings provisional: **Shiraz** new ★★ **05** jammy nose, lightish palate make this a soft, quaffing wine (albeit at 14.2% alc). **Ruby Cabernet-Merlot** new ★★★ **04** ripe & rich, dry tannins touch abrasive, need steak. Should soften/hold ± 2 yrs. **Chardonnay** ★★★ Friendly food-styled **05**; tropical notes, smooth acidity. Moderate 13.4% alc. **Chenin Blanc** ★★ Lovely green apple & pear hints on **05**, weightier than pvs at 13.5% alc. **Sauvignon Blanc** ★★★ **05** subdued passionfruit nose/palate, leaner than pvs; lacking acid, length. **Chenin Blanc-Chardonnay** new **05** too unformed to rate, seems promising, with Golden Delicious apple character, yeasty middle. **Reef Red** discontinued. – *MM/IvH*

Mount Vernon Farm

Paarl ▪ Est/1stB 2003 ▪ Visits by appt ▪ Closed Easter Fri/Sun, Dec 25/26 & Jan 1 ▪ BYO picnic ▪ Walks ▪ Mountain biking ▪ Owners David & Debbie Hooper ▪ Winemaker Debbie Hooper, with Anele Mangene ▪ Viticulturist Phillip du Toit ▪ 28 ha (cab, malbec, merlot, petit v, pinotage, shiraz, chard) ▪ 200 tons 7 000ℓ ▪ mountvernon30@hotmail.com ▪ PO Box 348 Klapmuts 7625 ▪ ***T/F 875-5073***

Buoyed by the bronze show medal received last year, vine- and wine-grower Debbie Hooper upped the production capacity for her Chenin by purchasing a new 3 000ℓ tank, and added an easy-drinking Pinotage Rosé to the range. Her reds were yet to be released at press time, but include a pinotage blend and a rhône-style red featuring grenache, shiraz and mourvèdre. With a 'good' 2005 harvest behind her, she aims to keep standards high and quantities low, growing only as demand increases.

Three Peaks range

Both **05**. **Pinotage Rosé** new ★☆ Sunset quaffer, for early enjoyment. Soft pear & gumdrop nose, tart fruit-shy palate. **Chenin Blanc** ★★★ Delicious, zesty sipper with passionfruit, dried fruit & quince notes; friendly 12.5% alc. From low-yielding bushvines. — *CvZ*

Mulderbosch Vineyards

Stellenbosch ▪ Est 1989 ▪ 1stB 1991 ▪ Sales: Mon-Fri 8-5; tasting by appt only ▪ Closed on pub hols ▪ Owner Hydro Holdings ▪ Cellarmaster Mike Dobrovic (1991) ▪ Winemaker Clinton le Sueur (Jun 2001) ▪ Vyd manager Desmond Hendriks ▪ 27 ha (cabs s/f, malbec, merlot, petit v, chard, chenin, sauvignon) ▪ 500 tons 30 000 cs 30% red 70% white ▪ PO Box 548 Stellenbosch 7599 ▪ info@mulderbosch.co.za ▪ www.mulderbosch.co.za ▪ ***T 865·2488*** *▪ F 865·2351*

In the 2005 vintage, nature's scale balanced a drought-reduced crop with smaller berries, flavour concentration — and 'impeccably behaved chardonnay'! The result: 'dynamic, delicious wines, each with their own flavour and personality'. Human intervention ranged from sterling viticultural work by Desmond Hendriks, to the efforts of an eclectic gathering of drama, psychology and law students, all cellar-ratting under the direction of philosopher/cellarmaster Mike Dobrovic. Invoking mystical influences no doubt also had an effect. In the words of Rumi, one of Mike D's favourite mystic philosophers: 'A white flower grows in the quietness/Try and let your tongue become that flower' ... and let the wines speak for themselves.

★★★★ **Faithful Hound** New blending angle from **03**; small but influential drop shiraz (6%) joins Bdx quartet cab, merlot, malbec, cab f (53/34/3/3), all beautifully meshed. Ample, soft, cedar-edged red-wine aromas; more cab structural presence on palate, confers seamless grip on creamily textured savoury/red fruit flavours. Good now; even better by 2009. 18 mths Fr oak 50% new. **02** (★★★☆) sans shiraz; tasty, understated; for shorter-term drinking. Earlier vtgs 90 pts *WS*.

★★★★ **Beta Centauri** Occasional 'stellar' offering (Alpha, sparkled in **98**). **02** equal parts cabs f/s with 12% petit v. More plush, modern than temperate 'Hound', though vibrant tannin needs few more yrs ageing. 18 mths new Fr oak effortlessly absorbed.

★★★☆ **Shiraz 03** (★★★★) better balanced, more charming than pvs; pretty floral/spicy notes, richer smoked meat undertones; supple, silky concentration; more marked effects of burly 14.6% alc freshened/diminished by 14% infusion petit v. 19 mths, 100% new Fr oak. Stanford grapes. WO W Cape. Maiden **02** WS 90 pts.

★★★★ **Chardonnay Barrel Fermented** Impressive New-World style; spirited but not superficial; regularly rewarded by show judges. Native yeast fermented, 9 mths new Fr oak (Mike D's '007' wine – barrels regularly rolled, not stirred); ±5g/ℓ sugar. **04** full hazelnut/lime mélange; balanced contrast between taut acidity & creamy texture; sleek, sinewy with usual expansive finish. Needs ±yr to fully settle; should improve till ±2009. **03**, nuanced, very contained, glossy. FCTWS trophy, *Wine* ★★★★★.

★★★★ **Chardonnay** This version a successful combo of tank & barrel-fermented, consistently combines elegance, depth of flavour. **04** usual attractive pickled lime/toast profile. Lightish, lively build, in harmony with well-layered fruit; clean, persistent finish. **03** mouth-filling, with refreshing minerally acid. 55% in Fr oak, 30% new. Partial native yeast ferment. *WS* favourite: **02**, **01** both 92 pts.

★★★★ **Steen-op-Hout** ✓ Maiden **96** of this oak-brushed chenin was considered daring; oak now regular partner to many SA chenins, few so tactfully handled as this (only 7% seasoned 4 mths in new Fr/2nd fill Am oak), as indicated by 'op-hout' labelling. Very food friendly. **04** (★★★☆) earlier developing than pvs; pleasantly full honeyed bouquet; palate more attenuated; needs drinking. **03** delicate yet persuasive. *Wine* ★★★★. From distinguished old hilltop bushvines.

★★★★☆ **Sauvignon Blanc** One of Cape's most consistent & sought-after. Notable for its verve, full-tilt dash. Sample **05** promises no disappointments; touch riper tropical fruit dimension to usual greengage/gooseberry tones, modest 12.5% alc; otherwise sprightly with resounding mineral crescendo. Regular *WS* 90+ pts. — *AL*

Muldersvlei *see* Westbridge

Muratie Estate

Stellenbosch ▪ Est 1685 ▪ 1stB ca 1920 ▪ Tasting & sales Mon-Fri 9-5 Sat & Sun 10-4 ▪ Fee R15, waived on purchase ▪ Closed Easter Fri, Dec 25 & Jan 1 ▪ Picnic baskets by appt ▪ Tours by appt ▪ Guest house ▪ Art gallery ▪ Owner Melck Family ▪ Winemaker Guillaume Nell (Apr 2003) ▪ Viti consultant Paul Wallace (1998) ▪ 38 ha (cabs, merlot, pinot, shiraz, chard, hanepoot, port varieties) ▪ 210 tons 6 000 cs own label 85% red 15% white ▪ PO Box 133 Koelenhof 7605 ▪ muratie@kingsley.co.za ▪ www.muratie.co.za ▪ ***T 865·2330*** *▪ F 865·2790*

Last year was the 320th anniversary of the emancipation of Ansela van der Caab, the slave who married the first owner of this farm, Lourens Campher. A rich patina of history colours Muratie, from the tasting room – one of the most atmospheric in the winelands, it hasn't changed since the 1950s – to a low-yielding block of shiraz, planted in 1975. But lest you think they're stuck in the past here, *au contraire*. Continuing cellar investment manifested in new stainless steel tanks and their new French oak barrel programme is starting to bring results. 'The wines have developed more fruit, even though the structure and backbone is still prominent,' says Rijk Melck. The contents in the bottles may have moved in a more contemporary, expressive direction but what won't change are the charming old-worldness of their origins and that tangible sense of history.

★★★★ **Ansela** Classically built **03** (★★★★☆) up with the best. Sultry dark charmer, fruit draped around discreet tannic backbone, shows burgeoning complexity. More relaxed, less overtly powerful than single varieties below. Merlot/cab 60/40 blend. 2+ yrs total in oak. Moderate 13.3% alc. Unfiltered. Terrific **02** half cab, + merlot, cab f. Cellar 5-7 yrs

★★★★ **Cabernet Sauvignon** After fine, seriously built **01**, **02** (★★★☆) invites with cedar & ripe mulberry, has ripe fruit, fine oak – all the good components, but also vintage's slightly gawky tannins; finish has dry tannic element over sweet hint. Yr Fr oak, 22% new. Could improve after yr/2. Like all major reds here, made in mix open fermenters/s steel.

★★★★ **Shiraz** Seductive fragrance of approachable **03** repeated in understated elegance of **04** (sample). Warm, spicy & welcoming, whiff oak vanilla (35% new, 20% Am); ripe black cherry fruit with supple tannins for dryness & subtle discipline. Cellar 3-5 yrs.

★★★★ **Isabella** Fine, bunch-pressed chardonnay. Sample **04** tasted last ed, sold out by time of this one: yeasty brioche, dried peach invitation; creamy breadth, long resonating finish. Fermented/8 mths Fr oak, 18% new. **05** unready for tasting mid-2005. Huge success: production now upped 30%.

★★★★ **Cape Vintage** After less satisfactory **01** (★★★☆), back on form with classy **02** from tintas b/r/f, souzão. Whiff brandy spirit, sweet fruitcake & plum flavours, surprisingly easy drinking – more LBV-style approachability (& oaking – 3 yrs). Correct 87g/ℓ sugar. For winter survival kit.

Melck's Red ☺ ★★★ Stylish quaffer with varying blend: **04** shiraz/merlot (60/40) ripe pruney fruit, some meaty richness, enough tannin for interest.

Merlot ★★★☆ **02** lead pencil, ripe cassis intro; developing minerally depth – savoury rather than dark choc, fine-grained tannins unravelling for classy dry finish. Well oaked, 28% new Fr. **Pinot Noir** ★★★☆ SA's first pinot vines planted here over 75 yrs ago. **02** hints forest floor, delicate redcurrant, damp compost, touch earth on finish; not quite silky soft yet, but on its way. Yr Fr oak, 30% new. **Cape Ruby** (Pvsly 'Port') ★★★ **NV** ever-popular bet from Muratie stable: dark prune ripeness, richer & weightier than classic Ruby, but good alc at 19%, not too sweet at 95g/ℓ RS. **Amber Forever** ★★★ Fortified muscat d'A, popular for over 75 yrs. **05** (sample) sees return to old style – 4 months in used Fr casks (like sewing diamonds on blue jeans). More breadth, less fragrance, has definitely put on weight. A meal-end bonbon. – *IvH*

Mystery Wine Corporation

*Cape Town ▪ 1stB 2002 ▪ Owner Saul Gorin ▪ 4 000 cs 40% red 50% white 10% rosé ▪ PO Box 281 Sea Point 8060 ▪ info@mysterywines.co.za ▪ www.mysterywines.co.za ▪ **T 083·628·5160** ▪ F 686·5404*

The only mystery that needs solving here is how Saul Gorin manages to pour this much value into these bottles, with their famously full-bodied labels. He's sticking to his guns when it comes sourcing the best possible wines for his growing base of customers, and heartened by selections of several of his wines by value-conscious Wine of the Month Club.

Dry Red ☺ ★★★ Lip smacking, unoaked **03**, fruity & juicy with just a hint of tannin for interest; balanced red berry flavours. Blend merlot/cab/shiraz.

Sauvignon Blanc new ★ Lightish (12% alc), faintly floral, zesty & short. Latest vintages of following not available for tasting: **Tickled Pink** ★★ **02** rosé from merlot; herbaceous rather than red fruit aromas, seemed a bit tired a yr ago. **Dry White** ★★★ Mainly chenin, jazzed up with 10% sauvignon; **03** attractive lemon cream aroma, tastily fresh & zingy-dry, hint passionfruit on finish. **Melon** ★★★ Shy in the flavour department, touch sweet for some palates. Clean & easy drinking, though — will win plenty of fans. Enjoy young. — *IvH*

My Wyn new

*Franschhoek ▪ Est/1stB 2001 ▪ Visits Mon-Fri 10–12:30 (Oct-Apr), otherwise by appt ▪ Fee R15 ▪ Closed pub hols ▪ Owner/winemaker Jacoline Haasbroek ▪ 200 cs ▪ 75% red 25% white ▪ PO Box 112 Franschhoek 7690 ▪ envision@wine.co.za ▪ **T 876·2518/083·302·5556** F 876·2518*

Rolling out the barrels from behind the old cellar doors on the Huguenot farm, La Bri, and certainly having a barrel of fun is the enthusiastic Jacoline Haasbroek. Here the freelance journalist, wine student and now amateur winemaker is getting hands-on experience with her *garagiste* style venture, experimenting with small batches of grapes bought in from La Motte and La Bri. With a little help and encouragement from friends and family, and served by some of the local restaurants, production has gone from 3 to 10 barrels. The wines are available for tasting and sales from La Bri, managed by her husband Johan.

My Wyn (Cabernet Sauvignon) ★★★ Frhoek fruit, only one barrel produced, 24 mths aged. **02** blackcurrant notes, ripe rounded tannins, unsurprising 15% alc. **My Wyn (Shiraz)** ★★★★ Barossa-style **01** with sweet raspberry notes, sumptuous tannins, confection tempered by ample acidity. Frhoek fruit, 14 mths 2nd fill barrels. **My Huiswyn** ★★★ **02** strawberry Kool-Aid whiffs belie firm-tannined, rustically textured, garnet-hued red from shiraz (85%), cab. 14 mths 3rd fill Fr barrels. Unfiltered. WO W Cape. **Chardonnay** ★★★ Tropical-style **04**'s flamboyance reined in by citrus finish (no malo), concealing 3.3g/ℓ sugar, rich leesy notes. **Viognier** ★★★★ **04** peach/apricot nose, pleasing & opulent floral palate (14.6% alc, 5g/ℓ sugar); oak (12 mths 3rd fill) & broadening effect of partial malo evident but integrated. **My MCC Brut** ★★★ **01** from chardonnay, base-wine old oak aged; developed appley/bready aromas, robust mousse. 42 mths in bottle, undosed yet well rounded. Disgorged Jun 2005. **My Eie Keur** ★ **02** unusual super-ripe Natural Sweet, 50/50 semillon/chardonnay, oxidatively handled. 3rd fill oak, alc (17%) & sugar (20g/ℓ) add complexity to maderised aromas. — *MF*

Nabygelegen Private Cellar

*Wellington ▪ Est 1712 ▪ 1stB 2002 ▪ Tasting & sales Mon-Fri 10–5 Sat 10–1 ▪ Tasting fee R10 incl glass ▪ Closed Easter Fri/Sun, Apr 27, May 1, Dec 25 & Jan 1 ▪ Tours anytime by appt ▪ BYO picnic ▪ Walks ▪ Owner Avalon Vineyards (Pty) Ltd ▪ Winemaker Charles Stassen (Jan 2003) ▪ Viti consultant Johan Wiese (May 2001) ▪ 18 ha (cab, merlot, petit v, tempranillo, chenin, sauvignon) ▪ 3 500 cs 60% red 40% white ▪ PO Box 302 Wellington 7854 ▪ avalonwines@icon.co.za ▪ www.nabygelegen.co.za ▪ **T 873·7534/ 082·829·1189** ▪ F 873·7534*

Aside from an expanded bottle storage area to house slightly higher output, there's 'no new news' from James McKenzie, public face of this characterful farm, with its buttress-walled cellar and vineyards spiced with Stone Age implements. Spicing up the wine portfolio is a new red blend featuring Spanish grape variety tempranillo. Now listed here is the joint-venture wine (with neighbour Graham Knox) At The Limiet, its 'home' recently having been relocated here from Knox's Siyabonga cellar. The production method remains unchanged: vinification in barrel, with nothing added until fermentation concludes all by itself after many months of stutters, starts and stops. The 04 version is currently incubating.

★★★★ **1712** More elegance & excitement in **04** incarnation of this characterful bdx blend thanks to beefed up portions cab & petit v (now 33% & 10%), balance merlot. Big mouthfeel, loads of berry fruit & serious structure, supported by yr Fr oak. 14% alc fairly modest for appellation. Unfiltered. Spicy & red-fruited **03** also carefully constructed; should develop few yrs still.

★★★★ **Scaramanga** new ✓ After Francisco S, the Man with the Golden Gun, suave, sophisticated million-dollar-a-shot nemesis to James Bond. But **04** funky Mediterranean blend cab, malbec & tempranillo is more Pedro Almodóvar than Cubby Broccoli with its exotic sweet berry fruit & spice. Great with jambon and Dalí.

★★★★ **At The Limiet Natural Sweet** Joint-venture with neighbour Graham Knox; moniker an allusion both to area's Limiet Mountains (extremity of the old Cape Colony) & boundary-pushing winemaking (last grapes whipped off vines as winter rains begin; 'hands-off' natural yeast ferment in barrel). Burnished **03** silky, well focused, fruity persistence mellowed by 58g/ℓ sugar. 100% hárslevelü; joined by semillon (19%), chenin (5%) in firmer, more tangy **02**. ±Yr *sur lie.* 500ml. Neither retasted.

Chenin Blanc ★★★ **04** dried peaches & honeysuckle notes, rich mouthfeel. **Sauvignon Blanc** ★★★ **05** victim of hot vintage: subtle fruit, shy nose, light alc (12%); lacks excitement of pvs. **Chenin Blanc-Sauvignon Blanc** ★★★ **05** not tasted. **04** flew with Aeroflot, entertaining passengers with melon & peach tones, sauvignon grassiness; honey & cream hint from dash semillon. *—NP*

Namaqua see WestCorp

Napier Winery

Wellington ▪ Est 1993 ▪ 1stB 1994 ▪ Tasting & sales Mon-Fri 9-5 Sat 10-4 Sun 11-4 pub hols by appt ▪ Cellar tours by appt ▪ Small conference facility ▪ Self-catering cottage (sleeps 4) ▪ Owners: Michael & Catherine Loubser, Leon Bester ▪ Winemaker/viticulturist Leon Bester (Apr 2000) ▪ 34 ha (five Bdx reds, shiraz, chard, chenin) ▪ ±5 500 cs 36% red 64% white ▪ PO Box 638 Wellington 7654 ▪ sales@napierwinery.co.za ▪ www.napierwinery.co.za ▪ ***T 873·7829*** *▪ F 864·2728*

Everything's running on smooth wheels at this recently upgraded cellar, crane and forklift operated from offloading of grapes through to pressing (the hand of Laurent Desfarges, builder of cellars both here and in the US, clearly evident). Complementing the contemporary cellar with its doubled capacity is the new tasting room, with winery and surrounding mountain views – well worth a visit as, expansion completed, this export-oriented winery intends focussing equally on the local market. New plantings of malbec and petit verdot are destined to add dimension to the red blend. Their first vintage brandy, Sir George (the name a tribute to Sir George Napier, the Cape governor who named the town of Wellington after the famous duke), and maiden Cabernet 03 were released.

Red Medallion ★★★★ Bdx-inspired blend cabs s/f, merlot (60/20/20). Plush **01** with dark choc & mocha tones, velvety ripe palate & dry savoury tannins; named 2005 FCTWS 'Discovery of Show'. 18-24 mths Fr barrels, ±30% new, 2 yrs bottle-matured at cellar. **Cabernet Sauvignon** new ★★★ Limited release **03** needs ± yr to show its true colours; now savoury with cedar hint, touch herbaceous. 18 mths Fr oak, 30% new, minimal filtration/fining prior to bottling. **St Catherine** ★★★ Barrel-fermented/aged chardonnay, **03** balanced, its 14% alc & 30% new Fr oak well integrated. Tropical fruits & walnuts lead the aroma/flavour spectrum. Promising. **Greenstone** ★★★ Unwooded chenin blanc, **05** aged *sur lie* 3 mths; waxy, leafy with core of zesty acidity. Poised & elegant, at 12% the ideal lunch time companion. *— CR*

Nature's Group see Oranjerivier Wine Cellars

Naughton's Flight new

Constantia ▪ 1stB 2003 ▪ Closed to public ▪ Owner Francis Naughton ▪ Vini consultant Ronell Wiid ▪ 5 000 btls ▪ 25 Willow Road Constantia 7806 ▪ naughts@mweb.co.za ▪ ***T 794·3928/ 082·571·3442*** *F 794·3928*

Francis Naughton's life path has emulated that of his 17th century ancestors, who fled Ireland to escape English domination – the so called 'flight of the wild geese'. A few of the now famous French châteaux were founded by these folk. Francis's flight was to SA in 1971, joining SFW, inspiring many successful brands. At age 55 he left the corporate nest to launch his own wine, Naughton's Flight Shiraz, made by Ronell Wiid. Fly the brand has! Sampled and imported by a Swedish agent, the first consignment sold out in 14 days, with positive Swedish press coverage and rated 'Best Buy' in one wine magazine. The secret of his success, per this spirited Irishman, is a sincere story and a good dram of Irish luck!

★★★★ **Shiraz** Bonhomous Francis N weighs in with surprisingly serious & structured offering; **03** shows good concentration of ripe berry fruit, subtle mocha & vanilla embellishments from oak (14 mths, 80/20 Fr/Am, 50% new). WO Paarl. – *NP*

Nederburg Wines

Paarl ▪ Est 1792 ▪ 1stB ca 1940 ▪ Tasting & sales Mon-Fri 8.30-5; Sat 10-2 (Apr-Oct); Sat 10-4 & Sun 11-4 (Nov-Mar) ▪ Informal tasting fee dependent on wine; tasting & tour: R25 ▪ Closed Easter Fri, Dec 25 & Jan 1 ▪ Tours in Afrikaans, English, French & German by appt ▪ Picnic lunches by appt Mon-Sun Nov-Mar ▪ Corporate & private lunches/dinners by appt ▪ 'Incredible Journey of Tastes' food & wine matching, by appt ▪ Tourgroups ▪ Gifts ▪ Conferences ▪ Conservation area ▪ Owner Distell ▪ Cellarmaster Razvan Macici (Jan 2001) ▪ Winemaker Elunda Basson (whites, reds, Jan 2000/2001), with Wellington Metshane & Pieter Badenhorst (reds, whites, Mar 2001/Jan 2003) ▪ Viticulturist Hannes van Rensburg ▪ 15 000 tons ▪ 1.1m cs ▪ Private Bag X3006 Paarl 7620 ▪ nedwines@distell.co.za ▪ www.nederburg.co.za ▪ ***T 862·3104*** *▪ F 862·4887*

Last year it was about the big picture. This year, cued by charismatic communicator, cellarmaster Razvan Macici, we focus on the small, though hardly less important, stuff. Romanian-born Razvan M questions modern preoccupations with new wood. Inspired by Nederburg's historic 5 000ℓ-plus vats, he's experimenting with slow vat-maturation of some 2004 cab and shiraz to express pure fruit, undominated by oak vanilla, for a niche range. Macici rates the 05 Sauvignon (a Nederburg focus variety) the best since 01. Look out also for the (increasingly rare in the Cape) Rhine Riesling. Planting plans include Spain's classic red variety, tempranillo – of course done in accordance with Nederburg's commitment to SA's new Biodiversity & Wine Initiative, something supported by Nederburg Auction 2005 guest, Loire Valley luminary and famous biodynamist, Nicolas Joly. An Auction era ends with auctioneer Patrick Grubb's retirement after 31 auctions/250 000 cases/R87-million. Moving, though not retiring, is winemaker Andrea Freeborough, who relocates to The Bergkelder. We recommend the 'Incredible Journey of Tastes' run by chef, lecturer and demonstrator Katinka van Niekerk, exploring food-and-wine pairings.

Private Bin wines for Nederburg Auction

The famous Nederburg Auction, now in its 32nd yr, is SA's biggest. It's open to any producer whose wine passes the selection process (Nederburg also subject to the screening). The Nederburg wines below are made in small quantities, usually from special vyd blocks, offered in lots of ±500 cs. Originally labelled under a meaningless Bin number, prefaced by a letter (R=dry red, D dry white, S dessert, C Cap Classique), they now also carry the variety/blend.

★★★★ **Cabernet Sauvignon Private Bin R163** 'New World' style – distinctive capsicum always on these. Excellent **03** (★★★★★) from Papkuilsfontein grapes. Fresh cedar, almost herbaceous; compact, concentrated dark-berried allure, tannin still taut, muscles & sinews showing. Will easily last 10 yrs. These 03 reds the first PB wines made in new Nederburg cellar. 10% juice removed after crushing to concentrate wine; mix open fermenters, steel tanks. All given 18 mths maturation in 300ℓ barrels on their way to auction.

★★★★ **Cabernet Sauvignon-Merlot Private Bin R109** Classic aromas/flavours on **03** – cassis, lead pencil, choc truffle with cab leading the way in 58/42 blend, giving frame, backbone for gentler attractions of merlot. Mid-weight, elegantly put together. More charm & approachability than R163 – almost ready.

★★★★ **Cabernet Sauvignon-Shiraz Private Bin R103** Sports-model version of the Baronne family sedan; **03** 60/40 blend, black, inky, inscrutable, matching black berries with touches toast & tar. Firm tannic backbone for tightly woven fruit – taut, compact, needs to unravel. Like below, Am oak for shiraz.

★★★★ **Shiraz-Cabernet Sauvignon Private Bin R115** Warm welcoming shiraz in charge: **03** ripe plum, black cherry with hint of cab's signature cassis, cedar. Softer, more relaxed than above. Fleshy fruit around firm cab core, more meat on the bone. Darling/ Dbnville grapes.

★★★★ **Merlot Private Bin R181** Fragrant cassis & lead pencil intro for **03**. Gorgeous blackcurrant flavours, some riper mulberry notes, soft fine-grained tannins; showing the variety's more rounded, 'feminine' persona here, stylishly groomed. Lovely dry finish, but no austerity. Ex-Dbnville.

★★★★ **Pinotage Private Bin R172 03**'s sleek fruit, groomed in oak, has emerged suave & stylish. Plum & tangy plum skins instead of pinotage sweetness; muscular tannins still firm, no signs of overweight, still very much a pinotage. Needs time to unravel, open. Trenchant, chewy **02** (★★★☆) a vintage victim.

★★★★ **Shiraz Private Bin R121** Black choc, veld fire, warm baked fruit on **03**, more savoury than sweet ripeness. Interesting crushed herb touches to dark fruit, attractive fruit/ tannin balance translates into early approachability. Elegantly proportioned & tailored outline, lengthy finish.

★★★★ **Sangiovese-Barbera-Nebbiolo Private Bin** Any Italian might shudder at the mix – until tasting it. Latest **03** intriguing truffly, choc, vanilla notes; combines cherry ripeness with savoury/meaty flavours. Wonderfully urbane, sleek, pleasingly soft – less tannic than cellarmates. 78/15/7 blend; mix Fr, Am, E Eur oak. No **02**.

★★★★ **Petit Verdot Private Bin R104** Such a charmer! **03** youthfully beguiling, whiff sweet ripe redcurrants complemented by vanilla oak; delicate cassis flavours clad in fine oak, soft & unobtrusive tannins. Grapes from Plaisir de Merle.

★★★★ **Sauvignon Blanc** Two distinct sources & styles, to appeal to different palates. **Private Bin D215** captures exotic tropical character of Dbnville; **05** a cornucopia of pineapple, pomelo, lime; expansive lime-tinged flavours explode, expand on palate. Big 14. 6% alc, saved from flab by good acid. **Private Bin D234** Delicate & refined, tender green aromas/flavours of fig, grass & nettles – sappy but suavely groomed along more classic lines.

★★★☆ **Sauvignon Blanc-Chardonnay Private Bin D253** Maiden **04** was rather closed in youth; **05** (★★★★) split personality – extraordinary bouquet features ripe fig of sauvignon with yellow peach of chardonnay & oak vanillin, not yet integrated (65% sauvignon winning mid-2005). Juicy, firm fleshed, tangy – the shrew should be tamed in time for 06 Auction. Chardonnay fermented/3 mths oak.

★★★☆ **Chardonnay Private Bin D270** Stony intensity & fabulous fruit on **03** (★★★★). Discreetly scented, elegant **04** repeats lime, citrus style with minerally, stony notes in lower key; still holding back, though all the components there. Needs another 2-3 yrs. Yr Fr oak. Stbosch, Dbnville sources.

★★★★ **Sauvignon Blanc-Semillon Private Bin D252** Last tasted was **03** 60/40 blend, tingling with sauvignon flint; no **04**.

★★★★ **Edelkeur** The botrytised chenin that gave rise to this country's NLH industry. **04** (★★★★☆) now bottled, taking on distinct chenin persona: honey, ripe quince, damp chalk – like a classic vouvray, but with SA ripeness, generosity giving honey & cream texture. Very sweet at 203g/ℓ RS. Superb concentration to this tangerine-tinged elixir, evident in long citrus finish. Huge concentration seen in **03** (VDG).

★★★★ **Semillon Noble Late Harvest** Always good value at Auction. No **03**. Last tasted was brooding, elegant **02**.

★★★★ **Weisser Riesling Noble Late Harvest Private Bin S316** Linden blossom, lime zest & eucalyptus honey on **04**. Exquisite sweetness buffed with botrytis, rich & heavy but never syrupy – lifted by clean citrus tang of acidity to glide across the palate. If chenin is taffeta, this is satin....

★★★★ **Eminence 04** suggests hand of master perfumier working with grapefruit, powder-puff, lime cordial, jasmine & wafting spice. Lively clean-cut citrus flavours a great cover-up for amazing 218g/ℓ sugar; lovely grapey sweetness, dances lightly across the palate. From muscat de F. **03** MIWA DG.

Following all rate ★★★✩. **Malbec Private Bin R101** Definitely something different. **03** showing smoked beef, charry oak, scrub & tar; still taut with tannin, savoury flavours, some youthful austerity on good dry finish. **Cabernet Franc Private Bin** Last was succulent **01**; next may be **04**. **Semillon-Viognier Private Bin D224** 'Having fun' embodied in maiden **03**, peach-pip aromas jest with full waxy spice in exotic 60/40 assemblage (both 2nd fill Fr oak). This & 3 next wines in abeyance; notes from last ed. **Semillon Private Bin D266 03** intensely reductive fruit to match brisk frame. **Viognier Private Bin 03** Poised muscat scents, ripe apricot-pip fruits & gentle oak (30% ferment in new Fr). **Gewürztraminer Private Bin D259** Macici's maiden **04** made to prevent grubbing-up of low-yielding old vines; alluring aromas, ripe, deeply concentrated & powerful palate. Refreshingly dry 2.5g/ℓ sugar, possible growth to ★★★★.

Other Private Bin wines (no numbers), more readily obtainable

★★★★ **Sauvignon Blanc** Outstanding **05** (sample) from home-grown grapes: figs, nettles, grass – full house of fresh sauvignon aromas. Lean, aggressive, tart, racy acidity, exciting – everything to make the aficionado's heart beat faster.

Following all rate ★★★✩. **Cabernet Sauvignon** Gorgeous mint, cedar & eucalyptus touches to dark mulberry/choc fruit in **03**, fine-grained tannins. These intended for earlier drinking though not without ambition. 18 mths new Fr/E Eur oak, same as for ... **Shiraz 03** roast beef, mocha, toasty oak give friendly welcome; ripe, rich & savoury, excellent fruit concentration. More accessible than R121 above. Blend Philadelphia, Dbnville fruit, as was radiant **02** (★★★★). **Chardonnay** Flamboyant modern style, a real show-off. **04** yellow peach, vanilla oak, butterscotch, leesy richness intro; expansive flavours, peachy fruit weight, complexity just starting – needs yr+. Fermented/yr new Fr oak.

Classic range

★★★★ **Edelrood** ✓ Quintessential Nederburg, firmly top of the heap. **03** woody balsamic notes to sweetly ripened cassis, touches of beef & tar, too; dry & meaty with firm savoury tannins, but already approachable. Perhaps (unusually) more approachable than Baronne this vintage. Cab/merlot blend 60/40.

★★★✩ **Rhine Riesling** ✓ Gorgeous whiff rose-petals announces gewürz in blend, upped to 15% (from enticingly aromatic **04**'s 10%) in delicately spicy **05** (★★★★). Off-dry with excellent sugar/acid balance; juicy lime dances prettily on the palate, twirls & disappears slowly to applause.

★★★★ **Noble Late Harvest** Credible alternative to special Auction offerings, some might even prefer. Latest **04** (★★★★✩) wafting honeysuckle, crème brûlée perfume; sweet glacé pineapple, peach & honey – with oh-so-elegant acidity to give balance & poise. All giving the longest finish this year. 151g/ℓ sugar, 9.7 g/ℓ acid. Blend chenin, muscat, semillon. 375 ml. FCTWS trophy/gold, Tri-Nations 2005 trophy. **03** upholstered peaches & cream opulence toned by cool tropical lines.

Paarl Riesling ☺ ★★★ Enduringly popular tipple from crouchen. **05** runs true to form: warm straw notes, crisply dry, with modest 12.1% alc – ideal for lunchtime pleasure. Enjoy fresh.

★★★✩ **Baronne** ✓ ★★★✩ Fragrant oak on **03**, pencil shavings, meaty aromas; tannic grip to savoury smoked beef palate, compact neatly tailored profile & very dry finish. Blend cab/shiraz 40/60. **Cabernet Sauvignon** ★★★✩ Oaky, mulberry-tinged **03**; firm still-taut tannins, but underlying fruit in abundance, hint herbaceous green character on finish. **Shiraz** ★★★☆ Variety Macici's bet for Nederburg's future. **03** deep & plummy with snatches of leather, burnt underbrush. Welcoming character; nice fleshiness of spiced plum, black cherry; tannins softening help towards lingering dry finish. **Pinotage** ★★★ Meaty, savoury intro, varietal exuberance held in check in this dry savoury version, with good whack of oak & mouth-watering acidity; long dry finish points to good fruit concentration. **Rosé** ★☆ More semi-sweet than off-dry in soft **05**, with curious animal-like aromas, meaty rather than berry flavours. **Sauvignon Blanc** ★★★☆ Ever-improving label, latest **05** (sample) a real show-off, nudging higher rating. Luscious tropical fruit around core of steely, dusty capsicum. Super concentration, loads of gooseberry, nettly flavours, crisp tangy acidity. A real achievement in such quantities – 40 000 cases. **Chardonnay** ★★★ Aromas, flavours lime, snatches wet chalk/damp cellar on very dry **04**; less nimble than previously, a bit rustic. 30% fermented/6 mths oak. **Sauvignon Blanc-Chardonnay** (Previously Prelude) ★★☆ **05** has tiny addition pinot blanc; fresh apple character in youth, will put on weight quickly; not so light at 13.8% alc. Seamless blend, chard briefly oaked. **Premier Grand Cru** ★★ Not your usual bleak dry white; latest bottling **NV** has ripeness & shapely build. Steely finish lifted by fruity tones from ripe chenin. Famously bone-dry.

Lifestyle range

Shiraz-Pinotage new ★★☆ **04** 60/40 blend is quite shy, with warm prune fruit, sweetness of pinotage. Staves 3 mths. **Duet** ★★☆ 55/45 pinot/cab **04** blend tasted last ed: smiling cherry fruit unobscured by wood or tannin. **Chenin Blanc-Chardonnay** new ★★☆ Chard component (40%) adds roundness, some breadth to crisp but balanced **05**; notes of peach, wet wool. **Lyric** ★★ **05** light-bodied, crisply off-dry cooling summer quaffer with lemony freshness and light 11.5% alc; blend sauvignon, chenin, chardonnay. **Stein** ★★ Ever-popular semi-sweet; tropical tones on **05** (sample), sweetness offset by crisp acidity. **Special Late Harvest** ★★★ Fragrant sweetie from chenin, gewürz, muscat, pure sun-ripened sweetness, tangy tropical nuances in **05**. Lively, fresh, 60g/ℓ sugar.

Sparkling

Premiere Cuvée Brut ★★☆ Ever reliable carbonated **NV** to put a spring in your step – it's crisply dry, & more about the bubbles than the flavour. — *IvH*

Neethlingshof Estate

*Stellenbosch ▪ Tasting & sales daily 9-7 (closes at 5pm Feb1-Nov 30) ▪ Fee R25 (R30 incl cellar tour) ▪ Closed Easter Fri & Dec 25 ▪ Tours by appointment ▪ Lord Neethling Restaurant, Palm Terrace ▪ Play area for children ▪ Tourgroups ▪ Conferences ▪ Owner Lusan Premium Wines ▪ Winemaker DeWet Viljoen, with Susan Wessels ▪ Vineyard managers Hannes van Zyl & Peet Blom ▪ Viticulturist Eben Archer ▪ 210 ha ▪ 50 000 cs 60% red 40% white ▪ PO Box 104 Stellenbosch 7599 ▪ info@neethlingshof.co.za ▪ www.neethlingshof.co.za ▪ **T 883·8988** ▪ F 883·8941*

From adopting screwcap for the Sauvignon ('the only way we can guarantee our wine 100%') to experimenting with fermenting red wines in barrel (Hungarian as well as French oak), young De Wet Viljoen has taken the winemaking helm at this 300 year old estate with great confidence (and some expert advice from Eben Archer, his former lecturer). The standout news from 2005 is the dual gong for the Lord Neethling Laurentius 01, named best Bordeaux blend and best red wine overall at the 2005 Trophy Show. Viljoen and new assistant Susan Wessels certainly make a young and vibrant team – and so, as if to keep up with them, Neethlingshof has upgraded its labels and visitors' centre.

Lord Neethling range

★★★★☆ **Laurentius** Refreshingly understated flagship red showing balance, refinement & length. **01** cab-dominated (70%) with cab f, merlot & shiraz. Deserved FCTWS 2005 trophy, yr oak, Fr:Am 90:10, 70% new. More tannic than meaty/mushroomy **00**, with fuller mouthfeel & warmer presence. Same wooding regimen.

★★★★ **Cabernet Sauvignon** Last tasted **00** (★★★) harks back to the more severe tones of **98**, which needed some yrs to open. The newer version unsophisticated, very dry with pronounced acidity. ±16 mths Fr oak.

★★★★ **Cabernet Franc 03** returns to form after vintage-impacted **02** (★★★). Floral bouquet with big dark fruits & serious structure, fine tannins. 14 mths Fr oak. Riper than **02**, with pronounced greenpepper character, very dry finish.

★★★★ **Pinotage** Usually has more style, personality than version below. Back on track with **02**, exuberant alc (15.2%), abundant red fruit & earthy notes with sweet tail. Richer than **01** (★★★) a fleeting diversion into quieter, sparser territory.

★★★★☆ **Chardonnay** Last tasted was show-stopping **02**. Barrel-fermented/aged 7 mths new Fr oak.

Standard range

★★★☆ **Cabernet Sauvignon 02** (★★★★) raises the bar with seriously structured cassis & dark choc, earthy tint. Yr Fr oak. Less woody than **01** with greenpepper nose & simple, sweet oak.

★★★★ **Shiraz** Brooding, introverted **01** needed time to develop, harmonise; good oaking. **02** (★★★), though big & mouth-filling, with plentiful bold ripe flavours, more extracted, less fresh than usual; grapples with some awkward tannins, finishing a little bitter.

★★★★ **Cape Blend** Mostly for export, though some available from estate. Last tasted was youthfully tannic **01**; mainly unwooded blend cabs s/f, pinotage (40/28/22) with dash cab.

★★★★ **Gewürztraminer** Lovely example, could even subvert those who only drink dry. **05** liquid Turkish Delight; huge floral bouquet of jasmine & honeysuckle. Specs (13% alc, 10g/ℓ RS) same as refined & elegant, well balanced **04**. Usually incl splash riesling.

★★★★☆ **Weisser Riesling Noble Late Harvest 04** returns to sweeter style (163g/ℓ RS) from drier **03** (118g/ℓ). Latest version just 9.5% alc, yet packs marvellous intensity into its small frame: fragrant granadilla plus apricot, honey & peach; even more flamboyant than **03**, showing tangerine peel, orange marmalade & honey tones.

Merlot ★★★☆ **01** nose of damp leaves, hints of mint & blackcurrant; serious oaking 17 mths (none new). **Pinotage** ★★★ **02** hefty alc (15%), sweet fruit & some tarry notes; seriously oaked – 17 mths Fr/Am (75/25) oak, 24% new. **Cabernet Sauvignon-Merlot** ★★★☆ **03** restrained style with prominent tannins, blackcurrant/black plum flavours. Low 13.% alc. 8 mths Fr oak. **Chardonnay** ★★★☆ **05** unwooded with steely character. Leesy nose, hint pears, bracing finish. **Sauvignon Blanc** ★★★☆ From False Bay-facing vyds; **05** (sample) classic grassy, lemon zesty character with undertones of tropical fruit, in style of pvs. — *NP/TJ/RK*

Neil Ellis Meyer-Näkel new

Stellenbosch ▪ Est/1stB 1998 ▪ Tasting/sales at Neil Ellis Wines (see entry) ▪ Owner Neil Ellis Meyer-Näkel (Pty) Ltd ▪ Winemakers Neil Ellis & Werner Näkel ▪ Viticulturist Pieter Smit ▪ 10 ha ▪ 3 500 cs 100% red ▪ PO Box 917 Stellenbosch 7599 ▪ info@neilellis.com ▪ ***T 887·0649*** *▪ F 887·0647*

Zwalu, which means 'new beginnings', is a joint venture brand started in 1987 between leading local winemaker Neil Ellis and Werner Meyer-Näkel, flamboyant German winemaker and red-wine specialist with a penchant for pinot – he owns vineyards in the Ahr valley, blessed with lime-rich shale and slate soils ideal for his favoured *spätburgunder*. The made-in-SA wines below are partly from a small own vyd on Helshoogte, and were originally intended for the German market only. But a demand, primarily from tourist-oriented restaurants, led to the decision to launch them locally too.

Zwalu ★★★☆ Traditionally-styled cab; **03** compact, firm; correctly dry, with more modern coffee/mocha enhancement to clean, fresh cassis fruit. Nicely balanced, not obviously big; persistent. Drink this, following wine, now & over ±2 yrs. **Z** ★★★☆ Genial **03** merlot/cab blend (67/33); quite advanced blood-red hue; fresher nose, flavours; not too dense, complicated but good presence to merlot-led bright, minty, red berry fruit. Noticeable but well meshed sappy tannins. Both WO Stbosch 14% alc. — *AL*

Neil Ellis Wines

Stellenbosch ▪ 1stB 1984 ▪ Tasting & sales Mon-Fri 9.30–4.30 Sat & pub hols 10–2 ▪ Fee R15 p/p, waived on purchase ▪ Closed Easter Fri/Sun, Dec 25/26 & Jan 1 ▪ Owner Neil Ellis Wines (Pty) Ltd ▪ Winemaker Neil Ellis, with Abraham de Klerk (Oct 2004) ▪ 40 000 cs ▪ 50% red 50% white ▪ PO Box 917 Stellenbosch 7599 ▪ info@neilellis.com ▪ www.neilellis.com ▪ ***T 887·0649*** *▪ F 887·0647*

'I'd like to put the fun and passion back into wine,' says Neil Ellis, looking back over the past five years of tough business conditions and unceasing international travel. 'And maybe take a long holiday.' For now, he seems too busy giving of his time and know-how to nurture a new generation (here on the Jonkershoek home farm and, lately, also as part of the KWV mentoring programme). What advice does he give his protégés? 'The four pillars: pride, passion, vision and technological competence.' On that other industry hot button, cool-climate winemaking, this pioneer has the inside track. He was first to reveal the potential of selected Groenekloof and Elgin sites back in the 80s. Now he has his own ten hectares of reds in Elgin, widely perceived as white-wine territory, and the young vines are producing exciting results: 'It's early days but what we're seeing is really encouraging....'

Vineyard Selection range

Single-vyd 'reserves', WO Jonkershoek Valley, for long maturation.

★★★★☆ **Cabernet Sauvignon** Pedigreed cab from home vyds expressing Neil E's long-time philosophy of power with elegance. More modern-style **03** very plush & richly fruited; luxurious cedar-dusted cassis/blackberry scents; still cocooned in oak/grape tannin — suggest leave until 2007; drink until at least 2013. No **02**. **01** showed more of Neil E's signature taut minerality; expressive dark-berry tones embellished with cedar fragrance from new wood (Fr, 18 mths). Breed recognised in numerous accolades, incl **01** 90 pts *WS;* **00** Wine ★★★★☆; *Decanter* ★★★★; IWC gold; VDG. 90 pts WS.

★★★★☆ **Syrah** (pvsly 'Shiraz') Offers more northern-Rhône spicy warmth than Premium version. **03** bigger than pvs under this label. Generous dark fruits/smoked meat endowments; lovely rich texture; firm yet unintrusive tannins; complementary toasty extras from 16 mths in Fr oak. Burly 15% alc harnessed by terrific fruit concentration, dry finish. Enjoy from 2008. No **02**. **01** proffered ambrosial allspice scents, ripe fine-grained tannins, 'cool' finish. **01**, **00** 90 pts *WS*.

★★★★☆ **Sauvignon Blanc** new Same vyd as Premium version below, crafted into more powerful, food-orientated style. Sophisticated & ultra-cool **04**; sleek chalky quality to usual gooseberry purity. Firmly built, uncompromisingly dry but with gorgeous weight, flavour penetration. 30% Fr oak fermented/matured 8 mths.

Premium range

★★★★☆ **Stellenbosch Cabernet Sauvignon** Ellis loses no opportunity to give full expression to wonderful vintage: **03** deep, cedar-dusted cassis/ripe blackberry scents; fruit intensity contrasted & freshened by light, compact texture, fine-grained tannins, plus usual moderate alc. A classic, promising impressive maturity around 2011/13. **02** agreeable, if less complex than usual; enjoy before **03**, brilliant **01**. ±18 mths Fr oak, 50% new. **01** 90 pts *WS*.

★★★★ **Stellenbosch Pinotage** ✓ **03** still in cask, not re-assessed. Last yr we noted healthy colour; refined, full flavour spectrum, medium body; structure for longevity. **02** svelte interplay of clove-spiked plums & well-meshed tannins. Polished ±15 mths Fr oak.

★★★★ **Stellenbosch Shiraz** Refined style with depth & substance. Retasted **03** hibernating; all original qualities in place (sleek mulberry/dark spice concentration, refinement, delicacy, freshness); just need yr/2 to relax. Promises fine evolution till ±2011-13. Subtly oaked; ±15 mths Fr barrels.

★★★★ **Stellenbosch Cabernet Sauvignon-Merlot** Sleek, chic 50/50 blend; traditional in its elegance & tight structure. **03** (★★★★☆), revisited, in quietish phase; will benefit from further ±2 yrs' maturation. Fine dusty grip, mineral length, blackberry/cassis richness. Beautifully composed, stylishly oaked. Growth possibilities till 2011/13. **02** broader palate with choc/meat notes, super finish. While usually approachable young, these better after ±5 yrs. Fr oak ±15 mths.

★★★★ **Stellenbosch Chardonnay** Always prime example (with Elgin version below) of the differences between sites & vintages. More powerful, richer chard yr (but usual ±13% alc) reflected in expansive though still elegant **04**. Less obvious oak on generous tropical fruit/lime nose; firmish mouthfeel; leesy richness on finish suggests earlier drinking (till ±2007) than supple, tapered **03**, which benefited from cooler than usual conditions in Stbosch. Always well oaked (Fr fermented/±9 mths). Home vyds.

★★★★ **Elgin Chardonnay** Fine, taut **04** speaks of cool, high vyds; initially reticent, mere glimpses of citrus peel on nose; on palate more forthcoming hazelnut, oatmeal savouriness, supple mineral freshness. Less ready than version above; may go yr/2 longer. But not as long-lived as **03** (★★★★☆), minerally, compact, with focused, tangy length. Potential till 2010-13. Fermented/matured Fr barrels, 10 mths.

★★★★ **Aenigma** new Part of Cape mini-trend to entice through non-disclosure. Minimalist front label gives away only origin (Stellenbosch) & vintage (**03**); we can reveal a Neil E experimental chardonnay, quite different from above versions, barrel-fermented with native yeasts, matured 10 mths (partial malo allowed). More complex vinosity, rich burgundy-like savoury decadence rather than New World fruitiness; Ellis's elegant touch a given. Lots of evolution potential.

★★★★☆ **Groenekloof Sauvignon Blanc** ✓ **05** first to be closed with smart-looking screwcap, the better to preserve quite stunning contents. Among the pick of variable vintage; cool & bracing as the Atlantic. Incisive, pure gooseberry/granadilla introduction; greengage/green fig extras unleashed with 'big wave' of flavour, even more explosive finish. Vivid, breathtaking stuff; set to entrench SA's sauvignon reputation internationally. **04** show-stopper in bigger, more luscious mode. WO Groenekloof.

—AL

Nelson Estate

*Paarl ▪ Est/1stB 1993 ▪ Tasting & sales Mon-Fri 9-5 Sat 9-2 Sun by appt ▪ Fee R10, waived on purchase of 6 btls ▪ Closed Easter Fri/Sun, Dec 25 & Jan 1 ▪ Tours Mon-Sat 10; Sun by appt ▪ Meals/refreshments by appt ▪ Facilities for children ▪ Tourgroups ▪ Gifts ▪ Walks ▪ Conference/function/lapa venue ▪ Conservation area ▪ Owner Alan Nelson ▪ Winemaker Jean van Rooyen, with Lisha Nelson (Dec 2003/Nov 2005) ▪ Viticulturists Lisha & Daniel Nelson (Apr 2005) ▪ 60 ha (cab, merlot, pinotage, shiraz, chard, sauvignon) ▪ 340 tons 20 000 cs own label 65% red 30% white 5% rosé ▪ PO Box 2009 Windmeul 7630 ▪ info@nelsonscreek.co.za ▪ www.nelsonscreek.co.za ▪ **T 869·8453** ▪ F 869·8424*

A champagne year for recently retired advocate Alan Nelson and his family, with a full house of Veritas medals awarded to the flagship Estate range; an international panel judging the estate SA's 'Best Business Tourism Destination' (a newly added 450-guest conference venue especially impressive to the judges); son Daniel joining taking over as viticulturist; and daughter Lisha graduating cum laude from Stellenbosch University and garnering the PJ van der Bijl medal for winemaking and viniculture. After doing a second season at Mulderbosch and a stint at Kendall-Jackson in California, Lisha joins the team as assistant winemaker for the 2006 harvest — 'but not before she gets to know every vine by name,' says Alan N.

Nelson Estate range

★★★★ **Cabernet Sauvignon-Merlot** To date the stylish **02**, 81/19 blend, all Fr oak, 18 mths, 80% new. (All estate's reds feature *saignée*-style drawing-off of some juice pre-fermentation, for heightened flavour concentration; here 30% was bled.) Last yr evinced classic cassis/cigarbox tones; firm, slightly grainy tannins; deftly applied wood. Begged couple of yrs to soften, unfold.

★★★★ **Pinotage 02** settled down with extra yr in bottle, initial big dry tannins last ed were less feisty; rich mocha/smoked meat character – appealingly showy. 18 mths Fr oak.

★★★★ **Chardonnay** Forceful, creamy style, lots of concentrated flavour & structure, extra complexity from native yeast fermentation, extended lie-in on lees (9-11 mths); **04** gets 100% new Fr oak, which it handles admirably; oozes very ripe lime fruit, butteriness, yet manages elegance. **03** (★★★★) somewhat quieter, also attractive.

Shiraz ★★★★ **02** last ed was noted as full-bodied/flavoured (14.8% alc) but not overpowering; well layered with peppery red fruit, warm toast & coffee tones. VDG.

Nelson's Creek range

Merlot ★★★ Lead pencils & cassis announce **03**, clean ripe fruit, very big dry wood tannins from yr 2nd/3rd fill Fr oak. **Pinotage** ★★★ Switches to wooded (9 mths Fr) for **03**, very different to silky pvs; this savoury & rustic, ±15% alc shows in tingly finish. **Cabernet Sauvignon** ★★★ **02**, with dash merlot, similar to pvs; meaty whiffs, dry, savoury, slightly earthy flavours, firm tannins. 8 mths new Fr staves. **Shiraz** ★★★★ Step-up **02** suave & supple; appetising dark choc/ black cherry flavours; fine pervasive smokiness. From single 'Stony Hill' vyd; 2nd-4th fill oak, 10% Am. **Albenet** ★★★ Blend changes to equal ruby cab, cinsaut, 20% merlot for **05** (sample), wine remains appealing pasta partner, juicy (& generous: 14.8% alc) unwooded mouthful. **Cabernet Sauvignon-Merlot Rosé** ★★★ Ideal summer picnic wine; **04** redcurrant jelly flavours, soft fruit-sweet (but technically dry) finish. **Chardonnay** ★★★ **04** no-frills version of the above; nice lime flavours, sharpish acidity. 'Great with garlic prawns' says Jean vR. 4 mths Fr staves. **Sauvignon Blanc** ★★★ **05** (sample) very gentle expression of the grape; bouncy fruity flavours, again sweetish slick from ±4g/ℓ sugar. **Triple Creek** ★★ Similar chenin, semillon, chardonnay composition as pvs; **04** (sample) more earthy, less complex, with whiff of honeycomb. **Marguerite** ★★★ Scented semi-dry blend chenin, muscat d'A (80/20); **03** not too sweet, persistent kiwi fruit flavour, good with spicy food. — *IvH/TM*

New Beginnings Wines

*Paarl ▪ Tasting & sales Mon-Fri 9-5 ▪ Fee R20 for groups ▪ Vineyard tours by appointment ▪ Owner Klein Begin Farming Association ▪ Winemaker Sollie Hendriks, assisted by Jean van Rooyen (Nelson Estate) since 2003 ▪ 13 000 cs 60% white 40% red ▪ PO Box 2009 Windmeul 7630 ▪ victor@nelsonscreek.co.za ▪ **T 869·8453** ▪ F 869·8424*

When New Beginnings produced their own wine for the first time in 1997, some thought this offshoot of Nelson Estate would not make it in the competitive wine business. But the farmworkers persevered and now their wines are beginning to come into their own. A new stylish label matches the much-improved wines, made from own vineyards now six years old. Last year young trainee winemaker, Solly Hendriks, a 3rd-generation worker on the estate, spent a season honing his skills in Burgundy. Not to be outdone by their husbands, the New Beginnings women have started their own bread-baking, catering and tourism business. Chairperson Mita Skippers says they have great aspirations of soon also running their own 'open fire' function and tourism venue.

No new releases. Last ed we noted a new seriousness throughout the range. **Cabernet Sauvignon** ★★★ More extract than pvs, **03** big (15% alc), deep blackberry flavour, assertive but good oak. **Pinotage** ★★★ **03** plump yet forceful (15% alc); banana whiffs, smoky complexity. Good potential. **Chardonnay** ★★★ 25% barrel-fermented, **03** attractive creaminess with baked apple whiff, nicely poised; alc well contained too (13.3%). — *TM*

New Cape Wines

*Worcester ▪ Est/1stB 2000 ▪ Tasting, sales & tours Mon-Fri 8–4.30 Sat 10–3 ▪ Owner/winemaker Christiaan Groenewald ▪ 80 ha ▪ 40% red 60% white ▪ PO Box 898 Worcester 6849 ▪ christiaan@ ncw.co.za ▪ www.newcapewines.co.za ▪ **T (023) 340·4112** ▪ F (023) 340·4132*

With a university degree in oenology/viticulture and a former career in financial management, an undeniably well-qualified Christiaan Groenewald is making a success of his own wine venture too. Born and bred on the family farm in the Worcester winelands, he continued farming after his father passed away on the nearly 600 ha farm, and is intent on building and expanding his export and local business for his Eagle's Cliff and Dwyka Hills ranges (Canada, Europe and the East). Facilities on the farm include tasting and conference areas and a small cellar.

Dwyka Hills Shiraz ★★★ Last tasted was **03**, well behaved, shy plum tones on nose, fairly open texture, sweetish finish tinged with fennel. Light oaking.

Eagle's Cliff Reserve range

Cabernet Sauvignon ★★★ Not retasted this ed; **02**'s initial charry oak became better meshed with time in bottle; now offers smoky cassis aromas, plump & juicy black plum fruit. **Shiraz** ★★★ **03** (sample) ripe juicy fruit, supple tannin – all elements in place for solid, flavourful easy drinker. **Chardonnay** new Unrated sample **05** boldly oaky, warmly ripe with obvious barrel character incl butterscotch & lees. **Sauvignon Blanc** ★★★★ **05** light but full flavoured; bright tropical fruit tinged with capsicum & gooseberry; firm, garden-fresh, with tingling mineral aftertaste. **Viognier** new ★★★★ **05** preview gorgeous wafts of apricot & nectarine, hint evening flower & greengage – real complexity, excitement here; rich, slightly sweet persistent flavours. Most auspicious debut.

Eagle's Cliff range

Merlot-Cabernet Sauvignon ★★★ **03** 70/30 blend, last yr noted as reticent on nose, hints smoky stewed prunes; sweet-sour character, muted fruity presence. **Shiraz-Pinotage** ★★★ Plummy **02** 70/30 blend, pvs ed was pleasantly sweet fruited, plump & silky. **Shiraz Rosé** new ★★★ Startling psychedelic pink **05**, light & attractively dry, tangy flavours, sweet-sour fruity aftertaste. **Chardonnay** ★★ **04** shy, light bodied, delicate & pleasant without too much varietal character. **Chenin Blanc** ★★ Pear-drop & guava tones this vintage; **05** (sample) fuller bodied, slightly short, very firm finish. **Sauvignon Blanc** ★★★ **05** again light bodied (12.6% alc) yet full of flavour, firmly dry with crisp mineral acidity. Super sundowner. Both ranges WO Wrcstr. *– IvH/TM*

Newton Johnson Wines

Walker Bay ▪ Est 1996 ▪ 1stB 1997 ▪ Tasting & sales Mon-Fri 9-4 Sat 10-12.30 (Sep 22-Apr 29 only, otherwise by appt) ▪ Closed pub hols ▪ Owners Dave & Felicity Johnson ▪ Winemaker Gordon Newton Johnson (Jan 2001) ▪ Viticulturists Christopher Cloete & Schalk du Toit (2004) ▪ 8 ha (pinot, shiraz, chard, sauvignon) ▪ 120 tons 6 000 cs 40% red 43% white 17% rosé ▪ PO Box 225 Hermanus 7200 ▪ wine@newtonjohnson.com ▪ www.newtonjohnson.com ▪ ***T (028) 312·3862*** *▪ F (028) 312·3867*

Winemaker Gordon Newton Johnson, struck by how radically interventions in the winemaking process affect the end-product, is fine-tuning his techniques with each passing vintage. This, he says, throws him back on a belief in the vineyard, and he finds himself being rewarded by more expressive and intriguing wines. Sale of their Cape Bay farm is funding the construction of a new gravity-fed cellar down the road, designed to complement this approach by minimising handling and allowing small batch vinification. Viticulturist Christopher Cloete has joined Schalk du Toit in N-J's own shiraz and pinot vineyards, where they aim to 'really start hitting the higher gears'.

★★★★ **Cabernet Sauvignon** Features dollop shiraz; this yr from H-en-A Vlly (pvsly Dbnville); cab as always ex-Bot River. Restrained, smoky, forest floor characters on **03**, black cherry palate with fine fruit tannins & persistent, cool adieu. **02** (★★★★) not very cab-like; chunky & chewy, needing time. ±Yr Fr oak, 40% new.

★★★★ **Pinot Noir** One of SA's more elegant pinots. Cherries, minerals & oak-toast mingle in bouquet of **04**, showing refreshing pinot acidity, grainy tannins. Silky cherry-fruit finish. Alc back down to ± 13.5% from solid 14.4% in **03**. 9-10 mths Burgundian oak, 35-40% new.

★★★★ **Shiraz-Mourvèdre** Exciting rhône-style blend from W Bay, Dbnville vyds. Modern but not sweet; in fact, tightly wound, needing time to relax, gain extra complexity. **04** black pepper, scrub, smoky plums; palate refreshed by raspberry acidity, supportive oak. Hints old leather on tail of Classic Wine Trophy Gold **03**. 12-13 mths Burgundy barrels, 40 % new.

★★★★ **Pour Mes Amis** Occasional label, when sense of adventure/need to experiment grips Gordon NJ. Typically small parcels fruit. **05** sauvignon (75%), semillon ex-W Bay. Slatey rather than fruity expression of the varieties; palate fleshed out by semillon's richness, 3 mths new Fr barriques. Harmonious, with zesty sauvignon core. Should gain complexity in bottle over 3-7 yrs.

★★★★ **Chardonnay** Endeavours to capture flint, grapefruit & lime profile of Vllrsdorp single vyd 'Kaaimansgat' ('Crocodile's Lair'); only partial malo for tighter mineral core; lees-stirring for creamier mouthfeel. Judicious use of Burgundian oak (40% new). **04** rich but not heavy; lemon cream, tangerine, lime flavours/aromas. **03** well-structured; overt sweetness (±6g/ℓ) cut by pervasive limy tang.

★★★★ **Sauvignon Blanc** ✓ From H-en-A Vlly, usually broadened by splash oaked Bot R semillon. **05** mineral nose, appetising grapefruit/apple flavours. Integrated & restrained, structure/flavour profile to keep ±3 yrs. **04** one of the more expressive that vintage. Modest ±13% alc.

Felicité ★★★★ Pinot, picked specifically for this sophisticated, food-friendly dry rosé. No **05** – fruit not up to std. Soupçon shiraz also featured in luminous coral-pink **04**, juicy, with firm zesty finish. – *CvZ*

New World see The Winery
Nicholas L Jonker Estate see Jonkheer

Nick & Forti's Wines

new

Est/1stB 2004 ▪ Closed to public ▪ Owners Fortunato Mazzone & Saronsberg ▪ Winemaker Dewaldt Heyns (2004) ▪ 200 cs 100% red ▪ PO Box 25032 Monument Park Pretoria 0105 ▪ ritrovo@mweb.co.za ▪ ***T (012)·460·4367*** *▪ F (012) 460·5173*

Collaboration between Nick van Huyssteen of Saronsberg and Forti Mazzone, chef and co-owner of acclaimed Ritrovo Ristorante in Pretoria, celebrating 'life, friendship and superb wine'.

Both **04**, attractively & appropriately packaged, eponymous N&F smiling benignly from the front label. **Shiraz** ★★★★ Fragrant, sippable & juicy; breadth & roundness imparted by the shiraz, weight & length lent by dollop (12%) malbec, petit v & cab. Spice, wild scrub & lavender whiffs; friendly tannins, subtle oak (yr Fr, 40% new). **Epicentre** ★★★★ Accessible, food-friendly bdx blend made to FM's specs. Suitably kitchenesque sniffs of tomato & black fruit; cassis palate focused by fine fruit/oak tannins (yr Fr, some new). Harmonious & silkily persistent. Cab, merlot, petit v, malbec (70/18/7/5). Widely sourced grapes (Coastal origin). – *CvZ*

Nico van der Merwe Wines

Stellenbosch ▪ Est/1st 1999 ▪ Closed to public ▪ Owners Nico & Petra van der Merwe ▪ Winemaker Nico van der Merwe ▪ 45 tons 3 500 cs 85% red 15% white ▪ PO Box 12200 Stellenbosch 7613 ▪ wilhelmshof@xsinet.co.za ▪ ***T/F 903·9507***

Reducing elevated alcohol levels is Nico van der Merwe's mission of the moment. Quite how he's not yet sure, this outspoken winemaker admits, but we'd bank on him figuring out this conundrum. He's sticking to his 'small but good' guns, believing that only quality will survive in a wine industry contending with difficult conditions like global gluts and a strong rand. With both his new label design and the wines well received, already 'out of the pipeline': his 20 hectares of Bot River vineyards and own cellar.

★★★★★ **Mas Nicolas** Nico vdM believes shiraz/cab is *the* 'Cape Blend', so his wines feature these two varieties; 55/45 blend in **02**, smouldering, smoky, savoury style, densely packed, not overtly fruity – too simple a descriptor for this multi-dimensional offering. Very dry & northern rhône-ish. Blended after maturation, 14 mths, cab in new oak, shiraz in 2nd fill, all Fr. Same vineyards since first 99 – K/River shiraz, Smnsberg cab.

Robert Alexander range

Merlot ★★★ Better-than-everyday maiden **03** now bottled: pleasing fruitiness, very accessible dark-berried charms, oak supportive & not overdone; decently dry. **Shiraz** ★★★★ Very attractive **04** step up from pvs. Waft of vanilla from Am oak (yr, used), ripe choc & prune flavours, creamy richness. Now all Stbosch grapes.

Nicolas van der Merwe range new

Red ★★★★ Blend merlot, shiraz, cab, intended both for maturation & to while away time waiting for Mas N above. **03** understated, with signature dry tannins, but more supple grace & rounded fruit, some chocolaty richness, slight sweetness to fruit, finishes dry. 14 mths Fr oak: cab all new, shiraz used. Stbosch grapes. **White** ★★★★ Maiden **04** sauvignon/semillon (58/42) seamlessly blended (sample tasted last ed), gooseberry notes mingling with peach, subtle oak. Semillon fermented/long on lees in wood, sauvignon not; blend briefly wooded. Previewed **05**'s 50/50 blend promises to be as well integrated. — *IvH*

Nico Vermeulen Wines

*Paarl ▪ Est/1stB 2003 ▪ Closed to public ▪ Owner/viticulturist Nico Vermeulen ▪ Winemaker Nico Vermeulen, with Judy & Izelle Vermeulen ▪ 1 000 cs ▪ 3 Pieter Hugo Str Courtrai Suider-Paarl ▪ 13657631@sun.ac.za ▪ **T/F 863·2048***

Havana Hills winemaker Nico Vermeulen wants these affordable own-label wines to be 'new and young in spirit' and 'have people dancing with excitement'.

The Right Two Reds ★★★★ **04** still a work-in-progress as the guide went to bed. **03** was earthy, firm yet supple, with satisfying finish. 63/37 merlot/cab blend; cool, pure Dbnvlle fruit seasoned 15 mths in Fr oak, 30% new. **The Right Two Whites** ★★★★ Aptly named 3:1 sauvignon/semillon alliance, latter oaked. Sample **05** fascinating litchi-laced guava shot with chilli sensation, really foxy. 13% alc. — *DS*

Niel Joubert Estate

*Paarl ▪ Est 1898 ▪ 1stB 1996 ▪ Visits by appt ▪ Walks ▪ Owner Joubert family ▪ Winemaker Ernst Leicht (May 2000) ▪ Viticulturist Daan Joubert ▪ 350 ha (cab, merlot, pinotage, shiraz, chard, chenin, sauvignon) ▪ 1 900 tons 40 000 cs own label 40% red 60% white ▪ PO Box 17 Klapmuts 7625 ▪ wine@nieljoubert.co.za ▪ www.nieljoubert.co.za ▪ **T/F 875·5936***

Last harvest 'the good was very good but not always plentiful', say the Joubert family of Klein Simonsvlei farm. Very good in general too, with further inroads into the Irish market and encouraging gains in the Western Cape (when they entered the local market a few years back, experienced Niel Joubert Snr wisely counselled that the wines had to offer very good value at all levels). This approach has paid off in a loyal and consistent customer base. Otherwise, things are much the same: menacingly named boerbull Byter still keeps watch over the werf. They have planted some exotic varieties, though, and plan to do 'something exciting' with these grapes.

Sauvignon Blanc ☺ ★★★ **05** Unassuming tropical aromas/flavours; friendly finish/ rounded mouthfeel helped by 4.2g/ℓ sugar. Drink up.

Cabernet Sauvignon ★★★ Last tasted was **01**, with eucalyptus-scented fruit, easy-ish tannins. **Merlot** ★★★ **03** tough tannin, hint bitterness & subdued fruit make this less than pvs vintages. 14.5% alc; 70% oaked. Could soften with 3–4 yrs cellaring. **Pinotage** ★★★ **03** similar to pvs vintages' with their generous dimensions (14.5% alc), plum/banana fruit but not as elegant. Latest earthy, not harmonious, only 12% oaked. **Chardonnay** ★★★★ Partially casked **04** tasted mid-2004 a step up; more structure, sweeter fruit with lively citrus tang. 2–3 yrs in store. **Chenin Blanc** ★★ Style change from pvs 8g/ℓ sugar, enormous alc (±15%) to 3.5g/ℓ & 14%. Tropical tones in **04**, short but concentrated, warm goodbye. **Sauvignon Blanc** ★★★ **04** racy-sweet passionfruit & guava tones, big flavour, modest alc (13% alc). Portion fruit ex-Rbtsn. **Viognier 04** unrated work-in-progress mid-2004, showed potential; beefy alc (15%), matched by structure, rich peaches & apricots. Combo barrels/staves. — *DH*

Niels Verburg see Luddite

Nietvoorbij Wine Cellar

Stellenbosch • Est 1963 • 1stB 1992 • Tasting & sales Mon-Fri 9-4; phone ahead on Sat • Fee R1/wine • Closed pub hols • Conferencing • Owner Agricultural Research Council • Winemaker Niel Strydom (2005) • Viticulturist Guillaume Kotze (Apr 2002) • 32 ha (cab, malbec, merlot, petit v, pinotage, shiraz, chard, sauvignon) • 150 tons 6 000 cs own label 54% red 45% white 1% port • Private Bag X5026 Stellenbosch 7599 • bosmand@arc.agric.za • www.heritagegarden.co.za www.heritagegarden-stellenbosch.com www.arc.agric.za • ***T 809·3091*** *• F 809·3202*

Some of the winelands' longest-kept secrets are about to be revealed if new winemaker Niel Strydom has his way. He has two cellars in which to ply his craft – one experimental, the other commercial – and he's intent on establishing Nietvoorbij wines on markets local and international. They've been around, untrumpeted, for at least 35 years. Prices across the range are reasonable in the extreme (the flagship Cape blend sells for R30). Also on the drawing board are cellar expansions, new presses, stainless steel tanks and a tasting locale. Nietvoorbij is owned by the Agricultural Research Council, giving Niel S access to some of the most advanced research available.

No new releases tasted for current ed; notes from pvs guide: **Cabernet Sauvignon** ★★★★ Satisfying cab with relaxed tannins for early drinkability plus 2/3 yrs cellaring potential. Yr oaked. Two vintages available mid-2005: **02** plump & sweet-fruited; **01** more complex, intense. **Pinotage** ★★★★ **02** fruitier, more structured than pvs, obvious pinotage mulberry tone. Yr older oak. **Dry Red** ★★★ **03** convivial pizza/pasta companion from trio cabs (sauv, franc, ruby) & pinotage; lightly oaked. **Sauvignon Blanc** ★★★ **04** (sample) forthcoming, bright & flavourful; medium-bodied. **Chardonnay-Sauvignon Blanc** ★★ **04** crisp, refreshing quaffable 60/40 blend. **Dry White** ★★ **03** blend chenin/chard with gewürz from Dbnville; with sweetish finish. – *TM*

Nieuwedrift Vineyards

Swartland • Est 1996 • 1stB 2003 • Visits Fri 2-6 Sat 8.30-12.30 Otherwise by appt (phone mobile no. below) • Light/buffet meals for groups of 5-74 by appt • B&B guesthouse • Facilities for children • Tourgroups • Conferences & weddings • Walks • Owners Johan & Teubes Mostert • Winemaker Johan Mostert, advised by Marais de Villiers • Viti consultant Jurie du Plessis • 29 ha (shiraz, chard, chenin, colombard) • ±7 tons 35% red 65% white • PO Box 492 Piketberg 7320 • nieuwedrift@telkomsa.net • ***T (022) 913·1966/082·824·8104*** *• F 913·1966*

For a taste of traditional Swartland hospitality and 'that real farm feeling', visit vinegrower and *garagiste* winemaker Johan Mostert. So visitor friendly, he promises to open the doors within five minutes of receiving your phone call if his normal opening times don't suit. The restaurant on the property hosts regular cabaret shows and wife Karen's paintings are on display. ('She almost makes more money out of her work than I do out of the wines.') Johan M intends staying exclusive at this small cellar – the rest of the crop is channelled to Porterville Cellars

Shiraz new ★★ Big, wood-driven style; **04** lots of luscious vanilla-caramel from yr 2nd-fill Fr wood, more body (14.8% alc) than flesh. **Chenin Blanc** ★★ **05** (sample) slightly less effusive & fleshy than last; shy watermelon/green apple whiffs, pronounced acidity. – *MM*

Nitida Cellars

Durbanville • Est 1992 • 1stB 1995 • Tasting & sales Mon-Fri 9-5 Sat 9.30-1 • Closed Easter Fri/Sun, Dec 25/26 & Jan 1 • Tours by appt • BYO picnic by request • Owners Veller family • Winemaker/viticulturist Bernhard Veller with Jacus Marais (1995/1999), advised by Eugene van Zyl & Johan Wiese • 15 ha (cab s/f, merlot, pinotage, shiraz, sauvignon, semillon) • 140 tons 7 500 cs own label 45% red 55% white • PO Box 1423 Durbanville 7551 • nitida@mweb.co.za • www.nitida.co.za • ***T 976·1467*** *• F 976·5631*

Bernard Veller marked 10 years of winegrowing here last year with another celebration: being invited to join the prestigious Cape Winemakers Guild. Looking ahead, he wants to keep making fruit-driven wines that are elegant – 'the sort of wine where you want to finish the bottle and wonder who drank the other half'. A concern is the quality-robbing effect of leafroll virus in the vineyards, which the Vellers are counteracting by replanting with varieties on more suitable sections of the farm. One grape which will not take root here, to Veller's disappointment, is Italian variety negroamaro. 'We could not obtain an export certificate from Italy and had to scrap the project. It would appear the Italians want to keep it for themselves.'

★★★★ **Cabernet Sauvignon 03** elegant cassis & perfume, palate light & lingering with cloves, cinnamon dominant. Quintessential cool-climate cab, modest 12.9% alc, serious wooding: 18 mths Fr oak, 40% new. Lighter than hefty (14.5% alc) **02** (★★★☆), with notes of cedar & black berries.

★★★☆ **Shiraz** Game, white pepper, leather & dark choc on **03** (★★★★); well-balanced, manages to finesse 15% alc. Poised & sharp. Riper than brambly, minty **02**.

★★★★ **Calligraphy 03** returns to form after vintage victim **02** (★★★). Equal parts merlot, cab f & s, modest 12.8% alc; meaty notes & barnyard influences, elegant; needs another couple of yrs.

★★★★☆ **Sauvignon Blanc Club Select** ✓ **04** last ed was hailed as another fine Dbnville example of the variety. Hugely enjoyable floral aromas with grassy back-up; subtle fruitiness & racy acidity. Very young – try to resist for few yrs.

★★★★ **Sauvignon Blanc 05** expressive tropical nose leads to a fruit salad of pineapple & limes with lingering aftertaste. Marginally bigger (13% alc) than elegant, drinkable **04**, a Kiwi clone with zingy acidity.

★★★★ **Semillon** ✓ **04** another stunner full of pears, wax & lanolin flavour behind a shyish nose; 50% tank fermented portion preserves freshness; insists on more time to develop lusciousness & honey character of expressive **03** (★★★★☆), best yet of these new-wave charmers.

Pinotage ★★★☆ **03** obvious bananas, huge 15.3% alc, exiting sweetness, chunky tannins. VDG. 10–12 mths Fr oak, none new. **Chardonnay** ★★★☆ Last tasted was **03**, dominated by oak (3 mths, 20% new). —*NP*

Noble Cape see Origin Wine
No Name see Pick 'n Pay

Nordale Winery 

Robertson ▪ Est 1950 ▪ Tasting & sales Mon-Thu 8-12.30; 1.30-5 Fri 8-12.30; 1.30-4 ▪ Closed pub hols ▪ Tours by appt ▪ BYO picnic ▪ Owners 31 members ▪ Winemaker Simon Basson (Dec 2001) ▪ Viti consultant Newald Marais ▪ 500 ha (shiraz, chard) ▪ 8 000 tons ▪ 1 500 cs own label + 5.8m litres bulk 15% red 85% white 1% other ▪ Ranges for customers: Rocco Bay (Sweden), Tabiso (Denmark) ▪ PO Box 105 Bonnievale 6730 ▪ info@nordale.co.za ▪ www.nordale.co.za ▪ ***T (023) 616·2050*** *▪ F (023) 616·2192*

First triumph for Newald Marais in his relatively new role as GM of this Bonnievale co-operative is the 'huge success' of the Sauvignon 04. Winemaker Simon Basson feels the same way: 'Anyone would be happy to see the words "Sold out" next to his wine,' he observes. It's too early to say but he has high hopes that the 05 will be equally well received. Meanwhile, he's had his first experience of an overseas harvest, doing a three-month stint in the US.

★★★★ **White Muscadel** Mouth-watering, lusciously smooth fortified; pvs was **02** VDG, from old vines on Gelukshoop farm. **04** (★★★) revisited this ed (last yr a sample) not as arresting; more 'summertime sweet' (poured over ice) than benchmark of style. 375ml.

Captain's Drift Shiraz Still-stocked **01** not retasted. Pvs ed rated as ★★★ but noted as starting to dry out, so drink soon. Next is **04**. **Double Cabernet** ★★☆ Sauvignon & ruby are alluded-to cabs, again 50/50 in **03**, unwooded; plump & juicy, tangy finish. **Vin Rouge** ★☆ Shiraz (50%) & merlot in **03**, rustic baked fruit, sweetish finish. **Captain's Drift Chardonnay** ★★★ Still selling **03**; last ed we featured **04** (still in barrel mid-2005), with eager butterscotch & marmalade-toast aromas, sweet finish. **Chenin Blanc** ★★ Dry version; light-bodied **05** honey-drizzled tropical fruit, zingy, good summer's day refreshment (within yr of harvest). **Steen** ★★ Sweeter this yr, again lightish; **05** undemanding, not too sugary, grape's 'wet wool' character in evidence. **Sauvignon Blanc** ★★ **05** soft greengage aroma & hint asparagus; light fruity flavours, undemanding & quaffable. **Red Muscadel** ★★☆ **04**, previewed last ed, now seems lighter-flavoured than pvs, some caramel/strawberry jam hints, tinge bitterness on finish. – *lvH/TM*

Norton Wines

Stellenbosch ▪ Est/1stB 2002 ▪ Closed to public ▪ Owner Anthony Norton ▪ Vini consultant Nicolette de Kock ▪ 50 cs 100% red ▪ PO Box 6045 Uniedal Stellenbosch ▪ ***T 082·807·4447***

No update available on this winery; contact details from previous edition.

Nuwehoop see Groot Eiland
Nuwe Wynplaas see Coppoolse Finlayson

Nuy Wine Cellar

Nuy (see Worcester map) ▪ Est 1963 ▪ 1stB 1967 ▪ Tasting & sales Mon-Fri 8.30–4.30 Sat 8.30–12.30 ▪ Fee R15 for groups of 10+ ▪ Closed Easter Fri/Sun, Dec 25 & Jan 1 ▪ Braai facilities ▪ Owners 23 members ▪ Manager/winemaker Christo Pienaar, with Juan Slabbert (Sep/Oct 2003) ▪ Viti consultant Newald Marais (Oct 2002) ▪ 9 500 tons ▪ 20% red 68% white 12% muscadel ▪ PO Box 5225 Worcester 6849 ▪ wines@nuywinery.co.za ▪ www.nuywinery.co.za ▪ ***T (023) 347·0272*** *▪ F (023) 347·4994*

In the smallest harvest since 1983, muscadel stole the show though chardonnay and shiraz, which habitually do well in the Nuy Valley, according to Christo Pienaar, also performed. The manager/winemaker's mantra is 'to make wines unique to your area, not to copy other regions' winners'. They're placing more emphasis on bottled wines (bulk production their historical forte) and, encouraged by their first export order for cork-closed products, are embarking on a vineyard selection programme to ensure only the best fruit ends up under NWC labels.

★★★★ **Red Muscadel** ✓ Deep, raisin-edged dessert, perfect winter companion, as flame-licked red hue suggests. **05** intense, muscat suffused aromas; waves of silky mouth-coating flavour wrapped, powerful but also elegant & lively. Moderate 16.5% alc already harmonious. Standout **03** (★★★★★) deep, complex, even more potential (these age brilliantly). ±261g/ℓ, 5g/ℓ acid .

★★★★ **White Muscadel** ✓ The wine that made cellar's name; revered among local fortified desserts. 24 carat gold **05** gleams as bright as array of medals to its ancestors. Rich & raisined, with lucid varietal tones of mint & cold tea. Seductive, silky, luscious but not over-heavy; upbeat tangerine peel tail. Can only improve over many yrs. Summer delicacy, chilled. Delicious in/with variety dishes. ±250g/ℓ sugar, 4.5g/ℓ acid.

Chant de Nuit ☺ ★★★ Exotic pineapple fragrance, from Ferdinand de Lesseps table grape, usual distinction on this **NV** (05). Lightish, juicy, delicious upbeat fruity finish. **Colombard Semi-Sweet** ☺ ★★★ Few more charming than **05**. Delicate honeysuckle scent; gentle sweetness offset by freshening fruity acids. Bring on the second bottle! 11.5% alc. **Sauvignon Blanc Sparkling Vin Sec** ☺ ★★★ Sauvignon & bubbles serendipitous partners; best well chilled. **05** ripe fig/tropical interest, lively fizz, just off-dry. **Chenin Blanc** ☺ ★★★ Brush honey on gentle tropical-toned **05**. Loads stimulating juicy fruit; lingering dryness. **Colombard Dry** ☺ ★★★ Characteristic ripe guava display, mouth-watering zest on **05**. Balance, moderate body helps refresh in summer.

Cabernet Sauvignon ★★★ **03** with bright ruby appeal; satisfying fruity substance; sound, rounded dry persistence. Fr oak influenced. **Rouge de Nuy** ★★ Shy **03** cab/merlot blend. Straightforward fruity touches; bit lean, drying tannins. Lightly oaked. **Chardonnay** ★★★ **05** invigorating steely pickled lime attractions. Clean, firm with just hint spicy oak. **Sauvignon Blanc** ★★ Floral/spring meadow daintiness on **05**. Lightish, bracingly fresh. **Fernão Pires** ★★ Off-dry **05** with gentle spicy hints; smoothly fruity. Uncomplicated quaffing. **Noble Late Harvest** Botrytised chenin/hanepoot. Unrated sample **04** not tasted as finished wine. Pvs ed noted ripe apricot-toned fruit; gentle flavours, slight citrus touch in tail. No **05** (insufficient botrytis). 10.8% alc. – *AL*

Oaklands Wine Exporters

*Est 2002 ▪ 1stB 2003 ▪ Closed to public ▪ Owner Danie Zeeman ▪ PO Box 12398 Die Boord 7613 ▪ info@oaklandswines.com ▪ www.deza.co.za ▪ **T 886·9626** ▪ F 887·0441*

Danie Zeeman, the man behind this negociant company, has extensive experience of winemaking and -trading, having worked at cellars like Longridge locally and as production director of a wine wholesaler in the Netherlands. He sources wines locally for clients in Europe for marketing under their own brands, and in some cases creates special blends to suit clients' requirements. Deza is his own label, and it flies to America, Switzerland and Singapore.

Deza Collection

Sauvignon Blanc ☺ ★★★ **05** riper, more mouth-filling & grainier than pvs; melon/pineapple on nose/palate, bone-dry goodbye.

Reserve Shiraz ★★★★ Last yr we erred when we said we tasted **03**, this was in fact the **02**. Modern-style; ripe black/plummy fruit, balanced, not over-extracted, lots of toasty wood (combo Fr/Am 80/20). Also tasted last yr: **Shiraz-Pinotage** ★★★ 55/45 mix, fruit ex-Wllngtn, not oaked; **03** melange red/black berry fruits & tobacco whiff; savoury/meaty tone, assertive but ripe tannins. **Chardonnay** new ★★★ Food-friendly addition to line-up; **04** (sample) fresh & balanced, weighty, permeated by lime marmalade aromas & flavours, sweet impression to finish possibly from biggish 13.7%. All WO W Cape. —*IvH*

Oak Lane see Beau Joubert
Oak Ridge see Shoprite Checkers

Oak Valley Wines

*Elgin ▪ Est 1898 ▪ 1stB 2003 ▪ Tasting & sales Mon-Fri 9-5, otherwise by appt ▪ Closed Easter Fri-Mon, Dec 25/26 & Jan 1 ▪ Conservation area ▪ Owner AG Rawbone-Viljoen Trust ▪ Winemaker Pieter Visser ▪ Viticulturist Pieter Visser, advised by Kevin Watt ▪ 35 ha (cabs s/f, merlot, pinot, chard, sauvignon) ▪ 5 800 cs 100% white ▪ PO Box 30 Elgin 7180 ▪ wines@oakvalley.co.za ▪ www.oakvalleywines.com ▪ **T 859·4110** ▪ F 859·3405*

Elgin pear, apple, cut-flower, beef and vine farmer Anthony Rawbone-Viljoen, whose family has worked these high-altitude, cool-climate sites since the 1890s, aims to produce 'elegant, deep and complex wines' that speak of their provenance. His debut Sauvignon (03) did just that, and received instant acclaim. Now an 'estate blend' of merlot, cabernet and cab franc is in the works (the latter variety showing 'consistent excellence' on this farm, ARV reports). (Experimental) pinot, typically tetchy, proved slightly disappointing in 2005 – but time will tell. No dabbling beginner, he. Vines were planted in the 1980s and Oak Valley was long a fruit source for Bouchard Finlayson, Rupert & Rothschild et al. The new tasting room complete, planting semillon is next on the list.

★★★★★ **Sauvignon Blanc** Fine gooseberry/green fig aromas on **04**; elegant, with delicate herbaceous notes, textured dry finish; marginally lighter, less intense than pvs, but similar lowish 13.5% alc, crisp, age-worthy profile. **05** (preview) a succulent successor. —*MF*

Oak Village see Omnia

Obikwa

Value-priced Distell brand, exported to North & South America, Europe and the Far East.

Cabernet Sauvignon ★★★ Generous unwooded **04**, dusty cassis tone; texture & bite from cab's tannins/astringency. Slightly sweet goodbye (4.5g/ℓ RS). Following mainly Fr oak, staves/barrels: **Merlot** ★★★ Savoury & gamey; better fleshed than Cab. **04** soft, smooth mulberry palate cut by clean tannin. **Pinotage** ★★★ **04** copybook pinotage with banana/strawberry aromas, cleansing acidity, youthfully abrasive tannins; ends fairly quickly. **Shiraz** ★★★ Quintessential bouquet of red fruit, black pepper. Broad red berries/currants in **04** brought into line by fresh acidity/furry tannins. **Chardonnay** ★★★ **04**. deftly part-oaked for texture rather than flavour; ripe tangerines, mellow peach flavours; unwooded portion keeps ripeness in check. **Chenin Blanc** ★★★ Delightful **05** with lemon blossom nose, Granny Smith apple palate; juicy & mineral. **Sauvignon Blanc** ★★★ Reticent **05**, fleeting gooseberry/nettle nose, crunchy palate. Delicate, light. All WO W Cape. — *CvZ*

Oddbins see Shoprite Checkers

Odyssey

These Natural Sweets by Robertson Winery/Vinimark targeting the youth market now discontinued.

Oewerzicht Private Cellar

Greyton ▪ Est/1stB 2002 ▪ Visits by appt ▪ Luxury guest cottages & tents ▪ Conference/function facilities for up to 40 delegates ▪ Mountain biking/hiking trails ▪ Owner/viticulturist/winemaker Kootjie Viljoen ▪ 3 ha (cab) ▪ 1 000 cs 100% red ▪ PO Box 18 Greyton 7233 ▪ oewerzicht@telkomsa.net ▪ ***T (028) 254·9831*** *F (028) 254·9968*

Hands-on winemaker Kootjie Viljoen is never happier than when working his Greyton vineyard. Using minimal intervention, he believes his wines express their origin and environment, so he's intrigued by the long-term impact of last year's wet season (while the rest of the Western Cape struggled with drought, the Overberg region suffered floods). Yield was similar to that of 2004, as was the approach: soft, gentle handling of grapes, using old-fashioned vinification equipment, and prodigious advice from cousin Wynand, who helps out when possible but has a day-job… as a winemaker elsewhere. You can now sample the results at Lapa, the new restaurant and tasting room Kootjie opened last year.

Cabernet Sauvignon ★★★★ Quality leap for **03**; showing softer side of this often austere-in-youth variety, thanks to gentle basket-press/deft oaking. Herbaceous & mulberry aromas & flavours, ripe & accessible tannins, juicy finish. Yr Fr oak. Low 13% alc. WO Overberg. — *IvH*

Old Bridge Wines

Closed to public ▪ Owner Paulinas Dal Farm Holdings (Pty) Ltd ▪ 20 000 cs 60% red 40% white ▪ PO Box 50002 Waterfront 8002 ▪ rickety@iafrica.com ▪ ***T 082·777·1519***

Export-focused producer and negociant sourcing wines for a variety of brands, including private labels for specialised corporate clients. The wines, untasted, include limited-edition African Gold Collection: Cabernet-Merlot, Shiraz, Merlot mainly for US, Europe and Far East; Big Six Collection: boxed sets of Cabernet, Merlot, Shiraz, Pinotage, Sauvignon, Chenin for local game lodges/retreats and for export; Old Bridge: Cabernet, Merlot, Shiraz, Pinotage, Sauvignon & Chenin.

Old Brown see Sedgwick's
Old Chapel see Robertson Winery

Old Vines Cellars

Cape Town ▪ Est/1stB 1995 ▪ Closed to public ▪ Owners Irina von Holdt & Françoise Botha ▪ Winemaker Irina von Holdt ▪ 11 000 cs own label + 2 500 cs for pvt client ▪ 30% red 70% white ▪ 50 Liesbeek Road Rosebank 7700 ▪ fran@oldvines.co.za ▪ www.oldvines.co.za ▪ ***T 685·6428*** *▪ F 685·6446*

Mother-and-daughter team Irina von Holdt, a taster for this guide, and Fran Botha were delighted to win a double-gold at Veritas for a well-aged vintage (98) of their speciality, Chenin. Says IvH: 'It proves what I've been saying for a long time: SA can make Chenins that stand the test of time.' The duo also scooped a string of Wine of the Month Club wins, especially for their women's empowerment range, Spring Valley. Not that the team is all-female anymore. Smiles Botha: 'The addition of three-and-a-half men has made the world of difference – the balance is better … ' (two marketers, a driver and part-time computer expert). New, apart from the wines listed below, is an NLH, unsurprisingly from chenin, not ready for tasting at press time.

★★★★ **Baron von Holdt** new Serious bdx-style blend from Hldrberg fruit, with distinct Old World mineral quality. **03** fronted by cab (70%), ±equal portions merlot/petit v. Brooding cassis & lead pencil; opulent dark fruit reined in by cab acidity, fine powdery tannins. Elegant rather than powerful, restrained 13% alc. 2 yrs combo new/old Fr oak.

★★★★ **Chenin Blanc** ✓ Standout in the unwooded genre: **04** (★★★★☆) notch up on elegant **03**. Packed with honeysuckle & elderflower; bruised apple finish more refined, with added mineral & 'wet slate' flavours/textures. Controlled 13.5% alc. Should gain waxy complexity with 4-7 yrs cellaring.

★★★★ **Barrel Reserve Chenin Blanc** The wooded version. Brilliant hue ushers in **04**'s opulent, creamy elderflower bouquet, elegantly firm lemon/mineral flavours. Slightly drier than **03** (2.3g/ℓ), longer in oak (10 mths Fr casks), 10% new wood (pvs none). Structure to develop ±8yrs, as had most pvs.

★★★★ **Vintage Brut** From chenin (unusual for MCC); 2 cool hillside Stbosch bushvine vyds. Currently available **01** last tasted mid-2004, made with help from 'Sparkling king', Villiera's Jeff Grier. Ebullient bubbles, easy, friendly, no brut-ish severity. 24 mths on lees. Degorged off lees, bottled on demand. 9.8g/ℓ sugar; 12.9% alc.

Blue White ★★★☆ ✓ 'Blue' bottle, 'White' chenin celebrate 10th anniversary with **05**; sample shows characteristic wet wool, floral & apple compôte tones. Hint sweetness leavens finish. Unwooded, portion from old Stbosch vines. 13.5% alc. This, most below, WO Coastal, otherwise Stbosch.

Spring Valley range

Shiraz-Merlot ★★☆ Lightly wooded (mix staves/oak) for accessibility. **04** friendlier alc (13%) than pvs. Lots of raspberry, cranberry fruit & juicy, easy goodbye. **Sauvignon Blanc** new ★★★☆ Attractive **05** sample has spicy/floral notes, refreshing grapefruit palate & persistent soft finish. **Chenin Blanc-Sauvignon Blanc** ★★☆ Happy-go-lucky blend, unfinished sample **05** with 80% chenin shows usual peach aromas, Granny Smith apple crispness to finish. **Stein Select** new ★★☆ From chenin, gently sweet (15g/ℓ sugar) with engaging honeycomb, hay & meadowflowers. — *CvZ*

Olsen Wines

Paarl ▪ Est/1stB 2002 ▪ Visits by appt ▪ Fee R10 ▪ Home-style light meals for groups of ±10 by appt ▪ Farm-style jams ▪ Owner Greg Olsen ▪ Winemaker Helene van der Westhuizen (2005) ▪ Viticulturist Armand Botha (2000) ▪ 30 ha ▪ 500 cs 90% red 10% white ▪ Eurepgap registered ▪ PO Box 9052 Huguenot 7645 ▪ olsenwines@mweb.co.za ▪ ***T 862·0781/862·3653*** *F 862·0781/862·2589*

American businessman Greg Olsen fell in love with SA and its wine while doing research here in 1971. His passion is shared by the staff at Olsen wines, a 180ha farm in the Du Toitskloof mountains. The 30ha of vines are divided into 31 smaller blocks, tended meticulously. About 8 tons of grapes are selected for the Olsen label, and hand-crafted in a modern cellar using old-fashioned techniques. The operation is small: only 500 cases, including exports to the USA (but excluding the Huguenot Tunnel baboons' share of Block 43 pinotage!). The latter being Greg O's favourite variety, it should attain unprecedented heights – he's training to become the world's third space tourist.

★★★★ **Cabernet Sauvignon 03** blackcurrant, plum & choc notes; ripe, well-balanced palate; fine, firm, slightly herbal tannins give structure to sweet finish; elegant despite 14% alc.

Cabernet Sauvignon-Shiraz ★★ Herbaceous green fruit aromas on **05**, intrusive tannins softened by well-managed sweet fruit. 11.4% alc. Released within 6 mths of vintage. **Pinotage** ★★★ Easy drinking **03** features attractive banana/black fruit whiffs spiced with nutmeg; surprisingly soft tannins for variety. From high-yielding (15t/ha) vineyard, 9 mths Fr oak. **Chardonnay** ★★ **05** tropical/marzipan aromas, fleeting flavours, curiously low alc (11.9%) for ripe Paarl fruit. — *MF*

Olyvenbosch Vineyards

new

Wellington ▪ Est 1990 ▪ 1stB 2003 ▪ Closed to public ▪ Owner/winemaker Otto G Schmidtke ▪ 20 ha (cab, merlot) ▪ 110 tons 572 cs own label 100% red ▪ PO Box 235 Wellington 7654 ▪ ogschmidtke@telkomsa.net ▪ ***T/F 864·1195***

'I bought Olyvenbosch when I was 55 and promised to produce my own wine before my 70th birthday,' says Otto Schmidke, who, with wife Dagi, made a successful career in clothing and textiles in the Far East. Well, they've done it. The first wine is bottled (the remaining grapes go to KWV) and, moreover, the newcomers are very happy with the quality. 'Everything about wine and winemaking fascinates me,' says Otto S, whose favourite wine is Châteauneuf-du-Pape. 'Our vines are between eight and 10 years old, the winemaking is hands on, and though the competition is fierce among SA as well as international wineries, our value proposition of quality and price will give us a fair fighting chance.'

Cabernet Sauvignon ★★★☆ **04** barrel sample shows concentrated blackcurrant tone, ripe & supple; new oak still intruding but harmony should come with bit of time. Single vyd. **Merlot** ★★★ **04** very ripe, even slightly raisined berry notes, soft succulent tannins, tasted from barrel uncomplex but easy drinking, 14% alc not intrusive. 12 months new Fr oak. *— MF*

Omnia Wines

Stellenbosch (see Stellenbosch & Helderberg maps) ▪ Est 2004 ▪ Tasting at two venues: Helderberg Winery Mon–Fri 9–5.30 Sat 9–5; Welmoed Winery Mon–Fri 9–5.30 Sat & pub hols 9–5 Sun 10–4 ▪ Both venues closed Easter Fri, Dec 25 & Jan1 ▪ Meals: Helderberg Restaurant Mon-Sat during tasting hours (T 842·2012); Welmoed: Duck Pond Restaurant daily during tasting hours (T 881·3310) ▪ Both restaurants available for after-hours functions by appt ▪ Play areas for children ▪ Tourgroups ▪ Owners: more than 200 shareholders ▪ Winemakers Nicky Versfeld, Morné van Rooyen, Celéste Truter, Stephan Smit & Danie van Tonder ▪ Viticulturists Francois De Villiers & PD Koegelenberg ▪ 15 000 tons 2.5m cs 70% red 30% white ▪ ISO 9001, BRC certified HACCP (for Koopmanskloof & Perdeberg cellars) ▪ PO Box 465 Stellenbosch 7599 ▪ info@omniawines.co.za ▪ http://www.omniawines.co.za ▪ ***T 881·3870*** *▪ F 881·3102*

Omnia was formed by the 2004 merger of Vinfruco and Stellenbosch Vineyards, which saw SV's chief winemaker Chris Kelly departing, and Vinfruco's Nicky Versfeld heading the winemaking team. Stephan Smit (ex Franschhoek Vineyards) has more recently replaced Carmen Kelly (née Stevens) at Welmoed. Versfeld is enthusiastic: 'It's a challenge to start making wines from scratch each year, and making 2.5m cases to suit various palates, regardless of climatic conditions.' Highlights of the year include tinkering in the Omnia R&D cellar at Welmoed, and a *Decanter* award for the 2004 Credo Sauvignon. Nicky V is quick to share the credit: 'I don't think it can be over-emphasised how important grower relationships are in achieving these accolades.'

Kumkani range

★★★★ **Shiraz** Well made **03** with broad, inviting canvas of mulberries, dark choc, loads of spice, juxtaposed by tightly reined tannins promising 5+ yr rewarding future. 15 mths Fr/Am oak (70/30). Elegantly structured **02**'s intermingling scents/tastes continual discovery, pleasure. Sealed with screwcap, as are others of existing range.

★★★★ **JJJ Shiraz** new **03** (sample, rating provisional) crammed with lush dark fruit, mint choc, easily cloaking sinewy structure from yr oaking. Try not to drink it all now, good for another 5+ yrs.

★★★★☆ **Pinotage** ✓ Multi-layered complexity confirms class. **04**'s opulent, spiced berry fruit draws you in, velvety palate seduces further. Ripe, fine-grained tannin structure promises 6+ yrs maturation. Aged 14 mths Fr/Am barrels, 30% new. WO Coastal. **03** sold only in USA.

★★★★ **Shiraz-Cabernet Sauvignon** Poised, integrated **02** (★★★★) not retasted; in traditional savoury, dry style. **01** was polished & taut.

★★★★ **Sauvignon Blanc** ✓ Comes after showy, mouth-filling **04**, but **05** (★★★★☆) even better. Sophisticated, fine, with sleek thoroughbred lines. Layered, delicious gooseberries, fennel & lime, with a green, nettly thread throughout adding tension, lift. WO Coastal. Great food wine (moderate 13% alc).

★★★★★ **Lanner Hill Sauvignon Blanc** new **05** powerhouse of asparagus, green figs, tinned peas fragrance, flavours; racy, intense, irresistible. Sauvignon at its expressive best. From single Groenekloof vyd.

★★★★ **VVS** Innovative blend viognier, verdelho, sauvignon. In **04** 61/29/10 mix, giving viogner's expected peachy/floral dominance. Beautifully balanced, crisp acidity, good palate weight, dab oak. *Wine* ★★★★. Delicious successor to seductive, big, modern **03**.

Viognier ★★★☆ **04** oaking deftly handled (half 4 mths on lees, half short period new Fr) so as not to interfere with variety's elegance, charm, peachy aromas. FCTWS gold. **Merlot-Cabernet Franc** discontinued.

Credo range

★★★★ **CWG Auction Reserve Groenekloof Sauvignon Blanc** new As befits cool-West Coast provenance, **04** has green edginess yet perfectly ripe fruit. Layered capsicum, gooseberries, litchis coupled with thoroughbred build, provides delicious, stylish experience.

Stellenbosch Cabernet Sauvignon ★★★☆ Only in top yrs. **03** bursts with blackcurrant/mulberry intensity, easily handles 18 mths new Fr/Am wood (incl partial oak ferment). Will drink even better in yr, good for 4+ more. **Stellenbosch Shiraz** ★★★☆ Manages power with subtlety **02** not retasted this ed; had black cherries, hints leather, choc-coated prunes, smooth ripe tannins. 18 mths Fr/Am oak, all new. **Groenekloof Sauvignon Blanc** ★★★☆ **04**, previewed pvs ed, delivers early promise: nervy, racy style; lithe structure, intense capsicum/asparagus aromas, long nettly finish. Sauvignon with attitude.

Arniston Bay range

Merlot Reserve ★★☆ **03** not retasted this ed. Pvsly showed minimal tannins & smooth, fleshy build, ripe mulberry fruit, hint leafiness. **Shiraz** ★★☆ **04** friendly & quaffable. Delivers smoky typicity, lush plums & black fruit. Unoaked. **Pinotage-Merlot** ★★☆ Last tasted **03** showy, juicy; high-toned fruit pastille flavours with sweet-sour twist. **Ruby Cabernet-Merlot** ★★★ Liquorice-spiked, dark-fruited **03**. Smooth drinkability veined with just enough grape tannin to handle food. Unwooded 70/30 blend. **Shiraz-Merlot** ★★★ **04** softly savoury, with merlot's 20% portion adding plummy flesh to shiraz's Karoo scrub tones. Delicious; not wooded. **Rosé** ★★☆ Cerise-hued dry **05**, redcurrant toned quaffer from pinotage **Chardonnay-Semillon** ★★★ **04** last available, had lemon & lime aromas/flavours, smooth silky texture. Unoaked. **Chenin Blanc-Chardonnay** ★★☆ Among biggest SA brands in Britain. Latest **05** pepped up from pvs. Pear-drop, guava freshness throughout; vibrant, juicy crowd pleaser. 80/20 blend. **Méthode Cap Classique** ★★★☆ Bottle-fermented sparkling last ed showed apple aromas, hints lemon/herb; full, creamy mouthful. Chardonnay & pinots blanc/noir, 36 mths on lees. **NV**. Fruit ex-Tlbgh.

Inglewood range

Export only. **Cabernet Sauvignon** ★★★ Peppered salami notes add interest to **03**'s cassis fruit core, toasty dry tannins from yr Fr/Am oak suggest 3–4 yr maturation potential. WO Coastal. **Shiraz** ★★★☆ Lots to admire about **03**: creamy macerated plum richness, whiff of liquorice; approachable & savoury, juicy palate, moreish finish. Yr Fr/Am oak. WO W Cape. **Chardonnay** ★★★ **05** slightly built & refreshing unwooded style with lemon zest, tropical fruit appeal. Charming. WO Coastal, as is ... **Sauvignon Blanc** ★★★ **05** step up on pvs. Lots of vibrant tasty freshness: gooseberry & capsicum aromas, flavours, long food-friendly finish.

Versus range

Red ★★★ Last tasted **03**, allsorts quaffer, essence of red berries, with dash oak adding firmness, flavour.

Rosé ☺ ★★☆ **05** simple but attractive fruit pastille/boiled sweets character, dry finish. Mainly pinotage, touch shiraz, cinsaut. Friendly 12.5% alc. This & rest of range in 1 litre, 500ml sizes. WO W Cape, as is ... **White** ☺ ★★★ Bright fruit, perky & lively **05** blend chenin/sauvignon drier than pvs; shows apple-dominant fruit, crunchy freshness, tasty drinkability.

Welmoed range

Cabernet Sauvignon ★★★ **04** continues in lighter style: red berries with meat extract, savoury shadings, a friendly, accessible palate despite yr Fr oak. **Merlot** ★★★☆ Good showcase for variety in **04**, with red berries, violets, herbaceous note. Partial Fr barrel maturation gives firm, dry finish, ±3 yr ageing potential. **Pinotage** ★★★ Partially oaked **04** less juicy, leaner than pvs. Has rhubarb, dark berry wildness, peppery note. **Shiraz** ★★★ Now a lighter style but still attractive: **04**'s brambleberry & smoky aromas, flavours vie for attention, gentle oaking leaves smooth accessibility intact. **Chardonnay** ★★★☆ Last tasted **03** had butterscotch/marmalade richness, oak firmness, weight & seriousness. 50% in Fr oak, 6 mths. **Sauvignon Blanc** ★★☆ **05** offers gentle but true version of sauvignon: asparagus aromas, flavours, with required palate freshness. **Chenin Blanc** ★★☆ An exuberant easy drinking **05**, with attractive melon & apple appeal. **Blanc de Blanc** discontinued.

Shamwari range

Merlot-Cabernet Sauvignon Last tasted **03** pre-bottling sample (provisional ★★★☆); impressed with 30% cab's dusty capsicum & cedar, merlot's fleshiness. **Shiraz** ★★★ **04** varietally true savoury, peppery styling, softly rounded body, just enough firmness to handle food. Unwooded. **Chardonnay** ★★★ Unoaked **04** (sample, not retasted) had ripe musk melon aromas/flavours, ample weight, smooth acidity.

Infiniti range

Brut MCC ★★★☆ Elegant, stylish **00** last ed showed honeyed bottle age on nose, bone-dry palate, biscuity texture. Mostly chardonnay, with 5% pinot.

Following ranges discontinued: **Genesis**, **Helderberg**, **Oak Village**; **Rock Ridge** for export only; untasted. — *CR*

Onderkloof

Stellenbosch (see Helderberg map) ▪ Est 1998 ▪ 1stB 1999 ▪ Tasting Mon-Fri by appt ▪ Sales & tours by appt ▪ Private functions (lunch/dinner) by appt ▪ Member of Schapenberg – Sir Lowry's Conservancy ▪ Owners Daniël Truter & Beat Musfeld ▪ Winemaker/viticulturist Daniël Truter, with Truter Willemse (May 2003) ▪ 25 ha (cab, pinotage, shiraz, chenin, crouchen, muscat d'A, sauvignon) ▪ 100 tons 4 000 cs own label 30% red 70% white ▪ PO Box 90 Sir Lowry's Pass 7133 ▪ wine@onderkloofwines.co.za ▪ www.onderkloofwines.co.za ▪ ***T 858·1538*** *▪ F 858·1536*

After 28 years of winemaking, Daniël Truter still finds tremendous inspiration each vintage 'at the first smell of fresh grapes starting to ferment'. The Schapenberg – Sir Lowry's Conservancy, of which Truter and Swiss partner Beat Musfeld are founders (rapid residential encroachment a big issue here) is 'up and running with great enthusiasm from the members'. Also in train is a policy of releasing Onderkloof whites earlier to show more fruit while retaining their hallmark ageability. And, true to the adage that good things come out of adversity, the unirrigated vineyards overcame dry conditions in 2005 to produce 'excellent' wines, shiraz and chenin being especially promising.

★★★★ **Chardonnay** Fast-forward from last-tasted **02** to **05**; barrel sample sleekly muscular, bold oaking adds savoury character to lemon zest/pomelo fruit; appealing vibrant freshness; **02** had similar racy concentration, build for few yrs ageing. Barrel-fermented/matured 5-8 mths.

Cabernet Sauvignon ★★★☆ This wine's signature raspberry tone evident on **02**, very well concentrated, more than match for energetic oaking (18 mths Fr); attractive, deserves yr/2 to settle, further few yrs to show best. Dryland vyd; balanced ±13% alc. **Pinotage** ★★★☆ **03**

made to enjoy rather than impress; packed with creamy black plum fruit, satisfyingly ripe & juicy, seamless oak (yr Fr). Upbeat wine – to quaff when your team's winning. **Shiraz** new ★★★★ First harvest from single vyd; **03** brazen New World styling: molasses whiffs, toasty dark fruit with vanilla slick (14 mths Fr oak); accessible now & probably for early enjoyment. **Floreal Rouge** new ★★★ Interesting & unusual **05**, unwooded malbec/merlot mix (55/45), 'easy drinking for everyday' says Truter; brambly flavours, light texture (±14% alc), refreshing acidity. **Chenin Blanc** ★★★ Well-applied oak chips add dimension, biscuity interest to **05**, lively greengage flavours, big alc (14.2%) cut by brisk acidity. **Sauvignon Blanc** ★★★ **05** sample much riper than pvs, rounder, broader, with softer acidity. Not unworthy at all – has its own appeal. From single vyd, est 1989. **Floreal** ★★★★ ✓ Floral semi-dry blend chenin, muscat de A, crouchen (55/40/5). **05** exuberant grapey perfume – chenin a mere delivery platform for pure hanepoot fragrance, scented gewürz-like finish. Gorgeous aperitif at a giveaway price. – *MM/CT*

Ondine see Ormonde Vineyards
Onyx see Darling Cellars

Oom Tas

One of SA's top-selling budget-priced brands (2m cases a year, all in returnable glass), produced 24x7 by Distell. Amber hue looks 'sweet', but latest (**NV**) ★ is decidedly dry, as always; nutty muscat aromas; leaner on palate than bouquet suggests, though no sharp edges. – *CvZ*

Open Sky see Premium Cape Wines

Opstal Estate

Slanghoek (see Worcester map) ▪ Est 1950 ▪ 1stB 1978 ▪ Tasting & sales Mon-Fri 9-5 Sat 10-2 ▪ Closed Christian holidays ▪ Tours by appt ▪ Restaurant Wed-Sun 10-3 ▪ Conference/function centre ▪ Owner Stanley Louw ▪ Winemakers Stanley Louw, with Jaco Theron (Jan 1999) ▪ 103 ha (13 varieties, r/w) ▪ 1 500 tons 10 000 cs own label 35% red 65% white ▪ PO Box 27 Rawsonville 6845 ▪ opstal@lando.co.za ▪ www.opstal.co.za ▪ ***T (023) 344·3001*** *▪ F (023) 344·3002*

With a winemaking tradition dating back to 1847, Opstal continued making its own wines in the 1950s instead of joining the newly founded local co-operative. Still leading the way, the Louws are active in the Breedekloof wine tourism initiative (Stanley L is its chair) and committed to uplifting the local community. With its new cellar facade and tasting facility, their estate has become a popular venue where guests come to relax, enjoy a meal at the restaurant, hold a conference or wedding, throw a birthday bash or simply enjoy a leisurely winetasting. And if you're looking for something different, book a haunted cellar tour which includes a medieval meal.

Chenin Blanc ★★★ 'Serious wine which will age that extra yr,' winemakers advise, though hard to imagine resisting **05**'s (sample) ample charms, incl fresh lemon flavour & youthful vibrancy. **Cabernet Sauvignon** ★★★ Characterful, lightish **02**, red berry flavours & plentiful dry tannins. ±Yr Fr oak. **Chardonnay** ★★★ Lightish **03** last yr showed tropical fruit tones & fairly obvious vanilla from oak staving; still finished fresh. **Hanepoot** ★★★ **03** was warming, appealingly smooth & fragrant last ed. **Merlot Blush** discontinued.

Carl Everson range

Cabernet Sauvignon-Shiraz ★★★ More traditional – not unappealing – style. **03** similar melange of black/green pepper as pvs, pronounced dry oak, full body but light texture. **Classic Red** ★★★ **01** still available, not retasted; engaging, rounded combo red berry, fresh herb & savoury. Blend shiraz, merlot, pinotage, ruby cab. **Sauvignon Blanc** ★★★ **04** shows positive bottle-age; guava & tropical tones; soft, but enough acid to refresh. – *DH*

Oracle

Distell export brand launched July 2002, initially into the UK retail market; the name an allusion to the 'ancient wisdom of Africa'.

Cabernet Sauvignon ★★★ **04** bouquet of bacon & spice over red berries, similar to pvs; austere, green tea palate a departure from pvs unaggressive tannins, light but not lean fruit. From Paarl/Stbosch vyds. Yr Fr oak staves/casks. **Pinotage** ★★★★ Dbnville/Hldrberg fruit in **04**; brooding savoury/tar notes leavened by lively fruit, racy acidity & lots of dry tannins. Friendly (4.5g/ℓ sugar, 12.7% alc), approachable. Combo barrels, Fr staves, unwooded. **Shiraz** ★★★ Challenging **04**'s aggressive acid & tough tannins at odds with its sweet, smoky berry aroma. Portion Fr oak staves. Has sufficient fruit to bed down acids/tannins; give ±1 yr. **Chardonnay** ★★★ **04** vibrant sipper; acacia, dust & nuts with ripe tangerine flavours, richness (from fermentation/ageing 6 mths on oak) offset by citrus freshness. **Sauvignon Blanc 05** not available for tasting. **04** was a promising sample last ed, possibly ★★★★ on release. All WO Coastal.—*CvZ*

Oranjerivier Wine Cellars

Lower Orange (see Northern Cape map) ▪ Est 1965 ▪ 1stB 1968 ▪ Tasting Mon-Fri 8-4.30 Sat 9-11.30 ▪ Fee R5 for 1-5 wines; R10 for 5+ wines ▪ Sales Mon-Fri 8-5 Sat 8.30-12 ▪ Closed pub hols except Easter Sat ▪ Tours Mon-Fri 9, 11 & 3 Jan-March ▪ Owners ±930 shareholders ▪ Winemakers Johan Esterhuizen (Upington cellar), Jan Steenkamp (Grootdrink), Chris Venter (Groblershoop), Deon Truter (Keimoes) & Bolla Louw (Kakamas), with (in same cellar order) Jopie Faul/Philani Gumede, George Kruger/Tinus Kotze, Henno Ludick, Christo Smit/Riaan Liebenberg & Johan Dippenaar/Mike du Toit ▪ Agricultural consultant Henning Burger (2005) ▪ 332 837 ha (pinotage, ruby cab, chenin, colombard) ▪ ±150 000 tons Export labels: River's Tale ▪ Ranges for customers: Vine Collection, Cape Fest & Liquor Boys (Liquor City); Country Cellars & Carnival (Spar); Nature's Group ▪ HACCP certification in progress ▪ PO Box 544 Upington 8800 ▪ marketing@owk.co.za ▪ www.owk.co.za ▪ ***T (054) 337·8800*** *▪ F (054) 332·4408*

Given the sheer size and scope of this operation — 900 growers; vineyards spread across 300km; a crop of ±150 000 tons (20% down on 2004!); five cellars; a flotilla of winemakers — the intention to feature as a good bottled-wine producer must be akin to turning an oil tanker on a tickey. Yet it's full steam ahead. They're testing new varieties to identify performers under hot, dry, irrigated conditions (petit verdot and tannat hold promise, as do reds in general, planted on the hillier edges of the Orange riverbank). Vintage 2005 was a white-wine year, though, with fruit-laden colombard, chenin and chardonnay. A two-year, R20m-plus cellar upgrade was followed by yet more investment in a bottling line, fermentation tanks and conversion to screwcaps. Also new premises for tastings & sales: not only is good wine on its radar screen; the good ship 'OWK' wants to land the tourist market.

All below lightish (12-12.5% alc unless noted), for earliest possible consumption. Mainly **NV**; most reds unwooded. **Cabernet Sauvignon** ★★★ Step above pvs; **04** fairly richly fruited, pleasant dry balanced tannin, easy to drink. **Pinotage** ★★★ Good everyday red. Comfortable & well-flavoured, medium-light bodied (13.5% alc). **Ruby Cabernet** ★★★ Always attractive here. **04** coffee & plum aromas, some thatch whiffs, juicy, supple tannins. Full bodied: 14% alc. **Shiraz** ★★★ Good everyday quaff, lightly & well oaked. Appealing white pepper sniff on **04**, juicy tannins. **Riverstale Classic Red** ★★★ Temporarily out of stock; **02** smoky/savoury blend cab, shiraz, pinotage, ruby cab, 6 mths oak-staved; light, slightly grainy dry flavours. **Rouge** ★★ From cab; smoky/savoury tone, hint oak (staves), berry fruit & undemanding dry tannins. **Rosé** ★ Shy, earthy semi-sweet pink from colombard, pinotage. **Blanc de Noir** ★★ Ruby cab does the business. Savoury this time; dryish & rounded despite ±17g/ℓ sugar. **Chardonnay** ★★ **04** bit honeyed & tired; reminds that these have evanescent charms. **Chenin Blanc** ★ Latest is vintaged (**05**) & dry, with rip-roaring acidity. **Colombard** ★★ Reprises semi-dry styling in **05**, soft 'blanc de blanc' style white, zesty acidity. **Grand Cru** ★ Water-white & bracingly dry, as expected. From colombard. **Blanc de Blanc** ★★ Three whites led by colombard; softer, fruiter than cellar mates; pleasant summer quaffing. **Nouveau Blanc** ★★ Popular talcum-powder-scented semi-sweet from chenin, very light though not too sweet. **Light** ★ Very ordinary off-dry from chenin; austere, fruit-free. 8% alc. **Stein** ★★ Pleasant & inoffensive, lots of sweetness to mask otherwise austere profile. Varieties as for ... **Late Harvest** ★ Colombard, chenin with very little to offer beyond sweetness. **Special Late Harvest** ★★ Delicately perfumed **04**, clean, with hint of fruit; varieties as for Late Harvest. **Sparkling Brut** ★★★ Sprightly carbonated dry bubbly with fine bead; clean, fresh & patently colombard. **Sparkling Doux** ★★ Big, bumptious bubbles; light & not too sweet. **White Jerepiko** ★★ Sultana stars in what tastes like liquidised raisins, with hot spirituous finish. **Sweet Hanepoot** ★★★ Foursquare version with pineapple/tropical fruit hint, clean spirit edge. **Red Jerepigo** ★★★ From ruby cab, as always; shows its thatchy character, sweetness tweaked into shape by 17% alc; lacks concentration for higher rating. **White Muscadel** ★★★ **04** hint of muscat, simple sweet-sour flavours, lacks silky charm of pvs. 16.5% alc. **Red Muscadel** ★★★ Invariably appealing, with well-judged sweetness & alc. **04** scented with muscat & cranberry. **Red Port** ★ Traditional-style fortified, usually from ruby cab; even lower in alc (17.5%) this yr, caramelised/medicinal flavours. N Cape & Lower Orange WOs for all these. *—DH/TM*

Org de Rac Domain new

*Swartland ▪ Est 2004 ▪ 1stB 2005 ▪ Visits Mon-Fri 8-5 Sat 9-1 ▪ Closed Easter Fri/Sun/Mon, Dec 16/25/26 & Jan 1 ▪ Tourgroups ▪ Conferences ▪ Owner Pieter Vercuiel ▪ Winemaker Hugo Lambrechts (Nov 2004) ▪ Viticulturist Pieter de Lange (Dec 2004) ▪ 42.5 ha (cab, merlot, shiraz) ▪ 210 tons 17 000 cs 95% red 5% rosé ▪ ISO certification in progress ▪ PO Box 268 Piketberg 7320 ▪ orgderac@mweb.co.za ▪ www.orgderac.com ▪ **T (022) 913·2397/3924** ▪ F (022) 913·3162*

Pieter Vercuiel, a Piketberg farm boy and grower of table grapes for 20 years, was inspired by his love of wine and belief in a healthy lifestyle to develop his own organic winery. He bought a neglected grain farm in 2001 and, 'after a lot of hard work', 42ha of organically grown and managed vineyards, a manor house, 400 ton winery, plus infrastructure have now been turned into reality. Vercuiel has an equally enthusiastic winemaker in the person of Hugo Lambrechts, ex-Windmeul. They and their wives are tackling marketing in similarly motivated fashion, with sound organic practices providing a point of difference in the crowded marketplace. Their launch offerings are a Cabernet Sauvignon, Merlot, Shiraz and Shiraz Rosé from the 2005 vintage, tasted in infancy and too unformed to rate.

Origin Wine

*Stellenbosch ▪ Est/1stB 2002 ▪ Closed to public ▪ Owner Bernard Fontannaz ▪ Winemakers Alain Cajeux & Theresa Bedeker (both Dec 2004) ▪ Viti consultant Thys Greeff (Jan 2003) ▪ 4m cs ▪ 55% red 40% white 5% rosé ▪ Export brands: African Horizon, Cape 1652, Cape Original, Noble Cape, Palm Grove, Sunbird & ranges below ▪ PO Box 7177 Stellenbosch 7599 ▪ reception@originwine.co.za ▪ **T 086·167·4446** ▪ F 865·2348*

'Survival of the fittest' is the philosophy guiding CEO Bernard Fontannaz in juggling changes and expansion at one of the Cape's largest (yet low-profile) wineries. Contracts with customers in a host of price-sensitive export markets, including biggies Holland and Germany, coupled with strong growth the past year necessitated extra capacity – pronto! In response, subsidiary Origin Bottling doubled its filling capability (to 2.4m cases) and expanded its warehousing and docking facilities, while sister company Origin Wine added an entire blending cellar. In six months flat. In between times Bernard F welcomed a former colleague, winemaker Alain Cajeux, into the fold.

Cape Original ★ Latest version of red 3ℓ bag in box not a patch on pvs; earthy & rustic, with huge dry tannins; shiraz & ruby cab; 10% oaked. NV/04.

African Horizon range

These **05**s destined for various European markets. **Pinotage** ★ new Touch ruby cab blended in; mainly banana character & puckering dryness. **Shiraz** ★★★ Robust, slightly smoky winter red; lacks charm & varietal character of pvs, but does a good warming job. **Pinotage-Ruby Cinsaut** ★ new Very little of cinsaut's fruity juiciness apparent, faint raisin notes & challenging dry tannins. **Cabernet-Pinotage-Ruby Cabernet** new ★★ Forthcoming cassis/vanilla notes, fruit restrained by dry tannins; drink with food or mature yr/2. **Shiraz-Pinotage** new ★ Savoury tones of smoked sausage, astringent & earthy. **Dry Red** new ★☆ Mainly pinotage – obvious from pleasant dried banana/wild berry sniffs; muted tannins make for comfortable anytime red. **Rosé** ★★ new Delicate dry pink from pinotage; subdued but easy strawberry flavours. **Chardonnay** ★☆ Bring back last yr's version! Retiring **05** insubstantial & unmemorable. **Chardonnay-Viognier** new ★★☆ 20% aromatic viognier lifts the blend, as does 10% Fr oak; welcoming ripe-peach/lemon butter character. **Colombard-Chardonnay** new ★☆ Chard potion oaked, adds butteriness, makes amiable pre-supper drink. **Chenin Blanc** new ★ Has varietal character (Golden Delicious apple) in slender, lightish package. **Chenin Blanc-Colombard** new ★☆ Crisp, dry, hints guava & other tropical fruits; subtly flavoured 70/30 blend. **White** new ★★ Cheerful chenin, colombard, muscat mix with delicate fruit salad aroma, light body.

Cape Nature Organic new

For Dutch market. All **05**. **Cabernet Sauvignon** ★☆ Herbaceous profile with leaves & damp earth; matching unfruity flavours/tannins. **Merlot** ★☆ A less than generous merlot; whiff nutmeg, unyielding stalky palate; decant well ahead of serving. **Shiraz** ★★☆ Lovely youthful purple colour; hint of new leather, softly spicy flavour. Nice! **Colombard** ★☆ Variety's signature guava character, ripe, dry & inoffensive.

Cape 1652 range new

Created for the Dutch market. All **05**. **Pinotage-Cabernet Sauvignon** ★☆ 70/30 blend, spicy/stalky red with earthy hint, food-friendly dry finish. **Pinotage Rosé** ★ Coral pink, with delicate petally bouquet & unexpectedly sharp dry finish. **Chenin Blanc-Chardonnay** ★ Your basic dry white – simple & subdued but clean.

Evolution range

Features redesigned labels & stylistic tweaks – perhaps not all for better, as in … **Merlot** ★☆ Incl 10% ruby cab in **05**, less engaging than pvs; stalky flavours, big dry tannins. 10% oaked. **Sauvignon Blanc** ★★☆ **05** again light-bodied, English gooseberry intro; some flinty hints; lively acidity. **Semillon-Chardonnay** ★★ **05** crisp, dry & minerally; light-bodied, for early enjoyment. Lower proportion (10%) Fr oaked. No follow-ups for remainder of range; notes from pvs ed: **Pinotage** ★★☆ Partly wooded **04** mingle of red fruits, gentle tannins for easy drinking. **Shiraz** ★★☆ Peppery touch to **04**, palate padded by touch sugar ±4g/ℓ. 20% Am oaked. **Rosé** ★★★ From pinotage; **04** plummy red berry character, crisp & refreshing, satisfyingly dry. **Merlot-Ruby Cabernet** ★★★ **04** rhubarb tartness to plum & choc flavours; firmish tannins; appealing; 15% Fr oaked. **Chardonnay** ★★☆ Portion wood-aged; **04** peaches & cream aromas, vanilla whiff, crisp liveliness. **Colombard** ★★☆ **04** tropical fruit aromas, crunchy, boiled-sweet aftertaste.

Fair Hills range new

Approved/certified by the Fair Trade Labelling Organisation (FLO). Both **05**. **Merlot-Shiraz** ★★ Starbucks special: mocha coffee & spice, lively flavours, youthful but balanced tannins. 10% oaked. **Colombard-Chardonnay** ★☆ 80/20 split, small portion oaked. Early evening aperitif with crisp, clean peach & apricot flavours.

Kaap Hollands range new

For Netherlands market. Both **05**. **Pinotage-Shiraz** ★☆ Undemanding & cheerful red, jammy wild berry flavours, generous but balanced tannins. **Chenin Blanc-Chardonnay** ★★ Fruity easy-drinker, apricot & orange zest aromas, clean – if quick – finish. 10% Fr oaked.

Lion's Gate range new

Range in development for UK & possibly other European markets. Both **05**. **Dry Red** ★☆ Enough robust berry flavours & tannins to match your favourite BBQ meat or full-flavoured Mediterranean food. 10% lightly oaked. **Dry White** ★★ As label says: dry, crisp, for no-frills party quaffing. Light-bodied; mainly chenin, with colombard & muscat.

Noble Cape new

For Netherlands market. All **05**. **Pinotage-Shiraz** ★★ For BBQ/outdoor days; well padded with strawberry flavour, tannins won't be bullied by a greasy chop; portion lightly oaked.

Chenin Blanc-Chardonnay ★★ Effortless casual quaff, with light pineapple & dried peach flavours. 5% Fr oaked. **Vonkel Wijn** ★★ Explosion of straw-toned bubbles in hugely festive brut-style sparkling; perfect for party animals on a budget.

Pier 42 range new

Styled for the UK market. All **05**. **Merlot** ★ Sappy, stalky, green tone only partly offset by dash fruity ruby cab. 10% oaked, as is ... **Chardonnay** ★★ Restrained, lightly buttery notes; dry & fresh, fairly soft flavours for comfortable quaffing. **Sauvignon Blanc** ★ More 'crisp dry white' than varietal hero; some wet wool character & racy acidity.

South Point range

Pinotage new ★★ Rustic **05** wild strawberry fruit & fairly severe tannins; decant if drinking early. **Sauvignon Blanc** new ★★ **05** greener-toned & lightish, crisp, dry, with hint of asparagus. Following **04**s not retasted: **Dry Red** ★★★ Pleasant BBQ/al fresco wine, smoothed by 4. 5g/ℓ sugar. Mainly pinotage & shiraz, with dash ruby cab. **Chenin Blanc** ★★★ Gentle, fresh-tasting guava flavours, styled for undemanding quaffability. All ranges WO W-Cape. — *CT*

Ormonde Vineyards

*Darling (see Swartland map) ▪ 1stB 1999 ▪ Tasting & sales Mon-Fri 9-4 Sat & pub hols 9-1 ▪ Closed Easter Fri, Dec 25/26 & Jan 1 ▪ Vineyard tours by appt ▪ Picnic baskets by appt or BYO ▪ Function hall ▪ Facilities for children ▪ Farm produce ▪ Walks ▪ Owners Basson family ▪ Winemakers Theo Basson & Wouter Pienaar ▪ Viticulturist Theo Basson ▪ ±400 ha (cabs s/f, merlot, mourvèdre, petit v, shiraz, chard, chenin, sauvignon, semillon) ▪ 2 000 tons 20 000 cs own label 40% red 60% white ▪ Also exported as Westerland & Ondine ▪ PO Box 201 Darling 7345 ▪ ormondevineyards@iafrica.com ▪ www.ormonde.co.za ▪ **T (022) 492·3540** ▪ F (022) 492·3470*

'In the past,' says Theo Basson, 'SA producers made a mistake in giving the world the perception that our wines were cheap. Now the mission is to prove ourselves with our premium and ultra premium wines, and this mission must keep its momentum.' He, for one, is doing his here in Darling, focusing on the Ormonde range as his 'world class wines' but still catering for the 'easy lifestyle' end with the Alexanderfontein wines. 'Both ranges are made using traditional techniques with modern equipment,' says Theo B, exhausted but upbeat after a tough 2005 season. 'It brought out a lot of character in our staff ... and our wines.'

Ormonde range

Cabernet Sauvignon-Merlot ★★★★ **03** vintage raises the bar. Classic bdx formula (45/45 cab/merlot remainder cab f & petit v); delightful breakfast nose of bacon & mushrooms, salty liquorice tang. Less wood (15 mths Fr oak) imparts more poise. **Chardonnay** ★★★ **03** retasted, fading, drink up. **Sauvignon Blanc** ★★★ **04** blush of youth fading into inoffensive drinkability, moderate 13% alc.

Alexanderfontein range

★★★★★ **Sauvignon Blanc** Pineapple & lime give zingy tropical dimension to **05** (★★★★); lots more power (14% alc) than stunning **04**, with racy acidity & concentration of flavours leading to long finish; lunch-friendly 12.9% alc.

Cabernet Sauvignon ★★★ **03** barnyard nose, earthy palate & full rustic flavours, excessive austerity. 9 mths Fr oak, 30% new. **Merlot** ★★★★ Marmite & dark choc tone to **04**, light & leafy with mint hints. **Chardonnay** ★★★ **04** barely wooded, light & fresh with subdued citrus flavours. Subtle wooding: fermented/6 mths older oak; some native yeasts. **Chenin** ★★★ **04** middle-aged vines (23 yrs avg) give oodles of boiled sweets/citrus tang, weighty 14% alc. — *NP*

Oubenheim Estate

*Olifants River ▪ Est/1stB 2002 ▪ Closed to public ▪ Owners DW Viljoen & Philip Viljoen ▪ Winemaker Philip Viljoen ▪ Merlot, pinotage, shiraz, chenin, sauvignon ▪ 500 cs 100% red ▪ PO Box 52 Vredendal 8160 ▪ oubenheim@telkomsa.net ▪ **T 083·509·9885** ▪ F (027) 213·5624*

No update available on this winery; contact details from previous edition.

Oude Compagnies Post

Tulbagh ▪ Est 1699 ▪ 1stB 2003 ▪ Tasting only by appt ▪ Owner Jerry Swanepoel Family Trust (Jerry & Henriette Swanepoel) ▪ Winemaker Jerry Swanepoel ▪ Viti adviser Hanno van Schalkwyk ▪ 18 ha (cab, merlot, pinotage, ruby cab, shiraz, chard, sauvignon) ▪ 80 tons 3 000 cs 100% red ▪ PO Box 11 Tulbagh 6820 ▪ swanepoel@intekom.co.za ▪ ***T (023) 230·1578/ 082·829·8404*** *F (023) 230·0840*

How many advocates does it take to make good wine? Only two (so long as plenty of passion is also involved), as owners Jerry and Henriette Swanepoel are determined to prove. With Jerry S using phrases like 'quality as opposed to quantity', 'as close to perfection as possible' and 'believe in your wine', it's no wonder wines coming out of his 'cathedral-like stone cellar', under the 'Compagnies Wijn' label, are drawing praise from as far away as Germany, Ireland and Sweden. Their roots are in eastern mountain slopes where, says Jerry (already with prizes to back him up), the terroir is ideal for red wine. 'I want to enjoy my wines', he asserts. So do many others, it seems.

★★★★ **Pinotage** Ultra-ripe **03** (★★★☆) decadent choc-, spice-coated fruitiness, soft tannin structure, oak flavours & sweetness (14 mths 50/50 Am/Fr), rather short. Brighter, livelier **04** much lauded at 2004 SANYWS, incl Nat. Champ; plenty of ripe rich fruit, good firm tannins. Also heavily oaked - rating given in hopes of some future harmony.

★★★★ **Merlot** Red/black berries, choc-mint notes on pleasantly approachable, fresh **04**. Succulently savoury, with smooth forceful tannins in good balance. 14 mths in Fr barrels not overwhelming.

Shiraz ★★★☆ Spicy, robust **04** has serious intentions, with firm structure & pleasant but rather evanescent flavour. 14 mths Am oak adds sweet dimension. **Cabernet Sauvignon** ★★★☆ Big, dark, brawny, very heavily oaked **04** with clear blockbuster aspirations - but not all will find it easy to actually drink. Ripe black fruit there, hiding under spicy tobacco notes, amongst the tannins, big 14.5% alc. **03** (★★★) similar aims & character, but lesser fruit amidst drier tannins. These ±14 mths Fr oak. WO Coastal, as is ... **Cabernet Sauvignon-Pinotage** ★★★☆ 80/20 blend in bold, forthright **03**; ripe mulberry aromas, good fruit albeit hollow-centred, firm structure — *TJ*

Oude Denneboom

Paarl ▪ 1stB 2003 ▪ Closed to public ▪ Owner Daniel de Waal ▪ Winemaker/viticulturist Hannes Aucamp ▪ 39 ha (cab, mourvèdre, pinotage, shiraz, viognier) ▪ 300 tons 100 cs 100% red ▪ PO Box 2087 Windmeul 7630 ▪ hannesaucamp@mweb.co.za ▪ ***T/F 869·8073***

This relative newcomer in the Perdeberg foothills already has a following thirsty for its Shiraz — the second vintage to be released (04) sold out within weeks. An additional 2ha each of viognier and mourvèdre have been added to the existing red-wine vines. 'Things are moving slowly but surely,' summarises Hannes Aucamp, who's working on plans for a future cellar to replace current makeshift — and largely outdoors — vinification facilities.

Shiraz ★★★ **04** balanced, with a sweet impression thanks to 14.5% alc. Spicy/savoury flavours & bluegum aromas; drop viognier for perfume. More restrained, less concentrated & complex than pvs. 100 cs. — *CT*

Oude Kaap

Range by DGB for export mainly to Germany, Scandinavia and the Low Countries.

Following three **03**s still in stock, not retasted: **Cabernet Sauvignon** ★★★ Fairly evolved aromas of roast meat & dried red fruit; soft, potpourri-scented palate. **Pinotage** ★★★ Meaty/savoury edge to sweet-berry fruit, comfortable dry tannins. **Cabernet Sauvignon-Merlot** ★★★ Tasty, harmonious equal partnership; bramble/game notes with food-cordial savoury finish. **Ruby Cabernet** new ★★ **04** lighter-style BBQ partner with strawberry flavour, touch of variety's stalkiness, some astringency. **Klassiek Rood** new ★★★ **04** good everyday red, mainly ruby cab & cinsaut; lively, rounded & juicy; enjoy over next yr/2. **Blanc de Noir** ★☆ Blue-tinged **05** again from pinotage, with variety's signature mulberry aromas, sweetish slightly grainy finish. **Chardonnay** ★★ Styled for the pop palate, though **04** will appeal more to lovers of an oaky style. **Chenin Blanc** ★★★ Lightish, softly dry **05** gorgeous white peach aroma, lively fresh flavours, good anytime glassful. **Elegant Wit** ★★ **04** equal chenin, colombard mix; shy, light, drier taste than 18g/ℓ RS would suggest. **Klassiek Wit** new ★ 10% muscat de A fails to lift this light, foursquare dry white, redeemed by some zestiness on finish. **NV**. All above WO W Cape. *— DH*

Oudekloof Private Cellar

Tulbagh ▪ Est 1752 ▪ 1stB 2000 ▪ Closed to public ▪ Owners Francois Rozon, Lyndsay Webster-Rozon, Paul & Lucille O'Riordan ▪ Winemaker TBA ▪ GM/viticulturist Bernardt Krüger ▪ 22 ha (cab, shiraz, chard, chenin) ▪ 1 000 cs ▪ 25% red 75% white ▪ PO Box 191, Oudekloof Farm, Tulbagh 6820 ▪ oudekloof@mweb.co.za ▪ ***T (023) 230·1925*** *▪ F 856·4595*

No update available on this winery; contact details from previous edition.

Oude Rust see Mooiuitsig

Oude Wellington Estate

Wellington ▪ Visits by appt ▪ Tasting fee R15 ▪ Closed Dec 25 ▪ A la carte restaurant ▪ Guest house & self-catering cottages ▪ Tourgroups ▪ Facilities for children ▪ Conferencing ▪ Owners/ viticulturists Rolf & Vanessa Schumacher ▪ Winemaker Vanessa Schumacher (Jul 1995) ▪ 13 ha (cab, ruby cab, shiraz, chard, chenin) ▪ 80 tons ±2 500 cs own label 60% red 20% white 20% rosé ▪ PO Box 622 Wellington 7654 ▪ info@kapwein.com ▪ www.kapwein.com http://estate.kapwein.com ▪ ***T 873·2262*** *▪ F 088021·873·4639*

With buildings dating back to the 1700s, upgrading, renovating and maintaining are part of the Rolf & Vanessa Schumacher's daily programme. The tasting room, where you can also sample Rolf S's potstill brandy, is in the 'new' building — which dates back to the 1800s. Next door is the kitchen, with whitewashed walls, gleaming wood and inviting fireplace. Glass-paned doors concertina back, creating an open-plan area which encourages *gemütlichkeit* at this winery-cum-guesthouse — no wonder they almost ran dry last year mainly through cellar door sales.

Cabernet Sauvignon ★★ Emphatic Wllngtn red, Fr oak aged, 2 yrs for barrel sample **03**. Mineral notes, very ripe dark fruits; lean tannins. **Shiraz** new **04** attractive smoke/spice permeates nose & palate, tannins currently dominant. Unrated sample needs time to knit. 13 mths combo Fr/Russian oak. **Blanc de Noir** ★ From ruby cab & in new livery! **04** coppery pink, light fruit & rasping acidity despite 7.5g/ℓ sugar. **Chardonnay Unwooded** ★★ **04** also with new label, understated peach & citrus tones; losing freshness. **Currant Abbey** ★★★ Anagram of ruby cabernet, from which it is made. Unwooded, fun-time wine; fruity, with game/meat aromas; sweet entry, sweet exit. Sample **05** tasted. No follow-ups in sight to the following; notes from pvs ed: **Ruby Cabernet** ★★★ **98** woody/earthy tones, nice dry tannins. **Chardonnay Barrique** ★★ **02** pleasantly honeyed, shows balanced wooding (Am oak, 8 mths, 2nd fill. **Gewürztraminer** ★★★ **03** sweetly rose-scented yet dry-tasting despite 6g/ℓ sugar, thanks to brisk acidity. Lowish 12% alc. *— CT*

Oude Weltevreden see Weltevrede
Our Founders see Bellingham
Out of Africa see African Terroir

Overgaauw Estate

Stellenbosch ▪ Est 1905 ▪ 1stB 1971 ▪ Tasting & sales Mon-Fri 9-12.30 2-5 Sat & pub hols 10-12.30 ▪ Closed Mar 21, Easter Fri-Sun, Dec 25/26 & Jan 1 ▪ Fee R10 ▪ Tours by appt ▪ Owner Braam van Velden ▪ Winemaker Chris Joubert (1990), with David van Velden Jnr (Nov 2002) ▪ Viti consultant Johan Pienaar ▪ 75 ha (11 varieties) ▪ ±360 tons 17 000 cs 60% red 40% white ▪ PO Box 3 Vlottenburg 7604 ▪ info@overgaauw.co.za ▪ www.overgaauw.co.za ▪ ***T 881·3815*** *▪ F 881·3436*

Celebrations last year of the 100th anniversary of the Van Veldens' tenure at Overgaauw in the Stellenbosch Kloof, while officially passing on (precisely) November 14, also included a celebratory special vertical tasting of four decades of Van Velden winemaking in August. The family records are unusually thorough — assistant winemaker David van V felt confident enough to offer the information that 2005 was the driest vintage since 1949. He's particularly enthused about the 03 version of the winery's flagship, Tria Corda ('Three Hearts', named by thirties Afrikaans poet WEG Louw), thinking it well worth its new redesigned label, and probably one of the best since the first attempt, the 1979, one of the Cape's earliest Bordeaux-style blends.

★★★★☆ **Tria Corda** Early 'Cape claret' blend & still a benchmark. **03** bears new livery & release aptly celebrates van Velden's centenary on Stbosch estate. Fantastic promise signalled by sample in pvs ed fully delivered by final version: sculpted huckleberry/blackcurrant fruits line up behind sweetly ripe, impossibly fine tannins. Now, more texture than taste, but flavour should fill out & be sensational around 2010. No **02**. **01** classic style with trademark leafiness for interest. VDG, JCWCA. **00** *Decanter* ★★★★. Cab, merlot, cab f (60/93/1), 18 mths new Fr oak.

★★★★☆ **Cabernet Sauvignon** Always strapping, with 18 mths in Fr oak, all new, for lavish **03**: asphalt warmth to concentrated forest-floor fruit & focused spice; imposing but soft tannins. Good maturation prospects. No **02**. **01** also impressively built, typical cab profile in classic dry finish.

★★★★☆ **Merlot** The first Cape bottling of this variety (1982), a seriously styled wine needing a few yrs cellaring, especially **03** (sample), with huge tannins well hung with butcher's block savouriness, will go a long way. **02** tasted pre-bottling showed deceptively open loganberry fruits, tight-grained tannins in support. Unobtrusive 18 mths used Fr oak.

★★★★ **Chardonnay** A consistent style that has done the family business for yrs. **05** not ready for review, no **04**. Last **03** was big & buttery, a rich mouthful freshened by acid seam.

★★★★★ **Cape Vintage** ✓ Pioneers of using Portuguese varieties locally, adherents to classic style – lower sugars, higher alcs. **97** still current. Tannic in youth, in true vintage style; also great balance, intensity & grip, promised long development. Blend touriga with tintas b/f/r, souzão & cornifesto. 2½ yrs 1 300ℓ casks.

Shiraz-Cabernet Sauvignon ★★★☆ Sweet bilberry flesh another arrow for cellar's 'Old World' quiver. Retasted **02** juicy berry nose, enough fruit but fades a tad in finish. 20% cab spine. 18 mths older oak. **Sauvignon Blanc** ★★★☆ **05** not ready at press time. Pvs **04** in new racier, pacier cut-grass mode, with lower alc (12%) than pvs. **Sylvaner** ★★★☆ A speciality since 1971, the sole Cape example of this grape. **05** distinctive waxy breadth to supple spicy style, refreshing finish. 12% alc.—*DS*

Overhex Private Cellar

Worcester ▪ Est/1stB 2002 ▪ Tasting & sales Mon-Fri 8-5 ▪ Closed pub hols ▪ Tours by appt ▪ BYO picnic ▪ Farm produce ▪ Owners George Smit, Gerhard van der Wath & Kobus Rossouw ▪ Winemakers Kobus & Johan Rossouw, with Willie Malan ▪ Viticulturist Pierre Snyman ▪ 10 000 tons ▪ Export brands: Balance, Five Senses & Yammé ▪ Ranges for customers: Cape Mist, Country Cellars, Marimba & Thorntree ▪ HACCP, BRC & ISO 9000 certification in progress ▪ PO Box 139 Worcester 6849 ▪ overhex@intekom.co.za ▪ www.overhex.com ▪ ***T (023) 347·5012*** *▪ F (023) 347·1057*

The 2005 vintage is one for the books, according to the Overhex team. They should know, as they source grapes from selected growers in most of the winegrowing regions. Last year they planted their first own-vineyard (sauvignon), and winemaker Kobus Rossouw vinified the maiden viognier, malbec, cab franc and mourvèdre. Other firsts include a Shiraz Port and semi-sweet Muscat (given the slew of recent awards, the variety is clearly his forte). With many new products planned for this year (including organic wines from the Nuy area), Kobus R must be relieved that his brother Johan, ex-Spruitdrift, has joined the team.

Overhex Soulo range

Lavida Cape Red ☺ ★★ Bright, red fruited quaffer; firmish & dry, unpretentious. **04** from mainly shiraz, plus merlot & pinotage, briefly oaked.

Foreign investment in SA wine, steadily on the rise since democracy in 1994, received a further fillip with the news that a leading figure from Bordeaux, **Hubert de Boüard de Laforest** of St-Emilion's top-rated Château Angelus, together with **Bruno Prats**, former owner of second-growth Château Cos-d'Estournel, had acquired an equal share of the Jooste family of Klein Constantia's heretofore low-profile Anwilka property. Pictured against Helderberg Mountain's distinctive domed silhouette are **De Boüard**, winemaker **Trizanne Pansegrouw**, viticulturist **Piet Neethling** and **Lowell Jooste**.

Charles Erasmus, raised among the wheatfields of Wolseley, has grass-roots credibility and well-honed experience for his role as CEO of the SA Wine Industry Trust (SAWIT), the organisation officially responsible for redressing past imbalances and promoting a vibrant and competitive wine industry. With him are **Veronica Campher** (left), marketing manager for Bouwland Wines, one of the first and most successful wine empowerment ventures, and **Dawne Johnson**, his personal assistant.

Established in November 2002, the voluntary, not-for-profit Wine Industry Ethical Trade Association (WIETA) has been lobbying quietly but effectively for a better deal for wine industry employees. WIETA's innovative code of good practice, allied to a social-auditing procedure, enjoys increasing local support and the endorsement of all major UK retailers. Driving the initiative are **Nicky Taylor**, CEO (left), **Anthea Flink**, office administrator, and **Peter Lewis**, audit co-ordinator, seen at their HO in Observatory, Cape Town.

SA, blessed with some of the planet's most ancient and diverse soils, has the potential to make some of its most interesting wines. Helping to realise this latent stellar quality are internationally respected scientists, researchers, viticulturists and specialised service providers such as (from left) **Francois Knight** and **Ryk Taljaard** (Agri Informatics), **Eben Archer** (Lusan farms), **Victoria Carey** (Stellenbosch University) and **Dawid Saayman** (Distell), here getting a feel for the 'good dirt' of Uitkyk Estate outside Stellenbosch.

A landmark on the road towards black economic empowerment (BEE) in the wine industry is the development of a BEE Charter and Industry Scorecard, providing practical guidelines and goals on aspects such as shareholding, land reform, training and skills development. Closely involved with formulating these blueprints for a more equitable future are Stellenbosch University's **Nick Vink** and **Mohammad Karaan**, seen here outside the elegant Agricultural Sciences building on campus.

Unlike in parts of the Old World, where the specialist wine steward has a long-established role in the selection and presentation of fine-wine, and in wine and food matching, the sommelier's contribution to the serving of wine in SA has historically been underplayed. Making a difference through professionalism and innovation are **Ricardo Roux** (left) of luxury estate hotel Grande Roche, and **Arnold Vorster**, originator of the new Roving Sommelier wine-service concept, pictured in the Paarl hotel's atmospheric cellar.

Shiraz ★★★ **04** smooth & drinkable, distinctly shiraz smoky fruit, sweet supple tannins – all necessary ingredients present & well wooded (yr 2nd/3rd fill Fr oak). **Chardonnay** Temporarily out of stock. **Sauvignon Blanc** ★★ Brisk, clean **05** with understated boiled sweet/pear-drop flavours. **Lavida Cape White** ★★ Early drinking **05** from chenin, 40% colombard; pleasantly rounded & gently dry. **White Muscadel** ★★ Powerfully sweet & muscatty **04**, with touch of lemon. Reserve champ at SAYWS. **Red Muscadel** ★★★ **04** lauded by Muscadel Assoc, SAYWS; well-balanced despite high alc (18.5%) & daunting sweetness (239g/ℓ RS); earthy touch, long lifted finish. Block since registered as single vyd. **Cape Rock Lizabelle** discontinued.

Balance range

Merlot-Cabernet Sauvignon ☺ ★★★ Juicily quaffable **04**, generous berry fruit balanced by gently effective cab tannins. 4 mths oaked.

04 reds tasted as samples last ed; bottled versions revisited this yr. **Shiraz-Merlot** ★★ Soft, balanced **04**, equal blend with pleasing spread of varietal attributes incl plum, berry & pepper. 5 mths oaked. **Pinotage-Shiraz** new ★★ Smooth, easy casual quaff; **04** light-textured ripe plum/berry fruit, supple tannins. **Pink** ★★ (Replaces 'Pinotage Rosé') Off-dry **05** ripe plum nose, berry flavours with touch banana, smooth & easy drinking. **Chenin Blanc-Colombard** ★★ Dry this yr, **05** again with guava & pineapple hints, lively no-frills white. **Colombard-Chardonnay** ★★ **05** even shyer than last vintage, with dry acidic finish. **Sauvignon Blanc-Semillon** new ★★ **05**'s underplayed tropical tones lifted by ±11g/ℓ sugar, well gauged for pleasurable quaffing. **Muscat d'Alexandrie Semi-Sweet** new ★ Understated in all respects; some muscat aromas & gentle sweetness. **05** guaranteed not to offend. **Vin Sec** new ★★ **04** pleasantly fresh & lively, light, with suggestion of fruit. **Vin Doux** new ★★★ Foaming fun for the sweeter-toothed. **04** fresh citrus blossom bouquet, light & sweet muscatty flavours. From sun-ripe hanepoot. Both ranges WO W Cape. – *DH*

Overmeer Cellars

No-frills quaffing range launched in 1996. All NVs in 5ℓ boxes, W Cape vyds. By Distell.

Selected Red ★★ Light-hued braai slosher; ripe fruit, earthy & rustic with some tannins. **Grand Cru** ★★ Zippy melon-toned quick-quaff, always with muted fruitiness. **Stein** ★★ Soft gulper for the sweeter toothed; gentle lemon flavours. **Late Harvest** ★★ Fractionally sweeter, fuller version of Stein; subdued candied pineapple note, quick finish. All alcs ±11%. – *CvZ*

Overvaal see Hartswater
Paarl Heights see False Bay Vineyards

Paarl Wine Company

Paarl ▪ Closed to public ▪ 9 Zuidmeer Str Huguenot Paarl 7646 ▪ winesales@ffbc.co.za ▪ ***T 862·0616*** *▪ F 862·6400*

Wine wholesalers and owners of, among others, the Fairbridge, Spencers Creek and Casa Portuguesa ranges.

Paddagang Wines

Tulbagh ▪ Est 1987 ▪ Tasting & sales daily 9–4 ▪ Fee R5 ▪ Paddagang Restaurant daily 8.30–4.30 ▪ Closed Easter Fri, May 1, Dec 25 & Jan 1 ▪ Guest house ▪ Gifts ▪ Owners Paddagang Vignerons ▪ Winemakers Carl Allen & Elsabé Roux (Aug/Dec 2002) ▪ Viticulturist Callie Coetzee (Dec 2002) ▪ 5 300 cs 52% red 21% white 27% other ▪ PO Box 303 Tulbagh 6820 ▪ paddagang@mweb.co.za ▪ www.tulbagh.net ▪ ***T (023) 230·0394*** *▪ F (023) 230·0433*

No update available on this winery; contact details and wine notes from previous edition.

All **NV**. **Paddarotti** ★★★ Appropriately wide-girthed blend shiraz/cab (60/40); jammy red fruit flavours, dry savoury finish. **Paddajolyt** ★★★ Easy unwooded *vin ordinaire* from pinotage & ruby cab (50/50); lightish, tangy dried-fruit finish. **Paddadundee** ★★ Chardonnay, latest subtitled 'Limited Release'; fragrant passionfruit hints; creamy dry finish.

Paddasang ★★ Lightish sauvignon, its apple/pear tones tinged with bottle-age. **Paddapoot** ★★★ Hanepoot, back in the froggy fold by popular demand; deliciously aromatic & fresh; very soft & sweet. **Brulpadda** ★★★ Good old-Cape port, from ruby cab & pinotage; soft, sweet, quite silky. Low 16.5% alc. —*TM*

Palm Grove see Origin Wine
Pangolin see MAN Vintners
Panorama see Lost Horizons
Papillon see Van Loveren
Papkuilsfontein see Tukulu
Paradyskloof see Vriesenhof

Patrys

Range by Woodlands Import Export of Somerset West, mainly for export to Europe. See Assegai for contact details. No new wines; notes from previous edition.

Cabernet Sauvignon ★★★ **02** tarry smoked meat aromas, scrubby palate, firm dry finish. ±9 mths Fr oak. **Merlot** ★★★ Light-textured **03**, sweetly fresh berry fruit, lacks intensity, finish. 6 mths equal Fr/Am oak. **Pinotage** ★★★★ ✓ **03** creamy/toasty palate with underlying sweet spice; nicely weighted & dry for variety; no hurry to drink up. 3-9 mths Fr/Am oak. 14.5% alc. **Shiraz** ★★★ **02** startlingly dark; concentrated, creamy black-fruit nose; strong tannins. 14% alc. 8 mths Fr oak. **Cinsaut-Ruby Cabernet** ★★★ **03** fruity but leaner & less amendable than pvs; very dry. **Chenin Blanc** ★★★ **04** Good summer refresher with Granny Smith apple nose, crisp, zesty palate. **Sauvignon Blanc** ★★ **04** delicate pear-drop aromas, leafy green-toned palate, not as much character as pvs. All WO Paarl. —*CR*

Paul Cluver Estate

Elgin ▪ Est 1859 ▪ 1stB 1997 ▪ Tasting & sales Mon-Fri 8-5 Sat & pub hols 9-2 ▪ Fee R10 for groups of 8-12 ▪ Closed Easter Fri/Sun, Dec 25 & Jan 1 ▪ BYO picnic ▪ Guest house ▪ Summer sunset concerts in amphitheatre ▪ Conservation area ▪ Owners Cluver family ▪ Winemaker Andries Burger (Nov 1996) ▪ Viticulturist Christiaan Cloete, advised by Kevin Watt (Feb 2005/ Mar 2003) ▪ 100 ha (cab, merlot, pinot, chard, gewürz, riesling, sauvignon) ▪ 300 tons 20 000 cs 50% red 50% white ▪ PO Box 48 Grabouw 7160 ▪ info@cluver.co.za ▪ www.cluver.com ▪ ***T 844·0605*** *▪ F 844·0150*

Neuro-surgeon Paul Cluver's Elgin farm is riding the crest of the wave, with winemaker son-in-law Andries Burger winning numerous decorations for his Chardonnay, Sauvignon and Noble Late Harvest. The NLH 03 was rated by top British consumer wineguide, The Wine List, as 'the best of its kind in SA and easily the finest in the New World'. Entrusted with the wellbeing of the vines is new viticulturist Christiaan Cloete. He and consultant Kevin Watt want to pursue 'a more hands-on and scientific approach to viticulture'. Their goal: 'even greater wines'. Vinification tweaks include 100% native yeast fermentation for the Chardonnay (up from 60%). Expect a Shiraz in the line-up in a few years: the first crop was harvested last season and has Andries B very excited about the future.

★★★★ **Cabernet Sauvignon** After cool & elegant **01**, a difficult vintage spoke in **02** (★★★★, not retasted); through slightly diminished substance, poise & length, & more obvious, dryer tannins, but still an attractive, savoury mouthful. Usual ±18 mths Fr oak, 60% new.

★★★★ **Pinot Noir** Has helped build reputation of cool Elgin over the years, but last yr **02** (★★★), while well structured, showed too much striving to overcome vintage. **03** returns to usual class: long, dark & handsome; rich fruit firmly supported, subtly oaked (Fr, third new, ±11 mths). 14.5% alc.

★★★★ **Gewürztraminer** Delicately aromatic **04** (★★★★★) shows real beauty after a yr: elegantly, subtly forceful, long-lingering multi-dimensionality marked by Turkish Delight & honeysuckle grace-notes. Finely poised & balanced – effectively dry, despite touch of sugar. Moderate alc (13%) adds to superb drinkability – alone or with lightly spiced food.

★★★★ **Chardonnay** Elegant, fine tones from Elgin's mild climate characterise these. Last ed we found toasty, spicy youthfulness on **03**, green lime flavours, in harmonious, silky ensemble. Big fresh acid should guard over few yrs' development. Fermented in Fr oak (75% new), partly with native yeasts, then 9 mths in barrel.

★★★★ **Weisser Riesling** Sophisticated **04** still offers the tingle of excitement that this great variety can give; it's partly inherent fineness, partly the subtle balance of fruit, 12% alc, acid & a little hidden sweetness (8.7g/ℓ sugar). Intense, peachy loveliness will develop complexity over 5+ yrs.

★★★★☆ **Weisser Riesling Noble Late Harvest** Splendid **03** (★★★★★) 'a hard act to follow' admits Andries B, but **04** does it well: as before, highlight is riesling's incomparably tense, exciting balance of sweetness, racy acidity in carrying the sumptuous fruit. Typical peach/muscat/pepper intermingling with honeyed botrytis. Should only grow more lovely for many yrs to come. **03** IWSC gold. No **02**.

The Elgin Blend ★★★★ Cheekily but proudly named maiden **03** blends home cab & bought-in Elgin merlot. Choc, berries to sniff. Fresh, with firm, savoury tannins. Typically sensitive oaking: 15 mths, 10% new. Should benefit from few yrs keeping. NE. **Sauvignon Blanc** ★★★☆ Last tasted was fresh, well balanced **04** with elegant 12.5% alc, earthy & green notes, lingering passionfruit finish. — *TJ*

Paul Wallace Wines new

Elgin ▪ Est 2004 ▪ Closed to public ▪ Vini adviser Inus Muller ▪ 3 tons ▪ 200 cs 100% red ▪ PO Box 141 Elgin 7180 ▪ wallovale@mweb.co.za ▪ T/F 848·9744

Paul Wallace, independent viticultural consultant, has contributed to the success of many SA brands, for a broad base of clients. After 25 years in the wine industry, he succumbed, not to *parskoors* or other vineyard-related ailments, but to the inevitable desire to launch his own label. Strongly influenced by Paul Pontellier of Chateau Margaux, he wanted to produce something different, a wine with magnificent structure, texture and fruit. His experience and inside knowledge of the Cape vineyards enabled him to source some prime red grapes from the Paarl area, and ensure the timing of the harvest at optimum ripeness.

★★★★ **Malbec** Densely fruited yet elegantly polished **04**; blackcurrant/cedar notes; rich soft tannins, persistent spicy finish. Paarl grapes, yr oak. — *MF*

Pax Verbatim Vineyards

*Stellenbosch ▪ Est 2004 ▪ Closed to public ▪ Owner/winemaker Richard Hilton ▪ 100 cs 100% red ▪ 21 Topaz Street, Heldervue, Somerset West 7130 ▪ info@paxverbatim.co.za ▪ www.paxverbatim.co.za ▪ **T/F 855·5244***

Last year was Richard Hilton's third harvest, and his toughest to date. Besides the usual pH problems (due to the low lime in West Coast soil where he sources his shiraz), rains led to uneven ripening, while high temperatures meant sunburn. But Richard is nothing if not resourceful — he has swopped his Rhône yeast for a Champagne one (it works better with low acidity), presses the grapeskins only very lightly, and plans a rather shorter barrel maturation. 'I set out wanting to make a deep, dark, opaque wine but the overall style has become a lot more svelte — smooth and elegant, with no harsh tannin.' Having mastered shiraz, he's now eager to work with sauvignon.

Blazing Hill Syrah ★★★ **04** sweet/sour cranberry flavours, touch austere palate. Leaner than pvs elegant version, yet remains unflamboyant with fine linearity. Groenekloof fruit. As with maiden **03**, needs few yrs to start showing its best. 35% new Fr oak 16–18 mths. — *MM*

Peacock Ridge see False Bay Vineyards
Pearl Springs see Cape Vineyards
Pearly Bay see KWV International
Pecan Stream see Waterford

Pella Wines

Stellenbosch ▪ Est/1stB 2004 ▪ Closed to public ▪ Owner Ingrid de Waal ▪ Winemakers Ingrid & Daniël de Waal ▪ Viticulturist Daniël de Waal ▪ 100 cs ▪ 100% red ▪ PO Box 89 Vlottenburg 7604 ▪ Pella@adept.co.za ▪ ***T 082·829·7509/881·3026***

It was pinotage that earned Daniël de Waal his Diners Club Winemaker of the Year status in 2002, and tempranillo in the form of 'unbelievably concentrated Circion from Rioja, Spain, that inspired him and wife Ingrid to attempt an SA equivalent of this 'ultimate' wine. But their real passion is shiraz, so they started searching for the specific site that would result in a 'peppery, spicy, smoky Côte Rôtie style of wine'. Eventually they found a 30 year old vineyard, yielding just 1.5 tons/ha, and the result is Pella, named after the Orange River town where Ingrid was born. Good ratings will be a bonus, they say, but at this stage they're happy simply to be making wine for their own pleasure.

Hoogland Shiraz ★★★☆ Striking **04** with northern Rhône-like peppery whiffs (though gamey nuance too), earthy mineral notes; concentrated & well extracted; tannins evident though integrated. 15 mths Fr oak, 20% new. – *MF*

Perdeberg Winefarmers' Co-operative

Paarl ▪ Est 1941 ▪ Tasting & sales Mon-Fri 8-5 ▪ Closed pub hols ▪ Tours by appt during tasting hours ▪ Owners 49 members ▪ Winemakers Kobus de Kock, Ewald Kellerman & Pieter Carstens (1989/1997/2004) ▪ Viticulturist Stephan Joubert (2001) ▪ 3 000 ha ▪ 20 000 tons 5 000 cs own label 60% red 40% white ▪ BRC accredited ▪ PO Box 214 Paarl 7620 ▪ info@perdeberg.co.za ▪ www.perdeberg.co.za ▪ ***T 869·8244/8112*** *▪ F 869·8245*

Setting out to prove you can please all the people all the time, this progressive co-op winery caters for 'those who enjoy a good glass of wine in the evening to the knowledgeable connoisseur'. MD and winemaker Kobus de Kock describes the wines as somewhere between the New and Old World, and promises great hospitality at Perdeberg's new tasting facilities: 'The people of the Boland are renowned for their warmth.' Other news is that Perdeberg has become a partner in MAN Vintners, while Bottelary Cellar (owned by Perdeberg) is once again open for tastings of its own labels (see separate entries).

Reserve range

★★★★ **Pinotage** We last tasted **01**, a retiscent Reserve, with evident but soft tannins. **04** is next.

Cabernet Sauvignon ★★★☆ Modern yet elegant **03**, pleasantly austere herbaceous tone, pencil shaving hint; still tight, begs yr/2 to show its best. 14 mths Fr/Am oak (ditto all Rsv reds). **Merlot** new ★★★☆ **02** mint & green leaf scents to ripe fruit, abundant dry tannins; still taut & nervy, needs time. **Shiraz** new ★★★☆ Most accessible of the reds; **02** spice, mint, pepper tinges to ripe black fruit, succulent tannins. **Chardonnay** ★★★☆ Shows refinement, breed. **04** vanilla butter tones well meshed with ripe fruit (citrus uppermost this yr); focused dry finish. New oak, Fr. **Chenin Blanc** new ★★★☆ Seriously styled **05** new-oak fermented/aged 5 mths. Wood, brawny 15% alc very well absorbed into ripe but vibrant pear/peach body. **Sauvignon Blanc** new ★★★ A characterful smoothie; **05** lots of flavour, zest; appealing gooseberry/tropical tones. **Viognier** new ★★★☆ These Rsv whites get serious rev of oak – new Fr/Am wood for **05** – but cope admirably. Bold, aromatic (incl signature apricot), fat & rich; brilliant with roast chicken or duck.

Perdeberg range

Cabernet Sauvignon ★★★ *Wine* 2004 value award for this wine. Juicy **03** well-made, honest, balanced. Unoaked, as are all these reds. **Shiraz** ★★★ **03** last yr showed good spread of black/red fruits, slight savoury pepperiness & chunky tannins. **Cinsaut** ★★★ Last tasted was bright & light textured **03**, with succulent cherry tone. **Pinotage** ✓ ★★★☆ A benchmark for the unwooded style. Cherry-fruited **05**'s stern tannins need yr/2 to relax; if impatient, tame with a hearty stew. **Cabernet Sauvignon-Merlot** ★★★ **04** modern fruity styling, satisfying, juicy, easier tannins than last yr. **Chenin Blanc Semi** ★★★ 'Semi' as in semi-sweet, though as always **05** not all that dulcet on analysis or taste (12g/ℓ sugar); otherwise similar to dry version. **Cinsaut Liqueur Wine** ★★ Unusual, attractive & potentially long-lived fortified dessert with lush cherry/strawberry tone; **05** uncharacteristically sweet & spiritous; possibly needs yr/2 to settle. 18% alc. 375ml. **Sauvignon Blanc** discontinued.

Cinsaut-Shiraz ☺ ★★★ **03** lively, quaffable 70/30 blend, lightish feel despite 14% alc; super braai wine. **Chenin Blanc Dry** ☺ ★★★ Honest, pleasant & reliable; **05** lively pear, apple & guava flavours; delivers balanced refreshment. — *JN*

Perold see KWV International

Peter Bayly

new

Calitzdorp (see Little Karoo map) ▪ Est 2002 ▪ 1stB 2004 ▪ Visits by appt ▪ Conservation area ▪ Owners Peter & Yvonne Bayly ▪ Winemaker Peter Bayly ▪ 1.2 ha (tinta b, touriga, souzão) ▪ 700 cs 100% port ▪ PO Box 187 Calitzdorp, 6660 ▪ info@baylys.co.za ▪ ***T (044) 213·3702*** *F (044) 213·3702*

A visit to Axe Hill in 1998 set Peter Bayly's dream of making 'a truly great Portuguese-style port' on the road to realisation. He and wife Yvonne recently left small Cape Town luxury hotel, Ellerman House, to become full-time growers. Peter B sees his manageably small vineyard area as an opportunity to apply meticulous attention to all aspects of production. Open lagars and the feet of friends and family are employed to tread grapes traditionally. Initially faced with stiff local competition — from birds and baboons — electric fences and netting now keep interlopers at bay. Otherwise, these untrained vintners are quick to acknowledge the selfless help and encouragement of Calitzdorp's port producers.

Cape Vintage Port ★★★★ Classically constructed **04** (20% alc, 95g/ℓ RS), from touriga, tinta, souzao, has very ripe, almost decadent nose with raisin, dried fruit notes. Soft & approachable, gentle tannic grip, fresh acidity. Unusual, notably pretty 500ml packaging. — *TJ*

Philip Jordaan Wines

Rawsonville ▪ Est/1stB 1998 ▪ Closed to public ▪ Owner/winemaker Philip Jordaan ▪ Viti consultant Leon Dippenaar ▪ 1 ha ▪ 500 cs 100% red ▪ PO Box 55 Rawsonville 6845 ▪ philipjordaan@intekom.co.za ▪ ***T (023) 349·1601*** *▪ F (023) 349·1581*

Philip Jordaan, by day cellarmaster at Du Toitskloof, makes a small quantity of Cab Franc for his own label.

★★★★ **Cabernet Franc** Establishing a name for silky refinement. **02** pleasant coffee character, notes of prune & mint, well-integrated tannins. **01** (★★★★★) particularly impressive; same coffee character but more elegance, balance. Yr oak; WO W-Cape. Neither retasted this ed. — *NP*

PicardiRebel

Est 1994 ▪ PO Box 18130 Wynberg 7800 ▪ mark.no@picardirebel.co.za ▪ ***T 700·5500*** *▪ F 700·5515*

Now full-time on board this well-established national drinks chain (90+ stores) as head of its wine division is widely experienced Mark Norrish, with a brief to 'build P-R into a wine retailing giant in the near future'. An ongoing facet of operations is sourcing value-wine for the own-label, Naked Truth (Cabernet Sauvignon, Pinotage, Dry Red, Dry White and Soetes); and the 5ℓ boxed range, filled for them by Robertson Winery (Red, Vin de Noir, Blanc de Blanc, Late Harvest and Stein). Also a 'tactical' label, Coast, used 'as exceptional opportunities arise'.

Pick 'n Pay

Enquiries Elsa Gray ▪ Bahrain Drive Extension, Airport Industria 7490 ▪ egray@pnp.co.za ▪ www.picknpay.co.za ▪ ***T 936·8400*** *▪ F 934·6355*

This national chain of supermarkets and hyperstores offers its house-brand No Name wines in 3ℓ and 5ℓ bag-in-boxes (the 500ml budget packs now discontinued). All commendably light (9.5–12.5% alc), made by Robertson Winery.

Dry Red ★★ Easy-quaffing berry-toned red, amenable tannins switch easily from standalone to table. **Rosé** ★★ Pale pink semi-sweet with lively berry fruit. **Dry White** ★☆ Smooth every-day white, not too dry. **Dry White Light** ★★ Juicy & smooth, good flavour for this genre. **Stein** ★☆ Honeyed semi-sweet, soft & gentle. **Late Harvest** ★★ Soft but perky semi-sweet, with tropical fruit salad flavours. — *DH*

Pick's Pick new

Stylish house wines of The Butcher Shop & Grill on Nelson Mandela Square, Sandton, ground-zero for big deal-making. Vinified to specs of wine-savvy owner Alan Pick by Paul Cluver Wines.

★★★★ **Cabernet Sauvignon-Shiraz-Merlot 03** soft, smooth blend (45/40/15); long, luscious fruit with mocha slick from yr small Fr/Am oak. WO W Cape; following wines both Elgin origin.

Cabernet Sauvignon ★★★☆ **04** big plummy flavours with soft tannins & savoury notes. Approachability & smoothness from dollop merlot; older oak aged. **Sauvignon Blanc** ★★★☆ Intended as slightly fuller, riper version of Paul C Sauv Bl, but no lack of racy bite on **05**; Elgin apple & green guava tastes, energising freshness. — *NP*

Pier 42 see Goedverwacht, Origin Wine
Pierre Jourdan see Càbriere
Pinecrest/Pinehurst see Môreson

Plaisir de Merle

Simondium (see Franschhoek map) ▪ Est 1993 ▪ 1stB 1994 ▪ Tasting & sales Mon-Fri 8.30-5 Sat 10-4 (Nov-Mar) 10-2 (Apr-Oct) ▪ Fee R20 (informal), R30 (tasting & tour) ▪ Closed Christian hols ▪ Tours by appt during tasting hours ▪ Small private functions by appt ▪ Overnight stays (B&B) by appt ▪ Tourgroups ▪ Conferencing ▪ Owner Distell ▪ Winemaker Niel Bester (Jan 1993) ▪ Viticulturist Hannes van Rensburg ▪ ±400 ha (cab, merlot, shiraz, chard, sauvignon) ▪ 900-1 000 tons 55 000 cs own label 80% red 20% white ▪ PO Box 121 Simondium 7670 ▪ nbester@distell.co.za plaisirdemerletours@distell.co.za ▪ www.plaisirdemerle.co.za ▪ ***T 874·1071*** *▪ F 874·1689 (sales) ▪ F 874·1488 (cellar)*

Cellarmaster Niel Bester clearly has things well in hand at this showpiece Distell winery. He found time to ride his fastest Argus Cycle Tour, set a new personal best in the Two Oceans Marathon (4:26) and train for the Comrades. Next he'll be dusting the cobwebs off his canoe ... Berg River, here we come! Similar pace and success in the cellar: testing the 'rack and return' technique on fermenting reds; a satisfying R2 800 per 6-bottle case for a special pre-release Nederburg Auction bottling of the 03 Cab Franc; an IWC gold for the 02 Merlot. Ongoing vineyard development incorporates gradual replacement of vines approaching 30 yrs, a process which should abet another Neil B goal: to raise the Grand Plaisir blend into a Plaisir de Merle 'icon'.

★★★★ **Merlot 00** splashed with shiraz. **01** took on 6% cab, 9% petit v. **02** returns to monovarietal; light, elegant, gently wooded. Attractive & restrained with well focused palate; more elegance than power in spite of gutsy 14.5% alc. 11–17 mths Fr oak, 1st-3rd fill. **03** not tasted; sold through Bergkelder Vinoteque.

★★★☆ **Shiraz** Modern **01** (★★★★), designed for obvious pleasure: lush, sweet-fruited, burly but gentle tannins. **02** soft & generously oaked, last yr needed time for wood to integrate, acidity to settle. 60% new & 2nd fill Am/Fr oak, 12–16 mths.

★★★★ **Grand Plaisir** This red launched ahead of Diners Club 'Cape Red' category with **97**, cab, merlot, shiraz, petit v (50/20/20/10); Soupçon malbec joins in **02** for final 50/24/10/10/6 make-up; big wine (14.6%) but classically taut last ed, promised red-fruit cornucopia few yrs hence. 16 mths Fr oak.

★★★★☆ **Cabernet Franc** new Specially bottled for Nederburg Auction; grapes from young (5 yrs) single-vyd; **03** incredible fragrance & delicate perfumed flavours. Elegant, has a real sense of mystery about it. 16 mths oak.

★★★★ **Sauvignon Blanc 05** (★★★) grapes from Paarl (66%) & West Coast; lemon sherbet character with slight medicinal nuance. **04** (sample) returned to aromatic style with fynbos whiffs, lots of soft-textured freshness.

Cabernet Sauvignon ★★★☆ **02** fairly typical of the vintage: elegant, soft, through not especially complex or intense; for early enjoyment. Not retasted for current ed. **Chardonnay** Always a fine, excellently wooded example. Light & delicate **03** last yr exhibited good citrus fruit, clever oak.—*NP*

Podium see Baarsma

Pongrácz

Popular and critically acclaimed brut-style cap classiques, named after late Desiderius Pongrácz (pronounced Pon-*grats*), aristocratic Hungarian army officer who became a much-loved Bergkelder viticulturist. By Distell (enquiries: **T 865·2590**).

Desiderius ★★★☆ Aristocratic packaging, boutique quantities for classic 60/40 chardonnay/pinot blend, bunch-pressed. Third-vintage **98** last ed had lively mousse, caramel & apple/quince nose & deep flavour from 5+ yrs on lees. *Wine* ★★★★. **Pongrácz** ★★★☆ Blend as above. Latest **NV** with delicate oyster shell hue, vibrant bubbles. Shorter time on lees (2 yrs), so not as rich as above, also for early drinking. Bracing acidity, persistent Granny Smith apple finish. *Wine* ★★★★, SAA 2005 Trophy. Both WO W Cape.—*CvZ*

Porcupine Ridge see Boekenhoutskloof
Porter Mill Station see Porterville Cellars

Porterville Cellars

Swartland ▪ Est 1941 ▪ Tasting & sales Mon-Fri 8-5 Sat 9-1 ▪ Closed Easter Fri-Mon, Dec 25/26, Jan 1 ▪ Tours by appt ▪ Picnics/light meals by appt or BYO ▪ Tourgroups ▪ Owners 94 members ▪ Winemakers André Oberholzer & Dico du Toit (Dec 1996/Sep 2004) ▪ Viticulturist Jurie du Plessis (Jun 2003) ▪ 1 380 ha (cab, pinotage, shiraz, chard, chenin, colombard) ▪ ±15 000 tons 12 000 cs own label 18% red 82% white ▪ Ranges for UK customers: Kumala & Porter Mill Station ▪ PO Box 52 Porterville 6810 ▪ info@portwines.co.za ▪ www.portervillecellars.co.za ▪ ***T (022) 931·2170*** *▪ F (022) 931·2171*

Hot, dry summers and hard winters, with snow on the mountains and Atlantic storms rolling in, leave winemaker André Oberholzer undismayed. 'Understand and value your own area,' he feels. 'You get into trouble when you try to copy another region's flavours and character, throwing other things into the wine as if you're cooking a soup.' It's a philosophy vindicated by the reception Porterville wines are getting locally and abroad. Including the swiftly growing Porter Mill Station brand, created in conjunction with Richard Kelley MW, which takes its name from the rail terminus which still ferries the grain away from the area at harvest time.

Unfiltered Reserve range

Cabernet Sauvignon ★★★ **04** soft, fruity & fairly easy red; hints dried leaves, distinct dry tannins. Yr Fr barrels, same for most following reds. **Pinotage** ★★ Medium-bodied **04**, savoury tone with pleasant sweet-sour twist, muted fruit & some astringency. **Shiraz** ★★★ **04** nothing like pvsly tasted version (02); light bodied (12.5) with restrained fruit, muted varietal character. **Visage** ★★★ Interesting blend shiraz (42%), pinotage, cab, grenache noir, merlot; **03** soft wild berry fruit & this range's vibrant tannin structure; low 13% alc. **Chardonnay** ★★★ Wooded **03** plumply forceful, enough stuffing, alc (14.7%), to stand up to full-flavoured food. Not retasted, ditto ... **Chenin Blanc Unfiltered** ★★★ Wood-fermented **03** lanolin & lime marmalade tone, suggestion butterscotch/caramel; full-bodied & balanced. **Chenin Blanc-Chardonnay-Grenache Blanc** ★★ (Pvsly 'Chanaché') **05** appealing peachy tone, good fresh mouthful of sweet fruit, open & accessible. Fr oak chips/barrels 7 mths. W Cape, Coastal, Swtlnd WOs for these.

Porter Mill Station range new

'Friendly & fruity drinking wines' are the goal for this eye-catching line-up. **Cabernet Sauvignon** ★★☆ **04** hints wet earth & wild berries; softer, more accessible character than range-mates. Yr Fr barrels, same for most following reds. **Pinotage** ★★ **04** similar sweet-sour zing, understated savoury/strawberry tone & dense tannin. **Shiraz** ★★☆ **04** smoky wild berries & bluegum whiff; leanish body with restrained fruit, pressy dry tannins. **Chardonnay** ★☆ Pleasant dry white, crisp & light (12.5%). **Chenin Blanc**★☆ **05** lightly fruity dry white with hint of winter melon. **Chenin Blanc-Chardonnay-Grenache Blanc** ★★ **05** appealing summer-evening drink; light (13% alc), undemanding, crisply dry. Lightly wooded. **Sauvignon Blanc** ★★ **05** grilled seafood partner; taut, wiry frame, firm acid backbone; asparagus & cuts grass whiffs. W Cape & Swtlnd WOs for these.

Disa range

Pinotage ★☆ Medium-bodied **03** last ed showed muted plum tones, some dusty tannins. **Cape Red** ★★ Friendly everyday red; **03** mainly pinotage with cab, ruby cab, shiraz; jammy fruit, spicy tannins. 12.5% alc. **Rosé** ★☆ Chug-a-lug style **05** from pinotage, fresh, succulent, strawberry-toned off-dry mouthful (in which big 14% alc well-hidden). **Chardonnay** ★★☆ **04** unwooded, lightish yet mouth-filling, generous. **Black Eagle Organic Chenin Blanc** ★ **05** uncomplicated, light dry quaffing white. **Sauvignon Blanc** ★ **05** austere dieter's friend (12% alc); faint asparagus character, bracing flinty acidity. **Chenin Blanc-Colombard** ★☆ ('Xation' pvs ed) **05** light off-dry white with hint sweetness lifting the palate. **Late Vintage** ★ new to the guide. Lightish semi-sweet **NV** white, shy raisin hints. Enjoy soonest after purchase. Neither of following full-sweet NV fortified desserts retasted: **Snakebite 02** (unrated) unusual fortified, leaning more towards sherry than port; quite spirity, sweet. **Red Jerepiko** ★★★☆ Pinotage, cab, cinsaut, fortified to 17%. Potpourri fragrance; silky, light-tripping palate with spiced herbs; firmer & drier tasting than … **Golden Jerepiko** ★★★ From hanepoot; Turkish Delight whiffs; smooth & honeyed with creamy finish. Above mostly WO Coastal. —*CT/TM*

Post House Cellar

Stellenbosch (see Helderberg map) ▪ Est/1stB 1997 ▪ Tasting & sales Mon-Fri 8.30–5 Sat by appt 8.30–1 ▪ Closed Easter Fri/Sun/Mon, Dec 25/26 & Jan 1 ▪ Owner/winemaker Nicholas Gebers ▪ Viti consultant Paul Wallace (1999) ▪ 37 ha (cab, merlot, petit v, pinotage, shiraz, chenin) ▪ ±200 tons 2 000 cs own label ▪ PO Box 5635 Helderberg 7135 ▪ ngebers@iafrica.com ▪ www.posthousewines.co.za ▪ ***T/F 842·2409***

Helderberg vintner Nick Gebers follows a minimal-intervention approach, ferments with native yeasts, uses as little sulphur as possible and refrains from filtering his wines before bottling. The winery's name and its eye-catching philatelic labels are linked to the small post office which served the tiny missionary community town of Raithby, now the winery office and residence.

★★★★ **Penny Black** new Sleek & supple red blend led by merlot, shiraz (equal 32%), cab & petit v (28/8). **03** lush with merlot's black fruits, hints iron & meat. Cab's tannin provides firm backbone, shiraz/merlot roundness & opulence. Persistent scrub/floral finale, moderate alc. Structure to age gracefully. 18 mths Fr oak, 35% new.

★★★★ **Chenin Blanc** Opens in glass to reveal thrilling Old World structure, complexity; **04** (★★★★☆) apple compôte, marzipan, apricot & more in fascinating bouquet, palate gripped by intense lime acidity & chenin's steely bite. Should develop with distinction. More modern **03** had opulent lemon flavours, creamy/leesy texture (from barrel-fermentation) & obvious biscuity oak. 9 mths Fr/Am oak, 14% new. Medium ± 13.5% alc.

Following trio not revisited: **Cabernet Sauvignon** ★★★☆ Middle-weight, dark-fruited **02** probably for drinking soon; lighter-textured than 14.3% alc suggests. Balanced oak (35% new, 20 mths). *Wine* ★★★★. **Merlot** ★★★ Workmanlike **01** seductive gamey nose; fairly austere texture (though backed by fleshy black fruit). 18 mths oak, 35% new. **Shiraz 03** with red fruit lushness, white pepper/lily fragrance. Oak (16% new) still rampant when previewed mid-2004; should have mellowed by now. Potential ★★★★. —*CvZ*

Post Stones see False Bay Vineyards

Premium Cape Wines

*Stellenbosch ▪ Est 2003 ▪ Closed to public ▪ Owner Premium Trust ▪ PO Box 12149 Die Boord 7613 ▪ ansgar@gravitywine.com ▪ **T/F 886·8515***

This young negociant company supplies wines to supermarkets and direct sales companies in Germany, selecting the wines from various Cape cellars. Ansgar Flaatten, who runs the local business, says a new Open Sky range is in the pipeline, as are sales into the SA market. Note: no new releases of the wines below; notes from previous edition.

Imvelo range

Cabernet Sauvignon ★★★ Undemanding but characterful **03**, not too full bodied, well pitched for earlier/easier drinking. **Sauvignon Blanc** ★★★ Zesty, crisp & dry **04**, food-cordial with leafy/nettly aromas & flavours.

De Sonnenberg range

Dry Rosé ★★★ Deeply coloured **03**, some appealing mature notes on palate, needing to be enjoyed fairly soon. **Natural Sweet Blanc** ★★★ **03** lovely sweet confectionary nose, light body, drier palate than expected, very soft. **Natural Sweet Rosé** ★★ Fruitgum aromas in ebullient **03**; semi- rather than full-sweet, slightly lacking in acidic grip. **Natural Sweet Red** ★★★ **02** warmly ripe basket of red fruit, more structured than others, even has touch tannin. Certainly doesn't need disguising, but a great base for Glühwein.

Uhambo range

Dry Red ★★★ Cinsaut/ruby cab blend, **02** uncomplicatedly juicy, though after the sweet-ripe fruit, the finish is unexpectedly dry. **Dry White** ★★★ Chenin-colombard mix, **03** youthful & fresh, zinging if somewhat curt appley finish. **Semi-Sweet White** ★★★ Same varieties as for Dry, more characterful on nose, appetising fruit salad tone, soft & easy to drink. **Natural Sweet White** ★★★ Repeat of above varieties, with more grip & flavour; a good quaffing style for the sweet of tooth. **Semi-Sweet Red** ★★ Same grapes as dry version, **02** fairly slender, much less sweet than name implies.—*CR*

Prospect 1870

*Robertson ▪ Est 1990 ▪ 1stB 1998 ▪ Closed to public (tasting & sales at The Wine Boutique, Main Rd, Ashton) ▪ Owners Louis, Chris & Nic de Wet ▪ Winemakers Johan van Wyk & Philip Louw ▪ Viti consultant Francois Viljoen ▪ 45 ha (cab, merlot, pinotage, shiraz, chard, sauvignon, viognier) ▪ 700 cs own label 80% red 20% white ▪ PO Box 141 Ashton 6715 ▪ nic@lando.co.za ▪ www.prospectwines.com ▪ **T 082·878·2884** ▪ F (023) 615·1913*

No update available on this winery; contact details and wine notes from previous edition.

Cabernet Sauvignon ★★★ **98** mature aromas with tobacco leaf & sandalwood; fruit starting to dry out. **Chardonnay** ★★★ **03** creamily assertive wood, finishes more than a shade oaky. 6 mths new Fr barrels. Early picked for moderate 12% alc.

Leatherwood range

Cabernet Sauvignon ★★★ **02** gentle ripe-fruit flavours, quite rich but firmed by mouth-coating tannin. **Shiraz-Viognier** ★★★ **02** spicy red fruit flavours, heavily accented by wood (6–12 mths Fr, 2nd fill). Incl 5% viognier. All WO W-Cape.—*JB*

Provin see Douglas Winery

Pulpit Rock Winery

*Swartland ▪ 1stB 2003 ▪ Tasting & sales Mon-Fri 8-5 Sat 9-1 ▪ Closed Easter Fri-Mon, Dec 25 & Jan 1 ▪ BYO picnic ▪ Tours by appt ▪ Tourgroups ▪ Walks ▪ Conservation area ▪ Owner Brinkshof Wines (Pty) Ltd ▪ Winemaker Piet Kleinhans (Dec 2003) ▪ Viti consultant Johan Viljoen (Jun 2004) ▪ 400 ha (cab, merlot, petit v, pinotage, roobernet, shiraz, chard, chenin, sauvignon) ▪ 570 tons 8 500 cs own label +300 000ℓ bulk 80% red 20% white ▪ PO Box 1 Riebeek West 7306 ▪ info@pulpitrock.co.za ▪ **T/F (022) 461·2025***

There may be 'no new toys' at this well-equipped cellar (operational since the 2003 crush) but, says winemaker Piet Kleinhans, 'we do have a new team member': Elzaan du Plessis, in sales and marketing. Launched last year was the Pulpit Rock flagship range, which takes its name from the distinctive geological formation behind the winery – fittingly, the first customer through their new tasting room doors was a dominee (minister). Having manoeuvred through a potentially difficult harvest, Piet K reports that fruit was fermented in any and every receptacle, even a trailer more accustomed to delivering grapes to the cellar. Varieties which really showed their colours were merlot and pinotage.

Cabernet Sauvignon ★★★ **04** attractive tannins, relatively low (for this producer!) 15% alc & luscious mulberry fruit make this a balanced, pleasing drink. Hint of oxidation a worry though, drink up. **Merlot** Towering 16% alc, dense cola/cassis aromas & flavours stymied our taster, who compared this to Crème de Cassis. Ripe tannins, integrated oak (same as above). How to rate? ★★★? Highly idiosyncratic as is... **Pinotage 04** porty, prune-like aromas & flavours, unctuous almost cloying mouthfeel, sweet impression to finish from 15.5 % alc. Respectable ripe tannins give focus, stop sprawl. Also ★★★? **Shiraz** A wine of extremes from leathery, date loaf & smoked beef nose to rich, Bovril, treacly palate to hot, 16% goodbye. 4 mths Fr oak, as are all above. Could rate ★★★. **Chardonnay** ★★★★ **04** chunky, sunkissed peach, pear & ginger compote; lacks grace at 14.8%, slightly higher acid would enliven/give better balance. Fr-oak-fermented/8 mths, partial malo.

Cape Haven range

Cabernet Sauvignon ★★ **04** balanced, for easy drinking. Baked plum pudding & cedar whiffs; full bodied 14.3% alc, dry finish. Slight bitter tail, as has ... **Merlot** ★★ **04** ripe plumy, almost porty nose, fat prune-like palate, impression of sweetness from 15% alc. **Pinotage** ★★★ **04** sweet/sour mulberry pinotage fruit on goodbye, subdued bouquet. Acidity standoutish but 14% alc integrated. **Shiraz** ★★★ **04** boasts pure berry notes unsullied by oak, palate similar; soft, juicy with touch tannic grip on finish. Undemanding 14% alc, well crafted. All these reds staved. **Chardonnay 05** flavoursome & concentrated sample. Lemon/lime marmalade, hint of oak. Good length, rounded. Possible ★★★★. **Chenin Blanc 05** sample too unknit to rate; 13.8% alc is active, gives impression of sweetness, overwhelms fruit at this stage. *—IvH*

Quagga Ridge see Horse Mountain

Quando

Robertson ▪ Est/1stB 2001 ▪ Visits by appt ▪ Owner Irene Bruwer Family Trust ▪ Winemaker Fanus Bruwer ▪ Viticulturist Martin Bruwer ▪ 80 ha ▪ 15 tons 1 100 cs own label 100% white ▪ EurepGAP certified ▪ PO Box 82 Bonnievale 6730 ▪ quandowines@mweb.co.za ▪ ***T/F (023) 616·2752***

'We are officially no longer *garagistes*,' announce Fanus & Martin Bruwer, following the completion of cellar extensions that brought about an increase in capacity. Despite their 5th year of production being one of the most difficult in years – rain during the harvest and disease in the vineyard – Fanus B is still buoyant: 'The vintage turned out surprisingly well.' In fact, the whole enterprise is riding a wave: exports are booming – Belgium and Sweden added to the list – and the Sauvignon sold out two months before release.

★★★★ **Sauvignon Blanc** ✓ **05** (★★★★) continues progress as vyds mature. Ultra-pale, but a whack of passionfruit-dominated flavour with asparagus undertones. Refreshingly, lightly elegant (dead-right 12.5% alc) rather than abrasively pungent. Like **04** & pvs, can mature beneficially few yrs. *—TJ*

Quantum see Lost Horizons
Quiriga see Rietrivier
Queen of Sheba see Eshkol

Quoin Rock Winery

Stellenbosch ▪ Est 2000 ▪ 1stB 2001 ▪ Visits by appt ▪ Owner Metlika Holdings ▪ Winemaker Carl van der Merwe (Jan 2002) ▪ Viticulturist Jaco van der Westhuizen (2000) ▪ 60 ha (cab, merlot, pinot, shiraz, chard, sauvignon) ▪ 180 tons 5 000 cs own label 70% red 30% white ▪ PO Box 1193 Stellenbosch 7599 ▪ wine@quoinrock.co.za ▪ www.quoinrock.com ▪ ***T 888·4740*** *▪ F 888·4744*

Juggling with different sites, Carl van der Merwe (now husband of Kathleen) did radical green-harvesting in Stellenbosch to remedy uneven flowering in hot, dry summer 2004/05, and in Agulhas had trouble deciding when to harvest because of wet, humid conditions. The results were reds with plenty of tannins and extract from the Boland but with less tannin and fruit from the Overberg, where 'elegant whites' resulted. Ever questing and testing, here and in France, CvdM has as his goal a site-specific culture and producing wines unique to the vintage. That means no more than 'spot treating' with chemical products, cutting down on tartaric acid and unnecessary filtration, experimenting with higher-density planting and natural fermentation, encouraging biodiversity in the vineyards and moving away from high sugars at harvest.

★★★★☆ **Merlot** Regal ruby robes of **03** matched by majestic structure: power with elegance, great fruit richness clad in fine, effective tannins; freshness alleviates heavier aspects of 14.5% alc. Shd see 2009 in great shape. Smart Fr oaking (50% new). Simonsberg/Agulhas vyds (so WO W Cape). **02** (★★★★) compact, dense, savoury; should flesh out over 4–5 yrs.

★★★★☆ **Syrah 03** vindicated our enthusiasm in last ed, taking gold/trophy on 2005 FCTWS. Resounding spice/smoked meat concentration; carefully oaked to enhance lovely textured mouthfeel. Well-defined tannin, seriously dry, savoury finish (and suitably flavoursome dish) all help downplay rumbustious 15% alc. 18 mths Fr oak, 25% new. This, Oculus below, WO Stbosch.

★★★★ **Oculus** Flagship dry white, aiming more to reflect character of Simonsberg site than (undisclosed) constituent varieties. **03** developing beautifully; intriguing suggestion of curds, roast nuts, in vinous rather than fruity mode. Broad, long with compelling presence that just begs for food. **02** full, grippy. Fermented/yr Fr oak, 20% new.

★★★★ **Chardonnay** As with following wine, cool Cape Agulhas site reflected in fruit purity, delicacy. **03** balanced lime/tangerine nose, brush of oak vanilla; rich, viscous texture; fine acid spine lends freshness, lightness to this big wine. Fermented/aged yr Fr oak, 80% new. Better potential (till 2008) than **02**, with already developed tropical tones.

★★★★ **Sauvignon Blanc** ✓ Pure gooseberry minerality on previewed **05** clear indicator of cool-climate origin. Lightish, lively but with appealing breadth of flavour, elegant dry finish. No **04**. **03** elegantly structured; food style par excellence.

Glenhurst range

Cape Blend ★★★☆ First release **01** shiraz, merlot, pinotage assemblage (41/31/28). Pleasantly mellowing winey character, chewy savouriness plus some noticeable tannin. Best enjoyed with hearty meat dishes. Fr/Am oak, 50% new. WO W Cape. **Sauvignon Blanc-Viognier** NEW Unusual though compatible 78/22 partnership; **05** (provisional ★★★☆) novel (figs/apricots) fruit salad nose; flavoursome, full bodied but balanced. Extra dimension from Fr oak fermentation/maturation 4 mths. WO Simonsberg. **Vine Dried Natural Sweet 04** unrated preview in last ed, not yet bottled. From sauvignon. Orange-blossom, honey scents; unctuous but uncloying 140g/ℓ sugar; 13.5% alc. —*AL*

R62 see Joubert-Tradauw

Raats Family Wines

Stellenbosch ▪ Est/1stB 2000 ▪ Visits by appt ▪ Owners Bruwer & Jasper Raats Jnr ▪ Winemaker Bruwer Raats ▪ Viticulturist Jasper Raats Snr (2003) ▪ 20 ha (cab f, chenin) ▪ 3 500 cs 15% red 85% white ▪ PO Box 2068 Stellenbosch 7601 ▪ braats@mweb.co.za ▪ www.raats.co.za ▪ ***T 881·3078*** *▪ F 885·1290*

Major kudos for Raats *père et fils* from US wine critic Richard Nalley, who included Raats Family Wines in his 20 Best New Wineries in the world listing on the sustained excellent showing of their Chenin. Further vindication of Bruwer R's belief in the potential for producing world-class chenin in the Cape. Cab franc is his other favoured variety, and B-R says the 2005 harvest was exceptional, showing 'ripe, juicy tannins from very small berries'. The tasting room on their Polkadraai area farm is now open and they welcome visitors by appointment.

★★★★ **Cabernet Franc** Intense garnet robe signals extraordinary quality of **03** (★★★★☆), choc nuance to dense berry fruit; pepper, clove & cinnamon whiffs; classy, elegant mouthful, round tannins, good length. Unfined/filtered, 19 mths Fr oak, 50% new. **02** (★★★☆) lifted bouquet, much lighter (13% alc), probably best drunk up. **01** superbly integrated standout wine which substitutes elegance for power.

★★★★ **Chenin Blanc 04** wood dominates genteel appley fruit mid-2005, needs time to settle. 6 mths Fr oak, 10% new; **03** oak more balanced; concentrated viscous palate, bone-dry finish, excellent restaurant wine.

★★★★ **Original Chenin Blanc** The unwooded version. **05** fresh pear-drops, well balanced, good length & finish, very promising. **04** same pear-drop tone, pleasant oily mouthfeel, good balance & length; all from mix of vertical hedge & bushvines 17 yrs & older. WO Coastal.—*NP*

Radford Dale see The Winery

Rainbow's End Estate

Stellenbosch ▪ Est 1978 ▪ 1stB 2002 ▪ Visits by appt ▪ Fee R15 refundable on purchase of 4+ btls ▪ Owners Jacques, Anton & Francois Malan ▪ Winemaker Anton Malan, with Francois Malan ▪ Francois Malan, with Anton Malan & Johan Pienaar ▪ 23 ha (cabs s/f, malbec, merlot, petit v, shiraz) ▪ 80 tons total 10 tons/850 cs own label 100% red ▪ PO Box 2253 Dennesig 7601 ▪ hbmeng@iafrica.com ▪ ***T 083·411·0170/082·413·7285/082·404·1085/885·1719*** *▪* ***F*** *885·1722*

Younger son Francois's always been the third member of this Malan team – only change is that he now has the letters BSc Agric (Viticulture & Oenology) behind his name. He shares a goal with father Jacques and brother Anton: 'To make a limited amount of red estate wines of unique style, drinkable within a year but with ageing potential of up to eight years'. And style should change only with the season's vagaries, declares paterfamilias Jacques, not with market trends. The trio's Shiraz has already won recognition; up for consideration next is their first blend, the Complexité, and, to follow, a single-vineyard Shiraz 05.

Shiraz ★★★☆ Elegant expression of extrovert modernity. **04**'s aromas are savoury – steak tartare, tar, smoke, fynbos – but its palate has attractive fruit flavours supported by firm & savoury acid/tannin structure. Combo Am/Fr oak. 14.5% well masked. Rustic, needs ± 3 yrs to show true colours. **Complexité** new ★★★☆ From lower yielding vineyards than stablemate. Aptly named bdx-style blend of cab/merlot cab f (39/31/30). Refined; ripe yet reined-in berry flavours, plenty of cab's firmer tannins; harmonious. Keep for at least a yr; potential for ± 5 yrs. Oaking as above.—*IvH*

Raka

Walker Bay ▪ Est/1stB 2002 ▪ Tasting & sales Mon-Fri 9-5 Sat 10-3 during peak season otherwise by appt ▪ Fee R10 for 4 wines ▪ Closed Dec 25 ▪ Tours by appt ▪ BYO picnic ▪ Walks ▪ Nature conservancy ▪ Owner Piet Dreyer ▪ Winemaker Tanya Rousseau (Oct 2004) ▪ Viti consultant Dawie le Roux ▪ 62 ha (five Bdx reds, pinotage, sangiovese, shiraz, sauvignon, semillon) ▪ 15 000 cs 75% red 17% white 8% rosé ▪ PO Box 124 Caledon 7230 ▪ rakawine@telkomsa.net ▪ www.rakawine.co.za ▪ ***T/F (028) 341·0676***

Piet Dreyer, a larger-than-life salty seadog with a parrot called kulula.com, is often likened to a pirate due to his previous incarnation as a fisherman. He bought the farm, which he named for his beloved fishing boat, from a naturalised Italian POW who, with his dying breath, swore him to the planting of grapes, and who now has a few rows of sangiovese planted in his memory. Theresa Fourie has spread her wings abroad, leaving the winemaking to Tanya Rousseau, herself the wiser for a couple of Italian vintages. Mrs Dreyer, who lists among her responsibilities 'taking the blame for everything that goes wrong', just wants 'to keep making good wine at affordable prices'.

★★★★ **Figurehead Cape Blend** new 14% pinotage joins Bdx quintet to add Cape flavour without distracting from finely tuned ensemble. **04** sample offers evolving layers of intrigue: gamey tints give way to bramble fruits, hint of pulpy red berries reined in by structured tension. Will reward cellaring 6 or so yrs from harvest. Yr 90% Fr oak, rest Am, mix new/used.

★★★★ **Quinary** Less overt cousin of above carrying cellar's elegant watermark. **03** lovely sappy fruit on mineral backdrop, lingering finish promises development over 3-5 yrs. MIWA Grand D'Or, SAA, VG. **02** supple, well-sprung. Cab s/f, merlot with dashes malbec, petit v. House grapes, plus Dbnville.

★★★★ **Best Barrique Merlot** new August selection of best Fr casks. **04** inky black, meaty flavours lurking behind brooding tannic curtain, interleaved structure suggests – demands – time: check from 2010. Kleinrivier home vyds.

★★★★ **Biography (Shiraz)** Real interest in market's sea of new-wave shiraz. Sample **04**: smoky spice ushers in purple mulberry fruits, good grip keeps tie-lines taught. **03** seamless integration of berry fruit in spiced frame, touch sweet on finish. **02** garnered VDG, SAA, SAYWS gold acclaim. Now yr mix new/seasoned Fr/Am (70/30) oak.

★★★★ **Sauvignon Blanc** ✓ Striking, individual option from cool Stanford: quintessential sauvignon but with focus, character. Fermentation aromas of **05** sample shroud svelte fruit mid-2005, racy tang revs up on palate. **04** herby, super body of melon & gunflint, intriguing stony finish. ±13% alc.

Pinotage ★★★ Unequivocal **04** brims with vanilla, purple plum fruit & spun candyfloss characters. Nice grip. Discontinued: **Shiraz**. New releases of wines below not ready for tasting, notes from pvs ed. **Spliced** ★★★ **03** clever blend cab, merlot, ruby cab & shiraz, rafts of accessible fruit licked into semblance of sophistication by yr oak. **Red** ★★★ **02** baked, earthy, rustic. **Cabernet Sauvignon-Merlot** ★★★ W Bay merlot joins own cab in juicy **02** marriage. **Rosé** ★★★ One of the nicest around, & dry to boot. **04** sangiovese adds body to cherry fruits. **Semillon-Sauvignon Blanc** ★★★☆ **04** unoaked 60:40 blend, muted savoury tones but full feel. Gentle 12% alc. May join Shannonea sibling in white blend in future. **Shannonea Sauvignon Blanc** ★★★ Semillon infusion & 2 mths new Fr oak bring spiky tickle to tropical character of **03**. – *DS*

R & de R-Fredericksburg see Rupert & Rothschild
R & R see Rupert & Rothschild

Ravenswood

Budget wines made by Robertson Winery for Vinimark. In 5ℓ packs; comfortably light-bodied (9.5-11% alc); all **NV**.

Dry Red ★★ Easy-quaffing *vin ordinaire*; latest version berry-toned with amenable tannins. **Rosé** ★★ Pale semi-sweet with lively berry fruit. **Grand Cru** ★★ Fruitily dry white with zesty finish. **Light** ★★ Dry white showing clean perky fruit. **Johannisberger** ★★ Quiet but pleasant fruity off-dry white. **Selected Stein** ★☆ Honeyed semi-sweet, gentle in every way. **Late Harvest** ★★ Soft but lively semi-sweet, with tropical flavour. – *DH*

Rawson's see Cape Vineyards
Ready Steady see Southern Sky
Red Wolf see Wolvendrift

Remhoogte Estate

Stellenbosch ▪ Est 1994 ▪ 1stB 1995 ▪ Tasting & sales Mon-Fri 9–4 Sep-Apr, otherwise by appt ▪ Tours anytime by appt ▪ Olives & olive oil for sale ▪ Conservation area ▪ Exhibition of SA hunting trophies ▪ Owners Murray Boustred Trust ▪ Cellarmaster Murray Boustred, advised by

Michel Rolland & Auguste Natter ▪ Viticulturist Jacques du Toit, advised by Johan Pienaar (Aug 2005/1994) ▪ 30 ha (cab, merlot, pinotage, shiraz, chenin) ▪ ±180 tons 6 500 cs own label 100% red ▪ PO Box 2032 Dennesig 7601 ▪ remhoogte@adept.co.za ▪ ***T 889·5005*** *▪ F 889·6907*

Remhoogte came through the 2005 harvest with the smallest crop ever, but Murray Boustred seems unperturbed. He's invested in some vibrating tables for berry-sorting, appointed full-time sales/marketing person Cathy Saunders, and extended the opening hours of the tasting room. Here visitors can view a collection of hunting trophies – a Murray B passion which he shares with winemaking partner and internationally renowned oeno-consultant Michel Rolland. Amid the challenges of the swift and dry harvest, the pair made time to toast Remhoogte's 10th vintage – winemaker Auguste Natter, who flies in from Sancerre for the crush, also raising a glass.

★★★★ **Bonne Nouvelle** Second release of Michel Rolland joint-venture wine, **03** more rigorously structured (cab – 46% – having edged out merlot from driving seat, demoted pinotage to 19%), yielding classically-styled though still sumptuously-fruited red; tannins evident though ripe, notwithstanding lower alc (14.5%) than super-ripe (15%) **02**, which was more showy (cf Concours Mondial gold, 90 points *WS*).

★★★★ **Estate Wine** Bordeaux-style red, robustly structured for prolonged ageing. **03** merlot-dominated (59%) though still with (decreasing, to 10%) pinotage component. Nutmeg & blackcurrant notes, ripe red berry fruits, persistent tannins; still evolving; follows similarly styled **02**, with more cab & less merlot, which evinced plum/cassia aromas & a fine texture. 15 mths Fr oak, all Smnsberg-Stbosch fruit.

★★★★ **Cabernet Sauvignon** No new release since classic & restrained **01**; with 12% merlot. 18 mths oak, third new, same as for ...

★★★½ **Merlot 01** (★★★★) still available, not retasted. Savoury plum/mulberry notes, dense dry finish, herbal whiffs. Incl 15% cab. **00** gold at IWC 2003.

Aigle Noir ★★★ Merlot-cab blend, 3% pinotage. **03** last ed showed almond/raspberry notes, tannic dry finish. **04** unready. – *MF*

Renosterbos see Hofstraat

Reyneke Wines

Stellenbosch ▪ Est 1863 ▪ 1stB 1998 ▪ Tasting & sales by appt ▪ Uitzicht B&B ▪ Owners Reyneke family ▪ Winemaker Tertius Naudé, with Johan Reyneke (2004 harvest) ▪ Viticulturist Johan Reyneke (1992) ▪ 20 ha (cab, merlot, pinotage, shiraz, sauvignon) ▪ 1 500 cs own label 70% red 30% white ▪ PO Box 61 Vlottenburg 7604 ▪ wine@reynekewines.co.za ▪ www.reynekewines.co.za ▪ ***T 881·3517/083·659·1826*** *▪ F 881·3451*

Owner and surfing buff Johan Reyneke has been spending more time in the cellar lately, with German winemaker Georg Meissner's SA sojourn having proved a brief one. But that's not why Johan R describes the 2005 vintage as unusual and difficult. Rather, this was due to drought as well as the toll the total conversion to biodynamic vinegrowing in 2004 had taken. 'But the wines came through with a lovely concentration of flavours, and we are proud and impressed with our vineyards.' On a personal note, a highlight was being invited to participate in the 'Return to Terroir' workshops and tasting in San Francisco, conducted by celebrated French biodynamic winemaker Nicolas Joly.

★★★★ **Reyneke Reserve** Rhône ranger Reyneke embraces 100% shiraz for the **04** flagship wine, with barnyard nose, spicy red fruit & slippery tannins. 15 mths mix Fr oak. **03**, with splash merlot, same wooding; shows explosive Guy Fawkes nose, big tannins well handled. Natural, non-interventionist approach: vyd in conversion to organic with biodynamic elements; native yeasts, no additives, unfined (as for Pinotage below).

★★★½ **Pinotage** From a small biodynamically farmed vyd; **04** sample shows granddad smells of leather, tobacco & smoke; typical pinotage grip. 15 mths older Fr oak toned down from electric, characterful **03** (★★★★½), with ripe loganberry fruit & excellent length. 18 mths oaked, 30% new.

Cornerstone ★★★★ Generously oaked (6 mths new Fr) & full-fruited blend cab, shiraz, merlot 40/40/20; merlot's plumminess makes for charm & approachability on **04** after **03**'s rather austere woodiness. **Sauvignon Blanc** ★★★★ **05** sample shows exotic perfumed melon nose & *bouquet garni* flavours; mild 13% alc. **Blanc Fume** NEW Fermented in 2nd fill barrels; plan is to wood mature for yr; **05** idiosyncratic character with greengage dominant; provisional ★★★. *—NP*

Rhebokskloof Private Cellar

Paarl ▪ 1stB 1989 ▪ Tasting & sales daily 9–5 ▪ Fee R25 (informal, incl bite-size foods); R45 (formal, booking essential); R75 (sunset tasting, booking required) ▪ Tours by appt ▪ Restaurant (see Eat-out section) ▪ Play area for children ▪ Tourgroups ▪ Gifts ▪ Conferences ▪ Conservation area ▪ Owner Rhebokskloof Farming & Trading ▪ Winemaker Daniël Langenhoven (May 1998) ▪ Viticulturist Magnus Joubert (Oct 2004) ▪ ±84 ha (cab, merlot, chard) ▪ 420 tons 28 000 cs 60% red 40% white ▪ PO Box 7141 Noorder-Paarl 7623 ▪ info@rhebokskloof.co.za ▪ www.rhebokskloof.co.za ▪ ***T 869·8386*** *▪ F 869·8504*

At Rhebokskloof they realise there's more to wine than sniffing and swirling. 'So we have introduced a few new things for visitors to do on our beautiful farm,' reveals director Tracey Thornycroft. These include walking trails, sunset tastings on top of Paarl mountain, horse riding trails and gourmet tastings with the winemaker and executive chef. There is also a new MCC in the line-up, and the Weisser Riesling Special Late Harvest stages a comeback after eight vintages. 'I think that our range is now complete, so my main aim is to build on this sound base and never compromise on quality,' says winemaker Daniël Langenhoven.

★★★★ **Cabernet Sauvignon** The flagship, grown in two vyds ±17 yrs old; only Fr oak, 20% new, 14 mths. Still-listed **00** last ed was approachable but showed potential for further cellaring. Luxuriously upholstered, deliciously round, full & mellow, enough tannin to continue improving 3–4 yrs or more.

★★★★ **Chardonnay Grande Reserve** More obvious wood than version below, thanks to barrel-fermentation/ageing in 100% new Fr oak, ±11 mths. **04**, like **03** at similar stage, still suffused with vanilla/butterscotch & spice, rounded fruit lurking, suggesting a much better wine a few yrs hence. Usual big alc (14%) would also benefit from bottle-maturation.

★★★★ **Chardonnay Barrel Selection** (Pvsly 'Sur Lie') Recently showing more elegance & restraint than New World flamboyance. **04** (★★★) positively demure by pvs stds: light citrus tone, oak a mild mid-palate enrichment, quiet leesy finish; **03**, though monsterish 15% alc, showed similar scaled-back barrel character, more lemon-lime tang. ±8 mths oak, only 30% new barrels, no malo.

Merlot ★★ **02** less beguilingly ripe than predecessors; sweet-sour tang to mulberry fruit, medium 13.5% alc. 70% oaked, 16 mths Fr, 2nd/3rd fill. **Pinotage** ★★★ **03** same plum/banana character as before, somewhat fuller, spicy oak (14 mths 2nd/3rd fill) a much more obvious presence; could do with yr/2 to settle. **Shiraz** ★★★ **03**, sampled for pvs ed, seemed fruitier then, more exciting; now leathery with fleeting mulberry whiff, savoury dry finish. 14 mths oak, 25% new, 10% Am. **Weisser Riesling** ★★ **05** same earthy/spicy profile as pvs, bone-dry ultra-crisp finish. **Tamay Sparkling** ★★ Fragrant not-quite-brut style fizz from chardonnay & riesling, splash hanepoot. Latest (NV) somewhat lower keyed, still lively, sippable, fairly racy finish. **Weisser Riesling Special Late Harvest** ★★★ Returns to guide with **05** from well-aged block (1988), still delivering enough racy acidity to carry the lemon/lime richness of the wine; attractive terpene/mineral quality, lovely up-tempo spicy finish. 375ml. **Cap Classique** Not ready for tasting. **Cabernet Sauvignon-Merlot** discontinued.

Rhebok range

Cabernet Sauvignon-Merlot ★★★ **03** not retasted; last noted as having a fresh-berry bouquet; choc-toned palate, savoury note in long finish. 9 mths Fr oak, 10% new. Also 250ml. **Dry Red** ★★★ Tangy, savoury-dry blend pinotage, gamay, cab; **02** last ed had softened, drank easily. **Chardonnay** ★★★ **05** not tasted. **04** light white-peach fragrance; clean apple-zest flavour, light 12.5% alc. **Chenin Blanc** ★ Back by popular demand; **05** refreshing if unremarkable dry white. **Sauvignon Blanc** ★★ **05** lightweight & tropical-toned, soft & undemanding. **Chardonnay-Sauvignon Blanc** ★★★ Varieties make a complementary combo in early-harvested **04**, chard adds juice, sauvignon verve. Also 250ml. Not retasted, ditto ... **Bouquet Blanc** ★★★ **04** lightly fragrant, crisply fruity everyday quaff from chenin. **Dry White** ★★★ **05** sample arrived after deadline. **04** was crisp, fresh & fruity, to be enjoyed young. Chardonnay/riesling blend (80/20). — *DH*

Rickety Bridge Winery

*Franschhoek ▪ Tasting & sales Mon-Sat 8-5 Pub hols 9-5 ▪ Closed Easter Fri, Dec 25/26 & Jan 1 ▪ Fee R10 refundable on purchase ▪ Cellar tours by appt ▪ BYO picnic ▪ Gifts ▪ Owner DS Sarnia (Pty) Ltd ▪ Winemaker Wilhelm van Rooyen, with Dawid Gqirana (Jan 2001/Jun 1998) ▪ Viticulturist Wilhelm van Rooyen ▪ 16 ha (cab, merlot, shiraz, chard, chenin, semillon) ▪ 120 tons 5 000 cs own label 65% red 35% white ▪ PO Box 455 Franschhoek 7690 ▪ sales@ricketybridgewinery.com ▪ www.ricketybridgewinery.com ▪ **T 876·2129/3669** ▪ F 876·3486*

The first vintage from new blocks of merlot and cab show great promise, and winemaker Wilhelm van Rooyen reports that the 2005 cabs generally have wonderfully ripe flavours and a classical structure. Last year, parent group DS Sarnia acquired the historic Zonnebloem Vineyards in the Simondium area, giving WvR extended options when sourcing fruit for his wines. The Rickety Bridge brand got international exposure during the Global Challenge Yacht Race (the prize-giving was hosted at the winery), the winetasting facilities were upgraded, and conversion of the Manor House into an upmarket guesthouse was begun.

★★★★★ **Shiraz** Cellar's polished signature. Hallmarks are concentrated black fruit, well-controlled by spicy oak. Typified by **02**, forthcoming, deep-flavoured & classy; **03** less extrovert but also very fine; subdued nose redeemed by rich, spicy/savoury palate, pleasantly chewy tannins. 20-24 mths Fr barrels, 20% new.

★★★★ **Paulinas Reserve** Limited-release barrel selections honouring farm's founder, Paulina de Villiers. **03** (★★★) continues bdx formula (cab-merlot, 68/32), lacks pvs's elegant generosity; Fr oak, 36% new. **02** (sample) signalled change in blend, to 66/34 cab/merlot; claret-like grip & feel; standout **01** (★★★★★) was unblended merlot from Stbosch.

★★★★ **Cabernet Sauvignon 01** (★★★★), with splash malbec, perfectly ripe, sleek & groomed; classic dry finish, which it shares with current **02**, more savoury, less overt berry character, but attractive & harmonious, food-friendly; 30 mths Fr oak, 25% new.

★★★★ **Chardonnay** Bright fruit-acid a signature of these deep-flavoured New World versions; **04** (★★★) leaner vintage, more mineral restraint than fruit richness, will peak earlier; new-oak (Fr) component wisely reduced to 12%, vs 17% for riper **03**. 10 mths barrelled.

★★★★ **Semillon** Serious, made to last, small-barrel style continues with **04** (★★★★) though in lighter, condensed mode. Honey/butterscotch notes & lively acidity. **03** was deliciously smooth & creamy. Fr oak, 18-30% new; 9-14 mths.

Merlot ★★★ Minty mocha aromas on **03**, meaty touch; more body than fruit this vintage, tautish tannins. 2 yrs Fr oak, 25% new. **Chenin Blanc 04** available, not tasted. **Sauvignon Blanc** ★★★ **05** big (±15% alc) but shy on nose; soft, easy flavours with fresh acidity. **Duncan's Creek Classic Red** ★★★ **04** recipe changes to shiraz (57%), cab & dollop malbec, Appealing, lightish & juicy fireside red (or, lightly chilled, summer picnic partner); ±13% alc. All these WO Frhoek or Coastal. — *CT*

Ridder's Creek

*Wellington ▪ Tasting by appt ▪ Owners George de Ridder & partner ▪ QC consultant Jeff Wedgwood ▪ PO Box 72 Wellington 7654 ▪ ridders@iafrica.com ▪ www.ridderscreek.co.za ▪ **T/F 873·7746***

Negociant George de Ridder and a partner launched the Ridder's Creek range, sourced and made to their specs, in 2002. Wines and blending components are sourced from various regions and assembled under the experienced eye of Jeff Wedgwood. The team also does bottling for clients as well as local and international bulk-wine trading. Also limited-release corporate gift packs yearly.

Cabernet Sauvignon ★★ Always a rather subdued wine: **03** with dark fruit nuances, stalky, fruit-shy palate. Not for long-term keeping but needs yr to soften. **Shiraz** ★★★ **04** approachable, despite firm tannins & 14.5% alc. Black pepper, brambleberry aromas & flavours. Following three wines tasted as samples: **Cape Red** ★★★ Grippier than usual **04** , with firm grape tannins & solid fruit core has structure for short term development. **Chardonnay** ★★★ Shy; muted tropical & citrus fruit on nose & palate, crisp finish. **Cape White** ★★★ Quaffable delight with appealing deciduous fruit & leafy tones. **Sauvignon Blanc** ★★ **05** not tasted for this ed; pvs lightish with peach & apricot accents. — *CR*

Rider's Valley see Ruitersvlei

Ridgeback Wines

Paarl ▪ Est 1997 ▪ 1stB 2001 ▪ Tasting & sales Mon-Sat 10-5 ▪ Fee R25 for 7 wines ▪ Closed Easter Fri, Dec 25/26 & Jan 1 ▪ Deli-style meals ▪ Tours by appt ▪ Owners Kilimanjaro Investments ▪ Winemaker Cathy Marshall (Jun 2000) ▪ Viti consultant Phil Freeze ▪ 35 ha (cabs/f, grenache, merlot, mourvèdre, petit v, shiraz, chenin, sauvignon, viognier) ▪ 200 tons ▪ 8 000 cs own label 79% red 21% white ▪ Eurogap certified ▪ PO Box 2076 Windmeul 7630 ▪ ridgeback@mweb.co.za ridgetasting@mweb.co.za ▪ www.ridgebackwines.co.za ▪ ***T/F 869·8068/082·554·0176*** *▪ F 794·1070*

Wrapped around a small ridge in warm Agter-Paarl, Ridgeback's vineyards are being given a complete make-over by international consultant Phil Freese, farm manager Jerry Parker (ex-Zimbawean tobacco farmer) and new viticulturist Toit Wessels. The mission: rich, complex wines. Full support comes from at-once cerebral and down-to-earth winemaker Cathy Marshall, a cellar minimalist intent on producing blends à la Pomerol and the Côtes-du-Rhône (2005 heralded the first: a syrah-viognier under the His Master's Choice label). She's experimenting with green and red 'verjus': natural wine-grape acids to replace tartaric, successfully tested on sauvignon. Owner, former Zim tobacco trader Vernon Cole, and his family concentrate on the whole wine and food experience. 'We'd like to communicate clearly and knowledgeably about our wines,' he says.

★★★★★ **Shiraz** In only 3 vintages has helped set new quality benchmarks for Paarl shiraz. Latest **03** muted but broad black pepper, wild scrub aromas; fine structure to elegant savoury richness. Complete & characterful without being showy. 16 mths small oak, some new. Concours Mondial gold; *Wine* ★★★★. **02** (★★★★); bold, rich & meaty with vigorous tannins. Paarl Shiraz champ.

★★★★ **Cabernet Franc-Merlot 03** still available. 54/46 blend shows spicy, leafy elegance; well-weighted fruit, serious ripe tannins. Most attractive; worth cellaring till 2008/10. Fr oaked 14 mths. Concours Mondial gold.

★★★★ **Merlot** Supple **03**, plum/green olive aromas enriched by 100% new Fr oak. Long, savoury. Harmonious now, good potential till 2007/09.

★★★★ **Viognier** Maiden **03** drew many appreciative comments. **04** (★★★★★) set to follow suit. More reined-in elegance, freshness, less oak influence, though also fermented/matured 15 mths in new Fr barriques. Fine apricot/honeysuckle fragrance; attractive mineral vitality, persistence. **03** sumptuous; richly dry. Bold but balanced 15.5% alc. Partial spontaneous ferment.

★★★★ **Sauvignon Blanc** Food-cordial **04** should benefit from ageing. Cool, sleek profile; good weight, concentration; 5g/ℓ sugar. Clearly defined fig/tropical fruit character on **05** (★★★★); less typical lowish acid should appeal to those who prefer an unassertive style. Still briskly fresh, vitality helped by bone-dry finish.

Vansha Red NEW ☺ ★★★ Everyday-drinking cinsaut blend with shiraz, cab franc. **04** tasty, warmingly full body eased by savoury dryness. Partially oaked.

His Master's Choice new ★★★★ New-wave shiraz/viognier blend; 94/6 in maiden **04**. Just post-bottling, viognier's apricot perfume/flavour override shiraz's spicy red fruits; needs time, too, for underlying delicacy to emerge from cloak dense tannins. 16 mths 85% new Fr oak. **Cabernet Sauvignon** new ★★★★ 'Warmer' style, expansive yet well-proportioned. **03** roast coffee bean/mulberry sweetness on nose; solid build; very dry tannins. 2 yrs Fr oak, some new. **Vansha Dry White** ★★★ Pvsly Chenin Blanc-Sauvignon Blanc. Juicily ripe **05**, touch botrytis on tropical fruit/fig flavours; balanced freshness. Fruitily dry for everyday enjoyment. *—AL*

Riebeek Cellars

Swartland ▪ Est/1stB 1941 ▪ Tasting & sales Mon-Fri 8-5 Sat 8.30-2 ▪ Closed Easter Fri/Sun, Dec 25 & Jan 1 ▪ Tours strictly by appt ▪ BYO picnic ▪ Farm produce ▪ Owners 63 shareholders ▪ Winemakers Zakkie Bester, Eric Saayman & Alecia Hamman (Dec 1999/Jan 1997/Dec 2004), with Kenneth Whiley ▪ Viticulturist Hanno van Schalkwyk (Sep 2000) ▪ 1 400 ha (cab, merlot, pinotage, shiraz, chard, chenin, colombard, sauvignon) ▪ 14 000 tons 45 000 cs own labels + 40 000 cs for customers, incl Rocheburg & Broken Rock (both UK) ▪ 35% red 60% white 5% rosé ▪ ISO certification in progress ▪ PO Box 13 Riebeek Kasteel 7307 ▪ riebeek@mweb.co.za ▪ www.riebeekcellars.com ▪ ***T (022) 448·1213*** *▪ F (022) 448·1281*

This co-operative group's marching to today's tune. First, there's the appointment of Alecia Hamman as the cellar's first female winemaker; a Swartlander, she worked at Oranjerivier Cellars, with stints in Bordeaux and Australia, before coming back home. Then there's progress at Highlands farm outside Malmesbury, where Riebeek Cellars' empowerment project is on its way to producing its maiden vintage under the Partnership label. The partnership in this case is between RC, producers and industry workers in the Riebeek Valley. Last season saw the producers' first small viognier crop which shows promise, according to cellarmaster Zakkie Bester, especially in a shiraz blend.

A Few Good Men range

These from selected vyds, their owners/growers being the eponymous Few Good Men. **Cabernet Sauvignon** ★★ **03** harks back to firmness of **01**; notes of dried leaves & damp earth; big dry tannins, will need time. Yr Fr oak, some new. **Merlot** ★★★ **03** As above, restrained fruit styling coupled with strong tannin structure; retains Swtlnd generosity in alc dept (14.1%). 9 mths 2nd fill oak. **Shiraz** ★★★ Portion new Am oak (30%, ±9 mths) distinguishes these; **03** subdued, slightly rustic incarnation, for early drinking; some 'milky' character, savoury tannins. **Chardonnay** ★★★★ 100% barrel-fermented/aged 6 mths, Fr/Am oak (50/50), none new; fruit ex-single vyd; well-crafted/judged **04** up to hgh std of pvs; deliciously ripe lime fruit, restrained leesiness, supple & juicy.

Riebeek range

Cabernet Sauvignon ★★★ Subdued **04** anthesis of ebullient pvs; light (but pleasant) dried-fruit characater, tight dry tannins. Low 13% alc. Fr oak 6 mths. **Merlot** ★★★ **04** has astringency under control; plummy fruit, medium-bodied, attractively taut for food-pairing. **Pinotage** ★★ **04** dried banana & sweet jammy fruit, savoury palate, slightly bitter tail. Oak-chipped. **Shiraz Reserve** ★★★★ **02** noted last ed as punchy, strapping; toast/mocha on finish. Still closed, but good prospects. 18-24 mths Fr/Am oak, some new. **Shiraz-Cabernet Sauvignon Reserve** new ★★★ 60/25 blend with petit v, merlot (10/5), no variety in command; savoury/smoked meat tone; restrained well-melded dry flavours; 6-24 mths, mix of blls. **Redneck** ★★★ Vibrant Mediterranean-style red, partly-oaked equal mix shiraz, malbec; savoury-dry **03** still avaialble, not retasted. **Cinsaut-Pinotage** ★★ **04** light-coloured/textured 60/40 blend, unwooded. **Pinotage Rosé** ★★★ Charming al fresco drink with strawberry/watermelon nose; plump, nearly-dry lingering flavours. Big 14% alc. **Chardonnay Reserve** ★★★ 100% Fr oak-fermented, lees-aged; **03** last ed notes as subdued fruit-salad flavours, sweetish impression though technically dry. **Chardonnay** ★★ Partly & subtly oaked **05**, pale & light, some elegance in friendly, undemanding package. **Sauvignon Blanc** ★★ **05** crisp, delicate & light (12.6% alc), with greenpepper hint. **Chenin Blanc Reserve** ★★★ **04** barrel-fermented in new Fr oak; same pleasingly restrained lees/oak character as pvs, so ripe tropical fruit gets the limelight. **Chenin Blanc** ★★ **05** rather less of the varietal statement we met last yr; more 'appealing dry white', for youthful enjoyment. **Stein** ★★ Soft, sweetish, undemanding quaffer with hints melon & honeysuckle. Light-bodied **NV** from chenin, muscadel. **Pinot2** ★★★ The renamed 'Brut' (**NV** carbonated sparkler), hinting at duo of pinots (blanc 60%, noir) in blend; similar easy, briskly dry refreshment as pvs, with green apple tones. **Red Jerepiko** ★★ Full-sweet winter-warmer from tinta. 17.3% alc. **NV**. Latest version very raisined, sweet & foresquare. **Cape Ruby** ★★★ Blend tinta, souzão (80/20), 50% small-oaked 24 mths; latest bottling old leather hints, sweet & tiring; not the vibrant, stylistically correct number we're used to. 19.8% alc. **NV**. Above mostly Coastal WO.

Montino range

Montino Petillant Light ☺ ★★ Lively, spritzy white with gentle grapey nose; chill well for instant summer refreshment. Light 9% alc. **NV**.

Off-Dry Rosé sold out.

Cape Table range

NV range of lowish-alc 1ℓ packs; **Cellar Red** ★★ Light, spicy dry *vin ordinaire*. **Cellar Rosé Semi-Sweet** ★★ Light, with balanced sweetness. **Natural Sweet Rosé** ★ Sweet strawberry tones, barley water chacacter. **Cellar White** ★ Simple dry quaff with guava hint. **Cellar Gold Late Harvest** ★★ Summer-sweet fruit character, melon finish. **Natural Sweet Low Alcohol White** ★ Sweetness, with rose-petal fragrance. **Cellar Lite** ★ Summer picnic wine; light pineapple flavour. — *CT*

Rietrivier Winery

Little Karoo ▪ Est 1965 ▪ 1stB 1990 ▪ Tasting & sales Mon-Thu 8-5 Fri 8-3 ▪ Closed pub hols ▪ Tours by appt ▪ Light meals daily 8-5; or BYO picnic ▪ Amenities/attractions: see intro ▪ Owners 46 members ▪ Manager/winemaker Chris-Willem de Bod, with Petrus Bothma (Oct 1999/Jan 1994) ▪ Viti consultant Willem Botha (Jan 2001) ▪ 300 ha (merlot, shiraz, chard) ▪ 5 700 tons 10 000 cs own label + 4m litres bulk 50% red 49% white 1% rosé ▪ PO Box 144 Montagu 6720 ▪ rietrivier@lando.co.za ▪ www.rietrivier.co.za ▪ ***T/F (023) 614·1705***

A wine route needs food stops to match its tasting venues and here's another for the much-travelled Route 62: Rietrivier's newly-opened farmstall and restaurant on the Montagu-Barrydale stretch. Manager/winemaker Chris-Willem de Bod reports that the winery's members brought in 10% less in 2005 but the flip side of the coin is the fine fruitiness of the wine. Raising the bar here is the regional Young Wine Show award winning Shiraz 04; recently launched to meet the same standards is a range of premium reds, labelled Quiriga.

Quiriga range new

Merlot Reserve 03 not tasted. **Shiraz Reserve** ★★★ Accessible, not-for-keeping **03**, malty on nose & palate; some pepper & mint, rich warm fruit. Tannins soft & dry; balanced. 18 mths Fr oak.

Rietrivier range

★★★★ **Montagu Red Muscadel** Made jerepiko-style (no fermentation), fortified to ±17.5%. **04** (★★) different bottle of wine to standout **02** with its billowing perfumes, fine fruity structure. Latest overly sweet & cloying with hint bitterness, spirit unintegrated. 250ml bottle.

Merlot ★★ **03** tasted for pvs ed youthful & fresh, prominent nose, needs time to mellow. **Pinotage** ★★ **04** cherry fruit, lightish tannins, medium body; 6 mths staves after fermentation. **Shiraz** ★★★ **04** leap up on pvs with dark cherry, spice & char aromas/flavours; dry finish, integrated 14% alc. **Petite Rouge** ★★ Rustic red from equal parts pinotage, ruby cab; unwooded. Latest (**NV**) shy, firm; tad coarse. **Route 62 Red** ★★ High-octane pinotage, merlot (90/10) mix, unwooded; overripe mulberry fruit on **03**, last tasted mid-2004. **Rosé** ★★★ Gracious member of the range; **05** from pinotage, straw/cranberry aromas, flavours; balanced, lifted semi-sweet (17g/ℓ sugar). **Sauvignon Blanc** ★★ Muted, lightish **05** showing quince & pears tones; just-dry summer sipper. **Colombar-Chardonnay** ★★ **04** tropically toned fruity blend, smooth & ripe, **05**

is next. **Petite Blanc** ★★ Crisp, light-bodied dry white; latest **NV** losing fruit, tiring. Equal dollops colombard, chardonnay, sauvignon. 500ml screwcap. **Late Harvest** ★★ **NV**; light, tropical sweetie which slides down easily. Latest bottling step up in quality, more obvious pear/apple fruit; same blend as Petite B. **Sparkling Vin Doux** ★★ Fresh, low-alc (11.5%) sweet fizz, red & white available, both **NV**. **Montagu White Muscadel** ★★★ Persistent, slightly raisined, silky **02**. Splash some into venison potjie, winemakers recommend, or over crushed ice for summer refreshment. 17.5% alc. **05** unready, ditto … **Montagu Hanepoot** ★★ **02** pleasant cream-textured full-sweet fortified with honeysuckle fragranc.e. Alc as above. **Montagu Ruby Port** ★★ from pinotage, **03** similar to pvs with idiosyncratic mulled wine character, touch tannin to finish. **Chenin Blanc** discontinued.—*JN/CR*

Rietvallei Estate

Robertson ▪ Est 1864 ▪ 1stB 1975 ▪ Tasting & sales Mon-Fri 8.30-5 Sat 9.30-1 ▪ Closed Easter Sat-Mon, Dec 25/26 & Jan 1 ▪ Cheese platters or BYO picnic ▪ Facilities for children ▪ Tourgroups ▪ Owner Johnny Burger ▪ Winemakers Johnny & Kobus Burger (1973/2001) ▪ Viti consultant Briaan Stipp (2000) ▪ 137 ha (10 varieties r/w) ▪ 2 040 tons ±20 000 cs own label 40% red 45% white 15% fortified ▪ Export brand: Wild Rush ▪ PO Box 386 Robertson 6705 ▪ info@rietvallei.co.za ▪ www.rietvallei.co.za ▪ ***T (023) 626·3596/4422*** *▪ F (023) 626·4514*

Winemaker Kobus Burger, now proud father of the first of the 7th generation of the family, remembers the last harvest as 'quick and wet' — but promising. With the help of newly-appointed marketer Colyn Truter, he hopes to grow Rietvallei's existing markets, of which there are now 13, the US representing the biggest newcomer. Burger's other ambition is to reduce bulk shipments and increase bottle sales: at the moment, only 20% of their wine goes into glass.

★★★★ **Chardonnay** ✓ **03** needed yr to reveal quality that pleased Chardonnay-du-Monde judges. Current **05** (★★★★) rich & creamy with appealing citrus notes. 40% wood-fermented, rest tank.

★★★★ **Red Muscadel** ✓ A Cape classic. Rooibos tea, raisins & dust on **04**. Much drier than pvs (200g/ℓ RS vs 265) but alc slightly up (17% vs 16%). Try as a cocktail: with soda, ginger, mint & slice lemon.

★★★★☆ **Muscadel 1908** From what's thought to be SA's oldest red muscadel vyd (tiny-yielding bushvines planted in 1908). **03** lighter & drier (15% alc, 209g/ℓ RS) than **02**. Same opulent raisiny nose, cooked apricot jam flavours with excellent complexity & concentration. Deserves time.

Cabernet Sauvignon ★★★☆ **04** sample shows sweet berry fruit on toasty bitter-choc platform, good ageing potential. Heavier & drier (14% alc, 4g/ℓ RS) than pvs. 7 mths Fr oak. **Shiraz** ★★★☆ **04** slippery ripe-fruit style with opulence & spice. Drier (3.5g/ℓ RS) than **03**. Both moderate 13.5% alc. Yr mix Fr/Am oak. **Juanita Rosé** ★☆ **05** sample shows cabbage nose & bitter finish atop a creamy palate. **Chardonnay Special Select** ★★★☆ Fresh & fruity **05** sample leads with gently wooded nose, nuts & vanilla. **Unwooded Chardonnay** new ★★★☆ **05** tropical fruit punch with excellent drinkability for those tired of overly tart sauvignon. **Sauvignon Blanc Special Select** new ★★★☆ Cool-climate Elim grapes star. Classic lemongrass nose on **05**, figs & grapefruit on palate, big acidity cushioned by sugar (5g/ℓ) & 3 mths Fr oak. **Sauvignon Blanc** ★★★ Shy nose, **05** pleasant lemon/lemon curd flavours on palate. Low 13% alc. **Rhine Riesling** new ★★☆ Cider-like apple & pear tones, high acids mask 12g/ℓ sugar. Abstemious 9.5% alc in **05** tank sample. **Gewürztraminer** discontinued.

John B range

Cabernet Sauvignon-Tinta Barocca ★★★ (Pvsly 'Bouquet Rouge') **04** smoky 70:30 blend with prunes & some wood character from oak staving. **Sauvignon Blanc-Colombar** ★★☆ The renamed 'Bouquet Blanc'. **05** refreshing 60:40 blend of sweaty sauvignon & vegetal colombard. Breathalyser-friendly 11.5% alc.—*NP*

Rijk's Private Cellar

Tulbagh ▪ Est 1996 ▪ 1stB 2000 ▪ Tasting & sales Mon-Fri 10-4 Sat 10-3 ▪ Fee R5/wine ▪ Closed Easter Fri-Mon, Dec 25 & Jan 1 ▪ Tours during tasting hours ▪ Country Hotel ▪ T (023) 230·1006 ▪

BYO picnic ▪ Tourgroups ▪ Conferencing ▪ Walks ▪ Owner Neville Dorrington ▪ Winemaker Pierre Wahl (Jan 2002) ▪ Viti consultant Johan Wiese (Mar 1996) ▪ 28 ha (cab, merlot, pinotage, shiraz, chard, chenin, sauvignon, semillon) ▪ ±180 tons 11 000 cs own label 70% red 30% white ▪ PO Box 400 Tulbagh 6820 ▪ wine@rijks.co.za ▪ www.rijks.co.za ▪ ***T (023) 230·1622*** *▪ F (023) 230·1650*

Established a decade ago in then unfashionable Tulbagh by leather goods manufacturer Neville Dorrington, the rise of this cellar has been meteoric. At this year's Trophy Show, it was the third-best performing entrant overall, winning a gold medal for its Cab. Other highlights included attaining Super Chenin status and two gold medals at the Swiss Awards. And the best is yet to come, predicts winemaker Pierre Wahl, now that production is up to the cellar's 10 000-case capacity: 'It puts me in a position to focus on the vineyard and the wine, and to produce top quality wine year after year.' Ongoing experimentation is yielding 'unbelievable' results.

★★★★ **Cabernet Sauvignon** Small block, intensively managed for ripe fruit – an objective convincingly attained with **02** (★★★★★); huge extract, booming fruit, colossal 15% alc for the whole 'Tulbagh does Down Under' number. Hugely showy – unsurprising FCTWS 2005 gold. 18 mths Fr oak, 70% new. **01** developed brilliantly; good mouthfeel, excellent balance despite massive 14.8% alc. Generously oaked 20 mths 70% new Fr barrels.

★★★★ **Cabernet Sauvignon-Merlot** new Bdx-style blend cab & merlot (65/35), 20 mths Fr oak, 40% new. **02** ripe fruit with excellent intensity & prominent alc (14.8%). Grippy & mouth-filling with slightly angular finish mid-2005. Swiss gold.

★★★☆ **Pinotage** Pinotage Top Ten 2003, VDG laurels for pvsly tasted **02**, mocha notes, rubber & choc, grainy tannins. Plenty of evidence of 18 mths largely new Fr/Am oak (65/35); 14.8% alc. Heavier than sleek, intense **01** (★★★★).

★★★★ **Shiraz 02** (★★★★☆) another explosive fruit bomb; incredible concentration & breadth, slippery tannins, liquid fynbos flavours, even more incendiary than fruit-driven **01** with rippling spiced fruit under guard of fine tannins. 16 mths Fr/Am oak, 30% new.

★★★☆ **Sauvignon Blanc 04** (★★★★) big flavours of cut grass & fresh hay; portion grapes ex-Mbury lends leesy/lemony dimension to own fruit; night-harvested, reductive style **03** had surprisingly gentle alc for house (13%). Neither retasted.

★★★★ **Chenin Blanc 04** one of their best yet; honey & lanolin notes, rich nutty flavours; 60% barrel fermented, 11 mths mix Hngrian/Fr barrels, 30% new. Drier & slightly lighter (4.6g/ℓ RS; 14% alc) than **03**, with fresh guava edge from tank component.

★★★★ **Semillon** Winning recipe of full mouthfeel, waxy lanolin & creamy honey, with good balance, length – & sweet element. **03** pvs ed continued the formula but eased up on alc & sugar (14.6%, 6.2g/ℓ) compared with rich, FCTWS trophy-winning **02**. Fermented/yr Fr oak, 20% new.

Bravado ★★★ Suitably bold name for house's first 'reserve' red; blend 60% cab, 30% merlot, 10% shiraz; **01** retasted for pvs ed, marked by porty notes & baked flavours. 20 mths Fr oak, 70% new. **Merlot** ★★★☆ Less rumbustious red. Last ed we revisited **01**: elegant bouquet, punchy but accessible minty fruit; 18 mths 60% new Fr oak. **Chardonnay** ★★★☆ Forcefully styled, with track record for pleasing show judges. Last ed **03** was rich & opulent; round full flavours, hefty 14.4% alc. Fermented/yr Fr oak, 70% new. – *NP*

Rising River see Cru Wines
River Grandeur see Viljoensdrift
River's Edge see Weltevrede

Riverstone Vineyards

Worcester ▪ Est 1963 ▪ 1st 1975 ▪ Tasting & sales Mon-Fri 8-12.30; 1.30-5 Sat 9-1 ▪ Fee R10 refunded on purchase ▪ Closed Easter Fri-Mon, Dec 25 & Jan 1 ▪ Merwida Country Lodge ▪ T (023) 349·1435 ▪ Owners Schalk & Pierre van der Merwe ▪ Winemakers Magnus Kriel (Dec 2000), with Sarel van Staden (Aug 1982) ▪ Viticulturist Magnus Kriel ▪ 630 ha (cab, merlot, shiraz, chard, chenin, sauvignon, semillon, viognier) ▪ 10 000 tons 20 000 cs own label 40% red 60% white ▪ PO Box 4 Rawsonville 6845 ▪ wines@merwida.com ▪ www.merwida.com ▪ ***T (023) 349·1144*** *▪ F (023) 349·1953*

An uneven harvest, was 2005, for this family-owned winery, but good semillon, chenin and reds resulted. Improvements continue apace with the building of a new barrel cellar and the launch of the second wine in the Family Reserve range, a promising Barbera from young vines. Best competitive performer of late has been the Muskadel, with golds at Veritas and the Young Wine Show, as well as Michelangelo silver.

Family Reserve range

Barbera new ★★★ Appealing & approachable **03**, dark wild-berry fruit & hint vanilla, sound dry tannins from 18 mths 2nd fill oak; good food wine. **Viognier** ★★★ Unoaked **05** (sample) pretty ripe-apricot & almond kernel whiffs, sweet ripe fruit & huge alc (15.1%), too overpowering for standalone enjoyment.

Riverstone range

Cabernet Sauvignon ★★★ **04** (sample) soft, sweet baked-fruit character, easy/early drinking, good pasta/pizza wine. **Shiraz** ★★★ Last tasted was muscled (15% alc) but benign **02**, with red berry fruit, scrubby touch. Our sample **04** too unformed to rate. **Sauvignon Blanc** ★★★ Drink-young **05** delicate capsicum/fig tones, lightish, with firm crisply dry finish. **Chardonnay-Viognier** ★★★ **05** step up this yr; lightish & lively (more so than Rsv above), dried peach/citrus flavours, characterful, complementary 60/40 blend, unoaked. **Muscadel** ★★★★ ✓ **03** last ed showed effusive aromas of honeysuckle & muscat, light toned & satin smooth, lovely citrus tail-end tang. 16.5% alc. **Cuvée Brut** ★★ Carbonated sparkling from sauvignon; **05** again lightish but not as fine, satisfying as pvs. **Port 00** available, not tasted. **Ruby Cabernet**, **Shiraz-Cabernet Sauvignon** discontinued. All ranges WO Brde Rvr Vlly/ Goudini unless mentioned.

Heron range

Shiraz-Petit Verdot ★★★ **03** rare varietal pairing (70/30) achieves friendly quaffability via exuberant plum fruit & balancing smoky/toasty note. Last ed noted as so fruity, you don't notice the high 14.5% alc. **Chenin Blanc-Viognier** sold out. *—IvH/DH*

Robertson Wide River Export Company

Joint venture between Robertson Winery and Vinimark, handling all Robertson Winery exports under brand names such as Kaapdal, Kleindal (mainly for Germany & UK), Silver Sands (chiefly UK), Sinnya (mainly Germany & Canada), The Veldt (primarily Scotland) and Vruchtbaar (The Netherlands). See Vinimark for contact details.

Robertson Winery

Robertson ▪ Est 1941 ▪ 1stB 1987 ▪ Tasting & sales Mon-Thu 8-5 Fri 8-5.30 Sat/Sun 9-3 ▪ Closed Easter Fri, Dec 25 & Jan 1 ▪ Tours by appt ▪ BYO picnic ▪ Gifts ▪ Tourgroups by appt ▪ Small wine museum ▪ Owners 43 members ▪ Winemakers Lolly Louwrens, Francois Weich, Jacques Roux (May 1995/Sep 1997/Jan 2000/Nov 2001) ▪ Viticulturist Briaan Stipp (Jan 2005) ▪ 1 900 ha (cab, merlot, pinotage, ruby cab, shiraz, chard, chenin, sauvignon) ▪ 29 000 tons ▪ 40% red 60% white ▪ No 1 Constitution Rd Robertson 6705 ▪ gaenor@vinimark.co.za ▪ www.robertsonwinery.co.za ▪ ***T (023) 626·3059*** *▪ F (023) 626·2926*

The third-largest wine producer in SA (1m cases a year), Robertson is gearing up for a new push into world wine markets. With the varietal mix on the 35 supplier farms in place, the winery has appointed its first full-time viticulturist, Briaan Stipp, charged with achieving the ideal balance between quality and productivity. Experienced (10 years with KWV, Vinpro), well travelled (US, South America, France, Australia), active (serving on national training, research and technology bodies), Stipp will assess world trends, ensuring Robertson meets consumer requirements. This efficient operation boasts a selective portfolio: good-value boxed wines (pioneering varietally-labelled, vintaged packaging); easy-drinking blends; (Old Chapel); single-varietal wines (Robertson); and Vineyard Selection, from quality vineyards nursed into bottle in a dedicated micro-cellar.

Vineyard Selection range

★★★★☆ **No. 1 Constitution Road Shiraz** Cellar's standard bearer, named after the Rbtson-town street address. Maiden **02** spicy & abundantly-fruited; loaded with potential – though latest **03** probably more so, given the quality of the vintage; same broad sweep of aromas/flavours (black cherry to Karoo scrub), same spirited oaking (2 yrs new Fr), but better honed, more refined. Wild yeast ferment; 22 blls made.

★★★★ **Phanto Ridge Pinotage** new Pvsly for US market, now in SA. Graceful & elegant expression of the often unruly grape; **04** sweet damson fruit, banana whiff; flavourful & supple. Ex-single vyd owned by Joh'burg accountant-turned-vinegrower Rupert de Vries. Yr oak, 20% Am.

★★★★ **Wolfkloof Shiraz** Maiden **02** excellent ripe shiraz; full & very rotund, comforting. Follow-up **03** noted last ed as also striking yet finer, more elegant; similar huge but balanced alc (15%), generous harmonious oak.

★★★☆ **Prospect Hill Cabernet Sauvignon** Warm-country cab with generous build, **02** ripe, meaty aromas, quite individual. **03** (★★★★) last yr unfolded slowly in glass to reveal more refined wine; real summer pudding melange, generous ripe tannins & vanilla oak.

★★★★ **Kings River Chardonnay** Gentle white peach wafts belied quite a forceful barrel-fermented **04**; last ed was layered with lime & lees, butterscotch & fudge; well focused & packaged. Probably could go another few yrs.

★★★☆ **Retreat Sauvignon Blanc** Grapes from eponymous farm owned by Jac de Wet. **05** (★★★★) one of their best; effusive super-ripe fruit with flinty spark; beefy & broad but balanced; **04** another attention grabber with fine weight & dry lip-smacking finish.

★★★★ **Almond Grove Weisser Riesling Noble Late Harvest** The original NLH in this line-up, from the eponymous farm, **03** genteel & understated – & all the better for it; beautiful sugar/acid balance; 10.5% alc. Not retasted.

★★★★★ **Wide River Reserve Noble Late Harvest** Tour de force took this Vyd Selection range to the next level last ed. **01**, from botrytised riesling, a deep golden nectar of remarkable richness, concentration; ample bracing acidity to ride out the wine's weight, viscosity. 9.5% alc. VDG.

Robertson range

Ruby Cabernet ☺ ★★★ Terrific, youthful **04**, robust, juicy & mouth-watering. Perfect quaffer; moderate alc (13.2%). No oak. **Beaukett** ☺ ★★☆ Invariably charming; **05** delicate, aromatic semi-sweet wafting Turkish Delight & honeysuckle. ±11.5% alc for this & following pair. **Colombard** ☺ ★★☆ Regional speciality shows extra verve this vintage; **05** sprightly semi-dry guava/jasmine appeal. **Gewürztraminer Special Late Harvest** ☺ ★★★ Delicious scented dessert, **05** billows honeysuckle & Turkish Delight; rich & smooth rather than sweet; enjoy in its beguiling youth.

Cabernet Sauvignon ✓ ★★★☆ Early drinking style. **04** offers usual smooth & soft approachability with some classy red berry fruit & whiffs spice & vanilla from 8 mths oak. **Merlot** ★★★ Shows some refinement in **04**; flowers & plums on nose; medium body, supple tannin support. **Shiraz** ✓ ★★★☆ **04** less boisterous than pvs; still well layered with dark berry flavour, sniffs of anise & toast from partial oaking 6 mths. **Pinotage** ✓ ★★★☆ **04** not quite the supercharged version of last year but most enjoyable; excellent with ostrich fillet. **Cabernet Sauvignon-Shiraz** ★★★ **04** near-equal blend sparingly oaked, smooth & balanced; a tasty berry-toned drop. **Chardonnay** ★★★ More bang for your buck this yr. **05** generously citrus-fruited, touched with toasty oak (well-handled Fr staves), generally rather nice. **Chenin Blanc** ★★ **05** satisfies with full, ripe tropical fruit in pleasingly compact body (12.5% alc). **Sauvignon Blanc** ★★★ Night-harvested to retain varietal zing; **05** tropical fruit salad with bits of grass, rounded yet crisp. Commendably low 12.5% alc. **White Muscadel** ★★★ **03** not retasted; last ed had apple & litchi fragrances, luscious sweetness enlivened by tangy acidity. 16.5% alc. **Cape Ruby Port** ★★☆ Last tasted was **02**, youthful, lively, dryish; light spirit (16.5%). Next is **05**.

Old Chapel range

Red ★★★ ☺ Pleasant everyday glassful from merlot (85%), ruby cab. Well juiced & fruited for instant enjoyment.

Rosé ★★ Light & lively colombard/chenin mix, pink blush courtesy of ruby cab; sweet, clean & fresh. Low ±11% alc; same for … **White** ★★★ Tropical-toned colombard, crisp & fruitily dry. All **NV**, & now also in 1.5ℓ containers.

Natural Light range

Low alc wines (7.5–9.5%), all **NV**, mainly Natural Sweet. **Red** ★★ Sweet ripe plums & berries with fresh acidity. **Rosé** ★★ Baby-pink hue; soft, fruity & gently sweet. **White** ★★ Delicate, light & easy. **Dry Light** ★★ Better this yr; decidedly dry but fruity, attractively fresh.

Sparkling wines

NV carbonated bubblies, usually with lightish alcs (10–11%). None retasted; pvs were all ★★. **Brut** Tart green-apple fruit, busy bubbles, firm dry acidity. **Sec** Pretty & aromatic; slight sweetness nicely balanced by fresh acidity. **Doux** Honeyed aroma (not bottle age), very sweet frothy bubbles.

Two-litre boxed range

Certified boxes with varietal labels & vintage dates for most.

Merlot ☺ ★★★ **04** partly oaked 6 mths, hence vanilla notes to sunny plum flavour; mellow & tasty. **Ruby Cabernet** ☺ ★★★ Epitome of an easy-swigger; **04** attractive warm plum fruit plus variety's cooler capsicum. 13% alc. **Shiraz** new ☺ ★★★ Surprisingly good varietal character for price; whole aromatic gamut plus oak hint, generous mouthfeel. **Chenin Blanc** ☺ ★★ **05** improved version; bright bouncy tropicality, slightly sweet send-off. **Johannisberger** new ☺ ★★ Friendly, perfumed easy-drinker; uncloyingly semi-sweet.

Chardonnay ★★ Broader build than other whites via brief Fr-oak staving; **05** rounded & gentle citrus flavours. **Sauvignon Blanc** ★★ Latest version step up, **05** fuller flavoured, zestier, bone-dry but easy. WO W Cape. **Extra Light** ★★ **NV** with attractive freshness, very light, almost dry; has charm. 9.7% alc. Also available in 3ℓ box: **Cabernet Sauvignon** ★★★★ ✓ Seriously good value **04**; delightfully soft & fruity, supple; equally pleasant solo or at table.

Vinipak range

Good-value anytime wines in 500ml/1ℓ packs (some now feature easier-opening 'push-down' tops). All **NV**, with low alcs (±7–11.5%). **Dry Red** ★★ Full flavoured, round, gratifying; could be chilled in summer. **Dry White** ★★ Smooth, easy, undemanding. **Light White** ★★ Extra-light (5.6% alc) & juicy, smooth acidity, tasty. **Stein** ★★ Light, with pleasing sweetness. **Late Harvest** ★★ As usual, drier than expected from this style, good fresh acidity. **Johannisberger Sweet Red** ★★ Light-bodied, soft acid, sweet plum-juice flavours, no tannins. **Natural Sweet Rosé** ★★ Pretty & floral, appealing full-ripe fruit & balanced sweetness. — *DH*

Robert's Rock see KWV International
Robusto see Rudera
Rocco Bay see Bottelary Winery, Nordale
Rocheburg see Arlington, Riebeek Cellars
Rockfield see Du Preez Estate
Rockhopper see Vinus Via
Rock Rabbit see International Wine Services
Rock Ridge see Omnia
Rodini see Goudini
Roland's Reserve see Seidelberg

Romansrivier Cellar

Wolseley (see Worcester map) ▪ Est 1949 ▪ 1stB 1976 ▪ Tasting & sales Mon-Fri 8-5 Sat 10-1 ▪ Closed Easter Fri-Sun, Dec 25/26, Jan 1 ▪ Tours by appt ▪ Tourgroups ▪ BYO picnic ▪ Conference facilities ▪ Owners 30 members ▪ Winemaker/viticulturist Francois Agenbag (2002) ▪ 500 ha (cab, chard, chenin, colombard) ▪ 8 000 tons 5 000 cs own label 40% red 60% white ▪ PO Box 108 Wolseley 6830 ▪ romans@cybertrade.co.za ▪ ***T (023) 231·1070/80*** *▪ F (023) 231·1102*

No update available on this winery; contact details and wine notes from previous edition.

Mountain Ridge range

Cabernet Sauvignon & **Shiraz**, both **04**, tasted as early barrel samples, too unformed to rate; both aged in 100% new Fr/Am oak; alcs ±14.5%. **Pinotage** ★★★★ Charming **03**, sweet-tasting fruit, soft, slightly smoky tannins. **Malbec-Pinotage** ★★★★ Unusual combo, unwooded; **03** thickly layered with plums & strawberries, slight smokiness adds interest. **Chardonnay Wooded** ★★★ **04** tropical fruit & spicy oak, crisp lime-tinged finish. **Chardonnay Unwooded** ★★★ Peaches-&-cream character, sprightly texture with crisp citrus finish in **04**. **Colombard-Chardonnay** ★★★ Attractive **04** combo peaches, guava & tropical fruit, light & vivacious, for early enjoyment. **Sauvignon Blanc** ★★★ **04** subdued nose but lively & bright fruity palate, clean finishing. All WO Brde Rvr Vlly. — *DH*

Romond Vineyards

Stellenbosch ▪ Est 1993 ▪ 1stB 2003 ▪ Visits by appt ▪ Walks ▪ Owners André & Rhona Liebenberg ▪ Winemakers André Liebenberg, advised by Inus Muller (Jan 2003) ▪ Viticulturist De Wet Theron (Oct 2002) ▪ 33 tons 2 500 cs ▪ 100% red ▪ PO Box 5634 Helderberg 7135 ▪ romondwine@iafrica.com ▪ ***T 855·4566*** *▪ F 855·0428*

'I enjoy pushing the envelope but embarking on major cellar construction during the harvest and a busy filming schedule tested my endurance and equanimity. However, the cellar is nearing completion, the wine is safely in barrel and the family are talking to me again ... ' says André Liebenberg, a commercials director who takes his role as custodian of these vineyards in the Helderberg foothills seriously. Their new tasting room is a place to enjoy 'informative and fun food-pairing experiences, serious philosophising about wine, open fireplaces and old-fashioned bonhomie' (initially by appointment only).

Rebus ★★★ Blend cab f (56%) & cab s. Quality grapes show in nicely concentrated flavours on youthfully vigorous **03**, oak now integrated well (20 mths staves); but tart finish — lower acidity would make for more generous profile. — *IvH*

Rondebosch Cellar *see* Alvi's Drift Private Cellar
Roodeberg *see* KWV International

Roodezandt Wines & Vineyards

Robertson ▪ Est 1953 ▪ Tasting & sales Mon-Fri 8-5.30 Sat 9-12.30 ▪ Closed Easter Fri-Mon, May 1, Dec 25/36 & Jan 1 ▪ Tours by appt ▪ Owners 54 members ▪ Winemakers Christie Steytler & Elmo du Plessis, with Piet Bruwer (May 1980/Oct 1999/Feb 1985) ▪ Viticulturist Anton Laas (Dec 2000) ▪ 1 400 ha (cab, merlot, pinotage, ruby cab, shiraz, chard, chenin, colombard, sauvignon) ▪ 23 000 tons ▪ PO Box 164 Robertson 6705 ▪ roodez@intekom.co.za ▪ www.roodezandt.co.za ▪ ***T (023) 626·1160*** *▪ F (023) 626·5074*

Production manager Christie Steytler, pretty much a part of the cellar equipment here after 25 years, firmly believes that good winemaking practices 'can only fulfil the circle', holding true to the old adage that a good wine is made in the vineyard. Last crush was off to a difficult start with grapes not in peak condition. Early ripening cultivars were beset by rot but later ripening varieties fared better. The return was 20% lower on average, lowest in the whites. 'Not the best, but not the worst of harvests,' was his pragmatic conclusion.

No new releases reviewed; notes from pvs ed: **Balthazar Classic Cabernet Sauvignon** ★★★ Limited release honouring winery's ex-chairman, Baltus Kloppers. Unfined/unfiltered.

±13% alc. **00** peaking, must drink. **Cabernet Sauvignon** ★★★ **01** herbal aromas with eucalyptus hint; quite soft, lean & leafy. Yr older Fr casks. **Syrah** ★★★ Cross between aromatic & wood-powered style; **03** pepper & spice over soft plum fruit, pervasive oakiness on palate (which not unappealing); light 13% alc. **Chardonnay** Pvs 'Balthazar Classic' to be replaced by another version, unavailable at press time. **Sauvignon Blanc** ★★ Usually from cooler river-fronting sites; ±13% alc. **04** soft, dry white-fruit palate, lacks zest. **Special Late Harvest** ★★★ From chenin, muscadel; **04** billows full-sweet honeysuckle, delicate 12% alc heightens the charm. **White Muscadel** ★★★ **02** huge Turkish Delight bouquet, zippy peach flavours & cleansing acidity. 17.5% alc. **Red Muscadel** ★★★ Appealing winter warmer, best in fragrant youth; **03** bright acidic lift for juicy effect. 18.5% alc. **Port** discontinued.

Keizer's Creek range

Both **NV**. **The Red** ★★★ Unwooded blend led by ruby cab; soft, full, juicy; quick but quaffable. 13.5% alc. **The White** ★★★ Just-off-dry, light-bodied, supple & juicy poolside tipple. — *TM*

Rooiberg Winery

Robertson ▪ Est 1964 ▪ 1stB 1974 ▪ Tasting & sales Mon-Fri 8-5.30 Sat 9-3 ▪ Closed Easter Fri/Sun, Dec 25 & Jan 1 ▪ Tours by appt ▪ Farmstall and tea garden with gift shop; also BYO picnic ▪ Facilities for children ▪ Tourgroups ▪ 4×4 trail ▪ Audio-visual on video/CD ▪ Owners 30 members ▪ Cellarmaster André van Dyk, winemaker Eduard Malherbe, vini consultant Newald Marais (all Oct 2002) ▪ Viti consultant Willem Botha (2004) ▪ 600 ha (cab, merlot, pinotage, ruby cab, shiraz, chard, chenin, colombard, sauvignon) ▪ 10 000 tons 75 000 cs own labels 20% red 70% white 10% rosé ▪ Export brands: African Collection, African Dawn, Amandalia, Cape Circle, De Sonnenberg, Goeie Tye, Signum, Umculi & Zebra Collection ▪ PO Box 358 Robertson 6705 ▪ info@rooiberg.co.za ▪ www.rooiberg.co.za ▪ ***T (023) 626·1663*** *▪ F (023) 626·3295*

It's not just a facelift (upgrading of entrance and grounds, enlargement of picnic area and playground, cellar renovations, introduction of a Reserve range and brand-new label design) that this familiar landmark on the road to Robertson has undergone, but also a makeover. The objective is to compete at the higher end of the market, and to that end they're focused on extracting the best quality from their top vineyard blocks, and starting to produce single-vineyard wines. Ultimately their ambition is to become the best co-operative cellar in the country — and to take on the 'icons' of the industry.

Reserve range

Cabernet Sauvignon ★★★ **03** unusually astringent & austere, slightly 'wild' black fruit still needs to unfold; give yr/2. 18 mths Fr oak, same for ... **Merlot** new ★★★ **03** solid red for earlier consumption; soft & very ripe-tasting. **Pinotage** ★★ **03** very different to pvs; rustic, jammy, plum pudding & raisin flavours, contrasting dry tannins. **Shiraz** new ★★ Delicate varietal character overpowered by wood (regimen as for Cab); **03** bramble notes, on palate fruit still latent. **Chardonnay** ★★★ Appealing lime marmalade/mineral combo; **04** well-integrated oak (fermented/9 mths Fr), lightish & understated (as opposed to gusty 'Rsv' style).

Standard range

★★★★ **Red Jerepiko** Last tasted was excellent unwooded fortified **96**, from single pinotage vyd; interestingly delicious, with a range of flavours (incl floor polish), racy acidity controlling the sweetness. 17.5% alc.

★★★★ **Red Muscadel** Scented, flowery, raisin aromas poured out a welcome in **03**; intense flavours no less good-hearted. **05** (★★) intensely sweet & unctuous yet little fruit substance/concentration behind the sugar. 16% alc.

Pinotage Rosé ☺ ★★ Crisply refreshing lunchtime (or midnight snack, for that matter) pale red quaffer; **05** lots of dried apricot flavour; shortish dry finish.

Cabernet Sauvignon ★★ **04** preview shows powerful dry tannins, fruit (smoky wild berries in this instance) cowering in a corner. Yr small oak. **Merlot** Cheerful, friendly pvs replaced with stern & austere **04**; mid-2005, pre-bottling sample not rated. Yr oak, 2nd-3rd fill.

Pinotage ★★ **04** (sample) tight, dry, youthfully austere tannin holding jammy fruit in check. Part wood aged (barrels/staves). **Shiraz** ★★★ **04** (sample) savoury rather than fruity this vintage; firm but ripe & juicy tannins. Yr barrels/staves. **Cabernet Sauvignon-Merlot (Roodewyn)** ★★★ Reliable steakhouse-type red. Touches leather & smoke on **04**, usual mild-tannined farewell. Yr older Fr oak. **Selected Red** ★★★ Generous, forthright & honest. **NV** lightly oaked blend with spicy/savoury dry flavours. **Chardonnay** ★★ Previewed **05** more outgoing than last yr's incarnation; juicy ripe fruit, hint lemon zest, full elegant mouthful. Brush of oak adds interest. **Chenin Blanc** ★★ Floral tones on **05**, light & dry; evanescent winter melon flavours. 12.9% alc. **Sauvignon Blanc** ★★ **05** step up; bit more substance/dimension; tinned green peas & cut grass, effortless. **Classic White** new ★★ Crisp, light & dry chenin/sauvignon; pineapple flavour in **05** (sample) quick-quaff. **Cape White** ★★ **05** from colombard, much drier-tasting than pvs; simple, crisp & clean; usual easy-going alc (11.8%). **Rhine Riesling** ★★★ Last was floral, spicy **04**; just-off-dry, with a quickening acidity marking the finish. **Natural Sweet Red** ★★★ **02** last ed, mouth-filling & juicy; cleverly balanced with some refreshing acid/tannin grip to complement sweetness (33g/ℓ sugar). **Natural Sweet Rosé** ★★ **04** switches to 100% red muscadel & shows absence of colombard's verve-imparting acidity. **Natural Sweet Blanc** ★ Last ed the grapey nose the best part of this soft-centred, insubstantial, insipidly sweet **04** white. Low 11.9% alc. **Brut Sparkling** ★★ Jovially frothy carbonated **NV** (as all these bubblies) from sauvignon, with its grassiness on light, dry palate. **Flamingo Sparkling** ★★ Soft, strawberry-toned pink fizz, white muscadel plus a dash of merlot for colour. **Vin Doux Sparkling** ★★ Festive (or anytime) sweetly foaming, with bright grapey aromas/flavours. **Hanepoot** ★★★ **00** was last vintage reviewed, floral, grapey & sweet – rather coarser, duller than Rooiberg's generally fine muscadels. 16.5% alc. **Vintage Port** ★★★ Pvs port was a Ruby; **03** enough acid/tannin to prop up the sugar but no real 'Vintage' structure or potential. **White Muscadel** discontinued. *—CT/TJ*

Roothman Wines see Jonkheer

Rose Garden Vineyards new

Paarl ▪ Est 1976 ▪ 1stB 2003 ▪ Visits by appt ▪ Cheese platters by appt; or BYO picnic ▪ Winemaker/viticulturist Hein Hesebeck (Jan 2004) ▪ 15 ha (pinotage, merlot, ruby cab, shiraz, chenin) ▪ 100 tons 8 000 cs own label 80% red 15% white 5% rosé ▪ PO Box 151 Wellington 7654 ▪ epstein@polka.co.za ▪ ***T 869·8211*** *▪ F 873·0871*

Shalom Epstein has vintning in the blood (his grandfather made wine in Romania for the French market) but for many years swam upstream as a liquor distributor in Botswana. Now here at last he's going with the family flow. 2004 saw him and Hein Hesebeck bottle the first Rose Garden vintage on the property, their 15 back-breaking hectares of bushvines (including 29 year old chenin) in the Windmeul area yielding 8 000 cases of wine. Some of which promptly swam cross-ocean to Brazil, Russia and the US.

Cabernet Sauvignon Reserve ★★ Rustic **03** with porty nose & sweet/sour palate, short. **Merlot** ★★★ Approachable & friendly (14.6% alc) **03** a braai-side sipper with green walnuts & ripe plumy fruit; soft & supple tannins for early drinking. **Pinotage** ★★★ Full ripe wild berry flavours coupled with strong tannins & bright acidity make this a wine with 3-5 yrs aging potential. Stewed fruit bouquet ideal match for hearty oxtail stew. Perfumed **Pinot Noir 04** ★★★ lacks varietal definition; sweet strawberry jam entry & dried peach goodbye. For early consumption. 15% alc. **Shiraz Reserve** ★★★★ Characterful **03** in the organic, earthy mould with mushroom/mud aromas; ripe, spicy berry palate from 16 mths new Fr oak. Bold & powerful with 'foxy' aromas. Drink up. **Shiraz** ★★ **03** Easy drinking with nuts/brambly fruit; dry, savory finish. **Maya's Red** ★★★ **03** Smooth, easy drinking ruby cab (81%) with splash shiraz. Attractive red cherry fruit, muted fruit tannins & enticing spicy top note. 14.5% alc goes unnoticed. **Shiraz Rosé Natural Sweet** ★ **05** sweetish (40g/ℓ) crowd pleaser with strawberry bouquet & palate, formidable 12.8% alc for the style. **Chardonnay Reserve 03** sample shows promising lime & toast/yeast aromas & flavours, interesting oxidative notes; finishes dry, body from 14 mths on lees in Fr oak. Could rate ★★★. **Chenin Blanc** ★★ **03**

mixes turpines/bottle age with pineapple & dried apricots. Palate initially fruity, buts fades fast. Mature. Drink soon. **05** sample not rated. — *CT*

Ross Gower Wines

Walker Bay ▪ Est 2003 ▪ 1stB 2004 ▪ Tasting & sales Mon-Fri 9-5 ▪ Closed pub hols ▪ Tours by appt ▪ Picnic baskets/light lunches by appt; or BYO ▪ Self-catering cottages ▪ Hiking ▪ Mountain biking ▪ Nature conservancy ▪ Owners Ross & Sally Gower/JM Family Trust ▪ Winemaker/viticulturist Ross Gower (Jun 2003) ▪ ±5 ha (shiraz, sauvignon) ▪ 1 500 cs 30% red 60% white 10% MCC ▪ PO Box 161 Elgin 7180 ▪ rossgower@worldonline.co.za ▪ ***T/F 844·0197***

'Things are progressing slowly.' says Ross Gower of his and wife Sally's own 'bare-hands' venture (a step beyond 'barefoot', he quips). 'We're doing everything ourselves, from throwing concrete to building walls.' Self-catering cottages and tasting room made visitor-ready (pre-booked picnics available), Gower turned his hand to building a 'rammed earth' cellar. This environment-friendly technique, picked up on a visit to Australia, provides natural insulation. Their first Cab from Elgin-sourced grapes is looking promising, as are 6 000 newly planted shiraz vines. The Gowers are delighted that their B Comm-graduate son Robert has joined the family business after a crash-course of four harvests in one year – here, in New Zealand, Burgundy and Germany.

★★★★ **Sauvignon Blanc Reserve** new **05** arresting. Not merely with lush fruit or tingling pyrazines, rather with breathtaking yet intricate power on palate. Elgin grapes crafted into refined grip; quintessential sauvignon without being overt. For food & (best) friends. 200 cs.

Shiraz new ★★★★ **04** perfumed tints to roast spice/pepper features, supple tannins ensure approachability in youth. Yr new Fr oak & 14% alc well integrated, don't jar. Stbosch grapes. **Sauvignon Blanc** new ★★★★ **05** unambiguous cool-climate Elgin offering loaded with asparagus, tinned-pea & bluegum character, not for the faint hearted, will attract followers. **Mankazana Sauvignon Blanc** ★★★ **05** nervy, grassy core lifts tropicality of Stbosch-fruited palate – for sun times & fun times within yr of harvest. — *DS*

Rotsvast see Baarsma
Route 101 see Du Preez Estate, Thirty-Two Degrees South
Route 303 see Ultra Liquors

Royle Family Vineyards

Paarl ▪ Est 2000 ▪ 1stB 2001 ▪ Closed to public ▪ Owner Noel Woods ▪ Vini consultant Ronell Wiid (2005) ▪ Viti consultant Paul Wallace (May 2000) ▪ 45 ha (cab, merlot, mourvèdre, pinotage, ruby cabernet, shiraz, viognier) ▪ 750 cs own label 100% ▪ PO Box 298 Klapmuts 7625 ▪ noelwoods@roylewines.com ▪ www.roylewines.com ▪ ***T/F 875·5363***

After an early tasting of his 2005 vintage, owner Noel Woods declared himself 'more than happy' with the first Royle wines produced by consultant Ronell Wiid – her predecessor Cathy Marshall having relinquished her post under pressure from other commitments. The other big event in harvest 2005 was the just-in-time baptism of the new cellar. 'This proved to be great fun,' chuckles Woods, 'but I'm glad we were dealing in relatively small volumes!' Next year, though, the expanded facility will have more to cope with.

Cabernet Sauvignon 03 Potential ★★★★; generous brambleberries, cassis whiffs followed by tart, savoury, focussed fruit & firm tannins. Clear cut flavours, smart oak detail, more sensible 14% alc than pvs. Needs ±3 yrs to show its true colours. 18 mths mainly Fr oak. **Syrah** ★★★★ **03** a step up on pvs, but same style: plum, choc, mocha, smoky roast beef nose. Soft, ripe tannin integrates harmoniously with rich beefy fruit. Elegant, showing promise. 13.5% alc. 10 mths mainly Fr oak. **Viognier** new Unrated **05** barrel sample showing delicate floral notes, ginger in bouquet; diffident fruit on palate. Elegant & attractive, on the right track. Only the first 450 ℓ/ton juice fermented/aged 6 mths old Fr oak. All above from Paarl fruit. — *IvH*

Rozendal

Stellenbosch ▪ 1stB 1983 ▪ Tasting, sales & tours by appt ▪ Luxury auberge with restaurant & amenities ▪ Conference facilities ▪ Walks ▪ Owners Kurt & Lyne Ammann ▪ Winemaker Kurt Ammann ▪ 6 ha (cabs s/f , merlot) ▪ 2-3 000 cs 100% red ▪ PO Box 160 Stellenbosch 7599 ▪ rozendal@mweb.co.za ▪ ***T 809·2621*** *▪ F 809·2640*

No update available on this winery and luxury auberge; contact details from previous edition.

Rozier Bay/Reef *see* Mount Rozier

Rudera Wines

Stellenbosch ▪ Est 1999 ▪ 1stB 2001 ▪ Closed to public ▪ Owners Teddy & Riana Hall ▪ Winemaker/viticulturist Teddy Hall ▪ 18 ha (cab, shiraz, chenin) ▪ 3 400 cs 45% red 50% white 5% NLH ▪ PO Box 2868 Somerset West 7129 ▪ info@rudera.co.za ▪ www.rudera.co.za ▪ ***T/F 852·1380***

Sidelined by a ruptured spinal disc, Teddy Hall had to hire another pair of hands to handle his 2005 crop. But this ever-positive lover of life greeted unseasonal late-harvest rain, resulting in widespread noble rot in his beloved chenin vineyards, as a big blessing – there had been no 2004 NLH. Besides the tiny amounts of powerful reds, his Rudera range, with three styles of chenin (a fourth finds expression under the new Teddy Hall label – see separate entry) is a textbook example of the extraordinary versatility of a variety once regarded as a commoner in the Cape. In ever-modest manner, Teddy H. describes his 2005 Chenin Blanc Challenge victory as 'nice'. Never mind that it was his fourth! (Previous wins were with Kanu).

★★★★☆ **Cabernet Sauvignon** Made in minuscule quantities (102 cs + a few 3ℓ bottles). **01** a beauty; cassis & black plums, sugared-violet nuances, richly oak-spiced. Beautifully balanced, well-served by firm yet ripe tannins. 8+ yrs to go. New Fr oak, 23 mths. 14.5% alc. *WS* 91. Maiden **00** excited international & local critics too: *Wine* ★★★★; MIWA gold. Off leased vyds in Stbosch, as are wines below. Like CWG wines, notes from last ed.

★★★★☆ **CWG Auction Reserve Cabernet Sauvignon B**ig, impressive, lots of depth in **02**; violets, lead pencils, wet heath nuances interplay with cassis core; cedar spice from oak (as for standard Cab). Supple, fine-grained tannins permit access, but will reward 8+ yrs cellaring. Unfiltered. 14.5% alc. Only 60 cs.

★★★★ **Syrah 03**, like its predecessor, bridges Old World & New: ripe plums, loganberries, big dollop of oak spice & an extra dimension of coffee grounds, woodsmoke. Elegant, already drinking well, but still an infant – has a 7-10 yr future. Unfiltered. 11 mths Fr barriques, 20% new. Dark-fruited **02** softly amenable, long creamy finish, also delicious in youth. 13.5% alc.

★★★★ **Chenin Blanc** From old bushvines, yielding small crops. **04** sleeker than pvs, with racy acidity (9g/l), an astonishing 3.02 pH, but no shortage of flavour, appetite appeal: peach & quince at core, with baked apple savouriness that sets it apart. Good 3-4 yr ageing potential. **03** voluptuous body (14% alc), mouthfilling intensity. *Wine* ★★★★. These native yeasts; 8 mths seasoned Fr barriques. 2

★★★★☆ **Robusto Chenin Blanc** 'Robust' but controlled, multiply gilded. Like scrumptious **02** (*Wine* ★★★★☆; Chenin Challenge Trophy), current **03** true to its name: a full flavoured, full bodied experience. Has honeyed botrytis, ripe pineapple & tropical fruit, but a savoury, almost meaty note makes it truly distinctive. Integrated oak adds texture to the dry-tasting 18g/ℓ sugar that is an integral part of this label's style. Easy 5-yr ageing potential. 8 mths Fr barriques, half new. Native yeasts. *Wine* ★★★★.

★★★★☆ **Chenin Blanc Noble Late Harvest** Hand-selected botrytised berries; 100% native yeast-fermented in new Fr barriques. Following in exalted footsteps of beautifully balanced, racy **03** (*WS* 92), comes **05** with its deep syrupy richness, nicely refreshed by 8 g/ℓ acidity, wide spectrum of flavours which include barleysugar, pineapple & a lemon zest piquancy. Complex, complete & irresistible. 140g/ℓ sugar. 12% alc.

★★★★☆ **CWG Auction Reserve Chenin Blanc Noble Late Harvest** Natural-yeast ferment in new Fr barriques for maiden **03** (tasted last yr). Concentration, complexity, balance:

sumptuous aromas assailing the nose, mouthfilling honeyed sweetness tempered by bracing acidity. Good 5+ yr cellaring potential. 132g/ℓ sugar; 12.5% alc. — *CR*

Rudi Schultz Wines

Stellenbosch ▪ Est/1stB 2002 ▪ Closed to public ▪ Owner/winemaker Rudi Schultz ▪ Viticulturist Dirkie Morkel ▪ 800 cs 100% red ▪ rudi@thelema.co.za ▪ ***T 082·928·1841***

Thelema winemaker Rudi Shultz makes this own-label wine at Thelema, from grapes sourced in Stellenbosch's Bottelary area. Here, Schultz feels, the slightly higher harvest temperatures yield a more full-bodied style. US *Wine Spectator* called it 'a gorgeous, modern-styled syrah' with a 'massive core' of fruit, and awarded the 2002 a massive 93 points (2nd highest ever for an SA wine). Most of the 100 cases go to America, where they are sold through select New York wine shops and Disney's Africa-themed Jiko restaurant. Self-effacing Rudi S, who maintains modest pricing for his current Syrah-only portfolio, hopes to add a Viognier and Rhône-styled blend, but production will in any case remain limited.

★★★★ **Syrah** Hand-crafted cult wine in rich but classical style. Standout **04** (★★★★★) heady white pepper, nutmeg, ground cassia notes, great focus & follow-through to sumptuously spiced yet restrained palate (notwithstanding 14.5% alc, 14 mths oak, 50% new), excellent persistence. Worthy successor to aromatic, succulent & fruit-driven **03**. Both less oaky & more refined than maiden **02**, all from Bottlry fruit. — *MF*

Ruiters see Fairseat Cellars

Ruitersvlei Wines

Paarl ▪ Est 1692 ▪ 1stB 1995 ▪ Tasting & sales Mon-Fri 9-5 Sat 9-3 Sun 11-3 ▪ Fee R10 (incl glass) ▪ Closed Easter Fri, Dec 25 & Jan 1 ▪ Italian-style lunches Tue-Sun 10-5; evenings by appt ▪ Tours by appt ▪ Farm produce ▪ Facilities for children ▪ Tourgroups ▪ Gifts ▪ Reception/ conference venue ▪ Conservation area ▪ Owner John Faure ▪ Winemaker Reino Kruger, with Jaco van Niekerk (Jan 2004/Dec 2004) ▪ Viticulturist Kobus Mostert (Nov 2001) ▪ 289 ha (cab, merlot, pinotage, shiraz, chard, chenin, sauvignon) ▪ 1 400 tons 50 000 cs own labels 70% red 29% white 1% rosé ▪ Export brand: Rider's Valley ▪ Ranges for customers: Vaughan Johnson, Steven Rom, Millers Thumb Restaurant & Casa do Mar ▪ PO Box 532 Suider-Paarl 7624 ▪ Sales@ruitersvlei.co.za ▪ www.ruitersvlei.co.za ▪ ***T 863·1517*** *▪ F 863·1443*

Reino Kruger, a diver and fisherman, is also determined to make his mark as a winemaker. He is convinced that only the strongest producers with strategies adapted to the meet the highly competitive world markets, among others, over-delivering on quality at reduced prices, will succeed. Lessons learned from the latest challenging harvest, which saw the drought and heat reduce volumes by between 10% and 30%, have resulted in new drip irrigation in dryland vineyard blocks and improved cooling machinery. He is excited by the potential of new members of his team: assistant winemaker, Jaco van Niekerk, and being a man of the sea, the best catch of Reino's life … his fiancé, Sheryl, daughter of Ruitersvlei owner, John Faure!

Reserve range

Cabernet Sauvignon Concentrated, delicious & easy to drink. **04** barrel sample seems firmer than pvs, but has ripe mul/cranberry fruit to match. Promising ★★★★. **Merlot** ★★★ **04** delicate & charming (rather than 'Rsv' quality); fresh herbs & dark berried fruits; soft tannins & unusually big acid (7g/ℓ). Yr Fr oak, 2nd-3rd fill. **Shiraz** new House's signature soft, fleshy fruit, though white pepper-tinged **04** sample suggests more class than range-mates, firmer, bigger concentration. Minimum ★★★★ on release. 2nd-3rd fill Fr oak. **Chardonnay** new 100% new Fr oak, 5 mths. Preview **05** too young to rate; full-flavoured (though only 13% alc), ripe citrus fruit & touch butterscotch, looking good. **Four Sisters MCC** ★★★ Brut sparkling from pinot, chardonnay, briefly bottle-aged; latest **NV** (02 vintage — 58/42 ratio) tasted prior to *dosage* pvs ed (final RS 7.5g/ℓ); creamy mousse, zingy lemon flavours, clean firm finish. **Port** ★★★ Ruby-style **NV**, varieties undisclosed; fortified with 3-10 yr old brandy spirit. Gorgeous pristine fruit; soft, juicy, not over-sweet; approachable as per style.

Ruitersvlei range

Cabernet Sauvignon ★★★ Shows some of variety's structure; **04** firm fleshy fruit, minty whiff; should soften to suppleness over next yr/2. 6 mths Fr staves. **Pinotage** ★★★ 'Fruit-driven for early consumption' winemaker's mantra **04** indeed discreetly oaked; redcurrant aroma, lively berry fruit, asks to be enjoyed in vibrant youth. **Shiraz** ★★★ **04** (pvs ed a sample) charming & appealing; youthful melange red/black & cherry fruit, touches roast beef/mocha; brush of oak rounding things off. Fr/Am staves, 4 mths. **Cabernet Sauvignon-Merlot** ★★★ Early-approachable 55/45 mix; cool cedar & meaty whiff; **04** (bottled – pvs ed a sample) balanced & satisfying. Unwooded. **Chenin Blanc** ★★ **05** delicate aromas; slender tropical fruit; light, clean & fresh. **Sauvignon Blanc** ★★ **05** (sample) boiled sweet aroma, tangy, dry, light fruit/body (12.7% alc).

Mountainside range

Red ★★ Unwooded merlot (44%) & 4 other varieties, sans usual smoothing grain sugar – & all better for it; **04** touch herbaceous; soft, easily quaffable. **Pink** new ★★ Pinotage gives the fuchsia pink colour; **05** light, sweet & soft, with boiled sweet flavours. **White** ★★ Colombard/sauvignon blend in **05**, semi-dry, light & delicately fruity. **Gold** ★★ new **05** similar to White but semi-sweet. – *CT*

Rupert & Rothschild Vignerons

Simondium (see Paarl map) ▪ Est 1997 ▪ 1stB 1998 ▪ Visits only by appt Mon-Fri 9-4.30 ▪ Fee R5/wine ▪ Closed Easter Fri-Sun, Dec 25 & Jan 1 ▪ Owners Rupert family & Baron Benjamin de Rothschild ▪ Winemaker Schalk-Willem Joubert (Jun 1997), with Clive Radloff & Yvonne Schröder (Jun 1997/Sep 2001) ▪ Viticulturist Renier Theron (Oct 2003) ▪ 90 ha (cab, merlot, chard) ▪ 500 tons 35 000 cs 95% red 5% white ▪ ISO 14001 certified; HACCP accreditation in progress ▪ PO Box 412 Franschhoek Valley 7690 ▪ info@rupert-rothschildvignerons.com ▪ www.rupert-rothschildvignerons.com ▪ ***T 874·1648*** *▪ F 874·1802*

The discreet public persona of this classy collaboration between two powerful family dynasties, the French Rothschilds (represented by Baron Benjamin de R) and the South African Ruperts (headed by second-generation Johann) may lead fans to believe R&R hides its light under a bushel. Young cellarmaster Schalk-Willem Joubert (another of the talented offspring of Barrydale's Joubert-Tradauw family) stays in sync with a calmly assured mien. 'Good terroir and attention to detail – precise viti- and viniculture – are the key to exceptional wines.' These usually are. Vintage 2005 was one of the best ever for merlot, pronounces S-W, who dealt with a Stellenbosch harvest nine days earlier and a Darling crop 22 days later than usual. A new cool-room now helps ensure prime fruit condition before destemming.

★★★★☆ **Baron Edmond** Opulent, ageworthy flagship, though **02** (★★★☆, not retasted) lacks gravitas of **01**. Same 66/34 cab s/merlot blend; solid ruby, oak nicely paced with light, fleshy feel, uncomplicated plummy, toffee sweetness; touch short, green. 15% alc. **01** had sound structure, fruit richness for evolution over next 3-7 yrs. Stbosch, Darling, Paarl, Dbnville vyds. 80% native yeast-fermented. 19 mths new Fr oak.

★★★★☆ **Baroness Nadine** Grand, complex chardonnay in classic style. **03** tasted last yr promisingly elegant; skilfully oak-enhanced fresh peach/roast nut character; creamy, rich; polished length. Likely 4-5 yr maturation. 80% fermented/yr Fr oak, third new. Simonsberg, Gr Drknstn, W Bay vyds. **02** first to show slightly fruitier, livelier approach.

Classique ★★★☆ Blend merlot (55% giving meaty note) & cab in elegantly structured **03**. Sweet fruit, solid core of smooth ripe tannin, dry finish. Accessible now, but no hurry. – *TJ*

Rustenberg Wines

Stellenbosch ▪ Est 1682 ▪ 1stB 1892 ▪ Tasting & sales Mon-Fri 9-4.30 Sat 10-1.30 Sat 10-3.30 (Dec/Jan) ▪ Closed Easter Fri, Dec 25, Jan 1 ▪ Farm-style cheeses ▪ Owner Simon Barlow ▪ Winemaker Adi Badenhorst, with Randolph Christians (Dec 1999/Oct 1995) ▪ Viticulturist Nico Walters (Nov 1999) ▪ 150 ha (cabs s/f, merlot, shiraz, chard, sauvignon, viognier) ▪ 900 *tons 55 000 cs 70% red 30% white ▪ PO Box 33 Stellenbosch 7599 ▪ wine@rustenberg.co.za ▪ www.rustenberg.co.za ▪ **T 809·1200** ▪ F 809·1219*

A dry winter and regulated stress levels in the vineyards (and presumably also in the cellar?) produced sought-after small berries, mitigating the challenges of an early and concentrated 2005 harvest for winemaking duo Adi Badenhorst and Randolph Christians. Rustenberg's viognier vines are now in full production and 'look spectacular', Adi B enthuses. Most of the grapes go into Brampton Viognier, though a portion has been used for spicing up the Rhône-styled Brampton Shiraz (which had its maiden vintage lauded at the Decanter World Wine Awards). Meanwhile involvement with a Stellenbosch non-governmental organisation helps prepare local women for jobs in the wine industry. And Simon Barlow's younger son, Murray (seen mucking out the calf pens in a recent Rustenberg newsletter), is learning that a career in the family business begins on the lowest rung. Talking straw, a recent tussle with authorities turned out to be 'The Last Straw' in a name change for what the team consider a superior *vin de paille*-style dessert wine.

Single Vineyard range

★★★★✰ **Peter Barlow** All-cab flagship as handsome as its venerable Smnsberg origin. Meticulous focus from grape (individually tagged bunches, stringent 3-pass harvest) to cellar (20 mths Fr barrels, 70% new, unfiltered). **03** boldly ripe; sultry cassis lurks under grainy tannin cloak mid-2005, sweet finish somehow keeps 15.5% alc at bay. **02** also bold, strong (15% alc): ripe blackberry fruit restrained from ungainly opulence by fine tannins. FCTWS gold. **01** riveting intensity, grand structure. 92 pts *WS*, as was **99** (★★★★★) among Cape's best, *Decanter* ★★★★★. No **00**: mountain fires singed vyd. Deserves cellaring up to 10 yrs.

★★★★ **Five Soldiers** Five stone pines guard the vyd, confer the moniker on this singular indulged chardonnay. **03** fuller, bigger; oak & fruit more obvious without losing individuality. **02** grew into a beauty of nuanced complexity. **01** mineral-rich palate. 91 pts *WS*. Natural fermentation in now all new Fr oak, 16 mths, full malo.

Regional range

★★★★✰ **Stellenbosch John X Merriman** Fine bdx-style red from 24 parcels of fruit, 20 mths Fr oak, 60% new. Latest **03** more modern than pvs; ripe, meaty, full-fruited, sweet tail. **02** (★★★★) oozed plump mulberries in ripe structure, not as elegant as **01**, 91 pts *WS*. 52:42 cab/merlot with splashes cab f, petit v. 15% alc.

★★★★ **Stellenbosch Chardonnay** Firm & ripe, a leader in its quality echelon. **04** treads middle road: not overt, not lean, rather elegant, fresh lemon/lime fillip in tail. **03** more oaky; apricot/almond depth in mineral chassis. Native yeast ferment/yr Fr oak, 40% new.

★★★★✰ **The Last Straw** Bought-in chenin wizened into raisiny sweetness on straw beds before yr-long barrel-fermentation with natural yeasts. **03** (★★★★) drier (relatively! – 300g/ℓ sugar), stronger (10% alc) but yard off electric pace of **02** (breathtaking ±400g/ℓ sugar, 6.5% alc). Similar styling: jasmine/tangerine-scents, explosive depth to dried apricot/mango flavours. 375ml. Release of both still to be decided.

Roussanne new Rare-in-SA white grape; **04** unrated preview quiet mid-2005, peanut brittle/orange pith interest to otherwise athletic palate, round finish. Unoaked but full (14.5% alc). **Brut** ★★★✰ MCC sparkling nicely pitched for conviviality, celebration. Languid bead, brioche nose, generous mousse with black-grape texture; 2/1 chardonnay/pinot; 11.5% alc. **NV**.

Brampton range

★★★★ **QF** Weighty NLH appears intermittently when nature affords good botrytis, which not since **00** (QF2), FCTWS trophy, from sauvignon; original **97** (QF1) ex chardonnay. Pvsly sampled **01** (QF3) not released, rerouted to Natural Sweet below.

Cabernet Sauvignon new ★★★ Provisionally rated sample **04** awkward marriage ripe blackcurrant fruit & exuberant Am oak (80% new); huge tannins, ends trifle coarse (14.5% alc). **Shiraz** ★★★✰ ('Shiraz-Viognier' pvs ed) Viognier (2%) edged out by mourvèdre (8%) in latest **04**; less perfumed than **03** (SAA) but tastes as 'purple' as the label flash! Bursting black cherry, warm clove, good tannic purchase on palate. 15 mths oak, 30% Am, 15% alc. **Old Vines Red** ★★★✰

Paarl, Darling grapes in **04** add red berry flesh; fuller, not as linear as wild-heather stamped & comparatively rustic pvs. Retains grip; altogether more interesting in newer format. **Unoaked Chardonnay** ★★★ **05** clever arrangement: oatmeal girth, richness (souped up with lees of pvs yr's Rustenberg sibling) drawn together by citrus tang. Fuller than the genre. **Sauvignon Blanc** ★★★ **05** leesy breadth of generous tropical fruit basket held together by fresh reductive zing. **Viognier** ★★★☆ Hip & happening, a wine to convert the in-crowd from their alcopops. **05** crammed with peach pip tang, boosted by oak, all rifled into focused order by electric acid seam. Great fun. 15.5% alc. Following **NV**s not retasted: **Natural Sweet** ★★★☆ Copper-toned with juicy apricot, fleshy peach, honeycomb flavours. Natural cask-fermented sauvignon, 190g/ℓ sugar, 13.5% alc. **Port** ★★★ Drier style from melange Portuguese varieties evoked images of smoking jackets (both cigar leaf and paisley), ended touch hard mid-2004.—*DS*

Rust en Vrede Estate

Stellenbosch ▪ Est 1694 ▪ 1stB 1979 ▪ Tasting & sales Mon-Fri 9-5 Sat: 9-5 Oct-Apr; 9-4 May-Sep; pub hols 9-4 ▪ Closed Easter Fri/Sat, Dec 16/25 & Jan 1 ▪ Gifts ▪ Walks ▪ Owner Jannie Engelbrecht Trust ▪ Winemaker Ettienne Malan (2005) ▪ Viticulturist Wessel Combrink (Jun 1998) ▪ 50 ha (cab, merlot, shiraz) ▪ ±350 tons 20 000 cs 100% red ▪ PO Box 473 Stellenbosch 7599 ▪ info@rustenvrede.com ▪ www.rustenvrede.com ▪ ***T 881·3881*** *▪ F 881·3000*

Former Springbok fly half Jannie Engelbrecht, who from 1978 transformed this 17th-century estate into a front-rank red-wine house, again wears the captain's jersey (son Jean now leading the Ernie Els and Guardian Peak packs). Into the winemaker slot comes former assistant Ettienne Malan, charged with maintaining the sort of quality that has garnered a Top 100 Wines of the World accolade (for the Estate Wine) from US *Wine Spectator* for four consecutive years. Daughter Angeline E, a qualified lawyer who 'understands the company and industry', lines up as general manager. Seasoned viticulturist Wessel Combrink remains in position, clearly an advantage given their conviction that 'it is the vineyards where the quality comes from'. Capacity is being increased, the cellar renovated and a new maturation hall built. 'Quality at all cost!' is the new haka.

★★★★★ **Estate Wine** Considered by many as an icon & one of SA's most prestigious reds, a reputation steadily built since mid-90s. Current **02** (★★★★) not quite in same league, though sensitively blended (58/33/9 cab/shiraz/merlot) to underplay difficult vintage & form homogenous whole. Similar truffle touch as Cab below, plus dark berries, usual understatement; light texture, pleasantly silky entry, just about enough concentration to hold prominent acid at bay. Will require careful monitoring to prevent over-ageing. **01** seamless fusion cab/shiraz/merlot (53/35/12), its richness sheathed in dense tannin. Usually 20 mths new Fr/Am oak. ±14% alc. These need ± 8–10 yrs. Also in magnum. Among numerous awards: **01** 91 pts WS; *Wine* ★★★★; **00** *Wine* ★★★★☆; 92 pts *WS*; FCTWS 2003 trophy.

★★★★☆ **Shiraz** Variety long associated with this Hldrberg estate. Since **00** has benefited from new-clone input. Current **02** (★★★☆) difficult yr. Fairly forward aromas of well-hung game, mushrooms; well-managed tannins but noticeable acid lends sweet/sour finish. Best consumed by 2007, while waiting for fine, understated **01**, with authoritative structure inviting ageing until 2007/10. 15 mths new Fr/Am oak effortlessly absorbed.

★★★★☆ **Cabernet Sauvignon 02** (★★★☆) yr that disfavoured this late-ripening variety, even with benefit of clean vine material. Quiet, rather truffly nose, open, sweetish palate. Pleasant enough, if short-lived. Drink by 2007 & before compact yet supple **01**. 18 mths new 300ℓ Fr oak.

★★★★ **Merlot** Consistently offers admirable breadth of flavour/texture with stylish restraint. Sample **04** sonorous dark choc/plum aromas, classy new oak augmentation. Similar contrasting ripe/fresh feel as in elegant, velvety **03**, delivered with more impact, concentration. Should sustain delicious drinkability for 5/6 yrs.—*AL*

Rusthof see Mooiuitsig

Rusticus Vintage Cellar

Robertson ▪ Est 2001 ▪ 1stB 2002 ▪ Tasting & sales Tue-Fri 9–4 Sat 10–2 Mon by appt ▪ Closed Easter Fri & Dec 25 ▪ Tours on request ▪ BYO picnic ▪ Self-catering cottages & guest houses ▪ Tourgroups ▪ Gifts ▪ Conferences ▪ Walks/hikes ▪ Game drives & conservation area ▪ 4x4 trail ▪ Owner Pat Busch Winemaker/viticulturist Stephan Busch ▪ 200 tons total, max 2 000 cs own label ▪ PO Box 579 Robertson 6705 ▪ patbusch@intekom.co.za ▪ www.patbusch.co.za ▪ ***T (023) 626·2033*** *F (023) 626·1277*

Last year Pat Busch relinquished the reins to youngest son Stephan, who, despite 'strange weather patterns', relished the new challenge, thanks in part to the help of winemaker friend Wade Metzer (Signal Hill). While the wines will remain hand-crafted and vinified using vintage machinery (the cellar is a living museum – 'worth visiting'), Busch Jnr has made a few changes and the 2005 vintage may prove to be quite different from previous. He plans to produce a first-class red blend in future but is being kept rather busy: the 2 000ha property includes a game reserve – now featuring new luxury self-catering cottages, and game drives by new ranger Willem Barnard.

Cabernet Sauvignon ★★★ Swashbuckling but well polished **03**; as pvs, displays port-like concentration of blackberry & choc flavours, masking the vast 16% alc. Combo Fr/Am wood. **Merlot** ★★★ Super-ripe **03** still in stock; massively fruited, intense plum character, expansive palate dominated by potent 15.5% alc. **Pinot Noir** ★★★ **03** last ed showed cherry aromas & intense berry flavours; unobtrusive older oak only. Next (**05**) not ready. **Pinotage** ★★★ Last ed, 02 reported as 03; the real **03** steps forward with varietally atypical cassis aroma, sweet impression (from massive 15.8% alc) not quite cushioning big dusty tannins. **Ruby Cabernet** ★☆ Robust **02** still current; gamey whiffs, chunky palate, 14.3% alc. **Shiraz** ★ **03** similar porty/jammy notes as pvs, rustic & unrefined, whereas ... **Shiraz Limited Release** new ★★☆ Shows some sophistication & typicity; **04** smoky bramble notes, full-ripe flavours, supple tannins; potential for development. 14 mths oak, mix new Fr, 2nd fill Am/Fr. All these WO Klaasvoogds. – *DH/MM/MF*

Sadie Family *see* he Sadie Family
Safeway *see* Daschbosch
Safiki *see* Goudini

Saltare

new

Stellenbosch ▪ Est/1stB 2003 ▪ Closed to public ▪ Owners Christoff & Carla Pauw ▪ Winemaker Carla Pauw ▪ 15 tons ▪ 250 cs ▪ 50% red 30% white 20% MCC ▪ PO Box 2290 Dennesig, Stellenbosch 7601 ▪ cpauw@mail.com ▪ ***T 883·9568***

Anura winemaker Carla Pauw felt it was time to make her own wines, starting with her beloved bubbly. In 2003, she invited some friends to help pick a ton of chardonnay and pinot: 'It was a joyous affair, we danced in the basket press' (and inspired the young venture's name). Next vintage she made a Syrah (her favourite red grape); next is a Chenin, instigated by a recent trip to the Loire.

★★★★ **Cap Classique Brut** Old-gold-tinted **03** from chard (60%) & pinot. Full-flavoured, full-bodied, rich & yeasty, with lingering flavours marmite & spicy baked apple; lively, dry. Old-oak barrel fermented. WO Smnsberg-Paarl, like Syrah below.

Syrah ★★★★ Only 25 cs of **04**. Ultra-ripe, fruity & slightly porty aromas/flavours; big 15% alc, but not brash, with bright acidity & lovely smooth tannins. Fermented old oak; 18 mths 2nd-fill Fr. – *TJ*

Sanctum Wines

Stellenbosch ▪ Est/1stB 2002 ▪ Closed to public ▪ Owners Mike & Alice Dobrovic ▪ Winemaker Mike Dobrovic ▪ 3.2 tons 240 cs 100% red ▪ PO Box 11 Koelenhof 7605 ▪ info@sanctumwines.com ▪ www.sanctumwines.com ▪ ***T 865·2483/082·882·2488*** *▪ F 865·2302*

Currently Stellenbosch-based Mike and Alice Dobrovic have joined the Elgin land-grab with the purchase of 16ha on this cool plateau. In the same breath as describing it as a farm 'for our retirement', he talks of embarking on planting (red and white) while sending out an appeal for any winemaking equipment that might be going begging! Tongue in cheek perhaps – this from a man who says he cultivates a different perspective on winemaking by occasionally standing on his head in the cellar. Above all, the guiding principle of the Elgin venture will be 'Keep things simple, small and fun'. This Mulderbosch winemaker's own-label Shiraz goes from strength to strength – his 2002 scored an impressive 92 in *Wine Spectator*.

★★★☆ **Shiraz** 'Most exceptional red-wine harvest ever', says Dobrovic of **03** (★★★★), from young Stanford vyds. Fresh, elegant, great savoury intensity; same oaking as pvs (18 mths new Fr barriques) complements pure spice/smoked meat aromas. Maiden **02** (incl Stbosch fruit) showed more obvious wood, tannins, needing time. 92 pts *WS*. Both WO W Cape. – *AL*

Sandy River see Zandvliet

Saronsberg Cellar

*Tulbagh ▪ Est 2002 ▪ 1stB 2004 ▪ Tasting & sales Mon-Fri 8.30-5 Sat 9-1 ▪ Closed Easter Fri-Mon, Dec 25/26 & Jan 1 ▪ BYO picnic ▪ Tours by appt ▪ Owner Saronsberg Cellar (Pty) Ltd ▪ Winemaker Dewaldt Heyns (Oct 2003) ▪ Viticulturist JP Dippenaar ▪ 27 ha (cab, grenache, malbec, merlot, mourvèdre, petit v, shiraz, viognier, chard, sauvignon) ▪ 65% red 35% white ▪ PO Box 361 Tulbagh 6820 ▪ info@saronsberg.com ▪ www.saronsberg.com ▪ **T (023) 230·0707** ▪ F (023) 230·0709*

Dewaldt Heyns is one happy man. Shiraz and shiraz-blends have always been a passion and Tulbagh, home of Saronsberg, looks highly promising. Vintage 2005 delivered a combination of blockbuster and less flamboyant wines, making blending a joy. Heyns has handed the 40 hectares of individually sited and managed blocks (all just 1ha in size) over to JP Dippenaar, who's also tending a motherblock of grenache (for the shiraz blend, of course), small pockets of chenin and semillon (for a straw wine) and some ancient muscadel (for a dessert). Leaving a still happy Heyns 'to get on with establishing Saronsberg as one of SA's top labels for generations to come, long after all of us have moved on to greener – or cloudier! – pastures.'

★★★★ **Full Circle** (Pvsly 'Epicentre') Powerful Rhône-style blend driven by shiraz, dollops mourvèdre & viognier (14%/5%) for 'feminine nuance', says Dewaldt H. **04** quite amazing complexity – black pepper, lavender, lilies, smoked bacon. Concentration & intense fruit masks 15% alc; 'take note' tannins provide structure for cellaring ±5-7 yrs. 16 mths 100% Fr oak.

★★★★ **Shiraz** Approachable, well-oaked & downright delicious **04**, pervasive & juicy red berry/black plum tone spiced up by soupçon (5%) mourvèdre, malbec, viognier. So delightfully fresh, almost an 'easy drinker' – but plenty gravitas. Mainly Fr oak, large % burgundian barrels ('better suited to our fruit').

★★★★ **Sauvignon Blanc** Serious wine, deserving of intellectual contemplation. Herbaceous & racy **04** maiden followed by slightly more tropical **05**, mirroring warmer vintage. Cleverly maintains pithy, zingy uplift via shorter lees contact; moderate alc & zesty grapefruit smack on finish.

Seismic ★★★☆ 'Bordeaux Blend' in pvs ed. Not quite earth-shattering perhaps, but ripe with promise. **04** claret-style red powered by cab. Very rich cassis/red berry fruit, whiffs lead pencil & Mochacino; tight, focused tannins needing probably 2 yrs to properly mesh. Charry touch from 100% new Fr barriques. **Chardonnay** new ★★★☆ Poised **04** with restrained oak; buttery, lemon/lime bouquet & creamy lime finish. Fermented/matured new Fr oak, 6 mths on lees. Extra zing from suppressed malo portion. **Muscat de Frontignan** new ★★★☆ 'Elixir to alleviate joint-numbing Tulbagh cold,' says Heyns. **05** fortified dessert with powerful muscat/nut character, delightful floral & apricot notes. Very sweet (209g/ℓ) but not unctuous. – *CvZ*

Savanha

*1stB 1997 ▪ Tasting, sales & tours at Spier ▪ Owner Winecorp ▪ Winemakers/viticulturists: see Winecorp ▪ 300 ha ▪ 200 000 cs 65% red 35% white ▪ ISO 9001 certified ▪ PO Box 99 Lynedoch 7600 ▪ winecorp@iafrica.com ▪ www.winecorp.co.za ▪ **T 881·3690** ▪ F 881·3699*

This Winecorp-owned label features fruit grown by contracted growers mainly in the Paarl and Darling areas and vinified at Winecorp's Spier cellar in Stellenbosch. The wines are now marketed in two ranges: premium and reserve, the latter for export only. Varietal reds – cab, merlot, shiraz – are usually a strong point.

Naledi Cabernet Sauvignon, **Sejana Merlot** in temporary abeyance. **Sulanga range** discontinued

Savanha (Premium) range

★★★★ **Merlot** Stylistic change, as part of brand realignment: **04** (★★★) lighter, easier drinking than pvs. Sweetly ripe plummy fruit, some briefly oaked. Enjoy within 2 yrs. **03** sold out before we could taste; followed rich, complex **02**. This & rest of range WO W-Cape.

Cabernet Sauvignon ★★★☆ Sinewy **04**, with 10% cab f, more athletic than red siblings; lovely cassis & spice layers, touch of mint; built for 4+ yr future. Lightly oaked, as is ... **Shiraz** ★★★ **04** back to **01**'s simpler styling: fruit the pleasure-giving hero, juicy & smooth, no hard edges. Flavour spectrum includes peppery nuances. With a touch cab. **Sauvignon Blanc** ★★★ Tasty, early-drinking **05** (sample) less concentration than pvs. Textbook gooseberry, green fig character; medium weight, refreshing palate. **Chardonnay** new ★★★ Flavourful quaffing style, with enough lemon peel/buttered toast depth in **04** to hold interest & satisfy. Small portion oaked.

Reserve range new

All WO Coastal; all ★★★☆; reds all **04**. **Cabernet Sauvignon** No shortage of fruit: intense cassis/cherries, overlaid with creamy vanilla spicing. Good length. These reds all with structure to age 3+ yrs. 8 mths oak, some new. **Merlot** Seductively perfumed, an array of red berries, candied violets. Svelte, accessible palate doesn't disappoint either. **Shiraz** Captures variety's essence – luscious dark fruit, smoky, well spiced, even fynbos notes. Sleek structure, firm but ripe tannins. **Sauvignon Blanc 05** delivers same fruit concentration as rest of this agreeable range: here passionfruit, litchi, supported by citric raciness. Great food partner. – *CR*

Savisa see African Terroir
Saw Edge Peak see Conradie Family

Saxenburg

Stellenbosch ▪ Est 1693 ▪ 1stB 1990 ▪ Tasting & sales Mon-Fri 9-5 Sat 9-4 Sun 10-4 (closed Sun-Tue in winter) Pub hols 10-4 (closed Easter Fri, Dec 25 & Jan 1) ▪ Fee R3-6 ▪ Guinea Fowl Restaurant & 'Lapa' (see Eat-out section) ▪ Farm produce ▪ Conferencing ▪ Miniature game park ▪ Owners Adrian & Birgit Bührer ▪ Winemaker Nico van der Merwe, with Edwin Grace (Nov 1990/Jan 2005) ▪ Viticulturist Len Coetzee (Jun 2001) ▪ 85 ha (cab, merlot, pinotage, shiraz, chard, chenin, sauvignon) ▪ 440 tons 50 000 cs 80% red 20% white ▪ Export brand: Bosman's Hill ▪ PO Box 171 Kuils River 7580 ▪ info@saxenburg.com ▪ www.saxenburg.com ▪ ***T 903·6113*** *▪ F 903·3129*

'Fifteen years in one job!' exclaims Nico van der Merwe, whose consistent success at Saxenburg means he doesn't have much time for winemakers who think overnight success entitles them to criticise their peers in public. 'It seems that some cannot handle their upliftment from zero to hero,' he comments wryly. But there's no resting on laurels here – in fact, quality looks set to continue improving, now that 100% of the grapes are farmed on the property. What's more, NvdM even has a solution for wines with high alcohol levels, such as those resulting from warm conditions in 2005: to use more American oak, whose richness 'harmonises with the very full ripe style of wine at present'. Something else new – following last year's successful launch of Guinea Fowl Red, look out for the equivalent 'serious but affordable' white blend of viognier and old-vine chenin.

Saxenberg Limited Release

★★★★★ **Saxenburg Shiraz Select** Pricey showpiece deserving 7-10 yrs' bottle-ageing. **01** firm, elegant, with perfectly ripe tannins. **02** seductive combination plush velvet &

fragrant vanilla bean, milk choc. Careful selection: grapes from choice section of 2 vyds, only free-run juice, best barrels chosen after maturation. New oak, 50/50 Fr/Am, 14 mths. Watch 15% alc.

Private Collection range

★★★★ **Cabernet Sauvignon** Elegant & generous **01** was first from all-home fruit. **02** packed with ripe mulberry, touches of delicate mulberry leaf, compact neat profile, profusion of ripe dark berries, smooth velvety tannins & enviable dry finish. Mid-2005 already approachable, but will repay cellaring. Yr Fr oak, 40% new. 14% alc. **00** *Wine* ★★★★.

★★★★ **Merlot 01** was quieter than pvs, but juicy with yielding tannins. **02** stylish aromas/flavours cassis & choc cherry fruit balanced by fine-grained tannins. Charming 'feminine' version with serene dark fruit, almost ready for drinking. Yr Fr casks, 30% new.

★★★★ **Pinotage** Already approachable **02** (★★★☆) shows signs of lesser vintage. Unlike charming **01** with fresh raspberry tones, this back to savoury style: beefy, biltong aromas matched by savoury meaty flavours, rather nice & chewy. Tannins manageable, good dry finish. Yr oak, 50/50 Am/Fr, 30% new.

★★★★☆ **Shiraz** Consistently & famously excellent. From difficult vintage, **02** (★★★☆) less exciting. Good ripe fruit marred by awkward tannins, but attractive spice, plum flavours; earthiness on finish. 50/50 Fr/Am oak, third new; 14.5% alc. Complex **01**, beautifully judged ripe tannins; *Wine* ★★★★☆. **93,96** both *WS* 90.

★★★★ **Chardonnay** After fat, rich, boldly flavoured **03**, quieter than usual **04** (★★★☆), but dried peaches & butterscotch, creamy caramel flavours, soft acidity, lots of oak showing (yr Fr, 20% new). 100% malo. Firmer acidity would aid focus & style – but always sells out, so why quibble?

★★★★ **Sauvignon Blanc Reserve** new **05** (sample) interesting contrast with version below. Where this has length, that has breadth, where this is Loire-ish, that is New World. Loads of tangy green peppers & ripe fig, excellent concentration of ripe figgy flavours, racy acidity; lip-smacking, almost breathtaking finish. A real show-off. 'The best of three vineyards,' says vdM.

★★★★ **Sauvignon Blanc 05** (sample) melange of passionfruit, grapefruit, gooseberry – against top notes of grass, capsicum. Plump & fleshy, big 14% alc, with firm acidity, mouth-watering. Picked 'when the vineyard seems to be ready, instead of waiting for full ripeness', says vdM. **04** friendly, charming tropical tones.

Le Phantom Brut Cap Classique ★★★ From 60/40 pinot/chard; last **NV** (96) tasted yrs back. **Le Rêve de Saxenbourg Natural Sweet** ★★☆ dusty, light-textured **NV** dessert from sauvignon, chenin; not retasted this ed.

Guinea Fowl range

Red (Last ed's sample called 'Guinea Fowl') ★★★ Deep mulberry fruit in ripe **03** blend shiraz, cab, merlot. In uncomplicated friendly style with slight grippiness on tail, lightly oaked. **White** new ★★★ **05** blends chenin (86%) & Wllngtn viognier, combines elegance with power, flavours white peach, marzipan. Just off-dry, aged in Am oak for extra oomph; 14.6% alc not obvious. Could grow in bottle.

Selection famille

These, only available from farm, not retasted this ed. Range named after Bührer children, completed by Ch Capion wines (so not tasted here): **Appollonia** (white blend), **Fiona** & **Adrianus** (both red).

★★★★ **Gwendolyn 01** blends 60/40 shiraz/cab for med-bodied mouthful, softly gathered by tannins, with warm spice, choc notes.

Manuel ★★★☆ After juicy **99**, Gear-up **00** (★★★★) unites cab (65%) & merlot: minty cassis, firm tannins.

Concept range

Two ★★★ **NV** wines, latest not tasted. Last **Grand Vin Rouge** was easy, fruity quaffer from range of reds, some ex-Capion. **Grand Vin Blanc** Fresh & rich; 50/50 home chenin, Capion chard. *– IvH*

Scali

Paarl ▪ Est/1st 1999 ▪ Visits by appt ▪ Olive oil ▪ B&B guest accommodation ▪ Owners/winemakers Willie & Tánia de Waal ▪ Viticulturist Willie de Waal ▪ 70 ha (cab, merlot, pinotage, shiraz, chardonnay, chenin, sauvignon, viognier) 910 cs 100% red ▪ PO Box 7143 Noorder-Paarl 7623 ▪ info@scali.co.za ▪ www.scali.co.za ▪ ***T 869·8340*** *▪ F 869·8383*

Mentors, movers and shakers behind the Voor Paardeberg ward's emerging reputation for ripping new reds, Willie and Tania de Waal were delighted to release their 2003 vintage under its new Wine of Origin designation. Almost as thrilled as they were to be selected as an SA representative in a tasting, showcasing five top red-wine cellars from key wine-producing countries at London's International Wine & Spirits Fair. With Scali now in full production (the name a play on the Afrikaans word for 'shale'), the De Waals are concentrating on upping value-adding quality. On a more personal note: 'We plan to keep the romantic side of winemaking – and wine farming – alive and well.'

★★★★ **Pinotage 03** (★★★★) atypical flavours (perhaps due to 13% cab), somewhat woody mid-2005 (yr oak, 50% new, 5% Am) but pleasing; lots of complexity lurking. Step up from **02**, fruity, well structured & balanced.

★★★★ **Syrah 03** (★★★★★) a standout shiraz; spectacular complex nose, exciting wild flavours holding expensive wood (2 yrs Fr, 50% new) & huge 15% alc in thrilling balance. Turns up volume on **02**, bursting with red fruit & spice; obviously deft use of wood. — *NP*

Scarborough see Cape Point Vineyards

Schalkenbosch Wines

Tulbagh ▪ Est 1792 ▪ 1stB 2002 ▪ Tasting & sales daily 9.30–4.30 ▪ Closed Dec 25/26 & Jan 1 ▪ Tours, meals & accommodation (B&B or self-catering) by appt ▪ Tourgroups ▪ Walks ▪ Conservation area ▪ Mountain biking ▪ Owner Platinum Mile Investments ▪ Winemaker Johan Delport (Jan 2005) ▪ Viti consultants Johan Wiese & Andrew Teubes ▪ 35 ha (cab s/f, merlot, mourvèdre, petit v, shiraz, chard, sauvignon, viognier) ▪ 100 tons 7 500 cs 80% red 20% white ▪ PO Box 95 Tulbagh 6820 ▪ info@schalkenbosch.co.za ▪ www.schalkenbosch.co.za ▪ ***T (023) 230·0654*** *▪ F (023) 230·0422*

Still in that enviable position: Sold Out. But plans to increase capacity and market locally (currently everything is exported to Germany and Sweden) are now well underway. By the end of the year a new red-wine cellar (working on gravity) and a new barrel-maturation cellar should be completed; by 2008 the current 120-tonne capacity should be running at 400. Last year was also the maiden vintage of the quietly confident Johan Delport (ex-Citrusdal Cellars), who says that dealing with co-op politics was distracting him from his true purpose in life – 'to make really good wines that are affordable to everybody'.

Edenhof range

Cabernet Sauvignon Barrel sample **04** dominated by new oak, too young to rate. Currently 14.5% alc. From Tulbagh fruit, yr Fr oak, 50% new shows is a style change. Pvs vintages only aged in older wood, have achieved ★★★★. **Shiraz** ★★★ Impressive **04** differs from pvs, rosé-like quaffers. Blackberry/savoury nose; dry, tad alcoholic palate (14.4%). Empathetic oaking – yr 2nd fill Fr – allows fruit to shine. **Cabernet Sauvignon-Merlot** Unfinished **04** not rated. Pvs received ★★. **Glen Rosa** ★★ From merlot/cab f/cab in 64/26/10 bend. New oak dominating **04**, too unkit to rate. **'Rhône-style Blend'** NEW Still to be named **04**, led by grenache & shiraz (43/33), dollop mourvèdre (**05** fruit)/cinsaut (± 10% each) & 2% splash cab. Not rated. **Sauvignon Blanc** ★★★ Similar tropical characters as pvs, acid more pronounced in **05**. Both ranges WO W Cape. **Merlot, Blanc de Blanc** discontinued.

Ibis range

Dry Red ☺ ★★☆ Cinsaut (45%) dominates unwooded 04 blend, this yr with ruby cab & merlot vs pvs cabs s & f. Fruity, fresh & firm. 13.3% alc. A favourite in Sweden as is ... **Dry White** ☺ ★★☆ **04** 74/19/7 blend of the blancs with dash hanepoot. Floral & lively, balanced, sensible 12% alc. **Rosé** ☺ ★★★☆ **03** delicious blend chenin, sauvignon, shiraz. Dry but not tart, ample texture & length. Moderate 12.7% alc helps make for lovely lunchtime drinking. **04**, not tasted by us, was selected for the Tri-Nations Taste-Off; **05** not ready for tasting. Above in 1ℓ bottles. — *MM*

Scholtzenhof see Ken Forrester

Schoonberg

Upper Langkloof ▪ Est 1999 ▪ 1stB 2002 ▪ Visits by appt ▪ Walks ▪ Mountain biking ▪ 4x4 trail ▪ Owner Morné Jonker ▪ 17 ha (cab) ▪ 200 cs 100% red ▪ PO Box 689 Oudtshoorn 6620 ▪ morné@schoonberg.co.za ▪ www.schoonberg.co.za ▪ ***T (044) 888·1707*** *▪ F (044) 203·3715*

No update available on this winery; contact details from previous edition.

Schoone Gevel see La Motte

Sedgwick's Old Brown Sherry

The original SA 'old brown' (launched 1886), & still the fisherman's friend (portion of sales go to long-running WWF-SA Fish Tagging Project). By Distell. NV blend jerepiko & dry sherry, from two muscats & chenin. Latest bottling ★★☆ redolent of raisins, prunes, coffee & malt. Clean, warm farewell. 16.8% alc. WO W Cape. — *CvZ*

Seidelberg Estate

Paarl ▪ Est 1692 ▪ 1stB 1989 ▪ Tasting & sales Mon-Fri 9-6 Sat/Sun & pub hols 10-6 ▪ Fee R10 ▪ Closed Dec 25 ▪ Tours daily (by appt for groups of 5+) ▪ De Leuwen Jagt Restaurant (see Eat-out section) ▪ Play area for children ▪ Farm produce ▪ Conferences/functions ▪ Tourgroups ▪ Gifts ▪ Walks ▪ Hiking trail ▪ Conservation area ▪ Tractor rides ▪ Bronze casting studio (with live demonstrations) ▪ Owner Roland Seidel ▪ Winemaker Cerina de Jongh (Jun 2002) ▪ Viticulturist Conré Groenewald (Nov 1999) ▪ 110 ha (cabs s/f, merlot, pinotage, shiraz, chard, chenin, sauvignon, viognier) ▪ ±500 tons ▪ 40 000 cs 70% red 20% white 10% rosé ▪ PO Box 505 Suider-Paarl 7624 ▪ info@seidelberg.co.za ▪ www.seidelberg.co.za ▪ ***T 863·5200*** *▪ F 863·3797*

Winning nine medals at the 2005 Michelangelo Awards was a feather in owner Roland Seidel's cap, and 'proof that the quality is increasing across the range'. Which is itself increasing, with the planting of malbec, mourvèdre and more viognier vines. Harvesting of the whites last time round was in 20kg baskets instead of bins, resulting in less oxidation and better flavour retention. A tweak in the cellar saw the installation of a conveyor sorter, allowing for better fruit selection. A new attraction on this supremely visitor-friendly estate is bronze-casting, bound to prove as popular as the glass-blowers in their open-to-view studio and the cuisine in the recommendable restaurant.

Roland's Reserve range

★★★★ **Merlot** Back to form & broad-shouldered style of **99**, **00**, with latest **03**; minty touch to lively, appealing medley of wild fruits, some jammy sweetness, choc thrown in for extra richness; seamless & delicious now & over few yrs. 16 mths Fr oak, 2nd-4th fill.

★★★★ **Syrah** Continues showy 'overripe' style of **02** in **03** (★★★☆), but without seriousness & structure for higher rating; almost quaffably soft; savoury meatiness to palate with sweet vanilla layers from 30% Am oak (18 mths, 2nd-4th fill). Fans will love, & should probably open before flamboyant, aromatic **02**.

★★★★ **Pinotage** Fast forward to **03**, textbook pinotage: cacophony of wild berry & banana, varnishy whiff; nicely synched oak (as for Syrah), impeccable tannins — not a jarring note. Must be enjoyed young while at wonderfully OTT best. Pvs tasted was **01**, pleasantly youthful with 3-4 yrs development potential.

Cabernet Sauvignon ★★★★ **04** less muscular than pvs (14% alc vs 15); attractive cedar tone to compôte of wild berries & cassis; sweet tannins hold potential for some development.

Seidelberg range

★★★★ **Un Deux Trois** ✓ Still the undisputed ruler of this roost; characterfully rustic bdx-style blend cab, merlot, cab f (58/31/11) in **02**, now barrelled (16 mths, mainly Fr wood) – pvsly oak-staved. Again the expensive cedarwood whiff (& 'lowly' farmyard sniffs too); bigger than pvs (14.3%) but retains **01**'s laudable grace & harmony.

Following reds mainly Fr oak-staved: **Cabernet Sauvignon** ★★★ **03** less refined than pvs; over-ripe raisin tone with hot (14% alc), dry savoury finish. Incl 5% 04 merlot. **Merlot** ★★★ **03** green walnut & ripe wild berry character, fairly soft & harmonious; earlier drinking style. **Pinotage** ★★ **04** very different to pvs; old-style aromas, dry, tannic, rustic. Demands time or food. 20% Am oak. **Shiraz** ★★★ Like pvs, **03** a wine on steroids: powerful, flashy; lots of zest & olfactory entertainment (incl bluegum, pepper, smoky meat). **Cabernet Sauvignon-Merlot** ★★★ Unwooded **03** 53/47 blend, cassis fruit & dry leaf hint; big pressy tannins suggest food rather than standalone drinking. **Rosé** ★ Dry this yr, again from red muscadel; **05** curiously tannic & firm, clashes with delicate floral fruit. **Chardonnay** ★★★★ Combo barrel/stave fermentation for **04**; well-crafted & harmonious; lemon butter & citrus leesiness impart classic flavour/structure. **Chenin Blanc** ★★★ Off oldest producing vyd on estate; **05** medium-bodied, Granny Smith apple tone, taut acidity invites food. **Sauvignon Blanc** ★★ **05** incl super-early-picked fraction (18°B), therefore lightish & austere; capsicum whiff; not the juicy easy-drinker we enjoyed last yr. **Viognier** ★★★ 2nd taste of **04** (pvsly a sample): much more subdued, shows little of the opulence & fruit we admired. Partly bunch-pressed; 30% 2nd fill Fr oak.

De Leuwen Jagt range

Mainly unwooded. **Cabernet Sauvignon** ★★★ **03** leesy/stalky character with touch cassis, balanced but firm-fleshed; a winter-sport supporter's red. **Merlot** ★★ **04** repeats the usual leafy character on nose, palate much more wiry than pvs; demands (rather than invites) food. **Pinotage** ★★ Dappled (rather than pvs vintage's bottled) sunshine in less ripe/juicy **04**; candyfloss aroma, wild fruit flavour, tastes taut & dry despite 6.1g/ℓ sugar. 2 mths oak chips, 20% Am. **Shiraz** ★★★ **03**, with dollop cab, continues middle-of-road style; honest, gently firm bramble flavours, medium-full body (14.2% alc). **Cabernet Franc-Merlot** ★★★ Less exuberant partnership in **04**, cab f's stalky minerality upfront, sturdy long-term tannins. **Leuwenrood** ★★★ Switches to straight cab in **03**; old-style nutty tones, pleasant, nostalgic, lightish; for rainy winter afternoons. **Rosé** ★★ Quaffable salmon-pink semi-dry **04** from own cab, Brde Rvr Vlly white muscadel; delightful berry/flower aroma, delicate strawberry palate. **Chardonnay** ★★ Unwooded **05** shy on nose yet quite effusive on palate; ripe fruit zested with clean lemon acidity. **Sauvignon Blanc-Chenin Blanc** new ★★★ Soft, fruity **05** lively mouthfeel, well-polished for easy sippability. Screwcap. **Leuwenblanc** ★★ Chenin from Rville. **05** cheerful pineapple flavour, satisfying pre-lunch glassful. **Nuance** ★★★ **05** fragrant semi-dry tipple from muscadel & crouchen. Potpourri nose, well-balanced acidity, fresh finish. **Stein** ★★ Light, charming white; **04** muscat, honey & raisin fragrances, creamy off-dry flavours. **Red Muscadel** ★★★ **NV** fortified dessert with developed tawny colour, raisin & treacle aromas, not too sweet. 17.4% alc. Some above NE; WO Paarl, W Cape. – *CT*

Semaya see Jonkheer
Sénga see MAN Vintners

Sentinel Vineyards

Stellenbosch ▪ 1stB 1995 ▪ Tasting & sales Mon-Fri & pub hols 9-4.30 Sat/ Sun 9-4 ▪ Fee R5 ▪ Closed Easter Fri, Dec 25 & Jan 1 ▪ Light meals Mon-Fri 10-4 Sat/Sun 9.30-4, or BYO picnic ▪ Facilities for children ▪ Conferences & functions ▪ Display of military artefacts ▪ Owners Rob Coppoolse, Walter Finlayson & Viv Grater ▪ Cellarmaster Jean-Claude Martin ▪ Winemakers Adele Dunbar & Danielle du Toit (Aug 1998/Apr 2002) ▪ Viti consultant Johan Pienaar (2001) ▪

23 ha ▪ 20 000 cs 75% red 25% white ▪ ISO 9001:2000, HACCP & BRC certified ▪ PO Box 4028 Old Oak 7537 ▪ wine@sentinel.co.za ▪ www.cfwines.co.za ▪ ***T 982·6175*** *▪ F 982·6296*

Winemaker Adele Dunbar, unlike most of her colleagues, had a relaxing 2005 harvest. A new sorting table made an 'unbelievable difference', both to the quality of grapes entering the cellar and to the morale of the sorting team. Vinification currently takes place at sister winery, Coppoolse Finlayson. The vineyards, nearer Stellenbosch town, are now managed by Johan Pretorius. Chardonnay has been established, and sauvignon, shiraz, merlot, cabs sauvignon and franc, mourvèdre and nebbiolo will follow. Overlooking the property is the castellated HQ-cum-tasting area, replete with a collection of antique muzzle-loading cannons (in good working order, too). A guesthouse is next up for attention, along with an upmarket restaurant to complement the function hall, which now accommodates up to 300 guests.

★★★★ **Shiraz 03** (tasted last ed) in established style of spicy, savoury fruit, wisp cigar smoke; broad expansive flavours – black plum, roast beef & dark choc richness, oak submerged (10 mths Am). Firm, yet approachable on release with potential to grow. **04** unready for tasting. **02** (★★★★☆) gold at FCTWS.

★★★★ **Pinotage** Seductive (& enormous alc) **03** loved by 2004 FCTWS & Top Ten judges. **04** (sample) also promises to deliver the 'Wow!' factor. Thrilling Satsuma plum, red cherry, vanilla pod intro; sweetly fleshy initially on palate, then good acid, dry tannins take over – to let you know this is serious, as well as a show-off. 10 mths oak.

★★★★ **Chardonnay** Lusty, delightful **03** tasted as sample. Very New Worldish **04** (★★★☆) shows ripe citrus, caramel; creamy texture with fleshy, lime-tinged flavours, slight sweetness on finish. 9 mths oak.

Cabernet Sauvignon ★★★☆ **02** (like Merlot not retasted) smooth ripe mulberry, touch of mint; supportive oak adding firmish tannins, dry finish. 14.8% alc. **Merlot** ★★★☆ **03**, slathered in dark choc, succulently ripe, slightly spicy. Yr+ Fr oak. 14.2% alc. **Sauvignon Blanc** ★★★ Sample **05** with all the right flavours from tropical spectrum: lime, passionfruit, grapefruit, against background of grass, fig. Juicy sweet/sour fruit interplay, though dry. **Cape Snort** ★★☆ Name grunts cellar's displeasure with EU banning of name 'port'. Last was **99** less sweet, alc a modest 17. 4%. Next may be NV; unavailable mid-2005. – *IvH*

Sequillo Cellars

new

Swartland ▪ Est/1stB 2003 ▪ Visits/amenities by appt only ▪ Owners Tymen Bouma & Eben Sadie ▪ Winemakers Eben & Niko Sadie ▪ 4 000 cs 100% red ▪ PO Box 1019 Malmesbury 7299 ▪ info@sequillo.com ▪ www.sequillo.com ▪ ***T 869·8349/875·5360*** *▪ F 875·5657*

Peripatetic Eben Sadie (sometimes in Priorat, sometimes in his beloved Paardeberg) pops up again, bringing typical dramatic poetry and passion to a collaboration with Anura's Tymen Bouma: Thinking sideways from the Sadie Family Columella and Palladius, Sequillo is his take on a southern Rhône wine made from Swartland grapes. His belief in the suitability of southern European varieties in the Cape's Mediterranean climate, best expressed in blends, is unshakeable. And, as in all his vinous adventures, Sadie remains committed to viticultural biodiversity (natural balance in unirrigated vineyards) and a basically peasant style of winemaking (cold soaks, *pigeage*, natural fermentation, traditional basket press, no fining/ filtration, gradual blending in of components).

Sequillo ★★★☆ **03** from Paardeberg (Swartland) fruit, blending 63% shiraz, 30% mourvèdre, 7% grenache, à la southern Rhône. Warm baked plum whiff hints at sweetness but, instead, nice savoury dry flavours with touch of earthiness on finish. Supple, ripe tannins. 18 mths in 500ℓ Fr barrels. No-nonsense workmanlike label. – *IvH*

Serengeti see Leidersburg
Seven Falls see Southern Cape Vineyards

Seven Oaks

new

Worcester ▪ Est 2003 ▪ 1stB 2004 ▪ Closed to public ▪ Owner Farmacres 27 (Pty) Ltd ▪ Vini consultant Francois Agenbag (Romansrivier) ▪ Viticulturist Danie Visser (Mar 2003) ▪ 26 ha (cab, cinsaut, pinotage, ruby cab, shiraz, chenin, sauvignon) ▪ 345 tons total 574 cs own label ▪

Brands for customers: Villa Verde & United Bulk ▪ *PO Box 11 Breerivier 6858* ▪ *jacqui@sevenoaks.co.za* ▪ *www.sevenoaks.co.za* ▪ ***T 083·639·0405***

Co-owner Jacqui Pols says she is well aware of the challenges of launching yet another boutique brand in a crowded market, particularly as this is not Seven Oak's primary focus: the vast bulk of the harvest goes to Waboomsrivier. Best, she believes, to keep it small, handing over only carefully selected parcels to winemaker Francois Agenbag of Romansrivier for vinification. The maiden vintage (04) was distributed mainly to restaurants nationwide.

Cabernet Sauvignon-Shiraz Reserve '6+1' ★★★ Welcoming vanilla /brambleberry intro to **04**, a rather unreserved Rsv – soft, silky & ready for immediate enjoyment. New Fr/Am oak 10 mths. **Cabernet Sauvignon-Shiraz** ★★★ Appealing easy-drinking style; **04** oak chipped, so wooding not as fine as above, but who's quibbling? Plenty of spicy red fruit to enjoy. Chenin Blanc ★★★ 05 super end-of-day glass – soothing, well-made & flavourful. All WO Brde Rvr Vlly. *– CT*

Shaka see Coppoolse Finlayson, Vinus Via
Shamwari see Omnia Wines
Shatot see Slaley
Shepherd's Creek see Clos Malverne
Sherwood-Berriman see High Constantia
Shibula see Freedom Hill

Ship Sherry

Not 'sherry', but a jerepigo-style fortified from two muscats & chenin. By Distell. Latest (**NV**) ★★ spirituous, raisiny, finishes with a firm, savoury, grip; warm goodbye from 16.8% alc. *– CvZ*

Shoprite Checkers

National wine-buyer Stephanus Eksteen ▪ *30 000 cs 60% red 35% white 5% rosé* ▪ *PO Box 215 Brackenfell 7561* ▪ *seksteen@shoprite.co.za* ▪ *www.shoprite.co.za* ▪ ***T 980·4000*** ▪ *F 980·4012*

A panel of winemakers, wine experts and consumers meets regularly under the aegis of national wine-buyer Stephanus Eksteen to select these well-priced in-house ranges for the nationwide retail chains Shoprite and Checkers.

Oak Ridge range

Cabernet Sauvignon ★★★ **03** still selling, not retasted; lightish bodied but shows variety's strong structure/tannins, mellowed somewhat by vanilla oak. **Merlot** ★★★ **02** still on shelves; last ed noted as jovial, with roly-poly profile matched by sweet ripe tannins. Should hold 2–3 yrs. Following samples too young/unformed to rate: **Cabernet Sauvignon-Merlot-Cabernet Franc 03** austere & tight, green walnut whiffs & mouth-clucking tannins. **Pinotage 04** robust, rustic, demandingly tannic. **Shiraz** ★★★ Honest to goodness *vin rouge*; **03** effortlessly drinkable mulberry fruit with leather/bluegum whiffs, balanced spicy tannins.

Oddbins range

Limited editions sourced directly from estates & private cellars; bin numbers change as batches are replaced by new lots.

Cabernet Sauvignon Bin 179 ★★ Medium-bodied **01** a food wine rather than standalone tipple, as was pvs; dusty dried-leaf character, dry stalky tannins. 2 yrs Fr oak. **Cabernet Sauvignon Bin 205** ★★ Second Cab in line-up dominated by massive stalky tannins, **00** will need 3–5 yrs to soften or decanting well in advance of serving. **Merlot Bin 196** ★★ Very soft commercial-style **04**, hints treacle & raisin, almost tannin-free. WO Brde Rvr Vlly. **Pinotage Bin 175** ★★ **01** well-matured, lighter-textured red with savoury/spicy undertone, just the thing for boerewors rolls. **Merlot Rosé Bin 198** ★★ Poolside quaffer with delicate strawberry fruit, **05** light & off-dry. **Chardonnay Bin 185** ★★ Soft, blowsy **04**, pear-drop flavours & lactic/oaky hints; burly 14.5% alc. W Cape origin. **Chenin Blanc Bin 192** ★★ Paarl fruit in **05**, with slight vegetal hint & easy, soft flavours. **Sauvignon Blanc Bin 202** ★★★ Lively &

racy **04**; nose of green grass & sundry vegetation; as pvs, on outer limit of dry (4.5g/ℓ), which lengthens the invigorating aftertaste. Both ranges WO Stbosch unless noted. – *CT*

Signal Hill

Cape Town ▪ Est/1stB 1997 ▪ Phone for opening hours ▪ Owners Ridon Family Vineyards ▪ Winemaker Jean-Vincent Ridon (1997), with Khulekani Laurence Buthelezi & Wade Metzer (1998/2005) ▪ Viticulturist Marietjie Marais (1997) ▪ 5 ha (cab, malbec, merlot, shiraz, pinot, muscat d'A) ▪ 45 tons ±3 000 cs ▪ 70% red 27% white 3% rosé ▪ PO Box 12481 Mill Street Cape Town 8010 ▪ info@winery.co.za ▪ www.winery.co.za ▪ ***T 461·9590*** *▪ F 465·0342*

'The French are always late; it's like a religion for us,' laughs Jean-Vincent Ridon, explaining his habitually late submission of wines for tasting. But he was quick off the mark in securing the bid for Cape Town's first inner-city winery at Mandela Rhodes Place, a R1-billion mixed-use development not far from J-VR's own 'city vineyard', Clos d'Oranje, in Oranjezicht. Expected to be up and running in time for the current harvest, the winery will be in Church Street, just a few metres from where the first vines were planted in SA. 'Visitors will be able to see the complete winemaking process before a wine tasting or a light meal.' Associate winemaker Laurence Buthelezi will also produce his Tutuka wines here.

★★★★ **Malbec** Cock-a-hoop **04**, previewed last ed, bulging sweet-and-sour cherry flavour, introduced by exotic bouquet of incense & vanilla. Zingy raspberry acidity, persistent fynbos finish. WO Smnsberg-Paarl. *Vive la Difference!* exclaims front label, accurately.

★★★★ **Petit Verdot 03** similar to pvs **01** (no **02**): seductive bouquet dark plums, scrub & fragrant toffee oak. Palate still tight, firm, tannins keeping fruit in check. Has structure to improve ±4–7 yrs.

★★★★ **Malwenn** From pinotage, off Paarl, Smnsberg vyds. **04** (★★★★) retasted/rated (sample last yr), shows pinot-like earthy tones, cinsaut strawberry & smoke; zesty cranberry palate. Tannins, alc in check. **03** sold out untasted by us. Yr Fr oak, 20% new.

★★★★ **Vin de l'Empereur** Natural Sweet from muscat d'A vyd on Smnsberg. Assertive **04** has choc hint to ripe apricot aromas & flavours; intense, slippery palate, clean exit. Arresting **03** (★★★★★) had 10% botrytis, boosting flavour & citrus acidity.

★★★★ **Crème de Tête Muscat d'Alexandrie NLH** Barrel-fermented & yr *sur lie*. Hedonistic **03** liberally touched by apricots (from botrytis), raisin, toffee & burnt sugar flavours. Silky, thanks to near-perfect sugar/acid balance (225/7g/ℓ). Probably best young. ±10% alc. No **01**; **02** untasted, but *Wine* ★★★★★.

★★★★ **Antica MM** From cab, **00** made with minimal intervention to express the essence of mature Smnsberg bushvine fruit. No new vintages of this, the following four wines, all tasted last yr. J-VR promises revival of all but Climat Chardonnay.

★★★★ **Climat de Corsaire Chardonnay 03** (★★★★) orange/lime, creamy flavours undimmed by exuberant alc (14.5%), caramel oak. No **02**. **01** firm, complex & limy finish. Bunch-pressed, fermented in Fr oak, 30% new.

★★★★ **Vin de Glacière** Extraordinary 'assisted icewine' – muscat d'A grapes coldroom-chilled to super-concentrate flavours. None since balanced, tangy **00**.

★★★★ **Mathilde Aszú 6 Puttonyos** Characterful orange-tawny Tokaji lookalike, again a Cape first. Botrytised Swtlnd furmint, Smnsberg sauvignon. MIWA DG; 91 pts *WS*. **02** long & racy, thanks to sugar/acid balance (185/14g/ℓ).

Pinot Noir ★★★★ Preview **05** shows classic pinot components in place: vibrant cherry, gripping fruit acidity, savoury/chalky tannins. Lighter in style than most. **Argile Rouge** Merlot from Smnsberg treated to 'Pomerol winemaking' (read: micro-oxygenation, lees lie-in). **02**, *still* a work-in-progress. Now savoury with slight high tones, even more choc/plum fruit; on track for ★★★★. **Clos de l'Oranje** new **05** first crop from tiny 'city vyd' in Cape Town, just 2 barrels of shiraz; modern, intense, brooding with dark fruit, mint & scrub, fine & focused tannins. Early sample tasted – potential high scorer. **Rosé de Saignée** ★★★ Possibly SA's first rosé from petit v (ex-Stbosch). Herbs & raspberries, **03** delightfully dry, firmer, thanks to fermentation in 3rd fill Fr oak. Ideal *charcuterie* accomplice. No **04**; **05** not available for tasting. **Viognier** new **05** unfinished sample too young to rate; heady fragrance of peach, nuts, almond blossom. As above, no new vintages of the following in sight: **Grand Rouge de**

Constance ★★★☆ Winter warming red, **02** mostly from Constia pontac, tinta & soupçon cab f. 18 mths older 500ℓ vats. 14% alc. **Tête Blanche** ★★★☆ Partly-oaked chenin, from selected low-yield Smnsberg, Plkadraai vyds. **03** melon & lemon fruit augmented with floral notes, cleansing lemon acidity. **Straw Wine** ★★★☆ Unknown field blend (possibly chardonnay, chenin, riesling), air-dried on straw mats as traditional *vin de paille* style demands. Only **01** so far, with nutty, sherry-like notes. 250g/ℓ sugar. Arduous, two yr fermentation, yielding just 10% alc. **Grenache** in this range discontinued.

La Siesta range

★★★★ **Grenache Blanc** Claims to be SA's first varietal bottling. Sample **05** similar to maiden **03** with dusty lemon blossom nose, almond & peach palate with rousing lime-rich acidity (7.5g/ℓ), juicy-fruit finish.

Grenache ★★★☆ **03** continues in southern Fr style: spicy red berry fruit, whiff lavender, chorizo sausage; friendly tannins & refreshing dry acidity. Fermented, aged in 20% new Fr wood. – *CvZ*

Signature Series see Jean Daneel
Signatures see Doolhof Estate
Signum see Rooiberg
Silver Myn see Zorgvliet
Silver Sands see Robertson Wide River
Simonay see Simonsvlei International

Simonsig Family Vineyards

*Stellenbosch ▪ Est 1953 ▪ 1stB 1968 ▪ Tasting & sales Mon-Fri 8.30-5 Sat 8.30-4 ▪ Fee R7/R10 (incl glass) ▪ Closed Easter Fri, Dec 25 & Jan 1 ▪ Tours Mon-Fri 10 & 3 Sat 10 (min 5; booking essential for groups) ▪ BYO picnic ▪ Play area for children ▪ Tourgroups by appt ▪ Walking trail ▪ Owners Malan brothers ▪ Winemaker Johan Malan (1981), with Van Zyl du Toit & Debbie Burden (Dec 97/Nov 99) ▪ Viticulturist Francois Malan (1980), with Ludwig Uys & Martin Farao, advised by Johan Pienaar & Di Davidson ▪ 205 ha (cab, merlot, pinotage, shiraz, chard, chenin, sauvignon) ▪ 2 000 tons 46% red 38% white 17% MCC ▪ HACCP certification in progress ▪ PO Box 6 Koelenhof 7605 ▪ wine@simonsig.co.za ▪ www.simonsig.co.za ▪ **T 888·4900** ▪ F 888·4909*

No wonder shiraz is Johan Malan's favourite variety. Not only does it help keep Simonsig in medals, but it also won him a trip to France (and enough to keep him in wine and bread while there). Cellar cat 'MD' – named for his occupation of the boss's chair whenever it's free – isn't the only one up-and-coming at Simonsig: assistant winemaker Debbie Burden claimed the SA Woman Winemaker of the Year 2005 title. Despite scoring his 25th vintage, Johan is still learning, bringing back from his travels an appreciation of what he calls 'immediacy' in wine, and a keener appreciation of the importance of a 'Cape Blend'. With a different kind of harvest in mind, the farm donated a classroom building to the neighbouring school, and have expanded their visitors' attractions with a 'grape variety garden' and 'vineyard labyrinth' walk.

★★★★ **Frans Malan** Stylish' Cape blend' tribute to visionary patriarch. Equal pinotage, cab, + 10% merlot in **03**. Most tightly structured of reds, but beguilingly perfumed, flavoured: wild berries, provençal herbs, campfire smoke. Firm tannins, more approachable in yr, will support long life, 10+ yrs. 16 mths Am/Fr 69/31, 80% new. **02** boldly flavoured, with juicy accessibility, but really designed for longer development. *Wine* ★★★★, *WS* 90 pts.

★★★★ **Tiara** Excellent bdx-style blend. **03**'s cab (87%), merlot partnership shows expected cassis dominance; is given extra dimension by oak's cedar, spice infusion. Elegantly structured with firm but ripe tannins, will easily hold 7+ yrs. 15 mths mainly Fr oak, touch Am, 60% new. **02** (71% cab, some cab f, petit v adding interest); bold 15.3% alc, but wine's depth, structure handles it. VDG.

★★★★☆ **Merindol Syrah** Frequently garlanded wine from single vyd in lighter sandy loam soils, specially groomed. In very classy **03**, seductive lush red fruit, roast vegetables, smoky spice aromas, taste sensations hide its true power, a sleek, fine-grained tannin structure allowing it to age effortlessly for 6+ yrs. 16 mths new Fr oak. 15.3% alc, cloaked by fruit concentration. Ultra ripe **02** with plush, velvet fruit punctuated by sinewy tannins from 16 mths new Fr/Am (68/32) barriques; tempting in youth. FCTWS, IWSC golds. **01** FCTWS trophy winner, VDG, MIWA double-gold, Shiraz Challenge winner.

★★★★☆ **Shiraz CWG Auction Reserve 03** (sample) marvellous complexity, dark fruit core with wafts prosciutto, campfire smoke, Karoo scrub, contributions from oak & terroir. Elegant with sheathed power; still coming together, has 7+ yr pleasure in store. 20 mths equal Fr/Am, all new. Single vyd. 15% alc masked by fruit.

★★★★☆ **Redhill Pinotage** From 40+ yr old bushvine vyd 'Rooibult'. Individual, modern, admirable **03** has pinotage's juicy mulberry/brambleberry fruit density perfectly partnering the serious oaking (18 mths new Fr, touch Am), exemplary concentration. Cigar-box, savoury layers already there, will deepen over next 6+ yrs. *Wine* ★★★★. **02** intensely perfumed, flavoured, benefiting by savoury overlay, lithe musculature. FCTWS gold.

★★★★ **Gewürztraminer** ✓ Frequent awards to this SLH (not labelled as such). Following pvs vintages' pattern, **05** fragrant & refined, good varietal expression; infused with rose-petal, softly sweet (28g/ℓ sugar) without losing any delicacy. Long, aromatic finish. Only 11% alc.

★★★★ **CWG Auction Reserve Valentine Viognier** NEW Name inspired by pressing date – 14 February. Gorgeous **04**, even in pre-bottling sample (so rating tentative), has lush peachy fruit, acacia flower fragrance, unblanched almond nuances. Voluptuous, textured richness aided by 7g/ℓ sugar, yet finishes fresh. Native yeasts; yr Fr barrels. WO Coastal.

★★★★ **Chenin Avec Chêne** NEW **04** (sample; rating provisional) impressive example of well-oaked chenin keeping its own personality; fruit in abundance, pears, melon, with creamy biscuit overlay. Full flavoured, nicely rounded (7g/ℓ sugar) & already delicious. Yr Fr oak, half new.

★★★★ **Cuvée Royale** Prestige sparkling in exceptional yrs. Last **96** (50/50 chard/pinot) proved ageability of good bubbly.

★★★★ **Kaapse Vonkel** ✓ SA's first bottle-fermented bubbly, over 30 yrs back. Chard/pinot noir, rare dash of pinot meunier. Following exuberantly zesty **03**, latest **04** same classy mould as predecessors: chalky, lemon-drop & biscuit tones, fine mousse, exceptional length. Dash oak adds complexity. 49/47/4 blend. Clean, fresh & very sophisticated. 12.2% alc. **01** Cap Classique Challenge ★★★★, VG. Also in magnum, 3ℓ, 9ℓ.

★★★★ **Encore** ✓ Off-dry sec-style MCC, with 3 yrs bottle-age evident in pronounced bready richness on maiden **00** (not retasted), tangy sweet-sour citrus; brisk acidity giving drier finish than 22g/ℓ sugar suggests. 12.3% alc.

★★★★☆ **Vin de Liza** Outstanding, elegantly presented NLH, honouring family matriarch. Concentration abounds on **04**; jasmine, dried peaches, botrytis honeycomb element, hardly subdued by 7 mths oak; but silky refinement, structural balance (74g/ℓ sugar, 7.2g/ℓ acid) impresses most. Gorgeous to drink. Semillon/chenin in almost equal parts. Step-up, irresistible **03** had evident botrytis; generous oaking (10 mths, 45% new). *Wine* ★★★★.

Chenin Blanc ☺ ★★★ Always eminently drinkable, **05** even better: more vibrant, tastier than pvs. Bursts with freshness, pears, crunchy Golden Delicious apples; palate-lengthening 6.9g/ℓ sugar offset by crisp acidity.

Cabernet Sauvignon ★★★★ **02** vibrant & muscular, with lovely deep cassis/cherry fruit, sweetly vanilla-spiced. Tannins already accessible but serious enough for 5+ yrs. 21 mths Am/Fr seasoned oak. **Pinotage** ★★★★ Steady performer stays resolutely unwooded. Smoothly appealing **03** had rhubarb & brambleberry typicity, arresting fruit-dominant body, long tasty finish, & 14.9% alc. Not retasted, nor was ... **Shiraz** ★★★★ Trademark campfire notes in **02**, spicy dark fruit, creamy texture. Integrated ripe tannins deliver accessibility but will continue to please 4+ yrs. Mainly seasoned barrels, 17 mths. 15.1% alc. **Cabernet Sauvignon-Shiraz** ★★★★ Export only. **04** has all the right ingredients, red berries, peppery spice, hint of liquorice, all bound together in a judiciously oaked, medium-weight structure.

Best within 3 yrs. **Chardonnay** ★★★★ Nicely made **04**, everything in balance: peach/citrus peel & buttered toast bouquet, flavours, a good, rounded mouthfeel. Finishes with verve. 10 mth oaking. **Sauvignon Blanc** ★★★ **05**'s styling is green figs, asparagus, summer meadow, backed by an appealing, food-friendly juiciness. **Vin Fumé** ★★★ Among SA's first wooded sauvignons. **04** again gets it right: the light oaking doesn't intrude, adds gentle savoury shading to vibrant asparagus/lime character. **Mustique** ★★★ Buket/riesling-driven off-dry blend laced with muscats (ottonel, morio). Off-dry **03** (not retasted) had charm, aromatics, drinkability in youth. Friendly 11.9% alc. **Franciskaner** ★★★ **05** chenin, morio muscat, colombard in 42/35/23 blend, but muscat takes centre stage in aromas, flavours. Semi-sweet (37g/ℓ RS), light 10.8% alc – a delightful summer quaffer.— *CR*

Simonsvlei International

Paarl ▪ Est/1stB 1947 ▪ Tasting & sales: Mon-Fri 8-6 (8-5 in winter) Sat 8.30-4.30 Sun 11-3 ▪ Fee R5 for 5 tastings ▪ Closed Easter Fri & Dec 25 ▪ Tours by appt ▪ Restaurant 101 ▪ Facilities for children ▪ Tourgroups ▪ Gifts ▪ Farm produce ▪ Function/conference facilities for small groups ▪ Owners 65 shareholders ▪ Cellarmaster Francois van Zyl (2000) ▪ Winemaker Rolanie Lotz (2002), with assistant Mari van der Rijst (2004) ▪ Viticulturist Jannie Underhay (Dec 2002) ▪ 1 200 ha (cab, shiraz, chard, chenin) ▪ 10 000 tons 220 000 cs own labels + 300 000 cs for customers, incl Long Neck (US) & others ▪ 50% red 50% white ▪ PO Box 584 Suider-Paarl 7624 ▪ info@simonsvlei.co.za ▪ www.simonsvlei.co.za ▪ T 863·3040 F 863·1240

'Strong and steady' best describe Simonsvlei after another year in the competitive environment of international wine. A 25% year-on-year growth over the past five years. Exports ever-climbing, particularly in Germany and Sweden where a new 3ℓ boxed Cab-Shiraz and Chenin have exceeded expectations. A 3ℓ box joins the 1ℓ and 5ℓ packs in the Simonay range, and a Light is added to the Lifestyle line-up. Backing all this up is an enlarged/upgraded red wine cellar, new brand manager Danie du Toit (ex-Distell), language courses for cellarhands and tasting room staff to up the service ante. Did we mention 'exciting new projects with Woolworths'?

Hercules Paragon range

Cabernet Sauvignon ★★★★ **03** classic cassis fruit with dark choc & mint extras; variety's tannins provide solid backbone for ripe flavours. 12–13 mths on oak; ditto … **Shiraz** ★★★ **03** combines early/flavourful drinkability with good varietal character (spicy smoked meat, hint cinnamon) & enough structure for few yrs maturation. **Sauvignon Blanc** ★★★★ Seldom disappoints; **05** again from Dbnville fruit, with signature aromas (dusty nettle, greenpepper), ripe fruit, crisp acidic grip.

Classic range

Following reds 6–9 mths on Eur oak: **Cabernet Sauvignon** ★★ **04** youthfully reticent & austere, earthy/dried leaf whiffs, needs yr/2 to unfold; if opening now, decant well head of serving. **Pinotage** ★★★ Mid-weight easy-drinker with spicy banana nuance, savoury smoked meat hint; **04** supple & well juiced. **Shiraz** ★★★ Hearty winter red with extraordinary spiced wet coconut nose, stalky tannins. **03** good with robust stews. **Cabernet Sauvignon-Merlot** ★★★★ ✓ Seamless, sensitively extracted red; minty **04** repeats successful 50/50 formula, tweaked for approachability with scope for few yrs cellaring. **Rosé** ★★ Semi-sweet **05** mainly chenin, with pinotage; latter lends fresh watermelon flavour. Very soft & pretty, will please widely. **Chardonnay** ★★★ **04** similar to pvs: dusty wood whiffs (from 2–4 mths oaking); full, ripe, leesy character, nicely fleshed. **Premier Chenin Blanc** ★★★ Appealing quaffer with hint of sweetness (3.5g/ℓ RS) in **05**, ripe guava flavour, slight grassy tint. **Sauvignon Blanc** ★★★ **05** restrained & leaner version of HP bottling above. Slightly 'hot' character, potent acidity. **Premier Bukettraube** ★★★ Characterful & full-flavoured Late Harvest style; pale but full flavoured **05**, fragrant, soft, uncloying. Following pair of fortifieds **NV**: **Humbro Hanepoot** ★★★ Jerepiko-style dessert with grapey/floral bouquet; current bottling fairly spirituous (±18% alc), accentuated by attenuated fruit. **Humbro Red Jerepigo** ★★★ Winter warmer from muscadel, ±17% fortification. Lovely rosy blush, Xmas cake & raisin lushness, shade sweeter than pvs.

Lifestyle range

Merlot new ☺ ★★★ **04** deliciously soft & balanced red with ripe wild-mulberry flavour & nutty hint, smoothly dry.

NV unless noted, unwooded. **Cabernet Sauvignon** new ★★★ **04**, like most in range, carefully made, satisfying, with well-managed tannins. **Pinotage** new ★★★ **04** interesting banana/biltong nose; dry, smoky, savoury tannins ideal for Italian food. **Shiraz** new ★★★ Aussie-style **03**, complete with bluegum whiffs, dense, slightly tangy flavours to enjoy with grilled steaks. **Simonsrood** ★★ Simple but flavoursome mediterranean-style red, for early enjoyment; four-way blend fronted by cinsaut, jammy wild-berry flavours, soft & dry. Also in 1.5ℓ. **Blanc de Blanc** ★★★ Latest bottling better balanced than pvs; well flavoured with tropical guava, light, fruity, softly dry. **Extra-Light** new ★★ Clean, light & refreshing, zippy acidity, not too dry, low 8.5% alc. From crouchen, hanepoot. **Simonsblanc** ★★ Simple off-dry chenin; our sample a bit tired, needs drinking soonest. **Stein** ★★ Straightforwardly sweet swig from chenin.

Simonay range

1, 3 and 5ℓ boxed wines; all **NV**, with low/lowish alc (11.5–13.5%). **Classic Red** ★★ Appealing cinsaut-led melange, braai wine deluxe with distinct sweet impression, jammy macerated fruit. **Blanc de Blanc** ★★ Chenin, colombard, crouchen, semillon mix (same blend for most of these), refreshingly clean & dry, well made. **Stein** ★★ Very soft fruity crowd-pleaser with balanced sweetness. **Late Harvest** ★ Summer-ripe flavours, simple & sweet. **Johannisberger** new ★ Floral-toned chenin, with white muscadel & hanepoot, sweet & soft. All ranges WO W Cape. **Zenzela**, **Charming Red** discontinued.—*CT*

Sinnya see Robertson Wide River
Six Generations see Rietvallei

Siyabonga

Wellington ▪ Est 1998 ▪ 1stB 1999 ▪ Closed to public ▪ Owners H Investments #121 (Pty) Ltd ▪ Owner Graham Knox ▪ Winemaker Corlea Fourie ▪ Viticulturist Andrew Pratt (2003) ▪ 15 ha (cabs s/f, merlot, pinotage, semillon, viognier) ▪ 3 000 cs own label ▪ PO Box 1209 Wellington 7654 ▪ doolhof@mweb.co.za ▪ ***T 864·3155*** *▪ F 864·1744*

This Wellington farm's precious old chenin and semillon vines remain in intensive care. Admitted in 2004, the three-decade-old bushvines underwent major surgery. Each was cut down to its original thick or spindly old stem and the new wood retrained. Now nursing staff (viticulturist Andrew Pratt and winemaker Corlea Fourie) keep meticulous record (in the 'census book') of a care and nutrition programme to bring weaker vines up to par with their stronger ward mates regarding ripening times and flavour intensity. Chief resident Graham Knox looks forward to checking out some healthy, productive bearers in a few years.

★★★★ **Cabernet Sauvignon-Merlot** Stylish composition: firm, but not too dense/tense for drinking on release, or keeping 4-6 yrs. **03** dusky echoes to dark, tarry tones; hyper-concentrated blackcurrant fruits under ripe-tannin wraps mid-2005. A wine with which to engage. **02** also complete & refined, with modulated finish. Young home vyd. 15 mths Fr oak.

★★★★ **Pinotage** Classical (Fr oak led) handling of sometime trenchant grape gets boost of added finesse in **03**: unmistakably pinotage with bold plummy fruit, but dusty tannin corset keeps the opulence in place; elegance retained. **02** gained extra pleasure in bottle; ripe gamey notes sit well with soft-tannined succulence, satiny finish. Low-yielding own vyd. Yr Fr barriques.

★★★★ **Severney** Serious white, designed to age; usually chenin, semillon from 30+ yr old vines. **04** not finished at press-time. Barrel-fermented 60/40 **03** blend last noted as well-structured, firm & dry.—*DS*

Slaley Estate

Stellenbosch ▪ Est 1957 ▪ 1stB 1997 ▪ Tasting & sales Mon-Sat & pub hols 10-4 ▪ Fee R20 refunded with purchase ▪ Closed Easter Fri, Dec 25/26 & Jan 1 ▪ Tours by appt ▪ Farm produce ▪ Owners Hunting family ▪ Winemaker Shaun Turnbull (Mar 2002) ▪ 70 ha (cab, merlot, pinotage, shiraz, chard, sauvignon) ▪ 350 tons 12-15 000 cs own label 90% red 9% white 1% rosé ▪ EurepGAP certified ▪ PO Box 119 Koelenhof 7605 ▪ info@slaley.co.za ▪ www.slaley.co.za ▪ ***T 865·2123*** *▪ F 865·2798*

The Hunting family-owned Simonsberg farm, on which this predominantly red-wine producer is based, has a long history. That is, if you take into account namesake Slaley Hall in Newcastle, where Lindsay Hunting's ancestor built the family shipping business from 1874. Not that age is limited to family history: last year saw their pinotage vines celebrating 50 yrs of production. It also saw the introduction of the Slaley Jazz Festival to keep everyone in the right spirit. Despite a focus on flagship reds, the Hunting Family Chardonnay 03 scored a bronze at the Challenge International du Vin in 2005. Clearly a year for filling their sails. Now it's all a race for line honours.

★★★★☆ **Merlot Reserve** So far only elegant, harmonious, silk-textured **99**; in magnums.

Hunting Family range

★★★★ **Merlot** After big, softly ripe **02**, **03** (★★★☆) has much lower alc (13.7% vs pvs 14.8). Dark choc, black cherry welcome; elegant blackcurrant fruit, firm tannins after extended stay in oak (all new Fr, 18 mths vs 12 mths 40% new pvsly). Highish acid gives fruit unnecessarily mean quality, but wine still manages elegance.

★★★★ **Pinotage** From single half-century-old vyd. **03** waft plum compôte, vanilla custard; supple ripe tannins, loads of sweet berry/plum flavours, better fruit-acid balance than cellarmates. Gorgeous oak integration (yr Fr/Am, 50% new). Re-jigging of ideas noticeable here too: harvested earlier for very manageable 12.8% alc – vs 14.6% in intensely powerful, tannic **02**. Cellar 5-7 yrs

★★★★ **Shiraz** Youthful, excellent **03** has all components for long life. Subtle spice to meaty, beefy fruit; muscular & trimmed down since rich **02** – more classic, with fine-textured dry tannins on long, resonating finish. Should keep well 3-7 yrs. 18 mths Fr/Am oak, 50% new.

Cabernet Sauvignon-Merlot ★★★☆ **03** 80/20 blend light-textured/-flavoured; tart, dry fruit, dry tannins, classy oak integration, like some clarets in style/flavour. Long finish with tang of acid. Welcome lowish 12.3% alc. **02** Gold at CWT. **Chardonnay** ★★★☆ Vanilla backdrop to juicy yellow peach repeated in **05** (sample). Luscious, generous fruit, firm acid & oaking (11 mths used Fr): authoritative wine-making. 11 mths used Fr oak.

Broken Stone range

Cabernet Sauvignon new ★★★ Mint & cool cedar intro to honest, light-bodied, dark-fruited **03**; dry tannins, freshened by tart acidity. Matured in oak. **Shiraz** ★★★ Robust & savoury **03** has baked plum, smoked beef aromas/flavours, tangy acid, dry finish. Yr Fr/Am oak, 10% new. **Cabernet Sauvignon-Shiraz** ★★★☆ ✓ **03** with 10% pinotage, which infuses attractive sweet plum character. Supple tannins, whiff vanilla custard, smooth juicy fruit, shows charm, grace. Alc a welcome modest 12.6%. **Pinotage** ★★☆ Latest **03** less successful than pvs; savoury Bovril whiffs, savoury & dry, firm tannins, not much joy. **Sauvignon Blanc** ★★☆ Sample **05** firm, steely, with hints fig, grass. Piercing acidity, bone-dry.

Shatot range

Lindsay's Whimsy ☺ ★★☆ Thoroughly accessible **03** blend pinotage/cab, shows generosity of home-grown variety; plump & pleasing, some warm plummy notes, nicely dry; ideal for chugging down around the braai.

Planque ★★ No-frills, everyday style **03** blend cab/pinotage has modest fruit, dusty tannins; very dry. **Plinque** ★★☆ Blue-ish pink from pinotage; **04** (sample tasted last ed) full-bodied yet fresh & lively. **05** unready for tasting. – *IvH*

Slanghoek Winery

Slanghoek (see Worcester map) ▪ Est 1951 ▪ Tasting & sales Mon-Fri 8–12.30; 1.30–5 Sat 10–1 ▪ Closed pub hols ▪ Picnic baskets by appt or BYO ▪ Tours 11 & 3 by appt ▪ Tourgroups ▪ Audio-visual presentation ▪ Gifts ▪ Conferencing ▪ Walks ▪ Conservation area ▪ Owners 25 members ▪ Cellarmaster Pieter Carstens (Aug 2002) ▪ Senior winemaker Nicolaas Rust, with Nico Grundling, Johan Jordaan & Jacques de Goede (Oct 2003/Dec 2002/Nov 2003/Dec 2001) ▪ Viticulturist Francois Nel (Dec 2000) ▪ 1 830 ha (17 varieties, r/w) ▪ 40 000 cs own label + 14m litres bulk 20% red 60% white 10% rosé 10% fortified ▪ Export brand: Zonneweelde ▪ PO Box 75 Rawsonville 6845 ▪ slanghoek@lando.co.za ▪ www.slanghoek.co.za ▪ ***T (023) 344·3026/7/8*** *▪ F (023) 344·3157*

Rising to the challenge of perpetuating growth while not sacrificing quality, Slanghoek last year expanded its cellar facilities to accommodate an extra 5000 tons. As it happened, harvest 2005 was slightly smaller (at 25 000 tons) than record 2004. Plans for the year ahead include a new barrel maturation cellar, which the public will be welcome to visit as part of the cellar's drive to market itself to a broader base of consumers.

Special Late Harvest ☺ ★★★ From hanepoot; good sugar-acid tension for effortless lightish sipping. **05** jasmine & powder puff prettiness on nose.

Camerca ★★ Bdx-style blend, equal cab/merlot; **03** sweet-sour cherry aromas, restrained fruitiness overtaken by big dry tannins & oak character (9 mths Fr, 20% new). **Cabernet Sauvignon** ★★ Hearty red, **03** sweet stewed fruit & caramel aromas, contrasting chewy dry tannins. Oak as above. **Merlot** ★★ Brawny (14.6% alc), savoury **04** reveals rather too much of its new-oak maturation (40%, Fr, 6 mths), too little of its sweet-sour fruit. **Pinotage** ★★★ **03** appealingly typical of variety, incl its high tone & strong tannin frame; supportively oaked (as for Camerca). **Shiraz** ★★★ **03** spicy oak (8 mths Fr oak, 20% new) better pitched than last, allows free rein to smoky berry fruit; lively dry tannins invite food. **Vinay Red** ★★ Four-way blend, fruity & drinkable. Red berry & plum flavours/aromas, light touch of oak. **Vinay Rosé** ★★ Latest from muscadel, with delicate rose-petal waft; sweeter than pvs but still with fresh acidic lift. Vinays above, below, in 1 000ml bottles, **NV**. **Chardonnay** ★★★ 40% oak-fermented in **05**, shows as engaging dusty wood backing to peach/tropical fruit; zesty, fresh, big alc (14.3%) encourages sipping, not swigging. **Chenin Blanc** ★ **05** not the superquaffer of last yr; simple & lean with standout 14% alc. **Sauvignon Blanc** ★ **05** not their best; tart, slight, very little varietal character. **Vin Doux** ★★★ **NV** carbonated sparkler with hanepoot's signature tones; energetic bubbles, delicate, not too sweet. Following six wines not retasted: **Vinay White** ★★ Supple, lightish off-dry quaffer (though string of three golds at Veritas!); last yr was blend sauvignon, chenin, colombard, with fresh pineapple & guava flavours. Newest bottling unready. **Semillon** ★★★ Fresh, lively **03** supportively oaked; new-clone nettles on nose, nicely rounded. **Riesling-Semillon** ★★★ Lightish 70/30 blend crouchen, semillon. **04** brisk & bone-dry; good food style. **Natural Sweet** ★★★ Dessert wine from hanepoot, chenin; vyds selected for high sugars & regular botrytis; noble rot character fairly evident in **03**, surprisingly dry at 91g/ℓ sugar. 500ml. **Noble Late Harvest** ★★★★ **03** shows laudable spread of flavours (incl vibrant pineapple), fine balance, albeit in more subdued form than predecessors (**01** lauded by Diners Club). Mainly chenin, dollop hanepoot; roughly 7g/ℓ acid, 160g/ℓ sugar, 12% alc. Unwooded. 375ml. **04** is next. **Red Jerepiko** ★★★ Penetratingly sweet fortified dessert from pinotage; **04** soft & grapey, 17% alc sure to warm the cockles. **Sweet Hanepoot** ★★★★ **05** samples unrateable. **04** last ed was light, delicate, well-made & clean. Good over crushed ice in summer, said Team S. 16.5% alc. **Red Muscadel** ★★★ Continues trend towards sweeter, more spirituous styling; **05** more muscat character than pvs, well-tweaked acidity & spirit for fleet-footed effect. 17.8% alc. **Cape Ruby** ★★★ Again mainly touriga in **04**, smidgen malbec; full, rich red berry & plum flavour, earthy undertone. Still traditional low alc (17.6%); small barrels 6 mths. — *MM/DH*

Smook Wines see Anthony Smook
Soek die Geluk see Goedverwacht

SoetKaroo

Prince Albert ▪ Est 2000 ▪ 1stB 2004 ▪ Visits Mon-Sat 8-6 ▪ Closed Easter Sun, Dec 25 & Jan 1 ▪ Self-catering cottage ▪ Owners Herman & Susan Perold ▪ Vini consultant Flip Smith ▪ Viticulturist Herman Perold ▪ 0.6 ha (petit v, red muscat d'A, red muscat de F, touriga) ▪ 3.4 tons 290 cs (375ml) 100% fortified ▪ 56 Church Str Prince Albert 6930 ▪ perold@netactive.co.za ▪ www.soetkaroo.co.za ▪ ***T (023) 541·1768***

Herman Perold, great-nephew of SA viticultural pioneer Abraham P, and wife Susan were drawn to winemaking after the purchase in 2000 of their home in the village of Prince Albert. The 150 year old property came with a hectare of virgin land and, seized with passion, the couple planted a mix of muscat vines and touriga. Four years later they carefully ferried the first cargo of grapes the 110km to Oudtshoorn's Kango Winery for vinification. Susan P, who claims she is no more than the gofer in this run-from-home business, says her husband communicates with his little vines on a molecular level. Seems to run in the family.

Red Muscat d'Alexandrie ★★★ As sweet as a Karoo 'tannie' ('auntie') & packaged in a bottle as plump! **05** delights with palest of ruby garnet hues, incense & Turkish Delight, dried currants. 16.2% alc; syrupy, cloying – at 216g/ℓ sugar, there's no need for dessert. —*IvH*

Solms-Delta

Franschhoek ▪ Est 1690 ▪ 1stB 2004 ▪ Visits daily 9-5 ▪ Closed Dec 25 & Jan 1 ▪ Light meals & selection of cheeses during opening hours; or BYO picnic ▪ Tourgroups ▪ Guest houses ▪ Gifts ▪ Walks ▪ Cultural museum (see intro) ▪ Owner 'Family trust' ▪ Winemaker Hilko Hegewisch (Mar 2003) ▪ Viti adviser Paul Wallace (Apr 2002) ▪ 12 ha (mourvèdre, shiraz, viognier) ▪ 3 500 cs ▪ 43% red 43% white 14% rosé ▪ PO Box 123 Groot Drakenstein 7680 ▪ info@solms-delta.com ▪ www.solms-delta.com ▪ ***T 874·3937*** *▪ F 874·3938*

The new partners in this steeped-in-history venture have dug deep to unearth the mysteries of winegrowing in the Cape. Co-owner, renowned neuroscientist Mark Solms, appointed viticulturist Paul Wallace and winemaker Hilko Hegewisch to establish Rhône varieties suited to the Franschhoek climate. In an ancient technique (used for the legendary 18th century Constantia sweet wines), bunch stems are strangled at ripeness to partially desiccate the berries and concentrate flavours without lowering acidity. Small portions of the current range are made this way, but the upcoming Solms-Hegewisch range is made exclusively from vine-dried fruit. To follow is the Solms-Astor range, in partnership with the English Astor family, new owners of neighbour farm Lübeck. This range will focus on traditional SA grapes and 'Cape blends'. An archaeological dig supervised by UCT is underway, and artefacts from the early Stone Age have been found. Along with details of the history of the valley, these can be seen at their cultural Museum van de Caab.

★★★★ **Hiervandaan 04** hugely promising debut. Authentic, tasty southern-Rhône-style blend; shiraz-led with mourvèdre, grenache noir, carignan, viognier (68/11/11/7.3/2.7). Fresh, elegant & comfortably structured; only medium-bodied yet with great multi-flavour richness, rounded dry persistence. Yr new Fr oak barely intrudes on overall harmony. Swtland/Frhoek vyds.

★★★★ **Lekkerwijn** Precisely named rosé; everything about **04** is delicious. Fashioned on traditional Fr style, reaches new level of quality, individuality in Cape. Twinkling peachy pink/gold glints; beautifully dry, firm; sound nip of tannin adds to overall food-friendliness. Mourvèdre, grenache noir, viognier, fermented/9 mths in older Fr oak . Stbosch/Swtlnd/Wrcstr vyds.

Amalie 05 twins Rhône varieties viognier & grenache blanc (80/20). Stems of latter's bunches twisted at ripeness leaving grapes to desiccate (and sugar/flavour to intensify). Unrated tank sample shows rich mouthfeel, satisfying vinosity, savouriness. All above WO W Cape. —*AL*

Somerbosch Wines

Stellenbosch (see Helderberg map) ▪ Est 1950 ▪ 1stB 1995 ▪ Tasting & sales daily 9-5 ▪ Fee R10 refundable with purchase of any wine ▪ Closed Easter Fri/Sun, Dec 25/26 & Jan 1 ▪ Tours by appt ▪ 'Die Fonteine' Bistro Tue-Sun 9-5 in season, otherwise 10-4 ▪ Facilities for children ▪ Owners Roux family ▪ Winemakers/viticulturists Marius, Japie & Wrensch Roux (1987/1995/ 2005) ▪ 80 ha (cab, merlot, pinotage, shiraz, cinsaut, chard, chenin, sauvignon) ▪ 60% red 40% white ▪ PO Box 12181 Die Boord 7613 ▪ enquiries@somerbosch.co.za ▪ www.somerbosch.co.za ▪ ***T 855·3615*** *▪ F 855·4457*

Now that the Roux brothers have bought their family farm, Die Fonteine, from their late father Wally's estate, Wrensch has become as involved as siblings Marius and Japie (though he's still doing consultancy work). All three have been caught up in the launch of a new flagship brand, Kylix, chosen for its classical associations – translated from the Greek, it means a drinking cup. Also new is a restaurant, Die Fonteine Bistro, attached to the wine-tasting facility (now open for longer and every day of the week). And with food in mind, don't miss the Roux strawberries, on sale in season.

Kylix new ★★★★ Serious & harmonious **02**, mainly cab lifted by 13% shiraz & by deft oaking (1st fill Fr wood 18 mths); classy mineral character; ripe, elegant tannin. Structure/stuffing to reward cellaring. **Cabernet Sauvignon** ★★★ **03** uncharacteristically rustic; notes of damp earth, green leaf tone to palate. Fr/Am oak, 2nd-4th fill, yr. **Merlot** ★★★ These usually firmly built, needing yr/2 to soften; **03** less fruity richness than pvs, giving leaner, drier feel. A food style. Fr/Am oak, 1st-4th fill, 6 mths. **Shiraz** ★★★ **03** well-balanced easy-drinker; smoky/meaty whiffs, oak (as for Cab) a pleasant background to soft berry flavours. **Pinotage** ★★★ **04** somewhat bolder, riper than pvs (though ±15% alc well concealed); savoury undertone will match a variety of hearty foods. Only 50% wooded (older Fr, yr). **Chardonnay** ★★★ **05** again unwooded; lemon zest on nose; crisp winey (rather than varietal) flavours, clean fresh send-off. **Chenin Blanc Barrel Fermented** ★★★★ **03** last ed noted as more complex, serious than version below, Fr-oaked component (80%, yr) showed attractively in rich toffee-toned flesh. 25 yr old bushvines. **Chenin Blanc** ★★ Ripe-picked **05** fruit-sweet, easy & uncomplex, for everyday drinking. **Sauvignon Blanc** ★★★ **05** riper & friendlier than pvs, less austere; still with good varietal zing & herbaceous typicity. **Late Bottled Vintage Port** ★★★ From cab, as was pvs, 5 yrs older oak; **NV**; raisin & treacle lushness glides down easily, as expected from style. 19.3% alc. **Cabernet Sauvignon-Merlot Limited Release** & **Pinotage Limited Release** sold out.

Seugnet range

Rouge ★★★ Another recipe change: **03** now shiraz/merlot (60/40), same easy drinkability; juicy plummy fruit & well disguised tannins. Portion oak-staved. **Blanc** ★★★ Latest version of bright outdoorsy tipple not ready; **04** 50/50 chenin/semillon mix was well-fruited & refreshing. – *CT/TM*

Somerlust see Viljoensdrift
Something Else see Cru Wines
Sommelier's Choice see Wine Concepts
Songloed see Coppoolse Finlayson
Sonop Organic see African Terroir
Soulo see Overhex

South African Premium Wines new

Est/1stB 2003 ▪ Closed to public ▪ PO Box 78973 Sandton 2146 ▪ norman@sapwines.com ▪ www.sapwines.com www.jabulani.com ▪ ***T/F (011) 462·0297***

What began as an MBA student's dream has turned into reality for strategy consultant Norman Celliers and the shareholders of this young Johannesburg-based negociant company. They've nurtured an innovative business model since 1998, and now, after a successful and massive capital gathering exercise, finally secured sufficient funding to implement their plans and fulfil orders for one million cases per annum, mainly from clients in Russia and the US.

Jabulani range

Merlot-Cabernet Sauvignon ★★★ Bright crimson **03**, ripe berry flavours in soft, balanced 60/40 blend, with subtle Fr oak influence. **Shiraz** ★★★ Animal motifs part of labelling for range. This is the leopard, appropriate given **03**'s meaty/gamey tones & savoury fruit flavours. **Chardonnay** ★★ Gentle tropical aromas on **04**, soft fruity flavours showing bit of age, so probably best enjoyed soon. Partly oak fermented. All WO Stbosch. — *CT*

Southern Cape Vineyards

*Little Karoo ▪ Barrydale cellar: Est 1940 ▪ 1stB 1976 ▪ Tasting & sales Mon-Fri 8-5 Sat & pub hols 9-3 ▪ Closed Easter Fri-Mon, Dec 25 & Jan 1 ▪ Book day ahead for tours ▪ BYO picnic ▪ Heritage garden ▪ Owners 25 members ▪ Winemaker Riaan Marais , with Ferdie Smit (Jan 1999/ May 1985) ▪ Viti consultant Willem Botha (2000) ▪ 152 ha (cab, merlot, ruby cab, shiraz, chard, colombard, sauvignon) ▪ 2 000 tons 50% red 35% white 5% other ▪ Range for customer: Decent Red ▪ PO Box 59 Barrydale 6750 ▪ sales@scv.co.za ▪ www.kleinkaroowines.co.za ▪ **T (028) 572·1012** ▪ F (028) 572·1541*

*Ladismith cellar: Est 1939 ▪ 1stB 1988 ▪ Tasting & sales Mon-Fri 8-5 ▪ Closed all pub hols except Easter Sat ▪ BYO picnic ▪ Tours by appt ▪ Conferencing ▪ Owners 75 members ▪ Winemaker Jim de Kock (Jan 2002) ▪ Viti consultant Willem Botha (Jan 2001) ▪ 600 ha (ruby cab, chard) ▪ 8 000 tons 4 200 cs own label + 3.2m litres bulk ▪ PO Box 56 Ladismith 6655 ▪ lkws@telkomsa.net ▪ www.kleinkaroowines.co.za ▪ **T (028) 551·1042** ▪ F (028) 551·1930*

The 2005 amalgamation of neighbouring co-ops, Barrydale and Ladismith, promises competitive spin-offs for the new parent company Southern Cape Vineyards (SCV). General manager Riaan Marais says: 'By joining forces, we are able to work smarter and contain costs more effectively. As far as we know, we are the first co-operative cellars in the region to pool resources. It seems like a logical conclusion for smaller players who want to increase competitiveness.' The cellar at Ladismith runs a methanol-free spirits production plant and Barrydale Cellar is the country's largest independent producer of potstill brandy. Despite the changes, the two facilities, situated 83 km apart, promise to retain their respective identities and protect vital local jobs, key to the tourism industry.

Barrydale range

Decent Red ★★☆ Appealing tutti-frutti style blend ruby cab, tinta, pinotage, unwooded; soft & gently dry with berry fruit ripeness all the way to the finish. **NV**. WO W Cape.

Misty Point range

Pinotage ★★☆ **02** pleasant quick-quaff with comfortably soft tannins. Not retasted. **Red** ★★☆ Ruby cab/merlot union, **02** last yr was extra-gulpable after further yr's softening in bottle. **White** ★☆ Slightly tweaked blend (chenin, chardonnay, gewürz) for **03**, plain but pleasant semi-dry white, with green pear hint. All WO W Cape.

Seven Falls range

White Muscadel ★★★☆ **00** a pudding in itself; very sweet & sticky, gorgeous tangerine/ honeysuckle wafts, richness relieved by clean citrus acidity, spirituous touch in tail. **Ruby Port** ★★★☆ More LBV-style than ruby, but attractive, well-made; prune & Albany choc richness matched by dry tannins, finishes almost dry. **NV**. Range to be discontinued when current stocks sell out.

Towerkop range

None of the reds oaked. **Pinotage** ★★★ **03** regional Young Wine Show winner; last ed showed hints of dried fruit, spice & pepper, reoccurring on lightish but pleasant palate. **Ruby Cabernet** ★★ Super little easy-drinker; **04** lightish but well-fruited, juicy, softly dry. **Rosé** ★ Semi-sweet **NV** with pale blanc-de-noir shade, low 10% alc. From pinotage, chardonnay. **Blanc de Blanc** ★☆ Uncomplicated **04** dry white from chardonnay, sauvignon, with dieter-friendly light alc (±11%) & low sugar (3g/ℓ). **Stein** ★☆ Supple, lightish summer drink with soft acidity; latest **NV** again dry for this style. **Amalienstein Muscadel** ★★★☆ Powerfully scented **02** red fortified dessert with abundant tangerine liqueur-like flavours. Not retasted. 16.5% alc. **Towersoet** ★★★☆ Fortified hanepoot, its name – literally 'Magic Sweet' – rather appropriate this vintage: **03** fine, complex & delicious. Muscat leaps out of glass, is joined by Oriental market smells (papaya, lemongrass, litchi), enlivened by acidic prickle.

Tradouw range

Cabernet Sauvignon ★★★ Second-release **02** last yr offered firm, sweet-fruited satisfaction; blackberries & minty whiffs; gentle oaking (new/2nd fill barrels); legs for 3/4-yrs. **Merlot** ★★★★ **03** (sample) well-structured & -layered with rich black cherry fruit; ripe, almost opulent profile; definite step up. **Pinot Noir** ★★★ **03** less outspoken vintage; soft raspberry/cherry tones, accessible tannins, finish not as warmly alcoholic. **Shiraz** new ★★★ Appealing & harmonious **03**, soft spicy tannins & dry finish good-inclined but equally amenable solo. 8 mths small oak. **Chardonnay** ★★ Blend barrelled & unwooded components; **03** last ed showed a peaches & cream character, lively elegance, brisk citrus acidity. **04** unready for tasting. **Sauvignon Blanc** ★★★ Balanced, lighter-styled **04** with dollop sugar to add roundness & breadth to fresh grassy/gooseberry tones. — *JN*

Southern Right

*Hemel-en-Aarde Valley ▪ Est 1994 ▪ 1stB 1995 ▪ Tasting & sales at Wine Village-Hermanus (see Specialist wine shops section) ▪ Owner Anthony Hamilton Russell ▪ Winemaker Hannes Storm ▪ Viticulturist Johan Montgomery ▪ ±13 ha (pinotage, sauvignon) ▪ 225 tons 17 000 cs 40% red 60% white ▪ PO Box 158 Hermanus 7200 ▪ hrv@hermanus.co.za ▪ **T (028) 312·3595** ▪ F (028) 312·1797*

2005 saw Southern Right celebrating its first decade of 're-defining pinotage' with the release of the 04 vintage, made entirely from estate-grown grapes. This theme of regionality follows through to the latest Sauvignon, now made entirely from Walker Bay fruit (some insourced). But this 'stay at home' philosophy translated into 'don't tread on our toes' with the release of Bastenburg last year. Following request of Rustenberg's Simon Barlow, the name has been changed to Ashbourne to avoid any confusion. Amid the local focus, Anthony Hamilton Russell has had time to look back and experiment – with clay amphoras! A local potter made two trial vessels, which were filled with pinotage. 'One is buried in clay-rich soil and one is in the cellar to monitor porosity and evaporation rates. The principle is to get the all-important air exchange without the foreign flavours of oak. We are also hoping to get an added dimension of minerality from our own soils.'

★★★★★ **Ashbourne** ('Bastenburg' in last ed) Maiden **01** (not retasted) from pinotage; bordelais in structure with distinct varietal edge. Next will be **04**. Anthony HR's ambitious vision is to redefine the variety: trials continue, including ageing in clay amphoras....

★★★★★ **Pinotage 04** immediate, forthcoming nose & palate, clear varietal character but positive secondary aromas. High toned, with pure fruit. Should evolve with 5+ years in bottle. 100% W Bay. Matured in 20% new oak. **03** needed time for wood & slightly grainy tannins to settle.

★★★★ **Sauvignon Blanc 05** all W Bay fruit for the first time. Powerful, concentrated, green fig & capsicum with mineral edge. **04** figgy, green fruit nose/palate, intense & weighty. — *RK*

Southern Sky Wines

*Paarl ▪ Est 2002 ▪ Tasting & sales at I Love Wine (see Wine shops section for opening hours) ▪ Coffee & light meals 9–4 ▪ Closed Dec 25/26 & Jan 1 ▪ Crafts, homeware & gifts ▪ Owner Andrew Milne ▪ Vini consultant Johann Jacobs (Mar 2004) ▪ 10 000 cs ▪ 80% red 20% white ▪ 40A Main Street Paarl 7646 ▪ sales@southernskywines.com ▪ www.southernskywines.com ▪ **T 871·1437/082·876·8878** ▪ F 863·0444*

Young Paarl wine entrepreneur Andrew Milne's eyes are focused eastwards. Not only does he eagerly report the opening of a Chinese restaurant on the premises of the I Love Wine tasting emporium where his various enterprises vinous may be sampled, but additionally, he's co-opted his father Peter's contacts and long experience in the SE Asian market to help market Marimba, his latest brand, in the Orient. The Marimba project is a joint venture between SSW & Overhex Private Cellar, which will be the 'home' of the brand. Kobus Rossouw of Overhex will manage the winemaking, and the project drivers anticipate large export volumes.

Tara Hill range

Cabernet Sauvignon ★★★ Suave dinner companion, **03** notes of sandalwood & cedar; slight nutty/leafy notes to succulent plum flavours; 16–18 mths Fr oak. WO Stbosch. **Sauvignon Blanc 04** sold out before we could taste.

Marimba range

Reds **04**; whites **05**. **Merlot-Cabernet Sauvignon** ★★ Effortless commercial style with jammy fruit, hints choc & treacle, sweetish finish. Briefly oaked. **Shiraz-Merlot** ★★ Light-coloured/textured with obvious oak & distinct tannins. Fr oak, 5 mths. **Sauvignon Blanc** ★★ Crisp, flinty/peppery aperitif with curt tropical fruit flavours. **Chenin Blanc-Colombard** ★★ Light (12.5% alc) but bouncy & flavourful, comfortably dry. **Sauvignon Blanc-Semillon** ★★ Equal partnership with neither dominant; zesty & refreshing beach-party type wine.

Ready Steady range

Both **NV**. **Red** ★★ Covers the whole spectrum (spice, hint bluegum, savoury, sweet-sour, red fruit), so food partnering's a cinch. **White** ★ Uncomplicated, softly dry blend chenin (70%), chardonnay, with peach nuance. All above new to guide; WO W Cape unless noted. — *CT*

South Point see Origin Wine

Spar SA

Est 1963 ▪ PO Box 1589 Pinetown 3600 ▪ ray.edwards@spar.co.za; livingworld@mweb.co.za ▪ ***T (031) 719·1900/1844*** *or (012) 998·4737 ▪ F (031) 719·1991 or (012) 998·4736*

When it comes to districts, wards, cellars, growers and varieties, one word fits all: 'various'. Add more than a dozen winemakers and millions of litres of wine, and you get an idea of the size of the Spar supermarket chain's wine-sourcing operation. 'Fruity, balanced, early accessible wines remain the aim,' says consultant Tinus van Niekerk, 'and of course value for money.' The group's private-label wines, Country Cellars and Carnival, are listed separately.

Special Selection see Laibach
Spencer Bay see WestCorp
Spencers Creek see Paarl Wine

Spice Route Wine Company

Swartland ▪ Est/1stB 1998 ▪ Tasting & sales at Fairview (see entry) ▪ Owner Charles Back ▪ Winemaker Charl du Plessis (Dec 2001) ▪ Viti adviser Andrew Teubes ▪ 123 ha (shiraz, mourvèdre) ▪ 450 tons ±18 000 cs 70% red 30% white ▪ PO Box 645 Malmesbury 7299 ▪ spiceroute@iafrica.com ▪ ***T (021) 863·2450*** *(office);* ***(022) 485·7139*** *(cellar) ▪ F (022) 863·2450/(021) 863·2591*

Golf-mad Charl du Plessis is equally at home in this Swartland cellar (owned by Fairview's Charles Back) as on the green, so his recent achievement of an excellent 6 handicap bodes well for a slew of top ratings. Despite a difficult 2005 harvest, both reds and whites (harvested from as early as January 21) show promise. A hotbed of experimentation and varietal adventure, Spice Route's future bottlings will feature a slew of unusual-in-SA grapes (tempranillo, tannat, souzão and nouvelle, to name a few) and these will certainly put CdP's driving skills to the test. But there's no doubt, given his abilities, he'll hole them all. And when the corks come out at the 19th, we know whose will be pulled first.

★★★★☆ **Malabar** Flagship blend, components dependent on vintage. **03** spicy & perfumed, thanks to elegant peppery contribution of shiraz (72%), here with pinotage (11%), mourvèdre (11%) & dashes grenache, viognier. Effusive Rhône-like aromas cloak 15.1% alc. All fruit hand picked/selected, Fr oak matured. Less striking than maiden **02**, bigger alc (15.4%) but elegant & textured. Blend shiraz, merlot, grenache (58/26/16) added cassia & pepper notes to red fruits tone.

★★★★ **Flagship Syrah** Super-ripe New-World style, substantially wooded. **03** sweet & silk-tannined; notes of raspberry & almond; seamlessly managed oak (45% new all Fr), malo in barrel; alc (15.3%) evident but not gauche. Probably just a shade finer than **02** where savoury meaty notes layer dense tannins. More in mould of flamboyant though elegant & multi-gonged **01**. Unfiltered.

★★★★ **Merlot** new Mega-ripe, almost raisin caramel notes, massive vinosity characterises **02**; already fully accessible though tannins/alc still evident, 16 mths Fr oak soaked up by sumptuous fruit.

★★★★ **Pinotage** High-toned raspberry aromas on **04**, also soft, supple, sweet banana cherry notes; boisterous pinotage aromas & tannins beautifully concealed; 13 mths 2nd fill oak, 80% Am; 'lower' 14.4% alc enhances elegance. Refined successor to **03** where high alc (15%) super-ripe fruit overwhelmed drinkability.

★★★★☆ **Chenin Blanc** Impressively handled wine, highlighting best of fully mature bushvines (27 yrs). 100% barrel fermentation (mainly 4th/5th fill), imparts gorgeous honeysuckle character to **04**, sumptuous yet restrained; fairly evolved bouquet with botrytis whiffs, slight funkiness; mouth-filling yet dry, persistent. 14.4% alc well concealed. Fresher than **03** with dried-fruit compôte aromas & tastes.

★★★★ **Viognier** new Beautifully executed **04**; more floral scents than usual peach, succulent yet elegant, oak well integrated (fermented in 3rd/4th fill cask, aged 10 mths), alc (14.4%) unobtrusively lifts fruit. From low-yielding Swtlnd vyds.

Mourvèdre new ★★★☆ **04** sweet fruited though lacking expected earthy/mineral tones; accessible black cherry whiffs, gentle tannins. Malo, aged in barrel 13 mths, Am oak. **Sauvignon Blanc** new ★★★ Greenpepper, green fig notes on elegant & composed **05**, with food-friendly textures (6.6% acid, 12.3% alc) & some ageing potential. **Flagship Merlot**, **Pinotage** discontinued. — *MF*

Spier

*Stellenbosch ▪ Est 1767 ▪ 1stB 1996 ▪ Tasting & sales daily 9–5 at Wine Centre ▪ Tasting fees: R8 (Spier), R12 (Winelands Select), R30 (Wine Experience) ▪ Tours by appt ▪ Meals, refreshments & picnics, see Eat-out section ▪ Luxury hotel & wide variety of attractions/amenities ▪ Owner Winecorp ▪ Winemakers/viticulturists: see Winecorp ▪ 300 ha (cab, merlot, pinotage, shiraz, chard, sauvignon) ▪ 200 000 cs 60% red 40% white ▪ PO Box 1078 Stellenbosch 7660 ▪ francoisvdw@spier.co.za winecorp@iafrica.com ▪ www.spier.co.za www.winecorp.co.za ▪ **T 809·1143** ▪ F 809·1144*

The home of Westcorp wine company (also owner of the Longridge winery and Savanha brand), Spier is much more than just a cellar and wine label. This historic 300-year-old wine farm is a mecca of leisure and entertainment. Its palette of pleasures includes a four-star hotel, conference centre, golf course, open-air amphitheatre, restaurants (including the decadent outdoor Afro-Arabian Moyo), wine centre (a shop showcasing SA), a deli (offering picnic hampers), outdoor activities such as horse-rides, wildlife encounters with cheetahs and raptors, and, to top it all, an annual arts festival. But back to its vinous delights. Says chief winemaker Frans Smit: 'Our objective is to create well-structured, fruit-driven wines and offer the wine lover consistent good quality and great value.'

Private Collection

★★★★ **Cabernet Sauvignon** Multi-faceted wine for keeping. Firm, ripe-tannined, 14.7% alc **02** followed by more elegant, charming **03**: bright-fruited cassis, cherry & savoury element that deepens on the palate. Tannins need more time, will reveal their potential over 5-7 yrs. Selection from Fr/Am barrels, 12-16 mths – similar oaking for all reds in range.

★★★☆ **Merlot** These always tightly structured but **03** (★★★★) has flesh for current accessibility. Complex nose: peppered salami, mulberries, wet heath, a hint of mint; sinewy tannins that will unfold, reward over ±6 yrs. Concours Mondial gold. **02** in tight-knit house style. VDG, MIWA Grand d'Or.

★★★★ **Pinotage** Sleek, supple, modern example. **03**'s seductive richness masks underlying svelte structure, deep muscle tone promises further 6 yr rewarding cellaring. The styling is savoury, cloves, underbrush, gamy, on a dark fruit core & enough varietal juiciness to drink beautifully. IWSC gold. Opulent **02** still an infant mid-2004, with firm fine-grained tannins. 14.7% alc.

★★★★ **Shiraz** As expected in this range, variety-true flavours in **03**: salty liquorice, roasted spice, dark fruit, deep & richly layered. Sleekly structured, with tannins still tight knit – just accessible now, will show better in yr, & drink well over 5+. Added dashes malbec, viognier. WO Coastal.

★★★★☆ **Chenin Blanc 04** (sample) has similar styling to the **03** – potentially same high rating. Has tropical/pineapple & crystallised citrus peel richness, refreshed by a limy tang. Harmonious oaking adds nutty flavours, weight, adding to the appetite appeal. Fermented/15 mths Fr oak. **03** raised bar on already acclaimed wine. Wonderfully perfumed, layers fruit, unwavering freshness.

★★★★☆ **Sauvignon Blanc** Powerful, full-flavoured. **05** is sauvignon with attitude: intense capsicum, asparagus aromas, flavours, a quivering green-yet-ripe style, lingering on after the glass is empty. Coupled with brisk acidity, approachable 12.6% alc, makes for perfect food wine.

★★★★ **Viognier** Delicious **04** (in similar style as **03**) has alluring scents honeysuckle, jasmine & variety's peach-pip note. Fr oaking adds to structure, doesn't detract from aromatics; further palate lengthening supplied by 8.6g/ℓ sugar. WO Coastal.

★★★★ **Noble Late Harvest** Not made every yr. Following on delicious **00** from riesling & chenin, a barrel sample **04** promises it will be worth the wait – potential ★★★★☆. From chenin, muscat d'A, riesling (64/32/4), multi-flavoured, with waves of litchi, honeyed pineapple, dried peach/apricot, in a satin-textured body. Sugar richness (158g/ℓ) offset by acidity, 12.3% alc & 18 mths Fr oak, making for great drinking pleasure. WO W Cape.

Malbec new ★★★☆ **03** peppery, gamy/smoked meat tones to the ripe plum fruit; velvety texture for immediate pleasurable drinking, with 5 yrs more development ahead for those who can wait. Unfiltered.

Spier range

Cabernet Sauvignon ★★★ **04**, with touch petit v, attractively youthful; red berry/plum fruit profile, already drinking well but 3+ yr cellaring future. All these reds 10 mths Fr oak. **Merlot** ★★★ Nicely balanced **04**, with accessible tannins for earlier drinking. Cigar-box, dark choc & ripe plums flavouring ensure it's a pleasurable experience. **Pinotage** ★★★ **04** has good fruit, wild berries, creamy rhubarb, with touch of seriousness in the structure – has 3 yr ageing potential. **Shiraz** ★★★ Light but not simple **04** has requisite shiraz styling of smoked beef, savoury spice, Karoo scrub, all harmoniously presented. Dab mourvèdre, malbec. **Sauvignon Blanc** ★★★ **05** Less vibrant, concentrated than pvs: herbaceous, summer meadow tones, light-textured palate minerality, brisk finish. WO W Cape, as is rest of range. **Chenin Blanc** ★★★ **05** varietally true, with cooler-character fruit: leafy freshness, Granny Smith apples, clean zesty finish. Food compatible styling. **Chardonnay** ★★★ Friendly & flavourful **04**: lemon peel, biscuit aromas, with palate a lightly oaked, tangy version of that. Smoothly drinkable, with 6.2g/ℓ sugar balanced by acidity, so finishes dry. **Bouquet Blanc** discontinued.

Vintage Selection range new

Malbec-Cabernet Franc-Petit Verdot ★★★☆ **03** blend (53/30/17) captures essence of the varieties: fennel, roasted vegetable savouriness, brambleberry piquancy; tannins are sinewy, still busy melding, will show better in yr, keep for 4–5. Am/Fr oak. WO Coastal, as is … **Shiraz-Mourvèdre-Viognier** ★★★☆ Compatible marriage of Rhône varieties on **03**. Café au lait, sweet spice tones to a soft red fruit core immediately attract, become more savoury on the plate & finish. Very ripe 14.9% alc fits with wine style. IWSC gold. **Sauvignon Blanc-Chardonnay-Viognier** ★★★☆ **04** tantalising interplay between sauvignon's leafiness, austere elegance & the floral, peach character of its main partners. 48/20/20 blend, also with dollop chenin, drop semillon 2%. 4 mths Fr oak. WO W-Cape, as is next range.

Discover range new

White ★★☆ Crisp, flavourful, early-drinking **05** blend chenin & colombard, with notes of pears, tangy lemon. **Red** ★★★ **05** smoothly accessible, characterful unwooded blend pinotage, shiraz (70/30). Dark fruit, hints of mocha, roasted vegetables. **Sweet** ★★☆ **05** A semi-sweet crowd pleaser: fruit gum, star-sweet attractions in a softly rounded package. 25 g/ℓ sugar.—*CR*

Spitz see Bellingham

Springfield Estate

*Robertson ▪ Est/1stB 1995 ▪ Tasting & sales Mon-Fri 8-5 Sat 9-4 ▪ Closed Easter Fri/Sun, Dec 25 & Jan 1 ▪ BYO picnic ▪ Owners Bruwer family ▪ Winemaker/viticulturist Abrie Bruwer, with Johan van Zyl (Jun 2000) ▪ 150 ha (cabs s/f, merlot, petit v, chard, sauvignon) ▪ PO Box 770 Robertson 6705 ▪ info@springfieldestate.com ▪ www.springfieldestate.com ▪ **T (023) 626·3661** ▪ F 626·3664*

Abrie Bruwer, challenger of convention, is reaping the results of his most recent projects, which, as one would expect, are taken on with not only passion but also dogged precision. Not many winemakers would uproot their (to die for) vineyards because they face the wrong way. However, AB has dived in with vim and vigour and realigned those facing north-south to run east-west, in the interests of more even ripening and advantageous cooling breezes. The latest project, started 4 years ago, involves densely planted sauvignon (7 000 vines per hectare vs the usual 5 000). The first crop came into the cellar in 2005, and immediately surprised/delighted one and (almost) all with its amazing complexity. Marketer/sister Jeanette is less sanguine, noting that 'planting is easy. You then realise you have to buy new tractors, implements and harvesting machines to fit into these tiny 1.5m rows.' But this is Springfield, and The Right Thing will be done. So JB good naturedly concedes: 'It makes sense to plant vineyards the width they should be, and not that of your tractor'.

★★★★★ **The Work of Time** Realisation of a 10 yr old dream to make a bdx-style red on the estate. **02** still not ready for tasting. Maiden **01** fleshy, fruit-crammed yet elegant blend cab f & merlot (40/40), with cab s & soupçon petit v. Smooth, seamless; marvellous concentration of ripe berry fruits (black-, logan-), hint of choc, fresh prune & savoury. 18 mths Fr oak, some new.

★★★★★ **Méthode Ancienne Cabernet Sauvignon** Steep, rocky, thorn-strangled site cleared 23 yrs ago for this vyd (abandoned ox wagon also removed); 'ancient' winemaking methods (100% native-yeast fermentation of whole berries in new Fr oak; ageing 2 yrs each on lees & in bottle; unfined/unfiltered). No follow-up to marvellous **99**, aromas of fresh berries & classy oak; intense chocolaty palate. Again the admirable purity of fruit seen in **98**, the same bright texture & ultra-soft tannins. Delicious on release, muted power hinting at great future.

★★★★★ **Whole Berry Cabernet Sauvignon** Cellar's quest for gentlest possible flavour/tannin extraction – via fermentation of uncrushed berries with native yeasts – reflected here too; **03** marvellously succulent & ripe, whiffs cherry & herbs; effortlessly maintains stellar quality of **02** with delightful fresh-crushed blackcurrant tone, cosseting tannins. These gorgeous on release, with potential to improve up to ±8 yrs. ±Yr Fr oak, some new.

★★★★★ **Méthode Ancienne Chardonnay** Bruwer-style extreme winemaking taken to the limit with this version, 'inspired by ancient Burgundy': native-yeast-fermented in barrels, all Fr, 80% new; yr on lees sans sulphur, bottled un-everything (-filtered, -fined, -stabilised). **99**, only the 2nd successful attempt in 5, followed by tour-de-force **02**, last ed noted as aromatic, open & lusciously creamy. 'Made to last (we hope) a lifetime,' winemakers say. **03** is next.

★★★★ **Wild Yeast Chardonnay** Unwooded, characterful version, off well aged block (23 yr); vinification mostly as above; 13 mths *sur lie*, 100% through malo, which shows in creamily rich texture. Standout **03** (★★★★★) redefines 'satin smooth'; ripe tropical flavours simply fold into the mouth with stunning concentration, persistence. Great prospects. **02** mid-2004 showed delightful bottle-age peeping though the ripe fruit & flower aromas.

★★★★ **Life from Stone Sauvignon Blanc** Striking & individual elixir eked from estate's rockiest soils. **04** showed extraordinary complexity in youth (spectrum covered cordite to fresh tropical fruit); **05** leads with full-blown bellpepper/mineral punch, then a tropical fruit caress, elegantly delivered, as ever, with moderate alc (12.2%). Abrie B believes this will continue to improve over several yrs.

★★★★ **Special Cuvée Sauvignon Blanc** From mature (20 yrs) extra-cool riverine vyd. Muscular style, usually distinct from 'extra-flinty' version above – though green-flecked **05** (★★★★) has distinct stoney undertone to pungent passionfruit/herbaceous tone. Bewitching intensity, easily finest of recent vintages. **04** ripeness kept in trim by bracingly fresh finish. Best in flush of youth. – *DH*

Springfontein

*Walker Bay · Est 1996 · 1stB 2004 · Visits Mon-Fri 9-5 Sat & pub hols by appt · Picnic baskets, meals & braais by appt; or BYO picnic · Facilities for children · Walks · 4 self-catering cottages (B&B by appt) · Owners Weber family & friends · Winemaker Anja Weber, advised by Kevin Grant & David Trafford · Viticulturist Albie du Toit, advised by Schalk du Toit · 25 ha (cab, merlot, mourvèdre, petit v, pinotage, shiraz, chard, chenin, sauvignon, semillon) · 20 tons 1 000 cs · 80% red 20% white · PO Box 71 Stanford 7210 · info@springfontein.co.za · www.springfontein.co.za · **T (028) 341·0651** · F (028) 341·0112*

With Germanic precision, Johst and Anja Weber from Essen, Germany, and a bevy of fatherland friends embarked on establishing their vineyards in the southernmost part of the Walker Bay district. They chose virgin land next to a nature reserve, distinguished by highly auspicious limestone soils. Aiming to produce bespoke wines, the Webers enlisted the help of two of the Cape's top hand-crafters, David Trafford and Kevin Grant. Despite volumes inching upwards (to 1000 cases for vintage 2005), the wines are still available only in 'homeopathic quantities'. The huge 500ha property welcomes guests and offers picnic baskets and braais by prior arrangement, as well as many attractions and amenities. As the guide went to press, an email from Anja W announced the appointment of Clinton le Sueur (Mulderbosch) as winemaker and farm manager.

★★★★★ **Jil's Dune Chenin Blanc** Hugely exciting debut from young maritime vines (5 yrs). Concentrated apricot & pear-drop aromas on **04**, well-crafted viscous palate with wonderful length – dry yet spicy & lifted all the way to the finish; uncompromising but far from austere. Ex-single vyd; 100% natural yeast fermentation in barrel, no malo; low 12.5% alc. After Weber daughter Amelie Jil.

★★★★ **Ikhalezi Chenin Blanc** Gorgeous **04** NLH-style dessert (but labelled 'Natural Sweet') with intense green-gold glimmer, botrytis-touched honeysuckle & peach aromas, succulent & sumptuous flavours; fruit richness balanced by youthful fresh acidity. 10 mths oak, 11.6% alc, 167g/ℓ sugar.

Jonathan's Ridge Pinotage ★★★★ Weber son Emil Jonathan lends his name to single-vyd **04**; dark, brooding & aromatic; black cherry & mulberry notes; fruity rather than estery bouquet (though some telltale varnishy whiffs on finish). Barrel fermented (incl malo), yr Fr oak, 30% new – same regimen for ... **Ulumbaza Shiraz** ★★★ Blockbuster **04** is luscious & concentrated, its polished tone punctuated by caramel & raspberry whiffs (& by big alc – 15% – noticeable on nose). – *MF*

Spring Grove see Zorgvliet
Spring Valley see Old Vines Cellars
Spruitdrift see Westcorp

Stanford Hills Winery

*Walker Bay · Est/1stB 2002 · Visits by appt · 3 self-catering cottages · Airstrip & flying school · Owner Stanford Hills (Pty) Ltd · Vini consultant Kevin Grant, with Peter Kastner (Jan 2002/Apr 2005) · Viti consultant Schalk du Toit (Jan 2002) · 4 ha (pinotage) · 30 tons 750 cs own label 100% red · PO Box 1052 Stanford 7210 · stanfordhills@maxitec.co.za · **T (028) 341·0841** · F (028) 341·0286*

Bought from retired airline pilot Maurice Jackson last year, the property formerly known as Mauroma is now Stanford Hills. The new owners are Hermanus restaurateur Peter Kastner and wife Jami. Additions since the purchase include 4ha of vines and a tasting area with views of the dam and vineyards. (Other attractions include an airstrip and flying school.) With two investor friends, the Kastners worked the 2005 crush with Maurice J (who happily handed over tougher tasks like the 2am and 4am punch-downs). Meanwhile adviser Kevin Grant (ex-Southern Right/Hamilton Russell) is putting his elegant stamp on the produce.

★★★★ **Pinotage** Consistently, attractively light-toned, alluding to grape's pinot parentage; **04** fruit character also pinot-like: earthy cherry & lavender, fine tannins, fresh acidity; elegant, long (if slightly acetone-lifted) finish. Delicious **03**, elegant & juicy, good taut acidity. 11 mths Fr oak, 33% new.—*CvZ*

Stark-Condé Wines

Stellenbosch ▪ Est/1stB 1998 ▪ Tasting & sales Fri 1-4.30 Sat 10-2 ▪ Owner Jonkershoek Cellars (Pty) Ltd ▪ Winemaker José Condé ▪ Viticulturist Pieter Smit ▪ 40 ha (cab, shiraz) ▪ 60 tons 3 000 cs 100% red ▪ PO Box 389 Stellenbosch 7599 ▪ info@stark-conde.co.za ▪ www.stark-conde.co.za ▪ ***T 887·3665*** *▪ F 887·4340*

2005 was the first vintage unaccompanied by the sound of building at this Jonkershoek property, known for its small volumes and big ratings. The new cellar was fully operational, handling close to the maximum 60 tons. An extremely low-yielding vintage, José Condé reports, with small berries, excellent concentration and robust tannins — well suited to his no-compromise approach. The concluded building has also provided a tasting area, open two days a week. Visitors will be able to sample the two labels produced here: Stark for varietal wines, Condé for single vineyard, both stylishly packaged by José C himself, wearing his graphic designer hat.

Condé range

★★★★★ **Cabernet Sauvignon** Prior hallmarks — restraint & harmony — jettisoned by riotous flavour of massive **03**: glistening wet-coal sheen, rich choc-laced blackcurrant fruits jostle alongside notable alc (15%) in sweet finish. Yet, balance also shows at this carnival: alarmingly drinkable in precocious youth. **02** brooding cassis aromas, ripe but reined-in palate, persistent. Gamier **01** (★★★★) more organic. 22 mths Fr oak, now mostly new.

★★★★ **Syrah** NEW Its Stark stablemate below looks south down the Rhône, this gazes north to Crozes: **03** cool, refined violet tones to spiced fruit, fine tannin structure sculpted for cellaring, balance tippled only by 15.5% alc. Single home vyd block with 15% sibling cab, hand-reared, 22 mths seasoned Fr casks.

Stark range

★★★★ **Cabernet Sauvignon** These are leafy rather than berry-fruited; **03** more accessible, supple & chewy than austere **02**, with 5% merlot & dash shiraz, unconcentrated, herbal finish. **01** spice, violets & black berry notes abound. 92 pts *WS*. Fr oak 22 mths, third new.

★★★★ **Syrah** ('Shiraz' pvs ed) **03** gears up: dense colour & choc-mulberry fruit pastille flesh arraigned by 15% alc. Sumptuous, as was succulent, sweet & ripe **02**; raspberry, allspice notes, not as grippy but elegant, polished. 14% cab, 22 mths seasoned Fr oak.

Merlot ★★★★ **02** pvs edition we noted minty, mulberry prelude to textured mouthful, with herbal notes. No **03**.—*DS*

St Clements see Daview Vineyards
St Dalfour see Lost Horizons

Steenberg Vineyards

Constantia ▪ Est 1990 ▪ 1stB 1996 ▪ Tasting & sales Mon-Fri 9-4.30 Sat & public holidays 9.30-1.30 ▪ Closed Easter Sun/Mon, Dec 25/26 & Jan 1 ▪ Fee R5 p/p for groups of 10+ ▪ Tours by appt Mon-Fri 10 & 3 Sat 10 ▪ Catharina's Restaurant; five-star Steenberg Hotel; championship golf course etc (see Stay-Over/Eat-out sections) ▪ Owner Graham Beck ▪ Cellarmaster John Loubser (Nov 2001) ▪ Winemaker Ruth Penfold (2003) ▪ Viticulturists Herman Hanekom & Johann de Swardt (1990/1999) ▪ 63 ha (cabs s/f, merlot, nebbiolo, pinot, shiraz, chard, sauvignon, semillon)

▪ *450 tons 50 000 cs 40% red 60% white ▪ PO Box 224 Steenberg 7947 ▪ info@steenbrg.co.za ▪ www.steenberg-vineyards.co.za* ▪ ***T 713·2211*** ▪ *F 713·2201*

In stark contrast with coolest-ever 2004, the heat of 2005, coupled with a dramatic fire in a neighbouring vineyard, threatened Steenberg's renowned cool-conditioned sauvignon and forced an earlier than usual harvest to capture those hallmark herbaceous flavours. An inspiring trip to Sancerre, and an invitation to join the prestigious Cape Winemakers Guild (offering him the chance to make small parcels of experimental wines), were highlights of the year for John Loubser. But the biggest excitement by far has been his former employer Graham Beck taking the helm as the new owner. 'We are extremely pleased to be part of a wine-focused organisation now, having previously been part of a hotel group.' Steenberg will maintain its own identity and, with the new expertise behind them, can only fly forward. 'Watch this space,' says Loubser, 'There are very exciting times ahead.'

★★★★ **Catharina** The flagship, after Catharina Ras, farm's founder; red quintet intended to express Steenberg identity. **03** may be closest to goal yet. Led by best performer, merlot, with shiraz, cabs s/f, (40/26/19/13) 'salted' with 2% nebbiolo. Still fairly closed but quality evident in balanced structure, fine tannin, creamy yet fresh mouthfeel, lingering savouriness. Give yr/2 to settle; potential to ±2009. **02** (★★★★☆) light-textured, deeply flavoursome. 20 mths new Fr barriques.

★★★★☆ **Merlot** Luxurious **04** turns up charm with greater nuance, depth, to trademark red-berried minty elegance. Crushed velvet richness; fresh acid backing; sleek polish from effortlessly absorbed 15 mths new Fr oak. Already delicious; probably even better around 2009. **03** cool, creamy, with lovely back-palate richness, telling mineral thread.

★★★★ **Nebbiolo** Stands out in range replete with distinctive individuals. Honest & well-executed; defined by clear-cut mineral, violet, tart wild-berry scents. **04** compact, taut, with arresting grip & acid, contrasting fragrant, sweet-fruited filling. Begs any Italian pork delicacy. **03** high-toned violet fragrance, reverberating mineral tannins. 13 mths used Fr oak.

★★★★ **Shiraz 04** big, punchy mouthful; nice freshness, well-modulated tannins. Youthfully exuberant still: coconut tones from new wood, spicy fruit currently apart; however, has concentration to harmonise over next few yrs; good prospects till 2008. **03** delicately handled fruit, tannins & oak. 13 mths new barrels, 60/40 Fr/Am. *Wine* ★★★★.

★★★★★ **Sauvignon Blanc Reserve** Recognised as Cape benchmark for over a decade. Noted for penetrating dried grass/passion fruit bouquet, emphatic presence & staying power. **05** true to type, though with more sophisticated restraint, less flamboyance. Full, rich mouthful; stately rather than agile but fine, rousing sauvignon finale. **04** a real powerhouse; penetrating mouthful delivered with flair, poise. *Wine* ★★★★☆. Ex-single vyd, 19 yrs old, on farm's propitious 'golden acre'.

★★★★ **Sauvignon Blanc** Perennial favourite; larger quantities than Reserve but also a fast seller. **05** maintains unflashy, ultra-fresh, bouncily dry feel, though pure gooseberry/lemon tones are touch riper, broader than pvs; excellent balance, remarkably sustained. Incl tiny but influential 7% semillon. **04** *Wine* ★★★★.

★★★★ **CWG Auction Reserve Barrel Fermented Sauvignon Blanc** new Fabulous introduction to **05**; trademark wild dried grass, minerals, citrus flamboyance lifted by suggestion of oak spice. More knife-edged austerity, tension. Not as big as either regular offering but with great concentration, expanse, length. All used Fr oak fermented/aged 4 wks.

★★★★★ **Semillon** This standout new-wave example a prominent factor in semillon's resurgence in Cape. Latest version is powerful, vibrant (as are all the farm's **05** whites). Also more sophisticated & complex than pvs, richer interplay of aromas & textures; subtle lemon/honey/tangerine fragrances melded with suggestion of toasty oak. Incl splash sauvignon (5%) for extra spine. More food compatible than exuberant **04** (★★★★☆) yet similarly concentrated, likely to improve over 4-5 yrs. Barrel-fermented in new Fr oak, 5 wks on lees. Single vyd. *Wine* ★★★★.

★★★★☆ **CWG Auction Reserve Barrel Fermented Sauvignon Blanc-Semillon** new Builds on (and convincingly trumps!) quality & potential of classic Graves varietal pairing pvsly attained with 'Catharina White' bottlings. Sophisticated **05** fresh citrus peel/honey complexity matched on palate by silky viscosity. Beautifully focused & clean-lined; even better in a few yrs. 60/40 blend, fermented/aged 4 wks in seasoned Fr barrels before blending.

★★★★ **Steenberg 1682 Brut** Dainty, fresh MCC, from traditional chardonnay & pinot; 70/30 mix in latest **NV** (04). Clean, biscuity nose with delicate raspberry top note from the pinot; unequivocal 'brut' palate softened by creamy, fine bead. Small portion barrel-fermented; 15 mths on lees (set to increase to 2 yrs for future releases). Comfortably low alc (11.5%) for solo sipping.

Unwooded Chardonnay ★★★☆ new to this guide & the local market (pvs exported). Loubser's 'fresh Golden Delicious apple' perfect description for **05**. Lees-aged for extra weight, vinosity; clean bone-dry finish. Food friendly.—*AL*

Stellar Winery

*Olifants River ▪ Est 1998 ▪ 1stB 2001 ▪ Tasting & sales Mon-Sat 8-5 ▪ Closed Easter Fri/Sun & Dec 25 ▪ Tours by appt ▪ Farm produce ▪ Tourgroups by appt ▪ Owner Stellar Winery (Pty) Ltd ▪ Winemaker Dudley Wilson (Jan 2002), with Berty Jones (2000) ▪ Viticulturist Dudley Wilson ▪ 100 ha (merlot, pinotage, shiraz, chenin, colombard, sauvignon, muscat d'A) ▪ 1 000 tons 45 000 cs own labels + 400 000ℓ bulk + 10 000 cs for clients, incl Peter Riegel Weinimport (Ger), Lovian (Hol), Triton Export Exchange (USA), Masuda Co (Japan), Les Caves de la Riviera (Côte d'Ivoire) ▪ 80% red 17% white 2% rosé 1% other ▪ HACCP & Eurepgap certified ▪ PO Box 4 Klawer 8145 ▪ info@stellarorganics.com ▪ www.stellarorganics.com ▪ **T (027) 216·1310** ▪ F (027) 216·1537*

Being situated on the outer fringe of the Cape's winegrowing area, with an aesthetic to match (see 'Heaven on Earth' below) doesn't preclude this Trawal winery from racking up some pretty mainstream achievements. Woolworths have brought some of the wines into their house Organic range and they've taken home gold medals from the BioFach 2005 organic products fair and Swiss International Airlines 2005 wine competition – this latter for their Shiraz. Winemaker Dudley Wilson is heartened but not surprised: 'These awards confirm our belief that our organically produced wines can compete with the best conventional wines.' The winery (which started out roofless, affording 'stellar' views) boasts a new sterile bottling room, grape seed oil production facility and fully operational tasting room.

The Sensory Collection

Cabernet ★★★ Wilson & co conducted complicated sounding experiments with Fr/Am oak before coming up with a formula for **03**, previewed last ed, still in thrall of wood, some black fruit lurking; give another yr to soften. **Merlot** new ★★★ **03** sweet-tempered, bit shy, hint of sweet mulberry fruit, youthful balanced tannins. **Shiraz** ★★★ Swiss gold for **03**, black cherry & dark choc whiffs; flavourful & balanced despite huge 15.4% alc, supportive oaking. **Pinotage** ★★ Full-bore wooding the norm here: **03**'s soft plum fruit struggles with great whack of vanilla oak, powerful wood tannins.

Stellar range

Cabernet Sauvignon ★★ **04** not tasted. **03** crème fraiche & black berry notes made for a most unusual cab. Fr/Am oak. **Shiraz** ★★★ **03** unready. **02** Rhône-style with leathery, gamey, savoury tones; well balanced. **Pinotage** ★★ **03** quite a beefy number (14.5% alc), shyish plum notes, strident tannins need food/time. **Merlot** ★☆ **03** rather different to easy-drinking pvs; very dry & astringent, suggestion of cassis on nose. **No-Sulphur-Added Chenin Blanc** new Quirky & individual, **04** with hint of lemon meringue pie. **Colombar** Last was **02**, past best. **Sauvignon Blanc** ★★★ **05** blended away. **04** good balance of fruit with crisp acidity; easy-going ±12% alc. **Colombard-Sauvignon Blanc** ★☆ **02**'s fruit was fading fast last ed. Next is **05**, unready. **Heaven on Earth Vin de Paille** Still current **03** a convincing statement from muscat d'A dried on straw & rooibos tea! Unctuous mouthfeel (300g/ℓ RS), weighty mid-palate of cooked apricot, cream & (what else?) rooibos. 11.5% alc. Sample, perhaps even ★★★★☆ on release. **Muscat d'Alexandrie** discontinued.

Live-A-Little range

Really Ravishing Red ★★ 100% shiraz in **03**, slightly ambitiously named: earthy, & touch austere, with hint of plum. Again low 12.5% alc. **Rather Revealing Rosé** new ★★ **03** from shiraz; light, dryish & gentle. Be wildly wicked & try with strawberries & cream. **Wildly Wicked White** ★★ **05** changes to mainly chenin (84%), sauvignon; slightly minty aroma, light, soft acidity; 'teasing' rather than 'wicked'. Some exported under Moonlight and Firefly labels. All ranges WO W Cape. — *IvH*

Stellcape Vineyards

Stellenbosch ▪ 1stB 2003 ▪ Tasting, sales & tours Mon-Fri 9-4.30 Sat 9-12 ▪ Fee R3/taste ▪ Closed most pub hols ▪ Farm-style platters; or BYO picnic ▪ Tourgroups ▪ Conferencing for 150+ delegates ▪ Art gallery ▪ Owners Kobie van der Westhuizen & Tertius Boshoff ▪ Winemaker Abraham Smith (2003), advised by Riaan Möller (2004) ▪ 200 ha (cab, merlot, pinotage, shiraz, chenin, sauvignon) ▪ 1 700 tons total 50 tons/2 000 cs own label 100% red ▪ PO Box 26 Koelenhof 7605 ▪ jjwines@mail.com ▪ ***T/F 865·2010***

Young guns Tertius Boshoff and Kobie van der Westhuizen, with help and advice from industry connections and freshly inspired by a grand tour of the Napa valley, promise to bring some serious excitement to the winelands. 'Expect something totally different' they say of the new Stellcape cellar and visitor facility in the Helderberg's viticulturally reputed 'Golden Triangle', replete with lounges, function area, art exhibitions and view-decks. The wines for the Stellcape range are made at Koelenhof (consultant is Riaan Möller, previously assistant winemaker at Ernie Els). Another aspect is JJ Wines, made on the VdW's farm Swartrivier in Koelenhof, and intended as a range of easy-drinkers. 'For the person who likes to drink *two* bottles comfortably,' explains Tertius B. This one of very few Cape wineries which welcomes members of the public (including large groups) to come and make their own wine on the premises.

Cabernet Sauvignon-Merlot 04 (barrel sample) flamboyant bdx-style blend, 60/40, matured 16 mths Fr oak. Hugely ripe & extracted, dense fruit & some lifted notes. Too young to rate.

JJ Wines

Red Blend ★★ Rustic shiraz/pinotage mix; **03** brambly/herby notes, distinct stalky character; strictly unserious. 14 mths 2nd fill Fr oak. Following tasted as samples: **Cabernet Sauvignon** Darkly brooding **04** gives away almost nothing except tight, gripping tannins. Ditto **Merlot**, both too unformed to rate. **Shiraz 04** early-drinking style with good varietal character (incl white pepper & anise); sweet, approachable tannins. Provisional ★★★. — *CT*

Stellekaya Winery

Stellenbosch ▪ Est/1stB 1999 ▪ Mon-Fri 10-4 Sat 11-3 ▪ Fee R10 (incl glass) ▪ Sales Mon-Sat 9-4 ▪ Closed pub hols ▪ Meals by appt ▪ Facilities for small tourgroups ▪ Owner Dave & Jane Lello ▪ Winemaker Nontsikilela Biyela, advised by Mark Carmichael-Green (2004/2005) ▪ 100 tons 100% red ▪ PO Box 12426 Die Boord 7613 ▪ info@stellekaya.co.za ▪ www.stellekaya.com ▪ ***T 883·3873*** *▪ F 883·2536*

It's been a while in the making but Bosman's Crossing, the 'wine village' Dave and Jane Lello and collaborators have created around the old KWV brandy site in Stellenbosch opens to the public this year. At the heart is the Stellekaya ('House of Stars') cellar and tasting area, where visitors can sample the full constellation, including the new limited-release Bordeaux-style blend. Mark Carmichael-Green now consults, bringing both wide experience and 'a more a scientific approach, which is important as volumes increase and the range grows'.

★★★★★ **Orion** new Attractively perfumed flagship; **03** cab-dominated bdx blend with merlot, cab f, (64:27:9), 2 yrs barrelled, 85% new; full fruity palate marked by depth & intensity; lingering, elegant finish.

★★★★ **Cape Cross** Assertive (unwooded) pinotage dominates **03** (★★★) fruity blend of merlot, pinotage & cab (45:30:25). Bigger alc than pvs (14% vs. 13.5%), less subtlety, finesse. 22 mths Fr oak. **02** attractive & well balanced, supported by tannin structure to ensure few yrs development.

★★★★ **Cabernet Sauvignon 03**'s restrained fruit somewhat overwhelmed by wood mid-2005 (though new wood fraction actually down 20% compared with pvs), usual elegance needs more time to emerge. 22 mths Fr barrels. Same fine-tannins & classical style as **02** (★★★★★), remarkable achievement in a weak vintage; 60% new oak.

★★★☆ **Merlot** Higher percentage alc (14.2%) helps propel **03** (★★★★) into higher league; classy aromas; flavours of cherries with mint hint. Goodbye leafiness, hello richness. **02**, with red plum & green olive notes, not for keeping. 22 mths Fr oak, usually 25% new.

Boschetto Rosso Red ★★★☆ Change of recipe to consummate pizza wine with addition of juicy sangiovese, in **04** kitchen sink blend with cab, merlot & shiraz (10:40:40:10); exotic sour cherry & dark choc flavours.—*NP*

Stellenbosch Hills 

Stellenbosch ▪ Est 1945 ▪ 1stB 1972 ▪ Tasting & sales Mon-Fri 8.30–4.45 Sat 9–12.15 (sales close 15 mins later) ▪ Fee R10 ▪ Closed Easter Fri, Dec 25 & Jan 1 ▪ Owners 20 members ▪ Winemaker PG Slabbert, with Suzanne Miller (Jan 1997/Nov 2003) ▪ Viticulturist PG Slabbert (Jan 1997), advised by Johan Pienaar ▪ ±1 000 ha (cab, merlot, pinotage, shiraz, chard, chenin, sauvignon, muscat de H) ▪ 8 000 tons 20 000 cs own label 65% red 35% white ▪ PO Box 40 Vlottenburg 7604 ▪ info@stellenbosch-hills.co.za ▪ www.stellenbosch-hills.co.za ▪ ***T 881·3828/9*** *▪ F 881·3357*

Until its metamorphosis into Stellenbosch Hills, Vlottenburg Cellars was selling all its branded wines from the cellar door: you'd be forgiven for thinking you'd chanced on a garage sale, with boots open and ready to be piled with bargains, particularly the Merlot, by savvy wine buyers. The aesthetics may have changed to the tune of an R15m investment – along with the name, which now better reflects the areas from which the grapes are sourced: Vlottenburg, Lynedoch and Stellenbosch Kloof. What hasn't changed, thankfully, is the price:quality ratio of what's in the bottle. Bulk sales to Distell are down and 25% of the wine is siphoned off for the local and international markets.

★★★★ **1707 Reserve** Classic Cape bdx-style blend (50/50 cab/merlot) intended as flagship; which stylish **01** clearly is. Tasted for pvs ed, densely packed dark choc core, hints mint, black cherry & lead pencil, not so much as a glimmer of tannin out of place. Keep 5+ yrs.

★★★★ **Cabernet Sauvignon** Needing 3/4 yrs in cellar to soften, **04** (★★★☆) herbaceous with puckering tannins. leaner, more alcoholic (13.9%) than **02** with its mulberry, savoury meaty fruit & touches of cool cedar, firmish tannins. 16 mths Fr oak, 30% new.

★★★★ **Merlot 03** (★★★) a bump in this variety's track record. Like pvs, classically styled with ripe cassis & coffee aromas/flavours but latest fruit-shy, lacking flesh & juicy to counter rasping tannins. **02** performed well in a difficult vintage. Standout **01** clinched two top 2003 FCTWS awards: Best Merlot & Discovery of Show.

★★★★ **Muscat de Hambourg** ✓ Fortified, jerepiko-style dessert wine. **05** attractive example of this unusual variety; 210g/ℓ sugar balanced by fresh acidity/16.5% alc. Elegant, old-fashioned tea-roses on farewell. **04** untasted. 375ml bottles.

Blanc de Blanc ☺ ★★ **NV** off-dry quaffer from chenin/sauvignon; soft tropical bouquet & palate. This, Rouge below, 1 000ml flagon screwcap.

Pinotage ★★☆ **02** skinny version of pvs, lacking flesh & fruit. Muted blue berry/cherry aromas/flavours, touch green on finish. Yr older Fr oak.

Shiraz ★★★ Medium-bodied with sweet lift at end thanks to Am oak. **02** enticing cassis/Xmas cake in bouquet, oak dominates palate. Ready now, with food, or 2-3 yrs. 16 mths oak, 50% new (Fr/Am), balance used Fr. **Rouge** ★★ **NV**; unwooded & unpretentious blend pinotage, merlot 50/50, scented with merlot's choc/game/blueberry. Pinotage delivers fresh acidity, hint bitterness in tail. **Chardonnay** ★★★☆ **05** (sample) delightfully ripe citrus/tropical notes, walnuts & honeysuckle; good minerality & vibrant acidity. **Chenin Blanc** ★★ **04** (sample) not as demure or as off-dry as pvs; still easy-drinking with candied ginger/pineapple aromas & flavours. Lacks **Sauvignon Blanc** ★★☆ **05** made reductively to preserve flavours/freshness; lemon/watermelon nose let down by dullish palate, hot/flat finish. —*JP*

Stellenbosch Vineyards see Omnia Wines

Stellenbosch Wine & Country Estate new

Stellenbosch ▪ Est 2004 ▪ 1stB 2005 ▪ Closed to public ▪ Owner Stellenbosch Wine & Country Estate (Pty) Ltd ▪ Winemaker Wynand Pienaar (Feb 2004), with Boschendal (James Farquharson) & Marklew Wines (Duan Brits) ▪ Viticulturist Wynand Pienaar ▪ 29.8 ha (cinsaut, pinotage, shiraz, chenin) ▪ 31 tons 1 450 cs ▪ 80% red 20% white ▪ PO Box 158 Elsenburg 7607 ▪ wynlpers@iafrica.com ▪ ***T 083·305·7332*** *▪ F 982·7925*

The long-held dream of owning a wine property has secured a very real piece of estate in the Muldersvlei area of Stellenbosch for Wynand Pienaar and partners. They've identified a gap in the market for wines from older vineyards, and plan to fill it by coaxing top quality from three 28 year old blocks on Klapmuts Hill. That, Pienaar & co concede, is the easy part. The challenge now is to position the brand in the market and promote it at the relevant level. The wines are made off-site at present, but in the pipeline are a cellar, with all facilities, and a further 50ha of vineyards.

Following **05**s sampled ex-barrel, none ready to rate. **Chenin Blanc** Robust, dry; power-packed ripeness commensurate with 14.9% alc. Fr oak, all used. **Pinotage** and **Shiraz** healthy colours, fruit/structure balance that augurs well. —*AL*

Stellendrift

Stellenbosch ▪ Est/1stB 1995 ▪ Sales via phone or from Hudsons on Vredenheim farm daily 9–5 (see separate entry) ▪ Closed Dec 25 ▪ Owner/winemaker/viticulturist Fanie Cilliers (SHZ Cilliers/Kuün Wines) ▪ 12 ha (cab, merlot, pinotage) ▪ ±5 000 cs 90% red 10% white ▪ PO Box 6340 Uniedal 7612 ▪ fcilliers@wam.co.za ▪ ***T 887·6561/082·372·5180*** *▪ F 887·6561*

Fanie Cilliers says he recently unearthed information that his family first made wine on the farm Kruispad in the Bottelary area just over 300 years ago. The tradition in its current Stellendrift/Cilliers Cellars form has just celebrated its 10th vintage, and Fanie C is well pleased with the recognition he's getting, particularly a *Wine* Best Value citation for his Merlot. He vinifies at Vredenheim farm where, among many other attractions, both his ranges can be bought.

Cabernet Sauvignon ★★★ **03** well-made lighter-style cab showing attractive ripe berry fruit & firm grip. Incl dash merlot; ±8 mths Fr/Am oak. **Cilliers Cellars Cabernet Sauvignon** ★★★ Returns to guide with **03**, approachable choc flavours, soft, easy, characterful. **Merlot** ★★ **03** *Wine* Best Value award, but to us very retiring compared with ripe, plummy **02**; some dry savoury tones, usual sweet-sour finish. 2nd fill oak. **Pinotage** new ★★ First under Stellendrift brand; **03** hints mulberry fruit & booming dry tannins. 4 mths 1st/2nd fill oak. **Cabernet Sauvignon-Merlot** ★★★ **04** ripe-fruited 70/30 blend, yr Fr oak; ripe red berry fruit, firm but balanced tannins/acidity, approachable but better in yr/2. **Merlot-Pinotage** new ★★★ 'A fluke,' avers Fanie C, amazed **04** turned out so well; 70/30 mix with ingrained food cordiality via lively acidity, dry savoury finish. **Special Select Dry Red** new ★★ **03** affable, undemanding; mainly cab, slugs pinotage, merlot, drizzled with soft vanilla oak (3rd fill Fr). **Cape White** ★★ new Rara avis in this red-wine portfolio; **NV** 80/20 chenin, chardonnay, unwooded, oxidative style, some lemon barley hints, medium body. —*DH*

StellenHills Wines

Stellenbosch ▪ Est/1stB 2001 ▪ Visits by appt ▪ Owner/winemaker Johann Slazus ▪ ±700 cs 36% red 64% white ▪ PO Box 415 Stellenbosch 7599 ▪ orders@stellenhills.co.za ▪ www.stellenhills.co.za ▪ ***T 083·252·2020*** *▪ F 887·7745*

The maiden vintage Barriques Nouveau 01 fared well on the Nederburg Auction: 'It's encouraging to know that there's a strong demand for matured Chardonnay,' says ophthalmic surgeon and chardonnay specialist Johann Slazus, who produces several styles of his chosen variety.

Charade ★★★★ Dry red from shiraz (60%) & cab, fermented in open wood vats, aged yr in new Fr oak. **01** tasted mid-2004 was soft & plump with meaty/plummy notes, powdery but harmonious tannins; modest 13% alc. New vintage not tasted for this ed. **Barriques Nouveau** ★★★★ Barrel-fermented/aged chardonnay, new Fr oak; from single Stbosch vyd. Toasty oak & vanilla dominate **04**'s bouquet, marmalade/nuts take over palate. Intense & weighty but with lively goodbye; 13.4% alc lower than pvs. Should improve with cellaring. **Chardonnay** ★★★★ Older oak for this version, 11 mths; vibrant & crisp; **04** a melange of orange peel/ Golden Delicious apple/lemon grass; succulent, elegant finish. *—MM*

Stellenvale see Ultra Liquors

Stellenzicht Vineyards

*Stellenbosch ▪ Tasting & sales Mon-Fri 9-5 Sat/Sun & pub hols 10-4 ▪ Fee R25 ▪ Owner Lusan Holdings ▪ Winemaker Guy Webber, with Ilse van Dijk ▪ Vineyard manager Johan Mong ▪ Viticulturist Eben Archer ▪ 70% red 30% white ▪ PO Box 104 Stellenbosch 7599 ▪ info@stellenzicht.co.za ▪ www.stellenzicht.co.za ▪ **T 880·1103** ▪ F 880·1107*

'As I get older – I turned 40 in December – I tend to strive more for elegance than power in my wines, Rhapsody being a good example,' says winemaker Guy Webber. Though his approach is evolving, his and assistant Ilse van Dijk's primary goal is to 'make a good wine before seeking varietal expression – balance always supersedes pure fruit'. Fruit will be uppermost in their mind, however, when they harvest young shiraz and sauvignon vineyards for the first time this season. Otherwise they'll be 'just following the same winning recipe'.

★★★★★ **Syrah** Set a new Cape shiraz benchmark with dramatic **94**; quality level sustained with **02**, but the real excitement will come only around turn of decade, when currently restrained, ripe, smoky fruit emerges from strong tannin sheath. Worth waiting for. IWC 2004 gold for **01**, with headily spicy bouquet & electrifying, sustained finish, lavish 15.8% alc. ±19 mths Fr, Am, Hungarian oak. From mature vyd named 'Plum Pudding Hill'. Not retasted.

★★★★ **Stellenzicht** Cab-dominated bdx-inflected blend (±50%), tempered by merlot (30%), equal parts cab f, malbec. None since **00**, which displayed a polished structure.

★★★★★ **Semillon Reserve** Usually serious dry white, though **03** (★★★★) somewhat less striking mid-2004; showed elegance but lacked definition of pvs; overt butteriness dominated palate, finished abruptly; whereas **02** retained usual complexity in spite of lesser yr. Recent alcs 14.5+%. 85% wooded, new/2nd fill Fr, Am, Hngrian oak 9 mths.

Rhapsody ★★★ Blend pinotage/shiraz (53/47), 16 mths mainly new oak, Fr/Am/Hngrian; **02** light coloured/fleshed, slightly earthy; very dry.

Golden Triangle range

Cabernet Sauvignon ★★★★ **01** textbook cassis & spearmint nose; nutty, approachable tannins from 30 mths maturation on lees in 67% Fr/33% Am oak; no racking. Ripe red/black fruit; warm goodbye from 14.4% alc. **Merlot** ★★★★ None sampled since **00**, with trademark clean-fruited succulence bolstered by ripe meaty frame. **Pinotage** ★★★★ **03** intense mulberry fruit, scrub & spice; firm acidity & charry oak. Slightly bitter lift to finish, alc – while lower than pvs (14.6%) – still stands out. **Shiraz** ★★★★ **03** brooding & reticent, strong tannins, ripe black fruit & powerful (14.9%) alc. *Wine* ★★★★, but probably for earlier enjoyment. ±15 mths mix new/seasoned oak, mostly Fr. **Chardonnay** ★★★ Not tasted for this edition. Barrel-fermented/matured **03** creamy, spicy & savoury; fair amount of sweet-sour acidity exposed in tail. **Sauvignon Blanc** ★★★ Unlike tropical-fruit-toned pvs, **05** sample more floral, subtle pink musk sweet, soft acidity & silky finish. Moderate 13% alc. *— CvZ*

Sterhuis

*Stellenbosch ▪ Est 1980 ▪ 1stB 2002 ▪ Visits by appt ▪ Closed Christian holidays ▪ Facilities for children ▪ Conservation area ▪ Owners Kruger family ▪ Winemaker Johan Kruger ▪ Viticulturist Hendrik de Beer, advised by Kevin Watt ▪ 48 ha ▪ 300 tons 2 500 cs own label 50/50 red/white ▪ PO Box 131 Koelenhof 7605 ▪ sterhuis@intekom.co.za ▪ **T 083·411·0757** ▪ F 906·1195*

Translated as 'Star House', the name of this farm on the high slopes of the Bottelary Hills was given by early colonists because it appears as if Venus rises above it. It's increasingly apt, however: last year the Krugers celebrated a quarter-century here and also international acclaim for their 04 Chardonnay. Rising talent Johan K (also making wine for Diemersdal) says the 2005 harvest was a classic case of good timing, with white grapes picked just before a major heatwave (chenin in particular shows 'huge promise') while the warmth ripened tannins in the reds. Assisted by new viticulturist Hendrik de Beer, JK plans to increase production, and is thinking of producing a cabernet-merlot blend.

★★★★★ **Chardonnay** new **04** well integrated, new Fr oak fermented version. Marriage of lemon & toasty oak, marmalade flavours, flinty textures, zesty goodbye. Ambitious 14.5% alc unobtrusive. *Wine* ★★★★★

★★★★ **Merlot 04** not ready for tasting, **03** (★★★) tasted for pvs ed showed some berry notes on palate, but now dominated by oak (16 mths Fr, 40% new), concealing 15% alc under dry tannins. Lacks more succulent savoury notes of elegant maiden **02**. 14% alc.

Sauvignon Blanc 05 a leap up on pvs. Flinty, with green notes of asparagus/capsicum, well defined palate with mouth-filling lees characters & crisp acidity. Lingering acidity. Unfinished sample showing ★★★★ potential. *—CT*

Stettyn Winery

Worcester ▪ Est 1964 ▪ 1stB ca 1984 ▪ Tasting Mon-Thu 8–4.30 Fri 8–3.30 ▪ Closed pub hols ▪ Tours by appt ▪ BYO picnic ▪ Walks ▪ 4x4 route ▪ Owners 11 shareholders ▪ Winemaker Albie Treurnicht (Nov 2000) ▪ Viti consultant Schalk du Toit ▪ 300 ha (cab, cinsaut, merlot, pinotage, shiraz, chard, chenin, colombard, sauvignon, semillon) ▪ ±4 600 tons 3 000 cs own label + 3.6m litres bulk ▪ 55% red 45% white ▪ Export brands: Baobab, Tyne & Dalby ▪ PO Box 1520 Worcester 6849 ▪ stettyncellar@telkomsa.net ▪ www.stettyncellar.co.za ▪ ***T/F (023) 340·4220***

No update available on this winery; contact details and wine notes from previous edition.

Millstone Pinotage ★★★ **01** satisfying ripe plum/red cherry flavours; charry touch to long fruity tannins. 14 mths 3rd fill oak. **Signature Reserve Shiraz-Cabernet Sauvignon** ★★★★ Elegant blend, shiraz 60%; **01** well rounded, big benign tannins in long mineral finish. **Sauvignon Blanc** ★★★ **04** with 5% oaked semillon for extra flavour; English gooseberries & nettles in lively, zesty, light-bodied package (11.5% alc). **Semillon-Chardonnay** ★★★ Fermented with Oregon oak; **03** bears its wood lightly, allowing citrus/tropical fruit plenty of leeway; attractively light 12% alc. **Vin de Paille** ★★★ **01** characterful dessert from air-dried hanepoot, botrytis whiff enlivening marmalade & apricot richness. Wrcstr & W Cape WOs. *—DH*

Steven Rom see Ruitersvlei
Steytler see Kaapzicht
Stoep see Main Street Winery
Stonebuck see Middelvlei
Stonecross see Deetlefs
Stonehurst see Excelsior

Stonewall Wines

Stellenbosch (see Helderberg map) ▪ Est 1828 ▪ 1stB 1997 ▪ Visits by appt Mon-Fri 9-5 Sat 9-1 ▪ Closed Easter Fri/Sun, Dec 25/26 & Jan 1 ▪ Conferencing ▪ Owner/viticulturist De Waal Koch ▪ Vini consultant Ronell Wiid (May 2000) ▪ 75 ha (cabs s/f, merlot, pinotage, shiraz, chard, sauvignon) ▪ 2 500 cs own label 90% red 10% white ▪ PO Box 5145 Helderberg 7135 ▪ stonewall@mweb.co.za ▪ ***T 855·3675*** *▪ F 855·2206*

Love and passion for the whole product, from vineyard to wine, are essential, says De Waal Koch as he continues to strive for top quality across his compact range. The recently enlarged underground barrel cellar is rich in character and atmosphere. But it's not just a pretty place — the humidity and temperature are 'exceptional' in the 177-year-old underground tanks.

★★★★ **Cabernet Sauvignon** Hallmark is great concentration from low-yielding (4-6 t/ha) old bushvines. **02** shrugged off difficult vintage with confident structure (more so than blend below). **03** (★★★★) dark plum/cassis aromas & flavours; lengthy, dusty, dry finish (drier than pvs). Ripe, firm tannins & black fruit core auger well for cellaring potential. 18 mths Fr oak. 14% alc.

★★★★ **Rubér** Forceful blend, structured for keeping. **03** (★★★★) rings the changes with merlot leading cab for the first time (57/43), alc up to 14.5%. Complex dark choc/spice/dust bouquet; rounded, soft tannin & mineral palate. Bountiful fruit supports generous oaking but not warm, alcoholic finish. 50% new Fr. **02** (★★★★) fruit-forward New-World styling.

Chardonnay ★★★★ **04** continues along upward path blazed by pvs. Bright lemon-gold colour; asparagus/lime aromas carry through to palate, this enriched/given buttery texture from ferment/maturation in mix new/old Fr oak by oak. Balance, poise benefiting from lower alc (13.5%). **Pinotage** discontinued. *—MM*

Stoney Croft

Stellenbosch ▪ Est 2000 ▪ 1stB 2001 ▪ Visits by appt ▪ Owner Sacramento Trading (Pty) Ltd ▪ Winemaker Danie Steytler, with Charl Coetzee (Jan 2001/Mar 2003) ▪ Viticulturist George Steytler (Mar 2000) ▪ 3 ha (shiraz) ▪ 25 tons 2 000 cs 100% red ▪ PO Box 239 Koelenhof 7605 ▪ cstone@absamail.co.za ▪ www.frontierlifestyle.co.za/stoneycroft.htm ▪ ***T/F 865·2360***

No update available on this winery; contact details and wine notes from previous edition.

★★★★ **Shiraz 02** appealing fynbos nose, herbal flavours brushed with peppermint, good mulberry fruit, tea-leaf character, supported by ripe tannin. 15 mths new Fr/Am oak (90/10). *—NP*

Stony Brook

Franschhoek ▪ Est 1995 ▪ 1stB 1996 ▪ Tasting & sales Mon-Sat 10-1 or by appt ▪ Closed Easter Fri/Sun/Mon, Dec 25/26, Jan 1 ▪ Fee R10 (refunded on purchase of 12 btls) ▪ Owners Nigel & Joy McNaught ▪ Winemaker Nigel McNaught ▪ Viti consultant Paul Wallace ▪ 14 ha ▪ 80 tons 5 500 cs 60% red 40% white ▪ ISO 14001 certified ▪ PO Box 22 Franschhoek 7690 ▪ info@stonybrook.co.za mcnaught@iafrica.com ▪ ***T/F 876·2182***

Judging by the line most often heard when entering the tasting room you'd swear Joy McNaught has become a pop singer. 'Don't let the dogs out!' has become her recurrent cry following the addition to her and husband Nigel's family of a pair of Jack Russells. In much the same runaway style, Stony Brook is celebrating its 10th vintage with extensions to their tasting room, a new barrel maturation cellar and a significant increase in spending on oak barrels. Embracing a philosophy of 'full oak integration with the wine' means consumers may have to wait a little longer than in the past. Says JMcN: 'We decided that the extra time spent in the cellar in new Fr oak barriques had really paid dividends.' There's a Ghost Gum already – watch out for it becoming a range in the future.

★★★★ **Cabernet Sauvignon Reserve 03** has distinctive eucalyptus to dense dark-berried fruit, plush texture ruffled by house's signature firm tannins. Needs good 5 yrs before opening, 8 for maturity. 22 mths Fr oak, 80% new.

★★★★ **Ghost Gum** A different, equally worthy take on cab; here 10% merlot, cab f & petit v add complexity. Selection of best barrels, 30 mths new Fr oak. Maiden **02** now bottled: packed with berries & cassis, oak integrating well, but mouth-coating tannins deter for next 5 yrs. Should last 10+. Fine wine, classically constructed. *Wine* ★★★★★.

★★★★ **Pinotage** ✓ **01**, tasted mid-2004, maturing with distinction; tannins smoothing out, fruit sweet, good length/potential. 13.5% alc. 10 mths Am/Fr oak.

★★★★ **Shiraz Reserve 02** (★★★★★) had exceptional vinosity, concentration, balance. **03**'s power discreetly cloaked in oak, with excellent concentration of dark meaty, smoky flavours; dry ripe tannins, touch of earthiness on finish. More subtlety than version below. From Mbury, Frhoek fruit. 14 mths oak, 22 mths.

★★★★ **Reserve** Blend mainly cab, merlot, dashes petit v, malbec, cab f in **03**. More approachable than most in range: attractive mulberry, lead pencil intro, neat classic build, fine-grained tannins not overwhelming, clean dry finish. 20 mths oak, 70% new. No **02**

Cabernet Sauvignon ★★★ **03** has all correct flavours, fine dark-berried fruit – & forbidding tannins: needs 5/7 yrs. 20 mths oak, new/used. **Merlot** ★★★★ **03** more firm, with more oak, than pvs, still daunting mid-2005: tough unyielding tannins unexpected in merlot – will they ever loosen? Warm choc & coffee; tight knot of dark-berried fruit. 20 mths mostly new Fr oak. **Shiraz** ★★★★ Hearty, 'masculine' **03** less ripe than pvs, more meaty, savoury style, whiff of veld-fire & scrub, firm savoury palate, twist of black cherry fruit to finish. 14 mths older oak. **Camissa** ★★★★ Maiden **03** blend merlot & cab with 10% shiraz, tasted last yr. Ripe black berry entry; firmly encased in sweet tannin & oak (Fr/Am oak, ±yr), needs few yrs to soften. **Chardonnay** ★★★★ Discreetly oaked **04**'s delicate peach aroma leads to firm, juicy peach flavours, with some delicacy & refinement, longish finish. Bunch-pressed, fermented/4 mths oak. **Semillon** ★★★★ Tangy, mouth-watering **04**, whiffs of vanilla, caramel, lemon/lime; lively citrus flavours to match, firm fleshed with exciting fruit-acid tension, lengthy finish. 3 mths new Fr oak. **Sauvignon Blanc** ★★★ **04**, as per last ed, tropical fruit tone, appealing herby touch. Moderate 12.5% alc. **05** not ready for tasting. **Annie's Wine** ★★★ Characterful uncertified NLH-style dessert; **02** blend 80% sauvignon plus semillon. Seville orange marmalade character, with distinct botrytis; light textured & not cloying, with clear oakiness & dryish finish. 2 yrs new Fr oak. – *IvH*

Stormhoek new

Owner Orbital Wines ▪ 13 Chapter Street, Pimlico, London SW1P 4NY ▪ nick@orbitalwines.co.uk ▪ www.stormhoek.com ▪ ***T +44 020·7802·5415*** *▪ F +44 020·7976·5376*

This zeitgeist-attuned brand, which uses the latest blog-marketing techniques to inform jaded consumers that 'Freshness Matters', is blowing up a storm in the UK. Launched at the end of 2003, last year it shifted some 100 000 cases. Mathew Jukes, a leading British winewriter, raved about the Pinot Grigio: 'You could spend a week on a Vespa in Friuli and not find a wine as joyous as this'. All the wines, which retail at £6-7, are made to spec in the Cape.

Cabernet Sauvignon-Shiraz ★★★★ **03** bearer of the 'freshness matters' standard, mellowed with time in bottle: richer, softer, more refined than cellar mates below. Ripe cassis with spiced edge introduces measured fruit/acid verve, medium tannins & alc: 13.5%) for table. Tank-fermented, 50% yr Fr oak. **The Storm Sangiovese-Merlot** ★★★ **04** pomegranate tints to earthy flesh; ripe palate carries the oak in easy yet interesting libation. Stave-fermented, portion then 7 mths older Fr casks. WO Darling, others W Cape. **Shiraz** ★★ **04** hot flush to ripe, confected character; chunky texture. 14% alc. **Cabernet Sauvignon 03** sold out; not tasted/rated. **Rosé** ★★★ **04** fully pigmented & aromatic; berry fruitiness retained in reductive style, rotund yet refreshingly dry send-off. **Semillon Reserve** ★★★★ **04** tangy lime edginess to candle-wax/paraffin nose, lip-smacking litchi gives crisp feel to smooth, plump mouthful, 13.5% alc peaks in tail. Grapes off 35 yr old Wllngtn vyd; Fr-barrelled 8 mths. **Chenin Blanc Reserve** ★★★★ **04** single vyd Wllngtn grapes given all-Fr cask treatment 8 mths: vanilla/waxy breadth to ripe peach character, opulence lifted by spiky citrus tang in sweet finish. Only 375 cs. **Pinot Grigio** ★★★ **05** novel herbal interest to medium/full body, nettle-like finish; fair grip in tail. **Sauvignon Blanc** ★★ **05** ripe gooseberry flesh cut into reductive grassy mould. Low 12% alc. – *DS*

Stormy Cape see Thelema
Stoumann's Wines see Excelsious
Strata Series see Flagstone
Suikerbosch see Zidela

Sumaridge Wines

Hemel-en-Aarde Valley (see Walker Bay map) ▪ 1stB 2001 ▪ Tasting & sales daily 10-3 ▪ Fee R10 ▪ Closed Easter Fri/Sun & Dec 25 ▪ Light lunches daily 12-2.30 ▪ Self-catering guest house (up to 6 people) ▪ Conferencing ▪ Walks ▪ Owner Brenda Harcourt-Cook ▪ Winemaker/viticulturist Gavin

Patterson ▪ ±25 ha (merlot, pinot, pinotage, shiraz, chard, sauvignon) ▪ 120 tons 6 000 cs own label 50% white 40% red 10% rosé ▪ PO Box 1413 Hermanus 7200 ▪ sumaridge@itec.co.za ▪ www.sumaridge.co.za ▪ ***T (028) 312·1097*** *▪ F (028) 312·2824*

It's taken Zimbabwean wine farmer Gavin Patterson 15 years, since completing his studies in Stellenbosch, to reach the 'personal milestone' of entering the SA wine industry. After working the 2002 harvest in California, he spent a season as vineyard manager at Hamilton Russell before moving here as winemaker and viticulturist. His aim is produce 'wines that are in balance with their environment'; wines that realise their full potential and earn Sumaridge recognition as 'the outstanding farm that it is'. Swiss Air Lines don't need any further persuasion about the white wines, having already listed the Sauvignon 04. But in 2005, GP notes, it's the reds which look 'particularly promising'.

★★★★ **Syrah 03** not retasted. Last ed we found a slightly imbalanced wine which few more yrs ageing should harmonise; Partly native yeast fermented. 16 mths Fr oak, half new. **02** had black berry fruit & herbal hints.

★★★★ **Merlot** Keeps getting better. **04** achieves marvellous spicy richness & power at medium 13.6% alc. 16 mths Fr oak, 40% new. Incremental progression from **03** (★★★★) with idiosyncratic milky aromas & leafy, herbal **02** (★★★).

★★★★☆ **Chardonnay 05** heralds a new confidence & seriousness for this label; 100% barrel fermented/aged 11 mths, small Fr oak, 40% new; rich, toasty butterscotch flavours with cinema foyer popcorn notes & buttery richness. Delicious. Light years from lightly appley **04** (★★★☆).

★★★★ **Sauvignon Blanc** Full-flavoured **05** lashed with asparagus & fig; fresher, vastly more appealing/satisfying than reductive **04** (★★☆) with sweaty nose.

Pinot Noir ★★★☆ Old-style SA pinot with savoury note; **04** smoked bacon & some sweet red fruit. 11 mths Fr oak, 40% new. **Pinotage** ★★★ **04** smoky nose leads to obvious tannins & pulpy red fruit, nicely framed by 11 mths Fr oak, 40% new. **Dry Rosé** ★☆ **05** from merlot; vegetal flavours & light 12% alc. *— NP*

Sunay see Wandsbeck
Sunbird see Origin Wine

Swartland Wine Cellar

Swartland ▪ Est 1945 ▪ Tasting & sales Mon-Fri 8-5 Sat 9-2 ▪ Closed Mar 21, Easter Fri/Sun, Dec 25/26 & Jan 1 ▪ Tours during tasting hours by appt ▪ BYO picnic ▪ Play area for children ▪ Tourgroups ▪ Gifts ▪ Farm produce for sale ▪ Conferencing ▪ Owners 56 members ▪ Cellarmaster Andries Blake ▪ Winemakers Andries Eygelaar, Sean Nieuwoudt & Hugo Truter ▪ Viticulturist Johannes Mellet (Jun 2000) ▪ 3 000 ha (cab, merlot, pinotage, shiraz, chenin, sauvignon) ▪ 21 000 tons ▪ 50% white 47% red 3% rosé ▪ Exported as Leeuwenberg & labels below ▪ BRC & ISO 9001 certified ▪ PO Box 95 Malmesbury 7299 ▪ andries@swwines.co.za ▪ www.swwines.co.za ▪ ***T (022) 482·1134/5/6*** *▪ F (022) 482·1750*

The winds of change have been blowing quite briskly here the past year. Cellar chief Andries Blake says they've created a new flagship wine named Idelia (untasted by us), changed to screwcaps for their d'Vine range and, thanks to many new blocks coming on-stream, are working with significantly higher quantities of red grapes than before. The premium Indalo and Eagle Crest ranges will see added attention, 'starting in the vineyards with precision farming practices, to meet the standards set for these wines'. Intent on constantly increasing quality across the board, they're 'investing in people with passion for wine and service' to look after their customers around the world.

Indalo range

★★★★ **Cabernet Sauvignon 03** (★★★★) elegant & balanced. Ripe black fruit jam aromas, dry tangy-savoury flavours, same firm but ripe tannins as suave **02**. 5 mths small oak.

Shiraz ★★★ **03** more workman than the high flyer we previewed last ed, but pleasant enough; smoked beef nuance to firmly dry savoury flavours. 8 mths oak. **Pinotage** ★★☆ **03** lacks zingy drinkability we noted on sample last ed; now more rustic, with ultra-ripe squishy fruit, rustic dry tannins. Yr Fr oak. **Chenin Blanc 05** too young to call: big wine, abundant peach richness, cut by variety's brisk acid. 14.9% alc. **Sauvignon Blanc** ★★☆ **05** (sample) tropical passionfruit tone, fleshy, ripely round; only vague hint of pvs' zinging greenness. **Cabernet Sauvignon-Merlot** discontinued.

Eagle Crest

Cabernet Sauvignon-Merlot 04 has attractive & food-cordial touch of cab's austerity & discipline; usual grain sugar (4.3g/ℓ) imparts suavity rather than sweetness. Likely ★★★☆. **Shiraz-Cabernet Sauvignon** Interesting contrast with above blend: **04** (sample) unrestrained, full-frontal-fruited, masses of concentration & punch (14.9% alc). Potential ★★★☆. **Chenin Blanc** Apricot-toned **05** preview appears more ambitious, offers more substance, character, vivacity. Possible ★★★☆. **Chenin Blanc-Chardonnay** Appealing **05** (sample) 4 mths oaked – shows more seriousness; toasted nut/dried apricot hints; good combo of chenin's length (80% of blend) & chard's breadth. Possible ★★★.

Swartland range

★★★★ **Vintage Port 03** (★★★☆) first under our scrutiny since **99**, which showed cellar's cross-over Portuguese/old-Cape styling. The new release again tinta (50%), shiraz, cab, 2 yrs small oak. Not quite as convincing as pvs, but very pleasant; rich, chocolaty, already well-integrated; purists would say 'LBV' rather than 'Vintage' – but why intellectualise?

Blanc de Noir ☺ ★★☆ Delightful. Pinotage, with carbonique-style chalky minerality on nose/palate, making **05** seem racier than 11g/ℓ RS indicates. **Sauvignon Blanc** ☺ ★★☆ **05** lots of fun & interest via wide-spectrum grass, fig & capsicum aromas, tangy sweet-sour flavour, quaffable 13.5% alc.

Reds unwooded unless noted. **Cabernet Sauvignon** ★★★ Honest unadorned **04**, lots of varietal attractions, touch capsicum to mulberry fruit, un-austere tannins allow standalone enjoyment. **Pinotage** ★★ **05** richer & less sprightly than pvs; soft, slightly raisined character with 14% alc evident. **Merlot** ★★ Similar nose/palate contrast to pvs; **04** beguiles with cassis wafts, surprises with lean herbal tannins. 4-6 mths small oak. **Shiraz** Herby/savoury notes of pvs replaced with grassy (but ripe) tone on **03**, full-flavoured, well-balanced tannins. 2 mths oak. Sample rates ★★★. **Tinta Barocca** ★★★ Unoaked **04** chunkily ripe, as always, with firm tannins. **05** sample too unformed to rate. **Cabernet Sauvignon Merlot** ★★☆ Out of stock mid-2005; last was attractive **02**; lightly fruity with spicy whiffs. **Shiraz-Malbec** new ★★ Zingy sounding combo (60/40) but styling's strictly middle-of-road, won't race any pulses; **04** faint stalky whiffs, quickish exit. **Dry Red** ★★ Seldom fails to appeal/satisfy; smoothly dry all-sorts red, low 12.5% alc adding to its cheerful quaffability. **Rosé** ★★ **NV**. Juicy, light (11% alc) summer swigger from pinotage, with generous maraschino cherry fruit, roundly dry finish. **Chardonnay** ★★☆ **04** unoaked; last ed bright, fresh & fruity, pleasing peach & lemon tones. **05** not tasted. **Bin 50 Viognier** new Good first effort; combines variety's weight & girth (14.5%) with real verve, generous glacé fruit flavour. Potential ★★★. **Chenin Blanc** ★★ Demure this time, no attention-getting flick-flacks; **05** smooth, easy tropical flavours. **Premier Grand Cru** ★★ Unlike pvs, new **NV** has some appetite appeal; rounder, bit fleshier, more character than most in genre. 12.2% alc. **Fernão Pires/Light** ★★ Good lunchtime tipple with low alc (10%). **05** ruby grapefruit hint, fresh, drier than ±8g/ℓ sugar suggests. **Bukettraube** ★★ Gentle, lightish sweetie; **05** lilting honeysuckle bouquet, lifted fresh finish. Great al fresco tipple for sweeter-toothed. Enjoy young. **Hanepoot** ★★★ Enduring favourite & one of the Cape's great fortified bargains; latest **NV** rich aromas of mimosa & stewed pineapple; vibrant acidity & alc (17.5%) ideal for winter cuddling or pouring over ice in summer. **White Jerepiko** ★★ Latest **NV** very simple, shy & spiritous; cellar & taste again in ±yr, when hopefully better meshed. From chenin. 16.6% alc. **Red Jerepiko** ★★★ Graceful, elegant **NV** from pinotage. Latest version youthfully unknit mid-2005, but already showing hints of velvety lushness of predecessors; good tannic grip augurs well for longevity. 15.7% alc. **Port** ★★ Recent releases (**NV**) have featured 'correct' tinta yet alcs remain non-classically low at ±17%. Latest is very sweet & rustic.

Sparkling range

Budget-priced carbonated **NVs**. **Cuvée Brut** ★★ Latest version lighter & more neutral in all depts; still refreshing & not quite as brut as label suggests. **Demi Sec** ★★ Brisk bubbles are highlight (& only light, really) of slender-fruited chenin/buket ensemble. **Rosette** discontinued.

D'Vine range

Untasted this ed; 500ml, 1.5ℓ glass, 2 & 5ℓ casks, all **NV**. **Dry Red**, **Rosé** , **Dry White**, **Johannisberger/Semi Sweet** & **Light**.

Cask range

2, 3 & 5ℓ packs untasted this ed; **Shiraz-Cabernet** new, **Grand Cru**, **Blanc de Blanc**, **Stein** & **Late Harvest**, all **NV**.—*IvH*

Sweetwell see Terroir Wines

SylvanVale Vineyards

*Stellenbosch ▪ Est 1997 ▪ 1stB 1998 ▪ Tasting & sales daily 11–7 ▪ Fee R15 refundable with any purchase ▪ Open pub hols ▪ Tours by appt ▪ Flavours Restauran, Vineyard Terrace & Cedarwood Lounge (see Eat-out section) ▪ Picnics by appt ▪ Luxury 38-room hotel (see Stay-over section) ▪ Conferences ▪ Tourgroups ▪ Play area for children ▪ Walks ▪ Owners LGI Hotels & Vineyards ▪ Vini consultant Mark Carmichael-Green (2002) ▪ Viti consultant Lorna Hughes (1997) ▪ 10 ha ▪ 4 600 cs 80% red 10% white 10% rosé ▪ PO Box 68 Stellenbosch 7599 ▪ info@sylvanvale.com ▪ www.sylvanvale.co.za ▪ **T 865·2012** ▪ F 865·2610*

Here's an idyllic winelands experience, where guests at the Devon Valley Hotel are 'friends of the vine' – the surrounding Sylvanvale vineyards are the protectorate of Lorna Hughes (wife of Dave, a taster for this guide), and the philosophy of 'handmade hospitality' is echoed in the credo 'handmade wines'. Transformation of the hotel into four-star boutique accommodation complete, labels and packaging have been freshened, the Vine-Dried Chenin renamed and a new red blend released. Agents are in place, so these vinous representatives of the valley are available further afield. The bar now includes a walk-in wine library (and big-game wall trophy, Chocolate Moose, still has pride of place).

★★★★ **Pinotage Reserve** Wild herb & mint overtones characterise these modern, partly new oak matured examples. Full-bodied **04** (★★★★) embroidered with sweet red cherries, splash vanilla; quite lush though variety's insistent tannin/nip of bitterness evident in sweet-fruited finish. Yr Fr wood, 70% new. Notch down on **03**, which displayed unblemished fruity lushness & fine tannin grip.

★★★★ **Chenin Blanc** Off 25+ yr old vines; from **04** (★★★★) includes wooded portion, which adds structure & richness to the soft flowery tones. **05** tropical notes; plump, satisfying; gently rounded into early, enjoyable drinking by partial oak fermentation.

★★★★ **Jewel of the Valley** Pvsly 'Vine Dried Chenin Blanc'. **02** last vintage to date of this unctuous dessert from desiccated chenin berries; not re-assessed. Good winey feel despite low 9% alc, though finishes a little tamely. 14 mths new Fr oak. ±30 yr old vines.

★★★★ **Vine Dried Pinotage** Broodingly dark dessert ultra-ripe grapes, fermented with native yeasts; buchu/spice-rack bouquet; smooth, balanced 16% alc. 18 mths in older Fr oak. 375ml. None between **00**, **04**; latter still evolving in barrel.

Dry Cabernet Sauvignon Rosé ☺ ★★★ Food-friendly **05**, bright cab cassis/fresh grass fragrance, satisfying weight, unassertive fruity length; ±20% barrel-fermented.

Cape Blend-Devon Valley new ★★★★ Pinotage-led **04** has house's wild herb/mint thumbprint; cab, shiraz (57/29/14) add extra spice/flesh, tame lead variety's more assertive tannins. Harmonised by yr 100% new Fr oak. **Cabernet Sauvignon** new ★★★★ Uncomplicated & approachable **04**; nicely harmonised fruit/oak; well-managed tannin; simple yet tasty sweet mulberry/strawberry flavours. Fr oaked, 75% new. **Shiraz** new ★★★★ **04** already drinks well.

Unshowy flower/spice/choc array; quite delicate texture; pliant tannins; some fruit-flattering oak aids harmony, length. Matured Fr/Am barrels 75/25, yr. **Ghost Tree Rosé** new ★★★ For the sweeter-toothed. **05** generous ripe strawberry/raspberry aromas, flavours. Pleasant, if little short on verve. Cab with chenin. — *AL*

Tabiso see Nordale
Table Bay see Ultra Liquors

Table Mountain

Distell range initially targeted at the Japanese market, now also available in the UK and Denmark.

Cabernet Sauvignon ★★★ **04** unoaked & friendly, blackcurrant/berry fruit with spice & dust; pleasantly austere tannins. **Merlot** ★★★ Easy drinking **04**, cherry/savoury aromas; smooth black fruit palate & refreshing acidity. **Chardonnay** ★★★ **04** carefully wooded to express fruit. Ripe peach/citrus notes, refreshing goodbye. Food friendly. **Chenin Blanc** ★★★ **05** has green-apple bounce & mouth-watering, lemon crispness. Pithy mineral goodbye. **Sauvignon Blanc** ★★★ **05** a fruit salad with nettles & lots of freshness. Light bodied (11.8% alc), uncomplex for comfortable summer imbibing. All WO W Cape. — *CvZ*

Talana Hill see Vriesenhof

Tall Horse new

DGB's slightly higher-priced version of the 'critter brands' (Yellowtail, Little Penguin) flying off US supermarket and cash 'n carry shelves. Colourful packaging, featuring a stylised giraffe, recently awarded an SA 'Wine Labels of Excellence' award.

Flattering dollops sugar a feature throughout. **Cabernet Sauvignon** ★★ **03** has some varietal character & structure propping up the sweetness (10.5g/ℓ RS) for overall balanced appeal. **Merlot** ★★ Underlying tannins rescue **03** from being a Slush Puppy. Sugar (10.7g/ℓ) lifts fruit, masks the astringency. **Shiraz** ★★ Ingratiating **03** offers marzipan & Demerara sugar flavours; rich & rotund, unctuous texture heightened by slick Am oak. Bound to be a pop hit. **Chardonnay** ★★ Quaffable & friendly **04**, creamy mouthfeel, ripe toffee-toned fruit. Perversely, driest (RS 7g/ℓ) of all these. W Cape all. — *DH*

Tamboerskloof see Kleinood

Tanagra Private Cellar

McGregor ▪ Est 2000 ▪ Tasting & sales daily 10-4.30 ▪ Closed Easter Sat/Sun, Dec 25 & Jan 1 ▪ BYO picnic ▪ Facilities for children ▪ Walks ▪ Conservation area ▪ Owners/winemakers/viticulturists Christoph Reinhold & Felicia von der Schulenburg ▪ 12ha (cabs s/f, merlot, pinotage, shiraz) ▪ 10 tons/480 cs own label ▪ PO Box 92 McGregor 6708 ▪ ffvdscar@lando.co.za ▪ ***T (023) 625·1780*** *▪ F (023) 625·1847*

Having designed an underground cellar, storage room and tasting venue for the family farm, Christoph Reinhold has gone back to his architecture practice and other people's dreams. Partner Felicia von der Schulenburg is 'running the overall circus' of assorted animals, four children and hired help, as well as making and marketing their wine, now in its second vintage and, in the winemaker's opinion, 'bolder and at the same time more elegant, more refined and more complex'. At least she has manager Hein Gerber playing the role of assistant ringmaster! They use traditional methods – slow fermentation and maturation, minimal racking and no fining or filtering.

Heavenly Chaos new ★★★ **04** merlot led blend for early enjoyment, says Felicia R. Soft & rounded with sofa tannins, wild brambles & warm plums. Shiraz/cab franc/cab (12/12/8) provide interest & structure. **Felicity** ★★★ **04** accessible bdx blend driven by cab, steered by merlot/cab franc (36/10). Harmonious – if unusual – with long almond finish; vegetal, dark choc/marzipan aromas & flavours. 14mths 1st/2nd fill Fr barrels. 66/34 cab/syrah blend **Carah** ★★ **04** not as impressive as pvs; over ripe, port-like nose & palate with char & rubber notes; jammy entry & unknit, dry goodbye. Appears lightweight even at 13.5% alc. **Rosé 05** from pinotage, too young & unformed to rate. **Chardonnay** ★★ New vintage not ready to taste. **04** rated for pvs ed, strident with vanilla-toast tone, ripe smooth peach & tropical fruit flavours, needing time to emerge. Taking a cue from mentor Abrie Bruwer: all above whole-berry, native-yeast fermentation. — *CT*

Tara Hill see Southern Sky

Tarentaal

Range by Woodlands Import Export of Somerset West, mainly for export to Europe. See Assegai for contact details. No new wines; notes from previous edition.

Pinotage ☺ ★★★ Unwooded charmer from Wrcstr fruit; **04** vibrant red berry aromas, appealing palate, modern & stylish. **Chenin Blanc** ☺ ★★★ **04** passionfruit/pineapple tones in flavourful, crisp-finishing package; slips down easily; could handle food well. **Sauvignon Blanc** ☺ ★★★ **04** light-bodied (12% alc) & well stocked with sauvignon character; value for your euro.

Shiraz ★★★★ ✓ Harmonious **03** proffers khaki bush & smoked meat, loads of spice, quite elegant, firm but not harsh. Fruit ex-Swtlnd, portion barrelled. **Shiraz-Cabernet Sauvignon** ★★★ Dark fruit-pervaded **03**, deftly blended for easy/early drinkability. 66/34 mix, unwooded. **Chardonnay** ★★★ **04** lively lemon-butter aromas; warm, ripe, appealing & definitely for early drinking. Most tasted as samples; all WO W Cape. — *CR*

Tarentaal Farm see Terroir Wines

Tassenberg

Dry red affectionately referred to as 'Tassies', launched 1936 & still associated with good times. Latest (**NV**) ★★ gluggable, very soft, light-textured with red fruit & dusty fruit-tannin tug. By Distell. W Cape vyds. — *CvZ*

Taverna Rouge

Juicy budget-priced red from Distell. **NV** blend technically off-dry (8g/ℓ sugar) but somehow not unctuous. Latest ★★ cherry aromas & flavours; light 12% alc, touch bitter lift to finish. W Cape vyds. — *CvZ*

Teddy Hall Wines new

Chenin champion (in cause and competition), Teddy Hall, has launched a new (for him) version of this versatile variety under an own-name label (his others form part of the Rudera range — see entry). The style emphasises chenin's fresh, fruity charms, is bottled with either cork or screwcap and, at under R35 a bottle, targets a lower price-point in answer to both local and international demand.

Chenin Blanc ★★★ **05** easy-drinking, but as you would expect from this producer, oodles of flavour, pineapple-laced fruit salad with a citrus tang. Rounded palate, dry crunchy finish. Eminently quaffable. — *CR*

Tempel Wines new

*Paarl ▪ Est 2000 ▪ 1stB 2003 ▪ Closed to public ▪ Owner Tuan Marais ▪ Vini consultant Neil Schnoor (2000) ▪ Viti consultant DeWet Theron (2000) ▪ 3 ha (pinotage) ▪ 11.8 tons 700 cs 100% red ▪ PO Box 7295 Noorder-Paarl 7623 ▪ tempelwines@lantic.net ▪ www.tempelwines.co.za ▪ **T 872·4065** F 872·3883*

Prompted by his homestead's history as a Jewish place of worship, and harassed into not retiring by his wife who 'married me for better or worse – but not for lunch', Tuan Marais lit upon the idea of growing kosher grapes and hasn't looked back. His bushvines – 'trellis systems looked expensive' – are tended and harvested according to kosher requirements, and the grapes sent to Neil Schnoor at nearby Zandwyk (Kleine Draken) for rigorous kosher vinification, including flash pasteurisation. Despite the challenges, Tuan M is determined to stick with the niche approach, abetted by the distinction of being the only English-speaking Catholic Afrikaner ever to have produced a kosher pinotage.

Pinotage ★★★★ Unique & rather good **03**; unmistakably pinotage: some stalky whiffs to toasty nose, sweet berry fruit flavours, spicy palate. Low sulphur a bonus. 8 mths Fr oak, some new.—*NP*

Terra del Capo *see* L'Ormarins

Terroir Wines of SA

Stellenbosch ▪ Est 2002 ▪ 1stB 2003 ▪ Closed to public ▪ Owners/viticulturists Inus Muller & Bennie Diedericks ▪ Winemaker Inus Muller (2002) ▪ 8 tons 600 cs 100% red ▪ PO Box 5435 Helderberg 7135 ▪ inus@terroirwines.net inusmuller@absamail.co.za bennad@telkomsa.net ▪ ***T 082·825·9001/082·452·7263*** *▪ F 842·2373*

This is a one-stop winegrowing advisory service owned and run by Inus Muller and Bennie Diedericks, providing assistance to a new generation of artisan winemakers. Clients include Devon Air, Kuikenvlei, Leeurivier Wines & Olives, Paul Wallace Wines, Romond, Sweetwell and Tarentaal Farm, some listed separately. Muller and Diedericks now also make small quantities of wine for their own account under the brand name Karmosyn, including a Cabernet 04, set for mid-year release.

These all new. **Sweetwell Cabernet Sauvignon** ★★★★ Appealing & well-made **03**, classic cab flavours with fine herbaceous note; soft & ripe tannins; classy, good prospects. Hldrberg fruit, 2 yrs in oak. **Karmosyn Shiraz** ★★★ Extroverted smoky/meaty varietal character on **03**, big-boned (14.5%) but unintimidating. Hldrberg & Paarl vyds; 16 mths oaked. **JWL Shiraz** ★★★ **03** scented *vin ordinaire* with freshness & flavour, lightly gripping tannins. Hldrberg fruit, 2 yrs barrelled.—*CT*

Teubes Family Wines

Olifants River ▪ Est/1stB 2003 ▪ Visits by appt (9-5.30 during wildflower season – Aug/Sep) ▪ Closed public holidays ▪ Self-catering/B&B guest house ▪ Tougroups ▪ Walking trails ▪ Owners Johan & Ella Teubes ▪ Winemaker Helene van der Westhuizen (Jan 2004) ▪ Viticulturist Johan Teubes ▪ 2 400 cs own label 100% red ▪ Also exported as Houmoed ▪ PO Box 791 Vredendal 8160 ▪ ella@teubeswines.co.za ▪ www.teubeswines.co.za ▪ ***T 083·274·4832/(027) 213·2377*** *▪ F (027) 213·3773*

Johan and Ella Teubes have pioneered a new genre: the industrial-strength *garagiste*. To stringent international standards, they supply 120 000ℓ of organically grown merlot, pinotage and shiraz for some of SA's largest wine exports, including Kumala, yet they have their own stable of hand-crafted wines which they market under their family banner and the brand name Houmoed. These are vinified by winemaker Helene van der Westhuizen in rented cellar space. This Olifants River farm near Spruitdrift has 62ha of organically grown red (including cabernet) vines plus some viognier. Another 54ha of 'conventional' vines comprise chardonnay, sauvignon and chenin.

Merlot ★★ **03** developed for age, esp blood-red colour; maintains some iron, red plum attractions, juiciness. Best drink soon before these fade. **Shiraz** ★ Sturdy, austere **04**; porty, drying with hot finish.—*AL*

Text

DGB range launched late 2003 in packaging calculated to appeal to 'fashion-conscious trendsetters in the 25 to 35 age group'. 15 000 cases.

Ruby Cabernet-Merlot ★★ 50/50 blend, similar to pvs with hint of mulberries; fruity entry to palate but the finish is lean; dry with slight tannic grip. **Chenin Blanc** ★★ Latest not as sexy, more assertive at 13.5% As pvs; faint deciduous fruit flavours, dry, uncomplex. Both NV, WO W Cape.—*DH*

Thabana Li Meli see Bartinney Cellars

Thabani Wines

*Stellenbosch ▪ Closed to public ▪ PO Box 1381 Stellenbosch 7599 ▪ thabani@iafrica.com ▪ www.thabani.co.za ▪ **T 412·9302** ▪ F 412·9305*

Jabulani Ntshangase remains *thabani* ('joyful') about his and partner Trevor Steyn's venture, the first wholly black-owned wine company in SA. Always fast-forward, JN decelerates long enough to shepherd groups of black oenology students though the system. (Protégé Mzokhona Mvemve has now joined JN as a taster for this guide.) Current Thabani releases are the Shiraz, Merlot and Cab-Merlot from the 03 vintage, and the Sauvignon 04.

Thandi Wines

*Elgin ▪ Est 1996 ▪ 1stB 1997 ▪ Tasting & sales daily 9-5 ▪ Fee R10 for groups of 10+ ▪ Closed Easter Fri/Mon, Dec 25/26 & Jan 1 ▪ Traditional home-cooked meals daily 9-5 ▪ Tours by appt ▪ Gifts, crafts & farm produce ▪ Owners Lebanon Fruit Farm Trust ▪ Winemakers Patrick Kraukamp (Jan 1997) & Nicky Versfeld ▪ Viticulturist PD Koegelenberg ▪ 26 ha (cab, pinot, chard) ▪ 260 000ℓ 90%red 10% white ▪ PO Box 465 Stellenbosch 7599 ▪ rydal@thandi.com ▪ www.thandi.com ▪ **T 881·3870** ▪ F 881·3102*

'Empowerment works' is the conclusion to be drawn from the success of this three-way wine and fruit farming venture, initiated ten years ago to protect jobs ahead of the privatisation of parastatal forestry giant SAFCOL's interests in the Elgin area. The workforce now own SAFCOL's shares in Thandi (Xhosa for love or cherish), and while they continue to use cellar space at neighbouring Paul Cluver Estate (their third original partner), they also have expanded winemaking and marketing operations at Omnia Wines in Stellenbosch. Successes reaped to date include being the first winery in the world to be Fairtrade certified. A clutch of IWC medals for their Chardonnay, coupled with a Veritas gold for their new Sauvignon-Semillon blend have given the owner-workers further reasons to celebrate.

Cabernet Sauvignon ★★★ Customary tobacco & red/black fruit notes on chunkily built, engagingly savoury **02**; 2 yrs Fr oak. **Pinot Noir** ★★★ **03**'s forward, ripely fruity nose leads to fresh, firm palate with sour-sweet element & powerful 15% alc. 10 mths in barrel. **Merlot-Cabernet Sauvignon** new ★★★★ **03** 70/30 blend more suave, elegant than straight Cab, fresh & juicy; clear fruit on firm foundation; integrated older Fr oak, 14 mths. WO W Cape. **Cabernet Sauvignon-Merlot** new ★★★★ **04** big & full-flavoured, stressing robust, ripe tannic cab element in roughly equal blend of Stbosch grapes; light wooding showcases sweet black fruit – though, like all these reds, savoury rather than simple fruitiness. **Chardonnay** ★★★★ Reliable, immediate attractiveness here: **04** packed with varietal flavour, fresh & dry-finishing, well calculated wooding – fermented/8 mths, 30% new. IWC gold for pvsly tasted **02**. **Sauvignon Blanc-Semillon** new ★★★ 50/50 blend in **05**, but sauvignon's grass & guava notes dominate; fresh, full-flavoured, round but dry.—*TJ*

The Berrio see Flagstone
The Blends see Bellingham

The Foundry

*Stellenbosch ▪ Est 2000 ▪ 1stB 2001 ▪ Visits by appt ▪ Owners Chris Williams & James Reid ▪ Winemaker/viticulturist Chris Williams, with selected growers ▪ 20 tons 1 000 cs 90% red 10% white ▪ PO Box 12423 Die Boord Stellenbosch 7613 ▪ thefoundry@mweb.co.za ▪ www.thefoundry.co.za ▪ **T 082·577·0491** ▪ F 843·3274*

Owner, viticulturist, winemaker, delivery boy. Meet Chris Williams (also the man helping Hannes Myburgh steer venerable Meerlust on a brave new wine course). Amazed that his and partner James Reid's winery is already five years old, Chris W continues 'the quest to identify those small elements which conjure greatness'. Such as? Fully knowing each of their growers' 'very special' sites; guiding vines/wines into natural balance; following a hands-off approach ('give the wine time!'); pushing the envelope with un-inoculated fermentations, long macerations. Eventually, bottling some single-vineyard wines illustrating terroir's massive impact. Judging from global rave reviews, many believe The Foundry's already conjuring greatness. For Williams, though, it's back to the books ... for his Master of Wine.

★★★★☆ **Syrah** Grows in stature, dimension each vintage, always with subtlety & finesse. **03** taken to impressive level by great red-wine year (& by 3% dash **04** viognier). Youthfully dark hue echoed in profound yet delicate spicy/floral aromas. Rich, long, with poised acid, tight tannin backing; agreeably understated oak. Deserves until 2007; should mature till at least 2013. 17 mths Burgundian oak, 10% new; unfiltered. 20% bottled under screwcap. **02** (★★★★☆) promising, though less immediately expressive; will reward 5–8 yrs patience. Classically-styled **01** (★★★★★) benchmark SA shiraz; Coastal WO (Stbosch, Paarl, Wllngtn vyds).

★★★★ **Viognier** Preview **05** promises greater varietal clarity, complexity, balance than maiden **04**. Same basic approach: used Fr oak-fermented, partial native yeast (vs 100% pvsly). Result is glorious ripe apricot nose with subtle earth notes. Rich yet not unctuous; prolonged & fruity. Lovely wine. **04** gorgeous heavy-silk texture; balanced though noticeable 5g/ℓ sugar. Coastal WO (Wllngtn vyd).

Double Barrel discontinued.—*AL*

The Goats do Roam Wine Company

Paarl ▪ Est/1stB 1998 ▪ 86% red 10% white 4% Rosé ▪ See Fairview for tasting/sales information

The edgy humour behind Fairview's innovatively branded stand-alone range belies the quality of the wines. Because, as the 'legend' points out, it was in search of the *choicest* grapes that members of the farm's goat herd first assailed the vineyards. Having provoked the displeasure of Rhône producers by cocking a snout at some of their most famous appellations with the Goat Roti and Goats do Roam in Villages labels, the goats are set to create fresh furores with their forthcoming jibes: a claret-style blend named Bored Doe and a Chardonnay, Goat Door. No doubt there's more impertinence waiting to be birthed.

★★★★ **Goat Roti** Shiraz plus seasoning white grape viognier calculated to deliver spicy tones of northern Rhône. **04** pre-bottling 2005 shows admirable complexity (black pepper, lilies, red fruits et al); juicy fruit, acidity, billy-goat-gruff tannins all need time to knit. Similar lifted fruit to **03**, also unready on release. **02** 91 pts *WS*. 12–14 mths Fr/Am oak, none new.

★★★★ **Goats do Roam in Villages Red** Serious blend shiraz, pinotage, mourvèdre & seasoning viognier. **04** (★★★★) lighter, easier drinking, with brisk acidity. **03** homogenous & well assembled. Fr/Am oak, none new.

★★★★ **Goats do Roam in Villages White** Maiden **03** was innovative, unwooded blend of widely sourced sauvignon, chard, clairette & grenache blanc. Full-flavoured **04** (★★★☆) also delightfully different from usual 'dry white'. Broad, even touch rustic coarseness to richness; shot through with lively freshness. Nice lick oak finds place in good balance.

Goats do Roam White ☺ ★★★ Distinctly workaday varieties clairette & crouchen whipped (with chenin, grenache bl) into perky drinkability in **04**, offering subtle but pristine muscat flavour.

Goats do Roam Red ★★★ Côtes-du-Rhône style red featuring Mediterranean varieties herded by shiraz; pinotage adds local dimension. Quaffable **04** light, soft & fruity with savoury edge. **Goats do Roam Rosé** ★★★☆ More dimension, seriousness in **05**; deep colour, positive tannic bite, powerful 14.5% alc. All Goats WO W Cape/Coastal; GdRs now under screwcap.—*RK/CvZ/TJ*

The Heads Collection see Knysna Cellars

The Juno Wine Company new

*Paarl • Est/1stB 2004 • Closed to public • Vini/viti consultant Newald Marais (Nov 2004) • ±13 500 cs 50% red 50% white • PO Box 68 Main Road Paarl 7622 • info@junowines.com • www.junowines.com • **T 872·0697** • F 872·1863*

This new negociant house in Paarl aims to create 'a playful brand with the potential to become a people's favourite'. Labels feature local artist Tertia du Toit's original oils on canvas. The wife of Johan du Toit, a partner in the business, her work also appears in many South African households, as designs on several food labels and on numerous book covers. Newald Marais, former head winemaker at Nederburg, sources these wines mainly from Robertson and Bonnievale.

Shiraz ★★★ 'Maiden' is an apt description for wines bottled as 'Cape Maidens' with suitably adorned label; **04**, plus a 15% dollop of cab, is approachable & unchallenging; ripe plum fruit, hints of cab herbiness, spicy choc/coffee & soft tannins. **Chardonnay** new ★★★ **05** unoaked; fruity nose & palate packed with pear/Golden Delicious apple/lime. Plump middle, easy drinking finish. — *MM*

Thelema Mountain Vineyards

*Stellenbosch • Est 1983 • 1stB 1988 • Tasting & sales Mon-Fri 9-5 Sat 9-1 • Closed pub hols • BYO picnic • Tourgroups by appt • Owners McLean & Webb Family Trusts • Winemakers Gyles Webb & Rudi Schultz (1983, Dec 2000) • Viti consultants Aidan Morton & Phil Freese • 50 ha (cab, merlot, shiraz, chard, sauvignon, riesling) • 25 000 cs 40% red 60% white • Export brand: Stormy Cape • PO Box 2234 Stellenbosch 7601 • wines@thelema.co.za • www.thelema.co.za • **T 885·1924** • F 885·1800*

Can Thelema aficionados be so lucky? Not one but two new wines from this iconic Helshoogte cellar (runner-up in *Wine*'s 2005 reader poll of SA's leading wineries). First, a new Sauvignon from the latest Thelema acquisition, Sutherland farm, a few kilometres south of Elgin. Managed by Chris and Alison Watermeyer, the property gives winemakers Gyles Webb and Rudi Schultz generally cooler conditions, its highest elevation being 245m above sea level. 'There are still some tasty apples being grown on the property – hope they don't become more popular than the wines,' quips middle son Thomas W, back from university in Adelaide and, as he puts it, 'general dogsbody but mainly sales and marketing'. Second, from the next-door in Elgin, Arumdale, a Shiraz which sold out in six weeks flat. At the home-farm on the slopes of the Simonsberg, 65 kms away, another press was added to what was needed for harvest 2005. 'We're not getting lazier,' TW assures, 'just preparing to handle more fruit in years to come.' Salivate, fans.

★★★★★ **Cabernet Sauvignon** Standard-bearer for the Cape since paradigm-shifting **89**, which inaugurated a more luscious, fruity, 'New World' style. In great yrs like **03**, indisputably world class. 100% cab; very complete, harmonious, nothing overdone; resonates with cassis richness, freshness supplied by vibrant tannins. Great maturation potential. Oaking to match: Fr barriques, 50% new, 20 mths. **02** troubled vintage handled with commendable sensitivity. Potential till 2008/9. *Wine* ★★★★ Regular 90+ pts *WS*. **00** (★★★★★) also sensational. *Decanter* ★★★★.

★★★★★ **Cabernet Sauvignon CWG Auction Reserve** new Five barrels of best cab, deemed worthy of 20 mths 100% new Fr oak enrichment. **03** as grand as vintage implies. Rich, sumptuous yet perfectly proportioned; sleek, freshening tannins framing perfectly ripe, soft, dark berry features. Min potential till 2013.

★★★★ **Merlot 03** so Thelema, so good! Limpid ruby hue matched by bright blackcurrant/herb aromas with savoury dimension. Concentrated, creamy; liveliness emphasised by dense, finely-grained tannins, perfectly poised acid. 20 mths Fr oak, 30% new. For those who can resist, should improve till ±2010. **02** finely tuned; good drinking till ±2007 while bigger vintages mature. *Wine* ★★★★, 90 pts *WS*.

★★★★★ **Merlot Reserve 03** (★★★★★) a show-stopper, possibly Thelema's best ever red. Elegant rather than ostentatious; marvellous concentration of blackcurrant, fennel, leaf flavours buffed by 20 mths in 100% new Fr oak. Ripe yet vibrantly fresh; lingeringly dry.

Limited 1400 bottle production, with excellent potential for at least a decade. **02** graceful & comfortably firm; augurs satisfying development till 2006/8. *Wine* ★★★★☆.

★★★★ **Shiraz** Those tired of over-oaked/-extracted shirazes will appreciate Webb's stand-back approach. Elegant **03** offers comfortable & characterful drinking. Finely textured, with ample mélange red fruits/lilies, spicy nuances too. Potential till ±2009. Fr/Am oak (90/10), 30% new. **02** earlier-maturing style; rounded & supple. *Wine* ★★★★; 91 pts *WS*.

★★★★ **Arumdale Shiraz** new First crop from Webb's Elgin neighbour. **03** most promising. As above, refined, unforced feel; soft, fluid texture, gentle dark berry/spice flavour. Doesn't lack form or length. Fr/Am oak (90/10), 30% new. Probably best enjoyed by 2008. NB: ref to Thelema on back-label only.

★★★★ **Chardonnay** Has stood the test of time both in consumer loyalty & in bottle. **04** powerful, tighter, less expressive in youth; mere hints ripe cinnamon-tinged citrus, hazelnut. Palate better conveys potential: great viscosity, layered flavours, harnessed by stiff mineral spine. Give another yr/2 to relax/unfold; possible peak ±2009. Distinctive **03** (★★★★☆) with more ready charm; seamlessly oaked; super-fine length. Will reward 8+ yrs' cellaring. Fermented/11 mths Fr oak, 33% new.

★★★★ **Ed's Reserve** Belies laconic label description 'A Dry White'. As recognisable as ageless materfamilias Edna McLean, pictured in childhood on label, still charming tasting room visitors. **04** with characteristic fruity generosity, well subsumed oak (regime as above). Sleek, supple with signature muscat tail. 'Enjoy for its exuberant self!' urges Webb.

★★★★ **Sauvignon Blanc** Always released July 1st, invariably eagerly anticipated. **05** similar cool greengage/winter-melon notes as **04**; bit fuller, few drops more juicy tropicality but not at expense of overall spirited dash, unequivocal dryness. Second bottle never a debate. **03** 90 pts *WS*.

★★★★ **Sutherland Sauvignon Blanc** new From youthful vines (3 yrs) on Webb's Elgin property, showing exhilarating potential. **05** cool, intense. Great precision, elegance to gooseberry/melon tones; lovely urgent acid propels whole to resoundingly dry, long finish.

★★★★ **Rhine Riesling 04** scintillating follow-up to racily brilliant **03**. Outspoken limey spiciness more New World than Old, but acid nervosity captures essence of variety's greatness. Wonderful balance. Bone dry. Will improve over 10 yrs, Webb predicts.

Muscat de Frontignan ☺ ★★★ Daintily fragrant quaffer. Charming **05** crisp & deliciously lingering. Beautiful poise highlights fruit rather than sweetness (21 g/ℓ sugar).

Pinotage ★★★★ Harmonious & rich **03** with characteristic plum/summer berry aromas; fine, well-integrated tannin; satisfying savoury tail. 18 mths Fr oak, 20% new. Coastal WO (fruit ex-Paarl). **Muscadel** ★★★★ Luscious dessert, now vintaged (pvs NV). **98** copper tinged; expressive salted roast nut/cream toffee bouquet. Quite powerful, but slides with warming, honeyed ease to memorable conclusion. 17% alc. **Blanc Fumé** resurrected in last ed, again laid to rest.—*AL*

The Marais Family new

Robertson ▪ Est ca 1884 ▪ Sales Mon-Fri 8.30-6 Sat 8.30-1 ▪ Tourgroups ▪ Conferencing ▪ Other attractions see intro ▪ Owner Paul René Marais ▪ Winemaker Stefan Bruwer (2002) ▪ Viticulturist Gert Visser, advised by Anton Laas (Jan 1997/Jan 2005) ▪ 240 ha (cab, merlot, pinotage, ruby cab, shiraz, chard, chenin, sauvignon, viognier) ▪ 5 500 tons 3 000 cs own label ▪ 10% red 80% white 1% rosé 9% fortified ▪ PO Box 4 Robertson 6705 ▪ law@lando.co.za ▪ ***T (023) 626·2212*** *▪ F (023) 626·2669*

Load up your 4x4 with family, friends and bikes, then leave the less adventurous to tend the braai at Lookout Lapa while you hit the Dirt Trail and explore the lovingly conserved Robertson farm Wonderfontein. Return for sundowners and share in the heritage of the Marais family through five generations. From the bottling of their first vintage in 1884 and the founding of Lake Marais (now known as Brandvlei Dam) by great-grandfather Kowie, to the current preservation of the farm's 100 year old vines. A particular challenge for Paul René, who took ownership at the tender age of 21, is to make a top-notch sauvignon.

La Bonne Vigne Sauvignon Blanc ★★☆ 'The Good Vineyard' gets a little help from staged picking (half early, half late) & flavour-concentrating cellar technology in **05**; light (12.5% alc) but juicy, appealing tropical fruit basket character, racy acidity great with crumbed calamari. —*IvH*

The Mask see Baarsma

The Mason's Winery

Paarl ▪ Est/1stB 2001 ▪ Visits by appt; tasting/sales also at I Love Wine (see Wine shops section) ▪ Owner Mason's Hill Wines (Pty) Ltd ▪ Winemaker Derek Clift ▪ 10 tons 700 cs 100% red ▪ PO Box 515 Suider-Paarl 7624 ▪ dehoop@mweb.co.za ▪ ***T 083·228·7855*** *▪ F 863·1601*

A case of old wine in new bottles: the name change to The Mason's Winery (from Mason's Hill Wines) coincides with owner Derek Clift's celebration of a hundred years of his family's quarrying business. The new 'Reserve' pays special homage to that occasion, but the continued presence of 'Shiraz' on the label says there's no deviation from the exclusive focus on Derek C's favoured variety. New multi-clone vineyards on Paarl Mountain spring from the long-range vision 'to make my mark in the bottle, to be drunk now or in 10 years' time by a discerning following'.

★★★★ **Shiraz** Barossa-style flamboyance & power (14+% alc) the hallmarks; **03** sweet, creamy strawberry whiffs, chewy savoury flavours, ends dry with peppery touch. Drinks well now, as did **02** at similar stage of evolution, but plenty in reserve.

★★★★ **Centenary Reserve Shiraz** new More elegant & svelte version of above, **03** similar creamy fruit, plentiful vanilla oak; appealing sleekness — 14.9% alc quietly tucked away; probably better prospects than std version but this so seductive, prognostications almost irrelevant.—*CR*

The Observatory Cellars

Cape Town ▪ 1stB 2000 ▪ Tasting by appt ▪ Owners Tom, Catherine, Elizabeth & André Lubbe ▪ Winemaker/viticulturist Tom Lubbe, with Catherine Lubbe (Jan 2000/Jun 2002) ▪ 15 ha (pinotage, shiraz, chard, chenin) ▪ 17 tons 700 cs 60% red 40% white ▪ PO Box 1098 Malmesbury 7299 ▪ syrah@netactive.co.za ▪ ***T/F (022) 487·3023***

Watch this space, tease the Lubbe quartet of Tom, Catherine, Elizabeth and André, when quizzed on cellar/tasting room news. We know they intend relocating their Culemborg winemaking facility in the centre of Cape Town to their Paardeberg farm within the year. But that's all they say. They're finding good global market reception for wines that adhere to firmly-held beliefs in organic, biodynamic farming principles and vinfication methods: simple, natural winemaking, whole berry fermentation, lower alcohols and no acidification. So, yes ... watch this space.

★★★★☆ **Syrah** Rigorously selected fruit from low-yielding, granitic Pdberg vyd. **01** fine, subtly gorgeous & harmonious; 60% new Fr oak. Remarkable **02** (not retasted) only older wood, intense grape purity & powerful delicacy untrammelled, giving perfumed spice, raspberries, lilies, with mineral depths. Fine acidity, supple tannins.

★★★★ **Carignan-Syrah** Maiden **02** sweet-fruited & touch jammy, with balanced & firmly constructed palate. We wondered: light-hearted seriousness or very serious fun? **03** (★★★★☆) has 79% shiraz, so **Syrah-Carignan**; definitely serious, even intellectual, but similarly joyous aromas with lavender, blackcurrant, mineral accents. A pure-fruited terroir wine, as far from blockbusterism as possible: 20% new light toast oak (rest much older), lowish alc (12.5%) playing role in light elegance — too light, perhaps, but harmonious, with smooth, subtle tannins.

★★★★ **Pinotage-Syrah** new Elegantly exuberant Pdberg nose on **04**: scrub, herbs, mineral. Almost easy to understand by Lubbe standards (& massive — 13% alc!), with bright, sweetly cheerful fruit. Refined; charming expression of pinotage (biodynamically farmed; 57% of blend; whole berry ferment), though forceful, with guiding, supple tannins in lovely balance.

★★★★ **Chenin Blanc-Chardonnay** new **04** made in oxidative style: unusual, but interesting & fine 50/50 blend, with incipient complexity (notes pear, baked apple, tropical fruit). Creamy texture helped by 15 mths on lees in old oak, with substantial poised acidity, good length. Mere 12% alc. WO Swtland, as all these are. – *TJ*

The Ruins see Bon Cap

The Sadie Family

Swartland ▪ Est 1999 ▪ 1stB 2000 ▪ Tasting & sales by appt ▪ Owners Sadie family ▪ Winemakers/viticulturists Eben & Niko Sadie ▪ 7 ha (grenache, mourvèdre, shiraz) ▪ 650 cs 90% red 10% white ▪ PO Box 1019 Malmesbury 7299 ▪ sadiefamily@mail.com ▪ ***T 869·8349*** *▪ F 869·8101*

Eben Sadie, following the rhythm of his own heartbeat, says: 'Winemaking becomes every day more a way of life ... we [wife, children, brother, friends] are continuing with bio-dynamics, getting more involved in truly integrated farming; in the cellar, we just keep things simpler and simpler as the years go by. The only way to truly produce great wines is to remove yourself and your ideals from the process of vinification and give the vineyards the true potential to become their own.' Thus he works wherever he finds himself: in the Swartland (in an unassuming little whitewashed building in the Perdeberg foothills), Spain (in a tiny self-built stone bodega in Priorat) and, now, in a southern Rhône-inspired Swartland venture, Sequillo Cellars, with Anura's Tymen Bouma (see separate entry under S-C).

★★★★★ **Columella** Superb & sophisticated expressions of Sadie's beloved Swtland, from shiraz with ±18% mourvèdre. **02** most obviously 'New World' to date, with sweet ripeness, roasted warmth. Savoury, supple tannins repeated in beautifully structured **03** (★★★★☆), which less ultra-ripe, more finely, densely, intensely packed – blackcurrant-toned approachability belying seriousness, delicate power & good devt potential. Native-yeast fermentation in open cask; 2 yrs very lightly toasted Fr oak, now up to 80% new – remarkably integrated already. Unfined, unfiltered.

★★★★☆ **Palladius** Swtland **04** (★★★★★) blend 40% viognier, equal parts chenin, chardonnay, grenache blanc. Peach/apricot aromas dominate; citrus notes. Flavours already developing complexity – soar in, cruise & glide on, buoyed by rich extract, moreish acidity, big alc (near 15%, in great balance). Lingering, serenely confident dry finish. 18 mths Fr oak, 30% new; imperceptible 3.7g/ℓ sugar. **03** (miscalled 02 last ed) also with depth & power, satin-textured intensity, long finish. These should mature few yrs at least. Unfined/filtered. – *TJ*

The Saints

Enduring range of easy drinkers by DGB. Quantities now top 280 000 cases a year, 60% white, rest equal portions red and rosé.

St Anna ☺ ★★ Perfumed Natural Sweet white; low alc (±8%). Delicate fruit salad flavours, honeysuckle aromas, always a lovely blend of perfumed varieties including gewürz.

St Raphael ★★☆ Muted black fruit aromas, smoky/mocha notes in salt-of-the-earth cinsaut, ruby cab (50/50) blend; latest bottling light textured, soft & dry for every day drinking. **St Celine** ★★ Same blend as St R, uncomplicated quaffing, bit jammy & sweet (13g/ℓ sugar). **St Claire** ★★ Appealing Natural Sweet rosé with low alc (8%); latest fresh & flirtatious, honeysuckle wafts, balanced. **St Vincent** ★★ Latest still sauvignon dominated but only just (40%), with equal portions chenin & colombard. Tropical aromas & flavours, refreshing & light bodied but uncomplex. **St Morand** ★★ More off-dry than semi-sweet, though technically the latter; current bottling from chenin/colombard/hanepoot; tad tired but still pleasing. All **NV**s, WO W Cape. Reds all lightly Fr oak chipped. – *DH*

The Sensory Collection see Stellar Winery

The Stables

KwaZulu-Natal ▪ Est 2004 ▪ 1stB 2005 ▪ Visits by appt ▪ Picnics by appt ▪ Self-catering luxury cottage ▪ Farm-style produce ▪ Owners/winemakers/viticulturists Tiny & Judy van Niekerk ▪ 2 ha (pinotage, shiraz, chard, nouvelle, viognier) ▪ 4 tons 170 cs 50% red 50% white ▪ PO Box 159 Nottingham Road 3280 ▪ Stables@telkomsa.net ▪ www.rox-prop.co.za ▪ ***T 082·441·3701*** *F (033) 266·6781*

Inspired by meeting leading Cape *garagistes*, Tiny and Judy van Niekerk returned to their Drakensberg former stud farm and converted their stables into a winery. Despite being in the Natal Midlands, more famous for its tourist-friendly Meander, the Van Ns pressed the wine authorities to add KwaZulu-Natal as an official 'geographical unit' – and won last year. Their maiden vintage (2005) was very small – only 170 cs – but plans include further plantings. 'Our philosophy is to make wine as naturally as possible, with as little interference as possible, which includes exceptionally low sulphur – the focus being on quality and not quantity.' The whites below are to be followed by (untasted) Cab, Merlot, Pinotage and Shiraz, briefly aged in French wood (barrels ex-Meerlust!).

Sauvignon Blanc ☆ This cool-preferring grape a tricky customer at best of times, in this climate a profound challenge; developed golden-hued **05** for early drinking (because of minimal sulphur content). **Blanc Fumé** ☆ **05** similar deep tints, boiled sweets/almond aroma, firm finish. – *MF*

Theuniskraal Estate

Tulbagh ▪ Est 1705 ▪ 1stB 1947 ▪ Tasting & sales Mon-Fri 9-12; 1-4 Sat 10-1 ▪ Fee R5 refundable on purchase ▪ Closed Easter Fri/Sun, Dec 25 & Jan 1 ▪ BYO picnic ▪ Tourgroups ▪ Owners Rennie & Kobus Jordaan ▪ Winemaker Andries Jordaan (1991) ▪ Viticulturists Jordaan brothers ▪ 140 ha (13 varieties, r/w) ▪ ±1 600 tons ±35 000 cs own label 10% red 90% white ▪ PO Box 34 Tulbagh 6820 ▪ tkraal@lando.co.za ▪ www.theuniskraal.co.za ▪ ***T (023) 230·0687/88/89/90*** *▪ F (023) 230·1504*

This historic Tulbagh estate has been in the Jordaan family for four generations, and the family is growing. Everybody is involved, so winemaker Andries's third child, a son born last July, is bound to be roped in. Famous for their (Cape) Riesling, which has been around since 1950, the estate continues to embrace the motto of good quality wines at affordable prices. Says AJ: 'One should be able to enjoy a glass of wine every day.' The farm also boasts a new tasting centre with fascinating old photographs of the historic Theuniskraal and its personalities.

Prestige ★★★ Still lone red in stable. **04** same blend as pvs (ruby cab/cab, 67/33); bursts with strawberry/raspberry flavour, tannic tug from cab, persistent savoury finish. Sip now & for ±2 yrs. **Riesling** ★★ Enduring brand, launched 1947; from crouchen, aka Cape riesling; **05** neutral, not showing variety's signature hay aroma; dry & fresh. **Semillon-Chardonnay** ★★★☆ ✓ Varieties seamlessly married in **04**, tasted this yr as finished wine, neither semillon freshness nor chardonnay fatness dominating; vibrant, eager to please with structure to improve ± 2 yrs. Unwooded 56/44 blend. **Natural Sweet** ★★★ Latest unavailable for tasting. Pvs **03** fragrant melange buket/gewürz (40/60); full-blown sweet bouquet, admirably restrained & uncloying palate. – *CvZ*

The Veldt see Robertson Wide River

The Winery

Stellenbosch ▪ Est/1stB 1998 ▪ Closed to public ▪ Owners Alex Dale, Edouard Labeye, Ben Radford, Heather Whitman, Stephen Ludlam, Andrew Openshaw & Craig Smith ▪ Winemakers Ben Radford, Edouard Labeye, Gus Dale (1998/1999/2002) & Clive Torr (advisor for pinot noir, 2004), with Tubby May (Feb 2003) ▪ ±120 ha (cab, carignan, grenache, merlot, shiraz, chard, chenin, sauvignon, viognier) ▪ ±850 tons 30 000 cs own label 50/50 red/white ▪ Ranges for customers: Churchaven, Three Gables (UK) ▪ Postnet Suite 124 Private Bag X15 Somerset West 7129 ▪ thefunwinery@thefunwinery.co.za ▪ www.thefunwinery.com ▪ ***T 855·5528*** *▪ F 855·5529*

Like Rome, The Winery will not be built in a day, avers chief architect Alex Dale. But progress is satisfying. With a 'brutally determined' team, the same winemaking philosophy, 'just more convinced' and a 'highly selective' modus operandi, the bar is continually being raised. As committed as they are to quality without compromise, the belief is still that sales remain key to success in a tough market. Thus, joining Team Winery is Stephen Ludlam. Formerly export director for Symington's, one of the world's leading port houses, Ludlam will concentrate on strategic development of export sales. The final member of Team Winery is a dedicated viticulturist (to be announced). And a new barrel cellar for 2006 will double maturation capacity (±1 000 barrels) and consolidate four production sites into a self-sufficient fermentation and maturation facility of their own at The Winery's Helderberg HQ.

Radford Dale range

★★★★☆ **Gravity** Name derives from vinification: even 'press' juice from pressure of grapes themselves, not machinery. **03** seamlessly combined merlot, shiraz, cab; impressed with pure savoury vinosity in soft frame; **04** just bottled when tasted; should gain depth, complexity & intensity with time; fine fruit, clean blueberry & blackcurrant flavours well defined & promising, provisional ★★★★. Partly barrel-fermented, ±14 mths wood.

★★★★ **Merlot 04** sample for release mid-2006, spicy black olives, good deep flavour, palate should catch up with nose with time; 18 mths Fr/Am oak 89/11; **03** previewed last ed more emphatic & striking than pvs. Hldrberg/Devon Vlly grapes.

★★★★ **Shiraz 04** (★★★★☆) glorious Old World nose, more Rhône than Rutherglen, flavours of meat & new leather, tobacco & smoke; superb tannin structure, great prospects. 15% alc. 14 mths 92/8 Fr/Am oak, 40% new. Even better than **03**, delicious rich mouthful dark spice/berries with fresh, lively core.

★★★★ **Chardonnay 04** (★★★★☆) big butterscotch & caramel nose leads on to somewhat restrained palate with minerals & crisp citrus; good definition & balance; finesse, elegance all round. Yr Fr oak, 20% new. Complex in subtle, understated manner, as was **03**. WO Stbosch, as are all above.

Pinot Noir 05 sample; release mid 2006; medicinal & slightly astringent (may dissipate with time), delicate redcurrant flavours; plenty of elegance, provisional ★★★☆; Fr oak, none new. Dijon clone, Elgin & Stbosch fruit. **Shiraz-Viognier** new Experimental sample of **05** plenty of fruit but unknit, some hard & chunky tannins, unfair to assess at this early juncture.

Black Rock range

★★★★☆ **Red 04** southern Rhône-inspired exotic red blend; gamey flavours & lavender whiffs; Old World elegance rather than knock-down, drag-out power. Shiraz, carignan, grenache (76/14/10). Yr Fr/Am oak, 90/10, 38% new.

★★★★ **White 04** blend dominated by old bushvine chenin (75%) with some fragrance from viognier (3%), chardonnay filling in the gaps. Not for the faint hearted, this is a powerful, idiosyncratic & full-bodied wine (14.5%); some wood character from barrel fermented chardonnay & chenin. Pdberg fruit.

Vinum range

★★★☆ **Cabernet Sauvignon 04** sample shows spicy Xmas cake nose, elegant perfumed cassis flavours, very good balance & length; needs time, provisional ★★★★. Yr 70/30 Fr/Am oak. Elegant **03** sleek, mouth-watering, harmonious. WO Stbosch.

★★★★ **Chenin Blanc** ✓ From old Hldrberg bushvines; **05** sample shows honey & apricot with generous acidity, nascent complexity. 7% wood matured. Previewed **04** riper than pvs, greater orange zest/honey intensity.

Winery of Good Hope range new

These all ★★★☆. WO Coastal/W Cape. **Cabernet Sauvignon-Merlot** Classy & complex **04**, fruit restrained & elegant, finishes sweet (3.5g/ℓ RS); 60:40 blend. **Chardonnay 05** unoaked; elegant citrus notes with persimmon nuance, good length. **Chenin 05** rich, fat palate, peach & pinenut hint, good length. Big 15% alc.

New World range

Shiraz ★★★ **05** sample shows boiled sweets & smoky 'matchstick' nose/palate, meaty hint. In same uncomplicated vein as pvs. **Sauvignon Blanc** ★★★ **05** sample shows hot climate sauvignon with slight topical pineapple & lunchtime-pleasing 12% alc. Following not retasted; notes from pvs ed: **Cabernet Sauvignon-Merlot** ★★★ **03** medium-bodied 60/40 blend. Light-textured, smoothed for readiness by wild strawberry/plum fruity sweetness. **Shiraz-Pinotage** ★★★ **04** peppy, easy-going 60/40 partnership. Substantial, expressive flavour richness, warmingly long. Unoaked. **Semillon-Chardonnay** ★★★ Satiny **04** unoaked 60/40 mix; flavoursome waxy lemony intensity, good zippy length. WO W Cape. — *NP*

Thierry's Wine Services see Cape Grace

Third World Wines

Est 2001 ▪ MD Jonathan van Blerk ▪ Vini consultant Kosie Möller ▪ The Stables, Westcot, Wantage, OX12 9QA UK ▪ wineorders@3rdworld.co.uk wineorders@gatsbyhotels.com ▪ www.3rdworld.co.uk www.gatsbyhotels.com ▪ ***T 0944·779·191·3044*** *▪ F 0944·123·575·1755*

No update available on this winery; contact details from previous edition.

33 Degrees South see Wamakersvallei

32 South Ltd

Stellenbosch ▪ Est 1998 ▪ Closed to public ▪ 100 000 cs 55% red 45% white ▪ UK office: Millennium Harbour, 202 Pierpoint Building, Westferry Rd, London E14 8NQ ▪ T 0944·0208 985·9700 ▪ F 0944·0870 487·5747 ▪ 32south@btconnect.com ▪ ***T/F 887·9112***

Noting that UK and mainland European retailers are moving towards buying in bulk, Louis Meyer gave his wine export company a fillip when he became a supplier of bulk as well as bottled wine. 'It seems the only way for retailers to reach their desired margins at the entry level is to bottle their product overseas,' he explains. Encouraged by overseas demand for his Fairtrade wines, particularly the Isabelo range, Louis M is now determined to get SA retailers interested too.

Bainskloof Merlot new ★★★ Fresh mulberry/cranberry provide nice sweet/sour character to **04**'s palate, vanilla notes in background, friendly but not for keeping. **Elephant Trail Pinotage-Shiraz** ★★★ **03** anytime sort of wine tasted for pvs ed; combo blackberries & sweet spice, soft, nice. 75/25 blend. **Limited Release Gewürztraminer** ★★★ Soft, semi-dry **04** with quince & sweet-spice aromas; lightish effortless quaffing. **Sweet Surrender Pudding Wine** ★★★ Scented NLH dessert from mainly chenin with furmint & buket. **03** tasted last yr, easy-sipping style for instant gratification; some quince, botrytis dustiness. **Cape American Oak Pinotage** & **Leopard Canyon Merlot** discontinued.

Isabelo range

Pinotage-Cabernet new ★★★ Inviting vanilla/plum notes on **05** lead to juicy palate; tannins fairly assertive, especially on finish. Great with steak. **Grenache-Shiraz-Cinsaut** new ★★ Subdued, austere style needing food to soften tannins. Brisk acidity, some sweet berries on finish. **Chenin Blanc** ★★ **05** like pvs, lively acidity & zest. Tropical, weight/texture for solo sipping or to enjoy with rich avo & feta salads. **Shiraz** & **Sauvignon Blanc**, & **Route 101** range discontinued. All above WO W Cape/Brde Rvr Vlly. — *DH*

Thomas Kipling see Makro
Thornhill see Veenwouden

Thorntree Wines

Est/1stB 2001 ▪ Closed to public ▪ Owner/winemaker André Badenhorst ▪ 70 000 cs 50/50 red/white ▪ Export brands: Cape Mist, Witteboomen ▪ Suite 310 Private Bag X16 Constantia 7848 ▪ andrebad@iafrica.com ▪ ***T/F 794·7679***

André Badenhorst has found a home for Thorntree Wines: Overhex Private Cellar, particularly convenient since he draws the bulk of his fruit from surrounding Worcester and Robertson. He's relishing the challenge of making affordable wines, having been involved with establishing vineyards in the premium Constantia valley for years (he was born on Groot Constantia). Having concentrated to date on supermarket brands in the US (Thorntree) and Europe (Cape Mist), he's considering entering the local market.

No new vintages tasted; following notes from pvs ed: **Cabernet Sauvignon** ★★★★ **03** inviting mulberry fruit, tannins nicely tamed. Good quality grapes, carefully put together. Staves for 4 mths, alc 14%. **Merlot** ★★★ Robust & rustic red. Dark plummy fruit, firm tannins on **03**, very dry. **Pinotage** ★★ **03** muscular & meaty, good concentration; some would find bitterness on finish. Unoaked. **Shiraz** ★★★ Good meaty red for winter tippling. Ripe pruney fruit & some leather of older-style shiraz in **03**. Very dry. **Chardonnay** ★★★ **04** shyish on nose; impressively fruity palate though, fullish body from extra time on lees. **Chenin Blanc** ★★★ **04** shows quality fruit – bouncy & ripe with greengage/melon flavours & twist lemon on finish. **Sauvignon Blanc** ★★★ Fresh & fruity **04**, grapes ex-Paarl, light citrus flavours, bone-dry. Low 13% alc. All WO W-Cape. – *IvH*

Three Anchor Bay see Cape First
Three Gables see The Winery
Three Peaks see Mount Vernon
Three Rivers see Bon Courage
Thys Drift see Goedverwacht

Tierhoek

Citrusdal ▪ Est 2001 ▪ 1stB 2003 ▪ Closed to public ▪ Owner Tony Sandell ▪ Winemaker Ian Nieuwoudt ▪ Viticulturist Johan Viljoen ▪ ±6 ha (chenin, sauvignon) ▪ ±2 000 cs 5% red 95% white ▪ 12 Ferndale Drive, Ottery, Cape Town 7800 ▪ tsrw@iafrica.com ▪ ***T 704·1122/ 082·536·7131*** *▪ F 704·1110*

From a modest 150 cases last year, owner Tony Sandell is now buying in grapes from the neighbouring property and upping production to 2000. But the growth spurt will not stop there. The plan is to plant 24 000 new vines, all white varieties; and in preparation of increased tonnages, erect a new cellar. Restoration of the historic homestead and yard is ongoing. When complete, Sandell says, Tierhoek will be the only example of an early 19th century Sandveld farm in fully restored condition, with all authentic stables, mill, saddlery, implements and virtually all items used for daily existence. Open to visitors? we wonder.

★★★★ **Chenin Blanc** Stylistic about-turn from semi-sweet maiden **03** to dry (just: 5g/ℓ sugar) **04** (★★★★); delicate lemon & fynbos bouquet enhanced by creamy oak; solid yet refreshing, lengthy; alc now unobtrusive 12.5%. Should improve 3-5 yrs.

Following both new: **Grenache** ★★ **04** enticing dried-fruit & cranberry bouquet & subtle oak spice, followed by unexpectedly tough, pressy tannins. **Sauvignon Blanc** ★★★★ **04** charms with forthcoming litchi/gooseberry nose & tropical palate, lemony acid & wet pebble finish. Medium bodied, promising. All WO Piekenierskloof. – *CvZ*

Timbili see Ernst & Co
Tin Mine see Zevenwacht
Todo see Helderkruin

Tokara

Stellenbosch ▪ Est/1stB 2000 ▪ Tasting & sales 9–5 Sat 9–1 ▪ Closed pub hols ▪ Tokara Restaurant for lunch & dinner Tue-Sat (T 808·5959) ▪ Farm-grown varietal olive oils from The Olive Shed ▪ Art exhibits (enquiries: Julia Meintjes ▪ T 083·675·1825) ▪ Owner GT Ferreira ▪ Winemaker Miles Mossop (Jan 2000), with Dumisani Mathonsi (Jan 2004) ▪ Viticulturist Aidan Morton (Nov 2000) ▪ 100 ha (cabs s/f, merlot, mourvèdre, petit verdot, shiraz, chard, sauvignon) ▪ 650 tons 40 000 cs ▪ 60% red 40% white ▪ PO Box 662 Stellenbosch 7599 ▪ wine@tokara.com ▪ www.tokara.com ▪ ***T 808·5900*** *▪ F 808·5911*

Perched on the crest of the spectacular Helshoogte Pass, Tokara has previously only released wines under the Zondernaam ('Nameless') label. But four flagship Tokara-branded wines have now been launched, obviously meeting big-businessman owner GT Ferreira's expectations of 'wines that could be considered among the best in the world'. Winemaker Miles Mossop, assisted by Dumisani Mathonsi and advised by neighbour Gyles Webb of Thelema, sources his 'exceptional' fruit (tended by viticulturist Aidan Morton) from the Simonsberg ward in Stellenbosch, Elgin and now, for the first time, the Hemel-en-Aarde Valley. Far from being forgotten, Zondernaam now sports a new look more consistent with the Tokara image. And joining the wine, fine food and olive oil this year is a five-year-old potstill brandy.

★★★★☆ **Red** The wait is over! Tokara's near-mythical top-of-the-line wines, years in meticulous gestation, finally released: 'Red' (and whites below) – well worth the wait, too. Behind the minimalist moniker a fine bdx-style blend, cab in lead with merlot, petit v. **03** classically styled (real Bordeaux does come to mind): elegant & dry, light-textured vinosity harmoniously meshed with fine grainy tannins. Sensitively oaked (Fr, 61% new, 20 mths). Already enjoyable; great pity to over-age (these are young vines); possibly best by 2008.

★★★★☆ **White** Name might be non-descript, but nothing featureless about **04**. In fact it's brilliant: unequivocal cool-climate sauvignon, Fr oak fermented, matured 6 mths, 13% new. Heady, refined gooseberry/granadilla tone; polished mineral mouthfeel, almost imperceptibly enriched by wood. Big, powerful but wonderfully controlled (15% alc).

★★★★ **Chardonnay** Cool, mineral style, impressively understated & balanced. **04** fruit seamlessly merged with oak for 'natural' feel; fine though plentiful substance; toasty/nutty finishing flourish hints at further complexity by ±2007/8. Incl 2% tank-fermented fraction; balance Fr oak fermented/aged, 50% new, 11 mths. Partial malo.

★★★★ **Sauvignon Blanc** Ethereal purity of W Bay's cooling sea influence calling card on **05**, from GTF's Hemel & Aarde vyds (so WO W Bay). Medium body perfectly sets off delicate passionfruit, deeper figgy features. Fine steely verve; great resurgence of flavour in uncompromisingly dry savoury finish. All above NEW.

Zondernaam range

★★★★ **Cabernet Sauvignon** Another **02** (★★★☆) reflecting difficult vintage for cab; somewhat disparate smoky/herbal character. Well-structured, oaked, if lacking depth. Probably best before ±2007. 40% new Fr barriques, 18 mths. **01** was graceful & serious, probably longer-lived. Own (Tokara), Devon Valley vyds.

★★★★ **Shiraz 03** (★★★★☆) epitomises delicacy (14.3% alc notwithstanding), shows off variety's beguiling red fruits/lilies fragrance to perfection. Supple, lissom palate, no sense of over-extraction. Oak in harmony with lovely fruit, structure; 18 mths Fr/Am casks, 23% new. Charming wine worth waiting for; should peak around 2009/10. **02** seamlessly refined, with fine grip & savoury finish. Stbosch, Paarl vyds. This, following wine, WO W Cape.

★★★★ **Sauvignon Blanc** ✓ **05** a crowd pleaser, should delight purists too. Good presence, not over-assertive; clear tropical fruit/fig ripeness, freshening greengage notes; zingy & deliciously sustained. 70/30 blend Hldrberg/Paarl/Vllrsdorp & home vyds.

Chardonnay ★★★☆ **03** delicate & carefully oaked to highlight bright, lime/lemon zest succulence; balanced 14.5% alc. Fermented/10 mths Burgundy barrels, 25% new. Home vyds. Still available. **Chenin Blanc** ★★★☆ Emphatic, bold **04**, strong honey-gold hue reflected in ripe honeysuckle, melon bouquet. Juicy; sweetish tone; alc kick in tail (14.8%). Bought-in Stbosch grapes; natural ferment; 20% new oak. *Wine* ★★★★☆. **Pinotage** discontinued. *—AL*

Tokolosh see International Wine Services
Tom Lubbe Wines see The Observatory

Topaz Wine

Stellenbosch ▪ Est/1stB 2000 ▪ Visits by appt ▪ Owners/winemakers Clive Torr & Tanja Beutler ▪ Viticulturists Willie de Waal & James Downes ▪ 0.04 ha 450 cs 100% red ▪ 26 Topaz Str, Heldervue, Somerset West 7130 ▪ topazwines@mweb.co.za ▪ ***T 855·4275*** *▪ F 855·5086*

Clive Torr (Cape Wine Master and taster for this guide) and partner Tanja Beutler are front-runners of *garagiste* winemaking in SA – though they're more correctly called *stoop-istes* (there's a veranda involved). Clive T's passion for Burgundy (he owns a share in a winery there) and Tanja B's for promoting the *garagiste* movement, make for a winning team. Most of the grapes for Topaz are bought in – pinot from Elgin, and shiraz from the Bottelary Hills and Perdeberg. But a few rows in the couple's garden add their own character (and at harvest time, yet another excuse for a party). Minimal intervention, gentle handling ('pump' considered a four letter word) and biodynamic principles are de rigueur. Says TB: 'Wine contains life forces. We try to preserve and nurture them, and deliver a beverage that is still alive in the bottle.'

★★★★ **Pinot Noir** Burgundy-inflected barnyard whiffs on **04**, strawberries in tight tannin jacket, raspberry/mushroom intrigues; lovely balance. Welcome trend to lighter alc continues (13% now vs 14.5% for **01**).

★★★☆ **Syrah 04** with just one extra % alc, strikes as more Aussie, less Rhône (& shade less stunning) than standout **03** (★★★★☆), which concealed cannabis notes (inter alia) within its fragrant depths. The new release marked by spicy white pepper & prune; smoked/roasted fruit more evident. 14 mths mixed Fr oak, third new. – *NP*

Towerkop see Southern Cape Vineyards
Tradouw see Southern Cape Vineyards
Travino see Klawer
Trawal see Klawer
Tribal see African Terroir
Trini Cella see Rooiberg

Tukulu

Groenekloof ▪ Est 1998 ▪ Tasting & sales at Bergkelder ▪ Owners Distell, Leopont 98 Properties, Maluti Groenekloof Community Trust ▪ Winemaker Adian Fry (2003) ▪ Viticulturist Hannes van Rensburg (1998) ▪ 245 ha (cab, pinotage, sangiovese, shiraz, chard, chenin, sauvignon, viognier) ▪ 4 500 cs own label ▪ 60% red 40% white ▪ PO Box 184 Stellenbosch 7599 ▪ info@tukulu.co.za ▪ www.tukulu.co.za ▪ ***T 809·7000*** *▪ F 883·9651*

Tukulu, the flagship black empowerment brand in the Distell stable, sources its grapes from the Papkuilsfontein vineyards near Darling (which supply other Distell-owned brands like Nederburg). Named after deep red vineyard soils, Tukulu has earned numerous kudos in competitions and panel tastings, and winemaker Adian Fry is keen to not only win more awards but ultimately 'make Tukulu an SA icon'. Expectations are that the initiative, in which a community trust has a sizeable share, is likely to make a bid for Distell's stake in the not too distant future. Perhaps this will be the catalyst for realising Adian F's dream of someday making wine in Papkuilsfontein's own cellar.

★★★★☆ **Pinotage 02** rich berried nose, opulent fruit & gentle tannins. Less arresting **03** (★★★☆) refuses to fly. Notably quiet on nose – some dusty plum-toned fruit, whiff smoked beef. Dry savoury palate with firm tannins, lighter style than pvs (13.6% alc vs 14.5 for pvs); yr mixed oak.

★★★★ **Chenin Blanc** Popularly styled **04** pleasant pineapple & melon, citrus notes; good dry finish. **05** sampled pre-bottling shows ripe fruit concentration; dry, but 15.6% alc lends sweetness as well as massive power; too unready to rate. – *IvH*

Tulani see Diemersfontein

Tulbagh Mountain Vineyards

Tulbagh ▪ Est 2000 ▪ 1stB 2003 ▪ Tasting, sales & tours by appt ▪ Owners Jason Scott & George Austin ▪ Winemaker/viticulturist Chris Mullineux (Dec 2002) ▪ 16 ha (cab, mourvèdre, shiraz) ▪ 19 tons 95% red 5% straw wine ▪ PO Box 19 Tulbagh 6820 ▪ winegrower@tmv.co.za ▪ www.tmv.co.za ▪ ***T (023) 231·1118*** *▪ F (023) 231·1002*

The denouement in this multi-act, real-life docu-drama (with comedic interludes), depicting 'The Making of a Micro-Organic Vineyard/Winery' (go backstage on their website), came last year with the launch of their maiden wines: 'Tulbagh Mountain Vineyards', from home-grown grapes; 'TMV' (partly) bought-in. Main characters: London investment bankers Jason Scott and George Austin. Supporting cast: wives, young children, a great cellar team led by emerging young star Chris Mullineux. Eye-catching props: 14 elevated concrete tanks, wax-lined, long and shallow for slow maceration, easy manual punch-downs (from walkways). Highlights: shiraz, continuing to look at home here; mourvèdre for blending. Emerging side-plots: cabernet and chenin. Continue watching this space.

★★★★ **Syrah-Mourvèdre** Lilies & spice aromas/flavours announce dominating shiraz (78%) in warmly harmonious but powerful (15%) **03** combo, good fruit well supported by firm ripe tannins, big succulent acidity & 22 mths Fr oak, 20% new. Like Theta: native yeasts, certified organic.

Theta ★★★★ Ambitious, dark, ripe-fruited **03** from shiraz – but variety less obvious than spicy-tobacco oak (22 mths Fr, 50% new) & touch of volatility. Strongly built; dry tannins; 14.5% alc. One to watch as young vines mature. All above, below, new.

TMV range

These from, or include, bought-in grapes. WO W Cape, **04** unless noted.

★★★★★ **Swartland Syrah** Rich, intense warm-country shiraz, typically Swtland in origin, with its scrubby, herbal notes, fine velvety tannins, inherent balance. Already showing character & interest, promising more complexity for those who resist the youthful charm. Judicious 16 mths Fr oak, 20% new.

★★★★ **Viktoria** Vibrant shiraz, with 10% cinsaut adding note of light jammy charm, and 10% cab focusing the fine tannins. Lovely warm-country blend with refined rusticity. Oaking as above.

★★★★ **Chenin Blanc** Interesting & serious – though very drinkable, with cool minerality threading the fruit. Fresh, lively, & weightier than moderate, elegant 12.5% alc suggests, richness from 9 mths old oak, extended lees contact.

Cabernet Sauvignon-Merlot ★★★★ **03** nice earthy, red berry notes; soft ripe tannins; well balanced but no great concentration. Well integrated oak – 20 mths, 40% new. Approachable now, but no hurry. **Syrah-Cabernet Sauvignon** ★★★★ Accessible but forceful, strong, dry; pleasingly combines leanness & generosity, earthiness & fruit. 16 mths Fr oak, 20% new. Balanced 14.5% alc. – *TJ*

Tulbagh Winery

Tulbagh ▪ Est 1906 ▪ Tasting & sales Mon-Fri 8-5 Sat 9-1 ▪ Closed pub hols except Easter Sat, May 1 & Sep 24 ▪ Gift shop ▪ Owners 32 members ▪ Cellarmaster Carl Allen (Aug 2002) ▪ Winemaker Elsabé le Roux (Dec 2002) ▪ Viticulturist Jan-Carel 'Callie' Coetzee (2002) ▪ 550 ha ▪ 5 200 tons 70 000 cs own label 70% red 20% white 7% rosé 3% other ▪ Range for customer: Paddagang ▪ PO Box 85 Tulbagh 6820 ▪ tkw@tulbaghwine.co.za ▪ www.tulbaghwine.co.za ▪ ***T (023) 230·1001*** *▪ F (023) 230·1358*

Set to celebrate their centenary this year, Tulbagh is the oldest co-op in the land. Festivities will be supported by both new packaging and a revamped semi-sweet to the Village Collection range. No doubt, the cheery spirit will dispel memories of the challenges of the 2005 harvest, down by 24% on the previous crop.

Unfortified reds in range lightly wood chipped. **Cabernet Sauvignon** ★★★ **04** not ready; **03** had some muscle & exuberance; spicy sweet jam intro, full flavour/body. **Merlot** ★★★ Inviting dark fruit/choc lead-in to easy-drinking **04**; juicy & ripe Satsuma plum flavour, ultra-soft tannin. **Pinotage** ★★ Baked fruit aromas on **04**, simpler, earthier than pvs. **Shiraz** ★★★ **03** quaffably ripe & friendly, juicy prune fruit, balanced oak & acidity. **Chardonnay** ★★★ **05** unwooded & appealing; lingering clean flavours, more varietal definition than last. **Chenin Blanc** ★★ **05** unoaked yet with spicy notes, compact & racy. **Sauvignon Blanc** ★★ Early-picked **05**, crisp, flinty & lightish (±12% alc), with khaki bush hint. **Port** ★★★ **NV** from pinotage & ruby cab; latest bottling hovers between old & new styles; dusty/earthy, not over-sweet, higher alc (18.4%) than pvs. **Brut** & **Vin Doux** discontinued.

Klein Tulbagh range

Unfortified reds barrel aged 9-12 mths; none retasted. **Cabernet Sauvignon Reserve** ★★★ Classically styled **03** rung above austere pvs; appealing redcurrant & green olive flavours, supple tannins. **Merlot Reserve** ★★★ Massively ripe, unsubtle style; **03** deeper coloured than pvs, more extracted; stewed plums & dried fruit, grainy tannins. **Pinotage Reserve** ★★★ **03** mulberry aromas & vanilla suggestion (from 47% Am oak); ripe, more satisfying than above wines. **Shiraz Reserve** ★★★ Last was **02**, shy strawberry nose, woodsmoke sniffs; soft & quaffable. **Vintage Port** ★★★ From pinotage; **02** (pvsly a sample) older style with lower alc, highish sweetness – but delicious; packed with succulent fruitcake flavour.

Tulbagh Magnums

NV in stylish 1.5ℓ bottles (untasted): **Cabernet Sauvignon**, **Merlot**, **Pinotage**, **Vin Rouge**, **Natural Sweet Red**.

Village Collection

Classic Red ☺ ★★★ Unwooded mix pinotage, ruby cab; masses of plump, soft & juicy berries to enjoy.

All in range **NV**, sold in 1, 3 & 5ℓ packs, & 500/750ml screwtops. **Natural Sweet Rosé** ★ Very demure, drier than expected pink with low 8.6% alc. **Crispy White** ★★ The renamed 'Blanc de Blanc'. Floral, delicately crisp blend colombard, sauvignon; fresh, quaffable. **Extra Light** ★★ Blend of 3 white grapes including fernão pires; zingier, crisper than Crispy, appropriately light (±9% alc) & bone-dry. **Simply Sweet** new ★★★ Replaces 'Late Harvest' & 'Stein'. Bouncy semi-sweet from trio of grapes incl hanepoot; fresh acidity prevents any cloy. *– IvH/TM*

Tutuka see Buthelezi Wines

Twee Jonge Gezellen Estate

Tulbagh ▪ Est 1710 ▪ 1stB 1937 ▪ Tasting & sales Mon-Fri 9-4 Sat & pub hols 10-2 ▪ Casual tasting: no charge; formal tasting: fee on request ▪ Tours Mon-Fri 11 & 3; Sat & pub hols 11 ▪ Closed Easter Fri-Mon, Dec 25-26 & Jan 1 ▪ Owner/winemaker Nicky Krone ▪ 120 ha (petit v, pinot, muscat de F, chard, chenin, riesling, sauvignon, semillon, viognier) ▪ 1 000 tons 7% red 85% white 8% rosé ▪ PO Box 16 Tulbagh 6820 ▪ tjg@mweb.co.za ▪ www.tjwines.co.za ▪ ***T (023) 230·0680*** *▪ F (023) 230·0686*

To say that Mary and Nicky Krone are crazy about bubbly wouldn't be an overstatement. Their latest special blend is biding time on its lees in the same elegant bottles that host Veuve Clicquot's Grande Dame. 'We felt this four-vintage *prestige cuvée* deserved special treatment,' says Mary K. But pursuing the French model doesn't cut them off from their local roots. 'We're proud to say that we are of Africa, and Africa is in our blood,' she philosophises. Neither are the Krones resistant to change: you'll see more elegant packaging over the course of the year across their restructured range, with the Krone Borealis flying the flag, followed by limited-volume Krone and the easy-drinking TJ ranges.

Krone range

★★★★ **Borealis Brut** Continues to impress, incl visitors from Champagne. Subtle, critically acclaimed MCC, blend 50/50 chard-pinot, traditional vinification incl bunch-pressing, free-run juice only. Latest **99** toasty, chard-dominated bouquet; crisp, dry biscuity feel, lengthy dry finish. Preview of **00** shows slightly more weight (within fine-boned TJ context), sweet red-berried pinot dominating in youth, very attractive. Tantalisingly close to Fr originals. Lightish alcs (11.5%), & getting dryer, now only 7-8 g/ℓ sugar.

Syrah ★★★★ **02** (tasted for last ed, as were next 2) with attractive dusty berry & dried prune quality, dry earthy tannins; sweetness from ripe fruit; carries 14.5% alc with ease. **Balm of the Night** ★★★ Fortified muscat de F ('Beaumes-de-Venise style' says Nicky K); **99** showed barley sugar sweetness balanced by clean acid, unorthodox heather/peat aftertaste; warming, soothing. Modest 15.5% alc. 500 ml, as is … **Engeltjipipi** ★★★ Delicate botrytised **01**

from semillon, chenin, riesling, ageing serenely. Honeyed citrus flavours, firm acidity, lovely balanced sweetness.

TJ range

The Rose (Pvsly 'Rose Brut') ☺ ★★★ 'Designer bubbly' in stylish new livery, now blend chard, chenin with pinot, shiraz; quite deep colour; more meaty, assertive (more like still wine) flavours; slight sweetness on finish. Great accessory for fancy picnics. **NV**, carbonated. **Light** ☺ ★★★ Wafting muscat a signature for these – **04**'s delicate dry palate comes as delightful surprise. Long approved by Heart Foundation: low 8.5% alc, low kilojoules too. Ideal lunchtime wine. **Night Nectar Natural Sweet** ☺ ★★★ **04** blend chenin, some viognier, slimmed down to RS of 59g/ℓ, low alc at 9.5%. Graceful sweetie with delicate acidity; not cloying – just the thing for lightly spiced Malay/Pacific rim cuisine.

Schanderl ★★★ **03** (not retasted) youthful honeysuckle/spice developed into lime & spice aromas. Off-dry, zesty & assertive. Perfect lunchtime tipple at 12% alc. 100% muscat de F. **Thirty Nine** ★★ Riesling dominated blend (39 = clone number), with sauvignon, chenin. **04** less convincing than pvs, some baked character, has lost aroma. These whites all delicate, slenderly built, with ultra-soft acidity. – *IvH*

Twin's Peak see Lateganskop
Two Cubs see Knorhoek

Two Oceans

Finland, New Zealand and Vietnam are among the newest markets for this aspirant global brand, owned by Distell. The Cab-Merlot and the Sauvignon are distributed locally and available for tasting at Bergkelder (see entry).

Sauvignon Blanc ☺★★★ Well-pitched & appealing, grain sugar for rounded mouthfeel; **05** grassy & juicy, fresh rather than crisp.

Pinotage ★★★ Early drinking **04**'s mulberry& plum fruit given texture/interest by combo oak barrels/staves. **Shiraz** ★★★ Fruit-shy bouquet on **04** has hints smoked meat & game, mid-2005 lacks fruit muscle to round out tannin skeleton. Fr staves/chips. **Cabernet Sauvignon-Merlot** ★★★★ ✓ Cut above these easy-drinkers; none since **04**'s 60/40 mix, classy clove & lead pencil whiffs, mineral touch; palate fruitier but fairly stern; should have settled by now. **Merlot-Shiraz** ★★★ Good middle-of-road style; 65/35 ratio, partly barrelled; **04** tasted last yr had expressive fresh-picked berry character with vanilla; agreeable dry finish. **Cape Red** ★★★ Aka Soft & Fruity Red. Minimally oaked blend, usually cab/pinotage/ruby cab. **04** heathery fragrance, vegetal touch; smooth & flavoursome. **Rosé** ★★★ Fresh & savoury **04** twins pinotage & carignan. Coral-hued with red-berried melange, best enjoyed soon. **Chardonnay** ★★★ Departure from usual lightish style in **04**. Ripe mandarin nose & palate, full-bodied & weighty, oak plush. 40% in older Fr barrels, 6 mths. **Chenin Blanc-Chardonnay** ★★★ Medium-bodied, subtly oaked **04** lemon zest aromas, approachable acidity. **Semillon-Chardonnay** ★★ **04** uncomplex quick-quaff with lemondrop flavours, texture & weight from touch oak. **Cape White** ★★★ Aka Soft & Fruity White. **04** pretty, floral chenin (85%), colombard fusion. Grassy; light-footed & light-hearted. All WO W Cape. Depending on country, available in 187 & 750ml, and 3ℓ bag-in-box. – *CvZ*

Tygerberg see Altydgedacht
Tyne & Dalby see Stettyn
Uhambo see Premium Cape Wines
Uiterwyk Estate see DeWaal Wines

Uitkyk Estate

Stellenbosch ▪ Tasting & sales Mon-Fri 9-5 Sat/Sun 10-4 ▪ Fee R20-R25 incl glass ▪ Picnics in summer ▪ Owner Lusan Holdings ▪ Estate manager Rudi Buys ▪ Winemaker Estelle Swart (2000) ▪ Viticulturist Eben Archer ▪ ±870 tons ▪ 20 000 cs ▪ PO Box 104 Stellenbosch 7599 ▪ info@uitkyk.co.za ▪ www.uitkyk.co.za ▪ ***T 884·4416*** *▪ F 884·4717*

Unseasonable rain in 2005 increased the likelihood of disease, particularly for sauvignon, but Estelle Swart – studied biophysics before realising she couldn't spend her life in a lab – picked the grapes just in time. While many reported lower yields, Uitkyk (literally 'Outlook') took in their biggest ever tonnage in one day, stretching the cellar to capacity and creating a logistical headache. Mere hiccups in an otherwise perfect environment: 'I have everything,' Estelle S says, 'excellent sites, healthy vineyards, beautiful views and a stunning manor house with excellent tasting facilities.' The Outlook remains sunny.

Cabernet Sauvignon ★★★ **99** lighter than pvs, delicate & leafy. **Shiraz Reserve** new ★★★☆ Slice of history – first shiraz from the property since 85, **03** the last from a 28-yr vyd now grubbed. Big hello with lilies, black pepper & red fruit; yielding tannins & dignified alc (13.4%) on palate. Mainly Fr oak with Am, some Hungarian, 60% new. Probably not for cellaring. **Cabernet-Sauvignon Shiraz** ★★★ **01** equal blend with some black fruits & light savouriness. Fresh juicy acidity, though touch dry on finish. Hearty 15% alc. 14–18 mths oak, mainly Fr, some new. **Chardonnay** ★★☆ **03** vinous rather than fruity, with firm acid finish. 9 mths oak, mainly Fr, 42% new. **Sauvignon Blanc** ★★★☆ A fruity, genteel version, smooth & easy-drinking. **04** well structured; fresh & attractive; enjoy young. More serious **05** preview hints at bigger concentration/amplitude of fruit. Possible ★★★★. Only Shiraz Rsv & Sauv Bl tasted for this ed. *– CvZ/RK/IvH*

Uitvlucht Co-op Winery

Little Karoo ▪ Est 1941 ▪ Tasting & sales Mon-Fri 8-5.30 Sat 9-1.30 ▪ Fee R5 for groups of 20+ ▪ Open pub hols ▪ Owners 41 members ▪ Winemaker/viticulturist Kootjie Laubscher (Jun 1993), with Johannes Mellet ▪ 325 ha ▪ 5 000 tons 12 000 cs 36% red 22% white 28% muscadel 14% sparkling ▪ PO Box 332 Montagu 6720 ▪ info@uitvlucht-wines.co.za ▪ ***T (023) 614·1340*** *▪ F (023) 614·2113*

Upgrades are usually cause for satisfaction but the recent changes made to the Uitvlucht cellar and tasting room were tinged with regret. For 63 years the Uitvlucht wines had been made under thatch – one of the last cellars to do so – but due to the staggering increase in insurance premiums, the character old *rietdak* was replaced with corrugated iron.

Cabernet Sauvignon in abeyance. **Merlot** ★★☆ Modest but appealing **03**, creamy red berry fruit, juicy, approachable, with sweetish finish. **Pinotage** ★★ Soft banana whiffs on **02**, tannins firm but undaunting, should last few yrs. **Shiraz** ★☆ Correct varietal qualities (incl smoke & red berries) present but in slighter form in **04**. **Derde Heuvel Rood** new ★★☆ **02** spicy, light-textured red with plum pudding character, toasty dry finish. **Rosé** ★★ Light-hearted, friendly **05**, quaffably smooth & not too sweet. **Chardonnay** ☆ new to guide yet already flagging; **04** restrained honey/peach tones. All whites here for earliest possible enjoyment. **Chenin Blanc** ★★ **05** Granny Smith apple & fruit salad flavours, crisply dry & fresh. **Blanc de Blanc** ★ **04** plain & simple dry white now coming off the boil. **Vin Sec Sparkling** Not ready for tasting. **Vin Doux Sparkling** ★★ Carbonated **NV** with well-controlled sweetness, soft muscatty bubbles, sherbet finish. **Red Muscadel** ★★☆ Fortified winter warmer; **05** fruit pastille/jellied sweet aromas, cloyingly sweet palate. **Muscadel** ★★☆ White (which not stated on label) fortified dessert, **NV**, flavours of honey-drizzled sultana, commensurably syrupy-sweet texture. 16.4% alc. **Muscat de Frontignan** ★★★ Another lusciously sweet fortified; **01** raisin & tea leaf whiffs, dried apricot flavours & enlivening savoury thread. **Port** ★ Workmanlike **04**, dusty liquorice hints, drier than expected. **Colombar**, **Late Harvest** discontinued. *– CR*

Ultra Liquors

Leading independent discount liquor chain, sourcing special parcels and value wines via a national buying team for its exclusive labels. See Specialist wine shops section for store locations and opening hours. Enquiries: Chris Minikin.

Stellenvale range

No newer vintages of following trio; notes from pvs ed: **Secret Cellar Barrel No. 25 Cabernet Sauvignon** ★★★ Meaty, earthy complexity in **00**; touch of mint-choc; yr new oak well integrated; ready, drink soon. **Secret Cellar Barrel No. 15 Cabernet Sauvignon-Merlot** ★★★ **99** stewed red plum & leather notes, evidence of some bottle-age complexity; needs drinking. **Secret Cellar Barrel No. 35 Cabernet Sauvignon-Merlot** ★★ **02** richer, more youthful than above; very ripe & sweet entry turns chunkily dry on finish; needs time or food. **Cabernet Sauvignon** ★★☆ **04** forthcoming plum jam/stewed fruit aromas, plump black fruit with tight minty edge; unwooded this vintage. **Merlot** ★★☆ Unoaked **04**, as pvs, attractive Xmas cake aromas, balanced & fresh, with flick of tannin. Following pair WO Rbtsn: **Chardonnay** ★☆ Unwooded, light-bodied **05** with sprightly acidity for summer refreshment. **Sauvignon Blanc** ★☆ **05** simple, bright & zesty with merest suggestion of tropical fruit; pleasantly light 12% alc.

Table Bay range

Dry Red ☺ ★★☆ Chunky, savoury all-sorts blend; dusty/leafy notes, hints mulberry & mocha. Unwooded, quaffable; low 13% alc.

Rosé new ★☆ Pinotage adds colour/berry flavour to chenin's flesh; **05** off-dry, easily quaffable. **Dry White** ★ From chenin; shy honeysuckle whiff, light 12% alc, simple dry white. Mainly **NV**, fruit ex-Paarl, as is following range.

Route 303 range

Latest bottlings of these **NV**s not ready; notes from pvs ed. **Dry Red** ★★☆ Savoury blend with dusty notes, hint mulberry. Unwooded, quaffable. **Dry White** ★ Mix of chenin, crouchen, colombard; bone-dry, verging on austere yet quite zesty.

Beaufort range

5ℓ bag-in-boxes, untasted: **Dry Red**, **Grand Cru**, **Johannisberger** & **Late Harvest**. All ranges W Cape unless noted. *—DH/TM*

Ulusaba see Keukenhof
Umculi see Rooiberg
Umfiki see Goudini

Umkhulu Wines

Stellenbosch ▪ Est/1stB 2000 ▪ Closed to public ▪ Owner Fiona Phillips ▪ 20 000 cs 80% red 20% white ▪ PO Box 132 Simondium 7670 ▪ info@umkhulu.co.za fiona@cybercellar.co.za ▪ www.umkhulu.com ▪ ***T/F 874·2106***

Making even more special the fifth anniversary of Fiona and Adam Phillips' wines was the 2005 release of their meticulously blended Ubuntu from the fine 2003 vintage, 'showing awesome potential'. Still concentrating on exports, they've doubled sales to the US and have started a pincer move on Europe via Spain and Ireland. 'Next stop Russia!' says Fiona P.

★★★★ **Tian** Bdx-style blend led by cab, with cab f, merlot, malbec, petit v. After extracted, modern **02**, latest **03** (★★★☆) rather shy, light feel & texture; subtle dark berries held in check by firm tannins, nothing overdone; stylishly oaked (yr Fr, 50% new), not excessive 13.4% alc. **01** *WS* 90 pts.

★★★★☆ **Pinotage** In bright, modern guise. **03** continues accessible trend: soft, plush, plummy fruit with wafting vanilla spice of Am oak. Slight sweetness to fruit hauled back by firmish oak tannins which add needed texture, dryness. Yr Am oak, 30% new. Drink now & over next 2-3 yrs.

Njalo new ☺ ★★★ Blend shiraz, merlot, pinotage well integrated in cheerfully plump **03**; juicy berries abound, touches mint & plum; soft tannins for immediate drinkability.

Ubuntu new ★★★★ Brave new 'Cape Blend', **03** pinotage-led, with 17% each petit v, malbec. Pleasing plumpness, slight sweetness from pinotage not out of place, soft velvety tannins. Good glassful, quietly idling at present, may still roar into action. Yr 100% new Fr oak. **Malbec** ★★★ Overwhelming mint on attractive, very dry **03**, with graceful cassis fruit; soft tannins for early drinking. Yr Fr oak. **Shiraz** ★★★★ Attractive ripe **03**, hints smoked beef, mint – the house signature – good oak; sweet black cherry, rich & cordial-like, tannins worked to early drinkability. Yr Fr oak, 50% new. **Akira** ★★★★ **03** (sample) blends cab, pinotage, petit v (49/34/17); pinotage sweetness adds generosity, plumpness to sturdy tannic backbone. Already approachable. **Dry Red** new ★★ Frisky unwooded blend cab, pinotage, petit v. **03** (sample) whiffs mulberry, plum; clean-cut flavours. **Sauvignon Blanc** ★★★ **05** capsicum/green fig character in lower key; firm acidity, bone-dry, suited to food. **Chardonnay** Unavailable for tasting. **Dry White** new ★★ **04** not distinguished or exciting, but soft, dry, quaffable. – *IvH*

Under Oaks

Paarl ▪ 1stB 2003 ▪ Visits by appt ▪ Fee R20 ▪ Owners Hans & Theresa Britz ▪ Winemaker Theresa Britz ▪ Viticulturist Hans Britz ▪ 30 ha (chard, chenin, crouchen) ▪ 2 000 cs 70% red 30% white ▪ PO Box 641 Wellington 7654 ▪ fresno@mweb.co.za ▪ T 872 6070 ▪ F 872 5575

From a table grape farming background, Hans and Theresa Britz, both enthusiastic cooks who love entertaining, decided to try their hands at winemaking because the romance intrigued them – and having their very own wines to serve with meals was of course part of the appeal. Their recently purchased farm in Paarl, Oaklands (circa 1695), is still a work in progress. 'It was very neglected. We've removed, replanted, and are now busy restoring buildings.' The grapes for their first wine, the Cabernet 03, came from their Wellington farm, with Bertus Fourie from nearby Diemersfontein the biggest influence on their winemaking.

Cabernet Sauvignon ★★ Well-balanced **04** with black fruit, forest floor flavours & aromas, sweet vanillas of Am oak prominent on nose & palate. Not for sipping solo, firm albeit ripe tannins require food. Yr Fr/Am barrels, 70% new. WO Paarl, as is … **Chenin Blanc** ★★ **05** powerful, 15.3% alc dominates nose & palate, remarkably viscous, blowsy for this variety. Lightish **Sauvignon Blanc** ★★★ **04** with delicious asparagus, fig & sherbet notes, fresh acidity & sherbety, dry finish. Tad short, drink up. WO Paarl. – *CvZ*

Unity see African Terroir
Unplugged 62 see Joubert-Tradauw
Upington see Oranjerivier Wine Cellars

Upland Estate

*Wellington ▪ Est/1stB 1998 ▪ Visits by appt ▪ 2 self-catering cottages ▪ Distillery ▪ Farm-grown/made olives & tapenade ▪ Owners Edmund & Elsie Oettlé ▪ Winemaker/viticulturist Edmund Oettlé ▪ 12 ha (cab, chenin, crouchen) ▪ 30 tons 500 cs 100% red ▪ PO Box 152 Wellington 7654 ▪ oettle@intekom.co.za ▪ http://organicwine.co.za ▪ **T 082·731·4774** ▪ F 873·5724*

'Environmentally friendly, home-spun, rural' evokes the impression of some hippie-styled existence. Not so. Off the beaten track, yes, but there is scientific, soundly principled and sustainable logic behind each piece of equipment and practice on this organically certified farm, owned by Edmund Oettlé (specialist vet + 2 PhDs, non-winemaking) and wife Elsie. Quality fruit, reflecting the true character of the site and each vintage, is their aim, and they go about this by sustainably nurturing the soil, vines and the environment. In his hand-crafted cellar, appearing ingeniously Heath Robinson (although complete with all necessary technology), experimentation continues with micro-oxygenation techniques for better tannin management of his seriously styled Cabernet.

Cabernet Sauvignon ★★★★ Authentic 'bio wine' from low-cropped, organic vyds; barrel-matured ± yr. **02** keeps good company with earlier cellarmates: ripe & curvaceous, even fleshy, soft tannins, showing a particularly amiable side of cab. Nudges next notch up. **Merlot** ★★★ Last tasted was **00** under 'Maske' label; grapes from neighbour's vyd; black cherries, touches tar, fragrant cigar in bouquet, easy palate. NE. — *IvH*

Urbane Wines

A restructure sees this easy-drinking range now exclusively made and bottled for export to the US by Porterville Cellars, where the wines may also be sampled. See separate entry for tasting hours.

Shiraz ★★ **04** spicy dry red with bluegum whiffs, fruit braced by tannin for comfortable BBQ partnering. Yr oak barrels. **Chardonnay** ★ Vinous, more than fruity, light (12.5%) & dry. **Sauvignon Blanc** ★ **05** straightforward light-bodied dry white. WO W Cape. — *CT*

Usana

Stellenbosch ▪ Est/1stB 2003 ▪ Tasting by appt ▪ Owner Joubert Family Trust ▪ Vini consultant Mike Dobrovic, with Clinton le Sueur (both Mar 2003) ▪ Viticulturists Joubert brothers ▪ PO Box 7087 Stellenbosch 7599 ▪ usana@xsinet.co.za ▪ www.usana.co.za ▪ ***T 082·896·3437/ 083·625·2301*** *▪ F 865·2441*

A firm believer that 'without outstanding grapes, one cannot produce a great wine', marketer Jennie Joubert's product is in good hands: her viticulturist brothers grow 80% of the grapes that go into Mulderbosch's acclaimed Sauvignon. The Jouberts, for many generations Stellenbosch-based, are expanding their horizons with the purchase of a farm in Elgin, where 8ha of sauvignon have been planted amid much excitement. More positive news is the imminent release of a trio of reds: a Cab, Merlot and Shiraz. Social issues being a theme here (Usana means 'New Beginning' in Xhosa), the family has decided to set up tertiary education funds for the farmworkers' children.

Sauvignon Blanc ★★★★ **04** raises the bar. Enticing bellpepper & tomato/blackcurrant notes herald fresh figgy palate with arresting acidity, gravelly finish. Food friendly & enjoyable on its own. 13% alc. — *CvZ*

Uva Mira Vineyards

Stellenbosch ▪ Est 1997 ▪ 1stB 1998 ▪ Mon-Fri 8:30–5 Sat 9.30–1 ▪ Closed Christian holidays ▪ Owner Denise Weedon ▪ Winemaker/viticulturist Matthew van Heerden (May 2003), advised by Kevin Watt ▪ 30 ha ▪ 5 000 cs 60% red 40% white ▪ info@uvamira.co.za ▪ PO Box 1511 Stellenbosch 7599 ▪ ***T 880·1683*** *▪ F 880·1682*

'There is no more beautiful spot to sip on quality wines in Stellenbosch,' reckons winemaker/ viticulturist Matthew van Heerden — and he's not exaggerating. Previously closed to the public, Uva Mira now welcomes visitors to experience its 'unmatchable views from high atop the Helderberg' while tasting its two tiers of cool-climate wine: the superior everyday Cellar Selection and the special occasion Vineyard Selection (including a yet-to-be-released red blend). 'We're over-delivering at prices accessible to the local consumer,' promises MvH, 'and aiming to produce a five star Chardonnay from an area traditionally associated with quality reds rather than whites.' His personal goal, meanwhile, is to finish in the top 20 in the Berg River Canoe Marathon … for the third time.

Vineyard Selection

★★★★☆ **Chardonnay** Gorgeous — all more so for being quiet & understated; **04** from a single vyd, rich & harmonious with pure acidity, great depth/elegance. Peach, butterscotch just two of many layers of aroma, flavour; discreetly oaked. 'Age-old burgundian methods' used, incl bunch-pressing; fermentation/ageing in Fr oak, 11 mths; light filtration. Restrained 13.5% alc.

Uva Mira Cab-led blend with 15% merlot, 5% shiraz; maiden **04** from Hldrberg vines. Barrel preview reveals intense flavours, dense tannins, silky texture, long & dry finish. Potential ★★★★ once bottled. 15 mths Fr oak, 30% 1st fill. Both new.

Cellar Selection

Merlot-Cabernet Sauvignon new ★★★★ 65/35 blend; introspective **03** only hints at the future; meaty/floral whiffs with hint tobacco, taut/fine tannins, lighter texture than above. Potential to improve over 3-5 yrs. 15 mths combo new/older Fr oak. **Sauvignon Blanc** ★★★ Last tasted was **03**, tropical-toned, sturdy, with some luscious filling. **04** untasted. Preview of understated & elegant **05** shows ★★★★ potential; lime/grapefruit bouquet & flavours, concentrated & long. *— IvH/AL*

Vals Baai see False Bay Vineyards

Van Loveren Private Cellar

*Robertson ▪ Est 1937 ▪ 1stB 1980 ▪ Tasting & sales Mon-Fri 8.30-5 Sat 9.30-1 ▪ Closed Easter Fri/Sun, Dec 25 & Jan 1 ▪ Tours on request ▪ Sweetcorn fritters available Sat 9.30-1 ▪ Tourgroups ▪ Conference/function venue ▪ Walks ▪ Owners Nico, Wynand, Phillip, Hennie, Bussell & Niel Retief ▪ Winemaker Bussell Retief ▪ Viticulturists Niel & Hennie Retief ▪ 220 ha (cab, red muscadel, sauvignon) ▪ 3 900 tons 300 000 cs 33% red 33% white 34% rosé ▪ PO Box 19 Klaasvoogds 6707 ▪ info@vanloveren.co.za ▪ www.vanloveren.co.za ▪ **T (023) 615·1505** ▪ F (023) 615·1336*

This value-orientated family cellar purposely bucks the trend towards specialisation and focus — and wins commendations for sticking to its populist paradigm. 'We want to offer each visitor a white, red, sweet, dry, sparkling and fortified, in an easy-drinking or more serious style,' says winemaker Bussell Retief. 'We also want to provide the best quality wines at the most affordable prices.' *Wine* magazine endorsed the Retief's efforts by naming Van Loveren 'Best Value Cellar' in its annual Value Awards, and Bussell R romped home with the Winemaker of the Year statuette from Wine of the Month Club. Now the family want to become the most popular winery among all South Africans....

Limited Releases

Cabernet Sauvignon ★★★ Fr oak adds hints vanilla & spice to quiet dark berry nose on **04**. Lean but smooth; agreeable if simple drinking over next yr. Barrelled yr. WO W Cape. **Shiraz** ★★★ **04** liberally adorned with coconutty Am oak; some spice, savoury flavours, smoothly drinkable; lacks concentration of pvs; best opened soon. Single-vyd. Yr oak, 70/30 Fr/Am. **Limited Release Reserve Chardonnay** ★★★★ ✓ Luscious butter/toast appeal on **05**; fleshy, flavoursome but firmly structured, citrus tang to solid dry tail. Fermented/aged 100% new Fr oak.

Van Loveren range

River Red ☺ ★★★ Red & ready **05**; sassy, spicy lip-smacker uncluttered by oak, tannin. Shiraz, merlot, ruby cab (50/30/20), also in 500ml under screwcap. **Blanc de Noir Shiraz** ☺ ★★★ Consistent & ever popular. **05**'s coppery blush contrasted by cheekily bright wine gum aromas, soft, juicy flavours. Fruitily dry. **Sauvignon Blanc** ☺ ★★★ Awarded wine, also eminently drinkable. **05** ripe varietal notes; lightish, refreshingly clean. **Colombar-Chardonnay** ☺ ★★★ Sound version of area's trademark blend. **05** with nutty/citrusy balance/weight both for light summer dishes, aperitif sipping. **Pinot Grigio** ☺ ★★★ (Pvsly 'Pinot Gris') Versatile food partner **05**; unshowy & defined spice/smoke character; rounded, fullish, dry.

Merlot ★★ Very ripe, sturdy **04**, with hints dark plum fruit, best opened soon. 60% barrel-aged, 4 mths. **Pinotage** ★★★ Instantly recognisable tart red berry/acetone nose on **04**; touch oak smoothes, plumps out sweetish palate. Big but unintrusive 14% alc. **Cabernet Sauvignon-Shiraz** ★★★ Happy partnership, as this often is. Soft, spice/cedar fragrance; savoury, fresh flavours in uncomplicated but satisfying, soundly dry **04**. **Blanc de Noir Red Muscadel** ★★★ Boudoir pink with dainty muscat scents; **05** trippingly fresh, light, attractively lingering fruity sweetness. **Colombard** ★★ **05** with ripe apple scents, fruit-lifting 13g/ℓ sugar. **Fernão Pires** ★★ Usually just off-dry, easy drinking. **05** not ready for tasting. **Cape Riesling** ★★ Tangy, bone dry **04** still available. **05** untasted. **Semillon** ★★ Still selling firm fleshed, concentrated **04**. **05** not tasted. **Chardonnay** ★★★ Ripe wheaten **05**, colour echoed in fleshy fullness, broad lime/tropical fruit. Unwooded; ex-single vyd. **Blanc de Blanc** ★★ Lively dry colombar/sauvignon blend; **05** lightish, pleasant fruity kick in tail. **Vino Blanc** ★★ Very brisk dry quaffer; gentle colombard fruit with dash sauvignon. **NV** (05). 500ml screwcap. **Special Late Harvest Gewürztraminer** ★★★ Pure, unshowy **05**; delicate spicy/floral fragrance; rounded sweetness balanced by clean acid. Easy characterful drinking. **Red Muscadel** ★★★★ ✓ **04** delicate, wafting muscat spice; good lift from freshening acid. **05** not ready. 17.5% alc. **Ruby Port** new ★★★ Colour as named. Loads of bright prune/fresh currant flavours; smoothly sweet, warming. From touriga. **NV** but blend 02/03. 18% alc.

Four Cousins range

All **NV**, uncertified handy party-size 1ℓ bottles. **Dry Red** ★★★ Friendly, uncomplicated blend; fresh, sappy red fruits styled for quaffability. Blend similar to above River Red. **Sweet Rosé** ★★ Muscat/hanepoot blend. Freshly picked strawberries strewn with generous 78g/ℓ sugar. Chill & quaff (preferably off bottling line). 7.5% alc. **River White** ★★ (Pvs 'Dry White') Tangy, lightish colombard/sauvignon blend, with juicy green apple core; further pep from dash muscat.

Four Cousins Natural Sweet range

All ★★, **NV**, uncertified. **Red** Mouthful juicy sweet plums, brush tannin, low 9.5% alc. Adaptable to chilled summer sipping, winter warmer mulled. **Rosé** Wild strawberries & cream sprinkled with 78g/ℓsugar. At appealing best very fresh & well chilled. 7.5% alc. **White** Muscat-scented, sun-sweet white muscadel/chenin blend with quaffable 8.5% alc.

Papillon sparkling range

Colour-coded butterfly labels on these budget-priced, lowish alc (11-11.5%) uncertified **NV** carbonated bubblies. All ★★. **Brut** Fresh fruit salad whipped up by sparky bubble, 12g/ℓsugar; alc at pick-me-up 11.5% level. From colombar & sauvignon. **Demi-Sec** Charming semi-sweet, gentle effervescence matched by fairy-light muscat tones. From riesling/muscat. **Vin Doux** Showy copper pink, sweet & fruity. 100% muscat de F. —*AL*

Vansha see Ridgeback

Van Zylshof Estate

Robertson ▪ Est 1993 ▪ 1stB 1994 ▪ Tasting & sales Mon-Fri 9-5 Sat 9-1 ▪ Closed Easter Fri, Dec 25 ▪ Tours by appt ▪ Owner Van Zylshof Trust ▪ Winemaker/viticulturist Andri van Zyl ▪ 32 ha (cab, merlot, chard, chenin, sauvignon) ▪ 10 000 cs 10% red 90% white ▪ PO Box 64 Bonnievale 6730 ▪ vanzylshof@lando.co.za ▪ ***T (023) 616·2401*** *▪ F (023) 616·3503*

A champagne year for chardonnay — that was 2005 for Andri van Zyl on the Bonnievale family farm, worth a visit particularly for flavourful, value-for-money whites. His Riverain Chardonnay was awarded Veritas gold; the latest vintage was a National Young Wine Show class winner; and Van Zylshof is flying KLM Business *and* First Class worldwide. The 2005 harvest, though, was as difficult here as elsewhere, AvZ reports: small, prone to rot, with selective picking the order of the day.

Cabernet Sauvignon-Merlot ☺ ★★★ Flavoursome blend with sound, understated oak. Preview medium-bodied **04** bright, straightforward cassis/blackberry fruits, squeeze softish tannin. **Chardonnay** ☺ ★★★ Modicum new Fr oak highlights characterful pickled lime/lemon peel notes of **04**. Plump, juicy, with balance & some spine. **Chardonnay Riverain** ☺ ★★★ Unwooded Rbtson chardonnay, with region's trademark lime minerality. Shiny straw-green **05**, delicate, lively flavours. Drink young. 14.2% alc. **Chenin Blanc** ☺ ★★★ **05** intense, lime-streaked ripeness suggests much fuller body than actual comfortable 12.1% alc; juicily mouth-filling, persistent. **Sauvignon Blanc** ☺ ★★★ Riper though unblowsy tropical-toned **05**; bright fruity acids tuned for those who prefer their sauvignons less overt. —*AL*

Van Zylskloof see Johan van Zyl Wines

Vaughan Johnson's Wine & Cigar Shop

Cape Town (V&A Waterfront Pierhead Cape Town) ▪ Est/1stB 1985 ▪ Sales Mon-Fri 9-6 Sat 9-5 Sun 10-5 ▪ Open pub hols ▪ Gifts, souvenirs, spirits & beer available ▪ Owner Vaughan Johnson ▪ PO Box 50012 Waterfront 8002 ▪ vjohnson@mweb.co.za ▪ www.vaughanjohnson.com ▪ ***T 419·2121*** *▪ F 419·0040*

By dint of its location and international clientele, Vaughan Johnson's wine shop on Cape Town's V&A Waterfront is something of a barometer for the local wine market. Because of the strengthening rand, V-J reports, only wines under R100 are moving in any volume, except where true cachet or branding can persuade consumers otherwise. 'So, producers should guard against excessive price increases taking them out of this bracket,' he opines. Cape speciality pinotage is not automatically attractive – there has to be exceptional quality or value to pique the interest, even among the Swedish and Norwegian visitors who are currently his greatest fans of SA wines. In straitened times such as these, Johnson's own value-for-money house wines unsurprisingly continue to pour off the shelves.

Mainly Paarl/Frhoek vyds. **Sunday Best Red** ★★ Blackcurrant cordial & smoky meat aromas from 50/50 blend cab/merlot in **04**. Very ripe berry fruit tussles with gruff tannins ... & comes second! **Good Everyday Cape Red** ★★ Still a hit in Ireland; **04** subtle cherry fruit, unchallenging tannins. Mainly merlot, splashes tinta, ruby cab, shiraz & carignan. **Good Everyday Cape White** ★★ At only R16/btl, the fastest seller in range. Subdued pear-drop aromas; unobtrusively dry finish, pleasant if quick. **NV**. **Sunday Best White** ★★★ A new blend in **05** for more fruit character, V-J notes; colombard (70%), sauvignon in, chardonnay, chenin out. Cheery tropical fruit, bubblegum finish. Enjoy young.

Waterfront Collection

Nautical labels distinguish this value-priced, quaffable duo. Both **NV**. **Captain's Claret** ★★★ Friendly everyday red. **04** 100% shiraz; typical black pepper/smoked ham aromas, ebullient red fruit, medium-bodied with firm, dry farewell. **Great White** ★★ Uncomplicated fun; **05** inviting floral nose & fruity sherbet finish. From Paarl chenin. – *CvZ*

Veelplesier see Baarsma
Veelverjaaght see Beau Joubert

Veenwouden Private Cellar

Paarl ▪ Est 1989 ▪ 1stB 1993 ▪ Tasting sales Mon-Fri 9-4.30 ▪ Fee R200/btl if no purchase made ▪ Closed pub hols ▪ Sales & tours by appt ▪ Owner Deon van der Walt ▪ Winemaker Marcel van der Walt, with Faried Williams (Jan 1994/1995) ▪ Viticulturist Marcel van der Walt, with Sias Louw (Jan 1994/1995) ▪ 14 ha (cabs s/f, malbec, merlot) ▪ ±80 tons 5 500 cs own labels 99% red 1% white ▪ PO Box 7086 Northern Paarl 7623 ▪ admin@veenwouden.com ▪ www.veenwouden.com ▪ ***T 872·6806*** *▪ F 872·1384*

It was 'hands off the tiller' in 2005 for Charles and Sheila van der Walt as they settled into retirement, but an established team was there to maintain continuity – their sons Deon and Marcel, owner and viti/vini man respectively (the latter's career on the home farm as old as SA's new democracy); Henriëtte Jacobs in charge of admin and marketing. Internationally renowned tenor DvdW had another celebrity event for his scrapbook in 2005, presenting a concert of songs by Schubert in the Vatican for Cardinal Joseph Ratzinger just before he became Pope Benedict XVI. Something else to sing about: their Merlot 01 was placed in the world's top 24 in a blind tasting by Swiss *Weinwisser* magazine. And brother Marcel is humming contentedly after the last harvest: 'An outstanding year for reds.'

★★★★☆ **Merlot** Introduced with fanfare & still prized a decade on: rightfully back on its pedestal with **03** after transient hiccoughs. Even fresh off bottling line & touch unsettled, enormously promising: beautiful flesh resting in sumptuous folds of powdery tannin, fine-toned structure reverberates with finesse. Finishes fuller than **02**, which had gamey hints among its layered tannins. Single low-yielding vyd on home farm with 10% cab. 2 yrs 70% new Fr oak.

★★★★☆ **Classic** Acclaimed Bdx-style red more retiring & intricate than above, also back to true form in **03**: striking Belgian-lace delicacy to the composition, a sleeper only likely to start rewarding an approach 5 yrs from harvest. **02** in ripe genre, opulent forest-floor fruits fleshed out with mocha, trademark tannins in restraint. Cabs s/f, merlot &, latterly, soupçon malbec. Oaking as above.

★★★★ **Vivat Bacchus** More considered, understated blend than above – & eminently delicious on release. **03** generous cassis sewn into firm yet pliable frame, finessed lingering exit. **02** had butcher-shop aromas, damson & red berry fruits. Now 60% merlot, with malbec, cabs f/s. 50% new Fr oak, 2 yrs.

★★★☆ **Thornhill Shiraz** Stylishly bold, fruity & dramatic. **03** (★★★★) measured in youth with promise of mineral spice in tapered, tangy finish. Seam of acid tension lifts it above **02**: gamey meat tones to tightly knit tannins. 10% cab stiffening. Latest 18 mths Fr oak, all 2nd fill.

★★★★☆ **Chardonnay Special Reserve** Some would pay the R250 cellar-door swing ticket for its rarity (just 30 cs); it's worth it for individuality. Neither merely opulent nor just elegant, it defies pigeon-holing: **04** Meursault-like apple pie with a tangerine twist. And moreish. **03** fine form with white truffle richness. New Fr oak fermented, *sur lie* ageing now 9 mths. Moderate 13% alc. *—DS*

Vendôme

Paarl ▪ Est 1692 ▪ 1stB 1999 ▪ Tasting & sales Mon-Fri 9.30–1 Sat 9.30–12.30 ▪ Fee R5 refunded on purchase ▪ Closed pub hols ▪ Tours on request ▪ Conferencing/functions for up to 60 ▪ Owner/viticulturist Jannie le Roux Snr ▪ Winemaker/viticulturist Jannie le Roux Jnr ▪ 70 ha (cabs s/f, merlot, shiraz, chard, chenin, colombard) ▪ 20 tons 1 400 cs own label 70% red 30% white ▪ PO Box 36 Paarl 7645 ▪ lerouxjg@icon.co.za ▪ www.vendome.co.za ▪ ***T 863·3905*** *▪ F 863·0094*

Jannie le Roux served his apprenticeship in Australia, Bordeaux and California before returning home to take over winemaking from a very busy dad – when Jannie Snr is not tending vines as viticulturist on the home farm, he's actively promoting SA wines abroad, among others as chair of Boland Kelders and a mover behind the Cape Coastal Vintners joint venture.

★★★★ **Cabernet Sauvignon** Features natural yeast fermentation & small portion cab f for complexity; standout **00** offered minerals & oak melded attractively with fruit. **01** (★★★) last ed showed elegant tomato cocktail-like tones; appeared to be peaking; moderate ±12.5% alc; yr Fr small-oak, 3rd-4th fill. No **02**.

Classique Red new Bdx-style blend, varieties/proportions/oaking similar to Le R version below; preview of **03** shows more concentration, punch; very ripe fruit coupled with strong tannins. Provisional ★★★☆. **Le Roux Merlot-Cabernet Sauvignon** ★★★ 54/42 blend (plus dash cab f) in **02**, with mocha/choc notes & quite firm elegant tannins. Yr Fr oak, 2nd-3rd fill, wild yeast ferment. **Chardonnay** ★★★ **04** an edgier version of the pvs ripe vintage's suppleness, thanks to racy lime acidity which firms the unoaked melon/papaya fruit; good persistent finish. *—MM*

Vera Cruz Estate see Delheim

Vergelegen

Stellenbosch (see Helderberg map) ▪ Est 1700 ▪ 1stB 1992 ▪ Tasting daily 9.30–4.30 (sales close at 5) ▪ Entrance fee R10pp ▪ Closed Dec 25, May 1 & Easter Fri ▪ Lady Phillips Restaurant: à la carte lunches daily; Rose Terrace: al fresco restaurant Nov-Apr; picnics Nov-Apr ▪ Guided winery tours daily 10.15, 11.30 & 3 Fee R2-R10/wine ▪ 'Interpretive Centre' depicting farm's history; also self-guided tour to the homestead ▪ Gifts ▪ Tourgroups ▪ Owner Anglo American plc ▪ Winemaker André van Rensburg (Jan 1998) ▪ Viticulturist Niel Rossouw, with Petrie Dippenaar & Dwayne Lotter ▪ 112 ha (cabs s/f, merlot, shiraz, chard, sauvignon, semillon) ▪ 47 000 cs 60% red 40% white ▪ ISO 9001/140001 & BRC certified ▪ PO Box 17 Somerset West 7129 ▪ vergelegen@vergelegen.co.za ▪ www.vergelegen.co.za ▪ ***T 847·1334*** *▪ F 847·1608*

'You need big balls to be winemaker at Vergelegen,' confides André van Rensburg somewhat indelicately, though probably accurately. This massive property (3 000 hectares in total) has an appropriately lofty reputation as SA's leading wine farm (reaffirmed, by a wide margin, in *Wine*'s latest Reader Poll), and pressure on the cellar chief to keep the brilliance flowing must be extreme. Yet eight years' tenure hasn't dampened his flagrant enthusiasm one bit. In fact, avers wife Maritza, he's so mad about the place, he'd gladly pay the R10 entrance fee to go to work. And, it must be said, Vergelegen loves him. The launch of the ultra-premium blend 'V' stole last year's limelight from the routine (stellar) accomplishments. 'V', according to AvR, is Vegelegen's – and owner Anglo American's – bid for global acknowledgement, palpable evidence that SA can stand on an equal footing with the very best in the world. Beyond the candle-lit celebrations, plans for transforming a full third of the property to tracts of indigenous fynbos continue apace, winning low-key but equally Vergelegen-passionate MD Don Tooth, marketer Eddie Turner and team the first Biodiversity & Wine Initiative Champion award.

★★★★★ **Vergelegen V** Maiden cult-styled **01** reflected luxurious price in its flavours: black plum/cassis lashed with wood; densely layered fruit waiting to unfold over the next 5-10 yrs. Follow-up **03**(★★★★☆) also single-vyd cab, also with ±10% merlot, dash cab f. More impressive, enormous & dramatic than lovely in its tight-sprung youth: needs yrs still for the concentrated sweet fruit to come out of its sombrely tannic, oak-dominated shell (2 yrs new barrels) – but already vibrant, deep & long. Elegance is quite beside the point here....

★★★★☆ **Vergelegen** For nearly a decade, Cape bdx-style blend showing its class in immaculate fruit, alluring texture, suave tannins. Mainly cab from relatively warmer Rondekop vyd, imparting fruity succulence, with 18% merlot & seasoning of cab f in superb **03**, whose beguiling, incipiently complex bouquet might even suffice – but there's more: fine cassis fruit lurking happily in velvet depths of darkly bright fruit, forceful ripe tannin. Plenty of showy oak (2 yrs new) yet to integrate, but it should, given the time deserved. **02** supple, rounded – thanks partly to lower (54%) fraction cab (half of crop wiped out).

★★★★★ **Vergelegen CWG Auction Reserve** Barrel selection of the above, & latest **02** (★★★★☆) reflects this, though cab now showing strongly (along with cedary wood) in powerful, long-lingering wine destined for good development over a decade or so. **01** was similarly tight, dense.

★★★★☆ **Cabernet Sauvignon** Tall, dark & handsome, confidently modern but with classic sympathies. **03** (with 8% cab f, 7% merlot) has youthful bouquet cedar, blackcurrants, powerful but smooth tannins: combo of fine deep fruit & structure signalling rewarding maturation over decade or so. Near 2 yrs oak, 70% new, well carried. No **02**. **01**, with smidgen merlot (★★★★★), had fine-boned velvet texture; focused, sweet fruit masking hefty 15% alc.

★★★★☆ **Merlot** After the **02** gap, **03** well worth the wait: with a new graceful elegance & fresh purity of fruit: but packed with mint-laced dark choc, hinting of meat, blackcurrant; fine structural support. **01** bold (15% alc) & beautiful, ingratiating tannins, long finish. 20 mths Fr oak, 60% new. ±10% cab most yrs.

★★★★☆ **Shiraz** In subtly refined rather than blockbuster style. After poor-vintage **02** (★★★☆) – not unattractive but with distinct 'green-stick' edge – **03** is perhaps the most precociously delicious of AvR's young premium reds, though still yrs to go (needs decanting if lure is irresistible in youth). Restrained & delicate red fruit follows on smoky, mocha, spicy nose, with ample & supply firm infrastructure. 18 mths Fr oak, 40% new.

★★★★ **Mill Race Red** ✓ Serious-minded 2nd-label blend merlot, cabs & f. 60/33/7 in firm, savoury **03**, with pleasing red fruit, forceful dry tannins. As usual, no scrimping on oak (± 30% new, 20 mths). **02** (★★★☆) herbaceous, less fruity.

★★★★★ **Vergelegen White 04** perhaps the most discreetly rich, serenely & subtly powerful yet in an already illustrious line. Follows **03** & **02** as best blend at FCTWS. Semillon (80% – most to date, rising since 22% in **01**) clearly dominant over sauvignon in youth, hinting at citrus, waxiness – though wood also assertive as yet, from 10 mths 60% new oak. Moderate 13% alc quite enough. Complexity promised, lovely aromas, lingering flavours already in attendance. Will benefit from few more yrs in bottle.

★★★★☆ **CWG Auction Reserve White** new **04** a barrel selection of above for going under the hammer: what could it be but similarly silkily, strongly elegant & thrilling?

★★★★☆ **Chardonnay Reserve** Vyd on lower Schaapenberg, delivering full-bodied fruit core & mineral finish. Bunch-pressed, native-fermented/yr matured in new oak. **04** wears this oak well; it's elegant & restrained, hinting at orange fruit, almost light in feeling, subtly forceful & quietly commanding. **03** showed ethereal white peach & orange blossom tones cosseted in creamy oak.

★★★★ **Chardonnay** Attractively rounded, subtly wooded **04** has notes of perfume, spice, citrus; silkily fresh, dry & refined. Like cream-textured **03**, wholly barrel-fermented, then ± 9 mths, 40% new oak; partial malo.

★★★★☆ **Sauvignon Blanc Reserve** Site-specific sauvignon from AvR's favoured, windswept Schaapenberg vyd – which will give its name to next-up **05** (not ready for tasting mid-2005). Skin contact mandatory to lower grapes' piercing acidity. **04** was a standout vintage, scintillating & rapier-sharp, lemongrass & wet slate character.

★★★★☆ **Schaapenberg Reserve** Says AvR with trademark restraint: 'I want this to be the best Sauvignon in the world.' Prestige bottling (50 cs) of Sauv Bl Rsv given weight, spice by oak (10 mths, no malo); grapes plucked from single rows. Rare (in SA) & haunting blackcurrant-leaf bouquet on **03**, tasted last ed also showed fynbos & honey, wonderfully cool 'river stone' palate. Should give pleasure up to or beyond 2010. **02** bottled as CWG Schaapenberg Auction Reserve. ±14% alc.

★★★★ **Sauvignon Blanc** ✓ **05** has now customary uplift of ±10% semillon. Generous, open nose/palate of ripe passionfruit, melon, with mineral undertone. Light-feeling & unaggressive, but tightly textured, with finely balanced acidity, dry finish. 10% of grapes from Koekenaap on West Coast, so WO W Cape. Small proportion of blend fermented in oak.

★★★★ **Semillon** new **04** another in cellar's occasional, protean guises for this grape. Subtle honey, citrus, blossom aromas, with incipient waxiness. 10 mths oak, but wood stays in background, lending richness to fine, acid-shot texture.

★★★★★ **CWG Auction Reserve Semillon 03** (not retasted) first since **99**, which took museum class trophy at FCTWS 2004. Minuscule bottling (75 cs – 50 for auction). Gorgeous honey/nougat & lime-zest flavours; persistent waxy 'wet-pebble' finish. Great structure, concentration for ageing. Bunch-pressed, barrel-fermented/10 mths Fr, 60% new, which shows in brush of caramel/spice.

★★★★☆ **Noble Late Harvest Semillon** Last were elegant, wooded **98**, **00**.

Vin de Florence ★★★☆ ✓ Chenin-based, softly curvaceous blend, though muscat de F's flower & grape aromas charmingly dominant (chard, semillon there too); just off-dry, but vibrantly fresh. WO W Cape. – *TJ*

Vergenoegd Estate

Stellenbosch ▪ Est 1773 ▪ 1stB 1972 ▪ Tasting & sales Mon-Fri 8-5 Sat 9.30-12.30 ▪ Closed pub hols ▪ Tours by appt ▪ Owners John Faure Family Trust & Strauss family ▪ Winemaker John Faure (1984) ▪ Vineyard manager Chris van Niekerk (May 2003), advised by Drikus van der Westhuizen ▪ 90 ha (cabs s/f, merlot, shiraz) ▪ 500 tons 10 000 cs own label 95% red 5% port ▪ PO Box 1 Faure 7131 ▪ enquiries@vergenoegd.co.za ▪ www.vergenoegd.co.za ▪ ***T 843·3248*** *▪ F 843·3118*

'No disappointments,' is the feedback on the 2005 harvest from John Faure, as selective with his words as he is of his grapes. 'Cab particularly good at this stage, followed by merlot and shiraz.' To more fully achieve his goal of 'red wines that are understated rather than overblown, that complement rather than overpower', Faure now maintains slightly lower temperatures during fermentation, and uses cultured yeasts to jump-start the critical process of converting malic acid into lactic. The estate name means 'Well satisfied', but there's no sign here of complacency.

★★★★☆ **Vergenoegd** Forceful cab-based blend, resisting market pressure for showy, simple fruitiness – as with all these; most also need & deserve maturing 5+ yrs yet. **01**, with 24% merlot, 8% cab f; rich, powerful, savoury & satisfying. Tasted last yr, **02** (★★★★)

reflected lesser vintage: lighter, perhaps more elegance to compensate, & readier earlier (probably shorter-lived). These 20+ mths in mostly new Fr oak, 11% Am in **02**.

★★★★ **Cabernet Sauvignon** Macho stuff, needing time to soften, develop. Deeply glowing **01**, with 8% merlot, sumptuously spread red berries, plums over serious dry tannins. **02** (★★★☆; not retasted) for earlier drinking: lighter, less intensity, also tannic but not the same rich fruit. ±20 mths oak, ± 60% new.

★★★★ **Shiraz** Handsome, muscular **01** had ripe fruit, notes of herb, leather, smoke. Unexaggerated, well-balanced, satisfying. 13.5% alc. 20 mths oak – over half new, mostly Fr, some Am. **02** tasted last ed more graceful, despite bigger alc (14.3%); roast coffee notes, red berries showing appealingly.

★★★★ **Old Cape Colony Vintage Port** Classically profiled – around 85g/ℓ sugar, 20% alc; fermented in open *kuipe,* old-wood-matured 18 mths. Now 66% tinta, with touriga. Rich, orange-zesty **01** (★★★★☆) was particularly good: refined, complex; needing min 5 more yrs. **02** (★★★) lighter-seeming, though same stats; only faintly echoing richness of pvs. **00** exclusively tinta, well balanced, with plum pudding aromas/flavours & firm structure.

Merlot ★★★☆ Recent vintages less concentrated, less weighty than **01** & earlier. **03**'s wooding (Fr, half new, 22 mths) still stands out, alongside choc-mint, green-edged notes – otherwise nicely balanced & dry. **Terrace Bay** ★★★☆ Serious-minded, modestly wooded 'second label', **03** blending farm's 6 varieties into attractive, well-balanced, vinous whole. – *TJ*

Versus see Omnia
Vertex see Bonnievale

Vilafonté

Paarl ▪ Est 1996 ▪ 1stB 2003 ▪ Closed to public ▪ Owners Mike Ratcliffe, Zelma Long & Phil Freese ▪ Winemaker Zelma Long, with Bernard Du Pré le Roux ▪ Viticulturist Phil Freese ▪ 15 ha (cabs s/f, malbec, merlot) ▪ ±80 tons 3 000 cs 100% red ▪ PO Box 64 Elsenburg 7607 ▪ mike@vilafonte.com ▪ www.vilafonte.com ▪ ***T 082·853·8737*** *▪ F 0866·81·7557*

Producing only premium reds, Vilafonté is a high-toned collaboration between American wine gurus Phil Freese and wife Zelma Long, Warwick's Mike Ratcliffe, and US distributor Bartholomew Broadbent (son of legendary English palate, Michael) – a team more than well-equipped to succeed in their targeted top-end market. Viticulturist Freese chose the virgin Paarl-Simonsberg slopes for their ancient, low-potential 'vilafontes' soils. He utilises a host of high-tech indicators for vineyard management, plus his own viticultural techniques to naturally limit yields and produce quality fruit. Production is both intensive and innovative – 'luxury winemaking, luxury wine', to quote Zelma L.

★★★★☆ **Series C** The 'C' is for cab, whose structure & power inform this masterly **03** bdx blend, its dark-berried opulence still swaddled in youthfully dense & austere tannins. Shows its size (& 15% alc), warm area origin more obviously than lighter-tripping 'M' below, but also absolute focus. One for the patient – should evolve into something majestic (around 2013?). 82% cab with merlot, cab f, malbec (9/7/2); Taransaud/Francois Frères barriques, 54% new, 18 mths. *Wine* ★★★★.

★★★★☆ **Series M** On paper, more of an equal-partner blend than 'C' above. But it's merlot's radiant ruby lights, bright red fruit fragrance & velvet accessibility which most striking features of **03**; extra nuances & mineral tautness imparted by blend partners cabs s/f, malbec, & subtle oaking. Very neat, 'cool' composition (despite 14.5% alc). Full of confident charm, though still way off its best. 41/39/16/4 blend; 18 mths small Fr cask matured, 19% new. Both above new. – *AL*

Viljoensdrift Wines

Robertson ▪ Est/1stB 1998 ▪ Tasting & sales Mon-Fri 8.30-5 (cellar); Sat 10-2 & 1st Sun of month 11-2 (riverside); every Sunday in Dec ▪ Closed Easter Fri, Jun 16 & Dec 25 ▪ Breede River cruises Wed, Sat & 1st Sun of month 12 noon, weather permitting; booking essential; additional weekday trips for groups of 15+ by appt ▪ Create your own picnic from the deli ▪ Tours by appt ▪ Owners

Fred & Manie Viljoen ▪ Winemaker Fred Viljoen ▪ Viticulturist Manie Viljoen ▪ 120 ha (cab, pinotage, shiraz, chard, chenin, sauvignon) ▪ 1 200 tons ±80 000 cs 50% red 48% white 2% rosé ▪ Export brands: Die Breedekloof, Elandsberg, Keurfontein & Somerlust (Netherlands & Belgium) ▪ PO Box 653 Robertson 6705 ▪ viljoensdrift@lando.co.za ▪ www.viljoensdrift.co.za ▪ ***T (023) 615·1901*** *▪ F (023) 615·3417*

The vineyards have been the main focus of attention this year for 40 year old Fred Viljoen and his brother Manie. The hospitality facilities of this ever popular tourist destination have also been fine tuned with a wheelchair-friendly extended riverside tasting deck, complete with semi-permanent tented covering, to ensure convivial tasting, regardless of the weather. A sleek new aluminium hulled 'Uncle Ben' took to the water last September – and of course there is no better way to celebrate your stylish river cruise than with a glass of their new maiden-vintage Bordeaux-style red 'Serenity' or limited release Cape Vintage Port.

River Grandeur range

★★★★ **Cabernet Sauvignon 04** (★★★★) same profile as **03**, **02**: rich cassis, mint, herbaceous flavours, hint of bouillon, cab's linear tannins. **04** finishes slightly greener/drier than fruit- & oak-sweet pvs. 14% alc unobtrusive. Structured for bottle aging ±3-5 yrs. **02** MIWA double-gold. Open fermenters for all reds in range, yr Fr oak. Amenable 13.5% alc.

★★★★ **Pinotage** Back-to-form **04**, intricate strawberry, floral, smoke, bacon notes; palate alive with fresh acidity, supportive tannins, juicy fruit. Savoury finish that really lingers. Spicier profile thanks to change from mostly Am oak to mainly Fr. **03** (★★★★) also well fruited but firmer.

★★★★ **Shiraz** Perfumed **04** (★★★★) a hedonist's delight: lily & lavender just some of the attractions; opulent fruit assaulted by gruff tannins, astringent lift to tail, alcoholic bite (14.5%). **03** in youth more approachable, with potential over ±3 yrs. Yr 50/50 Fr/Am oak.

Chenin Blanc ★★★★ ✓ Bunch selection ensures fruit quality. **05** aromas of dried apple & musk sweets; lovely dry floral palate. Restrained, with excellent balance; alc a moderate 13%; at 3.6g/ℓ driest of the whites. **Chardonnay** ★★★ Re-engaging last yr's sample, **04** shows hints lavender & macadamia nuts, rich palate courtesy of judicious oak (2 mths) & touch sugar – all given zip by fresh acidity. 30% new Fr oak fermented/matured. Warming 14.5% alc. **Sauvignon Blanc** ★★★ Delicate **05**, restrained alc (±12.5%) & reticent cut grass & floral aromas/flavours. Touch breadth from mth *sur lie*.

Viljoensdrift range

★★★★ **Serenity** new The wine Fred V has 'always wanted to make'. Bdx-style blend cab, merlot, cab f, petit v (40/30/20/10) fermented separately in open fermenters, matured separately 24 mths 100% new Fr before bending. **03** elegant & restrained with exceptional fruit quality, concentration. Supportive tannins, integrated alc. Drinks well & should gain complexity over 5–7 yrs.

Merlot-Shiraz ★★★★ ✓ **04** different blend to one tasted last ed. Now merlot, shiraz, petit v (62/26/12), Fr oak, yr. Savoury/mineral aromas, tomato/plum palate; bold but not overpowering; properly dry & long 'tea-leaf' finish. Drinks well now. **Rosé** ★★★ ✓ **04** made from juice bled off shiraz. Bright raspberry/blackberry notes; pleasing dry finish & gentle grip from fruit tannins. **Colombar-Chenin Blanc** ★★★ **05** (sample) bursts with spice, grapefruit, hay flavours for poolside refreshment. **Cape Vintage Reserve** new ★★★★ **03** as the Portuguese would have it: relatively high alc (±18%) & dry (79g/ℓ RS). From souzão/tinta (65/35). Dark & brooding choc, cherry & caramel flavours. Very ripe palate; bold, assertive finish. – *CvZ*

Village Collection see Tulbagh Winery

Villiera Wines

Stellenbosch ▪ Est/1stB 1983 ▪ Tasting & sales Mon-Fri 8.30-5 Sat 8.30-1 ▪ R7.50 p/p for groups ▪ Closed Easter Fri/Sun, Dec 25, Jan 1 ▪ Self-guided tours anytime during tasting hours; guided tours by appt ▪ Annual St Vincent's Day dinner (closest Sat to Jan 22) ▪ BYO pic-

*nic in summer ▪ Owners Grier family ▪ Winemakers Jeff Grier, with Anton Smal (Oct 1992) ▪ Viticulturist Simon Grier ▪ 260 ha (13 varieties, r/w) ▪ 1 800 tons 110 000 cs own label + 14 000 cs for Woolworths + 8 000 for Marks & Spencer (UK) ▪ 32% white 42% red 4% rosé 22% sparkling ▪ PO Box 66 Koelenhof 7605 ▪ wine@villiera.com ▪ www.villiera.com ▪ **T 865·2002/3** ▪ F 865·2314*

Perhaps this family business's greatest strength is the balance, sincerity and pragmatism of its approach to quite simply everything it does. As winemaker Jeff Grier says, it's all about team work: 'Our philosophy of offering natural wines, expressive of terroir, at an affordable price has worked for us. Our personal service and family presence has helped a lot in a competitive environment. One has to continue adding value and we are constantly tweaking to stay ahead.' Future plans are to take advantage of growth opportunities in the successful categories of the range, and 'to consolidate while still offering interest in an innovative manner'. Recent milestones? 'Discovering how important friends and family are.' Only natural that Villiera should commit to a BEE project with M'hudi Wines (see separate entry/photo gallery).

★★★★ **Monro** Flagship red coming out of '21 yrs experience to identify vyd blocks capable of achieving greatness'. Varying blend merlot/cab successfully & stylishly straddles conservative/modern divide. **01** 50/50 blend rich, sweetly ripe; gently firm tannins. Calyon Trophy winner – runner up was **02**, with 63% merlot offering fine red-berry fruit, supportive wooding; perhaps a little more austere than pvs, marked by still-prominent savoury, dry tannins. These up to 2 yrs mostly new Fr oak. Will mature beneficially over 5+ yrs yet.

★★★★ **Cellar Door Merlot** new C-D prefix indicates made in best years only. From 'Robin's block' vineyard. Quietly elegant aromas mocha, dark fruit on **03**, perfumed spice. Still youthful, with ripe tannins & prominent acidity, well integrated oak – yr mostly new. Trifle 'hot' on finish from 14.6% alc.

★★★★ **Chenin Blanc** ✓ Another fine bargain with characterful, earth-toned **05 (★★★★)**, perhaps a little more austere than **04**, but full-fruited, well-textured – enriched by 20% barrel-fermented part & a little sugar, though effectively dry. **04** *Wine* ★★★★.

★★★★ **Cellar Door Chenin Blanc** Characterful example fermented/matured on lees in mostly new Fr oak 7 mths. **04** worthy successor to fine **03** (VGG): spicy, rich, well balanced with good fresh acidity – actually off-dry, but finishes essentially dry. Will develop, keep at least few yrs. No **02**.

★★★★ **Traditional Bush Vine Sauvignon Blanc 05** notably pale in colour, but enticing aromas of melon, passionfruit. Elegantly focused, almost steely in its clean, clear dryness. Officially recognised single-vineyard wine.

★★★★ **Inspiration** NLH from hand-selected botrytised chenin. **03** hints of raisin, with honeyed, marmaladey yellow-gold rich silkiness. Refined style, with 115g/ℓ sugar, 12.6% alc. No **04**. Sample **05** also offers clean, airily elegant touch, though bigger: 176g/ℓ sugar, 13.9% alc – but excellently vibrant acidity. Incipient complexity now dominated by honey, beeswax. These fermented/aged ±9 mths Fr oak. Will keep/develop well, though delicious in youth. 375ml.

★★★★ **Cellar Door Rhine Riesling Noble Late Harvest** new Probably a one-off, says Grier – 'a high level of botrytis caught us by surprise in **05**' – but a very acceptable one, with lingering tinned pineapple & marmalade notes & integrated acidity on light, fine richness. 103g/ℓ sugar, 13.2% alc. 500ml.

★★★★ **Tradition Rosé Brut** Salmon pink **NV** with copper glints – colour from ripe pinotage added to blend of pinot, pinotage, chardonnay juice (45/40/15). Latest back on song: appetisingly tangy & refreshing, with ripe strawberry, earth notes & dry, soft finish. Uncertified.

★★★★ **Monro Brut** 'Monro Première Cuvée Brut' pvs ed. Pale old-gold colour presages mature baked apple & yeasty biscuit bouquet on **00**. Richly, silkily elegant blend of barrel-fermented/matured chardonnay (55%) & pinot, disgorged after 5 yrs on lees. Lingering savoury dry finish – low 7.5g/ℓ sugar. WO Paarl.

★★★★☆ **Brut Natural** ✓ Notably dry & refined MCC from chardonnay – no dosage, & no sulphur or other additives apart from sugar, yeast for 2nd, bubble-forming fermentation.

03 has almost decadent ripe-apple, brioche, spice bouquet/flavours, & usual creamy, bone-dry richness, fine acidity & lingering finish: a lavish austerity. These, including standout **01** (★★★★★), need even more careful storage than sulphur-protected wines if beneficially matured more than yr/2.

Sonnet ☺ ★★★ Sample **05** promises usual simple, undeniable off-dry pleasure from muscat ottonel/chenin. Big 14.5% alc.

Cabernet Sauvignon ★★★☆ ✓ Brilliantly reliable wine, textbook varietal expression, well-structured, honest & good. **03** flavourful & well-mannered as ever; ready but will keep few more yrs. Supported by yr Fr/Am oak (like Pinotage, Shiraz). **Pinotage** ★★★ **03** friendly rustic treat, with bold bright fruit, satisfying & freshly balanced, moderate tannins. **Shiraz** ★★★☆ **03** has excellently characteristic, immediately appealing aromas violets, lilies, mocha; less showy to taste, but decent, well-balanced, dry-finishing. **Merlot** ★★★ Unflashy, modest **03** fresh from nose to tail, quiet plummy fruit, choc-mint hints, prominent acidity, big 14.4% alc. Unobtrusive yr Fr oak, 25% new. **Sauvignon Blanc** ★★★☆ Zippily fresh **05** with dollop semillon as ever; bright but non-lingering tropical fruit/grassy aromas, flavours; satisfyingly dry. **Rhine Riesling** ★★★☆ Last example of this usually graceful, fresh, dry offering was **03**. **Gewürztraminer** ★★★☆ ✓ **05** more subtle, serious than usual, but as delightful; understated rose-petal exuberance, unnoticeably off-dry, alcoholic (14.6%). **Tradition Brut** ★★★☆ Splash of pinot meunier added to chard, pinot, pinotage in latest **NV**, ever-reliable, MCC. Pleasing, dry & lively, lightly rich. Also in 1.5ℓ & 375ml. Uncertified. **Fired Earth** ★★★☆ ✓ In LBV port style, **01** from 18% shiraz with touriga, pinotage, tinta. Deliciously ready (but will keep ages), with mocha, pruney spicy notes; grip more from acid than tannin. 3 yrs in older oak. 85g/ℓ sugar; 20% alc. **00** P Schultz trophy. WO Coastal.

Down to Earth range

Red ☺ ★★★ 5 varieties consort in safe, pleasant **05**. Toasty baked aromas, warmly friendly palate. Yr oaked; 14% alc. **White** ☺ ★★★ Reliably tasty fresh quaffer, sauvignon-based blend with semillon, chenin; tasted ex-tank **05** zippily follows suit. **Rosé** NEW ☺ ★★★ Completing the trio, the best of the lot: succulent & dry **05**, mostly pinotage (plus gamay, shiraz); earth & red berry flavours – all very satisfying.

Discontinued: **Cellar Door Cape Blend**. – *TJ*

Villiersdorp Cellar

Worcester ▪ Est 1922 ▪ 1stB 1980 ▪ Tasting Mon-Sat 8-5 Sun 9-3 ▪ Sales Mon-Sat 8-5 ▪ Fee R10 for groups of 7+ ▪ Closed Easter Fri & Dec 25 ▪ Fully licensed restaurant, farm stall & gift shop ▪ Owners 55 growers ▪ Winemaker WS Visagie ▪ Viticulturist Ryan Puttick ▪ 500 ha ▪ 5 600 tons 10 000 cs own label 20% red 60% white 6% rosé 14% fortified ▪ PO Box 14 Villiersdorp 6848 ▪ info@vilko.co.za ▪ www.vilko.co.za ▪ ***T (028) 840·1151*** *▪ F (028) 840·0957*

There's a new infusion of energy, resolve and investment to run this co-operative cellar like an 'estate'. The aim is to apply all that's best in vineyard and winemaking practices to upgrade the quality of the entire range. Acknowledging that not all grapes are suitable for good-wine production, the initiative also involves diversifying into grape concentrate and spirit production. The fruits of all this effort can be tasted at the ever-welcoming (and recently revamped) Kelkiewyn Farmstall & Restaurant, which doubles as the winery's tasting area and provides a refreshment station for visitors to the next-door antique tractor museum. Clarifying our report last ed, GM Ben Klindt says cellar tours are unavailable but tourgroups are welcomed to Kelkiewyn with the proverbial red carpet.

Chardonnay ★★☆ Citrus & tropical fruit in **04**, fresh, whistle-clean dry finish; unwooded. **Bouquet Blanc 03** from chenin/hanepoot, untasted. Following NVs (04) tasted as samples: **Hanepoot Jerepiko** ★★★☆ Full-sweet fortified dessert with fresh honeysuckle aroma, lifted palate, finishes with a very attractive spirity tang. 17% alc. **Port** ★★☆ Traditional Cape-style fortified with fruity/jammy character.

Cabernet Sauvignon ★★★ **03** notes of plums & cherries, full, generous, subtly oaked; good spicy length. Could happily be cellared few yrs. **Chenin Blanc** ★★★ **04** (sample) lovely fresh, clean tropical aromas, smoothly dry, quaffable. **Sauvignon Blanc** ★★★ **04** (sample) basket of sweet tropical fruit on nose/palate, lively light texture & poised acidity. Enjoy in yr of vintage. — *DH*

Vine Collection see Oranjerivier Wine Cellars
Vineyard Selection see Blaauwklippen, Kleine Zalze, Neil Ellis, Robertson Winery
Vinfruco see Omnia Wines

Vinimark

Stellenbosch ▪ Closed to public ▪ Directors Tim Rands, Cindy Jordaan, Geoff Harvey & Guys Naudé ▪ PO Box 441 Stellenbosch 7599 ▪ info@vinimark.co.za (exports: Brad Gold, bradg@vinimark.co.za) ▪ www.vinimark.co.za ▪ ***T1 883·8043/4*** *▪ F 886·4708*

Wine merchants marketing, selling and distributing various ranges with local partners, including Jonkerskloof, Kleindal, Long Beach, Ravenswood, Silver Sands and Zomerlust, listed separately.

Vins D'Orrance

Constantia ▪ Est/1stB 2001 ▪ Tastings by appt 8.30–4.30 ▪ Closed Easter Sun, Dec 25 & Jan 1 ▪ Owner Christophe Durand ▪ Winemaker Christophe Durand ▪ 530 cs 70% red 30% white ▪ 10 Squirrels Way Newlands 7735 ▪ christophe@vinum.co.za ▪ ***T 683·7479 ▪ F*** *683·7489*

Frenchman Christophe Durand, no longer involved in The Winery, is now focusing on his own label, established in 2001 with his Cuvée Ameena Syrah (from Simonsberg grapes). The latest addition, named after his baby daughter, is the Cuvée Anaïs Chardonnay (from Constantia), though his ultimate aim is a Rhône blend. Working in High Constantia's winery, he follows traditional vinification methods, including basket pressing and manual punch-downs (only two a day, to extract flavour and tannin gently). Small quantities go to the US, Sweden and France. Selective stuff, this.

★★★★ **Syrah 'Cuvée Ameena' 03**, revved with 100% new Fr oak, more dramatic than elegant, textured pvs. Rich concentration of dark-spiced, savoury Simonsberg fruit emphasised by fleshy tannins, bone-dry finish. Will need 2/3 yrs to emerge from oaky cocoon but unlikely to match refinement of **02**. Both 14.5% alc. WO Stbosch.

★★★★ **Chardonnay 'Cuvée Anais'** new **04** impressive debut. Stylish, with discernible classic influence. Polished interplay between tight lime freshness, mineral core, complementary new Fr oak; belies 14% alc. Tops off with great length. *Wine* ★★★★. — *AL*

Vintage International Brands

PO Box 19049 Wynberg 7824 ▪ info@vib.co.za ▪ ***T 762·5975*** *▪ F 761·8536*

Independent producing wholesaler based in Cape Town, importing wines and spirits for the retail trade and producing their own-label wines, Hippo Creek and Simply Red & White (see Hippo Creek).

Vinum see The Winery

Vinus Via

Stellenbosch ▪ Est/1stB 2004 ▪ 10 000 cs (projected) 50/50 red/white ▪ 21 Topaz Street, Heldervue, Somerset West 7130 ▪ info@vinusvia.co.za ▪ www.vinusvia.co.za ▪ ***T/F 855·5244***

It's been almost two years since Richard Hilton launched this easy-drinking, good-value range; sales targets have been met, but the highly competitive nature of the market at this end of the price spectrum means things can only get tougher. Richard knows that the key is to seek out really good quality grapes at even better prices but it's not an easy challenge to meet – last year the price of white grapes went up, and there is the ever-present fear of market saturation. But the wine marketer-cum-maker remains upbeat for 2006, with plans to extend the range as soon as the market is ready.

Wild Lily Chardonnay ☺ ★★★**05** crisp & diverting marmalade, citrus aromas & flavours. Unoaked, juicy & delicious.

Red Bishop Cabernet Sauvignon new ★★★ Agreeable dinner companion with ripe, plum jam nose; brisk acidity. Unoaked. Drink soon. **Shaka Zulu Shiraz** ★★★ A lighter, more accessible style of this sometimes powerful grape. Unoaked **04** shows crushed black pepper, spice & savory. Round, soft tannins; versatile, quaffable. More alcoholic at 13.5% than pvs. **African Jack Chenin Blanc** ★★ Pvs called 'Jackass'. Easy drinking, sherbety with hints of lemon. 12.4% alc up on easy going pvs. **Rockhopper Pinotage** discountinued. – *MM*

Vin-X-Port

Paarl • Est 2001 • Closed to public • Directors Hennie van der Merwe & Maretha Waso • 191 Main Rd Paarl 7646 • marketing@x-port.co.za • www.x-port.co.za • ***T 872·0850*** *• F 872·0849*

Negociant house specialising in procuring, producing and shipping quality wines, and in creating and marketing new brands. Its extensive portfolio includes African Treasure, Cape Circle and BunduStar, exported to various countries.

Virgin Earth

Little Karoo • Tasting by appt • Postnet Suite 57, Private Bag X18, Milnerton 7435 • sales@havanahills.co.za • ***T/F 972·1110/05***

This unorthodox project of Kobus du Plessis and Nico Vermeulen (both of Havana Hills) in the rugged Langeberg sees one of the area's larger farms (13 000 ha) now partly planted with five noble varieties. The rustic sandstone cellar also hides an unusual experiment. Without a pump in sight, barrels are fed by gravity only, and then lowered into a lake to mature underwater for up to a year.

High 5ive ★★★★ Unique: rugged Karoo grapes fermented in open vats, then matured in barrel underwater in natural lake for 'velvety smoothness'. **04** earthy rusticity reflects terroir; stamped, appropriately, with remarkably soft finish. Cab s & f, merlot, shiraz & petit v; yr oak, 30% new. WO W Cape. **Sauvignon Blanc** new ★★★ Very different **05**, tropical tones well fleshed in baby's-bottom smooth texture. 4 mths lees ageing, no wood. Gentle 12.7% alc. Sample tasted. – *DS*

Virginia

One of SA's long-standing big-volume white brands; now in 2ℓ as well as 4.5ℓ flagons. Semi-dry, lightish (11% alc) **NV** ★ with tropical fruit gluggability. By Distell. W Cape vyds. – *CvZ*

Vlottenburg Winery see Stellenbosch Hills
Volmaak see Baarsma

Von Ortloff

Franschhoek • 1stB 1994 • Tasting, sales & tours by appt • Owners/winemakers/viticulturists Georg & Eve Schlichtmann • 15 ha (cab, merlot, shiraz, chard, sauvignon) • 6 000 cs own label 60% red 40% white • PO Box 341 Franschhoek 7690 vortloff@mweb.co.za • ***T 876·3432*** *• F 876·4313*

No update available on this winery; contact details and wine notes from previous edition.

★★★★ **Cabernet Sauvignon-Merlot** These have style & presence, showing attention to detail: only free-run juice, individual oaking for components. **01** blend 76% cab, 24%

merlot; ripe cassis fruit, less taut, continues trend to easier accessibility. Cab 24-26 mths barriques, 60% new; merlot 24 mths, 50% new, all Fr.

★★★★ **No. 7** From merlot. Brilliantly fruity **03**, forthcoming cassis, mint choc/mocha introduction to meaty dry palate, manageable tannins. 9 mths Fr oak, 10% new.

★★★★ **Chardonnay** Elegant barrel-fermented example since **93**. Latest **03** in more consumer-friendly style (★★★★), misses some of the classic restraint of earlier vintages. Riper at 14.5% alc, fruit centre-stage, oak in the wings. **02** had a tangy palate & extraordinary length. 12-14 mths, all Fr, 70% new.

No. 5 ★★★★ From sauvignon. Delicious **04** bright-fruited; whiffs fig, gooseberry & passionfruit; exciting sweet/sour play on palate. **No. 3** ★★★★ Unwooded chardonnay, showing remarkable intensity in **03**; ripe, yellow peach juiciness & flesh to match. Rounder, looser weave than wooded version. — *IvH*

Voorspoed see Baarsma

Vooruitsig

Paarl ▪ Est 1998 ▪ 1stB 2002 ▪ Closed to public ▪ Owner Mozelle Holdings (Pty) Ltd ▪ Vini consultant Jean-Vincent Ridon (2002) ▪ 3ha (merlot) ▪ 500 cs 100% red ▪ PO Box 6080 Uniedal 7612 ▪ www.prime-invest.co.za/vooruitsig.htm ▪ vooruitsig@prime-invest.co.za ▪ ***T 082·566·4700/082·564·3231*** *▪ F 855·3028*

New cabs sauvignon and franc, malbec and shiraz vines join the 3ha of merlot at this venture neighbouring Veenwouden. With not much else to report, Francis Vanderlinden, MD of the consortium which owns the property, maintains that time in bottle has improved the 02, the wines in barrel are tasting good (all made by Signal Hill's Jean-Vincent Ridon), and that he expects the 2005 grapes — smaller, fewer, with soft, rich tannins — to produce an excellent wine.

Merlot ★★★★ Individual, brooding versions deserving further maturation. Last ed's provisional rating for **02** sample confirmed: rich & savoury, intense damson bouquet, ripe mouthfilling tannins, slight stalky lift from new Fr oak, 25%, 30 mths. **03** untasted; **04** barrel sample too unknit to rate. — *CvZ*

Vrede En Lust Wine Farm

Paarl ▪ Est 1996 ▪ 1stB 2002 ▪ Tasting & sales daily 10-5 ▪ Fee R10 ▪ Closed Dec 25 & Jan 1 ▪ Tours 10-4 by appt ▪ Cotage Fromage Deli & Restaurant ▪ Guest accommodation in two cottages & manor house ▪ Play area for children ▪ Tourgroups by appt (max 26 people) ▪ Gifts ▪ Farm produce ▪ Conferences & functions ▪ Owners Dana & Etienne Buys ▪ Winemaker Stephåne de Saint Salvy, with Bongani Shandu (Dec 2001/2002) ▪ Viticulturist Etienne Buys (Jun 1998) ▪ 42 ha (cab, malbec, merlot, petit v, shiraz, chard) ▪ 20 000 cs own label ▪ ISO 14001 certified ▪ PO Box 171 Groot Drakenstein 7680 ▪ info@vnl.co.za ▪ www.vnl.co.za ▪ ***T (021) 874·1611*** *▪ F (021) 874·1859*

With a successful background in computer software, it's no surprise that Dana Buys' Simondium farm embodies the latest trends — in both technology and wine. Picking up on the lifestyle/tourism groundswell, he and brother Etienne have created a multi-faceted destination which includes wine, of course, by amiable French expat Stephåne de Saint Salvy, gourmet food and cheese, a stay-over, conferences, functions and more. One indication of the public's hearty response is that their Cotage Fromage deli/restaurant has been extended so visitors can be hosted when the main venue is booked (45 weddings last year!). Needless to say a website features prominently (and sophisticated software to keep visitors returning for more) — all to deliver 'a level of customer experience that exceeds all expectations'.

Vrede en Lust range

Barbère ★★★ Rosé made from 5 varieties including cinsaut, yet sample **03** more vinous than fruity; acidity fairly prominent this yr — needs food. **Marguerite 03** from chardonnay, as pvs whole-bunch pressed, Fr cask fermented/matured 10 mths. Still woody mid-2005, core of citrus/stone fruit needs opportunity to unfold. Sample rates ★★★. **Karien** new ★★ Chenin

(85%) & semillon union, lees-aged in tank a lengthy 10 mths; **04** powerful *sur lie* character – all but overwhelms chenin's delicate fruit/acid; will have its adherents.

Jacques de Savoy range

Classic ★★★ Bdx-style blend switches to cab-based in sample **03**, with merlot, malbec & petit v (65/26/5/4). Where (merlot-led) pvs was suave & smooth, this still tight & unyielding; needs, say, 2-3 yrs to come round. Yr Fr oak, 10% new. **Cara** ★★★ Same varieties as pvsly for **03**, slightly altered ratio: cab, shiraz, merlot (39/37/24), less new oak (10% vs. 25); sample shows same robust profile, with strong tannins. **Simond** ★★★ Different formula for **03** red blend: merlot in lead with shiraz, cab, malbec & pinotage (44/35/10/7), now oaked (6 mth). More sprightly feel, juicier, wood a restrained presence. All above WO Smnsberg-Paarl. – *DH*

Vredendal Winery see Westcorp

Vredenheim Wines

Stellenbosch ▪ Tasting & sales Mon-Fri 9-5 Sat 9.30-2 (Dec 9-5) ▪ Fee R2/tasting ▪ Closed Easter Fri, Dec 25 & Jan 1 ▪ Barrique Restaurant ▪ T 881·3001 ▪ Hudson's Coffee Shop ▪ T 881·3590 ▪ Other amenities: see intro ▪ Owners Bezuidenhout family ▪ Winemaker Elzabé Bezuidenhout, advised by Fanie Cilliers ▪ 80 ha ▪ 10 000 cs 60% red 40% white ▪ PO Box 369 Stellenbosch 7599 ▪ trendsetter@vredenheim.co.za ▪ www.vredenheim.co.za ▪ ***T 881·3637*** *▪ F 881·3296*

No update available on this winery; contact details and wine notes from previous edition.

Reserve 214 ★★★★ Pick of this crop. **03** cab, shiraz & merlot (46/37/17), tidily packaged & tasty; ripe & supple. Yr Fr oak, further 18 mths in bottle. **Shiraz** ★★★ **01** allspice aromas with smoked ham hints; fullish, integrated but assertively fresh finishing. 3 yrs (!) Fr oak. **Pinotage** ★★★ WO Coastal (Paarl fruit); **03** aromas of mulberries & strawberry-yoghurt (creaminess from yr new Fr oak); ripe red fruits, healthy tannins. **Rosé** ★★★ Ostensibly chenin & cab, but definite muscat whiffs, fairly intense grapey palate; well balanced. NV/uncertified; low 11.5% alc. **Chenin Blanc** ★★★ **04** light & unsophisticated; soft stone-fruit aromas, Golden Delicious apple flavours. **Angel's** ★★ Returns to guide with **04**, still in Natural Sweet style, from chenin; summer meadow scents; sweet, lightish grapey flavours. **Vredenvonkel** ★★★ Demi-sec style sparkling from chardonnay; lots of exuberant bubbles; apple-crumble nuance to its mild sweetness. 12% alc. **NV**. – *JB*

Vreughvol see Baarsma

Vriesenhof Vineyards

Stellenbosch ▪ Est 1980 ▪ 1stB 1981 ▪ Tasting Mon-Fri 8.30-4 Sat 9-2 (groups of 10+ by appt only) ▪ Tours & meals/refreshments by appt ▪ Owner Landgoed Vriesenhof (Pty) Ltd ▪ Winemaker Jan Coetzee, with Richard Phillips (2001) ▪ Viticulturist Hannes Coetzee ▪ 37 ha (cabs s/f, merlot, pinot, pinotage, chard) ▪ ±500 tons 85% red 15% white ▪ PO Box 155 Stellenbosch 7599 ▪ info@vriesenhof.co.za ▪ www.vriesenhof.co.za ▪ ***T 880·0284*** *▪ F 880·1503*

Amid the plethora of ritzy new wineries are the few blue-bloods, sometimes underplayed, even undiscovered (by the new-generation wine lover). One such is Vriesenhof, celebrating a quarter century with the 2005 vintage, rated (with 2003, 1995, 1989 and 1982) by Jan Coetzee, winegrower and '70s Springbok rugby star, as the finest in his 30 years' experience. Though still active in industry business – agitating for new 'estate' legislation; serving on wine certification panels – this wellspring of expertise and anecdote has curtailed his consulting. The focus is Vriesenhof (note the return to the winery's original name). After decades of meticulous experimentation, this tough, charming individualist believes Vriesenhof's arrived at the pinnacle of quality, especially regarding Coetzee's passion: pinot noir. Time to revisit.

Vriesenhof range

★★★★ **Enthopio** Greek for 'truly indigenous', alluding to pinotage's starring role in this supple, seductive blend. Tiny quantities shiraz, cab f & merlot pique nose & palate. Preview **03** generously proportioned with dark glacé fruit whiffs, muscular tannins. Needs time to knit/gain complexity. **02** (★★★★☆) more open, harmonious, persistent. Pinotage's Burgundian parentage apparent in dense, earthy/savoury berry tones, lively acidity, crafted tannins. Fermentation in new oak then ± yr used barrels.

★★★★ **Pinot Noir** Pinotphile Jan C harvests just 2.7 kg/vine to super-concentrate variety's hallmark aromas & flavours. **04** (★★★★☆) quintessential pinot: truffles & cherries, poised tannins, rapier acidity. Perfect now, but plenty potential for growth. **03** similarly ethereal yet firm. Dijon clones in varying soils. Compassionately oaked – 10 mths 2nd fill Fr. Relatively slender ±13.5% alc.

★★★★☆ **Kallista** Flagship bdx-style blend usually led by merlot; dominated in **02** by cabs s/f (46/30). Baskets of fruit, liquorice & pencil shavings paired with gossamer tannins, judicious alc (13.5%). Structured for long-term. Moreish, merlot-ish **01** savoury, plummy with signature earthy finish & fine sour-cherry twist. Generously oaked: ±18 mths Fr, 50% new.

Talana Hill range

★★★★ **Royale** Established blend cabs s/f & merlot. **01** initial oak-vanilla attack balanced by opulent black fruit. 8 mths Fr oak, new/2nd fill. **02**, tasted as sample last yr, loses cab s but retains lavish berry ice-cream flavours. Now also with mocha/coffee, fatty biltong aromas & savoury tannins, still grippy but softened by yr in bottle.

Chardonnay ★★★★ Bunch-fermented in barrel. **04** similar to **03**, with dash citrus zest to cut buttered scone richness, alc nudge (13.5%) to finish. Both above single vineyard wines worth cellaring a few yrs.

Paradyskloof range

Following all NE. **Pinotage** ★★★ **03** step above easy drinking pvs. Lanolin, raspberry, smoke aromas with slight acetone whiff; robust earthy/organic flavours. Low 13% alc. **Cabernet Sauvignon-Merlot** ★★★ **03** soft tannins, unobtrusive alc & loads of fruit for solo sipping. Unwooded. **Chardonnay** ★★★ **04** notch up on pvs, delicate lemon/grape flavour with pithy finish. – *CvZ*

Vruchtbaar Boutique Winery new

*Robertson ▪ Est/1stB 2001 ▪ Visits by appt ▪ BYO picnic ▪ Tourgroups ▪ Guest house ▪ Owners Alwyn & Francois Bruwer ▪ Winemaker Francois Bruwer ▪ Viti adviser Briaan Stipp (2005) ▪ 35 ha (cab, pinotage, merlot, ruby cab, chenin, chard, colombard, sauvignon) ▪ 400 tons 100 cs own label ▪ 75% red 25% white ▪ PO Box 319 Robertson 6705 ▪ vruchtbaar@mweb.co.za ▪ T **(023) 626·2334** ▪ F (023) 626·4081*

'Good grapes make good wine, which results in good friendships,' believes Francois Bruwer, who can expect to make many new friends now that Vruchtbaar, for many years a co-op supplier, is keeping five of its best tons for its own wines (made with advice from brother Naudé, Boland Kelder winemaker) and welcoming visitors to the farm. 'Our aim is not to make a lot of wine but to let people share our passion for good wine, hospitality and the romance of winemaking'. Having been a literal *garagist* since 2001, F-B is justifiably proud of his new cellar, barrel store and tasting room, housed in the original stable dating back to the early 1900s.

★★★★ **Cabernet Sauvignon 03** distinguished by restrained flamboyance; blackberry fruits & slight herbal whiffs; fine spicy tannins; elegant sweet finish. Less showy & more classic than maiden **02**, blackcurrant/plum aromas, sweet coconut notes (from 50% Am oak), ample full-ripe tannins. Juicy & persistent. 18 mths barrel aged. Both from single block.

Sauvignon Blanc ★★★ Single-vyd **05** super-fresh style with green fig/greenpepper notes, racy lime/citrus palate. Crisp & food friendly; undaunting 13.5% alc. Sample tasted. – *MF*

Vruchtbaar see Robertson Wide River

Vuurberg Vineyards

Stellenbosch ▪ Est 2000 ▪ 1stB 2003 ▪ Visits by appt ▪ Owner Sebastiaan Klaassen ▪ Winemaker Miles Mossop, with Sebastiaan Klaassen (both 2003) ▪ Viti adviser Aidan Morton

(2002) ▪ 10 ha (cab s/f, malbec, merlot, petit v, chenin, grenache blanc, roussanne, viognier) ▪ 1 500 cs 100% red ▪ PO Box 449 Stellenbosch 7599 ▪ helshoogte@mweb.co.za ▪ www.vuurberg.com ▪ ***T 885·2334*** *▪ F 885·2714*

Young Dutchman Sebastiaan Klaassen, who interrupted a Cape kite-surfing holiday to buy this precipitously steep property (listed previous ed under its old name, Helshoogte Vineyards), obviously has the travel bug. Hepatitis contracted during a pre-harvest trip to India laid him low, leaving partner Anna Poll to labour through the night, having seen four small children to bed, to deliver their latest baby – a barrel fermented chenin. The pair is looking to an exciting future with new viognier, grenache blanc and roussanne plantings. The full complement of Bordeaux varieties will join them – the aim: a single white and red Vuurberg. Cellar practice is low-tech, employing only gravity and a basket-press. Committed to the community, they (with some sponsors) have built two after-care centres, locally and in Stellenbosch's Kayamandi township.

★★★★ **Vuurberg** ('Isa' last ed) **03** cab-merlot blend dominated by cab's classy cassis, hint lead pencil; stylish dark velvet texture, unobtrusive tannins, dry finish with fine-grained tannins, lingering oak. Half with corks, half screwcaps: latter bottles now shy, those with cork showing some nice development. **04** (sample) seems richer, more opulent within confines of classic structure, though still taut. 18 mths Fr oak, 30% new.

Tridente new Merlot-dominated blend, with 40% cab s, 10% cab f in **04** (sample). Sumptuous black-berried fruits disciplined in fine oak – compact & stylish, shows classic restraint, fruit groomed to perfection – just needs careful assistance into bottle. 18 mths Fr oak, 60% new. Potential ★★★★. **Chenin Blanc** new Big whack oak on tank sample **05**, but also variety's melon & dried apricot fruit; rich, tangy flavours, ripeness balanced by fresh acidity, decent finish. Oak 50% new. ★★★ or higher after bottling. – *IvH*

Waboomsrivier Co-op

Worcester ▪ Est 1949 ▪ 1stB 1950 ▪ Tasting & sales Mon-Fri 8-12.30; 1.30-5 Sat 8-10 ▪ Closed pub hols ▪ Cellar tours by appt ▪ BYO picnic ▪ Owners 40 members ▪ Winemaker Chris van der Merwe (Oct 1987), with Wim Viljoen (Sep 1991) ▪ ±15 500 tons 40% red 42% white 8% rosé 10% other ▪ PO Box 24 Breede River 6858 ▪ wabooms@mweb.co.za ▪ ***T (023) 355·1730*** *▪ F (023) 355·1731*

No update available on this winery; contact details and wine notes from previous edition.

Cabernet Sauvignon ★★★ **03** friendly, approachable, with mineral touch; bright red berry flavours; enough structure for some bottle development. **Pinotage** ★★☆ **02** full, decidedly alcoholic (14.4% alc), strong tannins. Quite unlike … **Ruby Cabernet** ★★☆ Unoaked **01** soft & rotund, light thatch/savoury touches, ready to drink. **Merlot-Ruby Cabernet** ★★★ **03** ripe plums touched with thatch & prune; sweet amenable tannins; drinks well now, should hold yr/2. **Roodewagen** ★★★ Rounded, accessible **03**, pinotage & cinsaut for succulence, cab for structure, merlot for fun. **Cabernet Sauvignon Rosé** ★★★ Fluorescent pink **03** rounded yet pleasingly crisp on finish. Enjoy soonest. **Blanc de Blanc** ★★☆ Last was lightish, dry **03**, from sauvignon/colombard. **Chenin Blanc Late Harvest** ★★★☆ **03** lovely honeyed tropical fruit flavours; still fairly brisk. **Rubellite Sparkling** ★★★ Last-tasted version of this blush-coloured **NV** carbonated bubbly was explosively fizzy, lightish & very sweet. **Hanepoot** ★★★☆ Last we tasted this **NV** fortified dessert, we noted unusual choc-mint whiffs & floral touch, enlivened by acidity. **Port** ★★★☆ **03** ruby-style fortified from ruby cab brims with sweet warming damson/cherry fruit. ±18% alc. – *DH*

Wamakersvallei Winery

Wellington ▪ Est 1941 ▪ Tasting & sales Mon-Fri 8-5 Sat 8.30-12.30 ▪ Closed pub hols except May 1 ▪ Tours by appt ▪ BYO picnic ▪ Conferences ▪ Owners 40 members ▪ Winemakers Bennie Wannenburg & André Swanepoel ▪ Viti consultant Johan Viljoen ▪ 1 400 ha ▪ 55% red 45% white ▪ PO Box 509 Wellington 7654 ▪ sales@wamakers.co.za ▪ www.wamakersvallei.co.za ▪ ***T 873·1582*** *▪ F 873·3194*

On balance, 2005 was a red-wine year, yielding lovely aromatic wines full of fruit, reflect Bennie Wannenburg and André Swanepoel, who espouse a non-interventionist approach to winemaking. In fact, all the wines turned out well, they believe, including the first Viognier, from vineyards planted only in the past few years (cab franc, malbec, mourvèdre and petit verdot are also coming on-line). A new conference centre is the latest in a series of modernisation moves, which include upgrading the tasting room, making the visitor amenities more wheelchair-friendly and, most importantly, beefing up the vinification facilities. These now include pneumatic tank presses and a fully mechanised red wine preparation system which, Wannenburg & co note, make the cellar one of the most modern in the Cape.

La Cave range

★★★★ **Pinotage** High-kicking/flying version (ABSA Top Ten, CWT, WOM), from a single vyd, 8 yrs old, taken to extremes of ripeness – 15% alc for current **03** (★★), with funky whiffs & overt wood character (9 mths Fr/Am); **02** last ed turning noticeably sweet, probably best enjoyed soon.

★★★★ **Shiraz** Blockbuster style with alc to match (14.5–15.5%); unfiltered. **03** (★★★) more in line with (**01** ★★☆), tannery whiffs, dry tannins & hot finish; **02** stepped into different league with plush fruit, chunky but supple tannins. Small oak matured.

Cabernet Sauvignon ★★ Pvs releases were striking, lauded by various show judges; 3rd vintage **03** marred by acute dryness, astringency accentuated by shy fruit. Yr oak. **Merlot** ★★★ **03** another bold but well-modulated statement (15% alc); attractive ripe/soft berry tone throughout, amenable tannins for current enjoyment, 2-3 yrs cellaring.

Bain's Way range

Pinotage Invariably the standout in range, though our (4) sample bottles of **04** all faulty; **03** (★★★☆) gently extracted, elegant & not too alcoholic at 13.5%. **Cinsaut** ★★☆ **02** last ed offered easy drinkabilty, showed some complexity in form of dried-fruit whiffs, tea-leaf nuance on finish. **Chenin Blanc** ★★ **05** easy, softly dry, light-bodied, tropical-toned quaffer. **Sauvignon Blanc** ★★☆ **05** crisply dry & light, whiffs of green vegetation & tropical fruit. **Sparkling Vin Sec** ★★☆ Latest **NV** from sauvignon not tasted. Pvs were zesty, refreshing any-occasion bubblies. **Viognier** new ★★ Gentle hint of white peach on **05**, uncomplex but pleasant, big 14.5% alc. Following current releases not retasted: **Cabernet Sauvignon** ★★★ **03** more elegant than pvs, better controlled alc (14%), grainy, by no means unpleasant, tannins. **Merlot** ★★☆ **03** extends the 'breakfast special' analogy of pvs into dinnertime with meat/bouillon/game tone to soft, sweet fruit. **Shiraz** ★★★ Sensitively extracted **03**; good varietal character, zingy dried fruit tang to leaven serious alc (14%). **Chardonnay** ★★★ **04** unwooded, with juicy acidity, lifted peach blossom & pear-drop aromas, sweetish finish from 14% alc.

33 Degrees South range

Both **NV**. **Dry Red** ★★ Latest not the soft pushover we met pvsly; more robust, firm pinotage tannins (here with cinsaut) show on finish. **Dry White** ★☆ Again 100% chenin for latest bottling; dry, slightly oxidised, drink soonest after purchase.

Dessert range

Both **NV**. **Fishermans Jerepigo** ★★★ Fortifying salty sea dogs since 1941; from hanepoot; very sweet & insinuating, hints of lemon meringue pie & marzipan. 16% alc. **Jagters Port** ★★☆ 'Hunter's Port', from cab. Latest bottling suave rather than rustic & earthy; for trophy seekers who wear Gucci. — *CT/TM*

Wandsbeck Wines

Robertson ▪ Est 1965 ▪ 1stB 1986 ▪ Tasting, sales & tours Mon-Fri 8-5 ▪ Closed Easter Fri-Mon, May 1, Dec 25/26 & Jan 1 ▪ Tours by appt ▪ Owners 22 members ▪ Winemaker Helmard Hanekom, with Tiaan Blom (Jan 1986/Dec 2003) ▪ Viti consultant Briaan Stipp (1995) ▪ 448 ha (cab, cinsaut, merlot, pinotage, semillon) ▪ 6 440 tons ±10 000 cs own label 50% red 50% white ▪ PO Box 267 Robertson 6705 ▪ akhwyn@lando.co.za ▪ ***T (023) 626·1103*** *▪ F (023) 626·3329*

Having geared up after 2004's record harvest, Wandsbeck's winemakers took in a crop substantially reduced by drought. But the wines are 'looking great', so no-one's complaining, says Helmard Hanekom, keen to start concentrating on single-block selections for special wines. Last year the co-op renamed itself Wandsbeck ('Agterkliphoogte' a tongue-tripper), released their maiden Cab, and modernised the cellar by replacing traditional cement tanks with a new-fangled mechanised system – inevitable changes tinged with regret for the nostalgic Helmard H.

Cabernet Sauvignon ☺ ★★ **02** BBQ-amenable quaffer with dark berry fruit, vanilla hint, dollop amenable tannins & sensible 13.4% alc. Yr Fr oak; extra yr bottle-aged. **Ruby Cabernet** ☺ ★★ **04** cheery & distinctive thatch & plum whiffs; supple tannin. Rounded palate (via 6.7g/ℓ sugar) but dry finish thanks to brisk acidity, fruit tannins (unwooded).

Shiraz ☆ Powerful & unsubtle **04**, 15% alc accentuates gruff tannins, giving harsh finish. **Chenin Blanc** ★ **05** tenuous tropical fruit flavours, zesty if short. **Sauvignon Blanc** ★☆ **05** light (12.5% alc), with restrained lime & lemon aromas, zippy acidity. **Muskadel** ★☆ Fortified sweet red, **04** pleasant muscat scent, syrupy finish – could do with splash more acidity. 17.5% alc big for style. – *DH*

Warwick Estate

Stellenbosch ▪ Est 1964 ▪ 1stB 1984 ▪ Tasting & sales Mon-Fri 10–5 Sat 10–4 (all year) Sun 10–4 (Oct to Apr only) ▪ Closed Easter Sun, Dec 25 & Jan 1 ▪ Tours by appt ▪ Mediterranean picnic baskets by appt, or BYO ▪ 'Wedding Cup' demonstrations ▪ Gifts ▪ Walks/hikes ▪ Owners Ratcliffe family ▪ Winemaker Louis Nel (Jun 2001) ▪ Viticulturist Ronald Spies (Aug 2001), advised by Phil Freese ▪ 65 ha (cabs s/f, merlot, pinotage, shiraz, chard, sauvignon) ▪ 300 tons 23 000 cs 70% red 30% white ▪ PO Box 2 Elsenburg 7607 ▪ info@warwickwine.co.za ▪ www.warwickwine.co.za ▪ ***T 884·4410*** *▪ F 884·4025*

A whirlwind year for Warwick. Planting continues (more cab and pinotage). New vineyards are close-planted (6 000+ vines/ha), trellised on metal poles, irrigated, minutely monitored using hi-tech imaging and water-stress readings. With his fifth Warwick vintage under the belt, winemaker Louis Nel has hit his stride. Raking in points (and praises) were Trilogy and Three Cape Ladies (the latter a *Wine Spectator* 'Top 100 Wines in the World' selection, first for a pinotage-based blend). The Ratcliffe family (pioneering woman winemaker Norma, son Mike and daughter Jenny) quietly celebrated a coming of age (their 21st vintage) with the re-introduction of a limited-release Cab called Stansfield, in honour of late father/founder Stan.

★★★★☆ **Trilogy (Estate Reserve)** Standout bdx-inspired blend dominated by the two cabs. **03** engaging nose of sunny plums, tea-leaf & lavender. Technically dry, but abundant fruit leaves impression of sweetness on finish. Tangy backbone, fine tannin, classy. **02** higher than usual merlot/cab f content (30/28) offers more diverse flavours than pvs. Elegant **01** 90 pts *WS*, Concours Mondial gold. 2 yrs Fr oak, 50% new.

★★★★ **Three Cape Ladies** Much admired – at home & abroad – pinotage blend with cab, merlot. **03** vibrant, warm summer pudding notes with some leather, vanilla. Chalky tannins, long goodbye. 2 yrs Fr, 20% new. **02** Concours Mondial gold. **01** 91 pts *WS*. **00** 92 pts *WS*.

★★★★ **Cabernet Franc** One of the Cape's benchmarks. Usually aged 24 mths Fr oak, 3rd fill. **03**'s bouquet of lilies & wild scrub continues on palate; dry, leafy tannins & refreshing acidity, refined structure. **02** sweeter raspberry fruit than pvs.

★★★★ **Old Bush Vines Pinotage** With bright strawberry fruit & acetone whiff, there's no mistaking parentage of lively **04** (★★★☆) early drinker, aged 14 mths older Fr wood. Uncomplex, bitter lift to tail. **03** plush, with signature flavour profile but tighter structure. NE.

★★★★ **Chardonnay** Intense yet smooth; pervasive lemon, cream & coconut tone. As with **03**, **04** fermented/9 mths on lees in Fr barrels, some new. Younger wine less alcoholic than pvs 14.5%.

★★★☆ **Professor Black Sauvignon Blanc** Rapier-like **05** (★★★★) step up on pvs, red grapefruit on nose & palate, minerally, very firm. Even better ±yr from harvest. Herbaceous, tropical **04** acidity toned & finish lengthened by touch sugar (3.5g/ℓ). Confirms class & stature of **03**, VDG & 91 pts *WS*.

Stansfield ★★★★ **03** named for late patriarch Stan Ratcliffe. Blackcurrant & sprinkling of spice; firm & determined tannin (from 24 mths 100% new Fr oak). Should gain complexity from ±5 yrs ageing; sweetness on finish unexpected. NE.—*CvZ*

Waterford Estate

Stellenbosch ▪ Est/1stB 1998 ▪ Visits Mon-Fri 9-5 Sat 10-3 ▪ Fee R20, negated on purchase ▪ Closed Easter Fri, Dec 25 & Jan 1 ▪ Wine & Chocolate Experience (see intro) ▪ Owners Jeremy & Leigh Ord, Kevin Arnold ▪ Winemaker Kevin Arnold ▪ Cellarmaster Francois Haasbroek (Jul 2004) ▪ Viticulturist Lombard Loubser ▪ 45 ha (barbera, cabs s/f, malbec, merlot, mourvèdre, petit v, shiraz, chard, sauvignon) ▪ 250 tons 35 000 cs 80% red 20% white ▪ PO Box 635 Stellenbosch 7599 ▪ info@waterfordestate.co.za ▪ www.waterfordestate.co.za ▪ ***T 880·0496*** *▪ F 880·1007*

This winery with its tinkling fountain and basking dogs may seem reposed, but behind the stone facade, hard work has been done over the past seven vintages (kudos garnered, too: recently, the 01 Cab became the third Waterford wine chosen to represent SA in the prestigious Tri-Nations Challenge). The focus of development is still firmly on the vineyards, where training of staff is a priority. Another educational avenue is an exchange programme whereby waiting staff at several bush lodges and restaurants experience this winelands gem firsthand, visit other wineries and dine at top Cape restaurants, in an endeavour to enhance their level of wine service. Partly educational, but mostly great fun, is the Waterford Wine & Chocolate Experience presented in conjunction with Von Gesau Chocolates of Greyton.

★★★★ **Cabernet Sauvignon** Quintessential cab with added élan from soupçons cab f, merlot, malbec; these total ±15% in **03** (★★★★☆). Restrainedly powerful red/black berry nose & palate augmented with spice, choc, coffee from 1st/2nd/3rd fill oak (10% Am, 40% new); taut tannins, excellent mineral finish; structured for 5+ yrs ageing. **02** has cab f etc seasoning in smaller measure (10%), similar oak treatment. Bouquet of sweet cassis, eucalyptus & herb; sensuous tannins.

★★★★☆ **Kevin Arnold Shiraz** Standout Cape Rhône-style red; usually includes small portion mourvèdre. This fraction down to just 6% in **03**, named after co-owner Jeremy Ord's daughter Katherine Leigh. Intoxicating bouquet of spice, lavender & leather; equally fine red-fruited palate reined in by tannins. Lowest Am oak fraction to date (30%). None of **02**'s strong farmyard whiffs, which initially obscured the fruit on nose. **02** VDG, *Wine* ★★★★. **01** VDG. All should improve with at least 5 yrs bottle age.

★★★★☆ **CWG Auction Reserve** 'In search of the best expression of the estate,' says Kevin A. Regal cab-dominated blend (40%) with 6 other Bdx/Rhône varieties incl petit v, shiraz. 2005 Auction sees second tranche of **03** under hammer; enticing, exotic spice/leather bouquet; layered red fruit palate; strapping tannin (12 mths Fr oak, some new); long fennel finish. Will reward cellaring.

★★★★ **Chardonnay** Refreshing alternative to the plump, buttery styles. Fine, focused fruit-acid (result of suppressed malo) the signature, as are exotic fruit, spice & toast. **04** (with 3% chenin) retiring but moreish tangerine/lime palate; needs time. Tauter than **03**, which gained honeyed complexity from bottle age. Fermented/matured in Fr oak, ±65% new. Drink these 3-5 yrs from harvest.

Sauvignon Blanc ★★★☆ Restrained, nervy **05**; water-white; muted on nose; some grapefruit pith flavours; 'wet pebble' finish. **Family Reserve 'Heatherleigh'** ★★★☆ **NV** dessert from muscat d'A (50%), chenin (40%), sauvignon. Billows beeswax & coconut, hints orange zest & apricot. Complex, slightly sweeter (88g/ℓ sugar) than pvs though still uncloying. Good prospects. 65% aged ±11 mths new Am oak. ±16% natural alc. 375ml.

Pecan Stream range

Stylishly attired 2nd label. **Cabernet Sauvignon-Shiraz** ★★★☆ Savoury blend cab/shiraz (90%) with equal dashes malbec, barbera; **04** approachable young thanks to juicy fruitiness, light wooding. Notch up on pvs. **Chenin Blanc** ★★★☆ ✓ **05** more than just easy-drinking fun wine; shows complexity in pear, apple, watermelon bouquet/palate; creaminess leavened by variety's racy acidity. — *CvZ*

Waterhof

Stellenbosch (see Helderberg map) ▪ Est 1997 ▪ 1stB 2003 ▪ Visits by appt ▪ Self-catering facilities ▪ Owner SWF Farming (Pty) Ltd ▪ 12 ha (cab, shiraz) ▪ 140 tons 100% red ▪ PO Box 1560 Somerset West 7129 ▪ info@waterhofestate.co.za ▪ www.waterhofestate.co.za ▪ ***T 842·3531*** *▪ F 842·2858*

When Pim and Annemarie de Lijster replanted their citrus orchards with cab and shiraz, they did so with a focus on diversity of flavour: the blocks claim 10 different clones between them. The wines are made offsite, and an export orientation means most bottles find their way to the US, China and Europe, though guests to their self-catering cottages can enjoy some too. A new philosophy embracing more subtle use of oak should make its debut from the 2005 vintage.

Shiraz Reserve ★★ Maiden **03** shows smoky campfire aromas, slightly vegetal whiffs & a fairly astringent finish. 18 mths oak. — *MF*

Waterkloof see False Bay Vineyards

WaverleyTBS

Est 2004 ▪ Closed to public ▪ SA consultant Jonathan Snashall (Jul 2003) ▪ ± 4m ℓ branded & own label exports 40% red 60% white ▪ UK office: Punchbowl Park, Cherry Tree Lane, Hemel Hempstead, Herts, HP2 7EU, UK ▪ T 09·44·1442·206800 F 09·44·1442·206888 ▪ SA office: PO Box 432 Franschhoek 7690 ▪ iwsinsa4@new.co.za ▪ www.waverley-group.co.uk ▪ ***T/F 876·3927; 082·322·3733***

The merger of Waverley and The Beer Seller in 2004 resulted in the creation of the UK's largest wholesale drinks distributor with over 25 000 on-trade customers. The off-trade arm of the company historically traded as (and was listed in this guide as) International Wine Services, pioneers of the 'flying winemaker' concept. Their locally-sourced wine range, Cape Promise (launched 2002), is one of the fastest-growing SA wine brands in the UK off-trade. (WaverleyTBS remains a big-volume business, creating own-label wines for many specialist and supermarket chains in the UK and mainland Europe.) 'We see ourselves as experts in developing SA wines to satisfy the evolving tastes of the UK consumer,' says accountant director Mark Jarman.

Cape Promise Reserve range

No new releases tasted for this, range below; notes from pvs ed: **Shiraz** ★★★★ **02** harmonious, complex nose of vanilla spice & white pepper; full silky flavour; pleasing integration of fruit, wood & alc (14%). Yr oaked. **Chardonnay** ★★★★ **03** full-on commercial crowd-pleaser: lashings peaches & cream, toasty oak, plump fruit, more richness via 6g/ℓ sugar. 30% barrel-fermented/6 mths aged. **Private Reserve Noble Late Harvest** ★★★★ From muscat & chenin; **03** appealing passionfruit, peach, apricot fruit. Silky, supple & delicious.

Cape Promise range

Cabernet Sauvignon ★★★ **03** warm aromas of damp earth, slight youthful edginess which should have settled by now. **Merlot** ★★★ Uncomplicated **03**, shy hints dried fruit & eucalyptus; soft jammy sweetness firmed by powdery tannins. **Pinotage** ★★★ **03** with splash merlot; banana & mulberry confirm pinotage is in charge; sweet palate-coating mulberry fruit, fairly robust but tasty. **Shiraz** ★★★ **03** good varietal nose with meaty/peppery whiffs, charred mocha wood to spice up the red fruit. 6 mths oak. **Ruby Cabernet-Pinotage** ★★★ Duo of fruity varieties abetted by dash of another smoothie, cinsaut; **04** thatchy smells from ruby cab, mulberries from pinotage; plummy in-your-face flavour. 60% oaked, 4 mths. **Chardonnay** ★★★ **04** pleasant spicy nose, hints vanilla & butterscotch; soft peach & lime flavours. 60% wooded 6 mths. **Chenin Blanc Barrel Fermented** ★★★ Sparingly oaked (70% 6 mths) & showing it in understated vanilla twist to **04**'s guava/passionfruit aromas, creamy apple flavours. **Chenin Blanc Unoaked** ★★★ Creamy, ripe baked-apple nose, touch honey in farewell. **04** shows some development potential. **Sauvignon Blanc** ★★★ Appealing **04**, spicy bouquet of capsicum & grapefruit, softly dry & juicy, generously flavoured. **Chardonnay-Colombard** ★★ 55/45 blend; **04** muted herby notes with lemon zest hints; simple fruity dry flavour. **Dry Muscat** ★★★ From muscat d'A. Turkish Delight & talcum powder billow from **04**; soft fruity tone, bone-dry flavour; satisfying & easy to drink. Above ranges sourced widely: WOs Stbosch, Dbnvlle, Wrcstr & W Cape. — *TM*

Webersburg Wines

Stellenbosch ▪ Est/1stB 1996 ▪ Visits by appt Mon-Fri 9-4 ▪ Closed pub hols ▪ Owner Fred Weber ▪ Winemaker Rudolf de Wet (Jan 2004), advised by Giorgio Dalla Cia (1997) ▪ Viticulturist Braam Steyn (Apr 1996) ▪ 20 ha (cabs, merlot) ▪ ±3 000 cs 100% red ▪ PO Box 3428 Somerset West 7129 ▪ weber@iafrica.com ▪ www.webersburg.co.za ▪ ***T 881·3636*** *▪ F 881·3217*

Restoration of the beautifully situated Helderberg farm's 1786 Cape Dutch homestead is now complete, and Fred Weber and Rudolf de Wet are considering the next big project – building a new cellar. With Giorgio Dalla Cia consulting, the wines listed below were made at Meerlust from Webersburg fruit. Both winemakers say they were so busy relocating from Weber's neighbouring farm (bought by Ernie Els) during the 2004 vintage that they only had time to make five barrels of wine. De Wet found the 2005 harvest – their 10th – very challenging. 'The grapes ripened simultaneously, so we were pushed for space.' An ideal year for muscular reds, he declares, claiming he has successfully maintained Webersburg's hallmark restraint.

★★★★ **Cabernet Sauvignon** Classicism & consistency, the antithesis of market-driven jolly immediacy. Expressing place & vintage, needs time to unfurl, especially meaty **00** (★★★★★) which still softening in cellar. Current release **01**; rich cassis fruit woven into plush frame, not revisited for this ed. No **02**. 18 mths Fr oak, 70% new.

★★★★ **Webersburg** (Pvsly Cabernet Sauvignon-Merlot) **02** bears standard with aplomb; piquant savoury edges to sumptuous fruit, all in refined genre. Elegance etched into echoing finish: singular. 70% cab, 18 mths Fr wood, two-thirds new. — *DS*

Wedderwill Country Estate

Stellenbosch (see Helderberg map) ▪ Est/1stB 1997 ▪ Visits by appt ▪ Owners Georg-Ludwig von Loeper & Neil Jowell ▪ Vini consultant Nico Vermeulen (2004), with Johan Manson ▪ Viticulturist Johan Manson, advised by Dawie le Roux (1997) ▪ 24 ha (cabs s/f, merlot, shiraz, sauvignon) ▪ 1 300 cs 90% red 10% white ▪ PO Box 75 Sir Lowry's Pass 7133 ▪ w@lfgang.de ▪ www.wedderwill.co.za ▪ ***T/F 858·1402***

No update available on this winery; contact details from previous edition.

Wederom new

Robertson ▪ Est 2002 ▪ 1stB 2003 ▪ Tasting & sales Mon-Sat 9-6 ▪ Fee R10 pp for groups of 10+ ▪ Closed Ascension Day, Good Friday ▪ Meals by appt during tasting hours ▪ Facilities for children ▪ Conference facilities ▪ Hiking/biking trails ▪ Guest house ▪ Owners Philip & Almien du Toit ▪ Vini consultant Newald Marais, with Philip du Toit ▪ Viticulturist Philip du Toit ▪ ±20 ha (merlot, shiraz, chenin) ▪ ±120 tons 500 cs 100% red ▪ PO Box 60 Robertson 6705 ▪wederom@myisp.co.za ▪ www.wederom.co.za ▪ ***T (023) 626·4139 ▪ F (023) 626·3306***

The boss became the apprentice the day veteran winemaker-turned-consultant Newald Marais walked in the cellar door, jokes Almien du Toit, wife of owner Philip. Together the couple tend 20ha of vineyard (one extremity of which abuts Graham Beck's standout block, 'The Ridge'), run a guesthouse and offer tastings (meals on request). Visitors are free to explore hiking and biking trails through 90ha of fiercely protected fynbos (no 4x4s allowed!) dotted with springbok. Recent restoration of the cellar (circa 1933) on this 4th generation landholding revealed murals painted by an Italian POW during his WW II internment.

Shiraz ★★★ Food friendly **03** raspberry/youngberry aromas; juicy, light & very soft; 14.5% alc evident as is 18 months Fr oak on finish. — *MF*

Weening & Barge Winery

Stellenbosch (see Helderberg map) ▪ Est 2003 ▪ 1stB 2005 ▪ Sales Mon-Fri 10-4 ▪ Guest villa ▪ Owners Edo & Veronique Weening-Barge ▪ Vini consultant Johan Joubert (2003) ▪ Farm manager Ken Nicholson (2003) ▪ 31 ha (cab f, pinot, shiraz, chenin, sauvignon) ▪ 160 tons 16 000 cs own label ▪ 44% red 56% rosé ▪ PO Box 3625 Somerset West 7129 ▪ info@weeningbarge.com ▪ www.weeningbarge.com ▪ ***T 842·2255*** *▪ F 842·3393*

Long before Edo and Veronique Weening-Barge were legally able to sample their bounty, they had visited most of Europe's major vinegrowing areas with their wine-loving parents. When the couple met years later, they kept up the tradition. Which helps explain why they leapt at the opportunity to purchase a farm in the Faure area with well-established vines, and let this deep-rooted passion loose in their own wines. Excited by the cool sea-exposition, they talk animatedly about producing 'limited quantities of balanced wines' (currently in conjunction with Kleine Zalze). 'Soon everybody will know our wines,' they promise.

★★★★ **Cuvée Lynette Pinot Noir** Earthy, wild strawberry aromas lead to **04**'s forceful but restrained palate, with some incipient complexity & fairly robust tannins. Appropriate support from 14 mths 2nd/3rd-fill barrels.

★★★★ **Cuvée Quint Shiraz 04** has ripe nose of creamy, smoky toffee. Dense, flavourful, big 14.5% alc; a little unyielding in youth but plentiful sweet red fruit, good tannic underpinning, well-balanced wood (14 mths older oak).

Cuvée Terry Lynn Shiraz Rosé ★★★ Deep onion skin colour, smoky/fruity aromas on dry **05**. Elegantly fresh & restrained but full flavours. — *TJ*

Welbedacht Wines

Wellington ▪ 1stB 2003 ▪ Tasting, sales & tours Mon-Fri 8.30-5 Sat 9-2 Sun by appt ▪ Fee R15 (incl glass) ▪ Closed Dec 25 & Jan 1 ▪ BYO picnic; also meals/refreshments for groups by appt ▪ Facilities for children ▪ Tourgroups ▪ Conferences ▪ Mountain biking ▪ Owner Schalk Burger Family Trust ▪ Winemaker Matthew Copeland, with Tiaan Burger (Sep 2004/Jan 2005) ▪ Viticulturist Jacobus de Bruyn (Jan 2002) ▪ 130 ha (cab, merlot, pinotage, shiraz, chard, chenin, sauvignon) ▪ 1 200 tons 100 tons/7000 cs own label ▪ 75% red 25% white ▪ PO Box 51 Wellington 7654 ▪ wine@welbedacht.co.za ▪ www.welbedacht.co.za ▪ ***T 873·1877*** *▪ F 873·2877*

Once a ramshackle cellar dating back to the 1800s, Welbedacht is now in the safe hands (or family trust) of former rugby Springbok Schalk Burger Snr. After selling grapes to high-profile producers with 'amazing results' for a few years (think ABSA Top 10 Pinotage), Burger last year decided to follow his dream of making his own wines. Describing the 2005 harvest as 'a roller coaster ride of gritted teeth and silent prayer', he and winemaker Matthew Copeland are particularly excited about the quality of their Pinotage and barrel-fermented Chenin, both from decades-old bushvines. But look out, also, for their 'very special, serious' blend named … no, not Rugby Field but Cricket Pitch, after the Welbedacht Oval situated alongside the beautifully restored homestead.

★★★★ **Cricket Pitch** Exciting newcomer; merlot-cab (60/40) blend, traditionally made (basket press, open fermenters etc). **03** first impression of raspberry fruit-sweetness quickly dispelled by savoury dryness, slight tangy astringency; firm elegant conclusion reveals little trace of 14.5% alc, or of 18 mths small oak, combo new-3rd fill (ditto all the reds). Pleads few yrs to show best.

Following quartet tasted pre-bottling, ratings provisional. **Cabernet Sauvignon** ★★★ **03** riper, plumper profile than above wine; pleasantly contrasting mineral & toffee/choc notes; softly ripe tannins. Well judged oak (here & throughout range). **Merlot** ★★★ Dense odours of black fruit & choc mirrored in **03**'s full-ripe flavours, pervasive sweet tone augmented by 14.5% alc; tannins still abrasive, need time to settle. **Chardonnay** ★★★ Fermented/6 mths sur lie in new oak, Hngrian ('more delicate'); attractively proportioned **05**, aromatic ripe pineapple whiffs, buttery flesh well supported by spicy oak; ends clean, with mineral flick. **Chenin Blanc Bush Vine** ★★★★ Oak as for Chard; ripe Golden Delicious apple notes on **03**, leesy breadth nicely curtailed by fresh, slightly sherbety acidity. All WO W Cape. — *MM*

Welgedacht *see* Baarsma, Dominion

Welgegund Farm

Wellington ▪ Est 1800s ▪ 1stB 1997 ▪ Tasting & sales by appt ▪ B&B ▪ Owners Alex & Sheila Camerer ▪ Winemaker Corlea Fourie (Siyabonga) ▪ Viticulturist Johan Smit (Winecorp, 2004) ▪ 30 ha (cab, carignan, cinsaut, merlot, pinotage, shiraz) ▪ 1 000 cs own label 100% red ▪ PO Box 683 Wellington 7655 ▪ alex.camerer@welgegund.co.za ▪ www.welgegund.co.za ▪ ***T 082·554·7871*** *▪ F 873·2683*

Alex Camerer claims that Corlea Fourie (abetted by friend and Siyabonga cellar owner Graham Knox) made the maiden Carignan Rosé behind his back. If so, perhaps he should keep his gaze averted. Having been invited onto the SA team for last year's Tri-Nations Challenge, 'you can bet your bottom dollar there will be more from the same old vineyard in the future'. With shiraz coming on stream and plans to plant grenache and viognier, Alex C feels Welgegund has a good future as a producer of Rhône-style blends. And with son Simon now also on board, his wishes seem Welgegund ('Well granted').

Cabernet Sauvignon ★★★ Re-engaged **04** (sample pvs ed) exuberant minty mulberry greeting, mint-choc flavour, finishes firmly tannic despite (4.4g/ℓ) sugar. Mix new/used oak. **Merlot** new ★★★ **04** smouldering black velvet hues, voluminous dark-fruit nose with savoury edge; tight 'green leaf' tannins. **Carignan Rosé** new ★★ Dusky rose-tinted **04**, light, raspberry-toned & properly dry with hint tannin; ex-27 yr old bushvines. **Carignan** ★★★★ Features dash shiraz for extra heft. **03** light bodied, juicy lunchtime wine, serve chilled. **04** sampled from barrel last ed, seemed slightly fuller, deeper coloured. Portion fruit ex-Swtlnd. *— CvZ/TM*

Welgeleë Vineyards

Paarl ▪ Est 1999 ▪ 1stB 2003 ▪ Visits by appt ▪ Owners/viticulturists Liris Trust (Chris & Lidea Meyer) ▪ Vini consultant Morné Kemp (Jan 2003), with owners ▪ 3 ha (shiraz) ▪ 300 cs 100% red ▪ PO Box 439 Klapmuts 7625 ▪ welgelee@absamail.co.za ▪ ***T/F 875·5726***

It's been a year of steady progress with hectic patches at this Paarl property, like when pet lovers Chris and Lidea Meyer's dogs produced 18 puppies all at once: 'T'was a nightmare!' An interesting harvest with shifting weather patterns reduced the crop but Meyer anticipates fine wines with quality further enhanced by the use of a sorting table, a time-consuming process but well worth it. Next up in the vinous pipeline is a Chardonnay 'asap!' A tasting venue was in the building too — they'll be open on Sundays, great news for weekend wine shoppers.

Shiraz Reserve ★★★★ Tasted last yr, **03** was elegant, offered nutmeg, cassia aromas, black berry fruit. Fine tannins, with good, unobtrusive support from 9 mths Fr oak. **04** has started on its promisingly spicy way. **Cabernet Sauvignon** ★★★ **04** ripe fruit tannins mingle with abundant blackcurrant fruit, mocha/coffee finish. Oak currently dominates, needs ± 2–4 yrs to knit with fruit flavours & textures. *— DH*

Welgemeend Estate

Paarl ▪ 1stB 1979 ▪ Tasting Wed 2–4 Sat 9–12.30 ▪ Sales during office hours only by appt ▪ Closed pub hols ▪ Privately owned ▪ Winemaker Louise Hofmeyr (Jul 1991) ▪ Manager/viticulturist Ursula Hofmeyr ▪ ±11 ha (cab s/f, grenache, malbec, merlot, 'petit mystery', pinotage, shiraz) ▪ 3 500 cs 100% red ▪ PO Box 1408 Suider-Paarl 7624 ▪ welgemeend@worldonline.co.za ▪ www.welgemeend.co.za ▪ ***T 875·5210*** *▪ F 875·5239*

This family-owned boutique winery, in so many ways a trend setter in the Cape (first Bordeaux-style red, first pinotage blend), is on the market. Fans will be severely disappointed, but both matriarch Ursula Hofmeyr and daughter Louise feel it is time to pack up and take a break. 'Ursula has put over three decades of her life into Welgemeend and, at 77, she deserves to retire,' says Louise H. For her part, the winemaker who in 1992 took over from her father Billy and shares his great reverence for classic, unshowy wines, feels the industry has lost its soul. 'Wines are being made for show,' she says, noting with alarm that thumping high alcohols are now the norm. She might, after a few years, lease a hectare or two and make a small quantity of wine, 'but this is a thought and not a given'.

★★★★☆ **Estate Reserve** ✓ The first Cape bdx blend – cab, merlot, cab f – with a loyal following around the wine world over 25 yrs. **02** sample (★★★★) shows return to cab dominance (85% s & f); well focused & refined, lighter fruit reflects vintage. **01** predominantly merlot, marked by signature elegance, finesse. Like pvs, needs time & patience to offers its best. Moderate ±13% alc. Oaked for the long haul (18 mths, 30% new).

★★★★ **Douelle** ✓ A fragrant, alternative nod to Bdx, mostly malbec with merlot, cab & soupçon cab f, 18 mths in oak. **02** displays quintessential Welgemeend stamp of tightly woven, supple tannins; sweet-fruit touch in well-judged finish. **01** savoury, herb-infused character to sappy scaffold. 13.5% alc.

Amadé ★★★★☆ ✓ Pioneering, idiosyncratic Cape interpretation of rhône-style blend. **02** 40/30/30 shiraz, pinotage & grenache ensemble: smoky, earthy warmth to tangy baked pudding features, tart finish. 13% alc. 18 mths older oak. **Soopjeshoogte** ★★★★☆ ✓ Cabs s/f with merlot; for earlier drinking than Reserve. **02** toffee/asphalt notes to lightly fruited texture, firm finish. All seasoned wood. 12.5% alc. Note: all **02**s tasted as pre-bottling tank samples. **Upelation** & **Pinotage-Shiraz** discontinued. – *DS*

Welgevonde see Daschbosch

Wellington Cooperative Cellar

Wellington ▪ Est/1stB 1934 ▪ Tasting & sales Mon-Fri 8-1; 2-5 ▪ Owners 49 members ▪ Winemakers Gert Boerssen, Koos Carstens & Andries de Klerk (1980/1990/2004) ▪ Viticulturist Andries de Klerk (Jun 2004) ▪ 1 600 ha (cinsaut, pinotage, chard, chenin, sauvignon) ▪ 12 000 tons ±6 500 cs own label ▪ PO Box 520 Wellington 7654 ▪ wellingtoncellar@iafrica.com ▪ www.wellingtoncellar@co.za ▪ ***T 873·1163*** *▪ F 873·2423*

The first harvest for new viticulturist Andries de Klerk in this Valley of the Wagonmakers was 'peculiar' due to unusual weather conditions. But the vineyards recovered well from heatstroke and the grapes ripened with lower sugars, resulting in fruity reds with lower alcohols and aromatic whites. The team have set their sights on making quality wines which reflect the character of warmer Wellington and, in the process, dispel the perception that varieties like sauvignon can be made into top-notch examples only in cooler climes.

Reserve range new

Cabernet Sauvignon ★★ Exuberant wooding obscures **03**'s attractive, rich cassis fruit; patience needed for 14 mths barrelling (same throughout this range) to be absorbed. **Pinotage** ★★★ **03** emerges from its rigorous oak schooling with more accessible fruit than cellar mates, hints ripe plum & dark fruits; will still need yr/2 to begin realising its potential. **Shiraz** ★★ **03** heavily influenced by oak; robust tannins & vanilla spice dominate fine but ethereal ripe plum fruit. **Chenin Blanc** ★★ Chunky **04** still sheathed in wood character from 3 mths oaking, unclear whether lurking fruit will emerge. This, range below, WO Paarl.

Wellington range

Cabernet Sauvignon ★★★ **03** similar wood-powered style as pvs – give plenty of time. 9 mths Fr oak. **Merlot** ★★★ Lively & ripe **03** last ed showed mix of red & black berries, healthy acid/tannin backbone. 9 mths Fr oak. **Pinotage** ★★ **04** good varietal aromas of red berry & cherry, fruit on palate less ripe & gripped by forbidding tannins. 3 mths Fr oak. **Shiraz** ★★★ **04** still middle-of-the-road style but lesser fruit concentration this vintage, 9 mths on Fr oak still needs to integrate. **Cinsaut-Ruby Cabernet** ★★★ 75/25 combo, partly Fr oaked. **03** last ed very light textured, chillable, for enjoying with a braai. **Pinotage Rosé** ★★★ Scented semi-sweet with firming touch tannin; **04** last yr was noted as tasting dry despite 10g/ℓ sugar. **Chardonnay** ★★★ None since lightly oaked **03**, full & lively, for early enjoyment. **Chenin Blanc** ★★★ **05** (sample) notes of pear, apple & guava; clean & easy to drink. **Sauvignon Blanc** ★★★ Bouncy, lightish **04** offers subtle gooseberry aromas/tastes, modest 13% alc. Not retasted. **Late Harvest** ★★★ **04** semi-sweet chenin with pear tones & hint of tangerine, not too sweet; light 12% alc. **Hanepoot Jerepiko** ★★★ Fortified dessert with delicate & charming floral aromas, **05** unusual steely/minerally streak not quite enough to neutralise the powerful sweetness. **Port** ★★★ Last was ruby-style **02** from tinta, fruity & balanced, with traditionally low fortification (17.5% alc).—*DH*

Welmoed see Omnia Wines

Weltevrede Estate

Robertson ▪ Est 1912 ▪ 1stB 1975 ▪ Tasting & sales Mon-Fri 8-5 Sat 9-3.30 ▪ Tours by appt ▪ Under the Vines Bistro for lunch Tue-Sat (closed Jun/Jul) or BYO picnic ▪ Weltevrede Guest Cottage (see Stay-over section) ▪ Conservation area ▪ Walks ▪ 4x4 trail ▪ Mountain biking ▪ Owner Lourens Jonker ▪ Winemaker Philip Jonker (1997), with Riaan Liebenberg (Sep 1999) ▪ Viticulturist Philip Jonker, advised by Francois Viljoen ▪ 100 ha (cab, merlot, shiraz, chard, colombard, sauvignon) ▪ 150 tons 25 000 cs own label 15% red 75% white 10% other ▪ PO Box 6 Bonnievale 6730 ▪ info@weltevrede.com ▪ www.weltevrede.com ▪ ***T (023) 616·2141*** *▪ F (023) 616·2460*

This year marks the 80th birthday of Weltevrede's designated national monument 'Oupa se Wingerd' – a vineyard originally (and still) planted with muscat de Hambourg, making the region's old staple, sweet muscadel. The Jonker family (itself a fourth-generation part of the local scene) have since moved on to exploit their greatest strength, chardonnay – in many guises, both still and bubbly, but with Philip J still covering all bases (reds included). A self-confessed chardonnay specialist, armfuls of awards attest to his expertise, but it's the wines' names (which allude to the soils) that betray his passion – to create site-specific wines, each with an individual personality, reflecting a particular location in the purest possible way.

★★★★☆ **Poet's Prayer Chardonnay** Impressive attention to an 'art wine' – wild yeast ferment (which can last full yr in barrel), 19 mths Fr oak, further yr in bottle, tiny 30 cs production. **03** individual in style: tropical aromas suggest plush richness of pvs, but tighter, more mineral, less obvious breadth to elegant textured structure. **02** golden patina, chalky aromas complex rather than bold; beautiful integration of fruit/oak in lingering 14.4% alc tail.

★★★★ **Rusted Soil Chardonnay** While above a poetic expression in a single barrel, this repositioned version ('Oude Weltevreden' in pvs eds) the senior of quartet of chardonnays in Jonker's pursuit of personality of terroir. Limestone origin of farm's oldest vyd site confers **03** with tropical, peach & passionfruit luxuriousness that stops just short of decadence. **02** 2005 Chardonnay-du-Monde gold. Fermented/10 mths Fr cask.

★★★★ **Place of Rocks Chardonnay** From broken shale rock, taut, less exuberant: **04** bristling lime fruit tingles in seam of bright acidity; mineral ring but full enough for, say, green curried chicken. **03** lovely stony citrus fruit integrated with wood (fermented/aged 10 mths), excellent length.

★★★★ **The Travelling Stone** ✓ Hand-harvested *vine* selection of sauvignon blanc from quartzite stone vyd which originally 'rolled down the surrounding hills'. **04** sampled pvs ed; nettley, herbaceous edge leavened by tropical flesh. **05** unready at press time.

★★★★ **Rhine Riesling** ✓ Verve, interest in (just-) dry & still current **01**, backed by Jonker for demure ageing. Was well-developed mid-2004; orange sheen, dusty dried herbs & dried apricots on honeyed palate; not retasted. 13% alc.

Bedrock Black Syrah ★★★★ New moniker for estate's first single-varietal red ('Syrah' pvs ed), now a finished wine, reflects commitment to expression of site, & muscularity of maiden **03**; purple plum/mulberry fruits laced with pepper spice; grippy tannins, generous frame. Yum! 14 mths oak, 80:20 Fr:Am. **Gewürztraminer** ★★★★ Cellar's 'undiscovered jewel', deserves table accompaniment. **05** aromatic rose-petal delicacy to litchi flesh, Turkish Delight viscosity in off-dry finish. **Ovation Rhine Riesling** ★★★ 'Natural Sweet' in pursuit of crossover style: botrytis richness but drier than NLH. **99** developed, gold hues; dried-fruit & terpene whiffs; cling-peach palate. Drink up. 32g/ℓ sugar; 12.5% alc. **Philip Jonker Brut** ★★★★ MCC from chardonnay, 3 yrs on lees. **00** in upgraded livery to reflect its hand-made identity; developed butterscotch tones, ready. **99** garnered Cap Classique Challenge applause. **Ouma se Wyn** ★★★ Consistently delicious, from single white muscat de F vyd; **03** grapey, honeycomb/dried peach notes; streamlined, less viscous style. 375ml. **Oupa Se Wyn** ★★★★ ✓ Succulent fortified dessert from red muscadel & muscat de Hambourg, partly ex-bushvines planted 1926. **01** light mahogany; enormous raisiny nose, rich, near-unctuous; orange-rind/roasted nuts in silky finish. VDG, MIWA gold. 17% alc. 375ml. Exported as 'Cape Muscat'.

River's Edge range

Chardonnay ☺ ★★★ Fourth in Jonker's terroir-quiver, this from alluvial soils. **05** billows summer melon/banana allure, delivers concentrated lemon freshness. Unwooded, pure fruit for enjoyment at altitude (SAA 2005) or beside the mountain stream.

Colombard ★★★ **04** not retasted; only available cellar-door & export. **Sauvignon Blanc** ★★ **05** perky poolside quaffer with lancing tingle to grapefruit tones.

Tricolore range

Duo of three-way blends crafted 'for my friends'. Both NE. **Red** ★★★ **03** black cherry tint to herby/earth tones, gentle tannins. Merlot, cab & syrah. **White** ★★★ **05** vibrant medley sauvignon, colombard fleshed out with semillon; fresh grassy grip to just-dry finish. Discontinued: **Oude Weltevreden Merlot-Cabernet Sauvignon**, **Privé du Bois**. *— DS*

Welvanpas

*Wellington ▪ Tasting & sales Mon-Fri 9-12.15; 1-5 Sat 9-1 ▪ Owners D Retief & Son Cellars ▪ Winemaker/viticulturist Dan Retief Jnr ▪ ±500 tons (15-30 tons for own range, 75% red 25% white) ▪ PO Box 75 Wellington 7654 ▪ welvanpas@xsinet.co.za ▪ **T 864·1238/082·498·5145/082·393·6268** ▪ F 864·1239*

Most of the grapes from this farm, in the Retief family for three centuries, go to nearby Bovlei Winery. A small, carefully selected quantity, however, are vinified by Dan R Jnr for release under the farm label. 'It was a good red wine year,' he reported post bottling the Pinotage 03, making a comeback after a few harvests' hiatus.

Cabernet Sauvignon ★ Artisinal **03** with smoky, oxidised & savory aromas & flavours. Chewy tannin. **Pinotage** ★ Rustic & reticent **03**, 15% alc gives a sweet impression to the lifted, bitter finish. **Chenin Blanc** ★ **04** Tropical, with burnt caramel/oxidised notes. *— DH*

Weskus see Winkelshoek

Westbridge Vineyards

*Stellenbosch ▪ Est 1998 ▪ 1stB 1999 ▪ Tasting & sales Mon-Sat 8-6 (phone ahead on pub hols) ▪ B&B & other amenities (see intro) ▪ Owner JC Starke & Muldersvlei Estates ▪ Winemaker Ian Starke ▪ Viticulturist Julian Starke ▪ 17 ha (cab, pinotage, chenin) ▪ 60 tons 4 000 cs 85% red 15% white ▪ PO Box 66 Muldersvlei 7607 ▪ wine@muldersvlei.co.za ▪ **T 884·4433***

The Starke family of Muldersvlei are tapping into wine tourism with a new tasting room in the old cellar – beautifully rustic, they say, opening onto shaded lawns for leisurely summer tastings – and a chapel/wedding venue to complement the guesthouse. (Nearby EagleVlei has also opened its doors to the public; another satellite wine route in the making?) 'Winemaking remains so exciting but also humbling as we rely on the gifts from above, not just on hard work and expertise,' says materfamilias Helen Starke. Last harvest they were blessed with abundant rains in January which upped the quality of the ripening berries; the rain's late arrival, however, meant volumes were down.

★★★★ **Pinotage Reserve** Two vintages to date: **99** characterful & full-flavoured with pronounced savoury edge; **00** attractively rustic profile.

No new vintages tasted; above/following notes from pvs ed. **Shiraz** ★★★ **02** characteristic shiraz spice, plus house's earthy touches, firm tannins. 3rd fill Fr oak. **Merlot 03** too young to rate but shows extraordinary concentration. **Pinotage** ★★★★ **03** individually styled, tropical fruit & whiffs tobacco/earth, tannins less daunting than pvs. Oak chip fermented/aged. **Juliette** Sparingly wooded blend changes with vintage; vinified/matured separately & blended just before bottling; **02** (★★★) cab, merlot, shiraz, appealingly round; **03** (★★★★) 22% pinotage injection, shows as fruitier, more satisfying. *— DH*

WestCorp International

*Olifants River (see Vredendal Cellar on Olifants River map) • Est 2002 • Tasting & sales Mon-Fri 8-5 Sat 8.30-12 (sales close 30 mins later) • Closed pub hols • Tours at 10 & 3 during harvest • Light meals by appt or BYO picnic • Tourgroups (±42 people) • Conferencing • Audio-visual presentation • Gifts • Owners 224 members • Winemakers Alwyn Maass, Pieter Verwey, Driaan van der Merwe & Len Knoetze (1997/1999/2000/2002), with Koos Thiart, Johan Weideman & Renier van Greenen (all Jan 2004) • Viticulturists Koos van der Merwe, Marina Bruwer & Hein Jansen van Rensburg (Dec 2002/Jan 2004/Jan 2004) • 4 990 ha (cab, merlot, pinotage, ruby cab, shiraz, chard, chenin, colombard, sauvignon, hanepoot) • 86 000 tons 610 000 cs 20% red 80% white • www.westcorp.co.za • Vredendal Cellar: PO Box 75 Vredendal 8160 • info@westcorp.co.za • **T (027) 213·1080** • F (027) 213·3476 • Spruitdrift Cellar: PO Box 129 Vredendal 8160 • **T (027) 213·3086** • F (027) 213·2937*

This massive wine-producing collaboration between West Coast cellars Vredendal and Spruitdrift has scored another marketing coup with its international best-seller Gôiya (stats say it's SA's No 2 brand in the UK; WestCorp's other mega-brand, Namaqua is No 5). A listing by supermarket chain Wal-Mart in Texas could see an eventual distribution of ±120 000 cases in 42 US states. Meanwhile, a sponsorship deal with the English cricket test side should convert some beer drinkers. Back home, the brand now includes the low-alcohol (9-10%), dry, Weigh-Less-approved 'D-Lite-Ful' Red, White and Rosé. Moves are also afoot to extend WestCorp's focus to premium wines. A joint project with the Institute for Wine Biotechnology is researching the measurement of grapes' chemical make-up as an early pre-harvest vine/fruit quality assessment.

Spencer Bay new

Special winemaker's selection; only in best vintages. **Shiraz Reserve** ★★★ Somewhat restrained **03**; ripe plummy/brambly fruit with smoky touch, obvious 18 mths oak; shows some elegance without real concentration. **Merlot Reserve 03** available but not tasted.

Gôiya range

Pronounced 'Hoya', meaning 'First'. **Merlot-Cabernet Sauvignon** ★★ Wooded **03** stern version of this habitually convivial duo; rustic tannins & savoury edge to choc-berry flavours. **Shiraz-Pinotage** ★★ Made in very large quantities; **04** shy game/smoked meat aromas; simple, undemanding. **D-Lite-Ful Red** new Vaguely vinous blend shiraz, pinotage. 10% alc. **NV**, as are the other D-Lites. **D-Lite-Ful Rosé** new Some floral notes, slightly savoury flavours, very plain. 9.5% alc. **Chardonnay-Sauvignon Blanc** ★★★ Winery's top seller; equal unwooded blend, off-dry; **05** fragrant floral bouquet, peachy fruit-salad flavours; limy acidity strikes good balance. **D-Lite-Ful White** new Very light & lean mix chenin, hanepoot; bone-dry. Pvsly featured **Merlot**, **Pinotage**, **Shiraz**, **Chardonnay**, **Sauvignon Blanc** & **Inanda Brut** all for export; no new versions tasted.

Namaqua range

Following all **NV**, available in 3 & 5ℓ bag-in-boxes. **Dry Red** ★ Latest rustic & savoury, bone-dry finish. Unwooded blend shiraz, pinotage, ruby cab, merlot. **Rosé** ★ Very simple & fairly dry-tasting (though 19g/ℓ sugar). **Grand Cru** ★★ Quite full & juicy, undemandingly dry mix chenin, colombard. **Stein** ★★ Shy, slight floral aromas; light but pleasant lifted flavours. **Late Harvest** ★★ Colombard, chenin (as are Stein, Grand-C), soft & semi-sweet. **Extra Lite** Weigh-Less approved for its low (9%) alc; our sample well past best. **Johannisberger** ★★ Hint of tropical flavour, simple but not over-sweet. **B4 Spumante Sparkling** ★★ Carbonated fizz from hanepoot ('B4 you start an occasion you have to drink some'); low-alc (±8%), **NV**; soft, pretty & sweet, energetic bubbles. **Johannisberger Red** ★ Same grapes as pvs version but much firmer, tannic, so tastes off-dry rather than full-sweet. Merlot, pinotage & ruby cab.

Spruitdrift range

New label designs throughout the range. **Cabernet Sauvignon** ★★★ **04** typical cassis with some leafy notes; house dryness though slightly fruitier than other reds. **Merlot** ★★ **04** smoked bacon & dried fruit on nose, lean & savoury, big dusty tannins. **Pinotage** ★★ More savoury than fruity this vintage; **04** lots of puckering astringency. **Shiraz** ★★ Uncomplicated

04, dusty plum notes, full-bodied with sweet finish. **Premier Grand Cru** ★ **NV** from chenin, colombard; (sample) hint of tropical fruit, challengingly dry. **Sauvignon Blanc** ★ new to guide; **05** bracingly fresh & insubstantial. Sample tasted. **Johannisberger** Not tasted. **Brut Sparkling** ★★☆ new Lively summer thirst quencher from colombard; lots of freshness, zing. Charmat method. **NV**, as is ... **Vin Doux Sparkling** ★★☆ Last featured in 2002 ed; returns with pleasant, light, salmon-pink summer fizz for the sweeter toothed. Chenin, hanepoot, pinotage. **Hanepoot Jerepigo** ★☆ Fortified dessert returns to guide with full-sweet, uncomplicated **04**, shortish flavours with alc kick (17%). **White Muscadel** ★★★ Muscadel Assoc gold medallist **04** simply billows muscat; big, luscious lemon-edged flavours, clean lengthy conclusion. 17% alc. new to this guide, as is ... **Red Muscadel** ★ Pale, shy **04**, sweet, grapey & bit thin. 17% alc. **Blanc de Noir** & **Natural Sweet** discontinued. — *DH*

Westerland see Ormonde Vineyards

Western Wines South Africa/Kumala

*Stellenbosch ▪ Est 1981 ▪ 1stB 1995 ▪ Closed to public ▪ Winemaker Ben Jordaan (Jul 2002) ▪ 25 ha (Journey's End — cab, shiraz, chard; Kumala — cab, cinsaut, merlot, pinotage, ruby cab, shiraz, chard, chenin, colombard, sauvignon, semillon) ▪ 5 500 cs (Journey's End) + 2.4m cs (Kumala) + 250 000 cs (Zenith) ▪ 45% red 50% white 5% rosé ▪ PO Box 769 Stellenbosch 7599 ▪ benj@western-wines.com jamesr@western-wines.com ▪ www.kumala.com ▪ **T 882·8177** ▪ F 882·8176*

This single company's sales represent a whacking 14% of SA wine exports worldwide. The Kumala brand, which has just celebrated its 10th anniversary and has risen speedily to 4th position among the UK's top wine brands. Western Wines UK was acquired in 2004 by Canadian wine-producing giant Vincor, who are spearheading Kumala's move into the US market, hoping to repeat this success there. The brand's sourcing and logistics in SA are handled exclusively by Origin Wine. Their Kumala Growers' Challenge recently acknowledged contributions to the Kumala range from Klawer and Daschbosch, joining previous winners Wamakersvallei and Du Toitskloof. Only the Kumala Reserve and the flagship Journey's End ranges are available locally. A recent collaboration with Charles Back, for an eponymous range featuring fruit from, among others, Sedgefield on the Cape's southern coast, sees another famous SA name on international shelves.

Journey's End range

★★★★ **Cabernet Sauvignon** Grapes for this range sourced from Journey's End farm in S/West. Classy yet unpretentious **03** (pvs ed a sample), fleshy & well rounded/meshed, attractive dry tannins on well-wooded finish (70% new Fr oak, rest 2nd/3rd fill Am). No **02**.

Shiraz ★★★☆ **03** still available; chunky & bold, big wild scrub bouquet with touch char to dark-cherry fruit, robust alc (14.5%) adds sweet note to long finish. **Chardonnay** ★★★☆ Well-upholstered **04**; ripe stone fruit, very attractive barrel character (toast, smoke), creamy/buttery texture refreshed by bright fruity acidity. ±9 mths oak, 50/50 new Fr/2nd fill Am. Above WO Stbosch; below W Cape unless noted.

Winemakers Selection

★★★☆ **Shiraz-Cabernet Sauvignon** ★★★☆ From selected vyds in Paarl, barrel-aged (contrast with ranges below, which staved/chipped), 20% new Am (rest older Fr). **03** 80/20 blend well-integrated & -balanced, big fruity tannins matched by healthy ripe fruit. Serious wine — deserves few yr to show its best.

Kumala Reserve range

Reds 20–50% Fr staved ±6 mths. **Cabernet Sauvignon** ★★★☆ Classically styled **04**, ripe cassis fruit checked by restrained dry tannins, well-applied oaking (incl some Am). WO Wllngtn, ditto ... **Merlot** ★★☆ Minty whiffs on **04**, attractive sweet but wood slightly apart mid-2004, needs time to mesh. **Pinotage** ★★★☆ Nicely tamed **03**, last ed noted as full & firm, flavourful, with approachable tannins. **Shiraz** ★★★ Ripe mulberry intro to **04**, touches choc & mocha, smooth & plump fruit held in place by supple tannins. **Chardonnay** ★★★☆ **04** last ed showed attractive toasty oak, citrus flavours, smooth acidity for soft silky palate. 30% Fr/Am oak staved. **Sauvignon Blanc** ★★★ **05** tropical tones this vintage; fruity, lightish (13% alc); ends firmly dry, with citrus nuance.

Kumala range

Cabernet Sauvignon-Shiraz ★★★ Drier & less overtly fruity than other reds, more serious; yet **05** approachably round & undaunting; to enjoy now & over 2-3 yrs. **Merlot-Pinotage** new ★★ Latter variety dominates despite only 30% of **05** blend; banana/plum whiffs, supple dry grip. Pleasant chilled. **Merlot-Ruby Cabernet** ★★★ Repeats pvs 60/40 assembly; **05** clean floral tones; mulberry/choc flavours; firm base of tannin for versatile food partnering. **Pinotage-Cinsault** ★★ **05** 80/30 formula, shows pinotage's sweet juicy fruit, balanced, undemanding. **Pinotage-Shiraz** ★★★ Oak-touched 60/40 mix tad more tannic than stablemates, hint of jamminess; **05** could do with yr/2 to soften. **Ruby Cabernet-Merlot** ★★★ Quaffable **05** again 80/20 blend, whiffs of ruby cab's signature grass/thatch, soft & smooth. **Chardonnay** ★★ **05** lively textured citrus fruit offset by subtle wood backdrop (20% oaked), soft finish. **Chardonnay-Semillon** ★★ Lightly oaked **05**, citrus & oak flavour profile, lively acidity, low 12% alc makes good lunchtime option. **Chenin Blanc-Chardonnay** ★★ **05** less plump than pvs, more zingy, suggestion of sweetness to pear-drop-tinged finish; usual modest oak. **Colombard-Chardonnay** ★★ Good lightish everyday dry white; 80/20 blend in **05**, delicate tropical tone, touch sweet tail. **Sauvignon Blanc-Semillon** ★★ Equal blend in light-textured, summery **05**, appealing tropical fruit/green grass combo. **Sauvignon Blanc-Colombard** ★★ **05** light citrusy 50/50 blend with markedly dry pithy finish.

Kumala Organic range

Pinotage-Shiraz ★★★ **04** pinotage dominant, taste-wise, in 60/40 blend. Ripe, plummy, brush of dry tannins on finish. Staves 2 mths. **Colombard-Chardonnay** ★★ **05** gentle dry white with zesty acidity, fresh & tasty, usual modest oak influence (Fr staves). — *DH/IvH*

Whalehaven Wines

Hemel-en-Aarde Valley (see Walker Bay map) ▪ Est/1stB 1995 ▪ Tasting & sales Mon-Fri 9.30-5 Sat & non-religious holidays 10.30-2 ▪ Fee R10 for groups of 10+ ▪ Closed Easter Fri/Sun, Dec 25 & Jan 1 ▪ Tours by appt ▪ BYO picnic ▪ Owners Bottega family ▪ Winemaker Paul Engelbrecht (Sep 2003) ▪ Viticulturist Tim Clark (Feb 2001) ▪ 80 tons 6 500 cs own label 70% red 25% white 5% rosé ▪ Private Bag X14 Hermanus 7200 ▪ wine@whalehavenwines.co.za ▪ ***T (028) 316·1633*** *▪ F (028) 316·1640*

What was one of the first wineries in the Hemel-en-Aarde Valley celebrated a decade of winemaking in 2005 and is now treading a path of what marketer Kath Simm terms 'quality that is not negotiable'. Sole owners since 2003, the Bottega family, who divert some grapes from their Hottentots Holland mountain farm, as well as buy in from Walker Bay, Villiersdorp and Elgin, are consolidating and streamlining. Cab and Unwooded Chardonnay have been discontinued. Cool-climate sites define the Whalehaven range, led by a consistently fine Pinot. Their promising Sir Lowry's Pass property, predominantly red (except for some viognier which has been teamed with chardonnay to sell-out success) is now reserved mainly for their new Idiom wines (see separate entry).

★★★★ **Pinot Noir** Elegant & restrained, but also succulent, well-wooded. Last tasted was **00** violets & delicate red-berry fruit well synchronised with oak's vanilla & tannins. Low ±13% alc. No **01**, **02** or **03**; next will be **04**.

Bord de Mer new ★★★★ **03** merlot/cab-based composition with cab f, shiraz, pinotage & mourvèdre filling the palette. Sultry tar nuances to shy black berry fruits just after bottling mid-2005, nicely grained tannins will protect their development over 3-5 yrs. WO W Cape. **Cabernet Franc** ★★★★ **04** true to variety: sappy, somewhat green; stern tannins mask savoury fruit mid-2005. Stbosch grapes, 50% new Fr oak. **Merlot** ★★★ Sample **04**, mulberry, smoked bacon features soften otherwise tight, hard structure & 15% alc. 40% new Fr wood, Stbosch vyds. **Old Harbour Red** ★★★ Chunky **NV** blend merlot, cab & shiraz; earthy, tarry fullness to firm tannins. **Rosé** ★★★ **04** crisp edge lifts off-dry mouthful; enjoy in flush of youth. Stbosch cab f & merlot; pinotage adds colour, viognier fragrance. **Chardonnay** ★★★★ Big, bold styling to sample **04**;

heavy oaking (80% new Fr) dominates tropical/citrus fruits mid-2005. W Bay grapes. **Viognier-Chardonnay** ★★★★ Novel 85/15 unoaked blend; maiden **04** sold out within 6 mths of release. **05**: aromatic jasmine, peach & pear angles to ripe mouthful; 16% alc unfettered in just-dry finish. Stbosch. — *DS*

White River see Bergsig
Wide River see Robertson Winery

Wildekrans Estate

Walker Bay ▪ Est/1stB 1993 ▪ Tasting & sales: Farm cellar Mon-Fri 9-5 (closed pub hols unless gate is open); Wildekrans Wine Shop & Art Gallery at Orchard Farmstall, Grabouw (T/F 859·5587), daily (except Dec 25) 8.30-5.30 (Sep-May) 9.30-5.30 (May-Sep) ▪ Cellar tours on request ▪ Meals, snacks, gifts, farm produce at farmstall, or BYO picnic to farm by appt ▪ Guest house ▪ Play area for children ▪ Conservation area ▪ Owners Bruce & Jo Elkin ▪ Winemaker Bruce Elkin, with William Wilkinson (2001/2003) ▪ Viticulturist Bruce Elkin ▪ 40 ha (cabs s/f, merlot, pinotage, shiraz, chard, chenin, sauvignon, semillon) ▪ 240 tons 10 000 cs own label 50% red 50% white ▪ PO Box 200 Elgin 7180 ▪ wines@wildekrans.co.za ▪ www.wildekranswines.co.za ▪ ***T (028) 284·9829*** *▪ F (028) 284·9902*

A busy year with a harvest of good-quality grapes, the release of their maiden MCC and Shiraz, as well as a new Merlot for the Caresse Marine range. And – finally! – the signposts are up, so no excuse not to visit. It was also a good year for William Wilkinson, who joined some years ago as a cellar hand and now finds himself a proud assistant winemaker. All part of Bruce Elkin's masterplan: 'To produce wines that reflect the life and personality of the farm, and for winemaking to be part of a simpler, uncomplicated way of life.'

Cabernet Sauvignon ★★★ Firm-tannined, spicy & herbal. **02** shows this wine's usual reticent fruit, dusty frame of dry tannins from oak (9 mths F, 10% new, rest 3rd fill), light 12.5% alc. **Merlot** Makes way for CM version below. **Pinotage Barrel Select** ★★★★ New oak (Fr/Am, 9 mths) still obvious mid-2005 on **03**, fruit understated, needs time to settle & fill out. Ripe, smooth, supportive tannins should facilitate. **Pinotage** ★★★★ **03**, only seasoned wood, more obviously fruity (ripe blueberry on nose), juicy, appealing; above version's sinew but shade more flesh, more generosity. **Shiraz** new ★★★ **04** displays house's restrained fruitiness, dry, food-accommodating savoury tannins, attractive spicy/earthy veneer. Wooding as for std Pinotage. **Warrant** ★★★★ Educated & classy bdx-style blend, 40/40/20 cab, merlot, cab f; last tasted was **01**, with dusty cedary fruit, sweet vanilla oak, grippy tannins from mainly new Fr oak. **Cabernet Franc-Merlot** ★★★ Curious tinned pea/asparagus extensions to **04**'s red-berried profile, dry tannins, not as well fleshed as pvs. 9 mths 2nd/3rd fill oak. **Chardonnay** ★★★★ (No longer labelled 'Reserve'.) **04** partly barrel-fermented/aged 3 mths, only seasoned oak; some toasty whiffs, orange rind & honey; smooth, lively, thanks to generous acidity. **Chenin Blanc** ★★ **05** very shy & light with aggressive acidity, which brief oaking (3 mths used barrels) fails to subdue. **Semillon** ★★★★ Broad-shouldered style, mouth-filling, oaky; bracing seam of acidity (8g/ℓ!) adds welcome counterpoint on **04**; 3 mths 2nd/3rd fill oak. **Sauvignon Blanc** ★★★ **05** cool-climate grassy/spicy tone, alc again pleasingly low (12.5%); despite high acidity (7.3g/ℓ) not as lively as pvs – perhaps just youthfully unsettled. **Méthode Cap Classique** new ★★ Characterful brut from chardonnay, 3 yrs on lees; **02** appley/lactic aromas (brie cheese?), clean dry mousse.

Caresse Marine range

Cape Red Blend ★★★ Shiraz (22%) from Elgin/W Bay enters picture in **03**, pinotage, cabs f & s; soundly & generously structured, dark berry/choc flavours, soft ripe tannin from barrelling 9 mths seasoned oak, Fr. **Merlot** new ★★★ Wldekrns's signature austerity imbues **04** newcomer, with underplayed red berry/spice; time/food needed to tame dusty dry tannins. **Dry White** ★★★ Lively blend chenin, sauvignon, portion lightly wooded; **04** sunny ripe flavours, touch green apple fruit, tart & zingy. To be enjoyed young. — *CR/IvH*

Wildfire see Vineyards
Wild Lily see Vinus Via
Wild Rush see Rietvallei

Wild Thing see Baarsma

Wilhelmshof see Nico van der Merwe

William Everson Wines

Paarl ▪ Est/1stB 2001 ▪ Tasting, sales & tours by appt ▪ BYO picnic ▪ Owner/winemaker William Everson ▪ 300 cs 80% red 20% white ▪ 7 Prospect Street Somerset West 7130 ▪ we@intekom.co.za ▪ ***T 082·554·6357*** *▪ F (021) 851·2205*

The archetypal *garagiste* winemaker, transport company owner William Everson says he enjoys 'making and managing' a small quantity of wine, and marketing it himself to wine lovers around the country. Currently only one of his reds, the Shiraz, is available (the Pinotage temporarily out of stock). With quality white grapes in short supply last harvest, William E struggled to get his share of chardonnay. The upside? 'Great quality in both reds and whites.'

Pinotage ★★★☆ No follow up vintage to flamboyant **02** from Mbury grapes, matured yr in Am oak. Tasted mid-2004, showy & appealing; cherry/banana tones, supportive oaking, earth undertone, juicy tannins. Should age well. ±14.7% alc. **Shiraz** ★★★☆ Cleverly crafted **03**, like pvs from Swtlnd fruit; unlike pvs with a more restrained 14.5% alc. Well composed; abundant fruit & spice/pepper/salty liquorice underpinned by dense but ripe tannins, for 5-6 yrs cellaring. 18 mths new/older Fr/Am. **Chardonnay** ★★★☆ **04** step up on pvs, now from Klapmuts fruit matured yr on gross lees in 3rd fill Fr barrels. Elegant, despite 14% alc, with lemon marmalade nose, tropical melon palate, lively acid backbone. *— CT*

Windfall

Robertson ▪ Est 2000 ▪ 1stB 2001 ▪ Closed to public ▪ Owner Rob Alexander ▪ Winemaker Helmard Hanekom (2001) ▪ Viticulturist Jaco de Wet (2001) ▪ ±14 ha 100 tons 2 000 cs own label 75% red 25% white ▪ PO Box 802 Robertson 6705 ▪ windfallwinefarm@webmail.co.za ▪ ***T (023) 626·4498*** *▪ F (033) 342·2531*

No update available on this winery; contact details from previous edition.

Windmeul Cooperative Cellar

Paarl ▪ Est 1944 ▪ Tasting & sales Mon-Fri 8-5 Sat 9-1 ▪ Closed pub hols ▪ Tours during tasting hours by appt ▪ Owners 48 members ▪ Winemakers Danie Marais & Danie Geldenhuys, with Francois van Niekerk (Dec 1999/Dec 2004/Dec 2004) ▪ Viticulturist Paul Malan (Dec 2001) ▪ 1 700 ha (cab, merlot, shiraz, chard, chenin, sauvignon) ▪ 11 013 tons 6 000 cs own label 55% red 45% white ▪ PO Box 2013 Windmeul 7630 ▪ windmeul@iafrica.com ▪ www.windmeulwinery.co.za ▪ ***T 869·8043/8100*** *▪ F 869·8614*

While their name may translate as 'Windmill', there's no time for tilting at them here – just honest, hard work poured into these wines, flagged by fans as good value. With 'double' Danies, Marais and Geldenhuys, now co-piloting the cellar, assisting is Elsenburg graduate Francois van Niekerk. The flight plan is simple. As Geldenhuys puts it: 'We give our full attention and time to each load of grapes which comes into the cellar to get the best out of every berry'. Upgraded tasting and sales facilities now include a conference centre which accommodates bigger groups.

★★★★ **Cabernet Sauvignon Reserve** Longer oaking distinguishes this from version below; **02** (sample) stylish, seductive; **03** (★★★), last yr as sample, now restrained; shows fruit on nose but not palate. Ripe tannins, lively acidity; may fill out with time. Yr new Fr barriques.

Cabernet Sauvignon ★★ Usually a crowd-pleaser with forward fruit, **03** less so; subtle mineral & organic notes, palate lean & fruit-shy. **Merlot** ★★★ Friendly & charming **03** with effusive black berry fruit, firm tannins. Charry/spicy oak noted on sample last ed has softened, melded nicely with fruit. Balanced 13.6% alc. **Pinotage** ★★★ **03** tasted for pvs ed lives up to provisional rating; dense, tarry/smoky aromas abound; dry, liquorice finish. This, above, yr Fr staves unless stated. **Shiraz Reserve** ★★★☆ **03** doesn't quite live up to sample ★★★★ prediction; does deliver promised creamy vanilla flavours but also less attractive sweet/sour twist. Yr oak, 45% Am. **Cabernet Sauvignon-Merlot** ★★★ Unpretentious 70/20 blend needing 2-3 yrs to show its true colours. **04** muted fruit, dry palate, almost cab f-like. A late developer? **Mill Red** ★★ Smoky 'floor polish' aromas, bit blunt; savoury/smoky flavours; usually blend of shiraz, cinsaut, cab f. Latest **NV** untasted. **Chenin Blanc** ★★★☆ ✓ **05** crisp & vibrant with pears, guavas & limes. Oodles flavour & concentration. Whopping 15% alc well absorbed. **Sauvignon Blanc** ★★ **05** soft, tropical fruit salad version, not as zippy as pvs. Drink soon. **Mill White** ★★☆ Typically melon & hay aromas, crisp tropical flavours. Latest **NV** not tasted. **Late Harvest** ★★ None since **03** from chenin (90%), white muscadel, with glacé pineapple scent; soft, rounded, uncomplicated. **Port** ★★★ ('Cape Ruby Port' pvs ed) They've beefed up the fortification for **03** since this tasted as sample, now a more healthy 18.6%. Still rich Xmas cake bouquet; concentrated, sweet/sour flavours, perhaps touch too sweet (102g/ℓ sugar) for classicists, more so the variety: ruby cab, yr older Fr barriques. WO Coastal, as are regular Cab & Pinotage; all others Paarl. — *MM/CR*

Winds of Change see African Terroir

Wine Concepts

*Cape Town ▪ Tasting & sales Mon-Fri 9-7 Sat 9-5 ▪ Cardiff Castle cnr Kildare & Main St Newlands 7700 ▪ sales@wineconcepts.co.za ▪ www.wineconcepts.co.za ▪ **T 671·9030** ▪ F 671·9031*

After years of planning, Cape Town fine-wine merchants and wannabe *garagistes* Mike Bampfield-Duggan and Murray Giggins made a Cab from Wellington grapes in 2005. It's a departure from their happy-go-lucky Sommelier's Choice range (still in abeyance), and will be available in limited quantities from their shops in Newlands and Kloof Street under a name yet to be announced at press time. See Specialist wine shops section for more details.

Winecorp

*Stellenbosch ▪ Closed to public ▪ Group winemaker Frans Smit ▪ Winemakers Kobie Viljoen (red) & Eleonor Visser (white), with Etienne le Roux ▪ Winemaker & procurement (Winepack) Johan de Villiers ▪ Viticulturists Johann Smit & Orlando Filander ▪ PO Box 99 Lynedoch 7603 ▪ winecorp@iafrica.com ▪ www.winecorp.co.za ▪ ISO 9001 & BRC certified ▪ **T 881·3690** ▪ F 881·3699*

This streamlined wine company seems on track to meet CEO Vernon Davis' stipulated goal of developing Winecorp into a prominent, leading player in the industry and establishing it as such internationally. Wines are carefully channelled into brands based on quality, site-specificity and price-point. The Longridge cellar concentrates on premium wines (Longridge, Bay View) from Helderberg slopes. The Spier ranges — Private Collection, Vintage Selection, Classic, Discover, Inspire — are mainly of Stellenbosch origin and produced in Winecorp's Spier winery. As are the Savanha Premium and Reserve ranges, from contracted growers in Paarl, Darling. Group winemaker Frans Smit is assisted by red wine specialist Kobie Viljoen (his red won the 2005 SAYWS overall trophy), and newly-married Eleonor Visser. See seperate listings for these brands. Winecorp's Simondium facility, Winepack, blends, bottles, labels, packages, manages for buyers. UK partner Private Liquor Brands (PLB) helps distribute the Dumisani range in the UK, Ireland and Scandinavia.

Dumisani range

Joint venture with PLB; now also distributed in the US & Ireland. Meaning 'Praise' in Xhosa. All these WO W Cape. **Pinotage** ★★☆ Uncomplicated, tasty. Last available **02** had berry piquancy, satisfying lively zestiness. Lightly oaked. **Pinotage-Shiraz** ★★☆ Early-drinking unoaked 70/30 blend. **04** best of both worlds: shiraz's rich, meaty, dark fruit influence, the juicy quaffability of pinotage. **Ruby Cabernet-Merlot** ★★ Quaffable 70/30 blend. Last was **02**, with red berry appeal, light-toned & juicy. **Pinotage Rosé** ★★☆ Charmer from top to toe. **05**'s fruit gum, softly rounded candyfloss appeal, touch sugar, makes it an ideal summer quaffer. **Chardonnay** ★★★ Last available **03** had tangy freshness, rounded peach-toast flavours from deft oaking. **Chenin Blanc** ★★☆ **04** not revisited this ed. Tasty, easy-drinking: guavas, crunchy apples, fresh & light (12.5% alc), roundly appealing. **Chenin Blanc-Chardonnay** ★★★ **05** unlike last, chenin (65%) major style player here: pears & lemony briskness, herbaceous whiffs. Crisply fresh, satisfying. Minimal oak.

Fat Ladies range

Uncomplicated, easy-drinking wines, all with screwcaps, all WO W Cape. Delightfully corpulent ladies on labels by local artist Roland West. **Cabernet Sauvignon-Merlot** ★★★ **04** fruit is main focus in this unwooded 60/40 blend; fresh-picked raspberries/mulberries, approachable, uncomplicated, tasty. **Pinotage Rosé** ★★ **05** (sample) friendly, easy to like; redcurrant aromas, flavours; off-dry with palate-lengthening sugar (12g/ℓ). **Sauvignon Blanc** ★★★ **05** (sample) shows less concentration than pvs, but lively pear & gooseberry appeal, light structure for earlier enjoyment. — *CR*

Wine 4U see Le Manoir de Brendell

Wine of the Month Club

Est 1986 ▪ Founder Colin Collard ▪ MD Tai Collard ▪ 200 000 cs 50% red 49% white 1% sparkling ▪ Private Bag X2 Glosderry 7702 ▪ wineclub@wineofthemonth.co.za ▪ www.wineofthemonth.co.za ▪ ***T 657·8100*** *▪ F 415·6385*

Colin Collard started this mail-order, door-to-door delivery wine venture two decades ago this year; it now handles some 200 000 cases per annum. Besides wines selected by the club's panel for distribution to 40 000 customers, WOM also supplies its own-label wines, including the Select Winemakers Collection Limited Release. The Paarl Cabernet Sauvignon 03 in this range, by Gesie Lategan (Domaine Brahms), is still available.

Winery of Good Hope see The Winery
Wines of Charles Back see Fairview, Goats do Roam, Spice Route, Western Wines

Wine Source South Africa new

Paarl ▪ Est/1stB 2002 ▪ Closed to public ▪ Owners Jason Gabriel & Linda Yancy Kidsley ▪ Winemaker Nelson Buthelezi, with Chris Leroux ▪ Viticulturist Johan Cronjé ▪ 95 ha in production (cab, malbec, merlot, pinotage, shiraz) ▪ 530 tons 35 000 cs 80% red 10% white 10% rosé ▪ jason@winesourcesouthafrica.com ▪ www.winesourcesouthafrica.com ▪ ***T/F (011) 804·3552***

The sophisticated elegance of a simple glass of wine and the lifestyle associated with it, made an indelible impression on Jason Gabriel as a teenager. This fascination developed into a hobby and after a captivating trip to France, it was career-change time. With hard work and perseverance, Johannesburg-based Gabriel launched a BEE venture, Wine Source SA, together with his Florida (US) based business partner, Linda Yancy Kidsley. Nelson Buthelezi, assisted by Chris le Roux, makes the wine, while Johan Cronjé looks after the 165ha of source vineyards in the Klein Drakenstein foothills. The wines, promoted via the SA consulates in America, Europe and the Far East, are currently listed on two airlines.

Following trio of reds tasted as samples, ratings provisional: **Cabernet Sauvignon** ★★★ **04** quite showy fruit, full-ripe red berries, but tannins are tight, not yet fully integrated; will show better over 1-3 yrs. Oaked yr Fr/Am. **Merlot** ★★★ **04** sweet-fruited style, offering softly rounded drinkability. Oaking (as above) in support role, promises up to 3 yrs ageing potential. **Pinotage** ★★★ **04** (sample) delivers variety's trademark sweet ripe red-fruit profile, backed by serious oaking, yr Fr/Am; has ageing potential for 3-4 yrs. **Shiraz** ★★★ **04** already accessible; full ripe-fruity style with some spice nuances. Oak backing (as above) provides framework for 2-3 yrs ageing. **Corundum** ★★★ Strikingly packaged cab/merlot blend with dollop pinotage (60/30/5). **04** still tightly structured, unyielding, needs few yrs to unfold. Has good red fruit in place, well spiced by yr Fr/Am oak treatment, show attractive hazel/walnut tones. **Daniel's Hat** ★★★ **05** light textured, melon/pear-toned blend chenin, chardonnay (50/50). Zesty acid backbone adds refreshing drinkability. All above WO Paarl. — *CT*

Wine Village-Hermanus

Walker Bay ▪ Est 1998 ▪ 1stB 2004 ▪ Tasting & sales hours: see Specialist wine shops section ▪ Owners Paul & Cathy du Toit ▪ ±1 000 cs 50% red 50% white

The housewines of this delightful country wine shop, owned/run by Paul and Cathy du Toit, are made back-stoep-style by the proprietors, some friends and enthusiastic staff members, and offered to wine lovers in a spirit of fun.

Both **NV**. Not retasted; notes from pvs ed. **Dry Red** ★★★ Elegant all-sort blend led by cab, with pleasant bottle-age hint. **Dry White** ★★★ Lively, light & refreshing, from semillon, 2 mths new Fr oak; attractive rhubarb twist to finish. — *TM*

Winkelshoek Wine Cellar

Piketberg (see Swartland map) • Tasting & sales Mon-Fri 9-4 Sat 9-12 • Fee R5 • Gifts • Owners Hennie Hanekom & Jurgens Brand • Winemaker Hennie Hanekom (1984) • PO Box 395 Piketberg 7320 • info@winkelshoek.co.za • ***T (022) 913·1092*** *• F (022) 913·1095*

This cellar's easy-drinkers are available for tasting and sale from the visitor centre at the intersection of the N7 and R44 roads near Piketberg. The wines, untasted for this edition, include the Weskus Dry Red, Grand Cru, Blanc de Blanc and Late Harvest; and the new Cap Vino Red (unwooded) and White (chenin).

Withoek

Calitzdorp (see Little Karoo map) • Est/1stB 1996 • Tasting & sales Mon-Fri 9-4 • Closed Mar 21, Easter Fri, Apr 27, May 1, Jun 16, Aug 9, Sep 24 • Tours by appt • Self-catering cottages • Farm produce • Walks • Conservation area • Owner/winemaker/viticulturist Koos Geyser, with Fanie Geyser (1996/2000) • 20 ha (cab, petit v, ruby cab, shiraz, tinta, touriga, chenin, colombard, hanepoot, muscadel) • ±300 tons 400 cs own label 50% red 50% fortified • PO Box 181 Calitzdorp 6660 • withoek@telkomsa.net stabilpave@mweb.co.za • ***T/F (044) 213·3639***

No update available on this winery; contact details and wine notes from previous edition.

Dry Red ★★★ Spicy, leafy notes on **03**, from tinta, ruby cab; dry, savoury, cinnamon/vanilla twist on finish from yr 3rd fill oak. **Cape Ruby** ★★★ Soft & friendly ruby-style port from above varieties, 2 yrs oaked. **01** ripe, spicy rum & raisin nose; soft, silky, medium-sweet. 17% alc, low for style. — *TM*

Withof *see* Cru Wines
Witteboomen *see* Thorntree
Wolvenbosch *see* Jason's Hill

Wolvendrift Private Cellar

Robertson • Est 1903 • 1stB 2002 • Tasting & sales Mon-Fri 9-4.30 Sat 10-1 • Closed Easter Fri-Sun, Dec 25/26 & Jan 1 • Tours by appt • Picnic baskets by appt or BYO • Farm produce • Walks • Owner Michael Klue • Winemakers Michael & Jan Klue (Jan 1973/Jan 2003) • Viticulturist Jan Swart (Jan 2000) • 120 ha (cab, merlot, chard, chenin, colombard, sauvignon) • 45% red 45% white 10% fortified • PO Box 24 Robertson 6705 • wolvendrift@lando.co.za • www.wolvendriftwines.co.za • ***T (023) 616·2890*** *• F (023) 616·2396*

The new barrel cellar with a view-deck overlooking river and vineyards — where you'll spot new petit verdot vines — is an attractive addition to this Robertson farm. The term 'chilled-out' springs to mind: not only are the grapes picked in the cool early morning, winemakers Michael & Jan Klue deliberately create 'a calm atmosphere in the cellar to ensure the grapes are handled with as little stress as possible'. More upbeat was the first live music concert on the riverbank, staged as part of the region-wide Wacky Wine Weekend.

Cabernet-Sauvignon-Merlot ☺ ★★★ Nothing menacing about this 60/40 blend, aka 'Red Wolf'; **04** juicy red berry fruit with toasty touch (8 mths Fr oak), agreeably firm tannins.

Chardonnay ★★★ Unshowy **04**, some citrus character & delicate touch oak; fairly compact package best enjoyed soon. **Sauvignon Blanc** ★ **05** quiet green apple aromas, lightweight with fresh acidity. **Muscadel** ★★★ Red (which it doesn't say on the charming label) muscadel, with unctuous texture despite fairly strenuous fortification (±17%); **04** barley sugar & sweet raisin whiffs.—*MM*

Wonderfontein see see The Marais Family

Woolworths

*Category manager William Fakude ▪ T 407·3683 ▪ Selection manager Allan Mullins ▪ **T 407·2777** ▪ F 407·3946 ▪ AllanMullins@woolworths.co.za ▪ Buying manager Ivan Oertle ▪ T 407·2762 ▪ IvanOertle@woolworths.co.za*

Allan Mullins' thumbnail philosophy – 'Total dedication to innovation and quality' – might trip off anybody's clipboard, but a look at his past year reveals plenty to back it up. He's flown to several countries to source wines, and continued to burrow into local cellars to create interesting and exclusive blends. As SA's premier upscale food chain, Woolworths is in a unique position to both reflect and influence SA's quality wine-purchasing trends. Explicitly acknowledging their close relationship with suppliers, they singled out, among others, Stellar Winery for their 'Innovation Of The Year' (for a preservative-free Organic Chenin), and Diemersfontein's Bertus Fourie for Winemaker Of The Year. Dedicated technologist Warren Dam has been appointed to drive the technical standards of the Woolies wine vehicle. And with Mullins promising more focus on unusual grape varieties, you'd be hard pressed to find anything stale in this range.

Signature Series

Flagship range, featuring special selections from exceptional vintages. Only one wine ready for tasting, to be joined by, among others, a Shiraz-Viognier from Boekenhoutskloof.

Neil Ellis Elgin Merlot ★★★ Long-time Wlwrths collaborator Neil Ellis here in almost easy-drinking mode – so possibly better showcased in new 'Classic' range below. **03** classic, certainly, in structure & flavour (ripe plums, hints mushroom & truffle), classic Neil E balance & elegance; but too open, uncomplex for flagship status. 16 mths Fr oak.

Reserve range

★★★★ **Founder's Reserve Cabernet Sauvignon** Special barrel selection from Diemersfontein, owned by Wlwrths' founding family. Impressive **01** deeply coloured, weighty & concentrated. No **02**. **03** (★★★) indisputably cab but less showy; pleasant damp earth character with forest smells; lively fruit/acid interaction, light oaking. For country stews & roasts. 60% new oak (70/30 Fr/Am), 15 mths.

★★★★★ **Pinotage** From Bellevue, usually highlighting that estate's singular essence-of-pinotage style, from vines up to 50 yrs old. Typified by stylish & perfumed **02**, only Am oak (10 mths small barrels, 50% new); **03** (★★★) same wooding, same pulpy macerated fruit character but much lighter, more like a pinot. Still, a very nice drink.

★★★★ **Groenekloof Shiraz** Full, rich, almost extravagant version from Darling Cellars. **02** had no rough edges, just creamy, delicious ripeness. **03** classic varietal aroma of black pepper, appealing ripe juiciness, salty liquorice mid-palate; powerful dry finish. 14 mths Fr oak, 60% new.

★★★★ **Cabernet Sauvignon-Merlot** Reflects vintage variations through mirror of Neil Ellis' classicism. Elegantly structured **02** (★★★★☆) hid its 5+ yr ageing potential behind easy accessibility. 61/39 blend; changes to 50/50 for **03**, a serious dinner wine; well built tannins, lingering silky flavours; mint & nutmeg whiffs to wild berry fruit. Also 4-5+ yr potential. 15 mths Fr barrels, ±25% new.

★★★★ **Chardonnay** All since **97** by Neil Ellis. Still selling **03**, last year noted as bold New World style at its best: tangy citrus peel & buttered toast, food-friendly acidity tempered by nutty overlay. 80% blend Fr oak-fermented/aged 9 mths, third new.

★★★★ **Barrel Chenin Blanc** ✓ By Ken Forrester; these delicious on release, sustain interest for good few yrs. **04** flew off shelves before we could taste. **05** (★★★☆) from old bushvines; effusive pineapple & peach welcome, sweet-ripe tone emphasised by dollop actual sugar (5.3g/ℓ). Tasty if more commercial. 50% barrelled 9 mths.

★★★☆ **Noble Late Harvest Chenin Blanc Barrel Reserve** From Ken Forrester. **04** not ready for tasting. Last yr **03** (★★★★) was deeply ripe, with tropical fruit, honeycomb

...made better!